Statistics for Economics

Statistics for Economics

Steven Proud

OXFORD
UNIVERSITY PRESS

OXFORD
UNIVERSITY PRESS

Great Clarendon Street, Oxford, OX2 6DP,
United Kingdom

Oxford University Press is a department of the University of Oxford.
It furthers the University's objective of excellence in research, scholarship,
and education by publishing worldwide. Oxford is a registered trade mark of
Oxford University Press in the UK and in certain other countries.

Published in the United States of America by Oxford University Press
198 Madison Avenue, New York, NY 10016, United States of America

British Library Cataloguing in Publication Data
Data available

Library of Congress Control Number: 2026930329

ISBN 9780198821038

Printed and bound by CPI Group (UK) Ltd., Croydon, CR0 4YY

The manufacturer's authorised representative in the EU for product safety is Oxford University Press España S.A. of El Parque Empresarial San Fernando de Henares, Avenida de Castilla, 2 - 28830 Madrid (www.oup.es/en or product.safety@oup.com). OUP España S.A. also acts as importer into Spain of products made by the manufacturer.

MIX
Paper | Supporting responsible forestry
FSC® C013604
FSC www.fsc.org

Acknowledgements

This book is the result of several years of development, and I am deeply grateful to my colleagues and to the undergraduate students at the University of Bristol for their valuable feedback on early drafts and teaching materials.

Throughout the text, I draw on data from the UK Labour Force Survey provided by the UK Data Service, as well as data from the OECD, the Federal Reserve Economic Data (FRED), and other sources. I also wish to acknowledge the developers of Maple, Stata, and Microsoft Excel, whose tools underpin many of the diagrams and code examples included in this book.

I am especially thankful to Caitlin Moreton-Lisle, and formerly Felicity Boughton and Amber Stone-Galilee, together with their colleagues at Oxford University Press, for their editorial guidance and support.

Finally, and most importantly, my deepest thanks go to my wife, Louise, and to our dog, Chase, for their constant love, patience, and encouragement throughout the writing of this book.

Outline Contents

Detailed Contents

Introduction

1

Learning outcomes for this chapter

At the end of this chapter, students will be able to:

- Explain where probabilities come from, and what they mean
- Characterize basic probabilities, and be able to construct probabilities based upon simple games, and represent probabilities using simple histograms
- Describe the concept of probability space, and represent probabilities relating to random variables, using Venn diagrams
- Determine when outcomes are mutually exclusive
- Formally define a random variable, in terms of a probability mass function
- Calculate a cumulative distribution function for a random variable, based upon the PMF
- Articulate the difference between populations and samples, and summarize how probability relates to populations and samples

Mathematical tools

- Arithmetic
- Simple sigma (Σ) notation for summations
- Frequency histograms

Introduction

Probability, statistics, and econometrics are absolutely core to an undergraduate study in Economics, or associated disciplines, such as finance and business. In this textbook, we will explore some of the fundamentals of these subjects, to develop an understanding of how we can analyse economic variables, both theoretically and empirically.

By the end of this book, we will develop tools for you to begin to be able to analyse relationships between economic variables. You will be able to evaluate the costs and benefits of using particular estimators to estimate relationships, and able to discuss whether or not the relationships you have estimated are causal relationships, or mere correlations.

In this book, we will begin by discussing basic probability theory. We will use this probability theory to develop our understanding of statistics. Statistics builds from probability, in that we will develop the concept of estimators, which follow probabilistic distributions, to make inferences about a population as a whole. Finally, we will move into a discussion of econometrics, which is the branch of statistics developed by economists to determine causal relationships between economic variables.

However, this is a long journey, and every journey begins with a single step, and our first step begins over 3,000 years ago.

1.1 A brief introduction to probability

In the physical world, there are certain concepts that we know will happen. If we push a child on a swing, then eventually, the child will start moving in the opposite direction. Similarly, if you drop a ball, it will eventually hit the floor. These are examples of deterministic relationships. We know that if we are holding a ball, and we let go of it, then it will start to fall.

However, many events are not deterministic, and instead occur with probability. For instance, if you were to flip a coin in the air, the coin has two sides—normally one side has a head on (representing the monarch, the president, or some other important person), and the other side has a design on. When we flip the coin, we don't know whether it will land with the head side up, or the design side (henceforth known as tails) upwards. It is uncertain whether it will land heads or tails upwards.

Games of chance have been played for thousands of years, where players compete against each other, based upon a random outcome. There is evidence that even in Ancient Greece, during the Trojan War, soldiers (such as Ajax and Achilles) would play games of dice, with the winner determined by the random outcome.

One of the results of games of chance is that gamblers begin to place bets upon the outcome of the game. If two players are playing dice, gamblers might place a bet on the outcome of the dice, or on the winner of the game. The most successful gamblers are going to be the gamblers who understand the game, and are able to identify the most likely winner.

To illustrate this, consider a very simple game of chance. Suppose that you have two six-sided dice. For illustrative purposes, suppose that one dice is blue, and the other dice is yellow. Both dice have the numbers 1 to 6 printed on the six sides, and each side is equally likely to land upwards. The players roll both dice, and the winner of the game is the player who correctly predicts (or gets closest to) the correct sum of outcomes on the dice (e.g. if the dice landed with a 2 and a 5 showing, the sum would be equal to 7).

We are not yet going to introduce any theory related to probability, other than that when we roll the dice, every pair of outcomes is as likely as each other. So for instance, the likelihood of the blue dice showing a 2 and the yellow dice showing a 3 is exactly the same as the likelihood of the blue dice showing a 6 and the yellow dice showing a 1.

Figure 1.1 shows all of the possible outcomes from rolling the two dice. Each cell represents a pair of outcomes, so for instance, the top left-hand cell indicates the blue dice scoring 1, and the yellow dice also scoring 1 (leading to a total score of $1 + 1 = 2$).

Each of these outcomes is equally likely, but if we look at the total scores, some of these occur more often than others. For instance, 2 only occurs once (when both dice score 1).

		Yellow dice					
		1	2	3	4	5	6
Blue dice	1	2	3	4	5	6	7
	2	3	4	5	6	7	8
	3	4	5	6	7	8	9
	4	5	6	7	8	9	10
	5	6	7	8	9	10	11
	6	7	8	9	10	11	12

Figure 1.1 Possible outcomes from rolling two (fair) dice.

Similarly, 12 occurs only once (when both dice score 6). However, the most likely score is 7, which occurs six times.

An understanding of probability would give a player of the game an advantage in this sort of game of chance; understanding that the most likely score was 7. In fact, we can see in this very simple example that a total score of 7 is six times more likely to occur than a score of 2.

However, the underlying mathematics was not formally recognized until much later. It wasn't until the seventeenth century that mathematicians really started to analyse games of chance, and to formalize the analysis of probability, and even to this day, probability is often seen by the general public as one of the least intuitive areas of modern mathematics.

Much of the initial work on probability was carried out in response to these sorts of parlour games. For example, in the seventeenth century, a problem, discussed by famous mathematicians such as Blaise Pascal and Pierre Fermat, posed the question of how to fairly split a prize pot in an incomplete game of chance, such as games of cards, or simple flips of a coin.

In these games, each player would have contributed an equal amount to a pot. Prior to the game, the players would agree on the number of rounds that needed to be won to win the overall pot; for example, they might agree before the game that the winner will be the first player to win ten games. In a complete game, the first player to reach ten games would win the entire pot. However, if the game is not completed, the question remains of how to fairly split the prize.

The solution to this problem was an elegant one, and underlies much of the probability and expectation theory that we use today, in that the split of the pot should be determined based on the likelihood of each player reaching the predetermined winning post.

1.2 What is a probability?

Put simply, a probability represents the likelihood of an outcome occurring. One way of visualizing this is by thinking about the relative frequency of different outcomes, if we repeatedly sample from a random variable. To illustrate this, let's consider what happens when we roll a single six-sided dice. If we roll the dice once, we will observe a single outcome, and that outcome might be a 1, 2, 3, 4, 5, or 6. However, now consider what would happen if you rolled this dice a very large number of times (say, 6,000,000 times).

If the dice is fair, then we would expect each side of the dice to be equally likely to occur. As such, if we repeatedly rolled the dice, we might expect to see roughly equal numbers of observations where the dice lands with a 1, 2, 3, 4, 5, or 6. In fact, we would expect approximately 1,000,000 of the outcomes to land with a 1, 1,000,000 to land with a 2, and so on, as illustrated in Table 1.1.

A probability tells us about the likelihood of each possible outcome. In the previous example, there are 6 outcomes, each of which occurs $\frac{1}{6}$th of the time. As such, the probability can be thought of as the relative likelihood of each of the outcomes.

So, the probability of gaining a 1 when we roll a single six-sided dice is equal to $\frac{1}{6}$th. Similarly, the probability of gaining a 2 would be $\frac{1}{6}$th. In the previous example, there are six possible outcomes, each of which has a probability equal to $\frac{1}{6}$th, illustrated in Table 1.2.

1.2.1 Formal notation for probabilities

When thinking about probability, we need to develop some key notation and terminology. The first key piece of terminology that we will introduce is that of a random variable. A random variable represents a variable where the outcome is uncertain.

Table 1.1 Approximate distribution of outcomes when we roll a dice 6,000,000 times

Outcome from rolling a single dice	Approximate frequency[1]	Proportion of outcomes
1	1,000,000	$\frac{1}{6}$
2	1,000,000	$\frac{1}{6}$
3	1,000,000	$\frac{1}{6}$
4	1,000,000	$\frac{1}{6}$
5	1,000,000	$\frac{1}{6}$
6	1,000,000	$\frac{1}{6}$

Table 1.2 Probabilities associated with each outcome from a fair dice

Outcome from rolling a single dice	Probability
1	$\frac{1}{6}$
2	$\frac{1}{6}$
3	$\frac{1}{6}$
4	$\frac{1}{6}$
5	$\frac{1}{6}$
6	$\frac{1}{6}$

[1] Important note: In reality, it is highly unlikely that you will see exactly 1,000,000 of each outcome. The key thing is that the outcomes will approximately be observed with each outcome represented $\frac{1}{6}$th of the time. As the number of rolls gets larger, the proportions will get closer and closer to exactly $\frac{1}{6}$th. By the time you have rolled the dice an infinite number of times, each outcome will occur exactly $\frac{1}{6}$th of the time. This is an application of a concept we will see later in the textbook, known as the law of large numbers.

We often denote a random variable in terms of a capital letter; for example, we might denote the random variable generated by rolling a dice as X.

Random variables have a set of possible outcomes, and we denote the general outcome of a random variable using a lower case letter; for example, we could denote the outcome from a roll of a dice as x. Each of the possible outcomes of a random variable occurs with probability, and we denote the probability that the random variable X takes on the particular value x as:

$$P(X = x)$$

That is, P represents the probability that the random variable X takes on the particular outcome x.

This is illustrated explicitly in Figure 1.2. We express this verbally as the probability (P) that the random variable (X) is equal to (=) the particular outcome x.

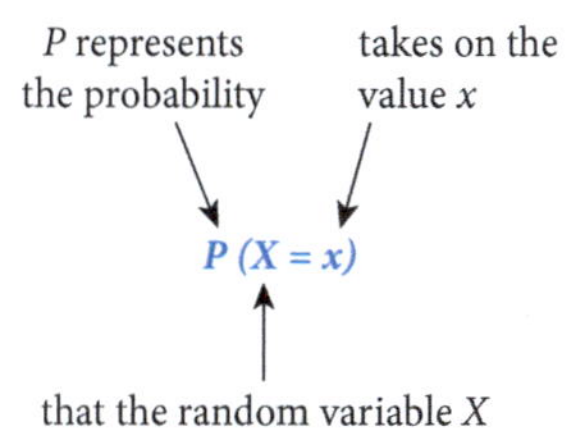

Figure 1.2 Explaining the notation of probabilities.

In the previous example, if we define the random variable representing the roll of a dice as X, then, for instance, we can write down the probability that the dice lands with a 6 as:

$$P(X = 6) = \frac{1}{6}$$

It should be noted that probabilities always lie between 0 and 1. If you carry out a calculation, and find a probability that is either negative, or greater than 1, then you know you have made a mistake!

Intuitively, the reason that probabilities must lie between 0 and 1 comes from our initial motivation behind probabilities; a probability represents the proportion of the time that a particular outcome occurs. If an outcome is certain (i.e. it occurs 100 per cent of the time), we can represent this proportionally as 1. If an outcome occurs 50 per cent of the time, then this is equivalent to saying that it occurs $\frac{1}{2}$ of the time (remember $\frac{1}{2} = 0.5$).

FORMAL DEFINITION OF A RANDOM VARIABLE

Formally, a random variable represents the mapping of a domain of possible outcomes to a range of real numbers. Because each of these outcomes is uncertain, we can assign a probability to those outcomes.

In the case of a toss of a coin, the domain of possible outcomes is {Heads, Tails}. Formally, a random variable would then map these outcomes to numerical values. For example, you might map heads as an outcome of 1, and tails as an outcome of 0.

The final mapping that takes place is to then map the probability associated with each of these outcomes; for example, if we represent the flip of a coin as X, then $P(X = 1) = \frac{1}{2}$, and $P(X = 0) = \frac{1}{2}$.

This is the same sort of language that mathematicians use for functions. When we consider a mathematical function, there is a domain of possible inputs (which are equivalent to the set of possible outcomes in a random variable), and a range, which represents the function applied to the members of the domain.

- Probabilities will always lie between 0 and 1.
- If you observe an outcome with a probability of 1, that means that it is certain to happen.
- An outcome that will never occur has a probability of zero.

1.2.2 Representing probabilities graphically

It is often useful to try to represent probability using a graph. In the case of rolling a dice, we could represent the outcomes using a frequency histogram. If we rolled a dice ten times, and observed the outcomes illustrated in Table 1.3, we could then represent the frequency of each outcome using a bar-chart, or more formally, a frequency histogram.

Table 1.3 Frequency of outcomes from rolling a single dice ten times

Outcome from rolling a single dice	Frequency	Proportion of outcomes
1	2	0.2
2	4	0.4
3	1	0.1
4	1	0.1
5	2	0.2
6	0	0

In a frequency histogram, the height of the bars represents the number of times we observe each outcome. So, in this example, we could plot a frequency histogram as in Figure 1.3.

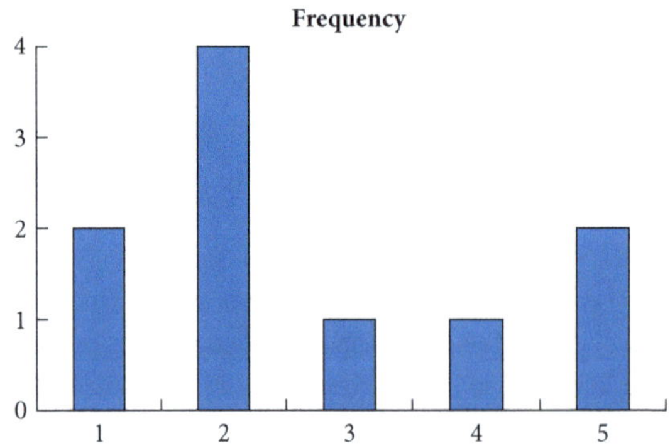

Figure 1.3 Frequency histogram from a simulation, rolling a six-sided dice ten times.

This example only considers ten rolls of the dice, and 6 has not occurred. However, as you roll the dice more and more, each outcome would become approximately equally represented. To illustrate this, I have simulated 6,000,000 dice rolls, and have observed the frequencies represented in Table 1.4.

As before, we can represent the frequency of the outcomes in a frequency histogram, shown in Figure 1.4.

As the number of rolls increases, we can see that the proportion of each outcome has converged to approximately $\frac{1}{6}$. If we did this again with a much larger number of rolls

Table 1.4 Frequency of outcomes from a simulation, rolling a dice 6,000,000 times

Outcome from rolling a single dice	Frequency	Proportion of outcomes
1	999,179	0.167
2	999,937	0.167
3	1,000,201	0.167
4	999,934	0.167
5	1,001,274	0.167
6	999,475	0.167

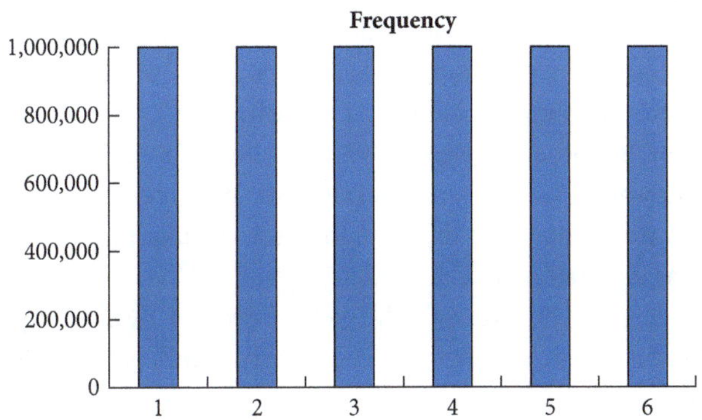

Figure 1.4 Frequency histogram from a simulation, rolling a six-sided dice 6,000,000 times.

(say, 6,000,000,000), then the proportion would be even closer to $\frac{1}{6}$. We can represent probability distributions in just the same way as frequency histograms; however, rather than illustrating them in terms of the number of outcomes, we can represent the probability by the likelihood of each outcome—that is, what proportion of the time we would expect each outcome to occur. For a roll of a single dice, each side of the dice is equally likely to occur; each side has a probability of $\frac{1}{6}$ of occurring, so we can represent the probability distribution as shown in Figure 1.5.

The height of the bar represents the probability or likelihood of each outcome. Any outcome that is impossible to achieve will have a probability of zero. So, since the dice can only

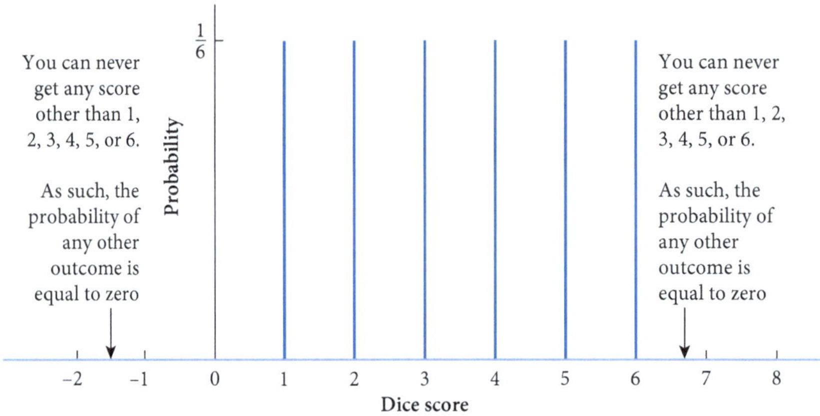

Figure 1.5 Probability distribution for a roll of a single dice.

ever produce integer outcomes 1, 2, 3, 4, 5, 6, then the probability of achieving, say, an outcome of −1 is equal to zero, and this is represented with the probability being equal to zero in Figure 1.5. Similarly, we cannot observe any outcomes between (say) 1 and 2. Therefore, the probability of getting a score of 1.5 will also be equal to 0.

This is a rather simple example, as each of the outcomes is equally likely, so the heights of the bars in the probability distribution are all the same.

This is not, however, an interesting example, because each of the possible outcomes is equally likely to occur. For most random variables it will not be the case that all of the possible outcomes have the same probability. To illustrate this, let's consider a slightly more interesting example. Suppose that we flip two coins. Each coin is equally likely to land heads upwards or tails upwards. We can represent the pairs of outcomes from the coins. It is relatively straightforward to show that there are four, equally likely possible outcomes from the flip of two coins, as illustrated in Table 1.5.

Each of the pairs of outcomes is equally likely to occur. However, suppose that you were not interested in the specific outcomes of coin 1 and coin 2, but were instead interested in the number of heads achieved. Here, there are three possible outcomes:

- When both coin 1 and coin 2 land heads upwards, you achieve 2 heads,
- when coin 1 and coin 2 both land tails upwards, you achieve 0 heads,
- but when one coin lands heads upwards, and the other tails upwards, you would achieve 1 head.

Table 1.5 Possible outcomes when we flip two coins

Coin 1	Coin 2	Number of heads
Heads	Heads	2
Tails	Heads	1
Heads	Tails	1
Tails	Tails	0

That is, out of the four possible pairs of outcomes, there is one way we could achieve two heads, one way that we could achieve two tails, but two ways we could achieve one head and one tail (see Table 1.6).

As such, since each pair of outcomes is equally likely to occur, $\frac{1}{4}$ of the time you would achieve 2 heads, $\frac{1}{4}$ of the time you would achieve 0 heads, but $\frac{1}{2}$ of the time you would achieve exactly 1 head. These likelihoods represent the probability of each of the outcomes; that is, the probability of getting exactly 1 head would be $\frac{1}{2}$. This is represented in exactly the same way in Figure 1.6.

Just as in Figure 1.5, the height of the bars represents the probability of each possible outcome: half of the time, when you flip two (fair) coins, you would expect to see exactly one head; one quarter (or 25 per cent) of the time, you would expect to see two heads; and one quarter of the time, you would expect to see two tails.

We could apply the same logic to the example we saw illustrated in Figure 1.1 at the beginning of this section, where we were interested in the total score obtained from rolling two dice. The total score in this game is obtained by adding together the score from the blue dice with the score from the yellow dice. Since these are fair dice, each of the outcomes is equally likely. Therefore, each of the pairs of outcomes across the blue and the yellow dice is also

Table 1.6 Probability of achieving 0, 1, or 2 heads when flipping two fair coins

Number of heads	Likelihood (probability)
2	$\frac{1}{4}$
1	$\frac{2}{4} = \frac{1}{2}$
0	$\frac{1}{4}$

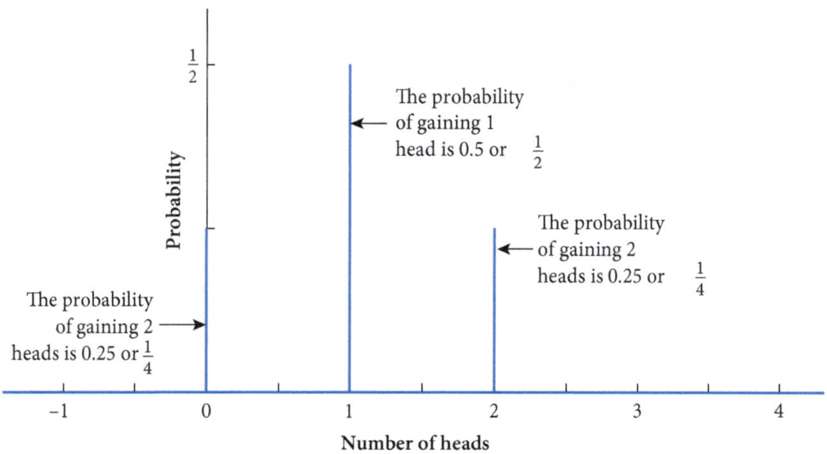

Figure 1.6 Probability distribution of the number of heads when we flip two (fair) coins.

equally likely. There are 36 possible pairs of outcomes, each with equal probability. So, for instance, the probability that the blue dice yields a score of 1 and the yellow dice also yields a score of 1 is equal to $\frac{1}{36}$. That is, one out of the 36 outcomes is represented by a score of 1 on the blue dice and 1 on the yellow dice (see Figure 1.7).

However, in this game, we are not interested in the score on each of the dice; instead we are interested in the total score when we add together the outcomes across the two dice.

We can see, from Figure 1.7, that some outcomes occur more often than others. For example, a total score of 7 is achieved six possible ways, a total score of 6 can be achieved five possible ways, and so on. In fact, there are 36 possible pairs of outcomes from the roll of two dice, of which six of the outcomes are 7. That means that we can write down that six out of 36 or $\frac{6}{36}$ of the (equally likely) outcomes are equal to 7. More formally, we can say that the probability that the total score in this game is equal to 7 is equal to $\frac{6}{36}\left(=\frac{1}{6}\right)$.

To represent this in formal probability notation, let's denote a random variable Y to represent the total score of the game. We can write down that:

$$P(Y = 7) = \frac{1}{6}$$

In other words, the probability that the random variable Y (which represents the score in this game) takes on the value 7 is equal to $\frac{1}{6}$. Using Figure 1.7, we can evaluate the probability of each of the possible outcomes for Y. Remember, there are 36 possible pairs of outcomes for the two dice, but, when we add together the scores, there may be multiple ways of achieving each score. Each of the pairs of outcomes are equally likely here. That is, the probability of observing both the blue and yellow dice landing on a 1 is the same as (e.g.) the probability of the blue dice landing on a 6, and the yellow dice landing on a 2.

		Yellow dice					
		1	2	3	4	5	6
Blue dice	1	2	3	4	5	6	7
	2	3	4	5	6	7	8
	3	4	5	6	7	8	9
	4	5	6	7	8	9	10
	5	6	7	8	9	10	11
	6	7	8	9	10	11	12

Figure 1.7 Possible outcomes from rolling two (fair) dice.

The probability of each score is calculated in Table 1.7. Since all of the pairs of outcomes are equally likely to occur, we can see that the probability of achieving a score of 7 can be achieved through six out a possible 36 combinations. Thus, the probability of achieving a score of 7 is six out of 36, or $\frac{6}{36}$, which is the same as $\frac{1}{6}$.

Table 1.7 Probabilities of each outcome when rolling two fair six-sided dice

Score	Description	Probability
1	No combination of the two dice outcomes leads to a score of 1	0
2	There is one combination (1,1) out of a possible 36 leading to a score of 2	$\frac{1}{36}$
3	There are two combinations (1,2) and (2,1) out of a possible 36 leading to a score of 3	$\frac{2}{36}=\frac{1}{18}$
4	There are three combinations (1,3), (2,2), (3,1) out of a possible 36 leading to a score of 4	$\frac{3}{36}=\frac{1}{12}$
5	There are four combinations (1,4), (2,3), (3,2), (4,1) out of a possible 36 leading to a score of 5	$\frac{4}{36}=\frac{1}{9}$
6	There are five combinations (1,5), (2,4), (3,3), (4,2), (5,1) out of a possible 36 leading to a score of 6	$\frac{5}{36}$
7	There are six combinations (1, 6), (2,5), (3,4), (4,3), (5,2), (6,1) out of a possible 36 leading to a score of 7	$\frac{6}{36}=\frac{1}{6}$
8	There are five combinations (2,6), (3,5), (4,4), (5,3), (6,2) out of a possible 36 leading to a score of 8	$\frac{5}{36}$
9	There are four combinations (3,6), (4,5), (5,4), (6,3) out of a possible 36 leading to a score of 9	$\frac{4}{36}=\frac{1}{9}$
10	There are three combinations (4,6), (5,5), (6,4) out of a possible 36 leading to a score of 10	$\frac{3}{36}=\frac{1}{12}$
11	There are two combinations (5,6), (6,5) out of a possible 36 leading to a score of 11	$\frac{2}{36}=\frac{1}{18}$
12	There is one combination (6,6) out of a possible 36 leading to a score of 12	$\frac{1}{36}$

One important thing to note that we haven't yet discussed is what happens when we add together the probabilities relating to each of the outcomes; you may have noticed that the sum of all of these probabilities is equal to 1:

$$1=\frac{1}{36}+\frac{1}{18}+\frac{1}{12}+\frac{1}{9}+\frac{5}{36}+\frac{1}{6}+\frac{5}{36}+\frac{1}{9}+\frac{1}{23}+\frac{1}{18}+\frac{1}{36}$$

The fact that all of the probabilities sum to equal 1 tells us that we have accounted for all of the possible outcomes. We will discuss this in more detail later in this book.

Finally, let's illustrate these probabilities diagrammatically in Figure 1.8, as we did earlier with the coin-tossing example. We have included the outcome where the score is equal to 1. However, if you look at Figure 1.8, you can see that the probability is equal to zero. This is because it is impossible to achieve a score of 1 based on the outcomes from two fair dice.

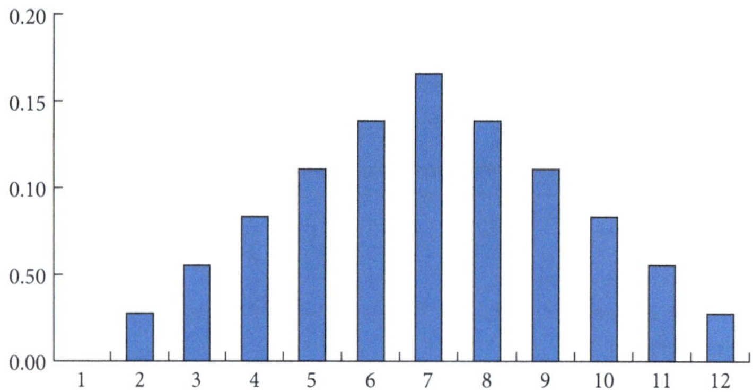

Figure 1.8 Probability distribution of scores from the sum of outcomes from rolling two (fair) six-sided dice.

Quick summary

- A random variable is a variable that takes a number of possible outcomes, and each outcome is uncertain.
- We represent the likelihood of any possible outcome within a random variable with a probability.
- Probabilities must lie between 0 and 1 (inclusive). If an outcome is certain (i.e. it will definitely happen), the probability of that outcome is equal to 1. If an outcome is impossible (i.e. it will never happen), the probability of that outcome is equal to 0.

TRY IT YOURSELF: FLIPPING A COIN

Flip a coin three times. Count how many heads you get. Repeat this ten times. How often did you get 1 head? 2 heads? 3 heads?
Each coin has equal chance of landing heads or tails upwards.

i) Write down the possible outcomes for each coin.

ii) Write down the possible sets of outcomes across the three coins (e.g. Head, Tail, Head).

iii) Hence, calculate the probability of gaining zero heads, one head, two heads, or three heads.

The probabilities you have calculated are unlikely to be exactly the same as those you gained from your experiment. Why do you think this is the case? What would happen if you repeated the experiment 10,000,000 times (instead of just ten times)?

1.3 Probability space

In Section 1.1, we saw that a random variable provides a map between a set of outcomes and their respective probabilities. We can think of these probabilities as being represented by a probability space.

The probability space (often represented as Ω) represents all of the possible outcomes for the random variable. The total area represented by the probability space will always be equal to 1, because this space represents all of the possible outcomes. Diagrammatically, the probability space is often represented as a rectangular space, which the domain of outcomes maps onto, as shown in Figure 1.9.

Within the probability space, the proportion of space taken up by each outcome represents the probability of that outcome. Let's think back to the example where we flipped a coin twice, and counted the number of heads achieved. There were three possible outcomes: gaining zero heads, gaining one head, and gaining two heads. We can represent the probabilities of each of these outcomes in the probability space, as illustrated in Figure 1.10.

The area covered by each outcome represents the likelihood, or probability, of each outcome. The top left quarter (shaded in dark blue), represents gaining two heads. The top right and bottom left corners (shaded in light blue) represents the outcome of gaining exactly one head, and the bottom right represents gaining zero heads.

Figure 1.9 A representation of the probability space.

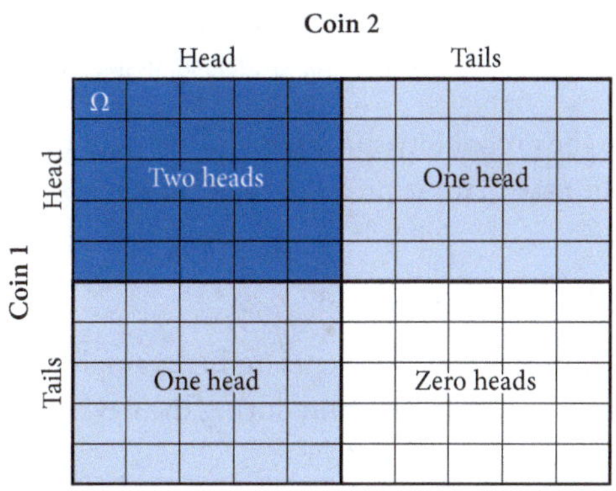

Figure 1.10 Probability space of all pairs of outcomes from flipping two coins.

As such, half of the probability space is devoted to gaining one head, one quarter to gaining two heads, and one quarter to zero heads. In this example, because it is impossible to gain both zero heads and two heads at the same time, the sum of all of these probabilities is equal to 1. In this example, all of the outcomes are mutually exclusive—that is, it is impossible to simultaneously achieve both two heads and one head at the same time. We will discuss what it means for outcomes not to be mutually exclusive later in the chapter.

1.3.1 Venn diagrams, probabilities, intersections, and non-mutually exclusive outcomes

Suppose that you are going on holiday, and you want to think about what clothes to pack. You might, therefore, be interested in the probability that on any given day of your holiday it is sunny, or on any given day it rains.

Suppose that the probability of rain on a given day is 20 per cent. For simplicity, we will denote the probability that a given day has rain as $P(Rain) = 0.2$. We can denote this probability in the probability space using a simple Venn diagram.

A Venn diagram represents the entire probability space as a rectangle (of area 1), and individual events as shapes (often circles) within the probability space. The size of the circle (relative to the total area of the probability space) represents the probability of that particular event occurring. The simple case of representing either the probability of Rain or No Rain is represented in Figure 1.11. The shaded area, in the circle, represents the outcome that a given day has rain; this makes up 20 per cent of the overall area of the probability space, representing a probability of 0.2. Similarly, the unshaded area outside of the circle represents the event of no rain on a given day.

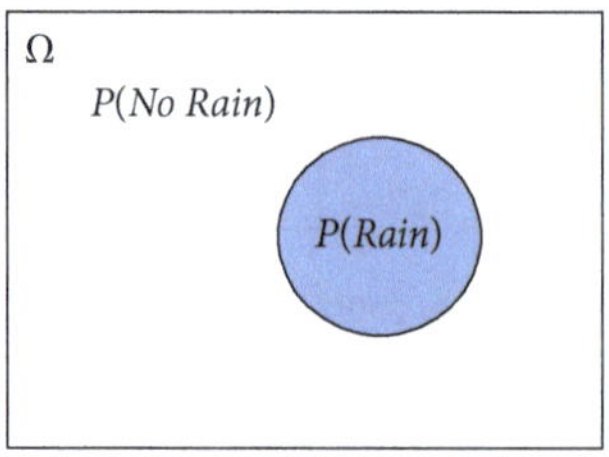

Figure 1.11 A simple Venn diagram representing the probability that a given day has rain or no rain.

Since the total area in the probability space is equal to 1, and the event of Rain takes up an area of 0.2, it must by the case that the probability of No Rain is equal to 1 minus the probability of rain:

$$P(No\ Rain) = 1 - P(Rain) = 1 - 0.2 = 0.8$$

We have defined two mutually exclusive events in this example: it cannot be the case that a day has both rain during the day, and no rain during the day. As such, the two events have no overlap, and their probabilities add up to 1.

We might also know that the probability of sun on any given day is equal to 30 per cent, or 0.3. Using the same notation as before:

$$P(Sun) = 0.3, \; P(No\ Sun) = 1 - P(Sun) = 1 - 0.3 = 0.7$$

Now, just because rain falls on a given day, this does not prohibit the possibility that you will also have some sunny spells during the day.

$$P(Rain) = 0.2$$

$$P(Sun) = 0.3$$

The notation that we are using here is very imprecise, as we are only really specifying outcomes, rather than relating to a random variable. We will also need to define the absence of Rain, or the absence of Sun.

Since on some days, there will be both Rain and Sun (e.g. it might rain in the morning, and then be sunny in the afternoon). We denote this outcome of both Rain and Sun using the symbol $\cap$. This is the known as the intersection of the two outcomes.

$$P(Rain \cap Sun)$$

We could represent this in our probability space by drawing a Venn diagram, which often represents different outcomes as circles (but could be any shape), and when both outcomes occur, the shapes overlap with each other.

In a Venn diagram, the size of the shape represents the probability of that particular outcome. So in Figure 1.12, because the probability of sun is larger than the probability of rain, the Sun circle is drawn 1.5 times larger than the Rain circle, and because the area of the probability space needs to be equal to 1, the size of the circle representing Sunny Days is 0.3.

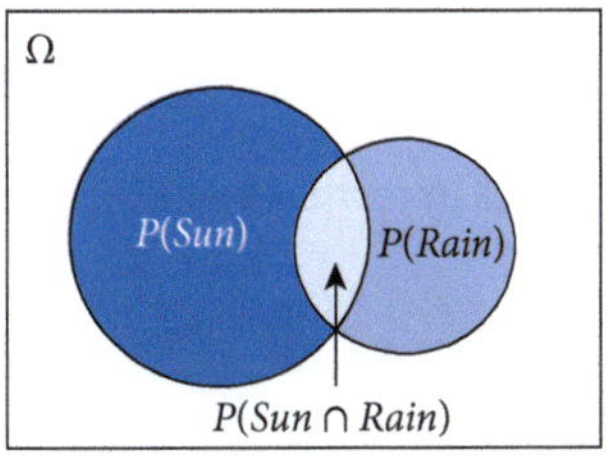

Figure 1.12 A Venn diagram, representing the probability that a given day has sun, and the probability that a given day has rain.

Since there are some days where it is both sunny and rainy, we can represent this event by the intersection between the two areas.

We can break down these probabilities further, by splitting the Venn diagram up into three sections, A, B, and C, represented in Figure 1.13. The probability of a day being sunny

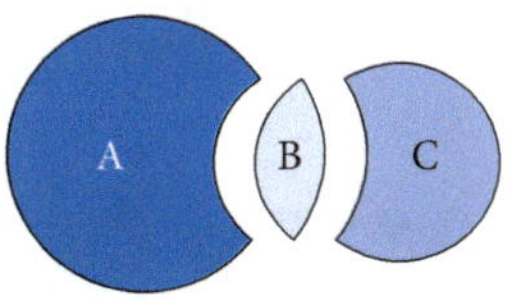

Figure 1.13 Breaking down the Venn diagram.

is represented by the area $A + B$. The probability of a day being rainy is represented by the area $B + C$.

- $P(Sun) = A + B$
- $P(Rain) = B + C$

If we wanted to calculate the probability that a given day was either rainy or sunny (i.e. if a day contained some rain, or it contained some sun, or it contained some sun and some rain), we would need to consider the total shaded area in the Venn diagram. We would denote the probability that it is sunny or rainy on a given day using a $\cup$ notation:

$$P(Sun \cup Rain)$$

This probability is known as the union of the two outcomes. In terms of Figure 1.13, this area would be equal to $A + B + C$:

$$P(Sun \cup Rain) = A + B + C$$

However, calculating this probability is a little more tricky, as we could not just add together the probability that a day contains sunny periods to the probability that a day contains rain, as we would include the intersection twice:

$$P(Sun) + P(Rain) = (A + B) + (B + C) = A + 2B + C \neq P(Sun \cup Rain)$$

If we wanted to calculate the probability of a day being either sunny or rainy, we would need to take account of the fact that area B is counted twice, and so we would need to subtract one B away:

$$P(Sun \cup Rain) = A + 2B + C - B = A + B + C$$

More formally, we can represent this in terms of our three probabilities:

- $P(Sun)$
- $P(Rain)$
- $P(Sun \cap Rain)$

If we added $P(Sun) + P(Rain)$, then the intersection, $P(Sun \cap Rain)$, would be included in both the sunny circle and the rainy circle. As such, if we wish to calculate the probability of the union of the two outcomes, we need to subtract the intersection:

$$P(Sun \cup Rain) = P(Sun) + P(Rain) - P(Sun \cap Rain)$$

You will hopefully have noticed that not all of the Venn diagram is shaded. Over half of the space is left empty; you may be asking what this represents. Well, in terms of the weather, that would represent all of those days when it is neither sunny or rainy. This would represent those cloudy days where it doesn't rain, but you don't see the sun all day!

1.3.2 An alternative way of representing Venn diagrams

Conventionally, Venn diagrams represent the probability of outcomes using circles, but sometimes it is difficult to ensure that they are drawn to scale. It can be more helpful to use rectangles to represent the possible outcomes.

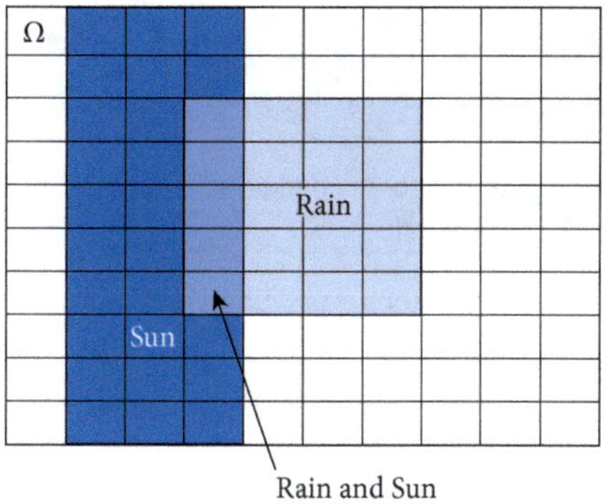

Figure 1.14 An alternative way of drawing a Venn diagram.

Let's focus on the example that we've just seen, but suppose that the probability of a day being both rainy and sunny is equal to 5 per cent.

In this simple example, illustrated in Figure 1.14, we have represented the probability space as containing 100 equally sized rectangles. Each small rectangle represents a probability of 0.01 (or 1 per cent of the space).

This helps us, because we can see that the outcome *Sun* takes 30 squares (i.e. 30 per cent of the total probability space), *Rain* takes up 20 squares (i.e. 20 per cent of the total probability space), and the intersection between the two takes up 5 squares.

In this example, we could then calculate the probability of the union of the two outcomes as:

$$P(Sun \cup Rain) = 0.3 + 0.2 - 0.05 = 0.45$$

We can check this answer, using our Venn diagram in Figure 1.14, and can see that, in total, 45 (out of 100) of the squares are shaded. That is, $\frac{45}{100} = 0.45$ are shaded.

The final thing to do would be to find the probability that it was neither sunny nor rainy. This outcome is represented by the unshaded portion of the Venn diagram; that is, where the diagram is not shaded, it represents days when there is neither rain nor sun.

If we know the probability of the union of the outcomes, then we can use the fact that the total area in the probability space is equal to 1, and so the probability that it is neither rainy nor sunny would be equal to:

$$1 - P(WEATHER = Sun \cup WEATHER = Rain) = 1 - 0.45 = 0.55$$

FORMAL DEFINITION

Suppose that there are a set of possible outcomes $\omega_1, \omega_2, \omega_3, \ldots, \omega_n$ that can occur within the probability space, Ω. Within the probability space $P(\Omega) = 1$; that is, the probability of all possible outcomes within the probability space is equal to 1. Therefore, if we have defined all of the possible outcomes within the probability space, the probability of the union of all of these outcomes is:

$$P(\omega_1 \cup \omega_2 \cup \omega_3 \cup \ldots \cup \omega_n) = 1$$

FORMAL NOTATION

$P(X = x)$	The marginal (or unconditional) probability that the random variable X takes on the value x
$P(Y = y)$	The marginal (or unconditional) probability that the random variable Y takes on the value y
$P(X = x \cap Y = y)$	The joint probability that the random variable X takes on the value x, and the random variable Y takes on the value y. This is often known as the intersection
$P(X = x \cup Y = y)$	The probability that either the random variable X takes on the value x, or the random variable Y takes on the value y

We will explore how to calculate joint probabilities in the upcoming chapters, when we also introduce the concept of marginal probabilities.

1.4 Mutually exclusive outcomes

In the previous section, we considered the weather on a particular day, and it was possible for a given day to contain both rain and sun. This complicates the analysis, as we need to take into account the overlap between days where it is rainy or sunny. In probability, it is often easier to consider random variables where the outcomes are mutually exclusive.

A random variable is said to have mutually exclusive outcomes if the outcomes cannot occur at the same time. So, for example, earlier in the chapter, we considered the number of heads achieved when we flipped two coins. There were three possible outcomes:

- Zero heads
- One head
- Two heads

It was impossible to gain zero heads and one head at the same time. Similarly, it was impossible to gain one and two heads, or zero and two heads at the same time. This is an example where the three possible outcomes are mutually exclusive.

More formally, suppose you had a random variable, X, which had two possible outcomes, x_1 and x_2. If these were mutually exclusive outcomes, then it wouldn't be possible for both x_1 and x_2 to occur at the same time. That would also mean that:

$$P(X = x_1 \cap X = x_2) = 0$$

When defining a random variable, it is usually best practice to define the random variable in terms of a set of mutually exclusive outcomes.

The reason for this is that it makes the mathematics easier to deal with. For instance, if we know that x_1 and x_2 are mutually exclusive outcomes then, since $P(X = x_1 \cap X = x_2) = 0$, it follows that:

$$\begin{aligned} P(X = x_1 \cup X = x_2) &= P(X = x_1) + P(X = x_2) - P(X = x_1 \cap X = x_2) \\ &= P(X = x_1) + P(X = x_2) - 0 \\ &= P(X = x_1) + P(X = x_2) \end{aligned}$$

That is, when the outcomes are mutually exclusive, we can find the probability that either occurs by simply adding together the probabilities.

We represent the random variable X in Figure 1.15. The two outcomes are mutually exclusive, as there is no overlap between the two outcomes. Equally, since these are the only possible outcomes from the random variable, and we know that the probability space must have area equal to 1, it must also follow that the sum of the probabilities here will equal to 1:

$$P(X = x_1) + P(X = x_2) = 1$$

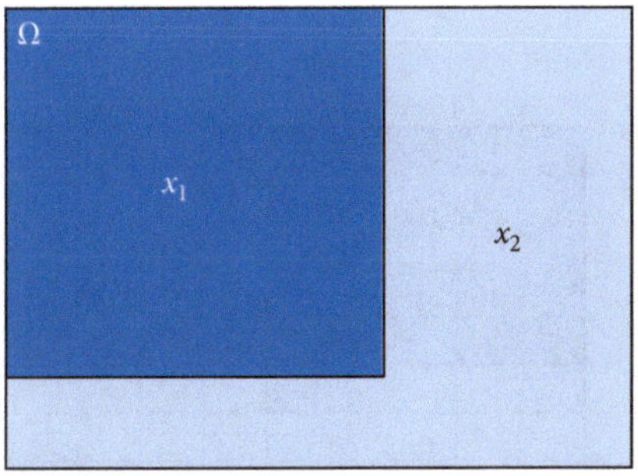

Figure 1.15 A Venn diagram illustrating a random variable with only two mutually exclusive outcomes.

More generally, if you have a random variable, Z, that can take up to n possible, mutually exclusive, outcomes, $z_1, z_2, z_3, \ldots, z_n$ then:

$$\sum_{i=1}^{n} P(Z = z_i) = P(Z = z_1) + P(Z = z_2) + P(Z = z_3) + \ldots + P(Z = z_n) = 1$$

When defining random variables, you will often need to think about how to choose mutually exclusive outcomes. In the example we saw of the weather earlier, the outcomes of Sun and Rain were not mutually exclusive, as it was possible on a given day for there to be periods of sun and periods of rain. In these circumstances, it will normally be better to set up two random variables, SUN and RAIN.

- SUN could take the value 'yes' if there are periods of sunshine on a given day, and 'no' otherwise
- RAIN could take the value 'yes' if there are periods of rain on a given day, and 'no' otherwise

Within the two random variables, the outcomes are now mutually exclusive. However, the outcomes of the two random variables are not mutually exclusive from each other.

TRY IT YOURSELF: DESIGN YOUR OWN RANDOM VARIABLE

Try to think of a random variable, where the outcomes are mutually exclusive.

- What are the outcomes?
- What is the probability associated with each outcome?

Remember, a random variable is a variable where the outcome is not certain, and occurs with some probability.

1.4.1 Example—Flipping two coins

Let's think back to the example we saw earlier in the textbook, where we flipped two coins. We were able to represent a random variable indicating the number of heads achieved in Figure 1.16.

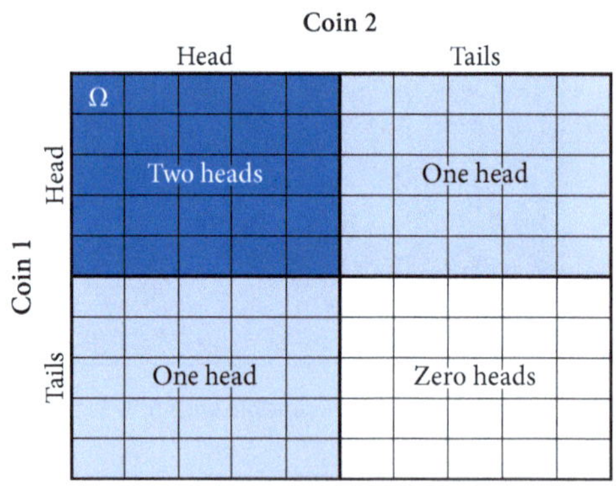

Figure 1.16 Probability space of all pairs of outcomes from flipping two coins.

For formality, let's represent the number of heads achieved as a random variable, H. We know that:

- $P(H = 0) = \frac{1}{4}$
- $P(H = 1) = \frac{1}{2}$
- $P(H = 2) = \frac{1}{4}$

These outcomes are mutually exclusive, and so if we add together all of the probabilities:

$$\sum_{i=0}^{2} P(H = i) = P(H = 0) + P(H = 1) + P(H = 2) = \frac{1}{4} + \frac{1}{2} + \frac{1}{4} = 1$$

the sum of all of the probabilities is equal to 1. Similarly, if we wanted to calculate the probability of either gaining 0 heads or 1 head:

$$P(H = 0 \cup H = 1) = P(H = 0) + P(H = 1) = \frac{1}{4} + \frac{1}{2} = \frac{3}{4}$$

Since the outcomes are mutually exclusive, the probability of gaining 0 heads and 1 head, $P(H = 0 \cap H = 1)$, is just equal to zero.

1.4.2 Example—Rolling two dice

The example when we roll two fair six-sided dice is a little more complicated, but again, if we are interested in the total score on the dice, then the possible outcomes are mutually exclusive. There are 11 possible (equally likely) outcomes: 2, 3, 4, 5, 6, 7, 8 , 9, 10, 11, 12. As before, we can write down the probabilities of each of these outcomes. These are represented in Table 1.8.

Table 1.8 Probabilities of each outcome when rolling two fair six-sided dice

Score	Description	Probability
1	No combination of the two dice outcomes leads to a score of 1	0
2	There is **one** combination (1,1) out of a possible 36 leading to a score of 2	$\frac{1}{36}$
3	There are **two** combinations (1,2) and (2,1) out of a possible 36 leading to a score of 3	$\frac{2}{36}=\frac{1}{18}$
4	There are **three** combinations (1,3), (2,2), (3,1) out of a possible 36 leading to a score of 4	$\frac{3}{36}=\frac{1}{12}$
5	There are **four** combinations (1,4), (2,3), (3,2), (4,1) out of a possible 36 leading to a score of 5	$\frac{4}{36}=\frac{1}{9}$
6	There are **five** combinations (1,5), (2,4), (3,3), (4,2), (5,1) out of a possible 36 leading to a score of 6	$\frac{5}{36}$
7	There are **six** combinations (1,6), (2,5), (3,4), (4,3), (5,2), (6,1) out of a possible 36 leading to a score of 7	$\frac{6}{36}=\frac{1}{6}$
8	There are **five** combinations (2,6), (3,5), (4,4), (5,3), (6,2) out of a possible 36 leading to a score of 8	$\frac{5}{36}$
9	There are **four** combinations (3,6), (4,5), (5,4), (6,3) out of a possible 36 leading to a score of 9	$\frac{4}{36}=\frac{1}{9}$
10	There are **three** combinations (4,6), (5,5), (6,4) out of a possible 36 leading to a score of 10	$\frac{3}{36}=\frac{1}{12}$
11	There are **two** combinations (5,6), (6,5) out of a possible 36 leading to a score of 11	$\frac{2}{36}=\frac{1}{18}$
12	There is **one** combination (6,6) out of a possible 36 leading to a score of 12	$\frac{1}{36}$

If we define the score gained across the two dice as a random variable, Y, then, for example, $P(Y=11)=\frac{1}{18}$

Again, since the outcomes are mutually exclusive, if we add together all of the probabilities, then because they represent all of the possible outcomes, the probabilities must add up to 1:

$$=\sum_{i=1}^{12}P(Y=i)=0+\frac{1}{36}+\frac{1}{18}+\frac{1}{12}+\frac{1}{9}+\frac{5}{36}+\frac{1}{6}+\frac{5}{36}+\frac{1}{9}+\frac{1}{12}+\frac{1}{18}+\frac{1}{36}=1$$

This is a useful check when we have mutually exclusive outcomes. If we get to a total probability that is less than (or greater than) 1, it means that either:

- we have made a mistake when calculating the probabilities, or
- if the sum is less than 1, then we might not have taken account of all of the possible outcomes.

Where the outcomes are all mutually exclusive, we can also calculate the probability of unions of outcomes simply by adding together the probability of the relevant groups.

For example, suppose we wanted to calculate the probability of scoring either 6 or 7, then this would be equivalent to:

$$P(Y = 6 \cup Y = 7) = P(Y = 6) + P(Y = 7) = \frac{5}{36} + \frac{1}{6} = \frac{11}{36}$$

Similarly, if we wanted to calculate the probability of getting a score of at most 6, from rolling two dice, we could add up the probability of getting a score of 1, 2, 3, 4, 5, or 6 together. This is equivalent to finding the union of the probability:

$$\begin{aligned} P(Y \le 6) &= P(Y = 1 \cup Y = 2 \cup Y = 3 \cup Y = 4 \cup Y = 5 \cup Y = 6) \\ &= P(Y = 1) + P(Y = 2) + P(Y = 3) + P(Y = 4) + P(Y = 5) + P(Y = 6) \\ &= 0 + \frac{1}{36} + \frac{1}{18} + \frac{1}{12} + \frac{1}{9} + \frac{5}{36} = \frac{15}{36} \end{aligned}$$

Important note

The only reason that we can find the probability of the union of the outcomes by adding together the marginal probabilities is because the outcomes are mutually exclusive. As we saw earlier in the chapter, if the outcomes are not mutually exclusive, then we would end up double-counting the intersection.

More generally, if outcomes are not mutually exclusive then:

$$P(X = x_1 \cup X = x_2) = P(X = x_1) + P(X = x_2) - P(X = x_1 \cap X = x_2)$$

It is often much easier to define our random variables such that the outcomes are mutually exclusive. Earlier in the chapter, we considered outcomes of *Rain* and *Sun* which were not mutually exclusive. It would have been easier to consider these as separate random variables, where the outcomes are mutually exclusive.

For instance, we could have defined one random variable as RAIN, with the possible outcomes as 'Yes' or 'No', representing whether there is rain on a particular day, or not. In this example, it is not possible for a day both to have rain on it, and to have no rain on it. As such, the two outcomes would be mutually exclusive.

Similarly, you could have a second random variable known as SUN, that takes the value 'Yes', if the day has any sunny periods, and 'No', if there are no sunny periods. We will see, in the next chapter, how we can use these sorts of variables to construct joint probabilities; that is, how we could go about calculating the probability that:

$$P(SUN = Yes \cap RAIN = Yes)$$

Often, it is much easier to construct random variables in such a way that the outcomes are mutually exclusive, even if this means that you need to construct more than one random variable. Throughout this book, when we construct, or describe, random variables, we will construct each random variable with mutually exclusive outcomes.

1.5 Formally defining a random variable

In probability theory, it's often important to think about how mathematical functions map a set of inputs to a set of outputs. Within this book, we do not go into much depth of formality in terms of probability theory, but as you develop your understanding of probability, statistics, and econometrics, it will be important that you consider this formal notation.

Mathematical notation

In this short section, we will use some mathematical notation, relating to sets, which will be useful in your future study. When dealing with functions, it is often useful to be able to denote ranges precisely. In set theory, brackets have very specific meanings:

- $[0,10]$ – By using closed brackets, we are denoting that we are looking at the range of numbers between 0 and 10, including both 0 and 10.
- $(0,10)$. By using round brackets, we are denoting that we are looking at the range of numbers between 0 and 10, excluding both 0 and 10.
- $(0,10]$ means that we exclude 0 and include 10.
- $\{0,1,2\}$. By using curly brackets, we are indicating that we are specifying a list of outcomes; in this case, we are restricted to $0,1$, and 2.
- $x \in [0,10]$. The $\in$ notation is also important, and means 'is an element of'. In this example, it would tell us that x could take any value between 0 and 10 (including both 0 and 10).
- Similarly, if we were to write $x \in \{0,1,2\}$, this would mean that x could take any outcome from the list 0, 1, or 2.

When we apply a function, we have a domain which is the input into the function, and a range which is the output of the function. So, if we were to consider the function $f(x) = x^2 + 5$, applied to any (real) number between 0 and 10, then the range would be the range of possible outcomes of the function; this would be between $0^2 + 5 = 5$ and $10^2 + 5 = 105$. For this function, we could denote the domain and range as a mapping from the domain of $[0,10]$ to the range of $[5,105]$:

$$\underset{x \in [0,10]}{\text{Domain}} \xrightarrow{\text{Function, } f(x) = x^2 + 5} \underset{x^2 + 5 \in [5,105]}{\text{Range}}$$

We can think of $x \in [0,10]$ meaning that x is an element of the domain between 0 and 10. So this function maps $x \in [0,10]$ to $f(x) \in [5,105]$.

Formally, a random variable is itself a mapping process, where we map a domain of possible outcomes first to a range of numeric outcomes, and finally to a set of probabilities within the probability space.

More formally, we define the set of possible outcomes as the sample space, S, and the random variable provides a mapping from this domain to the range representing the probability of each possible outcome.

So, for the example where we are interested in the number of heads achieved when we flip two coins, the domain is the set of outcomes $\{0, 1, 2\}$, and the random variable maps these outcomes onto a set of probabilities in the range $[0,1]$.

1.5.1 Probability distributions

An important concept, which we will keep returning to, is the idea of a probability mass function (PMF).[2] Every discrete random variable has a probability mass function, and this tells us about all of the possible outcomes of the random variable, and the probabilities of each of the possible outcomes. The probability mass function acts to map the outcomes of the random variables to probability space.

The random variables we have looked at so far are known as discrete random variables. This means that there are a finite number of discrete outcomes (e.g. heads and tails for the flip of a coin would be two discrete outcomes). Discrete random variables[3] can be described in terms of the PMF, which describes the probability of each of the possible outcomes. For the sake of this book, we will define the PMF of a random variable to be well defined if:

- all of the outcomes are mutually exclusive
- all of the probabilities lie between 0 and 1.
- all of the outcomes are defined, and hence, the sum of the probabilities is equal to 1.

To illustrate this, let's consider a really simple random variable, representing the outcome from a flip of a coin, which we will represent using the random variable C. This random variable can take two possible outcomes: 'heads' or 'tails'. If this is a fair coin, the likelihood of landing heads upwards will be exactly the same as the likelihood of landing tails upwards.[4]

We can represent the PMF as follows:

$$C = \begin{cases} Heads, & P(C = Heads) = \dfrac{1}{2} \\ Tails, & P(C = Tails) = \dfrac{1}{2} \end{cases}$$

[2] Probability mass functions are often also known as probability distribution functions. We use the term mass as the weight of the probability is placed on particular values for the random variables.

[3] There is a second type of random variable, known as continuous random variable, that we will look at later in this book, where there are an infinite number of possible outcomes. The notation and mathematics related to continuous random variables are slightly different from discrete random variables.

[4] Some smart students always point out that, in principle, it is possible for a coin to land in a crack on the floor, and become wedged, so that the coin is neither heads nor tails upwards, but instead lands on its edge. While this is in theory possible, we are ignoring this possibility.

So, if we want to check that this is a well-defined PMF, we need to check the three conditions. These are relatively trivial to show:

1.	All of the outcomes are mutually exclusive.	The coin cannot land with both the heads and tails side of the coin facing upwards at the same time, so the outcomes are mutually exclusive.
2.	All of the probabilities lie between 0 and 1.	Both probabilities are equal to 0.5, so these both lie between 0 and 1.
3.	All of the outcomes are defined, and hence, the sum of the probabilities is equal to 1.	If we add the probabilities together, $\frac{1}{2}+\frac{1}{2}=1$, so we have defined all of the possible outcomes; that is, there is no 'missing' probability.

As we move into discussing statistics, we will often care more about numerical outcomes, so we could instead consider a second random variable, representing the roll of a single six-sided dice.

However, this dice is a loaded dice, where the dice lands with a 1 for 50 per cent of the time, and the other five outcomes have equal probabilities. Let's represent the roll of this dice as a random variable that we will denote D. There are six possible outcomes, each of which is mutually exclusive. (You cannot have the dice landing with both 1 and 2 on the top of the dice.)

We can represent the PMF as:

$$D = \begin{cases} 1, & P(D=1) = \frac{1}{2} \\ 2, & P(D=2) = \frac{1}{10} \\ 3, & P(D=3) = \frac{1}{10} \\ 4, & P(D=4) = \frac{1}{10} \\ 5, & P(D=5) = \frac{1}{10} \\ 6, & P(D=6) = \frac{1}{10} \end{cases}$$

In this example, it's less clear that we've correctly written down the PMF. However, we can do exactly the same checks as before, and we can see immediately that the outcomes are mutually exclusive, and similarly that all of the probabilities are between 0 and 1.

The only thing to check is whether we have accounted for all of the probabilities:

$$\frac{1}{2}+\frac{1}{10}+\frac{1}{10}+\frac{1}{10}+\frac{1}{10}+\frac{1}{10}=1$$

Since the sum of the probabilities relating to the (mutually exclusive) outcomes is equal to 1, we can see that the PMF is well defined.[5]

Worked example 1.1: Hair colour of native Scots

We are presented with an incomplete PMF, representing the hair colour of native Scots.[6] The random variable HAIR takes four possible outcomes: Black, Brown, Fair, and Red. However, one of the probabilities is missing.

$$HAIR = \begin{cases} Black, & P(HAIR = Black) = 0.18 \\ Brown, & P(HAIR = Brown) = 0.47 \\ Fair, & P(HAIR = Fair) = 0.21 \\ Red, & P(HAIR = Red) = ???? \end{cases}$$

We need to calculate the probability that a randomly chosen native Scot has red hair. However, to do so, we will need to make two key assumptions:

1. That hair colours are mutually exclusive. That is, an individual can't have both Black and Brown hair. This is not a particularly controversial assumption.
2. That we have fully described all possible outcomes. While there may be bald or grey-haired individuals in the population, this random variable is describing their hair colour before they either lost their hair or became grey.

To calculate the missing probability, we know that the total probability must sum to 1. That is, since we have defined all of the outcomes, and those outcomes are mutually exclusive:

$$P(Hair = Black) + P(Hair = Brown) + P(Hair = Fair) + P(Hair = Red) = 1$$

Thus, we can substitute in the probabilities to give us:

$$0.18 + 0.47 + 0.21 + P(Hair = Red) = 1 \Rightarrow P(Hair = Red) = 0.14$$

[5] This is, indeed, a strange dice. We normally assume that dice are fair, and have equal probabilities of gaining any possible outcome. Indeed, earlier in this chapter, the dice we considered were fair, and the probability of gaining any outcome was equal to $\frac{1}{6}$. We have introduced a loaded dice simply to illustrate what a PMF would look like when the probabilities are not equal.

If you are playing a game of chance with someone which involves rolling a (single) dice, and you note that one number is coming up much more often than any of the others (say, half of the time) after a very large number of throws, then you should probably excuse yourself and leave the game.

That being said, when you roll a dice 10 times, the probability that 5 of the rolls land with a 1 is equal to 0.013. This is a small probability, but would be expected to occur once every 77 games, so it is not *that* unlikely.

[6] This data is constructed from J. Mengel-From et al. (2009), 'Genetic Determinants of Hair and Eye Colours in the Scottish and Danish Populations', *BMC Genetics*, 10(88).

1.5.2 Applying numerical values to categorical variables

A categorical variable is one that takes on qualitative descriptions of the outcome, rather than a quantitative outcome. For instance, the outcomes of a flip of a coin are categorical: the coin either lands heads upwards or tails upwards.

If we want to treat the variable as a numerical variable, we could assign values to the possible outcomes. Conventionally, this might be to assign 1 or 0 to the outcomes; for example, we could assign a value of 1 if the coin lands heads upwards, and a value of 0 if the coin lands tails upwards.

Thus, if we define a random variable C as taking the value 1 if a coin lands heads upwards, and 0 if the coin lands tails upwards, we can write the PMF as:

$$C = \begin{cases} 1, & P(C = 1) = 0.5 \\ 0, & P(C = 0) = 0.5 \end{cases}$$

This trick is useful, as we can then also use these same values to apply to 'counts' of heads. Earlier in the chapter, you were asked to write down all of the possible outcomes from flipping two coins. We can see the (equally) likely pairs of outcomes in Table 1.9.

Table 1.9 Outcomes from flipping two coins

		Coin 2	
		Heads	Tails
Coin 1	Heads	Heads, Heads	Heads, Tails
	Tails	Tails, Heads	Tails, Tails

We can use this table to help us calculate the probabilities of the possible outcomes. Effectively, there are three outcomes:

- two tails
- one head, one tail
- two heads.

Since each of the pairs of outcomes is equally likely, we can see that two tails occurs once, two heads occurs once, but one head and one tail occurs twice. The probabilities are shown in Table 1.10.

Table 1.10 Probabilities of different outcomes from flipping two fair coins

Outcome	Probability
Two tails	$\frac{1}{4}$
One head, one tail	$\frac{1}{2}$
Two heads	$\frac{1}{4}$

If we think back to the previous example, where we assigned a value of 1 to a head, we could do the same thing here, and essentially, add up the values on the coin. So if we obtained two heads the random variable would take the value 2; if we obtained one head, it would take the value 1; and if we obtained zero heads, it would take the value 0.

As such, let's define a random variable H_2 as being the number of heads we obtain when we flip a (fair) coin twice. We can write down the PMF for H_2 as:

$$H_2 = \begin{cases} 0, & P(H_2 = 0) = \frac{1}{4} \\ 1, & P(H_2 = 1) = \frac{1}{2} \\ 2, & P(H_2 = 2) = \frac{1}{4} \end{cases}$$

H_2 is an example of a random variable that follows the binomial distribution. Random variables that follow the binomial distribution are constructed based on a sum of observations from a simple random variable that takes only the values 0 or 1. We will explore the properties of the binomial distribution later in this textbook.

1.6 Cumulative distribution functions

We have seen the PMF tells us the marginal probability of any particular outcome. Where a random variable has a set of numerical outcomes, we can also write down the cumulative distribution function (CDF).

The CDF simply tells us the probability of being less than or equal to a particular value. So, suppose that we roll a single fair dice, we might be interested in calculating the probability that the dice scores less than 4.5, for instance. More generally, the CDF will tell us the probability that a random variable is less than or equal to any particular value we wish to choose.

To illustrate this concept, let's start by defining a random variable, Y, as the outcome from a single roll of a standard, six-sided fair dice.[7] As such, we can write down the PMF of Y. Each side is equally likely, and since there are six possible outcomes, the probability of each of the outcomes is equal to $\frac{1}{6}$.

$$Y = \begin{cases} 1, & P(Y = 1) = \frac{1}{6} \\ 2, & P(Y = 2) = \frac{1}{6} \\ 3, & P(Y = 3) = \frac{1}{6} \\ 4, & P(Y = 4) = \frac{1}{6} \\ 5, & P(Y = 5) = \frac{1}{6} \\ 6, & P(Y = 6) = \frac{1}{6} \end{cases}$$

[7] This is not like the dice from earlier in the chapter; in this case, each side is equally likely to be rolled.

We could also illustrate this PMF graphically, by including a line to represent the probability of each possible outcome, illustrated in Figure 1.17.

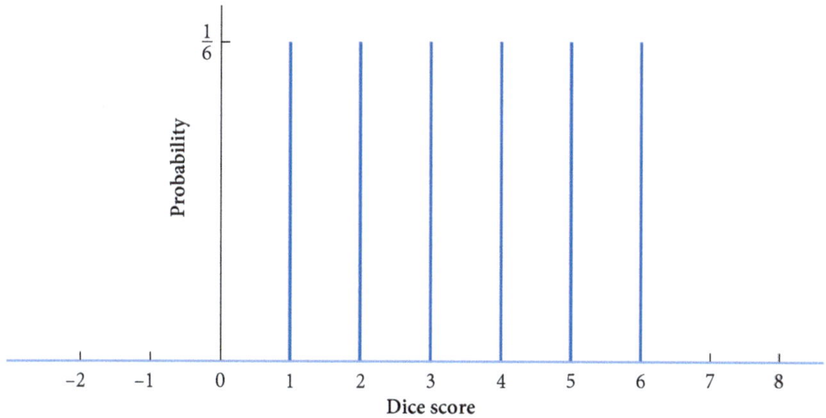

Figure 1.17 Probability mass function (PMF) of a fair six-sided dice.

Now, the thing to note here is that the set of possible outcomes is {1,2,3,4,5,6}—it is not possible to roll a dice and it to land on, for example, 2.5. Similarly, it is impossible to obtain a score less than 1, or a score greater than 6.

Therefore, if we wanted to calculate the probability of getting an outcome less than 4.5 (for example), we would need to add up all of the probabilities relating to the outcomes which satisfy the relationship. So, to calculate $P(Y \leq 4.5)$, the outcomes which satisfy $Y \leq 4.5$ are $Y = 1$, $Y = 2$, $Y = 3$, and $Y = 4$. As such, the probability would be equal to the sum of those relevant probabilities:

$$\begin{aligned} P(Y \leq 4.5) &= P(Y = 1) + P(Y = 2) + P(Y = 3) + P(Y = 4) \\ &= \frac{1}{6} + \frac{1}{6} + \frac{1}{6} + \frac{1}{6} = \frac{2}{3} \end{aligned}$$

Similarly, if we wished to calculate the probability that Y was less than or equal to 2.5, for example, we would add up all of the probabilities relating to outcomes of Y less than or equal to 2.5:

$$P(Y \leq 2.5) = P(Y = 1) + P(Y = 2) = \frac{1}{3}$$

More generally, if you want to find the probability that Y is less than or equal to some value, y^*, we would add up the probabilities that meet that criterion:

$$P(Y \leq y^*) = \sum_{y=1}^{y^*} P(Y = y)$$

We can represent the CDF by writing down where the probabilities change. So, in this case, we know that $P(Y \leq 2.5) = P(Y \leq 2.6) = P(Y < 2.7) = \frac{1}{3}$, but the second we get to $P(Y \leq 3)$,

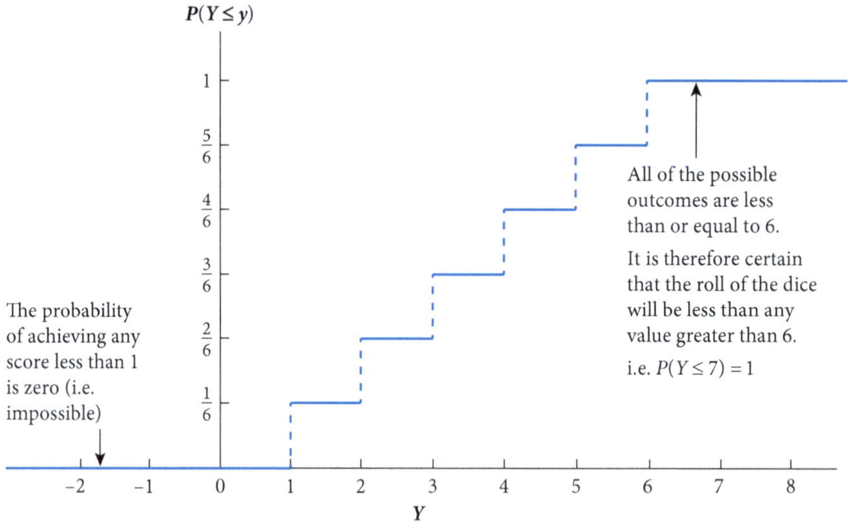

Figure 1.18 Cumulative distribution function (CDF) for a fair six-sided dice.

then the probability will increase, as $P(Y \leq 3) = P(Y = 1) + P(Y = 2) + P(Y = 3)$, as the next outcome ($Y = 3$) is now included.

Figure 1.18 shows a graphical representation of the CDF. The dotted lines at 1, 2, 3, 4, 5, and 6 indicate that the (cumulative) probability jumps at each of these points. So, for instance, $P(Y < 1) = 0$, whilst $P(Y \leq 1) = \frac{1}{6}$. As such, the cumulative probability jumps by $\frac{1}{6}$ at each of the possible values. That is, there is a discontinuity in the CDF at 1, 2, 3, 4, 5, and 6.

It is usually easier representing CDFs graphically, but when we do need to think about them mathematically, we can represent them in a similar way to PMFs: we need to detail the probabilities related to any possible outcome of the random variable. For completeness, Table 1.11 indicates the probability of gaining any possible value for y.

Table 1.11 Cumulative distribution function in mathematical form

Value of y	Cumulative probability, $P(Y \leq y)$	Explanation
$y < 1$	$P(Y \leq y) = 0$	The probability of achieving any outcome less than 1 is zero (impossible).
$1 \leq y < 2$	$P(Y \leq y) = \frac{1}{6}$	The probability of achieving any outcome that is less than or equal to any value between 1 and 2 (excluding 2) is equal to $\frac{1}{6}$. E.g. $P(Y \leq 1.9) = P(Y \leq 1.1) = P(Y \leq 1) = \frac{1}{6}$
$2 \leq y < 3$	$P(Y \leq y) = \frac{2}{6}$	The probability of achieving any outcome that is less than or equal to any value between 2 and 3 (excluding 3) is equal to $\frac{2}{6}$. E.g. $P(Y \leq 2.9) = P(Y \leq 2.1) = P(Y \leq 2) = \frac{2}{6}$

Value of y	Cumulative probability, $P(Y \leq y)$	Explanation
$3 \leq y < 4$	$P(Y \leq y) = \frac{3}{6}$	The probability of achieving any outcome that is less than or equal to any value between 3 and 4 (excluding 4) is equal to $\frac{3}{6}$. E.g. $P(Y \leq 3.9) = P(Y \leq 3.1) = P(Y \leq 3) = \frac{3}{6}$
$4 \leq y < 5$	$P(Y \leq y) = \frac{4}{6}$	The probability of achieving any outcome that is less than or equal to any value between 4 and 5 (excluding 5) is equal to $\frac{4}{6}$. E.g. $P(Y \leq 4.9) = P(Y \leq 4.1) = P(Y \leq 4) = \frac{4}{6}$
$5 \leq y < 6$	$P(Y \leq y) = \frac{5}{6}$	The probability of achieving any outcome that is less than or equal to any value between 1 and 2 (excluding 2) is equal to $\frac{5}{6}$. E.g. $P(Y \leq 5.9) = P(Y \leq 5.1) = P(Y \leq 5) = \frac{5}{6}$
$y \geq 6$	$P(Y \leq y) = 1$	The probability of achieving any outcome that is less than or equal to any value between 1 and 2 (excluding 2) is equal to 1. E.g. $P(Y \leq 7.9) = P(Y \leq 6.1) = P(Y \leq 6) = 1$

Worked example 1.2: PMF relating to the number of heads when we flip two fair coins

Let's consider the PMF relating to the number of heads that we will observe when we flip two fair coins. We will represent the number of heads as a random variable, H_2:

$$H_2 = \begin{cases} 0, & P(H_2 = 0) = \dfrac{1}{4} \\ 1, & P(H_2 = 1) = \dfrac{1}{2} \\ 2, & P(H_2 = 2) = \dfrac{1}{4} \end{cases}$$

We can calculate the CDF by, for every possible outcome, h, adding up the probabilities of all outcomes less than or equal to that particular value:

$$P(H_2 \leq h^*) = \sum_{h=0}^{h=h^*} P(H = h)$$

So, for example, the probability of getting an outcome less than or equal to 1 would be:

$$P(H_2 \leq 1) = P(H = 0) + P(H = 1) = \frac{1}{4} + \frac{1}{2} = \frac{3}{4}$$

We can draw the CDF as follows:

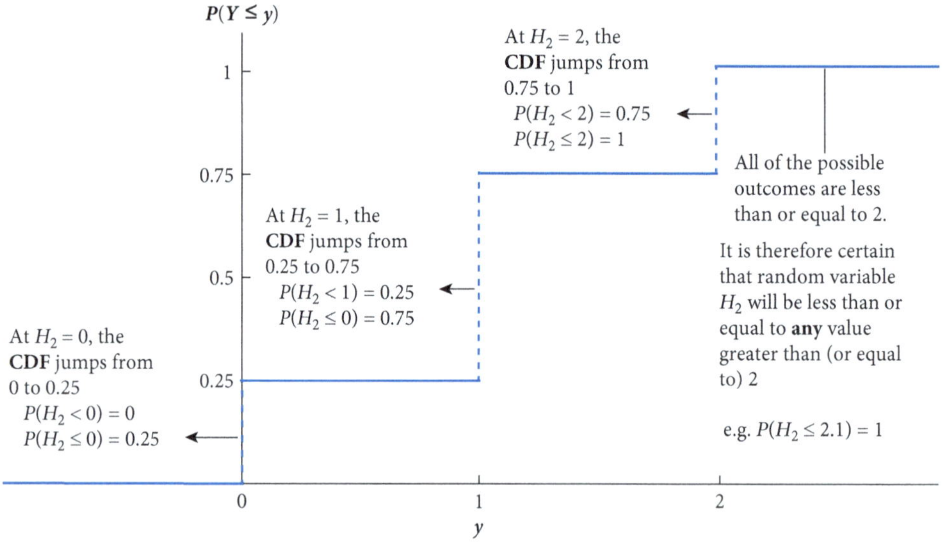

The examples that we see here are relatively simple, but illustrate how we go about calculating a CDF. These become much more important as we introduce statistics. For instance, if we are interested in inequality within a population, we might be interested in the ratio between the 10th and the 90th percentiles of earnings. We could calculate these by finding the values of y_{10} and y_{90}, such that $P(Y \leq y_{10}) = 0.1, P(Y \leq y_{90}) = 0.9$, and of course to do this, we need the CDF.

1.7 Populations and samples

In the following sections we consider populations and samples. On reading this final section of the chapter you should be able to compare populations and samples and summarize how probability relates to populations and samples. What is a population?

An important question, whenever you are carrying out statistical analysis is what the population we are interested in is. This may seem like a strange question, but it is a very important question, and is very important to how we both analyse probabilistic outcomes and make inferences using statistics. How we define a population will help us define how we need to design experiments, and also what inferences we can make about that population.

In short, the population contains all of the individuals that we are interested in. Linking this to the probability space, Ω, this represents the probability, and all of the individuals within the population sit within that probability space.

For instance, we might be interested in wages of all individuals within the USA (including children, retirees, and those who don't work). Then the population we are interested in would be all individuals within the USA.

However, we could equally have only been interested in the wages of female full-time workers in the USA. In that case, the population we would be interested in would have been only female full-time workers, working in the USA.

Populations can also relate to things other than living creatures. When we roll a dice, we are taking observations from the population of possible dice rolls. For a standard six-sided dice, there are six possible outcomes, and provided the dice is fair (i.e. each side has the same probability of occurring), then the population consists of all of the possible outcomes from the roll of the dice, and each of the possible outcomes makes up $\frac{1}{6}$ of the population.

Whilst, intuitively, we might think of populations as being large, in reality, populations can be any size from very small (i.e. 1 individual) to very large (infinite), and how we define the population will matter for our analysis. For example, if we considered the average wages of the entire population of the USA (including all those who don't work, such as children and retirees), then this would be much less than the average wages of only female full-time workers.

To think about how populations can be of different sizes, you might be interested in analysing characteristics of economics students. However, to do so, you will first need to decide what population you are interested in. Is it:

- Anyone who has ever studied economics at any institution in the world?
- Students who are currently studying economics degrees in the world?
- Students who are currently studying economics degree in the UK?
- Students who are currently studying economics degrees in your institution?
- Students who are currently in the final year of economics degrees at your institution?

We have defined five possible populations, but there are many more. As an economist, and a statistician, you will first need to think about what population you are interested in. In this example, there is no single, correct answer, as your definition of population will depend on what question you are asking. However, it is always important to remember that the more restrictive your definition of the population, the less representative the population will be, to be applied to other populations.

For instance, if you were interested in the earnings of Economics graduates, and you defined your population as only graduates of Harvard University, you can only really apply any findings to graduates of Harvard University, and no other institution. However, if you have a broader definition of the population, then the results may be more generalizable.

It may be the case that Harvard graduates earn more (or less) than, say, MIT graduates, but unless the population includes both Harvard and MIT graduates, we cannot say anything about that comparison.

1.7.1 What is a sample?

In statistics, we will regularly talk about samples from a population. Put simply, a sample is a subset of a population. We will often use samples to try to make inferences about the population as a whole.

Since populations often are very large (or may be infinite), statisticians use sampling to try to estimate characteristics of that population; for example, they may try to calculate the probability of particular outcomes occurring within that population (such as the eye or hair colour of individuals), and sampling can be a very powerful way of doing this.

In later chapters, we will introduce this idea of estimating characteristics, based upon a sample from the population, and we will see that how we sample from the population is very important for how we make inferences about the population.

Summary

In this chapter, we have introduced the idea of probability, and have set out a formal way of representing random variables, through the PMF and the CDF. In this chapter, all of the variables that we have seen are what is known as discrete random variables. This means that the outcomes which the variable takes are all discrete values (e.g. 1, 2, 3, 4, 5, 6), and there are a finite number of possible outcomes. This means that we can assign a discrete probability to each of the outcomes.

It should be noted that random variables need not take distinct, discrete outcomes; in fact, many random variables are what is known as continuous random variables. This means that they can take any value within a range. We will meet continuous random variables later in the book.

Key definitions

Term	Definition
Random variable	A variable where the outcomes are uncertain, and the mapping between the outcomes and the probabilities can be represented using a probability mass function.
Mutually exclusive outcomes	Outcomes which cannot occur at the same time. For a random variable to be well defined, it needs to be the case that all of the outcomes of the particular random variable are mutually exclusive.
Probability mass function	The PMF represents all of the possible outcomes (and their associated probabilities). For a PMF to be well defined, we need all of the possible outcomes to be represented, the probabilities for each outcome must be between 0 and 1, and as the outcomes are mutually exclusive, the sum of the probabilities should be equal to 1.
Marginal probability	The marginal probability tells us the probability of any particular value of the random variable, $P(Y = y)$.
Cumulative distribution function	The cumulative distribution function tells us the probability that a random variable takes a value less than or equal to any particular value, $P(Y \leq y)$.

Conditional Probabilities, Joint Probabilities, and the Chain Rule of Probability

2

Learning outcomes for this chapter

At the end of this chapter, students will be able to:

- Understand the key concept of conditional probability
- Represent and calculate conditional probabilities using tree diagrams
- Represent and calculate conditional probabilities using Venn diagrams
- Calculate joint probabilities based upon marginal and conditional probabilities
- Apply the chain rule of probability to calculate joint probabilities in simple games, such as the Monty Hall problem
- Calculate joint probabilities using the chain rule of probability, including more than two random variables

Mathematical tools

- Simple arithmetic
- Addition of fractions
- Multiplication involving fractions and decimals
- Indices (powers) of fractions

Introduction

In the previous chapter, we introduced the concept of **probability** relating to individual random variables. So for example, we examined the probability mass function relating to a **random variable** in terms of the score achieved when adding together the scores shown on two dice. Similarly, we considered the probability mass function related to the number of heads achieved.

However, in both of these examples, the random variable we examined was actually created by two random variables acting together; for example, when we roll two dice, the outcome on each of the dice is itself a random variable. In the case of rolling two dice, or flipping a coin twice, knowing the outcome of one roll will tell you nothing new about the likely outcome of the other dice, or the other coin.

However, in lots of pairs or groups of random variables, by observing the outcome of one random variable, we can update our beliefs about the likely outcome of the second random variable.

2.1 An introduction to conditional probability

In Chapter 1, we considered a simple example of the weather; we represented the weather on any given day by a Venn diagram, illustrated in Figure 2.1. We saw that the probability of it being sunny on a given day was 0.3, the probability of it being rainy was 0.2, and the probability of it being both rainy and sunny was equal to 0.05.

In the context of this book, this Venn diagram represents two random variables. Let's define *SUN* as a random variable that takes the value 'yes' if a given day has periods of sunshine, and 'no' if a given day has no sunshine, and a second random variable *RAIN* that takes the value 'yes' if it rains on a given day, and 'no' if it does not rain on a given day.

$$SUN = \begin{cases} yes, & P(SUN = yes) = 0.3 \\ no, & P(SUN = no) = 0.7 \end{cases}, \quad RAIN = \begin{cases} yes, & P(RAIN = yes) = 0.2 \\ no, & P(RAIN = no) = 0.8 \end{cases}$$

When looking at more than one random variable, it is often useful to consider the conditional probability. In the context of this example, we might ask the following question: suppose that it has been sunny today; conditional on this, what is the probability that it rained?

In the Venn diagram illustrated in Figure 2.1, we can see that:

- 30 squares are shaded for days that it is sunny
- 20 squares are shaded for days that it rains
- of the 30 squares representing sunny days, 5 squares represent days where it rains.

So, if we restrict ourselves only to the days where it is sunny, we can see that five out of thirty days would have rain. Or alternatively, if we only restrict ourselves to days on which it is

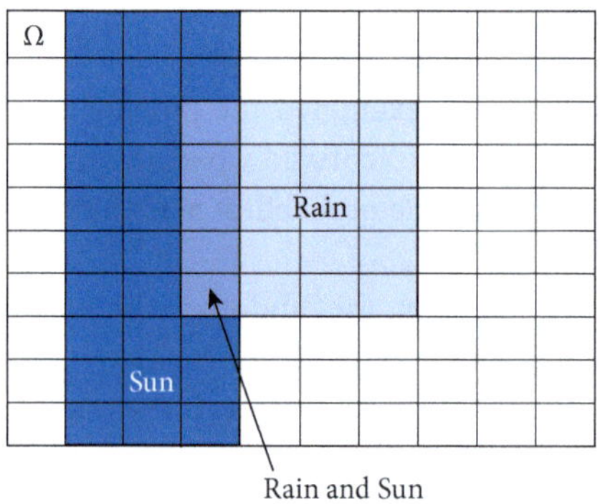

Figure 2.1 Venn diagram showing Sun and Rain.

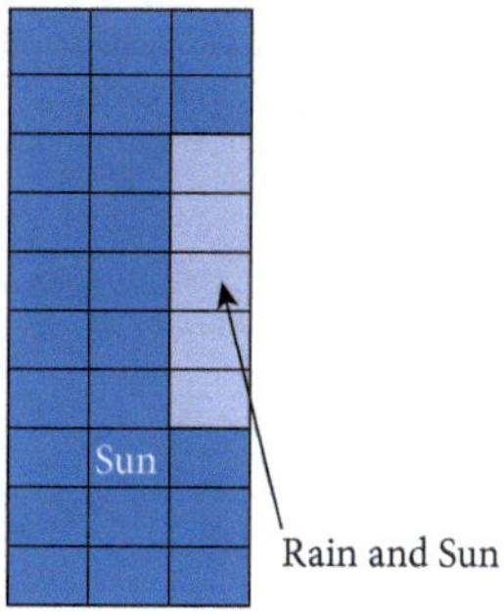

Figure 2.2 Restricting the Venn diagram to only the days where SUN=yes

sunny, the probability that we see rain would be equal to $\frac{5}{30} = \frac{1}{6} = 0.16$. Diagrammatically, the sunny days are represented in Figure 2.2.

This is what is known as a conditional probability. Conditional on knowing that a day is sunny, the probability that it rains is equal to $\frac{1}{6}$.

KEY NOTATION: CONDITIONAL PROBABILITIES

Suppose that you have two random variables, X and Y. We denote conditional probabilities using the following notation:

$$P(X = x|Y = y)$$

This notation translates to mean that we are looking at the probability that the random variable, X, takes on the particular value x, conditional on the random variable Y having taken on the particular value y.

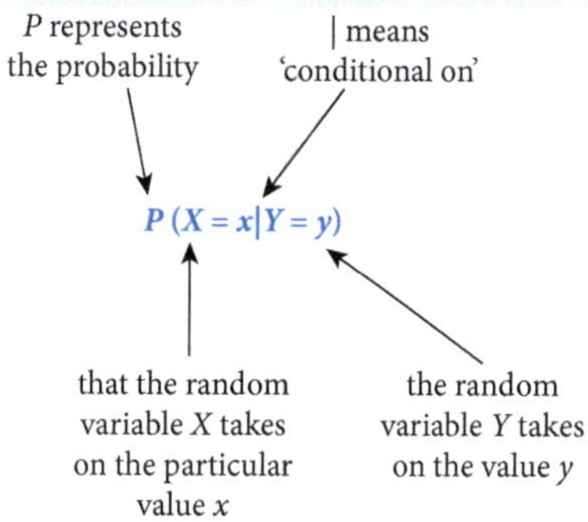

For example, if we were to write $P(X = 2|Y = 1)$, this would mean that we were looking for the probability that the random variable X takes on the value 2, conditional that the other random variable, Y, takes on the value 1.

A conditional probability simply tells you the probability of an event occurring, conditional on another event having occurred.

Applying the key notation to the case of our example relating to the weather, we can write down the conditional probability that a given day has rain, conditional upon the fact that the day also had sunny periods.

$$P(RAIN = yes|SUN = yes) = \frac{1}{6}$$

2.2 Representing games using tree diagrams

It is often helpful to illustrate games of chance using tree diagrams. If you go on to study game theory in microeconomics, you will often see many different types of games illustrated as a tree diagram. This is particularly useful when games are played sequentially, as we can improve our understanding and intuition of a game by drawing out the sequence of the game.

To illustrate this, let's begin with an example. Suppose that I have a bag containing ten balls: six of the balls are green, and four of the balls are orange.

Suppose that I randomly draw two balls out of the bag without replacement. That is, I randomly draw one ball out of the bag, look at the colour, and then, without replacing the first ball drawn back into the bag, I randomly choose a second ball from the bag, and look at the colour.

Formally, to represent this game, we need to begin by defining two random variables, representing the two balls that are drawn out from the bag. Let's define our two variables as B_1 and B_2, where B_i represents the ith ball drawn:

- B_1 is the first ball drawn out of the bag. We will denote the possible outcomes as $B_1 = O$ if the first ball is orange, and $B_1 = G$ if the first ball drawn is green.
- B_2 is the second ball drawn out of the bag. Again, we denote the outcomes as $B_2 = O$ if the second ball is orange, and $B_2 = G$ if the second ball is green.

For the first ball, there are two possible outcomes: B_1 could be green (i.e. $B_1 = G$) or B_1 could be orange. The (conditional) probability relating to the second ball will change depending on whether the first ball is green or the first ball is orange.

1. If the first ball drawn is green ($B_1 = G$)

There are ten balls in the bag initially, six of which are green. The marginal probability that the first ball drawn is green is $\frac{6}{10} = 0.6$. That is:

$$P(B_1 = G) = 0.6$$

If the first ball that I draw is a green ball, then there are nine balls left in the bag, only five of which are green. So, the probability that the second ball is green, given that the first ball is green, is $\frac{5}{9}$. Similarly, since there would be nine balls in the bag, four of which are orange, the probability that the second ball is orange, given that the first ball is green, is $\frac{4}{9}$.

$$P(B_2 = G|B_1 = G) = \frac{5}{9}, \quad P(B_2 = O|B_1 = G) = \frac{4}{9}$$

2. If the first ball drawn is orange ($B_1 = O$)

Initially, there are ten balls in the bag, four of which are orange. The marginal probability that the first ball drawn is orange is $\frac{4}{10} = 0.4$. That is:

$$P(B_1 = O) = 0.4$$

If the first ball that I draw is an orange ball, then there are nine balls left in the bag, only six of which are green. So, the probability that the second ball is green, given that the first ball is orange, is $\frac{6}{9} = \frac{2}{3}$. Similarly, since there would be nine balls in the bag, three of which are orange, the probability that the second ball is orange, given that the first ball is orange, is $\frac{3}{9} = \frac{1}{9}$.

$$P(B_2 = G|B_1 = O) = \frac{2}{3}, \quad P(B_2 = O|B_1 = O) = \frac{1}{3}$$

These conditional probabilities are represented in Table 2.1.

Table 2.1 Conditional probabilities when drawing two coloured balls from a bag

Conditional probability that the second ball is:	First ball is Green ($B_1 = G$)	First ball is Orange ($B_1 = O$)
Green ($B_2 = G$)	$P(B_2 = G\|B_1 = G) = \frac{5}{9}$	$P(B_2 = G\|B_1 = O) = \frac{2}{3}$
Orange ($B_2 = O$)	$P(B_2 = O\|B_1 = G) = \frac{4}{9}$	$P(B_2 = O\|B_1 = O) = \frac{1}{3}$
Sum of conditional probabilities	1	1

Hopefully, you notice that, within each column, the sum of the conditional probabilities is equal to 1. This is because, intuitively, the conditional probability is asking the following question:

> Conditional on (say) the first ball being green, what proportion of the time would the second ball be orange?

That is, the conditional probability $P(B_2 = O|B_1 = G)$ is telling you about the proportion of time that the second ball is orange, when the first ball is green.

Constructing a tree diagram

In games like the ones illustrated in this example, we can often represent them in a tree diagram.

We begin at the left-hand side with the first node. From this node, we represent all of the possible outcomes of the first stage of the game. In the example in Table 2.1, the two possibilities are Green or Orange. However, if there are more outcomes, we would have more lines coming from the first node (as in Worked example 2.1).

In the second stage of the game, there are two possible starting locations: Green or Orange. Emanating from the Green node, we represent all of the possible outcomes for the second stage of the game (Green or Orange in this example), and similarly, from the Orange node, we would represent all of the possible outcomes for the second stage of the game.

If there were a third stage, we could repeat this process, and represent all of the possible outcomes.

In games with multiple stages, and multiple possible outcomes at every stage, the tree diagrams can become very complex.

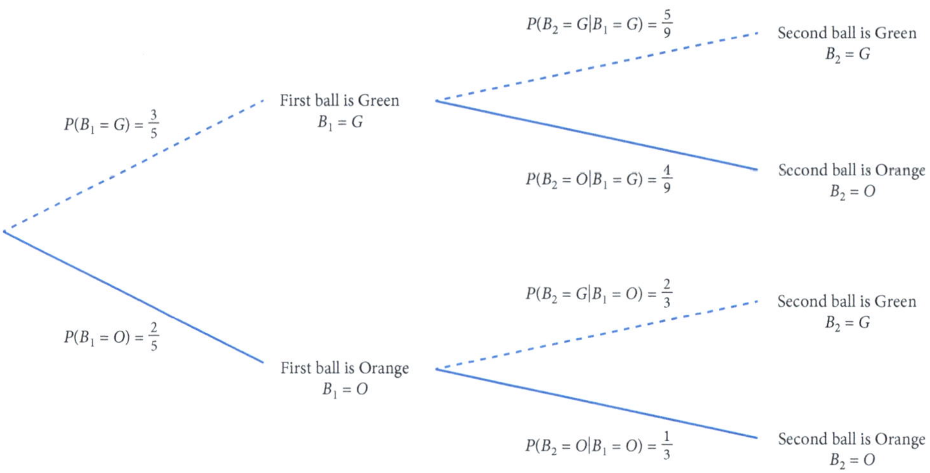

Figure 2.3 Tree diagram representing the draw of two balls, without replacement, from the bag.

The game where we randomly sample two balls from a bag containing six green balls and four orange balls is represented in Figure 2.3. Each of the pathways on the tree diagram represents a possible set of outcomes for the game as a whole; in this case, there are four possible routes, or outcomes:

1. $(B_1 = G \cap B_2 = G)$ – the first ball is green and the second ball is green.
2. $(B_1 = G \cap B_2 = O)$ – the first ball is green and the second ball is orange.
3. $(B_1 = O \cap B_2 = G)$ – the first ball is orange and the second ball is green.
4. $(B_1 = O \cap B_2 = O)$ – the first ball is orange and the second ball is orange.

We will return to this example later in the chapter, where we will use our knowledge about the conditional probabilities to calculate the joint probabilities associated with each of these pairs of outcomes.

Worked example 2.1: The English FA Cup Semi-Final Draw

In the English FA Cup, the teams who will play each other are determined by drawing numbered balls out of a bag without replacement. In 2023, the teams who qualified for the semi-finals were Manchester United, Manchester City, Brighton, and Sheffield United. The balls are illustrated in Table 2.2.

If the first ball drawn was number 1, and the second ball drawn was number 4, then this would mean that in the first semi-final, Manchester City would play Sheffield United.

Table 2.2 The balls for the 2023 FA Cup Semi-Final Draw

Club	Ball number	Location
Manchester City	1	Manchester
Manchester United	2	Manchester
Brighton	3	Brighton
Sheffield United	4	Sheffield

In this example, we can see that two of the clubs involved are from Manchester; therefore, the probability that the first ball drawn is from one of the Manchester clubs is 2/4 or 0.5. However, the probability relating to the second ball will change, depending on what the first club drawn was. If the first ball related to a Manchester-based club, then there will only be one Manchester club left in the bag (out of 3), leading to a probability of $\frac{1}{3}$ that the second ball relates to a Manchester Club, whilst if the first ball was either Brighton or Sheffield United, then there would be two Manchester clubs left in the bag, giving us a probability of $\frac{2}{3}$. The probabilities that we have calculated here are conditional probabilities; the probability that the second ball is a Manchester club, conditional on the first ball being a Manchester club, is equal to $\frac{1}{3}$.

Let's try to formalize our notation a little. We might be interested in the probability that the first and second balls drawn out of the bag were both from Manchester. To analyse this, let's define two random variables:

1. Y_1 representing the first ball drawn out of the bag.
2. Y_2 representing the second ball drawn out of the bag.

The outcome that we are interested in is the location of the club. So, the domain of both Y_1 and Y_2 is {Manchester, Brighton, Sheffield}.

In this example, the outcome observed for the first ball will affect the (conditional) probability relating to the second ball. Before any balls are drawn from the bag, there are four balls: two of the balls relate to clubs located in Manchester, and the other two relate to Brighton or Sheffield.

The unconditional probability that the first ball is a Manchester-based club is $\frac{1}{2}$.

$$P(Y_1 = Manchester) = \frac{1}{2}$$

When it comes to drawing the second ball, there will only be three balls left in the bag, and the probability that the second ball drawn is a Manchester club will depend on whether the first ball was a Manchester club (or not).

- If the first ball drawn was a Manchester club, $Y_1 = Manchester$, then there will be three balls left in the bag, only one of which is a Manchester club, so the probability that the second ball is a Manchester club is $\frac{1}{3}$. That is, $P(Y_2 = Manchester|Y_1 = Manchester) = \frac{1}{3}$.

- If the first ball drawn was not a Manchester club (so either $Y_1 = Brighton$ or $Y_1 = Sheffield$), then there will be three balls left in the bag, with two of the balls being a Manchester club. So, the probability of drawing a Manchester club is $\frac{2}{3}$. That is, $P(Y_2 = Manchester|Y_1 = Brighton) = P(Y_2 = Manchester|Y_1 = Sheffield) = \frac{2}{3}$.

When we are considering the second ball drawn, there are three possible starting positions, depending on what the first ball drawn was. Because of this, we need to consider the outcomes based on each of the possible outcomes of the first ball drawn.

In the case of the first two balls drawn for the FA Cup Semi-Final Draw, because the balls are drawn sequentially, without replacement, we can represent the two balls as two sets of 'branches' of the tree.

The first branch, on the left-hand side of Figure 2.4, represents the first ball drawn. The probability that the first ball is a Manchester club is equal to $P(Y_1 = Manchester) = 0.5$. Similarly, the probability that the first ball is a club based in Sheffield is $P(Y_1 = Sheffield) = 0.25$. These probabilities are represented on the individual branches.

The second set of branches (on the right-hand side of Figure 2.4) represents the second ball drawn. In a tree diagram, the second set of branches continues from what has happened

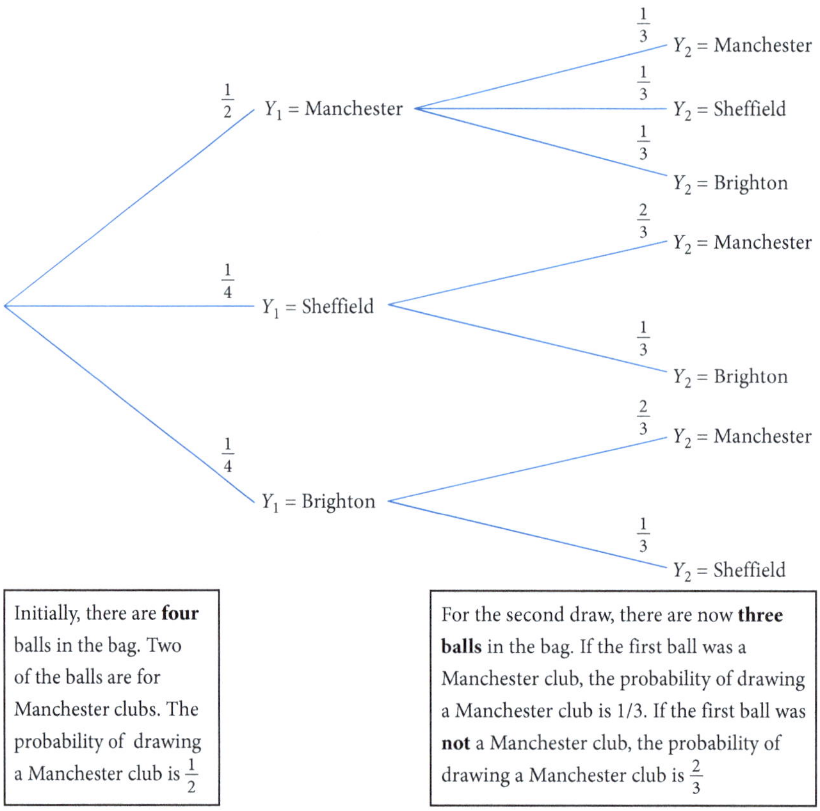

Figure 2.4 Tree diagram illustrating the probabilities related to the first two balls drawn in the English FA Cup Semi-Final Draw.

in the first set of branches. So, the top set of branches represents the possible outcomes, conditional on the first ball having been drawn being a club from Manchester (i.e. either Manchester United or Manchester City). If the first ball drawn was Sheffield United, then $Y_1 = Sheffield$. However, of the three balls left in the bag, none of them would be Sheffield. As such, there would be two possible outcomes for the second ball in this case: either a club based in Manchester or a club based in Brighton. The probabilities on the individual branches represent the conditional probabilities.

In reality, the first ball drawn was Brighton, and the second ball drawn was Manchester United. To calculate the conditional probability that the second ball was a Manchester-based club, conditional on the first ball relating to Brighton, we would consider that:

- If the first ball drawn is Brighton, i.e. $Y_1 = Brighton$
- There are now three balls left in the bag, of which two are Manchester-based clubs. As such, the conditional probability that the second ball relates to a Manchester club, conditional on the first ball being Brighton, is:

$$P(Y_2 = Manchester | Y_1 = Brighton) = \frac{2}{3}$$

Of course, something that we are interested in calculating, which we will see later in this chapter, is how we calculate **joint probabilities**. That is, in this context, what was the probability that the first ball was Brighton, and the second a Manchester club? Or in the context of the green and orange balls example, what is the probability that the first ball is green and the second ball is orange? Conditional probabilities are necessary to be able to calculate joint probabilities, and tree diagrams can help to visualize the problem.

In the case of the FA Cup Draw, if we look back at the tree diagram in Figure 2.4, we can see that:

- $\frac{1}{4}$ of the time, we would expect to see Brighton drawn as the first ball.
- Having drawn Brighton, $\frac{2}{3}$ of the time, we would expect to see a Manchester club drawn, and $\frac{1}{3}$ of the time we would expect to see Sheffield.

That is, one quarter of the time, we would draw Brighton as the first ball; two thirds of this one quarter would then be followed by a Manchester ball. So, the probability of drawing Brighton and then a Manchester club would be:

$$= \frac{1}{4} \times \frac{2}{3} = \frac{1}{6}$$

More generally, if we want to know the joint probability, we can calculate the product of the marginal probability relating to the first ball, and the conditional probability related to the second ball:

$$P(B_1 = Brighton \cap B_2 = Manchester) = P(B_1 = Brighton) \times P(B_2 = Manchester | B_1 = Brighton)$$

This rule is known as the **chain rule of probability**, and we will explore it in more detail later in the chapter.

2.3 Illustrating conditional probabilities using Venn diagrams

Tree diagrams are very useful when trying to illustrate complicated games, based upon lots of steps (or lots of random variables). However, when we are considering two random variables, it can be much easier to consider a Venn diagram.

Usually, we think of Venn diagrams represented by overlapping circles, but at its simplest, a Venn diagram is merely a graphical representation of a pair of random variables, where the area represents the probability. To illustrate this, let's consider the example where we have six green and four orange balls in a bag, and randomly draw two balls without replacement, as we saw in Section 2.2.

In Figure 2.5, the probability space, Ω, is split into four areas, representing the four possible combinations from the two balls. We have drawn this probability space graphically, so the vertical axis represents the marginal probability relating to the first ball, whilst the horizontal axis represents the conditional probability of the second ball (conditional on the first ball drawn).

- When the first ball drawn is orange, there are nine balls left in the bag, six of which are green, and three orange. This determines that the width of the 'Orange, Green' box is six (representing the six green balls for the second choice), whilst the 'Orange, Orange' box is only three wide.
- When the first ball is green (i.e. the top of Figure 2.5), there are only five green balls left, so the 'Green, Green' box is five squares wide.

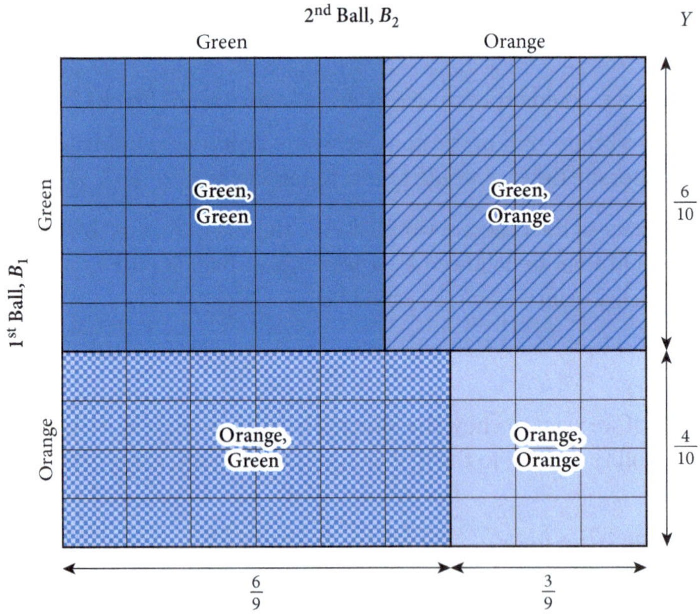

Figure 2.5 Venn diagram illustrating the outcomes from sampling two balls.

This diagram also allows us to visualize a second property; that is, the probability of pairs of outcomes. The relative size of each shaded area shows us the probability of each pair of outcomes. For instance, the area shaded dark blue in the top left hand corner consists of 30 squares. In total the shaded area consists of 90 squares. Therefore the probability of drawing a green ball for the first and the second draw is equal to $\frac{30}{90}$ or $\frac{1}{3}$.

When we are looking at a conditional probability, we are restricting ourselves to a particular outcome relating to one of the random variables. So, for example, we might be looking at the probability that the second ball is green conditional on the fact that the first ball drawn is green. However, we know that the first ball is green only 60 per cent of the time; so when we look at a conditional probability, it is telling us what proportion of that 60 per cent of the time the second ball would be green.

Thinking of this mathematically, we know that 60 per cent of the time the first ball that we draw would be a green ball. Of that 60 per cent of the time, we know that 5/9ths of the time the second ball would be green.

So, if we want to calculate the probability that the first ball is green and the second ball is green, we would consider that $\frac{5}{9}$ of 60 per cent of the time, we would draw a green ball. More formally:

$$P(B_1 = G \text{ AND } B_2 = G) = \frac{5}{9} \times \frac{3}{5} = \frac{1}{3}$$

What we have calculated here is known as a joint probability. This is a probability relating to pairs of outcomes from two (or more) random variables occurring.

KEY DEFINITION: JOINT PROBABILITY

The joint probability tells us the probability that two random variables take on particular values.

$$P(X = x \cap Y = y)$$

This notation represents the joint probability that the random variable X takes on the particular value x, and the random variable Y takes on the particular value y.

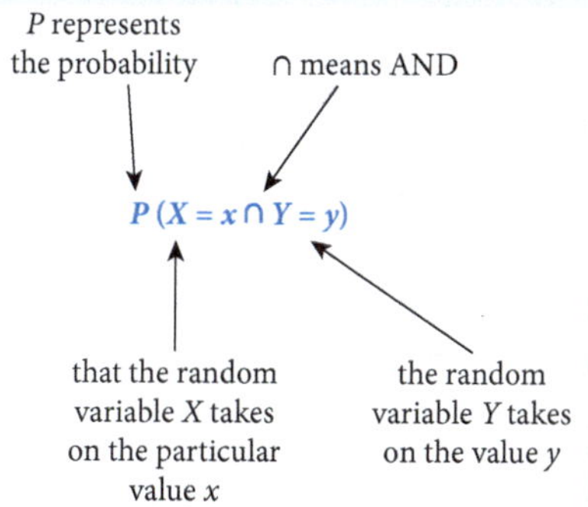

The $\cap$ notation indicates that we are saying 'and', and is sometimes known as the intersection. This is equivalent to the intersection between the two events.

We can think of this again in Figure 2.6, intuitively applied to this example; we can represent the probabilities related to the first and second ball separately. The joint probabilities are what we would achieve when we merge the two diagrams, and lay one on top of the other.

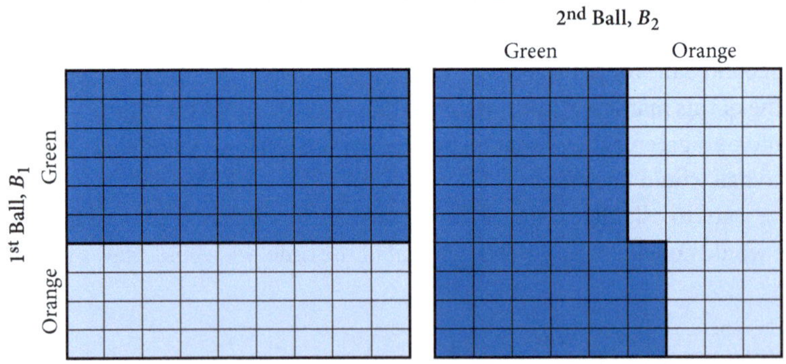

Figure 2.6 Representing the probabilities relating to the first and second ball drawn.

Without realizing it, we have already created a rule for calculating joint probabilities. In the previous example, we constructed the joint probability by multiplying together the conditional probability and the marginal probabilities:

$$P(B_1 = G \cap B_2 = G) = P(B_2 = G|B_1 = G) \times P(B_1 = G)$$

In fact, this is a general rule. If you know the conditional probability relating to one variable, and the marginal probability relating to the other variable, you can use this to calculate the joint probability. More generally:

$$P(X = x \cap Y = y) = P(Y = y|X = x) \times P(X = x)$$

That is, the probability that the random variable X takes on the value x and the random variable Y takes on the value y is equal to the product from multiplying together the conditional probability that Y is equal to the particular value y given that the random variable X is equal to the particular value x and the marginal probability that the random variable X is equal to the particular value x.

To apply this to the example in the Key definition box, suppose we wanted to calculate the probability that the first ball was orange and the second ball was green. We know that:

- $P(B_1 = O) = \frac{2}{5}$
- $P(B_2 = G|B_1 = O) = \frac{2}{3}$

So, we can calculate the probability that the first ball is orange and the second ball is green by finding the product:

$$P(B_1 = O \cap B_2 = G) = P(B_2 = G|B_1 = O) \times P(B_1 = O) = \frac{2}{3} \times \frac{2}{5} = \frac{4}{15}$$

In fact, we can do this for each of the pairs of possible outcomes, as shown in Table 2.3.

Table 2.3 Calculating joint probabilities based upon drawing two balls (without replacement) from a bag

	First ball	Second ball	Probability calculation	Probability
i)	Green	Green	$P(B_1 = G \cap B_2 = G) = P(B_2 = G\|B_1 = G) \times P(B_1 = G)$	$= \frac{5}{9} \times \frac{3}{5} = \frac{1}{3}$
ii)	Green	Orange	$P(B_1 = G \cap B_2 = O) = P(B_2 = O\|B_1 = G) \times P(B_1 = G)$	$= \frac{4}{9} \times \frac{3}{5} = \frac{4}{15}$
iii)	Orange	Green	$P(B_1 = O \cap B_2 = G) = P(B_2 = G\|B_1 = O) \times P(B_1 = O)$	$= \frac{2}{3} \times \frac{2}{5} = \frac{4}{15}$
iv)	Orange	Orange	$P(B_1 = G \cap B_2 = G) = P(B_2 = G\|B_1 = G) \times P(B_1 = G)$	$= \frac{1}{3} \times \frac{2}{5} = \frac{2}{15}$
	Total probability			$= 1$

An important thing to note here is that, if we have correctly calculated our joint probabilities, then these should add up to 1—as we would be looking to explain all of the possible (pairs) of outcomes, and the pairs of outcomes are mutually exclusive. That is, it is not possible to simultaneously gain the first ball being Orange and the second ball Green, with the first ball being Green and the second ball Orange!

Having calculated the joint probabilities, we will often represent them in a tabular form, as in Table 2.4.

Table 2.4 Representing the joint probabilities

Joint probabilities		Second ball, B_2	
		Green	Orange
First ball, B_1	Green	$\frac{1}{3}$	$\frac{4}{15}$
	Orange	$\frac{4}{15}$	$\frac{2}{15}$

2.4 The chain rule of probability

In the last section, we introduced the chain rule of probability, which allows us to calculate joint probabilities, based upon the product of marginal and conditional probabilities.

As we saw earlier in this chapter, we can represent sequential games using a tree diagram. The joint probability relating to the first and second ball can be thought of here as the

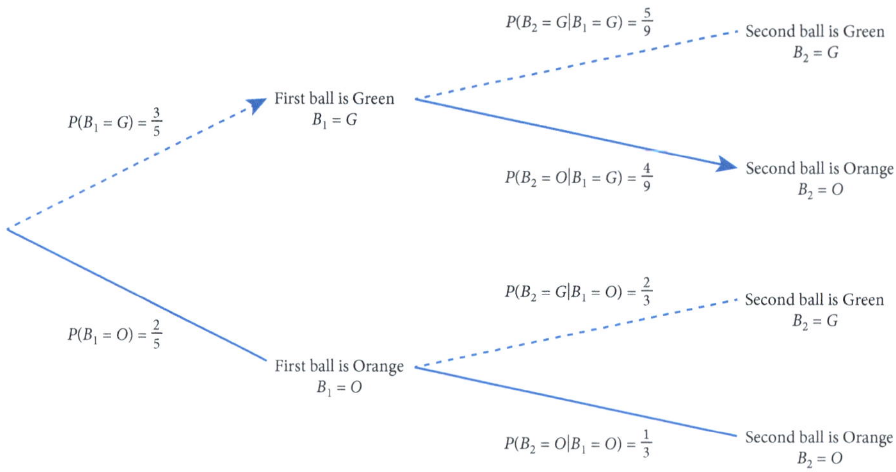

Figure 2.7 Tree diagram representing two balls drawn out of a bag.

probability of taking a particular route through the tree diagram. So, if we wanted to find the probability of the first ball being green and the second ball being orange, we are looking at the probability of following the route indicated by the solid arrows in Figure 2.7.

We know that $\frac{3}{5}$ of the time, the first ball will be green, $P(B_1 = G) = \frac{3}{5}$. Having gone down this route, we know that $\frac{4}{9}$ of the time, the second ball will be orange $P(B_2 = O|B_1 = G) = \frac{4}{9}$. Thus, four-ninths of three-fifths of the time, we will draw Green, and then Orange.

$$P(B_1 = G \cap B_2 = O) = \frac{3}{5} \times \frac{4}{9} = \frac{4}{15}$$

That is, to calculate the joint probability, we have multiplied together the marginal and the conditional probabilities:

$$P(B_1 = G \cap B_2 = O) = P(B_1 = G) \times P(B_2 = O|B_1 = G)$$

This is a general rule that you can apply. It applies to any pair of random variables and is called the chain rule of probability.

KEY NOTATION: THE CHAIN RULE OF PROBABILITY

Suppose we have two random variables, X and Y, each of which has a number of possible outcomes. Then the joint probability that X takes on a particular value x and that Y takes on a particular value y can be written as:

$$P(X = x \cap Y = y) = P(X = x) \times P(Y = y|X = x)$$

However, this could also be written as:

$$P(Y = y \cap X = x) = P(Y = y) \times P(X = x|Y = y)$$

2.4.1 Calculating conditional probabilities

Of course, since we have a formula that links joint probabilities with marginal and conditional probabilities, we can rearrange this to provide a formula for a conditional probability:

$$P(X = x|Y = y) = \frac{P(X = x \cap Y = y)}{P(Y = y)}, \quad P(Y = y|X = x) = \frac{P(X = x \cap Y = y)}{P(X = x)}$$

One way to remember this is that the vertical line in the conditional notation | can be thought of as being a bit like dividing.

So for example, if we have random variables X and Y, and we wanted to know the conditional probability that $X = 2$, given that $Y = 3$, this would be equivalent to dividing the joint probability that $X = 2$ and $Y = 3$ by the marginal probability that $Y = 3$.

$$P(X = 2|Y = 3) = \frac{P(X = 2 \cap Y = 3)}{P(Y = 3)}$$

Worked example 2.2: Probabilities and the weather

In Chapter 1, we saw a (fictitious) example of probabilities related to the weather. To further illustrate calculating conditional and joint probabilities, let's consider a similar example, based upon real data from the Met Office. The Met Office defines a 'rain' day as a day on which at least 1mm of rain has fallen. Let's also define a sunny day as one on which there is at least one hour where the sun is not obscured by clouds.

Good data exists for rainfall, so we can estimate this probability accurately. However, sunshine data is less easy to come by for the UK, so we will use the author's best guess for this data.

At Heathrow airport, on a randomly chosen day, there is a 30 per cent chance that at least 1mm of rain falls.[1] Suppose that the probability of there being at least one hour of sunshine at Heathrow airport is 0.6. Given this information, we cannot, yet, calculate the probability of a randomly chosen day having either rain or sun (or both). The reason is that we still do not know the joint probability that a randomly chosen day has both one hour of sunshine and at least 1mm of rain.

We have two random variables, *Rain* and *Sun*. Suppose that we also know that on days when it rains, there is a 0.5 probability that there is also at least one hour of unobscured sunshine. We can represent these probabilities a little more formally:

- $P(RAIN = yes) = 0.3$
- $P(SUN = yes) = 0.6$
- $P(SUN = yes|RAIN = yes) = 0.5$

First, let's illustrate these two random variables on a Venn diagram. We can see that the conditional probability that a day has at least one hour of sunshine, conditional on it being a 'rain' day is 0.5; that is, 50 per cent of rainy days have at least one hour of sunshine.

[1] Data from Met Office Climate Data.

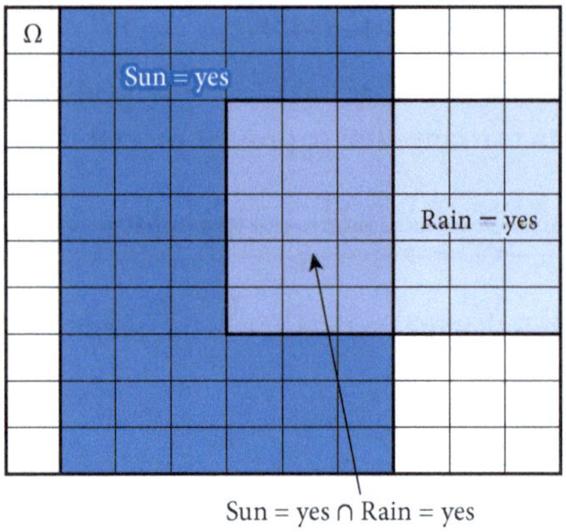

Figure 2.8 Venn diagram representing the Sun and Rain random variables.

That tells us that, on the Venn diagram, 50 per cent of the $Rain = Yes$ area will overlap with the $Sun = Yes$ area. This is illustrated in Figure 2.8.

We have scaled this diagram so that the probability space is represented by 100 small squares: 30 of the squares represent the rain days, and of those rain days, 15 are days where there is sun. Intuitively, we can see that the probability of a randomly chosen day being both sunny and rainy is 15/100 = 0.15.

Formally, we can use the chain rule of probability to calculate the probability that a given day has both at least 1mm of rain and at least one hour of unobscured sunshine. To calculate this joint probability, we need to multiply together the marginal probability that it rains, $P(Rain = Yes)$, with the conditional probability of sunshine, given that the day has rain, $P(Sun = Yes|Rain = Yes)$.

$$P(RAIN = yes \cap SUN = yes) = P(SUN = yes|RAIN = yes) \times P(RAIN = yes)$$
$$P(RAIN = yes \cap SUN = yes) = 0.5 \times 0.3 = 0.15$$

That is, in this example there is a probability of 0.15, or 15 per cent of days, having at least 1mm of rain and one hour of unobscured sunshine.

We can see that 50 per cent of the rain days overlap with the sun days. Since we know that 30 per cent of days are 'rain days', then 50 per cent of those 30 per cent of days are both rain and sunny days, so that gives us 15 per cent of days, or a probability of 0.15 having both rain and sun.

From Figure 2.9, we can also see that the probability of a randomly chosen day being a rain day is made up of two parts. The first part is labelled as $SUN = yes \cap RAIN = yes$. The other part consists of days where it rains, $RAIN = yes$, but it is not sunny, $SUN = no$. That is, the second area (on the right) consists of $SUN = no \cap RAIN = yes$.

As such, the probability of a randomly chosen day being a rain day can be seen as the sum of these two areas:

$$P(RAIN = yes) = P(RAIN = yes \cap SUN = yes) + P(RAIN = yes \cap SUN = no)$$

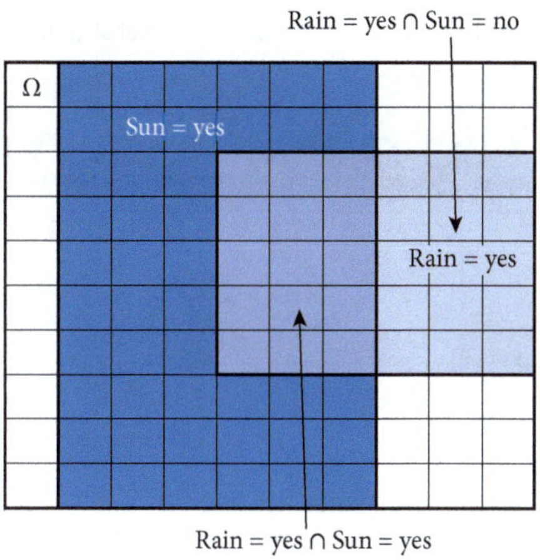

Figure 2.9 Venn diagram representing the Sun and Rain random variables.

That is, we can calculate the probability of a given day being rainy by adding together all of the joint probabilities which involve $RAIN = yes$. This is an application of the law of total probability, which we will discuss in more detail in the next chapter.

Using the same logic, we can also calculate the conditional probability that a day is rainy, given that there is at least one hour of sunshine. Since we know that:

- $P(RAIN = yes \cap SUN = yes) = 0.15$ and
- $P(SUN = yes) = 0.6$

to calculate the conditional probability, we can simply divide the joint probability by the marginal probability that it is sunny:

$$P(RAIN = yes|SUN = yes) = \frac{P(RAIN = yes \cap SUN = yes)}{P(SUN = yes)} = \frac{0.15}{0.6} = 0.25$$

That is, for the days where it is sunny, 30 per cent of those days also have at least 1mm of rain. We can equally see this in Figure 2.9. There are 60 squares representing the sunny days; of those, 15 are representing days when it is raining. That is, 15 out of the 60 sunny squares are also rainy squares (or $\frac{15}{60} = 0.25$).

Worked example 2.3: Hair and eye colour

Mengel-From et al. (2009)[2] collected data on the hair and eye colours of 133 Scots. Their data is presented in Table 2.5. For this example, we are going to treat this group of 133 individuals as the population we are interested in.

[2] This data is constructed from J. Mengel-From et al. (2009), 'Genetic Determinants of Hair and Eye Colours in the Scottish and Danish Populations', *BMC Genetics*, 10(88).

Table 2.5 Distribution of eye and hair colour, from Mengel-From et al. (2009)

		Hair colour				Total
		Black	Brown	Fair	Red	
Eye colour	Blue/grey	3	19	21	7	50
	Brown/hazel	18	31	2	7	58
	Green	2	13	4	6	25
	Total	23	63	27	20	133

Let's begin by trying to interpret what the data in Table 2.5 represents. In the bottom right-hand corner, we can see the total number of individuals (133). Each cell represents the number of individuals with a particular characteristic; as such, we can see that, for example, 19 individuals have blue/grey eyes and brown hair.

The bottom row (Total) represents the total number of individuals with each hair colour (so 63 individuals have brown hair), and the final column (Total) represents the number of individuals with each eye colour (so 58 individuals have brown/hazel eyes). This total is just calculated by adding up the number of individuals with brown/hazell eyes, across each hair colour (so $58 = 18 + 31 + 2 + 7$).

Restricting ourselves to this population of 133 individuals, we can see that 19 of the 133 individuals have both blue/grey eyes and brown hair.

If we were to randomly sample one individual from the population (of 133 individuals), then the probability that they would have both blue/grey eyes and brown hair would be $\frac{19}{133} = 0.1429\,(4dp)$ or 14.29 per cent.

Implicitly, we have calculated a joint probability here. For simplicity, let's define the random variable representing eye colour as EYE, and the random variable representing hair colour as $HAIR$. For simplicity of notation, we will also denote brown/hazel eyes as simply brown eyes, and blue/grey eyes as simply blue eyes.

$$P(EYE = Blue \cap HAIR = Brown) = \frac{19}{133} = 0.1429\,(4dp)$$

Intuitively, we can also construct conditional probabilities; for example, if we wanted to calculate the probability that an individual with brown hair had brown eyes. We know that 63 individuals in this population have brown hair; of those 63 individuals, 19 individuals have blue eyes.

As such, the conditional probability is just:

$$P(EYE = Blue|HAIR = Brown) = \frac{19}{63} = 0.30\,(2dp)$$

However, this looks like a different method to what we saw previously; we know that the formula for calculating the conditional probability is:

$$P(EYE = Brown|HAIR = Brown) = \frac{P(EYE = Brown \cap HAIR = Brown)}{P(HAIR = Brown)}$$

We could check our answer by using the joint probability we calculated previously, and construct the marginal probability that an individual has brown hair; we know that (from our population), 63 individuals have brown hair (out of 133 individuals in total). So, the marginal probability is just:

$$P(HAIR = Brown) = \frac{63}{133} = 0.4737\,(4dp)$$

We now have the joint probability $(EYE = Blue \cap HAIR = Brown) = \frac{19}{133}$, and the marginal probability $P(HAIR = Brown) = \frac{63}{133} = 0.4737\,(4dp)$, and we can combine these to give us that:

$$P(EYE = Brown|HAIR = Brown) = \frac{P(EYE = Brown \cap HAIR = Brown)}{P(HAIR = Brown)}$$

$$= \frac{19\,/\,133}{\frac{63}{133}} = \frac{19}{63} = 0.30\,(2dp)$$

That is, conditional on an individual having brown hair, the probability that they have blue eyes is 0.3—or 30 per cent of individuals with brown hair have blue eyes (in our population).

2.5 An application: The Monty Hall problem

An interesting probability problem can be seen, based on a round of the game show 'Let's make a deal', which ran in the USA from the 1960s onwards, which provides a counterintuitive result which is, nonetheless, true.

In the Monty Hall problem, a contestant is offered the chance to win a prize, often a sports car, which is hidden in one of three garages, labelled, say, A, B, and C. However, in the other two garages, there are pictures of goats (indicating that the contestant wins nothing). Initially, the contestant is offered the chance to choose one of the three garages.

Following this choice, the gameshow host (Monty Hall), who knows where the car is located, opens one of the other garages to reveal a goat, but keeping the initial choice of garage closed. (Note that since there are two goats, the gameshow host can always reveal a goat.) Following this reveal, the host then offers the contestant the chance to change their choice of garage.

To illustrate, let's consider what will happen in the game. Suppose that the car is contained behind door 3, and behind doors 1 and 2 are goats. To understand the game better, let's consider what Monty Hall would do. In each case, the contestant will be offered the choice of either sticking with the original door, or switching to the other unopened door.

Case 1: Contestant chooses door 1

Since the contestant has chosen door 1 (which hides a goat), Monty Hall will open door 2, revealing a goat. The contestant does not know whether door 1 contains a car or a goat, but will be offered the choice of either sticking with door 1, or instead opening door 3. If the contestant switches, then they will win the car.

Case 2: Contestant chooses door 2

Since the contestant has chosen door 2 (which hides a goat), Monty Hall will open door 1, revealing a goat. The contestant does not know whether door 2 contains a car or a goat, but will be offered the choice of either sticking with door 2, or instead opening door 3. If the contestant switches, then they will win the car.

Case 3: Contestant chooses door 3

Since the contestant has chosen door 3 (which hides a car), Monty Hall has a choice, and will either open door 1 or door 2, revealing a goat. The contestant does not know whether door 3 contains a car or a goat, but will be offered the choice of either sticking with door 3, or instead opening the other unopened door (either door 1 or door 2). Irrespective of which door Monty Hall opened, if the contestant switches, then they will not win the car.

The key question to be considered here is what is the best overall strategy if the contestant wants to maximize the probability of winning the car? There are three possible strategies:

1. Always stick with the original garage.
2. Always change to the one remaining garage.
3. Randomly decide whether to stick with the original garage, or to change to the other garage.

When this problem was first published[3], many very highly educated people (including some with PhDs) believed that the strategy should not matter, and whether you follow strategy 2 or 3, the probability of winning would be 0.5. However, these individuals were wrong. We are going to explore together why they are wrong.

We are going to solve this problem by taking each strategy one at a time, and then calculating the probability of winning. To formalize this problem, we are going to consider two random variables: X and Y. The variable X will take the value of what is behind the initial door that the contestant chooses. Since the contestant is randomly choosing between three doors, two of which contain goats, and the third containing a car, we can write down the probability distribution of X straightaway:

$$X = \begin{cases} Goat, \; P(X = Goat) = \dfrac{2}{3} \\ Car, \; P(X = Car) = \dfrac{1}{3} \end{cases}$$

That is, the probability that you initially choose the car is $\frac{1}{3}$.

The second variable Y represents the final winnings from the game—again, this could either be a goat or a car. However, the (conditional) probabilities will depend very much on what strategies are being played. To illustrate which strategy is optimal, we will use the chain rule of probability, which states that we can construct the joint probability by multiplying the conditional probability by the marginal probability.

$$P(X = x \cap Y = y) = P(X = x|Y = y) \times P(Y = y) = P(Y = y|X = x) \times P(X = x)$$

Let's begin with strategy 1.

[3] Selvin, S (1975). 'A Problem in Probability (letter to the editor)'. *The American Statistician*, 29(1), 67–71.

2.5.1 Strategy 1: Always stick with the original garage

We saw earlier that if you always choose to stick with the original garage, your winnings are determined purely by the original choice of garage. As such, if you have originally chosen a door containing a goat, then you will be certain to win the goat. Similarly, if you have originally chosen the car, then following this strategy, you will always win the car.

$$P(Y = Car|X = Car) = 1, \quad P(Y = Goat|X = Car) = 0$$
$$P(Y = Car|X = Goat) = 0, \quad P(Y = Goat|X = Goat) = 1$$

We also know that the probability of initially choosing the car is $P(X = Car) = \frac{1}{3}$, and the probability of initially choosing the goat is $P(X = Goat) = \frac{2}{3}$. We can ignore the cases where the conditional probabilities are equal to zero, indicating that the outcome is impossible. As such, there are two joint probabilities we can consider: the probability of winning the car, and the initial choice being the car, and the probability of winning the goat, and the initial choice being the goat.

$$P(Y = Car \cap X = Car) = P(Y = Car|X = Car) \times P(X = Car) = 1 \times \frac{1}{3} = \frac{1}{3}$$

Similarly,

$$P(Y = Goat \cap X = Goat) = P(Y = Goat|X = Goat) \times P(X = Goat) = 1 \times \frac{2}{3} = \frac{2}{3}$$

$$P(Y = Car \cap X = Goat) = P(Y = Car|X = Goat) \times P(X = Goat) = 0 \times \frac{2}{3} = 0$$

$$P(Y = Goat \cap X = Car) = P(Y = Goat|X = Car) \times P(X = Car) = 0 \times \frac{1}{3} = 0$$

We have calculated the joint probabilities, but what we really want to know is, using this strategy, what is the probability that we win the car? To calculate this, we can appeal to a new rule, the law of total probability.[4] The law of total probability tells us that when pairs of outcomes are mutually exclusive if we wish to calculate the marginal probability, we can do this by adding together the joint probabilities involving the outcome we are interested in. So:

$$P(Y = Car) = P(Y = Car \cap X = Car) + P(Y = CAR \cap X = Goat) = \frac{1}{3} + 0 = \frac{1}{3}$$

Using the same method, the probability of winning the goat is:

$$P(Y = Goat) = P(Y = Goat \cap X = Car) + P(Y = Goat \cap X = Goat) = 0 + \frac{2}{3} = \frac{2}{3}$$

So, using this strategy, the probability of winning the goat is $\frac{2}{3}$, whilst the probability of winning the car is $\frac{1}{3}$.

[4] We will discuss this rule in more detail in the next chapter.

2.5.2 Strategy 2: Always switch to a different garage

We saw earlier that if we always switch to a different garage, then if we initially chose the goat, we will always end up winning the car, similarly, if we initially chose the car, we will always end up winning the goat. So, we can construct the conditional probabilities in the same way:

$$P(Y = Car|X = Car) = 0, \quad P(Y = Goat|X = Car) = 1$$
$$P(Y = Car|X = Goat) = 1, \quad P(Y = Goat|X = Goat) = 0$$

These probabilities simply have the 1s and 0s switched over from the previous strategy. We can calculate the joint probabilities in the same way as before:

$$P(Y = Car \cap X = Car) = P(Y = Car|X = Car) \times P(X = Car) = 0 \times \frac{1}{3} = 0$$

$$P(Y = Goat \cap X = Goat) = P(Y = Goat|X = Goat) \times P(X = Goat) = 0 \times \frac{2}{3} = 0$$

$$P(Y = Car \cap X = Goat) = P(Y = Car|X = Goat) \times P(X = Goat) = 1 \times \frac{2}{3} = \frac{2}{3}$$

$$P(Y = Goat \cap X = Car) = P(Y = Goat|X = Car) \times P(X = Car) = 1 \times \frac{1}{3} = 0$$

We can again use the law of total probability to calculate the probability of winning the car as:

$$P(Y = Car) = P(Y = Car \cap X = Car) + P(Y = Car \cap X = Goat) = 0 + \frac{2}{3} = \frac{2}{3}$$

Similarly, the probability of winning the goat would be:

$$P(Y = Goat) = P(Y = Goat \cap X = Car) + P(Y = Goat \cap X = Goat) = 0 + \frac{1}{3} = \frac{1}{3}$$

By always switching, we have increased the probability of winning from $\frac{1}{3}$ using the first strategy to $\frac{2}{3}$ using the second strategy. This leaves one final strategy, randomizing between the two doors.

2.5.3 Strategy 3: Randomly choosing between the two unopened doors

Intuitively, people often think that randomly choosing between the two unopened doors should have the same probability of winning as strategy 2, but in fact, the likelihood of winning the car is lower in strategy 3 than in strategy 2.

In this case, irrespective of whether you've originally chosen the goat or the car, after one of the doors containing a goat is opened, there are two doors available, one of which contains a goat, while the other contains the car. If you re-randomize, and choose one of the two unopened doors at random, the probability of choosing the door with the car behind it is 0.5, whilst the probability of choosing the door with a goat behind it is also 0.5:

$$P(Y = Car | X = Car) = P(Y = Goat | X = Car) = P(Y = Car | X = Goat) = P(Y = Goat | X = Goat) = 0.5$$

We can, once again, use the chain rule of probability to illustrate the joint probabilities in this game:

$$P(Y = Car \cap X = Car) = P(Y = Car | X = Car) \times P(X = Car) = \frac{1}{2} \times \frac{1}{3} = \frac{1}{6}$$

$$P(Y = Goat \cap X = Goat) = P(Y = Goat | X = Goat) \times P(X = Goat) = \frac{1}{2} \times \frac{2}{3} = \frac{1}{3}$$

$$P(Y = Car \cap X = Goat) = P(Y = Car | X = Goat) \times P(X = Goat) = \frac{1}{2} \times \frac{2}{3} = \frac{1}{3}$$

$$P(Y = Goat \cap X = Car) = P(Y = Goat | X = Car) \times P(X = Car) = \frac{1}{2} \times \frac{1}{3} = \frac{1}{6}$$

Using the law of total probability, we can calculate the probability of the final prize being a car, $Y = Car$, by adding together all of the joint probabilities where $Y = Car$.

$$P(Y = Car) = P(Y = Car \cap X = Car) + P(Y = Car \cap X = Goat) = \frac{1}{6} + \frac{1}{3} = \frac{1}{2}$$

By the same process, we can see that the probability of winning the goat via this strategy is also $\frac{1}{2}$.

2.6 The chain rule of probability—continued

So far, we have only considered cases where we are looking at the joint probability relating to two random variables. However, let's think back to the example from Section 2.2, where we were randomly drawing balls out of a bag. The bag contained ten balls, six of which were green, and four were orange.

We considered the probabilities related to drawing two balls out of the bag, sequentially, where we did not return the balls to the bag. We defined the first ball drawn as B_1, and the second ball as B_2, and the joint probabilities of each possible pair of outcomes is represented in Table 2.6.

The first pair of outcomes is that the first ball drawn is green, and the second ball drawn is also green. Explicitly, we can think of the first probability as $P(B_1 = Green \cap B_2 = Green) = \frac{1}{3}$, and we calculated this probability using the chain rule of probability:

$$P(B_1 = Green \cap B_2 = Green) = P(B_2 = Green | B_1 = Green) \times P(B_1 = Green)$$

Table 2.6 Joint probabilities when drawing two balls out of the bag

	B_1	B_2	Probability
i)	Green	Green	$P(B_1 = Green \cap B_2 = Green) = \frac{1}{3}$
ii)	Green	Orange	$P(B_1 = Green \cap B_2 = Orange) = \frac{4}{15}$
iii)	Orange	Green	$P(B_1 = Orange \cap B_2 = Green) = \frac{4}{15}$
iv)	Green	Green	$P(B_1 = Orange \cap B_2 = Orange) = \frac{2}{15}$
	Total probability		1

Now, suppose that we now introduce a third draw from the bag, which we will represent as B_3. We can visualize the process of the game using a tree diagram, as illustrated in Figure 2.10.

Remember, there are ten balls initially in the bag, six of which are green, and four of which are orange, and we are drawing balls from this bag without replacing them each time. If the first and the second ball are green, then there will be eight balls left in the bag, four of which are green, and four of which are orange. So, at this stage, the probability that the third ball is green is $\frac{4}{8}$ or $\frac{1}{2}$.

$$P(B_3 = Green|(B_1 = Green \cap B_2 = Green)) = \frac{1}{2}$$

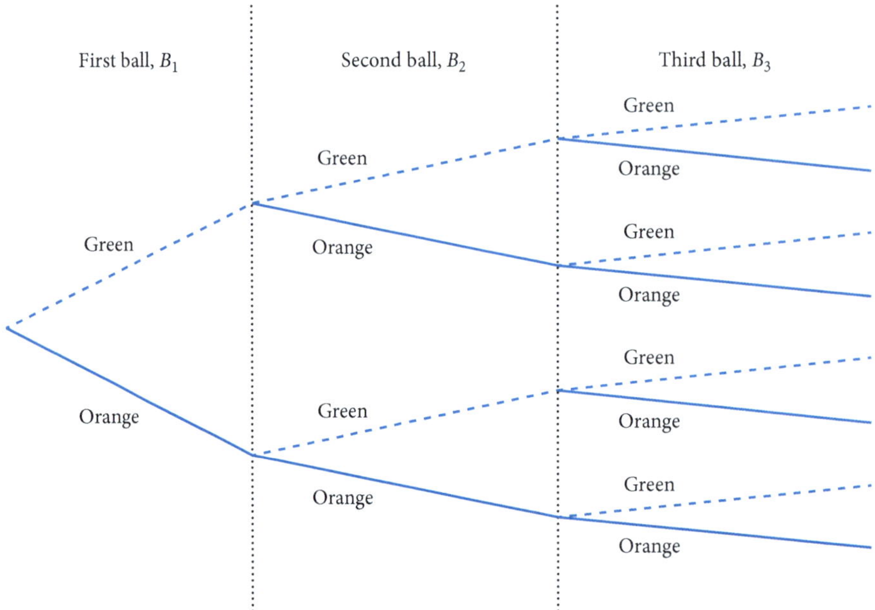

Figure 2.10 Tree diagram representing three balls drawn from a bag.

Similarly, if the first and the second ball were orange, there would be eight balls left in the bag, but now six of the balls would be green, and only two orange. As such, the probability of drawing a green ball would be $\frac{6}{8}$ or $\frac{3}{4}$.

$$P(B_3 = Green|(B_1 = Orange \cap B_2 = Orange)) = \frac{3}{4}$$

We can write down the conditional probability of every possible outcome for B_3 given every possible combination of B_1 and B_2 (Table 2.7).

Table 2.7 Conditional probabilities relating to the third ball drawn from the bag

	Marginal probability	First ball	Second ball	Third ball (conditional probability)	
				Green	Orange
i)	$\frac{1}{3}$	Green	Green	$\frac{1}{2}$	$\frac{1}{2}$
ii)	$\frac{4}{15}$	Green	Orange	$\frac{5}{8}$	$\frac{3}{8}$
iii)	$\frac{4}{15}$	Orange	Green	$\frac{5}{8}$	$\frac{3}{8}$
iv)	$\frac{2}{15}$	Orange	Orange	$\frac{3}{4}$	$\frac{1}{4}$

Suppose that we wanted to calculate the probability that the first ball is green, the second ball is orange, and the third ball is green. We could represent this probability as:

$$P(B_3 = Green \cap B_2 = Orange \cap B_1 = Green)$$

And we can calculate this using the chain rule of probability. That is, if we know the conditional probability that the third ball is green, conditional on the first ball being green and the second ball being orange, then this joint probability is just the product of the conditional probability and the probability of what we are conditioning upon.

So here, we can think of this joint probability as being the probability that $(B_3 = Green)$ and $(B_2 = Orange \cap B_1 = Green)$. So, we can use the chain rule of probability to say that:

$$\begin{aligned} P(B_3 &= Green \cap (B_2 = Orange \cap B_1 = Green)) \\ &= P(B_3 = Green|(B_2 = Orange \cap B_1 = Green)) \\ &\quad \times P(B_2 = Orange \cap B_1 = Green) \end{aligned}$$

So, substituting the numbers in gives us:

$$P(B_3 = Green \cap B_2 = Orange \cap B_1 = Green) = \frac{5}{8} \times \frac{4}{15} = \frac{1}{6}$$

2.6.1 Formalizing the chain rule of probability

More generally, if we had random variables, X, Y, and Z, and we wanted to calculate the (joint) probability that $X = x, Y = y$, and $Z = z$, we could represent this joint probability as:

$$P(X = x \cap Y = y \cap Z = z) = P(X = x \cap Y = y) \times P(Z = z|(X = x \cap Y = y))$$

That is, we would multiply the joint probability that $X = x$ and $Y = y$ by the conditional probability that $Z = z$, given that $X = x$ and $Y = y$.

However, we also know that the first joint probability term, $P(X = x \cap Y = y)$ can be further broken down using the chain rule of probability to be:

$$P(X = x \cap Y = y) = P(X = x) \times P(Y = y|X = x)$$

So, the overall probability can be written as the product of three terms:

$$\begin{aligned} P(X = x \cap Y = y \cap Z = z) = P(X = x) \times P(Y = y|X = x) \\ \times P(Z = z|(X = x \cap Y = y)) \end{aligned}$$

Similarly, we are not limited to calculating joint probabilities relating to three random variables. We can, in fact, calculate joint probabilities relating to as many random variables as we like. We simply need to take a systematic approach, taking account of the relevant conditional probabilities.

So far, we have thought about this approach only through a sequential game, where X goes first, then Y and then Z. However, this approach is valid whenever you have conditional distributions.

We could, for instance have calculated:

$$\begin{aligned} P(Y = y \cap Z = z) &= P(Z = z) \times P(Y = y|Z = z) \\ &= P(Y = y) \times P(Z = z|Y = y) \end{aligned}$$

That is, the joint probability that $Y = y$ and $Z = z$ can be calculated in two ways:

1. The marginal probability that $Z = z$ multiplied by the conditional probability that $Y = y$ given that $Z = z$.
2. The marginal probability that $Y = y$ multiplied by the conditional probability that $Z = z$ given that $Y = y$.

The order of the random variables in the joint probability does not matter. What matters is that when constructing the joint distribution, we multiply the marginal probability by the conditional probability, conditioning on the variable (and outcome) included in the marginal probability.

Worked example 2.4: Simple probability example

To illustrate the chain rule of probability, let's consider a really simple example relating to medical testing. When you take a medical test for a disease, such as the lateral flow tests for

COVID-19, there are two random variables. Let's define X as whether you are infected with the disease or not, such that:

$$X = \begin{cases} Yes, & P(X = Yes) = 0.04 \\ No, & P(X = No) = 0.96 \end{cases}$$

In this simple example, 4 per cent of the population are infected with the disease, so if you randomly sample an individual from the population, then the probability that they have the disease is 0.04.

Similarly, the result from the test is also a random variable. We may expect the test to be much more likely to deliver a positive test if the individual is infected with the disease, but ultimately, the result is itself a random variable. You might know that 5 per cent of the population obtain a positive test for the virus. Let's define Y as the results from the lateral flow test:

$$Y = \begin{cases} Positive, & P(Y = Positive) = 0.05 \\ Negative, & P(Y = Negative) = 0.95 \end{cases}$$

We want to find the probability that an individual, randomly sampled from the population, both is infected with the virus, $X = Yes$, and yields a positive test for the virus. Based on the information that we currently have, we cannot calculate this probability. To do so, we will need the conditional probabilities. We are told that 98 per cent of individuals with the virus yield a positive test; this means that conditional on an individual having the virus, the probability of a positive test is 0.98:

$$P(Y = Positive|X = Yes) = 0.98$$

Similarly, we are told that the lateral flow test is an imperfect test, and some people who do not have the virus obtain a positive test for the virus. In fact, you are told that conditional on observing a positive test, the probability that an individual actually has the virus is 0.784:

$$P(X = Yes|Y = Positive) = 0.784$$

We can now calculate the joint probability that, for a randomly chosen individual, they both have the virus ($X = Yes$) and have a positive test ($Y = Positive$). We will calculate this in both directions.

Firstly, if we use the marginal probability that an individual has the virus, $P(X = Yes) = 0.04$, and the conditional probability of a positive test, given that the individual has the virus, $P(Y = Positive \mid X = Yes) = 0.9$.

a) $P(X = Yes \cap Y = Positive) = P(X = Yes) \times P(Y = Positive|X = Yes) = 0.04 \times 0.98 = 0.0392$

It doesn't matter which way round we write a joint probability, so $P(X = Yes \cap Y = Positive) = P(Y = Positive \cap X = Yes)$, and so, we can also flip round the marginal and conditional probabilities:

b) $P(X = Yes \cap Y = Positive) = P(Y = Positive) \times P(X = Yes \mid Y = Positive) = 0.05 \times 0.784 = 0.0392$

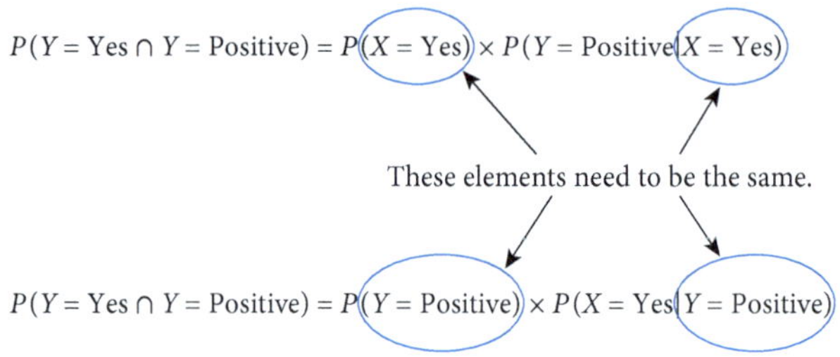

Figure 2.11 The chain rule of probability.

In both cases, we have found that the joint probability is 0.0392. That is, a randomly chosen individual from the population would have a probability of 0.0392 of both being infected with the virus and experiencing a positive test.

The key point in this calculation is that the 'thing' that we are conditioning for is the marginal probability that we begin with. So in case a), we take the marginal probability that $X = Yes$, and multiply it by the conditional probability that $Y = Positive$ given that $X = Yes$. This is illustrated in Figure 2.11.

Worked example 2.5: The birthday puzzle

Suppose there are n individuals in a room. What is the probability that at least two of the individuals share the same birthday? In order to analyse this sort of problem, we can think of the inverse. That is, what is the probability that none of the individuals share a birthday? That is:

$$P(At\ least\ 2\ share\ a\ birthday) = 1 - P(No\ individuals\ share\ a\ birthday)$$

In order to calculate the probability that none of the individuals share a birthday, it is often convenient to consider the individuals arriving in order. When the first individual arrives, the probability that no one has the same birthday is just 1 (i.e. when he or she arrives, it is guaranteed that no one could share their birthday, as they are the only person there).

When the second individual arrives, the probability that (s)he has a different birthday to the first individual, given the realization of the first birthday, is $\frac{364}{365}$ (if we ignore leap years). That is, for a year with 365 days, there are 364 other days when no one else has a birthday. This is a conditional probability.

So the probability that the first two individuals have different birthdays is:

$$P(Both\ unique) = P(1st\ unique) \times P(2nd\ unique \mid 1st\ birthday) = 1 \times \frac{364}{365} = \frac{364}{365}$$

Similarly, the probability that they share a birthday is $1 - \frac{364}{365} = \frac{1}{365} = 0.00274$.

When the third individual arrives, if the first two have unique birthdays, the probability that the third has a different birthday to the first two is $\frac{364}{365}$.

So the probability that at least two of the first three individuals share a birthday is:

$$1 - \left(1 \times \frac{364}{365} \times \frac{363}{365}\right) = 0.008204$$

Table 2.8 Probabilities of two (or more) individuals sharing a birthday

Number of people	Probability of at least two sharing a birthday
5	0.027
6	0.040
7	0.056
8	0.074
9	0.095
10	0.117
11	0.141
12	0.167
13	0.194
14	0.223
15	0.253
16	0.284
17	0.315
18	0.347
19	0.379
20	0.411
21	0.444
22	0.476
23	0.507

In fact with n individuals, we can find the probability that at least two share a birthday is equal to:

$$P(at\ least\ 2\ share) = 1 - \frac{(365) \times (365 - 1) \times (365 - 2) \times \ldots \times (365 - (n - 1))}{365^n}$$

So, if n = 4, the probability of at least two sharing a birthday is 0.016356. It turns out that when there are 23 individuals in the room, there is a greater than evens chance of two sharing a birthday. This is quite a counterintuitive result (Table 2.8).

This is an example of the chain rule of probability in action. We have used the product of marginal and conditional probabilities to calculate the joint probability relating to up to 23 different random variables.

We could represent the birthday of the ith person who enters the room using the random variable B_i. We are not interested in the actual birthday of the individual, only whether it is unique, or a duplicate; as such, B_i has two possible outcomes:

$$B_i = \begin{cases} u, & \text{If } i\text{'s birthday is unique} \\ d, & \text{If } i\text{'s birthday is a duplicate} \end{cases}$$

So, for instance, to calculate the probability that the first four individuals have unique birthdays, this is equivalent to B_1, B_2, B_3, and B_4 all being unique:

$$= P(B_1 = u \cap B_2 = u \cap B_3 = u \cap B_4 = u)$$

Using the chain rule of probability, this can be written as the product of marginal probabilities $P(B_1 = u)$ and conditional probabilities:

$$= P(B_1 = u) \times P(B_2 = u|B_1 = u) \times P(B_3 = u|B_1 = u \cap B_2 = u)$$
$$\times P(B_4 = u|B_1 = u \cap B_2 = u \cap B_3 = u)$$

In words, this is the product of:

- the probability that B_1 is unique, multiplied by
- the conditional probability that B_2 is unique, given that B_1 is unique, multiplied by
- the conditional probability that B_3 is unique, given that both B_1 and B_2 are unique, multiplied by
- the conditional probability that B_4 is unique, given that B_1, B_2 and B_3 are all unique.

Summary

In this chapter, we have introduced the idea of conditional probability, and used this to calculate joint probabilities, relating to more than one random variable.

In the next chapter, we will build upon this, and formally discuss the concept of joint probability mass functions; that is, probability mass functions telling you about the likelihood of combinations of outcomes from two (or more) random variables. However, these joint probabilities are constructed based upon the conditional probabilities we have observed here.

Similarly, we have used joint probabilities to construct conditional probabilities. We will apply this further in the next chapter, to a rule known as Bayes' rule. This is an important rule in probability, as based on observed characteristics about an individual, or a situation, it allows you the opportunity to update your beliefs about other characteristics of that individual. This has very important applications, such as the hunt for missing aircraft, and more frivolously, gamblers implicitly use this rule to update their beliefs about whether an individual is bluffing in a game of poker.

Key definitions

Term	Definition
Conditional probability	The conditional probability tells you the probability of one outcome, conditional on having observed another outcome. For example, you might be interested in the probability of a day being sunny, given that the previous day had a bright red sunset. We denote conditional probabilities using the following notation: $P(X = x \mid Y = y)$ This indicates the probability that the random variable X takes on the particular value x, conditional on the fact that the random variable Y has taken on the particular outcome y. Similarly, $P(X = 2 \mid Y = 3)$ would give you the conditional probability that X was equal to 2, given that we've observed that $Y = 3$.
Joint probabilities	The joint probability tells you the probability of two outcomes (from two random variables) occurring together. For example, we might be interested in the probability that a given individual, randomly chosen from the population, had both blue eyes and brown hair. We denote joint probabilities using the following notation: $P(X = x \cap Y = y)$ This indicates the probability that the random variable X takes on the outcome x and that the random variable Y takes on the outcome y. Similarly, $P(X = 2 \cap Y = 3)$ would indicate the probability that X is equal to 2, and $Y = 3$. It should be noted that with joint probabilities, it does not matter which way round you write the variables: $P(X = 2 \cap Y = 3) = P(Y = 3 \cap X = 2)$ In both of these cases, $X = 2$ and $Y = 3$, so the probabilities will be the same.

Key formulae

1. The chain rule of probability

   To calculate a joint probability, we consider the product of the marginal probability and the conditional probability:

$$P(X = x \cap Y = y) = P(Y = y) \times P(X = x \mid Y = y)$$

Similarly,

$$P(X = x \cap Y = y) = P(X = x) \times P(Y = y|X = x)$$

Note: The important element is that the marginal probability is related to the outcome that we are conditioning upon. For example:

$$P(X = 2 \cap Y = 3) = P(X = 2) \times P(Y = 3|X = 2)$$

2. Calculating conditional probabilities

We can rearrange the chain rule of probability to give us a formula for conditional probabilities:

$$P(X = x|Y = y) = \frac{P(X = x \cap Y = y)}{P(Y = y)}, \quad P(Y = y|X = x) = \frac{P(X = x \cap Y = y)}{P(X = x)}$$

Joint Probability Distributions and Bayes' Rule

3

Learning outcomes for this chapter

By the end of this chapter you will be able to:

- Recognize joint probability distributions, and use these to calculate both marginal and conditional probabilities
- Calculate marginal probabilities using the law of total probability from constituent joint probabilities
- Be able to interpret the intuition and mathematical derivation of Bayes' rule
- Apply Bayes' rule in a number of different settings, including medical testing

Mathematical tools

- Simple arithmetic
- Addition of fractions
- Multiplication involving fractions and decimals
- Summations using sigma (Σ) notation
- Summations involving more than one summation sign

Introduction

In the last chapter, we were introduced to the **chain rule of probability** as a way of calculating **joint probabilities**. The chain rule of probability links together **conditional probabilities**, marginal probabilities, and joint probabilities. We will also introduce a key rule to draw all of these elements together, known as Bayes' rule. As we will see later in the chapter, Bayes' rule allows us to update our beliefs about an individual, based upon characteristics we observe of that individual.

This chapter will begin by formally defining joint probability distributions, and we will then move on to discussing Bayes' rule, which we will motivate using the context of false positives and false negatives in medical tests.

3.1 Joint probability distributions

Suppose that you were to flip two coins, and you were interested in the combination of outcomes that you achieve. Each coin can be assumed to be a fair coin, with the probability that it lands heads upwards as 0.5 or $\frac{1}{2}$. Similarly, the outcome of the first coin can be assumed to be unrelated to the outcome of the second coin (and vice versa). That is, knowing that the first coin lands heads upwards does not affect the likelihood that the second coin lands heads (or tails) upwards.

Formally, let's define C_1 as the outcome of the first flip of the coin, and C_2 as the outcome of the second flip of the coin. We can write down the marginal probability mass functions relating to the two flips:

$$C_1 = \begin{cases} Heads, & P(C_1 = Heads) = 0.5 \\ Tails, & P(C_1 = Tails) = 0.5 \end{cases}, \quad C_2 = \begin{cases} Heads, & P(C_2 = Heads) = 0.5 \\ Tails, & P(C_2 = Tails) = 0.5 \end{cases}$$

Similarly, we could write down the conditional probabilities:

$$P(C_2 = Heads \mid C_1 = Tails) = P(C_2 = Heads \mid C_1 = Heads) = 0.5$$

That is, the probability that the second coin lands heads upwards will be equal to 0.5, irrespective of whether the first coin landed tails or heads upwards.

We could use the chain rule of probability to calculate any of the joint probabilities. For example,

$$P(C_1 = Heads \cap C_2 = Heads) = P(C_2 = Heads \mid C_1 = Heads) \times P(C_1 = Heads)$$
$$= \frac{1}{2} \times \frac{1}{2} = \frac{1}{4}$$

I'll leave it as an exercise for you to calculate all of the other joint probabilities, but in this example, it is trivial to show that the probability of any combination of outcomes from the flip of two coins will be equal, and equal to $\frac{1}{4}$. We illustrate these probabilities in Table 3.1.

Each probability in this table represents a joint probability; for example, the bottom left element (identified in **bold** type) is the probability that the first coin lands tails upwards and the second coin lands heads upwards, $P(C_1 = Tails \cap C_2 = Heads)$. This is an example of a joint probability mass function; we are representing the probability of every possible (pair of) outcomes. Since all of the pairs of outcomes are mutually exclusive, the sum of these probabilities must be equal to 1.

Table 3.1 Joint distribution relating to the outcomes from flipping two (fair) coins

		Coin 2, C_2	
		Heads	Tails
Coin 1, C_1	Heads	0.25	0.25
	Tails	**0.25**	0.25

More generally, let's suppose that we observe two different random variables, say X and Y. These random variables could be an individual's height and weight, they could be the results of two flips of a coin, or they could be the interest rate and the growth rate for a country.

Let us consider a simple example where X and Y are both *discrete* random variables, which only take two possible outcomes. The possible outcomes that X takes are x_1 and x_2, whilst for Y, the possible outcomes are y_1 and y_2. We can represent the joint distribution as follows.[1]

Table 3.2 A general joint probability distribution for random variables X and Y

		Y	
		y_1	y_2
X	x_1	$P(X = x_1 \cap Y = y_1)$	$P(X = x_1 \cap Y = y_2)$
	x_2	$P(X = x_2 \cap Y = y_1)$	$P(X = x_2 \cap Y = y_2)$

In Table 3.2, $P(X = x_1 \cap Y = y_1)$ denotes the probability that the random variable X takes on the value x_1 and that the random variable Y takes on the value y_1.

KEY DEFINITION: JOINT PROBABILITY MASS FUNCTION

The joint probability mass function for two discrete random variables, X and Y, provides the joint probabilities of all of the possible combinations of outcomes for these random variables:

$$P(X = x_i \cap Y = y_j)$$

The probability mass function is well defined if:

- Each of the joint probabilities is between 0 and 1 ($0 \leq P(X = x_i \cap Y = y_j) \leq 1$).
- The sum of all the joint probabilities is equal to 1 (provided the pairs of outcomes are mutually exclusive)

$$\sum_i \sum_j P(X = x_i \cap Y = y_j) = 1$$

Worked example 3.1: Distribution of hair and eye colour in Scotland

Recall from the previous chapter, Mengel-From et al. (2009) collected data on the hair and eye colours of 133 Scots.[2] Here, I have converted the number of individuals with each combination of hair and eye colour into a proportion of the population. So, if we randomly

[1] It should be noted that this is a simple example with only two possible outcomes for each measure; however, we can generalize this to multiple outcomes.

[2] This data is constructed from J. Mengel-From, et al. (2009), 'Genetic Determinants of Hair and Eye Colours in the Scottish and Danish Populations', *BMC Genetics*, 10(88).

Table 3.3 Joint distribution of eye and hair colours, derived from Mengel-From et al. (2009)

		Hair colour			
		Black	Brown	Fair	Red
Eye colour	Blue/grey	0.02	0.14	0.16	0.05
	Brown/hazel	0.14	0.23	0.02	0.05
	Green	0.02	0.10	0.03	0.04

sampled an individual from the population, the probability that they would have green eyes and brown hair would be 0.10. Each of the numbers in Table 3.3 represents a joint probability.

We saw earlier that, in order for a joint PMF to be well defined, it needed to be the case that:

1. Each of the joint probabilities is between 0 and 1 ($0 \leq P(X = x_i \cap Y = y_j) \leq 1$).
2. The sum of all the joint probabilities is equal to 1 (provided each of the pairs of outcomes are *mutually exclusive*) $\sum_i \sum_j P(X = x_i \cap Y = y_j) = 1$.

We can see, trivially, that the first condition holds; all of the joint probabilities are between 0 and 1. We can also check the second condition. Interpreting the notation, for each hair colour (black, brown, fair, red), we will add up the joint probabilities, and then add up that sum across each of the hair colours.

$$= (0.02 + 0.14 + 0.02) + (0.14 + 0.23 + 0.10) + (0.16 + 0.02 + 0.03) + (0.05 + 0.05 + 0.04)$$
$$= 0.18 + 0.47 + 0.21 + 0.14$$
$$= 1$$

We have also, implicitly, applied a rule that is known as the law of total probability. If we want to calculate the proportion of individuals with black hair, we simply need to add together each of the joint probabilities (which also represent proportions, remember) where individuals have black hair.

$$\begin{aligned} P(HAIR = Black) = {} & P(HAIR = Black \cap EYE = Blue) \\ & + P(HAIR = Black \cap EYE = Brown) \\ & + P(HAIR = Black \cap EYE = Green) \\ & = 0.02 + 0.14 + 0.02 = 0.18 \end{aligned}$$

3.2 The law of total probability

In the previous example, we implicitly applied a rule, known as the law of total probability. Before we formally define this rule, let's motivate it graphically. Remember the example we saw in Chapter 2, illustrating the probability of a given day being a 'sun day', or a 'rain day'. The distribution is illustrated in Figure 3.1.

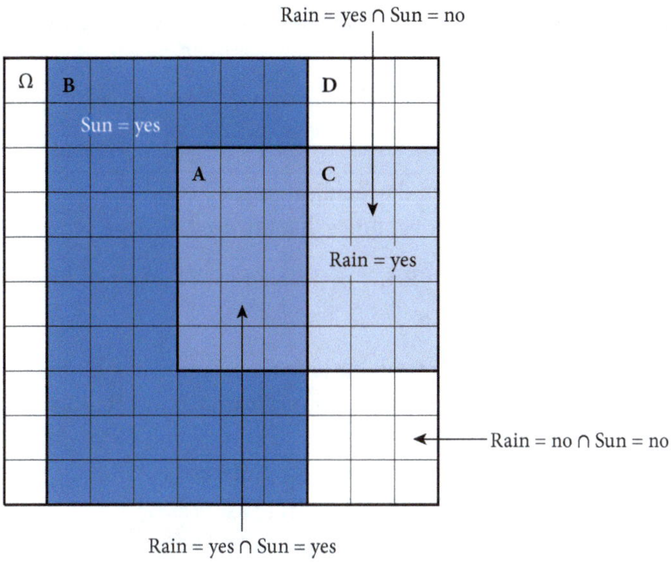

Figure 3.1 Venn diagram showing probabilities of rain and sun at Heathrow airport.

The Venn diagram in Figure 3.1 represents a joint probability mass function for two random variables:

$$SUN = \begin{cases} yes, & P(SUN = yes) = 0.6 \\ no, & P(SUN = no) = 0.4 \end{cases}, \quad RAIN = \begin{cases} yes, & P(RAIN = yes) = 0.3 \\ no, & P(RAIN = no) = 0.7 \end{cases}$$

We were also told the conditional probability $P(SUN = yes \mid RAIN = yes) = 0.5$. Graphically, this Venn diagram can be seen to represent the joint distribution of the two random variables, *SUN* and *RAIN*.

The entire probability space is made up of 100 squares, and we can think of this probability space as being made up of four possible combinations:

- $SUN = yes$ **and** $RAIN = yes$ (A – 15 squares, probability = 0.15)
- $SUN = yes$ **and** $RAIN = no$ (B – 45 squares, probability = 0.45)
- $SUN = no$ **and** $RAIN = yes$ (C – 15 squares, probability = 0.15)
- $SUN = no$ **and** $RAIN = no$ (D – 25 squares, probability = 0.25)

We have chosen to represent the probability space as being made up of 100 squares, so that it is easy to think about each small square representing a probability of 0.01.

As such, if we wanted to construct the probability of a given (randomly chosen) day being a rain day, we could add together all of the squares where $RAIN = yes$. That is, we would add together:

$$(RAIN = yes \cap SUN = yes) + (RAIN = yes \cap SUN = no)$$

This would be equivalent to 15 + 15 = 30 squares. Similarly, we can treat the probabilities in the same way:

$$P(RAIN = yes) = P(RAIN = yes \cap SUN = yes) + P(RAIN = yes \cap SUN = no)$$
$$= 0.15 + 0.15 = 0.3$$

To calculate the probability of a given day being sunny, we could do exactly the same thing by adding together all of the joint probabilities that involved $SUN = yes$:

$$P(SUN = yes) = P(SUN = yes \cap RAIN = yes) + P(SUN = yes \cap RAIN = no)$$
$$= 0.15 + 0.45 = 0.6$$

This may be more intuitive by writing out our joint distribution in a numerical form, rather than just relying on the graphical interpretation, as illustrated in Table 3.4.

Table 3.4 The joint distribution of *SUN* and *RAIN*

Joint probabilities		*RAIN*	
		yes	no
SUN	yes	0.15	0.45
	no	0.15	0.25

We can use this table of joint probabilities to calculate the marginal probabilities relating to either *RAIN* or *SUN*, simply by adding together the joint probabilities, either within a single column, or within a single row. So, $P(SUN = no) = 0.15 + 0.25 = 0.4$, $P(RAIN = no) = 0.45 + 0.25$, and so on.

More generally, suppose that we have a joint probability mass function for two random variables, X and Y. The domain of X is $\{x_1, x_2, x_3, \ldots, x_n\}$, while the domain of Y is $\{y_1, y_2, y_3, \ldots, y_m\}$, with each of the pairs of outcomes mutually exclusive (e.g. you couldn't observe x_1 and y_2 occurring at the same time as x_2 and y_4). The joint probability distribution will tell us the probability of every possible combination of x_i and y_j. If we wished to calculate the probability that $X = x_1$, we would need to add together all of the joint probabilities where $X = x_1$

$$P(X = x_1) = P(X = x_1 \cap Y = y_1) + P(X = x_1 \cap Y = y_2) + P(X = x_1 \cap Y = y_3)$$
$$+ \ldots + P(X = x_1 \cap Y = y_m)$$

More concisely, we can represent this with summation (sigma) notation as:

$$P(X = x_1) = \sum_{i=1}^{m} P(X = x_1 \cap Y = y_i)$$

Similarly, we can calculate the marginal probability relating to any particular outcome of Y by adding together all of the joint probabilities where, for instance, $Y = y_2$

$$P(Y = y_2) = \sum_{i=1}^{n} P(Y = y_2 \cap X = x_i)$$

Worked example 3.2: Calculating the marginal distributions of eye and hair colour

The law of total probability is most easily understood using a concrete example; in this case, we will think back to the example of eye and hair colour in Scotland.

Table 3.5 Joint distribution of eye and hair colours, derived from Mengel-From et al. (2009)

		Hair colour			
		Black	Brown	Fair	Red
Eye colour	Blue/grey	0.02	0.14	0.16	0.05
	Brown/hazel	0.14	0.23	0.02	0.05
	Green	0.02	0.10	0.03	0.04

Table 3.5 represents the joint probabilities relating to each of the possible pairs of outcomes of eye and hair colour. We have made the simplifying assumption that individuals cannot have different colour eyes,[3] so that each pair of outcomes is mutually exclusive.

If we wish to calculate, for example, the marginal probability of a randomly chosen individual having fair hair, we would calculate this by adding together all of the joint probabilities relating to fair hair:

$$\begin{aligned} P(HAIR = Fair) &= P(HAIR = Fair \cap EYE = Blue) + P(HAIR = Fair \cap EYE = Brown) \\ &\quad + P(HAIR = Fair \cap EYE = Green) \\ &= 0.16 + 0.02 + 0.03 = 0.21 \end{aligned}$$

So, this would tell us that the probability of a randomly chosen individual from the population having fair hair would be 0.21, or 21 per cent of our population has fair hair.

It is often convenient, whenever confronted with a joint probability mass function, to calculate the marginal probabilities relating to each column and row (Table 3.6).

Table 3.6 Joint distribution with calculated marginal probabilities of eye and hair colours, derived from Mengel-From et al. (2009)

		Hair colour				
		Black	Brown	Fair	Red	Total
Eye colour	Blue/grey	0.02	0.14	0.16	0.05	0.37
	Brown/hazel	0.14	0.23	0.02	0.05	0.44
	Green	0.02	0.10	0.03	0.04	0.19
	Total	0.18	0.47	0.21	0.14	

[3] This is a simplifying assumption, but in reality, life is not quite so neat; approximately 1 per cent of the population experience heterochromia. This includes celebrities such as Jane Seymour, Dan Aykroyd, and Kate Bosworth.

From this, we can formally write down the probability mass functions relating to the eye and hair colours:

$$EYE = \begin{cases} Blue, \ P(EYE = Blue) = 0.37 \\ Brown, \ P(EYE = Brown) = 0.44, \\ Green, \ P(EYE = Green) = 0.19 \end{cases} HAIR = \begin{cases} Black, \ P(HAIR = Black) = 0.18 \\ Brown, \ P(HAIR = Brown) = 0.47 \\ Fair, \ P(HAIR = Fair) = 0.21 \\ Red, \ P(HAIR = Red) = 0.14 \end{cases}$$

3.2.1 The law of total probability and conditional probabilities

The law of total probability is very important when it comes to calculating conditional probabilities. We know that, to calculate a conditional probability, we divide the joint probability by the marginal probability:

$$P(X = x \mid Y = y) = \frac{P(X = x \cap Y = y)}{P(Y = y)}$$

We can apply this to the Worked example 3.2, and can use the joint probability distribution and the marginal probability distribution to calculate conditional probabilities. For example, having observed that an individual has black hair, to calculate the (conditional) probability that the individual has green eyes:

$$\begin{aligned} P(EYE = Green \mid HAIR = Black) &= \frac{P(EYE = Green \cap HAIR = Black)}{P(HAIR = Black)} \\ &= \frac{0.02}{0.18} = 0.11(2dp) \end{aligned}$$

Again, intuitively, we are restricting ourselves to the 18 per cent of individuals with black hair, and we are asking what proportion of the time we would expect to see green eyes. More generally, we could calculate the conditional distribution, given a particular eye (or hair) colour. So, suppose we wanted to write down the conditional distribution of

Table 3.7 Calculating conditional probabilities (conditional on having green eyes) using joint and marginal probabilities

Hair colour	Calculation	Probability
Black	$= \frac{P(EYE = Green \cap HAIR = Black)}{P(EYE = Green)} = \frac{0.02}{0.19}$	$= \frac{2}{19} = 0.105\,(3dp)$
Brown	$= \frac{P(EYE = Green \cap HAIR = Brown)}{P(EYE = Green)} = \frac{0.10}{0.19}$	$= \frac{10}{19} = 0.526\,(3dp)$
Fair	$= \frac{P(EYE = Green \cap HAIR = Fair)}{P(EYE = Green)} = \frac{0.03}{0.19}$	$= \frac{3}{19} = 0.158\,(3dp)$
Red	$= \frac{P(EYE = Green \cap HAIR = Red)}{P(EYE = Green)} = \frac{0.04}{0.19}$	$= \frac{4}{19} = 0.211\,(3dp)$

hair colour, knowing that an individual has green eyes. To calculate this, we would divide each joint probability by the marginal probability that an individual has green eyes (Table 3.7).

So, if we randomly sample an individual from our population, and observe that they have green eyes, the probability that they have fair hair will be equal to $\frac{3}{19}$.

I will leave it as an exercise for you to calculate the other conditional probabilities, but these are trivial to calculate using the same methodology.

3.3 Bayes' rule

Economists often want to try to make inferences about individuals, or populations, based upon observed characteristics of that individual, or population. For instance, if you are a gambler, you might want to look for indications that your opponent is bluffing. Similarly, if you are trying to strike a business deal, you might try to make conclusions about the profitability of your prospective partner, based on their observed characteristics.

So far, in this book, we have considered a number of examples related to the weather, and to continue the theme, let's consider an ancient saying:[4]

Red sky at night, sailor's delight

Red sky in the morning, sailor's warning

The motivation behind this saying is that, if you see red sky at night, it is likely to be a sunny day the next day. However, if you observe a red sky in the morning, you might expect rain to fall during the day. This is an example where you are able to observe a characteristic (whether the sky is red in the evening, or in the morning) that allows you to update your beliefs about the probability that the weather will be fair. If you observe a red sky at night, that tells you that the probability that the following day will be fair is higher. Conversely, if you observe a red sky in the morning, this decreases the probability that the day will be fair.

We naturally, and implicitly make conclusions about individuals based on their observed characteristics,[5] but we need to develop a mathematical framework to allow us to do this formally. A framework for this was developed by the Reverend Thomas Bayes in the eighteenth century, and by using conditional probabilities, this allows us to update our beliefs about individuals based on observations of their characteristics, along with knowledge about the marginal and conditional probabilities in the population.

'Red sky at night' is an example of Bayes' rule in action. Having observed a characteristic (in this example, the colour of the sky in the evening or the morning), you can update your beliefs about the likelihood of a second random variable, the weather the next day!

[4] This saying is particularly apt for discussing the Reverend Bayes' rule, as this may be derived from biblical verses. See, for instance, the Gospel of Matthew, Chapter 16, Verses 2 to 3.

[5] Sometimes, these conclusions can lead to individuals discriminating for, or against, individuals based upon observable characteristics, such as skin colour.

3.3.1 A mathematical introduction to Bayes' rule

In the previous chapter, we introduced the chain rule of probability. This allows us to construct a joint probability from a combination of conditional and marginal probabilities. Remember that, if you have two random variables, X and Y, then:

$$P(X = x \cap Y = y) = P(X = x) \times P(Y = y \mid X = x)$$
$$P(X = x \cap Y = y) = P(Y = y) \times P(X = x \mid Y = y)$$

This result initially may look counterintuitive, but the reason that both relationships hold is that it doesn't matter in which order you write a joint probability $P(X = x \cap Y = y) = P(Y = y \cap X = x)$. If it is true that $X = x$ and $Y = y$, it doesn't matter which one you write first.

However, from this, we can also write that:

$$P(X = x) \times P(Y = y \mid X = x) = P(Y = y) \times P(X = x \mid Y = y)$$

and we can rearrange this to give us that:

$$P(X = x \mid Y = y) = \frac{P(X = x) \times P(Y = y \mid X = x)}{P(Y = y)}$$

What we have derived here is known as Bayes' rule, and is a really important rule in medicine, economics, statistics, and many different fields. Bayes' rule is important, as it allows us to update our beliefs about individuals, based upon observed characteristics. For example, as we will see in the next section, we will often know about how many false positives or false negatives a medical test has. However, as an individual facing a positive test result, what you really want to know is whether, based upon the positive result, it is likely that you have the illness (or do not have the illness).

KEY DEFINITION: BAYES' RULE

Mathematically, if you have two random variables, X and Y, and you know $P(X = x \mid Y = y)$, for all possible values of y, but do not know the conditional distribution of Y given X, you can use Bayes' rule to construct any of these conditional probabilities:

$$P(Y = y \mid X = x) = \frac{P(Y = y) \times P(X = x \mid Y = y)}{P(X = x)}$$

Bayes' rule can be applied in a wide range of circumstances, but we will begin by trying to motivate Bayes' rule through the lens of medical testing.

3.4 Applying Bayes' rule in medical testing

Medical tests often lead to false positive or false negative results. A false positive result is when a patient who does not have the disease tests positive for the disease in the test. A false negative result is when a patient who does have the disease tests negative for the disease in the test.

In 2020, the planet faced a new pandemic with the COVID-19 virus. Many countries required citizens to remain at home and not socialize with others outside of their household groups as a means of trying to stop the spread of the virus. Even after lockdown was relaxed, in 2021, individuals who tested positive for the virus were required to self-isolate. COVID-19 was a new coronavirus that for some led to severe respiratory distress and, according to the World Health Organization, has led to approximately 7 million deaths.

The first line of testing for the virus in many countries was through cheap, lateral flow tests that could be carried out within the home. Many workplaces required workers to take regular lateral flow tests before coming into the workplace. However, as with almost all medical tests, these tests were imperfect, and suffered from both false positive results (i.e. someone who did not have COVID testing positive for the virus) and false negative results (i.e. someone with the virus who gains a negative test). See Table 3.8.

Table 3.8 Possible outcomes for a medical test

		Test result	
		Negative for disease	Positive for the disease
Patient's condition	**Does not have the disease**	Correct diagnosis	False positive
	Has the disease	False negative	Correct diagnosis

Dinnes et al. (2021)[6] used results from a range of researchers' studies to estimate the precision of lateral flow tests, and found that the probability of a false positive was approximately 0.4 per cent, or 0.004, whilst the probability of a false negative was approximately[7] 40 per cent, or 0.4. That is, approximately 0.4 per cent of individuals without the virus would receive a positive test, whilst 40 per cent of individuals with the virus would receive a negative test.

The lateral flow test was useful as it could pick up symptomless COVID-19 infections (or infections before the symptoms emerged, but while an individual was infectious). As such, if you have no symptoms, but observe a positive (or negative) test result, you cannot say, with certainty, whether you have COVID-19 (or not), but the test result allows you to update your beliefs. Before carrying out the test, your belief might be that the probability of having COVID might be equal to the proportion of individuals in the population with COVID at

[6] Dinnes J. et al. (2021) 'Rapid, Point-of-care Antigen Tests for Diagnosis of SARS-CoV-2 Infection', *Cochrane Database of Systematic Reviews*, Issue 3.

[7] The actual point estimate was 0.419, but we will use 0.4 to make the maths slightly easier.

that time (so if, for example, 5 per cent of the population had COVID-19, then you might believe that the probability that you have COVID yourself is 5 per cent, or 0.05). However, after the test, a negative test is likely to mean that your probability of being infected with COVID is less than 0.05, whilst a positive test is likely to mean that your probability of being infected with COVID-19 is more than 0.05. However, precisely how much greater (or less) this probability will be will depend on how informative the test is.

To calculate the (updated) probability of being infected given a positive (or negative) test result, we will appeal to Bayes' rule. However, since the probabilities in this example are quite small, we will begin by considering a simpler, worked example, and then will return to this example about COVID-19 later in the chapter.

Worked example 3.3: A simple medical test

Suppose that there are 100 individuals in the population; 80 per cent of the population are healthy, but 20 per cent of the population have a disease, which has no external symptoms. However, there exists a test for the disease. A positive test is used as a signal that the individual has the disease, and a negative test is used as a signal that the individual does not have the disease.

This test, however, is imperfect, and sometimes gives the wrong result. The test has a probability of giving a false positive of 5 per cent, whilst the test has a probability of a false negative of 40 per cent. That is, if you do not have the disease, the probability of receiving a positive test for the disease is 5 per cent (or 0.05), whilst if you do have the disease, the probability that you receive a negative test (suggesting you don't have the disease) is 40 per cent, or 0.4. How could we calculate the probability that an individual has a disease, given that we observe a positive test?

In this information, we have implicitly been presented with some conditional and marginal probabilities. We know the marginal probability that an individual, randomly chosen from the population, has the disease is 0.2, whilst the probability that they do not have the disease is equal to 0.8. Let's define our first random variable, *DISEASE*, to indicate whether the individual has the disease, or not:

$$DISEASE = \begin{cases} yes, & P(DISEASE = yes) = 0.2 \\ no, & P(DISEASE = no) = 0.8 \end{cases}$$

Similarly, we have a second random variable, which is the result of the medical test; we know that the test can be either positive or negative. Let's define this second random variable as *TEST*, with the possible outcomes being *positive*, or *negative*.

We do not know the marginal probabilities, but we do know the conditional probabilities relating to this second random variable. Firstly, we know that if the individual does not have the disease, the probability of a positive test is 0.05 (and hence the probability of a negative test is 0.95):

$$P(TEST = positive \mid DISEASE = no) = 0.05,$$
$$P(TEST = negative \mid DISEASE = no) = 0.95$$

Similarly, if the individual does have the disease, we know that the probability of a negative test is equal to 0.4 (and hence the probability of a positive test is 0.6)

$$P(TEST = positive \mid DISEASE = yes) = 0.6,$$

$$P(TEST = positives \mid DISEASE = no) = 0.4$$

We can also illustrate these random variables diagrammatically. We can begin with the distribution of whether individuals have the disease (or not). The random variable *DISEASE* is represented in Figure 3.2.

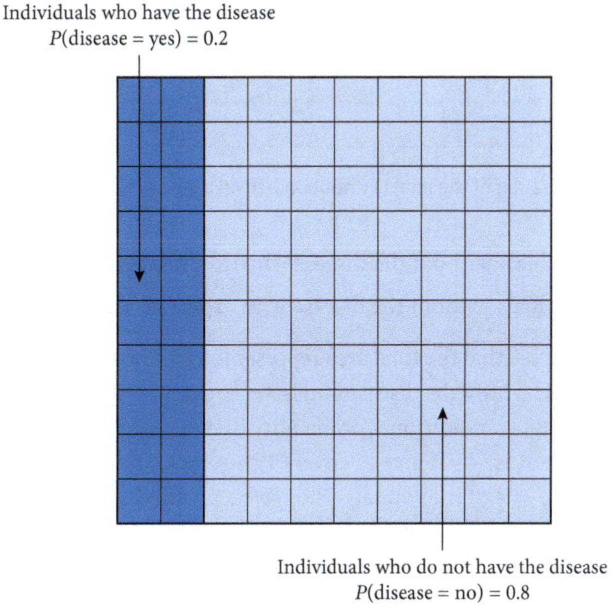

Figure 3.2 Distribution of individuals with the disease in the population.

Building on Figure 3.2, we can also include the positive and negative tests. We know that, amongst those without the disease, 5 per cent will experience a positive test. In this example, the individuals without the disease make up 80 per cent of the population; if there are only 100 people in the population, that means that 80 will not have the disease, and 5 per cent of these 80 (or $0.05 \times 80 = 4$ individuals) will experience a positive test. Similarly, amongst those with the disease, 60 per cent will experience a positive test. Again, in this example, if the population is made up of 100 individuals, 20 per cent of whom have the disease, this would be equivalent to 20 individuals. Since 60 per cent of these 20 individuals would have a positive test, 12 of the individuals would have a positive test. The joint distribution of our two random variables is illustrated in Figure 3.3.

We can see in Figure 3.3 that we have four areas, each of which represents a joint probability:

- A represents individuals with the disease who experience a positive test.
- B represents individuals with the disease who experience a negative test.

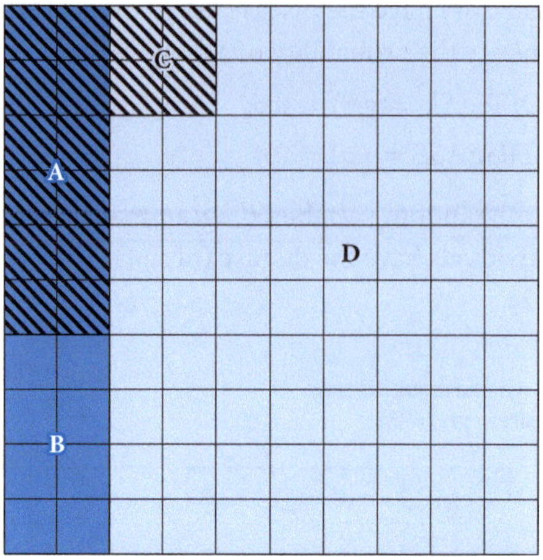

Figure 3.3 Graphical illustration of the joint distribution between DISEASE and TEST.

- C represents individuals without the disease who experience a positive test.
- D represents individuals without the disease who experience a negative test.

In this diagram, we can see that the total area represented by a positive test is equal to $A + C$, whilst the individuals who have the disease and have a positive test are represented by area A. As such, we can see that the conditional probability that an individual has the disease given that we see a positive test is $\frac{A}{A+C}$. Since A covers 12 squares, and C covers 4 squares, intuitively, we can see that $\frac{12}{16} = \frac{3}{4}$ of individuals who have a positive test have the disease.

If we think of these areas as the proportion of the area that is covered, these can be converted into probabilities. (This is dead easy, since the total area is made up of 100 small squares; as such, each small square represents a probability of 0.01.) So, what do these areas represent, and how are they calculated?

- A is the joint probability that an individual has the disease, and has a positive test. Out of the 100 squares in Figure 3.3, A represents 12 squares. This is equivalent to a probability of 0.12. Representing this joint probability using the chain rule of probability:

$$\begin{aligned} &P(DISEASE = yes \cap TEST = Positive) \\ &\quad = P(DISEASE = yes) \times P(TEST = Positive \mid DISEASE = yes) = 0.12 \end{aligned}$$

- C is the joint probability that an individual does not have the disease, and has a positive test. Out of the 100 squares in Figure 3.3, C represents 4 squares. This is equivalent to a probability of 0.04. Representing this joint probability using the chain rule of probability:

$$\begin{aligned} &P(DISEASE = no \cap TEST = Positive) \\ &\quad = P(DISEASE = no) \times P(TEST = Positive \mid DISEASE = no) = 0.04 \end{aligned}$$

- Intuitively, we can also see that $A + C$ is just the probability of a positive test. The positive tests cover 16 squares out of the 100, so we can see that the probability of a positive test is 0.16. As we are adding together all of the joint probabilities where we have a positive test, we are applying the law of total probability.

$$P(TEST = Positive) = P(DISEASE = yes \cap TEST = Positive) + P(DISEASE = no \cap TEST = Positive)$$

Combining all of these elements, if we wish to calculate the conditional probability that an individual has the disease, given a positive test:

$$P(DISEASE = yes \mid Test = Positive) = \frac{P(DISEASE = yes) \times P(TEST = Positive \mid DISEASE = yes)}{P(TEST = Positive)}$$

If we wish to substitute our numbers in, let's remind ourselves about the probabilities we know:

$$P(DISEASE = yes) = 0.2$$
$$P(TEST = Positive \mid DISEASE = yes) = 0.6$$
$$P(TEST = Positive \mid DISEASE = no) = 0.05$$

We can calculate the probability of a positive test by adding together the joint probabilities involving a positive test:

$$P(TEST = Positive) = P(TEST = Positive \cap DISEASE = yes) + P(TEST = Positive \cap DISEASE = no)$$

We calculated these joint probabilities earlier, giving us that:

$$P(TEST = Positive) = 0.12 + 0.04 = 0.16$$

Thus, the probability an individual has the disease, given a positive test, is equal to:

$$P(DISEASE = yes \mid Test = Positive) = \frac{0.2 \times 0.6}{0.16} = \frac{3}{4}$$

In terms of a medical test, this is useful, as the positive test does not provide certainty that you actually have the disease. If the treatment for the disease is very costly, or if it has significant side effects, then you wouldn't want to take the treatment unless you actually have the disease.

Before you had the test, you knew that the probability that you had the disease was 0.2. However, knowing that you have a positive test allows you to update your beliefs, so that you now believe that the probability you have the disease is $\frac{3}{4}$ or 0.75. By knowing this, you are able to make a better informed decision about whether you begin the treatment or not.

What about if you receive a negative test?

In this example, there is a substantial risk of receiving a false negative: 40 per cent of the time individuals with the disease receive a negative test. So, how could we calculate the probability that the individual does not have the disease, subject to a negative test? Well, again, we can use Bayes' rule:

$$P(DISEASE = no \mid TEST = Negative) = \frac{P(DISEASE = no) \times P(TEST = Negative \mid DISEASE = no)}{P(TEST = Negative)}$$

We know that the probability of not having the disease is equal to 80 per cent, or 0.8. Similarly, we know that the probability of a positive test for those with the disease is equal to 0.05. This must mean that (since there are only two possibilities for the test result) the probability of a positive test result for those without the disease is equal to 0.95.

Finally, we know that the probability of a positive test is 0.16. Therefore, the probability of a negative test is 0.84. Substituting these numbers in gives us:

$$P(DISEASE = no \mid TEST = Negative) = \frac{0.8 \times 0.95}{0.84} = \frac{76}{84} = \frac{19}{21} = 0.904\,(3dp)$$

This result is what we would intuitively expect: we can see that there are 84 squares representing a negative test in Figure 3.3 (= $B + D$), of which 76 are represented by individuals without the disease (area D).

Before you have the test, your prior belief that you do not have the disease is 0.8. However, by taking the test, and utilizing Bayes' rule, you can update your beliefs. That is, having observed a negative test, you can now update your belief about the probability that you do not have the disease to 0.904. You are still not certain that you don't have the disease, but knowing that you have had a negative test result means that you are more confident that you do not have the disease.

3.4.1 Lateral flow tests and COVID-19

Returning to the lateral flow test example we saw earlier in the chapter. Suppose that 5 per cent of the population have COVID-19. If we randomly sample an individual from the population, the probability that they have COVID-19 is 0.05. However, using a lateral flow test, we can revise our beliefs about the probability that the individual has COVID-19.

We know that the probability of a false positive is 0.004, whilst the probability of a false negative is 0.4. These are conditional probabilities. Let's define two random variables: *COVID*, which takes the value *yes* if the individual has COVID-19, and *no* if they do not, and *TEST*, which takes the value *positive* if they experience a positive test, and *negative* if they experience a negative test.

From the probabilities we have here, we can see that:

$$P(TEST = positive \mid COVID = no) = 0.004, \quad P(TEST = negative \mid COVID = yes) = 0.4$$
$$P(TEST = negative \mid COVID = no) = 0.996, \quad P(TEST = positive \mid COVID = yes) = 0.6$$

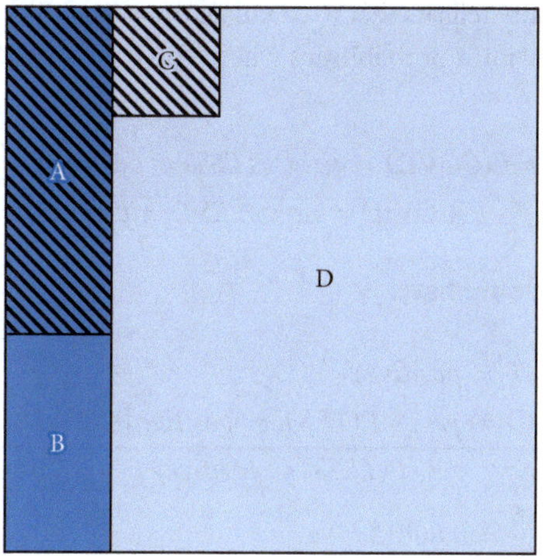

Figure 3.4 Diagram to help us think about the intuition of Bayes' rule (not to scale).

Suppose we see a positive test. What is the probability that the individual actually has COVID? Similarly, if we see a negative test, what is the updated belief that the individual does not have COVID?

Whilst we don't need to draw a diagram, it is often helpful to think about these sorts of probability questions diagrammatically, as shown in Figure 3.4.

We can think of this diagram as representing the four possible cases:

A	$COVID = yes \cap TEST = positive$
B	$COVID = yes \cap TEST = negative$
C	$COVID = no \cap TEST = positive$
D	$COVID = no \cap TEST = negative$

If you observe a positive test, that means that you are certain you are in either A or C. The probability that you have COVID-19 is then the proportion of positive tests that are made up of individuals who actually have COVID-19. That is $\frac{A}{A+C} = P(COVID = yes \mid TEST = positive)$

Area A is the joint probability $P(COVID = yes \cap TEST = positive)$, which we can calculate using the chain rule of probability:

$$P(COVID = yes \cap TEST = positive) = P(COVID = yes) \times P(TEST = positive \mid COVID = yes) = 0.05 \times 0.6 = 0.03$$

Similarly, area C is the joint probability $P(COVID = no \cap TEST = positive)$, which again, we can calculate using the chain rule of probability:

$$P(COVID = no \cap TEST = positive) = P(COVID = no) \times P(TEST = positive \mid COVID = no) = 0.95 \times 0.004 = 0.0038$$

The law of total probability tells us that to calculate the probability of a positive test we need to add together all of the joint probabilities where you have a positive test. In this example, this is made up of areas $A + C$.

$$P(TEST = positive) = P(COVID = yes \cap TEST = positive) + P(COVID = no \cap TEST = positive) = 0.03 + 0.0038 = 0.0338$$

Now, applying Bayes' rule, we have:

$$P(COVID = yes \mid TEST = positive) = \frac{P(COVID = yes) \times P(TEST = positive \mid COVID = yes)}{P(TEST = positive)} = \frac{0.05 \times 0.6}{0.0338} = 0.888\,(3dp)$$

Similarly (and I will leave this as an exercise for you to check), it's possible to show that the conditional probability that an individual does not have COVID, given a negative test, is equal to 0.978 ($3dp$). That is, having observed a negative test, the probability that you wouldn't be infected is 97.8 per cent.

As you can see, a positive test does not give you certainty that you have the virus, but it allows you to substantially update your beliefs. Without any information, the probability that you were infected was 0.05. However, having observed a positive test, the probability that you are infected is 0.888.

In this example, we have assumed that the marginal (or unconditional) probability is 0.05. However, during the COVID pandemic, this proportion increased, and decreased over time. If this marginal probability falls, then, the informativeness of the signal from a positive test also falls. If 0.5 per cent of the population (rather than 5 per cent) were infected with COVID-19, then your updated belief that you were infected would also fall substantially (in this case to 0.430 ($3dp$)).

Worked example 3.4: To bet, or not to bet? That is the question

In microeconomics, you will often read about agents providing signals about their type. For example, you might be playing poker with a friend called Steve. The size of bet that Steve places provides a signal for whether he has a good hand or a bad hand.

Suppose that we have a simple game of cards, where Steve can only gain a good hand or a bad hand, and can place a bet which is either large or small. The probability he gains a good hand is 0.2, and the probability of gaining a bad hand is 0.8.

If Steve has a good hand, he will always place a large bet (as he is more likely to win). However, he doesn't want to signal to you with certainty when he has a poor hand (as then you could place a large bet and win). As such, Steve will sometimes bluff, and place a large bet, even though he has a bad hand.

Suppose that you have played poker with Steve a very large number of times, and that you know that he places a large bet 40 per cent of the time. Can you calculate the probability that he has a good hand, given that he has placed a large bet?

The information we know is:

$P(Good\ hand) = 0.2$

$P(Bad\ hand) = 0.8$

$P(Large\ bet) = 0.4$

$P(Large\ bet\,|\,Good\ hand) = 1$

As such, if we observe a large bet, we can use Bayes' rule to calculate the posterior probability that Steve has a good hand:

$$P(Good\ hand\,|\,Large\ bet) = \frac{P(Good\ hand) \times P(Large\ bet\,|\,Good\ hand)}{P(Large\ bet)}$$

$$= \frac{0.2 \times 1}{0.4} = 0.5$$

Thus, 50 per cent of the time, when you observe a large bet, Steve has a good hand.

Real world application: The search for MH370

One of the most famous usages of Bayes' rule has been in the search for aeroplanes that have gone missing during their flights, with little indication of where they may have been lost.

On 8 March 2014, Malaysian Airlines flight MH370 between Kuala Lumpur and Beijing disappeared from radar screens, with its position unknown. However, air-traffic control experts do know that the plane must have been flying on a particular trajectory, either to the north, or to the south. To this day, the wreckage of the aircraft has not been found. However, the search techniques being used to find the plane build on usage of Bayes' rule, which had been used to find previous crashed aircraft, most famously Air France Flight AF447 between Rio de Janeiro and Paris in 2009.

Searching for crashed airlines can be like searching for a needle in a haystack. When planes crash in the sea, there is not always an obvious crash-site for investigators to find, the resting place of the fuselage is usually not visible from the air, and if any debris is found, this can have been carried hundreds, or even thousands, of miles. Furthermore, in the case of MH370, following the disappearance of the flight from RADAR, it is believed that the aeroplane may have flown for up to seven hours, covering thousands of miles in this time.

In the hunt for crashed aircraft, the application of Bayes' rule is relatively straightforward. Investigators begin with a set of beliefs about the probability mass function (PMF) of the likelihood of an aeroplane's crash-site. This PMF is based upon what is known about the flight—for example, where the flight disappeared from RADAR, the trajectory and flight plan of the aircraft before it disappeared, and the impact of known currents within the water. This *anterior* probability density function provides guidance for where to begin the search for the aircraft, with searching beginning at the most likely locations.

Having observed those locations, and any other evidence that emerges, the investigators are able to update their beliefs, and create a posterior probability mass function. For example, if investigators thoroughly search a one-square mile area of seabed, and find no evidence of the fuselage, or any wreckage, it would be possible to update the beliefs about the likelihood of it having crashed in nearby areas (as wreckage would often be distributed over a wide range, centred on the plane). Similarly, finding wreckage allows the investigators to update their initial beliefs based on the new evidence presented.

For example, suppose that you know that a plane has crashed in a certain area. The investigators may have initial beliefs about the probability that the plane came down in each possible area, represented in Figure 3.5.

0.025	0.025	0.025	0.025	0.025
0.025	0.025	0.1	0.025	0.025
0.025	0.1	0.1	0.1	0.025
0.025	0.025	0.1	0.025	0.025
0.025	0.025	0.025	0.025	0.025

Figure 3.5 Initial probabilities (anterior probabilities)

The investigators may begin their search in the centre area (shaded light blue), but if they found no debris in that area, it would allow them to update their beliefs: having searched the centre square, they know that the plane did not come down in that area. However, having found no debris in that area, it would also allow them to update their beliefs about the likelihood of it coming down in the surrounding area. If the plane had come down in one of the surrounding areas (shaded dark blue), then we might expect to see debris in the light blue area. This might allow the investigators to update their beliefs, so that the probability looks something like Figure 3.6. Having searched the light blue square and found no debris, the investigators are now able to update their beliefs to the most likely crash site being in the outside areas, shaded white.[8]

0.05	0.05	0.05	0.05	0.05
0.05	0.02	0.03	0.02	0.05
0.05	0.03	0	0.03	0.05
0.05	0.02	0.03	0.02	0.05
0.05	0.05	0.05	0.05	0.05

Figure 3.6 Possible set of updated beliefs (posterior beliefs) having searched the centre square.

[8] The author has, in this example, made up both the anterior and posterior probabilities for illustrative purposes.

The case of AF447 is an interesting one, as initially, one of the beliefs that was used to create search areas was incorrect. Aircraft are equipped with black boxes, which record data about the plane and the flight, and in the event of a crash, these black boxes are expected to send out an audible beacon. Initially, when searching for the crashed aircraft, investigators searched for the beacons without success. The assumption was, then, that it was very unlikely that the plane was located in the areas that had already been searched. However, the research team decided to relax this assumption, allowing for the possibility that both beacons failed, and a new location was suggested as a likely resting place for the plane. Within one week of searching, the investigators found the downed aircraft.

While Bayesian analysis can provide guidance in the hunt for missing aircraft, it is not a 'magic bullet'. In the case of MH370, the possible resting places of the plane are much larger than in the case of AF447, and so the anterior (prior) belief is likely to be weak. With a weak anterior belief, and potentially weak signals (the few pieces of debris that have been found have been washed thousands of miles in shifting currents through the oceans) to update beliefs, it remained difficult to find the overall resting place of the aircraft.

Reference

L. D. Stone et al. (2014), 'Search for the Wreckage of Air France Flight AF447', *Statistical Science*, 29(1), 69–80.

Summary

In this chapter, we have formalized our definitions of joint distributions, and seen how we can update our beliefs, based upon Bayes' rule.

Joint probability distributions tell us about the relative likelihood of *pairs* of outcomes from two (or more) random variables. Just as with marginal probability distributions, a well-defined joint probability distribution will have all of the probabilities between 0 and 1, and the sum of the probabilities will be equal to 1.

Where we know the joint distribution between two random variables, we can also use this to calculate the conditional probabilities. Similarly, if we know one set of conditional probabilities, we can use these to update our beliefs about an individual, based upon observed characteristics.

Key formulae

1. The law of total probability

To calculate any conditional probability, we will need to (implicitly) know both the joint probability distribution and the marginal probability. If we know the joint probability distribution between two variables, we can use this to calculate the marginal distribution of *either* variable. For example, to calculate $P(Y = y_j)$, we could sum all of the possible joint probabilities where $Y = y_j$:

$$P(Y = y_j) = \sum_i P(X = x_i \cap Y = y_j)$$

That is, we are taking all of the possible outcomes of X, and adding up all of the joint probabilities where $Y = y_j$.

2. Calculating conditional probabilities

If we know the joint probability mass function, then we can use this to calculate conditional probabilities. First, we would need to calculate the marginal probability distribution of Y, using the law of total probability, and then:

$$P(X = x | Y = y) = \frac{P(X = x \cap Y = y)}{P(Y = y)}, \quad P(Y = y | X = x) = \frac{P(X = x \cap Y = y)}{P(X = x)}$$

3. Bayes' rule

Bayes' rule allows us to update our beliefs about an observation, based upon observed characteristics of that observation. For example, if we observe an individual with blonde hair, we can update our beliefs about the likely colour of their eyes, and if we observe a red sky at night, we can update our beliefs about the likely weather that we will see the following day.

To calculate Bayes' rule, we need to know one set of conditional probabilities and the marginal probability distribution:

$$P(Y = y | X = x) = \frac{P(Y = y) \times P(X = x | Y = y)}{P(X = x)}$$

Independent Random Variables

4

Learning outcomes for this chapter

By the end of this chapter you will be able to:

- Recognize examples where random variables are dependent on each other
- Formally define what it means for random variables to be independent
- Use logic to be able to explain whether pairs of random variables are independent or not
- Calculate joint probabilities based upon independent random variables
- Apply the concepts of independence to random sampling
- Recognize the difference between independent random variables and mutually exclusive outcomes
- Formally show that two random variables are independent

Mathematical tools

- Simple arithmetic
- Addition of fractions
- Multiplication involving fractions and decimals
- Indices (power) of fractions
- Summations using sigma (Σ) notation

Introduction

In the last chapter, we saw that we can use Bayes' rule to update our beliefs about individuals based upon observed characteristics; for example, if we observe a gambler placing a large bet, we can update our beliefs about whether they have a good or bad hand. Similarly, if we see a positive medical test, we can update our beliefs about whether an individual has a disease (or not).

However, it is not always the case that when we observe a joint probability distribution, knowing the value of one random variable gives us any more information about the other random variable. For instance, think about when we flip two coins. Knowing that the first coin lands heads upwards does not make it more, or less, likely that the second coin will land heads upwards. This is because the flips of the coin are independent.

Independence of (certain) random variables is an important characteristic that we will rely upon later in this textbook when we introduce topics such as the binomial distribution, and statistical testing, but for now, in this chapter, we will introduce what it means for random variables to be independent, and what some of the implications of independence are.

4.1 Revisiting an example where two variables are not independent

To motivate independent random variables, let us begin by considering an example where two variables are not independent. In Chapter 3, we saw the joint distribution of hair and eye colour from a population of 133 Scots, collected by Mengel-From et al. (2009).[1] See Table 4.1.

Table 4.1 Joint distribution of hair and eye colour

		Hair colour				
		Black	Brown	Fair	Red	Total
Eye colour	Blue/grey	0.02	0.14	0.16	0.05	0.37
	Brown/hazel	0.14	0.23	0.02	0.05	0.44
	Green	0.02	0.10	0.03	0.04	0.19
	Total	0.18	0.47	0.21	0.14	

Suppose that you randomly sampled an individual from this population, and you observed that they had fair hair. Before you observe their hair colour, you would have a prior belief (i.e. a marginal probability) that the probability that they had blue/grey eyes is equal to 0.37 ($P(EYE = Blue) = 0.37$).

Conditional on observing fair hair, we can construct the conditional probability that an individual has blue eyes, given that they have fair hair:

$$P(EYE = Blue|HAIR = Fair) = \frac{P(EYE = Blue \cap HAIR = Fair)}{P(HAIR = Fair)}$$
$$= \frac{0.16}{0.21} = \frac{16}{21} = 0.762\,(3dp)$$

Having observed that the individual has fair hair has more than doubled the posterior, or conditional, probability that the individual has blue eyes. Knowing the hair colour of the individual tells you something about their likely eye colour; in this population, 37 per cent of the individuals have blue eyes, but, when we restrict the population to only those with fair hair, this proportion increases to 76.2 per cent.

[1] This data is constructed from J. Mengel-From et al. (2009), 'Genetic Determinants of Hair and Eye Colours in the Scottish and Danish Populations', *BMC Genetics*, 10(88).

This is an example where two random variables are not independent; the **conditional probability** changes depending on the values we observe of the other random variable. We could calculate the conditional probabilities of having blue eyes given brown hair (0.298), black hair (0.111), or red hair (0.357). The conditional probability changes, depending on the colour of the hair.

What is different about independent random variables is that when two variables are independent, the conditional probability does not change across the different values of the random variable; that is, in this example, were hair and eye colour independent random variables, the conditional probability of having blue eyes would be the same, irrespective of the colour of hair we condition upon.

Similarly, if we think back to the example of medical tests we saw in Chapter 3, the likelihood of observing a positive test changed depending on whether an individual had a disease or not; again, the variables are not independent from each other.

4.2 Formal definition of independent random variables

In the real world, there are lots of examples of random variables that are independent from each other. Intuitively, this means that, if we observe the outcome of one random variable, it has no impact on the observed outcome of a second independent random variable.

For example, suppose that you rolled a dice in your home; the outcome of that roll of the dice would have no impact on the likelihood that it rains that day in Sydney, Australia. Today's weather in Sydney is independent from the outcome of the dice roll.

More formally, observing the outcome of the dice roll tells us nothing about the probability of it raining in Sydney today. The conditional probability that it rains will be the same, whether the dice roll yields a 1, 2, 3, 4, 5, or 6. So, for example:

$$P(Rain = Yes|Dice = 1) = P(Rain = Yes|Dice = 2) = \ldots = P(Rain = Yes|Dice = 6)$$

That is, the conditional probability of rain is the same, irrespective of the outcome from the dice, and similarly, the conditional probability of rain will be the same as the marginal probability of rain.

Intuitively, this means that observing the outcome from the roll of the dice tells us nothing about the likelihood of it raining. If two variables are independent, knowing the outcome of one variable tells us nothing about the likely outcome of the other variable.

This leads us to a formal definition of independence: two random variables, X and Y, are independent if for all possible outcomes of X and Y the conditional probability distribution of X is equal to the marginal distribution of X, and similarly, the conditional distribution of Y is equal to the marginal distribution of Y:

- $P(X = x|Y = y) = P(X = x)$ for all x, y
- $P(Y = y|X = x) = P(Y = y)$ for all x, y

KEY DEFINITION: INDEPENDENT RANDOM VARIABLES

If you have a random variable X and Y, then X and Y are said to be independent random variables if:

$$P(X = x) = P(X = x|Y = y), \text{ for } all\ x,y$$

That is, the random variables X and Y would be independent if the marginal distribution of X is equal to the conditional distribution of X for all possible outcomes of X and Y.

To understand the intuition, it may be helpful to think about under what circumstances we could say that two variables are not independent from each other.

For example, consider height and shoe size. We know that height is correlated with shoe size; as someone gets taller, on average, their feet get bigger. That is, the probability that someone who is 6ft 2inches (188cm) has large feet is much larger than the probability that someone who is 5ft (152.4cm) has large feet. Therefore, since we can make inferences about the likely foot size having observed an individual's height, then these two random variables are not independent.

4.3 Examples of independent random variables

There are lots of examples of independent random variables. As we will see, we observe independent random variables when the realization of one random variable has no impact on the other random variable. That is, we can think of the variation in one random variable being completely random when compared to the other random variable.

4.3.1 Simple coin toss experiment

Suppose that you flip a (fair) coin 10 times. Each time you flip the coin, the probability that it lands heads upwards will be 0.5, irrespective of what you have observed in previous flips. Even if you have seen nine heads in a row, the probability that the tenth flip is a head still remains 0.5.

This is because the flips of a coin are independent from each other; that is, knowing the value of one flip will tell us nothing about the likelihood of obtaining a head on the other flips. We can define this a little more formally: suppose that C_i represents the ith flip of the coin (so C_{10} would be a random variable, representing the 10th flip of the coin).

$$P(C_{10} = Head) = 0.5, \quad P(C_{10} = Head|C_9 = Head) = 0.5$$

In this example, the marginal probability relating to C_{10} is the same as the conditional probability.

This concept of each flip of a coin being independent from all previous (and future) flips of the coin is sometimes referred to as the coin having no memory. Unless the act of observing the coin landing heads upwards in a previous flip somehow changed the nature of the coin, then, provided the action of flipping the coin is the same each time, the probability will always remain the same, no matter how many heads that you observe.

Gambler's fallacy

In a casino, just like the coin-tossing game, games such as roulette are set up such that every draw is independent from all of the other previous draws (and all future draws as well).

In the game of roulette, a croupier will spin the roulette wheel and release a small ball, and gamblers will bet upon where the ball lands. In the UK, roulette wheels consist of 37 separate possible outcomes: the numbers 1–36 will either be coloured red or black (18 are red, and 18 are black), and the 37th outcome, 0, is coloured green.

Gamblers will often place bets on whether the ball lands on a red number, or a black number. Gamblers will often observe that there is a 'run' of outcomes, where, for instance, the ball lands on a red number ten times in a row.

The gambler's fallacy is that, having observed such a run, then it is more likely than not that the run must come to an end, and that the 11th ball must be black (or at the very least is much more likely to be black).

However, each spin of the roulette wheel is separate from the previous spin; the wheel has no memory, and so cannot remember whether the previous spin yielded a red or a black number. As such, even if the previous 1,000 spins were all red,[2] the probability that the 1,001st spin is black is still $\frac{18}{37}$.

This could be applied to the flip of a coin as well. Intuitively, we might think that if we flip a coin twice, if the first flip is heads upwards, this somehow increases the likelihood that the second flip will land tails upwards. However, this is our intuition misleading us. The probability of the second flip landing heads upwards will be the same as the probability of the first flip landing heads upwards, which (if the coin is fair) will be equal to $\frac{1}{2}$.

4.3.2 Tossing a biased coin

In the previous example, we assumed that the coin that we were considering was a fair coin; that is, the probability of gaining a head was 0.5. Suppose instead that we have a biased, or a rigged, coin, whereby the probability of gaining a head is 0.95.

Just because the coin is biased does not mean that the flips will not be independent. When tossing a biased coin, like the one described here, the conditional and marginal probability relating to any flip, that the coin lands heads upwards, will be 0.95.

[2] If the roulette wheel is a fair wheel, then the probability of 1,000 spins all yielding a red number would be $\left(\frac{18}{37}\right)^{1000} = 1.2 \times 10^{-313}$. This probability is so close to zero that if you did observe this happening, you might be justified in assuming that the roulette wheel was rigged, and get out of that casino as quickly as you can!

If you saw a coin-tossing game, and the coin landed heads upwards ten times in a row, this would not be an indication that the flips were not independent, but instead, it may be a signal that the coin is a biased coin.[3]

4.3.3 Drawing balls with replacement

In Chapter 2, we discussed the concept of drawing balls out of a bag; the bag contained ten balls, six of which were green, and four of which were orange.

If we define B_i as the ith ball drawn from the bag, we saw that, if we did not replace the balls in the bag between draws, then the conditional probabilities of drawing a green ball as the second ball were:

$$P(B_2 = Green|B_1 = Green) = \frac{5}{9}, \ P(B_2 = Green|B_1 = Orange) = \frac{6}{9} = \frac{2}{3}$$

Because, by drawing a green ball out of the bag, you reduce the proportion of balls in the bag which are green, you change the conditional probability, depending on what colour the first ball drawn was. This is an example where the two random variables are not independent.

However, this game can be changed, so that the balls drawn are independent, by making a very simple change to the game. Suppose that you were to return the balls to the bag between each draw. When you draw the first ball, the probability of getting a green ball is $\frac{3}{5}$. If the first ball drawn is green, and then you return it to the bag, then there will be ten balls in the bag, six of which are green, and (provided you are drawing randomly) the probability of getting

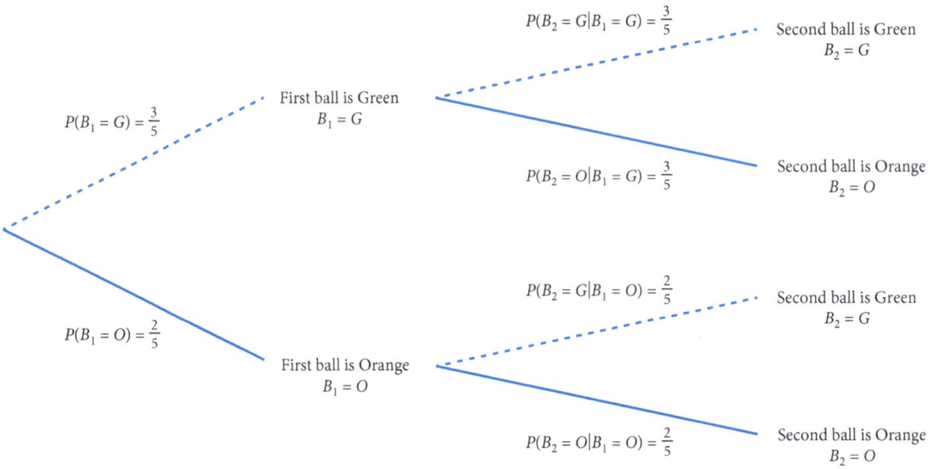

Figure 4.1 Tree diagram of game drawing balls from a bag, with replacement.

[3] The probability of observing ten heads in a row from a fair coin is 0.00098. However, for this biased coin, the probability of ten heads in a row is 0.59874. Whilst it is possible that a fair coin could produce ten heads in a row, it is much more likely from a biased coin. Having observed ten heads in a row, you could use Bayes' rule to update your belief that the coin is actually a biased coin.

a green ball is $\frac{3}{5}$. By the same argument, if the first ball is orange, the conditional probability that the second ball is green is $\frac{3}{5}$. The realization of the first ball has no impact on the conditional probability of the second ball.

Here, the conditional and marginal probabilities will be the same:

$$P(B_2 = Green) = P(B_2 = Green|B_1 = Green) = P(B_2 = Green|B_1 = Orange) = \frac{3}{5}$$

By making this small change, and sampling with replacement, the balls drawn are now independent random variables. We can adapt the tree diagram we saw in Chapter 2 to represent these new probabilities, when we draw with replacement (Figure 4.1).

4.3.4 Unrelated variables

If you have two completely unrelated variables, then these are likely to be independent random variables. For example, we could think about the proportion of babies born in the UK with blue eyes in a year, and the weight of rice imported into Australia in that same year.

Both of these can be treated as random variables; each year, there will be variation year-on-year in the proportion of babies born with blue eyes, and similarly, there will be variation in the amount of rice imported into Australia.

These are likely to be independent random variables, as there is no feasible linkage between eye colour of babies in the UK and the supply and demand of rice in Australia. For these variables not to be independent, either there would need to be a direct linkage between the two variables, or the two variables would need to be linked through one (or more) other random variables.

These sorts of unrelated random variables are very difficult to write down because there are often linkages between variables that you might not immediately think about. For instance, you might think that the weather is unrelated to the returns on a pension fund.

However, a pension fund tries to grow the capital invested by the workers by investing in both bonds and equities. Suppose that the pension fund had invested in bonds taken out by a farming consortium. If the weather is particularly bad in a given year, this is likely to lower the yield of the farms, which will lower the profitability of the farms. In extreme cases, this might mean that the farming consortium defaults on its debts, and hence doesn't pay the bond to the pension fund.

Whilst this is only part of the return on the pension fund, this reduction in income is likely to lead to a reduction in return for that pension fund. As such, the returns on the pension fund, and the weather, are not independent random variables.

4.3.5 Lotteries

In the UK, the main National Lottery (known as Lotto) is held twice a week, on a Saturday and a Wednesday. During the draw, 59 numbered balls (numbered from 1 to 59) are dropped into a lottery machine, and six numbers are drawn out of the machine (without replacement). Players buy a ticket, and choose six numbers, and if their numbers match all (or at least two) of the balls, then the player wins a prize, with the jackpot for matching all six numbers usually in the order of several million pounds.

The UK National Lottery can be used as an example of both independent and dependent random variables. Let's begin with thinking about a single lottery draw, and the balls that are drawn out of the machine. The machine randomly chooses six balls, one at a time. Let's define the ith ball drawn as B_i. The domain of B_i is $\{1, 2, \ldots, 58, 59\}$. Suppose that you are interested in the probability that the second ball is equal to 1, i.e. $P(B_2 = 1)$. If the individual draws from the machine were independent, it wouldn't matter what the first (or 3rd, 4th, 5th, or 6th) balls were, the conditional probability would always be equal to the marginal probability. But, now let's suppose that we know that the first ball is equal to 15:

$$P(B_2 = 1 | B_1 = 15) = \frac{1}{58}$$

Since there's already been one ball drawn out of the machine ($B_1 = 15$), there are 58 balls left in the machine, each of which is equally likely. As such, the probability that the second ball is 1 (conditional that the first ball is 15) is just $\frac{1}{58}$. This conditional probability would be the same for any value of B_1 other than $B_1 = 1$. Suppose now that the first ball drawn was equal to 1. Now, the number 1 ball is no longer in the machine, and so the conditional probability that the second ball drawn is a 1 is going to be zero:

$$P(B_2 = 1 | B_1 = 1) = 0$$

Two random variables are independent if the conditional probability distribution is equal to the marginal distribution, for all possible outcomes; this is equivalent to saying that the conditional probability of B_2 is the same for any given value of B_1.

Worked example 4.1: Calculating the marginal probability $P(B_2 = 1)$

We can calculate the marginal probability $P(B_2 = 1)$ using a combination of the chain rule of probability and the law of total probability. The probability of the second ball drawn being 1 is the same as the sum of all of the joint probabilities involving $B_2 = 1$. We will calculate this using a trick; there are essentially two possibilities for the first ball. Either $B_1 = 1$, or $B_1 \neq 1$.

We can use this trick because the conditional probability relating to the second ball doesn't change across all of the other possible values for B_1 other than $B_1 = 1$. $P(B_2 = 1 | B_1 = 2) = P(B_2 = 1 | B_1 = 3) = P(B_2 = 1 | B_1 = i) = \frac{1}{58}$ for all $i \neq 1$.

So,

$$P(B_2 = 1) = P(B_2 = 1 \cap B_1 = 1) + P(B_2 = 1 \cap B_1 \neq 1)$$

Both of these probabilities are trivial to calculate. We know that the marginal probability that the first ball is equal to 1 is just $P(B_1 = 1) = \frac{1}{59}$. Similarly, to find the probability that the first ball is not equal to 1, there are 58 possible, equally likely, values, out of 59 in total, where $B_2 \neq 1$. As such, $P(B_1 \neq 1) = \frac{58}{59}$.

$$P(B_2 = 1 \cap B_1 = 1) = P(B_1 = 1) \times P(B_2 = 1|B_1 = 1) = \frac{1}{59} \times 0 = 0$$

$$P(B_2 = 1 \cap B_1 \neq 1) = P(B_1 \neq 1) \times P(B_2 = 1|B_1 \neq 1) = \frac{58}{59} \times \frac{1}{58} = \frac{1}{59}$$

Then, completing the calculation gives us:

$$P(B_2 = 1) = 0 + \frac{1}{59} = \frac{1}{59}$$

This may seem counterintuitive, as when drawing the second ball, there are only 58 balls left in the machine. However, it may be easier to think of it like this. Suppose that you don't see the first ball that is drawn, but only the second. There are 59 possibilities, each of which is equally likely. When considering across lottery draws, you would expect each of those 59 possibilities to be equally represented. As such, the marginal probability that the second ball is equal to 1 is just the same as the marginal probability that the first ball is equal to 1.

It is also possible to show (using similar techniques) that the marginal probability is the same for the 1st, 2nd, 3rd, 4th, 5th, and 6th ball drawn:

$$P(B_1 = 1) = P(B_2 = 1) = P(B_3 = 1) = P(B_4 = 1) = P(B_5 = 1) = P(B_6 = 1) = \frac{1}{59}$$

In Worked example 4.1, we have shown that, for Lotto, the relevant probabilities are:

$$P(B_2 = 1) = \frac{1}{59}$$

$$P(B_2 = 1|B_1 = 1) = 0, \; P(B_2 = 1|B_1 \neq 1) = \frac{1}{58}$$

We have shown that, irrespective of the value of B_1, the conditional probability of B_2 is not equal to the marginal probability, and so, formally, we have shown that the balls drawn are not independent from each other. In fact, B_1, B_2, B_3, B_4, B_5, and B_6 are not independent from each other. Intuitively, this is because the realized value of any of the balls drawn affects the potential outcome of the other five balls. If we know that the sixth ball drawn was 43, then this would mean that it would be impossible (i.e. probability equal to zero) for B_1 to be 43 (or in fact, for any of the other balls to be equal to 43).

Each separate lottery is an independent random variable

We have said earlier that there are elements of the UK National Lottery that can be seen as independent random variables, but we have already seen that the balls drawn are not independent from each other. So a key question is, what can we treat as a random variable that is independent?

When considering the overall draw results from Lotto, each draw is independent from all other draws. To explain this, we need to think about the detail a little more. It is possible to show that the probability of any particular combination of six numbers from the UK national lottery is 1 in 45,057,474.[4]

[4] We will show this in the next chapter.

So, suppose that, in the last draw, the machine drew out 1, 2, 3, 4, 5, 6. This may look like an unlikely combination, but it is as likely as any combination of numbers, and would occur with probability $\frac{1}{45,057,474}$. In the next draw, it is possible that exactly the same combination of numbers (1, 2, 3, 4, 5, 6) could be drawn out, and the probability would still be $\frac{1}{45,057,474}$. The previous lottery has no impact on future lottery draws. Just because you've seen a combination of numbers before does not mean that they are any less, or more, likely to occur in the future.

How could we make each ball drawn from a lottery machine independent?

There are two main ways that the balls drawn from a lottery machine could be made independent: firstly, the balls could be returned to the machine after each number is drawn, and secondly, each ball could be drawn from a separate machine.

1. Returning the balls to the machine after each ball is drawn

Suppose that the lottery looked a little different, and after each number is drawn, the ball is returned into the lottery machine. The impact of this is that, having drawn the number 1, for example, as the first ball, this does not change the (conditional) probability of drawing 1 as the second ball. In the original lottery, having drawn the ball numbered 1 as the first ball, then this number was no longer in the machine, meaning that it couldn't be drawn.

Probability without replacement	Probability with replacement
$P(B_1 = 1) = \frac{1}{59}$, $P(B_2 = 1) = \frac{1}{59}$	$P(B_1 = 1) = \frac{1}{59}$, $P(B_2 = 1) = \frac{1}{59}$
$P(B_2 = 1 \mid B_1 = 1) = 0$	$P(B_2 = 1 \mid B_1 = 1) = \frac{1}{59}$
$P(B_2 = 1 \mid B_1 \neq 1) = \frac{1}{58}$	$P(B_2 = 1 \mid B_1 \neq 1) = \frac{1}{59}$

So, having returned the ball to the machine, the marginal and the conditional probabilities relating to the second ball are the same, irrespective of what the first ball drawn is. So, drawing balls with replacement allows the balls drawn to be independent.

2. Using a different machine for each ball

A second way of making the balls drawn independent would be to draw each ball from a separate machine; for example, you could design a lottery with 60 balls. Balls 1–10 are dropped into machine one, balls 11–20 into machine two, and so on until balls 51–60 are dropped into machine six.

One ball is then drawn from each of the machines, but the realization of the first ball drawn has no impact on subsequent balls drawn, because the draw of a particular ball does not affect the probabilities of any subsequent (or previous) ball drawn.

For example, suppose that ball 5 is drawn from machine one. Irrespective of what is drawn from machine one, the probability that ball 5 is drawn out of machine two will be 0 (as there is no ball 5 in machine two). Similarly, irrespective of what is drawn out from machine one, the probability that the ball 15 is drawn out of machine two will be 1/10.

An (almost) infinite lottery machine

In the UK National Lottery, we have a limited population, consisting of 59 balls, where we randomly draw six balls from the machine. Suppose that, instead of having only 59 balls, there were 59,000,000 balls, but with each number between 1 and 59 appearing 1,000,000 times.

The balls drawn will still not be purely independent. Having drawn one ball from the machine, if the first ball drawn is a 1, then there will only be 999,999 balls with a 1 on them, but if the first ball was not a 1, then there would be 1,000,000 balls left (from the 58,999,999 balls in the machine) with a 1 printed upon them:

$$P(B_2 = 1|B_1 \neq 1) = \frac{1{,}000{,}000}{58{,}999{,}999} = 0.0169491528\,(10dp)$$

$$P(B_2 = 1|B_1 = 1) = \frac{999{,}999}{58{,}999{,}999} = 0.0169491359\,(10dp)$$

The conditional probabilities are not the same, but we can see that, numerically, the probabilities are almost identical. To find a difference between the two probabilities we need to go to the eighth decimal place.

In this example, the realization of the first ball has no noticeable impact on the conditional probability relating to the second (or other) balls drawn. Whilst, technically, the balls drawn are not independent random variables, because the conditional and marginal probabilities are almost identical, we can treat the balls drawn from the machine as effectively independent from each other. As the number of balls in the machine increases, the impact of removing one ball from the machine is negligible when it comes to thinking about the distribution of outcomes within the machine.

4.3.6 Summary of lotteries

In most lotteries, the balls drawn are not independent random variables. In a way this is deliberate, because it can make it much less likely for players to win. For example, suppose that the ball was returned to the machine after each draw. This would introduce a whole set of new possible outcomes, which were not previously available. For example, it is possible that all six balls drawn could be 1. This would mean that, due to the increased number of possible outcomes, the probability of players correctly selecting the correct six numbers would be greatly reduced.

There are three main ways in which lotteries could have independent outcomes, in terms of the balls drawn from the machine.

1. The first is to draw each ball from separate machines.
2. The second is to draw balls, and then replace them in the machine after each ball is drawn.
3. The third is to have an (almost) infinite number of balls within the machine.

There are some lotteries in existence where separate machines are used for different numbers. For instance, in the UK, there is a second lottery, called 'Thunderball'. The first five numbers are drawn in much the same way as with the original Lotto game we discussed (with the exception that there are 39 balls in the machine, rather than 59). However, the sixth ball drawn is taken from a second machine—which draws the Thunderball. The second machine contains numbers 1 to 14. The probability that the Thunderball is equal to, say, 7 will always remain $\frac{1}{14}$, irrespective of whether the numbers drawn from the first were {1,2,3,4,5}, or {7, 14, 21, 28, 35}.

The number drawn from the second machine is independent from the combination of five numbers drawn from the first machine.

4.4 Calculating joint probabilities with independent random variables

We have seen in earlier chapters that the chain rule of probability allows us to calculate joint probabilities from marginal and conditional probabilities:

$$P(X = x \cap Y = y) = P(X = x) \times P(Y = y|X = x)$$
$$P(X = x \cap Y = y) = P(Y = y) \times P(X = x|Y = y)$$

Where two random variables, X and Y, are independent, it follows that the marginal distribution of X is equal to the conditional distribution of X given any particular value of Y (and similarly, the marginal distribution of Y is equal to the conditional distribution of Y).

$$P(X = x) = P(X = x|Y = y),\; P(Y = y) = P(Y = y|X = x)$$

It follows from this that, where two random variables are independent, we can write the joint probability as:

$$P(X = x \cap Y = y) = P(X = x) \times P(Y = y)$$

That is, where two random variables are independent, we can calculate the joint probability by finding the product of the two marginal probabilities. This is a special case, and does not hold when the variables are not independent.

Worked example 4.2: Flipping a (fair) coin three times

Suppose you flip a (fair) coin three times. You can calculate the probability that the first, second, and third flip is a head by:

$$P(C_1 = Head \cap C_2 = Head \cap C_3 = Head)$$
$$= P(C_1 = Head) \times P(C_2 = Head) \times P(C_3 = Head) = 0.5^3 = 0.125$$

In fact, in this instance, there are eight possible permutations that we could consider. Denoting a head as H and a tail as T, these are:

- HHH
- HTH
- HTT
- HHT
- THH
- TTH
- THT
- TTT

It is trivial to show that the probability of any of these permutations is equal to $\frac{1}{8} = 0.125$. What is more interesting here, and what we will see in future chapters, is that, if we are interested in the number of heads achieved, rather than the precise order of the number of heads, there are four possibilities: zero, one, two, or three heads. From the list, you can see that there are three cases where there is one head achieved: HTT, THT, TTH. Each of these has probability of 0.125 of occurring, so the probability of gaining exactly one head when we flip a coin three times will just be $0.125 + 0.125 + 0.125 = 3 \times 0.125 = 0.375$.

Worked example 4.3: Flipping a biased coin

Consider a biased coin. You are told that the probability of it landing heads upwards on any given flip of the coin is $\frac{2}{3}$. If we were to flip the coin twice, then we might be interested in calculating the probability of gaining two heads. That is, if we define the first flip as C_1 and the second flip as C_2, we are looking for the probability $P(C_1 = Heads \cap C_2 = Heads)$.

Since each flip of the coin is independent from the previous (and future) flips, the joint probability is just equal to the product of the marginal probabilities. Further, the probability of any given flip being heads upwards is $\frac{2}{3}$, the probability of landing tails upwards is $\frac{1}{3}$.

$$P(C_1 = Heads \cap C_2 = Heads) = P(C_1 = Heads) \times P(C_2 = Heads) = \frac{2}{3} \times \frac{2}{3} = \frac{4}{9}$$

So, the probability of gaining two heads is equal to $\frac{4}{9}$, whilst the probability of gaining two tails would be $\frac{1}{9}$.

Worked example 4.4: A random draw, with replacement

Returning to the example we saw in Section 4.2.3, if we have a bag of ten balls, six of which are green, and four orange, if we sample two balls from the bag, replacing the ball we select each time, we have seen that B_1 is independent from B_2, where B_i is the ith ball drawn from the bag.

We can see that:

$$P(B_1 = Orange) = \frac{3}{5}, \quad P(B_2 = Orange | B_1 = Orange) = \frac{3}{5}$$

Because the balls drawn are independent, the marginal and conditional probabilities relating to the second ball will be the same, and so $P(B_2 = Orange) = \frac{3}{5}$.

If we want to calculate the probability that both the first and second balls are orange, we can simply multiply together the two probabilities:

$$P(B_1 = Orange \cap B_2 = Orange) = P(B_1 = Orange) \times P(B_2 = Orange) = \frac{3}{5} \times \frac{3}{5} = \frac{9}{25}$$

Worked example 4.5: Will monkeys ever write the complete works of Shakespeare?

It is often said that if you give a monkey a typewriter and an infinite amount of time, eventually, just by choosing random letters, it will type the complete works of William Shakespeare. In order to illustrate the probability of this occurring at any given time, let us consider the likelihood of a monkey correctly typing the first two lines of *Richard III*:

Now is the winter of our discontent
Made glorious summer by this sun of York

If we assume that the monkey has a typewriter only consisting of letters (and a space bar), and we ignore punctuation, capital letters, and line breaks (for simplicity), what would be the probability that the first 15 words typed were from *Richard III*?

There are 27 possible keys for the monkey to press (26 letters and the space). As such, if the monkey is drawing letters randomly (and we assume to be independently), the probability that the first letter is an n is $\frac{1}{27}$.

In order to calculate the probability that the second letter is an o and the first letter is an n, we need to consider the conditional probability that the second letter is an o:

$$P(1st = n \cap 2nd = o) = P(1st = n) \times P(2nd = o | 1st = n)$$

Since the letter draws are assumed to be independent, $P(2nd = o | 1st = n) = P(2nd = o)$, and so the probability of gaining the first two letters correctly is:

$$P(1st = n \cap 2nd = o) = \frac{1}{27} \times \frac{1}{27} = \left(\frac{1}{27}\right)^2 = \frac{1}{729}$$

Now, there are 76 letters (or spaces) in this first line, so the probability of correctly picking all 76 is:

$$P(all\, correct) = \left(\frac{1}{27}\right)^{76} = \frac{1}{6.07 \times 10^{108}}$$

In other words, there are 6.07×10^{108} possible outcomes of these first 76 letters (i.e. 6 with 108 zeros after it). To provide a comparison, it is estimated that there are approximately 10^{80} particles within the observable universe.

However, the infinite monkey theory does not say that the monkey will write *Richard III* immediately, just that at some time in its infinite lifespan, it will almost surely write the entire works of Shakespeare. Given that the monkey has an infinite timescale, we would eventually expect all of the 6.07×10^{108} possible outcomes to be written out.

Important health warning

It is important to note that this trick of multiplying together marginal probabilities to construct joint probabilities only works when the random variables are independent.

It is much safer to remember that to calculate a joint probability, you need to use the chain rule of probability; that is:

$$P(X = x \cap Y = y) = P(X = x) \times P(Y = y \mid X = x) = P(Y = y) \times P(X = x \mid Y = y)$$

When Y and X are independent random variables, we have the special case that the marginal and conditional probabilities are the same, such that $P(Y = y \mid X = x) = P(Y = y)$ and $P(X = x \mid Y = y) = P(X = x)$.

4.5 Independent sampling in statistics

When we introduce statistics later in this book, we will consider samples of individuals, randomly sampled from the population, and we will treat each observation as being independent from all of the other observations. That is, knowing the characteristics of one individual does not impact the likelihood that we will observe particular characteristics of the other individuals.

For instance, if we are interested in estimating the average height in the population, we will randomly take a sample of the population and measure their heights, and use this to estimate the average height in the population. The assumption that the observations are independent means that if we know the height of any individual within the sample, this will give us no additional information about the other individuals within the sample. If the observations were not independent, then the height of one individual would affect the distribution of heights in the rest of the sample.

In many cases, this is not a bad assumption, provided one of two conditions holds: either the population is very large compared with the size of the sample, or individuals are sampled with replacement.

4.5.1 The population is very large compared with the size of the sample

If the population is very large compared with the size of the sample, then the random draws from the population are a little like our almost infinite lottery machine. Drawing one individual from the population does not affect the distribution of characteristics within the (remaining) population, and so knowing that (say) the first individual we draw has blue eyes is not going to affect the probability that the second, third, fourth (and so on) individual has a particular colour eyes. As such, in these circumstances, we will treat the random observations as being independent from each other.

4.5.2 Sampling with replacement from the population

If the individual sampled is returned to the population each time, then every time you (randomly) draw an individual from the population, the distribution of characteristics in the population you are sampling from will remain the same.

For instance, if you have 100 individuals, 20 per cent of whom have blue eyes, the probability of randomly drawing an individual with blue eyes is $\frac{1}{5}$. If you randomly draw an individual with blue eyes and do not return them to the population, then the conditional probability that the second person has blue eyes would be $\frac{19}{99}$. However, by returning the first individual to the population, there would still be 100 individuals in the population we are sampling from, 20 of whom have blue eyes, and the probability of randomly sampling someone with blue eyes would be $\frac{1}{5}$.

Of course, this does mean that, when sampling from our smaller population (with replacement), we are likely to see the same individuals more than once in samples.

4.5.3 Observations in data we observe will not always be independent

That being said, when dealing with data in statistics, it will not always be the case that the observations are independent from each other, and the lack of independence can be created by a number of routes. We will discuss some of these in more detail later in the book, but will provide a few examples here.

If we are using observational data on heights of individuals within the UK population, we can end up with observations that are not independent, depending on how we sample from the population. Suppose that a researcher samples users of a local sports facility to measure heights, and on the day that the researcher is measuring the heights, there is a professional basketball tournament being held at the facility. In basketball, there may be an advantage to being taller than average, and so the observations may not be representative of the population as a whole.

Similarly, if you are interested in data that gradually changes over time, such as data on share prices, then you wouldn't expect to see large changes over time. For example, if we look at the unemployment rate (as depicted in Figure 4.2), we can see that, month-on-month, we do not see very large, random changes in the unemployment rate. The unemployment rate moves fairly smoothly over time.

This means that one of the best indicators of the unemployment rate at time t (e.g. March 2020) is the unemployment rate in the previous month (time $t-1$). So, knowing the unemployment rate in a previous month gives you an indication of what the unemployment rate would be expected to be in the next month. As such, the observations of the unemployment rate over time would not be independent random variables.

This is an example of a particular type of data called time series. Time series data will often have the problem that data does not change randomly month-on-month, and as such, the observations will rarely be independent from each other.

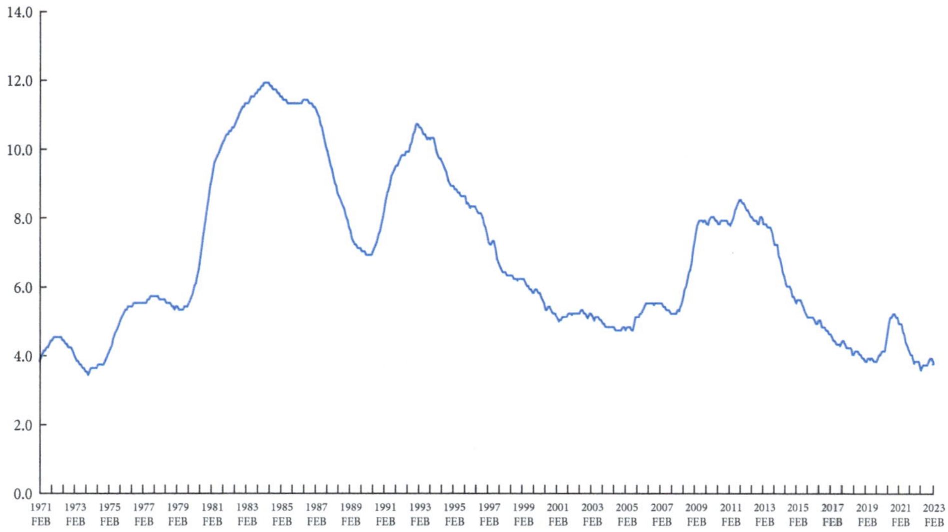

Figure 4.2 Unemployment rate (%) between February 1971 and March 2023 (data from the ONS).

4.6 Independence versus mutually exclusive events

Students often get confused about the difference between independent random variables and mutually exclusive outcomes.

Outcomes are mutually exclusive if two possible outcomes of a random variable cannot occur at the same time. For example, if you toss a coin, the two possible outcomes are that the coin lands heads upwards or tails upwards. It is not possible for the coin to land both heads upwards and tails upwards. As such, the outcomes that a single coin toss lands heads upwards and that a single coin toss lands tails upwards are mutually exclusive.

Independence relates to the individual random variables. For example, if you flip a coin twice, the two flips of the coin are two random variables. Each flip could land heads or tails upwards, but the two flips are independent from each other. The outcome of the first flip of the coin does not affect the outcome of the second flip of the coin!

KEY DEFINITION: MUTUALLY EXCLUSIVE OUTCOMES AND INDEPENDENT RANDOM VARIABLES

Random variables have a number of different possible outcomes. For example, when you flip a coin, the two possible outcomes are heads and tails. In thinking about mutually exclusive outcomes and independent random variables, it is important to understand the difference between a random variable and outcomes within a random variable:

- Two random variables are independent if knowing the outcome of one random variable tells us nothing about the likelihood of outcomes of the second random variable. Independence relates to separate random variables.
- Two outcomes are mutually exclusive if they cannot take place at the same time.

4.7 Detecting independent random variables from joint distributions

If you know the joint distribution between two random variables, you can use this to check whether two random variables are independent (or not), by evaluating whether the conditional probability distribution is equal to the marginal probability distribution.

For example, suppose that we are given the joint probability distribution relating to the example we saw in Section 4.3.3. If we have ten balls in a bag, six of which are green and four orange, and we draw two balls from the bag, with replacement, then we can see the joint probability distribution relating to the pairs of outcomes in Table 4.2.

Table 4.2 Joint probability distribution relating to drawing two balls from a bag

Joint probabilities		Second ball drawn, B_2	
		Green	Orange
First ball drawn, B_1	Green	$\frac{9}{25}$	$\frac{6}{25}$
	Orange	$\frac{6}{25}$	$\frac{4}{25}$

By definition, the two balls drawn will be independent if the marginal probability distribution is equal to the conditional probability. That is, the two balls will be independent if knowing that (for example) the first ball drawn is green tells us nothing about the likelihood that the second ball is also green. More formally, the balls drawn are independent if:

$$P(B_2 = Green \mid B_1 = Green) = P(B_2 = Green \mid B_1 = Orange) = P(B_2 = Green)$$
$$P(B_2 = Orange \mid B_1 = Green) = P(B_2 = Orange \mid B_1 = Orange) = P(B_2 = Orange)$$

Given the joint probabilities, we can use the law of total probability to calculate the marginal probabilities, by simply adding together the joint probabilities. For example, the probability that the first ball is green can be calculated by adding $P(B_1 = Green \cap B_2 = Green) + P(B_1 = Green \cap B_2 = Orange) = \frac{9}{25} + \frac{6}{25} = \frac{15}{25} = \frac{3}{5}$ (see Table 4.3).

Table 4.3 Joint probability distribution relating to drawing two balls from a bag

Joint probabilities		Second ball drawn, B_2		
		Green	Orange	Total
First ball drawn, B_1	Green	$\frac{9}{25}$	$\frac{6}{25}$	$\frac{3}{5}$
	Orange	$\frac{6}{25}$	$\frac{4}{25}$	$\frac{2}{5}$
	Total	$\frac{3}{5}$	$\frac{2}{5}$	

So, we can see that the marginal probabilities are $P(B_1 = Green) = \frac{3}{5}$, $P(B_1 = Orange) = \frac{2}{5}$, and similarly $P(B_2 = Green) = \frac{3}{5}$, $P(B_2 = Orange) = \frac{2}{5}$.

Revision from Chapter 3: Calculating conditional probabilities

Suppose that we have two random variables, X and Y. If we want to calculate the conditional probability that $X = 1$ given that $Y = 4$, we can calculate this by dividing the joint probability that $X = 1$ and $Y = 4$ by the marginal probability that $Y = 4$:

$$P(X = 1|Y = 4) = \frac{P(X = 1 \cap Y = 4)}{P(Y = 4)}$$

More generally, if we wish to calculate the conditional probability that $X = x$ given that $Y = y$, we would take the joint probability and divide by the marginal probability:

$$P(X = x|Y = y) = \frac{P(X = x \cap Y = y)}{P(Y = y)}$$

We can use the joint and marginal probabilities from Table 4.3 to construct the conditional probabilities, by dividing through the joint probability by the marginal probability, such that, for example:

$$P(B_1 = Green|B_2 = Orange) = \frac{P(B_1 = Green \cap B_2 = Orange)}{P(B_2 = Orange)} = \frac{6/25}{2/5} = \frac{3}{5}$$

Table 4.4 shows what happens when we calculate the conditional distribution of B_1, given the observed outcomes of B_2.

Table 4.4 Calculating the conditional probabilities

	Conditional that $B_2 = Green$	Conditional that $B_2 = Orange$
$P(B_1 = Green\|B_2 = b)$	$= \frac{9/25}{3/5} = \frac{3}{5}$	$= \frac{6/25}{2/5} = \frac{3}{5}$
$P(B_1 = Orange\|B_2 = b)$	$= \frac{6/25}{3/5} = \frac{2}{5}$	$= \frac{4/25}{2/5} = \frac{2}{5}$

So, we have shown that the conditional probability that $B_1 = Green$ is always equal to $\frac{3}{5}$, irrespective of what colour is realized for B_2. It is also trivial to see that the marginal probability that $B_1 = Green$ is also equal to $\frac{3}{5}$.

For the variables to be independent, it must be the case that all of the conditional probabilities are equal to the marginal probabilities, so for completeness, let's also examine the probabilities relating to the first ball being orange. Again, the conditional probability is always equal to $\frac{2}{5}$, as is the marginal probability.

Because the conditional probabilities relating to all of the outcomes of B_1 are equal to the respective marginal probabilities, we can conclude that the two variables are independent.

You may note that we have only shown that the conditional probabilities are equal for B_1, and you may be worried that we have only shown that B_1 is independent from B_2 (and not vice versa). However, if we have two random variables, we only need to show independence in one direction, and this will be sufficient to prove that the two variables are independent.

Proof that we only need to prove independence in one direction

If we have two random variables, X and Y, it is sufficient to show that if the conditional distribution of X given all possible values of Y is constant (and equal to the marginal distribution) then X and Y will be independent. It will automatically follow that the conditional distribution of Y given all possible values of X will equal the marginal distribution of Y.

That is, to show that two random variables are independent, it is a sufficient condition to show that:

$$P(X = x \mid Y = y) = P(X = x)$$

for all possible values of x and y.

As such, it will automatically follow that

$$P(Y = y \mid X = x) = P(Y = y)$$

Proof

In general, we know that:

$$P(X = x \mid Y = y) = \frac{P(X = x \cap Y = y)}{P(Y = y)}$$

However, if we have shown that $P(X = x \mid Y = y) = P(X = x)$ for all values of x and y, then we can rewrite this as:

$$P(X = x) = \frac{P(X = x \cap Y = y)}{P(Y = y)}$$

This can be rearranged to give:

$$P(Y = y) = \frac{P(X = x \cap Y = y)}{P(X = x)}$$

However, this is, by definition, the formula for the conditional probability:

$$P(Y = y \mid X = x) = \frac{P(X = x \cap Y = y)}{P(X = x)}$$

So, by definition, it must follow that:

$$P(Y = y) = P(Y = y \mid X = x)$$

Worked example 4.6: Evaluating whether two random variables are independent

When examining whether two random variables are independent (or not), it is very important that you check all of the pairs of possible outcomes. Suppose that we have two random variables, X and Y. The random variable X can take the possible outcomes 1, 2, or 3. More formally,[5] we can write this as $X \in \{1,2,3\}$. Y can take the outcomes 4, 5, or 6. Again, more formally, we can write that $Y \in \{4,5,6\}$.

We wish to evaluate whether X and Y are independent random variables or not. That is, we want to know whether observing the outcome of X tells us anything about the likely outcome of Y. The joint distribution of X and Y is denoted in Table 4.5. Remember, this table tells us the probability of pairs of outcomes of X and Y. So, the probability that X takes the value 2 and Y takes the value 6 is equal to $P(X = 2 \cap Y = 6) = 0.05$.

Table 4.5 Joint distribution (PMF) of the random variables X and Y

		Y		
$P(X = x \cap Y = y)$		4	5	6
	1	0.1	0.25	0.15
X	2	0.05	0.2	0.05
	3	0.05	0.05	0.1

If we wish to examine whether X and Y are independent random variables, we need to evaluate whether the conditional probability is equal to the marginal probabilities.

A good place to start, before doing any calculations, is to check that this is a well-defined joint **probability mass function** (PMF). Remember, for a joint distribution to be well defined, it needs to be the case that all of the probabilities are between 0 and 1, and the sum of the joint probabilities must be equal to 1. In this case, it is trivial to see that this is a well-defined joint distribution.

Having checked that this is well defined, we can now move to calculate the marginal probabilities, using the law of total probability. The law of total probability means that, since the pairs of outcomes are mutually exclusive, we can calculate the marginal probability by adding up all of the joint probabilities where a particular outcome is observed.

$$P(X = x) = \sum_y P(X = x \cap Y = y)$$

So, to calculate the probability that $X = 1$, we would need to add up all of the joint probabilities that involve $X = 1$. That is, we would add up the probability that $X = 1$ and $Y = 4$, the probability that $X = 1$ and $Y = 5$, and the probability that $X = 1$ and $Y = 6$.

[5] You can think of the notation $X \in \{1,2,3\}$ as meaning that the possible set of outcomes of X is 1, 2, or 3. That is, X is an element ($\in$) of the set of outcomes 1, 2, or 3. The curly brackets $\{\ldots\}$ indicate a set of possible outcomes. Similarly, $Y \in \{4,5,6\}$ indicates that the outcome of Y is an element of the set of outcomes 4, 5, or 6. If you read other textbooks, you may see this notation, so it is useful to understand what this means.

Applying this to the probabilities in Table 4.5, this gives us:

$$P(X = 1) = P(X = 1 \cap Y = 4) + P(X = 1 \cap Y = 5) + P(X = 1 \cap Y = 6)$$
$$= 0.1 + 0.25 + 0.15 = 0.5$$

We can repeat this for $P(X = 2)$ and $P(X = 3)$. The marginal probability mass functions for X and Y, calculated from the joint distribution, are given in Table 4.6.

Table 4.6 Joint and marginal distributions of X and Y

$P(X = x \cap Y = y$		Y 4	5	6	Total
X	1	0.1	0.25	0.15	0.5
	2	0.05	0.2	0.05	0.3
	3	0.05	0.05	0.1	0.2
	Total	0.2	0.5	0.3	

Now, we can calculate the conditional probabilities relating to Y by dividing the joint probabilities by the marginal probability of X:

$$P(Y = y \mid X = x) = \frac{P(X = x \cap Y = y)}{P(X = x)}$$

If we simply look at the conditional probability of Y, given that $X = 1$ (illustrated in Table 4.7), we can see that the conditional probability is equal to the marginal probability.

However, this is only for one value of X. We have not shown that X and Y are independent yet, as we would need to condition on all of the possible values of X. See Table 4.8.

Now, having conditioned that $X = 2$, and $X = 3$, we can see that the conditional probabilities are not always equal to the marginal probability. So, for example, $P(Y = 4 \mid X = 2) = \frac{1}{6}$, whilst $P(Y = 4 \mid X = 3) = 0.25$, both of which are different from the marginal probability $P(Y = 4) = 0.2$. As such, we can conclude that X and Y are not independent random variables.

Table 4.7 Calculating the conditional probability distribution of Y, given that $X = 1$

	Y 4	5	6
Conditioning that $X = 1$	$= \frac{0.1}{0.5} = 0.2$	$= \frac{0.25}{0.5} = 0.5$	$= \frac{0.15}{0.5} = 0.3$
Marginal probability	0.2	0.5	0.3

Table 4.8 Conditional probability distribution of Y

	Y		
	4	5	6
Conditioning that $X = 1$	$= \frac{0.1}{0.5} = 0.2$	$= \frac{0.25}{0.5} = 0.5$	$= \frac{0.15}{0.5} = 0.3$
Conditioning that $X = 2$	$= \frac{0.05}{0.3} = \frac{1}{6}$	$= \frac{0.2}{0.3} = \frac{2}{3}$	$= \frac{0.05}{0.3} = \frac{1}{6}$
Conditioning that $X = 3$	$= \frac{0.05}{0.2} = 0.25$	$= \frac{0.05}{0.2} = 0.25$	$= \frac{0.1}{0.2} = 0.5$
Marginal probability	0.2	0.5	0.3

This is a very important example, because it illustrates that when considering whether variables are independent (or not), you need to work through all of the possible pairs of outcomes of both variables.

Summary

In this chapter, we have introduced the concept of independent random variables; random variables are independent when knowing the value of one random variable tells you nothing about the likely outcome of another random variable. More formally, random variables are independent if the conditional probability distribution is equal to the marginal probability distribution.

Independence of random variables will become increasingly important as we discuss statistics later in this textbook, and in particular, we will often assume that observations from a population are themselves independent from all of the other observations.

Key formulae

1. If two random variables, X and Y are independent, then the conditional distribution is equal to the marginal distribution:

   $P(X = x_i \mid Y = y_j) = P(X = x_i)$, for *all* x_i, y_j

2. If two random variables are independent, then the joint distribution is equal to the product of the marginal distributions:

   $P(X = x_i \cap Y = y_j) = P(X = x_i) \times P(Y = y_j)$

Combinations and Permutations

5

Learning outcomes for this chapter

By the end of this chapter you will be able to:

- Calculate the number of permutations when randomly sampling from a population without replacement
- Describe the difference between combinations and permutations, and be able to calculate the number of possible combinations when randomly sampling from a population without replacement

Mathematical tools

- Simple arithmetic
- Addition of fractions
- Multiplication involving fractions and decimals
- Indices (powers) of fractions
- Products, using Pi (Π) notation
- Factorials (!)

Introduction

In 1994, the UK government introduced a National Lottery, which offered the opportunity to win multi-million pound prizes to ticket holders. As we've seen in the last chapter, the mechanics of the National Lottery are such that the draw machine contains 59 balls (numbered from 1 to 59), and the machine randomly draws out six balls.

If your ticket matches the balls that are drawn out of the machine, then you win the jackpot. However, since you have to pay for tickets, it will be important for players to know what the probability is of winning the jackpot. This probability can vary depending on the precise design of the game.

The way that the lottery is organized in the UK, it doesn't matter what order the balls come out in. So if you bought a ticket, choosing the numbers 1, 2, 3, 4, 5, 6, if those numbers were drawn out of the machine in any order, you would win the jackpot.

Of course, the lottery could have been designed in a different way, such that players had to select not only the winning numbers but also the order in which the numbers came out of the machine. What we will see in this chapter is that, if the order of the numbers matters, the probabilities can change significantly.

5.1 Permutations without replacement

We will begin this chapter by discussing permutations. Let's suppose that there is a simple lottery. In this lottery, there are three numbered balls (numbered from 1 to 3). In the draw, two balls are randomly chosen from the machine, without replacement. In this lottery you will only win if you predict both:

- the numbers that are drawn from the machine, and
- the order in which they are drawn.

Because there are only a small number of balls, we can represent all of the possible outcomes of this lottery by writing down each of the pairs of outcomes, as in Table 5.1.

Table 5.1 All of the possible outcomes from the lottery

First ball	1	2	1	3	2	3
Second ball	2	1	3	1	3	2

Here, we can see that there are six possible outcomes, each of which is equally likely. As such, if you bought a ticket for this lottery, the probability of winning would be one sixth. The number of possible outcomes here is also known as the number of possible permutations of outcomes.

Permutations relates to the number of possible outcomes, when the order of the outcomes matters. In the game in Table 5.1 the outcome of the first ball being 1 and the second ball being 2 is different from the outcome where the first ball is 2 and the second ball is 1.

As we will see, when the order of outcomes matters, the number of possible permutations can become very large. For instance, if in the UK national lottery, you had to guess not just the numbers that are drawn from the machine, but also the order in which the numbers are drawn, then the probability of winning would be one in 32,441,381,280 (i.e. one in 32 billion). Since we are interested in probabilities, we need to understand how we can calculate the number of possible permutations. As such, we need to develop some mathematical tools.

Whilst we will return to the lottery later in the chapter, we can begin by considering a relatively simple example, to help us find a general rule to calculate the number of possible permutations.

5.1.1 Sampling without replacement

Let's begin with a really simple example. Let's suppose that you have a bag containing three balls—a red ball, a green ball, and a blue ball. A key question is, how many ways can we draw the three balls out of the bag? To motivate this, it might be easiest by trying to draw out a

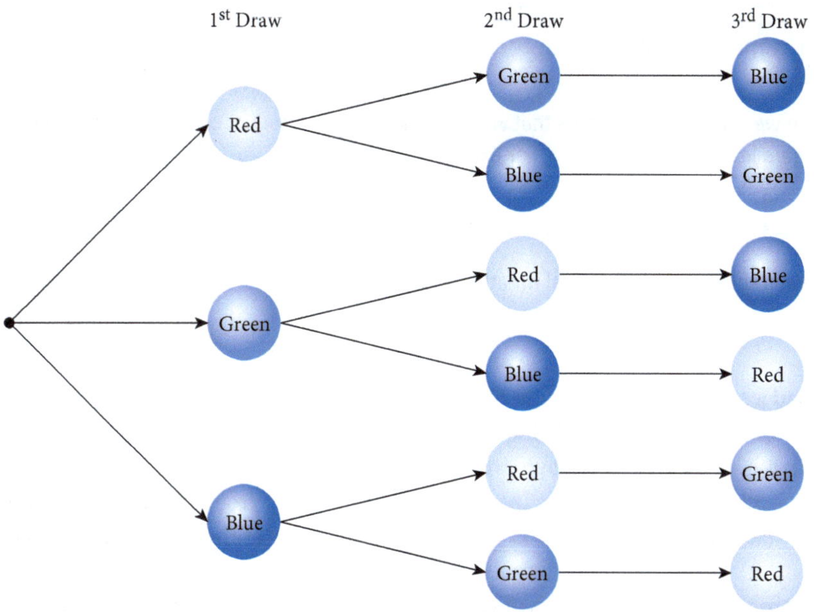

Figure 5.1 Possible permutations of balls drawn out of the bag.

tree diagram, which we represent in Figure 5.1 There are three, equally likely, outcomes for the first ball: red, green, or blue.

However, since the bag only contains three balls, in the second draw, there are only two possible outcomes. If the first ball were red, then the second ball must be either green or blue (each of which occurs with equal probability). Similarly, if the first ball were green, there are two possible outcomes for the second ball—red or blue. Finally, for the third draw, there is only one possibility, as there will only be one ball left in the bag.

So, what this tells us is that:

- There are three possibilities for the first ball.
- For each of the three possibilities, there are two possibilities for the second ball. This means that there are $3 \times 2 = 6$ routes to the second ball.
- For each of the possible routes to the second ball, there is one outcome for the third ball. This means that there are $3 \times 2 \times 1 = 6$ routes to the third and final ball.

When we draw all three balls from the bag, we have shown that there are six possible permutations in which to do so; that is, there are six possible orders that we can draw the three balls from the bag. If we represent a red ball as R, green as G, and blue as B, then the six orders are RGB, RBG, GRB, GBR, BRG, BGR.

More formally, we can calculate the number of permutations by using factorials. We can represent $3 \times 2 \times 1 = 3!$

Mathematical revision: Factorial notation

When we see $n!$, this indicates that we are looking at the product of all of the (positive) integers less than or equal to n. For example:

$$5! = 5 \times 4 \times 3 \times 2 \times 1 = 120$$
$$8! = 8 \times 7 \times 6 \times 5 \times 4 \times 3 \times 2 \times 1 = 40{,}320$$

We will repeatedly use factorial notation within this chapter.

If we had a simple game, where we had to predict the order of the balls drawn from the bag, then, since there are six equally likely outcomes, the probability of correctly identifying the order in which the balls are drawn would be one in six, or $\frac{1}{6}$.

We can check this probability by using the chain rule of probability. Let's define B_i as the ith ball selected. Suppose that you guessed that the order of the balls would be red, green, blue.

The probability that the first ball is red is $P(B_1 = Red) = \frac{1}{3}$, since there are three balls, of which only one is red. Similarly, for the second ball, conditional on the first ball being red, $P(B_2 = Green \mid B_1 = Red) = \frac{1}{2}$. There are two balls left in the bag, of which one is green. Finally, the conditional probability that the third ball is blue, given that the first ball is red and the second ball is green, is $P(B_3 = Blue \mid B_1 = Red \cap B_2 = Green) = 1$ since there is now only one ball left in the bag, and it's blue.

To calculate the joint probability, using the chain rule of probability, we have:

$$\begin{aligned} P(B_1 = Red \cap B_2 &= Green \cap B_3 = Blue) \\ &= P(B_1 = Red) \times P(B_2 = Green \mid B_1 = Red) \\ &\quad \times P(B_3 = Blue \mid [B_1 = Red \cap B_2 = Green]) \\ &= \frac{1}{3} \times \frac{1}{2} \times 1 = \frac{1}{6} \end{aligned}$$

Reassuringly, having calculated the probability using the chain rule of probability, we have achieved the same answer as when we simply considered the number of (equally) likely outcomes.

5.1.2 What happens if you have a bigger bag?

Suppose you now have a bigger bag, with seven coloured snooker balls in. This time, the balls are coloured red, yellow, green, brown, blue, pink, and black. Suppose that you randomly draw seven balls from the bag, without replacement (Figure 5.2).

If we are playing a game, where once again we need to predict the order in which the seven balls are drawn from the bag, we want to calculate the probability of correctly predicting the order of the balls. To understand this game, suppose that the first ball drawn was the red ball,

Figure 5.2 The possible balls from the bag.

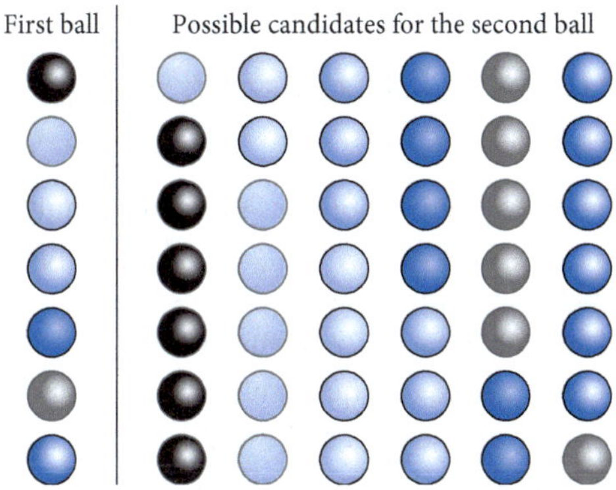

Figure 5.3 Possible candidates for the second ball, conditional on the first ball drawn.

then the second ball could not be red, but there would be six possible outcomes for the second ball. That is, the second ball could be yellow, green, brown, blue, pink, or black.

Similarly, if the first ball were yellow, again there would be six possible (equally likely) outcomes for the second ball (red, green, brown, blue, pink, or black). In fact, it will be the case for every possible first ball drawn that there will be six possible outcomes for the second ball. All of the possible second balls, conditional on the colour of the first ball, are illustrated in Figure 5.3.

So, this means that there would be $7 \times 6 = 42$ possible permutations for the first two balls. With seven balls, we could draw a tree diagram (as we did in the previous example), but hopefully you can see that, having just considered the first two balls drawn from the bag, the number of routes would be very large, and the diagram would very quickly become unmanageable.

We have seen that, since there are seven possible choices for the first ball, and for each of these seven possibilities there are six possible second balls, there are 42 possible permutations of the first two balls.

For each of those 42 possible permutations, there are five possible outcomes for the third ball; for example, if the first ball is red, and the second yellow, then the third could be any from green, brown, blue, pink, or black. This means that there would be $7 \times 6 \times 5$ possible permutations for the first three balls, and so on.

If we carry on this logic, it would tell us that:

- For the first ball, there are seven possibilities.
- For each of the possible first balls, there are six possible outcomes for the second ball.
- For each of the possible permutations of the first two balls, there are five possible outcomes for the third ball.

- For each of the possible permutations of the first three balls, there are four possible outcomes for the fourth ball.
- For each of the possible permutations of the first four balls, there are three possible outcomes for the fifth ball.
- For each of the possible permutations of the first five balls, there are two possible outcomes for the sixth ball.
- For each of the possible permutations of the first six balls, there is only one possible outcome for the final ball.

To calculate the total number of permutations, we would then multiply together the possible number of outcomes, giving us $7 \times 6 \times 5 \times 4 \times 3 \times 2 \times 1$. We can represent this as $7!$, or seven factorial possible outcomes. This would mean that, if we have seven (differently coloured) balls, there are $7! = 5{,}040$ possible ways of arranging the balls.

Since each of the possible outcomes is equally likely, this would mean that the probability of correctly guessing the order of the seven balls would be one in 5,040, or $\frac{1}{5040}$.

More generally, if you want to know how many ways there are of ordering n outcomes, then this can be calculated by simply looking at the factorial, $n!$

Worked example 5.1: The FA Cup Draw

In England, for each round of the Football Association (FA) Cup, all of the remaining competing teams are given numbered balls, and then the balls are drawn out of a pot to determine which sides play each other.

In the third round of the FA Cup (where the Premier League teams enter the competition), there are 64 teams who are in the pot.

This means that for the first ball drawn, there are 64 possibilities; for each of those 64 possibilities, there are 63 possibilities for the second ball and so on.

This means that there are 64 factorial (64!) possible orderings of balls that can be achieved through the third round draw for the FA Cup.

$$64! = 1.27 \times 10^{89}$$

However, this is not the number of possible combinations of teams. In the real FA Cup Draw, the order in which pairs of teams are drawn out makes no difference. For example, if Arsenal were drawn to play Aston Villa, it wouldn't matter if they were the first pair of teams drawn out (i.e. the first and second ball drawn), or the final pair (i.e. the sixty-third and sixty fourth pair).

What this tells us is the number of possible orders that those 64 balls could be drawn out of the pot.

5.1.3 What if you don't draw out all of the balls?

So far, we have considered what happens when we draw out all of the balls from the bag. In a lottery, however, the machine would rarely draw out all of the balls, but might, instead, draw out a sub-sample of the balls.

Let's look at the example in the previous section, where we have seven different coloured balls in a bag, but this time we will only draw out three balls (again from red, yellow, green, brown, blue, pink, and black).

Just as before, if we randomly choose the first ball, there are seven possibilities: having chosen the first ball, there are only six colours remaining, so for each of the seven possible balls first chosen, there are six possibilities for the second ball, then for each of the $7 \times 6 = 42$ possible pairs of first and second balls, there are five possible outcomes for the third ball, giving $7 \times 6 \times 5 = 210$ possible permutations from the three balls sampled. This also means that the probability of any given permutation is $\frac{1}{210}$. For instance, the probability of observing a red ball, then a green, and then a blue ball would be:

$$P(B_1 = Red \cap B_2 = Green \cap B_3 = Blue) = \frac{1}{210}$$

Just as before, we can represent the number of permutations using factorial notation. We know that $7! = 7 \times 6 \times 5 \times 4 \times 3 \times 2 \times 1$. However, the number of permutations is just equal to $7 \times 6 \times 5$, so we can construct this by dividing through $7!$ by $4 \times 3 \times 2 \times 1$, or four-factorial (4!).

$$\text{Number of permutations} = \frac{7!}{4!}$$

Finally, note that when we are drawing three balls from a bag containing seven balls, we divide through by 4! (which we can also think of as the factorial of seven minus three).

$$\text{Number of permutations} = \frac{7!}{4!} = \frac{7!}{(7-3)!} = 210$$

This notation will be helpful to bear in mind when we introduce more complicated cases.

5.1.4 A more general case

More generally, if there are n different balls that we are selecting from, and we are selecting k balls, then:

- There would be n possible outcomes for the first ball.
- For each of the n possible first balls, there will be $n - 1$ possible second balls, giving $n \times (n - 1)$ permutations of the first two balls.
- For each of the $n \times (n - 1)$ possible permutations, there will be $n - 2$ possible third balls, and so on.
- For the kth ball, there will be $n - (k - 1)$ possibilities, for each of the routes up to that kth ball.

This means that, if you draw k balls from the bag, we can calculate the number of permutations by considering the following product:

$$\text{Number of permutations} = n \times (n-1) \times (n-2) \times \ldots \times (n-(k-1)) = \prod_{i=0}^{k-1}(n-i)$$

That is, to find the number of permutations, we find the product of all of the integers between n (the number of balls in the bag) and $(n - k)$.

Alternatively, we can simplify the notation by using factorial notation. Just as in the case in Section 5.1.3, we can write $n \times (n - 1) \times (n - 2) \times \ldots \times (n - (k - 1))$ in terms of $n!$ and $(n - k)!$ This is just the same as:

$$\text{Number of permutations} = \frac{n!}{(n-k)!}$$

Similarly, since each of these orderings is equally likely, the probability can just be calculated as:

$$\frac{1}{\text{Number of orderings}} = \frac{(n-k)!}{n!}$$

Permutations notation

Formally, we will often write the number of permutations from drawing k balls from a population of n balls as P_k^n.

$$P_k^n = \frac{n!}{(n-k)!}$$

Most scientific calculators have a permutations button to allow you to calculate the number of possible permutations. This is often denoted as nPr on calculators, where n represents the size of bag, and r the sample size.

Worked example 5.2: Playing cards

A regular deck of playing cards contains 52 cards, arranged in four suits (spades, clubs, hearts, and diamonds). Each suit contains 13 cards, including the Ace, 2, 3, 4, 5, 6, 7, 8, 9, 10, Jack, Queen, and King. This means that, within the deck of cards, there are 52 unique cards.

If you randomly sample one card (without replacement), the probability of drawing any given card is $\frac{1}{52}$. Suppose that you shuffle the deck, to ensure that the cards are in a random order, and then deal five cards. We want to calculate the probability of obtaining the 10, Jack, Queen, King, and Ace of diamonds in that order.

We could use the chain rule of probability to calculate this, but it is easier to simply use our permutation notation. We are randomly sampling $k = 5$ from a population of $n = 52$. So, the number of possible outcomes is:

$$= P_5^{52} = \frac{52!}{(52-5)!} = 311{,}875{,}200$$

That means that there are 311,875,200 possible orderings of five cards drawn from a deck of 52, of which the 10, Jack, Queen, King, and Ace of diamonds in that order is just one.

Therefore, the probability of drawing out the 10, Jack, Queen, King, and Ace of diamonds is just equal to:

$$= \frac{1}{311{,}875{,}200} = 3.206 \times 10^{-9}\ (4sf)$$

5.2 Combinations without replacement

In Section 5.1.3, we showed that, if we randomly picked three snooker balls from a bag containing seven balls, then there were 210 different permutations of the balls. This meant that the probability of correctly guessing the balls that are drawn out, and the order in which they are drawn out, was $\frac{1}{210}$.

So, for instance, we showed that:

$$P(B_1 = Red \cap B_2 = Blue \cap B_3 = Green) = \frac{1}{210}$$

However, in many cases, we will not be interested in the precise order that observations are drawn from a population, but instead will only be interested in the combination of outcomes that we actually observe. For instance, in the UK National Lottery, ticket-holders win the jackpot if they match all six numbers, irrespective of the order in which the balls are drawn.

Similarly, if we are randomly sampling individuals from the population, to estimate the proportion of individuals with a particular eye colour, all that we are interested in is the number of people in our sample with that eye colour, and not the precise order in which we observe those individuals.

In this section, we will examine how to calculate probabilities, where all that matters is the combination of outcomes that we see, and the order does not matter.

5.2.1 Simple example: Randomly choosing snooker balls

Let's begin by re-examining the example where we have seven snooker balls in a bag, and we are interested in the probability of drawing out a red, a green, and a blue ball. If the order that the balls are selected doesn't matter, then all that matters is that, when sampling three balls from the bag, you randomly choose a red, a green, and a blue ball.

Just by sequentially working through the possible permutations of these three balls, as shown in Figure 5.4, we can see that there are six possible ways that we can obtain a red, green, and blue ball. However, if we do not care about the order the balls are drawn, (A)–(F) would be treated as the same outcome.

In fact, it will be the case that for any combination of three balls, there will be six equally likely orders they could be drawn. When we examined the total number of permutations of three balls drawn from seven, we found 210 possible permutations, but each combination will be repeated six times, in different orders.

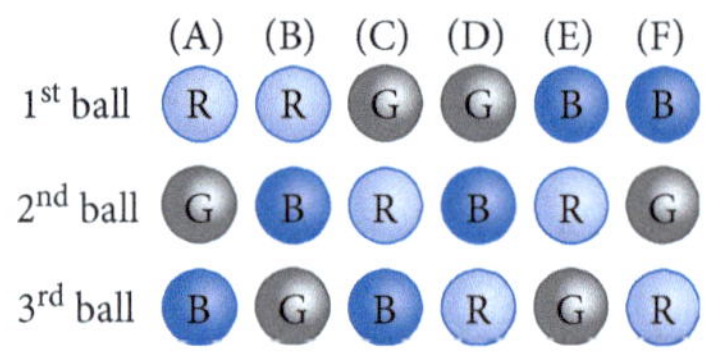

Figure 5.4 Possible orderings of a red, green, and blue ball when drawing this combination of balls.

Remember, in this example we only care about the combination of balls drawn out, and not the order in which they are drawn, so each of the outcomes (A)–(F) is equivalent when examining the number of combinations.

To calculate the number of combinations of three balls drawn from a population of seven, we just need to divide the total number of permutations by the number of ways each combination of balls is repeated. In this case, we know that there are 210 different permutations, but each possible combination will appear six times.

As such, to calculate the number of possible combinations, we can take the possible number of permutations of three balls, and divide it by the number of ways we can arrange the three balls in each combination. Therefore, we can conclude that there are $\frac{210}{6}$ possible combinations.

Obviously, we don't want to rely on having to write down each possible ordering sequentially when we wish to calculate the number of ways we can arrange each different combination, so we need a mathematical trick to be able to evaluate this. If you think back to Section 5.1.1, we were considering how many ways we could draw three coloured balls from a bag that contained three balls, and we concluded that the answer was $3! = 6$.

The problem of the number of ways each combination can be rearranged is actually identical to the previous problem. Suppose that we are looking for the number of ways that we can order a red, a green, and a blue ball. We are effectively restricting ourselves to only thinking about the red, green, and blue balls. If we were to have a bag containing only a red, green, and blue ball, and there were six ($= 3!$) different ways we could draw those balls out of the bag—the act of drawing the balls out of the bag is simply about establishing an order of the three balls. As such, the number of different orderings of the combination of red, green, and blue balls (i.e. the number of different permutations that we could achieve) will just be equal to $3!$ (i.e. 3 factorial).

We know, generally, that if we randomly draw three balls from a population of seven (without replacement), there are $P_3^7 = \frac{7!}{(7-3)!} = 210$ different permutations of the balls (where the order matters). We have also seen that each combination of three balls will be repeated $3! = 6$ times within the list of possible permutations, and as such, the total number of combinations will just be:

$$= \frac{P_3^7}{3!} = \frac{7!}{(7-3)!3!} = 35$$

So, by calculating the number of combinations, each of which is equally likely, we can also calculate the probability of each combination, which will just be $\frac{1}{35}$.

5.2.2 A more general case

More generally, suppose that we wanted to know the probability of correctly predicting a draw of k balls from a population of n balls. We saw in Section 5.1.4 that if we sample k balls from a population of n balls, there are $P_k^n = \frac{n!}{(n-k)!}$ possible permutations; however, this counts each separate ordering as a different outcome.

Since there are a range of different orderings of the k balls, the number of combinations of k balls drawn from a population of n is equal to the number of permutations, divided by the number of orderings of the k balls:

$$\text{Number of combinations} = \frac{P_k^n}{\text{number of orderings of k balls}}$$

However, the denominator here, the number of orderings of k balls, is itself a permutation. For a given set of k balls, we are looking at the number of permutations that k balls can be sampled from a set of k balls.

Thus, the number of orderings of the k balls can be written as: $P_k^k = k!$

Thus, if we choose k balls from a population of n balls, the number of available combinations is equal to:

$$\text{Number of combinations} = \frac{P_k^n}{P_k^k} = \frac{n!}{(n-k)!k!}$$

Since each of the combinations is equally likely, we could calculate the probability of any particular set of k balls being drawn out of a bag of n balls as 1/Number of combinations $= \frac{(n-k)!k!}{n!}$.

Combinations notation

Formally, we will often write the number of combinations from drawing k balls from a population of n balls as C_k^n.

$$C_k^n = \frac{n!}{(n-k)!k!}$$

Most scientific calculators have a permutations button to allow you to calculate the number of possible combinations.

This is often denoted as nCr on calculators, where n represents the size of bag, and r the sample size.

5.2.3 Combinations without replacement: Pascal's triangle

A very useful tool, when it comes to remembering and thinking about combinations is Pascal's triangle. In Pascal's triangle, each of the elements of the $n + 1$th row is calculated by adding together the corresponding two elements, directly above, in the nth row. Figure 5.5 shows the first ten rows of Pascal's triangle.

n	
0	1
1	1 1
2	1 2 1
3	1 3 3 1
4	1 4 6 4 1
5	1 5 10 10 5 1
6	1 6 15 20 15 6 1
7	1 7 21 35 35 21 7 1
8	1 8 28 56 70 56 28 8 1
9	1 9 36 84 126 126 84 36 9 1

Figure 5.5 The first ten rows of Pascal's triangle.

You have probably come across Pascal's triangle when learning how to expand expressions involving powers; for example, if you are trying to expand $(X + Y)^3$, then the coefficients in front of each term can be found by looking at row $n = 3$ of Pascal's triangle (1 3 3 1):

$$(X + Y)^3 = X^3 + 3XY^2 + 3X^2Y + Y^3$$

However, it may be easier to adapt Pascal's triangle, so that the left-hand diagonal is a vertical. This will represent choosing the number of ways of choosing zero from a population of size n. Figure 5.6 presents Pascal's triangle as a grid.

Pascal's triangle is also very useful when it comes to calculating combinations; each element of Pascal's triangle also relates to a number of combinations relating to the row number. So, if we wanted to calculate the number of combinations of outcomes when we

n \ k	0	1	2	3	4	5	6	7	8	9
0	1									
1	1	1								
2	1	2	1							
3	1	3	3	1						
4	1	4	6	4	1					
5	1	5	10	10	5	1				
6	1	6	15	20	15	6	1			
7	1	7	21	35	35	21	7	1		
8	1	8	28	56	70	56	28	8	1	
9	1	9	36	84	126	126	84	36	9	1

Figure 5.6 Presenting Pascal's triangle as a grid.

C_k^n	0	1	2	3	4	5	6	7	8	9
0	1									
1	1	1								
2	1	2	1							
3	1	3	3	1						
4	1	4	6	4	1					
5	1	5	10	10	5	1				
6	1	6	15	20	15	6	1			
7	1	7	21	35	35	21	7	1		
8	1	8	28	56	70	56	28	8	1	
9	1	9	36	84	126	126	84	36	9	1

Figure 5.7 Calculating C_k^n using Pascal's triangle.

randomly sample k from a population of n, we could calculate C_k^n, or alternatively look at the kth column, and the nth row of Pascal's triangle (see Figure 5.7).

The row number is equivalent to n, whilst the entry along the row relates to the value of k. However, it should be noted that in Pascal's triangle, the first value of n and k is equal to 0. That is, at the apex of Pascal's triangle, this value relates to $C_0^0 = 1$. That is, there is 1 way of sampling 0 elements from a total of 0. Similarly, if we looked at the row labelled $n = 5$, the third element along relates to $C_2^5 = 10$. That is, there are 10 possible combinations where we randomly draw two equally likely elements from a population of five. Pascal's triangle not only provides us with insights into combinations and permutations, but is useful for dealing with power, binomial distributions, and more.

Worked example 5.3: Sushi restaurants

Sushi restaurants provide a really interesting way of trying to apply combinations. In a sushi restaurant, there is normally a very wide range of possible dishes that you can eat, and diners will tend to choose a number of options.

A popular Sushi restaurant has introduced a competition whereby you get to choose six different dishes from their menu. If you are the first person (during the competition period) to choose a particular combination of dishes, then they will give you your meal for free. Otherwise, you will have to pay for your meal. This restaurant has 50 dishes available on the menu. This raises two questions:

1. How many combinations of dishes are there on the menu?
2. If everyone chooses dishes randomly, what is the probability of winning?

This is an example of a combination. For the competition, it does not matter what order you select your six dishes; for example, you might order miso soup as one item, but it wouldn't matter whether it was the first item, or the sixth item that you order.

Calculating the number of possible combinations is very easy, as we simply need to apply the formula:

$$C_6^{50} = \frac{50!}{(50-6)!6!} = 15{,}890{,}700$$

Calculating the probability of winning is a little more difficult, as you would need more information about the promotion. Initially, when no one has taken part in the competition, the first person to enter would be guaranteed of winning (as no one had previously chosen a meal), so their probability of winning would be 1.

However, as the number of previous winners increases, the number of untried combinations will decrease. After there are 100 winners, the probability that you randomly choose a combination that has already been chosen would be $\frac{100}{15{,}890{,}700}$, and similarly, the probability of winning would be $1 - \frac{100}{15{,}890{,}700}$.

If there had already been 10,000,000 winners, then the probability of winning would be much smaller $(= 1 - \frac{10{,}000{,}000}{15{,}890{,}700})$.

Of course, people rarely choose randomly from a menu, which would mean that not all combinations are equally likely, meaning that some combinations might be less likely to occur than others.

Worked example 5.4: The UK National Lottery

The UK's National Lottery is drawn by randomly selecting six balls, without replacement, from a set of 59 balls, numbered 1–59. Players can either choose six balls themselves, or can ask for a 'lucky dip' where six numbers were chosen, randomly, for them.

Initially, jackpots were approximately £10 million per draw, with the jackpot split between all ticket-holders who had chosen the six winning numbers.

There are a number of interesting questions relating to the lottery, but let's start by asking what is probability of any given combination of six numbers winning the jackpot?

What is the probability of winning the jackpot in the National Lottery?

In the first instance, we could simply use the formula we have developed in the UK National Lottery example, where each of the balls has an equal probability of being selected. We are choosing six balls from a population of 59 possible balls, so if we calculate C_k^n, where n is equal to 59 and k is equal to 6, this will give us the number of combinations.

$$C_6^{59} = \frac{59!}{(53)!6!} = \frac{59 \times 58 \times 57 \times 56 \times 55 \times 54}{6 \times 5 \times 4 \times 3 \times 2 \times 1} = 45{,}057{,}474$$

Thus, there are 45,057,474 possible combinations of six balls drawn out of a population of 59 balls, and the probability of winning if you buy one ticket is 1 in 45,057,474.

That is, the probability is:

$$\frac{1}{C_6^{59}} = \frac{6 \times 5 \times 4 \times 3 \times 2 \times 1}{59 \times 58 \times 57 \times 56 \times 55 \times 54} = \frac{1}{45{,}057{,}474}$$

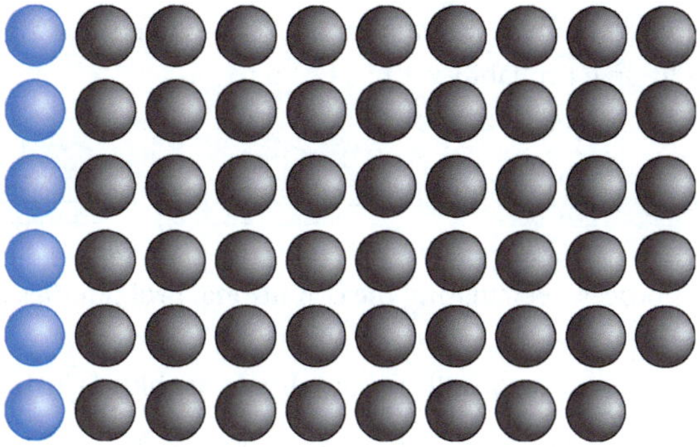

Figure 5.8 Lottery balls, replacing our chosen numbers with balls painted blue.

An alternative method

We have calculated the probability of winning the National Lottery by thinking about the number of possible combinations, using C_6^{59}. This is not, however, the most intuitive way of calculating this probability, and an alternative way might be to try to take advantage of the chain rule of probability.

If we think of this problem using numbered balls, this makes the problem unnecessarily cognitively complex, so let's simplify things. Suppose that, prior to the draw, we have painted the six balls corresponding to the numbers we have chosen blue, and painted all of the other balls black (see Figure 5.8). The lottery machine will then randomly select six balls from the machine. In order to calculate the probability of winning the lottery, this is equivalent to calculating the probability of the lottery machine choosing all six blue balls from the machine.

Let's begin with a simple question: What is the probability that the first two balls drawn from the machine will be blue?

To solve this, let's define B_i as the ith ball drawn. We know that, since there are 59 balls in the machine, six of which are blue, the probability that the first ball is blue is just $P(B_1 = Blue) = \frac{6}{59}$. Then, to calculate the probability that the second ball is also blue, we need to apply the chain rule of probability:

$$P(B_1 = Blue \cap B_2 = Blue) = P(B_1 = Blue) \times P(B_2 = Blue | B_1 = Blue)$$

Having drawn out one blue ball, there are 58 balls left in the machine, of which five are blue. As such, the conditional probability that the second ball is blue (given that the first ball is blue) is just $\frac{5}{58}$. So, the joint probability is:

$$\begin{aligned} P(B_1 = Blue \cap B_2 = Blue) &= P(B_1 = Blue) \times P(B_2 = Blue | B_1 = Blue) \\ &= \frac{6}{59} \times \frac{5}{58} = \frac{6 \times 5}{59 \times 58} \end{aligned}$$

Similarly, the probability that the first three balls are blue is just:

$$\begin{aligned} &P(B_1 = Blue \cap B_2 = Blue \cap B_3 = Blue) \\ &\quad = P(B_1 = Blue \cap B_2 = Blue) \times P(B_3 = Blue | [B_1 = Blue \cap B_2 = Blue]) \end{aligned}$$

Again, if the first two balls are blue, then there are 57 balls left in the machine, of which, four are blue. So the conditional probability is just equal to $\frac{5}{57}$.

Our joint probability then becomes:

$$P(B_1 = Blue \cap B_2 = Blue \cap B_3 = Blue) = \frac{6}{59} \times \frac{5}{58} \times \frac{4}{57} = \frac{6 \times 5 \times 4}{59 \times 58 \times 57}$$

We can carry on this process, calculating the conditional probabilities for the 4th ($= \frac{3}{56}$), 5th ($= \frac{2}{55}$), and 6th ($= \frac{1}{55}$) balls drawn.

As such, the joint probability that all six balls drawn are blue is just:

$$P(B_1 = Blue \cap B_2 = Blue \cap B_3 = Blue \cap B_4 = Blue \cap B_5 = Blue \cap B_6 = Blue)$$
$$= \frac{6}{59} \times \frac{5}{58} \times \frac{4}{57} \times \frac{3}{56} \times \frac{2}{55} \times \frac{1}{54} = \frac{6 \times 5 \times 4 \times 3 \times 2 \times 1}{59 \times 58 \times 57 \times 56 \times 55 \times 54} = \frac{1}{45{,}057{,}474}$$

So, using this second method, we have again found that the probability that all six blue balls are drawn out (or equivalently, the probability of winning the UK National Lottery) is 1 in 45,057,474.

What is the probability of winning smaller prizes in the National Lottery?

A more interesting (and more widely applicable) question is what is the probability of winning smaller prizes in the UK National Lottery? For example, players win a cash prize if they match three balls.[1] To calculate the probability of matching three balls exactly, we are going to need to use a combination of techniques that we have seen, both in this chapter and in previous chapters.

Just as in the previous section, we are going to treat the balls we have chosen as if they have been painted blue, and the balls that we have not chosen as if they have been painted yellow. So, there are 59 balls, and we are randomly choosing six balls, and we want to calculate the probability of exactly three of the balls being blue.

If we draw six balls from the population (without replacement), it is very easy to calculate the probability that the first three balls are blue. We will simply use the chain rule of probability to calculate:

$$P(B_1 = Blue \cap B_2 = Blue \cap B_3 = Blue \cap B_4 = \text{Black} \cap B_5 = \text{Black} \cap B_6 = \text{Black})$$

To calculate this probability, we will need to know the following conditional probabilities:

First ball	The (marginal) probability that the first ball is blue is $\frac{6}{59}$.
Second ball	Having initially drawn a blue ball, there are 58 balls in the machine, five of which are blue, giving a conditional probability of $\frac{5}{58}$.
Third ball	Having two blue balls, there are 57 balls in the machine, four of which are blue, giving a conditional probability of $\frac{4}{57}$.

[1] From November 2018, the standard prize was £30 for matching three numbers.

Fourth ball	Having drawn blue balls for the first three draws, there are 56 balls in the machine, 53 of which are black, giving a conditional probability of $\frac{53}{56}$.
Fifth ball	Having drawn three blue balls and one black ball, there are 55 balls in the machine, 52 of which are black, giving a conditional probability of $\frac{52}{55}$.
Sixth ball	Having drawn three blue balls and two black balls, there are 54 balls in the machine, 51 of which are black, giving a conditional probability of $\frac{51}{55}$.

As such, the probability of drawing the first three balls as blue, and the remaining three as black, is given by finding the product of these probabilities:

$$= \frac{6}{59} \times \frac{5}{58} \times \frac{4}{57} \times \frac{53}{56} \times \frac{52}{55} \times \frac{51}{54} = \frac{6 \times 5 \times 4 \times 53 \times 52 \times 51}{59 \times 58 \times 57 \times 56 \times 55 \times 54} = \frac{11{,}713}{22{,}528{,}737}$$

However, this is only one way in which we can achieve exactly three balls. We could also calculate the probability that the first three balls were black, and the fourth, fifth, and sixth were blue, using the same arguments. The probability would be:

$$= \frac{53}{59} \times \frac{52}{58} \times \frac{51}{57} \times \frac{6}{56} \times \frac{5}{55} \times \frac{4}{54} = \frac{6 \times 5 \times 4 \times 53 \times 52 \times 51}{59 \times 58 \times 57 \times 56 \times 55 \times 54} = \frac{11{,}713}{22{,}528{,}737}$$

The first thing to notice is that these two probabilities are exactly the same. In fact, the probability of drawing exactly three blue and three black balls in any permutation will be the same, and equal to 1 in 1,923. However, we are not interested in the probability that the first (or the last) three balls are blue, but instead, the probability of obtaining exactly three balls which are blue.

To calculate the probability of gaining exactly three blue balls, we will need to add up all of the probabilities where we gain exactly three blue balls. However, as we have seen, the probability of any particular arrangement of three blue balls and three black balls in this example is the same. As such, since multiplication is equivalent to adding the same values repeatedly, we simply need to calculate the number of ways that we can arrange three blue and three black balls, and multiply this by the probability of any particular arrangement of three blue and three black balls.

Figure 5.9 shows all of the possible ways in which we could draw exactly three blue balls and three black balls. Counting up the number of possible arrangements gives us 20 possible arrangements; however, once again, this is just an application of combinations.

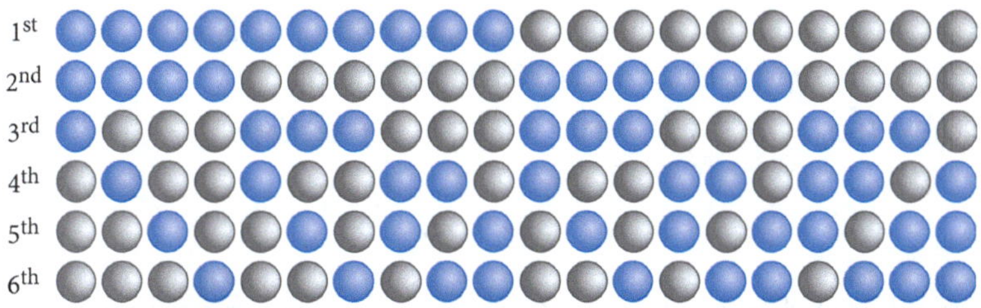

Figure 5.9 All of the possible arrangements with exactly three blue and three black balls.

If we assign the position of the blue ball numbers, when the first three balls are blue, then this is equivalent to thinking about the blue balls in positions 1, 2, 3.

Similarly, in the second case, the blue balls are in positions 1, 2, 4, and so on. Calculating the number of ways in which we can rearrange the balls is just like asking how many ways we can sample three numbers out of six, where the order doesn't matter.[2]

But we already know how to calculate this, by using our combinations notation. This is equivalent to finding $C_3^6 = \frac{6!}{(6-3)!3!} = \frac{720}{6\times 6} = 20$.

Since there are 20 ways of gaining exactly three blue balls (out of the six selected), we can calculate the probability of gaining exactly three blue balls (and three black balls) by multiplying the probability we constructed earlier by 20:

$$\begin{aligned}\text{Probability of gaining exactly three blue balls} &= 20 \times \frac{11{,}713}{22{,}528{,}737} = \frac{234{,}260}{22{,}528{,}737} \\ &= 0.0104\,(4dp)\end{aligned}$$

So, the probability of obtaining exactly three blue balls and three black balls is equal to 0.0104, or approximately 1 in 96.

5.2.4 Where else can combinations be applied?

There are lots of applications of combinations which are important in both probability and statistics. For example, when sampling from a population, you might want to know the probability of gaining a particular outcome.

This will become particularly important in statistics, where we might not know anything for certain about a population, but we might have an initial hypothesis about the characteristics of that population. In statistical testing, we begin with a hypothesis and then ask what is the likelihood of obtaining a sample that we have observed, if that hypothesis were true.

Worked example 5.5: Sampling with replacement from a population

Suppose that you were to flip a biased coin ten times. The probability of gaining a head from this biased coin is 0.2 (and the probability of gaining a tail is 0.8). How can we calculate the probability of seeing exactly three heads?

Let's define C_i as the outcome from the ith flip of the coin, and we will denote a head as h and a tail as t. Each of the flips of the coin is an independent random variable, so the conditional (and marginal) probability for each flip being a head is:

$$P(C_i = h) = P(C_i = h|C_j = h) = P(C_i = h|C_j = t) = 0.2 \text{ for all } i \neq j$$

[2] Saying that the blue balls lie in the first, second, and third positions is exactly the same as saying that the blue balls lie in the third, second, and first positions.

It is relatively straightforward to calculate the probability that the first three flips land heads upwards, and the remaining seven as tails upwards as:

$$\begin{aligned} P(C_1 &= h \cap C_2 = h \cap C_3 = h \cap C_4 = t \cap C_5 = t \cap C_6 = t \cap C_7 = t \cap C_8 \\ &= t \cap C_9 = t \cap C_{10} = t) \\ &= 0.2 \times 0.2 \times 0.2 \times 0.8 \times 0.8 \times 0.8 \times 0.8 \times 0.8 \times 0.8 \times 0.8 = 0.2^3 \times 0.8^7 \end{aligned}$$

Since the flips of the coin are independent, we can calculate the joint probability by multiplying together the marginal probabilities.

However, this is only one order where we could observe exactly three heads; the three heads could be the last three flips of the coin; they could be the second, fourth, and sixth flips, and so on. Irrespective of the positions that the three heads are in, the probability of each specific case where we observe three heads will be equal to $0.2^3 \times 0.8^7$.

To calculate the number of ways that we could obtain three heads, we need to think about how many ways we could arrange three heads out of ten outcomes. The order of the outcomes doesn't matter here, so we can use our combinations formula:

$$= C_3^{10} = \frac{10!}{(10-3)!3!} = 120$$

So, there are 120 possible ways we could observe three heads when we flip a coin 120 times. To calculate the probability of gaining exactly three heads, we will need to multiply the joint probability by the number of ways we can arrange three heads out of ten:

$$= 0.2^3 \times 0.8^7 \times 120 = 0.201326592$$

That is, if the probability of gaining a head is 0.2, then if we repeatedly flip the coin ten times, approximately 20.1 per cent of the time, we would obtain exactly three heads.

We will come back to similar examples later in the book, when we introduce the binomial distribution.

Worked example 5.6: Sampling without replacement from a population

To illustrate sampling without replacement, let's consider the following example. We have a population of 100 first-year undergraduate students at the University of Erewhon.[3] We might know that 60 per cent of the students (i.e. 60 students in the population) are first-generation university attenders (i.e. their parents did not attend university), and the remaining 40 per cent have at least one parent who attended university.

Suppose that you randomly sample ten students from the population (without replacement). We might want to calculate the probability that exactly k of the students have parents who attended university. In this case, let's set $k = 2$.

[3] Erewhon is not a real place, and credit needs to be given to Samuel Butler's novel of the same name from 1872. That being said, this university has quite a small economics programme.

It is relatively straightforward to calculate the probability that, say, the first two of the ten students sampled have parents who attended university; for the first student sampled, there are 100 students in the population, of whom 40 had parents who attended university. As such, the probability that the first student sampled has parents who attended university is $\frac{40}{100}$. Similarly, the conditional probability that the second student drawn has parents who attended university is $\frac{39}{99}$.

Conditional on these two observations, the probability that the third student is a first-generation student is $\frac{60}{98}$; there are 98 students left, of whom 60 are first generation, and so on. This allows us to calculate the probability that the first two students observed have parents who attended university, and the remaining eight are first generation, as follows:

$$= \frac{40}{100} \times \frac{39}{99} \times \frac{60}{98} \times \frac{59}{97} \times \frac{58}{96} \times \frac{57}{95} \times \frac{56}{94} \times \frac{55}{93} \times \frac{54}{92} \times \frac{53}{91}$$

However, this is only one order in which we can observe exactly two students who have parents who attended university. If we were to calculate the probability that only the ninth and tenth students sampled had parents who attended university, then the probability would be exactly the same.[4]

As such, we need to calculate the number of ways we could have exactly two out of ten; this means that we need to consider the number of combinations of positions that the two students could be drawn in; for example, they could be drawn in first and second, first and third, third and fourth, and so on. Therefore, we need to calculate the number of combinations of two drawn out of ten:

$$= C_2^{10} = \frac{10!}{(10-2)! \times 2!} = 45$$

So, the probability of drawing exactly two students with at least one parent who attended university, and the remaining eight as first generation students, would be:

$$= 45 \times \frac{40}{100} \times \frac{39}{99} \times \frac{60}{98} \times \frac{59}{97} \times \frac{58}{96} \times \frac{57}{95} \times \frac{56}{94} \times \frac{55}{93} \times \frac{54}{92} \times \frac{53}{91} = 0.115\,(3dp)$$

In statistics, effectively we begin with a prior belief, or a hypothesis, about a population. In this example, we might not know the exact proportion of individuals who are first generation. However, we might hypothesize that the true proportion is 60 per cent.

We would then randomly sample a set of observations from the population, and we might, for example, observe exactly eight individuals who are first generation (and two who have at least one parent who attended university). We could then calculate the probability of achieving the observed sample, if our hypothesis were true.

This is very much a simplification of what we do in statistical testing, but we will flesh this out in more detail in future chapters.

[4] You can check this as an exercise.

Summary

In this chapter, we have shown that when we are dealing with repeated sampling from a population, the design of the problem really matters; the probability of particular outcomes is very different if you care about the order in which observations are seen, from if you simply care about the overall outcome. For example, the probability of gaining the numbers 1, 2, 3, 4, 5, 6 from the UK National Lottery would be much smaller if we had not only to match the numbers that came out from the machine, but also to predict the order in which the numbers are drawn.

Key formulae

We have seen two key formulae. When calculating the number of possible outcomes from a random trial, where we are interested in the probability of choosing k possible options from a population of n individuals, then:

1. If the order in which the k options are drawn does not matter, we can calculate this as a combination, and the number of possible combinations can be calculated as:

$$= C_k^n = \frac{n!}{(n-k)!k!}$$

2. If the order in which the k options does matter, we can calculate this as a permutation, and the number of possible permutations can be calculated as:

$$= P_k^n = \frac{n!}{(n-k)!}$$

Sample Averages

6

Learning outcomes for this chapter

By the end of this chapter you will be able to:

- Explain the difference between a population and a sample
- Explain what it means to be average
- Calculate arithmetic and geometric mean averages, medians, and modes, based on a sample of data
- Explain that the mean, median, and mode may be different
- Choose appropriate averages based on the type of data used

Mathematical tools

- Summations using sigma (Σ) notation
- Simple arithmetic
- Square roots and powers

Introduction

You will often read in news articles about 'averages'. This might be about average wages, average house prices, average inflation rates, and so on. For example, in March 2023,[1] the BBC reported of the UK population:

> The wage of an average full-time employee stood at about £33,000 in the year to March 2022, having risen by about a quarter over the ten years until then. At this point wages had risen above inflation by about £1,250.

However, an important question is what is meant by 'average'? Averages are a group of measures that represent the 'centre' or the 'middle' of a distribution, which you will sometimes hear described as a measure of central tendency. We have seen both samples and populations in this book; this chapter will focus on averages within samples, and in the next chapter, we will discuss averages within populations.

[1] BBC News (2023), 'What has happened to pay in the UK?', https://www.bbc.co.uk/news/business-64944262 (accessed 16 July 2023).

6.1 What are populations and samples?

In statistics, we will often need to think about the difference between a sample and a population. We introduced the concept of a population in the first chapter; a population consists of all of the possible individuals we could consider. What we define as 'the population' will vary depending on what question we are asking.

For example, a roadrunner is a fast-running ground bird, native to the USA and Mexico. If we were interested in the (ground) running speed of roadrunners in the USA, our population would include all of the roadrunners who live in the USA.

Alternatively, we might be interested in the ground speed of birds native to the USA more generally. In this case, our population would include all of the birds in the USA.

The two populations we have described here would be very different from each other. Whilst the population of roadrunners would be part of both populations, the second population (all birds in the USA) would be likely to have far more variation in ground speed than the first population.

In the same way, a population might consist of:

- all of the people in the world
- all of the working-age men living in the USA
- all of the left-handed people studying economics.

However, populations don't need to consist of living beings. If we think about the examples in the previous chapter of lotteries, one population of interest might be all of the numbered balls contained within the machine. A second population might be the set of all possible draws (of six numbers) from the machine.

In the UK National Lottery, the first population consists of 59 balls, so the population contains 59 individual outcomes. The second population, however, is much larger, and consists of 45,057,474 individual outcomes. Both of these are interesting populations in their own right, and may be of interest to analyse. Similarly, a population might consist of every game of chess ever played in the history of time, or every outcome from a flip of a particular coin.

An important distinction is between a sample and a population. A sample is merely a smaller subset of the larger population. Often, we will construct samples so that the observations are randomly drawn from a population, because by doing so, the sample is more likely to be representative of the population as a whole.

Populations have characteristics that are often unknown. Statisticians use these representative samples to try to estimate these characteristics of the population. For instance, they may wish to estimate the proportion of the UK population that is left-handed, and so might randomly sample 1,000 people, and calculate the proportion of their sample who are left-handed. This would give an estimate of the proportion of the population as a whole who are left-handed. The reason for doing this is that when a population is large, statisticians rarely get the opportunity to observe the entirety of the population; there are exceptions, such as the census of the population that, in the UK, is carried out every ten years, but often, collecting data about the entirety of the population is difficult and costly.

We will talk about using samples to estimate population parameters in more detail in future chapters, but in this chapter, we will begin to discuss the characteristics of a sample, and will apply the same concepts to populations in Chapter 7.

6.2 What is an average?

In probability and statistics, we will often observe populations where outcomes are uncertain. For example, if we randomly observe an individual of working age from the UK population, their weekly wage is uncertain. Where outcomes are uncertain, we need to have measures to describe the population as a whole, providing information about where the data is centred, what the spread of the data is, and the likelihood of observations lying within different parts of the distribution.

An average is a measure telling us about where the data is centred, and is often referred to as a measure of central tendency of the data. There are lots of different types of averages, and we will talk about averages for both populations and samples. Put simply, an average is a measure of the 'middle' of the data.

6.3 Sample averages

We will begin by discussing sample averages. Remember, a sample is merely a subset of a population; it could consist of a very small number of observations (e.g. 1–2) or a very large number of observations (e.g. 1,000,000), but a sample is still merely a subset of that larger population.

You may well have come across sample averages in your prior education; a sample average provides a measure of the middle, or centre, of the data within your sample, and there are several different forms of sample average. In this section, we will discuss four such measures:

a) The sample (arithmetic) mean

b) The sample (geometric) mean

c) The sample median

d) The sample mode

6.3.1 Arithmetic mean

It is likely that you have already come across the concept of an average in your previous education, and it is likely that you have some experience of the arithmetic mean. The arithmetic mean is calculated by adding together all of the (numerical) observations, and dividing through by the number of observations. For example, suppose that you randomly selected five individuals on the high street, and measured their heights. You might observe data that looks something like this:

Individual	1	2	3	4	5
Height (m)	1.87	1.55	1.65	1.88	1.83

We can calculate the arithmetic mean by adding up the heights of the five individuals, and dividing through by five:

$$\text{Arithmetic mean} = \frac{1}{5} \times (1.87 + 1.55 + 1.65 + 1.88 + 1.83) = \frac{1}{5} \times 8.78 = 1.756$$

So, the arithmetic sample mean is equal to 1.756. The arithmetic mean provides us with an indication that the 'centre' of the data is equal to 1.756; it is not the case that any particular observation is equal to 1.756, but the sample mean is using information from all of the available observations to give us an indication of where the centre of the data is.

FORMAL NOTATION: ARITHMETIC MEAN

Formally, if we were to observe n observations of a variable X, with the ith observation represented as X_i, then the sample mean would be defined as:

$$\overline{X} = \frac{1}{n}\sum_{i=1}^{n} X_i$$

We normally denote a sample mean of a variable by drawing a bar over the top of it. In the example in Section 6.3.1, $\overline{X}$ is the sample mean of observations of X.

Intuitively, when we are calculating a sample mean, we are constructing a value for a representative individual from the sample, where that representative individual is 'average'.

When we divide through by the number of observations (n), this is equivalent to dividing through each observation by n; this is equivalent to placing an equal weight on each observation.

$$\overline{X} = \frac{1}{n}\sum_{i=1}^{n} X_i = \frac{X_1}{n} + \frac{X_2}{n} + \frac{X_3}{n} + \ldots + \frac{X_n}{n}$$

The sample mean is essentially a function that takes all of the information from the n observations, and re-scales those n observations to be equivalent to 1 representative individual, with all of the observations providing an equal weight.

Worked example 6.1: Average spending (per capita) on healthcare

The Organisation for Economic Co-operation and Development (OECD) publish data on a range of economic indicators. We are interested in the average spending on healthcare across the world. To that end, we have collected data from 50 countries, using the OECD database, of per-capita spending on healthcare in 2019. The observations are illustrated in Figure 6.1 and in Table 6.1[2]

[2] This data is available to download from Data Sets and Exercises at the end of the chapter.

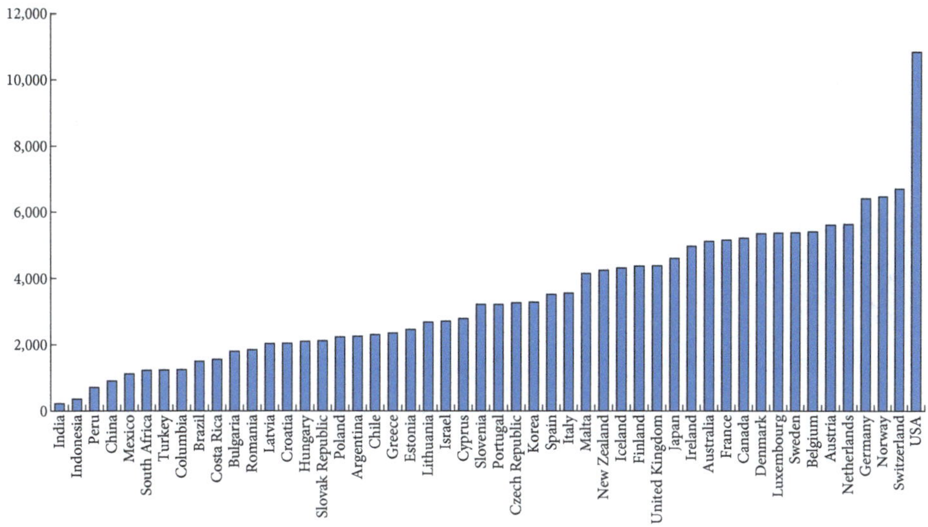

Figure 6.1 Spending per capita in 2019 on healthcare (US$, data from the OECD).

Table 6.1 Spending per capita in 2019 on healthcare (US$, data from the OECD).

Country	Spending	Country	Spending	Country	Spending	Country	Spending
Argentina	2254.047	Czech Republic	3272.224	Italy	3565.324	Portugal	3223.676
Australia	5126.653	Denmark	5359.776	Japan	4610.794	Romania	1844.269
Austria	5625.442	Estonia	2453.074	Korea	3290.825	Slovak Republic	2115.452
Belgium	5423.676	Finland	4383.634	Latvia	2025.57	Slovenia	3221.895
Brazil	1497.734	France	5163.421	Lithuania	2682.067	South Africa	1222.202
Bulgaria	1795.621	Germany	6418.323	Luxembourg	5379.663	Spain	3528.382
Canada	5222.644	Greece	2349.574	Malta	4154.13	Sweden	5387.733
Chile	2296.988	Hungary	2095.186	Mexico	1117.235	Switzerland	6708.349
China	901.854	Iceland	4318.27	Netherlands	5643.59	Turkey	1231.634
Columbia	1239.66	India	219.575	New Zealand	4249.593	United Kingdom	4389.038
Costa Rica	1556.168	Indonesia	356.262	Norway	6476.378	USA	10852.838
Croatia	2043.652	Ireland	4976.129	Peru	702.355		
Cyprus	2783.252	Israel	2709.984	Poland	2232.347		

We can see that in the data set, the country with the lowest spending per capita is India with \$219.575 per capita, and the highest with \$10,852.838 per capita. However, we are interested in the average, and particularly the mean average. To calculate this we need to add together all of the observations, and divide by the number of countries within our sample.

You can replicate this for yourself, but the sum of the per-capita healthcare spending across the 50 countries was 171,698.2. That is:[3]

$$\sum_{i=1}^{50} x_i = 171{,}698.2$$

Thus, we can calculate the sample mean by dividing this sum by the number of observations (50).

$$\bar{x} = \frac{1}{50}\sum_{i=1}^{50} x_i = \frac{171{,}698.2}{50} = 3{,}433.963$$

For comparison, in Great Britain, the per-capita healthcare spending was above average, at \$4,380.038, whilst Greece was below average at \$2,349.574 per capita.

Calculating mean averages in Excel

Microsoft Excel can calculate mean averages very easily, by using the formula =AVERAGE(. . .). You can replicate the calculation we have made here, using the healthcare data, by choosing an empty cell and then typing:

= AVERAGE(C2:C51)

This will calculate the mean average of the observations in cells C2 to C51.

Omitting outliers

Outliers can cause sample means to become unrepresentative. An outlier is simply an observation that is a long way away from the rest of the data; in this example we can see that the USA looks a little bit of an outlier, when compared with the other countries in the data. The USA's spending on healthcare is \$10,852.838 per capita, over \$4,000 more per capita than the next highest spending nation, Switzerland.

A sample mean is meant to provide a measure of the 'centre' of the distribution of the data. However, because of the way that it is calculated, if there are outliers, this could cause the sample mean to be skewed upwards (or downwards). In this example, because the USA's spending is so much higher than the rest of the data, including the USA in the sample mean will pull the sample mean upwards, and leads to the sample mean not being representative

[3] Note that we have used a lower case x_i here, as we are thinking about specific observations of the random variable.

of the population as a whole. We could repeat the process, and calculate the sample mean, omitting the USA from the data (so we will only have 49 countries):

$$\bar{x} = \frac{1}{49}\sum_{i \neq USA} x_i = \frac{1}{49} \times 160{,}845.324 = 3{,}282.558$$

By omitting the USA, the sample mean has dropped by $150 per capita, or by over 4 per cent. Because the USA was such an outlier, this mean average is now a much more representative measure of the per-capita spending in the rest of the world.

Weighted averages

As we have seen, outliers can cause sample means to be unrepresentative. However, simply using a standard sample mean can also lead to the average being unrepresentative. When we calculate a sample mean, we know that the formula is:

$$\bar{X} = \frac{1}{n}\sum_{i=1}^{n} X_i$$

But we could also write this formula in the form $\bar{X} = \Sigma_{i=1}^{n} w_i X_i$ where w_i is a series of weights applied to each observation. With the simple sample mean, the weights applied to each observation would just be equal to $w_i = \frac{1}{n}$ for all i. However, we could apply different weights and still get a measure of an average, provided the weights sum to 1:

$$\sum_{i=1}^{n} w_i = 1$$

A weighted mean allows you to place more emphasis on a particular set of observations. This might be because some observations are more representative of the population as a whole, or it might be because some observations represent a different-sized constituency.

For example, in the healthcare data we were looking at, we knew the per-capita healthcare spending for each country; however, that spending figure is spread across different numbers of people in each country; the data includes observations for China (1.4 billion population) and Iceland (0.4 million population), but in calculating the sample mean, these two countries are given equal weighting. That is, in China, the data represents the spending (on average) on each of the 1.4 billion population, whereas in Iceland, the data is only spent on each of the 0.4 million. A more representative measure might be to weight the observations by the relative population of each country.

Suppose we wanted to know the average spending on healthcare per person across the world. We could take account of the fact that each of the countries is a different size, and weight the samples by the populations of those countries. To take a very simple example, let's just consider two of these countries: the UK and Ireland (Table 6.2).

Table 6.2 A sub-sample of data from the healthcare data set (OECD)

Country	Spending per capita on healthcare	Population (millions)
Ireland	4976.129	4.9
United Kingdom	4389.038	66.8

We can calculate the weighted average of the spending on healthcare by constructing a set of weights, w_i, such that $\sum_{i=1}^{n} w_i = 1$, which allows us to take account of the fact that the UK population is 13.6 times larger than that of Ireland.

To construct the weights, we can simply create a fraction, where the denominator is the sum of the populations, and the numerators are equal to the populations in Ireland and the UK. So, our weights would be:

$$w_{Ireland} = \frac{4.9}{4.9 + 66.8} = 0.06834, \quad w_{UK} = \frac{66.8}{4.9 + 66.8} = 0.93166$$

You can check, but the weights we have constructed will add up to 1, and the difference in the weights accounts for the difference in the sizes of the UK and Ireland. As such, when we construct a weighted average, the UK will be given more weight than Ireland, simply because it has a larger population.

$$\begin{aligned}\text{Weighted average} &= w_{Ireland} \times X_{Ireland} + w_{UK} \times X_{UK} \\ &= 0.06834 \times 4{,}976.129 + 0.93166 \times 4{,}389.038 = 4{,}429.16\,(2dp)\end{aligned}$$

So, our weighted average of healthcare spending in the UK and Ireland provides an average spending (per capita) of $4,429.16. Of course, this is only for two countries. You could repeat the process, including all of the countries with data for both health expenditure and population from the OECD,[4] and this would give a weighted average of spending per capita of $1,987.64. The reason that this is now so much lower is because by weighting by population you are placing more weight on countries such as China and India, which have very large populations but relatively low expenditure per capita on healthcare. However, by calculating the weighted average, this gives a better indication of expenditure on healthcare per capita across the world.

Worked example 6.2: Average growth rates

The Office for National Statistics (ONS) continuously estimates the UK's Gross Domestic Product—that is, the total value of goods and services produced (and provided) in the UK in every year. A key indicator of the health of the UK economy is the growth rate of GDP.

The growth rate of GDP between, say, 2017 and 2018 can be measured as:

$$\text{Growth} = \frac{GDP_{2018}}{GDP_{2017}} - 1$$

[4] OECD figures do not include a population for Peru, but do provide healthcare spending per capita.

Table 6.3 GDP growth rate in the UK 2013–2022 (data from the ONS)

Year	2013	2014	2015	2016	2017	2018	2019	2020	2021	2022
Growth rate (%)	1.8	3.2	2.4	2.2	2.4	1.7	1.6	−11.0	7.6	4.1

So, if the ONS announced a growth rate of +5 per cent (0.05), then that would indicate that GDP was 5 per cent larger in 2018 than in 2017. Similarly, if the growth rate were −5 per cent, this would indicate that UK GDP was 5 per cent smaller in 2018 than 2017. The UK growth rates between 2013 and 2022 are illustrated in Table 6.3.[5]

Table 6.3 shows the annual growth rate of UK GDP across ten years from 2013 to the end of 2022. If we wanted to calculate the arithmetic mean, we would simply need to add these growth rates together and divide by the number of observations. We will represent our sample mean as $\overline{g}$.

$$\overline{g} = \frac{1}{10} \times (1.8 + 3.2 + 2.4 + 2.2 + 2.4 + 1.7 + 1.6 - 11.0 + 7.6 + 4.1) = \frac{16}{10} = 1.6\%$$

So, the arithmetic mean of the growth over the ten-year period from 2013 to 2022 is equal to 1.6 per cent. However, as we will see in the next section, this is a little misleading, and sometimes it will be better to calculate an alternative form of average, such as the geometric mean.

6.3.2 Geometric means

Whilst the arithmetic mean is the most commonly used form of sample average, there is a second form of mean average which may be more appropriate in contexts where we are considering growth rates, for example, called the geometric mean.

To motivate the geometric mean, let's consider a simple example. Suppose that you saved £100 in a bank account, with an interest rate of 3 per cent; this would mean that each year, the bank pays you 3 per cent of the value held in the account. At the end of the first year, the bank would pay 3 per cent of the amount held in the bank, or £3, giving you a total of £103. Mathematically, we can find the amount that is held in the bank account after 1 year by multiplying the initial amount (£100) by $(1 + r)$ where r is the interest rate; in this case, this would mean multiplying £100 by 1.03.

$$\text{Amount in bank after 1 year} = 100 \times (1 + r) = 100 \times 1.03$$

At the end of the second year, the bank would again pay interest of 3 per cent, but this time, it would not just be interest on the £100, but also on the £3 interest from the first year. So, now we can write this as:

$$\text{Amount in bank after 2 years} = 103 \times (1 + r) = 103 \times 1.03 = 106.09$$

But this is the same as multiplying the initial deposit by 1.03 twice (or 1.03^2). The fact that the interest is applied to both the original deposit and the interest from the first year is known as 'compounding'. Most bank accounts which pay interest use a form of compound interest.

$$\text{Amount in bank after 2 years} = 100 \times (1 + 0.03) \times (1 + 0.03) = 100 \times 1.03^2$$

[5] Data is accessible from https://www.ons.gov.uk/economy/grossdomesticproductgdp/timeseries/ihyp/pn2 (accessed 20 July 2023).

Suppose now that the bank increased the interest payable in the third year to 6 per cent. The amount in the account in the third year is now $106.09 \times 1.06 = 112.4554$.

KEY DEFINITION: COMPOUND INTEREST

Compound interest occurs when interest is paid on both the initial deposit, and interest that has been paid in previous years.

If you were to save £X in a bank account for n years, with a (constant) interest rate of r, then the amount you will have after n years is:

$$= X(1+r)^n$$

We might be interested in finding the average interest gained across the three years that the money has been saved in the bank. If we were to find the arithmetic mean of the interest gained across the three years, we would just add together the interest rates and divide them by 3: (3% + 3% + 6%) / 3 = 4% = 0.04. However, if we were to then apply this interest rate for three years to the initial deposit (using the compound interest formula):

$$= 100 \times (1 + 0.04)^3 = 112.4864$$

Whilst this figure is close to the actual amount in the account, it is marginally different. As such, can we find a better way of illustrating the average interest?

We have shown that if we had initially saved £100 in a bank account, which paid 3 per cent, 3 per cent, 6 per cent over three years, then we would have:

$$100 \times 1.03 \times 1.03 \times 1.06 = 112.4554$$

But this is just the same as multiplying the £100 by the product of 1.03, 1.03, and 1.06, giving a total of 12.4554 per cent interest over the three years. If we wish to find the average interest rate, this would be equivalent to asking what value of r would be equivalent to growing our initial £100 by 12.4554 per cent over three years.

So, using the compound interest formula, since the money is in the bank for three years, we will multiply £100 by $(1 + r)^3$

$$100(1 + r)^3 = 112.4554$$

Dividing left and right by 100 gives us:

$$(1 + r)^3 = 1.124554$$

So, if we were to find the cube root of 1.124554, we would effectively get $1 + r$ where r is the average level of interest over the three years:

$$\sqrt[3]{1.124554} = 1.124554^{\frac{1}{3}} = 1.03990445\ldots = 1 + r$$

That is, the amount in the bank after three years is equivalent to 100×1.03990445^3. We can use a geometric mean when we are looking at values that are multiplied together.

Typically, geometric means are most commonly used when examining growth rates, and we want to know what the average rate of growth was for each year in the sample.

FORMAL NOTATION: GEOMETRIC MEAN

The geometric mean is constructed by taking the *n*th root of the product of the *n* observations.

$$= \left(\prod_{i=1}^{n} X_i\right)^{\frac{1}{n}}$$

We would most commonly use the geometric mean when considering rates of change of variables; so X could be how many times larger GDP is in 2018 than in 2017 in the UK, for instance. That is, in this case, $X_i = 1 + g_i$, where g is the growth rate in year *i*.

Worked example 6.3: Average growth rates

We saw an example of trying to calculate an average growth rate for an economy over a ten-year period in Section 6.3.1. However, because a growth rate is like multiplying by a factor each year, it would be more informative to calculate a geometric mean.

Looking at the data in Table 6.4,[6] let's think about what these numbers mean; first of all, a percentage means out of 100, so we would need to divide each of these by 100, to give a proportional impact. So, for example, $1.8\% = \frac{1.8}{100} = 0.018$.

Similarly, a growth rate of 1.8 per cent means that the economy would be 1.8 per cent larger in the following year; this is equivalent to multiplying GDP at the beginning of 2013 by $1 + 0.018 = 1.018$. Similarly, a -11 per cent growth rate would be equivalent to multiplying GDP by $1 - 0.11 = 0.89$.

To illustrate this, suppose that GDP was 100 at the beginning of 2013; a 1.8 per cent growth would be equivalent to multiplying this by $1 + 0.018 = 1.018$.

$$= 100 \times 1.018 = 101.8$$

Similarly, to calculate GDP at the end of 2014, we would multiply this new figure by $1 + 0.032 = 1.032$.

$$= 101.8 \times 1.032 = 105.0576$$

Table 6.4 GDP growth rate in the UK 2013–2022 (data from the ONS)

Year	2013	2014	2015	2016	2017	2018	2019	2020	2021	2022
Growth rate (%)	1.8	3.2	2.4	2.2	2.4	1.7	1.6	−11.0	7.6	4.1

[6] Data is accessible from https://www.ons.gov.uk/economy/grossdomesticproductgdp/timeseries/ihyp/pn2 (accessed 20 July 2023).

Of course, we could write this out to take account of the growth in both 2013 and 2014 explicitly, by including the two growth rates:

$$= 100 \times 1.018 \times 1.032 = 105.0576$$

So, if the economy started at a size of 100 at the beginning of 2013, by the end of 2014, it would have grown to a size of 105.0576. To find the total growth over the two-year period, we could divide the new GDP figure by the original value:

$$= \frac{105.0576}{100} = 1.050576$$

Thus, the two years of growth at 1.8 per cent and 3.2 per cent is equivalent to a total growth over two years of 5.0576 per cent. To find the geometric mean of the growth rate, we would need to take the 2nd root (or square root) of this multiplier. For simplicity, let's denote the geometric mean growth rate as g^*.

$$(1 + g^*)^2 = 1.050576 \Rightarrow (1 + g^*) = \sqrt{1.050576} = 1.02498$$

So, the average growth over the two-year period could be calculated as $(1 + g^*) = 1.02495 \Rightarrow g^* = 0.02498$ or 2.498%. Of course, this is only the growth over a two-year period, but we want to know the average growth over the ten-year period. So, the overall growth can be calculated as shown in Table 6.5.

Table 6.5 Equivalences between growth rates and multipliers

Year	2013	2014	2015	2016	2017	2018	2019	2020	2021	2022
Growth rate (%)	1.8	3.2	2.4	2.2	2.4	1.7	1.6	−11.0	7.6	4.1
Equivalent to multiplying GDP by:	1.018	1.032	1.024	1.022	1.024	1.017	1.016	0.89	1.076	1.041

We can calculate the geometric mean growth rate by multiplying together these multipliers, and then taking the 10th root.

$$(1 + g^*)^{10} = 1.018 \times 1.032 \times 1.024 \times 1.022 \times 1.024 \times 1.017 \times 1.016 \times 0.89 \times 1.076 \times 1.041$$
$$\Rightarrow (1 + g^*)^{10} = 1.159701$$
$$\Rightarrow (1 + g^*) = \sqrt[10]{1.159701} = 1.014927$$

So, over that ten-year period, the average growth rate can be seen as $g^* = 0.014927$ or 1.4927 per cent.

When would you use a geometric mean?

You would only ever want to use a geometric mean when it makes sense to think about elements being multiplied together. For example, when we are looking at economic growth, a 4 per cent growth rate in 2022 would be equivalent to multiplying the size of the economy at the end of 2021 by 1.04. Similarly, a 1 per cent growth rate in 2023 would be equivalent to multiplying the size of the economy in 2022 by 1.01. If the size of the economy at the end of 2021 was 100, then we could find the size of the economy at the end of 2023 by multiplying 100 by the growth across the two years:

$$= 100 \times 1.04 \times 1.01$$

The total growth is then 1.04×1.01, and in this case, because we are multiplying elements together, when we're thinking of an average growth rate, the geometric mean makes sense.

So, the geometric mean is given by $= \sqrt{1.04 \times 1.01} = 1.02489$. That is, the average growth over two years would be 2.489 per cent.

6.3.3 Median averages

One of the problems with mean averages is that outliers can skew our estimate. In the healthcare spending example, earlier in the chapter, the USA's very high spending per capita on healthcare pulled the average upwards. In small samples, or where there are very significant outliers (i.e. outliers that a very long way from the rest of the data), then this can cause significant skew to our estimates.

We've already seen that we can estimate sample means by removing outliers, but an alternative route might be to use a different form of average. One possibility is to consider the **median**. The median average is, literally, the middle value in the sample. That is, the median observation in a sample is the value that has exactly the same number of observations that are bigger than it as it has that are smaller than it.

In order to construct the median, the data needs to be ordered from smallest observation to the largest observation. If there are n observations in the sample, then the median value will be the $\frac{n+1}{2}$th observation. For example, if there are five observations, then the median would be the third largest observation; there are two observations that are smaller than it, and two observations that are larger than it. If the number of observations, n, is odd, then $\frac{n+1}{n}$ will always take an integer value, and it is easy to calculate the median. However, if the number of observations, n, is an even number then there will not be an explicit middle value. In this case, we would need to take the mean average of the two observations either side of the $\frac{n+1}{2}$ case.

The median can also be related to other concepts in statistics; namely quantiles and percentiles. If an observation lies at the qth percentile, that tells you that q per cent of the observations are smaller than the observed value. Since the median is the middle value, this must mean that 50 per cent of the distribution is smaller than the median, and 50 per cent of the distribution is larger than the median; as such, the median lies at the 50th percentile.

Worked example 6.4: Median height in a sample

Suppose that we sample ten individuals from the population, and measure their height. We want to calculate an indication of the average height in the sample. The heights, in the order that the individuals were measured, are shown in Table 6.6.

Table 6.6 Heights of ten individuals

Individual	1	2	3	4	5	6	7	8	9	10
Height (m)	1.87	1.65	1.83	1.88	1.65	1.64	1.78	1.82	1.76	1.54

To find the median height, first, the data needs to be sorted, from smallest to largest. If we sort the data from smallest to largest, the distribution will be as shown in Table 6.7.

Table 6.7 Heights, sorted from smallest to largest

Individual	1	2	3	4	5	6	7	8	9	10
Height (m)	1.54	1.64	1.65	1.65	1.76	1.78	1.82	1.83	1.87	1.88

In order to find the median, we first need to calculate what value (in order) would be the middle value. This will be determined by the $\frac{n+1}{2}$th observation. Since there are ten observations, this would be:

$$\frac{10+1}{2} = 5.5$$

However, there is no such thing as the 5.5th observation. As such, we would want to take the *average* of the two values either side of the 5.5th observation—that is, we take the arithmetic mean of the 5th and the 6th observation.

The 5th observation is 1.76m, and the 6th observation is 1.78m. Thus, our median would be the mean average of these two observations; that is, our median is:

$$\frac{1.76 + 1.78}{2} = 1.77\text{m}$$

Worked example 6.5: Healthcare spending per capita by country

As a second example, let's consider the spending per capita on healthcare across countries. When we calculated the mean average, we noticed that the USA was an outlier, and so including this led to the mean average being skewed, or pulled upwards.

The median does not suffer from the same problem, in that it merely looks for the observation in the 'middle' of the data. There are 50 countries in the data set, and so there will be 25 countries below the median, and equally 25 countries above the median; formally, to find the point at which the median lies, we could use our formula:

$$\frac{50+1}{2} = 25.5$$

So, our median will be halfway between the 25th and the 26th ranked countries for spending on healthcare. Graphically, this is illustrated in Figure 6.2. Spending per capita on healthcare has been ordered from the lowest spending country in the data set (India) up to the highest spending country (USA), and we are looking for the median.

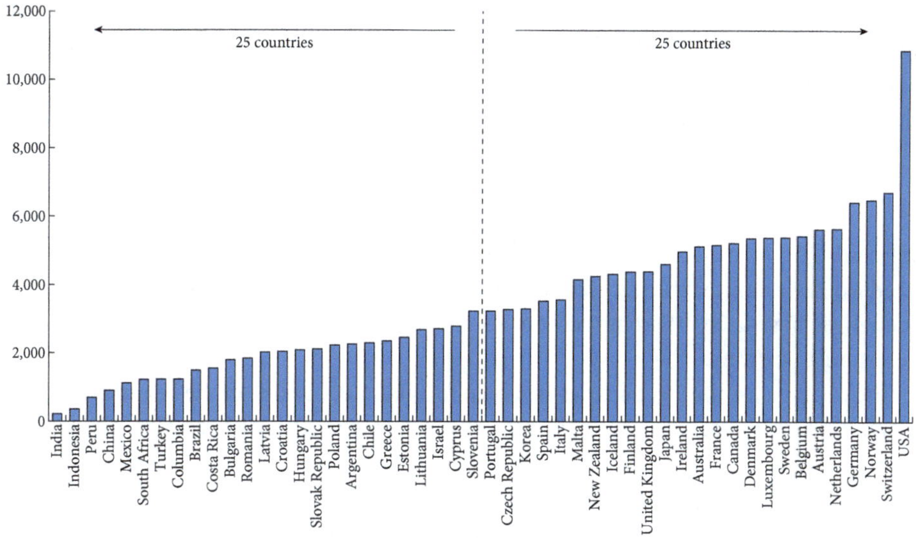

Figure 6.2 Spending per capita in 2019 on healthcare (US$, data from the OECD).

Table 6.8 Spending per capita in 2019 on healthcare (US$) (Source: OECD)

Country	Spending	Country	Spending	Country	Spending	Country	Spending
Argentina	2254.047	Czech Republic	3272.224	Italy	3565.324	Portugal	3223.676
Australia	5126.653	Denmark	5359.776	Japan	4610.794	Romania	1844.269
Austria	5625.442	Estonia	2453.074	Korea	3290.825	Slovak Republic	2115.452
Belgium	5423.676	Finland	4383.634	Latvia	2025.57	Slovenia	3221.895
Brazil	1497.734	France	5163.421	Lithuania	2682.067	South Africa	1222.202
Bulgaria	1795.621	Germany	6418.323	Luxembourg	5379.663	Spain	3528.382
Canada	5222.644	Greece	2349.574	Malta	4154.13	Sweden	5387.733
Chile	2296.988	Hungary	2095.186	Mexico	1117.235	Switzerland	6708.349
China	901.854	Iceland	4318.27	Netherlands	5643.59	Turkey	1231.634
Columbia	1239.66	India	219.575	New Zealand	4249.593	United Kingdom	4389.038
Costa Rica	1556.168	Indonesia	356.262	Norway	6476.378	USA	10852.838
Croatia	2043.652	Ireland	4976.129	Peru	702.355		
Cyprus	2783.252	Israel	2709.984	Poland	2232.347		

Twenty-five countries lie to the left of the dotted line, and twenty-five countries lie to the right of the dotted line; so the median will lie halfway between the spending per capita in Slovenia ($3,221.895) and Portugal ($3,223.676). As such, the median will be the mean of these two values (or halfway between these two values):

$$\text{Median} = \frac{3{,}221.895 + 3{,}223.676}{2} = 3{,}222.7855$$

Interestingly, the median in this example ($3,222.7855) is very close to the mean we calculated when we omitted the USA from the data ($3,282.558). This is interesting, because, even though we have used different methods to measure the 'centre' of the data, we have gained very similar answers.

The full data for the 50 countries is shown in Table 6.8, but one of the beauties of the median is that we do not need to use all of this data to calculate the median. All we need to do is find the middle-ranked observations, and this allows us to calculate the median.

The fact that the median does not use all of the data is a benefit, in that it is less likely than a mean to be affected by outliers; however, it is also a cost, because it does not reflect all of the available information about the data as a whole. This may mean that the median is less susceptible to outliers, but is less informative about the data set we are observing than the sample mean.

6.3.4 The mode

The third, and final, type of sample average that we consider here is the mode. The mode indicates the most commonly occurring outcome. The modal value is useful when we have discrete data with a limited set of outcomes, and outcomes are repeated within the sample.

Worked example 6.6: Shoe sizes

Suppose that you were interested in the distribution of men's shoe sizes within your university. You might randomly sample 100 individuals from the population, and obtain a distribution of (UK) shoe sizes (Table 6.9).

Table 6.9 Shoe sizes, distributed by frequency

Size	5	6	7	8	9	10	11	12	13	14
Frequency	2	5	10	15	23	22	12	7	3	1

The mode would be the most commonly occurring outcome; in this case, the mode would be a size 9. We can also see this graphically if we plot a frequency histogram of the data (Figure 6.3). In a frequency histogram, the height of the bars represents the number of times that observation occurs; here, the tallest bar is for size 9 shoes, indicating that size 9 is the mode within this data.

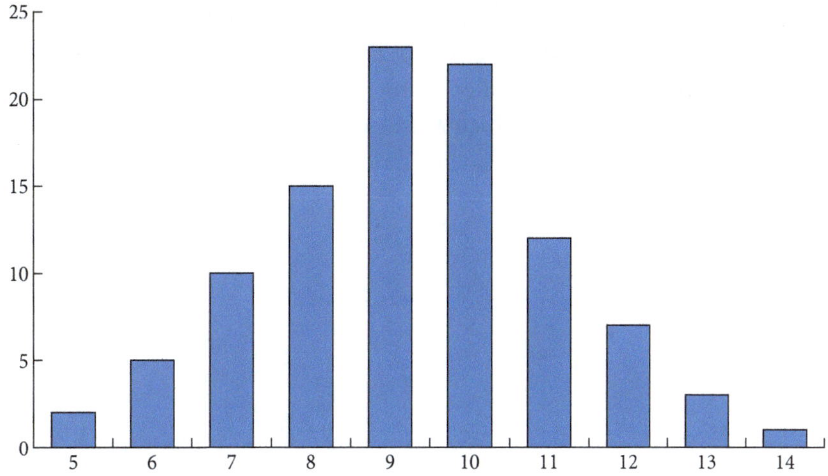

Figure 6.3 Frequency histogram.

For this data, there are three possible averages we could have looked at:

- the mean
- the median
- the mode.

We have seen that the mode is equal to a size 9, but what about the mean and the median? The mean is relatively easy to calculate; we can see that there are two individuals with size 5 feet, five with size 6, ten with size 7, and so on. A sample mean is calculated by adding together all of the observations, and dividing by the number of observations; however, we don't need to find $(5 + 5 + 6 + 6 + 6 + 6 + 6 + 7 + \ldots)$ as we can take advantage of the fact that we have multiple observations of each shoe size. Multiplication is just the same as repeated adding, and so, the mean average is just equal to:

$$\begin{aligned}\bar{x} &= \frac{1}{100} \times (2 \times 5 + 5 \times 5 + 10 \times 7 + 15 \times 8 + 23 \times 9 + 22 \times 10 + 12 \times 11 + 7 \times 12 + 3 \times 13 \\ &\quad +1 \times 14) \\ &= \frac{1}{100} \times 926 = 9.26\end{aligned}$$

Similarly, the median can be calculated by finding the 'middle' value of our observations. We have 100 observations, so the median observation would be $\frac{100+1}{2} = 50.5$th observation. Again, we can use the frequency distribution to find this. Moving from left to right, we can add the number of observations less than or equal to a particular shoe size, to construct the cumulative frequency (Table 6.10).

Table 6.10 Calculating the median shoe size

Size	5	6	7	8	9	10	11	12	13	14
Frequency	2	5	10	15	23	22	12	7	3	1
Cumulative frequency	2	7	17	32	55	77	89	96	99	100

Since the cumulative frequency tells us how many individuals have shoe sizes less than or equal to a particular shoe size, we can see that 32 individuals have shoe sizes of 8 or smaller, whilst 55 have shoe sizes of 9 or smaller. As such, both the 50th and 51st observations lie within the size 9 group. Thus, the median will also be equal to a size 9. We could also see this by plotting the cumulative frequency graph, illustrated in Figure 6.4.

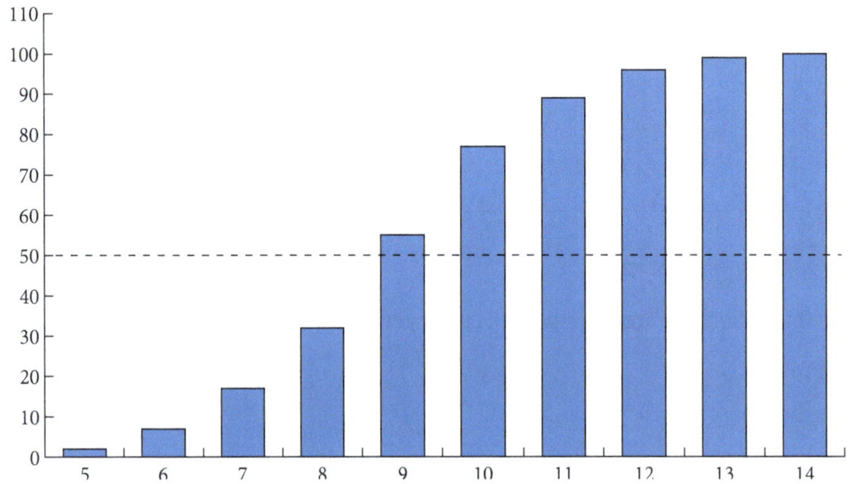

Figure 6.4 Cumulative frequency plot for shoe sizes.

We can see that the median (i.e. 50.5th) observation, as represented by the dotted line, first intersects with size 9; this indicates that the median occurs within the size 9 group.

Worked example 6.7: Finding a modal range

The mode is useful only when you have a way of indicating that particular observations are the 'most likely' to occur. When you don't have repeated observations, you could think about a modal range within the data. For example, if we look at individuals' heights, we wouldn't expect to see two people of exactly the same height. However, we could plot a frequency histogram to represent the number of individuals within a particular height range. To illustrate this, I have collected a random sample of 100 individuals, and rather than being interested in their exact height, I've considered the range in which their height lies, and banded these in 5cm bands. The distribution of the heights is illustrated in Table 6.11 and Figure 6.5. As you can see, the most common range observed is 165–170cm. There are no two individuals in the data with exactly the same height, but we still can calculate a mode, based upon the range in which observations occur. In this case, the modal range would be 165–170cm.

In this (and the previous) example, the mode is roughly in the middle of the distribution; in this example, there is an outlier (of 200–205cm), but the modal value is roughly in the middle of the distribution; it is also relatively straightforward to show that the median also lies in the range of 165–170cm in this distribution.

Table 6.11 Distribution of heights

Height range (cm)	Frequency
150–155	5
155–160	9
160–165	16
165–170	21
170–175	18
175–180	19
180–185	9
185–190	2
190–195	0
195–200	0
200–205	1

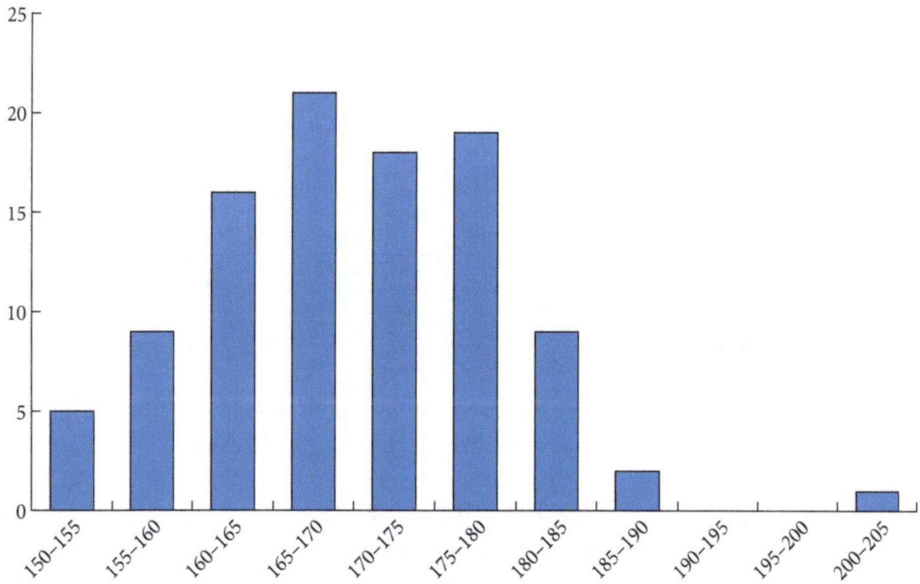

Figure 6.5 Frequency distribution of heights within the sample.

Bimodal, trimodal, and more

The mode need not be unique within a sample (or a population). It is perfectly possible to have more than one mode. Since the mode tells us the most commonly occurring outcome, it is not impossible to have two, three, or even more modes.

When we start looking at continuous random variables, we will also see that we can have local modes. The mode indicates the peak of the distribution, but you can have more than one peak within a single distribution.

6.4 Are the mean, median, and mode always different?

We have seen three key types of averages: the mean, the median, and the mode. An obvious question is which should you use in any particular case?

Sometimes, it will not matter which average you use, as it is possible that all three types of average will yield the same answer. To understand this, it's important to understand some of the properties of data that we observe.

In lots of data that you will see, the most common observations will be in the middle of the distribution, and the least common observations will be towards the edges of the distribution. This was illustrated in our shoe size example (Figure 6.6).

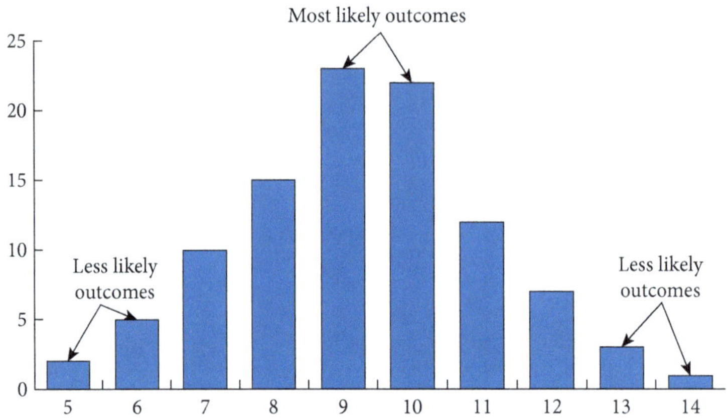

Figure 6.6 Distribution of shoe sizes.

In a population, it is often the case that there are more individuals who are 'close to average'—that is, close to the middle of the distribution, and fewer who are in the tails of the distribution.

Where we see characteristics distributed like this, then the mean, median, and mode will be approximately in the same place. Sometimes distributions will be symmetric around the median—that is, the distribution to the left and the right of the median is exactly the same. Where we have a symmetric distribution, with the mode in the middle of the distribution, the mean, median, and mode will be exactly the same.

To illustrate this, consider the following simple example. I have a four-sided dice, with the numbers 1, 2, 3, 4 printed on each side. I roll the dice twice, and note the total score (e.g. if the dice lands on a 1 and then a 4, then the total score would be 5). I have then repeated this 100 times, and gained the sample of total scores seen in Table 6.12.[7]

[7] It is highly unlikely that you would gain a distribution of scores like this from 100 rolls; this is a (fictitious) example that can illustrate symmetric distributions.

Table 6.12 Distribution from rolling two four-sided dice 100 times

Total score	2	3	4	5	6	7	8
Frequency	6	13	19	24	19	13	6
Cumulative frequency	6	19	38	62	81	94	100

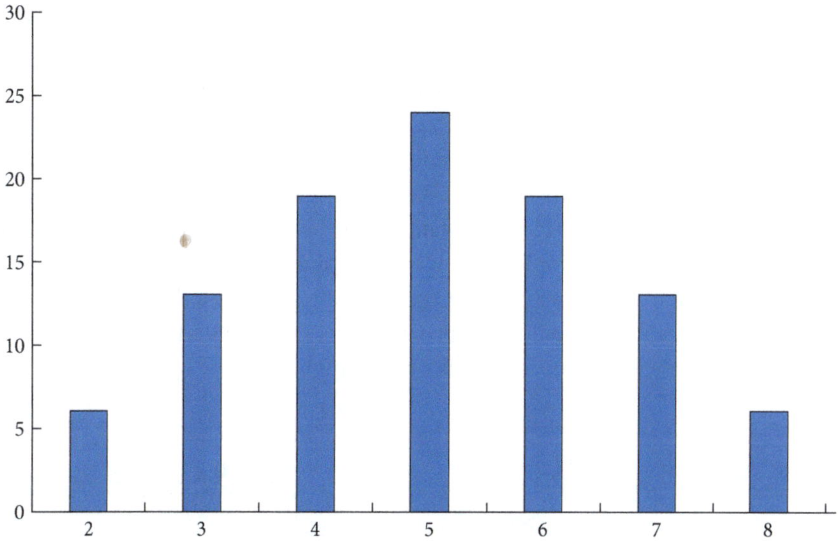

Figure 6.7 Frequency histogram of scores from game of dice.

If we plot the frequency histogram (shown in Figure 6.7), we can see that we observe 4 and 6 nineteen times each. Similarly, we see 3 and 7 thirteen times each, and we see 2 and 8 six times each. This is an example of a symmetric distribution—if we drew a line in place of the score of 5, the frequencies would be mirrored on either side of the line. The mode is obviously equal to 5 here (as the most common outcome). The median would be halfway between the 50th and 51st largest observations; from the cumulative frequency, we can see that this occurs in the middle of the total score equal to 5.

Finally, we can calculate the mean by dividing the sum of the observations by the number of observations:

$$\bar{x} = \frac{1}{100} \times (2 \times 6 + 3 \times 13 + 4 \times 19 + 5 \times 25 + 6 \times 19 + 7 \times 13 + 8 \times 6) = \frac{500}{100} = 5$$

That is, in this example the sample mean is also equal to 5.

The distribution of dice rolls in this experiment is actually highly suspicious, as the distribution is perfectly symmetric around 5. In the real world, we would expect these outcomes to be much more messy, particularly built around relatively small sample sizes (such as 100). If you try it for yourself, sometimes you will find that you get more 6s than 4s; sometimes the reverse will be true. If you are playing a board game, and see a distribution of dice rolls looking exactly like Figure 6.7 after 100 rolls, it may be the case that your opponent is cheating.

In the real world, it will be very rare for the mean, median, and mode from a dice rolls experiment with a relatively small number of trials to be the same.

6.5 When should we use each type of sample average?

The sample mean is the most commonly used average, in part because it represents all of the data within the sample. However, as we have seen, there are potential problems with the mean average as a measure of central tendency; if there are observations in your sample which are significant outliers, then this could have a big impact on your measure of central tendency using the mean.

For example, suppose that you are calculating the sample mean of annual salaries within a small firm with ten employees. Nine of the employees earn between £20,000 and £30,000 per annum. However, the chief executive (and owner) of the firm rewards themselves handsomely for the profits of the firm, and pays themselves £10,000,000 per year.

A good estimate of the centre of the data would be somewhere between £20,000 and £30,000. However, since the sample mean places the same weight, or emphasis, on all of the observations, then the one outlier (the CEO) will significantly skew the results; in this example, the mean average wages would be approximately £1,025,000, which does not represent the wages of the average employee. In this case, it might be more appropriate to appeal to the median value.

KEY DEFINITION: TYPES OF DATA

There are two key classes of numerical data that we could see: discrete data and continuous data. These two classes may need to be treated differently when thinking about sample averages.

Discrete data

Discrete data is data which has a limited number of possible outcomes. For example, discrete data might take only the values 1, 2, 3, 4, 5, with nothing in between.

Continuous data

Continuous data can take an infinite number of outcomes; an example of continuous data might be any sort of measurement; for instance, a length variable could take the value 1.23cm, 1.24cm, or any value in between 1.23 and 1.24.

Similarly, we have seen that the mode can be useful to determine the most commonly occurring outcome; for discrete data, where there are a finite number of outcomes, it is not unlikely that you will see some outcomes multiple times. However, if the data is continuous, then there are an infinite number of possible outcomes. For example, if we are looking at heights, there are an infinite number of possible measurements between, say, 1.75m and 1.76m. As such, the probability of observing two, exactly equal, outcomes is equal to zero.

When dealing with continuous data, in order to represent a mode, statisticians will often look for a modal range. For example, if randomly sampling from a range between 0 and 1, the statistician might group the outcomes in bins of width 0.1, so between 0 and 0.1, 0.1 and 0.2, 0.2 and 0.3, and so on. The modal range would then be the bin, or the range, with the largest number of observations. Of course, care would need to be taken when designing the bins; the size of the bins could affect the choice of the modal range!

CASE STUDY **The gender pay gap at Newcastle United Football Club**

A good way of illustrating the difference between median and mean averages is to consider the (publicly available) data about the gender pay gap.

In 1970, the UK government introduced the Equal Pay Act, which prohibited firms from providing any less favourable treatment, in terms of pay and contracts, for female workers than male workers. In spite of this legislation existing for over 40 years, the mean average of female workers' earnings is still significantly lower than the mean average of male workers' earnings. In 2017, the UK government introduced the Equality Act 2010 (Gender Pay Gap Information) Regulations 2017, which required firms with more than 250 employees to publish data on the percentage difference between the average male wages (A) and average female wages (B). The percentage difference is then calculated thus:

$$\frac{A-B}{A} \times 100$$

Thus, a positive figure indicates that male workers are being paid on average more than female workers in that firm; a negative figure indicates that female workers are being paid on average more than male workers.

The data published considered both the difference in mean average wages and the difference in median average wages, and also published the proportion of workers who are female (and the proportion who are male) in each **quartile** of the wage distribution. The pay gaps observed are not evidence, per se, that firms are paying male and female workers different amounts for the same job, but as we shall see, they may suggest that some firms are more likely to employ male workers in higher paid jobs than female workers.

In 2023, Newcastle United Football Club's gender pay gap report[8] stated that:

- the pay gap based on median pay was 0 per cent, and
- the pay gap based upon mean pay was 84.8 per cent.

What this means is that median wages for male and female workers at Newcastle United are the same, but the arithmetic mean of female wages at Newcastle United is 15.2 per cent of the arithmetic mean of male workers.

[8] Available from https://www.nufc.co.uk/media/75582/pay-gap-report_march2023.pdf. Government publication of gender pay gap information is available from https://gender-pay-gap.service.gov.uk/ (accessed 29 July 2023).

On the face of it this appears to be a contradiction, as one measure of the average suggests that there is no difference, whilst another suggests that male workers at Newcastle United are paid much more than female workers. So how do we solve this dichotomy?

The key difference is, unsurprisingly, the wages of first-team footballers. Many Premier League footballers will earn salaries of tens of thousands of pounds per week. However, first team footballers only make up a small fraction of the employees at a Premier League football club. Premier League rules mean that clubs may only name a squad of 25 senior players who are eligible to play for the club. But Newcastle United reports that it has between 1,000 and 4,999 employees. Most of the employees are paid significantly less than the footballing superstars.

It should be noted at this point that many Premier League football clubs have both male and female teams. Analysis by the BBC suggested that, in 2022, the average Women's Super League player earned £47,000 per year.[9] Male Premier League footballers may earn that amount in a week.

To illustrate the impact of the male first-team players' salaries on the mean gender pay gap, let's consider a simple example. Suppose that a firm employed 20 men and 20 women. All of the women were paid exactly £20,000 per annum. Nineteen of the men were paid £20,000 per annum, but one of the men was paid £1,000,000 per annum.

In this simple example, the median pay for both male and female workers is £20,000, and so the median pay gap would be equal to 0.

However, if we were to compare the mean averages, the male mean average wage would be £69,000, whilst the female mean average would be £20,000; using the methodology above, this suggests that the wage gap, based on mean wages, would be:

$$\frac{69{,}000 - 20{,}000}{69{,}000} \times 100 = 71\%$$

However, the £69,000 figure would not be representative for the vast majority of male employees, and so the difference in means would also not be representative of the difference between male and female earnings. This is not just a Newcastle United phenomenon. A similar story is seen when you examine almost any Premier League team. In fact, for the clubs in the Premier League in 2023/24 (based on their previous year's gender pay gap), the median wage for female staff at Arsenal FC was higher than the median wage for male staff, yet, when comparing the mean averages, all of the clubs have substantial gender pay gaps, caused by the data being skewed by the inclusion of very highly paid football players (Table 6.13).

Some clubs do try to take account of this in their reporting. Returning to the example of Newcastle United, when they exclude their managers and players, the pay gap based on median pay remains at 0 per cent, but the pay gap based upon mean wages is 18.1 per cent.

What this case study shows is that mean averages can be skewed by a relatively small number of 'outliers' that lie well outside the normal data range for other employees of a firm. If you wish to examine an average wage, the choice of measure will depend on whether you want to consider a 'typical' employee of the firm, or want to reflect all of the available data in the figure.

[9] See https://www.bbc.co.uk/news/business-62378095 (accessed 29 July 2023).

Table 6.13 Median and mean pay gaps of Premier League football clubs

	Median pay gap (%)	Mean pay gap (%)
Arsenal	−10.5	69.2
Aston Villa	4.4	84
Bournemouth	7.5	76.9
Brentford	33	87
Brighton and Hove Albion	1	76.2
Burnley	9.5	88.6
Chelsea	9.3	89.8
Crystal Palace	0	77
Everton	9	84
Fulham	9	78.1
Liverpool	7	85.8
Luton Town[10]	5.6	36.2
Manchester City	1.6	84.9
Manchester United	0	82.8
Newcastle United	0	84.8
Nottingham Forest	0	64.3
Sheffield United	4.5	69.7
Tottenham Hotspur	7	79
West Ham	14.5	80.7
Wolverhampton Wanderers	17.8	82.5

Summary

When we observe a sample of data from a population, we can make inferences about the middle of the data by observing the average. There are three main forms of averages that we use: the mean, the median, and the mode. For the mean, we often consider either the arithmetic mean or the geometric mean.

The characteristics of the sample will determine which form of average is most informative. If there are big outliers in the data (i.e. observations that are very large or small in

[10] Figures for 2019, as the club has not been required to produce this data since then.

comparison with the rest of the data set), then these observations will cause the mean to be skewed upwards or downwards. In these cases, the median might be a better measure.

Similarly, if you have discrete data—that is, data that only takes a limited number of possible outcomes—the modal outcome may be informative, as this shows the most likely outcome. In the case of discrete data, the mean may be somewhat uninformative, as there is no mechanism that forces the mean to take one of the possible outcome variables.

Key formulae

There are three key formulae that we have seen in this chapter: the arithmetic mean, the geometric mean, and the median.

1. If you observe n observations of X_i, then the (arithmetic) sample mean is calculated as:

$$\bar{X} = \frac{1}{n}\sum_{i=1}^{n} X_i$$

2. If you observe n observations of X_i, then the (geometric) sample mean is calculated as:

$$= \left(\prod_{i=1}^{n} X_i\right)^{\frac{1}{n}}$$

   You should only consider the geometric mean when you have a prior that the observations are normally multiplied together in some form.

3. If you observe n observations of X_i, then to find the median, you need to order the observations from smallest to largest. The median is the middle value, and you can find the position of the median by calculating:

$$= \frac{n+1}{2}$$

   If n is odd (e.g. 9), then this will be a whole number. So for $n = 9$, the median will be the 5th largest observation.

   If n is even, then this will not be a whole number. So for $n = 10$, the median would be the 5.5th largest observation. To find this, we would find the value of the observation that is halfway between the 5th and the 6th observation.

Expectations and Population Averages

7

Learning outcomes for this chapter

By the end of this chapter you will be able to:

- Identify the difference between populations and samples, and how this applies to averages
- Calculate expected values based on probability mass functions
- Calculate the expectation of a linear combination of random variables
- Calculate the expected values of random variables based on probability mass functions when non-linear transformations are applied
- Apply Jensen's inequality to non-linear functions
- Apply the law of large numbers to recognize that sample means converge to the population average as sample sizes tend towards infinity

Mathematical tools

- Summations using sigma (Σ) notation
- Double summations
- Simple arithmetic
- Square roots and powers

Introduction

In the last chapter, we introduced the concept of averages within samples. However, statisticians are often much more interested in averages within a population, rather than simply averages within samples. As we will see in later chapters, statisticians can use sample averages as a way of estimating the population average, but a key question we need to address is what is a population average, and how do we calculate it?

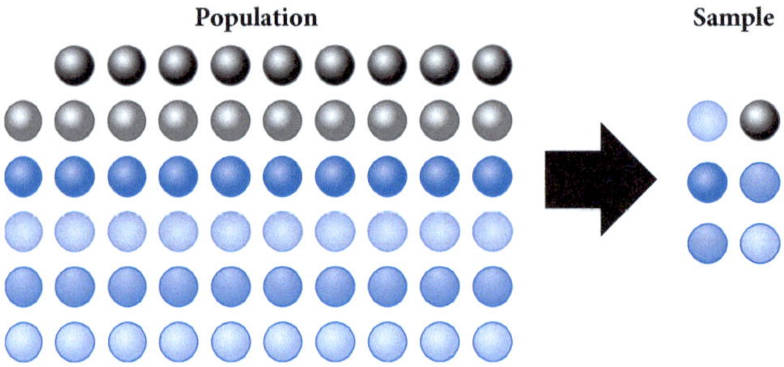

Figure 7.1 Sampling from a population.

7.1 What are populations and samples?

As we saw in the previous chapter, the population consists of all of the individuals that we are interested in, and a sample is merely a subset of that population (Figure 7.1). For example, one population could be all of the possible balls in the UK National Lottery (59 numbered balls), and a sample from that population could be the **six** numbered balls that are drawn out in a particular draw.

Every population has a particular set of underlying, characteristics. For example, we could consider the voting population of the UK as an underlying population, and the voting preferences of the population as an underlying characteristic. This characteristic may be the average wage, or the proportion of the population who vote for a particular political party, or the spread of data.

Provided a sample is representative of the population as a whole, we would expect it to have similar characteristics to the population as a whole. However, the average of a sample will almost always be different from the average (or expected value) within the population as a whole.

7.2 Population averages, expectations, and the expected value

So far, all of our measures of central tendency have been related to samples from a population. That is, the sample mean, median, and mode are all related to a sample from a population, and not the population as a whole.

In this section, we will discuss measures of central tendency for a population as a whole. The key measure of central tendency within a population is the **expected value**.

Let's begin by considering a simple example. Suppose that we roll a fair six-sided dice. With a fair six-sided dice, there is an equal probability that any single roll of the dice will yield any one of the numbers from 1 to 6.

Effectively, when we roll a dice, we are choosing a number from an infinite population. Since the probability of gaining a 1 is $\frac{1}{6}$, this means that $\frac{1}{6}$ of the population will be outcomes equal to 1. Similarly, $\frac{1}{6}$ of the population will be outcomes equal to 2, $\frac{1}{6}$ equal to 3, and so on.

If we roll the dice once, we get one observation from the population, and the outcome would be equally likely to take any value from the set of 1, 2, 3, 4, 5, and 6. However, suppose we were to repeatedly roll the dice.

- What would be the arithmetic mean if we rolled the dice ten times?
- What about 100 times?
- What about an infinite number of times?

Whilst we could never do this, if we were to roll the dice an infinite number of times, we would effectively be observing every member of that population. When we roll a dice, we can think of the dice acting to randomly select a number from a population, where the possible outcomes are 1, 2, 3, 4, 5, and 6, each of which has a probability of $\frac{1}{6}$ of occurring. Say we rolled the dice 6,000,000 times. How many of each number would we expect to roll? Since there is an equal probability of drawing each individual number, we would expect, roughly, for $\frac{1}{6}$ of the rolls to be a 1 (so about 1,000,000), $\frac{1}{6}$ of the rolls to be a 2 (about 1,000,000), and so on.

TRY IT YOURSELF: ROLLING A DICE

- **Find a simple, six-sided dice. Roll it once and record the number that you roll. If you can't find a dice, if you type 'Roll Dice' into Google, it will simulate a roll of a six-sided dice.**
- **Repeat ten times. What is the average of the ten rolls?**
- **Continue rolling the dice for 50 rolls.**
- **What is the average of the 50 rolls?**
- **Continue to 100 rolls. What do you notice?**

Note: 100 rolls is still a small number of rolls. It is perfectly possible to have over-representation of one number or another.

Assuming that we do gain exactly 1,000,000 observations of each number, what would the (arithmetic mean) average of the rolls be?

$$\overline{x} = \frac{1{,}000{,}000 \times 1 + 1{,}000{,}000 \times 2 + \ldots + 1{,}000{,}000 \times 6}{6{,}000{,}000}$$

But we can simplify this to give $\overline{x} = \frac{1}{6} \times 1 + \frac{1}{6} \times 2 + \frac{1}{6} \times 3 + \frac{1}{6} \times 4 + \frac{1}{6} \times 5 + \frac{1}{6} \times 6 = 3.5$. In reality, even with 6,000,000 rolls of the dice, it is very unlikely that we will gain exactly 1,000,000 observations of each possible outcome, but as the sample size gets increasingly large, we would expect the proportions of each outcome across our 6,000,000 observations to get closer and closer to the probabilities relating to those outcomes. So, after a very large number of trials, we would expect $\frac{1}{6}$ of the observations to be a 1, $\frac{1}{6}$ of the observations to be a 2, and so on.

The value of 3.5 that we have constructed here is effectively the population average, or the expectation. If we denote the random variable represented by the roll of a dice as X, then the expected value would be denoted as $E(X)$.

More formally, if we define the outcome from rolling a dice once as a random variable, X, then X will follow the probability mass function (PMF):

$$X = \begin{cases} 1 & P(X = 1) = \frac{1}{6} \\ 2 & P(X = 2) = \frac{1}{6} \\ 3 & P(X = 3) = \frac{1}{6} \\ 4 & P(X = 4) = \frac{1}{6} \\ 5 & P(X = 5) = \frac{1}{6} \\ 6 & P(X = 6) = \frac{1}{6} \end{cases}$$

As we saw, the expected value is equal to the sum of the products of each of the outcomes and their respective probabilities. That is:

$$\begin{aligned} E(X) = {} & P(X = 1) \times 1 + P(X = 2) \times 2 + P(X = 3) \times 3 + P(X = 4) \times 4 \\ & + P(X = 5) \times 5 + P(X = 6) \times 6 \end{aligned}$$

However, writing this out in full is somewhat cumbersome. Since the possible outcomes are the integers from 1 to 6, we can write this as:

$$E(X) = \sum_{i=1}^{6} P(X = i) \times i$$

Another, intuitive, way to think about this would be to think about the expectation as the average if we were to observe the entire population. However, it should be noted that the sample average and the expected value are not the same thing. These are concepts that are often mixed up.

More formally, let us denote the probability of observing an outcome x from a random variable X as $P(X = x) = p$. If we randomly sample observations from the population, as the sample size gets increasingly large, then the proportion of outcomes that are x would tend towards p.

In fact, if there are k possible outcomes of a random variable, and we randomly sample observations from the population, as the sample size tends towards infinity, the proportion of each outcome observed should tend towards their respective probabilities. Hence, we would also expect the sample mean to converge towards the expected value.

More generally, we can find the population average, or expectation, of a random variable by finding the sum of the products of the individual probabilities and the individual outcomes. So, if a random variable X has a range of outcomes, which we will denote x, then the expected value, $E(X)$, will be equal to:

$$E(X) = \sum_{x} P(X = x) \times x$$

That is, the expectation is equal to the sum over all possible values that x could be of the product of the probability $P(X = x)$ and each individual outcome x.

Another way of thinking about the expectation, or the population average

When we construct the expectation, effectively we are weighting each of the possible outcomes by their relevant probabilities. This is because the probability represents the proportion of the 'population' that is made up of a particular outcome.

One way of thinking about this is considering what would happen if we randomly sampled an infinite number of observations from a population (with replacement). The probability here would represent the proportion of the observations represented by each of the outcomes.

Suppose, for example, we had a random variable X which took two possible values, $X = 1$ and $X = 4$, and we knew that $P(X = 1) = 0.2$, and $P(X = 4) = 0.8$. This would tell us that, if we repeatedly randomly chose an observation from X, 20 per cent of the time, the observation would be equal to 1 (as a proportion, this is equivalent to $\frac{20}{100} = 0.2$), whilst the other 80 per cent of the time, the observation would be equal to 4. Thus, with the population average, where we take an infinite number of observations of X, we would weight each of the outcomes by their relative probabilities:

$$E(X) = P(X = 1) \times 1 + P(X = 4) \times 4 = 0.2 \times 1 + 0.8 \times 4 = 3.4$$

Worked example 7.1: Flipping two coins

Suppose that you have two (fair) coins that you flip, and you wish to find the population average, or expected number of heads that you achieve.

To evaluate this, we can assign a head a score of 1, and a tail a score of 0. So, if you achieve two heads, you achieve a score of 2, if you achieve one head, you achieve a score of 1, and if you achieve zero heads, you achieve a score of zero. Let's define the score from the game as Y, and we can write down the PMF of Y:[1]

$$P(Y = y) = \begin{cases} 0, & P(Y = 0) = 0.25 \\ 1, & P(Y = 1) = 0.5 \\ 2, & P(Y = 2) = 0.25 \end{cases}$$

So, to calculate the expectation, we will need to find the sum of the products of the probabilities with the outcomes.

$$E(Y) = \sum_y P(Y = y) \times y = P(Y = 0) \times 0 + P(Y = 1) \times 1 + P(Y = 2) \times 2$$
$$= 0.25 \times 0 + 0.5 \times 1 + 0.25 \times 2 = 0 + 0.5 + 0.5 = 1$$

[1] Remember that the outcomes of the two flips are independent from each other. The only way of achieving zero heads would be for both coins to land tails upwards. Therefore, if we define C_1 as the first coin, and C_2 as the second coin, then $P(Y = y) = P(C_1 = T \cap C_2 = T) = P(C_1 = T) \times P(C_2 = T) = 0.5 \times 0.5 = 0.25$.

So, if you played this game an infinite number of times, then the average score, or the average number of heads that we would expect to gain across those infinite games, would be 1.

Worked example 7.2: A risky investment

Suppose that you are interested in investing in a financial product. This is a very strange financial product, in that there are only four possible outcomes: you will either make a profit of £100, a profit of £0, a loss of £50, or a loss of £1,000. Let's denote the financial return as a random variable Y, and the probabilities associated with each outcome are denoted here:

$$Y = \begin{cases} 100, & P(Y = 100) = 0.5 \\ 0, & P(Y = 0) = 0.1 \\ -50, & P(Y = -50) = 0.38 \\ -1{,}000, & P(Y = -1{,}000) = 0.02 \end{cases}$$

We can calculate the expected profit from this financial product by finding $E(Y)$. This will tell you how much, on average, you would gain if you repeatedly made this investment. Remember that the expectation can be calculated as the sum of the products of the outcomes with the relevant probabilities.

$$E(Y) = \sum_y P(Y = y) \times y = 0.5 \times 100 + 0.1 \times 0 + 0.38 \times (-50) + 0.02 \times (-1{,}000)$$
$$= 50 + 0 - 19 - 20 = £11.00$$

So, the expected profit from this investment is £11.00. Because the outcomes are uncertain, this doesn't mean that you would be certain to make a profit of £11.00, but instead that this is the average profit (if you repeatedly invested in this financial product) that you could expect to make from the investment.

Worked example 7.3: Finding the expected score when we roll two dice

Suppose we roll two fair dice—a blue and a white dice—and add up the respective scores. What would be the expected score that we gain? In order to find this, first we need to find the probability of each discrete outcome. Since the outcomes on the two dice are independent, we know that the probability of gaining, say, a 1 on the blue dice and a 1 on the white dice is just $\frac{1}{6} \times \frac{1}{6} = \frac{1}{36}$. We also know that this is the only way of producing a score of 2.

However, if we were to consider the probability of scoring 3, this could be gained by either the blue dice landing on 1 and the white dice landing on 2 (probability $= \frac{1}{36}$), or vice versa. So the total probability of gaining a score of 3 would be $\frac{1}{36} + \frac{1}{36} = \frac{1}{18}$. That is, there are two available cases where we score 3. Similarly, there are three cases where we score 4, and so on.

The overall probability of each score is represented in Table 7.1.

We know that the expected value can be calculated as:

Table 7.1 Probabilities of each outcome from rolling two fair six-sided dice

Total	2	3	4	5	6	7	8	9	10	11	12
Probability	$\frac{1}{36}$	$\frac{1}{18}$	$\frac{1}{12}$	$\frac{1}{9}$	$\frac{5}{36}$	$\frac{1}{6}$	$\frac{5}{36}$	$\frac{1}{9}$	$\frac{1}{12}$	$\frac{1}{18}$	$\frac{1}{36}$

$$E(X) = \sum_{i=1}^{n} P(X = x_i) \times x_i$$

From this, we could calculate the expected value from the roll of two dice:

$$E(X) = 2 \times \frac{1}{36} + 3 \times \frac{1}{18} + 4 \times \frac{1}{12} + 5 \times \frac{1}{9} + 6 \times \frac{5}{36} + 7 \times \frac{1}{6} + 8 \times \frac{5}{36} + 9 \times \frac{1}{9} + 10 \times \frac{1}{12}$$
$$+11 \times \frac{1}{18} + 12 \times \frac{1}{36} = 7$$

So, intuitively, this means that if we were to observe the (infinite) population of all realizations of two dice rolls, then the mean average would be equal to 7.

7.3 Expectations of linear combinations of random variables

Returning to expectations, in Worked example 7.3 we saw that the expected value of the score when we added up the outcomes across two fair six-sided dice was equal to 7. Similarly, we know that when we roll a single six-sided dice, the expected outcome is equal to 3.5. Equally, we could show that the expected outcome from rolling three dice would be 10.5, and from rolling four dice would be 14.

It is no coincidence that the expected value we gain from rolling two dice is just the sum of the expected value from each of the individual dice. In fact, this demonstrates a fundamental rule relating to linear combinations of random variables.

To express this a little more formally, let's define three random variables. Suppose that we define X as the outcome from the first six-sided dice, Y as the outcome from the second six-sided dice. We will then use the outcomes from the two dice to construct the total score, Z, where Z is the sum of the outcomes from the first and the second dice:

$$Z = X + Y$$

We know that $E(X) = 3.5$, and $E(Y) = 3.5$. We saw in Section 7.2.3 that $E(Z) = 7$, which is just equal to $E(X) + E(Y)$.

More formally, what we have done is show that finding $E(Z)$ is equivalent to finding $E(X + Y)$, and we have seen in this example that $E(X + Y) = E(X) + E(Y)$.

This may seem like a surprising result, but, in fact this will always hold, because the expectation is a linear function. We construct an expectation by constructing a linear combination of the products of the outcomes and their corresponding probabilities.

More generally, there are a number of rules that we can apply when we are creating new random variables, based on a linear combination of other existing random variables.

7.3.1 Rules for finding the expectations of linear functions of random variables

Suppose that you have two random variables, X and Y, and constants a and b. The expectations of X and Y can be denoted as $E(X)$ and $E(Y)$ respectively.

1. The expectation of a constant is always equal to that constant.

   $$E(a) = a$$

2. The expectation of a constant multiplied by a random variable is equal to that constant multiplied by the expectation of the original random variable:

   $$E(aX) = aE(X)$$

3. The expectation of a sum of random variables is equal to the sum of the expectations:

   $$E(X + Y) = E(X) + E(Y)$$

4. By combining rule 1 and rule 3, we can see that, if we add a constant to a random variable, the resulting expectation is equal to the constant plus the expectation of the original random variable:

   $$E(a + X) = a + E(X)$$

   Intuitively, what is happening here is that every outcome of X is being shifted by an amount a, so we would expect that since every outcome is shifted by a distance a, it must also follow that the (population) average also shifts by that same amount.

5. By combining rule 2 and rule 3, we can see that if we have a linear combination of random variables, such as $Z = aX + bY$, then the expectation of Z will be equal to the same linear combination of the expectations:

   $$E(aX + bY) = aE(X) + bE(Y)$$

More generally, if we construct a random variable, W, based on a linear combination of k random variables $X_1, X_2, \ldots, X_k$ and constants $a_1, a_2, \ldots, a_k$, then the expectation of W will just be equal to a linear combination of the expectations of the X_i:

$$W = \sum_{i=1}^{k} a_i X_i$$

$$\Rightarrow E(W) = E\left(\sum_{i=1}^{k} a_i X_i\right) = \sum_{i=1}^{k} a_i E(X_i)$$

Proofs of the five rules relating to expectations are available in the appendix to this chapter. In the rest of this section, we will see a number of examples illustrating the application of these rules, and we will reassure ourselves, by example, that the rules we have constructed hold.

Worked example 7.4: Multiplying a random variable by a constant

Let us return to the example of a risky investment, discussed in Worked example 7.2. The profit made by an investor was defined by the random variable Y, where the PMF of Y is given by:

$$Y = \begin{cases} 100, & P(Y = 100) = 0.5 \\ 0, & P(Y = 0) = 0.1 \\ -50, & P(Y = -50) = 0.38 \\ -1{,}000, & P(Y = -1{,}000) = 0.02 \end{cases}$$

We calculated that expected value of Y, $E(Y)$, was equal to £11.00. Suppose that Ahmed is an investor who has bought three shares in this investment. This means that when the investment yields a profit of £100, he will realize this profit three times, and make an overall profit of £300. Similarly, when the investment yields a loss of £1,000, he will make a loss of £3,000.

In essence, by purchasing three shares, what we have done is to multiply the original random variable by 3. So, we have created a new variable, which we will call $Z = 3Y$.

Using rule 2, we know that the expectation of any constant multiplied by a random variable is equal to that constant multiplied by the expectation of the original random variable:

$$E(Z) = E(3Y) = 3E(Y)$$

Since $E(Y) = 11.00$, this means that $E(Z) = 3 \times 11 = 33.00$.

Verifying our calculation

The act of multiplying the random variable Y by 3 means that every outcome will be multiplied by 3. However, because we have this one-to-one translation of outcomes from Y to Z, the probabilities relating to the outcomes of Z will align with the probabilities of Y. So, for instance, if $Y = 100$, it automatically follows that $Z = 300$, so we can write that $P(Z = 300) = P(Y = 100) = 0.5$. We can repeat this process for all four possible outcomes of Y:

i) $Y = 100 \Rightarrow Z = 300$ $\quad P(Z = 300) = P(Y = 100) = 0.5$

ii) $Y = 0 \Rightarrow Z = 0$ $\quad P(Z = 0) = P(Y = 0) = 0.1$

iii) $Y = -50 \Rightarrow Z = -150$ $\quad P(Z = -150) = P(Y = -50) = 0.38$

iv) $Y = -1{,}000 \Rightarrow Z = -3{,}000$ $\quad P(Z = -3{,}000) = P(Y = -1000) = 0.02$

So, the PMF of our new random variable, Z, is:

$$Z = \begin{cases} 300, & P(Z = 300) = 0.5 \\ 0, & P(Z = 0) = 0.1 \\ -150, & P(Z = -150) = 0.38 \\ -3{,}000, & P(Z = -3{,}000) = 0.02 \end{cases}$$

Calculating the expectation of Z is now easy, as we just need to find the sum of the products of the outcomes and their corresponding probabilities:

$$\begin{aligned} E(Z) &= \sum_z P(Z = z) \times z = 0.5 \times 300 + 0.1 \times 0 + 0.38 \times (-150) + 0.02 \times (-3{,}000) \\ &= 33.00 \end{aligned}$$

So, as we calculated, the expected profit from this investment is now £33.00.

Worked example 7.5: Calculating expected wealth after an investment

Suppose that we are now not interested in the profit that an investor makes, but instead the wealth that they have at the end of the game. Beverly is an investor who begins with an initial wealth of $W_0 = £1{,}000$, and buys a single share in the investment, so the PMF of her investment is given by Y:

$$Y = \begin{cases} 100, & P(Y = 100) = 0.5 \\ 0, & P(Y = 0) = 0.1 \\ -50, & P(Y = -50) = 0.38 \\ -1{,}000, & P(Y = -1{,}000) = 0.02 \end{cases}$$

If Beverly invests, her final wealth is just going to be equal to her initial wealth, plus the profit that she makes from the investment. Let's define W as Beverly's final wealth:

$$W = 1{,}000 + Y$$

Based on the rules in Section 7.3.1, the new random variable, W, is just equal to the original random variable, Y, plus a constant. As such, if we wish to calculate the expectation of W, we can simply find:

$$\begin{aligned} E(W) &= E(1{,}000 + Y) \\ &= 1{,}000 + E(Y) \end{aligned}$$

That is, the expectation of a random variable plus a constant is just equal to the random variable plus the constant. We know that $E(Y) = 11.00$, so we would expect $E(W) = 1{,}000 + 11 = 1{,}011.00$.

Verifying our calculation

We have applied the rules in Section 7.3.1, but to verify that the rules are valid, it is useful to manually calculate the expectation of W. We know that every possible outcome of W is just equal to $W = 1{,}000 + Y$. So, when $Y = 100$, W will automatically be equal to $W = 1{,}100$. Similarly, whenever $Y = -50$, $W = 950$.

Because we have this simple one-to-one relationship between W and Y, we can also write down the probability relating to each of the possible outcomes of W:

i) $Y = 100 \Rightarrow W = 1{,}100$ $\quad P(W = 1{,}100) = P(Y = 100) = 0.5$

ii) $Y = 0 \Rightarrow W = 1{,}000$ $\quad P(W = 1{,}000) = P(Y = 0) = 0.1$

iii) $Y = -50 \Rightarrow W = 950$ $\quad P(W = 950) = P(Y = -50) = 0.38$

iv) $Y = -1{,}000 \Rightarrow W = 0$ $\quad P(W = 0) = P(Y = -1{,}000) = 0.02$

So, we can formally write down the PMF for W:

$$W = \begin{cases} 1{,}100, & P(W = 1{,}100) = 0.5 \\ 1{,}000, & P(W = 1{,}000) = 0.1 \\ 950, & P(W = 950) = 0.38 \\ 0, & P(W = 0) = 0.02 \end{cases}$$

Now, having constructed the PMF, it is very easy to calculate the expected wealth for Beverly:

$$E(W) = \sum_{w} P(W = w) \times w = 0.5 \times 1{,}100 + 0.1 \times 1{,}000 + 0.38 \times 950 + 0.02 \times 0$$
$$= 1{,}011.00$$

On average, Beverly will increase her wealth by investing in this financial product. However, as you develop your understanding of microeconomics, you are likely to come across the idea that investors are often risk averse. In this example, risk averse investors may prefer not to invest in the financial product, because of the risk of losing £1,000. We will explore this possibility in Worked example 7.9 later in this chapter.

Worked example 7.6: A linear combination of two random variables

Suppose that you are engaging in a competition. Your winnings in the competition are determined by the score you achieve in a game X_1, and the score that your competitor achieves in the game X_2. The prize you win is increasing as your score increases, but, as the other player's score increases, your prize decreases, and this may lead to you losing money (see Table 7.2).

Table 7.2 Joint PMF of X_1 and X_2

Joint probability		X_2: 6	X_2: 20
X_1	10	0.2	0.1
	15	0.2	0.5

The prize that you win will be calculated by multiplying the score you gain by 10, and subtracting seven times the score gained by player 2. Let's define the prize as Q.[2] We can then write down a mathematical expression for the prize in terms of the random variables X_1 and X_2:

$$Q = 10X_1 - 7X_2$$

The question of interest is what is your expected prize? There are two methods that we could use. Firstly, we could use our rule that the expectation of a linear combination is equal to the linear combination of expectations, so:

$$E(Q) = E(10X_1 - 7X_2) = 10E(X_1) - 7E(X_2)$$

We could also use the joint probabilities to calculate the expectation.

Method 1

To calculate $E(Q)$, we will first need to calculate $E(X_1)$ and $E(X_2)$, by calculating the marginal probability distribution of X_1 and X_2. Since we have the joint PMF, we can appeal to the law of total probability to calculate that:

$$P(X_1 = x_1) = \sum_{x_2} P(X_1 = x_1 \cap X_2 = x_2)$$

That is, for each possible outcome of X_1 (say, $X_1 = 10$), we would add up all of the joint probabilities where that outcome occurs. So, for example, to calculate the probability that X_1 is equal to 10, we would add up all of the joint probabilities where $X_1 = 10$. That is, we would add the probability that $X_1 = 10$ and $X_2 = 6$ to the probability that $X_1 = 10$ and $X_2 = 20$. That is:

$$P(X_1 = 10) = P(X_1 = 10 \cap X_2 = 6) + P(X_1 = 10 \cap X_2 = 20) = 0.2 + 0.1 = 0.3$$

We calculate all of these marginal probabilities in Table 7.3. So, the probability that $X_1 = 10$ is equal to 0.3, whilst the probability that $X_2 = 6$ is equal to 0.4.

More generally, we can write down the marginal probability distribution of X_1 and X_2 as:

$$X_1 = \begin{cases} 10, & P(X_1 = 10) = 0.3 \\ 15, & P(X_1 = 15) = 0.7 \end{cases}, \quad X_2 = \begin{cases} 6, & P(X_2 = 6) = 0.4 \\ 20, & P(X_2 = 20) = 0.6 \end{cases}$$

Table 7.3 Calculating the marginal distribution of X_1 and X_2

Joint probability		X_2: 6	X_2: 20	Total
X_1	10	0.2	0.1	0.3
	15	0.2	0.5	0.7
	Total	0.4	0.6	

[2] We have used Q here arbitrarily. It might have made more sense to use P to represent the prize won, but then we would have had the distinctly unpleasant notation $P(P = p)$, which the author felt was confusing.

Now, we can use these marginal probabilities to calculate the expected values of X_1 and X_2:

$$E(X_1) = P(X_1 = 10) \times 10 + P(X_1 = 15) \times 15 = 0.3 \times 10 + 0.7 \times 15 = 13.5$$
$$E(X_2) = P(X_2 = 6) \times 6 + P(X_2 = 20) \times 20 = 0.4 \times 6 + 0.6 \times 20 = 14.4$$

Now, we wish to find $E(Q)$ where $Q = 10X_1 - 7X_2$. Using rule 5, we can write that:

$$E(Q) = E(10X_1 - 7X_2) = 10E(X_1) - 7E(X_2) = 10 \times 13.5 - 7 \times 14.4 = 34.2$$

Method 2

Since the prize won is constructed based on a linear combination of X_1 and X_2, we can write down the possible outcomes for Q, and use the joint **probability mass function** (PMF) to calculate the probabilities of each possible outcome of Q.

For example, we know that $P(X_1 = 10 \cap X_2 = 6) = 0.2$. However, we also know that, when $X_1 = 10$ and $X_2 = 6$, the prize that we will win will be equal to:

$$= 10 \times 10 - 7 \times 6 = 100 - 42 = 58$$

We can calculate the possible outcomes of the prizes for each of the pairs of outcomes of X_1 and X_2 (see Table 7.4).

Table 7.4 Possible prizes for player 1/possible outcomes for Q

Outcome of Q		X_2 = 6	X_2 = 20
X_1	10	58	–40
	15	108	10

There are four distinct outcomes for Q, and we can use the joint distribution to calculate the probability of each possible outcome.[3] So, for instance, since when $X_1 = 10$ and $X_2 = 6$, then $Q = 58$, we can immediately write down that $P(Q = 58) = P(X_1 = 10 \cap X_2 = 6) = 0.2$. We can thus write down the PMF of Q:

$$Q = \begin{cases} -40, & P(Q = -40) = 0.1 \\ 10, & P(Q = 10) = 0.5 \\ 58, & P(Q = 58) = 0.2 \\ 108, & P(Q = 108) = 0.2 \end{cases}$$

Now, calculating the expectation of Q is trivial:

$$E(Q) = \sum_q P(Q = q) \times q = 0.1 \times (-40) + 0.5 \times 10 + 0.2 \times 58 + 0.2 \times 108$$
$$= 34.2$$

[3] If there were repeated outcomes of Q, we could calculate the marginal probability of each outcome by adding together all of the joint probabilities that lead to the repeated outcomes.

Reassuringly, having used two separate methods to calculate the expectation, we have achieved the same answer.

Worked example 7.7: Calculating average exam marks

In all of the examples we have considered so far, we have known the underlying probability distribution of the original random variables. However, because the rules relating to expectations we have constructed in Section 7.3.1 will always hold, if we construct a new variable from a linear combination of existing variables, all we need to construct the expectation is the expectation of the underlying random variables.

Consider the following example. In many educational environments, the grades for a particular course may be constructed by creating a weighted average of the grades in different papers. Suppose that for your statistics course, the final grade is made up from three papers: paper A, paper B, and paper C. We will treat the marks individuals gain in the three papers as random variables A, B, and C.

Each paper is marked out of 100, with the population average mark for paper A equal to 67 per cent, and paper B 55 per cent. Paper C was a much harder paper, with the population average equal to 35. Formally, we can represent these population averages in expectation notation:

$$E(A) = 67, \quad E(B) = 55, \quad E(C) = 35$$

However, to calculate the final grade, these marks are combined as a linear combination. Paper A counts for 50 per cent of the final grade, paper B counts for 30 per cent of the final grade, and paper C counts for 20 per cent of the final grade. Thus, the final grade, G, can be calculated as the linear combination of the marks in the three papers:

$$G = 0.5A + 0.3B + 0.2C$$

Since G is merely a linear combination of A, B, and C, we can calculate the expected final grade by applying rule 5:

$$E(G) = E(0.5A + 0.3B + 0.2C) = 0.5E(A) + 0.3E(B) + 0.2E(C)$$

Substituting in the values for the expectations gives us:

$$\Rightarrow E(G) = 0.5 \times 67 + 0.3 \times 55 + 0.2 \times 35 = 57$$

So, the average score in this examination will just be equal to 57.

7.4 Non-linear transformations of random variables

In the previous section, we have seen that if we apply a linear transformation (e.g. adding a constant, or multiplying by a constant) to a single random variable, or construct a new variable based upon a linear combination of two or more random variables, then the expectation of the new variable can be calculated based upon the same linear function applied to the expectations. For example, $E(X + Y) = E(X) + E(Y)$.

However, often we will be interested in either non-linear transformations (such as taking a logarithm, or raising a random variable to a power), or a non-linear combination of random variables (e.g. multiplying random variables together), and in general, it will not be the case that the expectation of the resulting random variable will be equal to the non-linear function applied to the expectation.

For example, if we have two random variables, X and Y, to which we apply non-linear transformations:

- If we square a random variable X, then the expectation of X^2 will generally not be equal to the square of the expectation of X: $E(X^2) \neq E(X)^2$
- If we take the natural logarithm of X, then the expectation of $\ln X$ will generally not be equal to the logarithm of the expectation of X: $E(\ln X) \neq \ln E(X)$.
- If we multiply together two random variables, X and Y, then the expectation of the product of X and Y will generally not be equal to the product of the expectations of X and Y, unless X and Y are independent random variables: $E(XY) \neq E(X) \times E(Y)$.

Worked example 7.8: Multiplying together two random variables

Let's consider the random variables we saw in Worked example 7.6. Here we had two random variables, X_1 and X_2, and we were presented with a joint probability mass function (see Table 7.5).

Table 7.5 Joint distribution of X_1 and X_2

Joint probability		X_2 = 6	X_2 = 20
X_1	10	0.2	0.1
	15	0.2	0.5

We saw that $E(X_1) = 13.5$, and that $E(X_2) = 14.4$. Let's suppose that we create a new variable Z, which is constructed based on the product of X_1 and X_2. That is:

$$Z = X_1 X_2$$

We wish to calculate the expectation of Z. We can calculate the outcomes of Z by multiplying together the possible outcomes of X_1 and X_2. So, for instance, if $X_1 = 10$ and $X_2 = 6$, then Z will be equal to $10 \times 6 = 60$. We also know the probability: $P(X_1 = 10 \cap X_2 = 6) = 0.2$ (from the joint PMF) (see Table 7.6).

Table 7.6 Possible outcomes of Z

Outcomes of $Z = X_1 X_2$		X_2 = 6	X_2 = 20
X_1	10	60	200
	15	90	300

Using the outcomes we have calculated, and the joint probability distribution, we can write down the PMF of Z:

$$Z = \begin{cases} 60, & P(Z = 60) = P(X_1 = 10 \cap X_2 = 6) = 0.2 \\ 90, & P(Z = 90) = P(X_1 = 15 \cap X_2 = 6) = 0.2 \\ 200, & P(Z = 200) = P(X_1 = 10 \cap X_2 = 20) = 0.1 \\ 300, & P(Z = 300) = P(X_1 = 15 \cap X_2 = 20) = 0.5 \end{cases}$$

The expected value of Z is trivial to calculate:

$$E(Z) = \sum_z P(Z = z) \times z = 0.2 \times 60 + 0.2 \times 90 + 0.1 \times 200 + 0.5 \times 300 = 200$$

Now, remember that $Z = X_1 X_2$, so $E(Z) = E(X_1 X_2)$. Let's compare this result we have calculated with the product of the expectations:

$$E(X_1) = 13.5, \; E(X_2) = 14.4$$
$$\Rightarrow E(X_1)E(X_2) = 13.5 \times 14.4 = 194.4$$

So, in this example, we have shown that $E(X_1 X_2) \neq E(X_1)E(X_2)$. This means that, when you are dealing with random variables constructed based on a product of two (or more) random variables, we have to be careful with how we calculate the expected value.

A general rule

- In general, if we multiply two random variables X and Y together, then $E(XY) \neq E(X)E(Y)$.
- Similarly, if we divide a random variable X by a second random variable Y, then $E(\frac{x}{y}) \neq \frac{E(X)}{E(Y)}$.

This is because the act of multiplying together or dividing by random variables is a non-linear transformation.

There is an exception to this rule, which we will explore in Section 7.4.1, where the random variables are independent from each other.

7.4.1 An exception—when random variables are independent

There is an exception, where the expectation of a product of random variables is equal to the product of the expectations,[4] and that is when the random variables are independent random variables. Let's suppose that we flip two fair coins, and we will denote the first flip as C_1 and the second flip as C_2.

[4] This is proven in the appendix.

Let's assign a value of1 whenever the coin lands heads upwards, and 0 if the coin lands tails upwards. As each flip is **independent and identically distributed**, we can write that:

$$C_i = \begin{cases} 1, & P(C_i = 1) = 0.5 \\ 0, & P(C_i = 0) = 0.5' \end{cases}, \quad \text{for } i = 1,2$$

It is now very easy to calculate the expectation of C_i:

$$E(C_i) = 0.5 \times 1 + 0.5 \times 0 = 0.5$$

That is, since each coin flip has exactly the same probability of landing heads upwards, it will be the case that $E(C_1) = E(C_2) = 0.5$.

Suppose we were to flip a coin twice, and then multiply together the outcomes of C_1 and C_2. If both coins land heads upwards, then the product would be equal to $1 \times 1 = 1$. Otherwise, the product would always be equal to 0. If we want to find $E(C_1C_2)$, we need to know the joint distribution of C_1 and C_2. However, since the flips are independent, the joint probability will also equal the product of the marginal probabilities.

Outcomes of $C_1 \times C_2$		C_2 = 0	C_2 = 1
C_1	0	0	0
	1	0	1

There are only two possible outcomes for our product: 0 and 1. 0 occurs whenever either $C_1 = 0$ or $C_2 = 0$ (or both equal 0).

As such $P(C_1C_2) = 0 = P(C_1 = 0 \cap C_2 = 0) + P(C_1 = 1 \cap C_2 = 0) + P(C_1 = 0 \cap C_2 = 1)$. Because the flips are independent, we can calculate these joint probabilities by multiplying together the marginal probabilities:[5]

$$P(C_1 = 0 \cap C_2 = 0) = P(C_1 = 0) \times P(C_2 = 0) = 0.5 \times 0.5 = 0.25$$
$$P(C_1 = 1 \cap C_2 = 0) = P(C_1 = 1) \times P(C_2 = 0) = 0.5 \times 0.5 = 0.25$$
$$P(C_1 = 0 \cap C_1 = 1) = P(C_1 = 0) \times P(C_2 = 1) = 0.5 \times 0.5 = 0.25$$
$$P(C_1 = 1 \cap C_1 = 1) = P(C_1 = 1) \times P(C_1 = 1) = 0.5 \times 0.5 = 0.25$$

So, using these joint probabilities, $P(C_1C_2 = 0) = 0.25 + 0.25 + 0.25 = 0.75$. Similarly, C_1C_2 will equal 1 whenever both $C_1 = 1$ and $C_2 = 1$, and so $P(C_1C_2) = 1 = P(C_1 = 1 \cap C_2 = 1) = 0.25$.

As such, the expectation of C_1C_2 can be calculated as:

$$E(C_1C_2) = P(C_1C_2 = 0) \times 0 + P(C_1C_2 = 1) \times 1 = 0.75 \times 0 + 0.25 \times 1 = 0.25$$

[5] This is an application of the chain rule of probability: $P(X = x \cap Y = y) = P(X = x) \times P(Y = y \mid X = x)$. However, when X and Y are independent, $P(Y = y \mid X = x) = P(Y = y)$, and so for an independent X and Y, the joint probability is equal to $P(X = x \cap Y = y) = P(X = x) \times P(Y = y)$.

Finally, let's compare this result with the product of the expectations. We saw that $E(C_1) = E(C_2) = 0.5$. If we were to multiply together these expectations we would get:

$$E(C_1)E(C_2) = 0.5 \times 0.5 = 0.25$$

So, in this example, where C_1 and C_2 are independent random variables, the expectation of the product of the random variables is equal to the product of the expectations of the random variables. This is a general result, proven in the appendix, such that the expectation of any product of two (or more) independent random variables will be equal to the product of the expectations of those random variables.

Important note

Generally speaking, when looking at a product of random variables (or a ratio of random variables), the expectation of the product will not be equal to the product of the expectations:

$$E(XY) \neq E(X)E(Y)$$

There are some exceptions, such as when X and Y are independent random variables. However, these are very much an exception, and generally, if you see a product of random variables, you should expect that $E(XY)$ will not be equal to $E(X)E(Y)$.

Worked example 7.9: Expected utility—A non-linear transformation

In microeconomics, you will see that individuals are likely to choose risky options, only if their expected utility is greater than the utility they would gain from not taking the risk. Utility can be thought of as the amount of 'happiness' or 'satisfaction' the individual gains from consuming their wealth. Economists will often analyse the behaviour of individuals by placing a mathematical function to represent their risk aversion:[6]

- An individual will be risk averse (i.e. prefer outcomes with certainty over equivalent risky outcomes) if their utility function is concave.
- An individual will be risk loving (i.e. prefer risky outcomes over equivalent outcomes with certainty) if their utility function is convex.
- An individual will be risk neutral if their utility function is linear.

Let's return to Beverly, whom we saw in Section 7.3.2. Beverly is risk averse (i.e. she does not like taking risks) and gains utility based on the amount she can consume based on her final

[6] Concave functions are functions whose second derivative is negative. That is, as the input increases, the slope of the function becomes less positive (or more negative). Examples of concave functions include the square root and a natural logarithm. Convex functions are functions whose second derivative is positive. As the input increases, the slope of the function becomes more positive. Examples of convex functions include squaring and exponentials. An easy way of remembering the difference is that con**cave** functions are shaped a little like a **cave** on the page.

wealth; she has a utility function $U(W) = \sqrt{W}$. That is, the utility she gains is equal to the square root of her final wealth.

If she does not purchase the financial product, her final wealth will be £1,000, and she can gain utility equal to $U_0 = \sqrt{1{,}000} = 31.623\,(3dp)$.

Now, we are applying a (non-linear) function to the wealth to construct the utility. However, we can use the same thought process as we did in Section 7.2.2 to calculate the expected utility. When the wealth is equal to £1,100, it will automatically follow that the utility is equal to $\sqrt{1{,}100}$. When the wealth is equal to £950, it automatically follows that the utility is equal to $\sqrt{950}$:

i) $W = 1{,}100 \Rightarrow U(W) = \sqrt{1{,}100} \quad P(U(W) = \sqrt{1{,}100}) = P(W = 1{,}100) = 0.5$

ii) $W = 1{,}000 \Rightarrow U(W) = \sqrt{1{,}000} \quad P(U(W) = \sqrt{1{,}000}) = P(W = 1{,}000) = 0.1$

iii) $W = 950 \Rightarrow U(W) = \sqrt{950} \quad P(U(W) = \sqrt{950}) = P(W = 950) = 0.38$

iv) $W = 0 \Rightarrow U(W) = \sqrt{0} \quad P(U(W) = \sqrt{0}) = P(W = 0) = 0.02$

So, we can write down the PMF of the utility:

$$U(W) = \begin{cases} \sqrt{1{,}100}, & P(U(W) = \sqrt{1{,}100}) = 0.5 \\ \sqrt{1{,}000}, & P(U(W) = \sqrt{1{,}000}) = 0.1 \\ \sqrt{950}, & P(U(W) = \sqrt{950}) = 0.38 \\ \sqrt{0}, & P(U(W) = \sqrt{0}) = 0.02 \end{cases}$$

To calculate the expected utility, we find the sum of all of the utilities, weighted by their respective probabilities:

$$\begin{aligned} E(U(W)) &= \sum_u P(U(W) = u) \times u \\ &= 0.5 \times \sqrt{1{,}100} + 0.1 \times \sqrt{1{,}000} + 0.38 \times \sqrt{950} + 0.02 \times \sqrt{0} \\ &= 31.4578 \end{aligned}$$

So, in this example, the expected utility, $E(U) = 31.4578$, is less than the utility that Beverly would gain from not making the investment ($U(1000) = 31.623$). Because the expected utility is lower than she would gain from not making the investment, she would choose not to make the investment.

An interesting result

In constructing the utility that Beverly gains, we have applied a non-linear function to her final wealth. In particular, the function we have applied is taking the square root of her wealth, which is a concave function, illustrated in Figure 7.2.

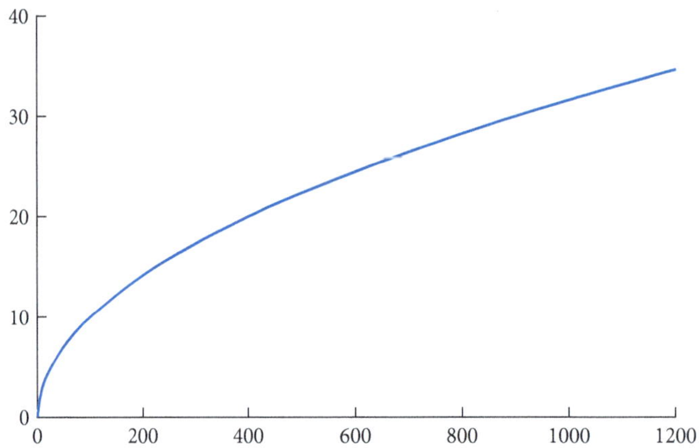

Figure 7.2 The utility function $U(W) = \sqrt{W}$

What is interesting about this is that if we consider the expectations we have calculated, we have calculated the expected wealth and the expected utility. Because the utility is calculated by just taking the square root of the wealth, we will write $E(U(W))$ as $E(\sqrt{W})$:

- $E(W) = 1{,}011$
- $E(\sqrt{W}) = 31.4578$

Suppose that we were to take the square root of $E(W)$. We would get:

$$\sqrt{E(W)} = \sqrt{1{,}011} = 31.7962$$

Formally, we can write that $\sqrt{E(W)} > E(\sqrt{W})$. This is interesting for two reasons:

1. We have shown that, when we apply a non-linear function to a random variable, the expectation of the resulting new random variable ($\sqrt{W}$ in this example) is not equal to the function applied to the expectation of the random variable.
2. We have seen that, for this particular case, where the function is a concave function, the expectation of $\sqrt{W}$ is strictly less than the square root of the expected wealth.

This is an example of something called Jensen's inequality, which states that, more generally, for a random variable X and any concave function denoted as f:

$$f(E(X)) > E(f(X))$$

7.4.2 A general rule for calculating the expectation of a non-linear transformation

So far, when considering a non-linear transformation of a random variable, we have created a new random variable. For example, if we start off with a simple random variable X, with possible outcomes $x_1, x_2, \ldots, x_n$, each occurring with probability $P(X = x_i)$, and we want to know the expectation of a non-linear transformation, we have created a whole new random variable, say Y, which applies this non-linear transformation.

So, for example, if $f(X) = X^2$, we might write down a new variable $Y = X^2$, and then write down all of the outcomes of Y as $x_1^2, x_2^2, \ldots, x_n^2$, each of which occurs with probability $P(Y = x_i^2)$. However, as we have a one-to-one transformation, the probability $P(Y = x_i^2) = P(X = x_i)$.

As such, there is no need to create the new variable. We could simply write down the distribution of $f(X)$ in terms of the probabilities of X, and hence the expectation of $f(X)$ can be calculated as:

$$E(f(X)) = \sum_{i=1}^{n} P(X = x_i) \times f(x_i)$$

That is, we find the sum of the products of each of the outcomes of $f(X)$, multiplied by the probabilities of each of the outcomes of X.

For example, suppose we have a random variable X, such that the PMF is:

$$X = \begin{cases} 0, & P(X = 0) = 0.25 \\ 1, & P(X = 1) = 0.5 \\ 2, & P(X = 2) = 0.25 \end{cases}$$

If we carry out a non-linear transformation to X, say $f(X) = X^2$, then all of the possible outcomes of X will be squared, but the related probabilities will be unaffected. As such, if we wish to calculate the expectation of $f(X) = X^2$, this will just be equal to:

$$\begin{aligned} E(f(X)) &= E(X^2) = \sum_x f(x) \times P(X = x) = \sum_x x^2 \times P(X = x) \\ &= f(0) \times 0.25 + f(1) \times 0.5 + f(2) \times 0.25 \end{aligned}$$

Now, applying that $f(X) = X^2$, we merely need to square the outcomes of X to apply the transformation:

$$\begin{aligned} &= 0^2 \times 0.25 + 1^2 \times 0.5 + 2^2 \times 0.25 \\ &= 0 + 0.5 + 1 = 1.5 \end{aligned}$$

So, the expectation of $f(X) = X^2$ from the random variable is equal to 1.5.

7.5 Jensen's inequality

Jensen's inequality is an important rule in microeconomics, particularly when thinking about choice under uncertainty. Jensen's inequality tells us about what happens to the expectation when we apply a (non-linear) transformation to a random variable. We saw, in Worked example 7.9, that having applied a concave function to transform our initial random variable, $f(E(X)) > E(f(X))$.

More generally, if we apply any function f to a random variable X, then:

- If f is a concave function then $f(E(X)) > E(f(X))$.
- If f is a convex function then $f(E(X)) < E(f(X))$.
- If f is a linear function then $f(E(X)) = E(f(X))$.

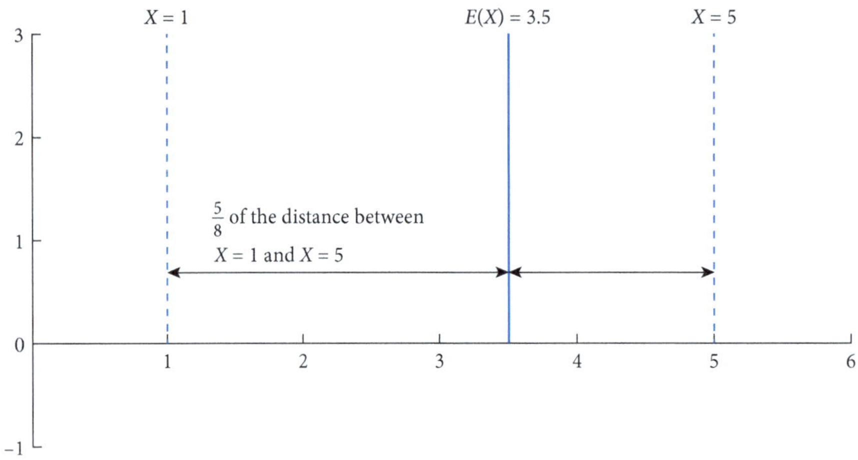

Figure 7.3 Plotting the points of X and the expectation.

To illustrate this, let's consider a simple random variable, X, which has two possible outcomes, $X = 5$ and $X = 10$:

$$X = \begin{cases} 1, & P(X = 1) = \dfrac{3}{8} \\ 5, & P(X = 5) = \dfrac{5}{8} \end{cases}$$

It is simple to calculate the expectation of X as $E(X) = 0.375 \times 1 + 0.625 \times 5 = 3.5$. Graphically, we can plot the points of X. As there are only two possible outcomes for X, we can think of the probabilities giving us the weight provided to each of the outcomes. As $P(X = 5) = \frac{5}{8}$, we are placing a weight of $\frac{5}{8}$ on the outcome 5, and $\frac{3}{8}$ on the outcome 1. Intuitively, this means that the expectation will be closer to 5 than to 1 (as we are placing more weight on 5), and more precisely, the expectation will be $\frac{5}{8}$ of the distance between $X = 1$ and $X = 5$ (see Figure 7.3).

Suppose that we apply a non-linear (and concave) transformation to X to create a new variable, Y, where:

$$Y = \ln X + 1$$

This is illustrated in Figure 7.4. The function $Y = \ln X + 1$ is plotted against the possible outcomes of X. There are only two possible outcomes of X, so equally, there will only be two possible outcomes of Y. If $X = 1$, then $Y = \ln 1 + 1 = 1$. Similarly, if $X = 5$, then $Y = \ln 5 + 1 = 2.609\,(3dp)$.

The expected value of Y will then lie along the solid line connecting these two points. In particular, just as the expected value of X lies $\frac{5}{8}$ of the way between 1 and 5, it will also be the case that the expected value of Y will lie $\frac{5}{8}$ of the way between these two points. This is because the expectation is simply finding a linear combination of the points at $Y = 1$ and

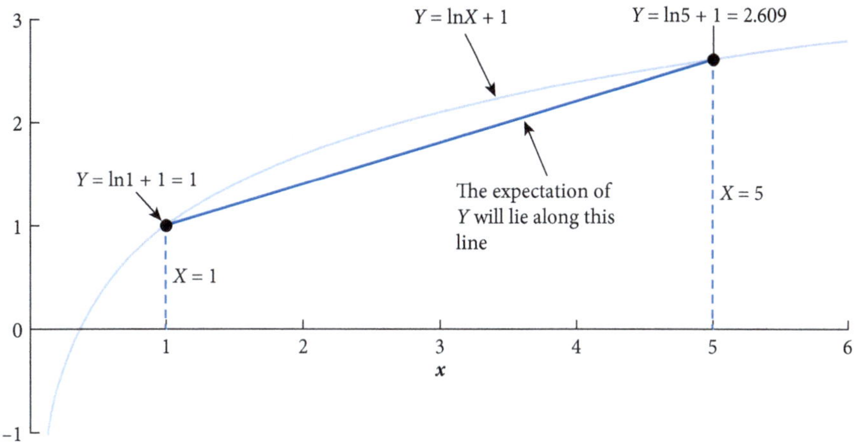

Figure 7.4 Plotting Y against X, with the possible outcomes identified.

$Y = 2.609$. The straight line represents this linear combination, and the distance along this straight line represents the weights placed upon each of the observations in the expectation.

This is illustrated in Figure 7.5 where the dashed horizontal line represents the expectation of Y, whilst the dotted horizontal line represents the non-linear function applied to the expected value of X.

Mathematically, we can calculate the expectation of Y, by first writing down the PMF of Y:

$$Y = \begin{cases} \ln 1 + 1 = 1, & P(Y = 1) = 0.375 \\ \ln 5 + 1 = 2.609, & P(Y = 2.609) = 0.675 \end{cases}$$

Then $E(Y) = 0.375 \times 1 + 0.675 \times (\ln 5 + 1) = 2.006$. Similarly, if we apply the concave function to $E(X)$, we would get $\ln E(X) + 1 = 2.253$. As you can see, both mathematically and

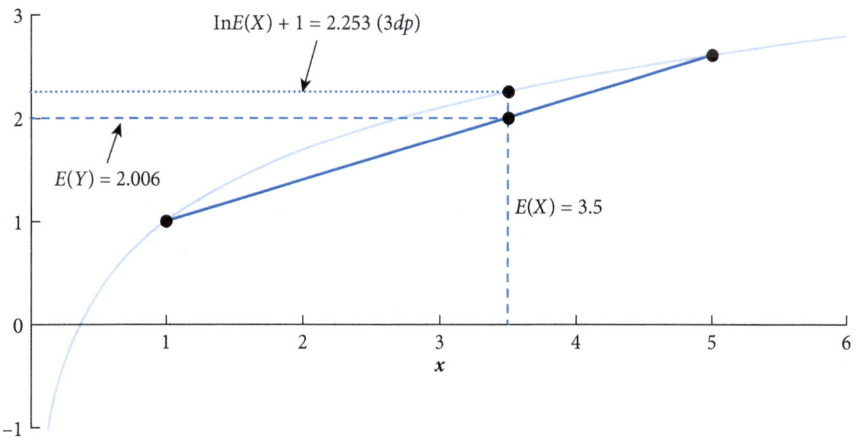

Figure 7.5 Expectation of Y, and the non-linear function applied to the expectation of X.

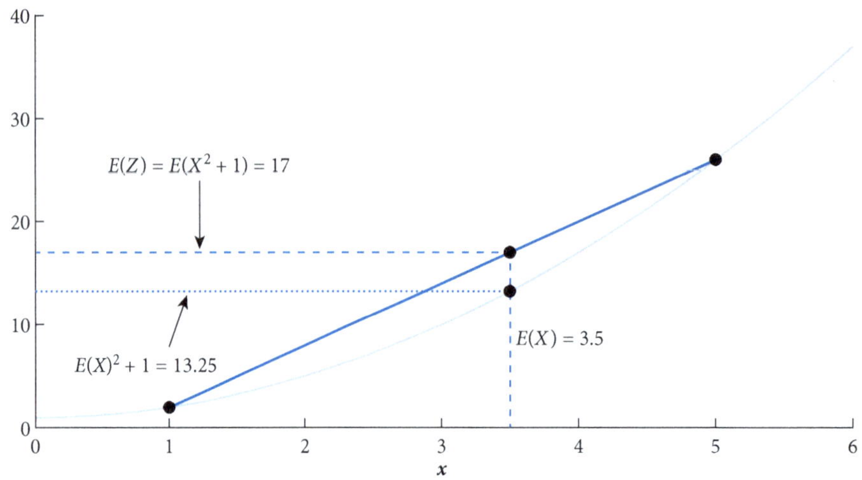

Figure 7.6 Applying a convex function to X.

diagrammatically, the expected value of Y is necessarily below the value we would get when we apply the non-linear function to the expectation of X.

This is because of the shape of the function; when we take expectations of Y, we are finding a linear combination of the outcomes of Y. In this simple example, that is equivalent to drawing a straight line between the points for $Y = 1$ and $Y = 2.609$. However, this line will take the average slope of the function between $X = 1$ and $X = 5$. Since the slope of Y is decreasing as X is increasing, this must mean that the average line of the average slope lies below the function.

Conversely, if we applied a convex function to X, such as $Z = X^2 + 1$, the reverse would be true; the expectation of Z would always be greater than the convex function applied to the expectation of X, as illustrated by Figure 7.6.

This concept will be very important as you study more microeconomics, but will also be important through this textbook, as later we will consider non-linear transformations of random variables, and will need to think about how we calculate the expectation.

KEY DEFINITION: JENSEN'S INEQUALITY

If we apply any function f to a random variable X, then:

- If f is a concave function then $f(E(X)) > E(f(X))$.
- If f is a convex function then $f(E(X)) < E(f(X))$.
- If f is a linear function then $f(E(X)) = E(f(X))$.

7.6 The law of large numbers

When introducing expectations in Section 7.2, we carried out a thought experiment of what would happen if we rolled a dice a very large number of times. Through our thought experiment, we expected that if we rolled the dice a very large number of times, eventually each outcome would occur with (approximately) its probability, and more importantly, the sample average we would construct would converge towards the population average (or the expectation).

More formally, we can write that:

$$\lim_{n\to\infty}\frac{1}{n}\sum_{i=1}^{n}X_i = E(X)$$

That is, the limit as the sample size n tends towards infinity of the sample mean ($\bar{X} = \frac{1}{n}\Sigma_{i=1}^{n}X_i$) is the population expectation.

7.6.1 Monte Carlo simulation to illustrate the law of large numbers

This may be easier to understand with an example. To illustrate this, I've carried out a Monte Carlo simulation. These are used by statisticians to explore the characteristics of measures and estimators, where they start with some assumed characteristics of the population, and they wish to explore the properties of that measure by repeatedly sampling from the population. In this case, we are going to explore the properties of the sample mean, as the sample size tends towards infinity.

To explore the properties of the sample mean, we will use a simple experiment. We have five dice—a red, orange, blue, purple, and black dice. Each of the dice is a fair six-sided dice, and we will roll each dice n times. After each roll, we calculate an updated sample mean for that dice.

So, for instance, for the red dice:

- The first roll was 2, so for $n = 1$, the sample mean is equal to 2.
- The second roll of the red dice is 5, giving a sample mean of $\frac{2+5}{2} = 3.5$ after two rolls.
- The third roll of the red dice is 6, giving a sample mean of $\frac{2+5+6}{3} = 4\frac{1}{3}$.

The results of the first five rolls, for each of the five dice, and the evolving sample mean are illustrated in Table 7.7.

Now, five rolls is not a very large sample, but we don't want to illustrate the evolution of our sample means by writing down the result of every single roll of the dice. To illustrate, let's consider the evolution of the sample means graphically. Figure 7.7 shows the evolution of the sample mean from $n = 1$ to $n = 10$ for each of the different coloured dice.

As you can see in Figure 7.7, the average of the rolls differs across the dice; this is not indicative that there's anything wrong with the dice—we should not be surprised that the rolls of the dice are different, and when n is small, this means that the average of the rolls will be different.

Table 7.7 Results and sample means from the first five rolls of the dice

	Red dice		Orange dice		Blue dice		Purple dice		Black dice	
n	Roll	Mean	Roll	Mean	Roll	Mean	Roll	Mean	Roll	Mean
1	2	2	3	3	1	1	5	5	2	2
2	5	3.5	2	2.5	3	2	2	3.5	6	4
3	6	4.333333	4	3	5	3	4	3.666667	2	3.333333
4	4	4.25	1	2.5	4	3.25	2	3.25	2	3
5	2	3.8	2	2.4	1	2.8	3	3.2	6	3.6

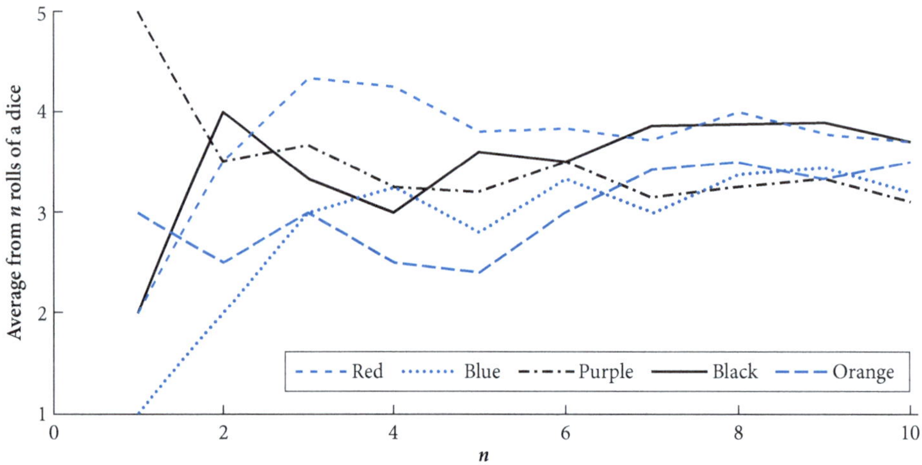

Figure 7.7 Evolution of mean average for $n = 1$ to $n = 5$.

However, as the sample size (n) gets larger, we would expect the outcomes for each dice roughly in the proportions equal to each of the probabilities. That is, in this example, when the sample gets very large, we'd expect each of the outcomes to occur in a proportion approximately equal to the probability. To illustrate this, let's consider how the proportion of each outcome evolves as the number of rolls increases. We will focus only on the red dice.

The first ten rolls that I observed when rolling the red dice are 2, 5, 6, 4, 2, 4, 3, 6, 2, 3. We can write down the frequency of each of the outcomes by counting up each of the outcomes, and then converting this into a proportion by dividing by the number of rolls. So, after ten rolls, we have observed zero 1s, three 2s, two 3s, two 4s, one 5, and two 6s. This gives the proportions shown in Table 7.8.

Initially, when n is small, the proportion of each outcome is a long way from the probability, but as n gets large, the proportion of each outcome gets closer and closer to $\frac{1}{6} = 0.16667$. The evolution of the proportions is easier to see graphically, as illustrated in Figure 7.8.

Table 7.8 Experimental distribution of outcomes from 10, 100, 1,000, 10,000, and 100,000 rolls of a fair dice

	Proportion of each outcome after *n* rolls					
n	1	2	3	4	5	6
10	0	0.3	0.2	0.2	0.1	0.2
100	0.12	0.18	0.21	0.14	0.15	0.2
1,000	0.173	0.168	0.164	0.163	0.173	0.159
10,000	0.167	0.1664	0.1718	0.1683	0.165	0.1615
100,000	0.16433	0.16778	0.1671	0.1663	0.1662	0.16829

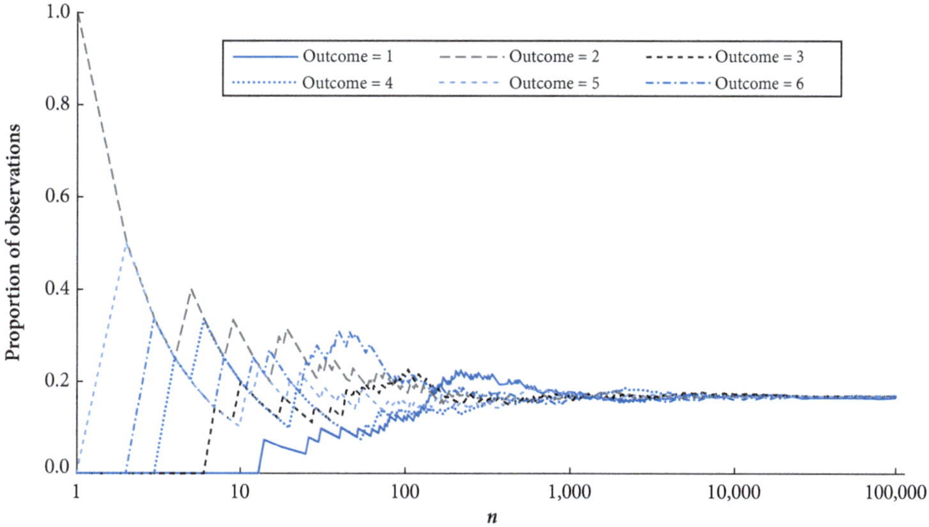

Figure 7.8 Experimental proportion of each outcome after *n* rolls for the red dice.

We can see that when the number of rolls is small, there is significant variation in the proportions across each of the outcomes.[7] However, as we move rightwards (i.e. increasing n), the proportion of each outcome tends towards the same value (and equal to approximately $\frac{1}{6}$).

This is just one experiment, where we have rolled the dice 100,000 times, and if we repeated it, when n is small, we would expect to see a different evolution of the probabilities, but as the number of rolls gets very large, we would expect the proportions to converge towards the probabilities of the respective outcomes.

This is illustrated in Figure 7.9. This figure shows the evolution of the sample mean of rolls for the red, blue, purple, black, and orange dice we saw earlier in this section. When n

[7] It should be noted that we have used a logarithmic scale on the horizontal axis, because most of the variation in the proportions occurs when n is small, but as n increases, the impact of an additional roll of the dice on the proportions decreases.

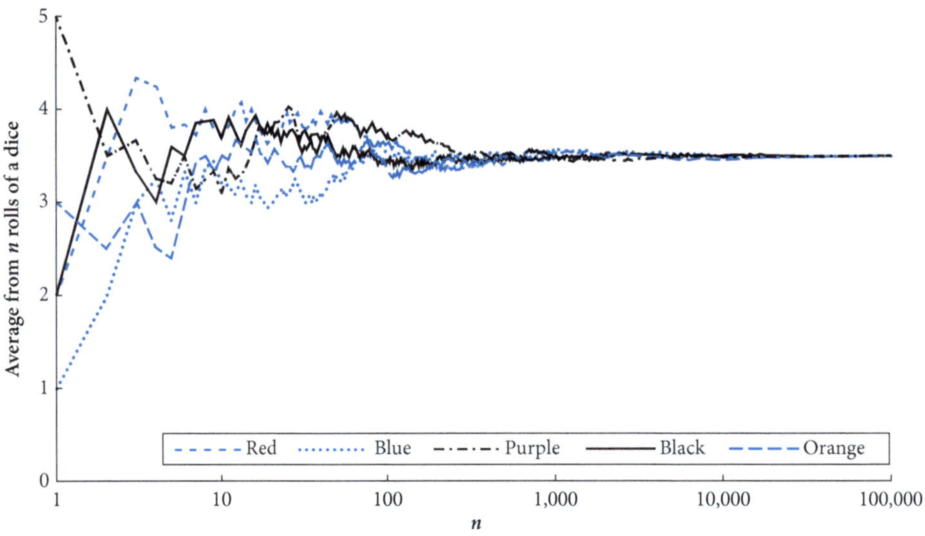

Figure 7.9 Evolution of average of rolls for five separate experiments.

is small, there is wide variation in the average of the n rolls across the five dice. However, as the number of rolls gets larger, the variation gets smaller, and for all five dice, by the time we have rolled them 100,000 times, the variation is close to zero, and in all five cases, the average of the n rolls is almost exactly equal to 3.5.

We saw earlier that if we define the roll of the dice as a random variable X, then $E(X) = 3.5$. As the sample size has become very large, we have seen that the sample mean has tended towards the expected value.

This is exactly what the **law of large numbers** predicts, as it states that as the sample size tends towards infinity, the sample mean will tend towards the expected value:

$$\lim_{n\to\infty}\frac{1}{n}\sum_{i=1}^{n}X_i = E(X)$$

We will use the law of large numbers in subsequent chapters, when analysing estimators of population parameters.

Summary

In this chapter, we have introduced the concept of population averages, or expectations. The expectation can be thought of as the measure of central tendency of the population as a whole. Expectations are important both as a concept in themselves, and as a tool that you will use, both within statistics, and in economics more generally.

When you start analysing the decisions that individuals make under uncertainty in economics, you will often need to consider the expected utility that they gain from their actions; rational agents will only choose an option if their expected utility from choosing that option outweighs their expected utility from any other option.

Similarly, we will need to consider expectations as we move further into statistics. Statisticians often use mathematical functions, known as estimators, applied to samples from a population to estimate properties of the larger population. However, the statisticians need to be able to calculate the properties of the estimators. One of the key properties that statisticians will need to construct is the expectation of the estimator.

This chapter has considered only the population expectation of discrete random variables. In the next chapter, we will introduce continuous random variables, and in Chapter 9, we will also consider calculating expectations conditional on observed characteristics of individuals.

Key formulae

The expectation of a discrete random variable, X is given by:

$$E(X) = \sum_x P(X = x) \times x$$

If we wish to find the expectation of a (non-linear) transformation of a random variable by applying a function $f(X)$, we can calculate this by finding the sum of products of the probabilities with the function applied to the outcomes:

$$E(f(X)) = \sum_x P(X = x) \times f(x)$$

For example, to find the expectation of X^2

$$E(X^2) = \sum_x P(X = x) \times x^2$$

Appendix

Proving the rules of expectations (Section 7.3.1)

Suppose that you have two random variables, X and Y, with expectations $E(X)$ and $E(Y)$. Variable X has n possible outcomes, $x_1, x_2, x_3, \ldots, x_n$ with probabilities $P(X = x_i)$ for $i = 1, \ldots, n$. Similarly, Y has m possible outcomes $y_1, y_2, y_3, \ldots, y_m$ with probabilities $P(Y = y_j)$ for $j = 1, \ldots, m$.

The joint PMF of X and Y is known, and the probabilities of each pair of outcomes can be denoted as $P(X = x_i \cap Y = y_j)$.

a and b are constants.

- The expectation of X can be calculated as $E(X) = \Sigma_{i=1}^{n} P(X = x_i) \times x_i$
- The expectation of Y can be calculated as $E(Y) = \Sigma_{j=1}^{m} P(Y = y_j) \times y_j$

1. The expectation of a constant is always equal to that constant.

$$E(a) = a$$

Proof 1

This proof is trivial, as by definition, $P(a = a) = 1$. Calculating the expectation:

$$E(a) = P(a = a) \times a = 1 \times a = a$$

2. The expectation of a constant multiplied by a random variable is equal to that constant multiplied by the expectation of the original random variable:

$$E(aX) = aE(X)$$

Proof 2

When we multiply X by a constant, a, the resulting random variable will have outcomes equal to $ax_1, ax_2, ax_3, \ldots, ax_n$. Because we are simply multiplying the outcomes by a constant, the probabilities are unchanged. That is:

$$P(aX = ax_i) = P(X = x_i)$$

So, calculating the expectation of aX:

$$E(aX) = \sum_{i=1}^{n} P(aX = ax_i) \times ax_i$$

Since $P(aX = ax_i) = P(X = x_i)$, we can rewrite this as:

$$\Rightarrow E(aX) = \sum_{i=1}^{n} P(X = x_i) \times ax_i$$

However, a is now a common multiplier in every single term, so we can take it outside of the summation:

$$\Rightarrow E(aX) = a \times \sum_{i=1}^{n} P(X = x_i) \times x_i$$

However, $\Sigma_{i=1}^{n} P(X = x_i) \times x_i = E(X)$, so we can substitute this back in to give us:

$$\Rightarrow E(aX) = aE(X)$$

Note: If you are a little confused as to why we can take the a outside of the summation, it may be useful to write out the summation, term by term:

$$\sum_{i=1}^{n} P(X = x_i) \times ax_i = P(X = x_1) \times ax_1 + P(X = x_2) \times ax_2 + \ldots + P(X = x_n) \times ax_n$$

a is a common multiplier in each of the terms, so we can factorize it out, giving us:

$$= a \times [P(X = x_1) \times x_1 + P(X = x_2) \times x_2 + \ldots + P(X = x_n) \times x_n]$$

However, we can rewrite all of the terms in the brackets using summation notation, giving us:

$$= a \times \sum_{i=1}^{n} P(X = x_i) \times x_i$$

3. The expectation of a sum of random variables is equal to the sum of the expectations:

$$E(X + Y) = E(X) + E(Y)$$

Proof 3

To calculate the expectation of $X + Y$, it is useful to think of creating a new variable Z. The variable Z will take the value $x_i + y_j$ when $X = x_i$ and $Y = y_j$, and so $P(Z = x_i + y_j) = P(X = x_i \cap Y = y_j)$. So, to find the expectation of Z, we will need to sum over all possible values of X and over all possible values of Y, giving us:

$$E(Z) = \sum_{j=1}^{m}\sum_{i=1}^{n} P(X = x_i \cap Y = y_j) \times (x_i + y_j)$$

Note: In a double summation as we have here, effectively, the order of the summation signs tells you the order to add up. The double summation here indicates that, for each of the possible values of j, we will first add up the expression over all possible values of i, and then add up the resulting sum across all of the values of j.
So, for example:

$$\sum_{j=1}^{2}\sum_{i=1}^{3} X_iY_j = (X_1Y_1 + X_2Y_1 + X_3Y_1) + (X_1Y_2 + X_2Y_2 + X_3Y_3).$$

The first bracket holds $j = 1$ constant, and adds up over the values of $i = 1,2,3$, and the second bracket does the same, but holding $j = 2$ constant.

We can multiple out the brackets, giving us:

$$\Rightarrow E(Z) = \sum_{j=1}^{m}\sum_{i=1}^{n} [P(X = x_i \cap Y = y_j)x_i + P(X = x_i \cap Y = y_j)y_j]$$

Because we have $[P(X = x_i \cap Y = y_j)x_i + P(X = x_i \cap Y = y_j)y_j]$ included in the summation, we can break this up into two separate summations. The order of the summation signs does not matter, as whatever order you add together values, you will always get the same answer. So, we can write this as:

$$= \sum_{i=1}^{n}\sum_{j=1}^{m} P(X = x_i \cap Y = y_j) \times x_i + \sum_{j=1}^{m}\sum_{i=1}^{n} P(X = x_i \cap Y = y_j) \times y_j$$

Since x_i remains constant as you change the value of j, and similarly, y_j remains constant as i varies, we can treat them as constant multipliers such that:

$$\sum_{j=1}^{m} P(X = x_i \cap Y = y_j) \times x_i = x_i \sum_{j=1}^{m} P(X = x_i \cap Y = y_j)$$

$$\sum_{i=1}^{n} P(X = x_i \cap Y = y_j) \times y_j = y_j \sum_{i=1}^{n} P(X = x_i \cap Y = y_j)$$

So, we can rewrite our expectation as:

$$E(Z) = \sum_{i=1}^{n} x_i \sum_{j=1}^{m} P(X = x_i \cap Y = y_j) + \sum_{j=1}^{m} y_j \sum_{i=1}^{n} P(X = x_i \cap Y = y_j)$$

We know, by the law of total probability, that since, for each value of x_i, we are adding up the joint probabilities across all of the possible values of Y_j, then:

$$\sum_{j=1}^{n} P(X = x_i \cap Y = y_j) = P(X = x_i)$$

Similarly,

$$\sum_{i=1}^{n} P(X = x_i \cap Y = y_j) = P(Y = y_j)$$

So, we can rewrite our expectation as:

$$\Rightarrow E(Z) = \sum_{i=1}^{n} x_i P(X = x_i) + \sum_{j=1}^{m} y_j P(Y = y_j)$$

But, by definition, these are just $E(X)$ and $E(Y)$:

$$\Rightarrow E(Z) = E(X) + E(Y)$$

4. By combining rule 1 and rule 2, we can see that, if we add a constant to a random variable, the resulting expectation is equal to the constant plus the expectation of the original random variable:

$$E(a + X) = a + E(X)$$

Intuitively, what is happening here is that every outcome of X is just being shifted by an amount a, so we would expect that since every outcome is shifted by a distance a, it must also follow that the (population) average also shifts by that same amount.

Proof 4

We have shown in proof 3 that $E(X + Y) = E(X) + E(Y)$. As such, if we are to find the expectation of $W = a + X$, then:

$$E(W) = E(a + X) = E(a) + E(X)$$

By proof 1, we know that $E(a) = a$ as a is a constant:

$$\Rightarrow E(W) = E(a + X) = a + E(X)$$

5. By combining rule 2 and rule 4, we can see that, if we have a linear combination of random variables, such as $Z = aX + bY$, then the expectation of Z will be equal to the same linear combination of the expectations:

$$E(aX + bY) = aE(X) + bE(Y)$$

Proof 5

We have shown that $E(aX) = aE(X)$, and that $E(X + Y) = E(X) + E(Y)$. We can combine these relationships to prove this relationship.

Suppose that $Z = aX + bY$. Then the expectation of Z can be expressed as:

$$E(Z) = E(aX + bY)$$

By rule 3, the expectation of a sum is equal to the sum of the expectations:

$$\Rightarrow E(Z) = E(aX + bY) = E(aX) + E(bY)$$

By rule 2, $E(aX) = aE(X)$ and $E(bY) = bE(Y)$ and so:

$$E(Z) = E(aX) + E(bY) = aE(X) + bE(Y)$$

Proving that the expectation of a product of independent random variables is equal to the product of the expectations of the random variables

Suppose that you have two independent random variables, X and Y. Since the random variables are independent, $P(Y = y|X = x) = P(Y = y)$ for all possible values of y and x, and similarly $P(X = x|Y = y) = P(X = x)$ for all possible values of x and y.

If we construct a new variable, $Z = XY$, by multiplying together the random variables X and Y, we can calculate the expectation of Z by finding:

$$E(Z) = E(XY) = \sum_x \sum_y P(X = x \cap Y = y) \times x \times y$$

Now, by the **chain rule of probability**, $P(X = x \cap Y = y) = P(X = x) \times P(Y = y|X = x)$. However, since X and Y are independent, it follows that $P(Y = y|X = x) = P(Y = y)$. So the expectation can be rewritten as:

$$E(XY) = \sum_x \sum_y P(X = x) \times P(Y = y) \times x \times y$$

Now, within the second summation ($\Sigma_y P(X = x) \times P(Y = y) \times x \times y$), we are essentially holding X constant, and allowing Y to vary. As such, $P(X = x)$ and x are fixed and can be taken outside of the summation. So we can rewrite the expectation as:

$$E(XY) = \sum_x P(X = x) \times x \times \sum_y P(Y = y) \times y$$

Now, we should recognize these two terms as $\sum_x P(X = x) \times x = E(X)$ and $\Sigma_y P(Y = y) \times y = E(Y)$, and so:

$$E(XY) = E(X)E(Y)$$

Important note

If X and Y are not independent, then it is almost certain that $E(XY) \neq E(X)E(Y)$.

Continuous Random Variables

8

Learning outcomes for this chapter

By the end of this chapter you will be able to:

- Recognize the difference between discrete and continuous random variables
- Evaluate whether a probability density function of a continuous random variable is well defined
- Calculate cumulative distribution functions (CDFs)
- Calculate the expectation of a continuous random variable
- Calculate percentiles of a distribution, based upon both a theoretical and a data-based distribution
- Manipulate joint distributions where the underlying variables are continuous

Mathematical tools

- Summations
- Integration
- Finding the area under a curve using integration between limits
- Double integrals

Introduction

In previous chapters, we have introduced random variables as a way of representing populations. We have discussed what it means for a random variable to be well defined, and how to use random variables to construct averages (or expected values) for a population as a whole. However, all of the variables we have analysed have had a finite number of possible outcomes, and all of the outcomes have been distinct. For example, when rolling a standard six-sided dice, there are only six possible outcomes (1,2,3,4,5,6), there are only a finite number of possible eye colours, and so on.

However, many variables have outcomes which are not finite and distinct. For example, suppose you are looking at heights of individuals; whilst we might measure an individual as 174cm to the nearest centimetre, we can infinitely subdivide the distance between 174cm and 175cm into smaller and smaller divisions. Where a random variable has these sort of infinite subdivisions, we describe them as continuous random variables.

However, where there are an infinite number of possible outcomes, the probability of any possible outcome is going to be equal to zero. As such, we will need a different way of describing and analysing these sorts of variables. In this chapter, we introduce continuous variables, and discuss how we can apply the same methods to continuous variables that we have used in previous chapters with discrete variables. The mathematics we will use is slightly different (we will use integration rather than summations), but the intuition behind it will be exactly the same as with discrete random variables.

8.1 Moving from discrete random variables to continuous random variables

In this chapter, we will introduce continuous random variables. However, to motivate this, let's begin with a quick revision of discrete random variables. All of the random variables we have seen so far have been discrete random variables; for discrete random variables, there are a finite set of distinct outcomes, each of which has a distinct probability. For instance, if we have a random variable, X, representing the roll of a fair six-sided dice, then the probability mass function (PMF) is given by:

$$X = \begin{cases} 1, & P(X = 1) = \frac{1}{6} \\ 2, & P(X = 2) = \frac{1}{6} \\ 3, & P(X = 3) = \frac{1}{6} \\ 4, & P(X = 4) = \frac{1}{6} \\ 5, & P(X = 5) = \frac{1}{6} \\ 6, & P(X = 6) = \frac{1}{6} \end{cases}$$

Rules relating to discrete random variables

In this chapter, we will discover a set of rules relating to continuous random variables that are all analogous to the rules you have already seen for discrete random variables. Let's begin by reminding you of the rules we have seen:

For a PMF to be well defined, two conditions need to be met:

1. All of the probabilities need to be between 0 and 1: $0 \leq P(X = x) \leq 1$ for all possible values of x.
2. If the outcomes are mutually exclusive, then the sum of the probabilities needs to be equal to 1: $\Sigma_x P(X = x) = 1$.

The **expectation** of a discrete random variable, X, can be calculated as the sum of the products of each outcome, multiplied by the corresponding probability:

$$E(X) = \sum_x P(X = x) \times x$$

If we apply a non-linear function to a discrete random variable, such as $f(X)$, then the expectation is equal to the sum of the products of the outcomes (having applied the function), multiplied by the probabilities:

$$E(f(X)) = \sum_x P(X = x) \times f(x)$$

Whilst these rules are for discrete random variables, an analogous set of rules exist for continuous random variables.

For example, we can calculate the expected score from a single roll of the dice as:

$$E(X) = \frac{1}{6} \times 1 + \frac{1}{6} \times 2 + \frac{1}{6} \times 3 + \frac{1}{6} \times 4 + \frac{1}{6} \times 5 + \frac{1}{6} \times 6 = 3.5$$

Similarly, if we wanted to find the expectation of the square of Y, then we would simply square each of the possible outcomes, and find the sum of the products of these squared outcomes of Y^2 with the probabilities of Y:

$$E(X^2) = \frac{1}{6} \times 1^2 + \frac{1}{6} \times 2^2 + \frac{1}{6} \times 3^2 + \frac{1}{6} \times 4^2 + \frac{1}{6} \times 5^2 + \frac{1}{6} \times 6^2 = 12.5$$

In statistics, many of the variables we observe are not discrete variables, but instead are continuous variables. Continuous variables are different from discrete variables, as instead of having a series of distinct outcomes, continuous variables can take any value within a given range, and so there are an infinite number of possible outcomes. As we saw earlier in the chapter, any sort of measurement (such as height, weight, distance, speed) could be a continuous random variable.

Time could be an example of a continuous random variable; we often measure time in discrete chunks, but between every measure, there will be an infinite number of possible outcomes. Let's consider the lap-times achieved by racing drivers. The lap-times in motor racing are often measured only to the thousandth of a second, so Max Verstappen might achieve a lap time of 1:46.168 (i.e. 1 minute, 46.168 seconds). It is perfectly possible for Lando Norris to gain the same lap time when measured to the same thousandth of a second (i.e. also 1:46.168). However, in reality, because each thousandth of a second could be split down into a further 1,000 microseconds (i.e. one millionth of a second), it is highly unlikely that both drivers would have exactly the same time.

In fact, we can go further and say that it is impossible for both drivers to gain exactly the same time, as even if the drivers gained the same time to the nearest microsecond, each microsecond can be infinitely divided down into smaller and smaller units of time. Eventually, you would find some way of distinguishing the two. Time is an example of a continuous variable, and we often only record to a certain level of accuracy because of the accuracy of the timing equipment available.

Statisticians also model variables where there are a very large number of possible outcomes across a large range, where the probability of any particular outcome is close to zero, as a continuous random variable, as the mathematics is often easier to analyse. For example, an economic statistician might treat the annual wages that individuals within the UK population earn as a continuous random variable, even though the wages can only be subdivided down to the nearest penny. However, there are a very large number of possible outcomes in the population, such that the probability of an individual having any particular annual wage will be close or equal to zero.

We need to find a way of formally representing continuous random variables. To illustrate this, let's begin with the discrete random variable of the roll of a six-sided dice that we saw earlier in the chapter. The PMF tells us that the probability of any of the six outcomes is equal to $\frac{1}{6}$. The probability of gaining an outcome equal to anything other than the integer values between 1 and 6 is equal to zero; for example, the probability of rolling a value of 1.5 is equal to zero. Similarly, the probability of rolling a seven is also equal to zero. We can represent the PMF mathematically, and graphically, as in Figure 8.1. The height of the bars represents the probability of any given outcome, and so we can see, at $Y = 1,2,3,4,5,6$, the height of the bars is equal to $\frac{1}{6}$, whilst for all other values of Y, the height of the distribution is 0.

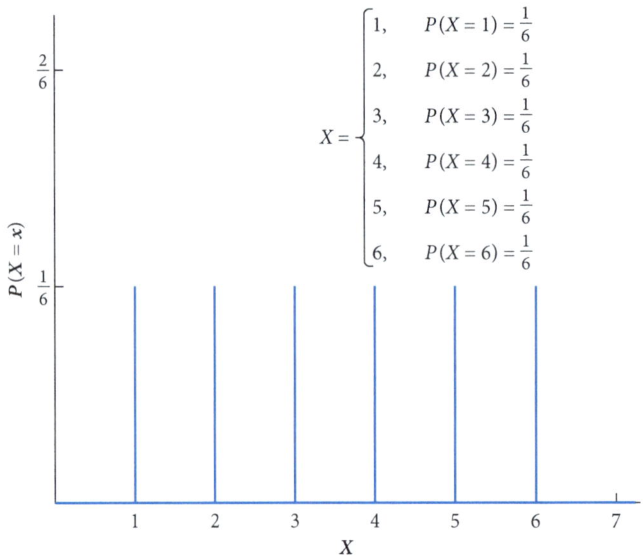

Figure 8.1 The probability mass function of a roll of a six-sided dice.

To generalize towards more continuous variables, let's consider that instead of a six-sided dice we now have an n-sided dice. If the dice is a fair dice, then the probability of any given outcome is $1/n$. So, for example, if $n = 12$, then the probability of any outcome is equal to $\frac{1}{12}$, and similarly if $n = 24$, then the probability of any outcome would be equal to $\frac{1}{24}$.

As n gets larger, intuitively, we can see that the probability of any given outcome occurring gets smaller and smaller. That is, as the number of sides on the dice increases, the probability of any given outcome gets smaller. In fact, as the number of sides on the dice tends towards infinity, the probability of any given outcome tends towards 0:

$$\lim_{n\to\infty}\frac{1}{n} = 0$$

With continuous variables, there is an infinite number of possible outcomes; for example, if we are measuring individuals' heights, for any possible pair of (different) heights, no matter how close the pair are, we can always write a possible height in between; for example, in between 1.82m and 1.83m, we could write 1.825m. In fact, in this example, there are an infinite number of possible heights in between 1.82m and 1.83m. Using the same logic as with the dice with an infinite number of sides, the probability of randomly sampling an individual with any particular height is going to be equal to zero. In fact, for any value, for a continuous random variable, the probability of any particular value is equal to zero! This raises a question: how do we represent continuous random variables?
However, the probability of randomly sampling an individual from the population who has a height between 1.82m and 1.83m will not be zero—you see people in this height range walking down the street every day. As such, we will need a new notation that takes account of the fact that the probability of any given outcome is zero, but that the probability of outcomes within a **range** will be non-zero. The solution that we will have is known as the probability density function (PDF).

8.2 Probability density functions

In continuous random variables, since there are an infinite number of possible outcomes, the probability of any given outcome is necessarily equal to zero. As such, we can't take the same approach to representing the variables as we did for discrete random variables by simply writing down the probabilities of each outcome. For example, if you have a continuous random variable, Y, where every outcome between 0 and 6 is equally likely, then $P(Y = 1) = P(Y = 2) = P(Y = 3) = 0$. The individual probabilities become meaningless.

Let's begin with a thought experiment. In the previous section, we discussed the PMF relating to a standard six-sided dice. We also saw that, as the number of sides of the dice tended towards infinity, the probability of any given outcome would be equal to zero.

Let's consider an infinite-sided dice, and each side of the dice corresponds to an outcome between 0 and 6. Each of the outcomes is equally likely, but we have already said that the probability of any given outcome is equal to 0. For example, if we represent this infinite-sided dice with a random variable $Y, P(Y = 2) = 0$.

However, what we can think about is the probability of observing an outcome within a particular range. If the random variable is equally likely to produce any outcome in the range between 0 and 6, we could calculate the probability that the outcome observed is (say) between 1 and 2:

- We know that the outcome is equally likely to occur anywhere between 0 and 6. This is equivalent to thinking of a width of possible outcomes as the distance between 0 and 6 (i.e. width = 6).

- If we wish to calculate the probability of observing an outcome between, say, 1 and 2, this would be equivalent of taking a width 1 out of the total width of 6 (or a probability of $\frac{1}{6}$).
- Similarly, the probability of observing an outcome between 3 and 5 (width = 2) would just be $\frac{2}{6}$.

With continuous random variables, what matters is not the probability of individual outcomes, but instead the probability density. The probability density is defined, such that the area under the probability density function represents the probability of ranges of outcomes occurring. The probability density represents the relative likelihood of outcomes occurring, such that a higher value of the probability density indicates that those outcomes are more likely to occur.[1]

So, for example, we could use a random variable, Y, to represent the infinite-sided dice. Since all outcomes between 0 and 6 are equally likely, the PDF will just be constant. The same rules of probability exist for continuous random variables, in that the total of all probability needs to be equal to 1. That means that the total area under the PDF must be equal to 1.

For our infinite-sided dice, the PDF is given by:

$$f_Y(y) = \begin{cases} 0, & y < 0 \\ \frac{1}{6}, & 0 \le y \le 6 \\ 0, & y \ge 6 \end{cases}$$

The PDF for our infinite-sided dice is illustrated in Figure 8.2. Since the PDF is equal to zero below the value of $Y = 0$ and above the value $Y = 6$, this tells us that we will never see

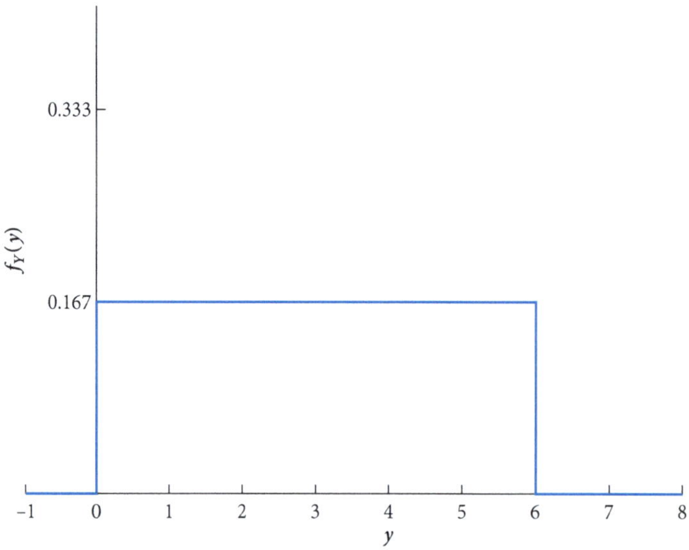

Figure 8.2 Probability density function for a uniform distribution.

[1] This may seem contradictory, because in a continuous random variable, the probability of any outcome is equal to zero. However, what really matters is the area under the curve. The reason that the probability of any given outcome is equal to zero is because, say, for $P(Y = 2)$, we are looking at an area with width equal to zero. Just as the area of a rectangle with zero width would be equal to zero, the probability of any particular outcome will be equal to zero as well.

an observation of the random variable below zero, or above 6. Similarly, we can say that, since the height of the PDF is the same for all values between 0 and 6, the likelihood of observing any particular outcome is equal.

Furthermore, as the area under the PDF represents the probability, the shaded area in Figure 8.3 represents the probability of observing a (randomly chosen) observation of Y that lies between 2.5 and 3.5. Intuitively, since the shape of the shaded area is a rectangle, we can calculate this probability geometrically, as equal to the width multiplied by the height. Here, the width is 1 and the height $\frac{1}{6}$, and so the area is $1 \times \frac{1}{6} = \frac{1}{6}$.

KEY DEFINITION: PROBABILITY DENSITY FUNCTIONS

We represent PDFs with the notation $f_Y(y)$. The (lower-case) f_Y indicates that we are looking at a PDF relating to the random variable Y.

The (y) indicates that we are evaluating this at the point $Y = y$. For example, $f_Y(2) = \frac{1}{6}$, whilst $f_Y(7) = 0$.

It should be noted that the distribution we see here is a special distribution, known as the **uniform distribution** (and is sometimes referred to as the 'rectangular distribution'). The uniform distribution is a distribution where the PDF is constant across a range of values, and zero elsewhere. Because of this, the PDF looks like a rectangle.

In this case, the PDF is constant at $f_Y(y) = \frac{1}{6}$ between 0 and 6, and $f_Y(y) = 0$ for all other values of x, and so we can say that the random variable is uniformly distributed between 0 and 6. We will revisit uniform distributions in more detail in later chapters.

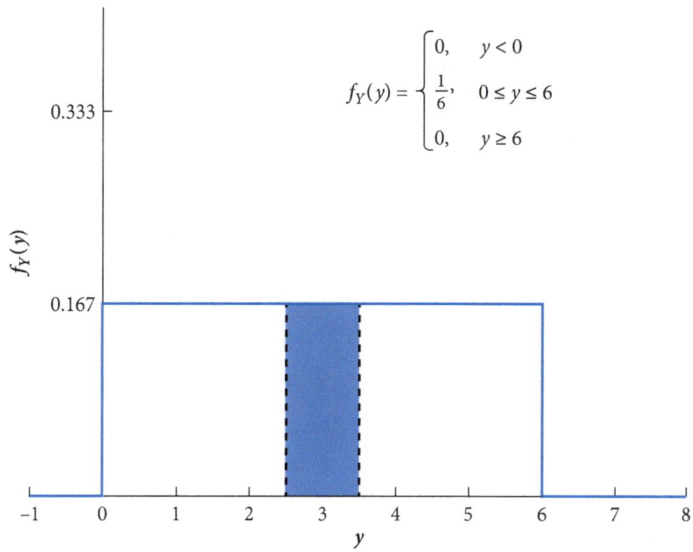

Figure 8.3 Probability density function for uniform distribution, with probability shaded.

8.2.1 Requirements for a continuous probability density function to be well defined

Just as with discrete random variables, it's important that the PDF of a continuous random variable is well defined. There are three key conditions for the PDF of the random variable to be well defined:

1. All of the outcomes must be mutually exclusive (i.e. it's impossible for two outcomes of the random variable to occur simultaneously).
2. The PDF must always be greater than or equal to zero. As we will see later in this chapter, it is possible for a PDF to be greater than 1. The key requirement is that $f_Y(y) \geq 0$ for all possible values of y.
3. The area under the PDF represents the probability of all possible outcomes. Therefore, the area under the probability density function must be equal to 1. More formally:

$$\int_{-\infty}^{\infty} f_Y(y)dy = 1$$

Worked example 8.1: Evaluating whether the PDF of our infinite-sided dice is well defined

Let's return to the example of the infinite-sided dice we introduced earlier in this section. Remember, this is an example where every possible value between 0 and 6 has equal likelihood of occurring, and the PDF was given by:

$$f_Y(y) = \begin{cases} 0, & y < 0 \\ \frac{1}{6}, & 0 \leq y \leq 6 \\ 0, & y \geq 6 \end{cases}$$

We want to check that this is a well-defined PDF. The PDF is represented diagrammatically in Figure 8.4.

Taking each requirement in turn:

1. **Mutually exclusive outcomes**

   In this example, by design, the random variable cannot deliver two separate outcomes simultaneously; we will not be able to observe both $Y = 2.34$ and $Y = 3.67$ (say) as a single observation. As such, by design, the outcomes of the random variable are mutually exclusive.

2. **The PDF must always be non-negative, $f_Y(y) \geq 0$, for all possible values of y**

   Similarly, it is trivial to see that the PDF is always greater than (or equal to) zero. For $Y < 0$ and $Y > 6$, $f_Y(y) = 0$, and for $0 \leq Y \leq 6$, $f_Y(y) = \frac{1}{6}$. So, the PDF is always non-negative.

3. **The area under the PDF needs to be equal to 1**

   Finally, it needs to be the case that the area under the PDF is equal to 1. We can see that for the points where the PDF is non-zero, the PDF is a rectangle, and the area of a

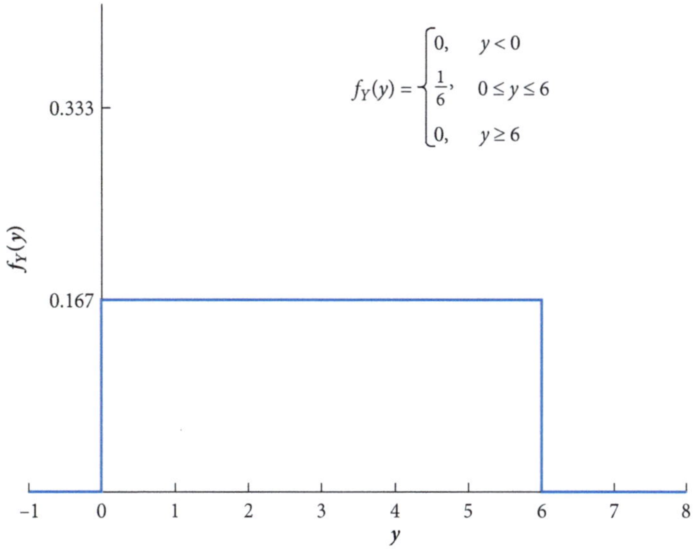

Figure 8.4 Probability density function for the infinite-sided dice.

rectangle is just equal to the width of the base times the height. Here the width is equal to 6, and the height $\frac{1}{6}$, and so the area is just equal to $6 \times \frac{1}{6} = 1$.

More formally, the total area under the PDF is equal to the integral over the full possible range of outcomes of Y:

$$= \int_{-\infty}^{\infty} f_Y(y)dy$$

To calculate this, we will need to split the PDF into three parts:

- For $Y < 0$, the PDF is equal to zero, $f_Y(y) = 0$
- For $0 \le Y \le 6$, the PDF is equal to $\frac{1}{6}$, $f_Y(y) = \frac{1}{6}$
- For $Y > 6$, the PDF is equal to 0, $f_Y(y) = 0$

To calculate the overall integral, we just need to add together the integrals for these three sections:[2]

$$\Rightarrow \int_{-\infty}^{\infty} f_Y(y)\,dy = \int_{-\infty}^{0} 0\,dy + \int_{0}^{6} \frac{1}{6}dy + \int_{6}^{\infty} 0\,dy = 0 + \left[\frac{y}{6}\right]_0^6 + 0$$

$$= 0 + \left[\frac{6}{6} - \frac{0}{6}\right] + 0 = 1$$

So, the area under the PDF is equal to 1, and so the PDF is well defined, as shown in Figure 8.5.

[2] The first and last elements are fairly trivial, since $\int_a^b 0\,dy = 0$. We have included these for completeness, but they make no difference to the overall area under the curve. You would gain exactly the same answer if you omitted $\int_{-\infty}^{0} 0\,dy$ and $\int_{6}^{\infty} 0\,dy$.

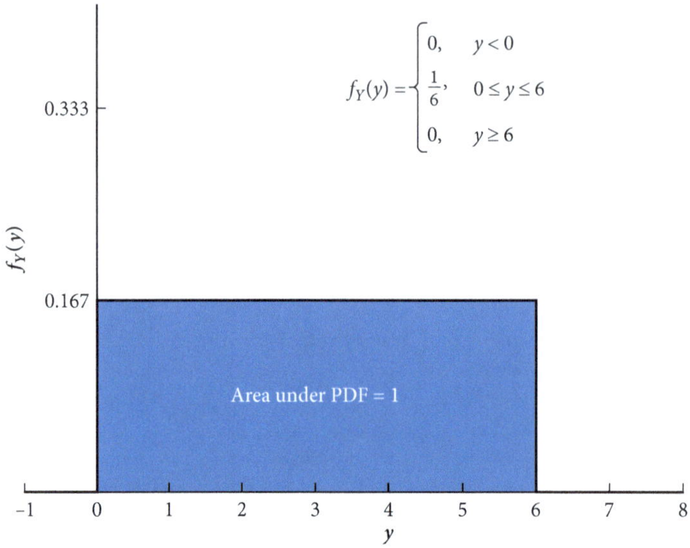

Figure 8.5 The area under the PDF must be equal to 1.

Of course, there is an easier way of checking that the area under the PDF is equal to 1 in this case. You know that the shape of the PDF is a rectangle, and you should remember that the area enclosed by a rectangle is just equal to the width times the height. In this case, the width is equal to 6, whilst the height is equal to $\frac{1}{6}$. As such, we can check our calculation as:

$$\text{Area} = 6 \times \frac{1}{6} = 1$$

This second method only works for relatively simple PDFs, but provides a much more intuitive way of checking the area under the PDF.

8.2.2 Comparison of discrete and continuous random variables

In the previous section, we introduced continuous random variables, and from these probability density functions. However, it's useful to compare both discrete and continuous random variables. Let's suppose that we have a discrete random variable, X, representing the roll of a fair, six-sided dice, and a continuous random variable, Y, with equal likelihood of outcomes *anywhere* between 0 and 6.

Figure 8.6 provides a comparison between discrete and continuous random variables, which have very similar properties.

For a discrete random variable, if we add up all of the probabilities, then (provided the distribution is well defined), the sum of all of the probabilities will be equal to 1:

$$\sum_x P(X = x) = 1$$

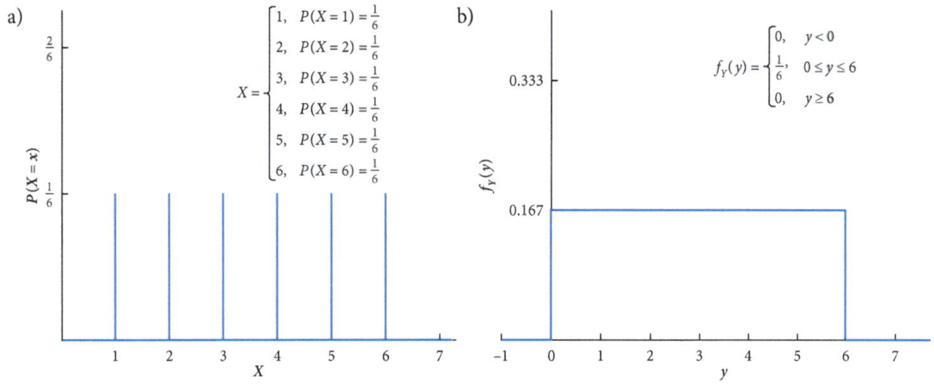

Figure 8.6 Comparing PDFs of discrete and continuous random variables.

Similarly, for a continuous random variable, integration is the equivalent to adding up all of the probabilities. If we integrate the PDF over the entire domain of Y, then (provided the distribution is well defined), the integral will be equal to 1:

$$\int_{-\infty}^{\infty} f_Y(y)dy = 1$$

Similarly, for both continuous and discrete random variables, we can calculate the probability of observing outcomes within a range. Suppose we wanted to know the probability that we randomly observed an outcome between 1.5 and 3.2. In the discrete case, we would just add together all of the probabilities relating to outcomes, where the range was met. So, in this example, this would be $X = 2$ and $X = 3$:

$$P(1.5 \le X \le 3.2) = P(X = 2) + P(X = 3) = \frac{1}{6} + \frac{1}{6} = \frac{1}{3}$$

For the continuous case, we would need to use an integration to find the area under the curve between $Y = 1.5$ and $Y = 3.2$:

$$P(1.5 \le Y \le 3.2) = \int_{1.5}^{3.2} f_Y(y)dy = \int_{1.5}^{3.2} \frac{1}{6}dy = \left[\frac{y}{6}\right]_{1.5}^{3.2} = \frac{17}{60}$$

By definition, this will just be equal to the area under the probability density function, bounded by 1.5 and 3.2, as illustrated in Figure 8.7.

Summations and integrals

Hopefully, you have noticed that whenever we are carrying out a calculation using a sum with a discrete random variable, the equivalent for a continuous random variable is to carry out an equivalent integral. In fact, whenever we have used a summation for a discrete random variable, we would use an integral to calculate the equivalent characteristics of a continuous random variable.

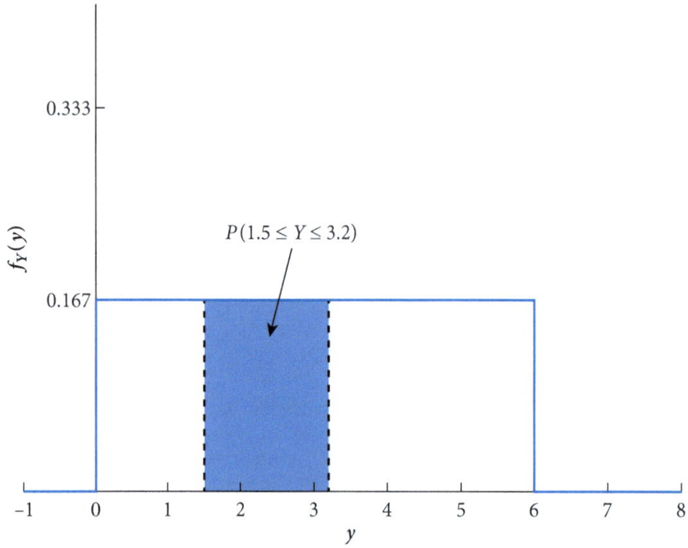

Figure 8.7 The probability of observing an outcome between 1.5 and 3.2.

8.2.3 Probabilities including less than, or less than or equal to

In many of the examples you have seen in previous chapters, it matters whether you consider whether a random variable is less than, or less than or equal to, a particular value. For instance, if you are rolling a standard six-sided dice, the probability that the outcome is less than or equal to 3 is equal to:

$$P(X \le 3) = \frac{1}{2}$$

whilst the probability that the outcome is strictly less than 3 is equal to:

$$P(X < 3) = \frac{1}{3}$$

The difference between these two cases is that in the first case, the outcome 3 is included in the range, whilst in the second case, the outcome 3 is excluded. So, for a discrete random variable, we calculate $P(X \le 3)$ by adding up all of the probabilities where the condition is met. This would mean that:

$$P(X \le 3) = P(X = 1) + P(X = 2) + P(X = 3) = \frac{1}{2}$$

Similarly, to calculate $P(X < 3)$, we would add up all of the probabilities where this condition is met, so:

$$P(X < 3) = P(X = 1) + P(X = 2) = \frac{1}{3}$$

The difference between these probabilities is simply that in the first case, where $X \leq 3$, we include $P(X = 3)$ in the calculation, whilst in the second case, because $X = 3$ is not within the range we are looking at, $P(X = 3)$ is excluded.

In general, we can write:

$$P(X \leq x) = P(X < x) + P(X = x)$$

This relationship also holds for continuous random variables. So, for our continuous variable Y, it will also follow that $P(Y \leq y) = P(Y < y) + P(Y = y)$. However, as we've already seen, the probability of any particular outcome for a continuous random variable is just equal to zero, so if we wanted to compare $P(Y \leq 3)$ and $P(Y < 3)$, since $P(Y = 3) = 0$, it must follow that $P(Y \leq 3) = P(Y < 3)$.

As such:

$$P(Y \leq y) = P(Y < y) + P(Y = y) \Rightarrow P(Y \leq y) = P(Y < y) + 0 \Rightarrow P(Y \leq y) = P(Y < y)$$

Since the probabilities are equal, we will always use the same method to calculate the probability of a range for a continuous random variable. So, for example:

$$P(Y \leq 3) = P(Y < 3) = \int_{\infty}^{3} f_Y(y)dy = \int_{-\infty}^{0} 0\, dy + \int_{0}^{3} \frac{1}{6} dy = [\frac{y}{6}]_0^3 = \frac{1}{2}$$

Of course, what we have effectively constructed here is a cumulative probability. In the next section, we will explore cumulative probability density functions for continuous random variables.

8.3 Cumulative distribution functions

The **cumulative distribution function** (CDF) for a random variable Y is defined as the probability of being less than or equal to any particular value of $P(Y \leq y)$. For a discrete random variable, the cumulative distribution is easy to calculate, as we simply add together all of probabilities of all of the outcomes less than or equal to the particular outcome we are interested in.

So, for example, in panel a) of Figure 8.8 we have the PDF for a fair six-sided dice. If we want to construct the CDF, we simply need to add together all of the probabilities up to $X = x^*$, for each possible value of x^*. Since there are no outcomes of $X < 1$, we know that the CDF must be equal to 0 for $X < 1$, and similarly, since all of the outcomes are less than or equal to 6, then the CDF must be equal to 1 for $X > 6$:

$$P(X \leq x^*) = \begin{cases} 0, & x < 1 \\ \sum_{x=1}^{x=x^*} P(X = x), & 1 \leq x \leq 6 \\ 1, & x > 6 \end{cases}$$

So, for example, to calculate the probability of a randomly chosen observation of X (or in this case a roll of a dice) being less than or equal to 3.5, we would just add together all the probabilities where $X \leq 3.5$:

$$P(X \leq 3.5) = P(X = 1) + P(X = 2) + P(X = 3) = \frac{1}{2}$$

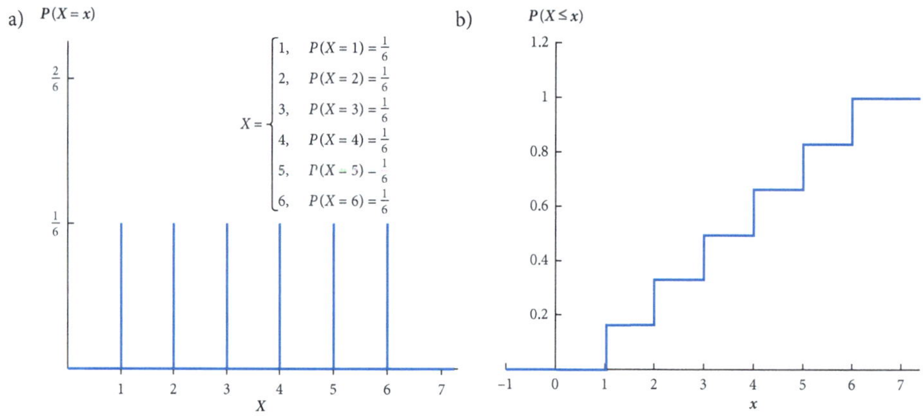

Figure 8.8 PDF and CDF for a fair six-sided dice.

For continuous random variables, since the probability of all outcomes is equal to zero, we can't just add together all the probabilities. However, integration is a continuous equivalent to the discrete case of summations, and so for continuous random variables, rather than adding together the probabilities less than or equal to a particular value, we will integrate the probability density function.

To illustrate, let's consider the uniform distribution between 0 and 6 we saw earlier in the chapter. We saw that the PDF $f_Y(y)$ is given by:

$$f_Y(y) = \begin{cases} 0, & y < 0 \\ 1/6, & 0 \le y \le 6 \\ 0, & y \ge 6 \end{cases}$$

So, if we want to find the probability of randomly observing a value of Y less than or equal to a particular value, y^*, say, we would need to integrate this expression over all possible values of y up to y^*:

$$P(Y \le y^*) = \int_{-\infty}^{y^*} f_Y(y)\,dy$$

Because the PDF is defined in three ranges, we will also need to construct the CDF in the same three ranges. First of all, for $y^* \le 0$, we know that $f_Y(y) = 0$ for all $y < 0$:

$$P(Y \le y^*) = \int_{-\infty}^{y^*} 0\,dy = 0$$

For values of y^* between 0 and 6, we need to consider both the PDF for $0 \le y \le 6$ and, because this is a cumulative probability, the PDF for $y \le 0$. We know that $f_Y(y) = \frac{1}{6}$ between 0 and 6, and so:

$$P(Y \le y^*) = \int_{-\infty}^{0} 0\,dy + \int_{0}^{y^*} \frac{1}{6}dy = 0 + \left[\frac{y}{6}\right]_0^{y^*} = \frac{y^*}{6}$$

Finally, for $y^* > 6$, we need to consider all three parts of the PDF:

$$P(Y \le y^*) = \int_{-\infty}^{0} 0\,dy + \int_{0}^{6} \frac{1}{6} dy + \int_{6}^{y^*} 0\,dy$$

$$= 0 + \left[\frac{y}{6}\right]_0^6 + 0 = 1$$

Formally, we can write down these probabilities using a CDF:

$$P(Y \le y) = \begin{cases} 0, & y \le 0 \\ \frac{y}{6}, & 0 \le y \le 6 \\ 1, & y \ge 1 \end{cases}$$

The PDF and CDF of our uniformly distributed random variable is illustrated in Figure 8.9.

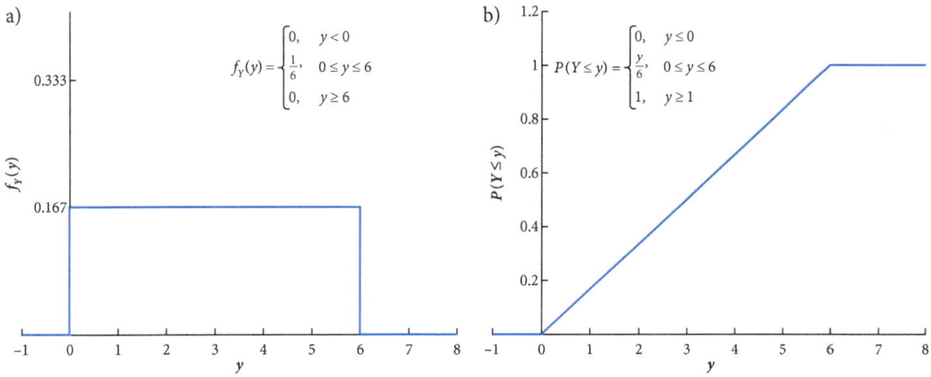

Figure 8.9 PDF and CDF for a uniform distribution.

This CDF has a lot of characteristics in common with the discrete distribution for the rolls of a single dice. For example, the probability that Y is less than or equal to any value greater than 6 is equal to 1, whilst the probability that Y is less than or equal to any value less than 0 is equal to 0. Similarly, for any value of x between 0 and 6, the probability of randomly observing a value less than or equal to y is just $\frac{y}{6}$. When we roll a standard six-sided dice, we are effectively using a random number generator that chooses an integer between 1 and 6 (inclusive). For this CDF, we could think of it as relating to a random number generator that chooses any number (not just limited to integers) between 0 and 6.

KEY DEFINITION: CUMULATIVE DISTRIBUTION FUNCTION

We can formalize this by setting a CDF of the continuous random variable Y, $F_Y(y)$. We formally define this CDF as:

$$F_Y(y) = P(Y \leq y)$$

That is, the CDF provides us with the probability that the random variable Y takes on a value less than (or equal to) a particular value y.

Key notation

We use a capital F to denote a CDF. The subscript Y indicates that we are looking at the density function of the random variable Y, and the (y) in parentheses indicates that we are evaluating this at the point $Y = y$.

So, for example, $F_Y(2) = P(Y \leq 2)$.

So, for example, by this CDF, we can see that $F_Y(1.5) = \frac{1.5}{6} = 0.25$; that is, $P(Y \leq 1.5) = 0.25$, or the probability of observing a value of Y less than or equal to 1.5 is equal to 0.25. Similarly, $F_Y(3.6) = \frac{3.6}{6} = 0.6$, or $P(Y \leq 3.6) = 0.6$.

So, we can use the CDF to calculate the probability of randomly observing an observation less than or equal to a particular value of y, but how about calculating the probability of observing an outcome within a particular range? We have already shown that:

$$P(Y \leq 3.6) = 0.6$$

$$P(Y \leq 1.5) = 0.25$$

However, suppose that we wanted to find the probability that a randomly drawn observation of Y was between 1.5 and 3.6. This would be equivalent to saying that it was less than 3.6, but not less than 1.5. This is relatively straightforward to calculate, as the CDF tells us the probability of being less than or equal to a particular value. $P(Y \leq 3.6)$ includes all of the possible values of Y, including those less than 1.5. However, if we want to exclude the values less than or equal to 1.5, we simply need to subtract the probability:

$$P(1.5 \leq Y \leq 3.6) = P(Y \leq 3.6) - P(Y \leq 1.5)$$

But this is just the same as $F_Y(3.6) - F_Y(1.5) = 0.35$.

It should be noted in this CDF that the maximum value it can ever take is 1, and the minimum value it can ever take is 0. This is for the obvious reason that this represents an explicit probability of an event, and probabilities can only take values between 0 and 1.

In fact, for any CDF, if we want to find the probability that an outcome lies between two points, a and b, where $b \geq a$, then:

$$P(a \leq Y \leq b) = F_Y(b) - F_Y(a)$$

Worked example 8.2: A simple example of using a CDF

Suppose that we considered the CDF:[3]

$$F_X(x) = \begin{cases} 0, & x < 0 \\ x/6, & 0 \le x \le 6 \\ 1, & x \ge 6 \end{cases}$$

We wish to find the probability that a random observation, drawn from X, is between 2 and 3. That is, we are looking for the probability that $P(2 \le X \le 3)$.

We can use the CDF to calculate this probability:

$$P(2 \le X \le 3) = P(X \le 3) - P(X \le 2) = F_X(3) - F_X(2) = \frac{1}{2} - \frac{1}{3} = \frac{1}{6}$$

Similarly, if we wanted to find the probability that X were to take a value between, say, 6.5 and 7, we could calculate this as:

$$P(6.5 \le X \le 7) = P(X \le 7) - P(X \le 6.5) = F_X(7) - F_X(6.5) = 1 - 1 = 0$$

This final result should not be surprising though. The CDF implies that all of the observations are between 0 and 6. It is not possible to get an observation greater than 6.

8.3.1 Comparison between discrete and continuous CDFs

We have seen examples of discrete and continuous random variables, and the differences between the CDFs allow us to see one of the key differences between discrete and continuous random variables. Let's begin by considering the CDFs of two random variables: the first is the CDF for a standard six-sided dice, and the second is the continuous random variable we defined in Worked example 8.2. Both of these CDFs are illustrated in Figure 8.10.

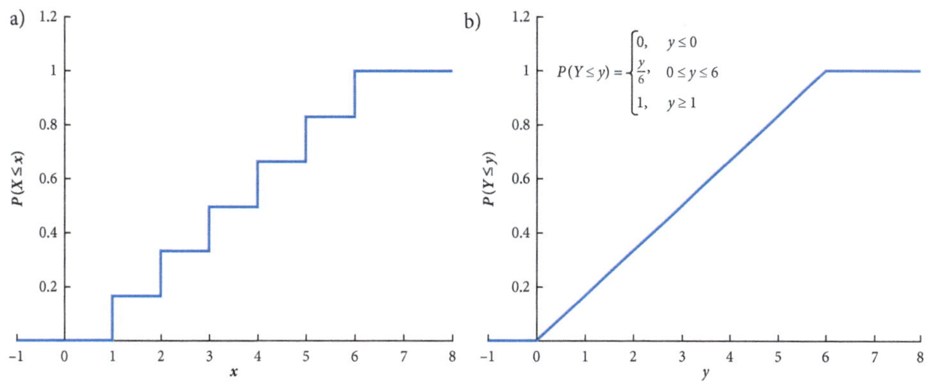

Figure 8.10 Comparing a discrete and continuous CDF.

[3] We have deliberately changed the notation here to illustrate that there's no reason why you have to stick with Y as a random variable. You can use any letter (or combination of letters) to indicate a random variable.

With the discrete CDF (panel a) of Figure 8.10), we have to be very careful about the difference between $P(Y < y)$ and $P(Y \leq y)$. As you can see from the CDF, there are discrete changes in the probability that occur at each of the outcomes. So at $Y = 2$, the CDF jumps from $\frac{1}{6}$ to $\frac{2}{6}$. If we are excluding 2 (i.e. we are interested in $P(Y < 2)$, so we are looking at the probability of being explicitly to the left of 2), then the probability will be $P(Y < 2) = \frac{1}{6}$. However, once we include $Y = 2$ in our probability, the CDF goes up the step, and so $P(Y \leq 2) = \frac{2}{6}$.

With the continuous CDF, there are no similar distinct steps. As such, there is no change in probability whether we include or exclude a particular value. For the continuous random variable, $P(Y \leq 2) = P(Y < 2) = \frac{2}{6}$.

Worked example 8.3: Constructing a CDF

Suppose that we have a continuous random variable, H. The probability density function $f_H(h)$ tells us the relative likelihood of particular outcomes occurring. The probability density function of H is given as:

$$f_H(h) = \begin{cases} \frac{h}{4}, & 1 \leq h \leq 3 \\ 0, & \text{Otherwise} \end{cases}$$

We wish to construct the CDF, $F_H(h)$.[4] The PDF is illustrated in Figure 8.11. We can see that the PDF is equal to zero for all values of $h < 1$, and also for all values of $h > 3$. This means that we already know that the probability of gaining an outcome less than 1 is equal to zero, and because all of the possible outcomes are less than 3, the probability of

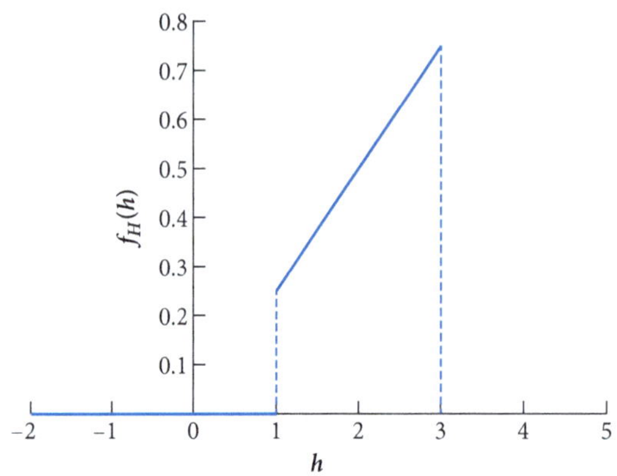

Figure 8.11 PDF of the random variable H.

[4] It is good practice to show that a PDF is well defined before you start trying to construct other measures such as the CDF. This is an example of a well-defined PDF, and I will leave it as an exercise for you to prove that in this case.

gaining an outcome less than or equal to any value of h greater than 3 will be equal to 1. That is, whenever randomly sampling from H, you will always gain an outcome less than or equal to 3!

Formally, we can find the CDF by integrating the PDF from minus infinity to some value h^*. As before, we will split this into three sections:

- $h^* < 1$
- $1 \le h^* \le 3$
- $h^* > 3$

For $h < 1$, we are only going to consider the first part of the PDF, where $f_H(h) = 0$:

$$F_H(h^*) = \int_{-\infty}^{h^*} f_H(h)dh = \int_{-\infty}^{h^*} 0\, dh = 0$$

Because the CDF is looking at the probability up to the point h^*, when considering the CDF for $1 \le h \le h$, we need to include both the PDF for $h < 1$ where $f_H(h) = 0$ and for $1 \le h \le h$ where $f_H(h) = \frac{h}{4}$. So, if we are looking for $F_H(h^*)$ for h^* between 1 and 3, we need to integrate $f_H(h) = 0$ between minus infinity and 1 (i.e. the full range of the first part of the PDF), and then $f_H(h)$ between 1 and h^*.

So, for $1 \le h^* \le 3$:

$$F_H(h^*) = \int_{-\infty}^{1} 0dh + \int_{1}^{h^*} \frac{h}{4}dh = 0 + \left[\frac{h^2}{8}\right]_1^{h^*}$$

Substituting in the limits of integration gives us:

$$F_H(h^*) = \frac{h^{*2} - 1}{8}$$

Similarly, for $h^* > 3$, we need to include all three sections of the PDF:

$$\begin{aligned} F_H(h^*) &= \int_{-\infty}^{1} 0\, dh + \int_{1}^{3} \frac{h}{4}dh + \int_{3}^{h^*} 0\, dh \\ &= 0 + \left[\frac{h^2}{8}\right]_1^3 + 0 \\ &= \frac{9}{8} - \frac{1}{8} = 1 \end{aligned}$$

So, we can write down the CDF for H as:

$$F_H(h) = \begin{cases} 0, & h < 1 \\ \dfrac{h^2 - 1}{8} & 1 \le h \le 3 \\ 1, & h \ge 3 \end{cases}$$

The PDF and CDF of H are illustrated in Figure 8.12.

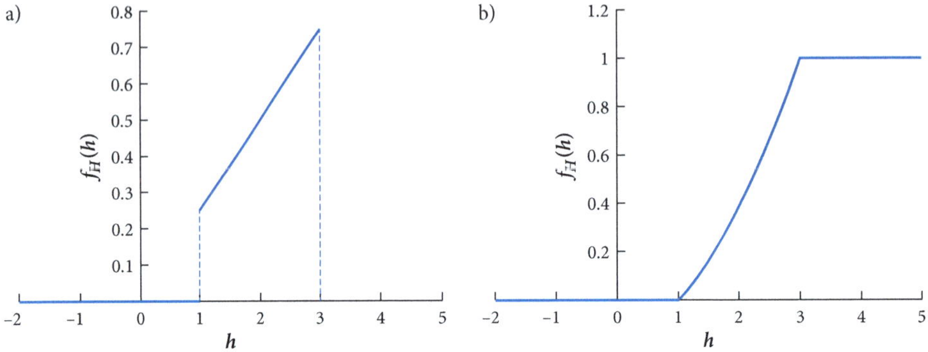

Figure 8.12 The PDF and CDF of H.

Summary of the mathematics

In this example, we have split the CDF up into three parts, taking account of the areas where the PDF is equal to zero, and the areas where it is non-zero.

- For $H < 1$, the PDF is always equal to zero, so it automatically follows that $P(H \le h) = 0$ for all values of h less than 1.

$$F_H(h^*) = \overbrace{\int_{-\infty}^{h^*} 0 \, dh}^{\text{This integral covers the range of } h<1}$$

When h^* is less than 1, calculating the CDF is trivial, as the PDF is always equal to zero.
In this case, we can carry out the integration, but the CDF is automatically going to be equal to zero.

$$F_H(h^*) = \underbrace{\int_{-\infty}^{1} 0 \, dh}_{\text{This integral covers the range of } h<1} + \overbrace{\int_{1}^{h^*} \frac{h}{4} \, dh}^{\text{This integral covers the range of } 1 \le h \le 3}$$

When $1 \le h^* \le 3$, the CDF is a little more difficult to calculate:

- We need to include the range from minus infinity to 1, but this is just equal to zero.
- The second integral covers the range from 1 to h^*.

This provides us with the probability $P(H \le h^*)$ when $1 \le h^* \le 3$

$$F_H(h^*) = \underbrace{\int_{-\infty}^{1} 0 \, dh}_{\text{This integral covers the range of } h<1} + \overbrace{\int_{1}^{3} \frac{h}{4} \, dh}^{\text{This integral covers the range of } 1 \le h \le 3} + \underbrace{\int_{3}^{h^*} 0 \, dh}_{\text{This integral covers the range of } h>3}$$

The final case is where $h^* > 3$. We know that, since the PDF is equal to zero beyond this point, the CDF must be equal to 1, as $P(H \le h^*) = 1$. Formally, we have included all three sections in the integral.

Now, suppose we wanted to calculate the probability of randomly observing an outcome of H between 1.5 and 2.5. We have two methods that we can use. Either we could integrate under the PDF between $H = 1.5$ and $H = 2.5$, or we could use the CDF, and the fact that $P(a \le H \le b) = F_H(b) - F_H(a)$.

Method 1: Integrating under the PDF

We know that the PDF for H is given by:

$$f_H(h) = \begin{cases} \frac{h}{4}, & 1 \le h \le 3 \\ 0, & \text{Otherwise} \end{cases}$$

If we wish to find $P(1.5 \le H \le 2.5)$, this is equivalent to finding the area under the PDF between 1.5 and 2.5. This is represented graphically where the shaded area represents the probability of randomly sampling an observation from H between 1.5 and 2.5 (see Figure 8.13).

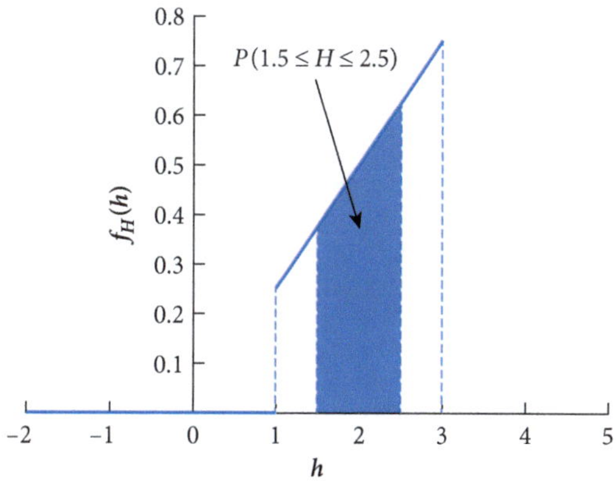

Figure 8.13 Using the PDF to find the probability of an outcome between 1.5 and 2.5.

Mathematically, we can calculate the probability as:

$$P(1.5 \le H \le 2.5) = \int_{1.5}^{2.5} f_H(h)dh = \int_{1.5}^{2.5} \frac{h}{4} dh$$

$$= \left[\frac{h^2}{8}\right]_{1.5}^{2.5} = \frac{6.25 - 2.25}{8} = \frac{1}{2}$$

So, using this method, we can see that the probability of randomly observing an outcome of H between 1.5 and 2.5 is equal to $\frac{1}{2}$ or 0.5.

Method 2: Using the CDF to calculate the probability

We know that the CDF of the random variable H is given by:

$$F_H(h) = \begin{cases} 0, & h < 1 \\ \frac{h^2 - 1}{8}, & 1 \le h \le 3 \\ 1, & h \ge 3 \end{cases}$$

We can use the CDF to calculate $P(1.5 \le H \le 2.5)$ by substituting in the values of h, and finding the difference between these two probabilities:

$$P(1.5 \le H \le 2.5) = F_H(2.5) - F_H(1.5) = \left[\frac{2.5^2 - 1}{8} - \frac{1.5^2 - 1}{8}\right] = \frac{6.25 - 2.25}{8} = \frac{1}{2}$$

So again, using this second method, we have, reassuringly, obtained the same answer as the first method.

It should be noted that these two methods are not really different methods, as the only difference is when we do the integration. In method 2, we are finding the area under the PDF by considering the difference between two areas.

This is illustrated in Figure 8.14. If we look for the CDF, evaluated at $H = 1.5$, this is equivalent to area A. That is, it is the area under the PDF to the left of $H = 1.5$. Similarly, $P(H \le 2.5)$ is represented by the area to the left of $H = 2.5$, which in our diagram is equal to area A + B.

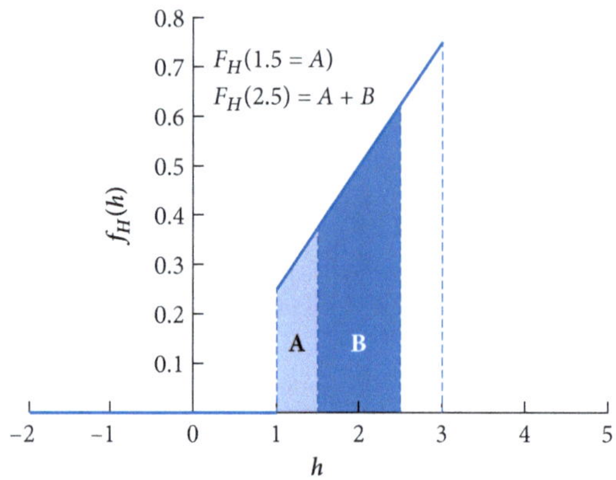

Figure 8.14 The relationship between the two methods.

Geometrically, we know that if we wish to find area B, then this is just the same as $(A + B) - A$, or in other words, $F_H(2.5) - F_H(1.5) = B$.

8.4 Expectations of continuous random variables

In the previous chapter, we discussed how we could construct measures of central tendency for discrete random variables. In particular, we constructed the expectation of a discrete random variable as the weighted average of the outcomes, weighted by their respective probabilities:

$$E(X) = \sum_X x \times P(X = x)$$

With a continuous random variable, since the probability of every possible outcome is equal to zero, and we have an infinite number of possible outcomes, we cannot just add up the products of the outcomes with their probabilities. As such, we need to use the analogous technique for continuous random variables. In other words, we integrate the product of the possible outcomes with the probability density function.

That is, if we have a random variable Y, with a PDF $f_Y(y)$, to find the expected value of Y, we need to calculate the following integral:

$$E(Y) = \int_{-\infty}^{\infty} y \times f_Y(y)dy$$

Effectively, we are weighting each of the (infinite) possible outcomes by their relative likelihood of occurring.

KEY DEFINITION: EXPECTATIONS OF CONTINUOUS VERSUS DISCRETE RANDOM VARIABLES

Even though continuous and discrete random variables look quite different, the methods for analysing the variables are very similar. The only key difference is that, when you use a summation for a discrete random variable, you would use an integral in the continuous case:

$$E(X) = \sum_X x \times P(X = x), \quad E(Y) = \int_{-\infty}^{\infty} y \times f_Y(y)dy$$

If X is a discrete variable, and Y a continuous variable, then comparing the formulae for the expectations, $E(X)$ and $E(Y)$, in both cases we are looking at the weighted average of the outcomes. In the discrete case, we are weighting by the explicit probability, whilst in the continuous case, we are weighting by the probability density.

Similarly, we know that if we apply a function to a random variable (say, squaring the random variable), then for a discrete variable we find the expectation of X^2 by finding the sum of products of the square of the outcomes with the respective probabilities of the original outcomes of X:

$$E(X^2) = \sum_x x^2 \times P(X = x)$$

We can use exactly the same logic to construct the expectation of a function applied to a continuous random variable; since a function provides a simple transformation from each possible outcome of y to y^2, then we can still use the original PDF of Y. So, for example:

$$E(Y^2) = \int_{-\infty}^{\infty} y^2 \times f_Y(y)dy, \quad E(e^Y) = \int_{-\infty}^{\infty} e^y \times f_Y(y)dy$$

Summary		
	Discrete variables	**Continuous variables**
Probability density function	$P(X = x)$	$f_X(x)$
Cumulative distribution function, $F_X(x)$	$\sum_{X \leq x} P(X = x)$	$\int_{-\infty}^{x} f_X(x)$
Expectation, $E(X)$	$\sum_{X} P(X = x) \times x$	$\int_{-\infty}^{\infty} x f_X(x) dx$
$E(X^2)$	$\sum_{X} P(X = x) \times x^2$	$\int_{-\infty}^{\infty} x^2 f_X(x) dx$
Expectation of a function of X: $E(g(X))$	$\sum_{X} P(X = x) \times g(x)$	$\int_{-\infty}^{\infty} g(x) f_X(x) dx$

Worked example 8.4: Calculating the expected height of an alien race

Suppose that you have received data about mankind's first contact with an alien species. You discover that the population has heights Y which follow a simple PDF (see Figure 8.15):

$$f_Y(y) = \begin{cases} 0, & y \leq 170\text{cm} \\ \frac{1}{20}, & 170\text{cm} \leq y \leq 190\text{cm} \\ 0, & y > 190\text{cm} \end{cases}$$

We wish to:

a) Verify that this is a well-defined PDF, and construct the CDF.

b) Calculate the expected height in the population.

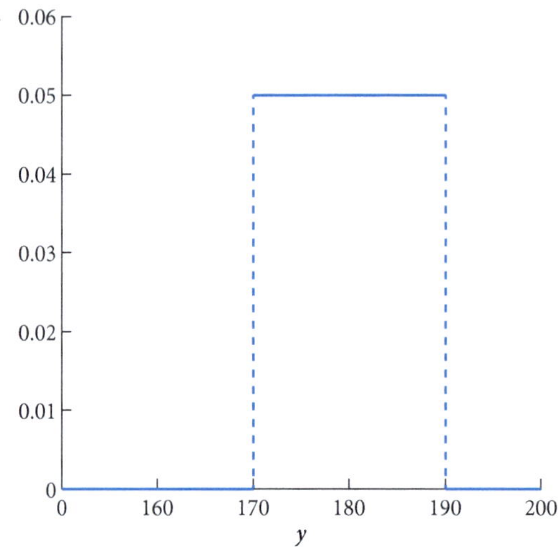

Figure 8.15 PDF of heights.

Let's begin with a), verifying that this is a well-defined PDF. For this to be a well-defined PDF, it needs to be the case that:

- the outcomes are mutually exclusive,
- the PDF is always non-negative, and
- the area under the curve is equal to 1.

Beginning with the mutually exclusive outcomes, it is not possible for an individual to simultaneously be two separate heights, so the outcomes are mutually exclusive. It is also clear (from Figure 8.15) that the PDF is never negative. To complete the proof, we would need to find the area under the curve:

$$\begin{aligned}\int_{-\infty}^{\infty} f_Y(y)dy &= \int_{-\infty}^{170} 0dy + \int_{170}^{190} \frac{1}{20}dy + \int_{190}^{\infty} 0dy = 0 + \left[\frac{y}{20}\right]_{170}^{190} + 0 \\ &= 0 + \left[\frac{190-170}{20}\right] + 0 = 0 + 1 + 0 = 1\end{aligned}$$

Since the area under the PDF is equal to 1, this is a well-defined PDF. Next, we need to calculate the CDF.

- We know that there are no observations for $y < 170$, and so the CDF will be equal to 0 for all $y < 170$.
- Similarly, we know that all outcomes are less than (or equal to) 190cm, so the CDF must be equal to 1 for all $y > 190$.

Finally, for the range of $170 < y < 190$, we can calculate the CDF by integrating between minus infinity and some y^*:

$$\begin{aligned}P(Y \le y^*) &= \int_{-\infty}^{y^*} f_Y(y)dy = \int_{-\infty}^{170} 0dy + \int_{170}^{y^*} \frac{1}{20}dy \\ &= 0 + \left[\frac{y}{20}\right]_{170}^{y^*} = \frac{y^* - 170}{20}\end{aligned}$$

So, for any y between 170 and 190, $P(Y \le y) = \frac{y-170}{20}$.

So the CDF, $F_Y(y)$, can be written as:

$$F_Y(y) = \begin{cases} 0, & y < 170\text{cm} \\ \dfrac{y-170}{20}, & 170\text{cm} \le y \le 190\text{cm} \\ 1, & y > 190\text{cm} \end{cases}$$

Similarly, the CDF is illustrated in Figure 8.16. Next we move on to calculating the expected value, or average heights within the population. To calculate the expected value, we need to integrate the product of the possible heights with the PDF:

$$E(Y) = \int_{-\infty}^{\infty} yf_Y(y)dy = \int_{-\infty}^{170} y \times 0dy + \int_{170}^{190} y \times \frac{1}{20}dy + \int_{190}^{\infty} y \times 0dy = 0 + \left[\frac{y^2}{40}\right]_{170}^{190} + 0 = 180$$

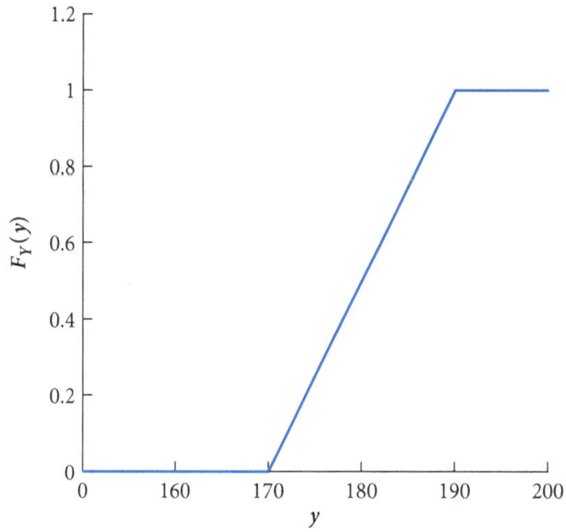

Figure 8.16 CDF of heights.

Worked example 8.5: A non-linear PDF

Probability density functions are rarely as simple as those seen in Section 8.5.1. Often, the height of the PDF will change as the outcome varies. To illustrate this, let's consider a slightly more complicated PDF for a random variable Z. Again, we will want to show that this is a well-defined PDF, and calculate $E(Z)$ and $E(Z^2)$.

$$f_Z(z) = \begin{cases} 3z - \frac{3z^2}{4} - \frac{9}{4}, & 1 \leq z \leq 3 \\ 0, & \text{Otherwise} \end{cases}$$

To show that this is a well-defined PDF, assuming that the outcomes are mutually exclusive, it needs to be the case that the PDF is always non-negative, and that the area under the PDF is equal to 1. In this case, the PDF is quite complicated, and there are a number of ways that you can check that $f_Z(z) \geq 0$ for all z. The easiest way of doing so is to draw the PDF, and check that the PDF never drops below the horizontal axis. This is shown in Figure 8.17, and as we can see, between 1 and 3, $f_Z(z)$ is always greater than or equal to zero, and for the rest of the possible outcomes, the PDF is equal to zero.

You might be worried that the PDF actually is infinitesimally below the axis at 1 or at 3. To reassure yourself, it is worthwhile substituting $z = 1$ and $z = 3$ into the PDF, to check that it is not negative at those points:

$$f_Z(1) = 3 \times 1 - 3 \times \frac{1^2}{4} - \frac{9}{4} = 3 - \frac{3}{4} - \frac{9}{4} = 3 - 3 = 0$$

$$f_Z(3) = 3 \times 3 - 3 \times \frac{3^2}{4} - \frac{9}{4} = 9 - \frac{27}{4} - \frac{9}{4} = 9 - 9 = 0$$

Because the PDF follows a negative quadratic, since we know that $f_Z(1) = f_Z(3) = 0$, it must follow that all of the PDF is greater than or equal to zero.

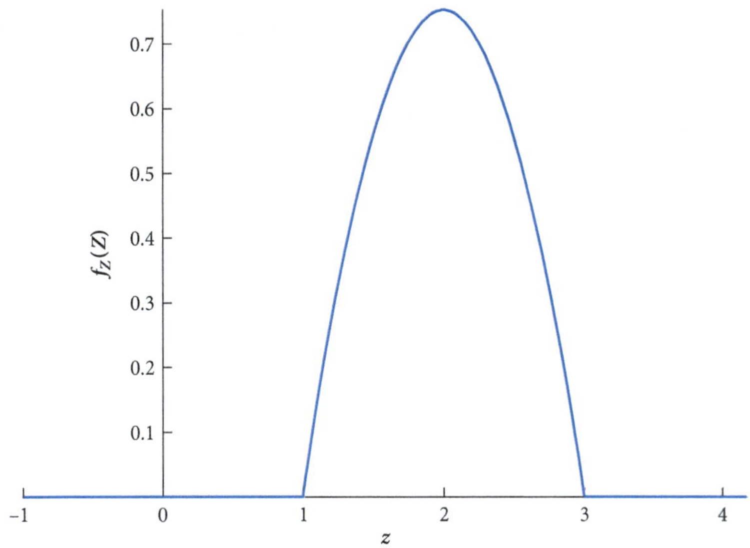

Figure 8.17 PDF of the random variable Z.

To find $E(Z)$, we just need to find the integral of the product of the PDF with all of the possible outcomes. Mathematically, this is calculated as:

$$E(Z) = \int_{-\infty}^{\infty} z f_Z(z) dz$$

Substituting in the three sections of the PDF gives us:

$$\Rightarrow E(Z) = \int_{-\infty}^{1} z \times 0dz + \int_{1}^{3} z \times \left(3z - \frac{3z^2}{4} - \frac{9}{4}\right)dz + \int_{3}^{\infty} z \times 0dz$$

The first and the third elements are just the integral of zero (which will itself just be zero), and so the expectation of Z will just be:

$$\Rightarrow E(Z) = \int_{1}^{3} z \times \left(3z - \frac{3z^2}{4} - \frac{9}{4}\right)dz = \int_{1}^{3} 3z^2 - \frac{3z^3}{4} - \frac{9z}{4}dz = \left[\frac{3z^3}{3} - \frac{3z^4}{16} - \frac{9z^2}{8}\right]_1^3$$

Substituting in the limits gives us:

$$= \left[3 \times \frac{27}{3} - 3 \times \frac{81}{16} - 9 \times \frac{9}{8}\right] - \left[3 \times \frac{1}{3} - 3 \times \frac{1}{16} - 9 \times \frac{1}{8}\right]$$

$$= \left[27 - \frac{243}{16} - \frac{81}{8}\right] - \left[1 - \frac{3}{16} - \frac{9}{8}\right] = \frac{27}{16} - \left[-\frac{5}{16}\right]$$

$$= 2$$

So, having integrated and substituted in the limits, the expectation of the random variable is equal to 2, which lies right in the middle of the distribution. This shouldn't be too surprising, as if we look at the PDF, we can see that it is symmetric. That is, if we drew a line at $E(Z) = 2$, we would have the same distribution of outcomes to both the left and right of the line of symmetry.

Finally, if we want to find $E(Z^2)$, we will use exactly the same method. The expectation of Z^2 is just the integral of the product of z^2 with $f_Z(z)$:

$$E(Z^2) = \int_{-\infty}^{\infty} z^2 \times f_Z(z)\,dz = \int_{-\infty}^{1} z^2 \times 0\,dz + \int_{1}^{3} z^2 \times \left(3z - \frac{3z^2}{4} - \frac{9}{4}\right)dz + \int_{1}^{\infty} z^2 \times 0\,dz$$

$$= \int_{1}^{3} 3z^3 - \frac{3z^4}{4} - \frac{9z^2}{4} dz = \left[\frac{3z^4}{4} - \frac{3z^5}{20} - \frac{9z^3}{12}\right]_1^3$$

$$= 4.2$$

This may seem like a curiosity, but in future chapters, we will use the expectation of the square of a random variable to construct a measure of variability of a random variable, known as the variance.

8.5 Percentiles and quantiles of a distribution

We are often interested in the spread of data within a distribution. One way of measuring this is by using percentiles or quantiles. Percentiles tell you values below which a particular percentage of the distribution lies. For example, the kth percentile of a distribution tells you the value below which k per cent of the distribution lies. To illustrate this, let's consider a simple example. In Section 8.2, we considered a random variable that followed the uniform distribution. Remember that a uniform distribution has a PDF that is fixed across a limited range, and is zero for all other possible outcomes.

Suppose that we knew that a variable X was uniformly distributed between 0 and 1 (see Figure 8.18). The PDF of X would be:

$$f_X(x) = \begin{cases} 1, & 0 \le x \le 1 \\ 0, & \text{Otherwise} \end{cases}$$

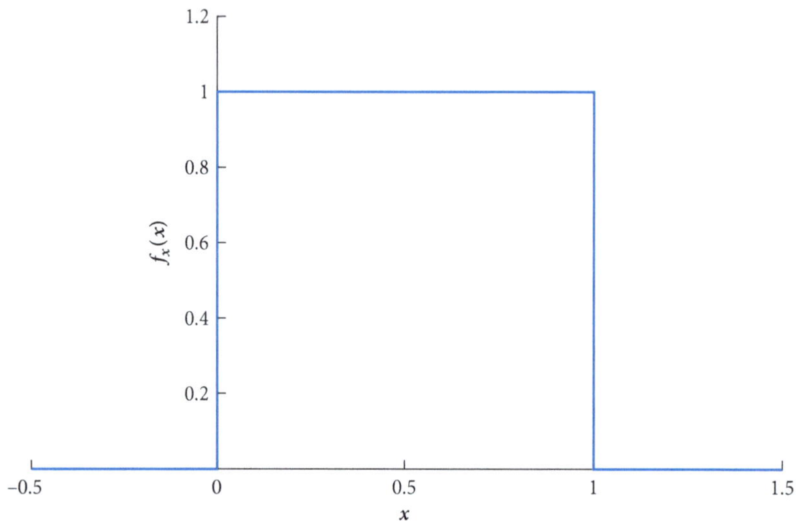

Figure 8.18 PDF of a uniform distribution between 0 and 1.

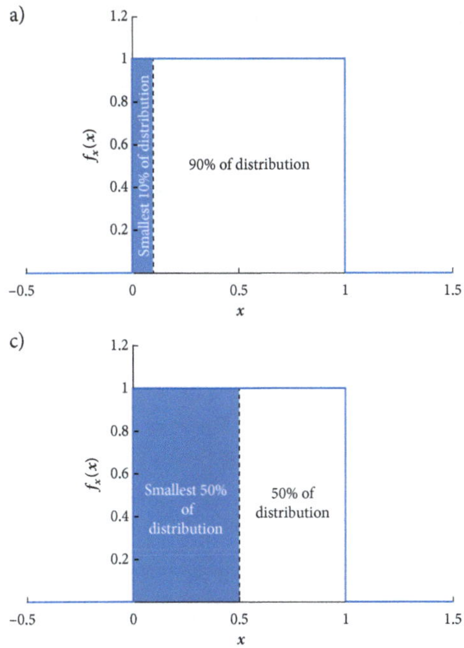

Figure 8.19 Percentiles of the uniform distribution.

It is possible that we might be interested in asking the following question: for what value of x would it be true that $P(X \leq x) = 0.5$? That is, for what value of x would we have a probability of 0.5 (or 50 per cent) of randomly observing a single observation of X, such that our observation was less than x; that is, what value of x would satisfy the equation $P(X \leq x) = 0.5$?

We could also define this value of x as the 50th percentile of X, or the **median** of X. It is the value of x such that 50 per cent of the distribution of X lies below it; that is, 50 per cent of the (probability weighted) observations would lie below x.

More generally, the kth percentile of a distribution tells you the value of x, below which lies k per cent of the distribution. So the 10th percentile has 10 per cent of the distribution below it, the 25th percentile has 25 per cent of the distribution below it, and so on.

The 10th, 25th, 50th, and 75th percentiles of the uniform distribution are illustrated in Figure 8.19. The 50th percentile should look familiar, as this is just the definition of a median—that is, the 50th percentile is the point where 50 per cent of the distribution is smaller than the value, and 50 per cent of the distribution is larger than the value. Intuitively, in the uniform distribution we have in Figure 8.19, we should be able to see that the 50th percentile of the distribution is 0.5, as 50 per cent of the distribution is smaller than 0.5, and 50 per cent is larger than 0.5. Similarly, the 10th percentile would be 0.1, the 25th percentile 0.25, and so on.

In order to calculate what the percentiles are in a distribution, we can take advantage of the fact that we know that the area under the PDF is equal to the probability of observing an outcome in the specified range. Therefore, if we wanted to find the kth percentile, we would need to solve for the value of x^* which satisfied:

$$\int_{-\infty}^{x^*} f_X(x)dx = \frac{k}{100}$$

So, for example, using the uniform distribution, if we wanted to find the 25th percentile, we would need to solve for the value of x^* which satisfied:

$$\int_{-\infty}^{x^*} f_X(x)dx = \frac{25}{100} = 0.25$$

So, substituting in the PDF gives us:

$$\int_{-\infty}^{0} 0dx + \int_{0}^{x^*} 1dx = 0.25$$

$$\Rightarrow [x]_0^{x^*} = 0.25$$

$$\Rightarrow x^* = 0.25$$

That is, in this distribution, the 25th percentile is equal to 0.25. That is, 25 per cent of the distribution lies below 0.25. Similarly, we can calculate other percentiles using exactly the same method:

10th percentile p_{10}	25th percentile p_{25}	50th percentile p_{50}	75th percentile p_{75}	90th percentile p_{90}	Expected value $E(X)$
0.1	0.25	0.5	0.75	0.9	0.5

Whilst we have not explicitly calculated it, the expected value $E(X) = 0.5$ is the same as the 50th percentile, or the median. This is because the distribution is symmetric; whenever faced with a symmetric distribution, the expectation and median will always be exactly the same.

When we move into statistics, it is very important that you understand percentiles, as we will use them extensively for statistical testing.

You will hopefully have noticed that, effectively, what we have been doing by integrating is constructing the CDF, and we are then finding what values of x correspond with different percentiles of our distribution.

Quantiles, quartiles, and deciles

A concept that is very closely linked to percentiles is the idea of quantiles. If we split a distribution up into q separate 'quantiles', we are effectively splitting the distribution up so that $1/q$ of the population lies within each quantile.

We have seen examples of quantiles. If we split the population up into four equally sized groups (i.e. into **quartiles**), then the 25th, 50th, and 75th percentiles are the dividers between the four quartiles of the population, as illustrated in Figure 8.20.

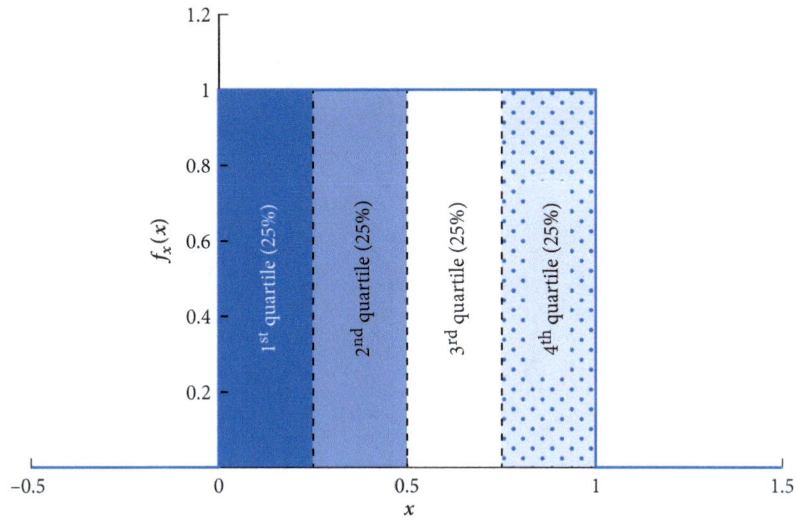

Figure 8.20 Quartiles of a uniform distribution.

Similarly, we could split the population into:

- three quantiles (tertiles)
- four quantiles (quartiles)
- five quantiles (quintiles)
- ten quantiles (deciles)
- 100 quantiles (centiles, or percentiles), and so on.

Percentiles are very useful to provide an indication of the spread of the data within a population; for example, one measure of inequality within the economy is to compare earnings at the 90th and 10th percentiles within the population. This allows a comparison between the marginal individual in the bottom 10 per cent of the earnings distribution and the marginal individual within the top 10 per cent of the earnings distribution. Equally, statisticians may look at the **interquartile range** (IQR) within a population, which measures at the distance between the 25th and 75th percentiles.

Worked example 8.6: Calculating percentiles from a probability density function

Suppose that we have a random variable T which follows the (strange) PDF shown in Figure 8.21, and we wish to calculate the 25th, 50th (median), and 75th percentiles:

$$f_T(t) = \begin{cases} \frac{t^2}{18}, & -3 \leq t \leq 3 \\ 0, & \text{Otherwise} \end{cases}$$

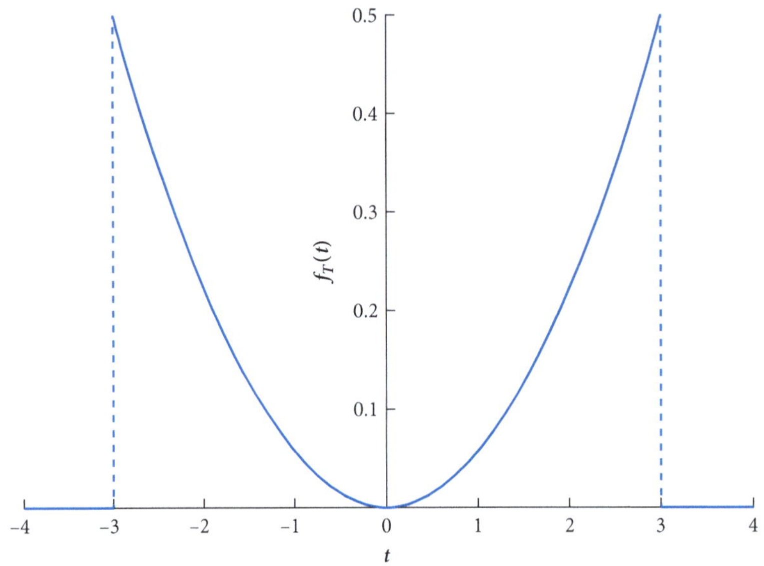

Figure 8.21 PDF of T.

In this example, outcomes which are a long way from the middle of the distribution (i.e. close to ±3) are much more likely to occur than outcomes near the middle of the distribution (i.e. close to zero). Many distributions that we will see will be the reverse of this, where the most likely outcomes are near the middle of the distribution.

However, these sorts of distributions might occur, for instance, when considering the temperature at the North Pole. During winter months, when the North Pole experiences no sunlight, we might expect temperatures to be much lower than the (annual) average. Similarly, in the summer months (when there is 24-hour sunlight), we might expect the temperature to be much higher than the annual average. Of course, in reality, the distribution of temperatures would look far less extreme than this.

There are multiple ways that we could construct the percentiles. Possibly the most general way of doing this is working from the CDF. Since the CDF tells us $P(T \leq t)$ for any possible value of t, it is useful in constructing the percentiles; we simply need to use the CDF, and solve which values of t correspond to probabilities of 0.25, 0.50, and 0.75.

We know that the CDF will be equal to zero for $t < -3$, and will be equal to 1 for $t > 3$ (as all of the non-zero PDF lies between −3 and +3), so we only really need to focus on the range between $-3 \leq t \leq 3$:

$$\begin{aligned} F_T(t) &= \int_{-\infty}^{t^*} f_T(t)dt \\ &= \int_{-\infty}^{-3} 0dt + \int_{-3}^{t^*} \frac{t^2}{18}dt \end{aligned}$$

Now, the first term will just be equal to zero, and for the second term, we merely raise the power by 1, and divide through by the new power:

$$= \left[\frac{t^3}{54}\right]_{-3}^{t^*} = \frac{t^{*3}}{54} + \frac{27}{54} = \frac{t^{*3}}{54} + \frac{1}{2}$$

So, we can write that, for a general t:

$$F_T(t) = P(T \le t) = \begin{cases} 0, & t < -3 \\ \frac{t^3}{54} + \frac{1}{2}, & -3 \le t \le 3 \\ 1, & t > 3 \end{cases}$$

Figure 8.22 shows the CDF of T. To find the 25th percentile, we can find this graphically by tracing a line horizontally from the vertical axis at 0.25 to the CDF curve to find the value of t which makes the *CDF* equal to 0.25. We can see here that this value of t is approximately equal to −2.4. However, this graphical method does not give us an exact value for the percentile; to do this, we would need to calculate the value for which the *CDF* is equal to 0.25.

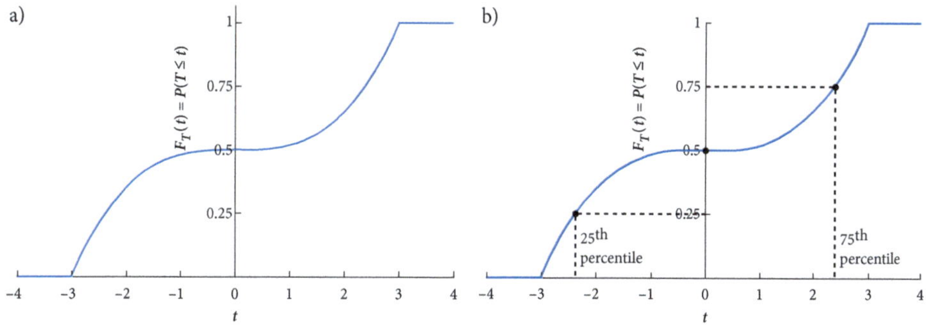

Figure 8.22 Cumulative distribution function of T.

So, if we wanted to find the value of t that satisfies $P(T \le t) = 0.25$, or $F_T(t) = 0.25$, we could simply solve the following equation:

$$F_T(t) = 0.25 \Rightarrow \frac{t^3}{54} + \frac{1}{2} = 0.25$$

If we subtract $\frac{1}{2}$ from both the left- and right-hand side, and multiply by 54, we have:

$$t^3 = -\frac{54}{4} \Rightarrow t = -2.3811(4dp)$$

Similarly, we can use the same methods to show that the 50th percentile (or median) is equal to 0, and the 75th percentile is equal to $2.3811(4dp)$.

Worked example 8.7: A non-symmetric distribution

Most of the distributions that we have seen so far have been symmetric distributions, where the expected value and the median (50th percentile) have been the same, and the percentiles have been symmetrically spread through the domain of the random variable. However, there's no reason that we should be restricted to symmetric probability distributions, and you will come across distributions later in the book, such as the F-distribution, where the PDF is not symmetric.

To illustrate this, consider the following PDF relating to a random variable X (see Figure 8.23).

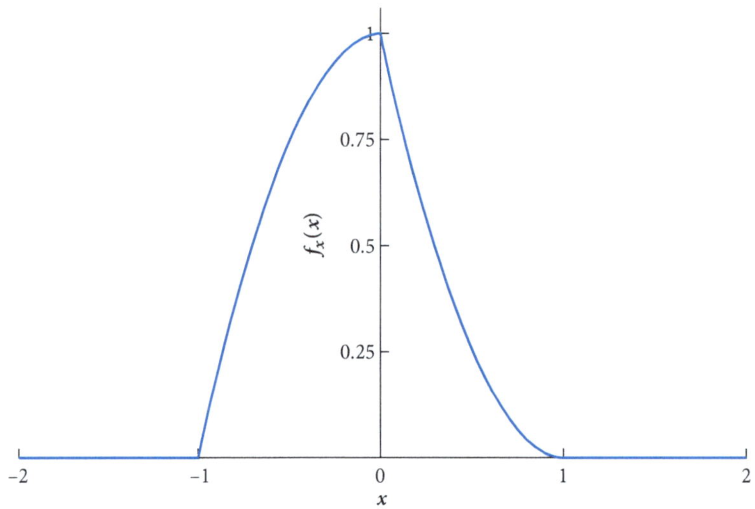

Figure 8.23 PDF of X.

$$f_X(x) = \begin{cases} 1 - x^2, & -1 \leq x \leq 0 \\ x^2 - 2x + 1, & 0 \leq x \leq 1 \\ 0, & \text{Otherwise} \end{cases}$$

We can use exactly the same methods to find the percentiles of the distribution, but let's begin by calculating the CDF. Remember that the CDF, $F_X(x)$, is calculated by integrating the PDF up to the value x. We know that for $x < -1$, the CDF must be equal to 0, whilst for $x > 1$, since there are no outcomes greater than 1, provided the PDF is well defined, then the *CDF* must be equal to 1.

$$F_X(x^*) = \int_{-\infty}^{x^*} f_X(x)dx$$

So, beginning with the first part of the PDF, for $-1 \leq x^* \leq 0$, we will need to include the PDF for $x < -1$, and for $-1 \leq x \leq 0$:

$$F_X(x^*) = \int_{-\infty}^{-1} 0dx + \int_{-1}^{x^*} 1 - x^2 dx$$

$$= 0 + \left[x - \frac{x^3}{3} \right]_{-1}^{x^*} = x^* - \frac{x^{*3}}{3} + \frac{2}{3}$$

Similarly, for the second part of the PDF, for $0 \le x^* \le 1$, we will need to include all of the PDF up to x^*. That means that we will need to include $f_X(x) = 1 - x^2$ for $-1 \le x \le 0$ and $f_X(x) = x^2 - 2x + 1$:

$$F_X(x^*) = \int_{-\infty}^{-1} 0dx + \int_{-1}^{0} 1 - x^2 dx + \int_{0}^{x^*} x^2 - 2x + 1dx$$

Integrating each expression in term gives us:

$$\Rightarrow F_X(x) = 0 + \left[x - \frac{x^3}{3}\right]_{-1}^{0} + \left[\frac{x^3}{3} - x^2 + x\right]_{0}^{x^*}$$

$$= \frac{2}{3} + \frac{x^{*3}}{3} - x^{*2} + x^*$$

So, we can now write down the CDF for X as:

$$F_X(x) = \begin{cases} 0, & x \ge -1 \\ x - \dfrac{x^3}{3} + \dfrac{2}{3}, & -1 \le x \le 0 \\ \dfrac{2}{3} + \dfrac{x^3}{3} - x^2 + x, & 0 \le x \le 1 \\ 0, & \text{Otherwise} \end{cases}$$

The CDF of x is illustrated in Figure 8.24. The mathematics needed to solve the 25th, 50th, and 75th percentiles is a little trickier (as this would involve solving a cubic equation), but it is possible to show that the percentiles are:

25th percentile (P25)	50th percentile (P50), median	75th percentile (P75)
-0.4463(4dp)	-0.1683 (4dp)	0.09144 (4dp)

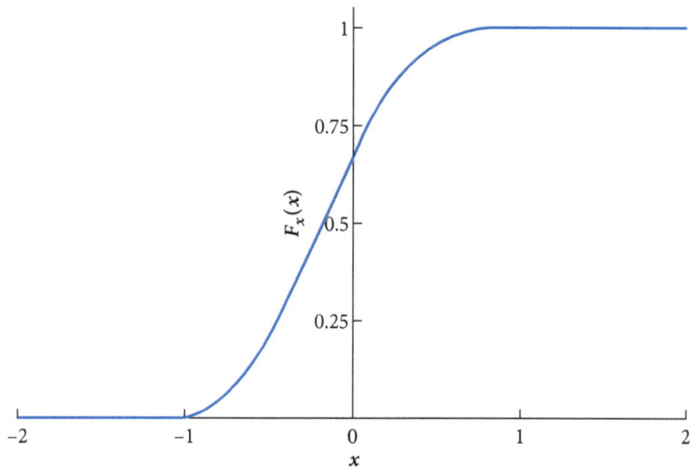

Figure 8.24 CDF of X.

We could also calculate the expectation of our random variable X:

$$E(X) = \int_{-\infty}^{\infty} x \times f_X(x)dx$$

Substituting in the four parts of the PDF gives us:

$$\Rightarrow E(X) = \int_{-\infty}^{-1} x \times 0dx + \int_{-1}^{0} x \times (1 - x^2)dx + \int_{0}^{1} x \times (x^2 - 2x + 1)dx + \int_{1}^{\infty} x \times 0dx$$

The first and last terms disappear, as the integral of zero is just zero, leaving us with:

$$\int_{-1}^{0} x - x^3 dx + \int_{0}^{1} (x^3 - 2x^2 + x)dx = \left[\frac{x^2}{2} - \frac{x^4}{4}\right]_{-1}^{0} + \left[\frac{x^4}{4} - \frac{2x^3}{3} + \frac{x^2}{2}\right]_{0}^{1}$$

$$= -\frac{1}{4} + \frac{1}{12} = -\frac{2}{12}$$

So, $E(X) = -\frac{2}{12}$ (which as a decimal is equal to $-0.1667\,(4dp)$). This is close to the median, but, unlike most of the distributions we have previously seen, it is not exactly the same. Whenever the distributions we are looking at are not symmetric, the expectation and the median are no longer equal.

Worked example 8.8: Data-based example

More often than not, you will not be faced with a theoretical distribution, but instead you will be more interested in trying to calculate percentiles based on observed data.

The file Weekly Wage.xlsx contains an extract of 200 observations of female, full-time workers aged 25–45 from the 2019 UK Labour Force Survey.[5] We can use Microsoft Excel to find different percentiles in the data, using the command =PERCENTILE.EXC(Range, Percentile).

In Figure 8.25, the percentile being found is the 20th percentile (i.e. it is finding the value below which the smallest 20 per cent of observations lie), where the data lies between cells A2 and A201:

Percentile	Value
0.1	277
0.2	327.6
0.3	393.2
0.4	462
0.5	522.5
0.6	577
0.7	638.5
0.8	736.8
0.9	962

[5] See Data sets and exercises at the end of this chapter.

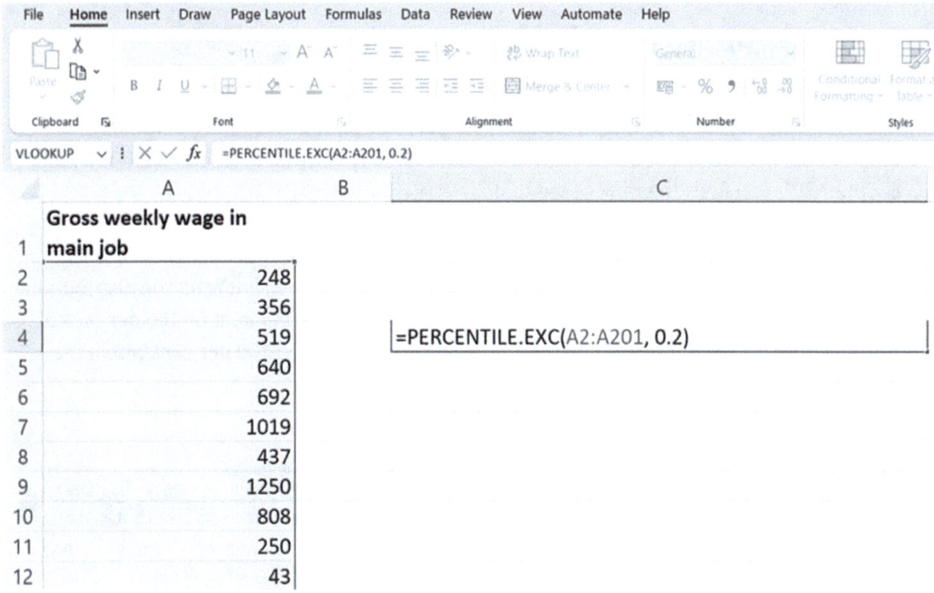

Figure 8.25 Using Excel to find percentiles.

If we use Excel, we can find the 10th, 20th, 30th, and so on percentiles. The data shows that 10 per cent of the observations are less than £277 per week, 20 per cent are less than £329.4, 30 per cent are than £394.8, and so on.

An alternative way that you could find the percentiles is to sort the data in order, from smallest to largest, and find the percentiles manually.

If there are n observations in the data, the kth percentile is calculated by finding the observation ranked:

$$(n + 1) \times \frac{k}{100}$$

For example, with 300 observations the 20th percentile would be the $(300 + 1) \times 0.2 = 60.2$th smallest observation.

However, this method raises a question; for example, when finding the median with 200 observations, we need to find the value that half of the data is smaller than, and half of the data is larger than. That is, we want the value below which 100 observations lie and above which 100 observations lie. Using the formula

$$(n + 1) \times \frac{k}{100}$$

we wish to find the 100.5th observation. However, there is no 100.5th observation; the 100th observation is £519, whilst the 101st observation is £526. To calculate the 50th percentile, since we wish to find the 100.5th observation we find the point that is 50 per cent (0.5) between the 100th and 101st observation; here the midpoint between the two observations is £522.50.

Important note about how Excel calculates percentiles

Microsoft Excel has two commands to calculate percentiles, which lead to (marginally) different answers. The first is the method we have already discussed, where =PERCENTILE.EXC(A2:A201, 0.2) finds the rank based upon $(n+1) \times \frac{k}{100}$.

However, there is a second formula in Excel, which is =PERCENTILE(A2:A201, 0.2) or =PERCENTILE.INC(A2:A201, 0.2). If you apply this formula, you will get a different answer. The reason for this is that the first method excludes 0 and 100 per cent from the distribution; that is, there is no value within the sample below which either 0 per cent or 100 per cent of the observations lie. The second method, however, includes 0 and 100 per cent within the distribution.

The rank for the second formula is calculated as $(n-1) \times \frac{k}{100}$.

Percentile	10	20	30	40	50	60	70	80	90
Excluding 0 and 100	277	327.6	393.2	462	522.5	577	638.5	736.8	962
Including 0 and 100	277	329.4	394.8	462	522.5	577	636.5	733.2	962

This table represents the values for the percentiles using the two different methods. Some of the differences are quite small, but it is always important to be aware of what method you are actually using.

8.6 Joint and conditional distributions

As with discrete variables, it is possible to have joint distributions with continuous variables. A joint probability density function tells us about the relative likelihood of pairs of outcomes from two variables. As with the marginal probability density function, the total *volume* under the joint distribution must equal to 1.

Figure 8.26 provides an example of a joint distribution. In this distribution, the height on the z axes represents the relative likelihood of pairs of outcomes. It should be noted again that the probability of any given pair is equal to zero, but looking at this figure, we can see that the most likely observation is at the peak of the distribution—that is, where $x = y = 0$.

The joint distribution, $f_{X,Y}(x,y)$ here, is analogous to the probability $P(X = x \cap Y = y)$ in the discrete case. Obviously, we can't have an individual probability (as, for example, the probability that X takes on the value exactly 2, and Y takes on the value exactly 3, say, is always going to be zero), but we can examine similar relationships to those we saw in the discrete case.

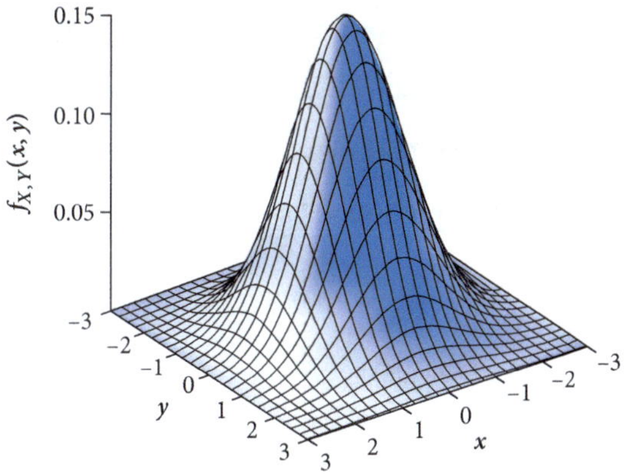

Figure 8.26 PDF of a joint distribution.

As such, we can use this joint distribution to calculate marginal distributions, using the **law of total probability**. Previously, when we had a discrete distribution, we had a joint distribution that told us the probability: $P(X = x \cap Y = y)$.If, say, we wanted to know the overall, or marginal, probability that X was equal to 2, we would add up all of these joint probabilities across all values of y, for the cases where $x = 2$.

$$P(X = x) = \sum_{Y} P(X = x \cap Y = y)$$

However, in a continuous distribution, we cannot just add up all the probabilities, so as before, we need to integrate across all possible values for Y:

$$f_X(x) = \int_{Y} f_{X,Y}(x, y)dy$$

This will give us the marginal, or unconditional, distribution of X.That is, it will tell us the overall likelihood of any given value of X occurring, unconditional on the value that Y takes.

Similarly, if we wanted to find the conditional distribution (i.e. the probability of Y taking a value, given X takes a certain value), then we divided the joint distribution by the marginal distribution. For continuous variables, we can write this in exactly the same way.

That is, if, for the random variables X and Y, we have a *joint* PDF $f_{X,Y}(x, y)$, and calculate the *marginal* PDF $f_Y(y)$, then we can construct the conditional PDF for x given a particular value of Y, $f_{(X|Y)}(x|Y = y)$, as follows:

$$f_{(X|Y)}(x|Y = y) = \frac{f_{X,Y}(x, y)}{f_Y(y)}$$

Alternatively, to find the conditional distribution of Y given a particular value of X:

$$f_{(Y|X)}(y|X = x) = \frac{f_{X,Y}(x, y)}{f_X(x)}$$

KEY DEFINITION: REQUIREMENTS FOR A JOINT PDF TO BE WELL DEFINED

For a joint PDF $f_{X,Y}(x, y)$ to be well defined, two conditions need to be met:

1. The value of the PDF needs to be greater than (or equal to) zero for *all possible combinations of* x *and* y:

   $$f_{X,Y}(x,y) \geq 0, \text{ for } \textit{all } x \text{ and } \textit{all } y$$

   That is, the PDF can never be negative.

2. The volume under the PDF needs to be equal to 1. We calculate the volume using the double integral:

   $$\int_{-\infty}^{\infty}\int_{-\infty}^{\infty} f_{X,Y}(x,y)dxdy = 1$$

   This tells us that all of the possible pairs of outcomes are defined.

Marginal PDF

The marginal PDF of X is the PDF irrespective of the value Y takes. We usually denote this as $f_X(x)$.

$$f_X(x) = \int_{-\infty}^{\infty} f_{X,Y}(x,y)dy, \; f_Y(y) = \int_{-\infty}^{\infty} f_{X,Y}(x,y)dx$$

Conditional PDF

The conditional PDF of X is the PDF conditioning that y takes a particular value, y. We usually denote this as $f_{(X|Y)}(x|Y = y)$:

$$f_{(Y|X)}(x|Y = y) = \frac{f_{X,Y}(x,y)}{f_Y(y)}, \quad f_{(Y|X)}(y|X = x) = \frac{f_{X,Y}(x,y)}{f_X(x)}$$

Worked example 8.9: Simple example of a joint distribution

Suppose that we are presented with the following (simple) joint PDF between two random variables, X and Y, and wish to examine the marginal PDF for X:

$$f_{X,Y}(x,y) = \begin{cases} 1, & 0 \leq x \leq 1, 0 \leq y \leq 1 \\ 0, & \text{Otherwise} \end{cases}$$

It should be noted that the joint PDF is defined for a range of X and Y. This PDF implies that there will never be any outcomes which lie outside of the range of X between 0 and 1, or Y between 0 and 1. So, for instance, in this random variable, it would be impossible to get an observation of X being equal to 0.5, with Y equal to 1.5, say.

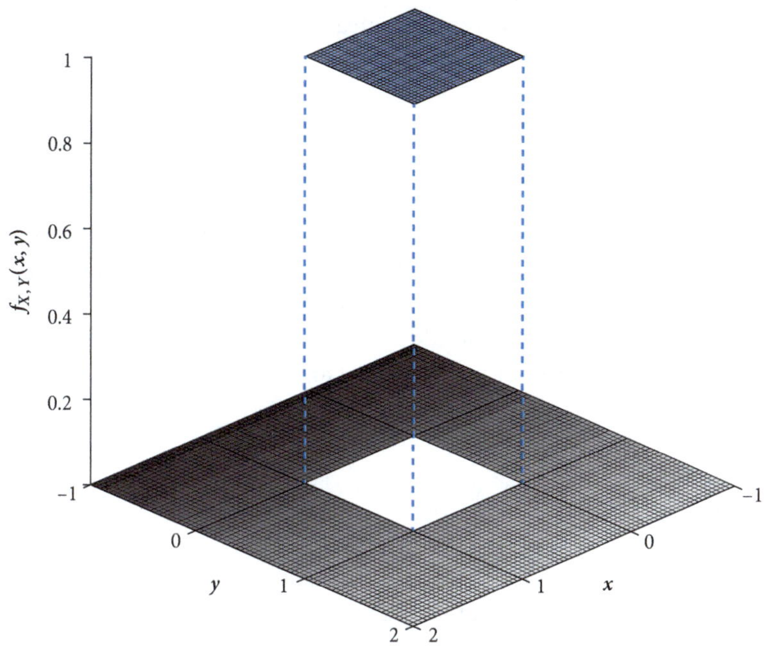

Figure 8.27 Joint PDF of X and Y

Joint PDFs are often difficult to visualize intuitively. To assist, the PDF is illustrated in Figure 8.27. The first thing we might want to check is that this is a well-defined PDF. As with marginal PDFs, it must be the case that:

i) the PDF is always greater than (or equal to) 0, and

ii) the volume under the PDF is equal to 1.

Since the PDF is always equal to 0 or 1, it is trivial to show that i) holds. However, to show ii), we need to consider the (double) integral of the joint PDF. For simplicity, we will ignore any areas where the PDF is equal to zero, as the integral will also be equal to zero here:

$$\int_{-\infty}^{\infty}\int_{-\infty}^{\infty} f_{X,Y}(x, y)dx\,dy = \int_{0}^{1}\int_{0}^{1} 1\,dx\,dy$$

Note: Solving double integrals

Solving double integrals is relatively straightforward; unlike cutlery at a posh banquet, you should start from the inside, and work outwards. For the example:

$$\int_{y=0}^{y=1}\int_{x=0}^{x=1} 1dxdy$$

First, integrate 1 with respect to x, and substitute in the limits of x. Then, and only then, move on to integrate with respect to y.

To solve this double integral, we begin by integrating with relation to x, and then substitute in the limits of X, then we integrate w.r.t. y, and substitute in the limits of y.

$$\int_0^1\left[\int_0^1 1\,dx\right]dy = \int_0^1 [x]_0^1\,dy = \int_0^1 1dy = 1$$

Thus, since the volume under the PDF is equal to 1, this is a well-defined joint PDF.

When we constructed the marginal PDF with discrete random variables, we saw that to calculate, for example, the probability that X was equal to a particular value, x, we added up all of the joint probabilities where $X = x$. For continuous variables, integration across all possible outcomes of y is analogous to adding up all of the probabilities where $X = x$. Thus, the marginal PDF, for X between 0 and 1, is equal to:

$$\begin{aligned} f_X(x) &= \int_{-\infty}^{\infty} f_{X,Y}(x,y)dy \\ &= \int_{-\infty}^{0} 0dy + \int_0^1 1dy + \int_1^{\infty} 0dy = 1 \end{aligned}$$

Note that since the joint PDF is equal to 0 for all values of X other than between 0 and 1, it follows that the PDF is also equal to 0 in those ranges. We can show that, because if we choose a value of $x < 0$ or $x > 0$, then $f_{X,Y}(x,y) = 0$, and $\int_{-\infty}^{\infty} 0dy = 0$:

$$f_X(x) = \begin{cases} 1, & 0 \le x \le 1 \\ 0, & \text{Otherwise} \end{cases}$$

Similarly, it is trivial to show, in this instance, that:

$$f_Y(y) = \begin{cases} 1, & 0 \le y \le 1 \\ 0, & \text{Otherwise} \end{cases}$$

In order to construct the conditional PDF, we are essentially asking the question about what the PDF looks like across a particular cross-section of the distribution, re-scaled so that the area under the curve is equal to 1. This is illustrated in Figure 8.28.

For example, as in Figure 8.28, we might be interested in the conditional PDF for the case where $Y = 0.5$. This would be equivalent to substituting $Y = 0.5$ into the joint PDF. However, this would only give us the shape of the conditional PDF, and not the magnitude.

Since this is only for a subset of Y, to construct the magnitude, we also need to re-scale the joint PDF to a range between 0 and 1 by dividing through by the probability density of Y taking the particular value (in this case 0.5).

So, to calculate the conditional distribution, conditioning that Y takes a particular value, y:

$$f_{(X|Y)}(x|Y = y) = \frac{f_{X,Y}(x,y)}{f_Y(y)} = \frac{1}{1} = 1$$

Of course, this will only be non-zero in the areas where the marginal probability density of X is non-zero, and it will be undefined for areas of the distribution where $f_Y(y) = 0$:

$$f_{(X|Y)}(x|Y = y) = \begin{cases} 1, & 0 \le x \le 1 \text{ and } 0 \le y \le 1 \\ 0, & \text{Otherwise} \end{cases}$$

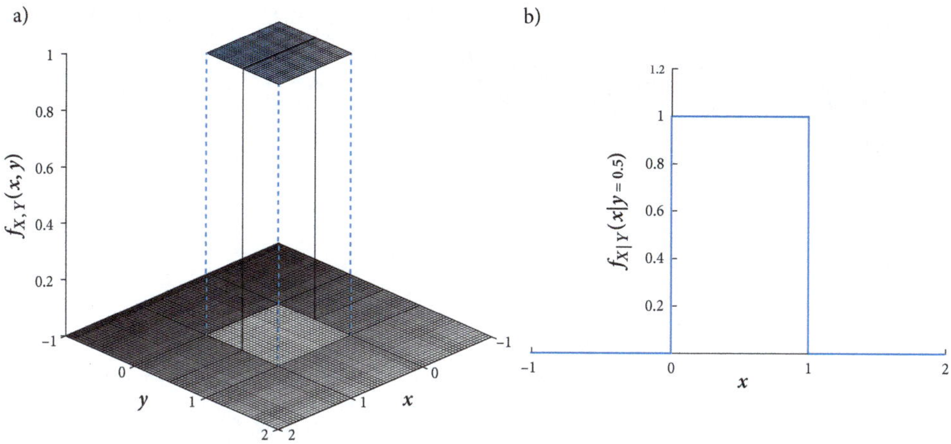

Figure 8.28 Constructing the conditional distribution.

The PDF of the conditional distribution is illustrated in panel b) of Figure 8.28. Reassuringly, this looks like the cross-section from the joint PDF, which is exactly as we would expect.

The other thing that we can note here is that the conditional and marginal distributions are the same. This means that X and Y are independent random variables.

Independent random variables

As with discrete variables, if the realization of a particular value of Y has no impact on the marginal PDF of X, then we can say that the two variables are independent. That is, if, for all values of X:

$$f_{Y|X}(y|X=x)=f_Y(y)$$

then the variables Y and X are said to be independent.

Summary of joint distributions		
	Discrete variables	Continuous variables
Joint density/distribution function	$P(X=x\cap Y=y)$	$f_{X,Y}(x,y)$
Total probability	$\sum_x\sum_y P(X=x\cap Y=y)=1$	$\int_{-\infty}^{\infty}\int_{-\infty}^{\infty} f_{X,Y}(x,y)dy\,dx=1$

(Continued)

Summary of joint distributions		
	Discrete variables	**Continuous variables**
Law of total probability (i.e. calculating marginal probabilities)	$P(X = x) = \sum_{y} P(X = x \cap Y = y)$ $P(Y = y) = \sum_{x} P(X = x \cap Y = y)$	$f_X(x) = \int_{-\infty}^{\infty} f_{X,Y}(x, y)dy$ $f_Y(y) = \int_{-\infty}^{\infty} f_{X,Y}(x, y)dx$
Conditional probabilities	$P(X = x \vert Y = y) = \frac{P(X = x \cap Y = y)}{P(Y = y)}$	$f_{(X\vert Y)}(x \vert Y = y) = \frac{f_{X,Y}(x, y)}{f_Y(y)}$
Independence	Two discrete random variables are independent if: $P(X = x \vert Y = y) = P(X = x)$ for all possible x, y	Two continuous random variables are independent if: $f_{X\vert Y}(x \vert Y = y) = f_X(x)$ for all possible x, y.

Summary

In this chapter, we have introduced continuous random variables. Continuous random variables are variables where the outcomes are on a continuum, rather than distinct separate outcomes. Because of this, we represent the distribution of continuous random variables using PDFs.

Any operation that we used for discrete random variables using a summation can be calculated for continuous random variables, with the adjustment that the summation is replaced by an integral.

Conditional Expectations and the Law of Iterated Expectations

9

Learning outcomes for this chapter

By the end of this chapter you will be able to:

- Calculate conditional expectations of continuous and discrete random variables based on the joint PDF or PMF
- Use the law of iterated expectations to calculate unconditional expectations
- Apply the law of iterated expectations to important statistical identities, such as calculating the expectation of a product of random variables
- Prove that when two random variables are independent, $E(XY) = E(X)E(Y)$

Mathematical tools

- Simple arithmetic
- Summations
- Integrations

Introduction

In previous chapters, we have introduced the idea of population averages, and also the idea of conditional probabilities for both discrete and continuous random variables. Conditional probability distributions relate to the probability distribution of one random variable, conditional on the value that another random variable takes.

However, if you can have conditional probability distributions, it also raises the question of whether you can have conditional expectations; that is, population averages, conditional on a particular characteristic. For instance, we might believe that average wages depend on whether an individual has been to university or not. A conditional expectation might be the average wages for individuals in the population, conditional that they have either

1. attended university, or
2. not attended university.

9.1 An introduction to conditional expectations

In 2016, the Institute for Fiscal Studies (IFS) provided estimates for the average wages for males and females, dependent on the subject in which they graduated.[1] We can treat these as estimates of the expected wages, conditional on the subjects that they studied. A subset of their estimates (in £000s) is presented below. The data is presented for earnings in 2011/12 and 2012/13, from students who began their study in 1999.

	Medicine	Engineering and Technology	Physical Sciences	Subjects Allied to Medicine	Mathematics and Computing	Biological Sciences	Veterinary and Agriculture
Average earnings (£000s)	45.5	28.0	25.6	23.0	24.7	22.2	18.9

We see figures like this in the news every day. However, these are effectively conditional expectations. Conditional on having studied Medicine at university (beginning in 1999), an individual's expected wage is equal to £45,500 per annum. Similarly, conditional on an individual having studied Mathematics or Computing, the expected wage is £24,700 per annum.

This provides an example of a conditional expectation, but we need to know how to calculate these conditional expectations from probability distributions. We have seen how to calculate an expected value for a population. However, in previous chapters, we have introduced the idea of a conditional probability—that is, the probability that a random variable (say, X) takes on a particular value (x), given that some other random variable Y takes on a particular value y.

Let's suppose that we are playing a two-player game. In this game, the score that player 1 gains is dependent on the score that player 2 gains, and the joint distribution of the scores is illustrated in Table 9.1. For simplicity, we'll denote player 1's score as X, and player 2's score as Y.

X and Y can take the possible outcomes of 5,10, and 20:

Table 9.1 Joint distribution of X and Y

$P(X = x \cap Y = y)$		Player 2, Y		
		5	**10**	**20**
Player 1, X	**5**	0.1	0.1	0
	10	0.2	0	0.2
	20	0.3	0.1	0

[1] J. Britton et al. (2016), 'How English Domiciled Graduate Earnings Vary with Gender, Institution Attended, Subject and Socio-Economic Background', IFS Working Paper W16/06.

Suppose that we want to find player 1's expected score, given that we've observed that player 2 has obtained a score of 10. That is, we wish to calculate $E(X|Y = 10)$. To calculate this, we can use the conditional probability distribution of X. That is, we can calculate: $P(X = 5|Y = 10), P(X = 10|Y = 10)$, and $P(X = 20|Y = 10)$, and then can use these conditional probabilities to calculate the conditional expectation.

We know that the (unconditional) expectation is calculated by finding the sum of the products of the outcomes and their respective probabilities. Similarly, the conditional expectation can be calculated by finding the sum of the products of the conditional probabilities and their respective outcomes:

$$E(X|Y = 10) = \sum_x P(X = x|Y = 10) \times x$$

KEY DEFINITION: CONDITIONAL EXPECTATION

A conditional expectation is the expectation of one variable conditional on the value that *another* variable takes. In the example in Section 9.1, when thinking about $E(X|Y = 10)$, we are restricting our population only to the cases when $Y = 10$, and then asking what the average score of X is for those games when $Y = 10$.

We could do the same with $E(X|Y = 5)$, which would ask what the (population) average value of X would be when $Y = 5$, or $E(X|Y = 20)$, which would ask what the (population) average value of X would be when $Y = 20$.

Where X and Y are independent random variables, knowing the value of Y tells you nothing about the value of X (and vice versa). As such, for independent random variables, the conditional expectation would always equal the unconditional expectation.

Of course, to find this, we will also need to construct the conditional distribution of X. We know that:

$$P(X = x|Y = y) = \frac{P(X = x \cap Y = y)}{P(Y = y)}$$

We have the **joint probabilities** above, but to construct the conditional probabilities, we will also need to find the **marginal probabilities** relating to Y. To do so, we will appeal to the law of total probability, which states that the marginal probability, $P(Y = y)$, is just equal to the sum of all of the joint probabilities where $Y = y$:

$$P(Y = y) = \sum_x P(X = x \cap Y = y)$$

This is equivalent to adding together all of the probabilities across each joint probability in a column within the joint probability distribution. Similarly, we can calculate the marginal probability distribution of X by adding together the joint probabilities within a row of the joint PDF (see Table 9.2).

Table 9.2 Joint and marginal probabilities of X and Y

$P(X = x \cap Y = y)$		Player 2, Y 5	10	20	Total
Player 1, X	5	0.1	0.1	0	0.2
	10	0.2	0	0.2	0.4
	20	0.3	0.1	0	0.4
	Total	0.6	0.2	0.2	1

So, having added together the joint probabilities, we have calculated the marginal probabilities relating to X and Y. For instance, the probability that $Y = 5$ is given as $P(Y = 5) = 0.6$. However, we are interested in the conditional expectation of X, given that $Y = 10$. Therefore, we need to divide the joint probabilities by the marginal probability. We know, from Table 9.2 that $P(Y = 10) = 0.2$, and so, we can calculate the conditional probabilities:

$$P(X = 5 | Y = 10) = \frac{P(X = 5 \cap Y = 10)}{P(Y = 10)} = \frac{0.1}{0.2} = 0.5$$
$$P(X = 10 | Y = 10) = \frac{P(X = 10 \cap Y = 10)}{P(Y = 10)} = \frac{0}{0.2} = 0$$
$$P(X = 20 | Y = 20) = \frac{P(X = 20 \cap Y = 10)}{P(Y = 10)} = \frac{0.1}{0.2} = 0.5$$

We could repeat the same process, conditioning on all of the possible values of Y, giving us the conditional distributions illustrated in Table 9.3.

Table 9.3 Distribution of conditional probabilities relating to X conditional on the value of Y

$P(X = x \| Y = y)$		Player 2, Y 5	10	20
Player 1, X	5	$\frac{0.1}{0.6} = \frac{1}{6}$	$\frac{0.1}{0.2} = 0.5$	0
	10	$\frac{0.2}{0.6} = \frac{1}{3}$	0	$\frac{0.2}{0.2} = 1$
	20	$\frac{0.3}{0.6} = \frac{1}{2}$	$\frac{0.1}{0.2} = 0.5$	0

Each element in Table 9.3 represents a conditional probability. For example, the top left element represents $P(X = 5 | Y = 5) = \frac{1}{6}$. We can use these probabilities to calculate the population average or expectation of X conditional on the value Y takes. So, if we wanted to calculate $E(X | Y = 10)$, we would weight the outcomes of X by the respective conditional probabilities:

$$\begin{aligned} E(X | Y = 10) &= \sum_x P(X = x | Y = 10) \times x \\ &= P(X = 5 | Y = 10) \times 5 + P(X = 10 | Y = 10) \times 10 \\ &\quad + P(X = 20 | Y = 10) \times 20 \\ &= 0.5 \times 5 + 0 \times 10 + 0.5 \times 20 = 12.5 \end{aligned}$$

So, in this game, if player 2 has a score of 10, the expected score for player 1 is 12.5. We can do the same for the other possible scores by player 2:

$$E(X\,|\,Y = 5) = \sum_x P(X = x\,|\,Y = 5) \times 5 = \frac{1}{6} \times 5 + \frac{1}{3} \times 10 + \frac{1}{2} \times 20 = \frac{85}{6} = 14.1667\,(4dp)$$

$$E(X\,|\,Y = 20) = \sum_x P(X = x\,|\,Y = 20) \times 20 = 0 \times 5 + 1 \times 10 + 0 \times 20 = 10$$

So, we can see that the conditional expectation of X changes, depending on the observed value of Y: $E(X\,|\,Y = 5) = \frac{85}{6}$, $E(X\,|\,Y = 10) = 12.5$, and $E(X\,|\,Y = 20) = 1$. In fact, as Y increases, the average score for X decreases. Immediately, this tells us that X and Y are not independent random variables, because as the value of Y changes, the changes in Y affect the likely or expected value of X.

Exercise

As an exercise, work through and construct the conditional expectations of Y given the values of X, and show that:

$E(Y\,|\,X = 5) = 7.5$

$E(Y\,|\,X = 10) = 12.5$

$E(Y\,|\,X = 20) = 6.25$

Returning to X, we can also use the marginal probabilities to calculate the overall expectation of X. We know (from Table 9.2) that $P(X = 5) = 0.2, P(X = 10) = 0.4$, and $P(X = 20) = 0.4$, so we can calculate the unconditional expectation of X as:

$$E(X) = \sum_x P(X = x) \times x = 0.2 \times 5 + 0.4 \times 10 + 0.4 \times 20 = 13$$

Again, we can see that $E(X)$ is not equal to the conditional expectations of X (which shouldn't be a surprise, as the conditional expectation changes according to the value that Y takes), indicating that X and Y are not independent, but there is an interesting relationship between the conditional expectations and the unconditional expectations.

From Table 9.2, we know that $P(Y = 5) = 0.6$. This means that Y takes on the value of 5 for 60 per cent of the time. Alternatively, we could think about the fact that when we consider the conditional expectation of X given that $Y = 5$ (i.e. $E(X\,|\,Y = 5)$, this is the average of X for 60 per cent of the population. Similarly, since $P(Y = 10) = 0.2$, then $E(X\,|\,Y = 10)$ represents the average of X for 20 per cent of the population, and since $P(Y = 20) = 0.2$, then $E(X\,|\,Y = 20)$ represents the average of X for the final 20 per cent of the population.

Since the expectation is a linear operator, this means that, if we wanted to calculate the overall expectation, we could simply find the weighted average of these conditional expectations, weighting each by the respective probabilities of Y:

$$\begin{aligned} E(X) &= P(Y = 5) \times E(X\,|\,Y = 5) + P(Y = 10) \times E(X\,|\,Y = 10) \\ &\quad + P(Y = 20) \times E(X\,|\,Y = 20) \\ &= 0.6 \times \frac{85}{6} + 0.2 \times 12.5 + 0.2 \times 10 = 8.5 + 2.5 + 2 = 13 \end{aligned}$$

This is an example of a rule known as the law of iterated expectations which we will discuss in more detail in Section 9.3.

A special case: When *X* and *Y* are independent random variables

Remember that two random variables are independent if knowing the outcome of one random variable tells you nothing about the outcome of the other random variable. Formally, two random variables X and Y are independent if the conditional probability distribution is equal to the marginal probability distribution for all possible outcomes of X and Y. More formally, the discrete random variables X and Y are independent if:

$$P(Y = y \mid X = x) = P(Y = y), \qquad \textit{for all } x \textit{ and } y$$
$$P(X = x \mid Y = y) = P(X = x), \qquad \textit{for all } x \textit{ and } y$$

Now, we know that the unconditional expectation of X can be calculated (for a discrete random variable) as:

$$E(X) = \sum_x P(X = x) \times x$$

Similarly, the conditional expectation of X, given a particular value of $Y = y$, can be calculated as:

$$E(X \mid y = y) = \sum_x P(X = x \mid Y = y) \times x$$

Now, if X and Y are independent random variables, then $P(X = x \mid Y = y) = P(X = x)$ for all values of x and y. As such, we can replace the conditional probability by the marginal probability:

$$\Rightarrow E(X \mid Y = y) = \sum_x P(X = x) \times x$$

However, this is just the same formula as $E(X)$, and as such, it must be the case that if X and Y are independent random variables then $E(X) = E(X \mid Y = y)$.

9.1.1 Continuous random variables

In this chapter, so far, we have only considered conditional expectations relating to discrete random variables. However, it is equally useful to consider conditional expectations using continuous random variables. We will use exactly the same methods, but where we used summations for discrete random variables, we will use integrals for continuous random variables.

Let's illustrate this with three worked examples.

Worked example 9.1: Calculating conditional expectations using continuous random variables

We can calculate conditional expectations for both discrete and continuous random variables (and even joint distributions where one dimension is continuous and the other dimension is discrete).

Let's suppose that we are interested in the population of a slightly strange country called Ecalpon. In Ecalpon, 45 per cent of the population attend university, and 55 per cent do not attend university. For those who attend university, their wages are equally, or uniformly, distributed between £30,000 and £40,000, with probability density $\frac{1}{10{,}000}$ between 30,000 and 40,000, and zero otherwise.

Similarly, for those who do not attend university, their wages are equally, or uniformly, distributed between £20,000 and £35,000, with probability density $\frac{1}{15{,}000}$ between 20,000 and 35,000, and zero otherwise.

What we have here are conditional distributions: conditional on having attended university, we know that individuals' wages will be between £30,000 and £40,000, whereas, for those who do not attend university, their wages will be between £20,000 and £35,000.

Let's define two random variables. U is a random variable that represents whether an individual has attended university or not. U will take the value 1 if an individual has attended university, and 0 otherwise:

$$U = \begin{cases} 1, & P(U = 1) = 0.45 \\ 0, & P(U = 0) = 0.55 \end{cases}$$

Our second random variable W will be the wages of individuals within the population, which we are treating as a continuous random variable. We are told that, conditional on attending university, W has a probability density of $\frac{1}{10{,}000}$ for W between 30,000 and 40,000, and 0 otherwise. Similarly, conditional on not attending university, W has a probability density of $\frac{1}{15{,}000}$ for W between 20,000 and 35,000, and 0 otherwise. We can write these down more formally, using the conditional probability density function (PDF), $f_{W|U}$:

$$f_{W|U}(w\,|\,U = 0) = \begin{cases} \dfrac{1}{15{,}000}, & 20{,}000 \le w \le 35{,}000 \\ 0, & \text{Otherwise} \end{cases}$$

$$f_{W|U}(w\,|\,U = 1) = \begin{cases} \dfrac{1}{10{,}000}, & 30{,}000 \le w \le 40{,}000 \\ 0, & \text{Otherwise} \end{cases}$$

We can use the conditional PDFs to also write down the conditional expectation. The only difference from our previous example is that, since W is a continuous random variable, rather than using a summation, we will use an integral:

$$\begin{aligned} E(W\,|\,U = 0) &= \int_{-\infty}^{\infty} f_{W|U}(w\,|\,U = 0) \times w dw \\ &= \int_{-\infty}^{20{,}000} 0 \times w dw + \int_{20{,}000}^{35{,}000} \frac{1}{15{,}000} \times w dw + \int_{35{,}000}^{\infty} 0 \times w dw \end{aligned}$$

Now, the first and last terms will just be zero (as we are integrating zero) and for the middle term we will raise the power of w by 1, and divide through by the new power:

$$= \left[\frac{w^2}{30{,}000}\right]_{20{,}000}^{35{,}000} = \frac{35{,}000^2 - 20{,}000^2}{30{,}000} = 27{,}500$$

So, in this population, the average wage for those who do not attend university is equal to £27,500. Similarly, we can calculate the average wage for those who do attend university:

$$E(W|U=1) = \int_{-\infty}^{\infty} f_{W|U}(w|U=1) \times wdw$$
$$= \int_{-\infty}^{30,000} 0 \times wdw + \int_{30,000}^{40,000} \frac{1}{10,000} \times wdw + \int_{40,000}^{\infty} 0 \times wdw$$

As before, the first and last terms will vanish, leaving us with:

$$= \left[\frac{w^2}{20,000}\right]_{30,000}^{40,000} = \frac{40,000^2 - 30,000^2}{20,000} = 35,000$$

So, we have an average wage for those who do attend university of £35,000. Formally, we can write:

$$E(W|U=0) = 27,500$$
$$E(W|U=1) = 35,000$$

Now, we know that 55 per cent of the population do not attend university ($U = 0$), and 45 per cent do attend ($U = 1$), and so $E(W|U = 0)$ represents the average wage across 55 per cent of the population, whilst $E(W|U = 1)$ represents the average wage across the other 45 per cent of the population.

As such, we can again calculate the overall average wage in the population by weighting these expected values by the probabilities relating to U. And so:

$$E(W) = P(U=0) \times E(W|U=0) + P(U=1) \times E(W|U=1)$$
$$= 0.55 \times 27,500 + 0.45 \times 35,000 = 30,875$$

So, the average wage in the population as a whole will be equal to £30,875. Again, we can conclude that in Ecalpon, attending university and the wages that individuals gain are not independent random variables, because the average wages differ across those who attend and those who do not attend.

Worked example 9.2: A further example using continuous random variables

Let's return to the example we saw in the previous chapter, of a simple pair of continuous random variables, X and Y, with the following PDF:

$$f_{X,Y}(x,y) = \begin{cases} 1, & 0 \le x \le 1, 0 \le y \le 1 \\ 0, & \text{Otherwise} \end{cases}$$

We want to find the conditional expectation of X given any particular value of Y. To calculate this, we will need to find the conditional distribution of X, which we know is calculated by dividing the joint distribution of X and Y by the marginal distribution of Y.

Remember that we calculate the marginal distribution of Y by integrating this PDF across the full range of X (w.r.t X). This is analogous to adding up all of the joint probabilities where Y takes a particular value.

So, we can find $f_Y(y) = \int_{-\infty}^{\infty} f_{X,Y}(x,y)dx$. We will need to consider three ranges, $x < 0, 0 \le x \le 1, x > 1$. However, in the first and the third of these ranges, the joint PDF is trivial to integrate (as it is equal to zero).

$$\begin{aligned} f_Y(y) &= \int_{-\infty}^{0} 0dx + \int_{0}^{1} 1dx + \int_{1}^{\infty} 0dx \\ &= [x]_0^1 = 1 \end{aligned}$$

This marginal PDF is only valid for $0 \le y \le 1$. For any other values of y, the joint PDF is always equal to zero, and so $f_Y(y) = \int_{-\infty}^{\infty} 0dx = 0$. As such, the marginal PDF of Y is given as:

$$f_Y(y) = \begin{cases} 1, & 0 \le y \le 1 \\ 0, & \text{Otherwise} \end{cases}$$

and equivalently, the conditional distribution of X given any particular value of Y is just equal to:

$$f_{X|Y}(x \mid y) = \frac{f_{X,Y}(x,y)}{f_Y(y)} = \frac{1}{1}, \quad 0 \le x \le 1, 0 \le y \le 1$$

So, the conditional PDF is given by:

$$f_{X|Y}(x \mid y) = \begin{cases} 1, & 0 \le x \le 1, \quad 0 \le y \le 1 \\ 0, & \text{Otherwise} \end{cases}$$

Similarly, we can illustrate the conditional distribution of X, conditioning that, say, $Y = 0.5$, as in Figure 9.1.

Using the same logic as in the previous examples, we can calculate the conditional expectation by replacing the PDF with the conditional PDF in the expectation formula. So, the conditional expectation of X will be:

$$E(X \mid Y = y) = \int_{-\infty}^{\infty} f_{X|Y}(x \mid y) \times x\,dx, \quad for\, 0 \le y \le 1$$

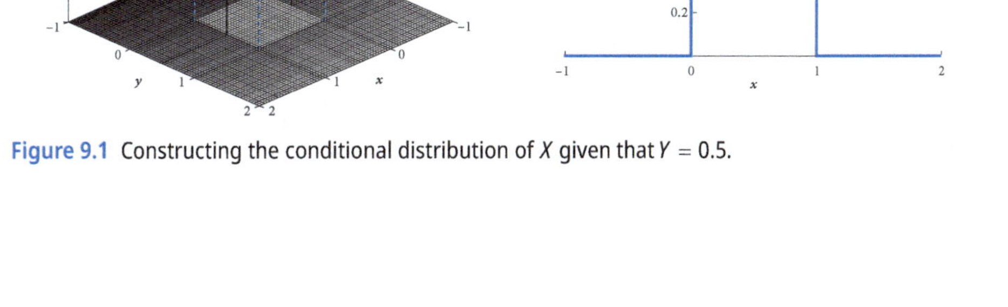

Figure 9.1 Constructing the conditional distribution of X given that $Y = 0.5$.

Substituting in the conditional PDF gives us:

$$\Rightarrow E(X\,|\,Y = y) = \int_{-\infty}^{0} 0 \times x + \int_{0}^{1} 1 \times x\,dx + \int_{1}^{\infty} 0 \times x\,dx$$
$$= \left[\frac{x^2}{2}\right]_0^1 = \frac{1}{2}$$

So, conditional on $Y = y$, $E(X\,|\,Y = y) = \frac{1}{2}$. Now, this value does not change as Y changes, and as such, we can conclude that X and Y must be independent random variables. This means that $E(X) = E(X \mid Y = y)$ for all possible values of y.

Worked example 9.3: A more difficult example

Let's consider a trickier example. In this final example, we will have a joint distribution of two random variables, W and Z, such that W and Z are both continuous random variables, and the variables are not independent. We wish to find the conditional expectation of Z given that $W = 0.5$

The joint PDF of W and Z is given by:

$$f_{W,Z}(w,z) = \begin{cases} 1.5(w^2 + z^2), & 0 \le w \le 1, \quad 0 \le z \le 1 \\ 0, & \text{Otherwise} \end{cases}$$

Before we carry out any calculations, because the joint PDF is equal to zero for all other values than for $0 \le w \le 1$ and $0 \le z \le 1$, the marginal and conditional distributions will also be equal to zero outside of these ranges. A visualization of the non-zero part of the distribution is illustrated in Figure 9.2.

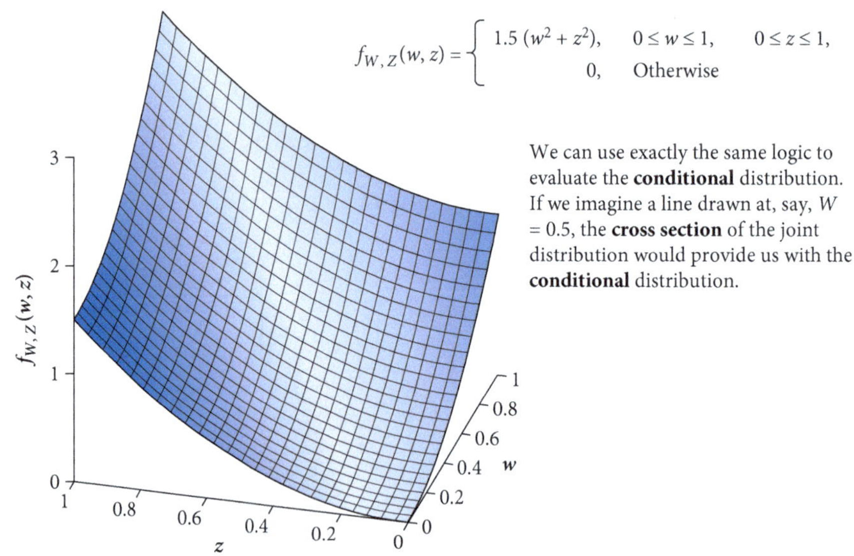

Figure 9.2 A joint distribution of two continuous random variables, Z and W.

To calculate the conditional expectation, we will first need to construct the conditional PDF of Z given W. To do this, we will first need to construct the marginal PDF of W, as:

$$f_{Z|W}(z|w) = \frac{f_{W,Z}}{f_W(w)}$$

The marginal PDF of W is calculated by integrating the joint PDF with respect to the other variable (Z) over the full range of Z, giving us:

$$f_W(w) = \int_{-\infty}^{\infty} f_{W,Z}(w,z)dz = \int_{-\infty}^{0} 0\ dz + \int_{0}^{1} 1.5(w^2 + z^2)dz + \int_{1}^{\infty} 0\ dz$$

Now, when we integrate the expression $w^2 + z^2$ with respect to z, the w is effectively just treated as a constant. As such, $\int w^2 dz = w^2 z$. Applying that to this example:

$$\Rightarrow f_W(w) = 0 + 1.5\left[w^2 z + \frac{z^3}{3}\right]_0^1 + 0$$

$$\Rightarrow f_W(w) = 1.5\left(w^2 + \frac{1}{3}\right), 0 \le w \le 1$$

Similarly, as before, since the joint PDF is equal to zero for all other possible values of w, then the marginal PDF will also equal zero for all other possible values of w.

So, we can construct the conditional PDF by dividing through the joint PDF by the marginal PDF:

$$f_{Z|W}(z|w) = \frac{f_{W,Z}(w,z)}{f_W(w)} = \frac{1.5(w^2 + z^2)}{1.5\left(w^2 + \frac{1}{3}\right)} = \frac{w^2 + z^2}{w^2 + \frac{1}{3}}, \quad 0 \le w \le 1, \quad 0 \le z \le 1$$

One thing that we can see, immediately, is that the conditional PDF is a function of w. This means that the PDF changes depending on the value of w, and as such, W and Z are not independent random variables.

Now, to find the conditional expectation of Z given $W = w$, we need to integrate the product of this conditional PDF with the outcomes of z:

$$E(Z|W = w) = \int_{-\infty}^{\infty} f_{Z|W}(z|w) \times z dz$$

Now, we are going to ignore the zero elements of the PDF, and only focus on the non-zero part, giving us:

$$\Rightarrow E(Z|W = w) = \int_0^1 \left(\frac{w^2 + z^2}{w^2 + \frac{1}{3}}\right) \times z\, dz$$

$$= \left(\frac{3}{3w^2 + 1}\right)\int_0^1 w^2 z + z^3 dz$$

Note that, because $\frac{1}{w^2+\frac{1}{3}}$ is only a function of w, we can treat it as a constant multiplier of all of the z-related terms, so we can take it outside of the integral. We have simplified the notation a little by rewriting this as $\frac{3}{3w^2+1}$.

Now, the integral is fairly straightforward to evaluate:

$$= \left(\frac{3}{3w^2+1}\right)\left[\frac{w^2 z^2}{2} + \frac{z^4}{4}\right]_0^1 = \left(\frac{3}{3w^2+1}\right)\left(\frac{w^2}{2} + \frac{1}{4}\right) = \frac{3}{4}\left(\frac{2w^2+1}{3w^2+1}\right)$$

So, if $w = 0.5$, we can calculate the expected value of Z conditional that $W = 0.5$ by substituting 0.5 in place of the w terms.

$$E(Z\,|\,W = 0.5) = \frac{3}{4}\left(\frac{2w^2+1}{3w^2+1}\right) = \frac{3}{4} \times \left(\frac{2\times 0.5^2+1}{3\times 0.5^2+1}\right) = \frac{9}{14} = 0.6429(4dp)$$

Similarly, we could substitute in $W = 1$:

$$E(Z\,|\,W = 1) = \frac{3}{4}\left(\frac{2w^2+1}{3w^2+1}\right) = \frac{3}{4}\left(\frac{2\times 1+1}{3\times 1+1}\right) = \frac{9}{16} = 0.5625$$

As you can see, the expected value of Z changes depending on the value of W. This indicates that W and Z are certainly not independent random variables. In fact, because we have a nice functional form of $E(Z\,|\,W = w)$, we can plot this expectation out for different values of w.

Figure 9.3 shows that the conditional expectation of Z is decreasing as W increases. This does not mean that whenever W is large, Z must be small, but instead when W is large (i.e. close to 1), it means that on average Z will be smaller than it would be when W is small (i.e. close to zero).

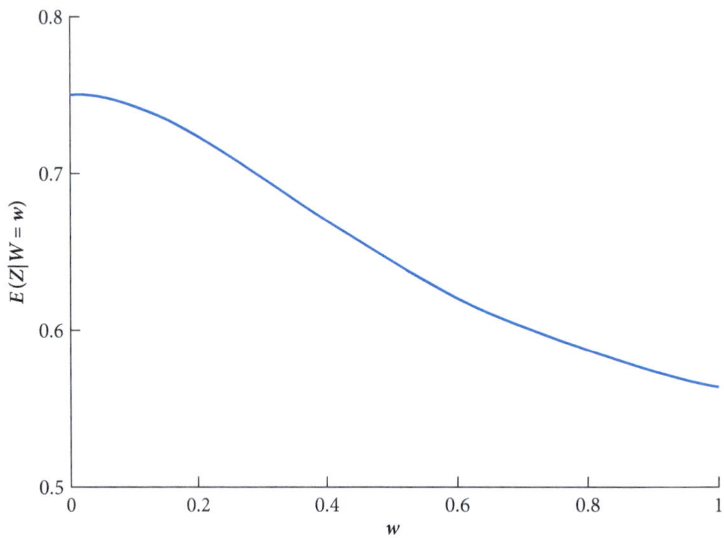

Figure 9.3 Conditional expectation of Z given $W = w$.

9.2 The law of iterated expectations

Let's return to the data we saw at the beginning of this chapter. The IFS provided estimates for average wages of graduates, dependent on the subject in which they graduated.[2] The authors used data from the Student Loans Company, representing 10 per cent of students who took out student loans in 1999, and evaluated their earnings in the 2012/13 tax year.

The data, illustrated in Table 9.4, shows earnings of graduates from STEMM (Science, Technology, Engineering, Mathematics, and Medicine) related subjects. For the sake of this example, we are treating our population as students who studied STEMM subjects, and are represented in the data used by the IFS.

Table 9.4 Average earnings, and proportion of the population, derived from Britton et al. (2016)

	Medicine	Engineering and Technology	Physical Sciences	Subjects Allied to Medicine	Mathematics and Computing	Biological Sciences	Veterinary and Agriculture
Average earnings (£000s)	45.5	28.0	25.6	23.0	24.7	22.2	18.9
Proportion of population	6.2%	13.0%	12.8%	19.0%	29.0%	16.6%	3.4%

Whilst these are all conditional averages, we can use these conditional averages to calculate the average earnings within the population as a whole.[3] We know from the data that graduates in Medicine make up 6.2 per cent of the population of STEMM graduates. Similarly, we know that, conditional on having studied Medicine, the average earnings in 2012/13 was £45,500. What we can do, to calculate the overall average of earnings within the population of STEMM graduates, is to find the weighted average of all of these conditional averages, weighting each of the average earnings by the proportion within the population; that is, the weight for Medicine would be equal to $0.062 = \frac{6.2}{100}$:

$$\begin{aligned} &= 0.062 \times 45.4 + 0.13 \times 28.0 + 0.128 \times 25.6 + 0.19 \times 23.0 + 0.29 \times 24.7 \\ &\quad + 0.166 \times 22.2 + 0.034 \times 18.9 \\ &= 25.5986 \end{aligned}$$

This weighted average tells us the overall average within the population of STEMM graduates, indicating that, on average, STEMM graduates who began their degrees in 1999 were earning by 2012/13 on average £25,598.60 per year.

[2] J. Britton, et al. (2016), 'How English Domiciled Graduate Earnings Vary with Gender, Institution Attended, Subject and Socio-economic Background', IFS Working Paper W16/06.

[3] Remember that this is a very carefully defined population, as only consisting of graduates from STEMM subjects, having attended university in 1999, and part of the 10 per cent sample used by the IFS.

What we have effectively done here is to weight the set of conditional expectations by their respective probabilities to calculate the overall expectation. If, in this example, we treat W as a random variable representing earnings, and Z as a second random variable representing subject studied, we know, for example, that:

$$E(W \mid Z = Medicine) = 45.5$$

We have calculated the overall $E(W)$ by weighting each of the conditional expectations by the probability of a (randomly chosen) individual studying each subject. This probability is equivalent to the proportion of the population. So, our overall $E(W)$ is calculated as the sum of the products of the conditional expectation of wages, for each subject ($E(W \mid Z = z)$), multiplied by the probability of studying each subject $P(Z = z)$:

$$E(W) = \sum_z E(W \mid Z = z) \times P(Z = z)$$

What we have defined here is what is known as the law of iterated expectations.

Important notation for the law of iterated expectations

When we take the expectation of a (discrete) random variable, we find the sum of products of the outcomes, multiplied by their respective probabilities:

$$E(W) = \sum_w w \times P(W = w)$$

In the example in Section 9.2, we have seen that we can also calculate $E(W)$ by calculating the weighted average of the conditional expectations, weighted by the relevant probabilities:

$$E(W) = \sum_z E(W \mid Z = z) \times P(Z = z)$$

These two expressions look very similar—in both, we are weighting outcomes by probabilities, but in the second case, we are effectively finding the expectation of a set of conditional expectations.

We can use a separate notation to denote the law of iterated expectations, such that:

$$E(W) = E_Z[E(W \mid Z = z)] = \sum_z E(W \mid Z = z) \times P(Z = z)$$

The E_Z term indicates that we are taking the expectation over z. That is, we are taking the term inside the brackets, and considering every possible $E(W \mid Z = z)$—e.g. if Z can take the values 1, 2, 3 then we would consider $E(W \mid Z = 1), E(W \mid Z = 2), E(W \mid Z = 3)$ and weight each of these conditional expectations by the probability of each value of z.

We could use this notation to write down the original expectation calculating we saw:

$$E(W) = E_W(w) = \sum_w w \times P(W = w)$$

The E_W term indicates that we are taking the expectation over all possible values of w—so we will weight every possible value of w (the term inside the brackets) by the probability of each possible value of w.

This rule is known as the law of iterated expectations as we are (effectively) taking expectations of an expectation. If we wish to find the expectation of wages in the population, we take the expectation of the conditional expectations, weighting each conditional expectation by the probability of each value that we are conditioning on.

$$E(W) = E_Z(E(W \mid Z = z))$$

KEY DEFINITION: THE LAW OF ITERATED EXPECTATIONS

The law of iterated expectations states that the (unconditional) expectation of a random variable X can be calculated based upon the conditional expectation of X given the outcomes of some other random variable Y by weighting each of the conditional expectations by the respective probabilities of Y.

More formally, the expectation of X is equal to the expectation over all possible values of Y of the conditional expectation of X given Y:

$$E(X) = E_Y[E(X \mid Y = y)]$$

Of course, the key weakness with the law of iterated expectations is that, to apply it, you need to know both the conditional expectations of the random variable, given any possible outcome of the second random variable, and also the probability distribution of that second random variable. As you will see in Section 9.4, the law of iterated expectations allows us to evaluate sometimes very complicated expressions.

Worked example 9.4: Simple example of the law of iterated expectations

Mathematically, the law of iterated expectations often confuses students, so it's often easier to visualize what is going on through a numerical example.

Let's suppose that we have two random variables X and Y. We do not know the joint distribution of X and Y, but we do know the following:

1. We know the marginal distribution of Y.

Y takes on three possible outcomes, and the PDF of Y is given by:

$$Y = \begin{cases} 1, & P(Y = 1) = \dfrac{1}{6} \\ 2, & P(Y = 2) = \dfrac{1}{2} \\ 3, & P(Y = 3) = \dfrac{1}{3} \end{cases}$$

2. We also know the conditional expectations of X, given each of the possible values of Y:

$$E(X \mid Y = 1) = -12$$
$$E(X \mid Y = 2) = 24$$
$$E(X \mid Y = 3) = 0$$

From this information, we want to calculate the unconditional expectation of X. That is, we want to calculate the population average of X. To do this, we can use the law of iterated expectations:

$$E(X) = E_Y[E(X|Y = y)]$$

Remember, what the E_Y notation means is that we are going to substitute in each of the values of Y, and weight each of these by the respective probabilities associated with those values of Y. This is what is known as taking the expectation over all possible values of Y.

So, applying the law of iterated expectations to this example:

$$E(X) = E_Y[E(X|Y = y)] = \sum_y P(Y = y) \times E(X|Y = y)$$

Substituting in the values of Y gives us:

$$\begin{aligned} E(X) &= P(Y = 1) \times E(X|Y = 1) + P(Y = 2) \times E(X|Y = 2) + P(Y = 3) \times E(X|Y = 3) \\ &= \frac{1}{6} \times (-12) + \frac{1}{2} \times 24 + \frac{1}{3} \times 0 = \frac{60}{6} = 10 \end{aligned}$$

This tells us that the population average or expectation of X is equal to 10. This is a very powerful result, because we know very little about the random variable X. We don't know the outcomes of X, and similarly, we don't know any probabilities relating to X. All that we know is the set of conditional expectations of X.

This is just like the case of the average earnings for graduates from different subjects we saw in Section 9.3. We did not know the distribution of earnings within the population, but because we knew the average of earnings for different graduates, we could still calculate the average earnings of STEMM graduates more generally.

Worked example 9.5: Applying the law of iterated expectations with a continuous random variable

In the previous example, we knew the conditional expectation of X, conditional on a discrete random variable, Y. However, we can also apply this to a case where we know the conditional expectation of (the same) X based upon a continuous random variable, Z.

We are told that the conditional expectation of X is equal to $E(X \mid Z = z) = 2z + 4$. We also know that Z has a PDF, $f_Z(z)$, such that:

$$f_Z(z) = \begin{cases} \frac{1}{6}, & 0 \leq z \leq 6 \\ 0, & \text{Otherwise} \end{cases}$$

Now, as before, we will apply the law of iterated expectation to calculate the expectation of X. This time, we will take the expectation over all possible values of z:

$$E(X) = E_Z[E(X|Z = z)]$$

The only difference between this example and the previous example is that, rather than finding the sum of the product of the conditional expectations with the respective probabilities of z, because Z is a continuous random variable, we will need to integrate the product of the conditional expectations with the PDF:

$$E(X) = E_Z[E(X|Z = z)] = \int_z E(X|Z = z) \times f_Z(z)dz$$

Now, since $f_Z(z) = 0$ for $z < 0$ and $z > 6$, this integral will also be equal to zero in this range, so let's only consider the domain where $f_Z(z) \neq 0$ (i.e. $0 \leq z \leq 6$):

$$= \int_0^6 \frac{1}{6} \times (2z + 4)\, dz = \frac{1}{6} \times [z^2 + 4z]_0^6 = \frac{1}{6} \times [36 + 24] = \frac{60}{6} = 10$$

Having used this alternative route, we have gained the same expected value for X.

9.3 Application of the law of iterated expectations—Evaluating expectations of products of random variables

The law of iterated expectations is incredibly useful, as we can use it to prove relationships relating to products and ratios of random variables.

For example, earlier in this book, we stated that generally $E(XY) \neq E(X)E(Y)$. It is often important to be able to evaluate these sorts of expectations, without knowing the joint distribution of X and Y, and under certain circumstances, the law of iterated expectations is very useful, as it provides us with a mechanism to evaluate these sort of expectations.

Remember, for a single random variable, X, if we know the conditional expectation of X given any outcome of a second random variable, Y, we can calculate the overall expectation of X by weighting all of the conditional expectations by the respective probabilities of Y. More formally, we might say that the expectation of X is equal to the expectation over all possible values of Y of the conditional expectation of X given Y:

$$E(X) = E_Y[E(X|Y = y)]$$

We can apply the same logic to calculating the expectation of XY. The product XY is also a random variable, and should we know the conditional expectation of XY, given all of the possible values of Y or all of the possible values of X, we could write that:

$$E(XY) = E_Y[E(XY|Y = y)]$$

or

$$E(XY) = E_X[E(XY|X = x)]$$

Remember that the E_Y notation simply means that we are effectively taking each of the possible values of Y in turn, and substituting them into the conditional expectation, and weighting each of the conditional expectations by the respective probabilities of Y.

Aside: Rules of conditional expectations

All of the rules relating to expectations that we saw earlier in this book also apply to conditional expectations. So for instance, if you multiply a random variable X by a constant, a, then the conditional expectation of aX, given some value of Y, will just be:

$$E(aX \mid Y = y) = aE(X \mid Y = y)$$

This is helpful when evaluating the conditional expectation of XY. Suppose that we are interested in the conditional expectation of XY, given that $Y = 2$. We can write the conditional expectation as:

$$E(XY \mid Y = 2)$$

However, by conditioning that $Y = 2$, we are effectively setting the random variable Y to be equal to 2. As such, we can rewrite this conditional expectation as:

$$E(XY \mid Y = 2) = E(2X \mid Y = 2)$$

However, now we are just looking at the conditional expectation of $2X$, where 2 is just a constant multiplier. As such, we can take it outside of the expectation:

$$\Rightarrow E(XY \mid Y = 2) = E(2X \mid Y = 2) = 2E(X \mid Y = 2)$$

This property will be very helpful when trying to evaluate the unconditional expectation of XY.

Let's return to the law of iterated expectations to evaluate $E(XY)$.We know that we can find this expectation by taking the expectation over all possible values of Y of the conditional expectation of XY given each possible value of Y:

$$E(XY) = E_Y[E(XY \mid Y = y)]$$

We can begin our analysis by just thinking about the conditional expectation (inside the square brackets), $E(XY \mid Y = y)$. We are conditioning that the random variable Y is taking a particular value y—this is just equivalent to conditioning that $Y = 2$ in the previous example, but, by setting $Y = y$, we are considering a general case:

$$E(XY \mid Y = y) = E(Xy \mid Y = y)$$

Since y is a constant we have conditioned, within this conditional expectation, we have effectively multiplied the random variable X by a constant y, and as such, we can take this outside of the conditional expectation:

$$\Rightarrow E(XY \mid Y = y) = yE(X \mid Y = y)$$

Now, applying the law of iterated expectations, this means that we can rewrite the unconditional expectation of XY as:

$$E(XY) = E_Y[yE(X \mid Y = y)]$$

That is, to calculate the expectation of XY, if we know the conditional expectation of X, and the probability distribution of Y, we can weight $y \times E(X \mid Y = y)$ by the respective probabilities of y.

Worked example 9.6: Example of calculating $E(XY)$

Let's return to the example we saw in Section 9.3.1. In this example, we know the probability distribution of Y and the conditional expectations of X. We can use these to calculate the unconditional expectation of XY.

1. We know the marginal distribution of Y

   Y takes on three possible outcomes, and the PDF of Y is given by:

$$Y = \begin{cases} 1, & P(Y = 1) = \frac{1}{6} \\ 2, & P(Y = 2) = \frac{1}{2} \\ 3, & P(Y = 3) = \frac{1}{3} \end{cases}$$

2. We also know the conditional expectations of X, given each of the possible values of Y:

$$E(X \mid Y = 1) = -12$$
$$E(X \mid Y = 2) = 24$$
$$E(X \mid Y = 3) = 0$$

Now, we know from Section 9.4 that $E(XY) = E_Y[yE(X \mid Y = y)]$. This means that we can consider the product of all of the outcomes of y multiplied by the conditional expectation of X, and then weight each of these products by the respective probabilities of y:

$$E(XY) = E_Y[yE(X \mid Y = y)] = \sum_y y \times E(X \mid Y = y) \times P(Y = y)$$

Substituting in $Y = 1$, $Y = 2$, and $Y = 3$ gives us:

$$= 1 \times (-12) \times \frac{1}{6} + 2 \times 24 \times \frac{1}{2} + 3 \times 0 \times \frac{1}{3} = 22$$

So, using this method, the expectation of the product of X and Y is equal to 22.

9.4 When two random variables are independent $E(XY) = E(X) \times E(Y)$

We said, earlier in this book, that generally, $E(XY) \neq E(X) \times E(Y)$. However, when X and Y are independent random variables, it turns out that we can calculate $E(XY)$ by multiplying together the two unconditional expectations. To prove this relationship, we are going to apply the law of iterated expectations.

We are interested in evaluating $E(XY)$ when X and Y are independent random variables. We saw, earlier in this chapter, that if two random variables are independent, then:

$$E(X \mid Y = y) = E(X), \text{ for } \textit{all } y$$
$$E(Y \mid X = x) = E(Y), \text{ for } \textit{all } x$$

Now, we saw in Section 9.4 that we can use the law of iterated expectations to evaluate $E(XY)$ as:

$$E(XY) = E_Y[E(XY \mid Y = y)]$$

Now, as before, within the square brackets, the conditional expectation $E(XY \mid Y = y)$ is treating $Y = y$ as a constant. As such, we can rewrite the expectation of XY as:

$$E(XY) = E_Y[E(Xy \mid Y = y)] = E_Y[y \times E(X \mid Y = y)]$$

Now, in this example, since X and Y are independent random variables, it follows that $E(X \mid Y = y) = E(X)$. The expectation of a random variable is itself a constant. The expectation is a measure of the population, and for a given population, that expectation does not vary. As such, we can treat the expectation of X as a constant multiplier and take it outside of the expectation:

$$\Rightarrow E(XY) = E_Y[y \times E(X \mid Y = y)] = E_Y[y \times E(X)] = E(X) \times E_Y[y]$$

Now, we are left with $E(X)$ multiplied by $E_Y[y]$. This is taking the expectation over all possible values that y could take. If Y is a discrete random variable, then $E_Y[y]$ would mean that we would take each of the possible outcomes of Y, and multiply them by the respective probability:

$$E_Y[y] = \sum_y P(Y = y) \times y$$

However, this formula should look familiar, as it is just the formula for the expectation of Y. That is:

$$E_Y[y] = E(Y)$$

As such, we can rewrite the expectation of XY as:

$$E(XY) = E_Y[y \times E(X \mid Y = y)] = E_Y[y \times E(X)] = E(X) \times E_Y[y] = E(X) \times E(Y)$$

Therefore, when X and Y are independent random variables, it follows that $E(XY) = E(X) \times E(Y)$.

Summary

Conditional expectations tell us the population average for individuals within a subgroup of a population with a particular characteristic. We started the chapter by considering average earnings for STEMM graduates who studied different subjects; each of those averages was a conditional average. The average earnings of STEMM graduates, conditional upon having enrolled in a Medicine degree in 1999, was £45,500 in the 2012/13 financial year.

These sorts of conditional expectations are useful for a number of reasons: they tell us the characteristics of different subsets of the population, but also can be very useful when it comes to evaluating the overall expectation of the population as a whole.

We have developed a new tool known as the law of iterated expectations in this chapter. This is useful in that it allows us to calculate expectations based upon conditional expectation. The law of iterated expectations is also a very important tool in statistics.

In coming chapters, we will start to develop the idea of using estimators to construct estimates of population characteristics (such as expectations). One of the questions we will need to ask is whether the estimator is a 'good' estimator or not. One of the tools we will use to evaluate this is the law of iterated expectations.

KEY DEFINITIONS

The conditional expectation of a random variable X is defined as the population average (or expectation) of X conditional on the outcome of some, second, random variable. For example:

$E(X|Y=2)$ indicates the conditional expectation of X given that $Y=2$

If we know the conditional expectations of a random variable X, we can use the law of iterated expectations to calculate the unconditional expectation of X:

$$E(X) = E_Y[E(X|Y=y)]$$

This notation means that:

E_Y indicates that we are taking the expectation over all possible values of Y of
$[E(X|Y=y)]$ the conditional expectation of X given $Y=y$

In practical terms, this means that we would find the weighted average of all of the conditional expectations, weighted by the relevant probabilities of the outcomes of Y. So:

$$E(X) = E_Y[E(X|Y=y)] = \sum_y P(Y=y) \times E(X|Y=y)$$

Properties of independent random variables

When two discrete random variables, X and Y, are independent, it automatically follows that:

$$P(X=x|Y=y) = P(X=x)$$
$$P(Y=y|X=x) = P(Y=y)$$
$$E(X|Y=y) = E(X),\ E(Y|X=x) = E(Y)$$
$$E(XY) = E(X)E(Y)$$

These properties only hold for independent random variables. In general, $E(XY) \neq E(X)E(Y)$.

Shapes of Distributions: Variation, Skew, and Kurtosis

10

Learning outcomes for this chapter

By the end of this chapter you will be able to:

- Calculate percentiles and the interquartile range, and be able to visualize these through box and whisker diagrams
- Calculate the variance of a random variable, and use these figures to compare the variability of different random variables
- Apply Chebyshev's inequality to provide an estimate of the maximum size of the tails
- Calculate the skew of a random variable
- Calculate the kurtosis of a variable
- Use statistical software to calculate the skew and kurtosis from a sample of data

Mathematical tools

- Simple arithmetic
- Summations
- Integrations

Introduction

In the previous chapters, we have examined measures of central tendency—that is, we have only examined different ways of measuring the middle of the data. This does not tell us anything about the overall shape of the data.

For example, when individuals are making decisions about what assets to purchase within a pension fund, they may have the choice between two assets, each of which has, on average, a 3 per cent return. However, the two assets may have different levels of risk: one asset (e.g. government bonds) may generate returns of 3 per cent with certainty, whilst the other asset (e.g. a risky share) might generate returns of 13 per cent with probability $\frac{1}{2}$, and also generate losses of 7 per cent, also with probability $\frac{1}{2}$.

Both of these assets have the same expected return, but the second is much riskier. If the investor is close to retirement, they may wish to invest in the less risky investment, as they do not wish to risk losing a big proportion of their savings. If the investor is a long way from retirement, they may be willing to take the risk, with the hope of gaining the higher level of return.

In this chapter, we will introduce some measures of variation. We will begin with simple measures of variation (including the interquartile range), and will then introduce standardized measures of variation, including the variance and the standard deviation.

10.1 Percentiles and the interquartile range

The simplest form of measure of dispersion of the data is the overall range of the data—that is, the difference between the largest and the smallest observation. However, if there are outliers in the data (i.e. a very few number of observations that lie a long way away from the main body of the data), this can cause the range to be unrepresentative of the overall trend in the data.

In Chapter 8, we introduced the idea of percentiles of a distribution. The kth percentile is the value below which k per cent of the observations lie. A simple measure of the spread of data within the population (or sample) is to consider the distance between the lowest 25 per cent of the population and the highest 25 per cent of the population—that is, the distance between the lowest quartile and the highest quartile of the distribution. This is known as the interquartile range. The interquartile range is generally a better measure of the spread of the data than simply looking at the overall spread, or range, of the data, because it is much less likely to be affected by outliers.

To illustrate this, let's consider the data on wages from the 2019 UK Labour Force Survey that we previously saw in Chapter 8.[1] Remember that this data represents a sample of 200 full-time female workers aged 25–45. The distribution of the data is represented in Figure 10.1. This frequency histogram shows the number of individuals within the sample who have weekly earnings between each of the values—for example, there are 66 individuals within the data with weekly earnings between £400 and £600.

There are 200 observations within the data, so if we wanted to find the median, we would need to sort the data from the smallest to the largest observation, and find the middle value. To find the rank of the median, we can apply the following formula:

$$\text{Rank of } k\text{th percentile} = \frac{k}{100} \times (n + 1)$$

In the case of the median, we'd be looking for the 50th percentile, so based on $n = 200$ observations, we would need to find the $\frac{50}{100} \times 201 = 100.5$th largest observation. We know from Figure 10.1 that the 100th and 101st observations (when ranked from smallest to largest)

[1] This data is available to download as Weekly Wages.xlsx from Datasets and Exercises at the end of this chapter.

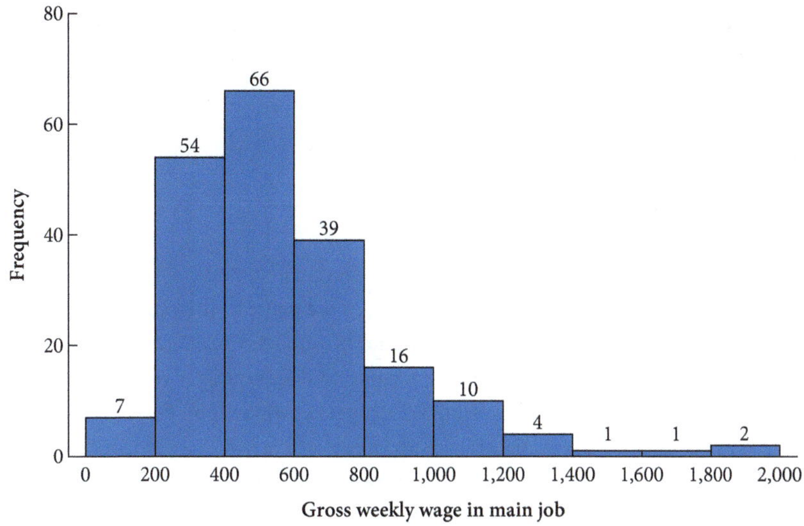

Figure 10.1 Histogram of earnings from (random sample) of 200 female full-time workers aged 25–45 from the 2019 UK Labour Force Survey.

will lie in the range between 400 and 600. If you look at the data more closely (as illustrated in Figure 10.2), you can see that the 100th ranked observation is £519, and the 101st is £526. As such, the median would be halfway in between £519 and £526, giving a median (or 50th percentile) of £522.50.

However, this is only a measure of the middle of the data. What about the spread of the data? One way we can measure the spread is through the interquartile range. That is, the difference between the 25th percentile and the 75th percentile.

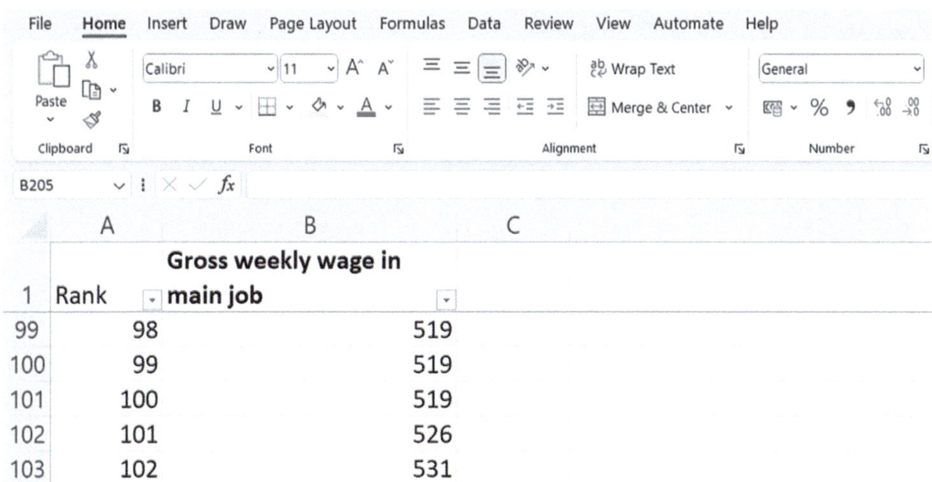

	A	B	C
1	Rank	Gross weekly wage in main job	
99	98	519	
100	99	519	
101	100	519	
102	101	526	
103	102	531	

Figure 10.2 Extract from LFS wage data, with rank illustrated.

In a sample, we can calculate the observation number we need to look at to find the kth percentile by considering $(n + 1) \times \frac{k}{100}$, where n is the number of observations in the sample:

$$\text{Rank of } p_{25} = 0.25 \times (100 + 1) = 0.25 \times 101 = 50.25$$
$$\text{Rank of } p_{75} = 0.75 \times (200 + 1) = 0.75 \times 201 = 150.75$$

So the 25th percentile will be equivalent to the 50.25th observation, and the 75th percentile will be equivalent to the 150.75th observation.

Using the data from the UK LFS sample, illustrated in Figure 10.3, the 50th observation is £365, and the 51st observation is £369. To find p_{25}, we want to find the observation ranked 50.25—that is, we will want to find the value that is a quarter (i.e. 0.25) of the way between the 50th and the 51st observation. Finding a value that is a quarter of the way between 365 and 369 gives us a value of £366. That is, the 25th percentile will be £366.

Similarly, for the 75th percentile, the 150th observation is 676, and the 151st is £692. To find the 75th percentile, we want the 150.75th ranked observation, so we consider the outcome that is 75 per cent of the way between the 150th and 151st observation. In this case, that will be £688.

The interquartile range for the data is then the difference between p_{75} and p_{25}. So, in the previous example, we saw that $p_{75} = 688$ and $p_{25} = 366$. Thus the interquartile range (IQR) is equal to £322.

$$IQR = p_{75} - p_{25} = 688 - 366 = 322$$

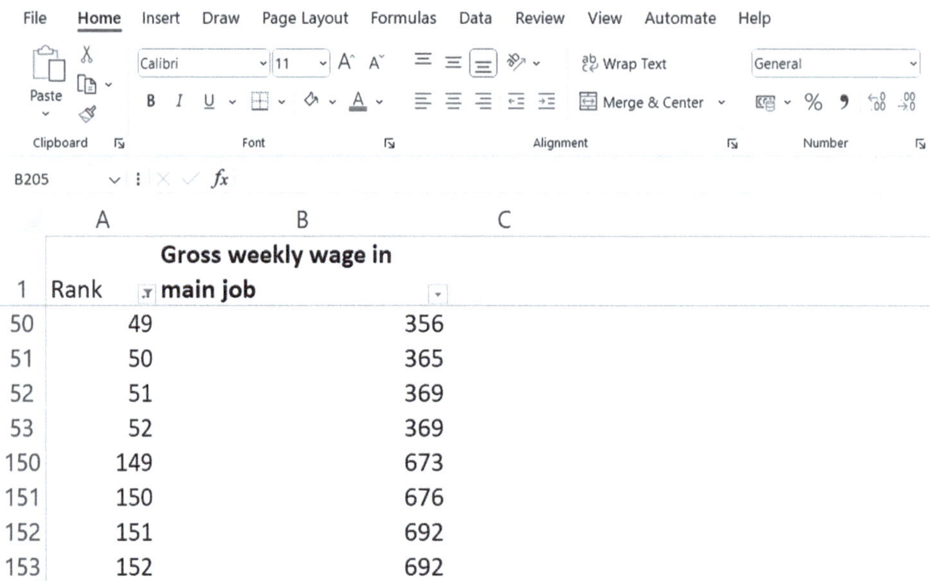

	A	B
1	Rank	Gross weekly wage in main job
50	49	356
51	50	365
52	51	369
53	52	369
150	149	673
151	150	676
152	151	692
153	152	692

Figure 10.3 Extract of data from the UK LFS to calculate the 25th and 75th percentiles.

10.1.1 Box and whisker diagrams

To make data easy to interpret, statisticians will often take advantage of graphical representations. In Figure 10.1, we saw the wages data represented in a frequency histogram. Alongside this, we can provide a simplified illustration of the shape of the data using a box and whisker diagram.

A box and whisker diagram will represent the median with a line, and the 'box' element will be bounded by the lower and upper quartiles. The 'whiskers' of the box and whisker diagram will illustrate the overall range of the data. Outliers (defined as being more than 1.5 times the interquartile range above p_{75}, or below p_{25}) are illustrated with dots.

The distribution of data from the Weekly Wages data set is illustrated in Figure 10.4. As before, the upper quartile is equal to £688, whilst the lower quartile is equal to £366. Of the 200 observations, we can also see that seven are defined as 'outliers'.

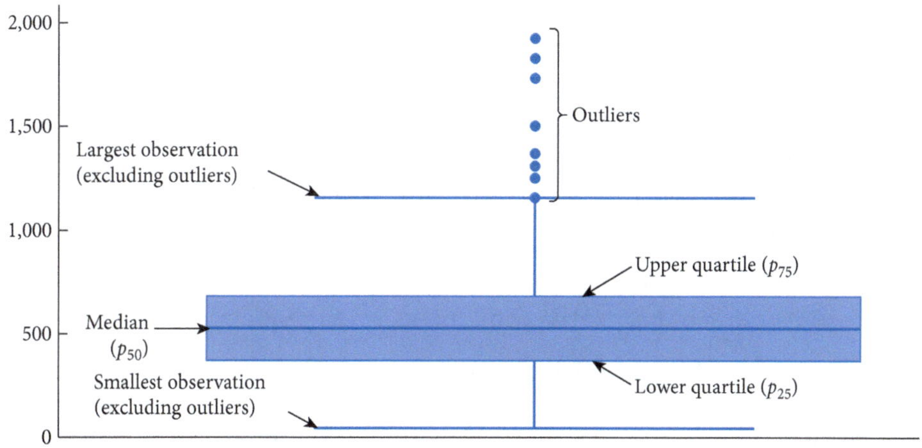

Figure 10.4 Box and whisker diagram representing earnings data from the UK LFS for female full-time workers aged 25–45.

That is, mathematically, they are more than 1.5 times the interquartile range above the upper quartile. Outliers are simply observations that are outside the main trend of the data, which may cause calculations (such as sample means) to be inappropriately pulled upwards (or downwards, depending on the direction of the outliers). Box and whisker diagrams are particularly useful when comparing data sets, as any number of samples (or populations) can be represented on the same set of axes. For example, we could plot the earnings of male and female full-time workers on the same set of axes to compare the distribution of earnings for male and female workers. Again, based upon a random sample of 200 observations of female workers and 200 observations of male workers from the UK Labour Force Survey, Figure 10.5 shows the distribution of male and female weekly earnings.[2]

[2] You can replicate this figure using the Excel data set Male and Female Weekly Wages.xlsx, available to download from Data sets and exercises at the end of this chapter.

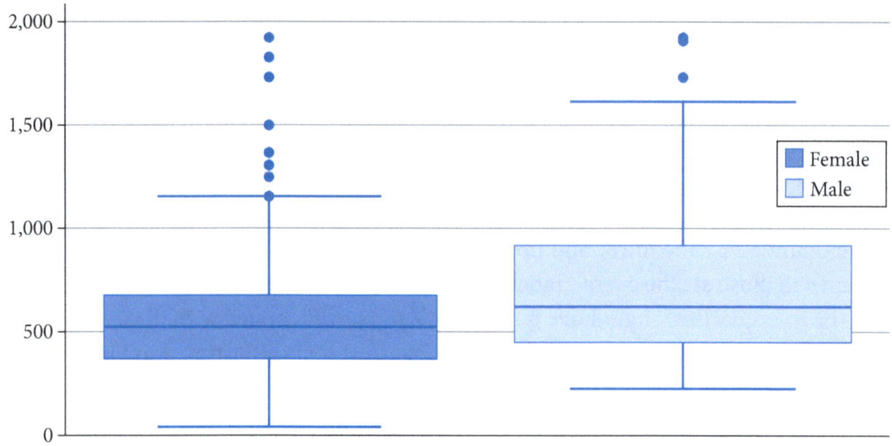

Figure 10.5 Comparing the distribution of male and female earnings (Source: UK Labour Force Survey).

Figure 10.5 allows us to compare both average earnings and the spread of the data. The median earnings are higher for male workers in this data set. Similarly, both the 25th and 75th percentiles are higher for male workers compared with female workers, and the overall spread of data is wider for male workers, as indicated by a higher interquartile range.

10.1.2 Application of percentiles and measuring inequality

Economists are often interested in measuring the level of inequality within a given country. This provides a measure of how equal (or unequal) income or wealth is within a country. In a country with a very unequal income distribution, there may be some individuals who live in luxury whilst there are others who live in abject poverty.

One measure that is often used is to compare the ratio of the earnings of the top 90 per cent of the population (i.e. p_{90}) of the earnings distribution with the earnings of the bottom 10 per cent of the population (i.e. p_{10}):

$$90/10\,\text{ratio} = \frac{p_{90}}{p_{10}}$$

The higher this 90/10 ratio, the higher the level of income inequality within the country. The OECD publishes data on household income inequality across countries.[3] A sample of the 90/10 ratios for 2019 are published in Table 10.1.

What this data tells us is that, in Slovakia, the marginal household in the top 10 per cent of the earnings distribution earns 2.9 times as much as the marginal household in the bottom 10 per cent of the earnings distribution. This is a relatively equal distribution, when compared with the UK (90/10 ratio is 4.5), the USA (6.3), and Costa Rica (9.8).

[3] Data is available from https://data.oecd.org/inequality/income-inequality.htm (accessed 8 August 2023).

Table 10.1 90/10 ratio of household earnings (Source: OECD)

Country	90/10 ratio
Slovakia	2.9
Norway	3.1
Ireland	3.5
Germany	3.7
United Kingdom	4.5
USA	6.3
Costa Rica	9.8

Of course, this measure is merely a measure of the level of inequality between high and low earners; the 90/10 measure tells us nothing about the absolute earnings of individuals. For example, it is possible for a country to have a very unequal income distribution, but still to have earners in the bottom 10 per cent of the population earning more than individuals earn in the top 10 per cent of Slovakia's earnings distributions.

For this reason, it's important when considering distributions not just to consider the spread of the data, but also the level of the data.

Similarly, on its own, the average only gives you the centre of the data, but doesn't tell you anything about the spread, or the inequality within a population. To get a fuller picture of a data set, it's always important to consider both the level and the variation of data.

Worked example 10.1: Interquartile range in a discrete random variable

Let's consider two possible games of chance, game 1 and game 2. Their payoffs and associated probabilities are illustrated in Table 10.2. We will define the payoff from game 1 as X, and the payoff from game 2 as Y.

These are interesting games to compare, as the expected payoff from both games is just equal to £20:

$$E(X) = \sum_x P(X = x) \times x = 0.03 \times 0 + 0.07 \times 10 + 0.8 \times 20 + 0.08 \times 30 + 0.03 \times 40 = £20$$

$$E(Y) = \sum_y P(Y = y) \times y = 0.3 \times 0 + 0.18 \times 10 + 0.04 \times 20 + 0.18 \times 30 + 0.3 \times 40 = £20$$

To compare the two distributions, we also need to consider the variability of the outcomes. In terms of investment, this would be thought of as the level of risk or uncertainty associated with the investment. Since the expected payoffs are the same in these two games, players will choose the game that best fits their attitude towards risk. If the player is risk averse, they will prefer the game with the lower level of variability in the outcomes, whilst a risk lover would prefer the game with the higher level of variability.

Table 10.2 Payoffs and probabilities associated with two games of chance

Game 1		Game 2	
Payoff (X)	Probability	Payoff (Y)	Probability
£0	0.03	£0	0.3
£10	0.07	£10	0.18
£20	0.8	£20	0.04
£30	0.07	£30	0.18
£40	0.03	£40	0.3

One way of measuring the risk of the two games is to consider the interquartile range. Remember that the interquartile range is the difference between the 25th and the 75th percentile. Now, p_{25} is the value (within the population) that 25 per cent of the population lies below. That is, $P(X \leq p_{25}) = 0.25$. Similarly, there is a probability of randomly drawing a value of X below p_{75} of 0.75 (or 75 per cent). That is, $P(X \leq p_{75}) = 0.75$.

If we take each game in turn, we can calculate the cumulative probability distribution, shown in Table 10.3.

Table 10.3 Cumulative probability distribution for game 1

Game 1		
Payoff (X)	Marginal probability, $P(X = X)$	Cumulative probability $P(X \leq X)$
£0	0.03	0.03
£10	0.07	0.1
£20	0.8	0.9
£30	0.07	0.97
£40	0.03	1

Examining this population, we can calculate the quartiles. Three per cent of the outcomes are less than (or equal to) £0. Then, 10 per cent of the outcomes are less than (or equal to) £10. When X increases to £20, the cumulative probability jumps up to 0.9.

$$P(X \leq 0) = 0.03$$
$$P(X \leq 10) = 0.1$$
$$P(X \leq 20) = 0.9$$

Therefore, if we are looking for the value p_{25} such that $P(X \leq p_{25}) = 0.25$, this must be contained within $X = 20$. That is, the smallest 25 per cent of observations within the population will include all of the observations from $X = 0, X = 10$, and 15 per cent of the observations from $X = 20$.

Similarly, for p_{75}, since 0.75 is also between 0.1 and 0.9, it must be the case that p_{75} is contained within $X = 20$ also. As such, the interquartile range is just:

$$IQR = p_{75} - p_{25} = 20 - 20 = 0$$

Similarly, we can repeat the same exercise with game 2 (Table 10.4).

Table 10.4 Cumulative probability distribution for game 2

Game 2		
Payoff (Y)	Marginal probability, $P(Y = y)$	Cumulative probability $P(Y \leq y)$
£0	0.3	0.3
£10	0.18	0.48
£20	0.04	0.52
£30	0.18	0.70
£40	0.3	1.00

Now, we can see p_{25} (i.e. the value for which $P(Y \leq p_{25}) = 0.25$ lies within the outcome of $Y = 0$. Similarly, p_{75} lies within the outcome of $Y = 40$. As such, the interquartile range is given as:

$$IQR = p_{75} - p_{25} = 40 - 0 = 40$$

This indicates that game 2 is the riskier game. Intuitively, this makes sense, as in game 1, 80 per cent of the time, you would have a payoff of £20, whereas in game 2, 30 per cent of the time you have a payoff of zero, but this is balanced by having a larger payoff of £40, 30 per cent of the time.

10.2 Variance and standard deviation (of a population)

The interquartile range gives us some idea about the spread of the data, but it is often useful to consider a standardized measure of the level of dispersion of data within a population. Commonly, statisticians will use one of two (linked) measures: the variance or the standard deviation.

To motivate these, let's return to the two games we saw in Worked example 10.1. We saw that both of these games have an expected payoff of £20, but that game 2 has a higher interquartile range, and hence a higher level of risk (Table 10.5).

One way of measuring the variability of a random variable is to consider the average deviation of the random variable away from the mean, or expected value. We can see that, in game 2, 30 per cent of the time, you will gain an outcome £20 below the average, and 30 per cent of the time, you will gain an outcome £20 above the average. In game 1, however, you would only be £20 below the average 3 per cent of the time.

Table 10.5 Payoffs and probabilities associated with two games of chance

Game 1		Game 2	
Payoff (*X*)	Probability	Payoff (*Y*)	Probability
£0	0.03	£0	0.3
£10	0.07	£10	0.18
£20	0.8	£20	0.04
£30	0.07	£30	0.18
£40	0.03	£40	0.3

By considering the average deviation from the expected value, you can gain a measure of whether most of the observations are likely to be close to the expected value (i.e. a small level of variability), or whether the outcomes are more likely to be a long way from the average (i.e. a high level of variability).

Figure 10.6 shows the probability distributions for game 1 and game 2. In game 1, the most likely outcome is equal to the expected value. However, for game 2 (where there is higher variability), there is a much higher probability of being either £20 above or £20 below the expected value. Let's define a new random variable *Deviation*, as the deviation of the random variable X away from the expected value of X. That is,

$$Deviation = X - E(X)$$

So, if $X = £40$, then the deviation is equal to $40 - E(X) = 40 - 20 = +20$. Similarly, if $X = 0$, then the deviation is equal to $0 - 40 = -40$.

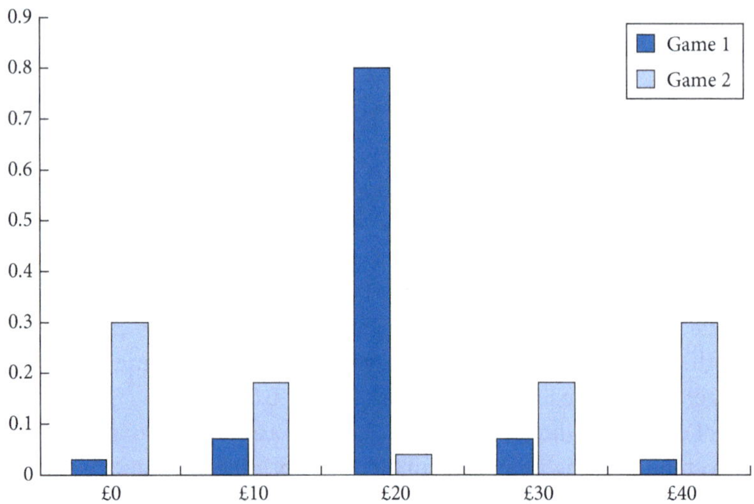

Figure 10.6 Probability distributions for game 1 and game 2.

Table 10.6 Calculating the average deviation of the game from the expected value

Game 1			Game 2		
Payoff (X)	Deviation $X - E(X)$	Probability	Payoff (Y)	Deviation $Y - E(Y)$	Probability
£0	−20	0.03	£0	−20	0.3
£10	−10	0.07	£10	−10	0.18
£20	0	0.8	£20	0	0.04
£30	10	0.07	£30	10	0.18
£40	20	0.03	£40	20	0.3

For the two games, we can write down the deviations, and the probabilities associated with each of the deviations (Table 10.6).

If we simply found the average of these deviations, we would not gain an interesting result, as for both games, the weighted average of the deviations would equal zero. That is, $E[X - E(X)] = E[Y - E(Y)] = 0$. This is because, by the very nature of averages, some of the observations will be below average, and some will be above average, and averaging the positive and negative deviations would leave us with an average of 0.

Proving that the average deviation will always equal to zero

In a population, the average deviation is defined as the expected value of $X - E(X)$. If we take expectations of $X - E(X)$, we have:

$$E(Deviation) = E(X - E(X))$$

By the rules of expectations, we know that the expectation of any sum is just equal to the sum of the expectations, and so:

$$E(X - E(X)) = E(X) - E(E(X))$$

Secondly, we know that $E(X)$ is a constant for any population, and the expectation of any constant is just equal to that constant:

$$= E(X) - E(X) = 0$$

Therefore, the expected deviation away from the population average is always equal to zero.

Therefore, to consider the average deviation away from the expected value, we are really interested in the magnitude of these deviations, so we need a method to ensure that these are always positive.

One way to create a measure that is always positive is to square each of the deviations. By squaring the deviation, this automatically maps any negative deviations onto a positive value, and if we calculate the average of the squares of the deviations, we can get a measure of the level of variability in our random variable.

That is, if the deviation is defined as $X - E(X)$, we are interested in finding the average of the square of this, so we are looking for the average of $(X - E(X))^2$. Table 10.7 shows the average square of the deviation calculated for game 1.

Table 10.7 Calculating the average square of the deviation for game 1

Game 1			
Payoff (X)	Deviation $X - E(X)$	Square of deviation $(X - E(X))^2$	Probability
£0	-20	$= (-20)^2 = 400$	0.03
£10	-10	$= (-10)^2 = 100$	0.07
£20	0	$= 0^2 = 0$	0.8
£30	10	$= 10^2 = 100$	0.07
£40	20	$= 20^2 = 400$	0.03

By squaring the deviation, you can see that when X is either 20 above (i.e. $X = 40$) or 20 below (i.e. $X = 0$) the expected value, the square of the deviation is the same. This means that we are treating observations above or below the expected value in the same way.

The measure of variability that we are constructing, looking at the average of the squares of the deviation, is one of the most commonly used measures, and is known as the variance of a random variable:

$$var(X) = E[(X - E(X))^2]$$

Applying this to game 1, if we wish to find the average square of the deviation, we will need to weight each of the squares of the deviations by the respective probabilities:

$$E(X - E(X))^2 = \sum_x P(X = x)(x - E(X))^2$$

So, for instance, $P(X = 0) = 0.03$, so we would multiply $(0 - 20)^2 = (-20)^2 = 400$ by 0.03:

$$= 0.03 \times 400 + 0.07 \times 100 + 0.8 \times 0 + 0.07 \times 100 + 0.03 \times 400 = 38$$

So, the variance of outcomes in game 1, i.e. the variance of X, is equal to $var(X) = 38$.

In the same way, we can calculate the variance of Y (i.e. the variance of payoffs in game 2) by finding the average of the squares of the deviations (Table 10.8).

Table 10.8 Calculating the average square of the deviation for game 2

Game 2			
Payoff (Y)	Deviation $Y - E(Y)$	Square of deviation $(Y - E(Y))^2$	Probability
£0	-20	$= (-20)^2 = 400$	0.3
£10	-10	$= (-10)^2 = 100$	0.18
£20	0	$= 0^2 = 0$	0.04
£30	10	$= 10^2 = 100$	0.18
£40	20	$= 20^2 = 400$	0.3

The outcomes and the deviations are the same in game 2 as in in game 1; the only thing that is different is the probabilities between the two games. To find the average, or expected, square of the deviation, we need to weight each of the $(y - E(Y))^2$ terms by their respective probabilities:

$$\begin{aligned} E\left[(Y - E(Y))^2\right] &= \sum_y P(Y = y) \times (y - E(Y))^2 \\ &= 0.3 \times 400 + 0.18 \times 100 + 0.04 \times 0 + 0.18 \times 100 + 0.3 \times 400 = 276 \end{aligned}$$

So, the variance of game 2, $var(Y) = 276$. As we would expect, the variance of outcomes from game 2 is larger than the variance of outcomes from game 1.

However, there is a problem with using the variance as a measure of variation. By squaring the deviations, the variance is no longer in the same units (or scale) as the original random variable. So, in this example, the payoff, X, is measured in £s. However, by squaring each of the deviations, the units of the variance would be in £^{2}s. A very simple way to fix this is to simply construct a new measure, by taking the square root of the variance. This new measure is known as the **standard deviation**, or *s.d.*:

$$s.d.(X) = \sqrt{var(X)} = \sqrt{38} = 6.1644\,(4dp)$$
$$s.d.(Y) = \sqrt{var(Y)} = \sqrt{276} = 16.6132\,(4dp)$$

By square-rooting, we convert the measure of variability into the same scale as the original random variable, and we can think of the standard deviation of X as a measure of the average magnitude of the deviation of the random variable X away from the expected value.

So, in summary, we have calculated the expectation, variance, and standard deviation of our two games (Table 10.9).

What this suggests is that if you were to play the games a large enough number of times, on average, you would expect to receive £20 from each of the games. However, the level of variation is much larger in game 2; you are much more likely to receive an extreme value in game 2 than in game 1. Economists often assume that individual agents are risk averse, and would prefer outcomes with certainty to the same expected outcomes with risk. In this case, economists would assume that a rational, risk averse agent would prefer to play game 1 than game 2.

We have seen that we can calculate the variance as the expected square of the deviation of the random variable away from its expected value. For discrete random variables, this can be calculated as:

$$var(X) = E\left[(X - E(X))^2\right] = \sum_x P(X = x) \times (x - E(X))^2$$

Table 10.9 Expectation, variance, and standard deviation of games 1 and 2

	Game 1	Game 2
Expectation	$E(X) = £20$	$E(Y) = £20$
Variance	$var(X) = 38$	$var(Y) = 276$
Standard deviation	$s.d.(X) = 6.16$	$s.d.(Y) = 16.61$

In the same way as we saw in previous chapters, whenever we have an operation for discrete random variables using a summation, we can replace the summation with an integration for continuous random variables. Therefore, if we have a continuous random variable, X, then the variance can be calculated as:

$$var(X) = E\left[(X - E(X))^2\right] = \int_x f_X(X)(x - E(X))^2\,dx$$

KEY DEFINITIONS: EXPECTATIONS, VARIANCES, AND STANDARD DEVIATIONS

In statistics and probability theory, there are some commonly used conventions to represent expectations, variances, and standard deviations:

- The expectation of a random variable is often denoted as a μ—pronounced 'mew'. Sometimes, if you have multiple random variables, you might denote the expectation of random variables X and Y as $E(X) = \mu_X$ and $E(Y) = \mu_Y$.
- The variance of a random variable is often denoted as σ^2—pronounced 'sigma-squared'. Again, sometimes, if you have multiple random variables, you might denote the variance of X by $var(X) = \sigma_X^2$.
- The standard deviation is just the square root of the variance, and so the standard deviation is often denoted as σ.

	Mathematical expression	Discrete random variable	Continuous random variable
Expectation	$E(X)$	$\sum_x P(X = x) \times x$	$= \int_x f_X(x) \times x dx$
Variance, σ^2	$var(X) = E[(X - E(X))^2]$	$\sum_x P(X = x) \times (x - E(X))^2$	$= \int_x f_X(x) \times (x - E(X))^2 dx$
Standard deviation, σ	$s.d.(X) = \sqrt{var(X)}$	$= \sqrt{var(X)}$	$= \sqrt{var(X)}$

10.2.1 An alternative way of calculating the variance

We have constructed a formula for the variance of a random variable, X, as:

$$var(X) = E\left[(X - E(X))^2\right]$$

However, it is sometimes quite fiddly to calculate $E\left[(X - E(X))^2\right]$, and it is very easy for students to make errors when calculating this expectation as the (population) average of the squares of the deviations of observations from the expected value.

There is, however, an easier way of calculating the variance. If you already know the expectation of X, the variance of X can be calculated by finding the difference between the expectation of the square of X and the square of the expectation of X.

That is, we can also write the variance of a random variable, X, as:

$$var(X) = E(X^2) - E(X)^2$$

This formula is often much simpler to calculate. However, we do need to prove that the two expressions are the same.

Proof

We know that the variance of X is defined as:

$$var(X) = E\left[(X - E(X))^2\right]$$

For ease of notation, let's define $E(X)$ as μ_X, so let's rewrite $var(X) = E[(X - \mu_X)^2]$. We can begin by expanding out the square, giving us:

$$\Rightarrow var(X) = E[(X^2 - 2X\mu_X + \mu_X^2)]$$

Now, we have the expectation of a sum of random variables, and we know that the expectation of a sum is just equal to the sum of the expectations:

$$\Rightarrow var(X) = E(X^2) - 2E(X\mu_X) + E(\mu_X^2)$$

Now, the expectation of X is a constant, so that means that μ_X is also a constant. This means that we can take this out (as a constant multiplier) from the second term, and the final term will just be μ_X^2.

$$\Rightarrow var(X) = E(X^2) - 2\mu_X E(X) + \mu_X^2$$

But, by definition, $E(X) = \mu_X$, and so:

$$\Rightarrow var(X) = E(X^2) - 2\mu_X \times \mu_X + \mu_X^2 = E(X^2) - 2\mu_X^2 + \mu_X^2 = E(X^2) - \mu_X^2$$

To complete the proof, we know that $\mu_X = E(X)$, and so, the variance of X can just be written as:

$$var(X) = E(X^2) - E(X)^2$$

Worked example 10.2: Using the alternative method of calculating the variance

We saw in the previous section that there are two ways of calculating the variance of a random variable, such that:

$$\sigma_X^2 = var(X) = E\left[(X - E(X))^2\right] = E(X^2) - E(X)^2$$

Let's look again at game 1 (X) from our previous example. We saw that $E(X) = 20$, and we also saw that the variance of X was equal to 38. Let's use our alternative method to check our answer. The probability distribution of X and X^2 is represented in Table 10.10.

Table 10.10 Distribution of X and X^2 in game 1

Game 1		
Payoff (X)	X^2	**Probability**
£0	$0^2 = 0$	0.03
£10	$10^2 = 100$	0.07
£20	$20^2 = 400$	0.8
£30	$30^2 = 900$	0.07
£40	$40^2 = 1{,}600$	0.03

We already know that $E(X) = 20$, and to calculate the variance, we only need to calculate $E(X^2)$. Remember that this will not be equal to the square of $E(X)$, but instead, we need to weight each of the outcomes of X^2 by the respective probabilities:

$$\begin{aligned} E(X^2) &= \sum_x P(X = x) \times x^2 \\ &= 0.03 \times 0 + 0.07 \times 100 + 0.8 \times 400 + 0.07 \times 900 + 0.03 \times 1{,}600 \\ &= 438 \end{aligned}$$

This is not the variance of X though. To calculate the variance of X, we need to find the difference between $E(X^2)$ and the square of the expectation of X, $E(X)^2$:

$$\Rightarrow var(X) = E(X^2) - E(X)^2 = 438 - 20^2 = 438 - 400 = 38$$

That is, $\sigma_X^2 = 38$.Reassuringly, we have gained the same answer using this second, simpler method of calculating the variance of X.

Worked example 10.3: Calculating the variance for a continuous random variable

In Chapter 8, we considered the example of an alien race, whose heights, Y, followed a continuous probability density function (PDF):

$$f_Y(y) = \begin{cases} \frac{1}{20}, & 170 \le y \le 190 \\ 0, & \text{Otherwise} \end{cases}$$

The variance of this random variable can be constructed by calculating both the expectation of Y and the expectation of Y^2. Now, we know that to calculate the expectation of Y, we can find the integral of the product of the PDF[4] with the outcomes of Y:

$$E(Y) = \int_y f_Y(y) \times y\, dy = \int_{170}^{190} \frac{y}{20} dy = \left[\frac{y^2}{40}\right]_{170}^{190} = 180$$

[4] We have ignored the parts of the distribution where $f_Y(y) = 0$. This is because the integral will automatically be equal to zero in this range as $\int_a^b 0 \times y\, dy = \int_a^b 0\, dy = 0$.

Similarly, to find the expectation of Y^2, we simply need to replace y with y^2 in the above integral. The *PDF* will be exactly the same though:

$$E(Y^2) = \int_{170}^{190} \frac{1}{20} \times y^2 dy = \left[\frac{1}{20} \times \frac{y^3}{3}\right]_{170}^{190}$$

We can now substitute in the limits to give us:

$$\Rightarrow E(Y^2) = \frac{1}{20} \times \left[\frac{190^3}{3} - \frac{170^3}{3}\right] = \frac{1{,}946{,}000}{60} = 32{,}433.3333\,(4dp)$$

Finally, to calculate the variance of Y, we simply need to combine the two results. Remember that the variance is just equal to the difference between the expectation of the square of Y, less the square of the expectation of Y:

$$var(Y) = E(Y^2) - E(Y)^2 = \frac{1{,}946{,}000}{60} - 180^2 = \frac{100}{3} = 33.3333\,(4dp)$$

Similarly, the standard deviation of our random variable can be calculated by taking the square root of the variance:

$$s.d.(Y) = \sqrt{var(Y)} = \sqrt{\frac{100}{3}} = \frac{10}{\sqrt{3}} = 5.7735\,(4dp)$$

In subsequent chapters, we will see that there is an easier way of calculating the variance of a random variable that follows the uniform, or rectangular, distribution.

10.2.2 Calculating variances and standard deviations using empirical data

When using empirical data, you need to be very careful in calculating variances, as there are two methods, which give different answers, depending on what you have actually observed. The two methods have different interpretations. The key difference between the two methods is whether you are interested in the variance (and standard deviation) of the sample you have observed or whether you are interested in estimating the variance of the population as a whole.

Suppose that you observe the entire population

Suppose that you observe n observations of a random variable (such as the weekly earnings of full-time workers), and you want to calculate the variance of earnings. We know that, for populations, the formula for the variance is given as the expectation of the square of the deviations away from the expected value:

$$var(X) = E\left[(X - E(X))^2\right]$$

If we observe an entire population, then the sample mean is exactly the same thing as the expectation. So, within this expression, we could convert anything that is stated as an expectation into a sample mean:

$$= \frac{1}{n}\sum_{i=1}^{n}[x_i - \bar{x}]^2$$

Note that $\bar{x}$ is just the sample mean of the n observations, such that $\bar{x} = \frac{1}{n}\Sigma_{i=1}^{n}\bar{x}$. That is, when we observe a population of data, we can calculate the variance of that population by finding the mean of the squares of the deviations of the observations away from the population average.

For example, let's suppose that you have a (very small) population of five individuals, and their weekly earnings are £400, £350, £600, £550, and £450. We can easily calculate the sample mean, by adding together the five observations, and dividing by 5:

$$\bar{x} = \frac{1}{5}[400 + 350 + 600 + 550 + 450] = £470$$

Similarly, we can calculate the square of the deviations of the observations away from the population average (Table 10.11).

So, the average of the squares of these deviations is equal to:

$$= \frac{1}{5} \times [4{,}900 + 14{,}400 + 16{,}900 + 6{,}400 + 400] = 8{,}600$$

Similarly, the standard deviation would be equal to the square root of this variance, so $s.d.(X) = \sqrt{var(X)} = \sqrt{8{,}600} = 92.7362\,(4dp)$

Table 10.11 Square of the deviations of the observations away from the population average

x_i	$(x_i - \bar{x})^2$
400	$= (400 - 470)^2 = (-70)^2 = 4{,}900$
350	$= (350 - 470)^2 = (-120)^2 = 14{,}400$
600	$= (600 - 470)^2 = 130^2 = 16{,}900$
550	$= (550 - 470)^2 = 80^2 = 6{,}400$
450	$= (450 - 470)^2 = (-20)^2 = 400$

Calculating the variance using a sample in Microsoft Excel

If you observe a population of data in Microsoft, then you can calculate the variance using the formula =var.p(. . .), and the standard deviation using the formula =stdev.p(. . .). By adding the .p at the end of the formula, you are telling Excel that you are observing a population, and you want the variance, or standard deviation, of the population that you have observed.

For example, if we assume that the data we observed earlier of female full-time earnings from the UK Labour Force Survey is a population, then we can calculate the variance of the data we have observed using the formula =var.p(A2:A201), indicating that the data is contained in cells A2 to A201, illustrated in Figure 10.7.

In this example, the variance is calculated as 89,302.66, and the standard deviation as £298.8355 (4dp). However, in reality, this is unlikely to be a population. At best, you can state that we have calculated an empirical variance and standard deviation for the sample we have observed. In reality, we will normally be interested in the variance of the population as a whole.

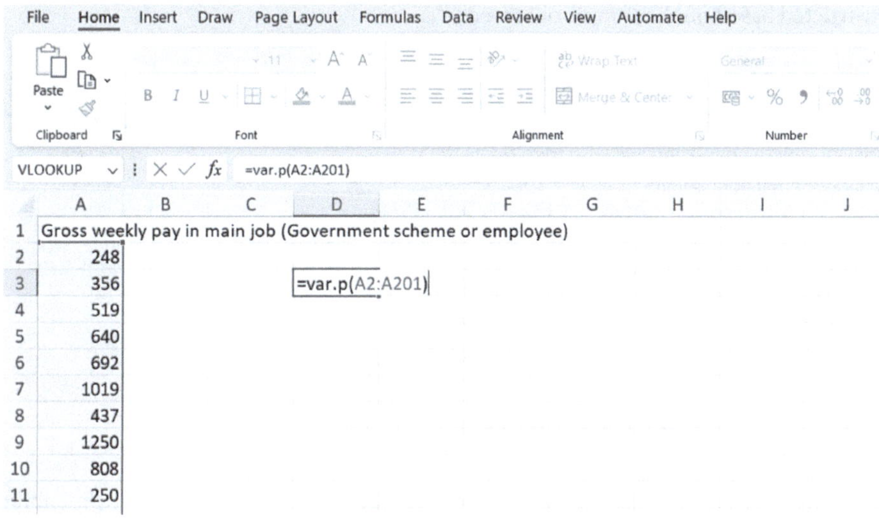

Figure 10.7 Calculating the variance based on observing a population within Excel.

Suppose that you observe a sample from a population

We will talk about using samples to create estimates of population parameters later in this book, but, if you observe a sample from a population, you may be interested in calculating an estimate of the population variance.

When we wish to estimate this, we use a slightly different formula, given by:

$$= \frac{1}{n-1}\sum_{i=1}^{n}(x_i - \overline{x})^2$$

In this formula, we divide by $(n - 1)$ rather than n as what is known as a degrees of freedom adjustment. This is because, when we observe a sample from a population, we do not know what the true expected value of X is, we merely have a sample average, which will (almost certainly) be different from the population average.

Whilst we are not going to discuss this in any great detail here, this is important, particularly if you are using Excel to calculate standard deviations and variances. If you use the formula =var(. . .) or =stdev(. . .), then Excel will automatically apply the previous formula as the variance formula. For example, if you used these commands on the earnings data, you would get a variance equal to 89,751.42, and standard deviation of £299.5854. These figures are marginally different, simply because these formulae calculate an estimate of the population variance and standard deviation, rather than the variance and standard deviation of the data you are observing.

This is an important distinction, and using statistical software often leads to students making small errors with the interpretation of the results. In later chapters, we will discuss why we need to use this formula, but for now, remember that if you use =var(. . .) in Microsoft Excel, it will assume that you want to see (an estimate of) the population variance, constructed based on the sample observed.

	Formulae to calculate	Excel command
If you observe a population and wish to calculate the variance of that population	$\frac{1}{n}\sum_{i=1}^{n}(x_i - \bar{x})^2$	= *var.p*(. . .)
If you observe a sample and wish to estimate the variance of the population	$\frac{1}{n-1}\sum_{i=1}^{n}(x_i - \bar{x})^2$	= *var*(. . .) = *var.s*(. . .)

10.3 Chebyshev's inequality

The standard deviation of a random variable can also help us understand the probability of observing an observation a long distance from the expected value. In the nineteenth century, Russian mathematician Pafnuty Chebyshev proposed a rule, which it is possible to prove[5] applies to most continuous random variables. It states that the probability of randomly observing an observation of a random variable greater than k standard deviations above or below the expected value will always be less than or equal to $1/k^2$ (see Figure 10.8). Formally, this can be written as:

$$P(|X - E(X)| \geq k\sigma) \leq \frac{1}{k^2}$$

To understand the inequality, if we have a random variable X, then we can find the maximum proportion of the population that lies greater than k standard deviations above or below the expected value. $P(|X - E(X)| \geq k\sigma)$ represents the probability that the magnitude of the deviation of the random variable X away from its expected value (i.e. $|X - E(X)|$) is greater than (or equal to) k times the standard deviation (i.e. $k\sigma$). The inequality states that this probability will always be less than (or equal to) $\frac{1}{k^2}$. So, if you wanted to calculate

[5] But the proof is well beyond the scope of this textbook.

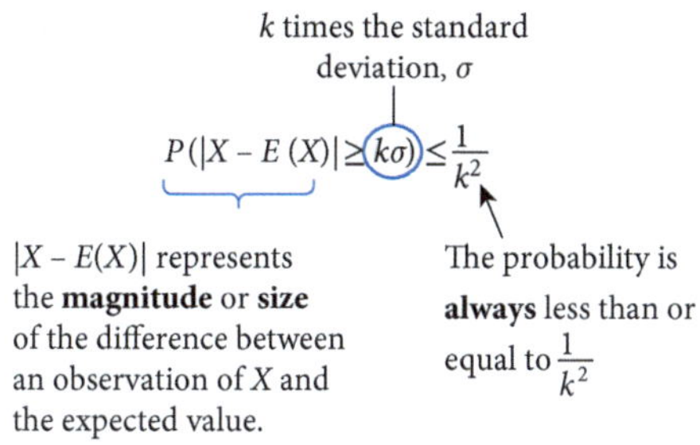

Figure 10.8 Explaining Chebyshev's inequality.

the maximum probability that an observation is two standard deviations above or below the expected value, then:

$$k = 2, \quad \frac{1}{k^2} = \frac{1}{2^2} = 0.25$$

Therefore, for (almost) any random variable, it will always be the case that the probability of observing an outcome at least two standard deviations above or below the expected value will be less than 0.25. In reality, in many distributions, this probability will be much smaller.

Let's illustrate this with an example. Suppose that we have a random variable, Z, with a PDF of $f_Z(z)$ (see Figure 10.9):

$$f_Z(z) = \begin{cases} 3z - \frac{3z^2}{4} - \frac{9}{4}, & 1 \leq z \leq 3 \\ 0, & \text{Otherwise} \end{cases}$$

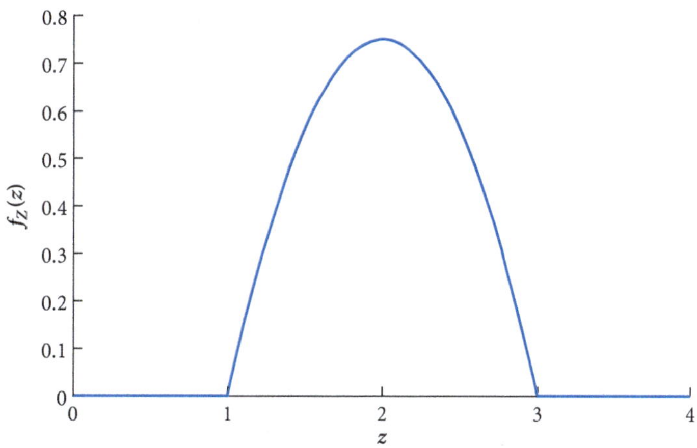

Figure 10.9 Probability density function of Z.

The expectation of Z can be calculated by integrating the product of $f_Z(z)$ and the outcomes of Z:

$$E(Z) = \int_1^3 f_Z(z) \times z dz = \int_1^3 \left(3z - \frac{3z^2}{4} - \frac{9}{4}\right) \times z dz = \int_1^3 3z^2 - \frac{3z^3}{4} - \frac{9z}{4} dz$$

$$= \left[z^3 - \frac{3z^4}{16} - \frac{9z^2}{8}\right]_1^3 = 2$$

Similarly, $E(Z^2)$ can be calculated as:

$$E(Z^2) = \int_1^3 f_Z(z) \times z^2 dz = \int_1^3 \left(3z - \frac{3z^2}{4} - \frac{9}{4}\right) \times z^2 dz = \int_1^3 3z^3 - \frac{3z^4}{4} - \frac{9z^2}{4} dz$$

$$= \left[\frac{3z^4}{4} - \frac{3z^5}{20} - \frac{9z^3}{12}\right]_1^3 = 4.2$$

Therefore, the variance of the random variable, $\sigma_Z^2 = E(Z^2) - E(Z)^2 = 4.2 - 2^2 = 0.2$, and the standard deviation is just the square root of the variance, so $\sigma_Z = \sqrt{0.2} = 0.4472$.

Using Chebyshev's inequality, suppose that we wanted to know the probability of observing an outcome at least one and a half times the standard deviation away from the expected value (i.e. $k = 1.5$). That would mean that we are looking at the probability that the magnitude of the deviation is greater than 1.5 times σ_z. This probability would always be less than or equal to 1 divided by 1.5^2:

$$P(|X - E(X)| \geq 1.5\sigma_X) \leq \frac{1}{1.5^2}$$

Calculating this would give us an upper bound for the probability of $\frac{1}{2.25} = 0.4444$. That is, the probability of randomly choosing an observation from Z that is more than 1.5 times the standard deviation away from the expected value would be less than 0.4444. We know that $\sigma = \sqrt{0.2}$ and so 1.5σ is just $1.5 \times \sqrt{0.2}$. Chebyshev's inequality tells us that if we randomly pick an observation from Z, the probability that the observation is at least $1.5 \times \sqrt{0.2}$ above or below the expected value, $E(Z) = 2$, is 0.4444. The actual probability in this case is represented by the shaded area in Figure 10.10.

We can calculate the actual probability by integrating under the PDF:

$$= 1 - \int_{2-1.5\times\sqrt{0.2}}^{2+1.5\times\sqrt{0.2}} \left[3z - \frac{3z^2}{4} - \frac{9}{4}\right] dz$$

I will leave it as an exercise for you to work through the mathematics here, but the actual probability of observing an outcome more than 1.5 times the standard deviation in this random variable is equal to 0.1447. This result validates Chebyshev's inequality for this particular distribution. However, this is a general rule that you can apply much more widely.[6]

[6] We will not provide a proof of Chebyshev's inequality in this book, but there are lots of proofs available online.

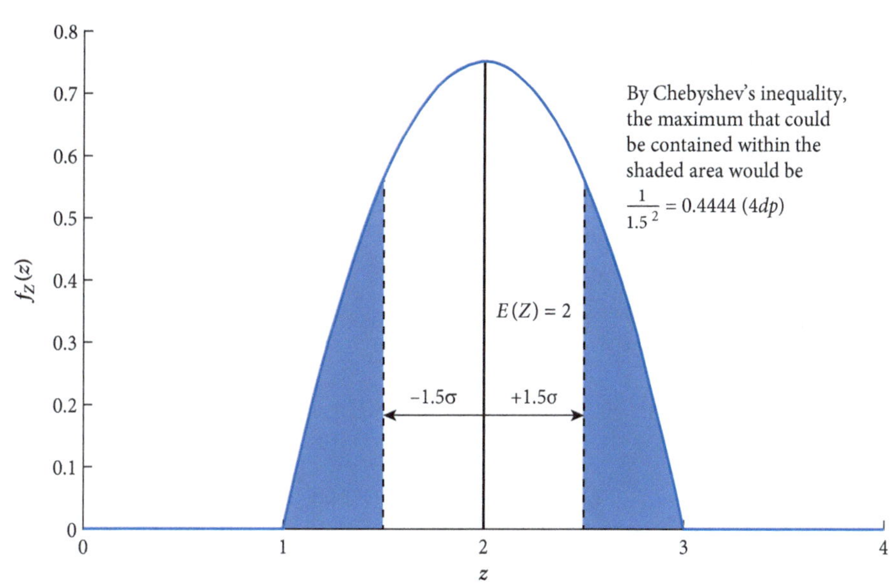

Figure 10.10 Illustrating Chebyshev's inequality.

10.4 **Skew of a population**

In populations, we often expect that a large proportion of the population will have values close to average, with fewer individuals having values a long way from the average. For example, if we think about the heights of humans, only a small proportion of the population will be either a long way above or a long way below the expected value. This sort of distribution will lead to a peak in the PDF close to the expected value, and much lower values for the PDF further away from the expected value. For example, a PDF for a population characteristic such as height might look like Figure 10.11.

The highest point (i.e. the most likely area to observe outcomes) within the PDF is in the middle of the distribution (which in this case is also the expected value and the median), and the extremes of the distribution have a much lower PDF; that is, you are much less likely to observe outcomes within the tails of the distribution, compared with close to the expected value.

However, in reality many random variables, and many population characteristics, do not follow neat and symmetric distributions like the one shown in Figure 10.11. In reality, many distributions are asymmetric, and may have large numbers of observations within the tails of the distribution. The skew of a population tells you about whether the distribution is symmetric or not.

For example, in Section 10.1, we saw data representing a random sample of the earnings of 200 female full-time workers from the 2019 UK Labour Force Survey (Figure 10.12). You can see that there is a peak to the histogram between earnings of £400 and £600 of the distribution (this is known as the modal area of the distribution).

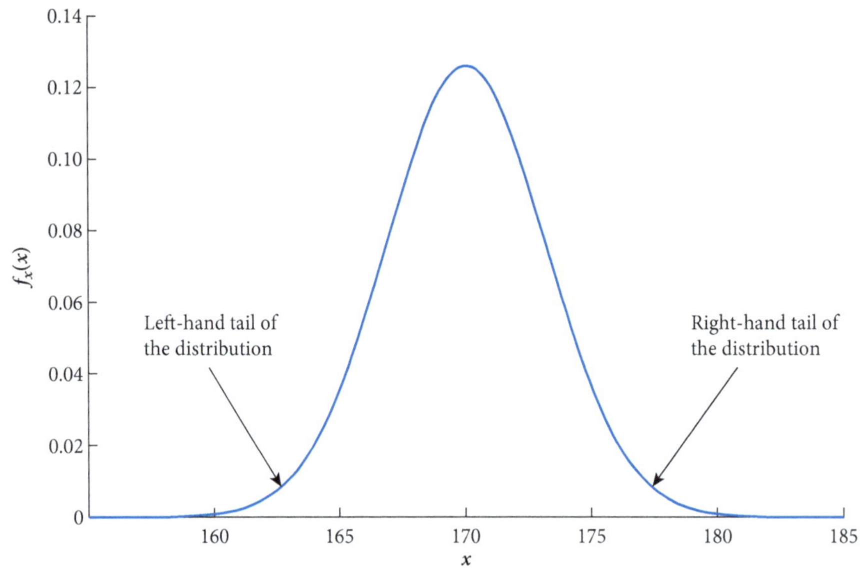

Figure 10.11 PDF of distribution with peak at the expected value, and fewer observations in the tails of the distribution.

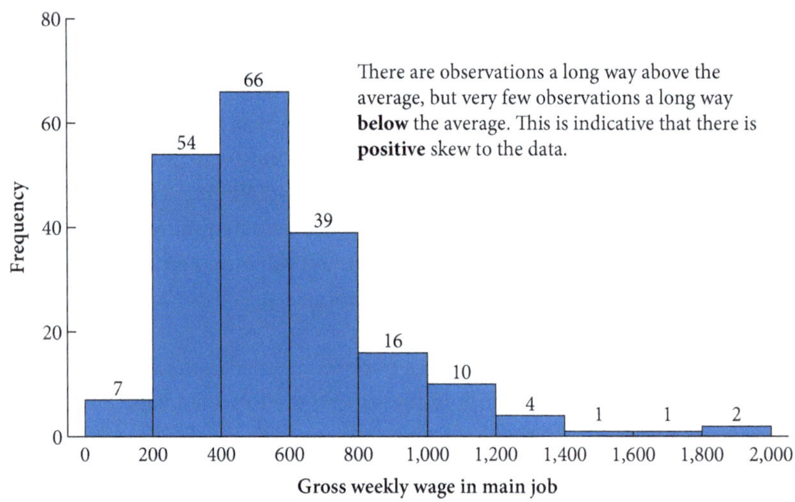

Figure 10.12 Histogram of earnings from (random sample) of 200 female full-time workers aged 25–45 from the 2019 UK LFS.

Because the amount that you can earn is bounded below at 0 (i.e. you can't earn less than zero pounds per week in a full-time job), it's impossible to see observations a long way below this modal region, but earnings are not bounded above. In principle, a full-time worker could earn thousands of pounds per week, which would place them a very long way above the modal region. This data displays what is known as positive skew. Where we have a long

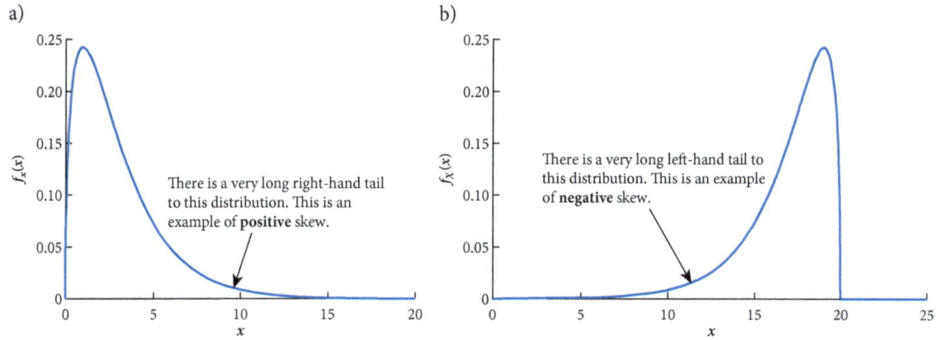

Figure 10.13 Examples of distributions with positive and negative skew.

tail to the distribution on the right-hand side, the data is said to be given a positive skew. The data we are looking at here relates to a sample, but skewness is more generally applied to a population. Figure 10.13 show examples of distributions with positive and negative skew.

For a population, the skew can be calculated as:

$$\text{Skew} = E\left(\frac{X - E(X)}{\sigma}\right)^3$$

Where a population has a PDF that is symmetric around its expectation (such as in Figure 10.11), then the skew will be equal to zero. When there is a long right-hand tail, then the skew will be positive, and if there is a long left-hand tail, the skew will be negative.

Worked example 10.4: Calculating the skew of a (symmetric) random variable

Earlier in the chapter, we considered a (uniformly distributed) variable, with a PDF of:

$$f_Y(y) = \begin{cases} \frac{1}{20}, & 170 \le y \le 190 \\ 0, & \text{Otherwise} \end{cases}$$

As you can see from Figure 10.14, this is a symmetric distribution, and so we would expect the skew to be equal to zero. We already know that $E(Y) = 180$ and the standard deviation, $\sigma = 10/\sqrt{3}$.

We can calculate the skew by finding the expectation of $(Y - E(Y))^3$ divided by the cube of the standard deviation of Y. To find $E(Y - E(Y))^3$, we will integrate the product of the PDF, and the difference between the observations and the expected value cubed, $(y - E(Y))^3$. We can also substitute in $E(Y) = 180$, and so the skew will be:

$$\text{Skew} = \frac{1}{\sigma^3}\int_y f_Y(y) \times (y - E(Y))^3\,dy = \frac{1}{\left[10/\sqrt{3}\right]} \times \int_{170}^{190} \frac{1}{20} \times (y - 180)^3\,dy$$

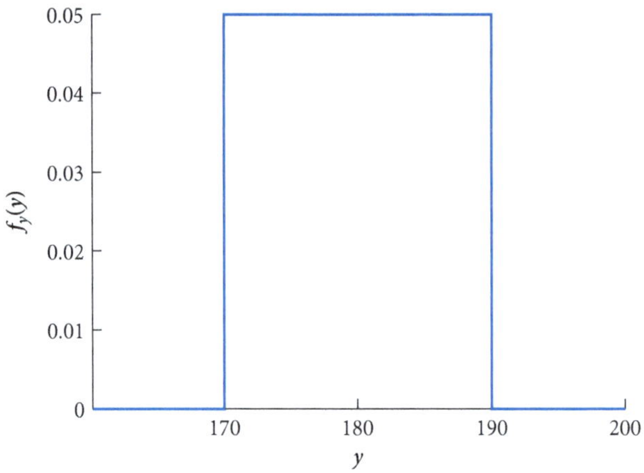

Figure 10.14 Probability density function of Y.

Now, we can simplify this problem a little by taking the $\frac{1}{20}$ out of the integral, giving us:

$$= \frac{\sqrt{3}}{200} \times \int_{170}^{190} (y - 180)^3 \, dy = \frac{\sqrt{3}}{200} \times \left[\frac{(y - 180)^4}{4} \right]_{170}^{190}$$

Substituting in the limits gives us:

$$= \frac{\sqrt{3}}{200} \times \left[\frac{10^4 - (-10)^4}{4} \right] = \frac{\sqrt{3}}{200} \times 0 = 0$$

Thus, as we had predicted, the skew of this distribution is equal to zero. This is not really a surprise because the distribution is symmetric, and therefore there is no skew of the data either to the left- or the right-hand side.

10.5 Kurtosis of a population

The skew of a random variable tells you about whether the distribution is symmetric, or whether there is a long tail, either to the right or the left of the distribution. The **kurtosis** is also related to the distribution within the tails of the distribution, and analyses whether there are 'fat tails' to the distribution. That is, the kurtosis of a distribution tells us about the proportion of the outcomes that are in the tails of the distribution.

The formula for calculating the kurtosis is very similar to the formula for the skew, but rather than cubing the $(X - E(X))$ term, we raise it to the power 4:

$$\text{Kurtosis} = E\left(\frac{X - E(X)}{\sigma} \right)^4$$

Whilst we do not calculate it here, it is possible to show that the distribution we found the skew of in Worked example 10.4 has a kurtosis of $\frac{9}{5}$ or 1.8.

When examining kurtosis, we often compare the kurtosis calculated with a standard kurtosis of 3; that is, we take the kurtosis calculated, and subtract 3. The resulting outcome is known as the excess kurtosis. In this example, the excess kurtosis would thus be −1.2. We can then think of the random variable in terms of the size of the tails of the distribution.

Excess kurtosis	Negative (less than 0)	Zero	Positive (Greater than 0)
	Platykurtic	**Mesokurtic**	**Leptokurtic**
Description	Outcomes rarely occur in the tails. The tails of the distribution are narrower than in the standard mesokurtic case.	Often used to model random variables; most common example is standard normal distribution (which we will see later in the book).	Tails are 'fat'. Outcomes a long way from the expected value are more likely than in the mesokurtic case.

In the example, there are no tails to the distribution, so it is not surprising that the distribution is platykurtic.

These concepts are very useful in finance. Excess kurtosis in the distribution of asset prices is one of the key reasons why banks mispriced risk in the run-up to the 2008 financial crisis. Standard financial models had assumed that asset prices followed a distribution with relatively low probabilities of extreme outcomes.[7] That is, they assumed that outcomes which were more than 3 standard deviations away from the expected value had an almost zero probability of occurring. However, in reality these 'Black Swan' events were much more likely, leading almost to the collapse of the worldwide financial sector.[8]

KEY DEFINITION: CENTRAL MOMENTS

Sometimes, you will read about 'moments' of a distribution in statistics, where a random variable X has expectation μ_X and variance σ^2. Then the kth moment is just defined as:

$$E[(X - \mu_X)^k]$$

That is, the kth moment is the expectation of the kth power of the difference between X and the expectation.

The variance is therefore the second central moment.

The skew is defined as $\frac{E[(X-\mu_X)^3]}{\sigma^3}$, and the kurtosis as $\frac{E[(X-\mu_X)^4]}{\sigma^4}$. By dividing through by the standard deviation, we are effectively constructing a standardized central moment for the distribution.

7 The models assumed that stock returns followed a normal distribution. We will revisit normal distribution in later chapters.

8 See, for example, N. Taleb (2008), *The Black Swan: The Impact of the Highly Improbable*, Penguin.

10.6 Data-based example of skew and kurtosis

We can demonstrate how to calculate skew and kurtosis for a sample using the sample from the UK Labour Force Survey that we saw earlier in the chapter (Figure 10.15).

By initially plotting a histogram of the weekly wages, we can see that the most common weekly wages are between £600 and £800 per week; however, we can also see that the distribution is not symmetric. The right-hand tail is much longer than the left-hand tail, and whilst there is a small probability of observing weekly wages a long way above the expected value, there is zero probability of observing weekly wages a long way below the expected value. That is, the data shows positive skew.

Microsoft Excel can estimate the level of skew in the random variable by using the formula:

= SKEW(A2:A201)

For this data, we get a measure for the skew of 1.604; as the initial histogram suggested, this distribution has positive skew. This illustrates the benefit of considering simple visualizations of data to make initial conclusions about that data.

Similarly, Excel can estimate the level of kurtosis in the random variable by using the formula:

= KURT(A2:A301)

The kurtosis here is 3.960. To find the excess kurtosis, we simply need to subtract 3 from this figure, to give an excess kurtosis of 0.960. This means that the variable is leptokurtic. That is, there is a relatively high probability of observing individuals with wages within the tails—in this case, this means that there is a relatively high probability of observing individuals with significantly higher than average weekly wages.

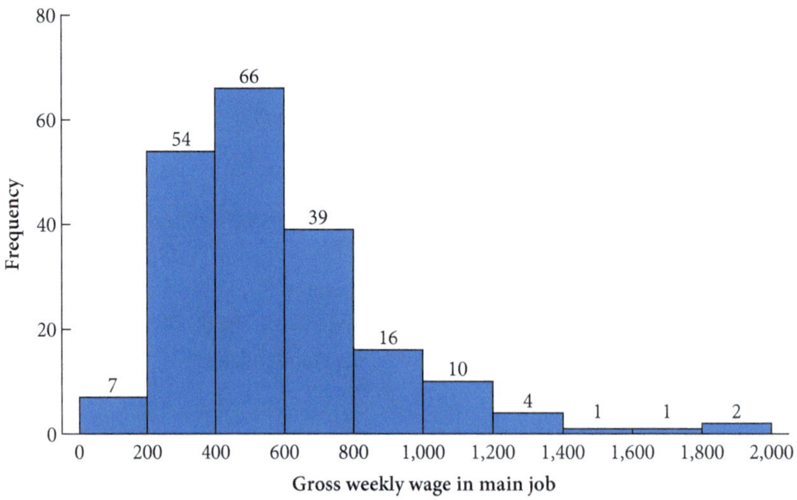

Figure 10.15 Histogram of earnings from (random sample) of 200 female full-time workers aged 25–45 from the 2019 UK LFS.

Summary

In this chapter, we have introduced a number of measures of both the level of variability and the shape of distributions.

The key measures of variability that we have explored are the interquartile range, the standard deviation, and the variance. For each of these, as the value increases, the level of variation within the population is also increasing. For risky assets, the higher the variance, the higher the level of risk associated with the asset.

However, we have seen that, on its own, the variance only tells part of the story of the distribution, as it's also important to consider the level of the random variable, or the expected value.

The skew and kurtosis add additional information about the distribution, as they give indications about the shape of the tails of the distribution. Having knowledge of these third and fourth moments is important in finance, weather-forecasting, and more, as they tell you about the likelihood of observing extreme events. For example, if we know the distribution of river levels, and we know that, in extremis, a river will flood a development, knowing the skew and kurtosis of the data will tell us about the likelihood of the extreme event that causes the development to be flooded: is it a one-in-ten-year event, a one-in-a-hundred-year event, or a one-in-a-thousand-year event?

Key formulae

Measure	Variance of *X*, σ_X^2 (second central moment)	Standard deviation of *X*	Skew of *X* (third, standardized, central moment)	Kurtosis of *X* (fourth, standardized, central moment)
Formula	$\sigma_X^2 = E[X - E(X)]^2$ $= E(X^2) - E(X)^2$	$\sigma_X = \sqrt{\sigma_X^2}$	$= \frac{E[(X - \mu_X)^3]}{\sigma^3}$	$= \frac{E[(X - \mu_X)^4]}{\sigma^4}$
Calculating in Excel	If you observe a population: =var.p(…) If you observe a sample and wish to estimate the population variance: =var.s(…)	If you observe a population: =stdev.p(…) If you observe a sample, and wish to estimate the population standard deviation: =stdev.s(…)	If you observe a population: =skew.p(…) If you observe a sample and wish to estimate the population skew: =skew(…)	=kurt(…)

Correlations and Covariances

11

Learning outcomes for this chapter

By the end of this chapter you will be able to:

- Construct measures of covariance between both discrete and continuous random variables
- Evaluate and interpret correlations between two random variables
- Apply the concept of covariances to evaluate the variances of linear combinations of random variables

Mathematical tools

- Simple arithmetic
- Summations
- Integrations

Introduction

So far, all of our measures of variation have focused on the variability of a single random variable. For example, if we are looking at the variance of weekly wages within an economy, all that this tells us is the level of variability there is between individuals' wages within the population. It doesn't tell us anything about how those wages might vary when compared with education levels, or job-type, or age.

Economists and statisticians are often interested in trying to evaluate relationships between economic variables—for example, an economist might be interested in the impact of a change in the interest rate on the unemployment rate or inflation, or the impact that increasing the amount that government spends on healthcare has on life expectancy.

The OECD regularly publish data on a range of country-level indicators, and also biennial publications examining an overview of health indicators. Here, we reproduce data used within the 2019 'Health at a Glance' publication to examine the relationship between health expenditures and life expectancy at birth.[1]

[1] OECD (2019), *Health at a Glance 2019: OECD Indicators*, OECD Publishing, Paris, https://doi.org/10.1787/4dd50c09-en

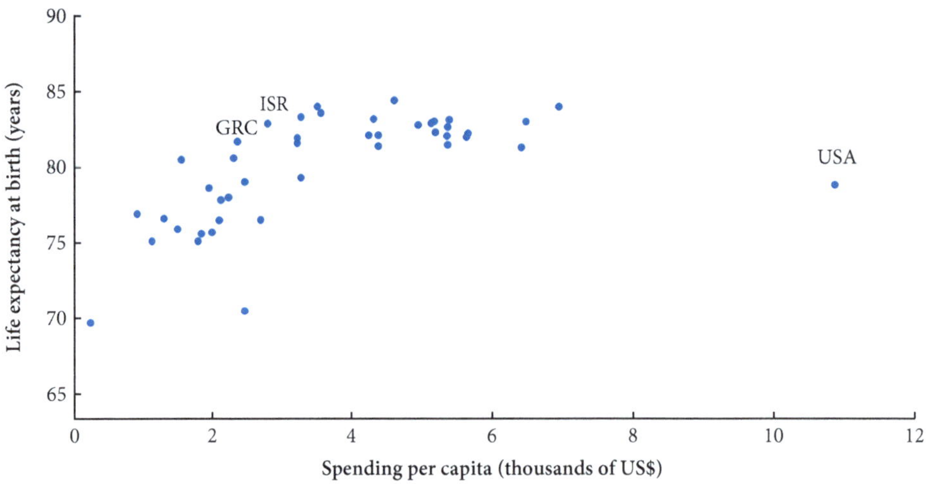

Figure 11.1 Life expectancy and expenditure on healthcare (data from the OECD).

We might expect that as spending on healthcare increases, life expectancy in the country might also increase; similarly, as spending on healthcare decreases, life expectancy might also decrease. Figure 11.1 replicates a figure from OECD (2019), and shows the spending per capita on healthcare, and life expectancy at birth in 2019, for a range of countries. Each dot here represents the spending per capita on healthcare (horizontal axis) and the life expectancy at birth (vertical axis) for a different country. Generally speaking, as spending per capita increases, life expectancy also increases. This suggests that as spending on healthcare increases, life expectancy also increases.[2]

Similarly, some economists postulate that, as unemployment falls, workers gain increased negotiating power and the ability to force up wages. In the medium to long term, this could lead to increased levels of inflation. (This relationship is often referred to as the Phillips curve.) As such, we might believe that there will be a negative relationship between unemployment and inflation; as unemployment increases, inflation might decrease.

Figure 11.2 shows a scatter plot of monthly data from the USA[3] with CPI inflation on the vertical axis, and unemployment on the horizontal axis, for data from 1 January 2000 until 1 December 2019. We can see that as the unemployment rate is increasing, in general, CPI inflation tends to be increasing. Whilst the relationship is less clear than for Figure 11.1, there is a general trend that seems to be sloping downwards.

We will see, in this chapter, that the level of correlation between two random variables can be measured with the correlation coefficient: the better the correlation between two

[2] The USA is a little bit of an outlier here, with exceptionally high expenditure on healthcare, but lower life expectancy than countries such as Israel (ISR) and Greece (GRC), which have significantly less spending on healthcare.

[3] Data downloaded from the Federal Reserve Economic Data, St Louis Fed: https://fred.stlouisfed.org/

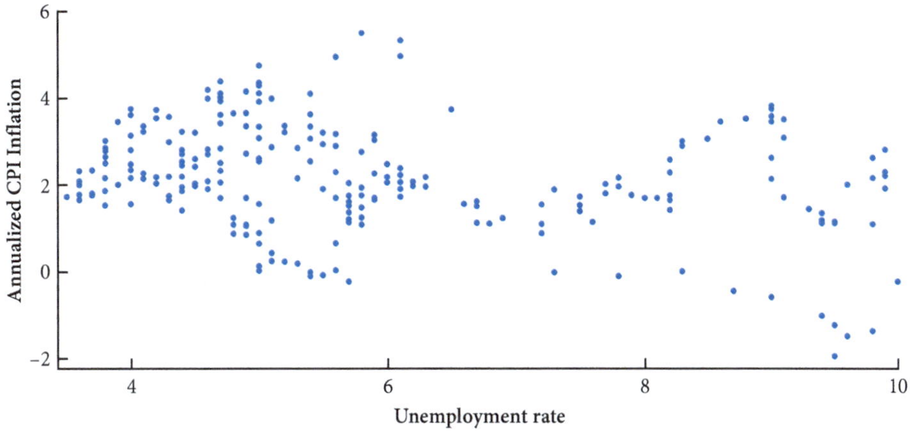

Figure 11.2 CPI Inflation and unemployment for the USA 2000–2020 (data from FRED).

variables, the closer the magnitude of the correlation will be to 1; if two variables are perfectly correlated (correlation coefficient equal to 1), then we could draw a straight line through the plotted data, and all of the data would lie exactly on the straight line.

At this stage, however, it is worth issuing a health warning. Econometricians are often interested in evaluating causal relationships between variables—for example, they might be trying to address whether spending on healthcare is genuinely causing an increase in life expectancy. Just because two variables are correlated does not mean that we can instantly conclude that, for example, an increase in spending on healthcare *causes* an increase in life expectancy. It is equally possible that an increase in life expectancy might be causing the increase in spending, or that the increase in life expectancy and the increase in spending are both caused independently by some other variable, such as the wealth of the country. It is always important to note that correlation does not equal causation.

11.1 Covariances

We saw, in Chapter 10, that we can measure the variability of one variable by calculating the variance of that variable. The variance is defined as the average square of the deviation of the random variable away from the expected value. That is:

$$var(X) = E\left[\left(X - E(X)\right)^2\right] = E(X^2) - E(X)^2$$

Now, we can use this as a starting point to think about how two variables move together. Suppose that we have two random variables, X and Y. We want to know about how X and Y deviate from their expected values together.

Remember, $X - E(X)$ measures the deviation of the random variable X away from its expected value, and $Y - E(Y)$ measures the deviation of the random variable Y away from

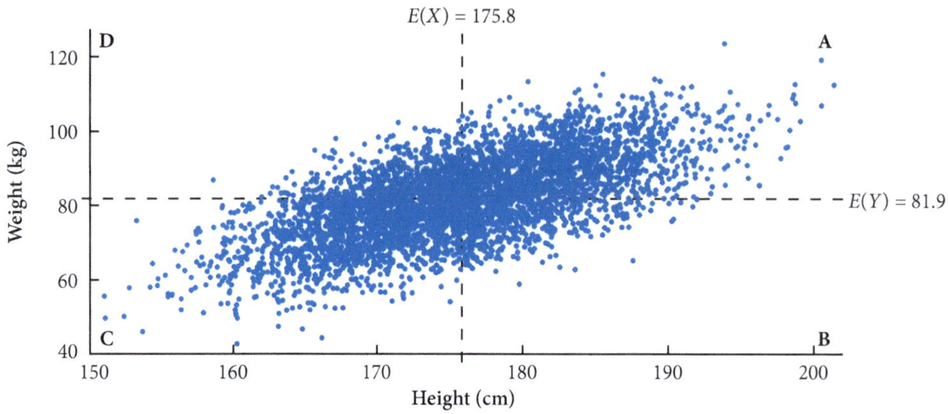

Figure 11.3 Height and weights of a fictional population of 5,000 people.

its expected value. We will begin by introducing a measure known as the covariance between X and Y, denoted $cov(X,Y)$:

$$cov(X,Y) = E\left[\left(X - E(X)\right)\left(Y - E(Y)\right)\right]$$

This covariance is then the average product of the deviations of the random variables X and Y from their respective expectations. To motivate this, let's begin with an example. Suppose that I observed a population of 5,000 men, and measured their height and their weight. We might obtain data that looks something like Figure 11.3.[4] For simplicity of notation, let's define individuals' heights as a random variable, X, and their weight as a random variable, Y. We would expect, as X increases, that on average, Y would also increase.

Each point on the scatter plot represents an individual, with the horizontal coordinate representing their height, and the vertical coordinate representing their weight. We have plotted the data so that the expected values are visible, and divided the data into four quadrants—A, B, C, and D.

- Quadrant A consists of individuals who are taller than average, and weigh more than average.
- Quadrant B consists of individuals who are taller than average, and weigh less than average.
- Quadrant C consists of individuals who are shorter than average, and weigh less than average.
- Quadrant D consists of individuals who are shorter than average, and weigh more than average.

In this (fictional) population, we can see that the vast majority of observations lie either in Quadrant A or Quadrant C. That is, for most of the population, if their height is above

[4] This data is available to download from Data sets and exercises at the end of this chapter. This is based on a fictional population of 5,000 individuals, with expected height of 175.8cm, and expected weight equal to 81.9kg (roughly 180lbs in imperial measures).

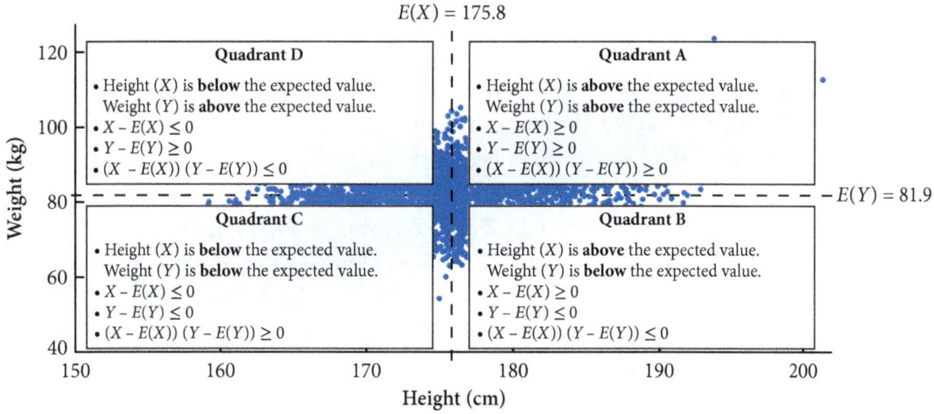

Figure 11.4 Summary of the products of deviations.

average, their weight is also above average. Similarly, if their height is below average, then their weight is also below average.

More formally, we can think about the values of $X - E(X)$ and $Y - E(Y)$, as denoted in Figure 11.4.

- If both $(X - E(X))$ and $(Y - E(Y))$ are positive, then it follows that the product of the deviations $(X - E(X))(Y - E(Y))$ will be positive (Quadrant A).
- Similarly, if both $(X - E(X))$ and $(Y - E(Y))$ are negative, then it follows that the product of the deviations $(X - E(X))(Y - E(Y))$ will be positive (Quadrant C).
- However, if $(X - E(X))$ is positive and $(Y - E(Y))$ is negative, then it follows that the product of the deviations $(X - E(X))(Y - E(Y))$ will be negative (Quadrant B).
- If $(X - E(X))$ is negative and $(Y - E(Y))$ is positive, then it follows that the product of the deviations will be negative (Quadrant D).

The covariance is then finding the average of these products.

Rule of thumb guide for covariances

- If most of the observations are in quadrants A and C, then the majority of the products of the deviations will be positive, and we would expect the covariance to be positive.
- If most of the observations are in quadrants B and D, the majority of these products will be negative, and so we would expect the covariance to be negative.
- If the observations are randomly distributed amongst all four quadrants, then we would expect the positive and negative products of the deviations to cancel out, and give a covariance equal to zero.

Returning to the example of height and weight, illustrated in Figure 11.3, we can see that most of the observations are in quadrants A and C. This means that, for most of the observations, the products of the deviations away from the expected values will, on average, be positive. This is associated with a positive covariance, meaning that as X increases, Y is also, on average, increasing. If, however, there had been a negative covariance, this would mean that, on average, as X increases, Y decreases.

The covariance between two variables X and Y is similar to the variance, in that it is a measure of how variables deviate from their expected value, but the covariance creates a measure of how the two variables deviate from their expected value together.

We have constructed the covariance as the average product of the deviations of the two variables away from their respective expected values:

$$cov(X,Y) = E\left[\left(X - E(X)\right)\left(Y - E(Y)\right)\right]$$

However, this can be fiddly to calculate directly. Just as with the variance, there is an easier route to calculating the covariance, such that:[5]

$$cov(X,Y) = E(XY) - E(X)E(Y)$$

Often, it is much easier to calculate a covariance for a theoretical distribution by finding $E(XY)$, $E(X)$, and $E(Y)$ separately, rather than trying to calculate the covariance directly.

Remember, generally speaking, the covariance measures the extent to which the two variables deviate from their expected value together:

i) If the covariance is positive, it means that when X is above its expected value, then on average, Y would also be above its expected value.
ii) If the covariance is negative, then it means that when X is above its expected value, then on average, Y would be below its expected value, and vice versa.

Worked example 11.1: Calculating a covariance from a joint probability distribution

Let's suppose that we have two discrete random variables, X and Y, with a joint probability mass function (PMF) shown in Table 11.1.

X is a random variable that takes the possible values 15 and 20, whilst Y is a random variable that takes the values 5 and 10. The covariance between X and Y is defined as $cov(X,Y) = E[(X - E(X))(Y - E(Y)) = E(XY) - E(X)E(Y)$.

Table 11.1 Joint probability mass function of X and Y

$P(X = x \cap Y = y)$		Y = 5	Y = 10
X	15	0.5	0.1
	20	0.1	0.3

[5] This is proved in the appendix to this chapter.

Reminder: The law of total probability

We have the joint PMF of two discrete random variables, *X* and *Y*, where the random variable *X* takes on the possible values $x_1, x_2, x_3, \ldots, x_n$, and the random variable *Y* takes the possible values $y_1, y_2, y_3, \ldots, y_m$

Provided each of the pairs of events are mutually exclusive from each other (i.e. cannot occur at the same time), then the probability that the random variable *Y* takes on a particular value, say y_j, is just the sum of all of joint probabilities where $Y = y_j$:

$$P\left(Y = y_j\right) = \sum_{i=1}^{n} P(X = x_i \cap Y = y_j)$$

To calculate the covariance, we will calculate three terms: $E(XY)$, $E(X)$, and $E(Y)$. However, to calculate $E(X)$ and $E(Y)$ we will need to first calculate the marginal distributions of X and Y. For example, to calculate the probability that $X = 15$, we will need to add together all of the joint probabilities where $X = 15$.

$$P(X = 15) = P(X = 15 \cap Y = 5) + P(X = 15 \cap Y = 10) = 0.5 + 0.1 = 0.6$$

If we repeat this for all of the possible outcomes of X and Y, we get the marginal probabilities (Table 11.2).

Table 11.2 Marginal distributions of *X* and *Y*

Marginal distribution of X		Marginal distribution of Y	
x	$P(X = x)$	y	$P(Y = y)$
15	0.6	5	0.6
20	0.4	10	0.4

To calculate $E(X)$, we simply need to find the sum of products of the outcomes and their respective probabilities:

$$E(X) = \sum_{x} P(X = x) \times x = P(X = 15) \times 15 + P(X = 20) \times 20 = 0.6 \times 15 + 0.4 \times 20$$
$$= 9 + 8 = 17$$
$$E(Y) = \sum_{y} P(Y = y) \times y = P(Y = 5) \times 5 + P(Y = 10) \times 10 = 0.6 \times 5 + 0.4 \times 10 = 7$$

The second step is to calculate $E(XY)$. We know the respective joint probabilities of each of the pairs of outcomes, $P(X = x \cap Y = y)$. Formally, we can find this expectation by finding the (double) summation:

$$E(XY) = \sum_{x}\sum_{y} P(X = x \cap Y = y) \times x \times y$$

Remember, what this notation means is that for every value of X, we will take each possible value of Y, and substitute in the respective probabilities, and the individual outcomes x and y.

$$\Rightarrow E(XY) = P(X = 15 \cap Y = 5) \times 15 \times 5 + P(X = 15 \cap Y = 10) \times 15 \times 10$$
$$+P(X = 20 \cap Y = 5) \times 20 \times 5 + P(X = 20 \cap Y = 10) \times 20 \times 5$$

So, we start with $X = 15$, and consider $Y = 5$ and $Y = 10$, and then move to $X = 20$, and consider $Y = 5$ and $Y = 10$ again.

$$= 0.5 \times 15 \times 5 + 0.1 \times 15 \times 10 + 0.1 \times 20 \times 5 + 0.3 \times 20 \times 10$$
$$= 122.5$$

We now have $E(XY) = 122.5$, $E(X) = 17$, and $E(Y) = 7$. We can combine these to calculate the covariance, such that:

$$cov(X,Y) = E(XY) - E(X)E(Y) = 122.5 - 17 \times 7 = 3.5$$

Since the covariance is positive, this indicates that as X increases, on average Y also increases.

Worked example 11.2: Calculating covariances for continuous random variables

When calculating covariances for continuous random variables, we need to follow exactly the same process as for discrete random variables. However, rather than adding together the products, we will need to integrate. To illustrate this, let's consider the following joint PDF for two random variables, W and Z, such that:

$$f_{W,Z}(w,z) = \begin{cases} \frac{w - z}{4} + \frac{1}{2}, & 1 \leq w \leq 3,\ 2 \leq z \leq 4 \\ 0, & \text{Otherwise} \end{cases}$$

Remember, for this to be well defined, it needs to be the case that the volume under the PDF is equal to 1. I will leave it as an exercise for you to show this. However, to calculate the covariance between W and Z, we need to find $cov(W,Z) = E(WZ) - E(W)E(Z)$.

That is, we will need three elements:

1. $E(W)$, which we can calculate from the marginal PDF of W.
2. $E(Z)$, which we can calculate from the marginal PDF of Z.
3. $E(WZ)$, which we can calculate from the joint PDF.

Let's start by constructing the marginal PDFs of W and Z. To do so, we will appeal to the law of total probability. Remember that, with discrete random variables, to construct the marginal probability that (say) $W = 2$, we added up all of the joint probabilities where $W = 2$ across all of the possile value of Z. Here, because $W$and Z are continuous random variables, each of the joint probabilities will be equal to zero, and so instead we will integrate the joint PDF across the domain of Z:

Marginal PDF of *W*	**Marginal PDF of *Z***
$f_W(w) = \int_z f_{W,Z}(w,z)dz = \int_2^4 \frac{w - z}{4} + \frac{1}{2}dz$	$f_Z(z) = \int_w f_{W,Z}(w,z)dw = \int_1^3 \frac{w - z}{4} + \frac{1}{2}dw$

Now, these integrals are relatively straightforward to evaluate. Remember, when you integrate with relation to z, you are effectively holding w fixed, and when you integrate with respect to w, you are effectively holding z fixed:

$$\Rightarrow f_W(w) = \left[\frac{wz}{4} - \frac{z^2}{8} + \frac{z}{2}\right]_2^4 \qquad \Rightarrow f_Z(z) = \left[\frac{w^2}{8} - \frac{wz}{4} + \frac{w}{2}\right]_1^3$$

Now, if we substitute in the limits of integration, we have:

$$\begin{aligned}\Rightarrow f_W(w) &= \left[\frac{4w}{4} - \frac{16}{8} + \frac{4}{2}\right] - \left[\frac{2w}{4} - \frac{4}{8} + \frac{2}{2}\right]\\ &= \frac{2w}{4} - \frac{12}{8} + \frac{2}{2}\\ &= \frac{w}{2} - \frac{1}{2}\end{aligned}$$

$$\begin{aligned}\Rightarrow f_Z(z) &= \left[\frac{9}{8} - \frac{3z}{4} + \frac{3}{2}\right] - \left[\frac{1}{8} - \frac{z}{4} + \frac{1}{2}\right]\\ &= 1 - \frac{2z}{4} + 1\\ &= 2 - \frac{z}{2}\end{aligned}$$

Now, remember that these PDFs are only non-zero for the range defined in the joint PDF—that is, for $2 \le z \le 4$ and for $1 \le w \le 3$. Therefore:

$$f_W(w) = \begin{cases} \frac{w-1}{2}, & 1 \le w \le 3 \\ 0, & \text{Otherwise} \end{cases} \qquad f_Z(z) = \begin{cases} 2 - \frac{z}{2}, & 2 \le z \le 4 \\ 0, & \text{Otherwise} \end{cases}$$

To calculate the expectation of W or Z, we need to integrate the product of the PDF with the outcomes of W (or Z). So for example, $E(Z) = \int_z f_Z(z) \times z dz$:

Expectation of W	Expectation of Z
$E(W) = \int_w f_W(w) \times w dw$	$E(Z) = \int_z f_Z(z) \times z dz$
$= \int_1^3 \left(\frac{w-1}{2}\right) \times w dw$	$= \int_2^4 \left(2 - \frac{z}{2}\right) \times z dz$
$= \int_1^3 \frac{w^2 - w}{2} dw = \left[\frac{w^3}{6} - \frac{w^2}{4}\right]_1^3$	$= \int_2^4 2z - \frac{z^2}{2} dz = \left[z^2 - \frac{z^3}{6}\right]_2^4$

If we now substitute in the limits of integration, this gives us that $E(W) = \frac{7}{3}$ and $E(Z) = \frac{8}{3}$.

Finally, we can calculate $E(WZ)$ by integrating the product of the joint PDF multiplied by the outcomes of W and Z across the full domain of both W and Z. That is:

$$E(WZ) = \int_w \int_z f_{W,Z}(w,z) \times w \times z \, dz \, dw = \int_1^3 \int_2^4 \left(\frac{w-z}{4} + \frac{1}{2}\right) \times w \times z \, dz \, dw$$

Because we are looking for the expectation of a product, we need to integrate over both W and Z here; remember, with a double integral, we begin in the middle and work outwards. It might be simplest to begin by multiplying out the brackets:

$$= \int_1^3 \int_2^4 \frac{w^2 z}{4} - \frac{wz^2}{4} + \frac{wz}{2} dz\, dw$$

We begin by integrating with relation to z, and we will leave all of the w terms as constants. This gives us:

$$= \int_1^3 \left[\frac{w^2 z^2}{8} - \frac{wz^3}{12} + \frac{wz^2}{4} \right]_2^4 dw$$

If we substitute in the limits of Z, we have:

$$= \int_1^3 \left[\left(w^2 \times \frac{16}{8} - w \times \frac{64}{12} + w \times \frac{16}{4} \right) - \left(w^2 \times \frac{4}{8} - w \times \frac{8}{12} + w \times \frac{4}{4} \right) \right] dw$$

$$= \int_1^3 \frac{3w^2}{2} - \frac{5w}{3} dw$$

In the same way, we now integrate with respect to w, giving us:

$$= \left[\frac{3w^3}{6} - \frac{5w^2}{6} \right]_1^3 = 6\frac{1}{3}$$

Finally, we can construct the covariance between W and Z by bringing all three elements together: $E(WZ) = \frac{19}{3}$, $E(W) = \frac{7}{3}$, $E(Z) = \frac{8}{3}$:

$$cov(W,Z) = E(WZ) - E(W)E(Z) = \frac{19}{3} - \frac{7}{3} \times \frac{8}{3} = \frac{19}{3} - \frac{56}{9} = \frac{1}{9}$$

As we can see, we have constructed a positive covariance, which means that on average as W increases, we would also expect Z to increase (and vice versa).

11.1.1 Empirical covariances

Suppose that you do not know the joint probability density or probability mass function of a pair of random variables, but instead observed the pairs of outcomes for every individual in the population; you can use this data to calculate the covariance and correlation for the population.

The covariance between two random variables, X and Y, is defined as:

$$cov(X,Y) = E\big(X - E(X)\big)\big(Y - E(Y)\big)$$

If you have observed the entire population, then $E(X)$ will be the same as the sample mean of the observations of X, whilst $E(Y)$ will be the same as the sample mean of Y. Therefore, if we observe all of the data within a population, then we can calculate the covariance as:

$$cov(X,Y) = \frac{\sum_{i=1}^{n} (X_i - \overline{X})(Y_i - \overline{Y})}{n}, \quad \text{where } \overline{X} = \frac{1}{n}\sum_{i=1}^{n} X_i \quad \text{and } \overline{Y} = \frac{1}{n}\sum_{i=1}^{n} Y_i$$

Important note

The formula given in Section 11.1.1 is only valid if you have observed a population. Just as with variances, when we observe a sample, and want to estimate the population covariance, we need to use a slightly different formula:

$$= \frac{1}{n-1}\sum_{i=1}^{n}(X_i - \bar{X})(Y_i - \bar{Y})$$

In Microsoft Excel, the formula =COVARIANCE.S(A2:A10, B2:B10) will apply this formula (2) to construct an estimate of the population covariance, based upon the pairs of observations within columns A and B from rows 2 to 10.

If you observe a population, and want to construct the covariance, then you will need to use the formula:

$$= \text{COVARIANCE.P}(\text{A2:A10, B2:B10})$$

This formula will construct the covariance by applying the following formula:

$$cov(X,Y) = \frac{\sum_{i=1}^{n}(X_i - \bar{X})(Y_i - \bar{Y})}{n}$$

If you simply use the formula =COVAR(A2:A10, B2:B10), then Excel will assume that you have observed a population, and use this latter formula (3).

Health warning

This is different from the default for the variance. Remember that if you use =VAR(A2:A10), then Excel will assume that you have observed a sample, and will divide by $n-1$ rather than n.

Worked example 11.3: Calculating an empirical covariance based on a very small population

To illustrate this, let's consider a very simple example. Let's suppose that we have a population consisting of only five individuals, and we observe each individual's height and weight (Table 11.3).

A good place to start, whenever you are interested in the relationship between two variables, is to plot this data on a graph, represented in Figure 11.5. We can see that, on average, as height increases, weight also increases.

Table 11.3 Height and weight of individuals in a population of five people

Individual	1	2	3	4	5
Height (*X*)	1.83m	1.78m	1.57m	1.65m	1.92m
Weight (*Y*)	78kg	82kg	54kg	68kg	88kg

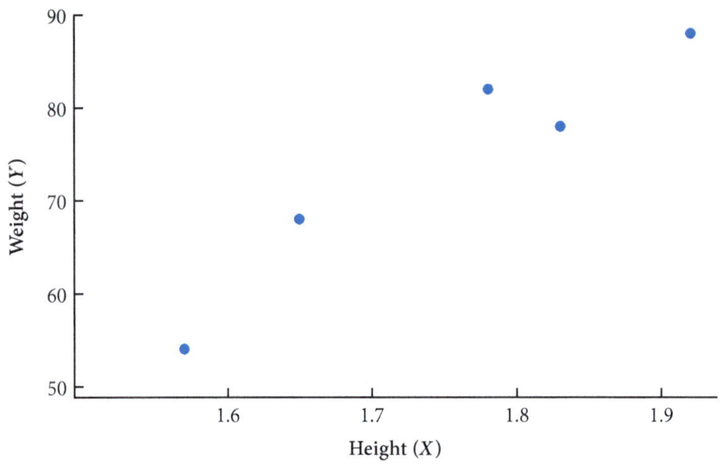

Figure 11.5 Scatter plot of weight against height in this small population.

Formally, to calculate the covariance, we need to begin by calculating the average height and the average weight. For simplicity of notation, let's define the random variable X as the individuals' heights, and let's define the random variable Y as the individuals' weights:

$$\bar{x} = \frac{1}{n}\sum_{i=1}^{n} x_i = \frac{1.83 + 1.78 + 1.57 + 1.65 + 1.92}{5} = 1.75$$

$$\bar{y} = \frac{1}{n}\sum_{i=1}^{n} y_i = \frac{78 + 82 + 54 + 68 + 88}{5} = 74$$

We can then calculate the deviations away from the expected value (average) (Table 11.4).

Then, we can calculate the covariance by substituting these into the formula:

$$cov(X,Y) = \frac{\sum_{i=1}^{n}(x_i - \bar{x})(y_i - \bar{y})}{n}$$

$$= \frac{0.08 \times 4 + 0.03 \times 8 + (-0.18) \times (-20) + (-0.10) \times (-6) + 0.17 \times 14}{5} = 1.428$$

As expected, this provides a positive covariance, indicating that, on average, as height increases, weight also increases (which is hardly a surprise).

Table 11.4 Deviations away from the expected value

Individual	1	2	3	4	5
$x_i - \bar{x}$	0.08	0.03	-0.18	-0.10	0.17
$y_i - \bar{y}$	4	8	-20	-6	14

Using Microsoft Excel to calculate the covariance between two random variables in a population

In large data sets, it can be very time consuming to manually calculate the covariance between two random variables in an observed population. However, Microsoft Excel will do this for you (see Figure 11.6). The formula COVARIANCE.P, or even just COVAR, will calculate the covariance, assuming that you are observing the entire population.

The command =COVAR(A2:A6, B2:B6) creates an entry in the cell which is equal to the covariance between Height and Weight. The term A2:A6 indicates that the first variable is located in the cells A2 to A6. The term B2:B6 indicates that the second variable is located in the cells B2 to B6.

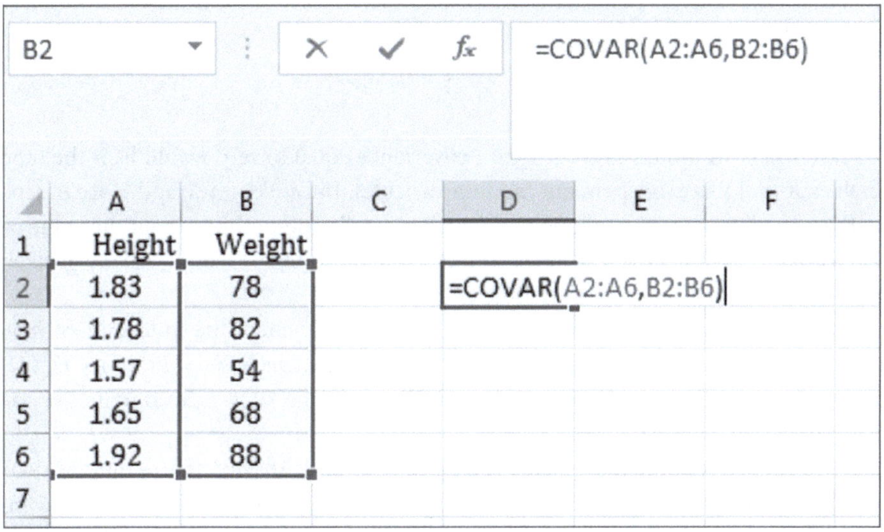

Figure 11.6 Using Microsoft Excel to calculate the covariance.

11.2 Cases where the covariance will be equal to zero

It is not always true that we will find a positive (or a negative) covariance between two variables. The covariance between two variables, X and Y, if knowing that X is above its expectation, does not affect the likelihood that Y is above (or below) its expectation. That is, if we observe an individual where $x_i > E(X)$, then we will not be able to make any prediction about that individual's value of y_i, as it will be random with relation to the value of X.

An example of this is illustrated in Figure 11.7. You can see that, unlike with the height and weight example, the observations lie equally distributed across the four quadrants. This means that the positive and negative products will end up cancelling each other out, leading to a covariance equal to zero.

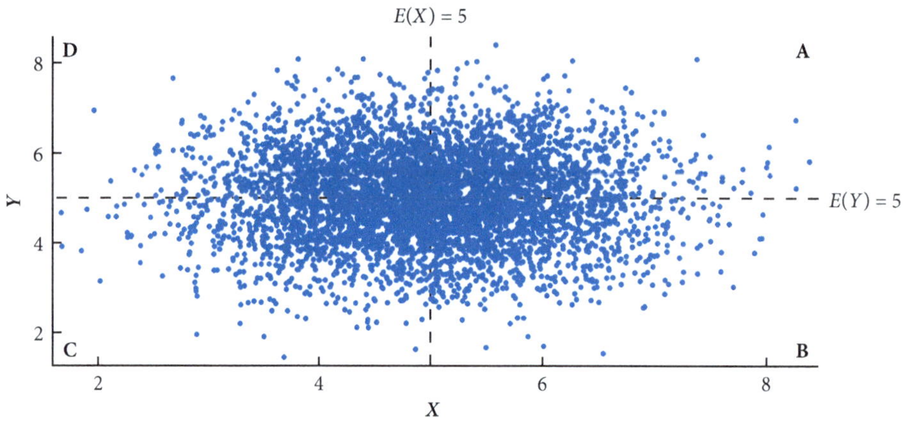

Figure 11.7 Scatter plot for two random variables with zero covariance.

A case where we would expect to see a covariance equal to zero would be if the random variables X and Y are independent random variables. Intuitively, if X and Y are independent, then knowing the value of one of the variables tells you nothing about the value of the other variable. That is, if you observe a large value of X, then Y could equally as likely be small, large, or somewhere in the middle!

Mathematically, we proved in earlier chapters that if X and Y are independent random variables, $E(XY) = E(X)E(Y)$. The covariance is defined as $cov(X,Y) = E(XY) - E(X)E(Y)$. Since, for independent random variables, $E(XY) = E(X)E(Y)$, we can rewrite the covariance as $cov(X,Y) = E(XY) - E(XY) = 0$.

As an example, suppose that you are rolling two fair dice. The outcomes from the two dice are independent from each other, so observing the outcome of one of the dice has no impact on the outcome of the other dice. If you gain a 6 from the first dice, you are still equally likely to gain any outcome from the second dice. Hence, since the outcomes are independent, the covariance will be equal to zero.

It should be noted that it is possible to obtain a covariance of zero even when two random variables are not independent. We will see some examples of pairs of random variables that are dependent but still produce a covariance equal to zero.

11.3 The role of covariances when finding the variance of a linear combination of random variables

We are going to take a little aside here, and return to discussing variances (which we saw in the last chapter). When we discussed expectations, we discussed how we could find the expectation of a linear combination of random variables. That is, if we have two random variables, X and Y, then:

$$E(aX + bY) = aE(X) + bE(Y)$$

However, when discussing the variance, we merely considered the variance of a single random variable. The reason for this is that, when you are calculating the variance of a linear combination of random variables, you may need to take into account the covariance between the pair of random variables as well.

There are a range of rules[6] that we can apply to evaluate the variance of a linear combination of random variables.

11.3.1 Adding a constant to a random variable

Firstly, if you add a constant to a random variable, the impact of this is merely to shift every outcome in the distribution by that constant. The variability of the random variable does not change; all that happens is that the distribution shifts to the right or left (depending on whether the constant is positive or negative).

For example, let's suppose we have a random variable X, whose PDF is illustrated in panel a) of Figure 11.8. We already know that adding a constant a to a random variable X will transform the expectation by adding a to the original expectation, $E(a + X) = a + E(X)$.

However, what happens to the variance? If we add a constant, all that happens is that every outcome will have that outcome added to it. In panel b) of Figure 11.8, we can see the impact of adding 5 to the random variable X. The impact is to shift the entire distribution 5 units to the right, so the new distribution is centred on 5 rather than 0. However, there is no impact on the variability, or the variance.

So our first rule is that, if you add a constant to a random variable, the resulting variance is just equal to the variance of the original random variable:

$$var(a + X) = var(X)$$

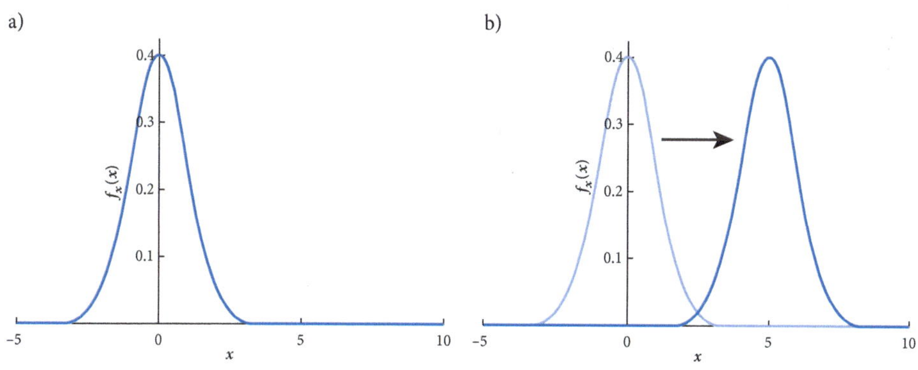

Figure 11.8 A linear transformation of a random variable.

[6] We provide mathematical proofs of these rules in the appendix to this chapter.

11.3.2 Multiplying a random variable by a constant

The impact of multiplying a random variable by a constant is a little less straightforward. Suppose that we have a random variable X where $E(X) = 0$. The impact of multiplying the random variable by a constant is to multiply every outcome by that constant. Therefore, every observation that is below the expected value is pulled further below the expected value, and every observation that is above the expected value is pulled further above the expected value.

To illustrate this, consider the following simple random variable, Y. Y can either take the value +1 or −1, each with probability $P(Y = 1) = P(Y = -1) = 0.5$. Now, if we multiplied Y by 2, this would mean that all of the outcomes of Y would also be multiplied by 2. The possible outcomes of $2Y$ would be equal to either +2 or −2, again, both with probability 0.5. However, by multiplying by 2, we have caused the distribution to spread out. That is, the variance will have increased.

We can also illustrate this for continuous random variables. Suppose that we think of the PDF of a random variable as being like a two-dimensional jelly on a perfectly flat plate. When we multiply the random variable by a constant a (for a greater than 1), this is a bit like pushing down on the jelly from the top; what ends up happening is that the probability density function spreads out along the axis.

This is illustrated in panel a) of Figure 11.9, which shows the original distribution of the random variable X. By multiplying the random variable by a constant (in this case 2), the impact is that the distribution is pushed downwards, and the data becomes much more spread out.

We can see that the variance must have increased when moving from X to $2X$; in fact, the variance is four times larger for the transformed variable than the original variable. That is, $var(2X) = 4 \times var(X)$.

More generally, if we multiply any random variable by a constant, then we know that $E(aX) = aE(X)$. However, the transformation of the variance is to multiply the variance by the square of the multiplier:

$$var(aX) = a^2 var(X)$$

This is because, since the variance is equal to $var(X) = E[(X - E(X))^2]$, we can think of this as being analogous to squaring a set of brackets. If you multiply everything within the brackets by a, then this is equivalent to multiplying the entire bracket by a^2.

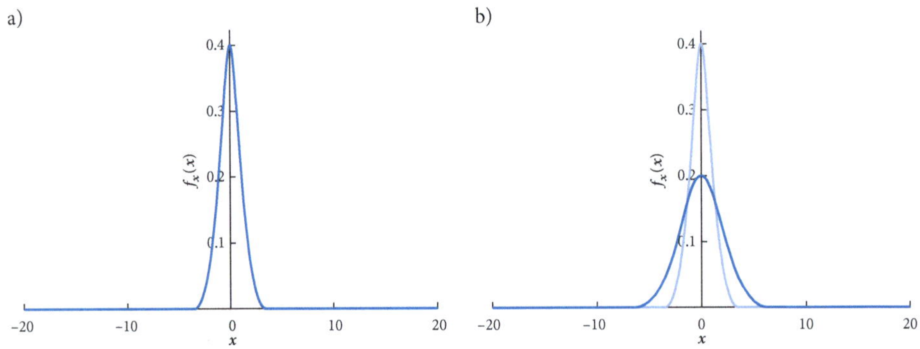

Figure 11.9 Impact of multiplying a random variable by a constant.

11.3.3 Adding together random variables

Suppose that we were to combine two random variables in a linear combination, to construct a third, Z, such that:

$$Z = aX + bY$$

An intuitive way to think about what happens when you find the variance of Z is to think about what happens when you square Z, because the variance is just the expectation of the square of Z less its expected value. We know that:

$$Z^2 = (aX + bY)^2 = a^2X^2 + b^2Y^2 + 2ab \times XY$$

When thinking of variances, we can think of any squared terms as being like a variance term. Similarly, we can think of any cross-product terms as being like covariance terms. In fact, it's possible to show that,[7] to find the variance of Z, this is just:

$$var(Z) = var(aX + bY) = a^2var(X) + b^2var(Y) + 2ab \times cov(X,Y)$$

The intuition is very useful to remember, because, as you study more statistics, you will need to find the variance of increasingly complicated sums. If you remember that the variance of that sum is like thinking about what happens when you square the sum:

- Any random variables that are squared become variance terms.
- Any random variables where you have cross products (e.g. XY) become covariance terms.

11.3.4 Summary of rules

If we have two random variables, X and Y, which have expectations $E(X)$ and $E(Y)$, and variances $var(X)$ and $var(Y)$:

Transformation	Expected value	Variance
Adding a constant to X $X \to a + X$	$E(a + X) = a + E(X)$	$var(a + X) = var(X)$
Multiplying X by a constant $X \to aX$	$E(aX) = aE(X)$	$var(aX) = a^2\, var(X)$
Creating a linear combination of two random variables $X,Y \to aX + bY$	$E(aX + bY) = aE(X) + bE(Y)$	$var(aX + bY) = a^2\, var(X) + b^2\, var(Y) + 2ab \times cov(X,Y))$

[7] There is a proof of this in the appendix.

Worked example 11.4: Calculating a module grade

Suppose that your mark for your statistics course was made up of two elements: a positive element consisting of the marks gained in an examination (X), and a negative element consisting of the number of classes missed during the year (Y). The lecturer wishes to calculate the expected score within the class, and the variance of the scores overall.

The overall, final grade, which we will define as Z for the unit, is given by:

$$Z = 5X - 2Y$$

That is, for every additional mark in the exam gained, the final grade increases by 5 marks. For every additional class missed, the final grade decreases by 2 marks. We know some of the characteristics of the exam mark (X) and the number of classes missed (Y), and the covariance between the two:

$$E(X) = 14, var(X) = 4$$
$$E(Y) = 10, var(Y) = 5$$
$$cov(X,Y) = -1.2$$

The covariance between X and Y is negative. This indicates that, as the number of classes missed increases, the grade in the exam falls. This might be a causal relationship, such that if you miss more classes (i.e. Y increases), then the impact is to lower the exam score. However, it might also be that those who gain lower marks in the exam might just be more prone to missing classes. Based on this information, it's impossible to say whether this is causal or not.

From this information, we want to find the expectation and the variance of the final grade, Z. Using our rules of expectations:

$$E(Z) = E(5X - 2Y) = 5E(X) - 2E(Y)$$
$$= 5 \times 14 - 2 \times 10 = 50$$

Similarly, we can use the rules of variances. We are looking for the variance of the final module grade, $var(Z)$, and we can calculate this by substituting in the generating process for this final mark:

$$var(Z) = var(5X - 2Y)$$

To calculate $var(5X - 2Y)$, we will need to apply our rules of variances, such that, if we have any linear combination of two random variables, we can calculate the variance of the linear combination as:

$$var(aX + bY) = a^2 var(X) + b^2 var(Y) + 2ab \times cov(X,Y)$$

In this example, $a = 5$, and $b = -2$, and so we can rewrite this as:

$$\Rightarrow var(Z) = var(5X - 2Y)$$
$$= 5^2 var(X) + (-2)^2 var(Y) + 2 \times 5 \times (-2) \times cov(X,Y)$$
$$= 5^2 var(X) + 2^2 var(Y) - 2 \times 5 \times 2 \times cov(X,Y)$$

Substituting the variances and covariances into the expression gives us the variance of the final grade, $var(Z)$:

$$\Rightarrow var(Z) = 25 \times 4 + 4 \times 5 - 20 \times (-1.2) = 144$$

From this value, we can see that the standard deviation of the final grade is equal to $\sqrt{144} = 12$.

11.3.5 More complicated linear combinations

As we introduce estimators in future chapters, we will need to calculate the variance of more complex linear combinations of random variables. The key thing to remember is that finding a variance is just like squaring an expression. For example, if you had four random variables, W, X, Y, and Z, and created a new variable, Q, as a linear combination of the four variables:

$$Q = aW + bX + cY + dZ$$

We can, intuitively, find the variance of the new variable Q by squaring the expression $(aW + bX + cY + dZ)$. Any terms that are left as square terms will convert into a variance, whilst any cross-product terms will become covariance terms:

$$Q^2 = (aW + bX + cY + dZ)^2$$

Squaring this expression, we will have terms involving the square of each of the variables (W^2, X^2, Y^2, Z^2), and we will have terms involving each of the possible cross-product terms (WX, WY, WZ, XY, XZ, YZ):

$$\begin{aligned} &= a^2W^2 + b^2X^2 + c^2Y^2 + d^2Z^2 \\ &\quad +2(ab \times WX + ac \times WY + ad \times WZ + bc \times XY + bd \times XZ + cd \times YZ) \end{aligned}$$

In the same way, if we want to construct the variance of Q, any of the variables that are squared will become variance terms, whilst any of the cross-product terms will become covariances:

$$\begin{aligned} var(Q) &= a^2 var(W) + b^2 var(X) + c^2 var(Y) + d^2 var(Z) \\ &\quad + 2 \times \begin{pmatrix} ab \times cov(W,X) + ac \times cov(W,Y) + ad \times cov(W,Z) + bc \times cov(X,Y) \\ + bd \times cov(X,Y) + cd \times cov(Y,Z) \end{pmatrix} \end{aligned}$$

11.4 Rules of covariances

We have seen a set of rules for how we calculate the variance of linear functions of random variables, but it is often very useful to be able to evaluate the covariance between variables which have had linear transformations applied.

11.4.1 The covariance of any constant with a variable is equal to zero

The first rule about covariances may seem relatively self-explanatory; if you have any random variable, and you wish to find the covariance with a constant, the covariance will always be equal to zero. The covariance is a measure of how the two variables vary together. If either one of those variables does not vary, then, by definition, there can be no covariance, and so the covariance is necessarily zero:

$$cov(a, X) = 0$$

11.4.2 The covariance of any variable with itself is just the variance of the variable

The next, important rule is that the covariance of any random variable with itself is just equal to the variance of that random variable. For example, if we are interested in the covariance of a random variable X with itself, we can write that:

$$cov(X,X) = E\left[\left(X - E(X)\right)\left(X - E(X)\right)\right] = E\left[\left(X - E(X)\right)^2\right]$$

However, this is just equivalent to the variance of X. So $cov(X,X) = var(X)$.

11.4.3 Multiplying a random variable by a constant

Suppose that we know the covariance between two random variables, X and Y, and we multiplied one of these random variables by a constant. We then might want to know the resulting covariance.

That is, if we transform a random variable X to a new variable, aX, by multiplying X by a constant, a, then:

$$cov(aX,Y) = a \times cov(X,Y)$$

In the same way, if we multiplied both X and Y by constants, a and b, then we could simply take the multipliers outside of the covariance:

$$cov(aX,bY) = a \times b \times cov(X,Y)$$

11.4.4 Finding covariances including a linear combination of random variables

Suppose that you multiply together $(aX + bY)Z$. We know, from simple algebra, that this expression would be equal to:

$$(aX + bY)Z = aXZ + bYZ$$

Now, just as in Section 11.3.3, we can think of covariances as a little like multiplying together pairs of variables. When we obtain cross-product terms (such as XZ, YZ, etc.) relating to random variables, these are equivalent to covariances. If you observe squared terms, these are equivalent to variances.

Through this logic, we can think of what we would get if we found the covariance between $aW + bX$ and $cY + dZ$. We would need to consider each possible pair of outcomes from the two brackets:

$$cov(aX + bY,Z) = acov(X,Z) + bcov(Y,Z)$$

More generally, if you wish to find the covariance between $aX + bY$ and $cW + dZ$, then:

$$cov(aX + bY, cW + dZ) = a \times c \times cov(X,W) + a \times d \times cov(X,Z)$$
$$= + b \times c \times cov(Y,W) + b \times d \times cov(Y,Z)$$

The terms that you obtain here are just as you would if you multiplied together $(aX + bY)$ and $(cW + dZ)$. This is a very useful rule to take advantage of when evaluating estimators later in this textbook.

11.4.5 **Summary of rules**

Rule	Covariance
The order of the variables does not matter	$cov(X,Y) = cov(Y,X)$
Covariance between a constant and a random variable	$cov(a, X) = 0$
Covariance of a random variable with itself	$cov(X,X) = var(X)$
Covariance between multiples of random variables:	$cov(aX,bY) = a \times b \times cov(X,Y)$
Covariance between linear combination of random variables	$cov(aW + bX, cY + dZ)$ $= a \times c \times cov(W,Y) + a \times d \times cov(W,Z)$ $+b \times c \times cov(X,Y) + b \times d \times cov(X,Z)$

Worked example 11.5: Covariances between exam results

In Section 11.3.5 we calculated the variance of exam scores, based on the variance and covariance of the component parts. That is, if there are two components, X representing the mark in the examination, and Y representing the number of classes missed during the year, then final grade, Z, for the module is given as:

$$Z = 5X - 2Y$$

If we know that $var(X) = 4, var(Y) = 5$, and $cov(X,Y) = -1.2$, then the variance of the final grade is just given as $var(Z) = 144$.

Now, because of the way the final grade is constructed, we would expect a positive covariance between the score gained in the X component and the final grade. That is, as X increases, we would expect the final grade to also increase. As such, we would expect a positive covariance between X and the final grade. However, before we calculate the covariance, let's consider what the data looks like, visually. To do this, I have simulated a population with the following characteristics:

- $E(X) = 14, E(Y) = 10$
- $var(X) = 4, var(Y) = 5$
- $cov(X,Y) = -1.2$
- $Finalgrade = 5X - 2Y$

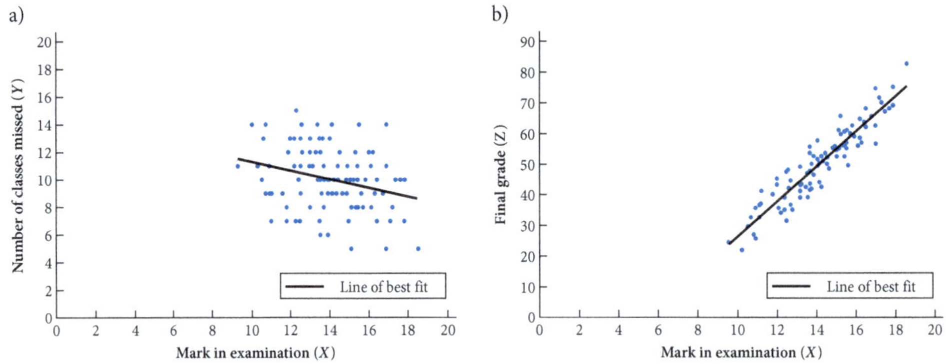

Figure 11.10 Scatter plot of simulated data of module marks and class attendance.

We have then randomly sampled 100 observations from this population. Figure 11.10 shows a scatter plot of the simulated data,[8] with a 'line of best fit' drawn through the data.[9] In panel a), we have the plot of the number of classes absent against the examination mark. We know, since the covariance is equal to $cov(X,Y) = -1.2$, that as X increases, then, on average, Y decreases. However, whilst we have drawn on a line of best fit, the data is not very close to the line. Without the line of best fit, it would be difficult to see the negative trend. In panel b) of Figure 11.10, we see a much clearer relationship between the final grade and the examination mark (X): as X increases, it is very obvious that the final grade also increases. It is also very clear that the increase is linear (i.e. the data looks like it is clustered around a straight line). This is because of the way that the final grade is created—by simply taking the mark in the examination, multiplying that by 5, and then subtracting twice the number of classes missed.

We still need to calculate the covariance between the final grade and the exam mark X. Remember that the final grade (Z) is just calculated as $Z = 5X - 2Y$, so applying the rules of covariances, we can construct the covariance between these two variables by substituting in $Z = 5X - 2Y$:

$$cov(Z,X) = cov(5X - 2Y, X)$$

From our rules of covariances, we know that we can split the $5X - 2Y$ up into two parts, and find the covariance relating to each element, so:

$$cov(5X - 2Y, X) = cov(5X, X) + cov(-2Y, X)$$

Where we have a constant multiplier of either term, we can take these outside of the covariance, giving us:

$$= 5 \times cov(X,X) + (-2) \times cov(Y,X)$$
$$= 5 \times cov(X,X) - 2 \times cov(Y,X)$$

[8] The data has been constructed so that Y is a discrete random variable, taking only whole numbers. This is because being absent from class is a discrete measure—even if you show up late to a class, you are still present for that class.

[9] You can add this line of best fit in Excel by creating a scatter plot, and adding a trendline. We will discuss how this line of best fit is constructed mathematically later in this book.

Now, we already know that $cov(X,X)$ is just the same as the variance of X, and so we can write this as:

$$= 5 \times var(X) - 2 \times cov(Y,X)$$

The other, potentially confusing, element is that in our formula, we have $cov(Y,X)$, but in the information shown, we are given $cov(X,Y)$. However, the order of variables within a covariance does not matter: $cov(X,Y) = cov(Y,X)$. We could think of this mathematically, as $cov(X,Y) = E\big[(X - E(X))(Y - E(Y))\big]$ and $cov(Y,X) = E\big[(Y - E(Y))(X - E(Y))\big]$. Because the order of the elements of a multiplication does not matter, these two covariances are exactly the same. So, we know that $var(X) = 4$ and $cov(Y,X) = cov(X,Y) = -0.35$. As such, we can calculate the covariance between the exam mark, X, and the final grade, Z, as:

$$cov(Z,X) = 5 \times 4 - 2 \times (-1.2) = 22.4$$

If you were to repeat this exercise, and plotted the final grade against the number of classes missed, you would expect to see a negative relationship. It is possible to show that the covariance between Y and the final grade will be equal to $cov(Y,Z) = -16$, but I will leave that as an exercise for you to prove.

11.5 Correlations

In Worked example 11.5, we saw three variables, each with different covariances between the variables. We saw that $cov(X,Y) = -1.2$, $cov(Z,X) = 22.4$ and $cov(Z,Y) = 16$. What this doesn't tell us is how 'strong' the relationship is between two variables. A positive covariance merely tells us that if one variable increases then, on average, the other variable also increases. Similarly, a negative covariance tells us that if one variable increases then, on average, the other variable decreases.

As such, we need to construct a new measure that tells us how strongly the two variables are related. Let's return to the example of per capita spending on healthcare and life expectancy (from OECD data) that we saw earlier in this chapter (Figure 11.11).[10]

We can see that as spending increases, then on average, life expectancy appears to increase. However, it is not the case that we can simply 'join the dots' to find a simple relationship between life expectancy and spending; that is, the observations do not all lie in a neat, straight line. Therefore, an important question that we might ask is how strongly these variables are related with each other, or more formally, how close is the data to lying on a straight line.

In Section 11.2, we saw that if there was an interrelationship between two random variables within a population, then we could calculate the covariance between these two populations. However, it is very difficult to interpret the meaning of the covariance, other than that a positive covariance indicates that, on average, as one variable increases, then the other variable is likely to increase. Similarly, a negative covariance indicates that as one variable increases, the other

[10] OECD (2019), *Health at a Glance 2019: OECD Indicators*, OECD Publishing, Paris, https://doi.org/10.1787/4dd50c09-en

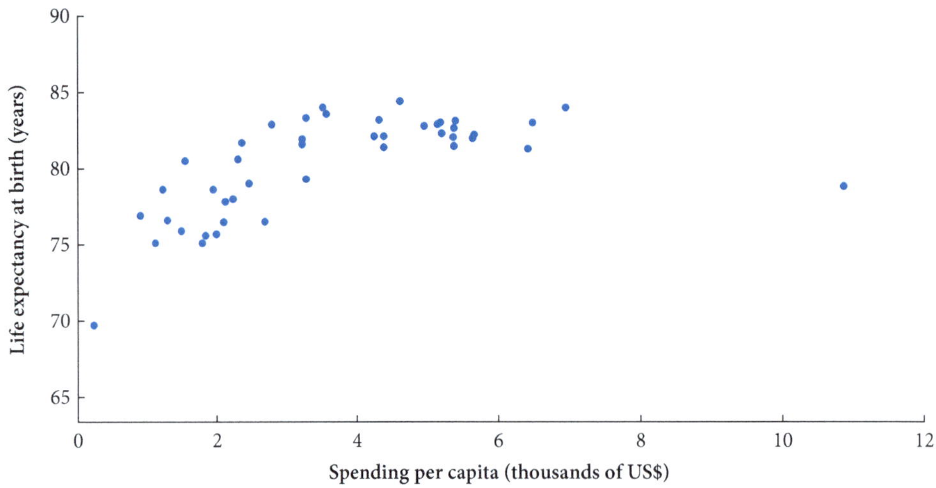

Figure 11.11 Life expectancy and expenditure on healthcare (data from the OECD).

decreases. However, this does not allow us to make any inferences about the strength of the relationship between the two variables, which we could compare with a different pair of random variables. If the underlying variance of the random variables is very large, we could see a very large covariance. Similarly, if the underlying variance of the random variables is close to zero, then the level of the covariance will also be small. As such, if we wish to compare the strength of the relationship between variables, we need to introduce a new measure which re-scales the covariance to a standardized measure. This measure is known as the correlation coefficient.

In order to motivate the correlation coefficient, let us begin by considering the units related to the covariance. In the example shown in Figure 11.11, spending is measured in USD, whilst life expectancy is measured in years. If we define the random variable X to represent spending on healthcare, and Y to represent life expectancy, the formula for the covariance is equal to:

$$cov(X,Y) = E\big(X - E(X)\big)\big(Y - E(Y)\big)$$
$$units = USD \times Years$$

The units for the covariance would be $USD \times years$. In order to compare strength of relationships between random variables, we would need a unitless measure. As such, we need to re-scale the measure to give a standardized measure of covariation, using the correlation coefficient, which is constructed based on the covariance we saw before. Remember that the covariance measures how much two variables deviate from their expected value together. That is:

$$cov(X,Y) = E\Big(\big(X - E(X)\big)\big(Y - E(Y)\big)\Big)$$

The units of the covariance will always be in the units of X multiplied by the units of Y. We can standardize the covariance, to construct the correlation coefficient by dividing the covariance through by the standard deviation of X and the standard deviation of Y.This has the effect of also making a unitless measure, which allows comparisons across different pairs of variables.

We generally represent the correlation between two variables X and Y as ρ_{XY}:

$$\rho_{XY} = \frac{cov(X,Y)}{s.d.(X) \times s.d.(Y)} = \frac{cov(X,Y)}{\sqrt{var(X)var(Y)}}$$

By dividing through by the standard deviations of X and Y, we create a standardized measure, which allows us to compare the level of *correlation* between different pairs of data.

Thus the correlation coefficient is unitless, and provides a standardized measure to compare the strength of relationships between two variables. It should be noted that the correlation coefficient must lie between −1 and 1.[11]

The two extremes are represented in Figure 11.12. In panel a), we can see there is an upward sloping relationship, with all of the points lying directly on the line. This is equivalent to a correlation equal to +1. In panel b), again, all of the points lie directly on a straight line, indicating a perfect correlation, but in this case, these are all on a downward sloping straight line.

Focusing on panel a), where we have a perfect positive correlation, $\rho_{X,Y} = +1$, we can see that every observation of Y is just a linear function of X. In this case, the equation of the line linking the two variables is just $Y = 3X + 2$. If you were to find the gradient of this line, you would see that for every 1 unit X increases, Y increases by 3 units. That is, the gradient of the line is equal to 3.[12]

Similarly, in panel b), we have a perfect negative correlation, $\rho_{X,Y} = -1$. Again, we can see that every observation of Y is a linear function of X. In this case, the equation of the line linking the two variables is just $Y = 7 - 2X$. That is, in this case, the marginal impact of increasing X by 1 is to decrease Y by 2.

Note that the correlation coefficient does not tell us anything about the slope of the line; we have had to calculate that ourselves. Instead, the correlation coefficient tells us about how close the points are to lying on a straight upward or downward sloping line.

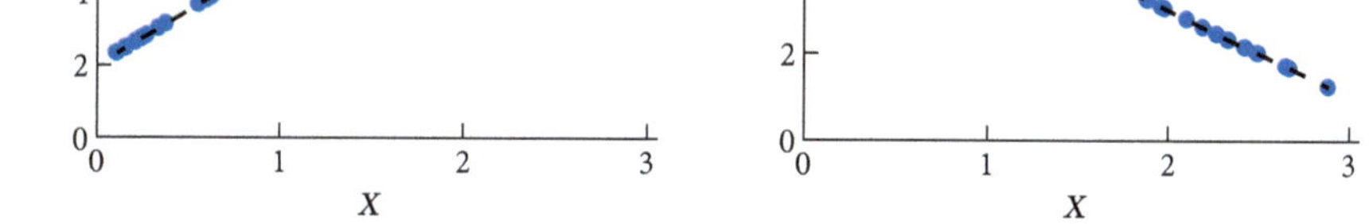

Figure 11.12 Perfect positive or negative correlations.

[11] The covariance will always be less than the product of the standard deviations.

[12] You could calculate this gradient by differentiating the equation of the line: $\frac{d}{YdX} = \frac{dd}{X}(3X + 2) = 3$.

Summary: Correlations

The correlation coefficient ρ_{XY} provides a standardized measure for the level of covariation between two random variables. The correlation coefficient is defined as the covariance divided by the product of the standard deviations of the two random variables.

$$\rho_{XY} = \frac{cov(X,Y)}{s.d.(X) \times s.d.(Y)}$$

The correlation coefficient will always lie between −1 and +1. It is a measure of how close the data from the pair of random variables are to lying on a straight upward or downward sloping line.

Figure 11.13 illustrates different correlations, ranging from $\rho_{X,Y} = 0.95$ to $\rho_{X,Y} = 0.25$. In each case, the slope of the data (illustrated by the line of best fit) is the same, and equal to 0.5. What we can see is that, when $\rho_{X,Y} = 0.95$, all of the observed points are very close to the line of best fit, but as the correlation tends towards zero, the spread of the data becomes much wider. By the time you reach $\rho_{X,Y} = 0.25$, it is difficult to easily discern the trend in the data, without the trendline being drawn in.

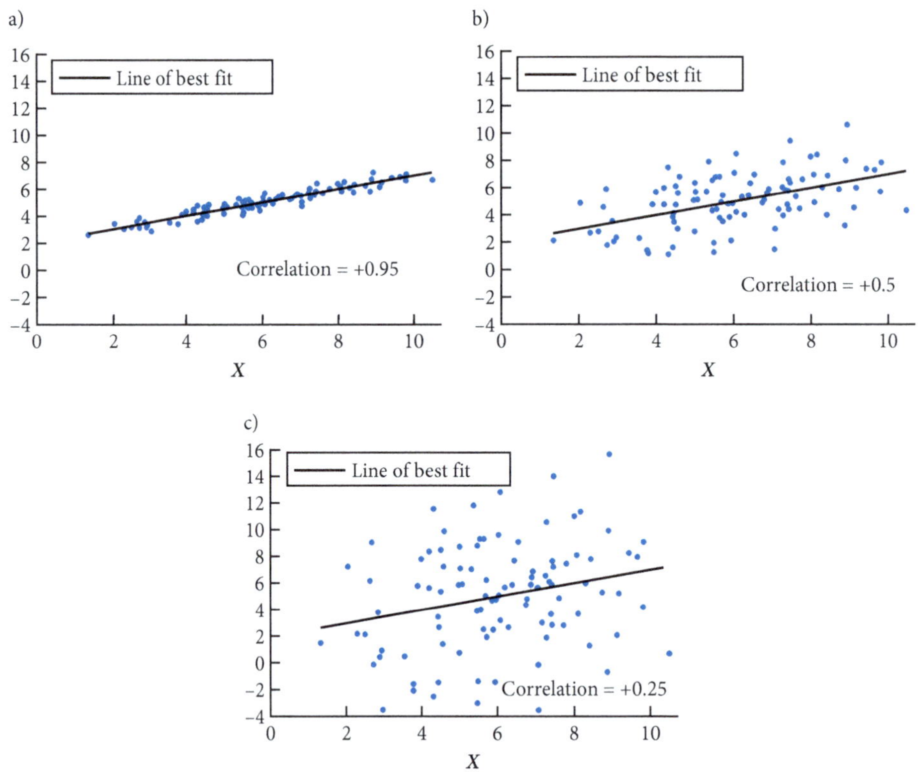

Figure 11.13 Different (positive) correlations.

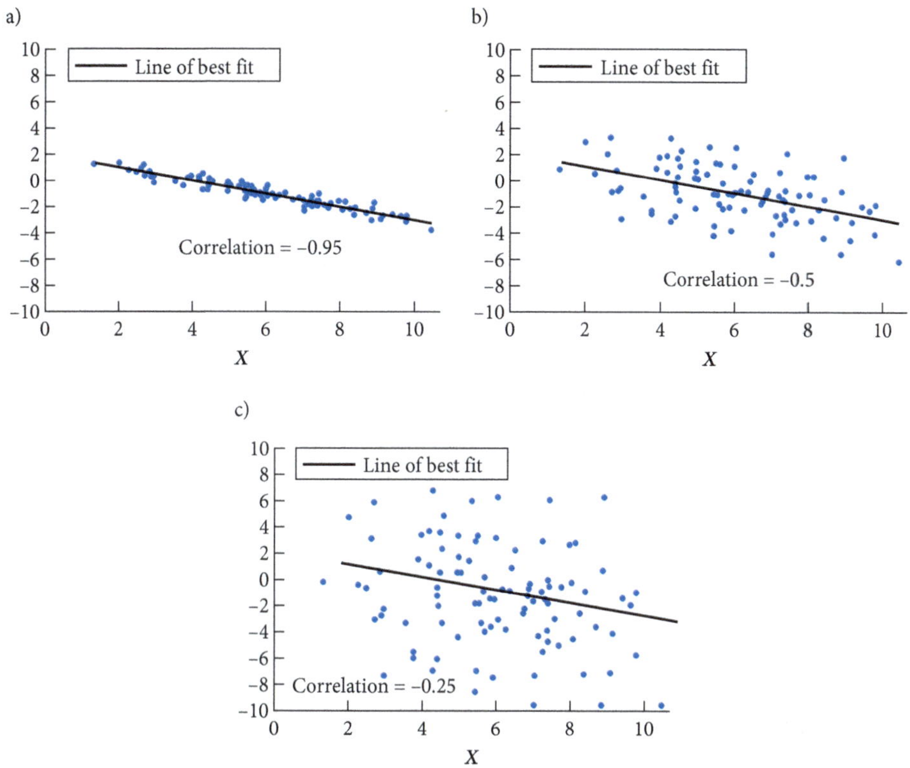

Figure 11.14 Different (negative) correlations.

A similar pattern is illustrated in Figure 11.14, but in this case illustrating different negative correlations. Again, each of the scatter plots is centred around a line of best fit, with a slope equal to −0.5. Even though it may be difficult to discern a relationship in panels c) of the two figures, this does not mean that there is no relationship between Y and X. In this case, because of the way the data has been generated, there is a deterministic relationship between X and Y, but there is a lot of 'noise' in panel c) that makes it more difficult to observe the relationship. Because of this, in cases where there is a lot of noise in the data, it will be important to appeal to estimators to provide estimates of relationships between economic variables.

Worked example 11.6: Calculating correlations from covariances

In Worked example 11.5, we considered the case of a unit mark that was constructed based upon the mark gained in an exam (X), and the number of classes missed (Y), where the final grade (Z) was calculated as:

$$Z = 5X - 2Y$$

We were told that:

- $E(X) = 14, E(Y) = 10$
- $var(X) = 4, var(Y) = 5$
- $cov(X,Y) = -1.2$

and we further calculated that $var(Z) = 144$ and that $cov(Z,X) = 22.4$. However, what we really want to know is how strongly correlated the variables are. Remember that the correlation coefficient tells us how close the data is to lying on an upward or downward sloping straight line. To illustrate the data, consider again the simulated data shown in Figure 11.15. The data appears closer to a straight line in panel b) than in panel a). As such, we would expect the magnitude of the correlation to be closer to 1 for the data in panel b) than in panel a).

a) Calculating the correlation between the mark in the examination (X) and the number of classes missed (Y)

We know that the correlation coefficient can be calculated as the covariance divided through by the square root of the product of the variances of the two variables. We know that $cov(X,Y) = -1.2$, $var(X) = 4$ and $var(Y) = 5$:

$$\rho_{X,Y} = \frac{cov(X,Y)}{\sqrt{var(X) \times var(Y)}}$$

As such, the correlation between the number of classes missed and the mark in the examination can be calculated as:

$$\rho_{X,Y} = \frac{-1.2}{\sqrt{4 \times 5}} = -0.268$$

b) Calculating the correlation between the mark in the examination (X) and the final module grade (Y)

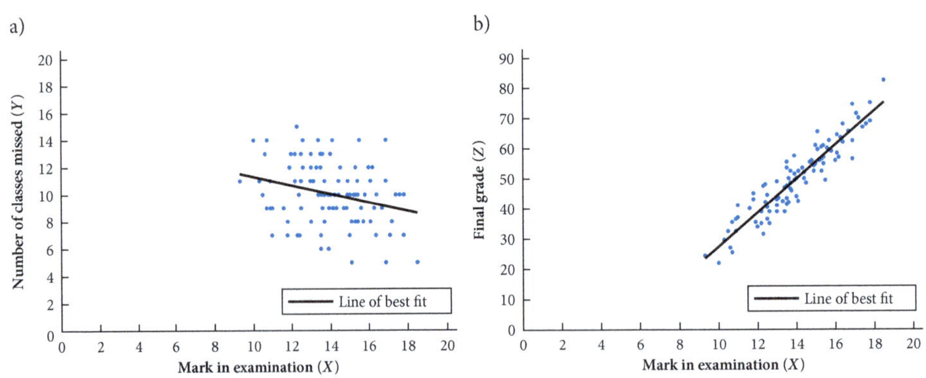

Figure 11.15 Scatter plot of simulated data of module marks, and class attendance.

Using exactly the same method as in part a), we know that $cov(Z, X) = 22.4$, and the variance of the final grade is equal to 144, whilst the variance of the exam mark was equal to 4:

$$\rho_{Finalgrade,X} = \frac{cov(Finalgrade, X)}{\sqrt{var(Finalgrade) \times var(X)}}$$

Substituting in the values for the covariance and variances gives us:

$$= \frac{22.4}{\sqrt{144 \times 4}} = \frac{22.4}{\sqrt{576}}$$

Before calculating the numerical value, this example highlights why the correlation is so important. If we simply compared the covariances between a) and b), we would see that the magnitude of the covariance is much larger when looking at the relationship between the final grade and the exam mark (= 22.4) than in the case of the covariance of the exam mark and the number of classes missed (= −1.2). However, this is, in part, due to the fact that there is much more variation in the final grade. We can see that the variance of the final grade is equal to 144; because of this, even if the correlation were identical, the covariance would automatically be higher in case b) than in case a).

Now, calculating the numerical value of the correlation gives us:

$$= \frac{22.4}{\sqrt{576}} = 0.9333$$

The correlation here is equal to 0.9333. This indicates a very strong correlation between the final grade and the mark gained in the examination, and a much stronger magnitude of correlation than between X and Y. This is reinforced visually by the simulated data in Figure 11.10, where we can see that the data is much more clustered around the line in panel b) than in panel a), indicating a stronger magnitude of the correlation.

11.5.1 Empirical correlations

Let's return to the example we saw at the beginning of the chapter, focusing on the Phillips' curve relationship between US unemployment and inflation.[13]

We can see from the scatter plot in Figure 11.16 that there appears to be a negative relationship between the two variables. If we draw a straight line through the data, it will not be the case that all of the observations lie on a straight line. The correlation coefficient can tell us how close the data is to an (imaginary) line of best fit through the data.

In this case, the correlation is equal to $\rho = -0.30418$. Whilst this is not a huge magnitude for a correlation coefficient, it is not trivial either. This indicates that there is certainly a trend to the data, and that on average, as unemployment increased, inflation decreased. However, this is not the same as stating that there is a causal relationship between the two variables. We will examine causality later in this book.

[13] You can download this data from Data sets and exercises at the end of this chapter.

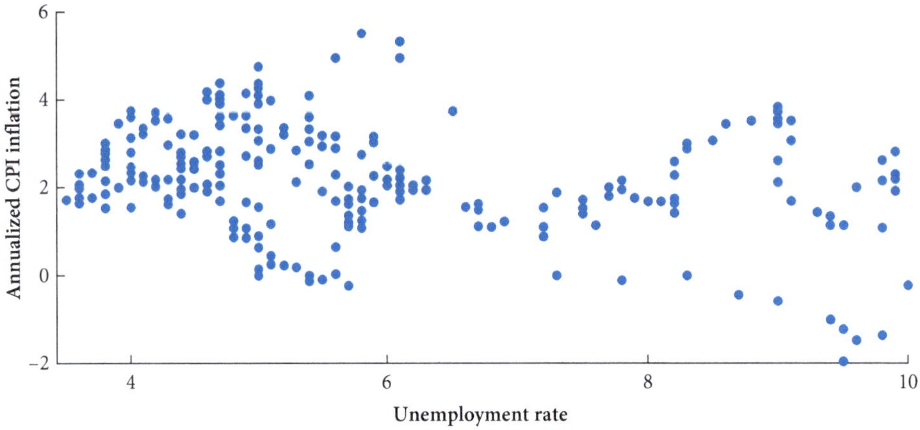

Figure 11.16 US inflation and unemployment rates between 2000 and 2019 (data from FRED).

11.6 Independent random variables and zero correlations

In previous chapters, we have discussed the concept of independent random variables. Two variables are independent if knowing the value of one of the random variables tells us nothing about the likely value of the other random variable. For example, if we flip a (fair) coin twice, just because the first flip lands heads upwards, the probability that the coin lands heads upwards on the second flip remains ½. The coin has no memory; as such, the flips of the coin are independent random variables.

As we move into statistics and the properties of estimators in future chapters, we will often make an assumption that successive observations from a population are independent. The implication of this is that the covariance, and hence also the correlation between the observations, is equal to zero.

In fact, it will always be the case that if two random variables are independent, they will have a covariance (and hence a correlation) equal to zero.[14]

However, an error that students often make is to observe zero correlation between two random variables, and assume that this also implies that the two random variables are also independent. We cannot make this jump.

Suppose that you have two random variables, X and Y. The first random variable, X, is uniformly distributed between −1 and +1. The second variable, Y, is constructed by squaring the observation of X. That is, $Y = X^2$. This is illustrated in Figure 11.17. We can see, very clearly, that there is a simple, deterministic relationship between X and Y. That is, X and Y are definitely not independent random variables!

[14] We will prove this in the appendix at the end of this chapter.

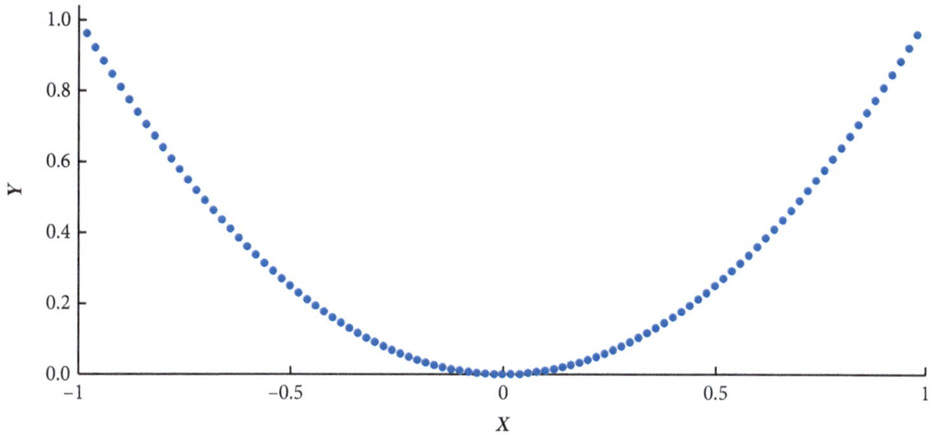

Figure 11.17 Plotting X^2 against X.

In this example, the correlation between the two variables will be exactly equal to zero. We can prove this, using the PDF of X. In this example, the PDF of X is:

$$f_X(x) = \begin{cases} 0.5, & -1 \le x \le 1 \\ 0, & \text{Otherwise} \end{cases}$$

The covariance between X and Y is defined as $cov(X,Y) = E(XY) - E(X)E(Y)$. However, since we know that $Y = X^2$, we can substitute this in, to give:

$$\begin{aligned} cov(X,Y) &= E(X \times X^2) - E(X)E(X^2) \\ &= E(X^3) - E(X)E(X^2) \end{aligned}$$

We can find $E(X)$ by integrating the product of $f_X(x)$ with the outcomes of x over the range of -1 to $+1$, giving:

$$E(X) = \int_{-1}^{1} 0.5x\,dx = \left[\frac{x^2}{4}\right]_{-1}^{1} = 0$$

Similarly, we can calculate $E(X^3)$ by finding the integral of the product of x^3 with the PDF of X:

$$E(X^3) = \int_{-1}^{1} \frac{x^3}{2}dx = \left[\frac{x^4}{8}\right]_{-1}^{1} = 0$$

So, we have that both $E(X^3) = 0$ and $E(X) = 0$, and so the covariance is just

$$cov(X,Y) = E(X^3) - E(X) \times E(X^2) = 0 - 0 \times E(X^2) = 0$$

So, here we have an example where two random variables are clearly not independent; there is a clear, deterministic relationship from X to Y, and so knowing the value of X tells us exactly what the value of Y will be. However, since the covariance is equal to zero, it must

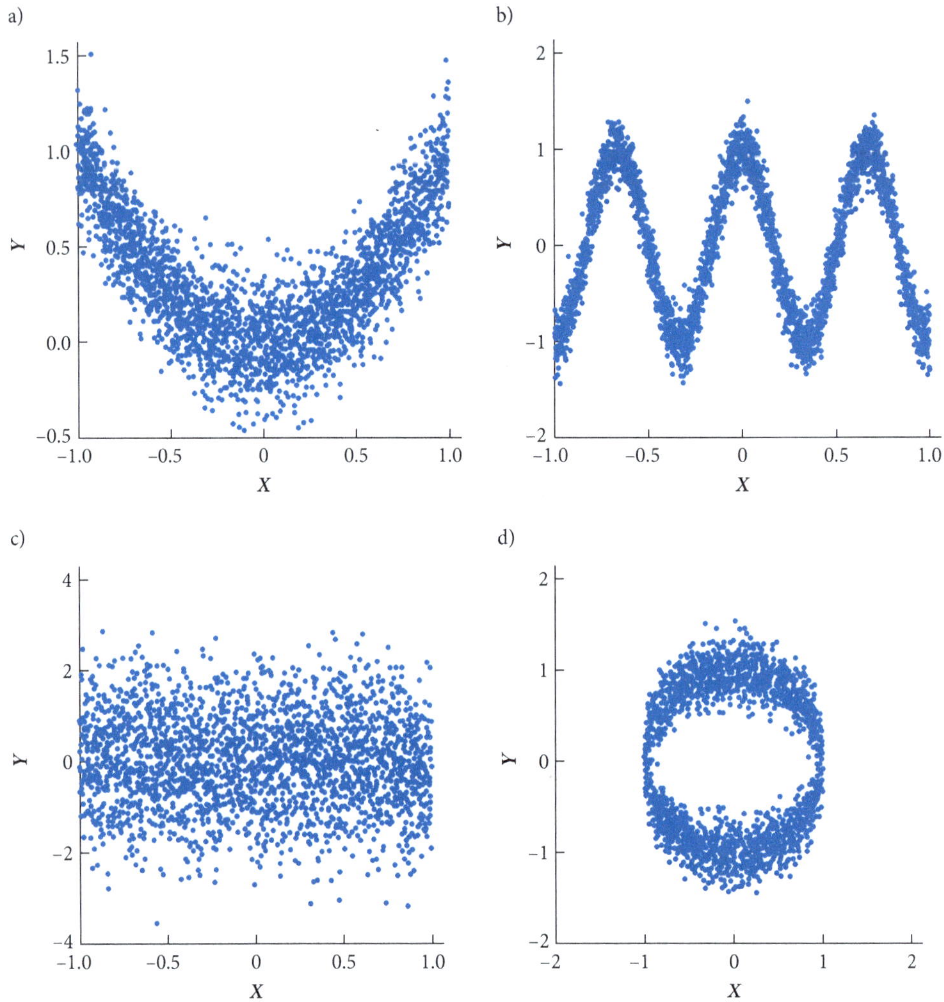

Figure 11.18 Pairs of random variables with zero correlation.

follow that the correlation is also equal to zero. Just because two variables have zero correlation does not mean that they are independent.

In Figure 11.18, all four diagrams illustrate two random variables, where there is a correlation equal to (approximately) zero between the two variables. However, the only case where the two random variables are independent is in specification a). In this case, all of the values of Y are random, irrespective of the value of X. In all of the other three cases, knowing the value of X tells you something about the value that Y will take.

In specification b), if X is negative, increasing X is associated with a decrease in Y. Similarly, if X is positive, an increase in X is associated with an increase in Y. We can see that the value that Y takes appears to be strongly related to the value that X takes. As such, X and Y are not independent.

Specification c) also shows an interdependence between two random variables: the relationship between X and Y follows a cyclical pattern, which could represent seasonal spending patterns or business cycles. Observing the data allows us to immediately see the relationship between the two variables, but if we merely relied on the correlation coefficient, it would be likely to suggest that there was no relationship.

As we move further into statistics, particularly thinking about estimators and statistical testing, it often becomes important to assume that random variables are independent. However, as we have shown, simply seeing that there is zero correlation is insufficient to prove that two variables are independent.

This illustrates a key weakness with the measure of correlation. The correlation merely measures how close the random variable is to lying on a linear, straight line. However, even when there is a clear, deterministic relationship, if the relationship is non-linear, the correlation will suggest that there is a less than perfect relationship between the two variables. For this reason, it is often important, particularly when using data to plot the data on a graph, to examine possible relationships.

It should be noted that if all of the observations lie on a horizontal (or vertical) straight line, then this means that one of the variables is simply constant. Because of this, there can be no covariation between the two variables, and so the covariance is equal to zero (and hence the correlation is equal to zero). This may seem a little odd, because all of the observations lie on a straight line, but the correlation is zero due to one of the variables being constant.

This is illustrated in Figure 11.19. In both cases, the correlation will be equal to zero. This is because there is no variation in the constant. This may seem unintuitive, since all of the observations lie on a straight line. The key element is that correlations will only be +1 if the straight line is upward sloping, whilst the correlation will be −1 if the straight line is downward sloping. In these two cases, the straight line is neither upward nor downward sloping.

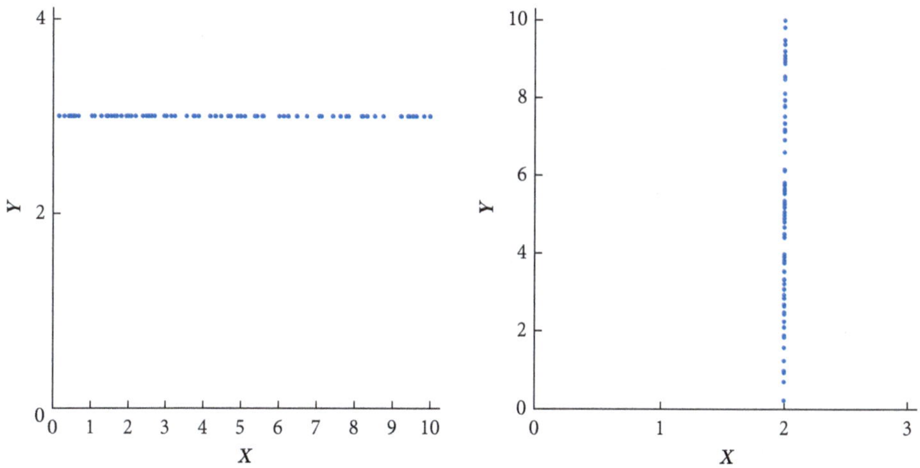

Figure 11.19 Zero correlation when one variable is a constant.

KEY NOTATION

Sometimes, statisticians use the following shorthand to represent measures of central tendency:

- $E(X) = \mu = \mu_X$
- $var(X) = \sigma^2 = \sigma_X^2$
- $s.d.(X) = \sigma = \sigma_X$
- Covariance between X and $Y = cov(X,Y)$
- Correlation between X and $Y = \rho = \rho_{XY}$

It is important to recognize these, as it will help you to understand more clearly what is going on!

Summary

In this chapter, we have introduced measures that evaluate how two random variables vary together. Whilst the variance of a random variable examines the average (square of the) deviation of the explanatory variable away from its expected value, the covariance measures how the two random variables deviate together from their expected values. If the covariance between X and Y is positive, then on average, as X increases, Y also increases (and vice versa). That is, if X is above the expected value, then, on average, Y will also be above the expected value.

Similarly, when the covariance is negative, then on average, as X increases, Y decreases. Similarly, on average, if X is above its expected value, then Y will be below the expected value (and vice versa).

The correlation between two random variables is, in essence, a standardized measure of the covariance, and tells you how close the observations are to lying on a straight line. Correlations will always lie between -1 and $+1$.

A correlation of $+1$ means that all of the observations will lie exactly on an upward sloping straight line. The smaller the magnitude of the correlation, the greater the variation of the observations around a straight line.

Measure	Covariance between X and Y, $cov(X,Y)$	Correlation between X and Y, ρ_{XY}
Formula	$= E[(X - E(X))(Y - E(Y))]$ $= E(XY) - E(X)E(Y)$	$= \dfrac{cov(X,Y)}{\sqrt{var(X)\,var(Y)}}$
Calculating in Excel	If you observe a population: =covar(. . ., . . .) =covariance.p(. . ., . . .) If you observe a sample and wish to estimate the population covariance: =covariance.s(. . ., . . .)	Whether you observe a sample or a population, the formula is always the same: =correl(. . ., . . .)

Appendix

Proving that $cov(X,Y) = E(XY) - E(X)E(Y)$

We have seen that the general formula for the covariance is given as the average product of the deviations of the two random variables away from their expected value:

$$cov(X,Y) = E\left[\left(X - E(X)\right)\left(Y - E(Y)\right)\right]$$

We can begin by multiplying out the brackets, to give us:

$$= E[XY - YE(X) - XE(Y) + E(X)E(Y)]$$

Now, we have the expectation of a sum of terms, and we know that the expectation of a sum is equal to the sum of the expectations, so we can rewrite this as:

$$= E(XY) - E\left(YE(X)\right) - E\left(XE(Y)\right) + E\left(E(X)E(Y)\right)$$

Now, $E(X)$ and $E(Y)$ are constants within a population, and where they are constant multipliers, they be taken outside of the expectation. That means that $E\left(YE(X)\right) = E(X)E(Y)$, and $E\left(XE(Y)\right) = E(Y)E(X)$. Finally, $E\left(E(X)E(Y)\right) = E(X)E\left(E(Y)\right)$. Now, because, $E(Y)$ is a constant, the expectation is just equal to $E(Y)$:

$$= E(XY) - E(X)E(Y) - E(X)E(Y) + E(X)E(Y)$$
$$= E(XY) - E(X)E(Y)$$

Since two of the $E(X)E(Y)$ terms cancel out, this leaves us with $cov(X,Y) = E(XY) - E(X)E(Y)$.

Proving the rules of variances

Suppose that we have two random variables, X and Y. We know that $E(X) = \mu_X$ and $E(Y) = \mu_Y$. Further, $var(X) = \sigma_X^2$ and $var(Y) = \sigma_Y^2$. We also have two constants, a and b.

The variance of a random variable is defined as $var(X) = E[(X - E(X))] = E(X^2) - E(X)^2$

$var(a + X) = var(X)$

Suppose that we create a new variable by adding a constant a to X:

$$var(a + X) = E\left[\left((a + X) - E(a + X)\right)^2\right]$$

Now, we can take the second term $E(a + X)$ and since the expectation of a sum is just the sum of the expectations, this gives us $E(a + X) = E(a) + E(X)$. Further, since a is a constant, $E(a) = a$. So we can rewrite the variances as:

$$\Rightarrow var(a + X) = E\left[\left(a + X - a - E(X)\right)^2\right]$$

The a and $-a$ terms cancel, leaving us with:

$$\Rightarrow var(a + X) = E\left[\left(X - E(X)\right)^2\right]$$

But this is just the equation for the variance of X:

$$\Rightarrow var(a + X) = var(X)$$

$var(aX) = a^2 var(X)$

Suppose that we create a new variable by multiplying X by a constant, a:

$$var(aX) = E\left[\left((aX) - E(aX)\right)^2\right]$$

Now, $E(aX) = aE(X)$ since a is just a constant multiplier:

$$\Rightarrow var(aX) = E\left[\left(aX - aE(X)\right)^2\right]$$

a is a common multiplier, so we can factorize it out of the brackets. Since the brackets are squared, then the a will also be squared:

$$\Rightarrow var(aX) = E\left[a^2\left(X - E(X)\right)^2\right]$$

Finally, since a is a constant multiplier of everything within the expectation, we can take it outside of the expectation:

$$\Rightarrow var(aX) = a^2 E\left[\left(X - E(X)\right)^2\right] = a^2 var(X)$$

$$var(aX + bY) = a^2 var(X) + b^2 var(Y) + 2ab \times cov(X,Y)$$

Suppose we create a new variable $Z = aX + bY$, then:

$$var(Z) = E(Z^2) - E(Z)^2$$

Substituting in for $Z = aX + bY$ gives us:

$$\Rightarrow var(aX + bY) = E[(aX + bY)^2] - [E(aX + bY)]^2$$

Let's take each term in turn. First, let's begin with $E[(aX + bY)^2]$. We know that:

$$(aX + bY)^2 = a^2X^2 + b^2Y^2 + 2abXY$$

So, we can rewrite the expectation as:

$$\Rightarrow E[(aX + bY)^2] = E[a^2X^2 + b^2Y^2 + 2abXY]$$

By the rules of expectations, we can now rewrite this as the sum of the expectations:

$$\Rightarrow E[(aX + bY)^2] = a^2E(X^2) + b^2E(Y^2) + 2ab \times E(XY) \qquad (1)$$

Similarly, the second element, $[E(aX + bY)]^2$, is the square of $E(aX + bY)$ which can be rewritten as $aE(X) + bE(Y)$, so the overall term can be rewritten as:

$$\Rightarrow [E(aX + bY)]^2 = [aE(X) + bE(Y)]^2$$

Squaring the brackets gives us:

$$\Rightarrow [E(aX + bY)]^2 = a^2E(X)^2 + b^2E(Y)^2 + 2ab \times E(X)E(Y) \qquad (2)$$

Combining (1) and (2) gives us:

$$var(aX + bY) = (a^2E(X^2) + b^2E(Y^2) + 2ab \times E(XY)) \\ -(a^2E(X)^2 + b^2E(Y)^2 + 2ab \times E(X)E(Y))$$

If we group terms, we have:

$$= a^2E(X^2) - a^2E(X)^2 + b^2E(Y^2) - b^2E(Y)^2 + 2ab \times E(XY) - 2ab \times E(X)E(Y)$$
$$= a^2[E(X^2) - E(X)^2] + b^2[E(Y^2) - E(Y)^2] + 2ab \times [E(XY) - E(X)E(Y)]$$

However, the first term is just the variance of X, the second term the variance of Y, and the third term the covariance between X and Y:

$$= a^2var(X) + b^2var(Y) + 2ab \times cov(X,Y)$$

Proving the rules of covariances

Suppose that we have four variables, W, X, Y, and Z, with expectations $E(W), E(X), E(Y)$, and $E(Z)$ respectively, and variances $var(X), var(Y), var(W)$, and $var(Z)$. The covariance between each of these variables exists and is finite.

The formulae for the covariance between two random variables, X and Y, is given as:

$$cov(X,Y) = E\left[\left(X - E(X)\right)\left(Y - E(Y)\right)\right] = E(XY) - E(X)E(Y)$$
$$cov(a,X) = 0$$

This first proof is relatively trivial. If you have a constant a and a random variable X, then the covariance is just:

$$cov(a,X) = E(aX) - E(a)E(X)$$

However, since a is a constant, $E(aX) = aE(X)$ and $E(a) = a$. As such:

$$cov(a,X) = aE(X) - aE(X) = 0$$
$$cov(X,X) = var(X)$$

This second proof is also trivial. If you are looking at the covariance of a random variable with itself:

$$cov(X,X) = E(XX) - E(X)E(X) = E(X^2) - E(X)^2$$

But this is just the formula for the variance of X:

$$cov(aX,Y) = a \times cov(X,Y)$$

Suppose that we multiply one of the random variables by a constant, a. Then, we can calculate the covariance as:

$$cov(aX,Y) = E(aXY) - E(aX)E(Y)$$

Now, a is a constant multiplier within the expectation, so it can be taken outside of $E(aXY) = aE(XY)$ and $E(aX) = aE(X)$, so the covariance can be rewritten as:

$$cov(aX,Y) = aE(XY) - aE(X)E(Y) = a[E(XY) - E(X)E(Y)]$$

However, the term in the square brackets is now just the covariance between X and Y:

$$\Rightarrow cov(aX,Y) = a \times cov(X,Y)$$

By the same argument, if we have $cov(aX,bY)$, this can be just rewritten as:

$$cov(aX,bY) = a \times b \times cov(X,Y)$$
$$cov(W + X,Y) = cov(W,Y) + cov(X,Y)$$

Suppose we construct a new random variable, based on the sum of two random variables, W and X, and we want to know the resulting covariance with Y:

$$cov(W + X,Y) = E[(W + X)Y] - E(W + X)E(Y)$$

Now, the first step is to multiply out the brackets in the first term:

$$E[(W + X)Y] = E[WY + XY]$$

However, the expectation of a sum is just equal to the sum of the expectations:

$$\Rightarrow E[(W + X)Y] = E(WY) + E(XY)$$

Taking the second term, $E(W + X) = E(W) + E(X)$, and so $E(W + X)E(Y) = E(W)E(Y) + E(X)E(Y)$.

Therefore, we can combine our terms to give:

$$cov(W + X,Y) = E(WY) + E(XY) - E(W)E(Y) - E(X)E(Y)$$

Grouping terms gives us:

$$cov(W + X,Y) = [E(WY) - E(W)E(Y)] + [E(XY) - E(X)E(Y)]$$

But these are just equal to the covariances:

$$= cov(W,Y) + cov(X,Y)$$

By combining the second and the rule of covariances, we can also write that:

$$cov(aW + bX,Y) = a \times cov(W,Y) + b \times cov(X,Y)$$

Finally, by the same argument, if you have a linear combination on both the first and the second term of the covariance:

$$cov(aW + bX, cY, dZ) = a \times c \times cov(W,Y) + a \times d \times cov(W,Z) + b \times c \times cov(X,Y) + b \times d \times cov(X,Z)$$

Proving that independent random variables will always have covariance (and correlation) equal to zero

Suppose that you have two random variables, X and Y. The random variables will be independent if the marginal PDF is equal to the conditional PDF. For ease of notation, we will denote X and Y as discrete random variables. Formally, X and Y are independent if:

$$P(X = x | Y = y) = P(X = x) \text{ for all possible values of } x \text{ and } y$$

Because the conditional distribution is equal to the marginal distribution, it follows that the conditional expectation of X will be equal to the unconditional expectation of X:

$$E(X | Y = y) = E(X) \text{ for all possible values of } y$$

Now, the covariance between X and Y is defined as:

$$cov(X,Y) = E(XY) - E(X)E(Y)$$

Let's begin by examining $E(XY)$. By the law of iterated expectations:

$$E(XY) = E_y[E(XY \mid Y = y)]$$

That is, the unconditional expectation of XY is equal to the expectation, over all possible values of y, of the conditional expectation of XY given $Y = y$. Now, if we are conditioning that $Y = y$, we can substitute this into the conditional expectation:

$$\Rightarrow E(XY) = E_y[E(Xy \mid Y = y)]$$

Now, y is a constant multiplier, so it can be taken outside the conditional expectation:

$$\Rightarrow E(XY) = E_y[y \times E(X \mid Y = y)]$$

We also know that, since X and Y are independent, then $E(X \mid Y = y) = E(X)$ for all possible values of y, and so we can substitute in to give:

$$\Rightarrow E(XY) = E_y[y \times E(X)]$$

However, now $E(X)$ is a constant for any value of y, and so we can take it outside as a constant multiplier:

$$\Rightarrow E(XY) = E(X) \times E_y[y]$$

The notation looks a little strange here, but $E_y[y]$ is equivalent to taking each of the outcomes of y and weighting them by their probabilities, and summing the products; that is, $E_y[y] = E(Y)$.

Thus, if X and Y are independent it follows that:

$$E(XY) = E(X) \times E(Y)$$

Thus, the covariance between X and Y is just

$$\begin{aligned} cov(X,Y) &= E(XY) - E(X)E(Y) \\ &= E(X)E(Y) - E(X)E(Y) \\ &= 0 \end{aligned}$$

Simple Distributions: Uniform and Binomial Distributions

12

Learning outcomes for this chapter

By the end of this chapter you will be able to:

- Evaluate the properties of the uniform distribution, including the expectation, variance, and standard deviation
- Evaluate the properties of the binomial distribution, including the expectation, variance, and standard deviation

Mathematical tools

- Simple arithmetic
- Summations
- Integrations

Introduction

So far, in this book, when we have looked at random variables, we have considered them in terms of their probability mass function (for **discrete random variables**), or **probability density functions** (PDFs) (for **continuous random variables**). However, there is a wide range of standard distributions that you are likely to come across in statistics. These include the **normal distribution** (which we will see in Chapter 13), the **uniform distribution**, the **binomial distribution** (which we will see in this chapter), and many more (some of which we will discuss later in this textbook).

When we introduced continuous random variables, we looked at a number of examples where the PDF looked like a rectangle. This distribution is known as the uniform (or rectangular) distribution.

In this chapter, we will begin by formally examining some of the characteristics of the uniform distribution, and will discuss an important discrete random variable, in the form of the binomial distribution.

12.1 The uniform (or rectangular) distribution

Suppose that you wanted to generate a random number between two particular values. If you want to ensure that any value in the range is equally likely, you could sample the observations from a distribution known as the uniform distribution.

In Chapter 8, we introduced continuous random variables by considering a random variable that produced outcomes that were equally likely between 0 and 6, with the PDF:

$$f_Y(y) = \begin{cases} 0, & y < 0 \\ 1/6, & 0 \leq y \leq 6 \\ 0, & y \geq 6 \end{cases}$$

This is illustrated in Figure 12.1. This distribution is known as the uniform distribution: all of the possible outcomes between 0 and 6 are equally (or uniformly) likely to occur, and the random variable will never produce an outcome outside of this range.

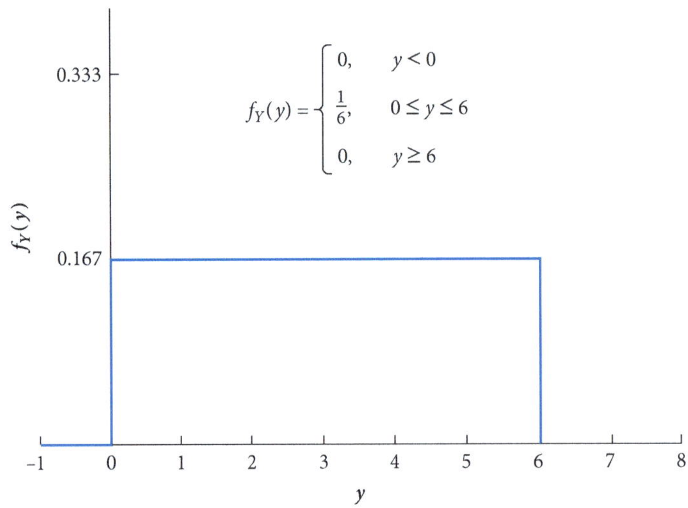

Figure 12.1 Probability density function for a uniform distribution between 0 and 6.

The distribution is also known as the rectangular distribution, due to the shape of the PDF. This is a specific example of the uniform distribution, whereby the outcomes were equally likely between 0 and 6. However, we can also consider the uniform distribution in a more general case, as illustrated in Figure 12.2.[1]

We want to define the PDF for this continuous random variable, so that we can evaluate the relative likelihood of any possible outcomes. It will be helpful to remind ourselves of the conditions that are necessary for a continuous random variable to be well defined.

[1] This case has all of the possible outcomes of X being positive. However, the uniform distribution can be specified for any range of real numbers. For example, we could define the uniform distribution between −5 and −1, or between −2 and 25.

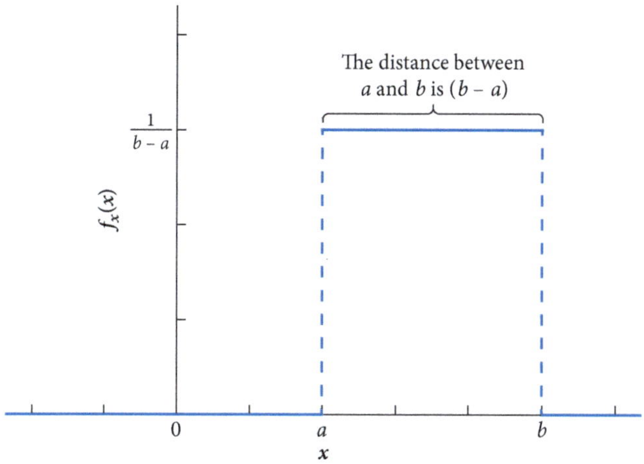

Figure 12.2 A more general example of the uniform distribution.

KEY DEFINITION: CONDITIONS FOR A (CONTINUOUS) RANDOM VARIABLE TO BE WELL DEFINED

For a (continuous) random variable to be well defined, two conditions need to be met:

1. The PDF must always be greater than (or equal to) zero. It is impossible to have a probability that is negative.
2. The area under the PDF must be equal to 1. Since the area under the PDF is the total probability, this is equivalent to saying that all of the possible outcomes are defined.

We can check the second condition by integrating the PDF over the full domain of the random variable:

$$\int_{-\infty}^{\infty} f_X(x)dx = 1$$

In the general case of a uniform distribution between a and b, the domain of possible outcomes is between a and b. For all values of x outside of this range, the PDF will necessarily be equal to 0, as these are outcomes that are not possible.

Between a and b, the PDF is constant, and we know two characteristics:

i) The PDF is shaped like a rectangle between a and b.

ii) The area under the PDF must be equal to 1.

From relatively basic geometry, we know that the area of any rectangle is just equal to the width multiplied by the height. So, in the case of the uniform distribution, the area of the PDF must be equal to the height multiplied by the width, as shown in Figure 12.3.

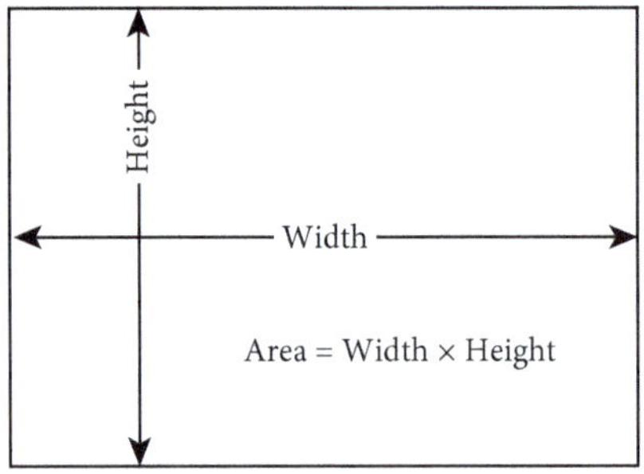

Figure 12.3 Calculating the area of a rectangle.

Of course, we already know two characteristics. The width of the rectangle in our uniform distribution is the distance between a and b, which is just equal to $b - a$. Similarly, we know that the area under the curve must be equal to 1.

So:

$$Area = Width \times Height$$
$$\Rightarrow 1 = (b - a) \times Height$$
$$\Rightarrow Height = \frac{1}{b - a}$$

Thus, by rearranging this equation, we can see that the height of the PDF is just equal to $\frac{1}{b-a}$ between $X = a$ and $X = b$ (and zero otherwise). Formally, this means that we can write the PDF as:

$$f_X(x) = \begin{cases} \frac{1}{b - a}, & a \leq x \leq b \\ 0, & \text{Otherwise} \end{cases}$$

That is, the probability density is equal to $\frac{1}{b-a}$ between a and b, and will be equal to 0 everywhere else.

Important note

In the example illustrated, both a and b are greater than zero, but a uniform distribution could be used for any range—you could have a uniform distribution that is defined over the domain of solely negative numbers, or both positive and negative numbers. The only constraint is that the PDF is constant across the full domain of the random variable.

For example, if we were writing down a uniform distribution between $a = 3$ and $b = 6$, then the width of the non-zero part of the PDF would be equal to 3, and the height would be equal to $\frac{1}{3}$.

The uniform distribution has some interesting, intuitive properties. For example, it is simple to see that this is a symmetric distribution. That is, if we were to find the middle value (the median), then there would be identical distribution both above and below the median (albeit in mirror image). In fact, the median is very easy to find in the uniform distribution (and in any symmetric distribution).

Since we know that the range of possible values for x is between a and b, then the median is necessarily the midpoint between a and b.

KEY NOTATION

If we observe a variable, X, which follows a uniform distribution, between limits a and b, we can denote this by:

$$X \sim U(a,b)$$

This means that the variable X is distributed (~) in a uniform distribution (U), between the values of $X = a$ and $X = b$. This corresponds to a PDF equal to:

$$f_X(x) = \begin{cases} \dfrac{1}{b-a}, & a \leq x \leq b \\ 0, & \text{Otherwise} \end{cases}$$

12.1.1 Properties of the uniform distribution

As with any random variable, there are a range of properties that we might be interested in calculating. For example, we might wish to examine:

1. The probability of observing an outcome between two possible values.
2. The cumulative distribution function (CDF), and percentiles of the distribution.
3. The expectation and variance of the distribution.
4. Higher moments including the skew and kurtosis.

Probabilities related to a uniform distribution and the cumulative distribution function

If we have a random variable, X, which follows a uniform distribution between a and b (i.e. $X \sim U(a,b)$), then the total area under the PDF between a and b is just equal to 1.

The probability of observing an outcome between two values (say, c and d) both of which lie between a and b is just the area under the curve between c and d, as illustrated in Figure 12.4.

Because the distribution is rectangular, the probability is just equal to the proportion of the distance between a and b that is represented by the distance between c and d. The distance between a and b is equal to $(b - a)$ and the distance between c and d is equal to $(d - c)$.

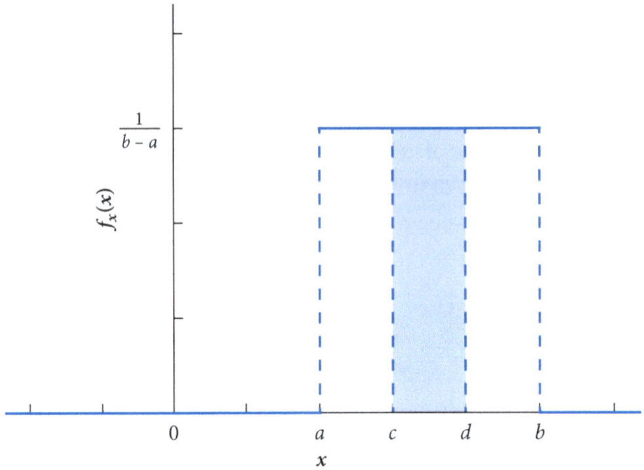

Figure 12.4 Probability of observing an outcome between c and d.

Thus, we can calculate the probability of randomly gaining an observation of X between c and d as:

$$P(c \leq X \leq d) = \frac{d-c}{b-a}$$

We could also show this by integrating the PDF between the limits of $X = c$ and $X = d$:

$$P(c \leq X \leq d) = \int_c^d \frac{1}{b-a} dx = \left[\frac{x}{b-a}\right]_c^d = \frac{d-c}{b-a}$$

Similarly, we can show that the CDF[2] for a uniform distribution between a and b (Figure 12.5) is given by:

$$F_X(x) = P(X \leq x) = \begin{cases} 0, & x \leq a \\ \frac{x-a}{b-a}, & a \leq x \leq b \\ 1, & x > b \end{cases}$$

We can use this CDF to also calculate percentiles of the distribution. Since the kth percentile is the value of x below which k per cent of the outcomes lie, we can construct this from the CDF. For example, if we wanted to find the 25th percentile, this is equivalent to $P(X \leq x) = 0.25$. As such, we could use the CDF to find what value of x corresponds to $F_X(x) = 0.25$

$$0.25 = \frac{x-a}{b-a}$$
$$\Rightarrow 0.25(b-a) = x - a$$

[2] This is proven in the appendix of this chapter.

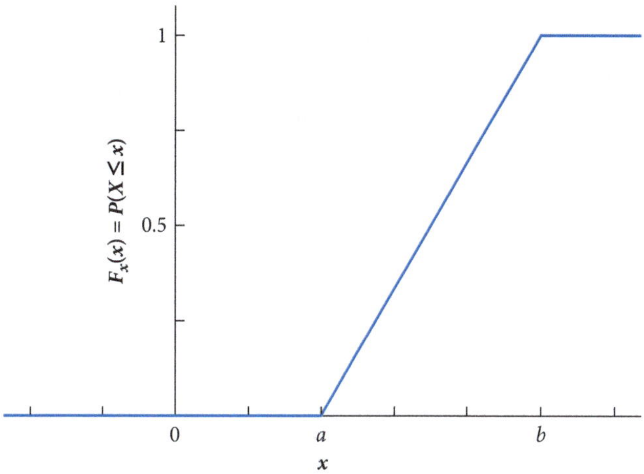

Figure 12.5 Cumulative distribution function of a uniform distribution between *a* and *b*.

We can rearrange this to give $x = a + 0.25(b - a)$. This is quite interesting, because the 25th percentile is effectively a point that is 25 per cent of the way between a and b. More generally, we can find the kth percentile as:

$$= a + \frac{k}{100} \times (b - a)$$

So, for instance, the median, or 50th percentile, is equal to $a + \frac{50}{100} \times (b - a)$, which rearranges to give us a median equal to $\frac{a+b}{2}$. This is just the same as the mid-point between a and b. This shouldn't be a surprise, since we can see that the CDF is a linear function. That is, it forms a straight line. We can see from Figure 12.6 that the 50th percentile lies exactly halfway between a and b.

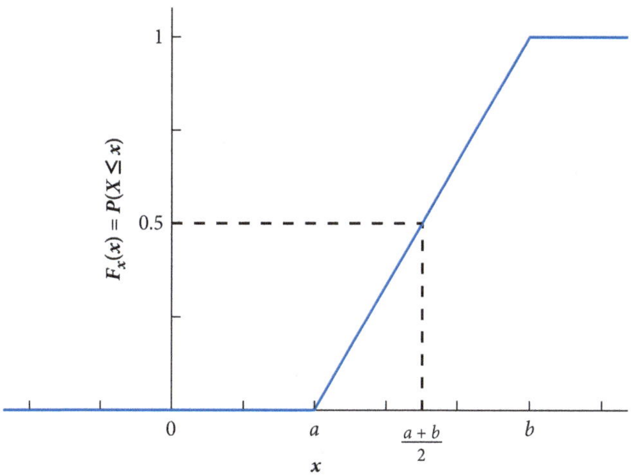

Figure 12.6 Using the CDF to find the median.

Expectation, variance, and higher moments of the uniform distribution

It is relatively straightforward to see that the expectation of the uniform distribution is also going to be equal to the mid-point of the distribution. This is because the expectation provides a measure of the average, and as such, since the distribution is symmetric around the median, we see the same shape of distribution to both the right and the left of the median. It therefore makes intuitive sense that the mid-point will be equal to the expected value. We can also see this, analytically, using our mathematical rules.

We know that, for a continuous random variable, we can calculate the expected value by integrating the product of the PDF multiplied by the outcomes of x across the full domain of X. In this case, if $X \sim U(a,b)$, then we know that the PDF is equal to $f_X(x) = \frac{1}{b-a}$ for the domain between a and b, and zero otherwise:

$$E(X) = \int_x x \times f_X(x)dx = \int_a^b x \times \frac{1}{b-a}dx = \left[\frac{x^2}{2(b-a)}\right]_a^b$$

Substituting in the limits of the integration, gives us:

$$= \frac{b^2 - a^2}{2(b-a)}$$

A relatively common factorization problem that we see is that for a difference of two squares, $(b^2 - a^2)$ can be rewritten as $(b - a) \times (b + a)$, and so we can rewrite the expectation as:

$$= \frac{(b-a)(b+a)}{2(b-a)}$$

Now, we can see that we have $(b - a)$ on both the top and the bottom of the fraction, and these cancel, giving us that:

$$E(X) = \frac{b+a}{2}$$

This is exactly what we expected. The expectation is just the same as we constructed for the median in the previous section, and this is just equal to the mid-point of the distribution.

The variance is a little more tricky to construct, but again, there is a relatively simple formula for the variance; in fact, it is possible to show[3] that for any uniform distribution, between the limits a and b, the variance is given by:

$$var(X) = \frac{(b-a)^2}{12}$$

So, we have shown that the expectation and median are the same in the uniform distribution, but what about the mode? The modal value is the most common, or most likely, outcome within the distribution. In the uniform distribution, all outcomes within the domain are equally likely, and so no modal value exists.

[3] This is shown in the appendix to this chapter.

Finally, we might be interested in constructing measures of the skew and kurtosis. We do not prove it in this book, but it is possible to show that the skew (which, remember, is equivalent to $\frac{E(X-E(X))^3}{\sigma^3}$) will be equal to zero, which again matches with the distribution being symmetric; there is equal weight both above and below the expectation. Similarly, the kurtosis, which provides a measure of how much weight of the distribution is contained within the tails of the distribution (or a measure of **outliers** within the distribution), is just equal to $\frac{9}{5}$.

Notation for a variable X that is uniformly distributed between a and b	$X \sim U(a,b)$
Probability density function	$f_X(x) = \begin{cases} \frac{1}{b-a}, & a \le x \le b \\ 0, & \text{Otherwise} \end{cases}$
Cumulative distribution function	$F_X(x) = P(X \le x) = \begin{cases} 0, & x \le a \\ \frac{x-a}{b-a}, & a \le x \le b \\ 1, & x > b \end{cases}$
Expectation $E(X)$	$E(X) = \frac{a+b}{2}$
Median	$\text{Median} = \frac{a+b}{2}$
Mode	Not applicable
Variance	$\frac{(b-a)^2}{12}$
Standard deviation	$\frac{b-a}{\sqrt{12}}$
Skew	0
Kurtosis	$\frac{9}{5}$

Worked example 12.1: Evaluating a simple uniform distribution

Suppose that you have a random variable, Y, which follows a uniform distribution between 2 and 5. We can think of Y as a random number generator that has equal likelihood of delivering any outcome between 2 and 5.

You wish to calculate the following quantities:

- the probability of randomly observing an outcome between 3 and 4
- the expected value of Y
- the variance of Y.

Since this is a uniform distribution between 2 and 5, we know that the width of the distribution is equal to $(5 - 2) = 3$. In order for the area under the PDF to be equal to 1, the height of the distribution must be equal to $\frac{1}{3}$ between 2 and 5, and zero otherwise. The PDF is illustrated in Figure 12.7.

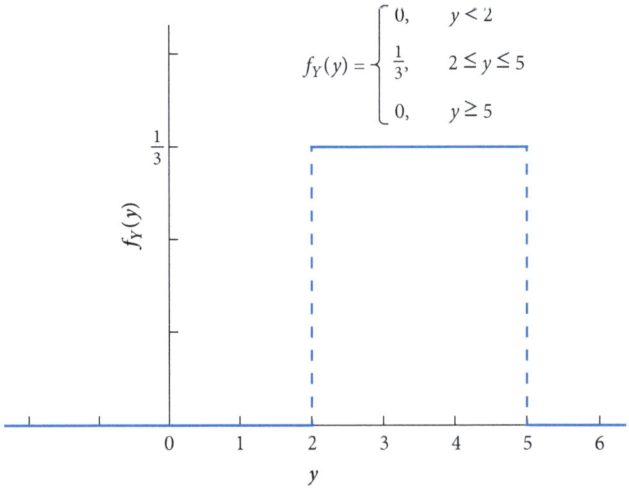

Figure 12.7 Probability density function of Y.

To calculate the probability of randomly observing an outcome between 3 and 4, $P(3 \leq Y \leq 4)$, this is equivalent to finding the area under the curve between 3 and 4. To find this, we could integrate the PDF between 3 and 4, but it is easier to simply find this intuitively. We know that the height of the rectangle is $\frac{1}{3}$, and similarly, the width of the area would be $4 - 3 = 1$, giving us an area equal to $1 \times \frac{1}{3} = \frac{1}{3}$. This is illustrated in Figure 12.8, showing that $P(3 \leq Y \leq 4) = \frac{1}{3}$.

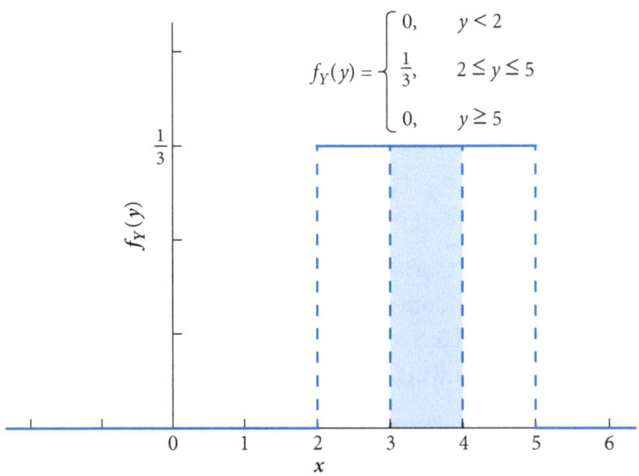

Figure 12.8 Finding the probability of randomly observing an outcome between 3 and 4.

We could also have calculated this probability using the cumulative probabilities. We know that finding the probability of observing an outcome between 3 and 4 is the same as finding the difference between the two cumulative probabilities:

$$P(3 \leq Y \leq 4) = P(Y \leq 4) - P(Y \leq 3)$$

We know that the CDF is given by $P(Y \leq y) = \frac{4-a}{b-a}$, where a is the lower bound of the uniform distribution, and b the upper bound. In this case, $a = 2$ and $b = 5$. So:

$$P(Y \leq 4) = \frac{4-2}{5-2} = \frac{2}{3}, \quad P(Y \leq 3) = \frac{3-2}{5-2} = \frac{1}{3}$$

So, this gives us that $P(3 \leq Y \leq 4) = \frac{2}{3} - \frac{1}{3} = \frac{1}{3}$.

Calculating the expectation and the variance

We can use the formulae we have developed in Section 12.1.1 to calculate the expectation and variance of the uniform distribution. We know that:

$$E(Y) = \frac{a+b}{2}, \qquad var(Y) = \frac{(b-a)^2}{12}$$

Substituting $a = 2$ and $b = 5$ in gives us:

$$E(Y) = \frac{2+5}{2} = 3.5, \qquad var(Y) = \frac{(5-2)^2}{12} = \frac{9}{12} = \frac{3}{4}$$

12.1.2 The uniform distribution as a random number generator

In experiments, you may often wish to generate random numbers, and the uniform distribution is a useful distribution to appeal to. Since all of the outcomes are equally likely, it can form the initial basis of any simulation.

Similarly, if you are constructing an experiment, and you want to randomly assign participants to (say) a control and a treatment group, you could randomly sample an observation from a uniform distribution between 0 and 1. If the randomly drawn observation is less than 0.5, then the individual could form part of the control group, and if it is greater than 0.5, the individual could form part of the treatment group. By using the uniform distribution, this also means that the control and treatment group will be approximately of equal size.

Using Excel to sample from a uniform distribution

If you use the formula:

= RAND()

in Microsoft Excel, then the result that you receive will be randomly drawn from a random variable X such that:

$$X \sim U(0,1)$$

12.1.3 Transformations involving uniform distributions

Just as with any random variable, we can apply linear transformations to variables that follow the uniform distribution. We already know some rules that apply to linear transformations of any random variable. Suppose that we have a random variable, X, which has expectation $E(X) = \mu_X$ and variance $var(X) = \sigma_X^2$.

	Impact on expectation	Impact on variance
Adding a constant	$E(a + X) = a + E(X) = a + \mu_X$	$var(a + X) = var(X) = \sigma_X^2$
Multiplying by a constant	$E(aX) = aE(X) = a\mu_X$	$var(aX) = a^2\ var(X)$

When we apply a linear transformation, what we are doing, in essence, is applying that linear transformation to every possible outcome from the random variable. This means that if we add a constant (say, 2) to a uniformly distributed variable, we are simply transforming every outcome so that it is 2 larger.

So, if $X \sim U(1,3)$, if we add 2 to every possible outcome, then this is equivalent to shifting the distribution, so that rather than being between 1 and 3, the transformed variable would be (uniformly distributed) between 3 and 5.

Similarly, if we multiplied a random variable by a constant, then this would be equivalent to multiplying every possible outcome by that constant. So if $X \sim U(1,3)$, then $2X \sim U(2,6)$.

In fact, any linear transformation (adding, subtracting, multiplying, dividing by a constant) that we apply to a uniformly distributed variable will result in a new variable that is also uniformly distributed.

Exercise

Suppose that you have a variable, $X \sim U(-1,5)$.

a) Calculate the expectation and variance of X.

b) Suppose that you generate a new variable $Y = X + 3$. Verify that $E(Y) = E(X) + 3$ and that $var(Y) = var(X)$.

c) Suppose that you generate a new variable $Z = 3X$. Verify that $E(Z) = 3E(X)$ and that $var(Z) = 9\ var(X)$.

12.2 The binomial (or Bernoulli) distribution

Let's begin with a simple experiment. Suppose that you flipped a coin. There are two possible outcomes—it could either land heads upwards or tails upwards. For a simple fair coin, the probability of it landing heads upwards would be 0.5, whilst the probability of it landing tails upwards would also be 0.5.

Now, suppose that instead of flipping the coin once, you flipped the coin three times. How could we calculate the expected number of heads? How could we evaluate the variability of the number of heads if you repeated the experiment?

What we have described is a very simple definition of a very useful distribution—that is, the binomial distribution (which is often referred to as the Bernoulli distribution).

To illustrate this further, let's represent the ith flip of the coin as X_i, and assign a numerical value to each possible outcome. If the coin lands heads upwards, let's assign the outcome as $X_i = 1$, and if it lands tails upwards, let's assign the outcome as $X_i = 0$.

Then, the **probability mass function** (PMF)[4] of each flip of the coin would be given as:

$$X_i = \begin{cases} 1 \ (Heads), & P(X = 1) = 0.5 \\ 0 \ \ (Tails), & P(X = 0) = 0.5 \end{cases}$$

Now, we have been quite devious when we allocated the numerical values for the outcomes. If we flip the coin three times, and we were to add up the numerical values of each of the flips, then each head would increase the sum by 1, and each tail would increase the sum by zero; that means that the sum of the X_i will give us the number of heads that we observe when we flip the coin three times. That is, if we flip the coin twice and get three realisations x_1, x_2, and x_3 then the number of heads would just be equal to:

$$\text{Number of heads} = x_1 + x_2 + x_3$$

Now, this is just the case for a specific set of realizations of the ten flips, but we can represent the number of heads more generally, as a random variable, constructed from ten random variables, representing the three flips of the coin. Let's define a new random variable, Y, as the number of heads achieved from three flips of a coin, and we can write that:

$$Y = \sum_{i=1}^{3} X_i$$

Now we know that Y is simply the number of heads obtained when we flip a coin three times, and we can use the methods we saw in Chapter 5 to calculate the **probability** associated with each possible outcome of Y. That is, if we flip a coin n times, then the probability of gaining k heads is just:

$$P(Y = k) = C_k^n \times P(Coin = Heads)^k \times P(Coin = Tails)^{n-k}$$

Since the probability of a head is 0.5, we can apply this formula to calculate the probability of gaining 0, 1, 2, or 3 heads. These probabilities are illustrated in Table 12.1.

We could then use these probabilities to calculate the expected number of heads (and the variance of the number of heads):

$$\begin{aligned} E(Y) &= \sum_y P(Y = y) \times y = 0.125 \times 0 + 0.375 \times 1 + 0.375 \times 2 + 0.125 \times 3 \\ &= 1.5 \end{aligned}$$

[4] Remember, this is sometimes referred to as the probability distribution function.

Table 12.1 Probabilities associated with the number of heads gained when flipping a fair coin three times

Number of heads	Probability
0	0.125
1	0.375
2	0.375
3	0.125

However, whilst this is relatively straightforward when dealing with a small number of flips, if we constructed the new variable based on (say) 100 flips of a coin, this would become a very cumbersome process, and we might hope that there is an easier way to analyse the distribution.

We can see that Y is constructed based upon three random variables. Each flip of the coin is itself a random variable, and the new variable Y is built based on a linear combination of the three flips:

$$Y = \sum_{i=1}^{3} X_i$$

Characteristics of the random variables representing each individual flip

Before we analyse Y any further, let's begin by looking at the distribution of the random variables that construct Y. Each of the flips of the coin can be thought of as an independent and identically drawn (*iid*) observation; that is, each of the flips has the same expected value, the same variance, and each of the flips is independent from all of the other flips. We can construct the expectation of X_i by finding the sum of the products of the outcomes with their corresponding probabilities:

$$E(X_i) = P(X_i = 1) \times 1 + P(X_i = 0) \times 0$$
$$= \frac{1}{2} \times 1 + \frac{1}{2} \times 0 = \frac{1}{2}$$

Similarly, the variance can be constructed by considering $var(X_i) = E\left(X_i^2\right) - E(X_i)^2$. We know that $E(X_i) = 0.5$, and so we just need $E\left(X_i^2\right)$:

$$E\left(X_i^2\right) = P(X_i = 1) \times 1^2 + P(X_i = 0) \times 0^2 = \frac{1}{2}$$

Thus, the variance of X_i is just equal to $var(X_i) = E\left(X_i^2\right) - E(X_i)^2 = \frac{1}{2} - \left(\frac{1}{2}\right)^2 = \frac{1}{4}$

Now, let's return to the distribution of Y. If we want to find the expectation of Y, we can simply use the rules of expectations we saw earlier in this textbook:

$$E(Y) = E\left(\sum_{i=1}^{3} X_i\right) = E(X_1 + X_2 + X_3)$$

Now, we know that the expectation of any sum is just equal to the sum of the expectations. So, we can rewrite the expectation of Y as:

$$E(Y) = E(X_1) + E(X_2) + E(X_3)$$

Since each flip is independent and identically distributed, $E(X_1) = E(X_2) = E(X_3) = 0.5$. Thus, the expectation of Y is just equal to:

$$E(Y) = 0.5 + 0.5 + 0.5 = 1.5$$

That is, if we repeatedly flipped the coin three times, then on average we would expect to see 1.5 heads. Similarly, we can construct the variance of the new variable Y:

$$var(Y) = var\left(\sum_{i=1}^{3} X_i\right) = var(X_1 + X_2 + X_3)$$

Now, we will need to appeal to our rules relating to the variance of a sum of random variables, and we can rewrite this variance as equal to the sum of the variances, plus all of the covariance terms:

$$= var(X_1) + var(X_2) + var(X_3) + 2 \times (cov(X_1, X_2) + cov(X_1, X_3) + cov(X_2, X_3))$$

However, since the observed flips are assumed to be independent from each other (they are assumed to be *iid*), the covariance terms will all just be equal to zero.

Similarly, $var(X_1) = var(X_2) = var(X_3) = var(X)$. We saw that the variance of X_i will just be equal to $\frac{1}{4}$, and so:

$$var(Y) = 3 \times var(X) = 3 \times \frac{1}{4} = 0.75$$

This example considers a relatively small number of trials (i.e. a relatively small number of flips of a coin), but provides us a framework to be able to examine a new type of variable, based on repeated trials.

12.2.1 The binomial distribution in general

In the previous section, we considered creating a new variable, based upon the number of heads achieved if we flip a fair coin three times. However, this is just an example of a random variable that follows a binomial, or Bernoulli, distribution.

A random variable that follows the binomial distribution is constructed based on a sum of independent and identically distributed random variables, each of which can take only two values, usually 0 and 1 (or alternatively success or failure).[5]

Each of the underlying building blocks is known as an individual Bernoulli (or binomial) trial, which we can denote as X_i. The probability that each trial is equal to 1 is constant, and defined as $P(X_i = 1) = p$ for all possible values of i.

To motivate the binomial distribution, let's begin with a simple variable X, which can take on two possible outcomes $X = 0$ and $X = 1$. The probability that $X = 1$ is given as $P(X = 1) = p$, and similarly $P(X = 0) = 1 - p$.

We can write down the PMF of X as:

$$X = \begin{cases} 1, & P(X = 1) = p \\ 0, & P(X = 0) = 1 - p \end{cases}$$

X might represent *anything* where there are two possible outcomes (with constant probability). For example, p could represent the probability an individual, randomly drawn from the population, has green eyes, and $(1 - p)$ would then represent the probability that an individual does not have green eyes.

Calculating the expectation and variance of *X*

The expectation of X can be calculated as the sum of the products of the outcomes multiplied by their respective probabilities. As such:

$$E(X) = \sum_x P(X = x) \times x = (1 - p) \times 0 + p \times 1 = p$$

Similarly, the variance of X is just equal to $var(X) = E(X^2) - E(X)^2$. We already know that $E(X) = p$, and so $E(X)^2 = p^2$:

$$E(X^2) = \sum_x P(X = x) \times x^2 = (1 - p) \times 0^2 + p \times 1^2 = p$$

Thus the variance of X is just equal to:

$$var(X) = E(X^2) - E(X)^2 = p - p^2 = p(1 - p)$$

Now, suppose that we randomly sample n independent and identically distributed observations from X. Each of these observations will have the same probability of being equal to $1\ (= p)$, and the same probability of being equal to $0\ (= 1 - p)$.

For simplicity, we will denote the ith observation as X_i, and based upon the n observations, $X_1, X_2, X_3, \ldots, X_n$, we will construct a new variable, Y which is the sum of the n observations:

$$Y = \sum_{i=1}^{n} X_i$$

KEY NOTATION

If we observe a variable, Y, constructed based on the sum of n independent Bernoulli trials X_i, each with probability $P(X_i = 1) = p$, $P(X_i = 0) = 1 - p$, such that:

$$Y = \sum_{i=1}^{n} X_i$$

[5] Bernoulli (binomial) trials are random variables with exactly two possible outcomes. They are named after Jacob Bernoulli, who analysed them in the seventeenth century. These trials are the building blocks of the binomial distribution.

Then, the Y variable would be said to follow a binomial distribution, based on n trials, with probability p. We would denote this as:

$$Y \sim Bin(n, p) \text{ or } Y \sim B(n, p)$$

This means that the variable Y is distributed (~) following a binomial distribution (Bin or B) based upon n trials, each with probability of success p.

Now, for example, if X_i represented whether an individual has green eyes (or not), then Y would represent the number of individuals within a sample of n individuals with green eyes. Similarly, if X_i represents a success (e.g. observing a head when we flip a coin), then Y would represent the number of successes.

Binomial formula

If we have a random variable Y, constructed based on n trials, each with probability p of success, the probability of gaining exactly k successes is:

$$P(Y = k) = C_k^n \times p^k \times (1 - p)^{n-k}$$

You can calculate this PMF in Microsoft Excel by using the formula:

=BINOM.DIST(k, n, p, FALSE)

where n represents the total number of trials, k is the number of successes, and p is the probability of success for each individual trial. The final term can be either FALSE or TRUE; this relates to whether you are interested in the cumulative distribution (TRUE) or the marginal probability (FALSE).

If you use =BINOM.DIST(k, n, p, TRUE), then Excel will calculate $P(Y \leq k)$.

We can represent the probability distribution for different values of n, as seen in Figure 12.9. The height of each bar represents the probability of that particular outcome. As you can see, when $p = 0.4$, the most likely outcomes are at 4, 20, and 40 for $n = 10$, 50, and 100 respectively, whilst for $p = 0.7$, the most likely outcomes are at 7, 35, and 70.

These most likely outcomes are also the expected values in the binomial distribution. Whilst we could use software such as Microsoft Excel to calculate the probability of each possible outcome, and then calculate the expected value by finding the sum of the products of the outcomes with the respective probabilities, there is an easier way, based on how the variables are generated.

We know that every individual observation, X_i, is equivalent to an independent and identically distributed (random) draw from a population, where $P(X_i = 1) = p$ and

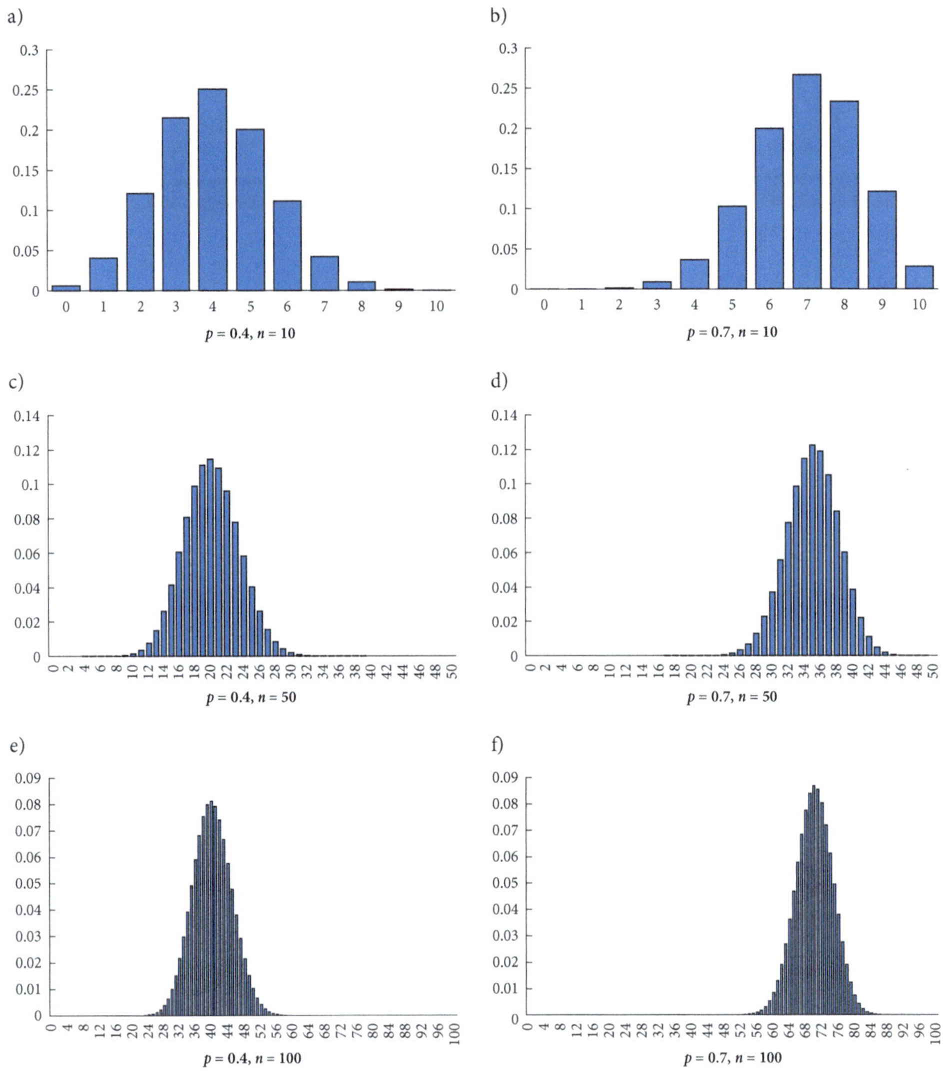

Figure 12.9 Probability distributions for the binomial distribution with $n = 10, n = 50$, and $n = 100$.

$P(X_i = 0) = (1 - p)$. As such, we have seen that $E(X_i) = p$ for all i and $var(X_i) = p(1 - p)$ for all i. Because the X_i are independent, it will also follow that $cov(X_i, X_j) = 0$ for all $i \neq j$.

Remember that $Y = \sum_{i=1}^{n} X_i$. We wish to find the expectation and variance of Y.

Calculating the expectation of a binomially distributed variable

Suppose that we have a random variable, Y, which follows a binomial distribution, based upon n trials, each of which has probability of success (i.e. = 1) equal to p. That is $Y \sim Bin(n, p)$.

Since Y is just the sum of the outcomes from the n trials, $Y = \sum_{i=1}^{n} X_i$, we can use our rules of expectations. Since the expectation of a sum is just the sum of expectations, we can write that:

$$E(Y) = E\left(\sum_{i=1}^{n} X_i\right) = \sum_{i=1}^{n} E(X_i)$$

However, since the X_i are iid, and $E(X_i) = p$ for all i, then:

$$E(Y) = \sum_{i=1}^{n} E(X_i) = \sum_{i=1}^{n} p$$

Now, p is a constant, and the sum is equivalent to $(p + p + \ldots + p)$. That is,

$$\sum_{i=1}^{n} p = np$$

Thus $E(Y) = np$.

Calculating the variance of a binomially distributed variable

Again, we will consider a random variable, Y, which follows a binomial distribution, based upon n trials, each of which has probability of success (i.e. = 1) equal to p. That is $Y \sim Bin(n, p)$.

Using the rules of variances, we know that:

$$var(Y) = var\left(\sum_{i=1}^{n} X_i\right) = var(X_1 + X_2 + X_3 + \ldots + X_n)$$

Remember that finding the variance of a sum of random variables is a bit like taking the square of the sum. Any terms that yield 'square' terms (e.g. X_1^2, X_2^2, and so on) would be equivalent to variance terms, and similarly, any cross-product terms are equivalent to covariance terms.

So, we can write that:

$$\begin{aligned} var(X_1 + X_2 + X_3 + \ldots + X_n) &= var(X_1) + var(X_2) + var(X_3) + \ldots + var(X_n) \\ &+ cov(X_1, X_2) + cov(X_1, X_3) + cov(X_1, X_4) + \ldots + cov(X_1, X_n) \\ &+ cov(X_2, X_1) + cov(X_2, X_3) + cov(X_2, X_4) + \ldots + cov(X_2, X_n) \\ &+ cov(X_3, X_1) + cov(X_3, X_2) + cov(X_3, X_4) + \ldots + cov(X_3, X_n) \\ &+ \ldots \end{aligned}$$

Now, hopefully, you can see that the covariance terms will include every possible pair of i and j, except where $i \neq j$. As such, we can denote the variance as:

$$var(Y) = \sum_{i=1}^{n} var(X_i) + \sum_{i \neq j} cov(X_i, X_j)$$

That is, we have the sum of all the variance terms, and the sum of all of the possible covariance terms. This notation is a little misleading though, as strictly speaking $cov(X_1, X_2) = cov(X_2, X_1)$. As such, we can be a little more precise with our notation to write:

$$var(Y) = \sum_{i=1}^{n} var(X_i) + 2\sum_{i=1}^{n-1}\sum_{j=i+1}^{n} cov(X_i, X_j)$$

However, since the observations are iid, it follows that $cov(X_i, X_j) = 0$ for $i \neq j$. Further, as we saw earlier in this section, it will follow that $var(X_i) = p(1-p)$ for all i:

$$var(Y) = \sum_{i=1}^{n} var(X_i) + 0 = \sum_{i=1}^{n} p(1-p) = np(1-p)$$

The binomial distribution can be applied in a wide range of cases. Whenever we repeatedly, randomly sample from a population where there are two possible outcomes, and we are interested in the number of individuals with one possible characteristic, we can model this using the binomial distribution. For example, we could apply this to the number of individuals from a random sample of the population whose education is at least at degree level, or the number of individuals from a random sample of the population who have a job, or the number of individuals in a random sample of the population with green eyes. Similarly, if we repeatedly play a game, each time with a constant probability of success, we can model the number of times that we win the game using a binomial distribution.

Summary of the binomial distribution

If we observe a random variable, Y, constructed from the sum of n IID realizations of a random variable X_i, such that:

$$X_i = \begin{cases} 1, & P(X_i = 1) = p \\ 0, & P(X_i = 0) = 1 - p \end{cases}$$

where:

$$Y = \sum_{i=1}^{n} X_i$$

Notation	$Y \sim Bin(n, p)$ or $Y \sim B(n, p)$
Expectation	$E(Y) = np$
Variance	$var(Y) = np(1-p)$
Probability mass function (sometimes referred to as the probability distribution function)	$P(Y = k) = C_k^n p^k (1-p)^{n-k}$

Worked example 12.2: How many people have a degree-level qualification in a sample?

Based on data from the 2019 UK Labour Force Survey, 43.1 per cent of the UK population aged 21–64 had completed some higher education (i.e. achieved a degree, a qualification such as a BTEC or HNC, or a qualification in HE lower than a degree).

Suppose we begin by defining a random variable X as whether an individual has achieved some higher education or not; as such, the probability distribution can be written as:

$$X = \begin{cases} HE, & P(X = HE) = 0.431 \\ No\ HE, & P(X = No\ HE) = 0.569 \end{cases}$$

So, if we sample one individual, randomly from the population, the random variable representing whether they have completed some higher education or not will be equivalent to a Bernoulli (or binomial) trial, whereby $X = 1$ if the individual has some higher education, and $X = 0$ if the individual has not completed any higher education.

As such, suppose that we randomly chose ten individuals (aged 21–64) from the population, and counted how many of these had completed some higher education. The number of people with a degree would follow a binomial distribution, based on ten trials ($n = 10$), and probability of success of 0.435 ($p = 0.431$):

$$X_i = \begin{cases} 1, & P(X_i = 1) = 0.431 \\ 0, & P(X_i = 0) = 0.569 \end{cases}$$

Let's represent the number of individuals who have completed some HE (from our random sample of ten) as a random variable Y, such that:

$$Y \sim B(10{,}0.431)$$

From this, we can calculate the expected number of individuals within our sample who have completed some HE, and the variance (and standard deviation) of this random variable:

$$E(Y) = np = 10 \times 0.431 = 4.31$$
$$var(Y) = np(1 - p) = 10 \times 0.431 \times 0.569 = 2.45239$$
$$s.d.(Y) = \sqrt{\text{var}(Y)} = \sqrt{2.45239} = 1.566$$

Simulation using real data

The UK Labour Force Survey is a very large survey of UK households, providing information about employment and other characteristics of the UK population. In this example, we are going to treat the data from the 2019 UK Labour Force Survey as our population.

In order to examine the example, we can model this through repeatedly sampling random samples of ten (between the ages of 21 and 64) from the Labour Force Survey, and count how many individuals' highest level of education is at least at the level of higher education.

If we take a single sample, we might find that six individuals had higher education. However, remember that there will exist **sampling variation**—every time we take a sample from a population, there will be some variation in the make-up of the sample, so sometimes there might be six individuals with higher education, sometimes eight, sometimes two.

By taking repeated samples from the population, we can find the distribution of this random variable. In order to simulate this, I have taken 100,000 repeated samples (each with ten observations) from the 2019 UK Labour Force Survey, and the distribution of the number of individuals with at least some higher education is illustrated in Figure 12.10.

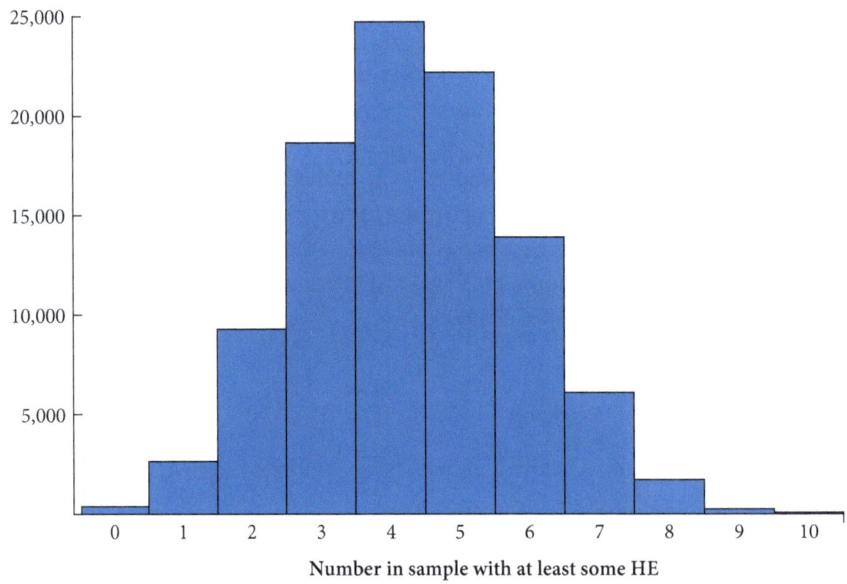

Figure 12.10 Distribution of number of individuals in sample with at least some HE from simulation.

We know, from the theory, that the expected number of individuals in the sample with at least some HE is 4.31. The most common outcomes across the 100,000 samples from the population was 4, with the second most common as 5. This suggests that the average from our trials is between 4 and 5. In fact, if we calculate the mean (average) and the standard deviation of the number of individuals with some HE across all 100,000 samples, the average is very close to the expected value (4.31), and the standard deviation and variance are exactly what would have been expected.

Number of trials	**100,000**
Average	**4.304**
Standard deviation	**1.566**
Variance	**2.452**

Had we repeated this experiment with a much larger number of trials (say 1,000,000), then we would expect the average of the trials to converge to the true population average.[6]

[6] This is an application of the law of large numbers.

12.2.2 Using the binomial distribution to calculate a probability within a range

So far, we've seen how we can calculate the expectation and the variance of a binomial distribution, but we may also be interested in calculating the probability of an outcome lying within a particular range. Suppose that you are playing a game of chance, each trial of which has probability of success of 0.6. Suppose that we played the game 1,000 times. Then we could define the number of successes using a binomial distribution.

That is, if we define X_i as the outcome from the *ith* game, with $P(X_i = 1) = 0.6$ and $P(X_i = 0) = 0.4$, then we can define a new variable, W (indicating the number of 'wins' from 1,000 games as:

$$W = \sum_{i=1}^{1000} X_i$$

Now, we know that $E(W) = np = 1{,}000 \times 0.6 = 600$, and $var(W) = np(1 - p) = 1{,}000 \times 0.6 \times 0.4 = 240$. However, suppose that we wanted to know the probability of winning at least 550 games, i.e. $P(W \geq 550)$, or the probability of winning at most 650 games, $P(W \leq 650)$. If we wanted to calculate these probabilities exactly, we would need to add up all of the probabilities related to outcomes where the condition is met.

With computer software packages, such as Microsoft Excel, this sort of calculation is relatively straightforward, as we can calculate the CDF for a binomial distribution using the =BINOM.DIST(. . .) formula in Excel.

Formula	Description	Value
=BINOM.DIST(550, 1000, 0.6, TRUE)	This would calculate $P(W \leq 550)$, where $W \sim B(1000, 0.6)$. The TRUE indicates that you are looking at the cumulative distribution function.	$P(W \leq 550) = 0.0007412$
=BINOM.DIST(650, 1000, 0.6, TRUE)	This would calculate $P(W \leq 650)$, where $W \sim B(1000, 0.6)$. The TRUE indicates that you are looking at the cumulative distribution function.	$P(W \leq 650) = 0.99948758$

So, we can immediately see that the probability of winning at most 650 games is equal to 0.99948758. However, it is slightly trickier to calculate the probability of winning at least 550 games, for two reasons:

1. The cumulative distribution function tells you the probability, $P(W \leq w)$, but in this case, we want to know $P(W \geq w)$.
2. The binomial distribution is a discrete random variable, and so $P(W \leq w) \neq P(W < w)$.

To calculate $P(W \geq 550)$, we would need to take account of the fact that the sum of all of the probabilities will be equal to 1, and that we would want to include $P(W = 550)$ in the probability. This is relatively straightforward to do, as we know that:

$$P(W < 550) = P(W \leq 549)$$

Thus, to ensure that we include $W = 550$ in our probability, we can calculate:

$$P(W \geq 550) = 1 - P(W < 550) = 1 - P(W \leq 549) = 0.999406$$

We can use exactly the same methods to calculate the probability of observing an outcome within a range. For example:

$$P(550 \leq W \leq 650) = P(W \leq 650) - P(W < 550)$$

Statisticians, however, often try to simplify the problem. Initially, this was because computers were not available to calculate exact probabilities using the binomial distribution, but also because it can often be useful to use continuous variables as a way to approximate the distribution of a discrete random variable.

If you remember the shape of the probabilities relating to the binomial distribution from earlier in the chapter, shown again in Figure 12.11, the distribution of probabilities looks very similar, irrespective of the number of trials, following a distinct bell-shape.

In fact, for a large number of trials, the PMF of the binomial distribution can be modelled using a continuous random variable known as the **normal distribution**, and we will introduce the normal distribution in the next chapter, and see how we can use this to answer questions relating to the binomial distribution.

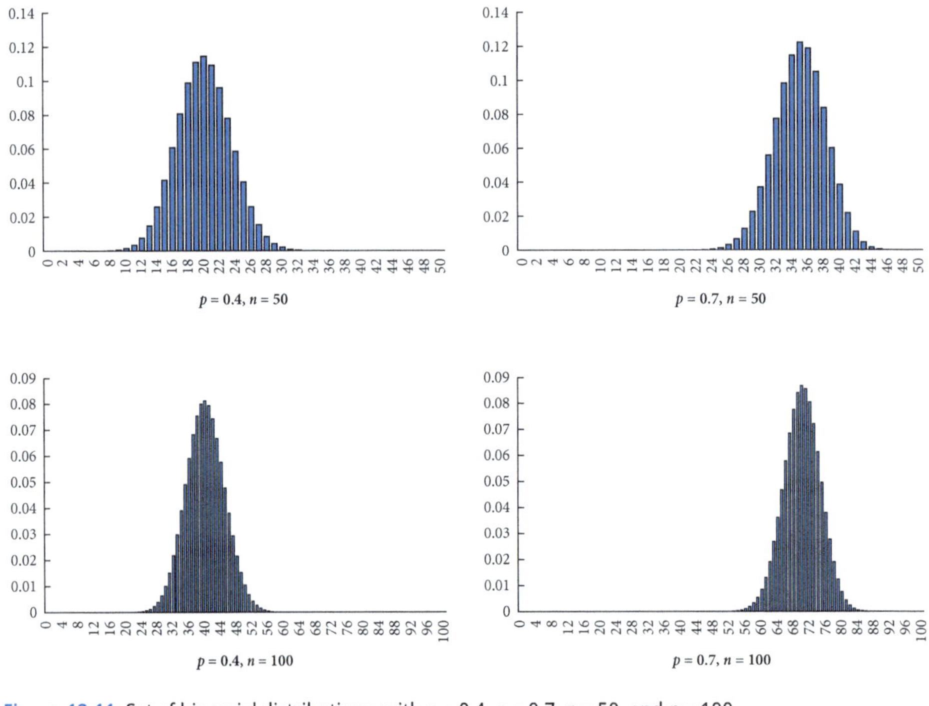

Figure 12.11 Set of binomial distributions, with $p = 0.4$, $p = 0.7$, $n = 50$, and $n = 100$.

Summary

In this chapter, we have seen two important distributions: the uniform distribution and the binomial distribution. Both of these distributions are commonly used in modelling outcomes, particularly in statistics, and so having a strong understanding of these distributions is important.

Key formulae

	Uniform distribution	Binomial distribution
Notation	$X \sim U(a,b)$	$Y \sim Bin(n,p)$ or $Y \sim B(n,p)$
PMF/PDF	$f_X(x) = \begin{cases} \frac{1}{b-a}, & a \leq x \leq b \\ 0, & \text{Otherwise} \end{cases}$	$P(Y=k) = C_k^n p^k (1-p)^{n-k}$
Expectation	$E(X) = \frac{a+b}{2}$	$E(Y) = np$
Variance	$var(X) = \frac{(b-a)^2}{12}$	$var(Y) = np(1-p)$

Appendix

Calculating the cumulative distribution function of a uniform distribution between *a* and *b*

If we are presented with a uniform distribution in the range a to b, i.e. $X \sim U(a,b)$, then we know that the PDF can be represented thus:

$$f_X(x) = \begin{cases} 0, & x < a \\ \frac{1}{b-a}, & a \leq x \leq b \\ 0, & x \geq b \end{cases}$$

The CDF is the probability of lying below a particular value of x and is equal to the area under the curve to the left of the value x. Since the PDF is defined in three parts, we will need to analyse the CDF in three sections: firstly for $x < a$, then for $a \leq x \leq b$, and then for $x > b$

For $x < a$:

$$F_X(x) = \int_{-\infty}^{x} 0dx = [0]_{-\infty}^{x} = 0$$

For $a \leq x \leq b$, to find the CDF, we will need to integrate between $-\infty$ and x:

$$F_X(x) = \int_{-\infty}^{x} f_X(x)dx$$

Because there are different functions between $-\infty$ and a, and between a and b, we will need to split this integral into two parts:

$$= \int_{-\infty}^{a} 0dx + \int_{a}^{x} \frac{1}{b-a}dx = 0 + \left[\frac{x}{b-a}\right]_a^x = \frac{x-a}{b-a}$$

For $x > b$, we need to use the same method again, but take account of the fact that the PDF is split into three sections!

$$F_X = \int_{-\infty}^{a} 0dx + \int_{a}^{b} \frac{1}{b-a}dx + \int_{b}^{x} 0dx = 0 + \left[\frac{x}{b-a}\right]_a^b + 0 = \left[\frac{b-a}{b-a}\right] = 1$$

So, the CDF is equal to:

$$F_X(x) = \begin{cases} 0, & x < a \\ \dfrac{x-a}{b-a}, & a \le x \le b \\ 1, & x \ge b \end{cases}$$

Constructing the variance of a variable following the uniform distribution

Suppose that we have a random variable, X, which is uniformly distributed between a and b, $X \sim U(a,b)$. We know that, for any random variable X, the variance is given by:

$$var(X) = E(X^2) - E(X)^2$$

We already know, from Section 12.2.1, that for a uniform distribution between a and b the expectation is given by: $E(X) = \frac{b+a}{2}$. As such, we will just need to find $E(X^2)$, and then combine this with the square of the expectation.

In general, we can construct the expectation of X^2 by integrating the product of the PDF of X, multiplied by the square of the observations of X, across the entire domain. That is, $E(X^2) = \int_x f_X(x) \times x^2 dx$

Substituting in the PDF, and the limits of $X = a$ and $X = b$, we have:

$$E(X^2) = \int_{a}^{b} \frac{x^2}{b-a}dx$$

This is relatively trivial to integrate (we merely raise the power of the x by 1, and divide by the new power), giving us:

$$E(X^2) = \left[\frac{x^3}{3(b-a)}\right]_a^b$$

Substituting in the limits, and factorizing, we have:

$$= \frac{b^3 - a^3}{3(b-a)} = \frac{(b-a)(a^2 + ab + b^2)}{3(b-a)}$$
$$= \frac{a^2 + ab + b^2}{3}$$

Now, we can combine $E(X^2)$ and $E(X)^2$, to give:

$$var(X) = E(X^2) - E(X)^2 = \left[\frac{a^2 + ab + b^2}{3}\right] - \left[\frac{a+b}{2}\right]^2$$

Which expands to give us:

$$var(X) = \left[\frac{a^2 + ab + b^2}{3}\right] - \left[\frac{a^2 + b^2 + 2ab}{4}\right]$$

We can put all of this over a common denominator (12), giving us:

$$var(X) = \frac{4a^2 + 4ab + 4b^2 - 3a^2 - 3b^2 - 6ab}{12}$$
$$= \frac{a^2 + b^2 - 2ab}{12}$$

However, we should recognize that the denominator is the same as $(b - a)^2$, so we can re-write the variance as:

$$var(X) = \frac{(b-a)^2}{12}$$

The Normal Distribution

13

Learning outcomes for this chapter

By the end of this chapter you will be able to:

- Define a normally distributed variable in terms of its expectation and variance
- Appreciate that there are a wide range of applications of the normal distribution
- Calculate probabilities based upon the standard normal distribution
- Find probabilities using the standard normal tables, and via Microsoft Excel
- Find probabilities relating to any normally distributed variable by standardizing the distribution
- Intuitively recognize probabilities relating to the normal distribution, based on the number of standard deviations away from the mean
- Use the normal distribution as a way of approximating the binomial distribution

Mathematical tools

- Integration is discussed, but not used
- Recognition of functions involving exponentials
- Simple summations

Introduction

One of the key distributions that you will encounter in statistics is often referred to as the normal or the Gaussian distribution. The normal distribution is extremely useful for evaluating the likelihood of events in statistical testing, and a sound understanding of the normal distribution is critical for understanding later topics, such as statistical testing. People often assume that random variables such as height, IQ, and returns on investments follow normal distributions, but in reality very few natural events follow exactly normal distributions. However, because of the central limit theorem (which we will see at the end of this chapter), it is possible to say that many estimators (such as the sample mean) will follow a normal distribution, which allows us, in future chapters, to introduce statistical testing.

13.1 Motivating the normal distribution

We saw, in Chapter 12, that when we examine the binomial distribution, when the number of trials becomes increasingly large, the probability distribution function begins to follow a characteristic bell shape, as illustrated in Figure 13.1.

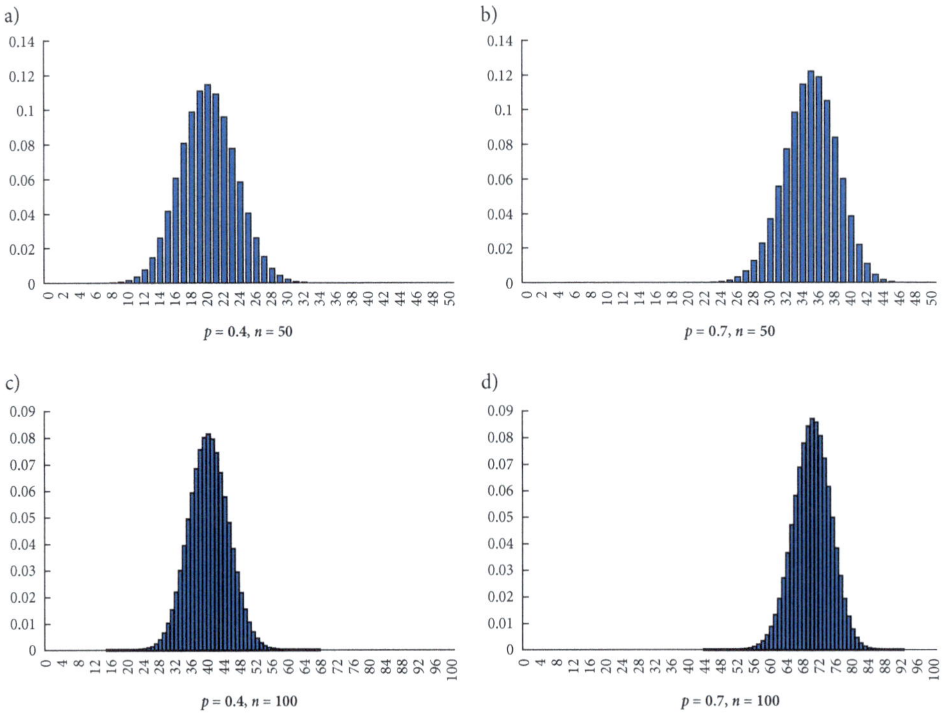

Figure 13.1 Set of binomial distributions, with $p = 0.4$, $p = 0.7$, $n = 50$, and $n = 100$.

As a characteristic of the binomial distribution, the most likely outcomes (with the highest probabilities) will be close to the middle of the distribution, whilst the least likely outcomes are in the tails of the distribution.

With the binomial distribution, it is relatively straightforward to calculate the probability of a particular outcome. So, for instance, if $Y_n \sim B(n, p)$, we can calculate the probability of getting exactly k successes (i.e. where the Bernoulli trial is equal to 1) as just equal to:

$$P(Y_n = k) = C_k^n p^k (1 - p)^{n-k}$$

However, we are often interested, not in the probability of gaining exactly k successes, but instead, the probability of gaining at least k successes. In principle, we could calculate this probability exactly by adding together all of the probabilities of the outcomes greater than (or equal to) k:

$$P(Y_n \geq k) = \sum_{i=k}^{n} P(Y_n = k)$$

For relatively small number of trials (n), this calculation will be trivial, but for larger number of trials, this sort of calculation can be computationally intensive.

For example, surveys are often carried out using large samples from the population. However, when carrying out a survey, you may worry that the sample you have observed is unrepresentative. Suppose that we had a sample of 10,000 individuals, randomly sampled from the population, and we have observed 5,600 females. We may want to examine whether obtaining 5,600 females in our sample would have been an unlikely event, so we could try to model this using the Binomial distribution.

We know that 51 per cent of the UK population is female, and so we could model the number of females (let's call this X) within our sample of 10,000 individuals using a binomial distribution:

$$X \sim B(10{,}000, 0.51)$$

If we wanted to calculate the probability of gaining at least 5,600 females, then we would need to calculate the probability of all of the possible outcomes from 5,600 females, all the way up to 10,000 females in the sample:

$$P(X \geq 5{,}600) = \sum_{i=5{,}600}^{10{,}000} P(X = i) = P(X = 5{,}600) + P(X = 5{,}601) + \ldots + P(X = 10{,}000)$$

However, this would involve calculating 4,401 separate probabilities, and if carried out by hand would be computationally intensive, and whilst software packages like Microsoft Excel can calculate these for you, historically, this was a relatively intractable problem, and it is often desirable to treat variables like this as being effectively **continuous random variables**. So, is there an easier way that we can analyse these sorts of problems?

In the eighteenth century, Abraham de Moivre, a French mathematician, was interested in this very problem. He observed that as n got larger, the distribution of a binomial variable, X_n, converged towards a consistent shape, which looked very like a bell shape.

We can see from Figure 13.1 how this **convergence** towards this shape occurs as n increases. De Moivre reasoned that if he were able to derive the probability density function (PDF) for this curve, he would be able to use this to find an approximation for the probability that $X_n \geq k$, when n becomes very large.[1]

This may seem like an odd thing to do as, essentially, he was looking for a continuous distribution to represent a discrete distribution, but as n gets large, it is clear that the distribution of the probabilities looks more and more like a continuous curve.

De Moivre was able to show that an approximation for the height of the probability density could be given by:

$$P(X_n = k) = C_k^n p^k (1 - p)^{n-k} \cong \frac{1}{\sqrt{2\pi np(1 - p)}} e^{-\frac{(k-np)^2}{2np(1-p)}}$$

In order to illustrate this, consider an example. In panel a) of Figure 13.2 we represent the probabilities of outcomes related to a random variable X, which follows a binomial

[1] De Moivre (1718), *The Doctrine of Chances*, Woodfall.

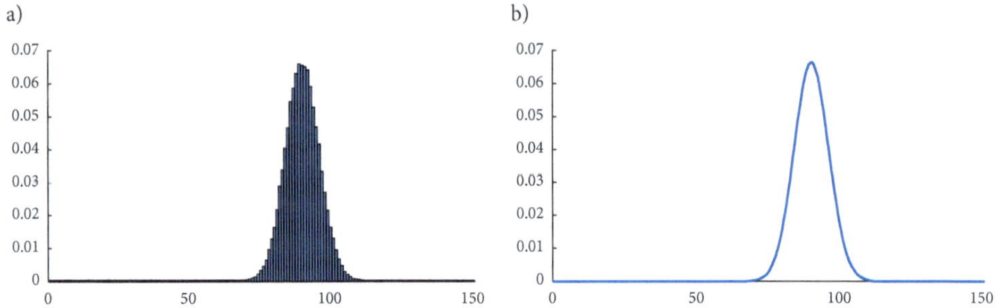

Figure 13.2 Binomial distribution and a continuous approximation

distribution, based on 150 trials, each with probability of success 0.6. Panel b) illustrates the continuous random variable, X_N, which has the PDF:

$$f_{X_N}(x) = \frac{1}{\sqrt{2\pi np(1-p)}} e^{-\frac{(x-np)^2}{2np(1-p)}}$$

If we plot these on the same set of axes, as illustrated in Figure 13.3, we can see that the continuous approximation is very close to the binomial distribution. As such, we could use the area under this continuous approximation as a way of calculating (approximate) probabilities relating to the binomial distribution.

Thus, if we are able to calculate a cumulative distribution function (CDF), we should be able to easily calculate the probability, $P(X_n \geq k)$.

Remember, if we want to find the probability that $X_n \geq k$, when we have a PDF $f_X(x)$, then we can find this by integrating between k and ∞.

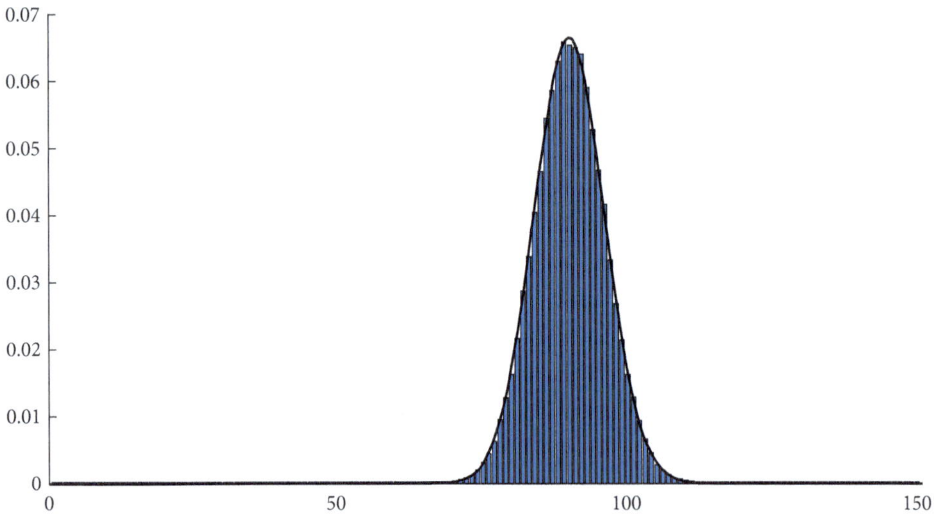

Figure 13.3 Plot of binomial distribution, and continuous approximation.

$$P(X_n \geq k) \cong \int_k^\infty f_{X_N}(x)dx$$
$$= \int_k^\infty \frac{1}{\sqrt{2\pi np(1-p)}} e^{-\frac{(x-np)^2}{2np(1-p)}} dx$$

Unfortunately, there is a problem with this idea, as there is no simple analytic solution to the integral of the PDF here, so we cannot simply write down a CDF. However, mathematicians *have* managed to calculate the CDF for this process using numerical methods, and tables illustrating the distribution of this density function are now commonplace. We will see later how to apply this.

If we look back at the PDF that we have used here to model the binomial distribution:

$$f_{X_N}(x) = \frac{1}{\sqrt{2\pi np(1-p)}} e^{-\frac{(x-np)^2}{2np(1-p)}}$$

remember that the expected value of our variable, X_n was equal to np, whilst the variance of the variable X_n was equal to $np(1-p)$. Both of these terms appear in our expression. If we now rewrite our expression, replacing the expected value of X_n with μ, and the variance as σ^2 (or the standard deviation as σ), we can see that our density function is:

$$f_{X_N}(x) = \frac{1}{\sigma\sqrt{2\pi}} e^{-\frac{(x-\mu)^2}{2\sigma^2}}$$

This probability density function is the PDF for what is known as the normal distribution, which is defined in terms of the expectation, μ, and variance, σ^2.

KEY DEFINITION: NORMAL DISTRIBUTION

The normal distribution is a continuous random variable which follows a bell-shaped PDF, and is defined in terms of its expectation (μ) and variance (σ^2), which is symmetric around the expected value.

If we have a random variable *X*, which follows a normal distribution with expectation μ and variance (σ^2), we would normally denote this as:

$$X \sim N(\mu, \sigma^2)$$

The PDF of *X* would be given as:

$$f_X(x) = \frac{1}{\sigma\sqrt{2\pi}} e^{-\frac{(x-\mu)^2}{2\sigma^2}}$$

The domain of the normal distribution is defined across all real values of x between $-\infty$ and ∞.

13.2 Gauss and the normal distribution

In the last example, the PDF is defined just in terms of the value of x, the expected value of the random variable (μ) standard deviation (σ). This general form of PDF is known as the normal distribution. Later in this chapter, we will return to using the normal distribution as an approximation for the binomial distribution, but let's first examine the properties of the normal distribution. A random variable that follows the normal distribution is characterized by a large probability that any given realization of the random variable is close to the variable's expected value, and the probability of gaining an outcome in the tails of the distribution is low.

Figure 13.4 provides an example of the PDF of a random variable X which follows a normal distribution, with expectation equal to 50, and variance equal to 100. That is, $X \sim N(50,100)$. The normal distribution is a symmetric distribution, centred on the expected value. In Figure 13.4, the expected value is 50, and there is a line of symmetry at $E(X) = 50$.

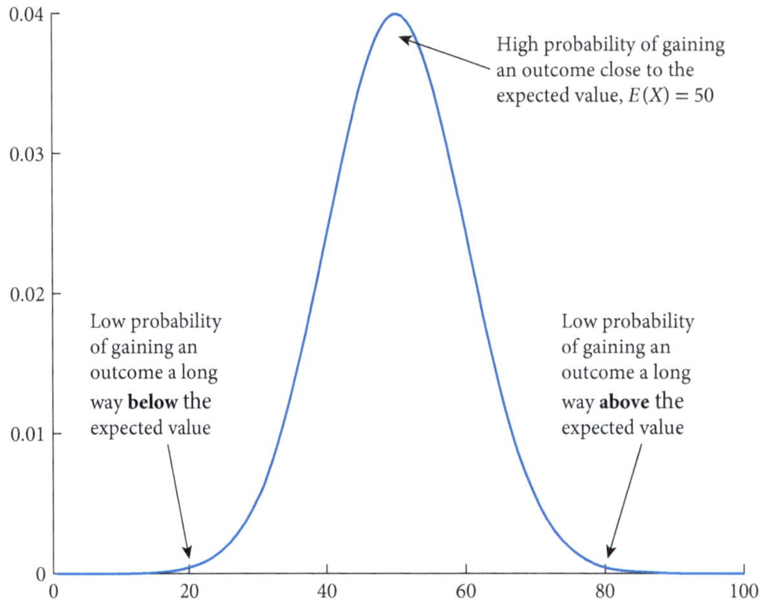

Figure 13.4 Normal distribution with expectation, $E(X) = 50$ and variance, $var(X) = 100$.

Random variables that follow the normal distribution are often referred to as following the 'Gaussian distribution'. This is not because Gauss invented the distribution, but rather because he made use of the distribution in an inventive and novel way.

In the nineteenth century, astronomers spotted a new dwarf planet in the heavens. This dwarf planet was Ceres, which lay between Mars and Jupiter. These astronomers plotted the movement of Ceres through the solar system, but when the dwarf planet moved behind the sun, the astronomers lost the planet, and could not find it again, even though they had some measurements of its orbit from observation, which could conceivably be used to predict where it would next appear. However, standard methods were fruitless, and the astronomers believed that without more data, it would be impossible to find Ceres again.

However, Carl Friedrich Gauss saw the problem differently. He reasoned that even though there were observations of where Ceres was in the night sky, it was highly likely that these observations were not exactly correct; that is, there was likely to be some error in the measurement. In some (rare) cases, the errors were likely to be very large, but in most cases, the errors would be close to zero. He reasoned that this sounded very like the standard normal distribution; the peak of the normal distribution is at zero, with large deviations from the expectation rare. Using the observations that had previously been gained, and the assumption that the measurement error followed this normal distribution, Gauss was able to predict the path of Ceres accurately, and astounded astronomers when Ceres appeared exactly where he predicted it would be.[2]

Not only is the normal distribution useful in astronomy, but because of its properties, it is fundamental to almost any statistical analysis that is carried out.

13.3 The 'standard' normal distribution

We have seen earlier in this chapter that the PDF of a normally distributed variable is given by:

$$f_X(x) = \frac{1}{\sigma\sqrt{2\pi}} e^{-\frac{(x-\mu)^2}{2\sigma^2}}$$

Suppose that we have a random variable, X, with expectation 10 and variance 100. That is,

$$X \sim N(10,100)$$

We might want to know the probability of randomly observing an outcome from X between −10 and 5. We can see this probability represented in Figure 13.5 as the shaded area under the normal curve between −10 and 5.

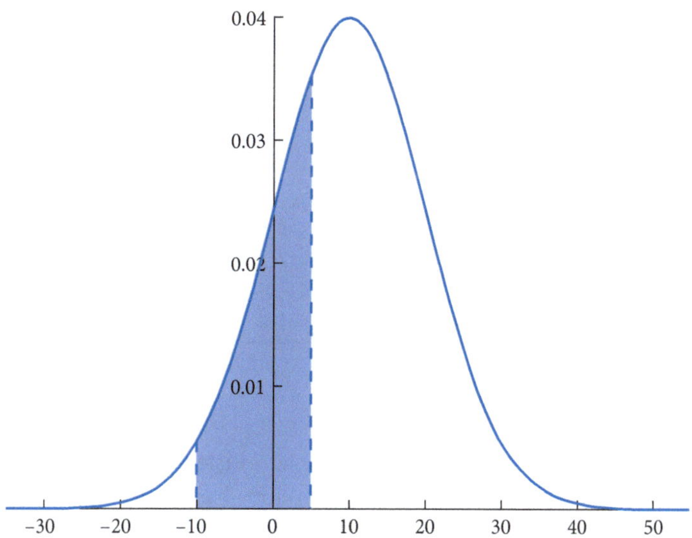

Figure 13.5 Shaded area represents the probability of observing an outcome between −10 and 5 from $X \sim N(10,100)$.

[2] I. Stewart (1977), 'Gauss', *Scientific American*, 237(1), 122–131.

Mathematically, we should be able to calculate this probability by integrating the PDF between the limits of −10 and 5. That is:

$$P(-10 \leq X \leq 5) = \int_{-10}^{5} f_X(x)dx$$

With $E(X) = \mu_X = 10$ and $var(X) = \sigma_X^2 = 100$, we can rewrite the PDF as:

$$f_X(x) = \frac{1}{10\sqrt{2\pi}} e^{-\frac{(x-10)^2}{2\times 100}}$$

However, if we were to substitute in this PDF, and try to integrate, we would not be able to find a solution. Similarly, if we tried to find the CDF of X:

$$P(X \leq x^*) = F_X(x^*) = \int_{-\infty}^{x^*} \frac{1}{10\sqrt{2\pi}} e^{-\frac{(x-10)^2}{2\times 100}} dx$$

Again, using standard methods, this integral would be insoluble, and so we would need a different method to evaluate it. However, whilst it is not possible to calculate this integral, statisticians have long known the characteristics of a random variable which follows a normal distribution with expectation 0 and variance 1.

We often refer to a random variable that is normally distributed with expectation 0 and variance 1 as a **standard normal distribution**, and this is normally represented as a random variable $Z \sim N(0,1)$ (see Figure 13.6).

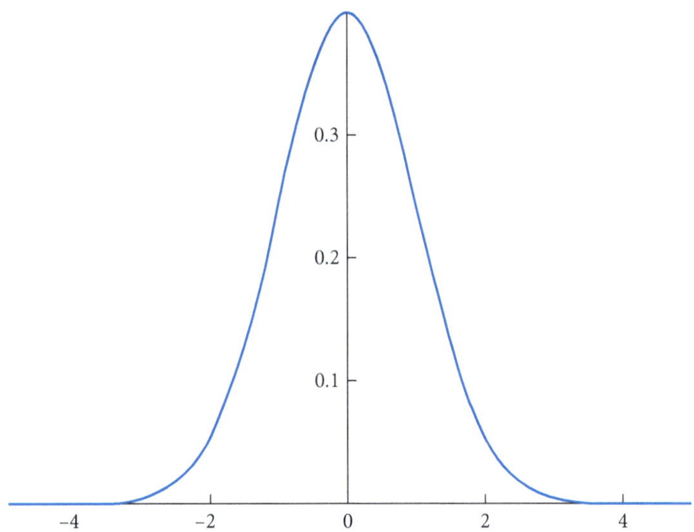

Figure 13.6 The PDF of a standard normal, Z~(0, 1).

Because the PDF cannot be integrated, statisticians instead used numerical methods to calculate the CDF, and we now rely on tables,[3] developed at the beginning of the twentieth century, which show the CDF.

[3] W. F. Sheppard (1903) 'New Tables of the Probability Integral', *Biometrika*, 2(2), 177–190.

In the standard normal distribution, the CDF is represented using $\Phi(z)$. This is the Greek capital *phi*, and it represents the probability of a random observation from a standard normal variable being less than the particular value z.

That is:

$$\Phi(z) = P(Z \leq z)$$

KEY NOTATION: STANDARD NORMAL DISTRIBUTION

For a random variable, Z, that follows a standard normal distribution, such that $Z \sim N(0,1)$, there is a set of standard notation that is often used.

Probability density function, $f_Z(z)$	$\phi(z)$
Cumulative distribution function (i.e. $P(Z \leq z)$)	$\Phi(z)$

To find probabilities relating to the normal distribution we need to look them up in the standard normal distribution tables.

Table 13.1 shows an extract from the cumulative standard normal distribution. For each of the values of z, the tables provide us with $\Phi(z)$, the probability of the observation being less than (or equal to) z.

Table 13.1 A simplified version of the cumulative distribution function, $\Phi(z)$, for a standard normal distribution

z	0	0.2	0.4	0.6	0.8	1	1.2	1.4	1.6	1.8	2
$\Phi(z)$	0.500	0.5793	0.6554	0.7257	0.7881	0.8413	0.8849	0.9192	0.9452	0.9641	0.9772

So, for example, if we wanted to find the probability of randomly observing a value of Z less than or equal to 1, we would merely need to look in the normal distribution function, and find $\Phi(1) = 0.8413$. This is illustrated in panel a) of Figure 13.7.

We can use similar methods if we wish to find the probability of randomly observing an outcome of z greater than or equal to (say) 2. The normal distribution tables provide us with the CDF. That is,

$$\Phi(z) = P(Z \leq z)$$

We can see from Table 13.1 that $P(Z \leq 2) = \Phi(2) = 0.9772$. However, if we wish to find $P(Z \geq 2)$, we will need to take account of the fact that the total area under the PDF must be equal to 1. This means that:

$$P(Z \geq 2) = 1 - P(Z \leq 2) = 1 - 0.9772 = 0.0228$$

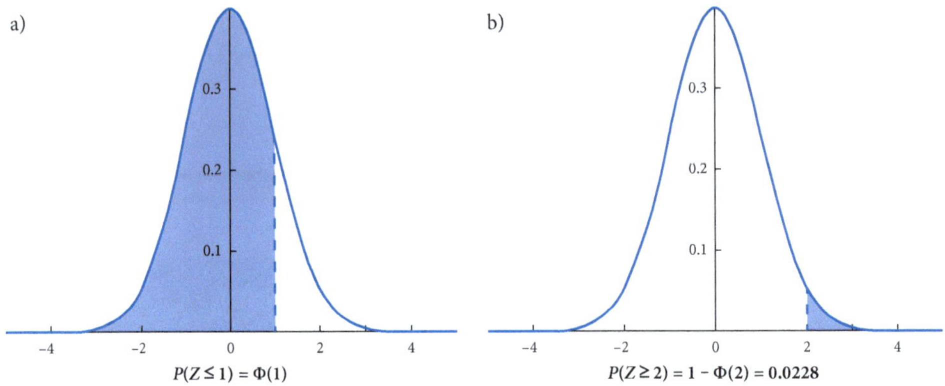

Figure 13.7 Calculating probabilities using the standard normal distribution.

A final difficulty with published tables for the standard normal distribution is that these tables normally start at $z = 0$. That is, they rarely provide $\Phi(z)$ for $z < 0$. However, this is not that tricky to calculate; the normal distribution is a symmetric random variable around the expectation. In the case of the standard normal, the distribution is symmetric around $E(Z) = 0$. What this means is that $P(Z \leq -2) = P(Z \geq 2)$.

More generally, it follows that $P(Z \leq -z) = P(Z \geq z)$. Thus, if we wish to find a probability like $P(Z \leq -2)$, we would first need to calculate $P(Z \geq 2)$. So, for example, $P(Z \leq -2)$ is just equal to 0.0228, as before.

This is illustrated in Figure 13.8. We can see that the shaded area to the left of −2 is just the same size as the shaded area to the right of +2.

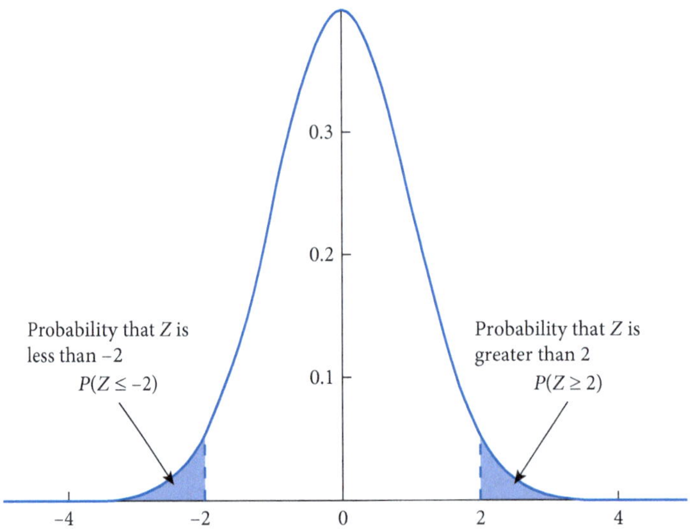

Figure 13.8 Illustrating that $P(Z \leq 2) = P(Z \geq 2)$.

Worked example 13.1: Calculating probabilities from the standard normal distribution

Suppose that we have a random variable, Z, which follows a standard normal distribution, $Z \sim N(0,1)$. Calculate the probability that a randomly chosen observation from Z lies between −0.4 and +1.2.

$$P(-0.4 \leq Z \leq 1.2)$$

To do this, we will need to calculate two probabilities. It is relatively simple to calculate the probability that we gain an observation of Z below 1.2. However, this will include some outcomes that lie below −0.4. Therefore, in order to omit these, we will need to subtract the probability of an observation below −0.4. These probabilities are illustrated in Figure 13.9.

$$P(-0.4 \leq Z \leq 1.2) = \Phi(1.2) - \Phi(-0.4)$$

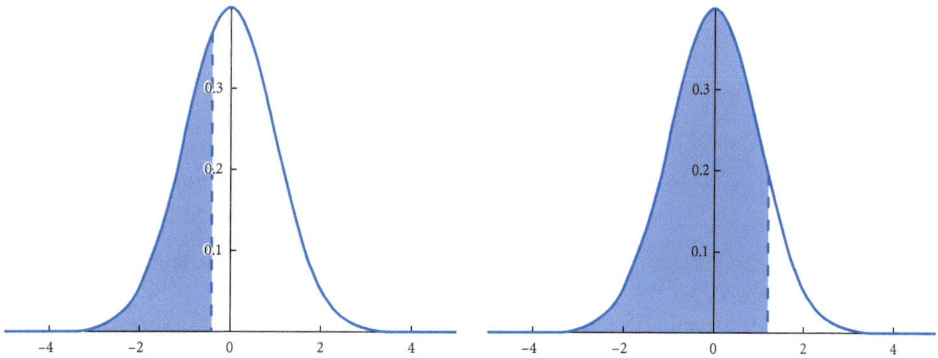

Figure 13.9 Calculating the probability of randomly observing an outcome between −0.4 and +1.2.

- By looking at the normal distribution tables, we can see that $\Phi(1.2)$ is just equal to 0.8849.
- To calculate $\Phi(-0.4)$, we will need to use the identity that $\Phi(-0.4) = 1 - \Phi(0.4)$.
- $1 - \Phi(0.4) = 1 - 0.6554 = 0.3446$

The probability of observing an outcome between −0.4 and 1.2 is then just the difference between these two probabilities. So, $P(-0.4 \leq Z \leq 1.2) = 0.8849 - 0.3446 = 0.5403$. This difference is illustrated in Figure 13.10.

13.4 The standard normal distribution tables

Whilst we can use Microsoft Excel (or other statistical software) to calculate probabilities relating to the normal distribution, you may also be asked to calculate probabilities relating to variables that follow the (standard) normal distribution. A simplified version of the tables is illustrated in Table 13.2.[4]

[4] These tables were produced using Microsoft Excel.

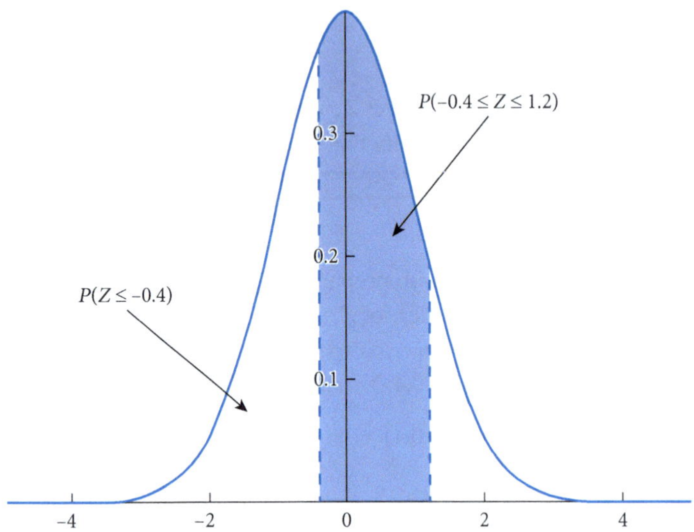

Figure 13.10 Probability of observing a standard normal between −0.4 and 1.2.

Using Microsoft Excel to calculate probabilities in the normal distribution

Microsoft Excel can calculate probabilities related to a standard normal distribution, using the formula =norm.s.dist.

The syntax of the formula is

=norm.s.dist(z, TRUE).

This will calculate $\Phi(z)$ for any value of z. The command 'TRUE' indicates that you are looking for the CDF.

If you used the formula =norm.s.dist(z, FALSE), this would provide the PDF at the particular value z.

Try it yourself

Using Excel, repeat the example to calculate $P(-0.4 \le Z \le 1.2)$.

Important information about the standard normal distribution

In the examples, we have considered a random variable Z, following a standard normal distribution:

$$Z \sim N(0,1)$$

The variance of the distribution is equal to 1, and hence the standard deviation is also equal to 1.

When we examine $P(Z \le 1)$, this is equivalent to calculating the probability that Z is less than 1 standard deviation above the expected value (0).

As a rule of thumb, over 99 per cent of all outcomes in the normal distribution are within ± 3 standard deviations of the expected value.

Table 13.2 A simplified set of tables for the standard normal distribution

z	$\Phi(z)$	z	$\Phi(z)$	z	$\Phi(z)$	z	$\Phi(z)$
0.00	0.5000	1.00	0.8413	2.00	0.9772	3.00	0.9987
0.05	0.5199	1.05	0.8531	2.05	0.9798	3.05	0.9989
0.10	0.5398	1.10	0.8643	2.10	0.9821	3.10	0.9990
0.15	0.5596	1.15	0.8749	2.15	0.9842	3.15	0.9992
0.20	0.5793	1.20	0.8849	2.20	0.9861	3.20	0.9993
0.25	0.5987	1.25	0.8944	2.25	0.9878	3.25	0.9994
0.30	0.6179	1.30	0.9032	2.30	0.9893	3.30	0.9995
0.35	0.6368	1.35	0.9115	2.35	0.9906	3.35	0.9996
0.40	0.6554	1.40	0.9192	2.40	0.9918	3.40	0.9997
0.45	0.6736	1.45	0.9265	2.45	0.9929	3.45	0.9997
0.50	0.6915	1.50	0.9332	2.50	0.9938	3.50	0.9998
0.55	0.7088	1.55	0.9394	2.55	0.9946	3.55	0.9998
0.60	0.7257	1.60	0.9452	2.60	0.9953	3.60	0.9998
0.65	0.7422	1.65	0.9505	2.65	0.9960	3.65	0.9999
0.70	0.7580	1.70	0.9554	2.70	0.9965	3.70	0.9999
0.75	0.7734	1.75	0.9599	2.75	0.9970	3.75	0.9999
0.80	0.7881	1.80	0.9641	2.80	0.9974	3.80	0.9999
0.85	0.8023	1.85	0.9678	2.85	0.9978	3.85	0.9999
0.90	0.8159	1.90	0.9713	2.90	0.9981	3.90	1.0000
0.95	0.8289	1.95	0.9744	2.95	0.9984	3.95	1.0000

Suppose that you wanted to find $P(Z \leq 1.75)$. What you would need to do is find 1.75 in the tables as a value of z, and then the corresponding value of $\Phi(z)$ is $\Phi(1.75) = 0.9599$. That is, $P(Z \leq 1.75) = 0.9599$.

As mentioned earlier, most printed versions of the tables only provide probabilities relating to positive values of z. This means that if you wanted to find the probability that $P(Z \leq -0.5)$, say, you would need to take advantage of the fact that the standard normal distribution is symmetric.

Equally, the tables do not tell us, directly, what $P(Z \geq 0.5)$ is. However, we can see from Figure 13.11 that the probability $P(Z \leq -0.5)$ is the same as $P(Z \geq 0.5)$. We also need to appeal to the **law of total probability**, which tells us that the area under the PDF must be equal to 1. As such, we can calculate $P(Z \geq 0.5)$ by finding $P(Z \leq 0.5)$ and subtracting that from 1:

$$P(Z \geq 0.5) = 1 - P(Z \leq 0.5)$$

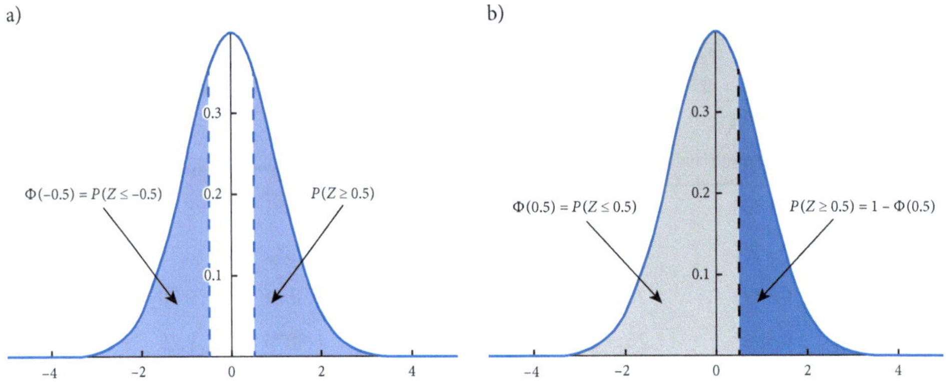

Figure 13.11 Calculating P(Z ≥ 0.5).

This is illustrated in panel a) of Figure 13.11. We can see from Table 13.1 that $\Phi(0.5) = 0.6915$. Therefore, $P(Z \geq 0.5) = 1 - \Phi(0.5) = 1 - 0.6915$. Similarly, it must follow that $P(Z \leq -0.5) = \Phi(-0.5) = 1 - 0.6915 = 0.3085$.

13.5 Standardizing the normal distribution

So far, we have only calculated probabilities relating to a standard normal distribution, with an expectation of 0 and variance of 1. However, the normal distribution can have any expected value and any variance. As we will see, we can convert any normally distributed variable into a standard normal distribution.

For a random variable Z, which follows the standard normal distribution, $Z \sim N(0,1)$, we know that $E(Z) = 0$, and $var(Z) = 1$. It therefore follows that the standard deviation, $\sigma = 1$.

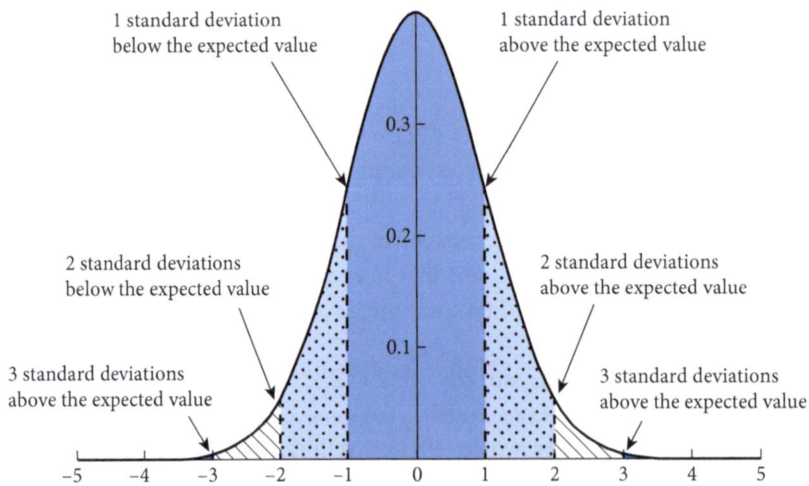

Figure 13.12 Standard normal distribution, considering standard deviations away from the expected value.

Figure 13.12 shows the standard normal distribution, considering the deviations of outcomes away from the expected value. When $Z = 1$, you are exactly 1 times the standard deviation above the expected value. Similarly, when $Z = -1$, you are 1 times the standard deviation below the expected value. Similarly, when $Z = 2$, you are exactly 2 times the standard deviation above the expected value, and so on.

If we look back at the PDF, this is defined in terms of a general expected value (μ) and a variance σ^2. This means that we can think about the normal distribution in a little more general terms; in the case of the standard normal distribution, we saw that $P(Z \leq 1) = 0.8413$, and similarly, $P(Z \leq 2) = 0.9772$.

However, suppose that we have a random variable, $X \sim N(\mu, \sigma^2)$. That is, the expectation of X is equal to μ and the variance equal to σ^2. For any normally distributed variable, we can write that the probability of observing an outcome of less than 1 standard deviation above the expected value will be equal to $P(Z \leq 1) = 0.8413$.

More formally, we can say that:

$$P(X \leq (\mu + 1 \times \sigma)) = P(Z \leq 1) = 0.8413$$

$$P(X \leq (\mu + 2 \times \sigma)) = P(Z \leq 2) = 0.9772$$

$$P(X \leq (\mu - 2 \times \sigma) = P(Z \leq -2)$$

and so on.

We can apply this thought process to any normally distributed variable. Irrespective of what the value of the standard deviation is, the probability of being less than 1 standard deviation above the expected value is always equal to 0.8413. Similarly, the probability of being less than 2 standard deviations above the expected value is always equal to 0.9772. This does not change with different μ or σ^2.

This occurs because of the characteristics of the normal distribution. If we perform any **linear transformation** (such as adding a constant, or multiplying by a constant) to a normally distributed variable, this also yields a normally distributed variable.

Rules related to linear transformations of variables

If we have a random variable X with expectation, $E(X) = \mu$ and variance, $var(X) = \sigma^2$, if we transform X by adding a constant, a:

$$E(a + X) = a + E(X) = a + \mu$$

$$var(a + X) = var(X) = \sigma^2$$

Similarly, if we transform X by multiplying by a constant, a:

$$E(aX) = a \times E(X) = a \times \mu$$

$$var(aX) = a^2\, var(X) = a^2 \times \sigma^2$$

As a preview, we can convert any normally distributed variable by applying two transformations: firstly, we can centre the distribution on zero by subtracting the expected value, and secondly, we can convert the variable to a standard (i.e. variance equal to 1) by dividing through by the standard deviation.

To illustrate this, let's suppose that we have a random variable X that follows a normal distribution with expectation 10 and variance 9. That is $X \sim N(10,4)$. This is illustrated in panel a) of Figure 13.13. Then by constructing a new variable, Y, which is constructed by subtracting the expected value of X, such that $Y = X - 10$, we can see in panel b) that the effect is to shift the distribution towards zero. In fact, by subtracting the expected value, the new variable, Y, is centred on zero (and hence has an expectation equal to zero).

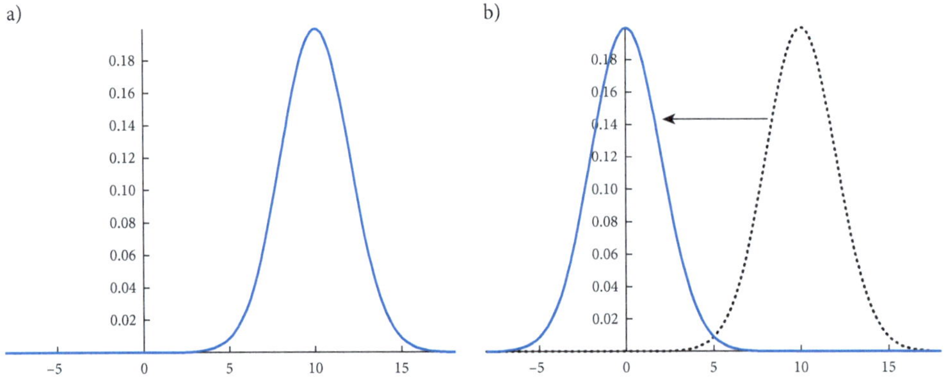

Figure 13.13 Transforming a normal distribution by subtracting the expected value.

Mathematically, we can see that, since $Y = X - 10$:

$$E(Y) = E(X-10) = E(X) - 10 = 10 - 10 = 0$$
$$var(Y) = var(X-10) = var(X) = 4$$

So, the new variable, Y, will also be normally distributed, with expectation 0. By subtracting (or adding) a constant, there is no impact on the variance, and so $Y \sim N(0,4)$.

We also wish to standardize the variance so that we have a new variable with variance equal to 1. We can do this by appealing to the rules of variances. We know that if we multiply a random variable Y by a constant a, then $var(aY) = a^2 var(Y)$.

Thus, if we have $var(Y) = 4$, we would want to know what value of Y we would multiply Y by so that:

$$var(aY) = 1$$

Since $var(aY) = a^2 var(Y)$, and $var(Y) = 4$, it must be the case that $a^2 = \frac{1}{4}$, and similarly, $a = \frac{1}{2}$. So, if we were to construct a new variable, Z, which is constructed by dividing Y by 2 (which is the standard deviation of Y), then the new variable will have a variance equal to 1.

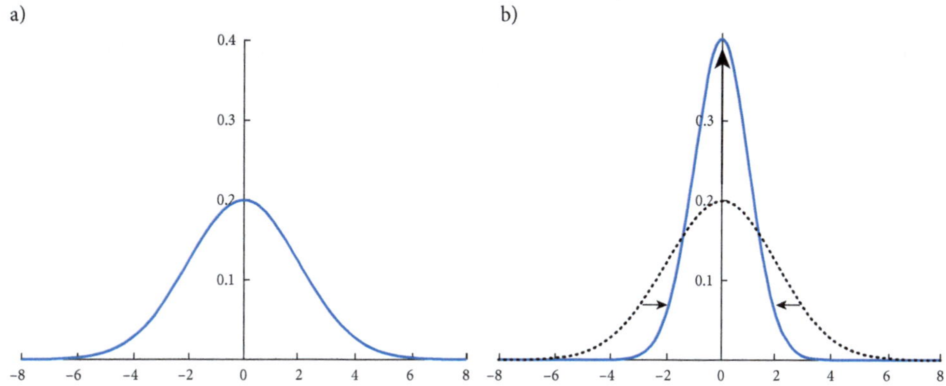

Figure 13.14 Transformation by dividing through by the standard deviation.

This transformation is illustrated in Figure 13.14. By dividing through by the standard deviation, we standardize the variable, such that the new variable, Z, has variance 1. In the illustrated example, since the original distribution had a variance greater than 1, the transformation has the effect of squeezing the distribution inwards. The effect is much like what happens if you squeeze a jelly—the extremes move inwards, but the peak moves upwards.

Standardizing any normally distributed variable

Suppose that we observe a variable, X, that is normally distributed with mean μ and variance σ^2:

$$X \sim N(\mu, \sigma^2)$$

1. Subtract the expected value μ from your variable X. Always do this step first!
2. Divide by the standard deviation.

The resulting variable, Z, will be normally distributed, with expectation 0 and variance equal to 1:

$$Z = \frac{X - \mu}{\sqrt{\sigma^2}}$$

Proof 1: Expectation of *Z*

We want to show that $E(Z) = 0$ and $var(Z) = 1$. First of all, let's consider the expectation:

$$E(Z) = E\left[\frac{X - \mu}{\sqrt{\sigma^2}}\right]$$

Now, we know that when we take the expectation of any variable multiplied by a constant, we can take the constant outside of the expectation. The variance is just a constant, giving us:

$$E(Z) = \frac{1}{\sqrt{\sigma^2}} \times E(X - \mu)$$

We also know that the expectation of a sum is just the sum of the expectations, and so $E(X-\mu) = E(X) - E(\mu)$. However, since μ is also a constant $E(\mu) = \mu$:

$$\Rightarrow E(Z) = \frac{1}{\sqrt{\sigma^2}} \times [E(X) - \mu]$$

Finally, we know that $E(X) = \mu$, and so we can rewrite this as:

$$\Rightarrow E(Z) = \frac{1}{\sqrt{\sigma^2}}[\mu - \mu] = \frac{1}{\sqrt{\sigma^2}} \times 0 = 0$$

Proof 2: Variance of *Z*

To find the variance of Z, we need to find:

$$var(Z) = var\left[\frac{X-\mu}{\sqrt{\sigma^2}}\right]$$

Now, we know that for any constant multiplier, we can take that outside of the variance (and square it):

$$\Rightarrow var(Z) = \frac{1}{\sigma^2} var[X - \mu]$$

We also know that the variance of any random variable plus a constant (or in this case less a constant) is just equal to the variance of the original random variable. As such, $var(X-\mu) = var(X)$.

$$\Rightarrow var(Z) = \frac{1}{\sigma^2} \times var(X)$$

Finally, we know that $var(X) = \sigma^2$, and so:

$$var(Z) = \frac{1}{\sigma^2} \times \sigma^2 = 1$$

Thus, since when we carry out any set of linear transformations to a normally distributed variable, the resulting variable is also normally distributed, it follows that:

$$Z \sim N(0,1)$$

That is, Z is normally distributed with expectation 0 and variance 1.

13.5.1 Why is it useful to standardize the normal distribution?

In the previous section, we have seen that any normal distribution can be standardized to a new variable, with expectation 0 and variance 1, by subtracting the expectation and dividing through by the standard deviation. That is, if we have a random variable $X \sim N(\mu,\sigma^2)$, then:

$$\frac{X-\mu}{\sqrt{\sigma^2}} \sim N(0,1)$$

This is useful because if we have a particular observation from a general normal distribution, we can use the standard normal distribution to calculate relevant probabilities relating to this.

Worked example 13.2: Estimating probabilities relating to a height

It is often assumed that the height of individuals within the population is approximately normally distributed (with separate distributions for men and women). We know that the expected height for men in England is 175cm (equivalent to 5ft 9ins in imperial measurements), and that the standard deviation is approximately 10cm. This means that the variance of heights is $10^2 = 100$. That suggests that we could model men's height as a variable:

$$Height \sim N(175,100)$$

From this, find the probability that a man, randomly drawn from the population, is less than 160cm. This probability is illustrated in Figure 13.15, with the shaded area representing the probability of a randomly chosen man being less than 160cm.

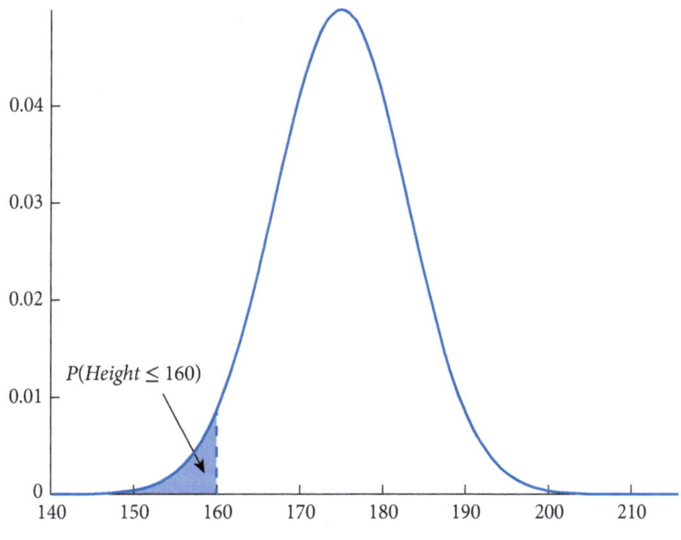

Figure 13.15 Distribution of heights.

If we begin with the probability that a randomly drawn man from the population is less than 160cm, the first step is to standardize this; that is, we need to calculate how many standard deviations this is below the expected value:

$$Z = \frac{Height - E(Height)}{\sqrt{var(Height)}} = \frac{160 - 175}{\sqrt{100}} = -\frac{-15}{10} = -1.5$$

That is, 160cm is 1.5 standard deviations below the expected height (175cm). As such, if we want to find the probability of observing a randomly chosen male who is less than 160cm

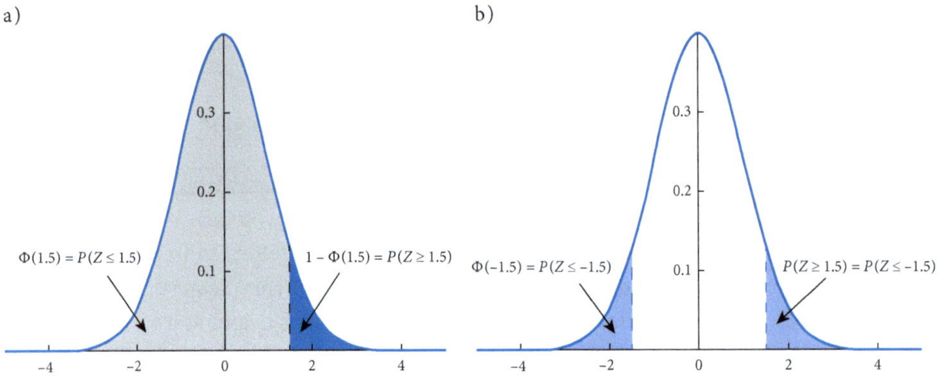

Figure 13.16 Calculating the probability using the standard normal distribution.

tall, we would need to find $\Phi(-1.5)$. Remember that the normal distribution tables only examine positive values of X, so we would need to find $\Phi(1.5)$.

Then, as seen in Figure 13.16, since the standard normal distribution is symmetric, it follows that $P(Z \leq -1.5)$ is the same as $P(Z \geq 1.5)$. Now, in panel a), we can see that $P(Z \geq 1.5) = 1 - P(Z \leq 1.5)$. We can either use Excel or look up the probability in the standard normal tables. Therefore to calculate $P(Z \leq -1.5)$, this will be the same as:

$$\Phi(-1.5) = 1 - \Phi(1.5) = 1 - 0.933193 = 0.066807$$

In this example, we have actually calculated two probabilities. Firstly, we have calculated the probability of randomly sampling an individual from this population with height less than or equal to 160cm. To calculate this, we standardized the variable, to give:

$$P(Height \leq 160) = P(Z \leq -1.5) = 0.066807$$

However, we also saw that $P(Z \geq 1.5) = 0.066807$ as well. We can follow the reverse process and show that this is equivalent to $P(Height \geq 190)$. This is equivalent to 1.5 standard deviations above the expected value.

Using Microsoft Excel to calculate probabilities in the (non-standard) normal distribution

Microsoft Excel can also calculate probabilities related to any normal distribution, using the formula =norm.dist.

The syntax of the formula is =norm.dist(x, mean, standard deviation, TRUE). This will calculate $P(X \leq x)$ for any value of x, where X is a normally distributed random variable, with expected value equal to 'mean', and standard deviation equal to 'standard deviation'. TRUE indicates that we are looking for the cumulative probability (rather than the probability density).

For example, we can check our answer to the height example. We saw that *Height* was normally distributed, with expectation 69 and variance 9:

$$Height \sim N(175,100)$$

As such, using the Excel formula we can calculate the probability of height being less than (or equal to) 160cm; that is, $P(Height \leq 160)$:

$$= \text{norm.dist}\left(160,175,10,\text{TRUE}\right)$$

(We would need to write the standard deviation as 10, because the standard deviation is just the square root of the variance: $\sqrt{var(X)} = \sqrt{10} = 10.$)

Reassuringly, Excel returns the same probability, equal to 0.066807.

13.6 The 68–95–99.7 rule

Since the probability density of the normal distribution is (in general) defined in terms of the number of standard deviations away from the expected value, it is also the case that there are some helpful rules about the (approximate) probability bounded within certain areas of the normal distribution. In particular, for any random variable that is distributed normally, approximately:

- 68 per cent of the distribution lies within ± 1 standard deviations of the expected value
- 95 per cent of the distribution lies within ± 2 standard deviations of the expected value
- 99.7 per cent of the distribution lies within ± 3 standard deviations of the expected value

These proportions are illustrated in Figure 13.17. The shaded area represents the proportion (or probability) of the distribution lying within ± 1, 2, or 3 standard deviations of the expected value.

Whilst this may seem like a curiosity, this does mean that, for normally distributed variables, we have an easy way of thinking about whether an outcome is unlikely (or not). When we introduce statistical testing, we will often ask the question about whether an observed outcome is likely, given an initial hypothesis. Since approximately 95 per cent of the distribution lies within ± 2 standard deviations of the expected value, the probability of (randomly) observing an outcome that is more than 2 standard deviations from the expected value will be less than 5 per cent. Similarly, the probability of observing an outcome that is more than 3 standard deviations away from the expected value will be less than 0.3 per cent.

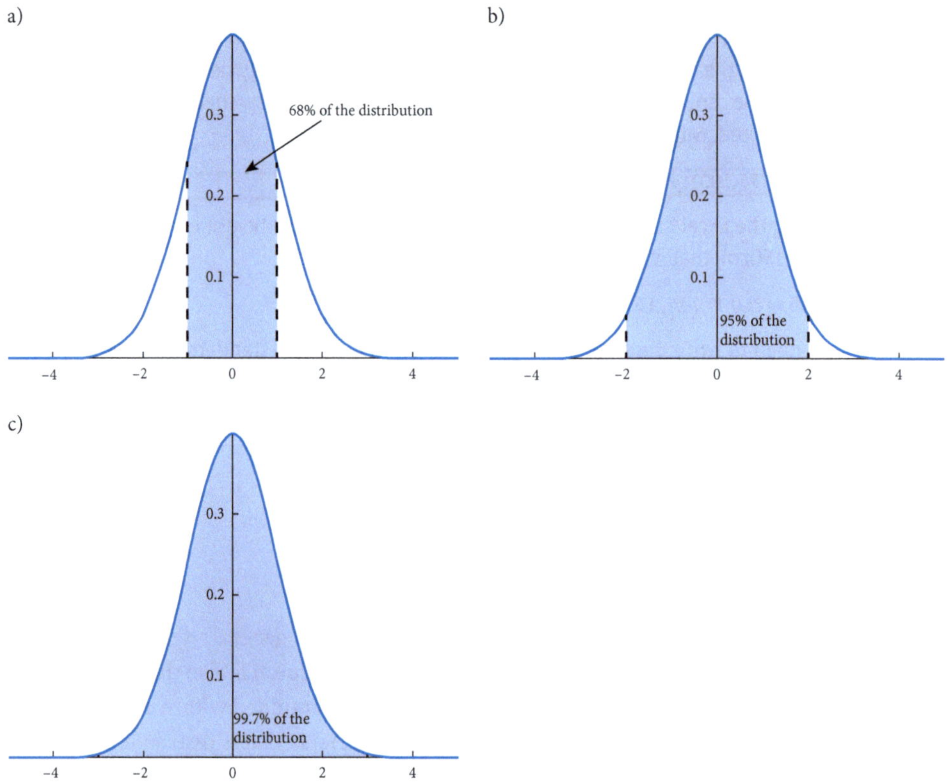

Figure 13.17 Proportion of the normal distribution lying within 1, 2, and 3 standard deviations of the expected value.

13.7 Normal approximation to the binomial distribution

We began this chapter by discussing that the normal distribution was developed (at least in part) as a way to try and model the binomial distribution using a continuous distribution, rather than having to deal with potentially computationally intense calculations of many separate binomial results. However, we are now in a position to be able to start using the normal distribution to address the binomial distribution.

We remember, from earlier, that if we have a binomial variable, X, constructed from n trials of a binomial variable with probability p, then we know the expectation and the variance of the variable are np and $np(1 - p)$ respectively.

Properties of binomial distribution

If $X \sim B(n, p)$, then:

Expectation:	$E(X) = np$
Variance:	$var(X) = np(1 - p)$

Since we know that the PDF of the normal distribution is approximately equal to the PMF of the binomial distribution, provided the number of trials (n) is large enough, we can approximately model a binomially distributed variable using a normally distributed variable, with the same expectation and variance.

That is, if $X \sim B(n, p)$, then we can model this with a normally distributed variable X_N, with the following distribution:

$$X_N \sim N(np, np(1 - p))$$

To illustrate this, let's consider the following example. Suppose we flip a fair coin ten times, and we want to find the probability of gaining at most five heads. If we define our random variable X as the number of heads we achieve, then:

$$X \sim B(10, 0.5)$$

Our approximation to the variable X is a continuous variable, Y, which follows a normal distribution:

$$Y \sim N(5, 2.5)$$

Figure 13.18 shows the probability distribution function for a binomial distribution associated with flipping a (fair) coin ten times (i.e. the distribution of X), and the PDF of the equivalent normal distribution (Y). In this figure, the bars represent the individual probabilities of achieving x number of heads. So, for example, the third bar (from the left) shows the probability of gaining exactly two heads.

When we use the normal distribution as an approximation for the binomial distribution, we need to take account of the fact that the binomial distribution is a discrete distribution, whilst the normal distribution is a continuous distribution.

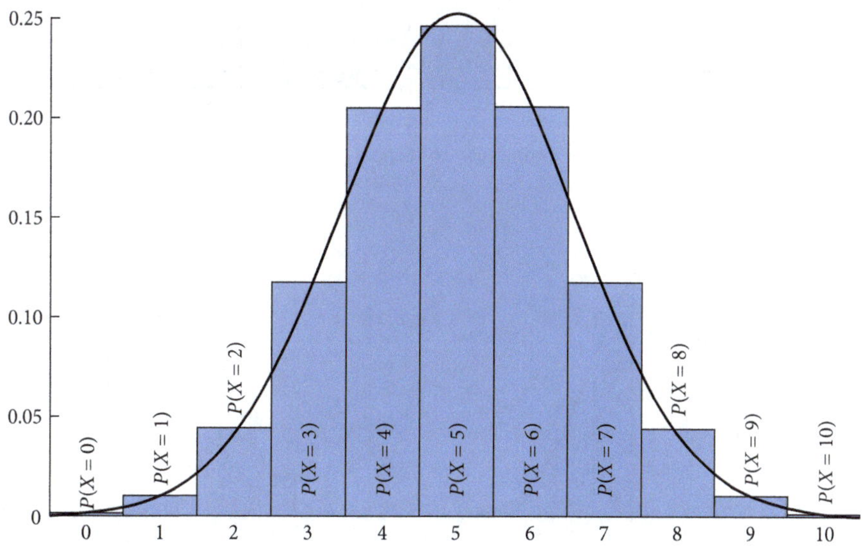

Figure 13.18 The binomial and normal distribution.

Suppose, for instance, you wanted to estimate $P(X \leq 5)$. You could calculate the area under the normal distribution to the left of $Y = 5$. However, we can see from Figure 13.19 that this would omit part of the probability that $X = 5$.

Intuitively, this is because for the binomial distribution the probability of getting less than five heads is different from the probability of gaining less than or equal to five heads:

$$P(X \leq 5) = P(X < 5) + P(X = 5)$$

In order to improve our estimates, and to differentiate between our estimates that $P(X \leq 5)$ and $P(X < 5)$, we need to introduce a continuity correction. This is illustrated in Figure 13.20. If we are interested in $P(X \leq 5)$, we need to ensure that $P(X = 5)$ is included. As such, if we find $P(X_N \leq 5.5)$, we have gone a little bit further within our normal distribution, to ensure that all of the probability related to $P(X = 5)$ is included.

Similarly, if we want to find $P(X < 5)$, we want to exclude $P(X = 5)$. To do this, we find $P(X_N \leq 4.5)$. By only going as far as $X_N = 4.5$, we ensure that we omit the $P(X = 5)$ from the probability. This is illustrated in panel b) of Figure 13.20.

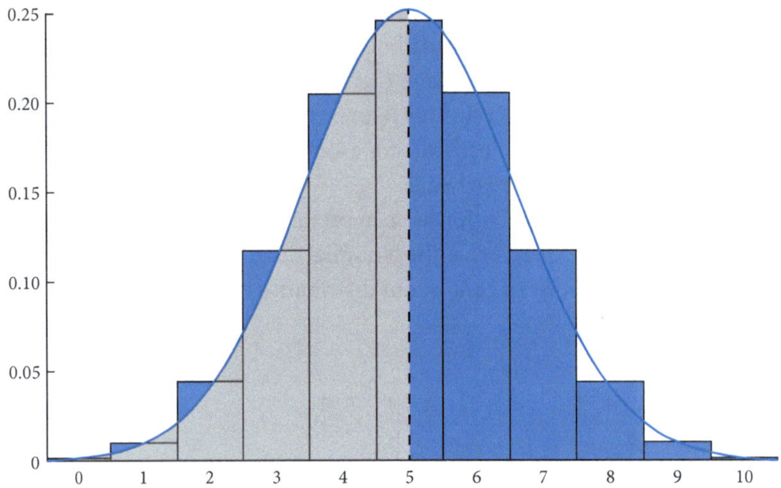

Figure 13.19 Motivating the need for a continuity correction.

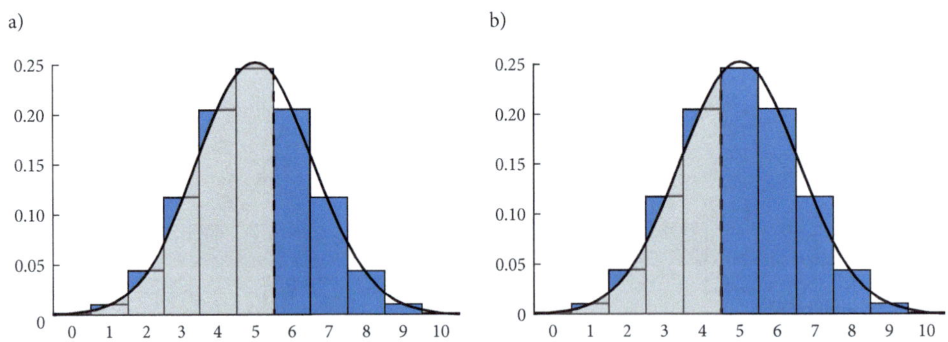

Figure 13.20 A continuity correction.

Continuity corrections

When using a continuous random variable as an approximation to a discrete random variable, we need to use a continuity correction.

As a general rule, we take the mid-point between the discrete categories to determine the appropriate threshold for our continuity correction.

Examples of continuity corrections

Example 1

Suppose we have a discrete variable, A, which takes the values 3, 4, 5, 6, 7, and we want to find the probability that A takes a value equal to 4 or higher. We have a variable B which is a continuous approximation to A.

Our approximation of the probability would be:

$P(A \geq 4) \cong P(B \geq 3.5)$

Example 2

Suppose we have a discrete variable, A, which takes the values 3, 4, 5, 6, 7, and we want to find the probability that A takes a value equal greater than 4. We have a variable B which is a continuous approximation to A.

Our approximation of the probability would be:

$P(A > 4) \cong P(B \geq 4.5)$

Example 3

Suppose we have a discrete variable, A, which takes the values 3, 4, 5, 6, 7, and we want to find the probability that A takes a value equal to 4 or lower. We have a variable B which is a continuous approximation to A.

Our approximation of the probability would be:

$P(A \leq 4) \cong P(B \leq 4.5)$

Example 4

Suppose we have a discrete variable, A, which takes the values 2.1, 2.2, 2.3, 2.4, 2.5, and we want to find the probability that A takes a value equal to 2.2 or lower. We have a variable B which is a continuous approximation to A.

Our approximation of the probability would be:

$P(A \leq 2.2) \cong P(B \leq 2.25)$

Note

In many cases, it does not make sense to use a continuous variable as an approximation to a discrete variable. For example, if there are large irregular gaps between possible realizations, then it may not be appropriate to attempt to use a continuous approximation. However, for the binomial distribution, with a large number of observations, it is usually fine to use a normal approximation.

Worked example 13.3: Doing the high jump

At a primary school sports day, there are 100 children initially competing in the high jump competition. For each child, there is an equal probability of them clearing the first height, and this probability is equal to 0.6.

Calculate the probability that at least 70 children clear the first height.

Obviously, this is an example where we might be stretching reality, but we need to assume that each individual is independent from all of the others, and they all have the same probability of clearing the height.

Thus, if we define the number of children who clear the first height as X, then:

$$X \sim B(100,0.6)$$

We want to calculate the probability that at least 70 children clear the first height. In order to do this, whilst we could calculate the probability of all of the options between 70 and 100, it is simpler to use the normal approximation to the binomial.

We can calculate both the expectation and the variance here:

$$E(X) = np = 100 \times 0.6 = 60$$

$$var(X) = np(1-p) = 100 \times 0.6 \times 0.4 = 24$$

So, let's use a continuous variable Y, which follows a normal distribution, such that $E(Y) = E(X) = 60$, and $var(Y) = var(X) = 24$. That is, $Y \sim N(60,24)$.

We are interested in $P(X \geq 70)$, but we can approximate this using our continuous variable Y. As we want to ensure that we include $X = 70$, we need to extend the range we are interested in, such that:

$$P(X \geq 70) \cong P(Y \geq 69.5)$$

This probability is illustrated in Figure 13.21. By considering $P(Y \geq 69.5)$, we ensure that we include $P(X = 70)$ and $P(X > 70)$.

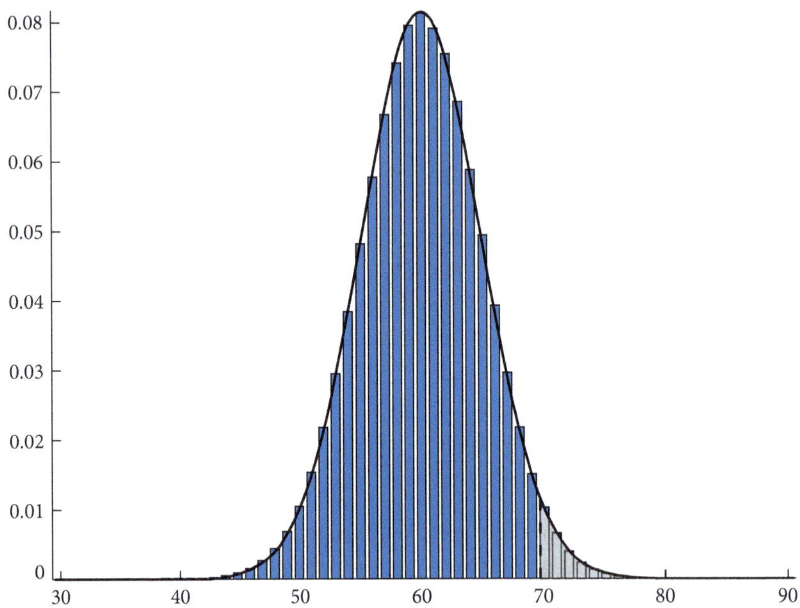

Figure 13.21 Normal approximation to the binomial.

In order to calculate this probability, we need to standardize our variable first. We are looking for $P(Y \geq 69.5)$. So, the first step is to find the value of z such that $P(Y \geq 69.5) = P(Z \geq z)$. We can calculate z by standardizing the distribution by subtracting the expected value ($\mu = 60$), and dividing through by the standard deviation, $\sigma = \sqrt{24}$:

$$z = \frac{y - \mu}{\sigma} = \frac{69.5 - 60}{\sqrt{24}}$$
$$= 1.939$$

So, $P(X \geq 70)$ is equivalent to looking for $P(Z \geq 1.939)$. Remember that the standard normal distribution, $\Phi(z)$, looks for $P(Z \leq z)$, so we need to find:

$$\begin{aligned} P(Z \geq 1.939) &= 1 - \Phi(1.939) \\ &= 1 - 0.9738 \\ &= 0.0262 \end{aligned}$$

Whilst the normal approximation to the binomial is a very useful tool, it should be noted that, firstly, this is an approximation, and secondly, when the number of trials is small, or the probability of success is close to 0 or close to 1, then the approximation performs much less well.

In the example, it is possible to show that the actual probability is equal to 0.02478. Whilst the probability is not exactly equal, this provides a good approximation to the actual probability, and is often used in economic modelling in place of the exact probabilities, because of the easy manipulability.

Further, the accuracy of the approximation improves as the number of trials increases.

Using Microsoft Excel to calculate exact binomial probabilities

Microsoft Excel can be used to calculate the exact cumulative probability related to the binomial distribution, using the formula:

$$=\text{BINOM.DIST}(\text{s}, \text{n}, \text{p}, \text{TRUE})$$

This will return $P(X \leq s)$, where $X \sim B(n, p)$. The TRUE indicates that you wish to calculate the cumulative probability. If you wished to calculate the probability $P(X = s)$, you would need to replace TRUE with FALSE.

Try it yourself

Suppose that $X \sim B(100, 0.6)$. Using Microsoft Excel, calculate the exact probabilities:

i) $P(X \leq 70)$

ii) $P(X < 70)$

iii) $P(X \geq 70)$

Compare your result to iii) with the estimate we obtained in the previous example. What do you notice?

Summary

As we move through this textbook, and introduce statistical testing, the normal distribution will become one of the (if not the) most important distribution. Whilst many people believe that the normal distribution exists inherently within nature, generally speaking, most variables in the population do not follow a normal distribution. For example, income is a very skewed distribution, with a long right-hand tail.

However, we will see in the coming chapters that provided we have large enough sample sizes, estimators such as the sample mean will approximately follow a normal distribution. Understanding the normal distribution allows us to understand the behaviour of estimators, and hence allows us to analyse what likely outcomes of estimators are!

Key formulae

If you have a random variable, Y, which follows a normal distribution with expectation $E(Y) = \mu_Y$ and $var(Y) = \sigma_Y^2$, then we denote this as:

$$Y \sim N(\mu_Y, \sigma_Y^2)$$

We can standardize the variable Y to a standard normal with expectation 0 and variance 1 by subtracting the expectation, and dividing through by the standard deviation (which, remember, is the square root of the variance):

$$Z = \frac{Y - \mu_Y}{\sqrt{\sigma^2}} \sim N(0,1)$$

Introduction to Estimators

14

Learning outcomes for this chapter

By the end of this chapter, students should be able to:

- Define the meaning of estimators, estimates, and population parameters
- Recognize that estimates will change every time we take a different sample from a population
- Calculate the bias of simple estimators both analytically and by using the results of Monte Carlo simulations
- Apply the concepts of biased and unbiased estimators to applied situations, like opinion polls
- Recognize that non-random sampling can lead to biased estimates
- Recognize a biased estimator of the population variance
- Recognize that s_{n-1}^2 is an unbiased estimator of the population variance
- Be able to apply the sample mean and s_{n-1}^2 to produce unbiased estimates of population parameters, based upon numerical data

Mathematical tools

- Summations using sigma (Σ) notation
- Algebraic manipulations using summations

Introduction

Mark Twain wrote, attributing British prime minister, Benjamin Disraeli (1874–1880), 'There are three kinds of lies: lies, damned lies, and statistics.' This phrase is omnipresent whenever raw statistics or statistical analysis are presented in the media to the general population. It illustrates a general lack of belief in the statistics that are presented, and the way that they are presented.

There are two major complaints that are often levelled at statisticians, both of which derive from the fact that statisticians are trying to make conclusions about particular parameters of a population, based on observations of a sample.

The first of these often arises when individuals wish to question the veracity of statistics. 'How can this be an estimate of the population? I've never been asked, so it can't be representative.' The whole aim of statistics is to make inferences about populations *without* having to ask everyone in the population. However, in order to do this, it needs to be the case that the observations are representative of the population as a whole, or that individuals are randomly sampled from the population.

The second complaint manifests itself in the fact that multiple statisticians can ask the same question, yet gain different answers. Since commentators can observe the differing results, this can actually reinforce the belief that the results cannot be meaningful. However, it should not be surprising that statisticians will often gain different results, as what statisticians are doing is trying to make inferences about a population, based on an (ideally random) sample from that population. If two separate statisticians ask the same question to different groups of individuals, then it is almost certain that, unless the sample is extremely large, there will be random variation in the characteristics of the samples, meaning that the answers obtained will be slightly different.

Statisticians use estimators to convert observations from a sample into an estimate of a parameter relating to the population. This parameter might be the population average (i.e. the expectation), or the population variance (or the skew, or kurtosis), and as we will see in future chapters, it might also be the relationship between multiple economic variables.

In this chapter, we will see that a good estimator is one that will, *on average*, produce the correct answer for the population characteristic, and provide results such that when multiple researchers ask the same question of different samples of people, there is little variation between their results.

14.1 Sampling from a population

In Chapter 7, we introduced the idea of sampling from a population. The population consists of all of the individuals that we are interested in, and a sample is merely a subset of that population. For example, one population could be all of the possible balls in the UK National Lottery (59 numbered balls), and a sample from that population could be the six numbered balls that are drawn out in a particular draw (Figure 14.1).

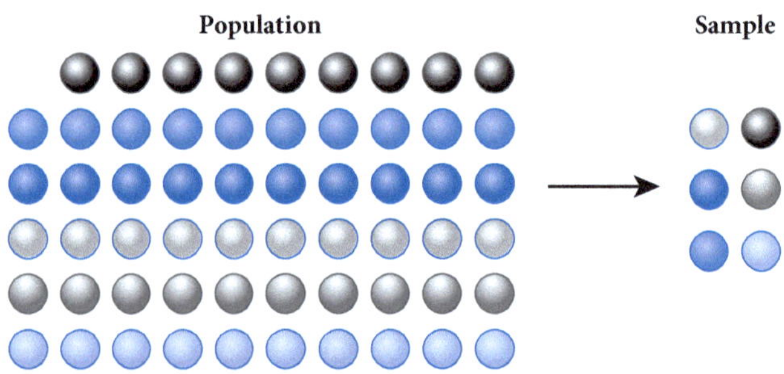

Figure 14.1 Sampling from a population.

In statistics, statisticians are usually trying to draw conclusions about the (unknown) parameters of a population, based on a sample that they have observed.

In general, individuals within populations may be represented by lots of different variables, which follow some distribution. For example, these variables could be the heights of individuals in the population, the voting intention, or the income of the population.

For instance, if the statistician is interested in the distribution of income within the population, theoretically, they could go and measure every individual in the population to assess the distribution of income. However, populations are usually very large. For example, in 2025, the population of the UK was approximately 69.3 million. As such, it would take a very long time to measure the income of all individuals within the population.

To overcome this, statisticians often try to use an estimator, applied to representative samples to estimate the parameters relating to the population as a whole.

If all individuals within the population had the same measure (e.g. if everyone were the same height), then estimating the population parameters would be easy. All you would need to do is measure one individual, and this would then be applicable to the entire population.

However, in reality individuals within a population are not all identical. Income, height, and voting intention within the population can be represented as **random variables**, which have a particular distribution. The distribution within the population can then be characterized by specific parameters, including the expected value (or average), the **variance** (and standard deviation), the **skew**, and the **kurtosis**. These population parameters are all characteristics of the population that a statistician may wish to estimate.

Many of the statistics that we see every day are estimates of a population parameter. For example, we see estimates of the unemployment rate, estimates of average earnings within the population, estimates of average house prices across the country, and so on. These are all based on observed samples from within a population, and use estimators to construct the estimate of the population parameter they are interested in, based on the observed characteristics of the sample.

KEY DEFINITIONS

There are a number of important terms that we will use regularly through this chapter. These terms (particularly estimators and estimates) sound very similar, so it is important to be clear what the difference is between them.

Estimator

An estimator is a mathematical operation that is applied to an observed sample of data to provide an estimate of a population parameter. For example, the sample mean is often used as an estimator for the expected value in the population.

Estimate

An estimate is a single realization of an estimator, using a single sample taken from the population. The estimate will provide us with an estimate of the population parameter being estimated. For example, we might use the (sample mean) average earnings from a sample to estimate the expected (average) earnings in the population.

Population parameter

A population parameter is simply a (fixed) characteristic of the population, which is often unknown. We apply an estimator to a sample of data from the population to gain an estimate of the unknown population parameter. Population parameters include the expected value, the variance, and the range of the random variable in the population.

14.2 Sampling variation

Suppose that you are trying to estimate the average (expected) earnings of full-time workers within the population, and are using an estimator based on an observed sample. What characteristics would make the estimator you are using a good estimator?

A naïve answer to this question would be that a good estimator would give the correct value for the population parameter we are trying to find. However, in statistics, unless we observe the entire population, we will never obtain the 'right answer'. Every time that we take a different sample from the population, there will be different individuals contained within the sample, and this will (almost certainly) lead to different outcomes.

To illustrate this, we will consider our first estimator—which you should already be very familiar with: the sample mean is an estimator. We can use the sample mean as a way to estimate the average (or expected) value in the population. Remember, the sample mean is obtained by adding up all of the values within the observed sample, and dividing by the sample size:

$$\bar{X} = \frac{\sum_{i=1}^{n} X_i}{n}$$

To illustrate the concept of sampling variation, let's consider an example, using real data and a simple estimator. One of the simplest estimators that we are familiar with is the sample mean. The sample mean is an estimator for the population expectation. To construct the sample mean, we simply add up the values of all of our observations and divide by the sample size.

We are going to use data taken from the 2019 UK Labour Force Survey to try to find an estimate of full-time workers in the population (i.e. we wish to use observations from a sample to find the average salary of full-time workers). Our population is therefore all full-time workers in the UK. We will further restrict the population to full-time workers aged 21–64.

To begin, I have randomly sampled 100 full-time workers from the Survey, and obtained their gross weekly wage in their main job. To estimate the expected weekly wage in the population, we calculate the sample mean of the observed salaries.

Using the sample of 100 individuals, the sample mean is calculated as £661.45. This provides us with an estimate of the population average gross weekly wage of full-time workers.

However, if we sampled a different 100 individuals from the population, the characteristics of the new sample would (likely) be different from the characteristics of the original sample. It is almost certain that you would obtain a different sample mean. This can be seen in Table 14.1, which illustrates the sample means from ten separate trials, where we randomly draw 100 observations from the population. The second sample yielded a sample mean of £611.49, whilst the third yielded a sample mean of £687.52.

Table 14.1 Outcomes from ten separate samples of 100 individuals from the population

Sample	Sample average
1	661.45
2	611.49
3	687.52
4	670.82
5	682.92
6	609.57
7	674.89
8	675.99
9	681.81
10	602.92

Based on ten separate samples from the population, we get ten different estimates. So, what is the true population average? From this, we cannot tell with certainty what the true average is, but each of the separate samples provides us with an estimate of that population average.

KEY DEFINITION: SAMPLING VARIATION

At its simplest, sampling variation is simply the variation in the statistic from sample to sample. Sampling variation occurs as the make-up of the sample varies from sample to sample.

We could, in fact, take this further. We have taken ten samples from the population, and have seen substantial variation in the estimates we obtained. Suppose that we repeated this process a very large number of times (say, 25,000), then what would the distribution of estimates look like? (see Figure 14.2).

Just as there is an underlying distribution of weekly wages within the population, there is also a distribution of sample means. Each random sample consists of different individuals, with different weekly wages, so each sample generates a different sample mean. This variation in sample means is known as sampling variation.

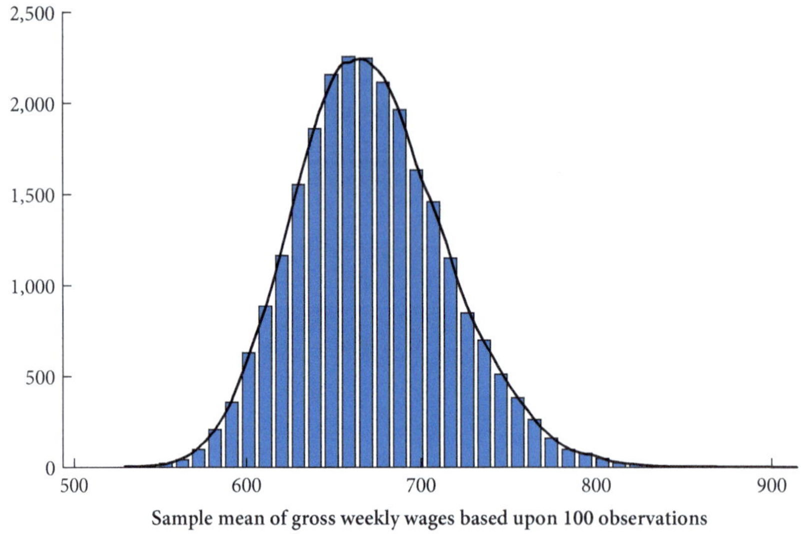

Figure 14.2 Histogram showing the distribution of estimates across 25,000 separate samples of 100 individuals from the 2019 UK LFS.

So, because of sampling variation, we cannot simply classify a 'good' estimator naïvely as one that gives the correct value every time, as this would, realistically, only occur if there were no variation in the underlying population variable.

We therefore need to construct a different measure of whether an estimator is 'good' or 'bad'. In reality, we will not be able to simply define an estimator as being 'good' or 'bad', but we will be able to compare estimators based on their characteristics. In future chapters, we will introduce a measure, known as the mean squared error, which provides a metric for the quality of the estimator. However, in order to construct this, we need to consider the bias and efficiency of estimators. We will discuss bias in this chapter, and introduce efficiency in the next chapter.

KEY NOTATION: ESTIMATORS

When we are estimating a population parameter, which we'll call μ, we will often identify the estimator for μ by putting a 'hat' on the parameter we are estimating:

- For example, $\hat{\mu}$ could be an estimator for the population parameter, μ.

Sometimes, we wish to be able to compare multiple estimators. In this case, we could use other indicators above the parameter, such as a 'tilde' (~) above the parameter. For example, $\tilde{\mu}$ could be an alternative estimator for the population parameter, μ.

This notation is not universal though. For example, one particular estimator that we will use regularly is the sample mean; $\overline{X}$ is an estimator for the population expectation of X, $E(X)$.

14.3 Bias and unbiasedness

The first metric that we will consider for whether an estimator is good is to question whether an estimator is biased or not. We saw in the previous section that due to sampling variation we observe variation in our estimates as we take repeated samples. The first metric that we could consider is whether, across repeated samples, the estimator gives the correct value for the population parameter, on average.

More formally, we consider the expectation of our estimator. An estimator is said to be unbiased if the expectation of the estimator is equal to the true population parameter being estimated. That is, if, on average, the estimator provides the correct value of the population parameter, then the estimator is said to be unbiased. Similarly, an estimator is said to be biased if the expectation of the estimator is not equal to the true population parameter being estimated.

KEY DEFINITION: UNBIASED AND BIASED ESTIMATORS

- An estimator, $\hat{\mu}$, of a population parameter, μ, is unbiased if $E(\hat{\mu}) = \mu$.
- An estimator, $\hat{\mu}$ of a population parameter, μ, is biased if $E(\hat{\mu}) \neq \mu$.

The size of the bias is defined as the difference between the expected value of the estimator and the true population parameter:

$$bias = E(\hat{\mu}) - \mu$$

14.3.1 Is the sample mean an unbiased estimator?

Earlier in this chapter, we introduced the idea that the sample mean is an estimator for the expectation of a random variable in the population. However, an important question is whether this is a good or a bad estimator. We have seen in Section 14.3 that when we repeatedly sample from the population, the sample mean varies due to sampling variation. However, the question is whether, on average, the sample mean provides the 'correct' answer. That is, if we repeatedly sampled from the population enough times, would the average of our averages be equal to the population average?

Formally, the sample mean $\overline{X}$ is an estimator of the population average (or expectation) of X, $E(X) = \mu_X$. If the sample mean is an **unbiased estimator** of μ_X, then $E(\overline{X}) = \mu_X$.

Monte Carlo simulations

As we progress through this chapter, we will begin to examine formally whether specific estimators are biased or unbiased estimators. However, it is often easier to think about this experimentally first. To evaluate whether the sample mean is an unbiased estimator of the population expectation, we will design a **Monte Carlo simulation**.

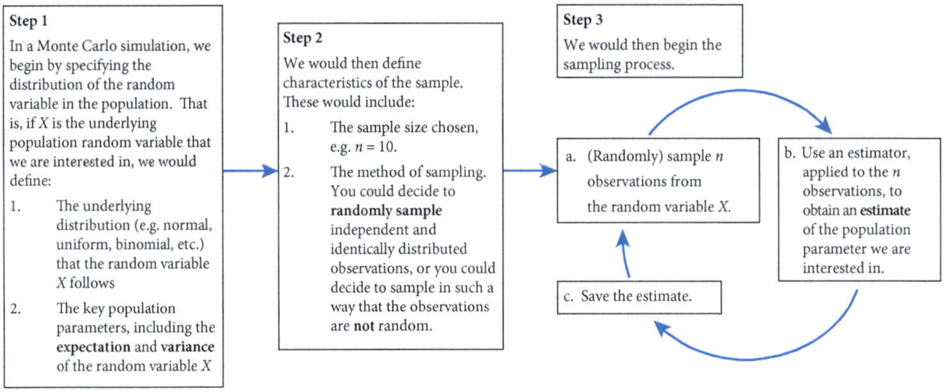

Figure 14.3 The process of a Monte Carlo simulation.

In a Monte Carlo simulation, we repeatedly use random sampling from a known population to examine the distribution of outcomes that we would gain from using an estimator.

The overall process for a Monte Carlo simulation is illustrated in Figure 14.3. Having defined the underlying population we are sampling from, we would repeatedly sample from that population to generate repeated observations (step 3). This could include randomly sampling upwards of 100,000 times, to generate an experimental distribution of our estimator. If we are interested in whether the estimator is an unbiased estimator, we would compare the average of our estimates to the true population parameter that we are estimating (which we defined in step 2 of the process).

Using a Monte Carlo Simulation to evaluate the properties of the sample mean

In this case, we wish to evaluate whether the sample mean is an unbiased estimator of the population expectation (or population average).

Step 1

Let's begin by defining a population random variable, X, which follows a uniform distribution between 0 and 1. That is, $X \sim U(0,1)$. It is relatively straightforward to show that:[1]

$$E(X) = 0.5$$

$$var(X) = \frac{1}{12}$$

Step 2

For each trial, we will randomly sample 50 (independent and identically distributed) observations from X, which we can denote as $X_1, X_2, X_3, \ldots, X_{50}$.

[1] Remember that for a variable $X \sim U(a,b)$, then $E(X) = \frac{a+b}{2}$ and $var(X) = \frac{(b-a)^2}{12}$.

Table 14.2 Fifty observations from a uniform distribution between 0 and 1

0.6583	0.9875	0.8916	0.5433	0.3747	0.6048	0.7984	0.1389	0.3992	0.0147
0.6815	0.6577	0.8756	0.4518	0.2691	0.2515	0.3270	0.8607	0.8745	0.7825
0.7992	0.2777	0.0929	0.9939	0.3491	0.5331	0.3285	0.8011	0.6064	0.6017
0.8229	0.0537	0.0286	0.8923	0.8627	0.4302	0.0392	0.7333	0.3741	0.7743
0.8157	0.9287	0.1987	0.5477	0.5134	0.3756	0.3656	0.9807	0.2860	0.9678

Step 3

So, for the first trial, the observations I gained are shown in Table 14.2.

The sample average of these 50 observations is 0.5564. We know that the true population average is equal to 0.5. Even if an estimator is unbiased, we would not expect any individual estimate to be equal to the true population average. However, what would make this an unbiased estimator would be if when we repeat this process (a large number of times), the average of our estimates is equal to the true population average.

So, we repeat this process of randomly sampling 50 observations from the population and gain a second estimate. We then keep on repeating this a very large number of times (100,000 times), to generate an (experimental) distribution of the sample means. It is this repeated sampling, and generating a distribution, that makes this experiment a Monte Carlo simulation.

Figure 14.4 shows the distribution of the sample means obtained in our simulation. The distribution of the sample means is approximately symmetric, and centred around 0.5 (which, remember, is the true value of the expected value of the random variable). In addition, the distribution of sample means looks like it approximately follows the normal distribution.[2]

We can be more precise by looking at the summary statistics. We can see that the average of the 100,000 estimates obtained is equal to 0.5000 (4dp). That is, whilst it is not the case that any given estimate is exactly equal to the true population average (0.5), when we take lots of samples, and then find the average of our estimates, we get a value almost exactly equal to the true population parameter being estimated.

That being said, the average of the estimates is not exactly equal to 0.5. In reality, based on the 100,000 simulations, the average was 0.4999869. If we repeat this experiment, we might get a different average (say, 0.500012), which would again be marginally different from 0.5. However, what we can see is that the average of our estimates is almost exactly equal to 0.5.

[2] We will see, later in this chapter, that provided the sample size is large enough (normally more than about 30), then the sample mean from any well-defined random variable will be approximately normally distributed. This result is known as the central limit theorem, and is probably the most important rule in the whole of statistics.

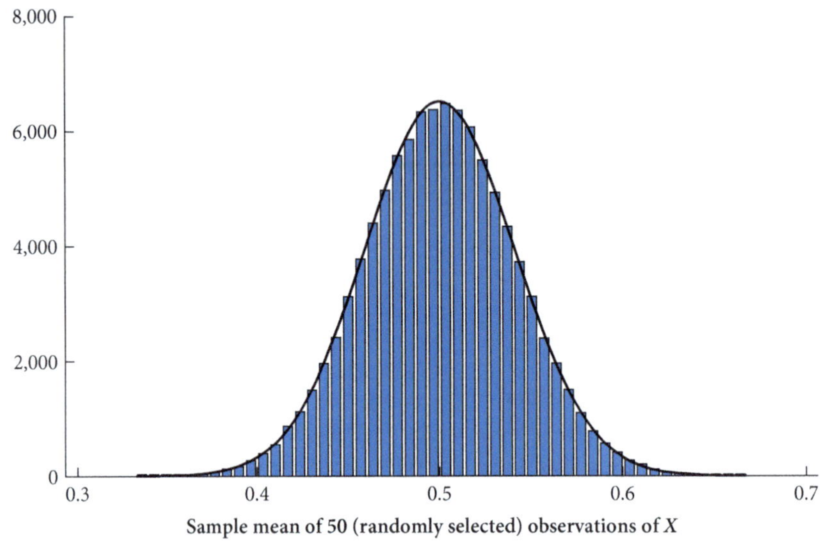

Average of estimates	0.5000
Variance of estimates	0.00167
Smallest estimate	0.3331
Largest estimate	0.6671

Figure 14.4 Histogram showing the distribution of sample means from our Monte Carlo simulation. Statistics reported to two significant figures.

Having found from the Monte Carlo simulation that the average of the estimates is almost exactly equal to the true population average (which is what we have been estimating), this is an indication that the estimator may be unbiased. However, to prove this beyond doubt we will need to analyse this mathematically.

Formally showing that the sample mean is unbiased

Suppose that we have a random variable, X, representing a particular characteristic of individuals within the population (e.g. individuals' income). We are interested in estimating the population average, $E(X)$, which is unknown, but we will denote it as μ_X.

We randomly sample n independent and identically distributed observations of X, which we will denote as $X_1, X_2, X_3, \ldots, X_n$, and construct the sample mean, as an estimator of the population average, μ_X. We will denote the estimator as $\hat{\mu}$:

$$\hat{\mu} = \frac{1}{n}\sum_{i=1}^{n} X_i$$

KEY DEFINITION: INDEPENDENT AND IDENTICALLY DISTRIBUTED

We will often make the assumption that observations are independent and identically distributed (*iid*). When we randomly sample n observations from a population $(X_1, X_2, X_3, \ldots, X_n)$, each observation, X_i, is itself a random variable, with an expectation and a variance.

We say that these observations are *iid* if:

- X_i and X_j (for all $i \neq j$) are independent random variables
- Each of the random variables is drawn from a population with identical distributions:
  - $E(X_i) = E(X_j)$ for all i, j
  - $var(X_i) = var(X_j)$ for all i, j

It is usually assumed that the expectation and variance of the observations is equal to the expectation and variance of the underlying random variable. That is, if $E(X) = \mu_X$ and $var(X) = \sigma_X^2$, then we will additionally assume that $E(X_i) = \mu_X$ and $var(X_i) = \sigma_X^2$.

Because the observations are *iid*, it will follow that $E(X_i) = \mu_X$ for all possible values of i. The sample mean, in this example, is our estimator of the population expectation. An estimator, μ, of a population parameter, μ_X, is unbiased if:

$$E(\hat{\mu}) = \mu_X$$

So, in order to investigate whether the sample mean is an unbiased estimator of the population expectation, we need to take expectations of our estimator:

$$E(\hat{\mu}) = E\left(\frac{1}{n}\sum_{i=1}^{n} X_i\right)$$

To evaluate this expectation, we will need to use our rules for manipulating expectations.

Reminder: Rules for manipulating expectations

Suppose that you have two random variables, X and Y, and constants a and b:

1. The expectation of a random variable multiplied by a constant is equal to the constant multiplied by the expectation of the random variable:

   $$E(aX) = aE(X)$$

2. The expectation of a linear combination of random variables is equal to the linear combination of the expectations:

   $$E(aX + bY) = a(E(X)) + b(E(Y))$$

Firstly, since the sum of the observations is, itself, a random variable, and the $\frac{1}{n}$ a constant, we can take the $\frac{1}{n}$ outside of the expectation:

$$\Rightarrow E(\hat{\mu}) = \frac{1}{n} \times E\left(\sum_{i=1}^{n} X_i\right)$$

Similarly, since the sum of the X_is is just a sum of random variables, $(\sum_{i=1}^{n} X_i = X_1 + X_2 + X_3 + \ldots + X_n)$, the expectation of the sum is just the sum of the expectations:

$$\Rightarrow E(\hat{\mu}) = \frac{1}{n} \times (E(X_1) + E(X_2) + E(X_3) + E(X_4) + \ldots + E(X_n)) = \frac{1}{n} \times \left(\sum_{i=1}^{n} E(X_i)\right)$$

Since all of the observations are drawn randomly and *iid* from the population, it follows that the expectation of each of these observations would be the same as the expected value in the population: that is, $E(X_i) = E(X) = \mu_X$:

$$\Rightarrow E(\hat{\mu}) = \frac{1}{n} \times \left(\sum_{i=1}^{n} \mu_X\right) = \frac{1}{n} \times n \times \mu_X = \mu_X$$

Worked example 14.1: Evaluating a biased estimator of the population average

As in Section 14.3.1, we have a random variable X representing a particular characteristic of individuals within the population (e.g. individuals' income). We are interested in estimating the population average, $E(X) = \mu_X$. We sample n independent and identically distributed (*iid*) observations from the population $(X_1, X_2, X_3, \ldots, X_n)$.

We use the following (strange) estimator, $\tilde{\mu}$ for μ_X:

$$\tilde{\mu} = \frac{2 + \sum_{i=1}^{n} X_i}{n}$$

To assess whether this is a biased or unbiased estimator, we take expectations of the estimator:

$$E(\tilde{\mu}) = E\left[\frac{2 + \sum_{i=1}^{n} X_i}{n}\right]$$

Using our rules of expectations, since $\frac{2}{n}$ is a constant, we can rewrite this as:

$$\Rightarrow E(\tilde{\mu}) = \frac{2}{n} + \frac{1}{n} \times \sum_{i=1}^{n} E(X_i)$$

Since the observations are *iid*, $E(X_i) = E(X_j) = \mu_X$ for all i, j:

$$\Rightarrow E(\tilde{\mu}) = \frac{2}{n} + \frac{1}{n} \times n \times \mu_X = \frac{2}{n} + \mu_X \neq \mu_X$$

Since $E(\tilde{\mu}) \neq \mu_X$, this is a biased estimator of μ_X. The bias is equal to the difference between the expected value of the estimator and the true, population, parameter being estimated:

$$\text{Bias} = E(\tilde{\mu}) - \mu_X = \left(\frac{2}{n} + \mu_X\right) - \mu_X = \frac{2}{n}$$

So, on average, this estimator would overestimate the population parameter by $\frac{2}{n}$. One thing to note though is that as the sample size (n) gets very large, the bias will tend towards 0.

14.4 Opinion polls as biased estimates: A case study

An example of researchers using a sample of data from the population to make conclusions about the beliefs in the population as a whole are opinion polls. Polling companies observe a sample of the population and (for example) ask them which political party they are planning on voting for. The polling company then uses an estimator to construct an estimate of the distribution of political views within the country. Ahead of general elections, polls are held almost daily to provide an indication of which political party is likely to win the election. Similarly, political parties use opinion polls to gauge public support for particular policies.

This raises a key question about whether or not the polls can be trusted; for example, polls might be untrustworthy if they produced biased estimates. That is, if the polls consistently estimated more public support for one party than there is in the country (as a whole), then the estimator may be biased.

To illustrate this, let's consider general elections in the UK. In particular, we will travel back in time to the 2015 general election to consider a case of biased estimates from an opinion poll.

The day before the election, YouGov,[3] an opinion pollster, published a poll suggesting that the Conservative Party and the Labour Party were neck and neck in Great Britain,[4] with both expected to gain 34 per cent of the vote. With this level of support, it was expected that no one party would command a majority in the House of Commons, and coalitions would have to be formed. However, in reality, the Conservatives gained 37.8 per cent of the vote, and Labour 31.2 per cent (Table 14.3). A key question, therefore, is how could the estimated results be so different from the results in reality?

14.4.1 Was the YouGov estimator biased?

An estimator is unbiased if the expected value of the estimator is equal to the true population parameter being estimated. Usually, it is difficult to simply look at estimates and consider whether an estimator is biased or not, as we don't know the true population value being estimated.

[3] I have chosen to look at YouGov, but other polling companies were also producing similar results.

[4] Whilst the UK parliament (and elections) cover both Great Britain and Northern Ireland, the political parties represented in Northern Ireland are very different from the parties in the rest of the UK (and in fact, the largest UK parties do not stand in Northern Ireland). I have only represented the results for Great Britain here.

Table 14.3 Comparison between final YouGov poll and the ultimate election results

Party	YouGov poll	Election result
Conservative	34%	37.8%
Labour	34%	31.2%
UKIP	12%	12.9%
Liberal Democrats	9%	8.1%
Green	5%	3.8%

In an election, the true population parameter is revealed on the morning after the election. In this case, 37.8 per cent of the voting public voted Conservative and 31.2 per cent of the voting public voted Labour. This was substantially different from the results of the final YouGov poll, which suggested that the vote share would be 34 per cent for each.

However, just because one poll result is different from the true population parameter does not mean that the estimator is a biased one. Remember that bias indicates that on average the estimator produces the wrong value for the population parameter. As such, we should look at the average of the poll results.[5]

Figure 14.5 shows the results from YouGov polling from the beginning of 2015, along with the actual election results. Up until the election day, there were 99 opinion polls published. On average, the polls overstated the Labour share of the vote and understated the Conservative share of the vote (in fact, none of the YouGov polls predicted the Conservatives would gain 37.8 per cent of the vote in Great Britain). If we take the average of the polls, we find that the average predicted vote share for the Conservatives was 33 per cent, whilst for Labour it was 34 per cent.

Since the opinion polls consistently understated the Conservative vote share in the population, and consistently overstated the Labour vote share in the population, it suggests that the estimator used for Conservative (and Labour) vote shares was biased.

14.5 What might cause bias?

When we are looking at an estimator relating to a single population parameter (relating to a single random variable), there are two key areas that could cause an estimator to be biased; that is, there are two key areas that could cause you to systematically over- or underestimate the true population parameter.

The first of these is simply that the mathematical operation leads to a biased estimate. For instance, we saw earlier in this chapter that if we used n independent and identically

[5] The data used here is freely available from Wikipedia: https://en.wikipedia.org/wiki/Opinion_polling_for_the_2015_United_Kingdom_general_election (accessed 27 October 2023).

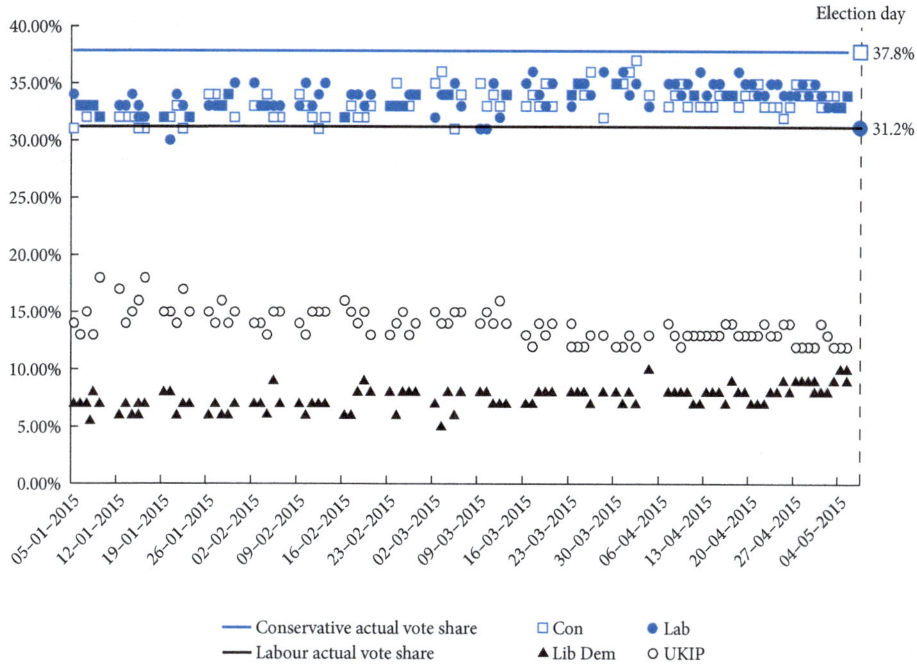

Party	YouGov poll	Election result
Conservative	34%	37.8%
Labour	34%	31.2%
UKIP	12%	12.9%
Liberal Democrats	9%	8.1%
Green	5%	3.8%

Figure 14.5 Opinion poll results ahead of the 2015 general election (Data source: Wikipedia).

distributed observations of a random variable, then the sample mean was an unbiased estimator, but a similar looking estimator,

$$\tilde{\mu} = \frac{2 + \sum_{i=1}^{n} X_i}{n}$$

is a biased estimator of the population parameter.

However, in order for the sample mean to be an unbiased estimator, we did need to make the assumption that the observations are randomly sampled from the population and identically distributed. If the observations are not randomly chosen from the population, then it is possible that the sample mean could become a biased estimator.

14.5.1 Selection bias

Suppose that you were interested in estimating the average wage in the UK population, but rather than randomly sampling from the population, you simply went and interviewed (medical) doctors. Because we know that doctors are (generally) paid substantially more than the average in the population, if we estimated the population average by based only on the average of medical doctors' wages, we would overestimate the average wage within the UK population as a whole.

We can show this formally. Suppose that salaries of individuals within the population are modelled by the random variable X. The (unknown) population average $E(X) = \mu_X$. The average salary for doctors is equal to $3 \times \mu_X$. Suppose that you randomly sample n doctors, and calculate their average wage. The sample of doctors can be assumed to be randomly sampled from the population of medical doctors, such that $E(X_i) = 3 \times \mu_X$:

$$\hat{\mu} = \frac{1}{n}\sum_{i=1}^{n} X_i$$

Now, if this is an unbiased estimator of the population average, $E(\hat{\mu}) = \mu_X$. We can evaluate this by taking expectations of our estimator:

$$E(\hat{\mu}) = E\left(\frac{1}{n}\sum_{i=1}^{n} X_i\right) = \frac{1}{n}\sum_{i=1}^{n} E(X_i)$$

In this case, even though the observations $X_1, X_2, X_3, \ldots, X_n$ are *iid*, they are not randomly drawn from the population as a whole; they are only drawn from the population of doctors. That means that $E(X_i) = 3 \times \mu_X$ for all i:

$$\Rightarrow E(\hat{\mu}) = \frac{1}{n} \times n \times 3 \times \mu_X = 3 \times \mu_X$$

This is not the same as the population average, and the bias is equal to $E(\hat{\mu}) - \mu_X = 3 \times \mu_X - \mu_X = 2 \times \mu_X$. That is, by randomly sampling only from doctors we will on average overestimate the population average salary, and the size of the bias is equal to $2 \times \mu_X$.

Worked example 14.2: What happens if we do not take a representative sample from the population?

The example in Section 14.5.1 shows us how, analytically, selection issues can cause bias. However, it might also be useful to think of this numerically.

Suppose that you are interested in estimating the average salary in the fictional city of Ecalpon. Ecalpon is made up of two districts, Uptown and Downtown. All of the richest inhabitants live in Uptown, and the poorest inhabitants live in Downtown.

Unbeknownst to you, the expected salary in Uptown is £2,000 per week, whilst the expected salary in Downtown is £400 per week. The demographic of Ecalpon is made up of 20 per cent living in Uptown, and 80 per cent living in Downtown. The expected salary in Ecalpon as a whole is thus £720. (This is merely the weighted average of the expected salaries in the two areas.)

In order to estimate the expected salary in Ecalpon, you try to randomly sample 100 individuals from the population. However, since you know that the average salary varies between Uptown and Downtown, you try to take account of this by sampling 50 per cent of the sample (i.e. 50 individuals) from Uptown, and 50 per cent of the sample from Downtown. Does this sample mean provide an unbiased estimate of the expected salary in Ecalpon?

Solution

We can show, mathematically, that the results you would gain are biased. Let's define the observed salaries in Uptown as X_i and the observed salaries in Downtown as Y_i. From the question, we know that $E(X_i) = £2{,}000$ and $E(Y_i) = 400$. Further, let's set $i = 1,2,\ldots,50$ as the observations relating to individuals from Uptown, and $i = 51,52,\ldots,100$ as the observations relating to the individuals from Downtown.

Our estimator is:

$$\hat{\mu} = \frac{1}{100}\left(\sum_{i=1}^{50} X_i + \sum_{i=51}^{100} Y_i\right)$$

Taking expectations, we can write this as:

$$E(\hat{\mu}) = E\left[\frac{1}{100}\left(\sum_{i=1}^{50} X_i + \sum_{i=51}^{100} Y_i\right)\right] = \frac{1}{100} \times \left[\sum_{i=1}^{50} E(X_i) + \sum_{i=51}^{100} E(Y_i)\right]$$

$$= \frac{1}{100} \times [50 \times E(X) + 50 \times E(Y)] = \frac{1}{100} \times [50 \times 2{,}000 + 50 \times 400] = 1{,}200$$

So, the expected value of our estimator is equal to £1,200, which is not equal to the expected value in the population as a whole. Therefore, our estimator is biased, and the bias is equal to £480.

Intuitively, the reason that the estimator is biased here is that the sample is not representative of the population as a whole. In the actual population, only 20 per cent of the population are from Uptown, but in this sample, 50 per cent of the sample are. As such, the over-representativeness of the higher income area pushes the estimates upwards.

14.6 A biased estimator of the population variance

So far, all of our estimators have been relating to the population average, or expected value. However, we will often want to estimate other parameters within the population, including the population variance. For example, if we are looking at the distribution of weekly incomes within the economy, we might get an estimate of £497.[6] However, this figure only tells us about the middle of the distribution. It does not tell us about the level of inequality, or even how spread out the data is. For example, the average £497 weekly wage could equally be constructed through everyone in the population earning £497 per week, or alternatively 10 per cent of

[6] This was the ONS estimate of average weekly, nominal wages before tax in February 2019. https://www.ons.gov.uk/employmentandlabourmarket/peopleinwork/employmentandemployeetypes/bulletins/averageweeklyearningsingreatbritain/april2019

individuals earning £4,970 per week, and the other 90 per cent earning £0 per week! As such, we need to be able to estimate the variance of the underlying random variable.

We have seen that, by definition, the variance of a random variable, X, is defined as:

$$\sigma_X^2 = E(X - E(X))^2$$

That is, the variance is defined as the average of the square of the deviations of observations of away from the its average. Intuitively, this provides a suggested estimator:

$$\sigma_x^2 = \underbrace{E(X - \overbrace{E(X)}^{\text{Population average of } X})^2}_{\text{Population average of } (X - E(X))^2}$$

We know that (provided the observations are randomly drawn and *iid*) the sample mean is an unbiased estimator of the population average. Since the variance is just defined in terms of population averages, intuitively, one route that we might be able to use to find an estimator for the population variance is to replace the expectations with sample means.

As such, there are two steps to constructing our estimator:

Step 1: Replace the population average of X with the sample mean of X:

$$= E\left(X - \frac{1}{n}\sum_{i=1}^{n} X_i\right)^2 = E(X - \bar{X})^2$$

Step 2: Replace the expectation of $(X - \bar{X})^2$ with the sample mean:

$$= \frac{1}{n}\sum_{i=1}^{n}(X_i - \bar{X})^2$$

This provides us with an estimator for the population variance, which we will define as $\hat{\sigma}_X^2$. The important question is whether this is an unbiased estimator of the population variance. As a preview, this estimator is a biased estimator of the population variance, but we will use the characteristics of this estimator to construct an unbiased estimator of the population variance.

Important health warning

Our initial estimator is:

$$\hat{\sigma}_X^2 = \frac{1}{n}\sum_{i=1}^{n}(X_i - \bar{X})^2$$

We will see later in this section that this estimator is a biased estimator of the population variance:

$$E(\hat{\sigma}_X^2) = \left(\frac{n-1}{n}\right)\sigma_X^2$$

As such, unless you have a very large sample, you should not use this estimator to estimate the variance!

The proof of this bias is found in the chapter appendix.

Table 14.4 Ten observations randomly sampled from the standard normal distribution

0.4077	−0.6765	0.2659	0.6756	0.4719	−1.5159	−0.6697	1.7041	0.8386	0.2650

In order to investigate whether this estimator is biased or unbiased, we will begin in the same way as we did with the sample mean. We will use a Monte Carlo simulation to evaluate, intuitively, whether the estimator on average produces the correct value (or not).

To begin the simulation, we need to define the population from which we are randomly sampling. For simplicity, we are going to consider n independent and identically distributed observations, randomly drawn from Z, where $Z \sim N(0,1)$. That is, Z is normally distributed with expectation 0 and variance 1.

We randomly sample ten (*iid*) observations from Z, and obtain the data (rounded to four decimal places) found in Table 14.4.

This set of observations provides us a sample mean of 0.1767, and if we apply the estimator for the variance, we obtain an estimate of $\hat{\sigma}_X^2 = 0.7486$. We know that the true variance is equal to 1. The estimate that we have obtained is different from the true variance, but this doesn't tell us anything about whether the estimator is unbiased (or not). In order to assess whether this is an unbiased estimator of the population expectation, we need to repeatedly sample from the population. If the estimator provides unbiased estimates of the population variance, then, since the true variance is equal to 1, the average of our estimates over a large number of trials should be equal to 1.

We repeat the process 250,000 times to obtain 250,000 estimates of the population variance. Figure 14.6 shows the distribution of these estimates. The mean average of our estimates is equal to 0.900. However, because we constructed the data, we know that the true variance in the population is equal to 1. As such, on average, our estimator does not produce the correct answer. In fact, the average of our estimates (0.900) is only 90 per cent of the true variance when there are ten observations.

One possibility is that the estimator may become better as the sample size gets larger. That is, as the sample size gets larger, it might be the case that the bias becomes smaller. To investigate this, let's repeat the experiment with larger sample sizes (of 100 and 1,000).

Figure 14.7 shows the results from this simulation. In each case, the average of all of our estimates of the variance is less than the true variance (remember that the true variance is equal to 1). We saw above that when $n = 10$, the average of all of our trials is equal to 0.90. Similarly, when $n = 100$, the average of all of our trials is equal to 0.99, and when $n = 1{,}000$, the average is equal to 0.999.

Sample size	Average of estimates	Relation to true variance
$n = 10$	0.900	Average of estimates is 90% of the true variance
$n = 100$	0.990	Average of estimates is 99% of the true variance
$n = 1000$	0.999	Average of estimates is 99.9% of the true variance

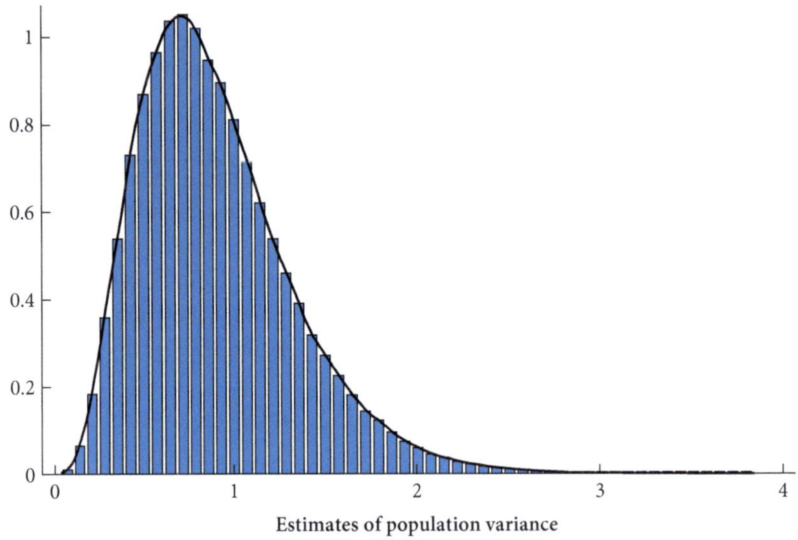

Average of estimates	0.900
Variance of estimates	0.180
Smallest estimate	0.033
Largest estimate	3.843

Figure 14.6 Distribution of estimates of population variance.

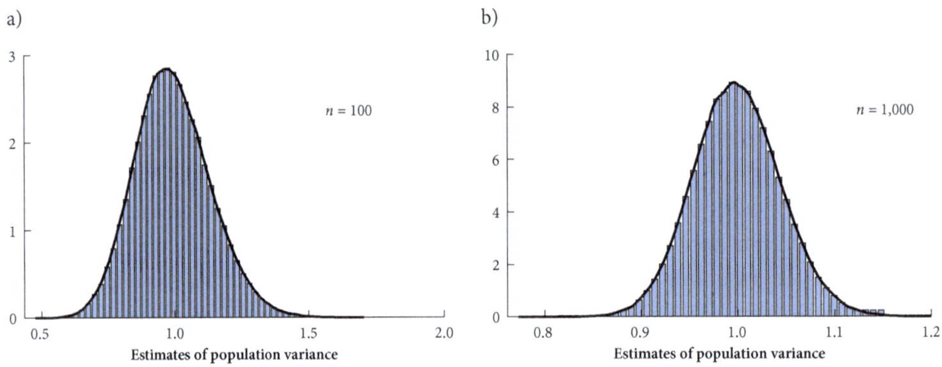

Average of estimates	0.990
Variance of estimates	0.020
Smallest estimate	0.474
Largest estimate	1.706

Average of estimates	0.9990
Variance of estimates	0.002
Smallest estimate	0.773
Largest estimate	1.200

Figure 14.7 Distribution of estimates for larger sample sizes.

As the sample size gets larger, the average of the estimates gets closer to the true variance, but is always less than that true variance. However, we can see that there is a pattern, in that the average of the estimates is always equal to:

$$\frac{n-1}{n} \times \sigma_X^2$$

That is, when we had ten observations ($n = 10$), the estimates were, on average, $\frac{9}{10} \times \sigma_X^2$; when we had 100 observations ($n = 100$), the estimates were, on average, $\frac{99}{100} \times \sigma_X^2$, and so on.

In fact, it is possible to prove[7] that the expectation of our estimator is equal to:

$$E(\hat{\sigma}_X^2) = \left(\frac{n-1}{n}\right)\sigma_X^2$$

Therefore, our initial candidate estimator for the variance of the population provides biased estimates. The bias becomes smaller as the sample size becomes larger, but we would still like to construct an unbiased estimator for the population variance.

14.7 An unbiased estimator of the population variance

We have seen that if we use $\hat{\sigma}_X^2 = \frac{1}{n}\sum_{i=1}^{n}(X_i - \overline{X})^2$ as an estimator for the population variance, then we get biased estimates, such that $E(\hat{\sigma}_X^2) = \left(\frac{n-1}{n}\right)\sigma_X^2$. However, this also provides us with a route to try to construct an unbiased estimator. We will examine if there is a transformation that we can apply to $\hat{\sigma}_X^2$ to provide us with an unbiased estimator.

Remember, from the rules of expectations, we know that if we multiply a random variable X by a constant, a, then the expectation of the resulting product will just be $E(aX) = aE(X)$. That is, this is equivalent to multiplying the expectation of X by the constant a. Estimators are themselves random variables. We have seen that they have distributions, and their outcomes are determined by the (random) sample from the population. As such, we can apply the rules of random variables to estimators as well.

Since we know that $E(\hat{\sigma}_X^2) = \left(\frac{n-1}{n}\right)\sigma_X^2$, a question is, what constant could we multiply $\hat{\sigma}_X^2$ by to make the resulting expectation equal to σ_X^2? So, if we multiply $\hat{\sigma}_X^2$ by a constant, a, then:

$$E(a \times \hat{\sigma}_X^2) = a \times E(\sigma_X^2) = a \times \left(\frac{n-1}{n}\right) \times \sigma_X^2$$

In order for this to be an unbiased estimator, it would need to be the case that $E(a \times \hat{\sigma}_X^2) = \sigma_X^2$. That is, it would need to be the case that $a \times \left(\frac{n-1}{n}\right) = 1$. The simple way to achieve this is to set $a = \frac{n}{n-1}$.

[7] A proof is provided in the appendix of this chapter.

So our new estimator is:

$$\left(\frac{n}{n-1}\right) \times \hat{\sigma}_X^2 = \left(\frac{n}{n-1}\right) \times \frac{1}{n}\sum_{i=1}^{n}\left(X_i - \overline{X}\right)^2 = \left(\frac{1}{n-1}\right) \times \sum_{i=1}^{n}(X_i - \overline{X})^2$$

The estimator that we have constructed here is often referred to as s_{n-1}^2, or just s^2. It is possible to show, algebraically,[8] that this is an unbiased estimator of the population variance.

$$s_{n-1}^2 = \frac{1}{n-1}\sum\nolimits_{i=1}^{n}(X_i - \overline{X})^2$$

KEY DEFINITION: UNBIASED ESTIMATOR FOR POPULATION VARIANCE

When we observe *n iid* observations from a population variable, X, whose variance is σ_X^2, the unbiased estimator of the population variance is:

$$s_{n-1}^2 = \frac{1}{n-1}\sum\nolimits_{i=1}^{n}(X_i - \overline{X})^2$$

That is:

$$E(s_{n-1}^2) = \sigma_X^2$$

The fact that we divide by $(n - 1)$ rather than n is known as Bessel's correction, and leads to an unbiased estimator of the population. The intuition for why we divide by $n - 1$ rather than n is that since we are using $\overline{X}$ as an estimator for $E(X)$ within our estimator, we have lost one linearly independent piece of information, so rather than having n independent pieces of information, we only have $n - 1$. This is often known as the number of degrees of freedom, and these will become important when we move into statistical testing.

If we repeat the Monte Carlo simulations that we used in the previous section with our new estimator, we can see that, irrespective of the sample size, the average of our estimates is always equal to 1. That is, our new estimator provides unbiased estimates of the population variance.

Figure 14.8 illustrates that, experimentally at least, our new estimator s_{n-1}^2 provides unbiased estimates of the population variance. Further than this, we can also prove that, provided the observations are drawn randomly from the population (and that, they are *iid*), then the estimator provides unbiased estimates of the population variance.

Whilst it is true to say that s_{n-1}^2 provides an unbiased estimator for the population variance, it is (generally speaking) not true that $\sqrt{s_{n-1}^2}$ provides an unbiased estimator for the standard deviation of the population variable, even though the standard deviation is simply equal to the square root of the variance.

[8] There are a number of proofs for this. We have constructed a proof, based upon the proof that $\hat{\sigma}_X^2$ is a biased estimator, in the appendix, but you can find numerous other proofs which examine the unbiasedness of s_{n-1}^2 directly.

a)

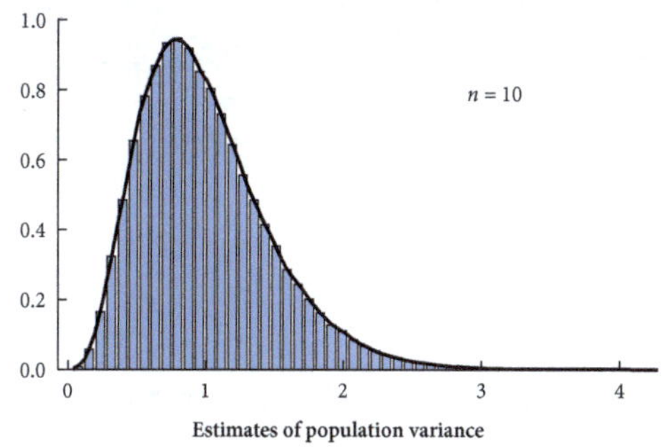

Average of estimates	1.00
Variance of estimates	0.222
Smallest estimate	0.036
Largest estimate	4.270

b)

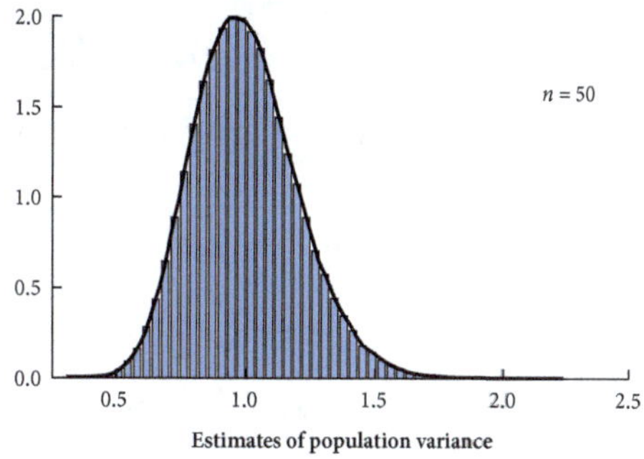

Average of estimates	1.00
Variance of estimates	0.041
Smallest estimate	0.309
Largest estimate	2.235

c)

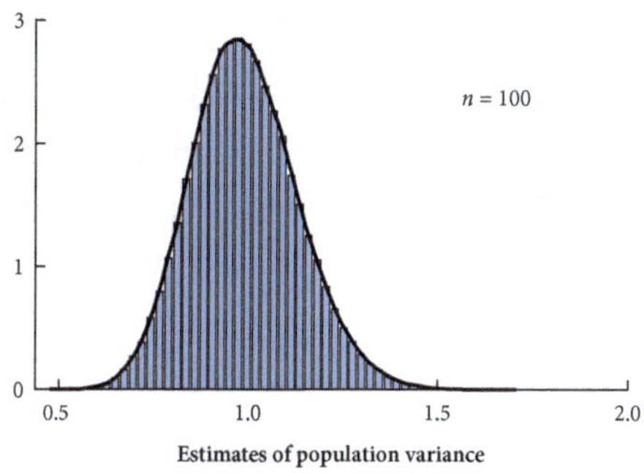

Average of estimates	1.00
Variance of estimates	0.020
Smallest estimate	0.479
Largest estimate	1.723

d)

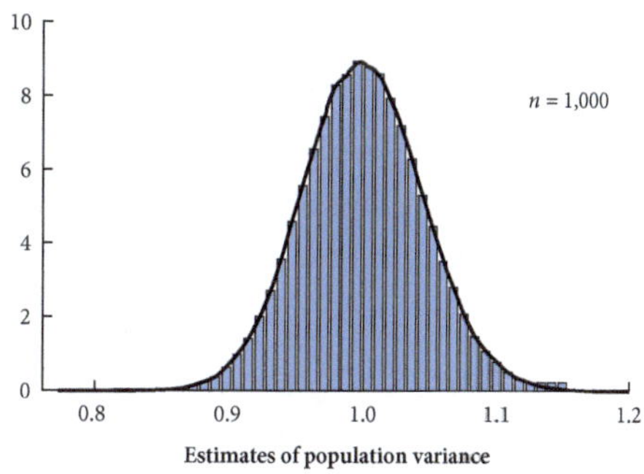

Average of estimates	1.00
Variance of estimates	0.002
Smallest estimate	0.773
Largest estimate	1.200

Figure 14.8 Distribution of estimates using s^2_{n-1} with $n = 10, 50, 100$, and $1{,}000$.

The reason for this is that, in line with Jensen's inequality, for non-linear functions, f:

$$E(f(X)) \neq fE(X)$$

So, in the case of s^2_{n-1}, we know that $E(s^2_{n-1}) = \sigma^2_X$, and we know that $\sqrt{\sigma^2_X}$ is the standard deviation of X. However, since $E(\sqrt{s^2_{n-1}}) \neq \sqrt{E(s^2_{n-1})}$, it will not be, generally, true that $\sqrt{s^2_{n-1}}$ is an unbiased estimator of the population standard deviation. However, in practice, when statisticians need to use an estimate the standard deviation, we usually use $\sqrt{s^2_{n-1}}$.

KEY DEFINITION: UNBIASED ESTIMATORS

We have seen that, if we observe n independent and identically distributed observations from a population variable, X, then:

1. The sample mean, $\overline{X}$, provides an unbiased estimator for the population expectation, $E(X)$:

$$E(\overline{X}) = E(X) \qquad \text{where } \overline{X} = \frac{1}{n}\sum_{i=1}^{n} X_i$$

2. The **sample variance**, s_{n-1}^2, provides an unbiased estimator for the population variance, $var(X)$:

$$E(s_{n-1}^2) = var(X)$$

$$\text{where } s_{n-1}^2 = \frac{1}{n-1}\sum_{i=1}^{n}(X_i - \overline{X})^2$$

14.8 Applying our unbiased estimators to data

Suppose that you randomly sample five observations of individuals' weekly wages. If we assume that the observations are randomly sampled from the population and are *iid*, use this data to calculate an unbiased estimate of the expected weekly wage in the population, μ_X, and an unbiased estimate of the variance of wages in the population, σ_X^2:

Observation	Value
1	£865
2	£240
3	£442
4	£418
5	£385

The sample mean, $\overline{X}$, is an unbiased estimator of μ_X:

$$\overline{x} = \frac{1}{5}\sum_{i=1}^{5} x_i = \frac{1}{5} \times [865 + 240 + 442 + 418 + 385] = 470$$

So, based on this data, our estimate of the expected (average) salary in the population is £470 per week.

To construct our estimate of the population variance, we need to use the s_{n-1}^2 estimator:

$$s_{n-1}^2 = \left(\frac{1}{5-1}\right)\sum_{i=1}^{5}(x_i - \overline{x})^2$$

$$= \frac{1}{4}[(865 - 470)^2 + (240 - 470)^2 + (442 - 470)^2 + (418 - 470)^2 + (385 - 470)^2]$$

Note: we subtract the sample mean from each observation before squaring!

$$= \frac{1}{4}[(395)^2 + (-230)^2 + (-28)^2 + (-52)^2 + (-85)^2] = 54{,}909.5$$

So, our estimate of the population variance is 54,909.5, which provides a (biased) estimate of the standard deviation of £234.33.

Estimators in Excel

You can use Microsoft Excel to calculate these unbiased estimates, using formulae.
For example, if you have a sample of data in cells A2 to A100, you can find an estimate of the population average using the sample average formula:

$$=\text{average}(\text{A2:A100})$$

Similarly, you can find an estimate of the population variance by using the var formula:

$$=var(\text{A2:A100})$$

Note carefully that there is a second formula for the variance, $=var.\text{p}(\text{A2:A100})$. If you use this formula, you are assuming that you are observing the entire population. The formula that Excel will use here will be $\hat{\sigma}^2 = \frac{\sum_{i=1}^{n}(X_i - \bar{X})^2}{n}$, which we have seen is a biased estimator of the population variance.

Of course, in this example, the estimates will only be unbiased if the data is randomly sampled from the population. If the sampling is non-random, so that, for instance, you only sampled from university graduates, our estimate would likely be biased due to selection bias.

Summary

An estimator is a mathematical operation that is applied to a sample of data to provide an estimate of a population parameter:

- An estimate is a single realization of an estimator using a single sample of data.
- Due to sampling variation we will observe different estimates of the population parameter for every different sample we take from the population.
- An estimator is unbiased if, on average, it gives the correct result. For example, if $\hat{\mu}$ is an estimator for some population characteristic, μ, the estimator is unbiased if $E(\hat{\mu}) = \mu$.

Key formulae

Assuming our observations are independent and identically distributed, then:

1. The sample mean, $\overline{X} = \frac{1}{n}\sum_{i=1}^{n} X_i$ is an unbiased estimator of the expected value of X, $E(X)$ for the population.
2. $\hat{\sigma}_X^2 = \frac{1}{n}\sum_{i=1}^{n}(X_i - \overline{X})^2$ is a biased estimator of the population variance, σ_X^2.
3. $s_{n-1}^2 = \frac{1}{n-1}\sum_{i=1}^{n}(X_i - \overline{X})^2$ is an unbiased estimator of the population variance, σ_X^2.
4. $\sqrt{s_{n-1}^2}$ is a biased estimator of the population standard deviation $\sqrt{\sigma_X^2}$.
5. An unbiased estimator for the covariance between two random variables, X and Y, is given as $\frac{1}{n-1}\sum_{i=1}^{n}(X_i - \overline{X})(Y_i - \overline{Y})$.

Appendix

Proof that the sample variance is a biased estimator of the population variance

Suppose that we have a random variable X, whose expectation is $E(X) = \mu_X$ and variance $var(X) = \sigma_X^2$.

We randomly sample n *iid* observations of X_i, and we wish to estimate the population variance. We are interested in evaluating whether the following estimator is unbiased:

$$\hat{\sigma}_X^2 = \frac{1}{n}\sum_{i=1}^{n}(X_i - \overline{X})^2$$

Let's begin by proving some identities:

1. We know that $\sigma_X^2 = E(X^2) - E(X)^2$. Since $E(X) = \mu_X$, we can rewrite this as:

   $$\sigma_X^2 = E(X^2) - \mu_X^2$$

   And thus:

   $$E(X^2) = \sigma_X^2 + \mu_X^2$$

   so that also means that: $E(X^2) = \sigma_X^2 + \mu_X^2$ where μ_X is the expectation of X, and σ_X^2 is the variance of X.

2. Provided the observations are *iid*, then:

   $$var(\overline{X}) = \frac{\sigma_X^2}{n}$$

   However, we could also write the variance of the sample mean as:

   $$var(\overline{X}) = E(\overline{X}^2) - E(\overline{X})^2$$

We know that the sample mean is an unbiased estimator of μ_X, and so $E(\overline{X}) = \mu_X$ and $E(\overline{X})^2 = \mu_X^2$

Thus, we can rewrite this as:

$$\text{var}(\overline{X}) = \frac{\sigma_X^2}{n} = E(\overline{X}^2) - \mu_X^2$$

$$\Rightarrow E(\overline{X}^2) = \frac{\sigma_X^2}{n} + \mu_X^2$$

Our estimator, $\hat{\sigma}_X^2$, is defined as:

$$\hat{\sigma}_X^2 = \frac{1}{n}\sum_{i=1}^{n}(X_i - \overline{X})^2$$

Let's begin by expanding the brackets:

$$= \frac{1}{n}\sum_{i=1}^{n}(X_i^2 + \overline{X}^2 - 2X_i\,\overline{X})$$

Now, we can break this sum up into three parts:

$$= \frac{1}{n}\left[\sum_{i=1}^{n}X_i^2 + \sum_{j=1}^{n}\overline{X}^2 - 2\sum_{k=1}^{n}X_k\overline{X}\right]$$

Now, for the second and third terms, $\overline{X}$ is just a constant, and so we can treat it as a constant multiplier. $\sum_{j=1}^{n}\overline{X}^2$ is just $(\overline{X}^2 + \overline{X}^2 + \ldots + \overline{X}^2)$ n times $(= n\,\overline{X}^2)$. So we can rewrite this as:

$$= \frac{1}{n}\left[\sum_{i=1}^{n}X_i^2 + n\overline{X}^2 - 2\,\overline{X}\sum_{k=1}^{n}X_k\right]$$

Now, we also know that $\overline{X} = \frac{1}{n}\sum_{i=1}^{n}X_i$, and so we can multiply left and right by n to give:

$$n\overline{X} = \sum_{i=1}^{n}X_i$$

So, our estimator is now:

$$\begin{aligned}\hat{\sigma}_X^2 &= \frac{1}{n}\left[\sum_{i=1}^{n}X_i^2 + n\overline{X}^2 - 2\,\overline{X}n\overline{X}\right]\\ &= \frac{1}{n}\left[\sum_{i=1}^{n}X_i^2 + n\overline{X}^2 - 2\,n\,\overline{X}^2\right]\\ &= \frac{1}{n}\left[\sum_{i=1}^{n}X_i^2 - n\overline{X}^2\right]\end{aligned}$$

Now, we can take expectations of this to examine whether this is an unbiased estimator:

$$E[\hat{\sigma}_X^2] = E\left[\frac{1}{n}\left[\sum_{i=1}^{n}X_i^2 - n\overline{X}^2\right]\right]$$

Now, because $\frac{1}{n}$ is a constant multiplier, it can be taken outside of the expectation:

$$= \frac{1}{n} E\left[\sum_{i=1}^{n} X_i^2 - n\bar{X}^2\right]$$

We can also break this up into two parts, as the expectation of a sum is just the sum of the expectations:

$$= \frac{1}{n}\left[E\left(\sum_{i=1}^{n} X_i^2\right) - nE(\bar{X}^2)\right]$$

Finally, we know that the expectation of a sum is the sum of the expectations, and that since the observations are *iid*, then $E(X_1^2) = E(X_2^2) = \ldots = E(X_n^2) = E(X^2)$:

$$= \frac{1}{n}\left[\sum_{i=1}^{n} E(X^2) - nE(\bar{X}^2)\right] = \frac{1}{n}[nE(X^2) - nE(\bar{X}^2)]$$

$$= E(X^2) - E(\bar{X}^2)$$

Substituting our identities from earlier in the proof, we know that:

- $E(X^2) = \sigma_X^2 + \mu_X^2$ and
- $E(\bar{X}^2) = \frac{\sigma_X^2}{n} + \mu_X^2$

$$= (\sigma_X^2 + \mu_X^2) - \left(\frac{\sigma_X^2}{n} + \mu_X^2\right) = \frac{\sigma_X^2(n-1)}{n}$$

$$= \left[\frac{n-1}{n}\right]\sigma_X^2 \neq \sigma_X^2$$

Thus $\hat{\sigma}_X^2$ is a biased estimator of σ_X^2, although the bias gets smaller as n tends towards infinity.

Proof that s_{n-1}^2 is an unbiased estimator of the population variance

We are interested in proving that $s_{n-1}^2 =\in \frac{1}{n-1}\Sigma_{i=1}^{n}(X_i - \bar{X})^2$ is an unbiased estimator of σ_X^2.

Let's begin with $\hat{\sigma}_X^2$ from the previous example:

$$\hat{\sigma}_X^2 = \frac{1}{n}\sum_{i=1}^{n}(X_i - \bar{X})^2$$

Now, we can transform $\hat{\sigma}_X^2$ into s_{n-1}^2 by multiplying by $\frac{n}{n-1}$. That is:

$$\left[\frac{n}{n-1}\right]\hat{\sigma}_X^2 = \left[\frac{n}{n-1}\right]\left[\frac{1}{n}\sum_{i=1}^{n}(X_i - \bar{X})^2\right] = \left[\frac{1}{n-1}\right]\sum_{i=1}^{n}(X_i - \bar{X})^2 = s_{n-1}^2$$

So:

$$\left[\frac{n}{n-1}\right]\hat{\sigma}_X^2 = s_{n-1}^2$$

In the previous proof, we calculated $E(\hat{\sigma}_X^2) = \frac{\sigma_X^2(n-1)}{n}$, so we can use this and the properties of expectations to find $E(s_{n-1}^2)$:

$$E(s_{n-1}^2) = E\left(\left[\frac{n}{n-1}\right]\hat{\sigma}_X^2\right)$$

Now $\frac{n}{n-1}$ is a constant multiplier, so it can be taken outside of the expectation:

$$= \left[\frac{n}{n-1}\right]E(\hat{\sigma}_X^2)$$

Since $E(\hat{\sigma}_X^2) = \frac{\sigma_X^2(n-1)}{n}$, we can write:

$$E(s_{n-1}^2) = \left[\frac{n}{n-1}\right]\frac{\sigma_X^2(n-1)}{n} = \sigma_X^2$$

Therefore our estimator is unbiased!

What Makes a Good Estimator? Efficiency and Consistency of Estimators

15

Learning outcomes for this chapter

By the end of this chapter you will be able to:

- Describe an estimator in terms of the variance of the estimates generated, and calculate the variance of a sample mean based on n independent and identically distributed observations
- Apply the central limit theorem to evaluate the distribution of the sample mean
- Construct the mean squared error of simple estimators
- Apply the mean squared error to show that estimators are consistent
- Use probability limits to show whether estimators are consistent or not

Mathematical tools

- Limits
- Summations using sigma (Σ) notation

Introduction

So far, we have defined an estimator as a mathematical function, applied to data, to provide an estimate of some population parameter.

Since an estimator is simply a mathematical operation applied to a sample of data, there are a wide range of estimators that could be applied to a set of data observed from the population.

The estimator that you are probably most familiar with is the sample (arithmetic) mean, but we could also use other estimators, such as the geometric mean, or the harmonic mean. These are all estimators that we could use to generate an estimate of the population average (or expectation). Later in the book, we will introduce other forms of estimator, which are used to estimate relationships between economic variables.

Arithmetic mean	$= \frac{\sum_{i=1}^{n} X_i}{n}$
Geometric mean	$= \left(\prod_{i=1}^{n} X_i \right)^{\frac{1}{n}}$
Harmonic mean	$= \left(\frac{\sum_{i=1}^{n} X_i^{-1}}{n} \right)^{-1}$

KEY DEFINITION: ESTIMATOR

An estimator is a mathematical operation that is applied to an observed sample of data to provide an estimate of a population characteristic. For example, the sample mean is often used as an estimator for the expected value in the population.

Since there are a range of estimators that could be used, statisticians need to be able to choose the 'best' estimator for estimating a particular population parameter. It should be noted that the 'best' estimator may change depending on the structure of the data, the observations that are observed, and precisely what type of population parameter is being estimated.

An unbiased estimator is one that, on average, produces the 'correct' estimate of the population parameter. More formally, an estimator is unbiased if the expectation of the estimator is equal to the population parameter being estimated. However, even if an estimator is unbiased, this doesn't necessarily mean that it is a good estimator.

Suppose that the true value of a population parameter being estimated was equal to zero (i.e. $\mu = 0$). You might have two estimators for the population parameter that you want to use, $\hat{\mu}_1$ and $\hat{\mu}_2$:

- $\hat{\mu}_1$ is an unbiased estimator, such that $E(\hat{\mu}_1) = \mu = 0$.
- $\hat{\mu}_2$ is a biased estimator which, on average, provides estimates of the population parameter which are 1 unit above the true value; that is, $E(\hat{\mu}_2) = \mu + 1 = 1$.

On the face of it, we might initially feel that $\hat{\mu}_1$ is the better estimator, because, on average, it will give the correct result. However, when we are using an estimator, we are usually only gaining one realization of the estimator (or a single estimate). As such, we also need to consider how close any particular realization of the estimator is going to be to the true population parameter. This is due to the fact that estimators are, themselves, random variables with an expectation and (more importantly) a variance.

You may discover that all of the possible realizations of $\hat{\mu}_2$ are between 0.5 and 1.5, whilst the range of $\hat{\mu}_1$ might be equally spread between −1,000 and +1,000. For a given realization of $\hat{\mu}_1$, you might be up to 1,000 above (or below) the true population parameter being estimated. In this case, you might conclude that even though it is biased—because for the majority of the possible realizations, $\hat{\mu}_2$ is closer to the true population parameter—we may prefer estimates from $\hat{\mu}_2$ to estimates from $\hat{\mu}_1$. $\hat{\mu}_1$ has a higher variance than $\hat{\mu}_2$, which may lead us to prefer $\hat{\mu}_2$.

In this chapter, we will further examine what makes a good estimator. In doing so, we will introduce three key concepts: the variance of an estimator, the mean squared error (MSE) of an estimator, and finally the consistency of an estimator.

15.1 Variance of an estimator

We have seen, in the previous chapter, that due to sampling variation, every time we apply an estimator to a new sample from the population, we gain a new estimate of the population parameter. For example, in the previous chapter, when we randomly sampled ten separate samples from the UK Labour Force Survey, we obtained ten different estimates of the average wage of full-time workers. The ten different estimates that we obtained from ten separate samples are presented in Table 15.1.

You can see that there is a relatively wide range of estimates, from £602.92 up to £687.52. Even though we have seen that the sample mean is an unbiased estimator of the population average, we still see substantial variation between samples in the estimates that are obtained.

Table 15.1 Estimates of average wage of full-time workers, based on ten separate samples of 50 individuals from the UK Labour Force Survey

Sample	Sample average
1	661.45
2	611.49
3	687.52
4	670.82
5	682.92
6	609.57
7	674.89
8	675.99
9	681.81
10	602.92

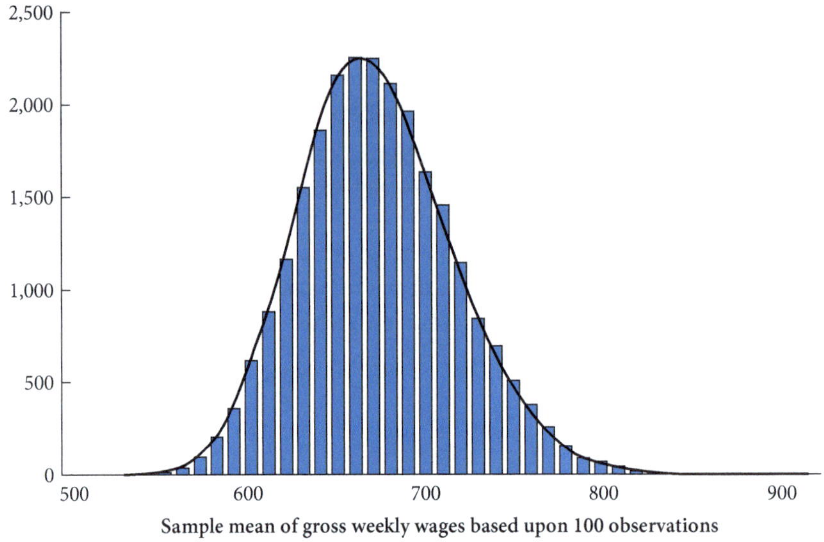

Figure 15.1 Histogram showing the distribution of estimates across 25,000 separate samples of 100 individuals from the 2019 UK LFS.

The distribution of estimates of the population average wage is illustrated in Figure 15.1. We can see that the estimates for the population average range from below 550 to above 800. This variability is a measure of the spread or the variance of the estimator.

To investigate the properties of the variance of the sample mean, let's begin with a Monte Carlo simulation. We are going to consider what the impact of taking different sample sizes is on the variance of our estimates. Let's begin by defining the population we wish to sample from. Let's define a population, represented by a random variable, X, which is normally distributed with expectation 10 and variance 100.

$$X \sim N(10,100)$$

We will randomly sample n independent and identically distributed observations (where $n = 25,50,100,200$), and calculate the sample mean to obtain (unbiased) estimates of the population average. We will then repeat this, until we have 250,000 estimates, and then will examine the distribution of our estimates.

The experimental distributions are illustrated in Figure 15.2. The histograms are presented as density plots, which means that the height of each bar is telling you about the relative probability of observing an outcome in that area. As the sample size increases, the sample mean remains unbiased. That is, in all four simulations, the average of the estimates is equal to the true population average (which we know to be equal to 10).

The variance of the estimator is a measure of how much variability we observe in the estimates. The larger the variance, the more variability in the observed estimates. What we can see, from our simulation, is that the variance of the estimates gets smaller as the sample size increases. That is, we can see that the distribution of estimates becomes squeezed as the sample size increases. Numerically, when we move from a sample size of 25 to a sample size of

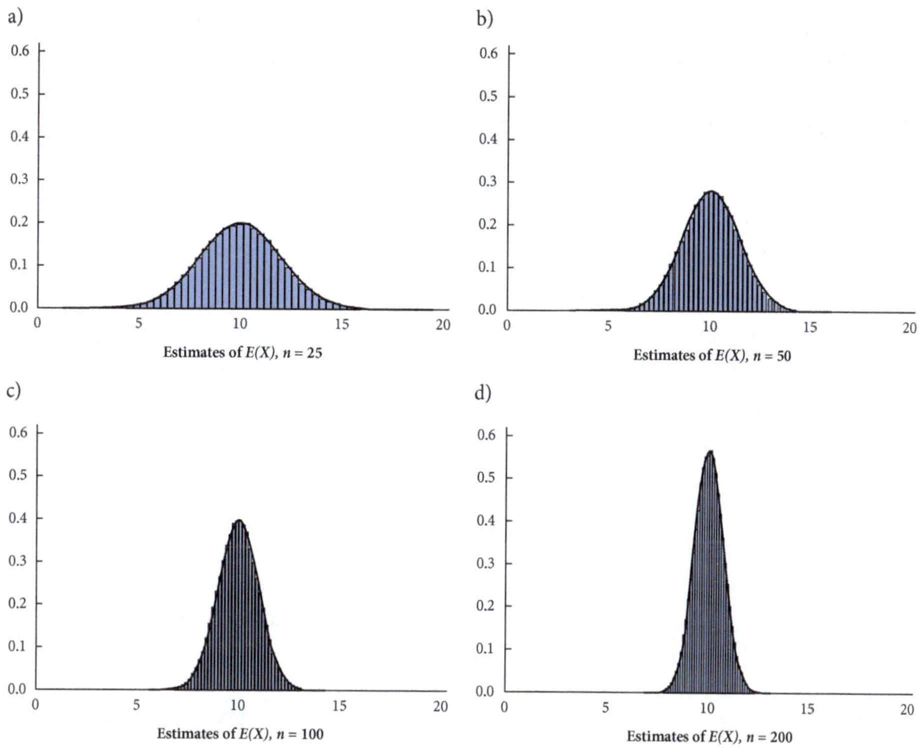

Figure 15.2 Distribution of sample means from Monte Carlo simulations, based upon samples of 25, 50, 100, and 200 observations.

50, the variance of the estimates halves from 4.00 to 2.00. If we double the sample size again to 100, the variance of the estimates halves again from 2.00 to 1.00.

In fact, we have shown that, for the sample mean, the variance of our estimates appears to be inversely proportional to the sample size. If we extended this simulation to include sample sizes of 400 and 800, we would obtain the distributions shown in Table 15.2.

Table 15.2 Expected distributions based on sample sizes from 25 to 800

Sample size	Average	Variance
25	10.00	4.0
50	10.00	2.0
100	10.00	1.0
200	10.00	0.50
400	10.00	0.25
800	10.00	0.125

Something else that is interesting is that we know the true variance of X. In this simulation, we have constructed the population such that the variance is equal to 100. If you look at the variance of our estimates, this is always equal to 100 divided by the sample size.

This suggests that (for this example at least), we can write that the variance of the sample mean is:

$$var(\overline{X}) = \frac{var(X)}{n}$$

An important question is whether this holds generally. In fact it is possible to prove that,[1] provided the observations are independent and identically distributed, and randomly sampled from the population, then the variance of the sample mean will be equal to the variance of the underlying random variable divided by the number of observations.

Distribution of sample mean

Suppose we observe n independent and identically distributed (iid) observations from a population, such that $E(X_i) = \mu_X$ and $var(X_i) = \sigma_X^2$ for all i. The distribution of the sample mean, $\overline{X} = \frac{1}{n}\Sigma_{i=1}^{n} X_i$, is given by:

Expectation	$E(\overline{X}) = E(X) = \mu_X$	The sample mean is an unbiased estimator of the population average, or expectation.
Variance	$var(\overline{X}) = \frac{var(X)}{n} = \frac{\sigma_X^2}{n}$	The variance of the sample mean is inversely proportional to the sample size.

The variance of our estimator is just telling us about how much variation we will observe when we repeatedly sample from the population, and apply our estimator. We have seen, for the sample mean, that as the sample size increases, the variability of the estimates gets smaller.

Intuitively, the reason that the variance of the estimator gets smaller as the sample size increases is because we are gaining more data about the population, and so we might expect the estimates to simply be closer to the true population parameter being estimated! It is not just the sample mean (as an estimator of the expectation) where the variance gets smaller as the sample size increases. If we repeat the simulation for s_{n-1}^2 (sometimes referred to as the sample variance, or the unbiased estimator for the population variance), we can see a similar pattern; as the sample size gets larger, the variance gets smaller.

$$s_{n-1}^2 = \left(\frac{1}{n-1}\right) \times \sum_{i=1}^{n} (X_i - \overline{X})^2$$

[1] This is proven in the appendix.

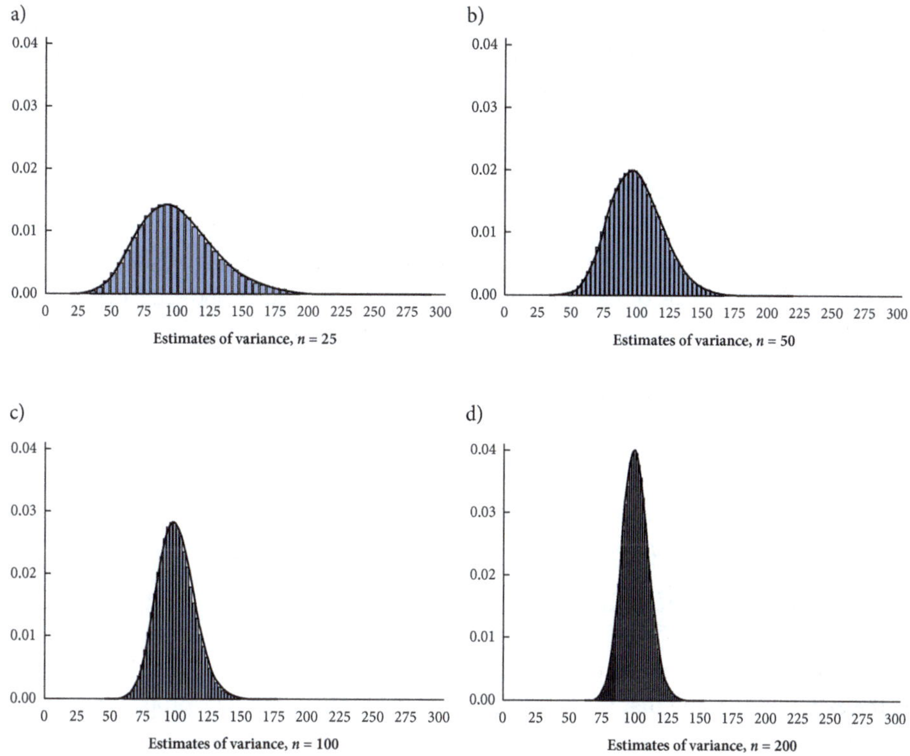

Figure 15.3 Distribution of estimates of the population variance using the s^2_{n-1} estimator.

Remember, we are randomly sampling n observations from a population that has a true variance equal to 100. We have already seen that s^2_{n-1} is an unbiased estimator, so the mean of the estimates should be equal to 100. What we are interested in is the variance of the estimates.

The variance of s^2_{n-1} is a little trickier to evaluate analytically. However, from Figure 15.3 we can see that, each time the sample size doubles, the variance of the estimates drops by (slightly more than) half. The fact that the variability drops by more than a half is because, when constructing the estimates, we are dividing by $(n-1)$, rather than n. As such, the degree of freedom $(n-1)$ more than doubles, leading to the reduction in the variability by more than half.

Distribution of sample variance

Suppose we observe n independent and identically distributed (*iid*) observations from a population, such that $E(X_i) = \mu_X$ and $var(X_i) = \sigma^2_X$ and $cov(X_i, X_j) = 0$ for all i, j. The distribution of the sample variance, $s^2_{n-1} = \left(\frac{1}{n-1}\right) \times \Sigma^n_{i=1}(X_i - \overline{X})^2$, is given by:

Expectation	$E(s^2_{n-1}) = var(X) = \sigma^2_X$	The sample variance is an unbiased estimator of the population variance, σ^2_X

We have now seen two estimators both of which demonstrate reduced variability (i.e. a lower variance) as the sample size gets larger. In general, estimators become more efficient (i.e. lower variance) as the amount of information used to create the estimates increases.

Consequences of an estimator having a large variance

Suppose that you have an estimator that is unbiased. This means that, on average, the estimator will produce the correct value of the population parameter being estimated.

However, if the estimator has a large variance, this means that any individual realization of the estimator may be a long way away from the true population parameter being estimated. With a large variance, the probability of gaining an estimate that is a long way from the true value is high.

15.2 The central limit theorem (or the most important theorem in statistics)

So far, we have seen that the sample mean is an unbiased estimator of the population average (i.e. the expectation), and that the variance of the estimator is inversely proportional to the sample size.

Reminder: Distribution of the sample mean

If we randomly sample n independent and identically distributed observations from a population X, such that $E(X) = \mu_X$ and $var(X) = \sigma_X^2$:

$$\overline{X} = \frac{1}{n}\sum_{i=1}^{n} X_i$$

Expectation	$E(\overline{X}) = E(X) = \mu_X$	The sample mean is an unbiased estimator of the population average (expectation).
Variance	$var(\overline{X}) = \frac{var(X)}{n} = \frac{\sigma_X^2}{n}$	The variance of the sample mean is equal to the variance of the underlying random variable, divided by the number of observations.

We have also seen that the distribution of the estimates follows a very familiar shape. From the Monte Carlo simulations, illustrated in Figure 15.4, we can see that the estimates follow a bell-shaped curve.

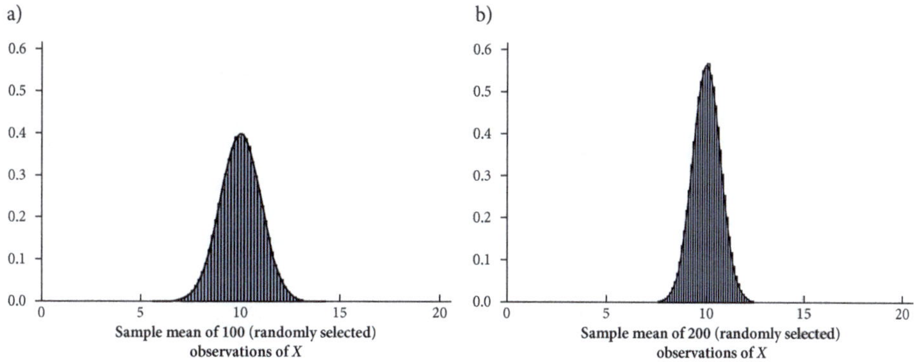

Figure 15.4 Distribution of sample means, randomly sampled from a population with expectation 10 and variance 100.

We can be more precise than that. Formally, we can say that, if we observe n independent and identically distributed observations from *any* distribution (albeit with a well-realized and finite expectation and variance), then provided n is sufficiently large, the sample mean (and other estimators) will be approximately normally distributed centred around the expectation of the underlying random variable.

For example, if you have a random variable X, which has expectation, $E(X) = \mu_X$ and variance, $var(X) = \sigma_X^2$, then for a large enough sample size, the sample mean will be approximately normally distributed:

$$\bar{X} \sim N\left(\mu_X, \frac{\sigma_X^2}{n}\right)$$

As a rule of thumb, in order for the sample mean to be treated as approximately normally distributed, the sample size would need to be greater than 30. As the sample size gets larger, the distribution of the sample mean will increasingly get closer to being normally distributed.

The intuition behind this is as follows. If we observe n realizations of a variable (and n is large enough), then we would normally expect the sample average that we compute to be close to the expected value. In fact, if we repeat this process, say 10,000 times, we would expect most of these sample averages to be close to the expected value. However, occasionally we might randomly get a sample average that is a long way away from the expected value, but these cases would be few and far between. In order to illustrate this, a Monte Carlo simulation is often useful.

15.2.1 Monte Carlo simulation to demonstrate the central limit theorem

We are interested in the properties of the sample mean. Let us consider a variable X, which is uniformly distributed between 3 and 6, as illustrated in Figure 15.5.

$$X \sim U(3,6)$$

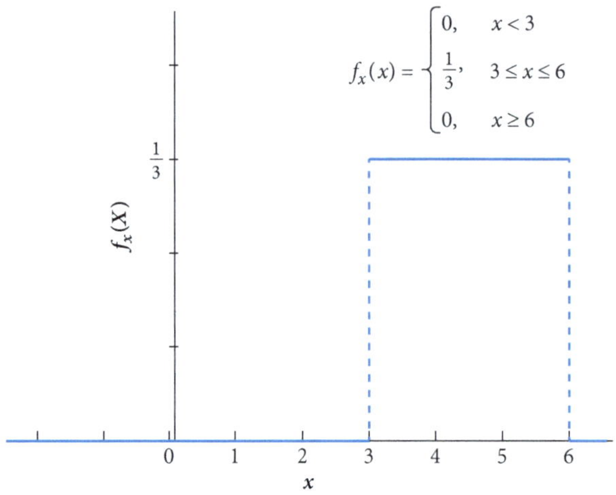

Figure 15.5 Probability density function for $X \sim U(3,6)$.

We know that for a variable, X, that is uniformly distributed between a and b, $E(X) = \frac{a+b}{2}$ and $var(X) = \frac{(b-a)^2}{12}$. Hence, in this example:

$$E(X) = \frac{3+6}{2} = 4.5, \quad var(X) = \frac{(6-3)^2}{12} = \frac{9}{12} = 0.75$$

We now randomly (and independently) sample 50 observations from this random variable, and find the (mean) average of all of our observations. From this, we have a single realization of a sample average. It is likely that this sample average will be close to the expected value, but there is a small probability that it will be a significant distance from the expected value. However, we know that this sample average will lie somewhere between 3 and 6.

In order to carry out a Monte Carlo simulation, we now need to repeat this process a large number of times. To illustrate this particular process, I have repeated the process 250,000 times. This repeated process allows us to find an experimental distribution, which is plotted here, along with the normal distribution.

Figure 15.6 illustrates the histogram of the sample averages achieved in the 250,000 trials, with a normal curve plotted over the top. Overall, the distribution of our sample means appears almost identical to the normal distribution.

Furthermore, the mean of all of the sample averages is exactly 4.5 (which is the same as the expected value for X), and the variance is equal to $0.015\left(= \frac{0.75}{50}\right)$. We could go further and show that the quantiles of the distribution are exactly the same as would be expected under the normal distribution, but I will leave that exercise for you to attempt yourself.

As we would expect, the variance of the sample average is exactly 1/50th of the size of the variance of the contributing variable, X:

$$\bar{X} \sim N\left(4.5, \frac{0.75}{50}\right)$$

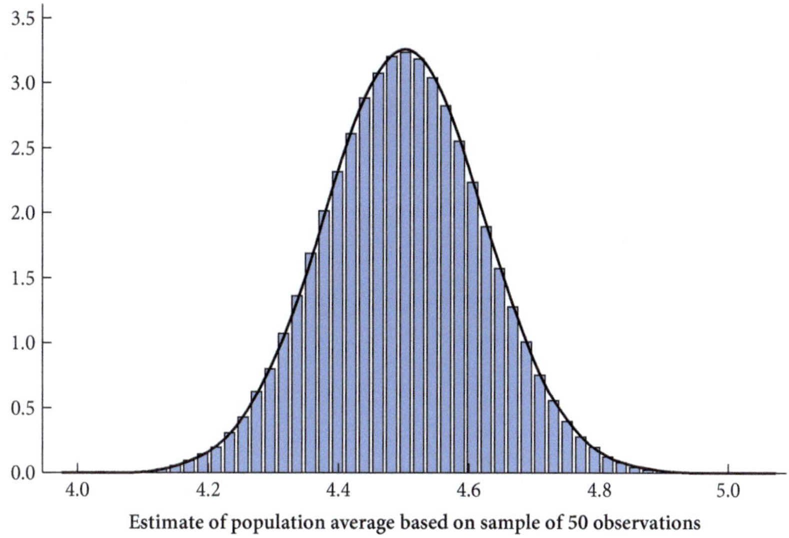

Figure 15.6 Distribution of sample means when randomly sampling 50 observations from the uniform distribution.

15.3 Mean squared error

So far, we have seen that estimators can be unbiased or biased. However, when we estimate a population parameter, we only see a single realization of the estimate. Due to sampling variation, all estimators have a variance. Depending on the variance of the estimator, we could gain an estimate that is a long way from the true population parameter.

Figure 15.7 illustrates the distribution of four separate estimators. We often need to choose estimators based upon their properties. In each instance, the population parameter that is being estimated is equal to 5. In this example, the estimators yield symmetric distributions, meaning that if the peak of the distribution is at the true population parameter being estimated, then this is an unbiased estimator. Because of this, we can see that the estimators used in panels a) and c) are unbiased estimators. That is, on average the estimator produces the 'correct' answer.

For an estimator to be good, we not only want the estimator to produce the correct answer on average, but also for any individual estimate to be close to the true population parameter. For estimator a), you can see that the distribution of the estimates is clustered closely around the true value (5), whereas for estimator c), the estimates are much more spread out. This means that for estimator a), you are much more likely to observe an individual estimate that is close to the true population parameter than for estimator c).

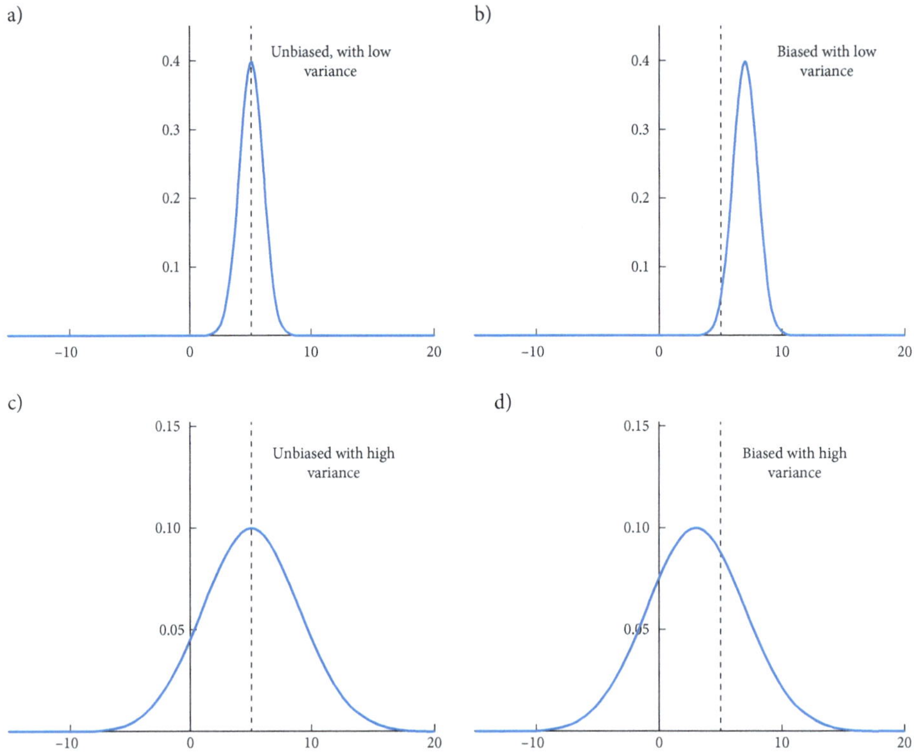

Figure 15.7 Distributions of estimates for four separate estimators; in each case, the population parameter being estimated is equal to 5.

How can we tell what the average of the estimator is?

We can see that in panels a) and c), the estimator is unbiased; that is, the average of the estimator is equal to the true population parameter. We can identify the average of the estimator because:

a) The distribution of the estimator is symmetric.

b) The peak of the distribution is in the middle of the distribution.

Whenever a distribution is symmetric, the middle of the distribution (which for a bell-shaped curve will also be the highest point) will also be the expected value, the **median**, and the **mode** of the distribution.

Similarly, looking at the estimators in panels b) and d), we can see that these are biased estimators—that is, on average, the estimator produces the incorrect answer—but in panel b), the estimator has a small variance, whilst in panel d), the estimator has a large variance. This means that in estimator d), not only will the estimator produce the 'wrong answer' on average, but also when you repeatedly sample from the population, you are likely to gain a lot of variability in your estimators.

The best of these estimators is the estimator in panel a). It is an unbiased estimator, and all of the estimates are close to the true population parameter being estimated. That is, it is also an efficient estimator.

This leaves the question of which of the other estimators we would prefer.

It is uncontroversial to say that the least favoured estimator would be the one in panel d). It is a biased estimator, and it has a high variance, so there is a high likelihood that any given estimate will be a long way from the true population parameter, and even if we repeatedly sampled from the population, the average of the estimates would not be equal to the true population parameter.

This leaves the estimators in panels b) and c). Even though the estimator in panel c) is unbiased, it often produces estimates that are a long way from the true population parameter. For the sake of illustration, let's define an inaccurate estimate (or an estimate that is a long way from the true population parameter) as one that is either 5 above or 5 below the true population parameter.

There is a high probability that you gain an estimate that is 5 above the true population parameter, or 5 below the true population parameter. This probability is represented by the shaded area in panel a) of Figure 15.8. If we compare the likelihood of gaining an estimate a long way away from the true population parameter for the biased estimator with a small variance (panel b) of Figure 15.8), you can see that even though the estimator is biased, the likelihood of gaining an estimate a long way from the true population parameter is very low.

As such, if we are relying on a single estimate, we might prefer a biased estimator with a small variance over an unbiased estimator with a large variance. This is because, on average, the biased estimator may make a smaller error in terms of the estimate of the population parameter. However, we need a way of measuring the average error.

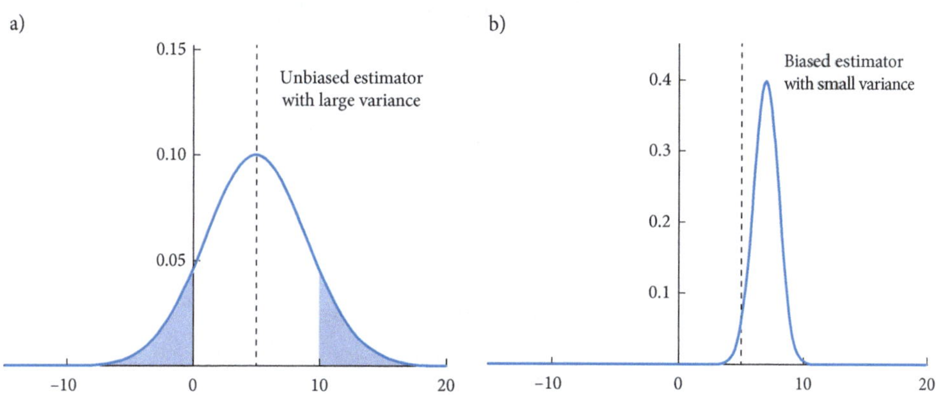

Figure 15.8 Representing the probability of gaining an estimate a long way from the true population parameter.

15.3.1 Constructing the mean squared error

In Section 15.3, we discussed that, in order for an estimator to be a good estimator, we wanted any given estimate of a population parameter to be close to the true population parameter being estimated.

As such, we need to construct a measure of how good an estimator is, and an intuitive way to do this would be to examine how far, on average, the estimator is away from the true population parameter being estimated. In this section, we will introduce a measure of how big, on average, is the error that an estimator makes when estimating a population parameter.

To motivate this, let's begin with an example. Suppose you flip a (fair) coin, but instead of the outcomes being 'heads' or 'tails', let's allocate the outcome as 1 if the coin lands heads upwards and 0 if the coin lands tails upwards. We will flip the coin twice and find the arithmetic mean of the outcomes. The mean is an estimator of the expected value in the population. So, if you gained two tails, you would score $(0, 0)$, and the average would be 0. Similarly, if you gained a head and a tail, you would score $(1, 0)$, and gain an average of $\frac{1+0}{2} = 0.5$.

When you flip the coin twice, the possible outcomes are (0,0), (0,1), (1,0), (1,1), each with probability ¼. If we calculate the average of the outcome in each case, these will be 0, 0.5, 0.5, and 1, respectively (see Table 15.3).

We can easily calculate the expected value of this simple estimator, by finding the sum of the averages, weighted by their individual probabilities:

$$= 0 \times 0.25 + 0.5 \times 0.25 + 0.5 \times 0.25 + 1 \times 0.25 = 0.5$$

We can write down the probability mass function for our estimator, along with the size of the error made in each case. We know that the true expected value would be equal to 0.5 (see Table 15.4).

Table 15.3 Probability distribution when flipping two coins

Outcomes	Mean average	Probability
(0,0)	0	0.25
(0,1)	0.5	0.25
(1,0)	0.5	0.25
(1,1)	1	0.25

Table 15.4 PMF of our estimator

Estimate of population average	'Error'	Probability
0	−0.5	0.25
0.5	0	0.5
1	0.5	0.25

- If your estimate is equal to 0.5, then the size of the error is 0.
- If the estimate is 1, then you have overestimated the true population average by 0.5.
- If the estimate is 0, then you have underestimated the true population average by 0.5.

Now, if we simply found the average of these errors for an unbiased estimator, we would always find that the average error was equal to zero. This is because for an unbiased estimator, some of the estimates will be below the true population parameter (i.e. a negative error), and some of the estimates will be above the true population parameter (i.e. a positive error). This is illustrated for our example in Figure 15.9.

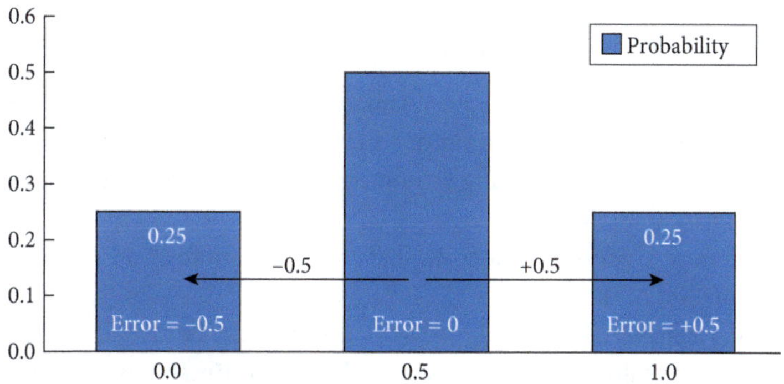

Figure 15.9 Distribution of estimates using the sample mean when flipping a coin twice.

To gain a measure of the average error, we need a mechanism to ensure that the 'size' of the error is always positive. To do this, we will use a similar trick to the one we used when constructing the variance of a random variable; that is, we will square the error so that we can find the average of something that is always positive.

In other words, we will construct the MSE, which is the expectation of the square of the difference between the estimator and the true population parameter being estimated:

$$MSE = E[(\hat{\mu} - \mu)^2]$$

Let's apply this to the example we have just seen. We will need to square the error made by the estimator. Since the true value of μ is equal to 0.5, when $\hat{\mu} = 1$, we overestimate the parameter by $\hat{\mu} - \mu = 1 - 0.5 = 0.5$. Therefore the square of the error is equal to $0.5^2 = 0.25$. Since the estimator creates discrete estimates, we can do this for all of the possible outcomes (see Table 15.5).

Table 15.5 PMF of the average squared error

Estimate of population average	*Error*	*Error*^{2}	Probability
0	−0.5	0.25	0.25
0.5	0	0	0.5
1	0.5	0.25	0.25

The average of these squared errors is then the MSE; that is, we can weight each of the errors squared by the relevant probability:

$$
\begin{aligned}
MSE = E[(\hat{\mu} - \mu)^2] &= P(\hat{\mu} = 0) \times (0 - 0.5)^2 + P(\hat{\mu} = 0.5) \times (0.5 - 0.5)^2 \\
&\quad + P(\hat{\mu} = 1) \times (1 - 0.5)^2 \\
&= 0.25 \times (-0.5)^2 + 0.5 \times (0)^2 + 0.25 \times (0.5)^2 \\
&= 0.25 \times 0.25 + 0.5 \times 0 + 0.25 \times 0.25 = 0.125
\end{aligned}
$$

Thus, in this example the average square of the error, or the MSE, is equal to 0.125.

15.3.2 How does the mean squared error relate to a 'good' estimator?

Since we normally only consider a single estimate of a population parameter, based upon a single sample of data, we want an estimator where every individual realization will be close to the true population parameter being estimated; that is, we want the estimator, on average, to produce a relatively small error.

In order to choose a 'good' estimator, in that case, we want to choose an estimator which produces the smallest MSE.

The method we have used in the previous section can be useful when dealing with relatively simple estimators, but for instance, where an estimator is a continuous random variable, it can be very complicated calculating the MSE through this route. However, it is possible to prove that the MSE can be rewritten as the sum of the square of the bias of the estimator, and the variance of the estimator:[2]

$$MSE(\hat{\mu}) = bias(\hat{\mu})^2 + var(\hat{\mu})$$

That is, the MSE is simply equal to the square of the bias of the estimator, plus the variance of the estimator. Intuitively, this provides a link between the average size of the error, and our two measures of 'goodness' of the estimators. Ideally, we want an estimator to be unbiased and have a small variance. If that is true, then the (square of the) bias will be equal to zero, and the variance will be small, so the MSE will also be small.

Worked example 15.1: Finding the mean squared error of the sample mean

Suppose that we randomly sample n independent and identically distributed observations from a random variable, X, where $E(X) = \mu_X$ and $var(X) = \sigma_X^2$.

We know that, since the observations are randomly drawn from the population, and are *iid*, the sample mean is an unbiased estimator of μ_X. That is:

$$E(\overline{X}) = E\left(\frac{1}{n}\sum_{i=1}^{n} X_i\right) = \mu_X$$

[2] This is proved in the appendix.

It follows from this that the bias is equal to zero. $bias = E(\overline{X}) - \mu_X = \mu_X - \mu_X = 0$. Similarly, we know that the variance of the sample mean is given by:

$$var(\overline{X}) = \frac{\sigma_X^2}{n}$$

Based on this, the MSE is just equal to the square of the bias, plus the variance:

$$\begin{aligned} MSE(\overline{X}) &= bias^2 + var(\overline{X}) \\ &= 0 + \frac{\sigma_X^2}{n} = \frac{\sigma_X^2}{n} \end{aligned}$$

Worked example 15.2: Using a different estimator

Suppose that you are trying to estimate the average wages within the population. You sample n independent and identically distributed observations from the population, where the true (unknown) average wage is μ_Y, and the true (unknown) variance of wages is equal to σ_Y^2. We assume that each observation is randomly drawn from the population such that $E(Y_i) = \mu_Y$, and $var(Y_i) = \sigma_Y^2$.

Since the observations are independent and identically distributed, it also follows that $cov(Y_i, Y_j) = 0$ for all $i \neq j$. We use a simple estimator, $\hat{\mu}$, to estimate the population average, where:

$$\hat{\mu} = \left(\frac{1}{n-1}\right)\sum_{i=1}^{n} Y_i$$

The easiest way to find the MSE is to, separately, calculate the bias of the estimator and the variance of the estimator, and combine these to construct the MSE. The bias of $\hat{\mu}$ is just the difference between the expectation of our estimator and the true population parameter being estimated:

$$bias(\hat{\mu}) = E(\hat{\mu}) - \mu$$

To calculate $E(\hat{\mu})$, we merely need to find:

$$E(\hat{\mu}) = E\left(\left(\frac{1}{n-1}\right)\sum_{i=1}^{n} Y_i\right)$$

Since the $\frac{1}{n-1}$ is just a constant multiplier, we can take it outside of the expectation:

$$\Rightarrow E(\hat{\mu}) = \frac{1}{n-1} E\left(\sum_{i=1}^{n} Y_i\right)$$

Secondly, since the expectation of a sum is just equal to the sum of expectations, we can rewrite $E(\sum_{i=1}^{n} Y_i)$ as the sum of the expectations, $\sum_{i=1}^{n} E(Y_i)$:

$$\Rightarrow E(\hat{\mu}) = \frac{1}{n-1}\left(\sum_{i=1}^{n} E(Y_i)\right)$$

Similarly, since the observations are *iid* observations, randomly sampled from the population, $E(Y_i) = \mu_Y$ for all i:

$$\Rightarrow E(\hat{\mu}) = \frac{n}{n-1}\mu_Y$$

The bias is then just the difference between the expected value of our estimator, less the true population parameter being estimated; that is, $bias = E(\hat{\mu}) - \mu$

$$\Rightarrow bias(\hat{\mu}) = \left[\frac{n}{n-1}\right]\mu_Y - \mu_Y = \left[\frac{\mu_Y}{n-1}\right]$$

To calculate the variance, we use a similar argument:

$$var(\hat{\mu}) = var\left(\left(\frac{1}{n-1}\right)\sum_{i=1}^{n} Y_i\right)$$

Since the $\frac{1}{n-1}$ is just a constant multiplier, we can take it outside of the variance (and square it):

$$= \left(\frac{1}{n-1}\right)^2 var\left(\sum_{i=1}^{n} Y_i\right)$$

The variance of a sum is just equal to the sum of the variances, plus all of the covariance terms:

$$= \left(\frac{1}{n-1}\right)^2 \left[\sum_{i=1}^{n} var(Y_i) + 2\sum_{i=1}^{n-1}\sum_{j=i+1}^{n} cov(Y_i, Y_j)\right]$$

Since the observations are *iid* $cov(Y_i, Y_j) = 0$, so:

$$var(\hat{\mu}) = \left(\frac{1}{n-1}\right)^2 \times n \times \sigma_Y^2 = \frac{n\sigma_Y^2}{(n-1)^2}$$

Now, to calculate the MSE:

$$\begin{aligned} MSE(\hat{\mu}) &= bias(\hat{\mu})^2 + var(\hat{\mu}) \\ &= \left(\frac{\mu_Y}{n-1}\right)^2 + \frac{n\sigma_Y^2}{(n-1)^2} fa \\ &= \frac{\mu_Y^2 + n\sigma_Y^2}{(n-1)^2} \end{aligned}$$

If there were another estimator, which had a lower MSE, then we would prefer to use that estimator. In fact, since we've seen, in the previous example, that the MSE for the sample mean is just given by:

$$MSE(\overline{Y}) = \frac{\sigma_Y^2}{n}$$

for any value of n it will be the case that:

$$\frac{\sigma_Y^2}{n} < \frac{\mu_Y^2 + n\sigma_Y^2}{(n-1)^2}$$

It therefore follows that $MSE(\bar{Y}) < MSE(\hat{\mu})$. That is, the MSE of the sample mean (which we examined in Worked example 15.1) will always be smaller than the MSE of this new estimator.

15.4 Consistency of estimators and the mean squared error

We have just seen that, provided our sample is based on n randomly sampled, *iid* observations from a population, then the MSE of the sample mean, as an estimator of the population average, is:

$$MSE(\bar{X}) = \frac{\sigma_X^2}{n}$$

We can see that, as the sample size gets larger, just as the variance will get smaller, it will also be the case that the MSE will get smaller.

Intuitively, this suggests that eventually, when the sample size gets large enough, the MSE might converge towards zero; that is, the average error of an estimator tends towards zero. More formally, we might expect that the *limit* as the sample size tends towards infinity of the MSE of the sample mean tends towards 0:

$$\lim_{n \to \infty} MSE(\bar{X}) = 0$$

If the MSE of an estimator does converge towards zero as the sample size tends towards infinity, then we can say that the estimator is a **consistent estimator**.

To illustrate this, let's consider an example. Suppose that we randomly sample n independent and identically distributed observations of a random variable X, such that $E(X) = \mu_X$ and $var(X) = \sigma_X^2$. We will use an estimator, $\hat{\mu}_1$, to construct an estimate of the population average, μ.

$$\hat{\mu}_1 = \left[\frac{1}{n-1}\right]\sum_{i=1}^{n} X_i$$

Now, let's begin our analysis with a **Monte Carlo simulation**, to examine the properties of this estimator, as the sample size gets larger. We will construct our population such that $X \sim N(10, 4)$, and examine the distribution of estimates that we would obtain when we construct our estimates based upon samples of size $n = 20, 50, 100,$ and $1{,}000$. Each Monte Carlo simulation is based upon 250,000 trials.

Figure 15.10 shows the distribution of estimates generated from $\hat{\mu}_1$ based on different sample sizes. The true expected value, $\mu = 10$, is marked on with a dotted line. Looking at panel a), we can see that as we move from a sample size of 20, to 50, to 100, two things

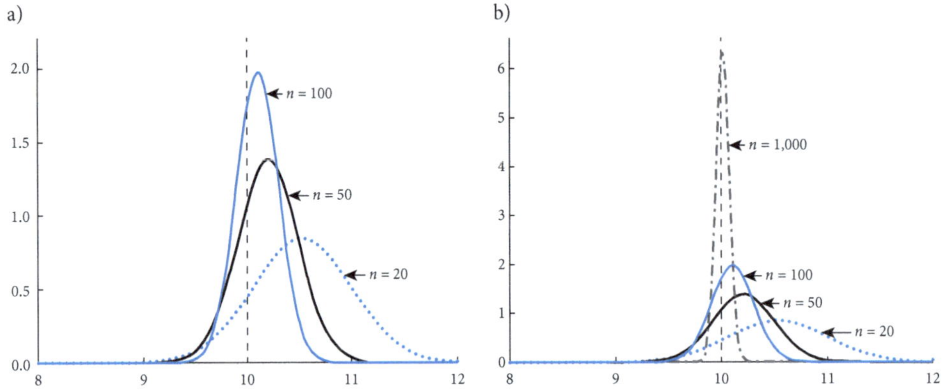

Figure 15.10 Distribution of estimates from $\hat{\mu}_1$ based on different sample sizes.

occur. Firstly, and most obviously, as the sample size gets larger, the spread of the estimates (i.e. the variance) gets smaller.

Secondly, the centre of the distribution moves leftwards, towards the true expectation. This suggests that, as the sample size gets larger, the average of the estimates is getting closer and closer to the true population average of $\mu = 10$. This is even more obvious in panel b) of Figure 15.10, whereby, once we are basing our estimates on 1,000 observations from the population, the centre, or the peak, of the distribution is only very slightly to the left of the true population average.

We saw, in the previous section, that this estimator was a biased estimator, and the size of the bias was given by:

$$bias(\hat{\mu}_1) = \left[\frac{\mu_X}{n-1}\right]$$

In this simulation, $\mu_X = 10$, and so the bias would be equal to $\frac{10}{19}, \frac{10}{49}$, and $\frac{10}{99}$ for $n = 20, 50,$ and 100, respectively. That is, we can see that the bias is getting smaller as the sample size gets larger. This means that the average of the estimates gets closer to the true population parameter as the sample size gets larger. As n gets very large, this bias will tend towards zero.

Similarly, the variance was equal to:

$$var(\hat{\mu}_1) = \frac{n\sigma_X^2}{(n-1)^2}$$

Again, it is relatively simple to see that, as n gets larger, whilst the n on the numerator will get larger, $(n-1)^2$ on the denominator will get larger much more quickly, and so the variance will also tend towards zero.

More formally, we saw that the MSE is given by:

$$MSE(\hat{\mu}_1) = \frac{\mu_X^2 + n\sigma_X^2}{(n-1)^2}$$

This will be a consistent estimator if $\lim_{n\to\infty} MSE(\hat{\mu}_1) = 0$. That is if:

$$\lim_{n\to\infty}\left(\frac{\mu_X^2 + n\sigma_X^2}{(n-1)^2}\right) = 0$$

Now, evaluating the limit of the MSE looks difficult, as both the numerator and the denominator will tend towards infinity. However, we can appeal to L'Hôpital's rule, to show that, in this case, as the sample size tends towards infinity, the MSE will tend towards zero. Therefore, this estimator is a consistent estimator.

L'Hôpital's rule

As an aside, you will often find yourself appealing to L'Hôpital's rule when evaluating what happens to the MSE as a sample tends towards infinity. If you are interested in finding the limit:

$$\lim_{n\to a}\frac{f(n)}{g(n)}$$

either $f(a)$ and $g(a)$ are equal to 0 or are both infinite, then the limit will be the same as:

$$\lim_{n\to a}\frac{f(n)}{g(n)} = \lim_{n\to a}\frac{f'(n)}{g'(n)}$$

In the example:

$$\lim_{n\to\infty}\left(\frac{\mu_X^2 + n\sigma_X^2}{(n-1)^2}\right)$$

Both $(\mu_Y^2 + n\sigma_Y^2)$ and $(n-1)^2$ will converge towards infinity as $n \to \infty$, and so we can use L'Hôpital's rule and differentiate both the top and the bottom with relation to n, giving us:

$$\lim_{n\to\infty}\left(\frac{\mu_X^2 + n\sigma_X^2}{(n-1)^2}\right) = \lim_{n\to\infty}\left(\frac{\sigma_X^2}{2(n-1)}\right)$$

Now, we can see that the numerator is a constant, and the denominator will converge to infinity. Anything divided through by infinity will be zero, and so the limit of the MSE will also be equal to zero.

We can also think about the limit of the MSE by thinking about the impact on both the bias and the variance as the sample size tends towards infinity. Since the MSE is just equal to:

$$MSE = bias^2 + variance$$

If both the bias and the variance converge towards zero as the sample size tends towards infinity, then the estimator can be said to be consistent.

This allows us to define two additional concepts, the **asymptotic bias** and the **asymptotic variance**. This is just the limit (as the sample size tends towards infinity) of the bias and the variance of the estimator.

In the example, we saw that the bias was equal to $bias(\hat{\mu}_1) = \left[\frac{\mu_X}{n-1}\right]$. The asymptotic bias is then just the limit as $n \to \infty$ of this bias:

$$\lim_{n\to\infty}[bias\,\hat{\mu}_1] = \lim_{n\to\infty}\left[\frac{\mu_X}{n-1}\right] = 0$$

So, the asymptotic bias is just equal to zero.

Similarly, we know that the variance is given by $var(\hat{\mu}_1) = \frac{n\sigma_X^2}{(n-1)^2}$. The asymptotic variance is just the limit of this variance as the sample size tends towards infinity, which again is equal to zero. Intuitively, this helps us to understand consistency. If, as the sample size tends towards infinity, the bias and the variance both converge towards zero, then the estimator is consistent. This tells us that if, as the sample size gets very large, both the bias and the variance tend towards zero, then this means that the estimates achieved will converge towards the true population parameter being estimated.

15.4.1 Showing the sample mean is a consistent estimator

We will repeat the simulation that we carried out in Section 15.5, but this time for the sample mean. If we randomly sample n observations from a population, and calculate the sample mean, does this provide consistent estimates of the population parameter being estimated?

We know that the sample mean is an unbiased estimator, and that the variance is given by $var(\overline{X}) = \frac{var(X)}{n}$. We begin by looking at the distribution of estimates when we simulate 250,000 samples from a population with $E(X) = 10$ and $var(X) = 4$.

The distribution of sample means is illustrated in Figure 15.11. As with the previous example of $\hat{\mu}_1$, the variance of the estimator (i.e. the spread of the estimates) decreases as the

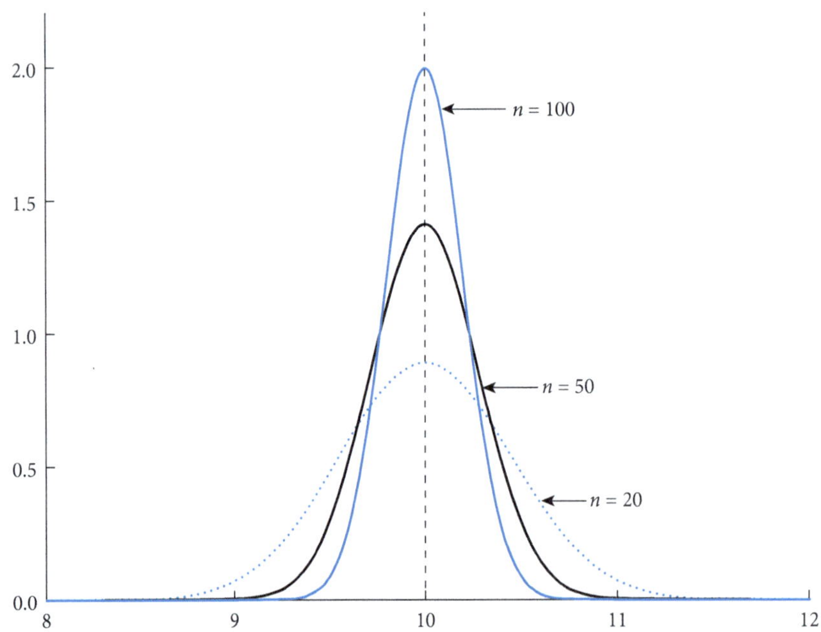

Figure 15.11 Distribution of sample means for $n = 20$, $n = 50$, and $n = 100$.

sample size decreases. However, since the sample mean is an unbiased estimator, each of the distributions is centred on the true population parameter, $\mu = 10$.

We have also seen that when we randomly sample n independent and identically distributed observations of X, the MSE of the sample mean is just equal to:

$$MSE(\overline{X}) = \frac{\sigma_X^2}{n}$$

In this case, the bias is always equal to zero, and so the limit, as the sample size tends towards infinity (or the asymptotic bias), will also be equal to zero. The variance is non-zero, but, as the sample size tends towards infinity, $\lim_{n\to\infty}\frac{\sigma_X^2}{n} = 0$. That is, the asymptotic variance is equal to zero. As the sample size tends towards infinity, the MSE therefore converges to zero, and so the sample mean is a consistent estimator.

KEY DEFINITIONS: CONSISTENT ESTIMATORS—DEFINITION 1

An estimator $\hat{\theta}$ of a population parameter θ is said to be consistent if the MSE converges to zero as the sample size converges towards infinity. That is, an estimator is consistent if:

$$\lim_{n\to\infty} MSE(\hat{\theta}) = 0$$

Note: whilst it is true that if the MSE converges towards zero an estimator is consistent, it is not the case that the opposite is true. That is, it is possible to have an estimator that is consistent, whilst not having **convergence** of the MSE.

15.5 Probability limits and consistency

Whilst an estimator can be said to be consistent if the MSE converges towards zero, there is also a set of estimators which are consistent, but do not satisfy the MSE condition. Formally, this means that, whilst the MSE converging towards zero as the sample size converges to infinity is a sufficient condition for consistency, it is not a necessary condition.

In practice, this means that we may observe estimators where the MSE does not converge towards zero but which are still formally consistent estimators. A more formal definition of a consistent estimator is one whereby, as the sample size gets very large, the probability that any given realization of the estimator is infinitesimally close to the true population parameter being estimated converges towards 1.

Mathematically, if we have an estimator, $\hat{\mu}$, estimating a population parameter, μ, the estimator is consistent if:

$$\lim_{n\to\infty}(P(|\,\hat{\mu} - \mu\,| < \varepsilon)) = 1$$

$\mid \hat{\mu} - \mu \mid$	For a single realization of the estimator, $\hat{\mu}$, this represents the absolute size of the difference between the estimate and the true population parameter being estimated.
ε	Some arbitrarily small value. This could be any (very small) value.

What this means is that as the sample size tends towards infinity, the probability that $\hat{\mu}$ is less than any choice of (very small) ε away from the true population parameter, μ, is equal to 1.

Intuitively, what this means is that if an estimator is consistent, then as the sample size gets very large, the probability that the estimate obtained is extremely close to the true population parameter converges towards 1.

15.5.1 Probability limits

In statistics, we will often talk about a **probability limit** or plim of an estimator. The probability limit of an estimator is the value which the estimator converges to with probability.

That is, suppose that we know that:

$$\lim_{n \to \infty} (P(\mid \hat{\mu} - A \mid < \varepsilon)) = 1$$

then we can say that the estimator $\hat{\mu}$ converges, in probability, to the value A. We can also write this as $plim(\hat{\mu}) = A$. That is, the probability limit of $\hat{\mu}$ is equal to A.

Intuitively, if the $plim(\hat{\mu}) = A$, what this means is that, as the sample size gets very large, the probability that the estimate $\hat{\mu}$ is within an infinitesimally small distance of the value A tends towards 1.

Probability limits and 10,000 hours

It is often said that it takes 10,000 hours to master something – whether it's to be a concert pianist or world champion snooker player (or a statistician).

Suppose that you were a pianist, attempting to play 'Flight of the Bumblebee' by Rimsky-Korsakov. This is a very fast piece, with very fast finger movements. The first time that you attempted to play the piece, it is likely that (if you played it at the correct speed), the probability of you getting all of the notes in the right order would be very low, or more precisely, the probability that the number of mistakes is very very small would be very low.

So, when you first play the piece, the probability of making fewer than ε mistakes might be equal to a very small number (for example, $= 0.000000000000000001$).

$$P(Number\ of\ mistakes < \varepsilon) = Something\ very\ small$$

Here, ε is just an arbitrarily small number of mistakes – it might be 1, it might be 2, but the key thing is that the probability of being within ε notes of playing the piece correctly is very close to zero.

However, as you practise the piece, the probability of you making mistakes will reduce. After you've practised for several hours, the probability of making fewer than ε mistakes will have increased. After you've practised more, the probability will increase a bit more.

Eventually, having practised for long enough, the probability of making fewer than ε mistakes will converge towards 1. This is not to say that you will *always* get all of the notes right, but that the probability will converge towards 1.

$$\lim_{n\to\infty}(P(Number\ of\ mistakes < \varepsilon)) = 1$$

The *plim* operator now gives us another tool to use when evaluating estimators. We saw in previous chapters that an estimator is unbiased if the expectation of the estimator is equal to the true population parameter being estimated.

For example, suppose you are using an estimator $\hat{\mu}$ to estimate the population parameter μ, then the estimator is unbiased if $E(\hat{\mu}) = \mu$. Similarly, an estimator can be said to be consistent if $plim(\hat{\mu}) = \mu$.

Conversely, an estimator is biased if $E(\hat{\mu}) \neq \mu$, and is inconsistent if $plim(\hat{\mu}) \neq \mu$. It should be noted that it is possible for an estimator to converge in probability to the true population parameter, but have the MSE not converge to zero. Therefore, it is important, if you conclude that an estimator is inconsistent, that you examine the probability limit, and don't just rely on the MSE.

Rules of plims

Plims are a little like expectations, and have their own specific rules. However, the rules of plims are much simpler than expectations.

• The plim of a sum of estimators is just equal to the sum of plims.	$plim(A + B) = plim(A) + plim(B)$
• The plim of a constant multiplied by an estimator is just equal to the constant multiplied by the plim.	$plim(aA) = a \times plim(A)$
• The plim of a product of estimators is equal to the product of the plims.	$plim(A \times B) = plim(A) \times plim(B)$
• The plim of a ratio of estimators is equal to the ratio of the plims (provided the denominator exists and is non-zer).	$plim\left(\frac{A}{B}\right) = \frac{plim(A)}{plim(B)}$
• The plim of a function applied to an estimator is equal to the function applied to the plim.	$plim(f(A)) = f(plim(A))$

The intuition behind why these rules work is simply that we are looking at what happens as the sample sizes get very large. By taking the plim overall, we are allowing the sample size to increase across the board. So, if we take the plim of a ratio, we are allowing the sample size to increase on both the numerator and the denominator.

Initially, the plim may appear to be difficult to use, but in reality many problems that we face can be solved using the weak law of large numbers, which simply states that (providing the observations are *iid*), the probability limit of a sample mean is equal to the expectation of the underlying population random variable.

KEY DEFINITION: WEAK LAW OF LARGE NUMBERS

The weak law of large numbers states that if we randomly draw n *iid* observations from a population random variable X, where $E(X) = \mu_X$:

$$plim\left(\frac{1}{n}\sum_{i=1}^{n}X_i\right) = plim(\bar{X}) = \mu_X$$

This means that, by the weak law of large numbers, the sample mean is automatically a consistent of the population average (or expectation).

But what about other estimators? Let's consider a simple example.

Worked example 15.3: Using plims to establish the consistency of a simple estimator

Let's return to the estimator we considered in Worked example 15.2:

$$\hat{\mu}_1 = \left(\frac{1}{n-1}\right)\sum_{i=1}^{n}X_i$$

If we wish to examine whether this is consistent or not, we need to consider what happens to this as the sample size tends towards infinity. That is, we need to take probability limits (or plims). Remember, this is an estimator for the population average (or expectation), where the true population average is equal to $E(X) = \mu_X$.

Before we take plims, it's often useful to examine an estimator, to see if you can write this in terms of sample means. If we were to multiply μ_1 by n/n (which is equivalent to multiplying by 1), then we could rewrite this as:

$$\hat{\mu}_1 = \left(\frac{1}{n-1}\right)\times\frac{n}{n}\sum_{i=1}^{n}X_i = \frac{n}{n-1}\times\frac{1}{n}\sum_{i=1}^{n}X_i$$

So, by using this trick of multiplying by 1, we have rewritten our estimator as a function of the sample mean.

So:

$$plim(\hat{\mu}_1) = plim\left[\frac{n}{n-1} \times \frac{1}{n}\sum_{i=1}^{n} X_i\right]$$

From the rules of plims, the probability limit of a product is equal to the product of the plims. Here we have the product between $\frac{n}{n-1}$ and the sample mean:

$$= plim\left[\frac{n}{n-1}\right] \times plim\left[\frac{1}{n}\sum_{i=1}^{n} X_i\right]$$

From the weak law of large numbers, we know that the probability limit of a sample mean is equal to the expected value. So, since $\frac{1}{n}\Sigma_{i=1}^{n} X_i = \bar{X}$, this means that $plim\left[\frac{1}{n}\Sigma_{i=1}^{n} X_i\right] = E(X) = \mu_X$, so we can rewrite the overall plim as:

$$= plim\left[\frac{n}{n-1}\right] \times \mu_X$$

The final step is to deal with the probability limit of $\frac{n}{n-1}$. Because this is only a function of n, and doesn't depend on the values of X observed, this is not a probabilistic entity; that is, it is not a random variable. The probability limit is thus the same as the standard limit.

Intuitively, as n gets very large, then $n - 1$ will get very close to n, so $\frac{n}{n-1}$ will converge towards 1. We could similarly show, analytically, using L'Hôpital's rule that this converges to 1.

$$= 1 \times \mu_X = \mu_X$$

So, without having to calculate the MSE, we have shown that this estimator is consistent.

KEY DEFINITION: CONSISTENT ESTIMATORS—A NECESSARY AND SUFFICIENT DEFINITION

An estimator $\hat{\theta}$ of a population parameter θ is said to be consistent if the estimator converges *in probability* to the true population parameter as the sample size tends towards infinity:

$$plim(\hat{\theta}) = \theta$$

Conversely, an estimator is inconsistent if the estimator does not converge in probability:

$$plim(\hat{\theta}) \neq \theta$$

Worked example 15.4: The consistency of estimators of the population variance

In the previous chapter, we saw that, if we observed n *iid* observations from a population, X, the following estimator, $\hat{\sigma}^2$ is a biased estimator of the population variance, σ_X^2:

$$\hat{\sigma}^2 = \frac{1}{n}\sum_{i=1}^{n}(X_i - \bar{X})^2$$

However, is this estimator consistent? The variance of this estimator is difficult to calculate, so trying to evaluate whether this is a consistent estimator using the MSE approach becomes very tricky. However, it is relatively straightforward to evaluate the consistency of this estimator using the probability limits approach:

$$plim(\hat{\sigma}_2) = plim\left(\frac{1}{n}\sum_{i=1}^{n}(X_i - \overline{X})^2\right)$$

The first thing that we can do here is that we can treat the plim as two parts:

$$plim\left(\frac{1}{n}\sum_{i=1}^{n}(X_i - \overline{X})^2\right) = plim\left(\frac{1}{n}\sum_{i=1}^{n}(X_i - plim(\overline{X}))^2\right)$$

This follows, because we are essentially letting the sample size tend towards infinity. This means that the sample size affecting $\overline{X}$ will also tend towards infinity. We can use the weak law of large numbers, which tells us that $plim(\overline{X}) = E(X)$. Thus, we can rewrite the overall plim as:

$$= plim\left(\frac{1}{n}\sum_{i=1}^{n}(X_i - E(X))^2\right)$$

We have a second sample mean now—by definition, the function in the plim is just equal to the sample mean of $(X - E(X))^2$. Thus, we can use the weak law of large numbers for a second time, and can write that this is equal to:

$$= E\left[(X - E(X))^2\right]$$

However, this is just the definition of the variance of X:

$$var(X) = \sigma_X^2 = E\left[(X - E(X))^2\right]$$

Therefore, since $\hat{\sigma}^2$ converges in probability to the true population variance (which is being estimated), we can say that $\hat{\sigma}^2$ is a consistent estimator of the population variance, σ_X^2.

Similarly, we could have calculated the MSE of $\hat{\sigma}^2$, and shown that this converges to zero, as the sample size tends towards infinity. However, the maths of calculating the variance of this estimator is a little trickier.

Exercise

We know that the estimator used in this example is a biased estimator of the population variance. We know that an unbiased estimator of the population variance is:

$$s_{n-1}^2 = \left(\frac{1}{n-1}\right)\sum_{i=1}^{n}(X_i - \overline{X})^2$$

It is relatively straightforward, using the same method as used in Worked example 15.4, to show that s_{n-1}^2 is also a consistent estimator. That is, it will be the case that:

$$plim(s_{n-1}^2) = \sigma_X^2$$

I will leave it as an exercise for you to prove this relationship.

15.5.2 Why can we not conclude inconsistency if the MSE does not converge?

The strict definition of inconsistency is that the estimator does not converge (with probability) to the true population parameter being estimated.

In the vast majority of cases, if an estimator is consistent, then the MSE will converge towards zero. However, it is possible that an estimator which doesn't have convergence in the MSE could still be consistent.

To examine this, let's consider a (very strange) example.

Suppose that you had an estimator $\hat{\theta}$ of some population parameter θ. You observe n *iid* random observations from the population. For some very strange reason, this estimator has a discrete probability distribution function, and only ever takes two values:

$$\hat{\theta} = \begin{cases} \theta, & P(\hat{\theta} = \theta) = \dfrac{n-1}{n} \\ \theta + n^2, & P(\hat{\theta} = \theta + n^2) = \dfrac{1}{n} \end{cases}$$

Now, in this example, we can't use the weak law of large numbers, but we can observe what happens to the probability that $\hat{\theta}$ is equal to the true population parameter, θ:

$$\lim_{n\to\infty} P(\hat{\theta} = \theta) = \lim_{n\to\infty} \frac{n-1}{n} = 1$$

Remember, the definition of a consistent estimator is one where:

$$\lim_{n\to\infty}\left(P(|\hat{\theta} - \theta| < \varepsilon)\right) = 1$$

In this case, we've shown that as the sample size tends towards infinity, the probability that the difference between the estimate and the true population parameter is equal to zero tends towards 1. Thus, the estimator is unambiguously consistent.

But what about the MSE? The MSE is just equal to the square of the bias added to the variance. Since both $bias^2$ and *variance* are greater than or equal to zero, if **either** does not converge towards zero, then the MSE **cannot** converge towards zero!

To construct the bias, we first find the expectation of our estimator:

$$E(\hat{\theta}) = P(\hat{\theta} = \theta) \times \theta + P(\hat{\theta} = \theta + n^2) \times (\theta + n^2) = \frac{n-1}{n} \times \theta + \frac{1}{n} \times (\theta + n^2)$$
$$= \theta + n$$

The bias is just equal to the difference between the expectation of the estimator and the true population parameter. That is:

$$bias = E(\hat{\theta}) - \theta = (\theta + n) - \theta = n$$

Thus, the estimator, on average, over-estimates the true population parameter by n. Thus, as the sample size gets larger, the size of the bias **also** gets larger. In fact, this is an extreme example, as the bias will tend towards $+\infty$ as the sample size converges towards infinity. Thus, without even calculating the variance of the estimator, we can tell that the mean square error will **also** be infinite. So, the estimator is consistent, **but** the MSE does **not** converge towards zero.

This is a very strange example, but it illustrates the possibility that an estimator can be **consistent**, whilst also having an MSE that does **not** converge towards zero. In reality, it is unlikely that you will ever come across an estimator that behaves in this way, **but** you should be prepared for the possibility.

	$plim(\hat{\theta}) = 0$	$plim(\hat{\theta}) \neq 0$
$\lim_{n\to\infty} MSE(\hat{\theta}) = 0$	Estimator is consistent	Impossible
$\lim_{n\to\infty} MSE(\hat{\theta}) \neq 0$	Estimator is consistent	Estimator is inconsistent

Summary

In the last two chapters, we've seen two key measures of 'accuracy' of estimators: the unbiasedness of estimators and the consistency of estimators.

It should be noted that an unbiased estimator is not necessarily consistent, and similarly a consistent estimator is not necessarily unbiased.

Unbiasedness refers to what happens when we repeatedly use the estimator to estimate the population parameter, using different samples from the population. An estimator is unbiased if on average the estimator gives the correct estimate of the population parameter. However, even if an estimator is unbiased, it is possible that any individual estimate may be a long way away from the true population parameter being estimated.

Consistency on the other hand relates to what happens when the sample size becomes very large. If an estimator is consistent, then it converges (in probability) to the true population parameter being estimated. An estimator can be both biased (in small samples) and consistent. All this means is that (when sample sizes are small), on average the estimator provides the wrong value for the population parameter being estimated. However, as the sample size gets very large, the estimates obtained converge (in probability) to the true population parameter. An example of an estimator that is both biased and consistent is $\hat{\sigma}^2$, the biased estimator of the population variance we saw earlier in the chapter.

KEY DEFINITIONS

Concept	Definition
Unbiasedness	An estimator $\hat{\theta}$ of a population parameter θ is unbiased if: $E(\hat{\theta}) = \theta$
Bias	The size of the bias is the difference between the expected value of the estimator and the true population parameter: $bias = E(\hat{\theta}) - \theta$
Asymptotic bias	The asymptotic bias is the limit of the bias, as the sample size tends towards infinity: $= \lim_{n \to \infty} bias = \lim_{n \to \infty} \left[E(\hat{\theta}) - \theta \right]$
Efficiency of an estimator	An estimator is more efficient if the variance, $var(\hat{\theta})$ is smaller.
Consistent estimators	An estimator is consistent if it converges, in probability, to the true population parameter: $plim(\hat{\theta}) = \theta$ Equally, if the limit of the MSE of the estimator is equal to zero as n tends towards infinity, then the estimator is consistent: $\lim_{n \to \infty} MSE = 0$

Appendix

Deriving the variance of the sample mean

Suppose that we randomly sample n independent and identically distributed observations X_i from a population, where $E(X_i) = \mu_X$ and $var(X_i) = \sigma_X^2$ for all i, where μ_X and σ_X^2 are the expectation and variance of the population random variable X.

The sample mean is calculated as:

$$\overline{X} = \frac{1}{n}\sum_{i=1}^{n} X_i$$

We wish to evaluate the variance of $\overline{X}$, so we will need to appeal to the rules of variances we saw earlier in this book:

$$var(\overline{X}) = var\left(\frac{1}{n}\sum_{i=1}^{n} X_i\right)$$

Using the rules of variances, we know that the variance of a random variable multiplied by a constant is equal to the square of the constant multiplied by the variance of the random variable $\left(var(aX) = a^2 var(X)\right)$:

$$\Rightarrow var(\overline{X}) = \frac{1}{n^2} var\left(\sum_{i=1}^{n} X_i\right)$$

Remember that the variance of a sum of random variables is equal to the sum of the variances, plus all of the covariance terms—for example, $var(X_1 + X_2) = var(X_1) + var(X_2) + 2cov(X_1, X_2)$. In this case $\sum_{i=1}^{n} X_i$ is a little more complicated than $X_1 + X_2$. When writing down the covariance terms, we simply need to think about all of the possible combinations of i and j.

For example, if we were looking at $var(X_1 + X_2 + X_3)$, this would be equal to:

$$\begin{aligned} &var(X_1 + X_2 + X_3) \\ &= var(X_1) + var(X_2) + var(X_3) \\ &\quad + cov(X_1, X_2) + cov(X_1, X_3) \\ &\quad + cov(X_2, X_1) + cov(X_2, X_3) \\ &\quad + cov(X_3, X_1) + cov(X_3, X_2) \end{aligned}$$

Now, since the order of the variables in a covariance doesn't matter (e.g. $cov(X_1, X_2) = cov(X_2, X_1)$), we can see that all of the covariance terms appear twice. As such, we can rewrite this variance as:

$$\begin{aligned} &= var(X_1) + var(X_2) + var(X_3) \\ &\quad + 2 \times [cov(X_1, X_2) + cov(X_1, X_3) \\ &\quad + cov(X_2, X_3)] \end{aligned}$$

Now, just examining the covariance terms, we know that there are three variables being combined. We can see that the first term in the covariances takes the values 1 and 2. Representing the covariance as $cov(X_i, X_j)$:

- When $i = 1$, j takes the values 2 and 3 $(cov(X_1, X_2), cov(X_1, X_3))$
- When $i = 2$, j only takes the value 3

We can represent this in double summation notation:

$$[cov(X_1, X_2) + cov(X_1, X_3) + cov(X_2, X_3)] = \sum_{i=1}^{2} \sum_{j=i+1}^{3} cov(X_i, X_j)$$

What this notation means is that we are going to take the value $i = 1$ to 2. For each of those i terms, we will consider the covariance with all of the js from $i+1$ to 3. So for $i = 1$, we will consider the covariance with $j = 2$, and $j = 3$. Similarly, for $i = 2$, we would consider the covariance with $j = 3$.

So:

$$var(X_1 + X_2 + X_3) = \sum_{(i=1)}^{3} var(X_i) + 2\sum_{i=1}^{2}\sum_{j=i+1}^{3} cov(X_i, X_j)$$

We can rewrite the previous term, using the double summation notation, as:

$$\Rightarrow var(\bar{X}) = \frac{1}{n^2}\left(\sum_{i=1}^{n} var(X_i) + 2\sum_{i=1}^{n-1}\sum_{j=i+1}^{n} cov(X_i, X_j)\right)$$

Explaining the double summation notation

Students are often confused by the double summation notation we have used here. To explain, consider the following:

Taking the sum for all values of i from $i=1$ to $i=n-1$. For example, if $n=10$, we would take the sum from $i=1$ to $i=9$.

$$\sum_{i=1}^{n-1}\sum_{j=i+1}^{n} cov(X_i, X_j)$$

We are taking the sum of the covariances here, taking into account all of the relevant combinations of i and j.

For each value of i you take the sum from $j=i+1$ to n. E.g, if $i=4$, we would take the sum from $j=5$ to $j=n$.

For example, if $n = 4$, then the summation would expand out to:

$$\begin{aligned}\sum_{i=1}^{n-1}\sum_{j=i+1}^{n} cov(X_i, X_j) &= \sum_{i=1}^{3}\sum_{j=i+1}^{4} cov(X_i, X_j)\\ &= cov(X_1, X_2) + cov(X_1, X_3) + cov(X_1, X_4)\\ &\quad + cov(X_2, X_3) + cov(X_2, X_4)\\ &\quad + cov(X_3, X_4)\end{aligned}$$

So, when $i = 1$, we combine with $j = 2, 3$, and 4, when $i = 2$, with $j = 3$ and 4 and when $i = 3$, with $j = 4$.

Since the observations are *iid*, it follows that $cov(X_i, X_j) = 0$ for all $i \neq j$. Therefore, all the covariance terms vanish, leaving us with:

$$\Rightarrow var(\bar{X}) = \frac{1}{n^2}\left(\sum_{i=1}^{n} var(X_i)\right)$$

From our assumptions, $var(X_i) = \sigma_X^2$:

$$\Rightarrow var(\overline{X}) = \frac{1}{n^2}\left(\sum_{i=1}^{n}\sigma_X^2\right) = \frac{n\sigma_X^2}{n^2} = \frac{\sigma_X^2}{n}$$

Proving the equality of the two forms of the MSE

When we are using an estimator, $\hat{\mu}$ of a population parameter, μ, the MSE is defined as:

$$MSE = E((\hat{\mu} - \mu)^2)$$

We can rewrite this, by adding and subtracting $E(\hat{\mu})$ as:

$$\begin{aligned} MSE &= E(\hat{\mu} - E(\hat{\mu}) + E(\hat{\mu}) - \mu)^2 \\ &= E((\hat{\mu} - E(\hat{\mu})) + (E(\hat{\mu}) - \mu))^2 \end{aligned}$$

Then, if we square the brackets, we will have a $(\hat{\mu} - E(\hat{\mu}))^2$ term, a $(E(\hat{\mu}) - \mu)^2$ term, and two times the cross-product, $(\hat{\mu} - E(\hat{\mu}))(E(\hat{\mu}) - \mu)$:

$$\Rightarrow MSE = E((\hat{\mu} - E(\hat{\mu}))^2 + (E(\hat{\mu}) - \mu)^2 + 2(\hat{\mu} - E(\hat{\mu}))(E(\hat{\mu}) - \mu))$$

We can take advantage of the rules of expectations, and break this expression down into three separate expectations:

$$\Rightarrow MSE = E[\hat{\mu} - E(\hat{\mu})]^2 + E[(E(\hat{\mu}) - \mu)^2] + 2E(\hat{\mu} - E(\hat{\mu}))(E(\hat{\mu}) - \mu)$$

Now, by definition, we can write down the first two terms, because:

- The variance of $\hat{\mu}$ is just equal to $var(\hat{\mu}) = E(\hat{\mu} - E(\hat{\mu}))^2$.
- Similarly, the bias is defined as $bias = E(\hat{\mu}) - \mu$. The bias is also a constant, so the expectation of the bias will just be equal to the bias!

$$\begin{aligned} \Rightarrow MSE &= var(\hat{\mu}) + E[bias^2] + 2E(\hat{\mu} - E(\hat{\mu}))(E(\hat{\mu}) - \mu) \\ &= var(\hat{\mu}) + bias^2 + 2E(\hat{\mu} - E(\hat{\mu}))(E(\hat{\mu}) - \mu) \end{aligned}$$

Now, the final term (the cross-product terms) just need to be multiplied out, giving us:

$$= var(\hat{\mu}) + bias^2 + 2 \times E[\hat{\mu}E(\hat{\mu}) - E(\hat{\mu})^2 - \mu\hat{\mu} + \mu E(\hat{\mu})]$$

Again, taking advantage of the rules of expectations, we can split this up into four separate expectations. However, note that $E(\hat{\mu}), E(\hat{\mu})^2, \mu$ are all constants. As such, this can be written as:

$$\begin{aligned} &= var(\hat{\mu}) + bias^2 + 2 \times [E(\hat{\mu})E(\hat{\mu}) - E(\hat{\mu})^2 - \mu E(\hat{\mu}) + \mu E(\hat{\mu})] \\ &= var(\hat{\mu}) + bias^2 + 2 \times [(E(\hat{\mu})^2 - E(\hat{\mu})^2) + (\mu E(\hat{\mu}) - \mu E(\hat{\mu}))] \\ &= var(\hat{\mu}) + bias^2 + 2 \times [0 + 0] \\ &= var(\hat{\mu}) + bias^2 \end{aligned}$$

An Introduction to Statistical Testing

16

Learning outcomes for this chapter

By the end of this chapter you will be able to:

- Describe the problem that sampling variation causes for making conclusions about statistical estimates
- Explain the concepts behind standard, critical-value-based statistical tests
- Carry out statistical tests with two-tailed tests
- Carry out one-tailed tests, and recognize the circumstances when one-tailed tests are appropriate
- Calculate p-values relating to simple statistical tests.

Mathematical tools

- Simple arithmetic

Introduction

Statisticians often get a raw deal from the general public. Whether it's Mark Twain writing about lies, damned lies, and statistics, or politicians stating that the country has 'had enough of experts', these sorts of statements undermine the important work that statisticians do. However, often, this lack of confidence in statistics comes from a misunderstanding about what statistics can actually tell us.

Because of sampling variation, there will always be variation in estimates. Therefore, one statistician may tell you that their estimate of the average wage of full-time workers in the UK is £610 per week, whilst another (using a different sample of the same population, but an equally valid method) could provide an estimate of £650 per week. It is this sort of variation that can lead the public to believe that statisticians merely manipulate statistics to tell the story that they want to tell.

It is perfectly possible for both of these estimates to be valid, but at the same time they cannot both be the truth; this is simply the nature of statistics. Because we don't observe the entire population, we rarely know anything with certainty. We can only make conclusions about the population based upon probabilities.

In this section, you will not learn how to manipulate statistics to tell a particular story. You will instead learn how to interpret statistics, and how to perform statistical tests.

Revision of important definitions

In Chapter 14, we introduced a number of definitions that we will build upon in this chapter.

1. Estimator

An estimator is a mathematical operation that is applied to an observed sample of data to provide an estimate of a population parameter. For example, the sample mean is often used as an estimator for the expected value in the population.

2. Estimate

An estimate is a single realization of an estimator, using a single sample, taken from the population. The estimate will provide us with an estimate of the population parameter being estimated. For example, we might use the (sample mean) average earnings from a sample to estimate the expected (average) earnings in the population.

3. Population parameter

A population parameter is simply a (fixed) characteristic of the population, which is often unknown. We apply an estimator to a sample of data from the population to gain an estimate of the unknown population parameter. Population parameters include the expected value, the variance, and the range of the random variable in the population.

4. Sampling variation

Sampling variation is the phenomenon that means that every time you take a (random) sample from a population, you will observe different individuals, meaning that the estimates we observe will vary across samples.

Because of sampling variation, an estimator is itself a random variable, with an expected value, a variance, and an overall distribution.

16.1 What is statistical testing for? The problem of sampling variation

Statisticians begin with hypotheses about a population, and then use estimates based upon samples of the population to test whether those hypotheses are likely to be true (or not). For example, a statistician may believe that the average wages in the economy are the same for men and women, or that on average 40 per cent of the population go to university, or that on average red cars are faster than blue cars.

In later chapters, we will talk about how we can test hypotheses about the relationship between different groups in the population, but let's begin by thinking about testing hypotheses about average earnings in the economy. We might begin with a very strong belief that the average earnings of full-time workers are £650 per week. To investigate this, we have randomly sampled 100 individuals from the 2019 UK Labour Force Survey, and we will use the sample mean as an estimator for the population average (expectation).

These figures represent the gross weekly wages of 100 randomly sampled, full-time workers from the 2019 UK Labour Force Survey. If we were to calculate the mean average of these 100 wages, by adding together these 100 observations, and dividing by the number of observations, we would gain an average of £661.45:

$$\frac{1}{100}\sum_{i=1}^{100} x_i = \frac{1}{100} \times (1250 + 298 + \ldots + 750 + 462) = 661.45$$

1250	298	462	1288	288	500	1000	846	485	1269
415	531	788	462	1058	1288	492	400	623	365
300	544	317	365	646	1923	808	566	615	308
827	1250	962	415	481	654	360	346	769	538
442	337	392	529	500	673	837	1442	481	508
673	250	519	510	1394	481	760	581	865	750
654	404	462	681	529	942	654	1154	1558	865
469	111	500	481	788	788	1750	577	750	462
500	87	400	508	1464	219	275	325	310	1288
500	423	827	323	712	346	485	1635	590	323

Now, the estimate that we have for the population average is equal to £661.45; this is not the same as our hypothesized value (£650).

- Is this enough to conclude that the average wage is not equal to £650?
- Could we, instead, conclude that the true average wage in the population was equal to £661.45?

The answer to both of these questions is no! To understand why, we need to think back to the concept of sampling variation.

Remember, the sample mean is an estimator of the population average, and the value of £661.45 is merely an estimate of that population average. As this is an estimator, it will also be subject to sampling variation. That is, when we repeatedly take samples from the population we will get different realizations of the sample mean, providing different estimates of the population average.

Table 16.1 Estimates of average wages in the population based on ten separate samples from the UK LFS

Sample	Sample average
1	661.45
2	611.49
3	687.52
4	670.82
5	682.92
6	609.57
7	674.89
8	675.99
9	681.81
10	602.92

To illustrate this, we have repeated the process[1] of randomly sampling 100 full-time workers from the UK Labour Force Survey ten times, to gain ten separate estimates of the population average. These estimates are represented in Table 16.1.

As we can see, every time we take a new sample from the population, we gain a different estimate of the population average wages of full-time workers; the estimates obtained range from £602.92 up to £687.52. These are all estimates of the population average, based on a random sample from the same population, but they cannot all be the true population average.

Based on a single estimate, without gaining more information, we cannot, with any certainty, state what the true population characteristic (in this case the expected value, or population average) is.

As such, we need a methodology to try to interpret what the true population parameter is, based on our observed estimate of the population parameter.

16.2 Statistical testing

Once we have an estimate of the population characteristic, we still cannot be sure what the true population characteristic is. For example, in the previous section, based on the first sample, our estimate of the average gross weekly wage in the population is £661.45. It is highly unlikely that this is the true population average (or expected value), but we can make inferences about the population average wage, based on this estimate.

[1] We saw these estimates in Chapter 14.

Statisticians often begin this process (before even constructing their first estimate) by hypothesizing a particular value for the population characteristic being estimated. In the example, we began by hypothesizing the population average of £650.

The hypothesized value will normally be based on a prior belief about the population parameter. This prior belief might be based on a previously known value of the population parameter, or may be based on a theoretical model. For example, suppose that you know that the average (real) wage last year for full-time workers was equal to £650. This might be a reasonable value to hypothesize what the average real wage this year would be.

Based on this hypothesized value, a statistician would then ask the following question:

> Suppose that the hypothesized value is the true population characteristic. If this were the true population characteristic, is it likely to (randomly) observe the particular estimate we have obtained (or is it very unlikely)?

In order to answer this question, we need to know how the estimates (in this case the sample means) would be distributed, if this hypothesized value were the true population characteristic.

To illustrate this, let's consider an example. Suppose that the true average gross weekly wage in the population was equal to £650 per week. In the example in Section 16.1, we randomly sampled 100 individuals and obtained a sample mean equal to £661.45. If the true population average was £650, would it be likely to have randomly observed a sample mean equal to £661.45?

For simplicity, let's also assume that we know the true standard deviation of gross weekly wages in the population and it is equal to £400.

If we were to randomly sample 100 observations from the population, the most likely outcomes for the sample mean would be close to £650, but because of sampling variation, sometimes we'd get sample means which are a long way away from £650.

Distribution of a sample mean (central limit theorem)

If you randomly sample n observations of a random variable X, with finite expectation, $E(X) = \mu_X$ and variance, $var(X) = \sigma_X^2$, then provided the sample size is large enough (a good rule of thumb is $n \geq 30$), then the sample mean of the n observations will be approximately normally distributed, with expectation equal to μ_X and variance equal to $\frac{\sigma_X^2}{n}$:

$$\overline{X} = \frac{1}{n}\sum_{i=1}^{n} X_i \sim N\left(\mu_X, \frac{\sigma_X^2}{n}\right)$$

By the central limit theorem, we know that, provided the sample size is large enough, the sample mean will be (approximately) normally distributed. So, in this case, where we have 100 observations, and we have hypothesized that $E(X) = 650$, and that $var(X) = 400^2$,

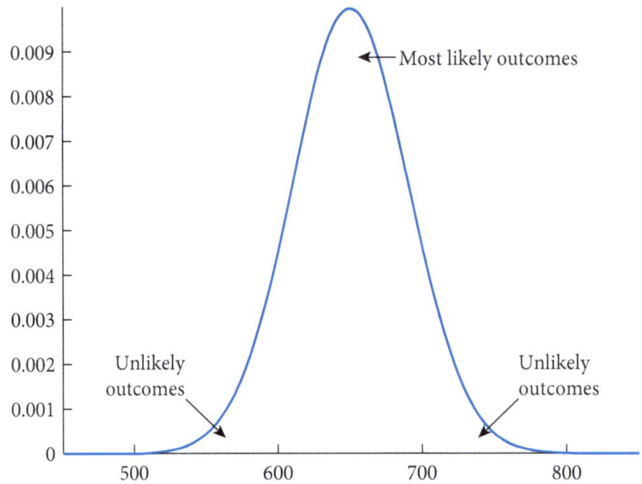

Figure 16.1 Distribution of sample means, if the true population average earnings are £650 per week.

we can write that, if the hypothesized value of the population average is the correct value (i.e. the true population average is equal to 650), then:

$$\bar{X} \sim N\left(650, \frac{400^2}{100}\right)$$

We can see this illustrated in Figure 16.1, which illustrates the distribution of sample means that we would achieve if we repeatedly randomly sampled 100 observations from a population where the expected value was 650, with standard deviation equal to 400.

The most likely outcomes to achieve for the sample mean of gross weekly wages is illustrated by the highest point on the probability density function (PDF). In this example, the most likely outcomes are those close to the population average (£650). Outcomes in the tails of the distribution are much less likely.

In statistical testing, given our hypothesized value of the population characteristic, we would seek to determine, what would be an unlikely outcome for our estimator to achieve randomly? In this example, we would be looking for what values for the sample mean we would be unlikely to achieve randomly if the true population average (expected value) was equal to £650.

If the sample mean that we achieve was an unlikely event, then we would reject our originally hypothesized value, in favour of an alternative hypothesis. However, if the sample mean we observe is not an unlikely event, we would be unable to reject our initially hypothesized value.

16.2.1 What do we class as an unlikely event?

In economics, it is often conventional to consider an unlikely event as one that occurs less than 5 per cent of the time (when our initial hypothesis is true). Applying that to the previous example, we would consider an unlikely event as being in the most extreme 5 per cent of

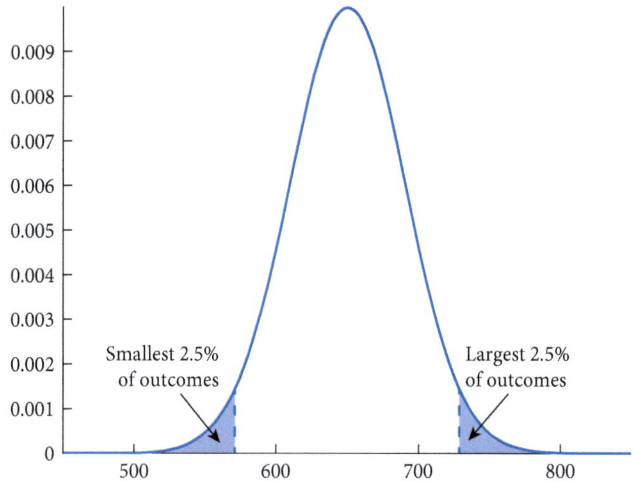

Figure 16.2 Distribution of sample means illustrating the least likely 5 per cent of outcomes.

the distribution. This is illustrated in Figure 16.2. If our hypothesis is true (i.e. $E(X) = 650$), we could randomly get either very large or very small estimates. Because of this, we normally define an unlikely outcome as one that lies in the most extreme 5 per cent of the distribution, split across the two tails of the distribution. So, in this example, the total shaded area represents 5 per cent of the distribution?

When testing a hypothesis, we can begin by examining the estimate we have achieved, and ask whether it lies within the 'unlikely' area; that is, if our hypothesis is true, is it unlikely to achieve an estimate of the magnitude that we have observed.

To apply that to this example, we can plot our estimate onto the distribution. This is illustrated in Figure 16.3. We can see that $\overline{X} = 661.45$ does not lie within the shaded region; that is, we could not define this as a rare event.

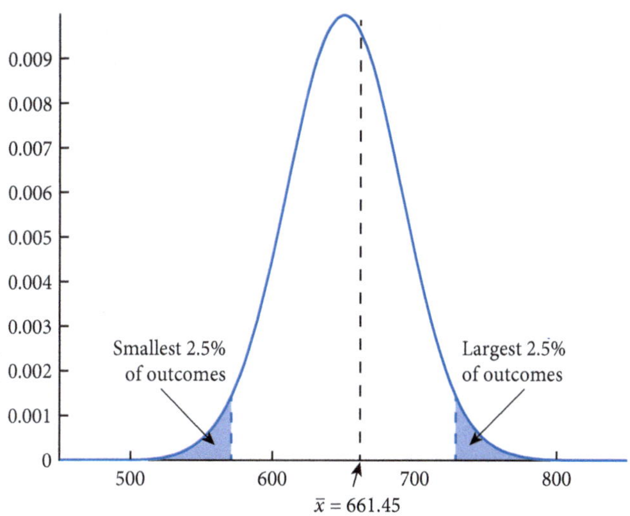

Figure 16.3 Plotting $\overline{x} = 661.45$ onto the distribution of sample means if the true $E(X) = 650$.

In the language of hypothesis testing, this would mean that we do not have enough evidence to reject our initial hypothesis. That is, if the true $E(X) = 650$, it is not unlikely to observe a sample mean equal to £650. Using 5 per cent as our definition of an unlikely event, we would only be able to reject our initial hypothesis if our sample mean was in the shaded area. These shaded areas are known as the rejection region. If we obtained an estimate within those shaded areas we would reject the null hypothesis.

However, there is nothing special about 5 per cent as a definition of an unlikely event. Some researchers will define a rare event as one that occurs less than 10 per cent of the time, others as one that occurs less than 1 per cent of the time. Other researchers will look for much lower probabilities of having achieved the estimate by chance; the probability that we look for depends on the context of the experiment. We will talk about why we choose these probabilities of rare events in later chapters, but for now, let's treat a rare event as one that occurs less than 5 per cent of the time, when our initial null hypothesis is true.

CASE STUDY Application of statistics—The hunt for the Higgs Boson

The Higgs Boson was a theorized particle which explained why particles have the masses that they do.

However, the particle itself could not be directly observed, and so, to prove its existence, physicists at the Large Hadron Collider (LHC) had to carry out a statistical test, based on collisions with other particles in the collider. However, even if the Higgs Boson didn't exist, there were other things that could cause collisions within the collider.

In order to test the existence of the Higgs Boson, the researchers started with the hypothesis that the Higgs Boson didn't exist, and under that hypothesis, looked for an unlikely event (i.e. collisions that would not have been expected to have been observed).

In 2012, when they announced 'proof' of the existence of the Higgs Boson, they had reduced this probability of an unlikely event to approximately 0.00006 per cent. That is, if the Higgs Boson did not exist, the probability that they would have observed the collisions that they did would be less than 0.00006 per cent.

16.2.2 Formal notation

In statistics, when we are defining a problem, we should always begin with what are known as null and alternative hypotheses. The null hypothesis tells us our position ex-ante, and is often denoted as H_0. In the example we have just seen, the null hypothesis was that the average weekly wage in the population was £650. This may not be true, but it is where we begin.

The alternative hypothesis tells us what we are going to test the null hypothesis against, and is often denoted as H_A. In the example we have just seen, the alternative hypothesis was that the average weekly wage was different from £650.

Based on the sample we have observed, and the distribution of the possible test statistics under the null hypothesis, we need to decide which hypothesis best fits the data. The sample mean ($\bar{x}$) of gross weekly wages that we observe is what is known as the test statistic, and is an estimate of the average gross weekly wage in the population.

As mentioned, we normally represent the null hypothesis using the notation H_0, and the alternative hypothesis using the notation H_A. So, in the example we have just seen, our null and alternative hypotheses would be defined thus:

$$H_0 : E(X) = 650$$
$$H_A : E(X) \neq 650$$

Whenever you are conducting a statistical test, it is important to start by defining the null and alternative hypotheses, and consider the distribution of test statistics if the null hypothesis were true:

- If our test statistic (in this case the sample mean) is within the most extreme, say, 5 per cent of the possible test statistics under the null, we say we reject the null hypothesis in favour of the alternative hypothesis.
- If our test statistic is not within the most extreme 5 per cent of the possible statistics, we fail to reject the null hypothesis.[2] This does not mean that the null hypothesis is necessarily true, but merely that we do not have sufficient evidence to reject that null hypothesis.

KEY DEFINITIONS

1. Null hypothesis (H_0)

This is the starting point for your test. This might be based upon your *ex-ante* beliefs about the population parameter you are estimating. In the example, we have begun with a null hypothesis that the average weekly wage is equal to £650.

2. Alternative hypothesis (H_A)

In most cases, the alternative hypothesis will simply be that the null hypothesis is not true. Unless you have very specific reasons to do so, you should always set your alternative hypothesis to be as general as possible. In the example, our alternative hypothesis is simply that the expected wages are not equal to £650.

[2] Many textbooks use the terminology 'accept the null hypothesis'. However, this is not good practice, because stating that we accept the null hypothesis suggests that we are accepting the null hypothesis to be true. It is best practice to think about failing to reject, because, whilst we aren't able to reject that null hypothesis, it still may not be true.

Table 16.2 Percentiles of the standard normal distribution

$\Phi(z)$	0.005	0.01	0.025	0.05	0.1	0.25	0.5	0.75	0.9	0.95	0.975	0.99	0.995
z	−2.58	−2.33	−1.96	−1.64	−1.28	−0.67	0	0.67	1.28	1.64	1.96	2.33	2.58

16.3 Carrying out a simple statistical test

Due to the central limit theorem (provided that we have a large enough sample), the sample means (and many estimators) seen in the previous examples will follow an approximately normal distribution.

Unless you have a computer available, we don't know the cumulative distribution function (CDF) of the general normal distribution (and we can't just integrate the PDF as a simple, analytic, solution for the integral doesn't exist).

However, the distribution of the standard normal distribution is well known; that is, the distribution for $Z \sim N(0,1)$ is well known, and percentiles of the distribution are illustrated in Table 16.2.

Normally, we define the most extreme 5 per cent of outcomes as consisting of the smallest 2.5 per cent of the distribution (in the left-hand tail), and the largest 2.5 per cent of the distribution (in the right-hand tail), as illustrated in Figure 16.4.

Returning to Table 16.2, to find the smallest 2.5 per cent of outcomes, we are essentially looking for the value of z such that $P(Z \leq z) = 0.025$. Remember, $\Phi(z)$ represents the CDF of a standard normal variable, so we $\Phi(z) = P(Z \leq z)$. Thus, to find the smallest 2.5 per cent of outcomes, we need to find the value of z such that $\Phi(z) = 0.025$.

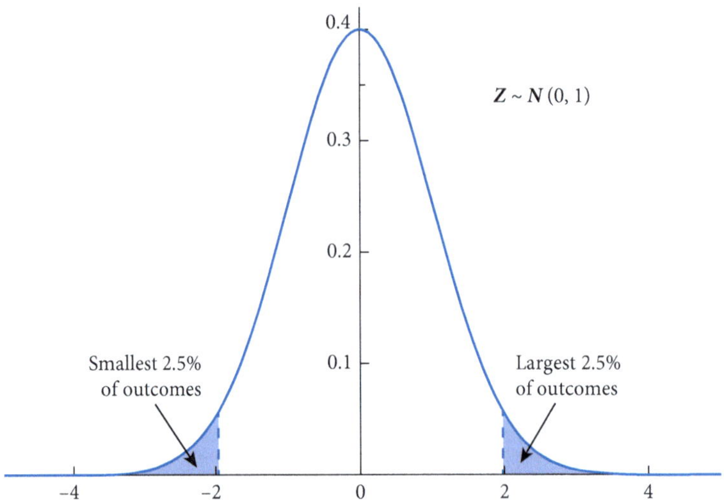

Figure 16.4 Illustrating the most unlikely 5 per cent of outcomes in a standard normal distribution.

From the table, we can see that, when $z = -1.96$, then $\Phi(-1.96) = 0.025$. This means that 2.5 per cent of possible outcomes lie to the left of -1.96. Similarly, if we want to find the largest 2.5 per cent of outcomes, we need to look for $P(Z \geq z) = 0.025$. The tables, however, report $P(Z \leq z)$, and so, we would want to find the value of z that satisfies $P(Z \leq z) = 1 - 0.025 = 0.975$.

You can see, from the table, that $\Phi(1.96) = 0.975$. As such, the largest 2.5 per cent of outcomes will be to the right of $+1.96$. We can see this illustrated in Figure 16.4. As before, the shaded area represents the most extreme 5 per cent of outcomes. You can see that the most unlikely 5 per cent of outcomes are to the right of $+1.96$, and to the left of -1.96.

Thus for a standard normal distribution, we define the shaded area (i.e. with magnitude greater than 1.96) as a rare event to occur randomly (i.e. less than 5 per cent of the time).

In order to apply this to statistical testing, we need to remember that we can standardize any normally distributed variable to a standard normal distribution. That is, for a normally distributed variable X, if we subtract the expected value of X and divide through by the standard deviation of X, we will gain a variable that follows a standard normal distribution, with expectation equal to 0 and variance equal to 1:

$$Z = \frac{X - \mu}{\sigma} \sim N(0,1)$$

We can apply this to the example we saw in the previous section. Let's represent the gross weekly wage of full time employees as a random variable X with expected value, $E(X) = \mu_X$ and variance, $var(X) = 400^2$.

We begin by writing down a null and alternative hypothesis. Again, let's begin with the null hypothesis that average full-time weekly wages in the population is equal to £650, and the alternative hypothesis that full-time weekly wages is not equal to £650.

$$H_0 : E(X) = 650$$
$$H_A : E(X) \neq 650$$

We have randomly sampled 100 **independent and identically distributed** (*iid*) observations of X, and obtained a sample mean as an estimate of the population average of $\overline{X} = 661.45$.

Now, since we have a relatively large sample[3] ($n = 100$), we can apply the **central limit theorem** to find the sampling distribution of the sample means. That is, by the central limit theorem, we know that, provided the observations are *iid* the sample mean of X will be approximately normally distributed, such that:

$$\overline{X} \sim N\left(E(X), \frac{var(X)}{n}\right)$$

Now, when we carry out statistical testing, the first question to ask is what the distribution of our estimator would be if the null hypothesis is true. In this case, we know that $var(X) = 400^2$, and if the null hypothesis is true, then $E(X) = 650$.

[3] Recall that in applying the central limit theorem, provided you have more than about 30 observations, the sample mean will be approximately normally distributed.

Therefore, if the null hypothesis is true (i.e. $E(X) = 650$), then the sample mean will be distributed normally, centred on 650, with variance equal to 400^2 divided by 100:

$$\bar{X} \sim N\left(650, \frac{400^2}{100}\right)$$

Standardizing an estimator

If we have an estimator, $\hat{\mu} \sim N(E(\hat{\mu}), var(\hat{\mu}))$, then we can standardize the estimator in exactly the same way as we do for a general normal distribution. That is, we subtract the expected value and divide through by the standard deviation of the estimator.

Often, you will hear the standard deviation of an estimator being described as the **standard error** of the estimator.

So, for an estimator, $\hat{\mu}$, we can standardize it thus:

$$\frac{\hat{\mu} - E(\hat{\mu})}{\sqrt{var(\hat{\mu})}} \sim N(0,1)$$

Standard error of the sample mean

We know that the **variance** of the sample mean is just given by:

$$var(\bar{X}) = \frac{var(X)}{n}$$

Therefore, the standard error of the sample mean, $s.e.(\bar{X})$, is just given by:

$$s.e.(\bar{X}) = \sqrt{\frac{var(X)}{n}}$$

So, if the null hypothesis is true, we can standardize the sample mean by subtracting the expected value (£650), and dividing through by the standard error of the sample mean:

$$\frac{\bar{X} - E(\bar{X} \mid H_0 \text{ is true})}{\sqrt{var(\bar{X})}} = \frac{\bar{X} - 650}{\sqrt{\frac{400^2}{100}}} \sim N(0,1)$$

We observed a sample mean of £661.45, and we want to know whether this lies within the area we have defined as a rare event:

$$z = \frac{\bar{x} - 650}{\sqrt{var(\bar{X})}} = \frac{661.45 - 650}{\sqrt{\frac{400^2}{100}}} = 0.28625$$

What this tells us is that, if the null hypothesis is true, then $P(\bar{X} \leq 661.45) = P(Z \leq 0.28625)$. We can clearly see, from Figure 16.5, that the standardized z does not lie within the shaded area. We would therefore fail to reject the null hypothesis.

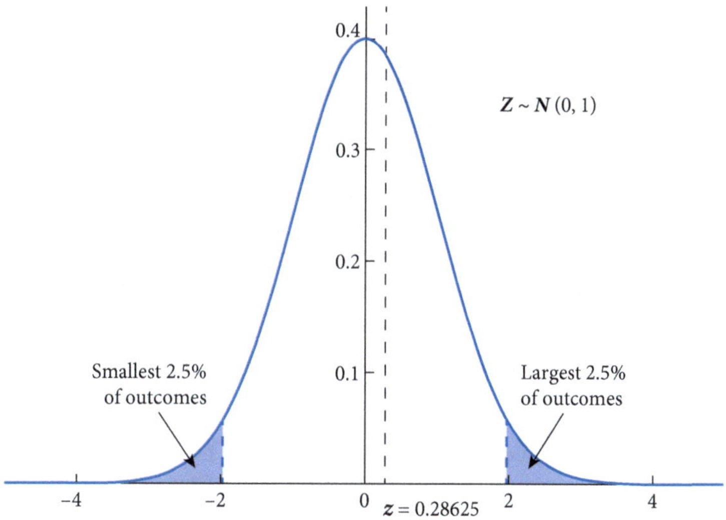

Figure 16.5 Plotting our standardized estimate onto the standard normal distribution.

The shaded area in this diagram is known as the **rejection region** at the 5 per cent significance level. This is the area for which you would reject your null hypothesis. When the null hypothesis is true, you will randomly find a test statistic in this shaded area 5 per cent of the time, and 95 per cent of the time, the test statistic will be in the unshaded area (where you fail to reject the null).

DEFINITION: CRITICAL VALUES

In statistics, we will often refer to critical values. These are the values beyond which we reject our null hypothesis.

We have seen that if we define an unlikely event as one that occurs less than 5 per cent of the time (when the null hypothesis is true), the critical values would be ± 1.96. That is, if the standardized test statistic has a magnitude greater than 1.96, we would reject the null hypothesis.

The critical values change, depending on the definition we use for an unlikely event:

- If we define an unlikely event as one that occurs less than 10 per cent of the time (when the null hypothesis is true), the critical values would be ± 1.64.
- If we define an unlikely event as one that occurs less than 5 per cent of the time (when the null hypothesis is true), the critical values would be ± 1.96.
- If we define an unlikely event as one that occurs less than 1 per cent of the time (when the null hypothesis is true), the critical values would be ± 2.58.

Definition: Significance level of a test

The significance level is just the probability that we define as relating to an unlikely outcome, if the null hypothesis were true:

- If we define an unlikely event as one that occurs less than 10 per cent of the time when the null hypothesis is true, we are testing at the 10 per cent significance level.
- If we define the unlikely event as one that occurs less than 5 per cent of the time when the null hypothesis is true, we are testing at the 5 per cent significance level.
- If we define the unlikely event as one that occurs less than 1 per cent of the time when the null hypothesis is true, we are testing at the 1 per cent significance level.

Some tests will be carried out at the 0.1 per cent significance level, whilst the test for the existence of the Higgs Boson was effectively carried out at the 0.00006 per cent significance level.

16.3.1 Algorithm for carrying out a simple statistical test

As you're gaining confidence with statistical testing, it is often easiest to begin with a simple algorithm that you apply. However, as you progress with statistics, it is important to understand precisely why you are doing at each step. A simple algorithm is illustrated in Figure 16.6.

Worked example 16.1: Simple numerical example

Suppose that we have randomly sampled ten independent and identically distributed observations from a random variable, X. We know that X follows a normal distribution, with variance 1, but we don't know what the true population average (expectation) is. Our prior belief is that the average in the population is equal to zero, and we wish to use our data to test this hypothesis.

We will test this hypothesis at the 10 per cent, 5 per cent, and 1 per cent significance levels.

Our null (and alternative) hypotheses are:

$$H_0 : E(X) = 0$$
$$H_A : E(X) \neq 0$$

The ten observations of X are denoted as:

Observation number	1	2	3	4	5	6	7	8	9	10
Observation of *X*	0.3	−0.1	1.6	3.5	0.2	4.5	2	3	−0.1	2.2

Step 1 Specify hypotheses and significance levels

Write down your null and alternative hypotheses. The null hypothesis will normally be based on some sort of prior belief, or theory. At this stage, you should also normally think about what a reasonable significance level should be. Normally, we specify this at 5% (i.e. we define an unlikely event as one that occurs less than 5% of the time when the null hypothesis is true), but we may specify a 10%, 1%, 0.1% (or even smaller) significance level.

For example, in the example we've just see, our prior belief was that the average wage in the population was £650:

$$H_0: \mu_x = £650$$
$$H_A: \mu_x \neq £650$$

Note: Here, μ_x represents the expected value of X.

Step 2 Collect data

Collect data and construct your estimate of the population parameter you wish to examine using an estimator (e.g. the sample mean is an estimator of the expected value).

For example, we might collect 100 observations of wages, and calculate an estimate $\hat{\mu}_x = \Sigma_{i=1}^{n1} X_i$.

Step 3 Write down the distribution of the estimator under H_0 (IMPORTANT)

Write down the distribution of the estimator used in Step 1, **based on the assumption** that the null hypothesis (H_0) is true.

Often, you will be able to appeal to the central limit theorem, which states that, provided the sample size is large enough, the sample mean will follow a **normal distribution**.

For example, in the example above:

$$\hat{\mu}_x \sim N\left(650, \frac{var(X)}{n}\right)$$

Step 4 Standardize your estimates

If the estimator follows a normal distribution (this will normally be the case), you can standardize the test statistic (again assuming that the null hypothesis is true) by subtracting the expected value of the estimator, and dividing through by the **standard error** of the estimator.

$$Z = \frac{\hat{\mu}_x - E(\hat{\mu}_x | H_0 \text{ is true})}{\sqrt{\left(\frac{var(X)}{n}\right)}}$$

Step 5 Compare with critical values

Having standardized your estimate, you should compare this with the critical values from the normal tables. At the 5% significance level, the critical value is 1.96. If the test statistic obtained in step 4 is larger in magnitude than the critical value, then you would reject the null hypothesis.

If the test statistic is **smaller** than the critical value, you would **fail to reject** the null hypothesis.

Figure 16.6 Simple algorithm for carrying out a statistical test.

In order to test this hypothesis, we need to construct an estimate of $E(X)$. We know that, provided the observations are randomly sampled from the population and *iid*, the sample mean is an **unbiased estimator** for $E(X)$:

$$\overline{x} = \frac{1}{10} \times \sum_{i=1}^{10} x_i = \frac{0.3 - 0.1 + 1.6 + 3.5 + 0.2 + 4.5 + 2 + 3 - 0.1 + 2.2}{10} = 1.71$$

The distribution of our estimator

We know that the underlying random variable X follows a normal distribution. One of the helpful characteristics of normally distributed variables is that, if you combine n independent variables that follow a normal distribution, the **linear combination** of these variables will also follow a normal distribution. In this case, since the sample mean is merely a linear combination of 10 *iid* observations of X_i, it will also follow that the sample mean will be normally distributed.

We know that $var(X) = 1$, and since the observations are *iid*, it also follows that $var(\overline{X}) = \frac{var(X)}{n} = \frac{1}{10}$. If the null hypothesis is true, then $\overline{X} \sim N(0, \frac{1}{10})$.

Important note

In this example, we can write down the distribution of the sample mean only because the underlying random variable, X, follows a normal distribution and, in general, if you construct a new variable as a linear combination of normally distributed variables, then the resulting random variable (here the sample mean) will also be normally distributed.

However, most of the time, when you carry out a statistical test, the underlying random variable will not follow the normal distribution. Instead, provided the sample size is large enough ($n \geq 30$), we normally need to appeal to the central limit theorem, and the sample mean will be (approximately) normally distributed.

In this simple example, as we only have ten observations, if the underlying X were not normally distributed, then the sample mean would not be normally distributed, and it would be much more difficult to carry out a valid statistical test.

Standardizing our test statistic

We have calculated that $\overline{X} = 1.71$. If the null hypothesis were true, then:

$$Z = \frac{\overline{X} - E(\overline{X} \mid H_0 \textit{ is true})}{s.e.(\overline{X})} \sim N(0,1)$$

Since the sample mean is an unbiased estimator for the population expectation, if H_0 is true, it follows that $E(X) = 0$, and so $E(\overline{X} \mid H_0 \textit{ is true}) = E(X \mid H_0 \textit{ is true}) = 0$. Similarly, the standard error of our estimator ($s.e.(\overline{X})$) is just equal to the square root of the variance of the sample mean:

$$s.e.(\overline{X}) = \sqrt{var(\overline{X})} = \sqrt{\frac{1}{10}}$$

Substituting in the numbers gives:

$$z = \frac{1.71 - 0}{\sqrt{\frac{1}{10}}} = 5.4075$$

Compare with critical values

To find the critical values at the 10 per cent, 5 per cent, and 1 per cent significance levels, we would need to look up the critical values in the normal tables (or in Excel). For the 10 per cent critical value, we would want to look up the 95th percentile of the standard normal distribution (as we would define a rare event as occurring in either the largest 5 per cent of outcomes or the smallest 5 per cent of outcomes).

Finding critical values using Microsoft Excel

10 per cent critical value

For the 10 per cent critical value, we would want to look up the 95th percentile of the standard normal distribution (as we would define a rare event as occurring in either the largest 5 per cent of outcomes, or the smallest 5 per cent of outcomes), as shown in Figure 16.7.

In Excel, we can find the 10 per cent critical value using the following formula:

$$= \text{norm.s.inv}\left(0.95\right) = 1.645$$

This provides us with the value of z such that $\Phi(z) = 0.95$; that is, the value of z such that $P(Z \leq z) = 0.95$. This means that 5 per cent of the outcomes lie to the right of $+1.645$. Since the distribution is symmetric, it must also mean that 5 per cent of the outcomes lie to the left of -1.645.

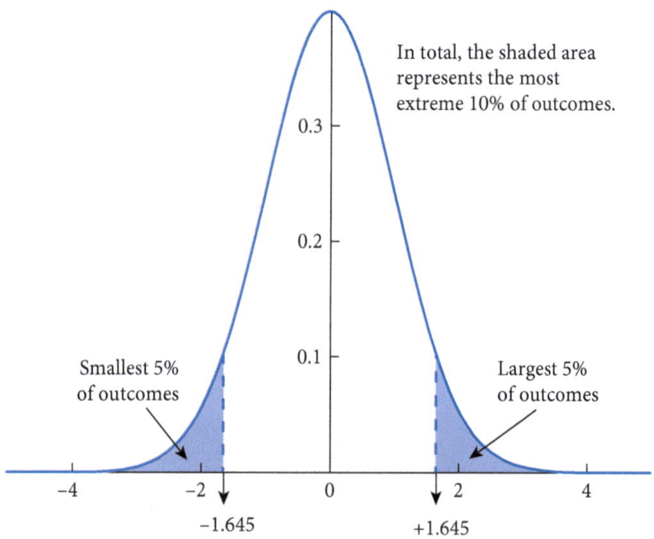

Figure 16.7 Finding the most extreme 10 per cent of outcomes.

5 per cent critical value

For the 5 per cent critical value, we would want to look up the 97.5th percentile of the standard normal distribution (as we would define a rare event as occurring in either the largest 2.5 per cent of outcomes, or the smallest 2.5 per cent of outcomes), as shown in Figure 16.8.

In Excel, we can find the 5 per cent critical value using the following formula:

$$= \text{norm.s.inv}\left(0.975\right) = 1.96$$

This provides us with the value of z such that $\Phi(z) = 0.975$; that is, the value of z such that $P(Z \leq z) = 0.975$. This means that 2.5 per cent of the outcomes lie to the right of $+1.96$. Since

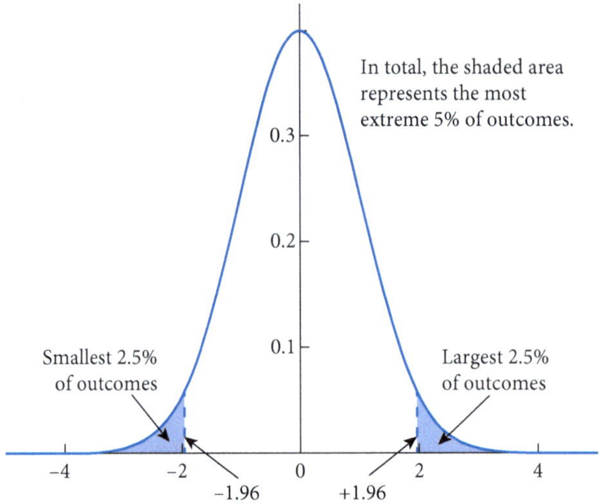

Figure 16.8 Finding the most extreme 5 per cent of outcomes.

the distribution is symmetric, it must also mean that 2.5 per cent of the outcomes lie to the left of -1.96.

1 per cent critical value

For the 1 per cent critical value, we would want to look up the 99.5th percentile of the standard normal distribution (as we would define a rare event as occurring in either the largest 0.5 per cent of outcomes, or the smallest 0.5 per cent of outcomes). See Figure 16.9.

$$= \text{norm.s.inv}\left(0.995\right) = 2.576$$

Since the distribution is symmetric, the upper critical value is $+2.576$, and the lower critical value is -2.576.

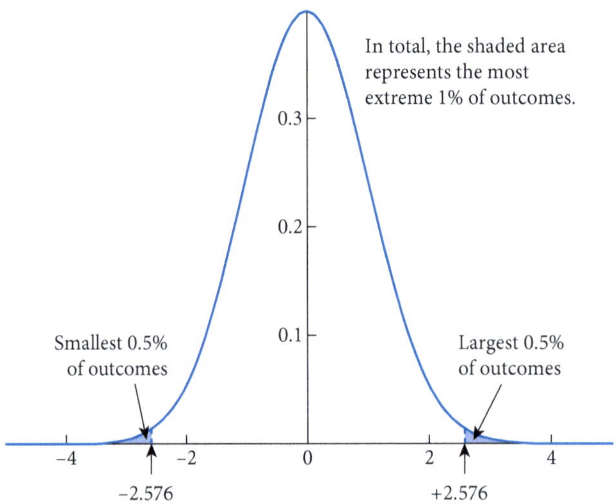

Figure 16.9 Finding the most extreme 1 per cent of outcomes.

Table 16.3 Critical values for our statistical tests at 1, 5, and 10 per cent significance levels

Significance level	Lower critical value	Upper critical value
10%	−1.645	+1.645
5%	−1.960	+1.960
1%	−2.576	+2.576

So that gives us the critical values illustrated in Table 16.3.

In this example, the (standardized) test statistic that we obtained was $z = 5.4075$. The magnitude of the standardized test statistic is larger than the magnitude of the critical value at the 10 per cent (1.645), 5 per cent (1.960), and 1 per cent (2.576) significance levels.

This is illustrated in Figure 16.10, where we can see that our standardized estimate, $z = 5.4075$, lies within the shaded rejection region. We therefore reject the null hypothesis in favour of the alternative hypothesis. What this means, intuitively, is that we have found sufficient evidence to suggest that the null hypothesis is false. We could repeat this exercise at the 10 per cent or 1 per cent significance level, and because the magnitude of our estimate is larger than the critical value (in each case), we would reject the null hypothesis.

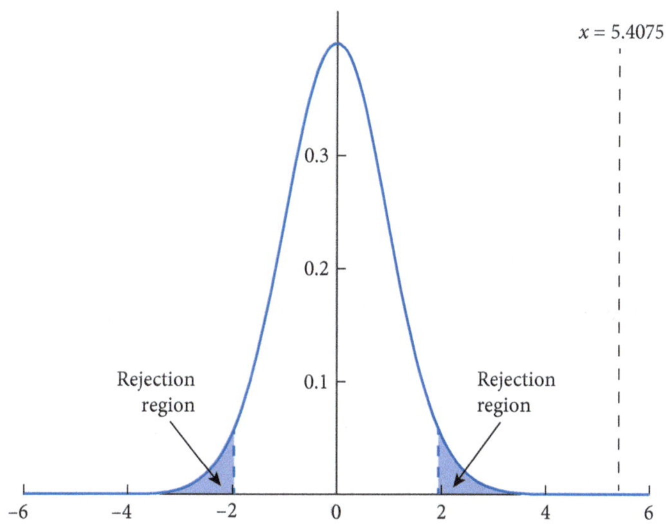

Figure 16.10 Comparing our estimate of $z = 5.4075$ with the 5 per cent critical values.

Common mistakes made by students

In this example, our estimate of the population average was $\overline{x} = 1.71$. We rejected the null hypothesis that $E(X) = 0$, and sometimes students make the error of concluding that the true value of $E(X)$ must be equal to our estimate.

This is incorrect. All that we can conclude, based upon the test, is what is defined in the alternative hypothesis. In this case, the alternative hypothesis is that $E(X) \neq 0$. As such, this is all that we can conclude with any reasonable level of certainty. It is almost certainly not the case that the true population average is equal to 1.71.

16.3.2 What if we don't want to standardize the distribution?

So far, all of our tests have involved standardizing the distribution of our estimator, and looking at whether the (standardized) values are greater than our critical values. However, we can also calculate the rejection regions without first standardizing the distribution. Suppose again that we want to test the hypothesis:

$$H_0 : E(X) = 650$$
$$H_A : E(X) \neq 650$$

We know that in a standard normal distribution, the most extreme 5 per cent of outcomes are less than −1.96, or greater than +1.96. However, because in a standard normal distribution $Z \sim N(0,1)$, ±1.96 relates to the number of standard deviations above or below the expected value. In the wages example we saw earlier in the chapter, we saw that if the null hypothesis were true, then:

$$\bar{X} \sim N\left(650, \frac{400^2}{100}\right)$$

That is, the expected value is equal to 650, and the variance is equal to $\frac{400^2}{100} = 1{,}600$. Since the standard deviation (or standard error) is just the square root of the variance of the estimator, we can easily calculate it:

$$s.e.(\bar{X}) = \sqrt{var(\bar{X})} = \sqrt{1{,}600} = 40$$

So, in this distribution, the most extreme 5 per cent of outcomes will also be within ±1.96 times the standard error of our estimator. If the null hypothesis were true, the upper critical value will be:

$$\text{Critical value} = 650 + 1.96 \times s.e(\bar{X}) = 650 + 1.96 \times 40 = 728.4$$

Similarly, the lower critical value will be:

$$\text{Critical value} = 650 - 1.96 \times s.e.(\bar{X}) = 650 - 1.96 \times 40 = 571.60$$

These critical values are illustrated in Figure 16.11.

You can also find these critical values directly in software such as Microsoft Excel, where the formula =norm.inv(. . .) will calculate cumulative probabilities from any normally distributed variable. Suppose you wanted to find the smallest 2.5 per cent of outcomes ($p = 0.025$) from a distribution with expectation 650 and standard deviation 40, you could use this formula:

$$= \text{norm.inv}\big(0.025, 650, 40\big) = 571.6014$$

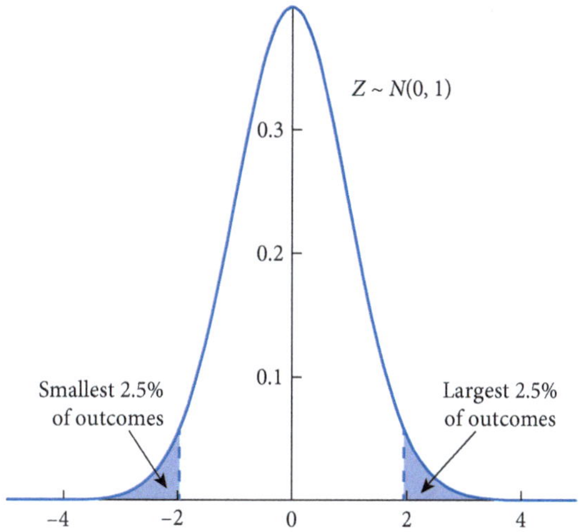

Figure 16.11 Critical values at the 5 per cent significance level.

In the same way, if you wanted to find the largest 2.5 per cent of outcomes, you would want to find the value below which $1 - 0.025 = 0.975$ (or 97.5 per cent) of outcomes lie. Again, Microsoft Excel will do this for you:

$$= \text{norm.inv}\left(0.975, 650, 40\right) = 728.3986$$

16.4 One-tailed tests

So far, whenever we have carried out a test, we have considered that an unlikely outcome could occur in either 'tail' of the distribution.

So, when we are testing at the 5 per cent significance level, we look for the most extreme 5 per cent of outcomes, and this would be made of the smallest 2.5 per cent of outcomes and the largest 2.5 per cent of outcomes (making 5 per cent in total).

However, sometimes, if the null hypothesis is false, it is only possible for us to have outcomes that lie within one of the tails of the distribution. In these cases, we would use what is known as a one-tailed test.

For example, in the examples we have seen previously, where we were testing whether the average wage in the population was £650, if the only possible alternative to the true average being £650 per week is that the true average was greater than £650 per week, then we would use a one-tailed test, and we would treat an unlikely event as being the most extreme 5 per cent of outcomes in the right-hand tail of the distribution.

We can see the difference between the two types of test by comparing Figures 16.12 and 16.13. In Figure 16.12, if you observe an outcome in the shaded area of either tail, you would reject the null hypothesis. However, in Figure 16.13, we can see that we would only reject the null hypothesis if the outcome lies in the right-hand tail. As we will see in Figure 16.14, you could also have a rejection region in just the left-hand tail.

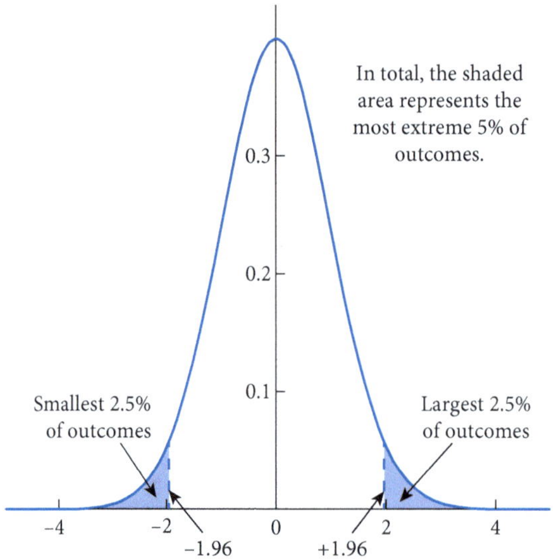

Figure 16.12 Critical values in a two-tailed test.

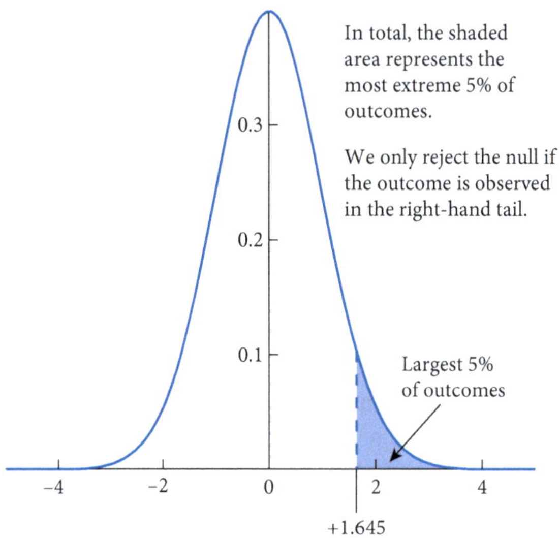

Figure 16.13 Critical values in a one-tailed test (right-hand tail).

We would denote a one-tailed test by using inequality notation. For example, if we wished to test the null hypothesis that the expected wage in the population was equal to £650 against the alternative that the expected wage was greater than £650, then we would denote this as:

$$H_0 : E(X) = 650$$
$$H_A : E(X) > 650$$

Alternatively, we could have a one-tailed test in the left-hand tail of the distribution.

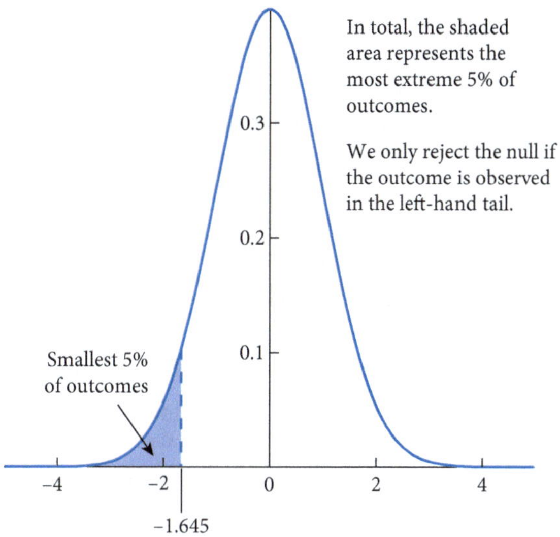

Figure 16.14 Critical values in a one-tailed test (left-hand tail).

In a one-tailed test in the left-hand tail of the distribution, if the null hypothesis is false, it can only be the case that the test statistic is smaller than it would be under the null hypothesis.

For example, if we wished to test the null hypothesis that the average wage in the population was equal to £650 per week against an alternative that the average wage was less than £650, then we would denote this as:

$$H_0 : E(X) = 650$$
$$H_A : E(X) < 650$$

Important statistical health warning

In general, unless there is good reason to believe that the only possibility under the alternative is that the test statistic is larger (or that the only possibility is that the test statistic is smaller), then you should always assume that you begin with a two-tailed test.

In statistics, there are certain classes of tests that are always carried out as one-tailed tests. For example, tests using the **chi-squared distribution** are always carried out using a one-tailed test.[4] The reason for this is that, since this distribution is constructed based on the sum of squares of a standard normal, each of the squared terms must be greater than (or equal to) zero. As such, the extreme outcomes can only exist in the right-hand tail of the distribution.

If you are ever in doubt, if you are testing using the normal distribution, you should err on the side of caution and always use a two-tailed test.

[4] A chi-squared distribution is constructed when we combine the square of n normally distributed variables, with expectation 0 and variance 1.

If $Z_i \sim N(0,1)$ for all i, then: $\sum_{i=1}^{k} Z_i^2 \sim \chi_k^2$

Where χ_k^2 represents a chi-squared distribution, based on k normally distributed variables.

Worked example 16.2: Using a one-tailed test relating to an ice-cream machine

Consider the case of an ice-cream machine which has two settings, large and small. You know that the expected mass of ice-cream under the small setting is 20g (but there is some variability in the actual size of ice-cream that the machine delivers). For the large setting, all you know is that the average serving size is larger than the average serving size for the small setting.

You notice one day that the switch to choose the setting is broken, and appears to be stuck on small, but you don't know whether the machine is actually dispensing small ice-creams, or large ice-creams (so you don't know what price to charge).

The null hypothesis that we have here is that the machine is dispensing small ice-creams (because that's what the switch says it is producing), and thus the expected mass is 20g. The alternative hypothesis is that the machine is producing large ice-creams.

In this case, this is clearly a one-tailed test. The expected mass under the alternative (the large ice-cream setting) can only be higher than the expected mass under the null. Thus, it makes no sense to look for a case when it could be smaller.

We could begin by defining our random variable Y as the mass of ice-creams, and specify our null and alternative hypotheses:

$$H_0 : E(Y) = 20\text{g}$$
$$H_A : E(Y) > 20\text{g}$$

If you sample n ice-creams, and your test statistic lands within the rejection region, then you would reject your null hypothesis, and conclude that the machine is on the large setting. Suppose that you randomly sample 50 ice-creams, and the mean average mass of the ice-cream is $\bar{y} = 22.7$. It is known that the standard deviation of the mass of ice-creams is 10g. We wish to formally test this hypothesis.

By the **central limit theorem**, since the sample size is (relatively) large, the sample mean will be approximately normally distributed, with expectation equal to $E(\bar{Y}) = E(Y)$ and variance equal to $\frac{var(Y)}{50}$. Since the standard deviation of ice-cream masses is known to be 10g, it follows that $var(Y) = s.d.(Y)^2 = 10^2 = 100$. As such, if the null hypothesis is true, then:

$$\bar{Y} \sim N\left(20, \frac{100}{50}\right)$$

Our observed sample mean is $\bar{Y} = 22.7$. We wish to evaluate whether this lies within the rejection region at the 5 per cent significance level. To evaluate this, we will first standardize the test statistic:

$$\frac{\bar{Y} - E(\bar{Y})}{s.e.(\bar{Y})} \sim N(0,1)$$

If the null hypothesis is true, then $E(\bar{Y}) = 20$. As such, we can standardize our estimate:

$$z = \frac{22.7 - 20}{\sqrt{\frac{100}{50}}} = 1.909$$

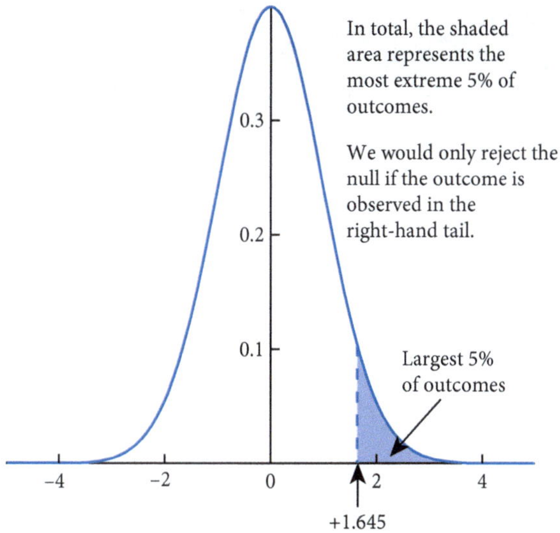

Figure 16.15 The critical value for a one-tailed test.

We know from above that the critical value will be equal to +1.645 (see Figure 16.15). Since the standardized test statistic lies within the rejection region, we can reject the null hypothesis at the 5 per cent significance level. This suggests that the machine is not set on small, but instead is set on large.

Note: As before, you do not know for certain whether it is on the large or small setting, just what the balance of probability tells you!

16.4.1 Differences between one-tailed and two-tailed tests

There are two major differences with one-tailed and two-tailed tests. The first difference is in the alternative hypothesis we use. If, for instance, we have a null hypothesis that, say, $E(Y) = 0$, we would denote this as:

$$H_0 : E(Y) = 0$$

For a two-tailed test, the alternative hypothesis would be that the expectation of Y was not equal to zero. That is, we are allowing for the true expectation to be either greater than or less than 0. In this case, our alternative hypothesis would be:

$$H_A : E(Y) \neq 0$$

In a one-tailed test, under our alternative hypothesis, it might be that if the null hypothesis is false, it is only feasible that the true expected value is greater than 0.[5] In that case, the alternative hypothesis would be:

$$H_A : E(Y) > 0$$

[5] Alternatively, if the only possibility where the null was false was for the expectation to be less than 0, we would denote the alternative hypothesis as:

$$H_A : E(Y) < 0$$

	Two-tailed test	One-tailed test (left-hand tail)	One-tailed test (right-hand tail)
Alternative hypothesis	$H_A : E(Y) \neq 0$	$H_A : E(Y) < 0$	$H_A : E(Y) > 0$
Rejection region	a) 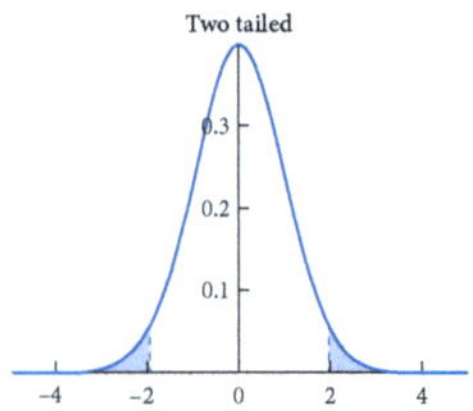	b) 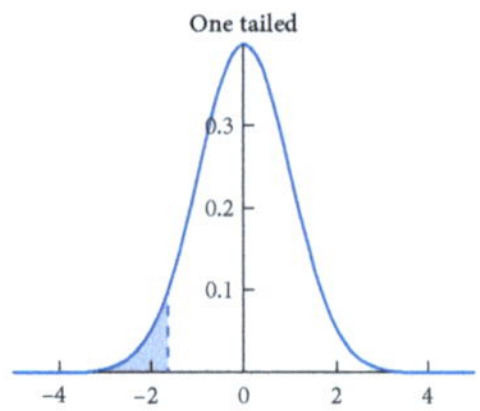	c) 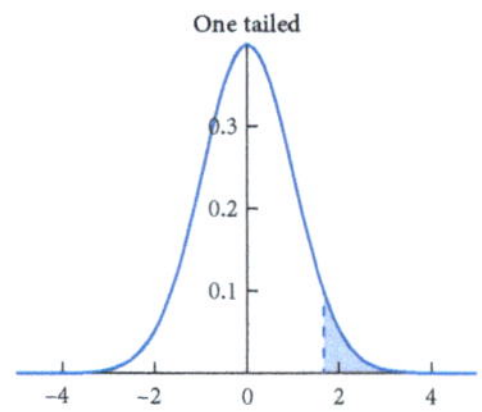
Critical values at:			
10%	±1.645	−1.282	+1.282
5%	±1.96	−1.645	+1.645
1%	±2.576	−2.326	+2.326
0.1%	±3.291	−3.090	+3.090

Figure 16.16 Two-tailed and one-tailed tests.

The second difference between one-tailed and two-tailed tests is the critical values that we use. If we are testing at the 5 per cent significance level, in a two-tailed test, that 5 per cent is split between the two tails of the distribution. However, in a one-tailed test, those 5 per cent of rare events would all appear in a single tail of the distribution.

Suppose that we are testing the null hypothesis that the expected value of Y is equal to 0:

$$H_0 : E(Y) = 0$$

Then we could construct our rejection regions at different significance levels using the critical values in Figure 16.16.

16.5 **P-values**

Historically, statisticians have used critical values at 1 per cent, 5 per cent, and 10 per cent significance levels, say, for carrying out statistical testing. However, with the advent of computers, it has become much easier to assign a value called a p-value (or probability value) to any test statistic that we generate. The p-value tells us the probability of gaining a test statistic of magnitude greater than or equal to the one we have achieved, if the null hypothesis were true.

KEY DEFINITION: P-VALUES

For any given test statistic, there will be a corresponding p-value. The p-value tells you the probability of randomly achieving a standardized test statistic at least as impressive as the one we have achieved, if the null hypothesis were true.

To illustrate this, let's consider the example we considered earlier in the chapter, where we collected 100 observations of individuals' weekly wages, and found an average wage of £661.45. The variance of wages was known to be equal to 400^2.

We wished to use this to test the hypothesis:

$$H_0 : E(X) = £650$$
$$H_A : E(X) \neq £650$$

using a two-tailed test.

To test this hypothesis, we began by standardizing our test statistic, to give a z-statistic:

$$z = \frac{661.45 - 650}{\sqrt{\frac{400^2}{100}}} = 0.28625$$

The p-value is equal to the probability of randomly achieving a z-statistic at least as impressive as the one that we have gained here, if the null hypothesis were true. This is illustrated in Figure 16.17.

Since this is a two-tailed test, if the null hypothesis were actually true, we would be equally likely to randomly gain a test statistic less than −0.28625, or greater than +0.28625.

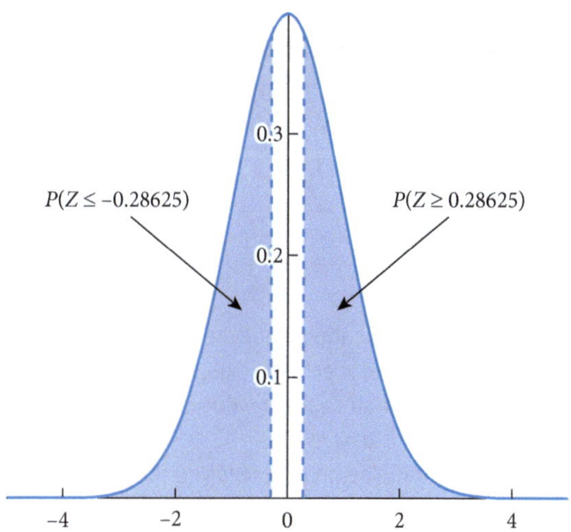

Figure 16.17 Calculating the p-value for $z = 0.28625$.

As such, we look for the probability of randomly gaining a test statistic larger (in magnitude). That is, we would want to know the probability of randomly gaining a z-statistic either less than –0.28625, or greater than +0.28625.

Finding a p-value with Excel

Microsoft Excel can calculate the p-value related to a particular test statistic. If you use the formula:

$= \text{norm.s.dist}\left(-0.28625, \text{true}\right)$

then Excel will report the probability of randomly gaining a test statistic less than or equal to –0.28625:

$P(Z \leq -0.28625) = 0.387343$

However, since this is a two-tailed test, the p-value will be twice this (as you need also to consider $P(Z \geq 0.28625)$. So, the p-value is equal to 0.774687.

In this example, the p-value is equal to 0.774687, and the corresponding sample mean was 661.45—that is, 11.45 above the hypothesized value (650). The p-value tells us that, in this example, if the null hypothesis were true, the probability of randomly achieving a sample mean that was £11.45 away from the expected value (either above or below) would be equal to 0.774687.

That is, if the null hypothesis were true, then 77.4687 per cent of the time, you would obtain a sample mean at least £11.45 above or below the expected value.

To convert this back to thinking about testing with particular significance levels (e.g. 5 per cent significance levels), then if you achieved a p-value less than 0.05, you would also have rejected the null hypothesis at the 5 per cent significance level. For a p-value less than 0.01, you would have rejected the null hypothesis at the 1 per cent significance level.

Bad statistics: p-values

Sometimes, newspapers or other publications indicate that the p-value relates to the probability that the null (or alternative) is actually true.

For example, they might write that 'since the p-value is 0.02, we can say that the probability that the null hypothesis is true is 2%'.

This is an incorrect interpretation. The p-value tells you the probability of gaining a test statistic as large as the one you have achieved, given that the null hypothesis is true.

These statements are not the same thing!

Summary

In this chapter, we have introduced statistical testing. In statistics, we don't know anything for certain, so we need to use statistical tests to make conclusions about population parameters. In statistical testing, we begin by hypothesizing a value for a population parameter, and look for evidence whether we can reject that hypothesis.

However, when a test statistic lies within the rejection region, there are two reasons why that might occur. Firstly, it might be that the null hypothesis is false and the alternative hypothesis is in fact true. However, it might also be that the null hypothesis is true and we have randomly gained a test statistic in the rejection region, and made an error in rejecting the null hypothesis.

In the next chapter, we will formalize the types of errors you can make in statistical testing (often referred to as type 1 and type 2 errors in statistics, or false positives and false negatives in medical trials). We will also introduce statistical testing where we do not know the true variance of the underlying population random variable, and we need to test using both an estimate of the expected value of the population, and an estimate of the variance of the underlying random variable.

17 Errors in Statistical Testing

Learning outcomes for this chapter

By the end of this chapter you will be able to:

- Recognize the possibility of type 1 errors, or false positives in statistical testing
- Recognize the possibility of type 2 errors, or false negatives in statistical testing
- Explain the trade-off that exists between type 1 and type 2 errors
- Evaluate the relative importance between power and size of a statistical test

Mathematical tools

- Simple arithmetic

Introduction

In the last chapter, we introduced the concept of statistical testing. When carrying out a statistical test, we begin by specifying a **null hypothesis**, based on our prior beliefs, and look for evidence to reject (or fail to reject) this null hypothesis.

When we test a hypothesis, we begin by constructing the distribution of test statistics that we would expect to achieve if the null hypothesis were true. Based on this distribution, we can define a **rejection region** as the set of *unlikely* test statistics we could achieve.

When we reject a null hypothesis, it could be for one of two reasons: either the null hypothesis is false, or the null hypothesis is true and we are making a statistical error.

Similarly, when we **fail to reject** the null hypothesis, again, it could be that the null hypothesis is **true**, or, we might be making an error, and in fact the alternative hypothesis might be true.

In this chapter, we will discuss statistical errors, and the trade-offs between different types of errors.

17.1 False positives, or type 1 errors

In statistical testing, the first thing that we need to note is that we never know anything with certainty. We construct tests that begin by assuming that the null hypothesis is true, and if we see an outcome that would have been unlikely (i.e. it lies in the rejection region), we reject the null hypothesis.

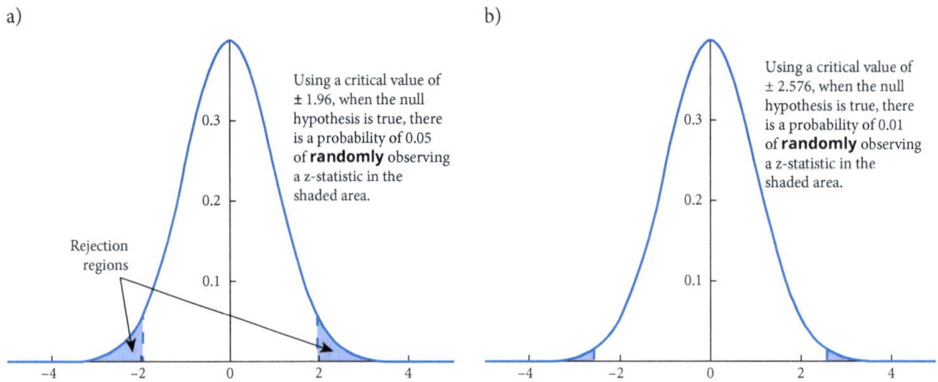

Figure 17.1 The probability of a type 1 error.

However, by convention, economists often define an unlikely event as one that occurs 5 per cent (or less) of the time, when the null hypothesis is true. That means that if the null hypothesis is actually true, there is a probability of 0.05 (or 5 per cent) of rejecting the null. This is an example of a false positive, which statisticians often refer to as a type 1 error (see Figure 17.1).

When we carry out statistical tests, we explicitly control the probability of a type 1 error by choosing the appropriate critical values. For example, with a standard normal distribution, if we chose a critical value of ± 1.96, then, if the null hypothesis were true, we would incorrectly reject that null hypothesis 5 per cent of the time. However, we could reduce that probability by simply increasing the magnitude of critical values.

For example, if, rather than using ± 1.96, we had, instead, used ± 2.58 as our critical values, then if the null hypothesis were true, we would incorrectly reject the null hypothesis 1 per cent of the time.

KEY DEFINITION: TYPE 1 ERROR

A type 1 error occurs when we (incorrectly) reject the null hypothesis, even though the null hypothesis is true. This is often referred to as a 'false positive'.

Statisticians control the probability of a type 1 error by choosing appropriate critical values. The probability of a type 1 error is often known as the 'significance level' or the 'size' of the test.

An example of a false positive would be in the context of a test for a disease, such as **COVID-19** or HIV. The 'null hypothesis' of the test would be that the individual did not have the disease. A false positive (or a type 1 error) would be where a doctor gained a positive test result, even though the individual did not have the disease.

What this means is that the probability of finding a false positive is effectively controlled by the statistician, based upon the critical values that they choose. We can reduce the probability of making a type 1 error (or finding a false positive) in statistical testing by increasing the magnitude of the critical values. This is illustrated in Table 17.1, where we can see that, if we used a critical value of ± 7, that would reduce the probability of a type 1 error to 0.000000000003.

Table 17.1 Probability of type 1 errors, based upon increasingly large critical values

Critical value	Probability of a type 1 error (false positive) if the null hypothesis is true
±3	0.0027
±4	0.00006
±5	0.0000006
±6	0.000000002
±7	0.000000000003

This raises the question of why we don't just choose extremely large critical values. As we will see in the next section, there is a second type of error that we can make in statistics: a false negative (or type 2) error. As we decrease the probability of making a type 1 error, we increase the probability of a type 2 error, so we need to choose critical values that achieve a balance between type 1 and type 2 errors.

TRY IT YOURSELF: THE IMPACT OF CHANGING THE CRITICAL VALUE ON THE PROBABILITY OF A FALSE POSITIVE

Suppose that you chose to use ±1.5 as your rejection region for a statistical test. That is, if you randomly obtained a (standardized) z-statistic either greater than +1.5, or less than −1.5, you would reject your null hypothesis.

You can use Microsoft Excel to calculate the probability of a type 1 error for different critical values that you might choose.

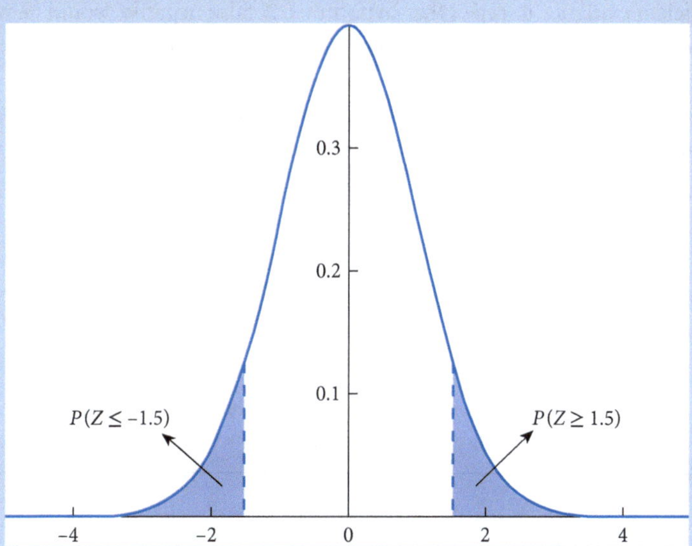

If you use the formula:

$$= \text{norm.s.dist}\left(-1.5, \text{TRUE}\right)$$

then Excel will return the probability of gaining a standardized normal (z-) statistic less than −1.5, $P(Z \le -1.5)$. In order to find the probability of gaining a test statistic either less than −1.5 or greater than +1.5, we would need to multiply this value by 2 (as we need to account for the probability in both tails)

Excel will output the probability 0.066807. This is telling you that:

$$P(Z \le -1.5) = 0.066807$$

Thus, to find the probability of randomly gaining a test statistic less than -1.5, or greater than $+1.5$, we can calculate this probability by multiplying the probability above by 2:

$$P(Z \le -1.5 \cup Z \ge +1.5) = 2 \times P(Z \le -1.5) = 0.133614$$

Therefore, if the null hypothesis is true, and we use a critical value of ± 1.5, then the probability of (falsely) rejecting the null is 0.133614 or 13.3614%.

Repeat this process for critical values of $\pm 1, \pm 3, \pm 4, \pm 8, \pm 10$.

17.2 False negatives, or type 2 errors

False positives are not the only type of errors that we can experience. We can also experience false negatives, or type 2 errors. This is when we fail to reject the null hypothesis, even though the null hypothesis is false.

An example of where these sorts of false negatives might occur would be in medical testing. Medical tests are often forms of statistical test, where the doctor begins with a hypothesis of not having a virus, and then looks whether observable markers (e.g. a blood test) indicate that there is sufficient evidence to reject that hypothesis. A false negative would be where the test tells you that you did not have the virus, even though you were, in fact, infected with the virus.

To illustrate type 2 errors, let's consider the wage example we considered in the previous chapter. Our null hypothesis was that the average weekly wage in the UK was £650, and variance equal to $400^2 = 160{,}000$.

$$H_0: \mu_X = £650$$
$$H_A: \mu_X \neq £650$$

Revision: Distribution of sample means

Suppose that you randomly sample n independent and identically distributed observations from a population with expectation equal to μ_X and variance equal to σ_X^2, and construct the sample mean, $\bar{X} = \frac{1}{n}\sum_{i=1}^{n} X_i$.

Then, by the **central limit theorem**, provided the sample is large enough, the sample mean will follow an (approximately) normal distribution, with expectation equal to μ_X and variance equal to $\frac{\sigma_X^2}{n}$:

$$\bar{X} \sim N\left(\mu_X, \frac{\sigma_X^2}{n}\right)$$

Based on 100 individuals, we used the sample mean of weekly wage as an estimate of the population expectation. If the null hypothesis were true, then, by the central limit theorem, the sample means would follow an (approximately) normal distribution. This distribution is illustrated in Figure 17.2.

$$\bar{X} \sim N\left(650, \frac{160{,}000}{100}\right)$$

The shaded area of Figure 17.2 represents the set of sample means for which we would reject the null hypothesis if that null hypothesis were true. That is, it represents the most unlikely 5 per cent of outcomes for the sample mean if the null hypothesis was true (and represents the rejection region). In this case, the smallest 2.5 per cent of sample means are smaller than 571.60, and the largest 2.5 per cent of sample means would be greater than 728.40. (i.e. we would reject the null hypothesis if we observed a sample mean greater than 728.40, or less than 571.60).

However, if the null hypothesis were false, then the sample means would certainly not follow the distribution in Figure 17.2.

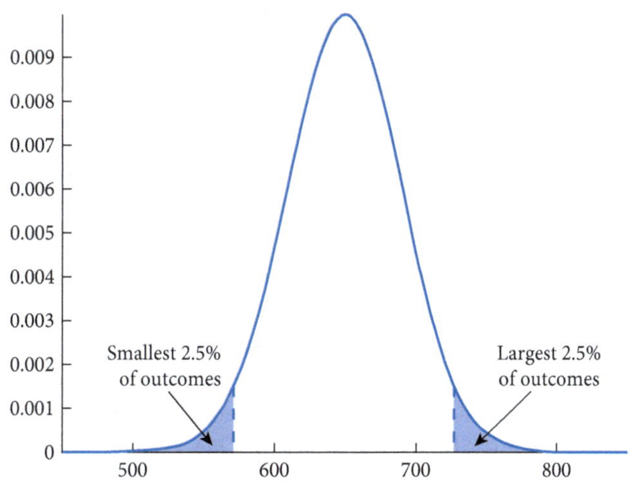

Figure 17.2 Distribution of sample means.

If, for instance, the true population average wage was equal to £700 per week (with the variance unaffected), then the sample means would instead follow a distribution of:

$$\bar{X} \sim N\left(700, \frac{400^2}{100}\right)$$

When we are carrying out a statistical test, we construct the critical values by assuming that the null hypothesis is true, so our rejection regions would be the same as above. That is, we would reject the null hypothesis, $H_0 : \mu_X = 650$ if we achieved a sample mean greater than 728.40, or less than 571.60.

Figure 17.3 illustrates the distribution of sample means if the true average wage was £700 in the population. The shaded area indicates the cases where you (correctly) reject the null hypothesis. However, the unshaded area indicates where you would fail to reject the null hypothesis, even though that null hypothesis is not true. That is, the unshaded area represents the false negative cases, or the cases where we are making a type 2 error.

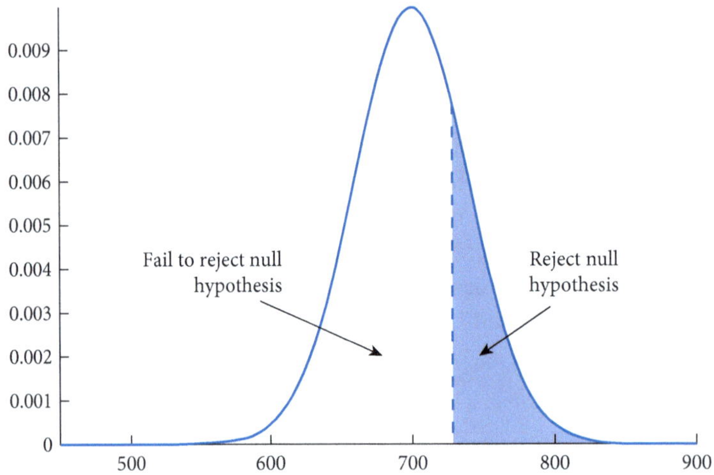

Figure 17.3 The distribution of sample means when the true expected value is equal to £700.

In this example, the null hypothesis is false, so we want a statistical test to reject the null hypothesis. Intuitively, we can see that the cause of the false negative cases is our choice of critical value. In this example, we are only rejecting the null hypothesis when the sample mean is above £728.40 (and a very small proportion of the time when the sample mean is less than 571.60).

We can also calculate this probability, by considering what proportion of the time we would fail to reject the null hypothesis when the true population average is equal to 700. Remember, we fail to reject the null hypothesis when the estimated statistic does not lie within the rejection region—that is, if the estimate lies between 571.60 and 728.40 (see Figure 17.4). So, we wish to find the following probability:

$$P(571.60 \leq \bar{X} \leq 728.40 \mid E(X) = 700)$$

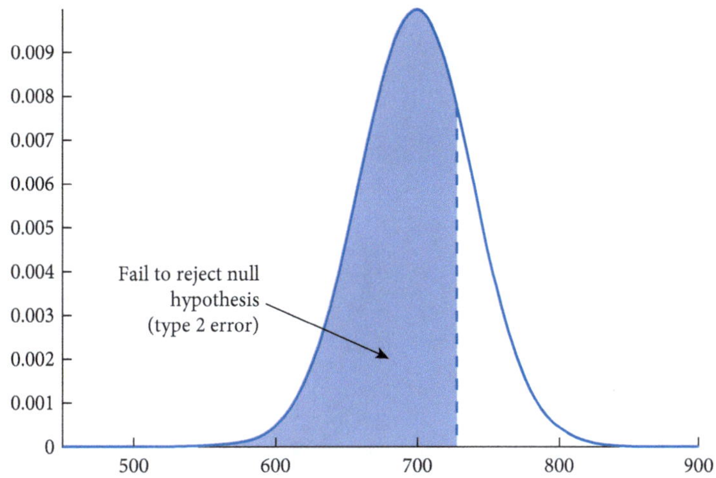

Figure 17.4 The probability of a type 2 error.

Conditional on the true average being $E(X) = 700$, we know that this probability will just be:

$$P(\overline{X} \leq 728.4) - P(\overline{X} \leq 571.60)$$

These probabilities are relatively easy to calculate in Microsoft Excel.

Probability	Excel Formula	Value
$P(\overline{X} \leq 728.4)$	=norm.dist(728.4, 700, sqrt(400^2/100), true)	0.761147
$P(\overline{X} \leq 571.60)$	=norm.dist(571.6, 700, sqrt(400^2/100), true)	0.000664

By finding the difference between these two probabilities, we can find the probability of failing to reject the null hypothesis:

$$= 0.761147 - 0.000664 = 0.76048$$

That is, the probability of making a type 2 error is just 0.76048.

Intuitively, we can see a (relatively) easy way of decreasing the probability of making a type 2 error. If we simply move the upper critical value leftwards, this will reduce the unshaded area; that is, we will increase the probability of correctly rejecting the (incorrect) null hypothesis, and decrease the probability of incorrectly failing to reject the null hypothesis.

Suppose that we changed the critical values to 700 and 600. The impact of this would be to squeeze the probability of making a type 2 error, as illustrated in Figure 17.5.

By moving the critical values inwards (i.e. towards the hypothesized value of £650), we have lowered the proportion of the time when we incorrectly fail to reject the null hypothesis.

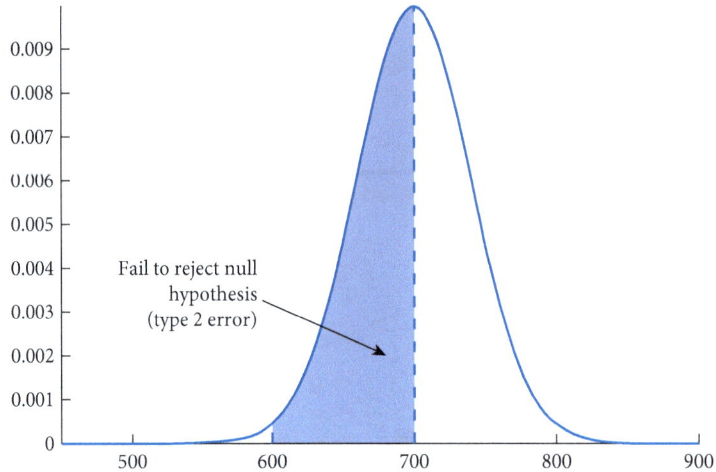

Figure 17.5 Probability of making a type 2 error, with revised critical values.

KEY DEFINITION: TYPE 2 ERROR

A type 2 error occurs when we (incorrectly) fail to reject the null hypothesis, even though the null hypothesis is actually false.

The choice of critical value for the test affects the likelihood of making a type 2 error, but because the true distribution of test statistics is usually unknown, it is much more difficult to calculate the probability of making a type 2 error.

So, why don't we just move the critical values towards each other? As we will see in the next section, there is a trade-off between type 1 and type 2 errors. Since both of these probabilities are determined by the choice of critical values, if we decrease the probability of a type 1 error, this automatically increases the probability of a type 2 error.

If we adjust the critical values to lower the probability of a type 2 error, this increases the probability of a type 1 error.

KEY DEFINITION: SIZE AND POWER

We will often talk about statistical tests in terms of their size and their power.

The **size of a statistical test** is simply the significance level of the test. This is equivalent to the probability of making a type 1 error. A statistician will choose an appropriate size for their test.

The **power of a test** is the probability of rejecting the null hypothesis when the null hypothesis is false. We know that a type 2 error is when you fail to reject the null when it is false. The power is therefore 1 minus the probability of a type 2 error.

$Power = 1 - P(Type\,2\,error)$.

17.3 Trade-offs between type 1 (false positive) and type 2 (false negative) errors

So far, we have seen that, if we change the critical values that we use, we automatically change both the probability of observing a false positive (i.e. a type 1 error), and the probability of observing a false negative (i.e. a type 2 error). In this section, we will see that there is a clear trade-off to be had:

- If by adjusting the critical values we decrease the probability of a type 1 error, we will increase the probability of a type 2 error.
- If by adjusting the critical values we decrease the probability of a type 2 error, we will increase the probability of a type 1 error.

To illustrate this, let's return to our example of wages. We tested the null hypothesis that the average full-time wage was £650 against the alternative that the average was not equal to £650:

$$H_0: E(X) = 650$$
$$H_A: E(X) \neq 650$$

We also considered the distribution of sample means if the true average wage was £700. If we are testing at the 5 per cent significance level, we would reject the null hypothesis if we observed a sample mean less than £571.60, or above £728.40.

Panel a) of Figure 17.6 shows the probabilities of type 1 and type 2 errors in the two cases where $E(X) = 650$ and $E(X) = 700$ when we test at the 5 per cent significance level. Panel b) repeats this process at the 1 per cent significance level. However, what we can see is that because the critical values have moved outwards, the probability of making a type 2 error has increased.

By lowering the probability of a type 1 error, we have the trade-off of increasing the probability of a type 2 error.

However, it is possible to lower the probability of a type 2 error (increase the power of the test) whilst simultaneously reducing the probability of a type 1 error.

The key determinant of the probability of a type 2 error is the level of overlap between the distribution of the test statistics when the null hypothesis is true, and when the alternative

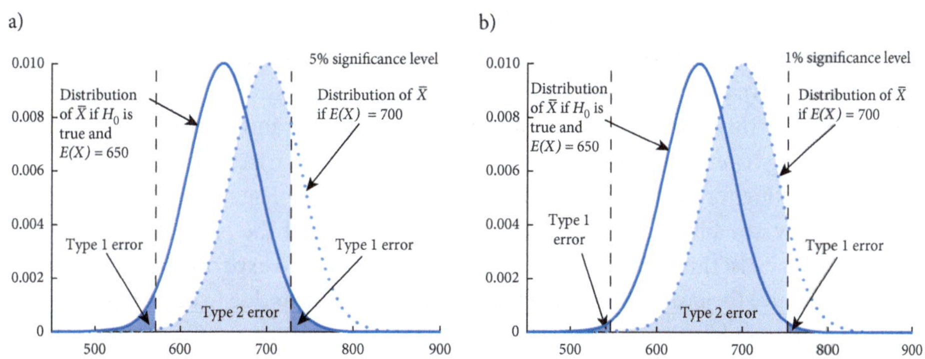

Figure 17.6 Type 1 vs type 2 errors at the 5 per cent and 1 per cent significance level.

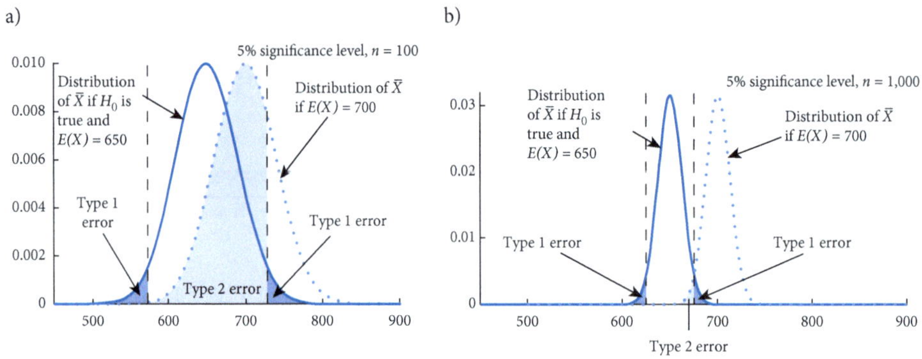

Figure 17.7 Probabilities of type 1 and type 2 errors for n = 100 and n = 1,000.

hypothesis is true, and this level of overlap is determined by the standard error (or standard deviation) of our estimator.

Remember that, if you sample n independent and identically distributed observations from the population with expectation μ_X and variance σ_X^2, and construct the sample mean, then the distribution of the sample means is given by:

$$\overline{X} \sim N\left(\mu_X, \frac{\sigma_X^2}{n}\right)$$

That is, the variance of the sample mean is inversely proportional to the sample size used. In Figure 17.7 we illustrate the distribution of test statistics under two circumstances: firstly, where there are 100 observations, and secondly with 1,000 observations.

Two things change when we increase the sample size. Firstly, because the variance of the estimator decreases, the spread of the estimates is compressed. This means that you are less likely to observe extreme outcomes. Because of this, to maintain the probability of a type 1 error at 5 per cent, the critical values have to change (these are still 1.96 times the standard error above and below 650).

However, the big impact is that there is much less overlap between the distribution under the null, and the distribution under an alternative hypothesis where $E(X) = 700$. As such, the probability of making a type 2 error is now much, much smaller.

By increasing the sample size, we are also effectively able to choose to use a lower significance level (i.e. reduce the probability of a type 1 error) and to lower the probability of gaining a false negative result (type 2 error).

It is precisely this trick that physicists have used at CERN in their hunt for the Higgs Boson. By using repeated experiments, they have carried out a large number of experiments, each time looking for evidence of the Higgs Boson. Since the Higgs Boson cannot be observed directly, the physicists need to look for the impact of the particle. However, that impact could be just through random chance. By using repeated experiments, the physicists are able to reduce the probability that what they are observing is due to anything other than the Higgs Boson to less than 0.000000000003.

CASE STUDY **Medical testing and COVID-19**

False positives and false negatives are often seen in the context of medical testing for diseases. In medical testing, statisticians often refer to the 'specificity and sensitivity' of tests:

- Specificity is the probability of correctly failing to reject the null hypothesis. That is, if an individual does not have the disease, the specificity is the probability of failing to find evidence of the disease (or failing to reject the null hypothesis). This is equivalent to $1 - P(type\,1\,error)$.
- Sensitivity is the probability of correctly rejecting the null hypothesis. That is, if an individual does have the disease, the sensitivity is the probability of rejecting the null hypothesis. This is equivalent to the power of the test.

In 2020, the world was hit by the COVID-19 pandemic. One of the key tools for reopening the economy was rapid testing of individuals to try to ensure that they did not have the virus (and were not inadvertently spreading the virus).

The UK introduced lateral flow tests, which were available for anyone to take themselves at home. Research from a Cochrane Review suggested that the specificity of the lateral flow test was 99.5 per cent, whilst the sensitivity was 57.5 per cent (for individuals without symptoms).[1]

That is, if you randomly tested someone with no COVID symptoms, if the individual was healthy (and did not have COVID), then the probability of a false positive would be 0.5 per cent. So, if you randomly carried out the test on 1,000 healthy individuals, you might expect to find 5 positive tests.

Similarly, if you randomly tested someone who had no COVID symptoms, if the individual actually had COVID, the probability of a false negative (type 2 error) would be 42.5 per cent. So, if you randomly carried out the test on 1,000 individuals who had COVID, but were asymptomatic, you would expect 425 to present negative tests.

Ideally, in a statistical test, we want to have high power (i.e. the probability of correctly rejecting the null hypothesis when it is false is high) and low size (i.e. the probability of incorrectly rejecting the null hypothesis when it is true is low).

17.4 Which is more important—high power or low size?

Because, for a particular sample size, when we adjust the size of a test, this has a direct bearing on the power of the test, statisticians and econometricians often need to make a decision about which is more important to them: having a small size or a large power. We have seen that one way of gaining a larger power without any impact on the size is to increase the sample size, but this is not always possible. Moreover, the answer is not always straightforward and depends completely on the situation that is being considered.

[1] J. Dinnes et al. (2021), 'Rapid, Point-of-care Antigen and Molecular-Based Tests for Diagnosis of SARS-CoV-2 Infection', *Cochrane Database of Systematic Reviews*, Issue 3. Art. No.: CD013705.

Reminder

Size of the test

The size of a statistical test is the same as the significance level you are working with. If you have defined a rare event as one that occurs less than 5 per cent of the time, then the size of the test is 5 per cent (or 0.05). This is the same as the probability of a type 1 error (or a false positive).

This is not the same as the sample size.

Power of the test

The power of the test is equal to the probability of rejecting the null hypothesis, when the null hypothesis is false. This can be calculated as $1 - P(type\,2\,error)$.

Keeping the size of the test constant (e.g. at 5 per cent), if we increase the sample size, the power of the test will increase (i.e. the probability of correctly rejecting the null hypothesis will increase).

When considering the trade-off between low size and high power, you need to consider which type of error is more problematic. As an economist, you might need to make judgements to advise governments about spending money.

Suppose that you are evaluating the impact of an educational intervention in schools (such as marginally changing class sizes). Your null hypothesis would be that changing classroom sizes has no effect on students' outcomes, but your alternative might be that changing classroom sizes does have an impact on students' outcomes.

- If you make a type 1 error (false positive), you would find an impact of classroom size on students outcomes, even though no impact exists.
- If you make a type 2 error (false negative), you would find no impact of classroom size on students' outcomes, even though an impact exists.

The consequence of these errors might be significant. If you make a type 1 error, you might commit the government to spending large amounts of (taxpayers') money to change the size of classrooms. If you make a type 2 error, you might deprive students of educational improvements through changes to classroom size.

As an economist, you would need to make a decision about which of these is more costly, or more problematic. A statistician will always need to weigh up the costs and benefits of lower size or higher power.

Summary

It is always important to note that, in statistics, we never know anything with certainty. If we reject a null hypothesis, it might be that the null hypothesis is false, or we could be incorrectly rejecting a null hypothesis. Similarly, if we fail to reject a null hypothesis, it might be that the null hypothesis is true, or that we incorrectly fail to reject said null.

	Null hypothesis is true	Null hypothesis is false
Fail to reject the null hypothesis	Correct conclusion	Type 2 error (false negative)
Reject the null hypothesis	Type 1 error (false positive)	Correct conclusion

If we fail to reject the null when the null is true, or we reject the null when the null is false, we have made the correct conclusion. However, if we reject the null hypothesis when the null hypothesis is true, we make a type 1 error, whilst if we fail to reject the null when the null hypothesis is false, we make a type 2 error.

If we adjust the critical values to make the probability of a type 1 error smaller, we automatically increase the probability of making a type 2 error. However, we can reduce the probability of a type 2 error, without affecting the probability of a type 1 error, by increasing the number of observations that we consider.

Key definitions

- Type 1 error—this is where we reject the null hypothesis, when the null hypothesis is true. This is often referred to as a false positive.
- Type 2 error—this is where we fail to reject the null hypothesis, when the null hypothesis is false. This is often referred to as a false negative.
- Size of the test—this is the probability of making a type 1 error. You choose the size of the test by choosing the appropriate significance level (e.g. 5%, 1%) for your test.
- Power of the test—this is the probability of correctly rejecting a false null hypothesis. This is calculated as $1 - P(Type\,2\,error)$.

The T-distribution, Confidence Intervals, and More on Testing

18

Learning outcomes for this chapter

By the end of this chapter you will be able to:

- Explain why you cannot use the normal distribution when testing hypotheses using estimates of the population variance
- Describe the t-distribution, and calculate the number of degrees of freedom
- Carry out simple tests using the t-distribution
- Calculate and interpret confidence intervals

Mathematical tools

- Algebra
- Inequalities
- Summations

Introduction

When carrying out a statistical test about a population characteristic, we start off by constructing an estimate of that population characteristic. So, in most of the examples that we've seen so far, we have been testing hypotheses about the population average, or expected value, and have used the sample mean as an (unbiased) estimator of the population average.

However, in order to carry out a statistical test, we have needed to know the distribution of the estimator that we have used. We know, for example, that if we randomly sample n observations from a population X, where $E(X) = \mu_X$ and $var(X) = \sigma_X^2$, then the variance of the sample mean is given by:

$$var(\overline{X}) = \frac{\sigma_X^2}{n}$$

That is, in order to construct the distribution of the sample mean, we need to know the true variance of the underlying random variable. So, if we wanted to test a hypothesis relating to the average wages in the economy, not only would we need to construct an estimate of the average wages (e.g. by sampling 100 individuals and constructing a sample mean) but also, to construct the standard deviation of that estimator, we would need to know what the true variance of wages was in the economy.

Since we don't know what the true average wage in the population is (we've estimated it, after all), it is highly unlikely that, in reality, we will know the true variance of the population. As such, in order to carry out a statistical test, it's important not only to estimate the population parameter we're trying to estimate, but also to estimate the variance of the estimator!

In this chapter, we will introduce statistical testing where you have to estimate the variance of the underlying random variable, and we will see that the standardized test statistics no longer follow the normal distribution, but instead, follow a new distribution known as the (Student's) t-distribution.

Revision: Definition of the standard error

Since an estimator is a random variable, there is an associated variance and standard deviation of the estimator. The standard error is just the same as the standard deviation of an estimator. We use the term standard error to indicate that this is relating to an estimator.

$$s.e.(\bar{X}) = \sqrt{var(\bar{X})} = \sqrt{\frac{\sigma_X^2}{n}}$$

18.1 Can we use the normal distribution when we don't know the true variance?

So far, we have been focusing on testing hypotheses using the sample mean as an estimator of the population average, or expectation. In Chapter 16, we saw that when we standardized our estimator by subtracting the expected value, and dividing through by the standard error, the resulting test statistic followed a normal distribution with expectation 0 and variance 1.

We have also seen that, if you randomly sample n observations from a population random variable, then the sample mean will follow an approximately normal distribution, and the variance of the sample mean will be equal to:

$$var(\bar{X}) = \frac{\sigma_X^2}{n}$$

That is, the standard error of the sample mean will be equal to the square root of the variance.

18.1.1 Standardizing a test statistic when we know the variance of the underlying population

Suppose that you have a population variable X with expectation μ_X and variance σ_X^2, and you randomly sample n independent and identically distributed observations of X.

Since the sample mean is unbiased, and because the observations are *iid*, we know that the expectation of the sample mean, $\overline{X}$, will be equal to the expectation of X, μ_X, and the variance will be equal to the variance of X divided by the number of observations:

$$E(\overline{X}) = E(X) = \mu_X, \quad var(\overline{X}) = \frac{var(X)}{n} = \frac{\sigma_X^2}{n}$$

Provided n is large (i.e. n greater than 30), then the central limit theorem also tells us that the sample mean will be approximately normally distributed. Therefore, we can write down the approximate distribution of $\overline{X}$ as:

$$\overline{X} \sim N\left(\mu_X, \frac{\sigma_X^2}{n}\right)$$

We can standardize the distribution of this estimator by subtracting the expected value, and dividing through by the standard error of $\overline{X}$ (i.e. the square root of the variance of $\overline{X}$):

$$Z = \frac{\overline{X} - \mu_X}{\sqrt{\frac{\sigma_X^2}{n}}} \sim N(0,1)$$

Then the resulting test statistic is normally distributed, with expectation 0 and variance 1. In this case, we can only standardize the test statistic because we know the true variance of X, σ_X^2. As we will see in the next section, normally, we will have to estimate the variance, and when we use an estimate of the variance, the resulting (standardized) test statistic follows a different distribution, which is known as the t-distribution.

18.1.2 Using an estimate of the variance to standardize a test statistic

In Section 18.1.1, when we standardized our test statistic, we needed to use the true variance of the random variable (in this case, we needed to know the true variance of $\overline{X}$). However, in most cases, we will not know the true variance of the underlying random variable, so instead, we will need to estimate it.

We know that an unbiased estimator for the population variance of X is s_{n-1}^2:

$$s_{n-1}^2 = \left[\frac{1}{n-1}\right]\sum_{i=1}^{n}(X_i - \overline{X})^2$$

We can use this estimator to also construct an estimate of the variance of the sample mean by dividing through s_{n-1}^2 by the number of observations.

That is, we can construct an estimator for the variance of the sample mean by combining s_{n-1}^2 with the fact that the true variance of the sample mean is $var(\overline{X}) = \frac{\sigma_X^2}{n}$. Thus, an estimator for the variance of the sample mean can be given as:

$$\widehat{var}(\overline{X}) = \frac{s_{n-1}^2}{n}$$

All that we have done here is that we've replaced the true variance of X, σ_X^2, with our unbiased estimator for the variance of X, s_{n-1}^2.

Note: Proving that we have an unbiased estimator of the variance of the sample mean

Since we know that s_{n-1}^2 is an unbiased estimator of the variance of X:

$$E(s_{n-1}^2) = \sigma_X^2$$

it follows that s_{n-1}^2/n is an unbiased estimator of σ_X^2/n:

$$E\left(\frac{s_{n-1}^2}{n}\right) = \frac{1}{n}E(s_{n-1}^2) = \frac{\sigma_X^2}{n}$$

Remember, $\widehat{var}(\overline{X})$ will not be exactly equal to the true variance of the sample mean, but it provides us with an unbiased estimate of the variance, which we can use in statistical testing.

We can use this estimate of the variance of the sample mean to try to standardize the sample mean as we did previously. However, now, as we are using an estimate of the variance of the sample mean, let's denote the test statistic as T:

$$T = \frac{\overline{X} - \mu_X}{\sqrt{\frac{s_{n-1}^2}{n}}}$$

When carrying out statistical tests, it is highly unlikely that you will ever know the true variance of the population random variable, so in reality you will almost always need to construct an estimate of the standard error of your estimator to be able to carry out any statistical tests.

However, you might ask whether this resulting test statistic, T, will still follow a normal distribution, or whether it follows some other distribution.

18.1.3 Monte Carlo simulations to illustrate the distribution of the test statistic

To investigate the distribution of the test statistics when we use s_{n-1}^2 as an estimator for $var(X)$, we will begin by using a Monte Carlo simulation. Remember that a Monte Carlo simulation uses repeated random sampling from a population (with known characteristics) to construct experimental distributions for estimators, or test statistics, when certain assumptions are made.

For the simulation, we are going to define an underlying population random variable, X, such that X follows a normal distribution, with expectation 5 and variance 25:

$$X \sim N(5,25)$$

We will randomly sample five independent and identically distributed (*iid*) observations from X, and construct the sample mean. We know that, since the underlying random variable X is normally distributed, $\overline{X}$ will also be normally distributed, and that:

$$var(\overline{X}) = \frac{var(X)}{n}$$

where n is the number of observations (five in this instance).

To compare the distribution of the test statistic when we use both the true variance and the estimated variance, we will construct our (standardized) test statistic in two ways:

Method 1: Using the true variance to standardize	Method 2: Using the estimated variance to standardize
We know that $var(X) = 25$, and so the variance of the sample mean will be equal to $\frac{25}{5}$. As such, we can standardize the sample mean by calculating: $z = \frac{\overline{x} - 5}{\sqrt{\frac{25}{5}}}$	In method 2, we estimate the variance using s_{n-1}^2 based upon our five observations: $s_{n-1}^2 = \left[\frac{1}{n-1}\right] \times \sum_{i=1}^{n}(X_i - \overline{X})^2$ Having estimated the variance of X, we substitute s_{n-1}^2 into the standardization formula: $t = \frac{\overline{x} - 5}{\sqrt{\frac{s_{n-1}^2}{5}}}$

In both cases, we subtract 5 from $\overline{X}$ on the numerator, as we are standardizing, based on the true expected value: $E(\overline{X}) = 5$.

To make this a Monte Carlo simulation, we will repeatedly sample from the population a very large number of times (1,000,000 times in this simulation), to obtain a distribution of test statistics, based upon the two methods.

The first five samples are illustrated in Table 18.1.[1]

[1] As an exercise, you should try to replicate these estimates. Note that the observations are reported to four decimal places; the true variables are continuous, and so may have any number of decimal places. If you put the observations for sample 1 in cells A1 to E1 in Excel, you can calculate the estimated variance, s^2, using the formula =*var*(A1:E1). Remember that this provides you with an unbiased estimate of the population variance of X.

Table 18.1 Estimates from the first five samples from the population

	Observations					Estimates			
	X_1	X_2	X_3	X_4	X_5	$\overline{X}$	S_2	Standardized statistic using **true variance**	Standardized statistic using **estimated variance**
Sample 1	11.0427	2.1472	−1.6976	4.4060	6.0275	4.385	22.257	−0.275	−0.291
Sample 2	7.2659	14.7092	1.2374	10.1525	4.7273	7.618	26.475	1.171	1.138
Sample 3	5.2124	8.1131	18.1082	5.7502	1.1128	7.659	40.469	1.189	0.935
Sample 4	5.8486	−1.6377	−0.2608	6.6525	7.5887	3.638	18.154	−0.609	−0.715
Sample 5	5.3006	14.1972	5.2821	−0.5413	7.1822	6.284	27.995	0.574	0.543

So, for instance, in the first sample, the sample mean of the observations was $\overline{X} = 4.385$, with an estimate of the variance of X as $s_{n-1}^2 = 22.257$. Using the two methods, we can construct the standardized test statistic:

Method 1: Using the true variance to standardize	Method 2: Using the estimated variance to standardize
$z = \frac{\bar{x} - 5}{\sqrt{var(\overline{X})}} = \frac{4.385 - 5}{\sqrt{\frac{25}{5}}} = -0.275$	$t = \frac{\bar{x} - 5}{\sqrt{\widehat{var}(\overline{X})}} = \frac{4.385 - 5}{\sqrt{\frac{22.257}{5}}} = -0.291$

If we repeat this a very large number of times, we will obtain a distribution of the (standardized) test statistics from the two methods. We know that method 1 should yield a standard normal distribution, but we do not know what distribution method 2 will yield. Will it be normal? Or will it be something else?

Figure 18.1 shows the distributions of the test statistics when we use the true variance, and the estimated variance to construct our test statistics. We know that, when we use the true variance to standardize, the distribution of test statistics should be normally distributed. However, the distribution when we use the estimated variance looks a little different.

What we can see is that when we use the estimated variance, we are much more likely to gain an outcome in the tails of the distribution than we would if we had used the true variance.

That is, if we use the estimated variance of Y, we are much more likely to gain (standardized) test statistics that are a long way away from zero. This also means that we are much more likely to gain test statistics whose magnitude is greater than 1.96.

We can go further and look at the percentiles of the distribution that we have simulated, illustrated in Table 18.2.

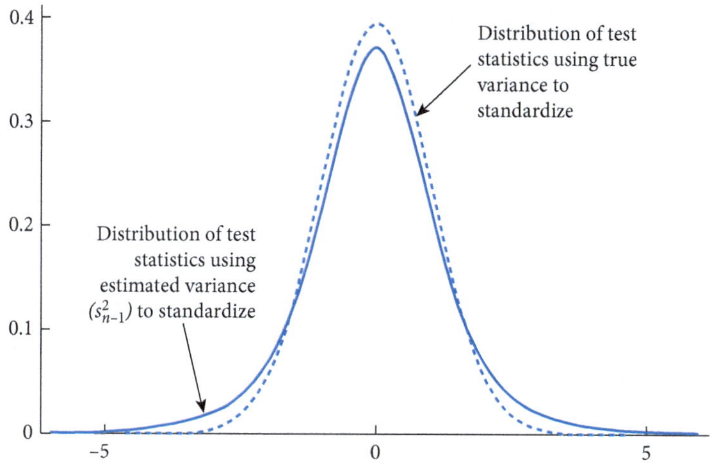

Figure 18.1 Distribution of test statistics using the true and the estimated variance.

Table 18.2 Percentiles of the standardized test statistics from the simulation

Percentile	2.5%	5%	10%	50%	90%	95%	97.5%
Using true variance (method 1)	−1.96	−1.64	−1.28	0	1.28	1.65	1.96
Using estimated variance (method 2)	−2.78	−2.13	−1.53	0	1.53	2.13	2.78

- When we use the true variance to standardize, we can see that the smallest 2.5% of the outcomes lie to the left of −1.96, and the largest 2.5% of the outcomes lie to the right of +1.96.
- Whereas when we use the estimated variance, the smallest 2.5% of outcomes lie to the left of −2.78, and the largest 2.5% of outcomes lie to the right of +2.78.

This would mean, if we wanted to carry out a two-tailed test at the 5 per cent significance level, our critical value would be ±2.78.

In fact in this simulation, when we used the estimated variance to standardize, we found 121,299 of the 1,000,000 simulations gained a standardized test statistic with magnitude greater than 1.96—that is, 12.1 per cent of the time.

What this tells us is that if we are using an estimate of the variance to standardize our test statistic, we are much more likely to observe 'extreme' values. In the example, if we used ±1.96 as the critical value, we would (incorrectly) reject the null 12.1 per cent of the time (rather than 5 per cent with the true variance).

As such, when we use the estimated variance of the estimator to standardize our test statistic, the resulting (standardized) test statistic is no longer normally distributed, and we will need to find different critical values to compare our test statistic against. The distribution that we will need to use to find our critical values is called the Student's t-distribution (often just referred to as the t-distribution).

Summary

When we use estimates of the variance of the estimator to standardize the test statistic, the resulting standardized distribution does not follow a standard normal distribution. Instead, the test statistic follows a t-distribution, and when we carry out statistical testing, we will need to use different critical values.

18.2 The t-distribution

So far, we have seen that, if we use an estimate of the population variance to standardize our estimates, then the resulting test statistic is no longer normally distributed. Instead, the test statistics will follow a distribution known as the t-distribution. The t-distribution is unlike the normal distribution, in that the distribution actually changes depending on the number of degrees of freedom in the model. In the examples we have seen so far, the number of degrees of freedom is just equal to the number of observations minus 1. That is, in this case, the degrees of freedom would be $n - 1$.

18.2.1 Degrees of freedom

In statistics, we often have to think about a concept known as the number of degrees of freedom. Formally, the number of degrees of freedom is the number of linearly independent elements used within the construction of the estimate of the variance. Intuitively, this is a count of the number of pieces of information that can be combined in a linear combination to construct the other elements.

To illustrate this, suppose we have n observations of a random variable, Y, and wish to estimate the variance of Y. We saw in an earlier chapter that the unbiased estimator for the variance of Y was:

$$s_{n-1}^2 = \frac{1}{n-1}\sum_{i=1}^{n}(Y_i - \overline{Y})^2$$

The $n - 1$ on the denominator represents the number of degrees of freedom; this comes from the fact that the $\overline{Y}$ is itself an *estimate* of the expected value of Y. The consequence of this is that we lose one piece of independent information.

The degrees of freedom are the number of linearly independent elements used in the construction of the estimate of the variance. That is, from the $(Y_i - \overline{Y})^2$ terms, the degrees of freedom are the number of elements that would be needed to be known to write down the other elements of the summation.

If all of the elements are linearly independent, we would not be able to perfectly predict $(Y_n - \overline{Y})^2$, based on the previous $n - 1$ elements $\{(Y_1 - \overline{Y})^2, (Y_2 - \overline{Y})^2, \ldots, (Y_{n-1} - \overline{Y})^2\}$. However, because $\overline{Y}$ is itself a linear combination of all of the observations of $Y_1, Y_2, \ldots, Y_n$, this automatically means that if you know $n - 1$ of the elements (and the sample mean), then the nth element can be constructed using a linear combination of the other elements.

You can, intuitively, think about this as the number of pieces of 'information' that are lost by using estimates within the estimator for the population variance. The true variance of Y is given by:

$$var(Y) = E\left[(Y - E(Y))^2\right]$$

However, in using s_{n-1}^2, we are essentially using the sample mean, $\overline{Y}$, as an estimator of $E(Y)$. Having used this estimate within the s_{n-1}^2 estimator, we lose one element of linear independence, because the $\overline{Y}$ automatically contains information from all of the observations. If we know $n - 1$ observations, and the sample mean, we can automatically write down the final observation.

The number of degrees of freedom in this example is the number of observations (n) minus 1 ($= n - 1$).

Worked example 18.1: Illustrating why knowing the sample mean loses a degree of freedom

To illustrate why knowing the sample mean causes a problem for linear independence, let's consider a simple worked example. Suppose we have three observations, 1, 5, and x (where x is unknown), but we know that the sample mean is 4. This automatically tells us that:

$$\frac{1}{3} \times (1 + 5 + x) = 4$$

Now, from this information, we can also write down that the sum of the three observations will be equal to 12. Therefore, the only possible value of x is equal to 6:

$$\Rightarrow x = 6$$

So, by introducing the sample mean, $\overline{X}$, we can automatically write down the value of the unknown observation; that is, we lose one degree of freedom.[2]

Worked example 18.2: What happens if you have one observation?

Suppose that you had one observation of Y_i and wanted to estimate the variance of Y. Intuitively, you would never be able to estimate the variance, as by only seeing one observation, you gain no signal about the variability of Y. However, it would also be the case that in constructing the sum of squares:

$$= \sum_{i=1}^{1}(Y_i - \overline{Y})^2 = (Y_1 - \overline{Y})^2$$

[2] Try this for yourself. If you have three observations 1, 2, and x, and are told that the mean average of the three observations is 3, calculate the value of x.

Since the sample mean is constructed based on the sum of the observations, it will always be the case that $Y_1 = \overline{Y}$; so by knowing $\overline{Y}$, we automatically also know Y_1.

In this case, we would have zero pieces of linearly independent information within the summation, or zero degrees of freedom.

More generally, whenever there are zero degrees of freedom, we are unable to provide any estimate of the variance.

18.2.2 The relationship between the t-distribution and degrees of freedom

Having motivated the idea of the number of degrees of freedom, we can now investigate what impact these degrees of freedom have on the t-distribution.

To illustrate this relationship, consider Figure 18.2, which illustrates the distributions based upon 5 and 100 degrees of freedom. As the degrees of freedom increase, the peak of the distribution is pulled upwards, and the tails become smaller. Intuitively, what this means is that as the number of degrees of freedom increases, it becomes less likely to gain very large outcomes (positive or negative) in the t-distribution.

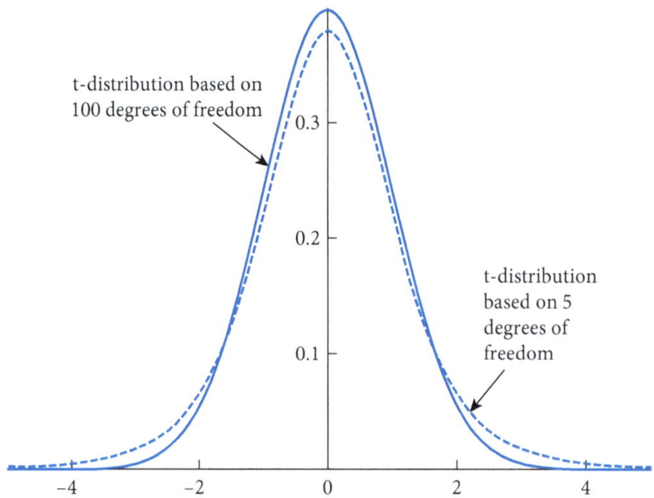

Figure 18.2 Illustrating the t-distribution based upon different degrees of freedom.

The change in shape of the distribution is shown even more strongly in Figure 18.3, where we see the most extreme 5 per cent of outcomes for the t-distribution with 5 degrees of freedom in panel a), and 100 degrees of freedom in panel b). As you can see, the distribution is squeezed inwards as the number of degrees of freedom increases, and so the critical value for a test at the 5 per cent significance level would be squeezed inwards as well.

In fact, as the number of degrees of freedom increase, the shape and distribution of the t-distribution converges towards the normal distribution. For very large numbers of degrees of freedom (more than about 500), the t-distribution is almost indistinguishable from the normal distribution, as illustrated in Table 18.3.

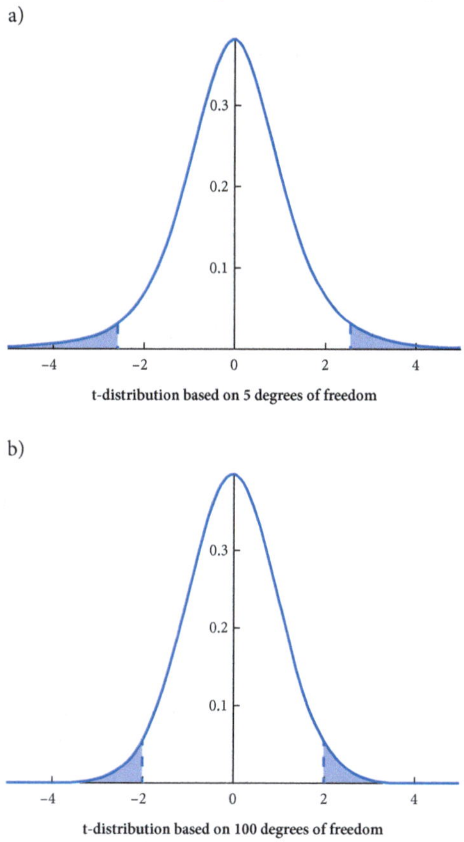

Figure 18.3 Distribution of t-distribution, illustrating the change in rejection regions.

Table 18.3 Comparing the percentiles of the t-distribution with different degrees of freedom

		Percentile								
		0.5	2.5	5	10	50	90	95	97.5	99.5
t-distribution with k degrees of freedom	$k = 5$	−4.03	−2.57	−2.02	−1.48	0	1.48	2.02	2.57	4.03
	$k = 10$	−3.17	−2.23	−1.81	−1.37	0	1.37	1.81	2.23	3.17
	$k = 100$	−2.63	−1.98	−1.66	−1.29	0	1.29	1.66	1.98	2.63
	$k = 1{,}000$	−2.58	−1.96	−1.65	−1.28	0	1.28	1.65	1.96	2.58
Normal distribution		−2.58	−1.96	−1.65	−1.28	0	1.28	1.65	1.96	2.58

When we carried out statistical testing with the normal distribution, the critical values at the 5 per cent significance level (for a two-tailed test) were ±1.96, representing the most extreme 5 per cent of outcomes. When we have 5 degrees of freedom, the most extreme 5 per cent of outcomes are observed beyond ±2.57, so we should only reject a **null hypothesis** (at the 5 per cent significance level) if the magnitude of the t-statistic was greater than 2.57.

Similarly, if there are 10 degrees of freedom, the most extreme 5 per cent of outcomes would be beyond ±2.23. So, when testing at the 5 per cent significance level, we would reject the null hypothesis if the magnitude of the t-statistic was greater than 2.23.

Revision: Two-tailed test

Remember, in a two-tailed test, we treat the unlikely events as occurring in either of the tails of the distribution. At the 5% significance level, we would look for the smallest 2.5% of outcomes and the largest 2.5% of outcomes to determine the least likely 5% of outcomes.

As the degrees of freedom increase, the shape of the t-distribution becomes indistinguishable from the normal distribution, and when we have 1,000 degrees of freedom, at any reasonable level of rounding, the percentiles of the distribution are more or less indistinguishable.

18.3 Testing using the t-distribution

If we do not know the true variance of our underlying population, then in order to find the standard error of the sample mean, we will need to use estimates of the population variance. We have seen, earlier in this chapter, that the resulting test statistic will not follow a normal distribution, but instead will follow the t-distribution.

Other than this distinction between the distributions of the test statistics, the methodology for carrying out statistical tests (when we don't know the true variance) is exactly the same as we have seen previously, except that since we don't know the true population variance we now need to estimate it to construct estimated standard errors of our estimator, and we need to compare the (standardized) test statistics we construct with the critical values from the t-distribution rather than the normal distribution (see Figure 18.4).

Worked example 18.3: Was the average weekly wage £650 in 2019?

In Chapter 16, we used data from the UK Labour Force Survey to test the null hypothesis that the average (weekly) wage in the UK was equal to £650, against the alternative hypothesis that the average wage was different from £650.[3]

When we looked at this previously, we were presented with a value of the variance of weekly wages, but in reality, we don't know what the true variance of weekly wages is, so we would need to estimate it. Let's repeat the test, but this time we will use estimates of the variance of weekly wages.

$$H_0 : E(X) = £650$$
$$H_A : E(X) \neq £650$$

[3] This data is available to download from Data sets and Exercises at the end of this chapter.

Step 1 Specify hypotheses and significance levels

Write down your null and alternative hypotheses. The null hypothesis will normally be based on some sort of prior belief, or theory. At this stage, you should also normally think about what a reasonable significance level should be. Normally, we specify this at 5% (i.e. we define an unlikely event as one that occurs less than 5% of the time when the null hypothesis is true), but we may specify a 10%, 1%, 0.1% (or even smaller) significance level.

For example, in the example we've just seen, our prior belief was that the average wage in the population was £650:

$$H_0: \mu_x = £650$$
$$H_A: \mu_x \neq £650$$

Note: Here, μ_x represents the expected value of X.

Step 2 Collect data

Collect data and construct your estimate of the population parameter you wish to examine using an estimator (e.g. the sample mean is an estimator of the expected value).

For example, we might collect 100 observations of wages, and calculate an estimate $\hat{\mu}_x = \frac{1}{n}\Sigma_{i=1}^{n} X_i$.

Step 3 Write down the distribution of the estimator under H_0 (IMPORTANT)

Write down the distribution of the estimator used in Step 1, **based on the assumption** that the null hypothesis (H_0) is true.

Often, you will be able to appeal to the central limit theorem, which states that, provided the sample size is large enough, the sample mean will follow a **normal distribution.**

For example, in the example above:

$$\hat{\mu}_x \sim N\left(650, \frac{var(X)}{n}\right)$$

Step 4 Construct an estimate of the variance of your estimator used in Step 2

Since we do not know $var(X)$, we cannot write down the true variance of $\hat{\mu}_x$, so we will need to estimate it. We can construct an estimate of $var(X)$ as:

$$s_{n-1}^2 = \frac{1}{n-1}\sum_{i=1}^{n}(X_i - X)^2$$

Then, an estimate of the variance of $\hat{\mu}_x$ would be:

$$\widehat{var}(\hat{\mu}_x) = \frac{s_{n-1}^2}{n}$$

Step 5 Standardize your estimates using the estimated variance from Step 4

If the estimator follows a normal distribution (this will normally be the case), you can standardize the test statistic (again assuming that the null hypothesis is true) by subtracting the expected value of the estimator, and dividing through by the estimated **standard error** of the estimator.

$$t = \frac{(\hat{\mu}_x) - E(\hat{\mu}_x | H_0 \text{ is true})}{\sqrt{\left(\frac{s_{n-1}^2}{n}\right)}}$$

Step 6 Compare with critical values from the t-distribution

Having standardized your estimate, you should compare this with the critical values from the **t-distribution.** The critical values change depending on the number of degrees of freedom (which in these tests is just equal to $n - 1$). If the magnitude of the test statistic is larger than the critical value, then you would **reject** the null hypothesis.

- With 20 degrees of freedom, the critical value at the 5% significance level is 2.086
- With 50 degrees of freedom, the critical value at the 5% significance level is 2.009
- With 100 degrees of freedom, the critical value at the 5% significance level is 1.984
- With 1,000 degrees of freedom, the critical value at the 5% significance level is 1.96

If the test statistic is **smaller** than the critical value, you would **fail to reject** the null hypothesis.

Figure 18.4 Algorithm for carrying out a statistical test using an estimate of the variance of $\overline{X}$.

Just as before, we have observed 100 independent and identically distributed observations of gross weekly wages of full-time workers, and calculate a sample mean equal to $\overline{X} = 661.45$. That is, our estimate of the population average is equal to £661.45. We know that, when we have n independent and identically distributed observations of X, the variance of the sample mean can be written as:

$$var(\overline{X}) = \frac{var(X)}{n}$$

Similarly, since we have a relatively large sample (greater than 30), we can appeal to the central limit theorem, telling us that the sample mean of X will be approximately normally distributed, centred on the expectation of X:

$$\overline{X} \sim N\left(\mu_X, \frac{var(X)}{n}\right)$$

We don't know the true variance of X. However, we can estimate this, using the unbiased estimator of the variance, s^2_{n-1}:

$$\begin{aligned} s^2_{n-1} &= \frac{1}{n-1}\sum_{i=1}^{n}(X_i - \overline{X})^2 = \frac{1}{99} \times 13{,}636{,}402.8 \\ &= 137{,}741.442 \end{aligned}$$

Estimating the variance in Excel

In Excel, you can use the formula:

$= var(\text{A2:A101})$

This will find s^2_{n-1} as an unbiased estimate of the population variance, based on the observations in cells A2 to A101.

Thus, we can construct an estimate of the variance of the sample mean as:

$$\widehat{var}(\overline{X}) = \frac{s^2_{n-1}}{n} = \frac{137{,}741.442}{100} = 1{,}377.41$$

When we standardize our test statistic, we begin by assuming that the null hypothesis is true, and then subtract the expected value of our estimator (conditional on that null hypothesis being true). We then divide through by the estimated standard error of the sample mean. Because we are using an estimate (and not the true standard error), the resulting test statistic will follow a t-distribution. Note that the notation $\widehat{s.e.}(\overline{X})$ indicates the estimated standard error (or standard deviation) of the sample mean:

$$T = \frac{\overline{X} - E(\overline{X} \mid H_0 \text{ is true})}{\widehat{s.e.}(\overline{X})}$$

Because the sample mean is an unbiased estimator, if the null hypothesis is true, then $E(\overline{X} \mid H_0 \text{ is true})$ will just be the hypothesized value under the null (= £650), and the estimated standard error, $\widehat{s.e.}(\overline{X})$, will just be the square root of the estimated variance of $\overline{X}$:

$$\widehat{s.e.}(\overline{X}) = \sqrt{\widehat{var}(\overline{X})} = \sqrt{\frac{s^2_{n-1}}{n}} = \sqrt{1{,}377.41} = 37.11$$

So, we now have the following estimates:

- $\overline{X} = 661.45$
- $\widehat{s.e.}(\overline{X}) = 37.11$
- $E(\overline{X} \mid H_0 \text{ is true}) = 650$

We can substitute these into the t-statistic formula, giving us:

$$t = \frac{661.45 - 650}{37.11} = 0.309$$

We need to look up the critical value from the t-distribution. However, the critical value changes depending on the number of degrees of freedom. In this example, we have 100 observations, and have effectively lost one of these, as we have used $\overline{X}$ as an estimate of $E(X)$ when constructing the estimate of the variance of $\overline{X}$. This leaves 99 degrees of freedom ($n - 1$).

Either reading from statistical tables, or from statistical software packages (such as Microsoft Excel), we can find the critical value with 99 degrees of freedom is equal to ± 1.984.

Since the magnitude of the t-statistic is less than 1.984, we would fail to reject the null hypothesis. That is, based on the data we have been presented with, we cannot reject the hypothesis that the average gross weekly wage in the population is equal to £650.

Finding the critical value in Excel

To find the critical value with 99 degrees of freedom, we could use the formula:

$$=\text{t.inv.2t}(0.05, 99)$$

This would find the critical value at the 5% (= 0.05) significance level, with 99 degrees of freedom for a two-tailed (2t) test. The critical value is 1.984.

18.3.1 Using the t-tables

In the example in Section 18.3, we used Excel to calculate the critical values, but often, traditionally, statisticians have used statistical tables to calculate the critical values from the t-distribution.

An extract of critical values from the t-distribution is illustrated in Table 18.4 as you will often see them in published tables.[4]

Table 18.4 An extract from the t-distribution critical values tables

Upper percentiles of the t-distribution		$P =$								
		50	40	30	20	10	5	2.5	1	0.5
Degrees of freedom	10	0.000	0.260	0.542	0.879	1.372	1.812	2.228	2.764	3.169
	20	0.000	0.257	0.533	0.860	1.325	1.725	2.086	2.528	2.845
	30	0.000	0.256	0.530	0.854	1.310	1.697	2.042	2.457	2.750
	60	0.000	0.254	0.527	0.848	1.296	1.671	2.000	2.390	2.660
	120	0.000	0.254	0.526	0.845	1.289	1.658	1.980	2.358	2.617
	∞	0.000	0.253	0.524	0.842	1.282	1.645	1.960	2.327	2.576

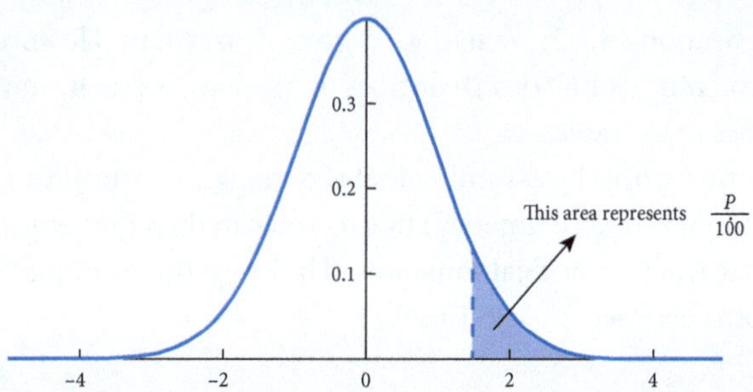

[4] A more extensive version is shown in the chapter appendix.

To find the critical value from the t-tables, there are two parameters: down the left-hand side, there are the numbers of degrees of freedom in the model (10, 20, 30, 60, 120), whilst the numbers along the top indicate the size of the right-hand tail you are considering. For example, 50 indicates that you are looking for the 50 per cent of largest values from the t-table.

So, if you are trying to find the critical value at the 5 per cent significance level, for a two-tailed test, you would want to find the most extreme 2.5 per cent of outcomes at either end of the distribution. With 10 degrees of freedom, this would be associated with a critical value of +2.228 and (because the t-distribution is symmetric) –2.228. This would represent the most extreme 5 per cent of possible outcomes.

Whilst you can access exact critical values using statistical software packages, if you are required to calculate critical values using tables, sometimes you will be confronted with difficulties. The tables do not provide critical values for all possible degrees of freedom. In the example we saw earlier, we had 99 degrees of freedom, but the extract from the t-tables (shown in Table 18.4) only provides critical values where we have 60 degrees of freedom and 120 degrees of freedom. As such, we cannot just look up the critical value at (say) the 5 per cent significance level.

Where you are provided with tables (e.g. in a closed-book examination), there are two key ways of determining whether you reject the null hypothesis (or not). Let's suppose that we have 99 degrees of freedom, and we have obtained a test statistic, which we'll denote t.

- At the 5 per cent significance level, with 60 degrees of freedom, the critical value[5] is ± 2.00.
- At the 5 per cent significance level, with 120 degrees of freedom, the critical value is ± 1.98.

What you can immediately say is that the critical value with 99 degrees of freedom must be somewhere between 1.98 and 2.00.

- If the magnitude of t is less than the smaller of these (i.e. if $|t| \leq 1.98$), then we would fail to reject the null at the 5 per cent significance level.
- If the magnitude of t is larger than the larger of these (i.e. if $|t| \geq 2.00$), then we would reject the null hypothesis at the 5 per cent significance level.

If $|t|$ lies somewhere between 1.98 and 2.00, this method would not tell us precisely whether we would reject the null (or not), and we would need to appeal to another method. One method that we could use is known as **linear interpolation**.

Finding critical values using linear interpolation

In the example in Section 18.3.2, we had 99 degrees of freedom. However, Table 18.4 only provides upper percentiles for 60 or 120 degrees of freedom. As such, you can't directly look up the critical values in the tables.

Linear interpolation works by assuming that the change in critical values between different degrees of freedom is (approximately) linear. You can then (either graphically or mathematically) calculate what the critical value would be by (in this example) finding the critical value that is 39/60ths between 2.00 and 1.98.

[5] Remember, the tables are showing you the probability of lying only in the upper tail. You are (normally) interested in a two-tailed test, so you want to find the most extreme 5 per cent of outcomes in either tail.

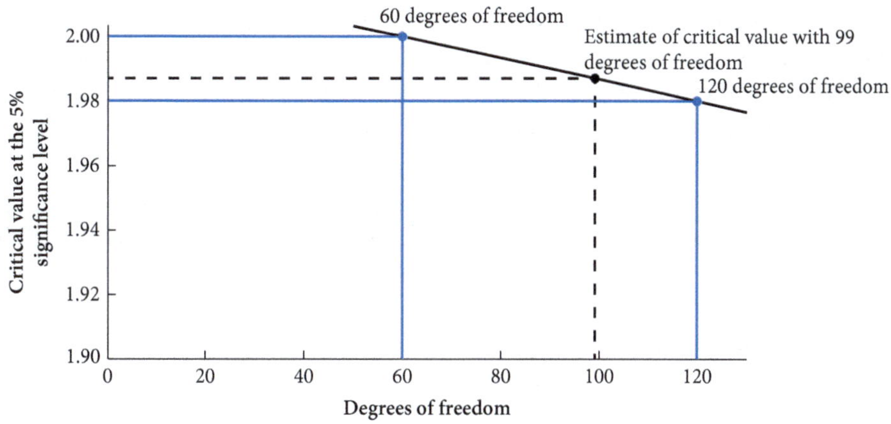

Figure 18.5 Linear interpolation.

This is often easier to visualize graphically. Figure 18.5 shows how we might go about carrying out linear interpolation to find the appropriate critical value in this case.

If we plot the known critical values (2.00 with 60 degrees of freedom, and 1.98 with 120 degrees of freedom) on a graph, with degrees of freedom on the horizontal axis, and the critical value on the vertical axis, we can then draw a straight line between these two points, to allow us to approximate the critical value for any degrees of freedom between 60 and 120.

To find the critical value with 99 degrees of freedom, you can simply draw a straight line up from the axis to the line, and find what critical value the fitted line predicts.

Mathematically, you can also do this implicitly, as you know that 99 degrees of freedom is 39/60ths of the way between 60 and 120. As such, your approximation of the critical value would be 39/60ths between 2.00 and 1.98. You could calculate this thus:

$$2.00 + \frac{39}{60} \times (1.98 - 2.00) = 1.987$$

It should be noted that the critical value is not linear in terms of the degrees of freedom, and so the critical value calculated from linear interpolation will be slightly wrong (in reality, with 99 degrees of freedom, the critical value is 1.984). However, for all but the most marginal cases, it will give you a reasonable guess at the critical value.

18.3.2 When can we use the normal distribution, and when the t-distribution?

All through this chapter, we've emphasized that if you are using an estimate of the variance of your estimator, you need to use the t-distribution. However, since the t-distribution converges to the normal distribution as the number of degrees of freedom gets very large, if you have a very large sample (more than about 500),[6] then it makes no difference whether you use the t-distribution to find your critical values, or the normal distribution.

[6] In practice, many statisticians assume that if $n > 200$, then they can appeal to the normal distribution. There is only a very slight difference between the critical values for the normal and the t-distribution with more than 200 degrees of freedom. For example, with $\nu = 200$, the 5 per cent critical value for a two-tailed test is 1.97. The 5 per cent critical value for the normal distribution is 1.96.

Thus, if you have a large number of observations (remember, in the tests we have seen, the number of degrees of freedom is just the number of observations minus 1), and you wish to test a hypothesis at the 5 per cent significance level, if you get a test statistic whose magnitude is greater than 1.96, you would reject the null hypothesis:

	Small sample	Large degrees of freedom (>500)
True variance is used to standardize	The test statistic will be normally distributed	The test statistic will be normally distributed
True variance is unknown, variance is estimated	You must use the t-distribution	The test statistic will be approximately normally distributed

Important: Statistical health warning

Students who are new to statistics sometimes get confused because we often see lots of different definitions of large samples. So far in this book, we have seen three mentions of large samples:

1. In the central limit theorem, for large enough samples, the sample mean will be approximately normally distributed.
2. In the t-distribution, as the sample size, and hence the degrees of freedom, become large, then the t-distribution converges to the normal distribution.
3. In the (weak) law of large numbers, as the sample size gets very large, the sample mean converges (in probability) towards the population average.

In these three cases, the meaning of large samples is very different.

Application	Central limit theorem	t-distribution	(Weak) law of large numbers
Meaning of large sample	$n > 30$ The central limit will approximately hold for *n* larger than about 30. The approximation improves as the sample size increases.	$n > 500$ The t-distribution approximately converges to the normal distribution with about 500 degrees of freedom. As with the CLT, as the degrees of freedom increase, the approximation improves.	$n = \infty$ The law of large numbers applies what happens as the sample size converges either to the size of the population or (for infinite populations) towards infinite numbers of observations.

These are important distinctions to be aware of, but they are often confused. If, say, you had 30 observations, and assumed this was large enough to appeal to the normal distribution, the probability of you rejecting a (true) null hypothesis would be greater than 5 per cent.

18.3.3 P-values

Just as when we were testing with the normal distribution, a more informative measure than simply whether you reject (or fail to reject) a null hypothesis is the p-value associated with a hypothesis test. Remember that the p-value tells you the probability of *randomly* achieving a standardized test statistic at least as impressive as the one we have achieved, if the null hypothesis were true.

In the example in Section 18.3.3, we obtained a t-statistic equal to 0.309. The p-value would tell us the probability of achieving a t-statistic with a magnitude at least as large as 0.309, if the null hypothesis was true.

We can easily calculate p-values with Excel. For a two-tailed test, we can use the formula:

$$= \text{t.dist.2t}(0.309, 99)$$

This will find the probability that you (randomly) observe a t-statistic either greater than 0.309, or less than −0.309, if the null hypothesis were true, when we have 99 degrees of freedom. The 2t in the formula indicates that you are considering a two-tailed test. This example corresponds with a p-value of 0.757971. That is, if the null hypothesis were true, 75.7971 per cent of the time, you would obtain a t-statistic at least as large as 0.309.

18.4 Confidence intervals

So far, we have seen how we can estimate population parameters, including the sample mean and the sample variance. We have also seen the concept of efficiency of estimators (i.e. the variance of an estimator), and we have seen how we can carry out statistical tests relating to population parameters. What we haven't discussed in any great detail is the concept of the precision of estimates.

We can begin to discuss the concept of precision of estimates using a new measure, which is the concept of confidence intervals. These are regularly discussed in scientific papers as a way of discussing the range of possible outcomes that are consistent with the estimates observed.

In the test that we carried out in Worked example 18.3, we hypothesized that the true population average weekly earnings were £650. Based on a sample mean of £661.45, we failed to reject the null hypothesis. However, this does not mean that the true population average was definitely equal to £650—we could have made a type 2 error, and found a false negative.

To illustrate this, let's carry out the test again, but this time, let's use a different hypothesized value: that the true population average was equal to £680:

$$H_0 : E(X) = 680$$
$$H_A : E(X) \neq 680$$

Statistics that we are going to use

Based on 100 observations, the estimate of the population average (sample mean) is:

$\bar{x} = £661.45$

Estimate of the standard error of the sample mean:

$$\widehat{var}(\bar{X}) = \frac{s_{n-1}^2}{n} = \frac{137,741.442}{100} = 1,377.41$$

We can construct a t-statistic in exactly the same way as before:

$$t = \frac{(\bar{x} - E(\bar{X}\,|\,H_0 \text{ is true}))}{\widehat{s.e.}\,(\bar{X})} = \frac{661.45 - 680}{\sqrt{1,377.41}} = -0.4998$$

As before, the critical value at the 5 per cent significance level with 99 degrees of freedom is ± 1.984. As the magnitude of the t-statistic is less than the critical value, we fail to reject the null hypothesis.

This may seem a little strange, because we have now seen that there are two null hypotheses that we would fail to reject:

1. $H_0: E(X) = 650$
2. $H_0: E(X) = 680$

It is not possible that both of these hypotheses can be true, yet statistical testing fails to reject either of these null hypotheses. In fact, because the values $E(X)$ can take are continuous, there is an infinite number of possible values for $E(X)$ that we would fail to reject the null hypothesis for. The range of values that we would fail to reject the null hypothesis for is known as the confidence interval of your estimate.

Remember that we fail to reject the null hypothesis at the 5 per cent significance level if the magnitude of the t-statistic (or z-statistic) is less than the critical value $(c.v.)$.[7] We can therefore write that we would fail to reject the null hypothesis if:

$$-c.v. < t < +c.v.$$

In the t-statistic, since the sample mean is an unbiased estimator, if the null hypothesis is true, then $E(\bar{X} \mid H_0 \text{ is true})$ will just be the same as the hypothesized value. Let's define the hypothesized value as μ_{H0}. So, substituting in the values, we would fail to reject the null hypothesis if:

$$-c.v. < \frac{\bar{x} - \mu_{H0}}{\widehat{s.e.}\,(\bar{X})} < +c.v.$$

[7] Many textbooks would represent this as $t_{\nu,0.975}$. This indicates that you are looking at the t-distribution with ν degrees of freedom, evaluated at the 97.5th percentile. That is, what value of t_ν would satisfy $P(T_\nu \leq t_{\nu,0.975}) = 0.975$.

Rearranging this, for a given sample mean, we can find the range of values of μ_{H0} for which we would fail to reject the null hypothesis:

$$\bar{x} - c.v. \times \widehat{s.e.}\,(\bar{X}) < \mu_{H0} < \bar{x} + c.v. \times \widehat{s.e.}\,(\bar{X})$$

In the example, where we had 100 observations, the 5 per cent critical value was 1.984, our estimated standard error was $\sqrt{1377.41} = 37.113$, and the sample mean was equal to 661.45. Therefore, we can construct our confidence interval for the average earnings in the population as:

$$£661.45 \pm 1.984 \times 37.113 = (587.8178, 735.0822)$$

That is, you could specify any value for $E(X)$ between £587.82 and £735.08 under the null hypothesis, and you would have failed to reject that null hypothesis.

KEY DEFINITION: 95 PER CENT CONFIDENCE INTERVAL

The 95 per cent confidence interval tells you the range of values for which you would fail to reject the null hypothesis when testing at the 5 per cent (= 100 − 95%) significance level.

When testing using the t-distribution (or the normal distribution), the confidence intervals will be symmetric around the estimated value, with the estimated value at the centre.

The 95 per cent confidence interval for a sample mean is given by:

$$\bar{x} \pm c.v. \times \widehat{s.e.}\,(\bar{X})$$

You could also consider a 99 per cent confidence interval, where you would replace *c.v.* with the critical value at the 1 per cent significance level. Alternatively, you could consider confidence intervals at any other significance level.

The confidence interval provides you with a range of values for the population parameter being estimated (in this case, the population average) that are consistent with your estimate. The confidence interval effectively provides you with an indication of the precision of your estimates. If the confidence interval is very wide, then there is a lot of uncertainty about what the *true* population average is. However, with a much narrower set of confidence intervals, we have a much more precise estimate of the population parameter.

18.4.1 Improving the precision of the estimates (narrowing the confidence intervals)

When providing advice to governments and the public, we want to be as precise as possible in terms of the estimates of population parameters. As you have seen in the previous section, the confidence interval is a measure of the precision of the estimates; the size of the confidence interval is determined by the standard error of the estimator:

$$95\% \text{ confidence interval } = \bar{x} \pm c.v. \times \widehat{s.e.}\,(\bar{X})$$

We also know that the variance of the sample mean decreases as the sample size gets larger. So, let's repeat the exercise, but this time we will randomly sample 200 observations from the UK Labour Force Survey,[8] rather than the previous sample of 100.

We gain the following data:

Sample mean, $\overline{X}$	$\overline{x} = 664.52$
Sum of squares: $\sum_{i=1}^{n}(X_i - \overline{X})^2$	$\sum_{i=1}^{n}(x_i - \overline{x})^2 = 30{,}913{,}816$
Estimate of population variance, s_{n-1}^2	$s_{n-1}^2 = \left[\frac{1}{n-1}\right] \times \sum_{i=1}^{n}(x_i - \overline{x})^2 = \frac{1}{199} \times 30{,}913{,}816 = 155{,}345.81$
Critical value from the t-distribution with 199 degrees of freedom	5% critical value: $c.v. = 1.97$

To calculate the confidence interval, we first need the (estimated) standard error of the sample mean. We know that $var(\overline{X}) = \frac{var(X)}{n}$, and so, the estimated variance of the sample mean will just be $\widehat{var}(\overline{X}) = \frac{s_{n-1}^2}{n} = \frac{155345.81}{200} = 776.72905$.

As such, the 95 per cent confidence interval will just be equal to:

$$664.52 \pm 1.97 \times \sqrt{776.72905} = (609.606, 719.424)$$

By increasing the sample size, we have a narrower range of possible population averages that are consistent with our sample mean:

- Based on 100 observations, the 95 per cent confidence interval was (587.8178, 735.0822).
- Based on 200 observations, the 95 per cent confidence interval was (609.606, 719.424).

Of course, as always with statistics, if you took a different sample of 200 observations from the population, you would get different estimates of the sample mean, and the variance, and thus the 95 per cent confidence interval, would be different. However, each time the interpretation of the confidence interval would be the same: the values in the confidence interval are the range of population parameters for which you would fail to reject the null hypothesis at the 5 per cent significance level.

Figure 18.6 provides a visual interpretation of how you calculate the 95 per cent confidence interval relating to an estimated population parameter, and what conclusions we can make.[9] The key thing to remember is that:

- any value, x, that lies within the confidence interval is a value that we would fail to reject the null hypothesis that the true population parameter is equal to x
- we would reject any null hypothesis at the 5 per cent significance level that the true population parameter is any value outside of the 95 per cent confidence interval.

[8] This data is available to download from Data sets and exercises at the end of this chapter.

[9] Note that the degrees of freedom determine the multiplier in the confidence interval: with 199 degrees of freedom, this is 1.97; with 99, this was 1.984. Where we use a normal distribution for the test, this would be 1.96.

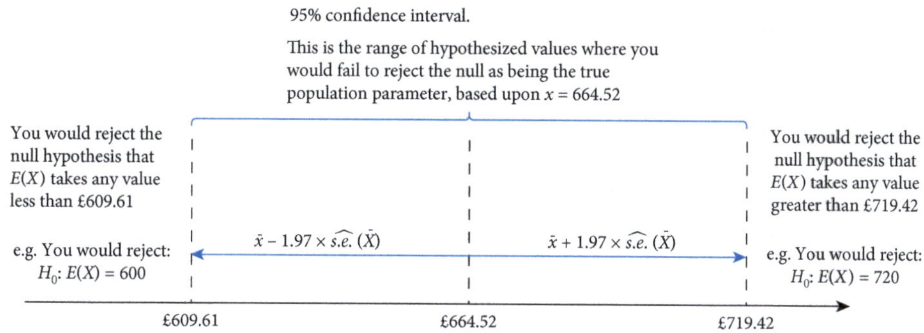

Figure 18.6 Visual interpretation of the 95 per cent confidence intervals with 199 degrees of freedom.

18.4.2 When are confidence intervals used?

Whilst we have introduced the confidence interval for a t-test, the methodology used here is equally valid if you were to carry out a test where the test-statistic is normally distributed. Confidence intervals are important, as they give you a sense for the range of possible values that your estimates might imply for the population.

For example, when the Bank of England produces estimates of GDP level and projected GDP, it often produces 'fan charts'. These fan charts provide confidence intervals for the estimated level of GDP, based on their point estimates. Remember that point estimates are not the true population parameter that you are estimating. They are merely estimates of the population parameter that you are estimating. The confidence intervals provide a range of values, within which you can be reasonably confident that the true population parameter is contained.

Summary

In this chapter, we have introduced testing when we do not know the true variance of the underlying population random variable. As a general rule, if you have a small sample, and you are using estimates of the population variance, then you will need to use the t-distribution. Alternatively, if you have a large sample, or you know the true population variance, then you can use the normal distribution.

In the next two chapters, we will introduce two additional forms of testing. We will introduce testing relating to proportions in the population, and we will introduce a form of testing that allows us to distinguish between population averages for different groups of individuals.

Key formulae

Standardizing the t-distribution	$t = \dfrac{\overline{x} - E(\overline{X})}{\sqrt{\dfrac{s_{n-1}^2}{n}}}$
Calculating a confidence interval	95% confidence interval $= \overline{x} \pm c.v. \times \widehat{s.e.}\,(\overline{X})$

Appendix
Upper tails of the t-distribution

	P									
	50	40	30	20	10	5	2.5	1	0.5	0.05
$v = 1$	0	0.325	0.727	1.376	3.078	6.314	12.706	31.821	63.657	636.619
2	0	0.289	0.617	1.061	1.886	2.920	4.303	6.965	9.925	31.599
3	0	0.277	0.584	0.978	1.638	2.353	3.182	4.541	5.841	12.924
4	0	0.271	0.569	0.941	1.533	2.132	2.776	3.747	4.604	8.610
5	0	0.267	0.559	0.920	1.476	2.015	2.571	3.365	4.032	6.869
6	0	0.265	0.553	0.906	1.440	1.943	2.447	3.143	3.707	5.959
7	0	0.263	0.549	0.896	1.415	1.895	2.365	2.998	3.499	5.408
8	0	0.262	0.546	0.889	1.397	1.860	2.306	2.896	3.355	5.041
9	0	0.261	0.543	0.883	1.383	1.833	2.262	2.821	3.250	4.781
10	0	0.260	0.542	0.879	1.372	1.812	2.228	2.764	3.169	4.587
11	0	0.260	0.540	0.876	1.363	1.796	2.201	2.718	3.106	4.437
12	0	0.259	0.539	0.873	1.356	1.782	2.179	2.681	3.055	4.318
13	0	0.259	0.538	0.870	1.350	1.771	2.160	2.650	3.012	4.221
14	0	0.258	0.537	0.868	1.345	1.761	2.145	2.624	2.977	4.140
15	0	0.258	0.536	0.866	1.341	1.753	2.131	2.602	2.947	4.073
16	0	0.258	0.535	0.865	1.337	1.746	2.120	2.583	2.921	4.015
17	0	0.257	0.534	0.863	1.333	1.740	2.110	2.567	2.898	3.965
18	0	0.257	0.534	0.862	1.330	1.734	2.101	2.552	2.878	3.922
19	0	0.257	0.533	0.861	1.328	1.729	2.093	2.539	2.861	3.883
20	0	0.257	0.533	0.860	1.325	1.725	2.086	2.528	2.845	3.850

	P									
	50	40	30	20	10	5	2.5	1	0.5	0.05
21	0	0.257	0.532	0.859	1.323	1.721	2.080	2.518	2.831	3.819
22	0	0.256	0.532	0.858	1.321	1.717	2.074	2.508	2.819	3.792
23	0	0.256	0.532	0.858	1.319	1.714	2.069	2.500	2.807	3.768
24	0	0.256	0.531	0.857	1.318	1.711	2.064	2.492	2.797	3.745
25	0	0.256	0.531	0.856	1.316	1.708	2.060	2.485	2.787	3.725
26	0	0.256	0.531	0.856	1.315	1.706	2.056	2.479	2.779	3.707
27	0	0.256	0.531	0.855	1.314	1.703	2.052	2.473	2.771	3.690
28	0	0.256	0.530	0.855	1.313	1.701	2.048	2.467	2.763	3.674
29	0	0.256	0.530	0.854	1.311	1.699	2.045	2.462	2.756	3.659
30	0	0.256	0.530	0.854	1.310	1.697	2.042	2.457	2.750	3.646
40	0	0.255	0.529	0.851	1.303	1.684	2.021	2.423	2.704	3.551
50	0	0.255	0.528	0.849	1.299	1.676	2.009	2.403	2.678	3.496
60	0	0.254	0.527	0.848	1.296	1.671	2.000	2.390	2.660	3.460
90	0	0.254	0.526	0.846	1.291	1.662	1.987	2.368	2.632	3.402
120	0	0.254	0.526	0.845	1.289	1.658	1.980	2.358	2.617	3.373
240	0	0.254	0.525	0.843	1.285	1.651	1.970	2.342	2.596	3.332
∞	0	0.253	0.524	0.842	1.282	1.645	1.960	2.326	2.576	3.291

The values in this table provide us with values from the t-distribution, such that $P(T \geq t) = \frac{P}{100}$.

Testing Related to Proportions of the Population

19

Learning outcomes for this chapter

By the end of this chapter you will be able to:

- Estimate proportions using random samples from populations
- Carry out exact tests relating to binomially distributed variables using statistical software
- Carry out tests using a normal approximation to the binomial
- Construct confidence intervals relating to binomial distributions

Mathematical tools

- Algebra
- Inequalities
- Summations

Introduction

In Chapters 12 and 13, we introduced the **binomial distribution**, and saw that we could approximate the binomial distribution using the **normal distribution**. The binomial distribution is a really useful way of modelling simple 'count' variables, where there are two possible outcomes. For instance, the binomial distribution can model:

- the number of heads obtained when we flip a coin n times
- the number of Labour voters in the 2024 general election when we sample n individuals from the UK population
- the number of people who are members of trade unions when we sample n individuals from the UK population.

In each of these cases, the distribution can be modelled using a binomial distribution, in which $X \sim Bin(n, p)$, where n is the number of trials and p is the probability, or proportion of individuals in the population. For example, p might be the proportion of the UK population who are members of trade unions. However, we rarely know the true value of p, and as such, we will need to estimate it.

In this chapter, we will explore two concepts:

1. How we can estimate the value of p.
2. How we can test hypotheses relating to the true value of p.

When we introduce testing, we will appeal to the normal approximation to the binomial. However, because we will be using a continuous random variable to model the behaviour of a discrete random variable, the test will not be exact.

19.1 Estimating *p*

Let's suppose we are interested in testing whether a coin is biased or not; that is, we are interested in testing whether the coin has equal probability of landing heads and tails upwards. If we flip a coin n times, and model outcome as $X_i = 1$ if the coin lands heads upwards, and $X_i = 0$ if the coin lands tails upwards, then the number of heads could be constructed as $X = \sum_{i=1}^{n} X_i$ and we could model the number of heads that we achieve by:

$$X \sim B(n, p)$$

where p is the (unknown) probability that we achieve a head on any given flip of the coin. We know that:

	Characteristic of each trial, X_i	Characteristic of binomial distribution X, based on n trials
Expectation	$E(X_i) = p$	$E(X) = n$
Variance	$var(X_i) = p(1-p)$	$var(X) = np(1-p)$

Suppose that we wanted to estimate p. An estimator for p would simply be the sample mean of the number of heads we achieve—that is, the proportion of times that we achieve a head. Let's define our estimator for p as $\hat{p}$:

$$\hat{p} = \frac{\sum_{i=1}^{n} X_i}{n} = \frac{X}{n}$$

We might be interested in whether $\hat{p}$ is an unbiased estimator of the population probability, p. Since $\hat{p}$ is just the number of heads (X) divided by the number of observations n, we can evaluate the expectation of $\hat{p}$ by taking expectations of $\frac{X}{n}$:

$$E(\hat{p}) = E\left(\frac{X}{n}\right)$$

By the rules of expectations, we know that, for a constant a multiplied by a random variable, X, then $E(aX) = aE(X)$. In this instance $\frac{1}{n}$ is a constant, and so:

$$\Rightarrow E(\hat{p}) = \frac{1}{n} \times E(X)$$

We know that $E(X) = np$, and so that means that:

$$E(\hat{p}) = \frac{1}{n} \times n \times p = p$$

19.2 Testing relating to the binomial distribution—the exact binomial test

Suppose that we are interested in testing whether a coin is a 'fair' or a 'biased' coin. To investigate this, you flip the coin 100 times and obtain 57 heads. Each flip is an independent and identically distributed (*iid*) trial, with the probability of landing heads upwards as an (unknown) p. This means that the number of heads then follows a binomial distribution based on 100 trials, each with probability p.

Based on the 100 flips, we can construct an estimate of the probability of the coin landing heads upwards as:

$$\hat{p} = \frac{X}{n} = \frac{57}{100} = 0.57$$

If we want to test that the coin is a fair coin, this is equivalent to testing the following null hypothesis and alternative hypothesis.

$$H_0: p = 0.5$$
$$H_A: p \neq 0.5$$

All of the tests we have seen so far have required us to estimate (or know) the variance of the random variable, but with the exact binomial test, this is unnecessary. Since we know n and we know p, we can construct a probability distribution for X if the null hypothesis is true. We can then use this to determine what a rare outcome is (e.g. what are the most extreme 5 per cent of outcomes), and compare this with the number of successes we have observed in this example.

We know that, for a standard binomial distribution, the probability of achieving k successes is equal to $P(X = k) = C_k^n p^k (1 - p)^{n-k}$. We also know that the probability of observing k or fewer successes is just equal to the sum of these probabilities:

$$P(X \leq k_l) = \sum_{i=0}^{k_l} P(X = i), \quad P(X \geq k_u) = \sum_{i=k_u}^{n} P(X = i)$$

Let's define k_l as the marginal value defining the smallest 2.5 per cent of the distribution, and k_u as the marginal value defining the largest 2.5 per cent of the distribution. We can plot out the distribution of X, with the most extreme 5 per cent of outcomes highlighted, in Figure 19.1.

Calculating the most extreme 5 per cent of outcomes would be quite time consuming, but statistical software packages such as Microsoft Excel can do this for you. If you wish to find the most extreme 5 per cent of outcomes (i.e. the most extreme 2.5 per cent of outcomes in either tail of the distribution), you could use the formula =BINOM.INV(n, p, α), where n

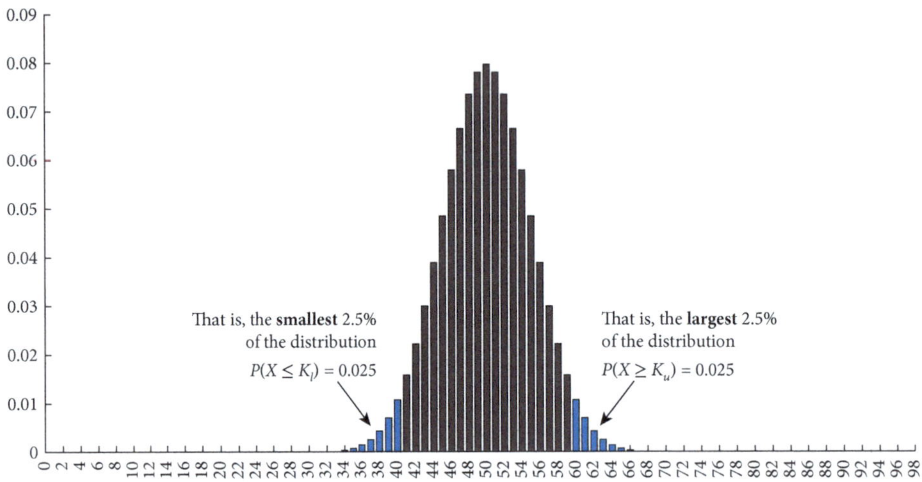

Figure 19.1 The most extreme 5 per cent of outcomes from a binomial distribution based on 100 trials, and $p = 0.5$.

is the number of trials, p the probability of success on each trial, and α the percentile. Since we want the most extreme 5 per cent of outcomes, we would set $\alpha = 0.025$ and $\alpha = 0.975$, to give us the most extreme 2.5 per cent of outcomes in either tail:

- =BINOM.INV(100, 0.5, 0.025)=40
- =BINOM.INV(100, 0.5, 0.975)=60

So, that is, the most extreme 5 per cent of outcomes lie to the left of 40, and to the right of 60. These would correspond with values of $\hat{p}$ of 0.4 and 0.6.

In this example, we observed 57 heads. This is between 40 and 60, so it is not within the most extreme 5 per cent of outcomes. That is, it is not in the rejection region, and so we would fail to reject the null hypothesis. This is therefore equivalent to saying that we would fail to reject the null hypothesis that $p = 0.5$.

Algorithm for the exact binomial test

Where we randomly sample n independent and identically distributed (*iid*) observations of a Bernoulli trial (i.e. one that takes only the values 1 or 0, with probabilities p and $(1 - p)$ respectively, we can test hypotheses relating to the population probability.

1. Write down a null and alternative hypothesis relating to the probability of success. This might be:

   $H_0: p = 0.4$
   $H_A: p \neq 0.4$

Normally, you would specify your alternative as merely contradicting the null hypothesis, but you could consider a one-tailed test, such as $H_A: p > 0.4$, or $H_A: p < 0.4$. This would simply change the rejection region.

2. Take a sample of size n, and count the number of 'successes'—i.e. the number of observations where $X_i = 1$.
3. Choose an appropriate significance level. This might be 10%, 5%, 1%, or 0.1%.
4. Using n, p, and your significance level, calculate how many successes would be an unlikely outcome; for example, what value of $X = \sum_{i=1}^{n} X_i$ would be in the most extreme 5% of outcomes?
5. Compare your observed number of successes with the critical values calculated in 4. If the number of successes is in this most extreme 5 per cent of outcomes, you would reject the null hypothesis.

Worked example 19.1: Individuals with at least some higher education

In 1997, the new Labour Prime Minister, Tony Blair, set a target of 50 per cent of young people attending university. A key question is whether this target was met. To answer this question, I have randomly sampled 500 individuals from the 2019 UK Labour Force Survey. Individuals who were 18 in 1997 would be 40 in 2019, so I have restricted the sample only to individuals aged 21–40 in 2019.

From the sample of 500 individuals,[1] we observe 238 who have obtained some higher education. This includes individuals who have not achieved a degree, but have received some education in university (or equivalent). We wish to test the hypothesis that 50 per cent of the population of individuals aged 21–40 have received some higher education.

So, our estimate of the proportion of the population with some higher education is:

$$\hat{p} = \frac{238}{500} = 0.476$$

Hypothesis 1

If 50 per cent of the population attended university, then the probability of randomly sampling someone from the population with some higher education would be 0.5. That is, we wish to test the hypothesis that half of the population is gaining some form of higher education.

$$H_0: p = 0.5$$
$$H_A: p \neq 0.5$$

[1] The sample is available to download from Data sets and exercises at the end of this chapter. The variable 'Has any Higher Education' takes the value 1 if the individual has *any* higher education, and 0 otherwise.

Let's define the number of individuals in the sample with some higher education as Y. Since Y is based on n independent and identically distributed draws from the population, each with a probability p of success, we can model Y using a binomial distribution:

$$Y \sim Bin(n, p)$$

More precisely, since $n = 500$, we can write that $Y \sim Bin(500, p)$.

If the null hypothesis is true, then the true population probability is equal to $p = 0.5$. From this, and $n = 500$, we can calculate what would be an unlikely value of Y at the 5 per cent significance level. That is, what are the values of k_l and k_u such that:

$$P(Y \leq k_l) = 0.025 \text{ and } P(Y \geq k_u) = 0.025$$

We will not attempt to calculate this manually, as there are a very large number of possible outcomes, but we will appeal to statistical software (Excel) to answer this question:

- To find the lower critical value: =BINOM.INV(500, 0.5, 0.025)=228
- To find the upper critical value: =BINOM.INV(500, 0.5, 0.025)=272

In this example, we have observed $Y = 238$. This is between k_l and k_u, and so we fail to reject the null hypothesis.

Hypothesis 2

Others have suggested that the true proportion attending university between 1997 and 2019 was closer to 40 per cent of the population. We can also test this hypothesis. If only 40 per cent of the population attended university, then the probability of randomly sampling someone from the population with some higher education would be 0.4:

$$H_0: p = 0.4$$
$$H_A: p \neq 0.4$$

If this null hypothesis were true, then the distribution of Y would be slightly different:

$$Y \sim Bin(500,0.4)$$

This would lead to different critical values:

- To find the lower critical value: =BINOM.INV(500, 0.4, 0.025)=179
- To find the upper critical value: =BINOM.INV(500, 0.4, 0.025)=222

Now, from our sample, we observed $Y = 238$. This is not between k_l and k_u and therefore lies within the rejection region. This rejection region is illustrated in Figure 19.2.[2]

We have observed a value of $Y = 238$; that is, we have seen 238 individuals in our sample of 500 individuals. Because this is within the rejection region we would reject the null hypothesis.

[2] We have deliberately only illustrated outcomes of Y between 159 and 243, because the probability of outcomes outside of this range is vanishingly small, and only serves to increase the width of the axis!

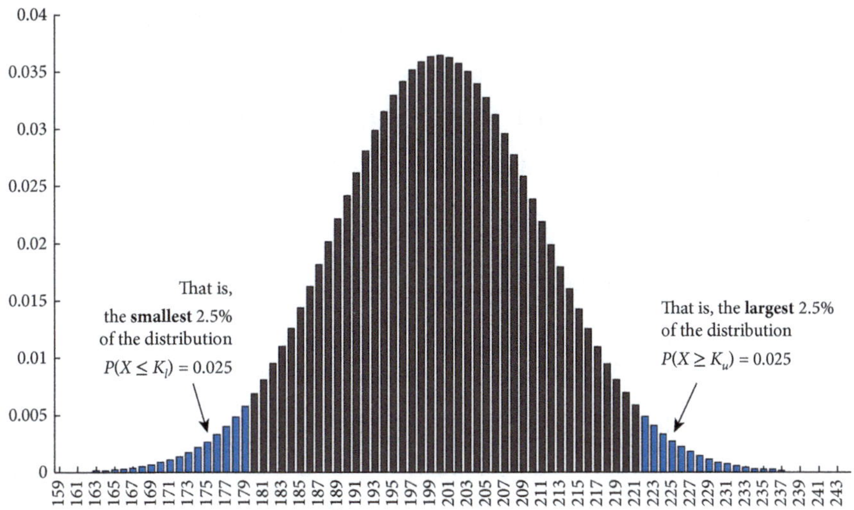

Figure 19.2 Rejection region if $n = 500$ and $p = 0.4$.

Using p-values

We can equally carry out statistical tests using **p-values** relating to the binomial distribution. If we repeat the second hypothesis from the previous example:

$$H_0: p = 0.4$$
$$H_A: p \neq 0.4$$

Based on 500 observations, if the null hypothesis is true, the expected number of individuals in the sample with some higher education would be:

$$E(Y \mid H_0 \; is \; true) = 0.4 \times 500 = 200$$

We have observed $Y = 238$, which is 38 above the expected value. The p-value tells you the probability of (randomly) gaining a test statistic at least 38 away from the expected value, if the null hypothesis were true:

$$p - value = P(|Y - 200| \geq 38)$$

That is, we are looking for the probability of randomly observing an outcome that is either:

- 38 or more above the expected value (i.e. greater than or equal to 238)
- 38 or more below the expected value (i.e. greater than or equal to 162)

We can once again appeal to statistical software to calculate this for us. The formula

$$=\text{BINOM.DIST}\left(\text{k}, \text{n}, \text{p}, \text{TRUE}\right)$$

will calculate the probability that a random variable Y which is binomially distributed based on n trials, each with probability p, gains (at most) k successes[3], $P(Y \leq k)$

[3] TRUE simply indicates that you are looking at the cumulative distribution.

So to calculate the p-value, if the null hypothesis is true, $Y \sim Bin(500,0.4)$

- $P(Y \leq 162)$=BINOM.DIST(162, 500. 0.4, TRUE)= 0.000267
- $P(Y \geq 238) = 1 - P(Y < 237)$=1-BINOM.DIST(237, 500, 0.4, TRUE)= 0.00034

Because Y is a discrete random variable, to find $P(Y \geq 238)$, we had to consider $1 - P(Y < 237)$, so that we ensured that $P(Y = 238)$ is included. The total p-value is then the sum of these probabilities:

$$= 0.000267 + 0.0034 = 0.000607$$

This is equivalent to saying that the probability of randomly gaining an outcome 38 above (or below) the expected value, when $p = 0.4$, based on 500 trials is equal to 0.000607.

- Because this is less than 0.1, you would reject the null at the 10 per cent significance level.
- Because this is less than 0.05, you would reject the null at the 5 per cent significance level.
- Because this is less than 0.01, you would reject the null at the 1 per cent significance level.
- Because this is less than 0.001, you would reject the null at the 0.1 per cent significance level.

These results may look a little surprising, not least because:

$$P(Y \leq 162) \neq P(Y \geq 238)$$

This is because, apart from $p = 0.5$, the binomial distribution is not exactly symmetric. As such, when you are looking for p-values, will have different values in either tail.

19.3 Testing when we do not have access to statistical software

When we don't have access to statistical software, we could use a normal approximation to the binomial. We know that, if $X \sim Bin(n, p)$, then since $E(X) = np$ and $var(X) = np(1 - p)$, we can approximate the binomial distribution using a random variable—let's call it X_N—that is normally distributed, with expectation np and variance $np(1 - p)$:

$$X_N \sim N(np,np(1 - p))$$

Now, we can use this to carry out statistical tests as well, in the same way as normal. However, as we are using a continuous approximation to a discrete random variable, we will need to carry out continuity corrections.

19.3.1 Testing a biased coin

To illustrate this, let's consider a simple example. Suppose that a salesperson in a novelty shop tries to sell you a 'trick coin'. The salesperson claims that the coin is a very special coin, and the probability of it landing heads upwards is not 0.5, but instead is 0.7. You decide that you want to test the salesperson's claim in a statistical test. As such, you flip the coin 100 times, and observe 60 heads. Based on this, using an appropriate approximation, can we reject the hypothesis that the true probability of gaining a head is 0.7? Let's define p as the probability of observing a head on any given flip:

$$H_0: p = 0.7$$
$$H_A: p \neq 0.7$$

The number of heads Y will follow a binomial distribution, and if the null hypothesis is true, $Y \sim Bin(100, 0.7)$. From this, if the null hypothesis is true, the expected number of heads is:

$$E(Y) = np = 100 \times 0.7 = 70$$

and the variance of the number of heads

$$var(Y) = np(1 - p) = 100 \times 0.7 \times 0.3 = 21$$

We can approximate the distribution of Y (conditional on the null hypothesis being true), with a normally distributed variable, Y_N, with expectation 70 and variance 21:

$$Y_N \sim N(70, 21)$$

We have observed 60 heads, and a simple way of testing our hypothesis would be to construct the p-value associated with 60. If the p-value is less than our chosen significance level (5 per cent), then we would reject the null hypothesis.

First, let's construct an estimate of the probability, $P(Y \leq 60)$—that is, the probability of observing Y in the left-hand tail. Because Y_N is a continuous random variable, approximating a discrete random variable, we will need to use a continuity correction, to ensure that we include $Y = 60$. So:

$$P(Y \leq 60) \cong P(Y_N \leq 60.5)$$

To calculate this probability, we can standardize the test statistic:

$$Z = \frac{Y_N - E(Y_N)}{\sqrt{var(Y_N)}} \sim N(0,1)$$

So, if we wish to standardize our observed value of Y_N, we can substitute in the expectation and variance, based on our hypothesized value of p:

$$z = \frac{60.5 - 70}{\sqrt{21}} = -2.07$$

Now, we have three values:

$$P(Y \leq 60) \approx P(Y_N \leq 60.5) = P(Z \leq -2.07)$$

Whilst many standard normal tables only consider positive values of z, we do know that $\Phi(-z) = 1 - \Phi(z)$, and $\Phi(2.07) = 0.981$. As such, $P(Z \leq -2.07) = 1 - P(Z \leq 2.07) = 0.019$.

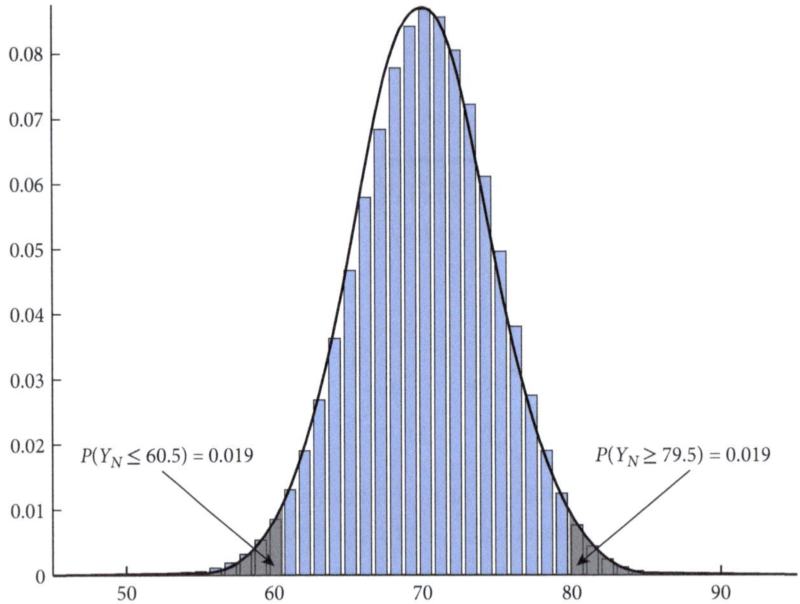

Figure 19.3 Distribution of possible outcomes if the null hypothesis is true.

This probability is illustrated by the shaded area in the left-hand tail of Figure 19.3, which shows the normal approximation to the binomial.[4] Because the normal distribution is a symmetric distribution and, by default, we would normally consider a two-tailed test, we don't just want to know the probability of being in that left-hand tail, but also the right-hand tail as well.

Comparing the approximation with the exact binomial test

We can check how well the normal approximation has performed by comparing the p-value with the exact binomial probability.

Using statistical software, such as Excel, it is relatively easy to show that $P(Y \leq 60) = 0.020989$, and that $P(Y \geq 80) = 0.016463$. This would create a two-tailed p-value equal to 0.037. For all intents and purposes, this approximation is close enough to be able to make clear conclusions:

$$P(Y \leq 60) = \text{BINOM.DIST}\left(60, 100, 0.7, \text{TRUE}\right)$$

$$P(Y \geq 80) = 1 - P(Y \leq 79) = 1\text{-BINOM.DIST}\left(79, 100, 0.7, \text{TRUE}\right)$$

It should be noted, though, that this approximation is only valid if n is relatively large, and p is not close to either 0 or 1.

[4] This figure focuses on the range between 45 and 90. Whilst it is possible for us to observe outcomes of Y less than 45, the probability is almost indistinguishable from zero. Having run a simulation with 10,000,000 observations, we saw zero outcomes less than 45. The probability $P(Y < 45)$ can be calculated as 5.85×10^{-8}. That is, for every $17{,}092{,}525.1\left(= \frac{1}{5.85 \times 10^{-8}}\right)$ observations, we would expect to see one observation of Y less than 45.

As such, if the null hypothesis were true, (i.e. $p = 0.7$), the probability of observing an outcome as extreme as $Y = 60$ would be approximately equal to $2 \times P(Y_N \leq 60.5) = 2 \times 0.019 = 0.038$. If we use our conventional significance level of 5 per cent, then the p-value is less than 0.05, which would mean that we would reject the null hypothesis.

Worked example 19.2: Data-based example—Individuals with at least some higher education

As a second example, let's consider the data from the UK LFS about individuals with at least some higher education. We randomly sampled 500 individuals (aged 21–40), and found 238 who had some higher education. We will repeat the second hypothesis we tested—that is, that 40 per cent of the population have some higher education:

$$H_0: p = 0.4$$

$$H_A: p \neq 0.4$$

Let's define the number of individuals within the sample (of 500) with some higher education as a random variable, X. Since each observation is assumed to be randomly drawn from a population, with a constant probability, p, of having some higher education, we can treat X as following the binomial distribution:

$$X \sim Bin(n, p)$$

So, if the null hypothesis is true, then and $X \sim Bin(500,0.4)$ and $E(X) = 200$, with $var(X) = 120$. As such, we can approximate the distribution using a normally distributed variable, X_N, with expectation 200 and variance 120:

$$X_N \sim N(200,120)$$

We have observed 238 individuals in the sample (of 500) who have at least some higher education. If the null hypothesis is true, what is the probability of randomly observing an outcome at least this far from the expected value? We can begin by calculating an approximation of $P(X \geq 238)$.

Using a continuity correction, as before, $P(X \geq 238) \approx P(X_N \geq 237.5)$. To calculate this, we can standardize the distribution, giving us:

$$Z = \frac{X_N - E(X_N)}{\sqrt{var(X_N)}} \sim N(0,1)$$

$$\Rightarrow z = \frac{237.5 - 200}{\sqrt{120}} = 3.423$$

That is, $P(X \geq 238) \approx P(X_N \geq 237.5) = P(Z \geq 3.423)$. We can calculate this probability as:

$$P(Z \geq 3.423) = 1 - \Phi(3.423) = 1 - 0.99969 = 0.00031$$

Similarly, as we are considering a two-tailed test, we want to find the overall probability of randomly being at least 38 above the expected value, so we will need to multiply this probability by 2 to give the p-value:

$$P(|Z| \geq 3.423) = 2 \times 0.00031 = 0.00062$$

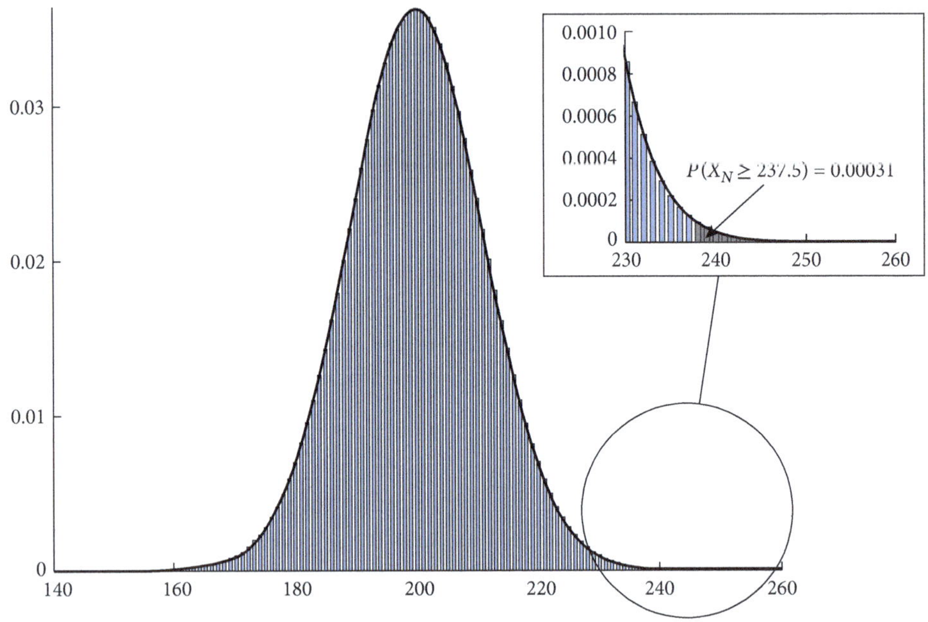

Figure 19.4 Normal approximation to the binomial if $p = 0.4$.

This p-value is a lot smaller than the standard significance level (0.05, or 5 per cent), so you would reject the null hypothesis at the 5 per cent significance level. This is illustrated in Figure 19.4. The probability in either tail is 0.00031, which is very, very small.

Is this a good approximation?

We calculated the p-values associated with $X = 238$ exactly in Worked example 19.1:

- We showed that the probability of observing an outcome at least 38 above (or below) the expected value was equal to 0.000607.
- Using the normal approximation to the binomial, we have achieved a p-value equal to 0.00062.

These p-values are, for all practical purposes, equal to each other. As such, we can make equivalent inferences using both the normal approximation and the exact binomial test. It is worth repeating, though, that this approximation breaks down when p is either very close to 0 or very close to 1. In those cases, you would need to consider the exact test.

19.4 Constructing confidence intervals

So far, we have not had to estimate the variance of a random variable following the binomial distribution for testing, but when we construct the 95 per cent confidence interval around an estimate, we do not have a hypothesized value for p, and so we cannot construct confidence intervals around an estimate.

In this section, we will build on the normal approximation to the binomial, but alongside estimating $\hat{p}$, we will also construct an estimate of the variance of $\hat{p}$.

For a random variable, X, which follows a binomial distribution, $X \sim Bin(n, p)$, our estimator, $\hat{p}$, will just be the underlying variable representing the number of successes, X, divided by the number of observations:

$$\hat{p} = \frac{X}{n}$$

Now, we already know that $var(X) = np(1-p)$. Since we have constructed $\hat{p}$ by multiplying X by a constant, $\frac{1}{n}$, we can use this to construct the variance of $\hat{p}$:

$$var(\hat{p}) = var\left(\frac{1}{n} \times X\right) = \frac{1}{n^2} \times var(X) = \frac{1}{n^2} \times np(1-p) = \frac{p(1-p)}{n}$$

All we have done here is taken advantage of the rules of variances; if we multiply a random variable, Y, by a constant, a, then $var(aX) = a^2 var(X)$. As such, we have shown that the variance of $\hat{p}$ is just equal to:

$$var(\hat{p}) = \frac{p(1-p)}{n}$$

We can also use our estimate of $\hat{p}$ to construct an estimator for the variance of $\hat{p}$. If we substitute $\hat{p}$ into the estimator, we will gain an estimator for the variance of $\hat{p}$:

$$\widehat{var}(\hat{p}) = \frac{\hat{p}(1-\hat{p})}{n}$$

Observation

If X is constructed based on n independent and identically distributed observations $X_1, X_2, \ldots, X_n$, then it is possible to show that:

$$\hat{p} = \frac{1}{n}\sum_{i=1}^{n} X_i, \quad \widehat{var}(\hat{p}) = \frac{\frac{1}{n} \times \sum_{i=1}^{n} (X_i - \overline{X})^2}{n}$$

That is, $\hat{p}$ is just a sample mean, and $\widehat{var}(\hat{p})$ is constructed based on a **biased estimator** for the variance of X_i divided by n, to construct a biased estimator for the variance of $\overline{X}$.

In principle, you could construct an unbiased estimate of the variance of $\hat{p}$ by dividing by $n-1$ rather than n. However, in practice, this makes little difference to the accuracy of your estimates for the following reasons:

- We are appealing to the normal approximation to the binomial. As such, the confidence intervals will not be exact.
- The approximation only holds for large values of n.
- The underlying random variable is a discrete random variable, and whether you divide by n or $n-1$ will make no difference to the observations included within the 95 per cent confidence interval.

Suppose we flip a coin 200 times and achieve 114 heads. What does this suggest the 95 per cent confidence interval for p is? We are going to use $\hat{p}$ as an estimator for p, and in this example:

$$\hat{p} = \frac{114}{200} = 0.57$$

From this, we can calculate an estimate of the variance of $\hat{p}$: $\widehat{var}(\hat{p}) = \frac{\hat{p}(1-\hat{p})}{n} = \frac{0.57 \times 0.43}{200}$ $= 0.0012255$. To construct a 95 per cent confidence interval, we will take the 5 per cent significance critical value from the normal distribution (as n is large):

$$= \hat{p} \pm c.v._{5} \times \widehat{s.e.}\ (\hat{p})$$
$$= 0.57 \pm 1.96 \times \sqrt{0.0012255} = (0.50139,\ 0.6386)$$

So, our approximation of the 95 per cent confidence interval for p is between 0.50139 and 0.6386. This suggests that, if we observed 114 heads when we flip a coin 200 times, we would reject the null hypothesis that $p = 0.5$ at the 5 per cent significance level.

It should be noted that the exact p-value associated with a two-tailed test that $p = 0.5$ is 0.056 (marginally above 5 per cent). This would mean that you would fail to reject the null hypothesis. As such, the 95 per cent confidence interval is not exact, but provides an indication of the range of p where you would fail to reject the null hypothesis.

Caution about this method

One problem immediately emerges when you gain estimates of $\hat{p}$ which are close to either 0 or 1. If we use the normal distribution as an approximation for the binomial, we will obtain confidence intervals that go beyond 0 or 1.

To illustrate, suppose that you flipped a coin 40 times, and obtained 38 heads. This would give an estimated $\hat{p} = \frac{38}{40} = 0.95$.

We would also have an estimate of the variance of $\hat{p}$ as $\frac{\hat{p}(1-\hat{p})}{n} = \frac{0.95 \times 0.05}{40} = 0.0011875$.

If we assume that $\hat{p}$ is approximately normally distributed, with 39 degrees of freedom, the critical value from the t-tables (at the 5 per cent significance level) is 2.023. As such, the naïve 95% confidence interval would be:

$$= 0.95 \pm 2.023 \times \sqrt{0.0011875} = (0.880, 1.020)$$

That is, the upper end of the 95 per cent confidence interval is beyond 1, which is impossible! This method works well for $\hat{p}$ that is in the middle of the distribution, but when we are very close to 0 or 1, then the method breaks down.

If you do need to estimate confidence intervals when p is close to 0 or 1, you would need to appeal to alternative methods, such as those developed by Agresti and Coull.[5]

[5] A. Agresti and B. Coull (1998), 'Approximate is Better Than "Exact" for Interval Estimation of Binomial Proportions', *American Statistician*, 52(2), 119–126.

Summary

In this chapter, we have introduced two ways in which we can test hypotheses relating to binomial distributions. The first is an exact method, where we rely on statistical software to calculate probabilities relating to observed outcomes, based upon hypothesized values of p. The second relies on the normal approximation to the binomial, which we first saw in how we can test proportions by appealing to the normal approximation to the binomial. The method we have discussed works well when the sample size is large, and the proportion is not very close to 0 or 1. However, when the sample size is small, or the proportion is very close to 0 or 1, then this method breaks down.

Further Testing: Equality of Means

20

Learning outcomes for this chapter

By the end of this chapter you will be able to:

- Explain why we need to develop a new method to test for the equality of means across populations
- Carry out statistical tests for the equality of means, both when the variance is assumed to be the same across groups, and when the variance is allowed to differ across groups
- Carry out tests for specific differences in population averages
- Carry out advanced tests for proportional relationships between population averages
- Explain the limitations of simple statistical testing for making wider conclusions

Mathematical tools

- Algebra

Introduction

So far, when we've carried out statistical testing, we have been interested in testing a hypothesis about a population parameter relating to a single **random variable**. However, we are often interested in whether that parameter is equal across more than one **population**.

One of the most fundamental questions an econometrician might ask is whether there is any underlying difference between two groups of people, or countries, or policies. For example, let's suppose we are looking at two separate groups of people, let's say men and women, and we are interested in examining whether men earn more or less (and how much more or less they earn) in the workforce than women. Similarly, you might ask the question about whether, on average, pupils gain higher GCSE scores in Free schools, or in standard community schools.

We will begin by focusing on the first question. Historically, it has been known that, on average, men are paid more in the workforce than women. However, since the 1970 Equal Pay Act, it has been illegal to offer any less favourable pay and conditions between men and women in employment. Nonetheless, it is often asserted that, on average, male employees are still earning more than equivalent female employees.

> 'The gender pay gap has been declining slowly over time; over the last decade it has fallen by approximately a quarter among full-time employees, and in April 2023 it stands at 7.7%.'
> Gender pay gap in the UK: 2023, ONS (2023)[1]

In this chapter, we are going to see how we can test these hypotheses across more than one population. We will introduce a test to examine, not whether a population parameter is equal to a particular value (e.g. whether $E(X) = 650$), but instead, whether that parameter is equal to the parameter in a different population. For example, if we represent an outcome amongst males as Y_M and amongst females as Y_F, we would be interested in testing whether $E(Y_M) = E(Y_F)$.

20.1 How might we test across groups?

Many countries across the world have introduced legislation that requires male and female workers to be paid the same wage for substantively the same job (e.g. in the USA, equal pay legislation was introduced in 1963, whilst in the UK, legislation was introduced in 1970).

Earlier in this book, we examined the published gender gap within firms, which looks at the median pay of male and female workers. However, this provides an indication of the pay gap within an individual firm, but it doesn't provide an indication at either an industry level or the country level.

You might, for example, want to test whether, on average, males and females are paid the same across the UK. As such, you might want to test that the expected wages for males are equal to the expected wages for females. You could do this by observing all of the wages in the population, and calculating the average male wage and average female wage, and then comparing the results, or you could use statistical testing.

Testing a hypothesis about a single population characteristic

We have seen that we can test a hypothesis about a single population characteristic using a simple t- or z-test.

We start by stating a hypothesis about the population characteristic. For example, we might hypothesize that the expected value (of a random variable, X) is equal to 5:

H_0: $E(X) = 5$

H_A: $E(X) \neq 5$

[1] https://www.ons.gov.uk/employmentandlabourmarket/peopleinwork/earningsandworkinghours/bulletins/genderpaygapintheuk/2023 (accessed 11 November 2023).

To test this hypothesis, we would need to construct a t- or a z-statistic, based on your estimate of the population parameter, and the (estimated) **standard error** of your **estimator**. So, for example, if you are using the sample mean of n observations of the random variable, X, then:

$$T = \frac{\overline{X} - 5}{\widehat{s.e.}(\overline{X})} \sim t_{n-1}$$

If we are using an **estimate** of the standard error of the sample mean, then the resulting test statistic will follow a **t-distribution**, with $n - 1$ degrees of freedom.

When investigating whether populations have equal expected values, it can often be tempting to look at an estimate of the population average from one population, and then test whether the average of the second population is equal to that estimate from the first population. For example, you might observe that the first sample has a sample mean of 100, and then for the second sample, you might try to test the hypothesis that the population average is (also) equal to 100. However, this would make two key errors:

1. Whilst the estimate of the population average relating to the first sample is equal to 100, this is almost certainly not the same as the true population average.
2. Due to sampling variation, you can observe two estimates of the same population average which are substantially different from each other.

Worked example 20.1: Why can't we test hypotheses based upon the estimate of a second population's expected value?

To illustrate this problem, let's consider the following example. A population random variable, X, has an expected value equal to 100, and a **variance** equal to 500. That is:

$$E(X) = 100$$
$$var(X) = 500$$

You randomly sample 50 **independent and identically distributed** (*iid*) observations from the population, and construct the sample mean. We know that, if the observations are *iid*, then the expectation of the sample mean is equal to the expectation of X, and similarly, the variance of the sample mean is given by the variance of X divided by the number of observations:

$$E(\overline{X}) = E(X) = 100$$
$$var(\overline{X}) = \frac{var(X)}{n} = \frac{500}{50} = 10$$

Similarly, since we have a relatively large sample ($n = 50$), we can apply the central limit theorem. This means that the sample mean will be approximately normally distributed. Thus, we can write down the approximate distribution of $\overline{X}$ as:

$$\overline{X} \sim N(100,10)$$

Suppose that you observe a sample mean equal to 95. The distribution of sample means is illustrated in Figure 20.1. The shaded area represents the most extreme 5 per cent of outcomes—that is, the most unlikely 5 per cent of sample means, based on a true population expectation of 100. Our observed sample mean is not within the shaded area, indicating that it is not an unlikely outcome to observe. However, it is close to the most unlikely outcomes in the left-hand tail.

Now suppose that a second statistician randomly samples 50 observations from the same population. However, this statistician believes that the second sample may have been taken from a different population. This statistician obtains a sample mean equal to $\overline{Y} = 104$.

The second statistician decides to test whether or not these samples are taken from the same population (with the same expected value), or not. They might be tempted to use the sample mean from the previous sample as a measure of the true population average of X,[2] and test whether the expected value of Y is different from this. That is, since we observed $\overline{X} = 95$, the second statistician might be tempted to test the hypothesis that $E(Y) = 95$. That is, they might test the following hypotheses:

$$H_0\text{: } E(Y) = 95$$
$$H_A\text{: } E(Y) \neq 95$$

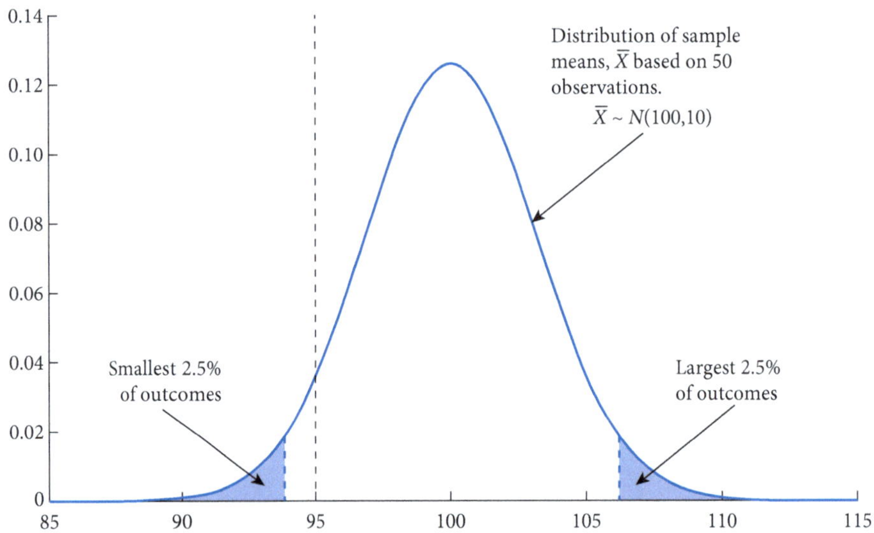

Figure 20.1 Distribution of sample means.

[2] However, this would be incorrect, and you would reject a (true) null of equal population averages much more than 5 per cent of the time.

If you were to do this, the standardized test statistic would be:

$$z = \frac{104 - 95}{\sqrt{10}} = 2.846$$

The critical value from the normal tables at the 5 per cent significance level is 1.96, so you would reject the **null hypothesis** that $E(Y) = 95$.

However, in reality these two samples were taken from the same population. This might seem slightly odd. Both of these sample means are taken from a population with the same expected value, and neither of the sample means is in the most extreme 5 per cent of the distribution, but based on $\overline{y} = 104$, we would reject the null hypothesis that $E(Y) = 95$ (which was our estimate of the population mean of X).

In fact, as you can see from Figure 20.2, the sample means are $2.846 \times s.e.(\overline{X})$ apart. There are a very large number of combinations of possible $\overline{x}$ and $\overline{y}$ that are more than 1.96 times the standard error apart, yet they are all drawn from the same population.

Because of this, if we followed this strategy, we would reject the null hypothesis 16.6 per cent of the time (rather than 5 per cent of the time).[3] The reason that this test yields the wrong answer is that $\overline{x}$ is not the true expectation of X. It is an estimate, and if you were to construct the confidence intervals around $\overline{x}$, the range of values of $E(X)$ that is consistent with $\overline{x} = 95$ is $95 \pm 1.96 \times \sqrt{10} = (88.80, 101.20)$.

To construct a valid test, we need to take account of the fact that the estimates $\overline{x}$ and $\overline{y}$ are imprecise estimates of the expectations, $E(X)$, $E(Y)$.

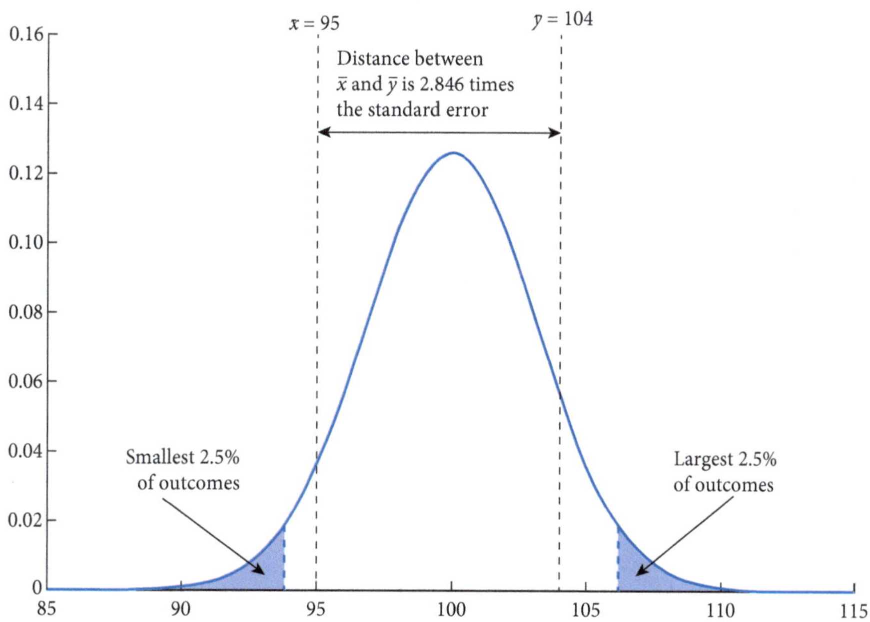

Figure 20.2 Two sample means taken from the same population.

[3] This is proven in the appendix to this chapter.

20.2 A formal method of testing for equality of expected values (equal population means)

As we have seen, when we are comparing population averages across two populations, we cannot just treat one of the estimates as a 'true' population average that we are comparing against. We need to construct a method to be able to take account of the sampling variation that exists when we construct estimates of the population average.

We need to try to create a formal method to test whether the expected values relating to two samples are the same, or different; that is, are the samples drawn from the same underlying population, or different underlying populations?

20.2.1 Constructing a hypothesis to test the equality of means across populations

Suppose we wanted to test the hypothesis that male and female full-time workers are, on average, paid the same. We would have two populations: the first population consists of male full-time workers, and the second population of female full-time workers. If these populations have different average wages, this might be prima facie evidence that discrimination may exist in the workforce.

To motivate a test to examine whether the (population) average is the same across two groups, we could begin by asking what conditions would be true. Let's suppose that we have two population random variables (which could represent male and female earnings, for instance), which we'll represent as X and Y. If the two populations have the same average (or expectation), then we could write that:

$$E(X) = E(Y)$$

But, if this is true, then, by rearranging, we could also write an identity that $E(X) - E(Y) = 0$. This provides us with a hypothesis that we could try to test.

Suppose that we observe (randomly sampled) data from X and randomly sampled data from Y, and we want to test whether the two populations have the same expected value. We could construct a null hypothesis based on this:

$$H_0: E(X) - E(Y) = 0$$
$$H_A: E(X) - E(Y) \neq 0$$

20.2.2 Distribution of estimators to test the equality of means across populations

As with any statistical test, to test the hypotheses, we need estimators of the population parameters we are estimating. In this example, the population parameter we are testing is $E(X) - E(Y)$. We already know that, provided our observations are *iid*, then the sample mean, $\overline{X} = \frac{1}{n}\Sigma_{i=1}^{n} X_i$, is an unbiased estimator of a population expectation:

$$E(\overline{X}) = E(X), \quad E(\overline{Y}) = E(Y)$$

Suppose we use $\hat{\mu} = \bar{X} - \bar{Y}$ as an estimator for $E(X) - E(Y)$. By taking expectations, we can see that:

$$E(\hat{\mu}) = E(\bar{X} - \bar{Y})$$

By the rules of expectations, the expectation of a sum is just the sum of the expectations, so:

$$E(\bar{X} - \bar{Y}) = E(\bar{X}) - E(\bar{Y})$$

So, the difference of the sample means is an unbiased estimator of $E(X) - E(Y)$.

Because $\bar{X} - \bar{Y}$ is an unbiased estimator of $E(X) - E(Y)$, we can use the observed differences of means to test the null hypothesis that the expected value is the same in the two populations. However, to carry out any tests relating to the difference in population averages, we would need to understand the distribution of $\bar{X} - \bar{Y}$.

Suppose that we have randomly observed n independent and identically distributed observations of X_i and m independent and identically distributed observations of Y_i to construct our sample means, then provided n, m are sufficiently large, then the sample means will be (approximately) normally distributed, such that:

$$\bar{X} \sim N\left(E(X), \frac{var(X)}{n}\right), \quad \bar{Y} \sim N\left(E(Y), \frac{var(Y)}{m}\right)$$

A characteristic of normally distributed variables is that, if we combine jointly normal random variables in a **linear combination**, then the resulting distribution will also follow a **normal distribution**. We also know that $E(\bar{X} - \bar{Y}) = E(X) - E(Y)$.

To finalize the distribution, we need to construct the variance of $\bar{X} - \bar{Y}$. Since the observations are drawn independently from the population, we can also assume that the sample means will be independent, and as such, $cov(\bar{X}, \bar{Y}) = 0$. Using our rules of variances:[4]

$$var(\bar{X} - \bar{Y}) = var(\bar{X}) + var(\bar{Y}) - 2cov(\bar{X}, \bar{Y})$$

Since the sample means are independent, then the **covariance** term will be equal to zero, and so:

$$var(\bar{X} - \bar{Y}) = var(\bar{X}) + var(\bar{Y})$$

We know that, if we have n observations of X, then $var(\bar{X}) = \frac{var(X)}{n}$, and similarly, if we have m observations of Y, then $var(\bar{Y}) = \frac{var(Y)}{m}$, so we can write down the variance of the difference of means as a function of the underlying variances of X and Y:

$$\Rightarrow var(\bar{X} - \bar{Y}) = \frac{var(X)}{n} + \frac{var(Y)}{m}$$

So, we can write down the (approximate) distribution of $\bar{X} - \bar{Y}$:

$$(\bar{X} - \bar{Y}) \sim N\left((E(X) - E(Y)), \frac{var(X)}{n} + \frac{var(Y)}{m}\right)$$

[4] In general, $var(aX + bY) = a^2 var(X) + b^2 var(Y) + 2ab\,cov(X, Y)$. In this example, $a = 1, b = -1$, and so $a^2 = b^2 = 1$, but $ab = 1 \times (-1) = -1$.

If we wish to test hypotheses related to the difference of the expectations, we can construct a test statistic in the same way as we have previously. That is, we subtract the hypothesized value (i.e. $\overline{X} - \overline{Y} = 0$), and divide through by the standard error of $\overline{X} - \overline{Y}$:

$$Z = \frac{(\overline{X} - \overline{Y}) - 0}{\sqrt{\frac{var(X)}{n} + \frac{var(Y)}{m}}} \sim N(0,1)$$

So, if we know the variance of the two underlying random variables, X and Y, then we can construct the variance of $\overline{X} - \overline{Y}$.However, it is unlikely that we will ever know with certainty what the true variances of our underlying population random variable are, and so we will need to estimate these.

Remember that if we are using an estimate of the standard error, then we will need to compare the test statistic with the t-distribution:

$$t = \frac{(\overline{x} - \overline{y}) - 0}{\sqrt{\widehat{var}(\overline{X} - \overline{Y})}} = \frac{(\overline{x} - \overline{y}) - 0}{\widehat{s.e.}(\overline{X} - \overline{Y})}$$

In order to test any hypotheses, we need to construct estimates of the standard error of $\overline{X} - \overline{Y}$.

20.2.3 Method 1: When the variances of *X* and *Y* are equal

The test that we are constructing is trying to evaluate whether the expected value, or average, is the same in two separate populations. For example, if we are testing whether or not average wages are the same for male and female workers, our two populations are male workers and female workers:

$$H_0: E(X) - E(Y) = 0$$
$$H_A: E(X) - E(Y) \neq 0$$

If the populations have different expected values, it is possible that other characteristics of the population random variables are different as well. For example, the variance, the skew, or the kurtosis of the random variables may also be different.

In the first method we will see for estimating the variance of the difference of means, we will begin with a (relatively benign) assumption that the variance of the two populations is equal.

That is, we are testing whether $E(X) = E(Y)$, but even if the alternative hypothesis is true, and $E(X) \neq E(Y)$, we are assuming that the variance is the same in both populations.

We don't know what $var(X)$ (or $var(Y)$ for that matter) is, so we will use data to estimate these. We already have an unbiased estimator of the population variance, and based on each of the samples, we can construct unbiased estimates of the variance of the population random variable. (Remember, we observe n observations of X and m observations of Y):

$$s_X^2 = \frac{\sum_{i=1}^{n}(X_i - \overline{X})^2}{n-1}$$

$$s_Y^2 = \frac{\sum_{i=1}^{m}(Y_i - \overline{Y})^2}{m-1}$$

If we believe there is a good reason that X and Y are drawn from populations with the same variance, we can combine the estimates of the variances to create one pooled estimate of the variance. Our new estimator s^2 for the overall population variance is essentially the weighted average of the two estimates of the population variances:

$$s^2 = \frac{(n-1)s_X^2 + (m-1)s_Y^2}{(n-1)+(m-1)} = \frac{(n-1)s_X^2 + (m-1)s_Y^2}{n+m-2}$$

$$\Rightarrow s^2 = \frac{\sum_{i=1}^{n}(X_i - \overline{X})^2 + \sum_{i=1}^{m}(Y_j - \overline{Y})^2}{n+m-2}$$

We divide by $n + m - 2$ as this is the total number of degrees of freedom now. We have used two estimates of population parameters, $\overline{X}$ and $\overline{Y}$, in our estimate of the population variance.

Important note

You might wonder why we use $\sum_{i=1}^{n}(X_i - \overline{X})^2 + \sum_{i=1}^{m}(Y_j - \overline{Y})^2$ on the top of the fraction, rather than combining this data all together.

The reason for this is that it is possible for data to have the same variance, even when the averages are different. This is illustrated in Figure 20.3. Within each population (X and Y),

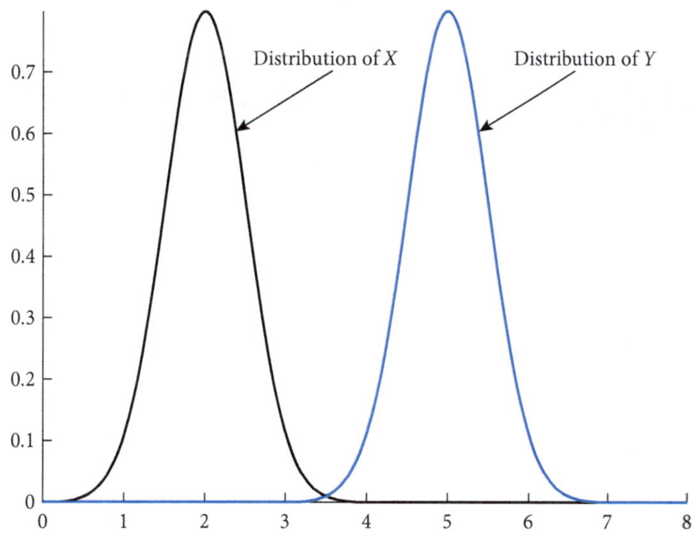

Figure 20.3 Distribution of two random variables, X and Y.

the expected values are different, but the variances (as illustrated by the spread of the data) are the same.

When we are estimating the variance of the random variables, we are interested in the variation within the population. By using information from both populations, we can get a better estimate of the variance, but we do need to take account of the possibility that the two populations have different expected values. If we simply pooled all of the data, we would gain an overestimate of the variance. By considering the data within the populations, we can take account of the possibility of there being different expected values.

Since we know that the variance of the difference of the sample means is given as $var(\overline{X} - \overline{Y}) = \frac{var(X)}{n} + \frac{var(Y)}{m}$, and since we are assuming that $var(X) = var(Y)$, then we can simply substitute our estimate of the variance (of X and of Y) into this formula, to give us:

$$\widehat{var}(\overline{X} - \overline{Y}) = \frac{s^2}{n} + \frac{s^2}{m}$$

Using this, we can construct our new test statistic as:

$$t = \frac{(\overline{x} - \overline{y}) - 0}{\sqrt{\frac{s^2}{n} + \frac{s^2}{m}}}$$

We would then need to compare the t-statistic we obtain with the critical value from the t-distribution with $n + m - 2$ degrees of freedom.

This methodology is valid even for sample means where the sample sizes are very different. However, because we rely on the fact that both sample means are normally distributed (by the central limit theorem), it is essential that each sample is large enough to ensure that the sample means will follow an approximately normal distribution. If the sample size is not large enough, then it is possible that the resulting test statistic we are examining will not follow a t-distribution, and we would be unable to make any inferences.

Key formulae when the variance of the groups is equal	
Unbiased estimator of the variance of X (and Y), based on n observations of X and m observations of Y	$s^2 = \frac{\sum_{i=1}^{n}(X_i - \overline{X})^2 + \sum_{i=1}^{m}(Y_j - \overline{Y})^2}{n + m - 2}$
Unbiased estimator of the variance of the difference of sample means, $var(\overline{X} - \overline{Y})$	$\widehat{var}(\overline{X} - \overline{Y}) = \frac{s^2}{n} + \frac{s^2}{m}$
Estimator for the standard error of the difference of sample means, $\widehat{s.e.}(\overline{X} - \overline{Y})$	$\widehat{s.e.}(\overline{X} - \overline{Y}) = \sqrt{\frac{s^2}{n} + \frac{s^2}{m}}$
Formula for t-statistic to test the null hypothesis that $E(X) = E(Y)$ (which is equivalent to $E(X) - E(Y) = 0$): H_0: $E(X) - E(Y) = 0$	$t = \frac{(\overline{x} - \overline{y}) - 0}{\widehat{s.e.}(\overline{X} - \overline{Y})} = \frac{(\overline{x} - \overline{y}) - 0}{\sqrt{\frac{s^2}{n} + \frac{s^2}{m}}}$
Degrees of freedom	$n + m - 2$

Worked example 20.2: Testing whether male and female workers are paid the same amount

To investigate whether males and females are, on average, paid the same amount, a researcher has randomly sampled 150 observations of male full-time workers aged 25–35, and 250 observations of female full-time workers aged 25–35 from the 2019 UK Labour Force Survey. We have chosen to have unequal sample sizes, so that we can illustrate how the sample sizes are used within this method. Let's define two random variables: X is defined as the wages of male workers, whilst Y is defined as the wages of female workers.

We wish to test whether the average wages of male workers, $E(X)$, is equal to the average wages of female workers, $E(Y)$.We will assume that the variance of wages of male and female earnings is equal. That is, we assume that $var(X) = var(Y)$.
Hypotheses:

$$H_0: E(X) - E(Y) = 0$$
$$H_A: E(X) - E(Y) \neq 0$$

Remember that $E(X) - E(Y) = 0$ is equivalent to stating that $E(X) = E(Y)$. We will use the difference in the sample means as an estimator for $E(X) - E(Y)$, and we know that:

$$(\overline{X} - \overline{Y}) \sim N\left((E(X) - E(Y)), \frac{var(X)}{n} + \frac{var(Y)}{m}\right)$$

where $n = 150$, the number of observations of male workers, and $m = 250$, the number of observations of female workers.

Remember that $E(X) - E(Y) = 0$ is equivalent to stating that $E(X) = E(Y)$. We will use the difference in the sample means as an estimator for $E(X) - E(Y)$, and we know that, if we observe n observations of X and m observations of Y, then:

- The mean average wage for males ($\overline{x}$) is £668.2267, with $\sum_{i=1}^{n}(x_i - \overline{x})^2 = 16{,}389{,}758.29$, $n = 150$
- The mean average wage for females ($\overline{y}$) is £569.032, with $\sum_{i=1}^{m}(y_i - \overline{y})^2 = 25{,}208{,}713.74$, $m = 250$

Since we have assumed that $var(X) = var(Y)$, we can construct $s^2 = \frac{\Sigma_{i=1}^{n}(X_i - \overline{X})^2 + \Sigma_{j=1}^{m}(Y_j - \overline{Y})^2}{n+m-2}$. Substituting in for $\Sigma_{i=1}^{n}(X_i - \overline{X})^2 = 16{,}389{,}758.29$ and $\Sigma_{i=1}^{m}(Y_i - \overline{Y})^2 = 25{,}208{,}713.74$, we have:

$$s^2 = \frac{16{,}389{,}758.29 + 25{,}208{,}713.74}{150 + 250 - 2} = 104{,}518.774$$

That is, our (unbiased) estimate of the variance of earnings for males is 104,518.774, and similarly, the estimate of the variance of earnings for females is 104,518.774.

The estimated gap between male and female earnings is equal to:

$$(\overline{x} - \overline{y}) = 668.2267 - 569.032 = 99.1947$$

Based on these estimates, we can construct our t-statistic:

$$t = \frac{(\bar{x} - \bar{y}) - 0}{\widehat{s.e.}(\bar{X} - \bar{Y})} = \frac{99.1947 - 0}{\sqrt{\frac{104{,}518.774}{150} + \frac{104{,}518.774}{250}}} = 2.97$$

We have 400 observations, but we have used estimators $\bar{X}$ and $\bar{Y}$ to provide estimates of $E(X)$ and $E(Y)$ in the estimate of the variance. This means that we have $400 - 2 = 398$ degrees of freedom. The critical value from the t-distribution is (approximately) equal to 1.96 at the 5 per cent significance level. As the test statistic is larger than the critical value, we therefore reject the null hypothesis. That is, we would reject the null hypothesis that the average weekly earnings are equal for both male and female full-time workers.

20.2.4 Method 2: When the variances of *X* and *Y* are allowed to be different

In the previous section, we considered the case where we assumed that the variances of the two underlying random variables were equal. However, in reality, it is unlikely that the variance of a random variable across populations is the same, and so we may need a slightly different method.

In order to test the hypothesis:

$$H_0: E(X) - E(Y) = 0$$
$$H_A: E(X) - E(Y) \neq 0$$

using the estimator $\bar{X} - \bar{Y}$, we need to be able to estimate $var(\bar{X} - \bar{Y}) = var(\bar{X}) + var(\bar{Y})$. If we have n observations of X and m observations of Y, we know that:

$$var(\bar{X}) = \frac{var(X)}{n}, \; var(\bar{Y}) = \frac{var(Y)}{m}$$

We also know that s_X^2 is an unbiased estimator of $var(X)$ and s_Y^2 is an unbiased estimator of $var(Y)$ where:

$$s_X^2 = \frac{1}{n-1}\sum_{i=1}^{n}(X_i - \bar{X})^2, \; s_Y^2 = \frac{1}{m-1}\sum_{i=1}^{m}(Y_i - \bar{Y})^2$$

If we allow the variances of X and Y to be different, we can simply use s_X^2 and s_Y^2 separately as estimators for the variances of X and Y respectively.

Thus, our estimator for $var(\bar{X} - \bar{Y})$ is just:

$$\widehat{var}(\bar{X} - \bar{Y}) = \frac{s_X^2}{n} + \frac{s_Y^2}{m}$$

And thus, our test statistic is just equal to:

$$t = \frac{(\bar{x} - \bar{y}) - 0}{\sqrt{\frac{s_X^2}{n} + \frac{s_Y^2}{m}}}$$

The only difference in the test statistic compared with the example in the previous section is that we use separate estimates for the variance of X and the variance of Y.

Why would you ever assume the variance is the same in both populations?

We have seen that we can construct the test statistic in two ways, depending on whether we assume that the variance is the same or different in the two populations.

The reason that we don't just use $\widehat{var}(\bar{X} - \bar{Y}) = \frac{s_X^2}{n} + \frac{s_Y^2}{m}$ in both cases is relatively simple. If we suspect that the variance in the two populations is the same, using data from both X and Y increases our effective number of observations, and thus, the estimate of the variance will become more efficient.

Degrees of freedom in the model

In all of the previous examples, we have had an analytical solution for the number of degrees of freedom. However, Welch (1947)[5] and Satterthwaite (1946)[6] demonstrated that since the overall distribution varies slightly with different variances in the populations, we need to estimate an appropriate number of degrees of freedom.

They developed the Welch–Satterthwaite equation:

$$df = \frac{\left(\frac{s_X^2}{n} + \frac{s_Y^2}{m}\right)^2}{\left(\frac{\left(\frac{s_X^2}{n}\right)^2}{n-1}\right) + \left(\frac{\left(\frac{s_Y^2}{m}\right)^2}{m-1}\right)}$$

That is, the degrees of freedom become a function of the estimated variances of $\bar{X}$ and $\bar{Y}$, along with the number of observations.

Key formulae when the variance of the groups is unequal

Unbiased estimator of the variance of X (and Y), based on n observations of X and m observations of Y	$s_X^2 = \frac{1}{n-1}\sum_{i=1}^{n}(X_i - \bar{X})^2,\ s_Y^2 = \frac{1}{m-1}\sum_{i=1}^{m}(Y_i - \bar{Y})^2$
Unbiased estimator of the variance of $\bar{X}$ and $\bar{Y}$	$\widehat{var}(\bar{X}) = \frac{s_X^2}{n},\ \widehat{var}(\bar{Y}) = \frac{s_Y^2}{m}$
Unbiased estimator of the variance of the difference of sample means, $var(\bar{X} - \bar{Y})$	$\widehat{var}(\bar{X} - \bar{Y}) = \frac{s_X^2}{n} + \frac{s_Y^2}{m}$

[5] B. L. Welch (1947), 'The Generalization of "Student's" Problem When Several Different Population Variances Are Involved', *Biometrika*, 34(1/2), 28–35.

[6] F. E. Satterthwaite (1946), 'An Approximate Distribution of Estimates of Variance Components', *Biometrics Bulletin*, 2(6), 110–114.

Estimator for the standard error of the difference of sample means, $\widehat{s.e.}(\overline{X}-\overline{Y})$	$\widehat{s.e.}(\overline{X}-\overline{Y})=\sqrt{\frac{s_X^2}{n}+\frac{s_Y^2}{m}}$
Formula for t-statistic to test the null hypothesis that $E(X)=E(Y)$ (which is equivalent to $E(X)-E(Y)=0$) H_0: $E(X)-E(Y)=0$	$t=\frac{(\overline{x}-\overline{y})-0}{\widehat{s.e.}(\overline{X}-\overline{Y})}=\frac{(\overline{x}-\overline{y})-0}{\sqrt{\frac{s_X^2}{n}+\frac{s_Y^2}{m}}}$

Worked example 20.3: Revisiting the equality of wages, assuming that the variance of wages differs across male and female workers

In Worked example 20.2, we made the assumption that the variance of male wages was the same as the variance of female wages. In reality this might be a very weak assumption. To illustrate the difference that this makes, let's revisit this worked example, and now allow the variance of wages to be different between male and female workers. As you will see, much of the methodology is identical to the previous worked example, but we will need to be careful when estimating the variance of the difference of the sample means, and when calculating the appropriate degrees of freedom.

To investigate whether males and females are, on average, paid the same amount, a researcher has randomly sampled 150 observations of male full-time workers aged 25–35, and 250 observations of female full-time workers aged 25–35 from the 2019 UK Labour Force Survey. We have chosen to have unequal sample sizes, so that we can illustrate how the sample sizes are used within this method. Let's define two random variables: X is defined as the wages of male workers, whilst Y is defined as the wages of female workers.

We wish to test whether the average wage of male workers, $E(X)$, is equal to the average wage of female workers, $E(Y)$.We will assume that the variance of wages of male and female earnings is equal. That is, we assume that $var(X)=var(Y)$.

Hypotheses:

$$H_0\text{: } E(X)-E(Y)=0$$
$$H_A\text{: } E(X)-E(Y)\neq 0$$

Remember that $E(X)-E(Y)=0$ is equivalent to stating that $E(X)=E(Y)$. We will use the difference in the sample means as an estimator for $E(X)-E(Y)$, and we know that, if we observe n observations of X and m observations of Y, then:

$$(\overline{X}-\overline{Y})\sim N\left((E(X)-E(Y)),\frac{var(X)}{n}+\frac{var(Y)}{m}\right)$$

Having randomly sampled 150 male workers and 250 female workers, we construct the estimates of the population averages:

- The mean average wage for males ($\overline{x}$) is £668.2267, with $\sum_{i=1}^{n}(x_i-\overline{x})^2=16{,}389{,}758.29$, $n=150$.

- The mean average wage for females $(\overline{y})$ is £569.0329, with $\Sigma_{i=1}^{m}(y_i - \overline{y})^2 = 25{,}208{,}713.74$, $m = 250$.

We can use these to construct estimates of the variance of X and Y:

$$s_X^2 = \left[\frac{1}{n-1}\right] \times \sum_{i=1}^{n}(x_i - \overline{x})^2 = \left[\frac{1}{149}\right] \times 16{,}389{,}758.29 = 109{,}998.38$$

$$s_Y^2 = \left[\frac{1}{m-1}\right] \times \sum_{i=1}^{m}(y_i - \overline{y})^2 = \left[\frac{1}{249}\right] \times 25{,}208{,}713.74 = 101{,}239.81$$

That is, our unbiased estimate of the variance of earnings for males is 109,998.38, whilst for females it's 101,239.81.

The estimated gap between male and female earnings is, as before,

$$(\overline{x} - \overline{y}) = 668.2267 - 569.032 = 99.1947$$

Based on these estimates, we can construct our t-statistic, remembering that the estimated standard error for $(\overline{X} - \overline{Y})$ is just the square root of the estimated variance of $\overline{X}$ plus the estimated variance of $\overline{Y}$:

$$t = \frac{(\overline{x} - \overline{y}) - 0}{\widehat{s.e.}(\overline{X} - \overline{Y})} = \frac{99.1947 - 0}{\sqrt{\frac{109{,}998.38}{150} + \frac{101{,}239.81}{250}}} = 2.94$$

Previously, when we imposed that the variance was the same in the two populations, we gained a t-statistic of 2.97, whilst here, where we've allowed the variance to be different across the two populations, the t-statistic is 2.94. This has made a minuscule difference in the estimated t-statistic. Where the variances are very different, we might expect to see big differences in our test statistic, but when the variances are similar, we see very little overall impact.

We haven't quite completed this example, as we need to find the critical value, but before doing that, we need to calculate the **degrees of freedom**, using Welch and Satterthwaite's formula:

$$df = \frac{\left(\frac{s_X^2}{n} + \frac{s_Y^2}{m}\right)^2}{\left(\frac{\left(\frac{s_X^2}{n}\right)^2}{n-1}\right) + \left(\frac{\left(\frac{s_Y^2}{m}\right)^2}{m-1}\right)} = \frac{\left(\frac{109{,}998.38}{150} + \frac{101{,}239.81}{250}\right)^2}{\frac{\left(\frac{109{,}998.38}{150}\right)^2}{149} + \frac{\left(\frac{101{,}239.81}{250}\right)^2}{249}} = 303.5997$$

The number of degrees of freedom needs to be an integer, and in this case, it will round to 304. The critical value from the t-distribution at the 5 per cent significance level with 304 degrees of freedom is 1.9678. Since the magnitude of the t-statistic is larger than this critical value, we therefore reject the null hypothesis.

20.2.5 **Performing t-tests for equality of expected values in Excel**

In reality, when we need to perform these tests, we can use a computer to do them. Whilst you can manually calculate the Welch–Satterthwaite degrees of freedom, often these sorts of programmes are already prepared. For example, Excel can carry out t-tests like the ones in Worked example 20.3 for arrays of data. However, in order to use these, you need to load the Analysis Toolpak.[7]

If the analysis toolpak is installed, when you click on the 'Data' tab, at the far right-hand corner, there should be a small icon called 'Data Analysis'. This will allow you to carry out data analysis in Excel.

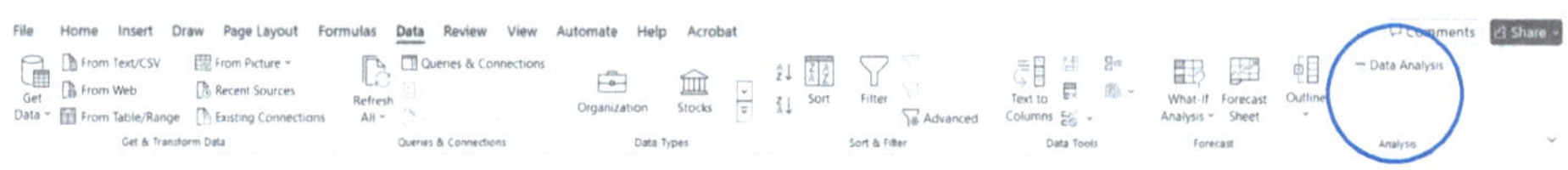

The three forms of tests of equal expected values are all available here:

- z-test: two-sample for means (*when we know the underlying variances of X and Y*)
- t-test: two-sample assuming equal variances
- t-test: two-sample assuming unequal variances.

When using Excel to test for equality of means, where the two populations have unequal variances, Excel will automatically estimate the appropriate degrees of freedom using the Welch–Satterthwaite methodology (see Figure 20.4).

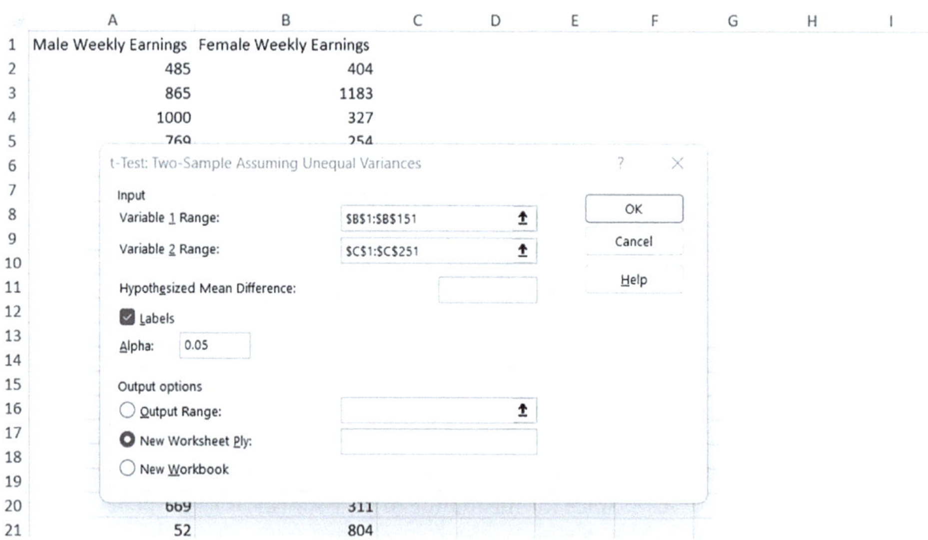

Figure 20.4 Using Excel to test the equality of means.

[7] Information about installing the Analysis Toolpak is available from Microsoft: https://support.microsoft.com/en-us/office/load-the-analysis-toolpak-in-excel-6a63e598-cd6d-42e3-9317-6b40ba1a66b4?ui=en-us&rs=en-us&ad=us (accessed 11 November 2023).

There are a number of options in Excel, that you should be aware of:

- Hypothesized mean difference: this is just the difference we hypothesize between the two populations. For example, for H_0: $E(X) - E(Y) = 0$, this hypothesized difference is just 0.
- Labels: this just tells Excel that the data has labels in the top observation.
- Alpha: this is the α of the test. This is equivalent to setting the significance level of a test.

Interpreting the results

When you ask Excel to carry out a test, it will generate a new worksheet, including lots of different statistics. It is important to be able to interpret what these statistics mean. To illustrate, I have carried out the t-test assuming unequal variances. That is, we are replicating Worked example 20.3 and the output from Excel is reproduced in Figure 20.5.

Most of the statistics in this table, you have already seen:

- $\overline{x} = 668.23$—the mean average of male earnings
- $\overline{y} = 569.03$—the mean average of female earnings
- $s_X^2 = 109{,}998.38$—the estimate of the variance of male earnings
- $s_Y^2 = 1{,}012{,}391.81$—the estimate of the variance of female earnings

In addition, we have $n = 150$ (the number of male observations) and $m = 250$ (the number of female observations):

- The hypothesized mean difference (= 0) is just the difference that we hypothesize under the null hypothesis. H_0: $E(X) - E(Y) = 0$
- df: These are the degrees of freedom. We calculated the Welch–Satterthwaite degrees of freedom and found them as 303.5997. These would round to 304.

t-Test: Two-Sample Assuming Unequal Variances		
	Male Weekly Earnings	Female Weekly Earnings
Mean	668.23	569.03
variance	109998.38	101239.81
Observations	150	250
Hypothesized Mean Difference	0	
df	304	
t Stat	2.94	
P(*T*< = *t*) one-tail	0.00	
t Critical one-tail	1.65	
P(*T*< = *t*) two-tail	0.00	
t Critical two-tail	1.97	

Figure 20.5 Output from Excel's t-test for equality of means, assuming unequal variances.

- t-stat: this is merely the t-statistic from the test, which as we saw before is equal to 2.94
- P(T<=t) one-tail: this provides the p-value for a one-tailed test relating to the t-stat. If $t > 0$, this calculates $P(T \geq t)$. If $t < 0$, this calculates $P(T \leq t)$
- t Critical one-tail: this is the 5 per cent critical value from the t-distribution for a one-tailed test
- P(T<=t) two-tail: this is the p-value associated with a two tailed test with the t-statistic we have achieved. This is equivalent to $P(|T| \geq |t|)$
- t Critical two-tail: this is the critical value from the t-distribution with 304 degrees of freedom for a two-tailed test.

20.3 Testing for specific differences between population averages

Across this chapter, we have seen tests whereby we are testing whether or not the expected value is equal across two populations. In particular, we have looked at whether or not we can reject the null hypothesis that weekly wages are equal across male and female full-time workers.

However, we can adapt the methodology seen here to test a wide range of hypotheses. When we were testing the null hypothesis of equality of means, we wrote that the null and alternative hypotheses were:

$$H_0: E(X) - E(Y) = 0$$
$$H_A: E(X) - E(Y) \neq 0$$

We would test this using the following (standardized) test statistic: $t = \dfrac{(\overline{x} - \overline{y}) - 0}{\widehat{s.e.}(\overline{X} - \overline{Y})}$

However, there is nothing to force us to test that the difference between the groups is equal to zero. We could, equally, have tested the null hypothesis that, on average, male workers earn £100 more per week than female workers, and would have written our null hypothesis as:

$$H_0: E(X) - E(Y) = 100$$
$$H_A: E(X) - E(Y) \neq 100$$

The estimator that we would use would still be the difference of the male average wages and the female average wages, and the estimated standard error of the estimator would remain the same. The only thing that would change would be how we construct the standardized

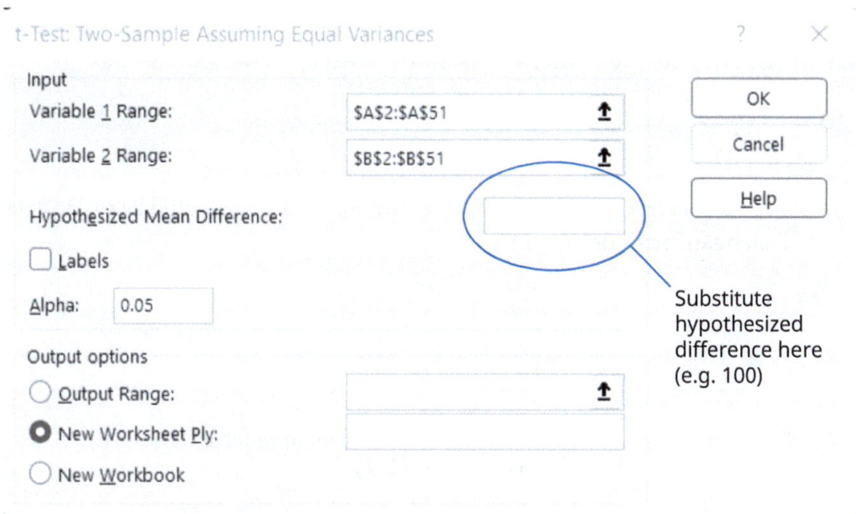

Figure 20.6 Testing a hypothesized difference between population means.

test statistic. On the numerator, we subtract the hypothesized value of $E(X) - E(Y)$, and so we would subtract 100 rather than 0:

$$t = \frac{(\bar{x} - \bar{y}) - 100}{\widehat{s.e.}(\bar{X} - \bar{Y})}$$

If you are using Microsoft Excel to test a hypothesis, then you can request that it tests any hypothesized difference between the two population averages (see Figure 20.6).

For example, if your null hypothesis was that the difference between $E(X)$ and $E(Y)$ was equal to 100, you could substitute '100' in the place of the Hypothesized Mean Difference.

20.4 More advanced tests

We can also use this methodology to test more advanced hypotheses. However, constructing appropriate standard errors (and hence test statistics) will require a little more thought.

Suppose that you suspected that across two populations, X and Y, the average of X was twice the average of Y; in other words: $E(X) = 2 \times E(Y)$. Remember, we could rewrite this as $E(X) - 2E(Y) = 0$.

We could use the same methodology as we've seen here to test this hypothesis. Our null (and alternative) hypotheses would be:

$$H_0: E(X) - 2E(Y) = 0$$
$$H_A: E(X) - 2E(Y) \neq 0$$

Provided the observations are *iid*, then an unbiased estimator for $E(X) - 2E(Y)$ would just be $\overline{X} - 2\overline{Y}$, and we could construct a test statistic based upon this estimator as:

$$t = \frac{(\overline{x} - 2\overline{y}) - 0}{\widehat{s.e.}(\overline{X} - 2\overline{Y})}$$

The numerator would be easy to construct, and the only challenge would be to construct the (estimated) standard error of $(\overline{X} - 2\overline{Y})$.

Rules of variances

Recall that the variance of a linear combination of random variables is given by:
$var(aX + bY) = a^2\ var(X) + b^2\ var(Y) + 2abcov(X,Y)$

By the rules of variances, we could write that:

$$var(\overline{X} - 2\overline{Y}) = var(\overline{X}) + 2^2\ var(\overline{Y}) - 2 \times 1 \times 2 \times cov(\overline{X},\overline{Y})$$

As before, provided the observations are *iid*, then $cov(\overline{X},\overline{Y}) = 0$, and so:

$$var(\overline{X} - 2\overline{Y}) = var(\overline{X}) + 4var(\overline{Y})$$

Using these methodologies, we could then construct an estimate of the variance of our estimator as:

$$\widehat{var}(\overline{X} - 2\overline{Y}) = \frac{s^2}{n} + 4 \times \frac{s^2}{m}$$

This methodology allows us to test hypotheses relating to any linear combination of two population averages. The only thing that you have to be careful with is how you go about estimating the standard error of your estimator (and also what the appropriate degrees of freedom are).

Worked example 20.4: Do female workers earn 90 per cent of what male workers earn?

We will return to comparing the earnings of male and female full-time workers. Suppose that you believed that female workers were underpaid compared with male workers, and wanted to test the hypothesis that female workers were paid on average 90 per cent of male earnings. That would mean that, if X represents the earnings of male workers and Y the earnings of male workers, if the hypothesis is true, then:

$$E(Y) = 0.9 \times E(X)$$

This would be equivalent to testing the hypotheses:

H_0: $E(Y) - 0.9E(X) = 0$

H_A: $E(Y) - 0.9E(X) \neq 0$

We have the same samples as before, and we will use the weighted difference between sample means as an estimator for $E(Y) - 0.9E(X)$. That is, our estimator will be:

$\overline{Y} - 0.9\overline{X}$

Using this method, the variance of the sample mean will just be:

$$var(\overline{Y} - 0.9\overline{X}) = var(\overline{Y}) + 0.9^2\ var(\overline{X}) - 2 \times 0.9 \times cov(\overline{X},\overline{Y})$$

With n observations of X and m observations of Y, provided the observations are *iid*, then $var(\overline{Y}) = \frac{var(Y)}{m}$, $var(\overline{X}) = \frac{var(X)}{n}$, and $cov(\overline{X},\overline{Y}) = 0$:

$$\Rightarrow var(\overline{Y} - 0.9\overline{X}) = \frac{var(Y)}{m} + 0.9^2 \times \frac{var(X)}{n}$$

As before, we will allow the variances to differ across the two samples, and we have 150 observations of male full-time workers, and 250 observations of female full-time workers.

- The mean average wage for males ($\overline{x}$) is £668.2267, with $\Sigma_{i=1}^{n}(x_i - \overline{x})^2 = 16{,}389{,}758.29$, $n = 150$.
- The mean average wage for females ($\overline{y}$) is £569.032, with $\Sigma_{i=1}^{m}(y_i - \overline{y})^2 = 25{,}208{,}713.74$, $m = 250$.

We can use these to construct estimates of the variance of X and Y:

$$s_X^2 = \left[\frac{1}{n-1}\right] \times \sum_{i=1}^{n}(x_i - \overline{x})^2 = \left[\frac{1}{149}\right] \times 16{,}389{,}758.29 = 109{,}998.38$$

$$s_Y^2 = \left[\frac{1}{m-1}\right] \times \sum_{i=1}^{m}(y_i - \overline{y})^2 = \left[\frac{1}{249}\right] \times 25{,}208{,}713.74 = 101{,}239.81$$

That is, our unbiased estimate of the variance of earnings for males is 109,998.38, whilst for females it's 101,239.81.

Applying the estimator:

$$\overline{y} - 0.9\overline{x} = 569.032 - 0.9 \times 668.2267 = -32.37203$$

We can equally calculate an estimate of the variance of our estimator:

$$\widehat{var}(\overline{Y} - 0.9\overline{X}) = \frac{s_Y^2}{m} + 0.9^2 \times \frac{s_X^2}{n} = \frac{101{,}239.81}{250} + 0.81 \times \frac{109{,}998.38}{150} = 998.95$$

Based on these estimates, we can construct our t-statistic:

$$t = \frac{(\overline{y} - 0.9\,\overline{x}) - 0}{\widehat{s.e.}(\overline{Y} - 0.9\,\overline{X})} = \frac{-32.37203 - 0}{\sqrt{998.95}} = -1.02$$

As before, the Welch–Satterthwaite degrees of freedom will be 304, so the critical value for a 5 per cent test is 1.97. As the magnitude of the t-statistic (1.02) is less than the critical value, we are unable to reject the null hypothesis that female workers are, on average, paid 90 per cent of what male workers are paid.

20.5 Discussion: Is this evidence of discrimination in the UK workplace?

In this chapter, we have considered two tests relating to average earnings, by comparing male and female workers. In the first test, we tested whether full-time male and full-time female workers had the same average weekly earnings (or not). Using two separate methods (assuming equal or unequal variances across males and females), we rejected the null hypothesis that men and women had equal earnings.

In the second test, we tested the hypothesis that female full-time workers earned on average 90 per cent of what male workers earned. Here we were sadly unable to reject the null hypothesis, suggesting that full-time female workers earn less than full-time male workers.

We have shown that, in the UK, it is likely that on average, female workers are paid less than male workers, but an important question is whether this is enough evidence to conclude that female workers are discriminated against. On its own, this is not sufficient to conclude (legal) discrimination between male and female workers. In the UK, the Equality Act (2010) states:[8]

> Equal pay means that men and women performing equal work, or work of equal value, must receive equal pay.

If there are differences between the types of jobs that male and female workers do, then even if there is no (legal) discrimination between male and female workers, we could expect to see differences between the earnings of male and female workers.

Some commentators argue that differences in average wages between male and female workers are not (necessarily) evidence of discrimination, but instead are caused by male and female workers having different propensities towards different careers. Legal discrimination occurs when male and female workers, doing the same job, in the same firm, are paid different amounts, but one way that we could see the significant difference between male and female earnings would be if, on average, female workers were more likely to work for firms that pay less, or female workers were more likely to work in careers that pay less.

However, if there are differences in the types of jobs that male and female workers work in, and a correlation between the salaries associated with those different types of jobs, this might be evidence of discrimination at a wider societal level. The financial rewards offered to different roles have evolved over time, and some roles gain higher financial rewards than others (despite requiring the same underlying skills and training). If the difference in financial rewards is related to the difference in the gender make-up of the workforce, then this could be evidence of discrimination at a societal level. This form of discrimination would not be picked up by the requirement for individual firms to publish salary information, as it would be represented by workers in different sectors being paid different amounts.

[8] https://www.gov.uk/government/publications/gender-pay-gap-reporting-guidance-for-employers/overview#:~:text=Equal%20pay%20means%20that%20men,holiday%20entitlement (accessed 11 November 2023).

Summary

We have seen in this chapter how we can test hypotheses relating to multiple random variables. The focus on this chapter has been on testing for equality of means, but the methodology can hold for equality of other population parameters. For a general population parameter, θ_i, which could represent the expectation, the variance, the kurtosis, the skew, etc., of a random variable, i, if we have an unbiased estimator, θ_i of θ_i, we can test for the equality of that parameter across different random variables by testing the hypothesis:

$$H_0: \theta_X - \theta_Y = 0$$
$$H_A: \theta_X - \theta_Y \neq 0$$

We can test this hypothesis using a t-test, based on the estimated standard error of $\hat{\theta}_X - \hat{\theta}_Y$.

$$t = \frac{(\hat{\theta}_X - \hat{\theta}_Y) - 0}{\widehat{s.e.}(\hat{\theta}_X - \hat{\theta}_Y)}$$

Provided the observations are *iid*, then:

$$var(\hat{\theta}_X - \hat{\theta}_Y) = var(\hat{\theta}_X) + var(\hat{\theta}_Y) - 2cov(\hat{\theta}_X,\hat{\theta}_Y) = var(\hat{\theta}_X) + var(\hat{\theta}_Y)$$

(as, if the observations are *iid*, then it follows that $cov(\hat{\theta}_X,\hat{\theta}_Y) = 0$).

It follows that we can write the t-statistic as:

$$t = \frac{(\hat{\theta}_X - \hat{\theta}_Y) - 0}{\sqrt{\widehat{var}(\hat{\theta}_X) + \widehat{var}(\hat{\theta}_Y)}}$$

Largely, this method will only be used to evaluate equality of means, but, provided you have an unbiased estimate of the variance of your estimator, in principle, you can use this method to test the equality of any population parameters across a range of explanatory variables.

Appendix

Calculating the probability of a type 1 error when using the method in Section 20.2

In Section 20.2 we considered a possible (but inaccurate) test whereby we considered if $E(Y)$ was significantly different from the point estimate of $\overline{X}$.

In this example, if we tried to use this method, it would lead us to reject the null hypothesis whenever $\left|\frac{\overline{Y}-\overline{X}}{s.e.(\overline{X})}\right| \geq 1.96$. We want to calculate the probability of this occurring, if the two samples are drawn from a population with the same expectation and variance, $E(X) = E(Y)$.

That is, we wish to find:

$$P(|\overline{Y} - \overline{X}|) \geq 1.96 \times s.e.(\overline{X})$$

Without loss of generality, we could consider the $var(\overline{X}) = var(\overline{Y}) = 1$. It will also follow that $s.e.(\overline{X}) = 1$ as well. Therefore, we are looking for:

$$P(|\overline{Y} - \overline{X}|) \geq 1.96$$

Now, to calculate this probability, we need to know the distribution of $\overline{Y} - \overline{X}$. If $E(Y) = E(X)$, and the observations are *iid*, it follows that:

$$E(\overline{Y} - \overline{X}) = E(\overline{Y}) - E(\overline{X}) = E(Y) - E(X) = 0$$

Similarly, if the two samples are independent, then $cov(\overline{X}, \overline{Y}) = 0$. As such:

$$var(\overline{Y} - \overline{X}) = var(\overline{Y}) + var(\overline{X}) - 2cov(\overline{X}, \overline{Y})$$

From before, we know that $var(\overline{Y}) = var(\overline{X}) = 1$ and that $cov(\overline{X}, \overline{Y}) = 0$:

$$\Rightarrow var(\overline{Y} - \overline{X}) = 1 + 1 = 2$$

Since $\overline{X}$ and $\overline{Y}$ are approximately normally distributed (by the central limit theorem), it will also follow that $\overline{Y} - \overline{X}$ will also be approximately normally distributed:

$$(\overline{Y} - \overline{X}) \sim N(0,2)$$

As such, we want to calculate $P(|\overline{Y} - \overline{X}|) \geq 1.96$ (see Figure 20.7).

Using Excel, we can show that $P(\overline{Y} - \overline{X}) \leq -1.96 = 0.083$, meaning that the total probability that the sample means are more than 1.96 apart is equal to $2 \times 0.083 = 0.166$.

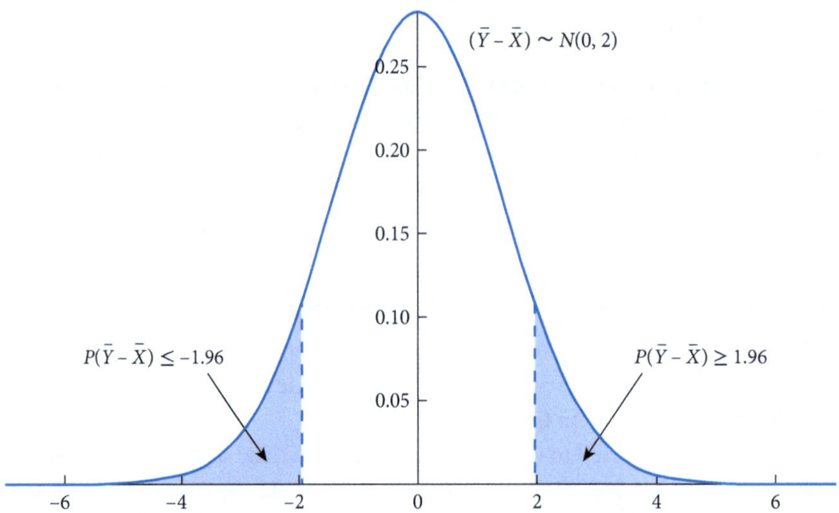

Figure 20.7 Distribution of $\overline{Y} - \overline{X}$.

Distributions Derived from the Normal Distribution

21

Learning outcomes for this chapter

By the end of this chapter you will be able to:

- Derive the distribution of a random variable constructed based on the sum of squares of k independent standard normal variables
- Recognize that the ratio of a standard normal and the square root of a chi-squared variable will follow a t-distribution, and apply this to the standard formula for statistical testing
- Construct an F-statistic based upon two variables following a chi-squared distribution
- Recognize the link between the t-distribution and the F-distribution

Mathematical tools

- Summations
- Algebra

Introduction

So far, we have introduced a range of probability distributions which are important for testing hypotheses. These include the normal distribution and the t-distribution. Intuitively, we can see that there is a link between these two distributions, as you know that, when you are testing relating to a population average:

- If you know the true variance, the standardized test statistic follows a normal distribution.
- If you are using an estimate of the variance, the standardized test statistic will follow a t-distribution.

In this chapter, we will introduce two new distributions, which are constructed from the normal distribution, in the form of the chi-squared χ^2 distribution and the F-distribution. We will also see how the t-distribution is linked to all three of these distributions.

The new distributions will be important when we introduce new statistical tests in Chapter 22, where we will introduce a new testing tool, known as ANOVA, which will allow us to test for equality of population parameters across more than two populations.

21.1 The chi-squared (χ^2) distribution

There are a range of distributions that build from the normal distribution. The first that we will discuss is known as the chi-squared (χ^2) distribution. This is constructed by considering a linear combination of the square of normally distributed random variables.

To illustrate, let's begin with an example. We know that s_X^2 is an unbiased estimator of the variance of the random variable X:

$$s_X^2 = \frac{\sum_{i=1}^{n}(X_i - \bar{X})^2}{n-1}$$

However, since s_X^2 is an estimator, it is itself a random variable and has a distribution, it may be interesting to investigate what distribution s_X^2 follows. As we can see, s_X^2 is based upon a sum of squares of random variables.

To discover what distribution the s_X^2 estimator follows, let's begin by thinking about a random variable Z, which follows a standard normal distribution; that is, $E(Z) = 0$ and $var(Z) = 1$. That is, $Z \sim N(0,1)$. We know that this variable is symmetric (around zero), and contains positive and negative values.

Thinking back to the s_X^2 estimator, we can see that the numerator contains the sum of squares of a random variable. What would happen if we constructed a new variable by squaring Z? What would the probability density function (PDF) of Z^2 look like?

First of all, because Z contains positive and negative values, by squaring the random variable, all of the negative values will become positive. Further, the spread of the distribution will move rightwards. Whilst the most extreme 5 per cent of outcomes in the standard normal are beyond ± 1.96, for the Z^2 distribution, the most extreme outcomes will be to the right of $1.96^2 = 3.841$. (This is because the most extreme outcomes from the left-hand tail of the normal distribution will become positive in the Z^2 distribution.)

The PDF of the resulting distribution is illustrated in Figure 21.1. The distribution that this follows is a chi-squared distribution, with one degree of freedom, which is often denoted as $\chi^2(1)$. The chi-squared distribution becomes interesting when we start to combine (the square of) multiple independent random variables (each of which follow a standard normal distribution).

Suppose that you randomly sampled k independent observations from a random variable, Z, which is normally distributed with expectation 0, and variance 1, and generate a new variable, which we'll call X_k:

$$X_k = \sum_{i=1}^{k} Z_i^2$$

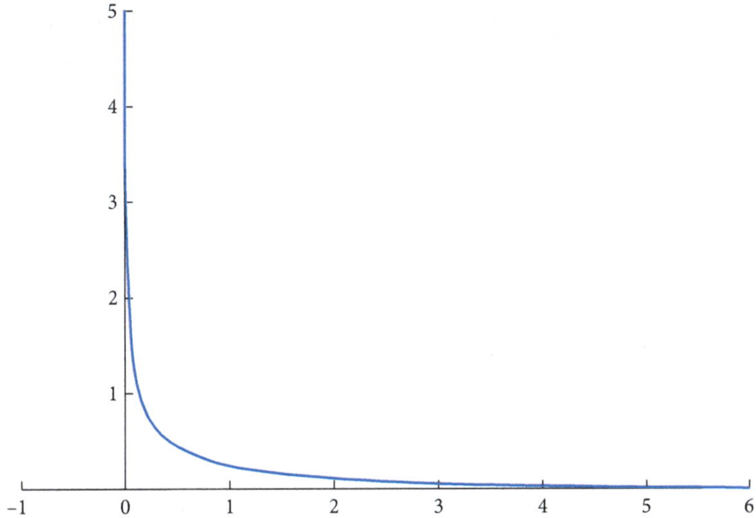

Figure 21.1 PDF of a chi-squared distribution, constructed based on the square of a standard normal variable.

Intuitively, when we combine the Z_i^2, the likelihood of obtaining an observation of X_k close to zero will be much lower. The reason for this is that in order to gain X_k close to zero, we would need each of the observations of Z_i to also be close to zero. When we combine an increasing number of Z_i^2, the likelihood of all of these being at, or close to, zero becomes very small, and so we would expect a greater probability of more extreme values of X_k. We can see this in the PDFs for $k = 4$, $k = 8$, and $k = 12$, illustrated in Figure 21.2.

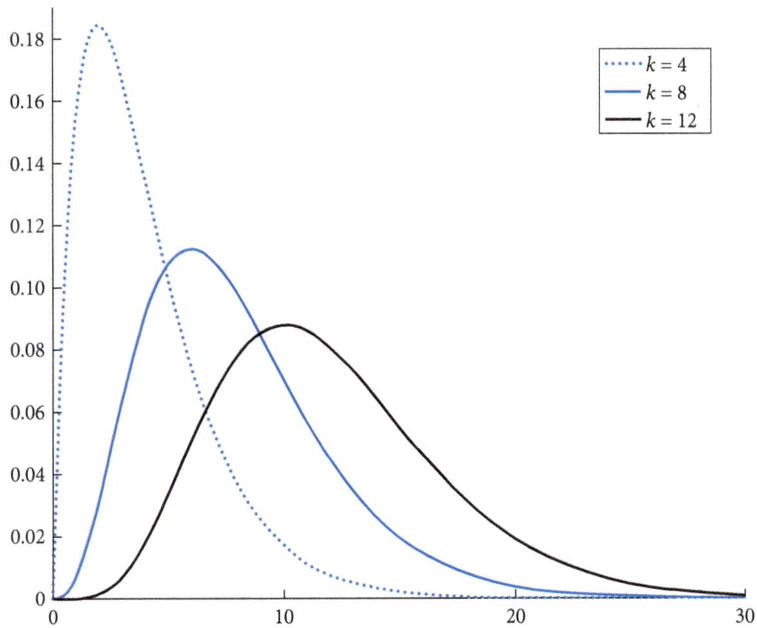

Figure 21.2 PDFs of $\chi^2(4)$, $\chi^2(8)$, and $\chi^2(12)$.

KEY DEFINITION: CHI-SQUARED DISTRIBUTION

A random variable follows a chi-squared distribution, with k **degrees of freedom** (represented $\chi^2(k)$) if it is constructed based on the sum of squares of k independent, normally distributed random variables (with expectation 0 and variance 1):

$$X_k = \sum_{i=1}^{k} Z_i^2 \sim \chi^2(k)$$

However, since the shape of the distributions varies depending on the number of degrees of freedom, the extreme values of this distribution are going to similarly vary depending on the number of degrees of freedom.

Suppose that you want to find the most extreme 5 per cent of observations within a chi-squared distribution. When we were looking at the normal distribution, we were interested in the most extreme 5 per cent outcomes, with 2.5 per cent of outcomes in either tail. However, since we have squared the normal variable, anything that had occurred in the left-hand tail (i.e. the negative values) of the normal distribution will now lie in the right-hand tail of the chi-squared distribution. As such, when we look for extreme values in the chi-squared distribution, we are only interested in the most extreme outcomes in the right-hand tail.

Using Excel to find percentiles of the χ^2 distribution

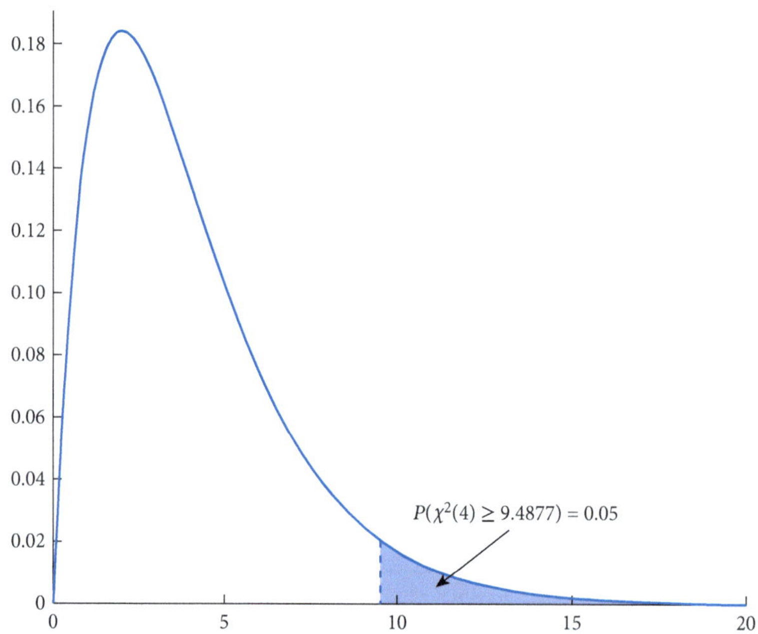

Figure 21.3 The most extreme 5 per cent of outcomes lie in the right-hand tail of the χ^2 distribution.

As with the t-distribution, or the normal distribution, we can find the most extreme p proportion of outcomes using Excel. If you use the formula:

$$=\text{CHISQ.INV.RT}\left(0.05,\text{k}\right)$$

this will deliver the most extreme 5 per cent of outcomes, when we have k degrees of freedom in the right-hand tail (RT) of the distribution. The diagram here represents a χ^2 distribution with 4 degrees of freedom, where the most extreme 5 per cent of the distribution lies to the right of 9.4877.

We will not discuss testing using the χ^2 distribution in any detail in this book, but you can find tables representing the upper tail of the chi-squared distribution in the appendix to this chapter.

The chi-squared distribution is used in various econometrics applications. However, one of the simplest uses is in the construction of the **F-distribution** and the t-distribution.

Worked example 21.1: Finding the distribution of s^2_{n-1}

We began our discussion of the χ^2 distribution by thinking about s^2_X, the unbiased estimator for the variance of X:

$$s^2_X = \frac{1}{n-1}\sum_{i=1}^{n}(X_i - \bar{X})^2$$

To evaluate the distribution of s^2, let's begin by focusing on the numerator:

$$\sum_{i=1}^{n}(X_i - \bar{X})^2$$

It is possible to show, via Cochran's theorem,[1] that with n independent and identically distributed (*iid*) observations of X, and with $var(X) = \sigma^2_X$:

$$\frac{\sum_{i=1}^{n}(X_i - \bar{X})^2}{\sigma^2_X} \sim \chi^2_{n-1}$$

That is, if we divide $\sum_{i=1}^{n}(X_i - \bar{X})^2$ through by the variance of X, the resulting random variable will follow a chi-squared distribution with $n-1$ degrees of freedom. As such, we can see that the s^2_X estimator would be expected to follow a distribution similar to the chi-squared distribution. However, if we wanted to standardize the estimator to ensure that it followed a standard χ^2 distribution, we would need to transform our estimator:

$$s^2_X = \frac{1}{n-1}\sum_{i=1}^{n}(X_i - \bar{X})^2$$

$$\Rightarrow \frac{n-1}{\sigma^2_X}s^2_X \sim \chi^2_{n-1}$$

[1] W. Cochran (1934), 'The Distribution of Quadratic Forms in a Normal System, with Applications to the Analysis of Covariance', *Mathematical Proceedings of the Cambridge Philosophical Society*, 30(2), 178–191, doi:10.1017/S0305004100016595

That is, by multiplying s_X^2 by $(n - 1)/\sigma_X^2$, the resulting variable would follow a chi-squared distribution, with $n - 1$ degrees of freedom.

21.2 The t-distribution

We have seen in earlier chapters that when we use an estimate of the variance, s^2, to test hypotheses about population parameters, the resulting test statistic follows a **t-distribution**, rather than the normal distribution. However, we have not talked about how the t-distribution is derived.

Formally, a random variable will follow a t-distribution if it is constructed based on a ratio relating to a normally distributed variable and a χ^2 distributed variable. For example, suppose that we have two random variables, Z and X_k. Z is distributed normally, with expectation 0 and variance 1, $Z \sim N(0,1)$, whilst X_k follows a χ^2 distribution with k degrees of freedom. Then we can define the t-distribution as the ratio:

$$\frac{Z}{\sqrt{\frac{X_k}{k}}} \sim t_k$$

That is, the t-distribution is constructed based on the ratio of a standard normal variable (Z) divided by the square root of a $\chi^2(k)$ variable, divided by the number of degrees of freedom (k).

Worked example 21.2: Standardizing a sample mean

We have, so far, taken it as read that when we use an estimate of the variance of the sample mean, the standardized test statistic will follow a t-distribution. However, given that we have now defined the meaning of a t-distribution, we should check this.

Suppose that we have a random variable X, with expectation μ_X and variance σ_X^2. If we randomly sample n independent and identically distributed observations, and construct the sample mean, $\overline{X}$, we know that, by the **central limit theorem**, the sample mean will be (approximately) normally distributed, with expectation μ_X and variance $\frac{\sigma_X^2}{n}$:

$$\overline{X} \sim N\left(\mu_X, \frac{\sigma_X^2}{n}\right)$$

When we standardize the test statistic, we subtract the expected value, and divide through by the standard error of the sample mean:

$$Z = \frac{\overline{X} - \mu_X}{\sqrt{\frac{\sigma_X^2}{n}}} \sim N(0,1)$$

In reality, we rarely know the true value of σ_X^2, and so have to estimate it, using s_X^2. We also know, from Cochran's theorem, that the distribution of s_X^2 is related to the χ^2 distribution:

$$\left[\frac{n-1}{\sigma_X^2}\right] s_X^2 \sim \chi_{n-1}^2$$

We know, from the definition of the t-distribution that:

$$T = \frac{Z}{\sqrt{\dfrac{\chi_{n-1}^2}{n-1}}} \sim t_{n-1}$$

Let's substitute in the elements that we know follow a standard normal and a χ_{n-1}^2 distribution:

$$\Rightarrow T = \frac{(\bar{X} - \mu_X) \Big/ \sqrt{\dfrac{\sigma_X^2}{n}}}{\sqrt{\left[\dfrac{n-1}{\sigma_X^2}\right] s_X^2 \Big/ (n-1)}}$$

Now, there are a few things that we can do to make this a little simpler: in the square root on the denominator, we have $n - 1$ divided by itself, so that cancels. In addition, we can bring the $\sqrt{\frac{\sigma_X^2}{n}}$ onto the bottom of the fraction:

$$\Rightarrow T = \frac{\bar{X} - \mu_X}{\sqrt{\dfrac{\sigma_X^2}{n}} \sqrt{\dfrac{s_X^2}{\sigma_X^2}}} = \frac{\bar{X} - \mu_X}{\sqrt{\dfrac{\sigma_X^2 \times s_X^2}{n \times \sigma_X^2}}}$$

Note that you have σ_X^2 / σ_X^2 which cancel, leaving us with:

$$T = \frac{\bar{X} - \mu_X}{\sqrt{\dfrac{s_X^2}{n}}} \sim t_{n-1}$$

However, this is just the formula we construct when we standardize the test statistic using an estimate of the variance. By definition, this must follow the t-distribution.

21.3 The F-distribution (sometimes known as the F-ratio)

In the next chapter, we will introduce the ANOVA test, which relies on a new distribution, known as the **F-distribution**. The F-distribution is named after Ronald Fisher, who was a key pioneer of statistics in the nineteenth century, and he developed the ANOVA test.

About Ronald Fisher

Alongside his work on statistics, Fisher also worked extensively in genetics, and was a key member of the Eugenics Society. As of 2023, because of this association, many institutions including the Committee of Presidents of Statistical Societies have distanced themselves from him. However, the F-ratio retains the link.

A summary of his work in the field of eugenics and his views of race is available from W. Bodmer et al. (2021), The Outstanding Scientist, R.A. Fisher: His Views on Eugenics and Race, *Heredity*, 126, 565–576.

A random variable will follow an F-distribution is constructed based on two random variables, each of which follows a chi-squared distribution. Formally, if we have two random variables, X and Y, both of which follow a χ^2 distribution, with j and k degrees of freedom respectively:

$$X \sim \chi^2(j),\ Y \sim \chi^2(k)$$

If we construct a new variable, W, based on the ratio of X divided by Y (each divided by their respective degrees of freedom):

$$W = \frac{X / j}{Y / k}$$

then W will follow an F-distribution, based on the degrees of freedom of the underlying random variables, X and Y. In this case, since X is constructed with j degrees of freedom, and Y is constructed with k degrees of freedom, then W, will follow an F-distribution based upon j and k degrees of freedom. Formally, we can represent this as:

$$W \sim F(j,k)$$

Care is needed when carrying out statistical tests using the F-distribution, as the shape of the distribution changes depending on the values of j and k used. Figure 21.4 illustrates the F-distribution based on a range of possible values for j and k. Even though k remains constant, the shape of the distribution changes for different values of j. As such, we will need to take care to look up the appropriate critical values when carrying out tests.

Since the F-distribution is constructed based on a ratio of two variables which follow a chi-squared distribution (and as such are necessarily positive), it also follows that the F-distribution is also necessarily positive, and as with the chi-squared distribution, we normally look for the most unlikely outcomes in the right-hand tail of the distribution.

In terms of notation, the 2 degrees of freedom are represented as ν_1 (representing the degrees of freedom on the numerator) and ν_2 (representing the degrees of freedom on the denominator). In this example:

$$\nu_1 = j,\ \nu_2 = k$$

Tables are available with critical values for the F-distribution. The critical values change based on the degrees of freedom of both χ^2 variables that form the F-distribution. As such,

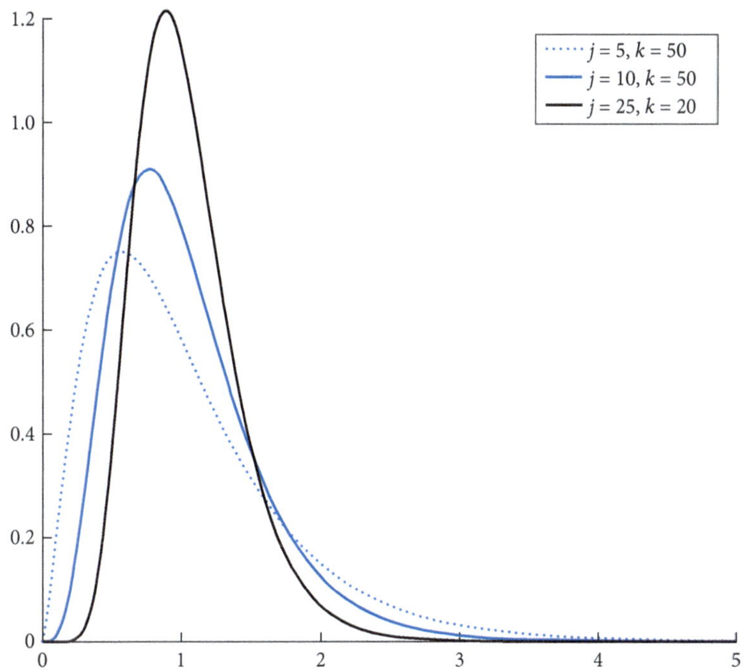

Figure 21.4 PDFs of F-ratios, based on chi-squared distributions with 5, 10, and 25 degrees of freedom on the numerator, and 50 degrees of freedom on the denominator.

to find the critical values, you need to consider both the degrees of freedom of the numerator and the denominator. Figure 21.5 shows an extract of the 5 per cent critical values for the F-distribution. Along the top of the table is the number of degrees of freedom represented by v_1, and down the left-hand side is the number of degrees of freedom represented by v_2. So, the 5 per cent critical value in an F-distribution, based on chi-squared distributions with 2 and 15 degrees of freedom (respectively) would be 3.682.

Unlike the t-distribution, or the chi-squared distribution, because the critical values are defined by two dimensions, it is not possible to provide a single table with a full range of critical values. Because of this, there are different tables for each significance level.

Using Excel to find percentiles of the *F* distribution

You can use statistical software such as Microsoft Excel to produce critical values from the F-tables. The most unlikely outcomes are normally considered only in the right-hand tail of the F-distribution. The formula =F.INV.RT(p, j, k) will deliver the most extreme proportion p in the right-hand tail of the F-distribution, based on a ratio of χ_j^2 over χ_k^2.

$$=\text{F.INV.RT}\left(0.05, 5, 50\right)$$

This formula will provide the value beyond which the most extreme 5% ($p = 0.05$) outcomes from the $F(5,50)$ distribution. For example, the 5% critical value from $F(5,50)$ is 2.400.

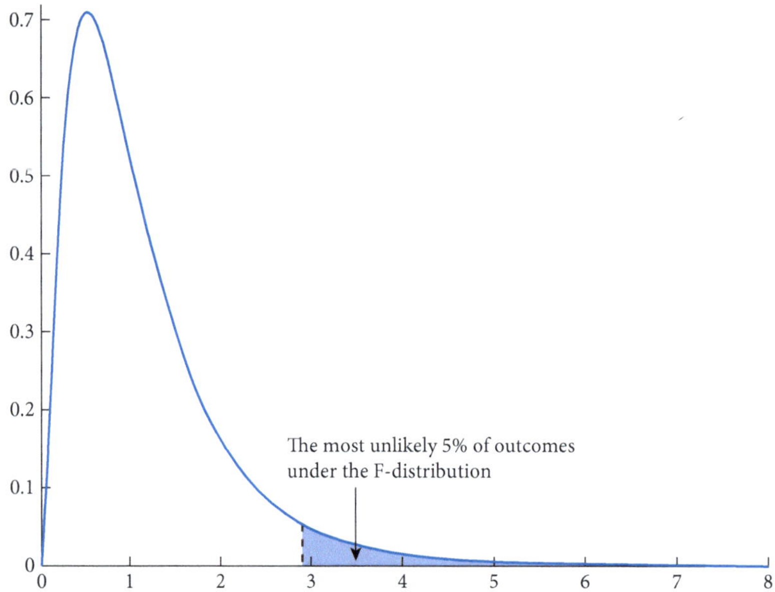

Figure 21.5 Extract from the 5 per cent critical values for the F-distribution.

21.4 The link between the t-distribution and the F-distribution

We have already seen that the t-distribution is constructed based on the ratio of a standard normal distribution and the square root of a chi-squared distribution (divided by the number of degrees of freedom):

$$T = \frac{Z}{\sqrt{\frac{\chi_k^2}{k}}} \sim t_k$$

That is, the ratio of any standard normal distribution, divided by the square root of the ratio of a chi-squared distributed variable, divided by its degrees of freedom, will follow a t-distribution. Similarly, we have seen that the F-distribution is defined by the ratio of two chi-squared variables, divided through by their respective degrees of freedom:

$$\frac{\chi_j^2 / j}{\chi_k^2 / k} \sim F(j,k)$$

Finally, we know that the chi-squared distribution with k degrees of freedom is based upon the sum of squares of k standard normal variables.

Suppose that we were to square a variable that follows the t-distribution:

$$T^2 = \frac{Z^2}{\chi_k^2 / k}$$

Now, by definition, Z^2 will follow a χ^2 distribution with 1 degree of freedom. As such we could rewrite this in terms of the distributions:

$$T^2 = \frac{\chi_1^2/1}{\chi_k^2/k} \sim F(1,k)$$

That is, if we square a variable that follows a t-distribution with k degrees of freedom, we will construct a new variable which follows an F-distribution, $F(1,k)$. For example, we know that with a very large number of degrees of freedom, the 5 per cent critical value in the t-distribution is 1.96. If we square this, we will find the critical value from the F-distribution: $1.96^2 = 3.84\,(2dp)$. If you compare that with the 5 per cent critical value from the $F(1,\infty)$ distribution, you will see that these values are the same.

Summary

In this chapter, we have introduced two new distributions, the Chi-squared and the F-distribution, constructed based upon the normal distribution. Further, we have seen how the t-distribution links all three distributions.

In the next chapter, we will introduce a new form of test, known as ANalysis Of VAriance, or ANOVA. This is a test built upon the F-distribution, which allows us to test multiple hypotheses.

We saw, in Chapter 20, that we could test the equality of means across two populations. This is quite a limited test, because you can only test that means are equal across two populations. However, you may often be interested in testing whether averages are equal across multiple populations. For instance, you might treat each high school in the country as a separate population, and then wish to test the hypothesis that average exam grades are the same across each of these schools. It is not possible to carry out this sort of test using a t-test, but, as we will see in the next chapter, we can test these sorts of multiple hypotheses using ANOVA.

Key formulae

Distribution	Explanation
Chi-squared distribution	The chi-squared (χ_k^2) distribution with k degrees of freedom is constructed based on the sum of squares of k independent variables, each following a standard normal distribution. If $Z_i \sim N(0,1)$ for all i, then: $Y = \sum_{i=1}^{n} Z_i^2 \sim \chi_n^2$ This is sometimes also denoted as $\chi^2(n)$.

Distribution	Explanation
T-distribution	A variable that is constructed based on the ratio between a standard normal and a chi-squared distribution will follow the (Student's) t-distribution. More precisely, if $Z \sim N(0,1)$ and $Y \sim \chi_k^2$, then if we construct a new variable, W, such that: $W = \frac{Z}{\sqrt{\frac{Y}{k}}} \sim t_k$ then W will follow a t distribution, based upon k degrees of freedom.
F-distribution	If we have two variables, X and Y, each of which follows the χ^2 distribution, such that: $X \sim \chi_j^2, Y \sim \chi_k^2$ and if we construct a new variable, F, based on the ratio of the two: $F = \frac{X / j}{Y / k} \sim F(j,k)$ then the resulting test statistic will follow the F-distribution.

Appendix

Upper tails of the chi-squared distribution

The table represents the probability of lying to the right of a value from the $\chi^2(k)$ distribution. For example, $P(\chi^2(3) \geq 4.878) = \frac{30}{100}$.

	$P\%$									
	50	40	30	20	10	5	2.5	1	0.5	0.05
$k = 1$	0.455	0.708	1.074	1.642	2.706	3.841	5.024	6.635	7.879	12.116
2	1.386	1.833	2.408	3.219	4.605	5.991	7.378	9.210	10.597	15.202
3	2.366	2.946	3.665	4.642	6.251	7.815	9.348	11.345	12.838	17.730
4	3.357	4.045	4.878	5.989	7.779	9.488	11.143	13.277	14.860	19.997
5	4.351	5.132	6.064	7.289	9.236	11.070	12.833	15.086	16.750	22.105
6	5.348	6.211	7.231	8.558	10.645	12.592	14.449	16.812	18.548	24.103
7	6.346	7.283	8.383	9.803	12.017	14.067	16.013	18.475	20.278	26.018
8	7.344	8.351	9.524	11.030	13.362	15.507	17.535	20.090	21.955	27.868
9	8.343	9.414	10.656	12.242	14.684	16.919	19.023	21.666	23.589	29.666
10	9.342	10.473	11.781	13.442	15.987	18.307	20.483	23.209	25.188	31.420
11	10.341	11.530	12.899	14.631	17.275	19.675	21.920	24.725	26.757	33.137
12	11.340	12.584	14.011	15.812	18.549	21.026	23.337	26.217	28.300	34.821
13	12.340	13.636	15.119	16.985	19.812	22.362	24.736	27.688	29.819	36.478

	P%									
	50	40	30	20	10	5	2.5	1	0.5	0.05
14	13.339	14.685	16.222	18.151	21.064	23.685	26.119	29.141	31.319	38.109
15	14.339	15.733	17.322	19.311	22.307	24.996	27.488	30.578	32.801	39.719
16	15.338	16.780	18.418	20.465	23.542	26.296	28.845	32.000	34.267	41.308
17	16.338	17.824	19.511	21.615	24.769	27.587	30.191	33.409	35.718	42.879
18	17.338	18.868	20.601	22.760	25.989	28.869	31.526	34.805	37.156	44.434
19	18.338	19.910	21.689	23.900	27.204	30.144	32.852	36.191	38.582	45.973
20	19.337	20.951	22.775	25.038	28.412	31.410	34.170	37.566	39.997	47.498
21	20.337	21.991	23.858	26.171	29.615	32.671	35.479	38.932	41.401	49.011
22	21.337	23.031	24.939	27.301	30.813	33.924	36.781	40.289	42.796	50.511
23	22.337	24.069	26.018	28.429	32.007	35.172	38.076	41.638	44.181	52.000
24	23.337	25.106	27.096	29.553	33.196	36.415	39.364	42.980	45.559	53.479
25	24.337	26.143	28.172	30.675	34.382	37.652	40.646	44.314	46.928	54.947
26	25.336	27.179	29.246	31.795	35.563	38.885	41.923	45.642	48.290	56.407
27	26.336	28.214	30.319	32.912	36.741	40.113	43.195	46.963	49.645	57.858
28	27.336	29.249	31.391	34.027	37.916	41.337	44.461	48.278	50.993	59.300
29	28.336	30.283	32.461	35.139	39.087	42.557	45.722	49.588	52.336	60.735
30	29.336	31.316	33.530	36.250	40.256	43.773	46.979	50.892	53.672	62.162
40	39.335	41.622	44.165	47.269	51.805	55.758	59.342	63.691	66.766	76.095
50	49.335	51.892	54.723	58.164	63.167	67.505	71.420	76.154	79.490	89.561
60	59.335	62.135	65.227	68.972	74.397	79.082	83.298	88.379	91.952	102.695
90	89.334	92.761	96.524	101.054	107.565	113.145	118.136	124.116	128.299	140.782
120	119.334	123.289	127.616	132.806	140.233	146.567	152.211	158.950	163.648	177.603
240	239.334	244.918	250.988	258.218	268.471	277.138	284.802	293.888	300.182	318.699

5 per cent critical values of the F-distribution

	5% critical values in the right hand tail									
	$\nu_1 = 1$	2	3	4	5	6	7	8	9	10
$\nu_2 = 1$	161.448	199.500	215.707	224.583	230.162	233.986	236.768	238.883	240.543	241.882
2	18.513	19.000	19.164	19.247	19.296	19.330	19.353	19.371	19.385	19.396
3	10.128	9.552	9.277	9.117	9.013	8.941	8.887	8.845	8.812	8.786
4	7.709	6.944	6.591	6.388	6.256	6.163	6.094	6.041	5.999	5.964

	5% critical values in the right hand tail									
	$v_1 = 1$	2	3	4	5	6	7	8	9	10
5	6.608	5.786	5.409	5.192	5.050	4.950	4.876	4.818	4.772	4.735
6	5.987	5.143	4.757	4.534	4.387	4.284	4.207	4.147	4.099	4.060
7	5.591	4.737	4.347	4.120	3.972	3.866	3.787	3.726	3.677	3.637
8	5.318	4.459	4.066	3.838	3.687	3.581	3.500	3.438	3.388	3.347
9	5.117	4.256	3.863	3.633	3.482	3.374	3.293	3.230	3.179	3.137
10	4.965	4.103	3.708	3.478	3.326	3.217	3.135	3.072	3.020	2.978
11	4.844	3.982	3.587	3.357	3.204	3.095	3.012	2.948	2.896	2.854
12	4.747	3.885	3.490	3.259	3.106	2.996	2.913	2.849	2.796	2.753
13	4.667	3.806	3.411	3.179	3.025	2.915	2.832	2.767	2.714	2.671
14	4.600	3.739	3.344	3.112	2.958	2.848	2.764	2.699	2.646	2.602
15	4.543	3.682	3.287	3.056	2.901	2.790	2.707	2.641	2.588	2.544
16	4.494	3.634	3.239	3.007	2.852	2.741	2.657	2.591	2.538	2.494
17	4.451	3.592	3.197	2.965	2.810	2.699	2.614	2.548	2.494	2.450
18	4.414	3.555	3.160	2.928	2.773	2.661	2.577	2.510	2.456	2.412
19	4.381	3.522	3.127	2.895	2.740	2.628	2.544	2.477	2.423	2.378
20	4.351	3.493	3.098	2.866	2.711	2.599	2.514	2.447	2.393	2.348
21	4.325	3.467	3.072	2.840	2.685	2.573	2.488	2.420	2.366	2.321
22	4.301	3.443	3.049	2.817	2.661	2.549	2.464	2.397	2.342	2.297
23	4.279	3.422	3.028	2.796	2.640	2.528	2.442	2.375	2.320	2.275
24	4.260	3.403	3.009	2.776	2.621	2.508	2.423	2.355	2.300	2.255
25	4.242	3.385	2.991	2.759	2.603	2.490	2.405	2.337	2.282	2.236
26	4.225	3.369	2.975	2.743	2.587	2.474	2.388	2.321	2.265	2.220
27	4.210	3.354	2.960	2.728	2.572	2.459	2.373	2.305	2.250	2.204
28	4.196	3.340	2.947	2.714	2.558	2.445	2.359	2.291	2.236	2.190
29	4.183	3.328	2.934	2.701	2.545	2.432	2.346	2.278	2.223	2.177
30	4.171	3.316	2.922	2.690	2.534	2.421	2.334	2.266	2.211	2.165
40	4.085	3.232	2.839	2.606	2.449	2.336	2.249	2.180	2.124	2.077
50	4.034	3.183	2.790	2.557	2.400	2.286	2.199	2.130	2.073	2.026
60	4.001	3.150	2.758	2.525	2.368	2.254	2.167	2.097	2.040	1.993
90	3.947	3.098	2.706	2.473	2.316	2.201	2.113	2.043	1.986	1.938
120	3.920	3.072	2.680	2.447	2.290	2.175	2.087	2.016	1.959	1.910
240	3.880	3.033	2.642	2.409	2.252	2.136	2.048	1.977	1.919	1.870
∞	3.841	2.996	2.605	2.372	2.214	2.099	2.010	1.938	1.880	1.831

Analysis of Variance, or ANOVA

22

Learning outcomes for this chapter

By the end of this chapter you will be able to:

- Interpret violin plots as a way of illustrating the distribution of data
- Carry out ANOVA tests based on grouped data
- Use Excel to carry out ANOVA tests
- Explain when t-tests are sufficient, and when ANOVA would be necessary

Mathematical tools

- Summations and double summations
- Algebra

Introduction

In Chapter 20, we introduced t-tests to test for equality of means. However, whilst we can use a t-test to test hypotheses, including multiple expected values, we cannot use it to test for equality of means across three or more populations simultaneously.

In order to do this, we will need a different tool. One tool that we can make use of is Analysis of Variance, or **ANOVA**.

To illustrate what ANOVA does, let's begin with an example. In the previous chapters, we have tested for the equality of average wages between male and female workers. ANOVA begins by estimating the overall **variance** of wages in the economy, and then tries to fit a model to the data to ask whether the variation between male and female wages is significant, compared with the overall variation in wages.

The power of ANOVA is that, because we are analysing the explained variance from a model, we can include more than two groups. For example, we could use this to analyse whether there are differences in test scores across different ethnicities, whether different areas of the country have different average house prices, or whether students studying Economics are, on average, the same height as maths majors, or law majors.

22.1 Interpreting 'violin plots' to visualize multiple samples or populations

In this chapter, we will make use of violin plots, which are an elegant way of representing the distribution of data, particularly across multiple samples.

An example of a violin plot, representing the distribution of weekly wages amongst full-time workers in the UK, is illustrated in Figure 22.1. The violin plot represents the distribution of the random variable (in this case, the gross weekly wage, based upon a sample). The width of the shaded area illustrates the relative frequency of observations. Included within the diagram is a box and whiskers to illustrate the median, and 25th and 75th percentiles (p25 and p75). The rare outcomes at the top of the distribution are likely to be outliers.

We have seen, in previous chapters, how we can use t-tests to test a single hypothesis. For example, we can test whether the average weekly earnings in the population are £650. Alternatively, we can test whether two populations have the same average. However, often, we might want to test whether population averages are equal across multiple groups. For example, we might be interested in testing whether average wages are equal across different

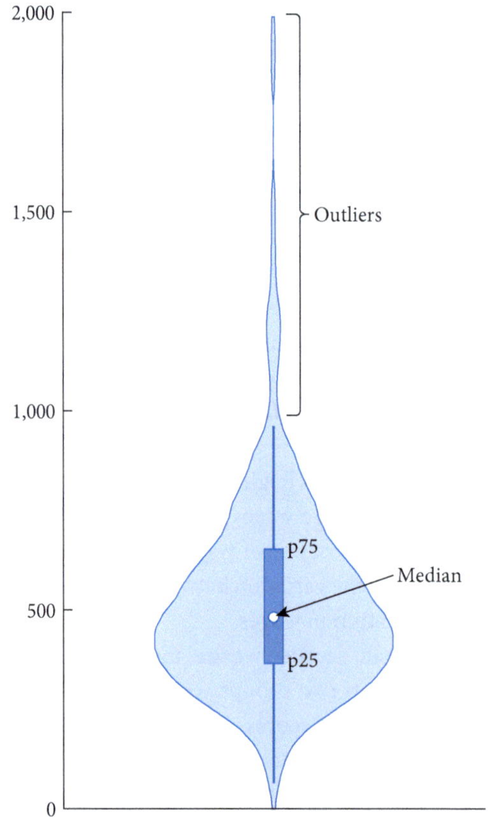

Figure 22.1 A simple violin plot.

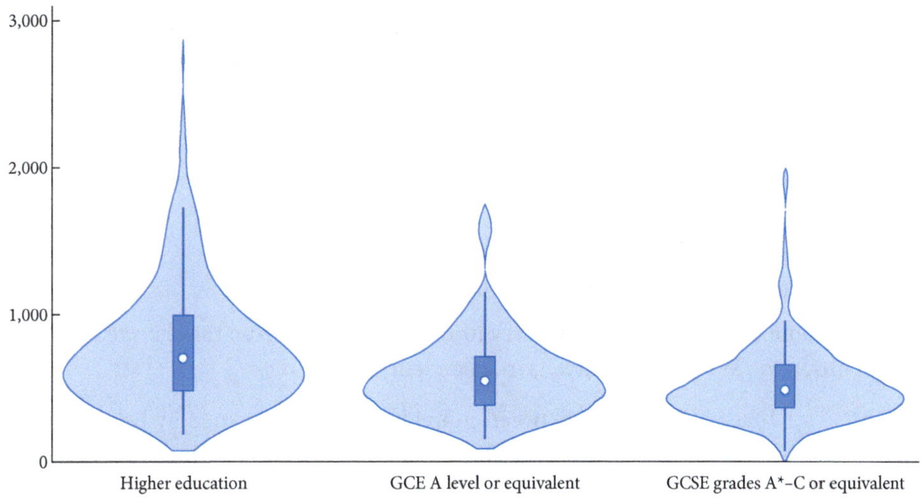

Figure 22.2 Violin plots illustrating the distribution of weekly wages for individuals with different levels of education.

age groups in the population, or across different industries, or across different levels of qualifications.

To investigate this, I have randomly sampled 600 individuals, in full-time employment, aged 25–45, from the UK Labour Force Survey, consisting of 200 individuals whose highest qualification is GCSEs (qualifications gained at age 16), 200 individuals whose highest qualification is A-level (qualifications at age 18), and 200 individuals who have some higher education, but which has not led to a degree. The distribution of weekly wages is illustrated in Figure 22.2.

Across the three groups, the distribution of wages appears very similar. However, it's not sufficient just to compare how the distributions look—we need a formal test to establish whether the average wages are equal, or different, across the three groups.

We will return to the example of highest education level later in the chapter, but for now, we will try to motivate ANOVA using a simpler example.

22.2 One-way ANOVA

As the name suggests, ANOVA is based on analysis of variance, and in particular, we are looking at analysing the variance of our variable of interest. To analyse the data, and in particular, to examine whether the samples are taken from populations with equal means, we will fit a model, which is based upon the group that an observation lies within.

Suppose that there are k groups. Within each group, there will be a number of individuals, with variation in outcomes, but there may also be systematic variation between groups in terms of outcomes.

If we represent the outcome that individual i within group j achieves as Y_{ij}, we can model the outcome Y_{ij} as consisting of two parts: a part that is determined by the group they are a member of, μ_j, and an individual (random) error term, u_{ij}. So, the individual outcome, Y_{ij}, can be modelled as:

$$Y_{ij} = \mu_j + u_{ij}$$

More precisely, we might define μ_j and u_{ij} as:

- μ_j – expected outcome for individuals in group j. i.e. $E(Y_j) = \mu_j$
- u_{ij} – random deviation of individual i, within group j, away from the expected value for that group, μ_j. We assume that u_{ij} is independent from μ_j.

$Y_{ij} = \mu_j + u_{ij}$. That is, differences between individuals are determined by between group differences (i.e. differences between μ_j) and differences between the individual level elements, u_{ij}.

If there is no significant difference between the individual groups, then this is equivalent to $\mu_1 = \mu_2 = \mu_3 = \ldots = \mu_k$. That is, the group average would be the same for all groups.

Formally, we could denote this as a **null hypothesis**:

$$H_0: \mu_1 = \mu_2 = \mu_3 = \ldots = \mu_k$$

The alternative hypothesis would be that there are differences in population averages between some of the groups. If the null hypothesis is true, then this is equivalent to saying that there is no variation in the μ_j between groups, or alternatively that the variance between groups is equal to zero. So, our null hypothesis is equivalent to:

$$H_0: var(\mu_j) = 0$$
$$H_A: var(\mu_j) \neq 0$$

That is, the variance of our μ_j is equal to zero. ANOVA is the 'analysis of variance', and as such, we are interested in the variance of the determinants. A good place to start might be to consider the variance of the overall outcome, Y_{ij}:

$$var(Y_{ij}) = var(\mu_j + u_{ij})$$

To evaluate this variance, we will need to appeal to the rules of variances.

Rules of variances

Remember, if we combine two random variables, X and Y, in a **linear combination**, using constant multipliers a and b, then:

$$var(aX + bY) = a^2\, var(X) + b^2\, var(Y) + 2ab \times cov(X,Y)$$

Since we modelled the individual outcomes, Y_{ij}, as determined by the between group elements, μ_j, and the individual (random) error term, u_{ij}, then we can decompose the variance of Y_{ij} into three parts:

$$\Rightarrow var(Y_{ij}) = var(\mu_j) + var(u_{ij}) + 2cov(\mu_j, u_{ij})$$

Since the individual error term, u_{ij}, is assumed to be random (and independent from group j's expected value, μ_j), it will follow that $cov(\mu_j, u_{ij}) = 0$. So, this allows us to simplify our expression for the variance of outcomes to:

$$var(Y_{ij}) = var(\mu_j) + var(u_{ij})$$

So, this means that we can decompose the overall variance of the outcome variables into two components:

- the variation within groups ($var(u_{ij})$). This is the variability that occurs when considering different individuals within the same group, and
- the variation between groups ($var(\mu_j)$). This is the variability between the group averages when we are looking across (or between) groups.

This is probably easiest to understand with a short example. Suppose that you are a teacher in a primary school class. The children have all decided where to sit (but have to sit there all term). You believe that the students have grouped themselves according to their natural ability, and each table has a different average or expected level of achievement. Within the classroom, there are three tables, each with four students. The results from the children, broken down by table, are illustrated in Table 22.1.

Table 22.1 Results of each student, by table at which they sit

	Table 1	Table 2	Table 3
Student 1	9	5	6
Student 2	8	4	7
Student 3	5	1	4
Student 4	6	2	3

Numerically, this might not tell us much, but if we illustrate this graphically, we can see the outcomes grouped, by table, in Figure 22.3. Each group of data represents a different table, and we also mark on the sample mean for each table.

You can see that there are two key sources of variability in terms of test scores:

1. Variation between the tables: this is seen because each table has a different average score. The variability between the average scores on the tables is represented by $var(\mu_j)$.
2. Variation within the tables: not everyone on the table has the same score. The variability within tables is represented by $var(u_{ij})$.

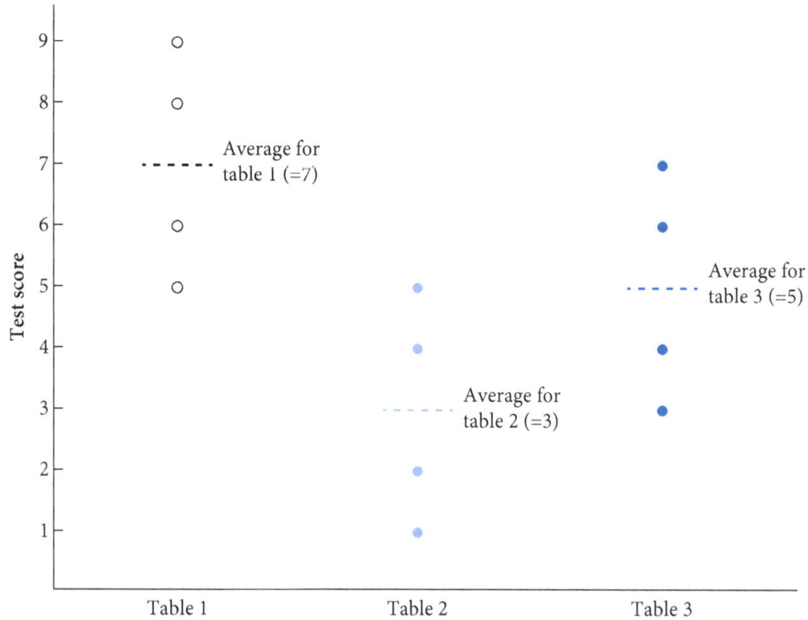

Figure 22.3 Example illustrating within and between group variation.

More formally we can represent the different variances as:

Type of variation	Mathematical notation	Description
Overall variation	$var(Y_{ij})$	This is the overall variation in outcomes.
Variation between groups	$var(\mu_j)$	This is the variation in outcomes between groups.
Variation within groups	$var(u_{ij})$	This is the variation in outcomes within groups.

Since we know that $var(Y_{ij}) = var(\mu_j) + var(u_{ij})$, if we divide left and right by $var(Y_{ij})$, we can represent this as the proportion of the variation of Y_{ij} that is made up of each element:

$$1 = \frac{var(\mu_j)}{var(Y_{ij})} + \frac{var(u_{ij})}{var(Y_{ij})}$$

Type of variation	Mathematical notation	Description
Variation between groups	$\frac{var(\mu_j)}{var(Y_{ij})}$	This is the proportion of the variance of Y_{ij} that is made up by the between group variation.
Variation within groups	$\frac{var(u_{ij})}{var(Y_{ij})}$	This is the proportion of the variance of Y_{ij} that is made up by the within group variation.

Finally, if we want to compare the relative contributions of the between and the within group variations, we can consider the ratio of these two elements:

$$\frac{var(\mu_j)/var(Y_{ij})}{var(u_{ij})/var(Y_{ij})} = \frac{var(\mu_j)}{var(u_{ij})}$$

This represents the relative weight of the between variation and the within variation. If the null hypothesis is true, then this ratio would be equal to zero.

Of course, we don't know what these variances are, so we would need to estimate them, and then use these estimates to test the hypothesis that $var(\mu_j) = 0$. Before we do that, let's remind ourselves of some definitions:

Y_{ij}	This is the outcome for individual i within group j.
$\bar{Y}_j$	This is the (sample) mean of outcomes of individuals within group j. If we have m individuals in group j, then the sample mean within group j will be: $\bar{Y}_j = \frac{1}{m}\sum_{i=1}^{m} Y_{ij}$ Note, in this summation, j does not change. This is because we are simply finding the sample mean of the individuals within a particular group j. If you have k groups, then you would obtain k group means, $\bar{Y}_1, \bar{Y}_2, \ldots, \bar{Y}_k$
$\bar{Y}$	This is the overall sample mean of observations of Y. If we had n observations, we would add up all of the observations, and divide by n. Since we are dealing with individuals nested within groups, it is worth writing this out, taking account of both the groups and the individuals within the groups. If we have k groups and m individuals in each group: $\bar{Y} = \left[\frac{1}{m \times k}\right] \times \sum_{i=1}^{m}\sum_{j=1}^{k} Y_{ij}$ For simplicity, let's define $m \times k = n$, and so we can write: $\bar{Y} = \frac{1}{n} \times \sum_{i=1}^{m}\sum_{j=1}^{k} Y_{ij}$

To test the hypothesis that the average scores are equal across tables, we will need to construct three new measures, based on the total sum of squares, the within sum of squares, and the between sum of squares. These measures are based upon the unbiased estimator for the population variance (s^2).

Unbiased estimator of population variance

Remember that $s^2 = \frac{1}{n-1}\Sigma_{i=1}^{n}(Y_i - \bar{Y})^2$ is an unbiased estimator of the variance of Y. We divide through by $n - 1$ as a **degrees of freedom** adjustment. Because we include the sample mean ($\bar{Y}$) as an estimate of $E(Y)$, we lose a degree of freedom.

22.2.1 The total sum of squares (TSS)

The total sum of squares (TSS) is equal to the sum of squares of the deviations of the observations of Y_{ij} from the average $\overline{Y}$. If we have m individuals within each of k groups, then we can write the TSS as:

$$TSS = \sum_{i=1}^{m}\sum_{j=1}^{k}(Y_{ij} - \overline{Y})^2$$

This is linked to the estimator for the variance of Y. As we are simply finding the sum of squares of the deviations of the observations of Y away from the (overall) sample mean of Y, if we divided the TSS by the total number of observations (less 1), we would have the s^2 estimator for Y as a whole.

For simplicity's sake, let's think of the total number of observations as n (which in this example would be equal to $m \times k$). So, we can represent the TSS as:

$$\frac{TSS}{n-1} = s_{n-1}^2$$

We can therefore think of the TSS as being linked to an estimator for the variance of Y as a whole.

22.2.2 The within sum of squares (WSS)

The within sum of squares is the sum of squares of the deviations within each group. Just as the TSS is linked to the estimator for the overall variance of Y, the WSS is linked to the within group variance, $var(u_{ij})$. The within sum of squares looks at the squares of the deviations of the observations away from their group mean:

$$WSS = \sum_{i=1}^{m}\sum_{j=1}^{k}(Y_{ij} - \overline{Y}_j)^2$$

This formula looks similar to the TSS, but note carefully that for each group (i.e. each j), we are subtracting the sample mean for that group. Later on, it will become important how many degrees of freedom there are in this expression. If you think back to when we introduced the s^2 estimator, because we had an estimate of the population average included, we lost a degree of freedom. However, in this case, as we have k groups, we will have used k different sample means (as estimates of the population average for individuals in group j) in this expression, and so, if we have n observations in total, we will have $n - k$ degrees of freedom.

It should be noted that we are, implicitly, assuming that the within group variance is the same for all groups. We are attempting to construct a single estimate of the within group variance for all groups. If we wanted to construct an estimate of the within group variance, this would be:

$$\widehat{\text{var}}(u_{ij}) = \left(\frac{1}{n-k}\right) \times \sum_{i=1}^{m}\sum_{j=1}^{k}(Y_{ij} - \overline{Y}_j)^2$$

Relating this back to the t-test for equal expected values

In Chapter 20, we tested the equality of means across two populations, which we represented by the random variables, X and Y. We saw that, when we assumed that the variance was the same in both X and Y, then:

$$s^2 = \left(\frac{1}{n-2}\right) \times \left(\sum_{i=1}^{n}(X_i - \overline{X})^2 + \sum_{j=1}^{m}(Y_j - \overline{Y})^2\right)$$

This formula is equivalent to $\frac{WSS}{n-2}$. We are looking at the sum of squares of the observations of X and Y away from their respective sample means in two groups. However, this is making the assumption that the within-group variance is the same in both X and Y.

If the within-group variance assumption is incorrect, then the simple one-way ANOVA we are developing here breaks down.

22.2.3 The between sum of squares (BSS)

The between sum of squares is the sum of squares of group averages away from the overall average. That is, the between sum of squares is related to $var(\mu_j)$. To ensure that this is in the same scale as the WSS and the TSS, it is important that the squared deviation is calculated for every member of every group.

$$BSS = \sum_{i=1}^{m}\sum_{j=1}^{k}(\overline{Y}_j - \overline{Y})^2$$

One important question is how many degrees of freedom we have here. In reality, we will have one value of $\overline{Y}_j$ per group (even though it is repeated m times in each group). That is, once you know the corresponding $\overline{Y}_j - \overline{Y}$ for one member of the group, you will know this for every member of the group.

By that reasoning, we only have k different values of $(\overline{Y}_j - \overline{Y})^2$. In addition, $\overline{Y}$ is simply an average of $\overline{Y}_j$, meaning that we lose a further degree of freedom. That means that, within BSS, we only have $k - 1$ degrees of freedom.

22.2.4 Constructing the F-statistic

It is possible to show that there is a linear relationship between the total, within, and between sums of squares, in that:

$$TSS = WSS + BSS$$

Reminding ourselves of the null hypothesis we want to test:

$$H_0: \mu_1 = \mu_2 = \ldots = \mu_k$$

If the null hypothesis is true, then we saw that this implies that $var(\mu_j) = 0$. The appropriate F-statistic can be constructed based on the ratio of the BSS and WSS. If the null hypothesis is true, then:

$$F = \frac{BSS\ /\ (k-1)}{WSS\ /\ (n-k)} \sim F(k-1, n-k)$$

So, in other words, if the null hypothesis is true, then the ratio of the between and within sum of squares, divided through by their relevant degrees of freedom, will follow an F-distribution.

We can then compare the F-statistic with the critical value from the F-tables. If the F-statistic is in the most extreme 5 per cent of outcomes in the right-hand tail, then we would reject the null hypothesis.

22.2.5 General formulae for one-way ANOVA

In general, suppose that you have n individuals, grouped into k groups, and you wished to test whether the (population) average was equal across all k groups of size m:

$$H_0\text{: } E(Y_1) = E(Y_2) = E(Y_3) = \ldots = E(Y_k)$$

Then, we can construct our relevant F-statistic using the following formulae, where j represents each of the k groups, $\bar{Y}$ represents the sample mean of all n observations, and $\bar{Y}_j$ represents the sample mean of scores for individuals in group j:

	Formulae	Degrees of freedom
Total sum of squares	$TSS = \sum_{i=1}^{m}\sum_{j=1}^{k}(Y_{ij} - \bar{Y})^2$	$n-1$
Within sum of squares	$WSS = \sum_{i=1}^{m}\sum_{j=1}^{k}(Y_{ij} - \bar{Y}_j)^2$	$n-k$
Between sum of squares	$BSS = \sum_{i=1}^{m}\sum_{j=1}^{k}(\bar{Y}_j - \bar{Y})^2$	$k-1$

The F-statistic can be calculated as:

$$F = \frac{BSS\ /\ (k-1)}{WSS\ /\ (n-k)}$$

and if the null hypothesis is true, then this F-statistic will follow an F-distribution based with $v_1 = k - 1$ and $v_2 = (n - k)$.

Note: In this example, we have imposed the conditions that all of the groups are the same size, m, and the total sample size is $n = m \times k$. ANOVA is powerful, in that the sample size need not be the same across all of the groups. So, for example, you could have 30 people in group 1, and 70 people in group 2, and the resulting test statistic would still be a valid F-statistic. The key assumption that is needed for one-way ANOVA to be valid is that the within-group variance is the same across all groups.

Worked example 22.1: Does it matter on which table you sit?

So far, the example of one-way ANOVA has been quite abstract, and we can make this more understandable by considering a concrete example. Let's begin by applying the ANOVA technique to the numerical example we saw earlier in the chapter.

Suppose that you are a teacher, teaching a primary school class. The children have all decided where to sit (but have to sit there all term). You believe that the students have grouped themselves according to their natural ability, and each table has a different average or expected level of achievement. Within the classroom, there are three tables, each with four students on. The results from the three tables are illustrated in Table 22.2 and Figure 22.4.

Table 22.2 Results of each student, by table on which they sit

	Table 1	Table 2	Table 3
Student 1	9	5	6
Student 2	8	4	7
Student 3	5	1	4
Student 4	6	2	3
Table average	$\bar{y}_1 = 7$	$\bar{y}_2 = 3$	$\bar{y}_3 = 5$

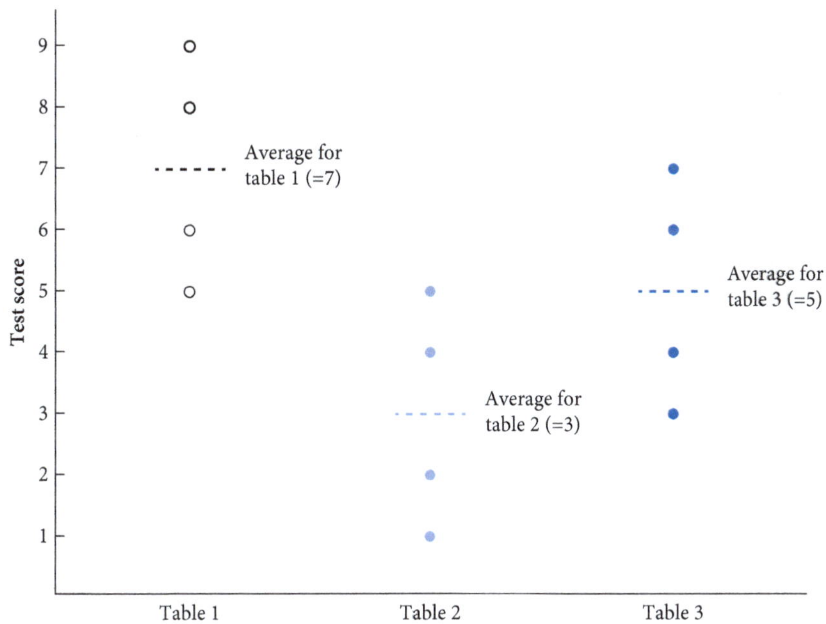

Figure 22.4 Example illustrating within and between group variation.

We are modelling that the score (Y_{ij}) of student i on table j is determined by a table effect μ_j and a random error u_{ij}, such that:

$$Y_{ij} = \mu_j + u_{ij}$$

We are interested in testing whether μ_j is the same across all three tables, or whether the underlying score varies across tables. That is, our null and alternative hypotheses will be:

$$H_0: \mu_1 = \mu_2 = \mu_3$$
$$H_A: \mu_1 \neq \mu_2 \; or \; \mu_1 \neq \mu_3 \; or \; \mu_2 \neq \mu_3$$

The alternative hypothesis contains all of the possibilities where the null hypothesis is not true. The key point is that, under the alternative hypothesis, the (population) average scores for the three tables are not the same.

In this example, we have three groups, each of which contains four individuals. This means that the total sample size (across all three groups) is $n = 12$. As such, the overall average score in the sample is given as:

$$\bar{y} = \frac{1}{12} \times \sum_{i=1}^{4}\sum_{j=1}^{3} y_{ij} = \frac{1}{12} \times [(9 + 8 + 5 + 6) + (5 + 4 + 1 + 2) + (6 + 7 + 4 + 3)] = 5$$

Calculating the total sum of squares

The TSS is calculated as the sum of squares of the observations away from the overall sample mean $\bar{Y} = 5$.

$$TSS = \sum_{i=1}^{4}\sum_{j=1}^{3}(Y_{ij} - \bar{Y})^2$$

We can tabulate each element of the TSS by considering $(Y_{ij} - \bar{Y})^2$ for every value of i and j. That is, we can calculate it for every individual on every table, as shown in Table 22.3.

Table 22.3 Calculating the total sum of squares

	Table 1		Table 2		Table 3		
	Test score	$(y_{i1} - \bar{y})^2$	Test score	$(y_{i2} - \bar{y})^2$	Test score	$(y_{i3} - \bar{y})^3$	
Student 1	9	$= (9 - 5)^2 = 16$	5	$= (5 - 5)^2 = 0$	6	$= (6 - 5)^2 = 1$	
Student 2	8	$= (8 - 5)^2 = 9$	4	$= (4 - 5)^2 = 1$	7	$= (7 - 5)^2 = 4$	
Student 3	5	$= (5 - 5)^2 = 0$	1	$= (1 - 5)^2 = 16$	4	$= (4 - 5)^2 = 1$	
Student 4	6	$= (6 - 5)^2 = 1$	2	$= (2 - 5)^2 = 9$	3	$= (3 - 5)^2 = 4$	
Average of student test scores							$\bar{y} = 5$

To find the total sum of squares, we can thus add up each of the $(y_{ij} - \bar{y})^2$ terms:

$$= 16 + 9 + 0 + 1 + 0 + 1 + 16 + 9 + 1 + 4 + 1 + 4 = 62$$

Because $\overline{Y}$ is just a linear combination of the 12 observations, and since we have used $\overline{Y}$ in the construction of the TSS, we have 11 linearly independent elements to the TSS. This means that we have $(12 - 1) = 11$ degrees of freedom.

Calculating the within sum of squares

The WSS is a proxy for the variance within each group, and calculates the sum of squares of the difference between observation Y_{ij} and the corresponding group average $\overline{Y}_j$. We can easily calculate the group averages for each table:

$$\overline{y}_1 = \frac{1}{4} \times (9 + 8 + 5 + 6) = 7,$$

$$\overline{y}_2 = \frac{1}{4} \times (5 + 4 + 1 + 2) = 3,$$

$$\overline{y}_3 = \frac{1}{4} \times (6 + 7 + 4 + 3) = 5$$

The WSS is then just calculated as:

$$WSS = \sum_{i=1}^{4}\sum_{j=1}^{3}(Y_{ij} - \overline{Y}_j)^2$$

and so, we can calculate our WSS as seen in Table 22.4.

Table 22.4 Calculating the within sum of squares

	Table 1 ($\overline{y}_1 = 7$)		Table 2 ($\overline{y}_2 = 3$)		Table 1 ($\overline{y}_3 = 5$)	
	Test score	$(y_{i1} - \overline{y}_1)^2$	Test score	$(y_{i2} - \overline{y}_2)^2$	Test score	$(y_{i3} - \overline{y}_3)^2$
Student 1	9	$= (9-7)^2 = 4$	5	$= (5-3)^2 = 4$	6	$= (6-5)^2 = 1$
Student 2	8	$= (8-7)^2 = 1$	4	$= (4-3)^2 = 1$	7	$= (7-5)^2 = 4$
Student 3	5	$= (5-7)^2 = 4$	1	$= (1-3)^2 = 4$	4	$= (4-5)^2 = 1$
Student 4	6	$= (6-7)^2 = 1$	2	$= (2-3)^2 = 1$	3	$= (3-5)^2 = 4$

To find the within sum of squares, we need to find the sum of all of the $(Y_{ij} - \overline{Y}_j)^2$ terms. As such, this is just:

$$WSS = \sum_{i=1}^{4}\sum_{j=1}^{3}(y_{ij} - \overline{y}_j)^2 = (4 + 1 + 4 + 1) + (4 + 1 + 4 + 1) + (1 + 4 + 1 + 4) = 30$$

In calculating the WSS, we have used three separate estimates of sample means, $\overline{Y}_1 = 7$, $\overline{Y}_2 = 3$, and $\overline{Y}_3 = 5$. We have 12 observations, but by using the three separate estimates we have lost 3 degrees of freedom. This means that we have 9 degrees of freedom in the WSS.

Calculating the between sum of squares

Finally, we are interested in the variation between groups, and we can estimate this, using the between sum of squares. The BSS is the sum of squares of the deviations of the group averages, $\overline{Y}_j$, away from the overall, sample average, $\overline{Y}$. (Note carefully the differences in subscripts between these two sample means.)

Formally, we can write the BSS as:

$$BSS = \sum_{i=1}^{4}\sum_{j=1}^{3}(\overline{Y}_j - \overline{Y})^2$$

That is, the BSS is the sum of squares of the table averages away from the overall average score. Remember, the average test score across all students is equal to $\overline{y} = 5$.

We can substitute in the numbers, and calculate the BSS, as shown in Table 22.5.

Table 22.5 Calculating the between sum of squares

	Table 1 ($\overline{y}_1 = 7$)		Table 2 ($\overline{y}_2 = 3$)		Table 1 ($\overline{y}_3 = 5$)	
	Average test score on table	$(\overline{y}_1 - \overline{y})^2$	Average test score on table	$(\overline{y}_2 - \overline{y})^2$	Average test score on table	$(\overline{y}_3 - \overline{y})^3$
Student 1	7	$= (7-5)^2 = 4$	3	$= (3-5)^2 = 4$	5	$= (5-5)^2 = 0$
Student 2	7	$= (7-5)^2 = 4$	3	$= (3-5)^2 = 4$	5	$= (5-5)^2 = 0$
Student 3	7	$= (7-5)^2 = 4$	3	$= (3-5)^2 = 4$	5	$= (5-5)^2 = 0$
Student 4	7	$= (7-5)^2 = 4$	3	$= (3-5)^2 = 4$	5	$= (5-5)^2 = 0$

As such, the BSS can be calculated as:

$$BSS = \sum_{i=1}^{4}\sum_{j=1}^{3}(\overline{y}_j - \overline{y})^2 = (4+4+4+4) + (4+4+4+4) + (0+0+0+0) = 32$$

Calculating this gives a BSS equal to 32. In reality, this estimate is based on three observations (each repeated four times), and we lose an additional degree of freedom, because we have used an estimate, $\overline{Y}$, in constructing the BSS. This leaves 2 degrees of freedom.

Using the WSS and BSS to test the hypothesis

Before we go any further, it is important to check our calculations. A useful check that we haven't made an error is that there should be a **linear relationship** between the TSS, the WSS, and the BSS in that:

$$TSS = WSS + BSS$$

We can check this here, as $TSS = 62$, $WSS = 30$, and $BSS = 32$. If we add $WSS + BSS$, we have $30 + 32 = 62$ as required. To summarize, let's display all of the results so far in a single table (Table 22.6):

The F-statistic can be calculated as:

$$F = \frac{BSS/(k-1)}{WSS/(n-k)} \sim F(k-1, n-k)$$

Table 22.6 Total, within, and between sum of squares

	Sum of squares	Degrees of freedom
Total	62	11
Within	30	9
Between	32	2

where n is the total number of observations ($n = 12$), and k is the number of groups ($k = 3$):

$$\Rightarrow F = \frac{32/(3-1)}{30/(12-3)} = \frac{32/2}{30/9} = 4.8$$

Now, if we look up the critical value from the F-tables based upon $\nu_1 = 2$ and $\nu_2 = 9$, we find a critical value, at the 5 per cent significance level, of 4.256. Since the F-statistic we have calculated (= 4.8) is larger than this critical value, we would reject the null hypothesis.

Based on our visualization of the data (illustrated again in Figure 22.5), the fact that we have rejected the null is quite reassuring, as we can see that there does appear to be a big difference in the performances across groups (in particular between the first table (table 1) and the second table (table 2)).

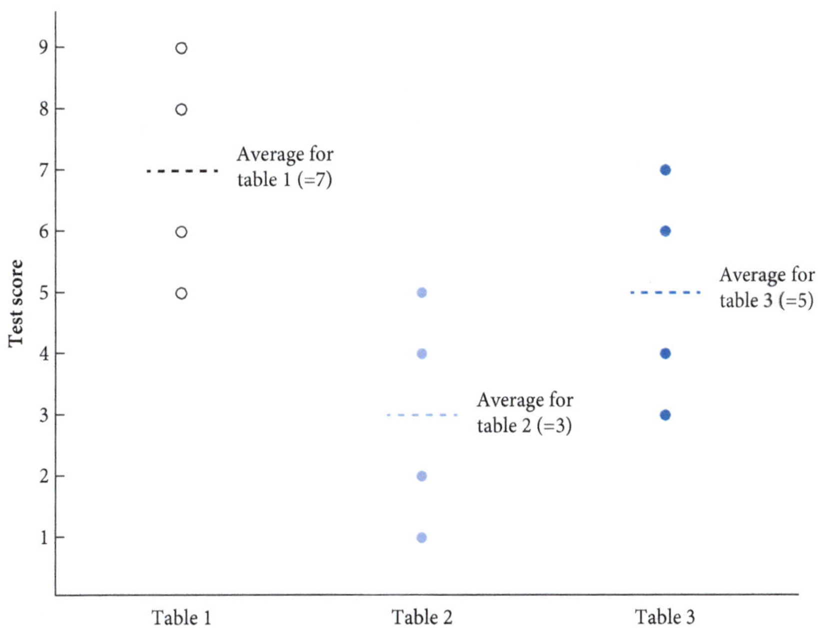

Figure 22.5 Example illustrating within and between group variation.

Important note

We have been quite courageous with our use of ANOVA in this instance. Just like when we tested single hypotheses, we rely on either there being a large enough sample to appeal to the central limit theorem, or that the underlying population is normally distributed.

In this example, we only have a small sample ($n = 12$), and it is highly unlikely that the data is normally distributed. As such, the F-statistic that we have generated may not be valid. In circumstances like these, researchers need to try to collect more data, in order to get more rigorous statistics.

Worked example 22.2: Are average earnings linked to qualifications?

Earlier in the chapter, we began to discuss whether we could test whether earnings were equal across all possible highest levels of education. In the UK, students complete education at different levels. For simplicity, we are considering the highest levels of education achieved, broken down into three separate groups:

1. GCSEs grade A*–C. Students complete GCSES at age 16, normally in 8–10 subjects.
2. GCE A-levels or equivalent. These are completed at age 18, and include academic qualifications (such as A-levels, Highers, or the International Baccalaureate), and vocational qualifications.
3. Higher education. This includes students who have gained any higher education (e.g. education at a university).

Let's begin by setting out some hypotheses. If we define X_1 as the income of the population whose highest qualification is GCSEs, X_2 as the income of the population whose highest qualification is A-level (or equivalent), and X_3 as the income population with some higher education, then our null hypothesis would be that the average wages for these three groups are equal. Similarly, our alternative hypothesis is that at least one of the averages is different. Formally, we can represent this as:

$$H_0{:}E(X_1) = E(X_2) = E(X_3)$$
$$H_A{:}E(X_1) \neq E(X_2)\,or\,E(X_1) \neq E(X_3)\,or\,E(X_2) \neq E(X_3)$$

To investigate this, I have randomly sampled 600 individuals, in full-time employment, aged 25–45, from the UK Labour Force Survey, consisting of 200 individuals whose highest qualification is GCSEs (qualifications gained at age 16), 200 individuals whose highest qualification is A-level (qualifications at age 18), and 200 individuals who have some higher education, but which has not led to a degree. Violin plots representing the distribution of earnings within the three groups are illustrated in Figure 22.6.

Looking at the violin plots, it is less obvious in this example whether there is a significant difference between the earnings across the three groups, but we can calculate the sample average weekly earnings for the three groups, as shown in Table 22.7.

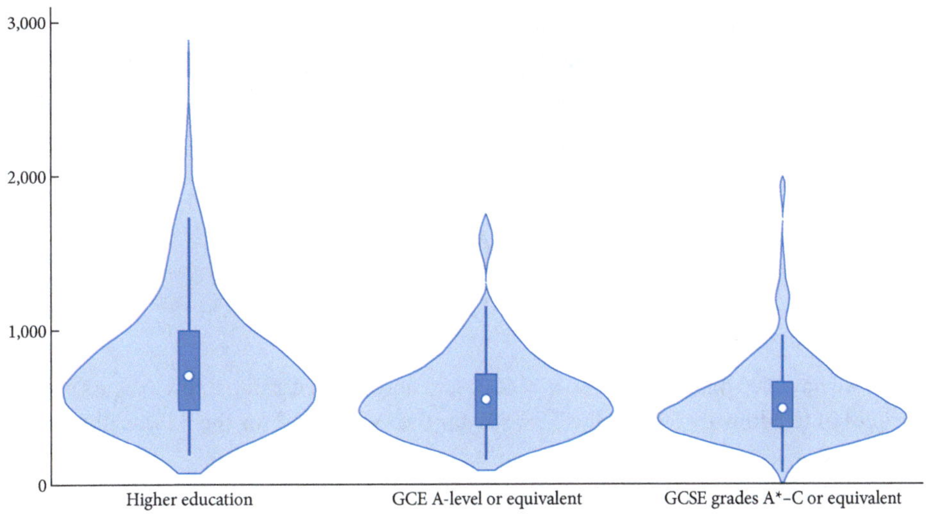

Figure 22.6 Violin plots illustrating the distribution of weekly wages for individuals with different levels of education.

Table 22.7 Average weekly earnings by highest level of qualification

Highest level of qualification	Average weekly earnings
Higher education	£811.24
GCE A-level or equivalent	£588.74
GCSE grades A*–C or equivalent	£535.48
Average across all 600 individuals	£645.15

Based on the sample averages, in our sample of 600 individuals, those with higher education have higher average earnings (£811.24) than those with A-levels or equivalent (£588.74), and those with GCSE grades A*–C (£535.48).

Of course, these averages hide a lot of variation within the groups: some individuals with only GCSEs have very high earnings, although in our samples, average earnings are highest for those with higher education (i.e. degrees), and average earnings are lowest for those with only GCSEs A*–C or equivalent. The key question is whether, based on this evidence, the population average earnings are significantly different across the three groups.

To carry out the test via ANOVA, we need to construct our sums of squares:

- The TSS tells us about how much variation there is in earnings overall.
- The WSS tells us about how much variation there is in earnings within the qualification.
- The BSS tells us about how much variation there is in earnings between qualifications.

Table 22.8 Total, within, and between sum of squares for the earnings data by qualification type

	Sum of squares	Degrees of freedom
Total	$TSS = \sum_{i=1}^{200}\sum_{j=1}^{3}(x_{ij} - \bar{x})^2 = 84{,}037{,}919.9$	$n - 1 = 599$
Within	$WSS = \sum_{i=1}^{200}\sum_{j=1}^{3}(x_{ij} - \bar{x}_j)^2 = 75{,}478{,}822.9$	$n - k = 597$
Between	$BSS = \sum_{i=1}^{200}\sum_{j=1}^{3}(\bar{x}_j - \bar{x})^2 = 8{,}559{,}097.01$	$k - 1 = 2$

Here, we have 600 observations, so $n = 600$, split across three groups, so $k = 3$. As such, the degrees of freedom are 599 for the TSS, 597 for the WSS, and 2 for the BSS, as illustrated in Table 22.8.

We can calculate the F-statistic as:

$$F = \frac{BSS / (k-1)}{WSS / (n-k)} = \frac{8{,}559{,}097.01 / 2}{75{,}478{,}822.9 / 597} = 33.85$$

At the 5 per cent significance level, the critical value from $F(2,597) = 3.01$. As the test statistic (33.85) is greater than the critical value (3.01), we can reject the null hypothesis in favour of the alternative. That is, we reject the null hypothesis that average earnings are equivalent across groups with higher education, A-levels, or GCSEs grade A*–C as their highest qualifications.

This is not very surprising, as we would expect gaining higher levels of qualifications either acts to increase an individual's productivity (i.e. education increases human capital), or acts as a signal of higher ability of the individual (see, for example, Spence's model of educational signalling[1]).

22.3 Using Excel to carry out ANOVA

Microsoft Excel can also carry out ANOVA (or analysis of variance) for you. If you have data where the observations are grouped by (say) highest qualification, or the table sat on in class, then the first step is to organize your data.

To make it easy for Excel, you should organize your data so that each column (or each row) represents the observations from one group. So, for example, this could be the first column represents earnings for individuals with higher education, and so on.

Having organized your data, you will need to click on the DATA tab in Excel, and there should be a button in the top right-hand corner called 'Data Analysis'.[2] To carry out an ANOVA test, click 'Anova: Single Factor' (see Figure 22.7).

1 M. Spence (1973), 'Job Market Signaling', *Quarterly Journal of Economics*, 87(3), 355–374.

2 If the data analysis button does not appear, you can activate it by (in Windows) going to the File menu, then clicking on 'Options', then 'Add-ins', and next to 'Manage: Excel Add-ins', click 'Go'. If you select 'Analysis ToolPak' and 'Analysis Toolpak – VBA', a range of additional data analysis tools will be made available for you.

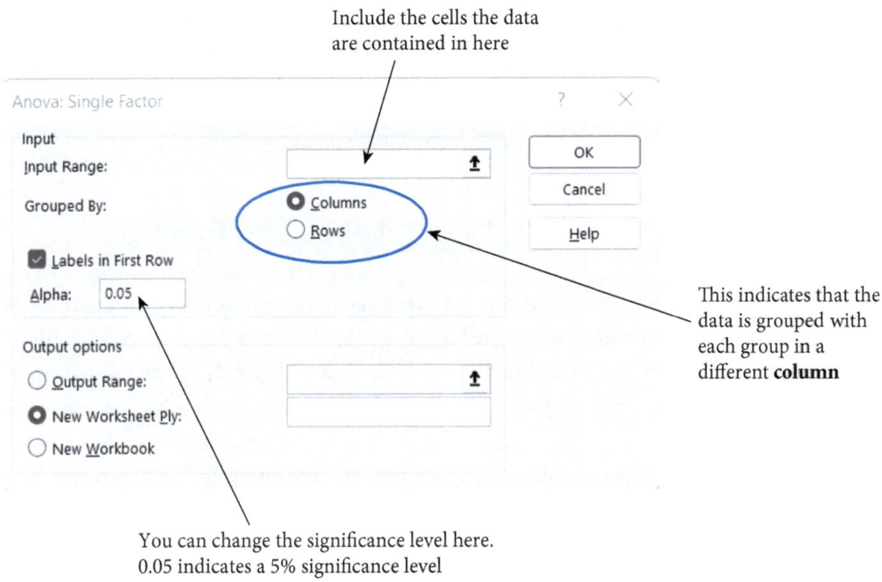

Figure 22.7 Dialog box in Excel for one-way ANOVA.

You will need to tell Excel what cells your data is contained in, but once you have done so, Excel will create a new worksheet containing the results of the ANOVA model.

Figure 22.8 illustrates the output from ANOVA from Microsoft Excel. Here, you can see that Excel does all of the hard work for us, and calculates the average wages in each of the groups, the sum of squares between and within groups, along with the relevant F-statistic

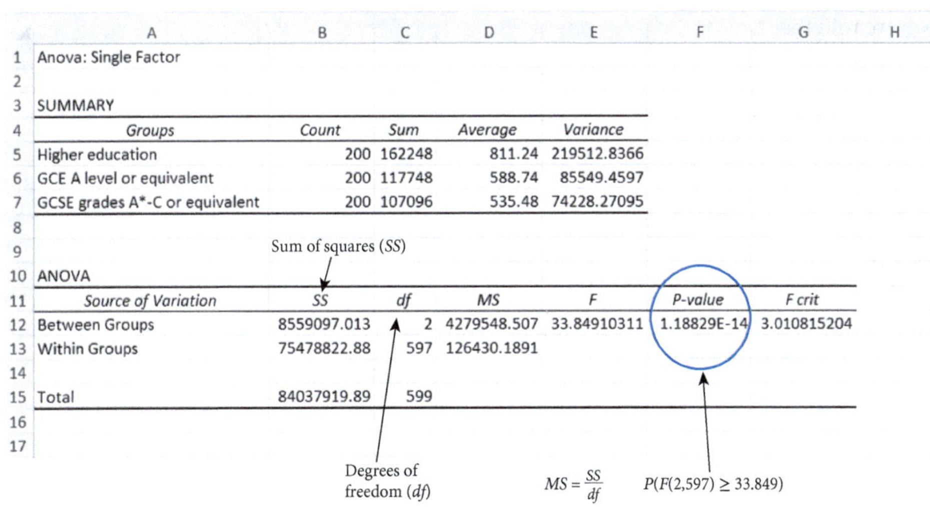

	A	B	C	D	E	F	G	H
1	Anova: Single Factor							
2								
3	SUMMARY							
4	*Groups*	*Count*	*Sum*	*Average*	*Variance*			
5	Higher education	200	162248	811.24	219512.8366			
6	GCE A level or equivalent	200	117748	588.74	85549.4597			
7	GCSE grades A*-C or equivalent	200	107096	535.48	74228.27095			
8								
9								
10	ANOVA							
11	*Source of Variation*	*SS*	*df*	*MS*	*F*	*P-value*	*F crit*	
12	Between Groups	8559097.013	2	4279548.507	33.84910311	1.18829E-14	3.010815204	
13	Within Groups	75478822.88	597	126430.1891				
14								
15	Total	84037919.89	599					
16								
17								

Figure 22.8 ANOVA output from Microsoft Excel.

(33.849). It also tells you the appropriate critical value from the F-distribution (3.01) and calculates the relevant p-value associated with the F-statistic of 33.849. Here, if the null hypothesis is true, the probability of achieving an F-statistic at least as large as the one we observe here is 1.188×10^{-14}.

22.4 Comparing the results of t-tests and F-tests

In Chapter 20, we saw that we could test for equality of means across two groups using a t-test. However, we have also seen (in Chapter 21) that if we square a variable that follows the t-distribution, we will obtain a variable that follows the F-distribution. This suggests that, if we test a single hypothesis using a t-test and using ANOVA, we should get the same result.

To illustrate this, consider the following example. We are going to use the same data as earlier in the chapter, based on the income of individuals, depending on their highest education level, but we will now restrict our analysis to the subgroup of individuals with highest qualifications consisting of A-levels (i.e. qualifications gained at age 18), and those with GCSEs grades A*–C as their highest qualification.

We wish to test only whether the average earnings for those with higher education is equal to the average earnings of those with GCSEs only. For simplicity, let's denote Y_{AL} as earnings of individuals with A-levels, and Y_{GCSE} as earnings of individuals with GCSEs as their highest qualifications:

$$H_0: E(Y_{AL}) = E(Y_{GCSE})$$
$$H_A: E(Y_{AL}) \neq E(Y_{GCSE})$$

22.4.1 Method 1: Using a t-test

We are told that:

$$\begin{aligned} \overline{y}_{AL} &= £588.74, & \overline{y}_{GCSE} &= 535.48 \\ s^2_{AL} &= 85{,}549.46, & s^2_{GCSE} &= 74{,}228.27 \\ n_{AL} &= 200, & n_{GCSE} &= 200 \end{aligned}$$

Remember that the null hypothesis is equivalent to: H_0: $E(Y_{AL}) - E(Y_{GCSE}) = 0$. We have an estimator for this as $\overline{y}_{AL} - \overline{y}_{GCSE} = 588.76 - 535.48 = 53.26$.

Similarly, based on the assumption that the variances are equal across the two groups, we can construct the pooled estimate of the variance as:

$$s^2 = \frac{(n_{AL}-1)s^2_{AL} + (n_{GCSE}-1)s^2_{GCSE}}{n_{AL} + n_{GCSE} - 2} = \frac{(199 \times s^2_{AL}) + (199 \times s^2_{GCSE})}{200 + 200 - 2} = 79{,}888.87$$

The estimated variance of our difference of means is thus:

$$\widehat{var}(\overline{Y}_{AL} - \overline{Y}_{GCSE}) = \frac{s^2}{n_{AL}} + \frac{s^2}{n_{GCSE}} = \frac{79{,}888.87}{200} + \frac{79{,}888.87}{200} = 798.8887$$

As such, we can construct the t-statistic as:

$$t = \frac{(\overline{y}_{AL} - \overline{y}_{GCSE}) - E(\overline{Y}_{AL} - \overline{Y}_{GCSE} \mid H_0 \; is \; true)}{\sqrt{\widehat{var}(\overline{Y}_{AL} - \overline{Y}_{GCSE})}} = \frac{53.27 - 0}{\sqrt{798.8887}} = 1.8843$$

The critical value from the t-distribution with 398 degrees of freedom is equal to 1.966. Since the magnitude of the test statistic is larger than the critical value, we therefore fail to reject our null hypothesis.

22.4.2 Method 2: Using ANOVA

We are also told the between, within, and total sum of squares, based on the data:

	Sum of squares	Degrees of freedom
Total	32,079,431.16	$= n - 1 = 399$
Within	31,795,768.4	$= n - k = 398$
Between	283,662.76	$= k - 1 = 1$

Note that there are two groups here ($k = 2$), and a total of 400 observations. We can construct our F-statistic, as:

$$F = \frac{BSS / df_{Between}}{WSS / df_{Within}} = \frac{283{,}662.76/1}{31{,}795{,}768.4/398} = 3.551$$

The critical value (at the 5 per cent significance level) from the $F(1,398)$ distribution is equal to 3.865. Since the test statistic is smaller than the critical value, we therefore fail to reject the null hypothesis.

Note, however, that using Method 1 we found that $t = 1.8843$. If we were to square this t-statistic, we would get $t^2 = 3.551$—which is exactly the same as the F-statistic obtained using the ANOVA test. As such, we have verified that using both tests yields the same result.

Based on both methods, we have been unable to reject the null hypothesis that earnings of individuals whose highest qualifications consist of GCE A-levels (taken at age 18) and of those whose highest qualifications consist of some grade A*–C (or equivalent) GCSE qualifications (normally taken at age 16) are the same. This suggests that there is little to no premium for students who achieve GCSEs at grades A*–C taking A-levels and then leaving education.

What we can see is that the value from A-levels may actually be in the form of providing access to higher education. We saw a statistically significant difference between average earnings when we included workers who had gained higher education. This may not be a surprise, as A-levels act as a gatekeeper for access to university, and a large number of studies have demonstrated that gaining a degree (particularly in subjects like Economics and Medicine) provides substantial earnings premiums for graduates.[3]

[3] See, for example, J. Britton et al. (2020), *The Impact of Undergraduate Degrees on Lifetime Earnings*. No. R167. IFS Report.

Important note

We can use a t-test to test the equality of means across two groups. For example, we could test the hypothesis that $E(X) = E(Y)$ using a t-test. However, you can only test one hypothesis using a t-test. You couldn't test a hypothesis of the form $E(X) = E(Y) = E(Z)$ as this would be two hypotheses. That is:

$$\begin{aligned} E(X) &= E(Y)\text{ and} \\ E(X) &= E(Z). \end{aligned}$$

If both of these hypotheses were true, it would follow that $E(X) = E(Y) = E(Z)$. If you have more than one hypothesis, then you cannot test this with a t-test, and you need to appeal to a different form of test, such as an F-test.

Similarly, ANOVA makes the (strong) assumption that the variance is the same with all of the groups we are testing across. We made a similar assumption when using the t-test in this chapter (Method 1). We have seen a method that allows us to estimate the equality of means across two groups, allowing the variance to vary across groups.

Summary

In this chapter, we have introduced one-way ANOVA as a way of testing whether population parameters (the expected values) are equal across multiple subgroups or multiple populations. In the data-based example we saw, we examined whether three separate populations (made up of those with highest qualifications consisting of at least some higher education, A-levels, or GCSEs) have the same expected earnings, and rejected this hypothesis.

Whilst we will not explore ANOVA in any more detail within this book, you should be aware that we have only considered a simple one-way ANOVA, where we are looking for variability in expected values across one dimension. In the examples we have considered here, we have looked at the variability across highest qualification gained.

However, there are more complicated versions of ANOVA that allow you to evaluate the impact of multiple explanators on your outcome variable; that is, if you were interested in the impact of, say, the sex of an individual and their highest educational qualification, on earnings, you could use an adaptation known as 'two-way ANOVA'. We will, instead, consider (in subsequent chapters) how we can achieve the same result using linear regression models.

In the next chapter, we introduce a new estimator, called the ordinary least squares estimator. We will use this estimator to estimate economic relationships between continuous random variables.

Key formulae

In general, suppose that we have n individuals, grouped into k groups, and we wish to test whether the (population) average is equal across all k groups of size m:

$$H_0: E(Y_1) = E(Y_2) = E(Y_3) = \ldots = E(Y_k)$$

We can construct our relevant F-statistic using the following formulae, where j represents each of the k groups, $\overline{Y}$ represents the sample mean of all n observations, and $\overline{Y}_j$ represents the sample mean of scores for individuals in group j:

	Formulae	Degrees of freedom
Total sum of squares	$TSS = \sum_{i=1}^{m}\sum_{j=1}^{k}(Y_{ij} - \overline{Y})^2$	$n - 1$
Within sum of squares	$WSS = \sum_{i=1}^{m}\sum_{j=1}^{k}(Y_{ij} - \overline{Y}_j)^2$	$n - k$
Between sum of squares	$BSS = \sum_{i=1}^{m}\sum_{j=1}^{k}(\overline{Y}_j - \overline{Y})^2$	$k - 1$

The F-statistic can be calculated as:

$$F = \frac{BSS \;/\; (k-1)}{WSS \;/\; (n-k)}$$

23 Introduction to Ordinary Least Squares

Learning outcomes for this chapter

By the end of this chapter you will be able to:

- Explain that the OLS estimator is a way of estimating a straight-line relationship between two economic variables
- Construct the OLS estimator with the intercept constrained to be zero
- Construct the OLS estimator, allowing the fitted line to pass through an intercept other than the origin, and estimate OLS using Microsoft Excel, and be able to interpret the estimated coefficients

Mathematical tools

- Summations
- Algebra
- Partial differentiation

Introduction

Economists are interested in estimating **causal relationships** between economic (and non-economic) variables. For instance, the Bank of England might be interested in estimating the causal impact of increasing interest rates on the inflation rate. That is, keeping everything else constant, what would be the impact of increasing interest rates?

In this chapter, we will introduce an **estimator** that can sometimes be used to estimate causal relationships between economic variables, known as the **ordinary least squares (OLS)** estimator. However, as we will see in future chapters, this estimator will only provide causal estimates under very strong assumptions, and when those assumptions are not met, the estimator merely provides further estimates of correlations between economic variables.

Remember that, just because you see a correlation between economic variables does not mean that one variable causes the other.

Revision: Equations of a straight line

In this chapter, we will introduce the ordinary least squares estimator, which fits a (straight) line of best fit through data.

In mathematics, you will have been introduced to the equation of a straight line (see Figure 23.1), possibly in the form:

$$y = mx + c$$

In this notation:

- c is the intercept of the line, and
- m is the gradient of the line.

In economics terms, we can think of m as the marginal effect of a change in x on y. In this straight line graph, as x increases by Δx, we can see that y also increases by Δy. The gradient is the ratio of the change in y (Δy) to the change in (Δx). The interpretation of this is that if x increased by 1, then y would increase by m.

Because this is a straight line graph, $\frac{\Delta y}{\Delta x}$ is just the same as the **derivative** of y with relation to x.

$$\frac{dy}{dx} = m$$

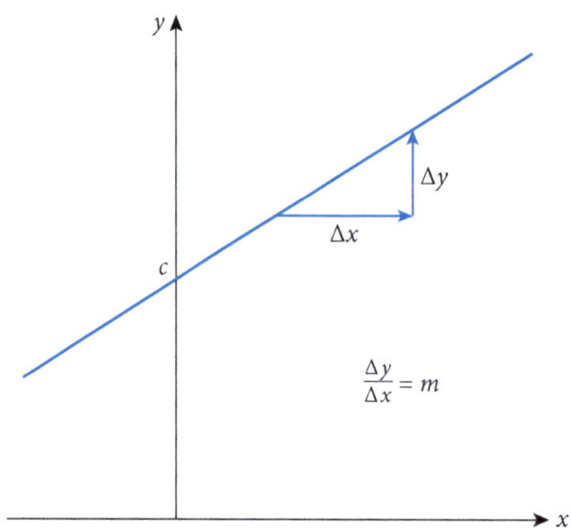

Figure 23.1 A standard straight line graph of the form $y = mx + c$.

23.1 What is the OLS estimator?

Fundamentally, the basis of the ordinary least squares (OLS) estimator is about trying to choose a (straight) line of best fit through some data.

In high school science, you may have plotted points on a graph, and then used your eye to choose the most appropriate line to pass through the data. Alternatively, you might have plotted the points in a software package, such as Excel, and asked it to plot the line of best fit for you.

If there is a simple, deterministic relationship between an outcome and an input variable, then we can draw a straight line that passes through all of the points. Suppose we have a relationship between an outcome variable Y and an input variable X, such that:

$$Y_i = 2 + 3X_i$$

That would mean that every observation of Y is equal to 3 times the value of X and then we add 2. So, if X were 1, then Y would be equal to 5, whilst if X were 3, Y would be equal to 11. This relationship is illustrated in Figure 23.2. As all of the observations lie on an upward sloping straight line, we can immediately say that the correlation between X and Y is equal to 1.

Note, however, just because you can plot all of the points on a straight line, this does not mean that we can conclude that there is a direct causal relationship between X and Y. We cannot say that a change in X causes an increase in Y. There are lots of reasons why you might see these sorts of relationship:

1. It may be the case that a change in Y causes the change in X.
2. There might be some other variable that determines both X and Y. For example, suppose that X is the number of pairs of wellington boots sold, and Y is the number of raincoats sold. Then it is not the case that the number of wellington boots sold affects the number of raincoats, but instead that if the weather is rainy, this causes both the sales of wellington boots and raincoats to increase.

The example in Figure 23.2 represents what we might expect to see in a perfect science experiment. However, economic data is rarely this tidy. In reality, even when there is a causal relationship between X and Y, there will be other factors that determine the outcome variable. Similarly, there may be random shocks leading to observations lying somewhat away from the straight line.

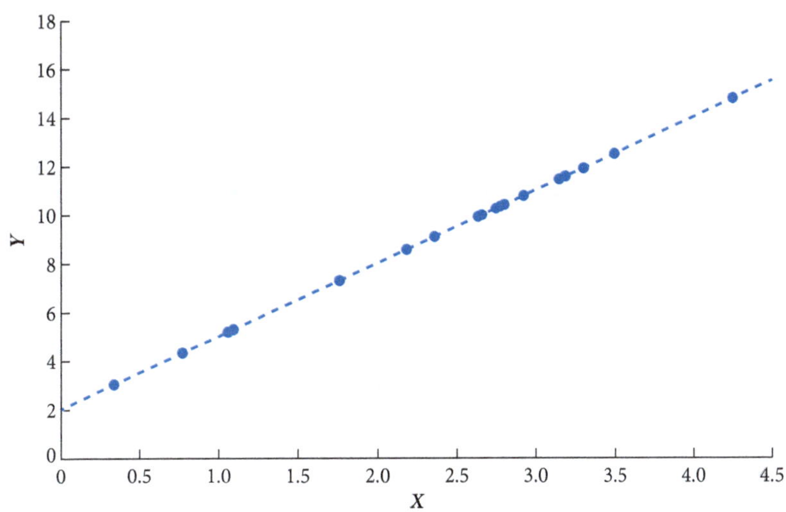

Figure 23.2 Example where all observations lie on a straight line.

To illustrate this, let's consider an example, using data from the OECD. We have plotted data of life expectancy at birth on the vertical axis, against per capita spending on healthcare on the horizontal axis.[1] Remember that per capita means that this is total spending on healthcare, divided by the size of the population. This is illustrated in Figure 23.3.

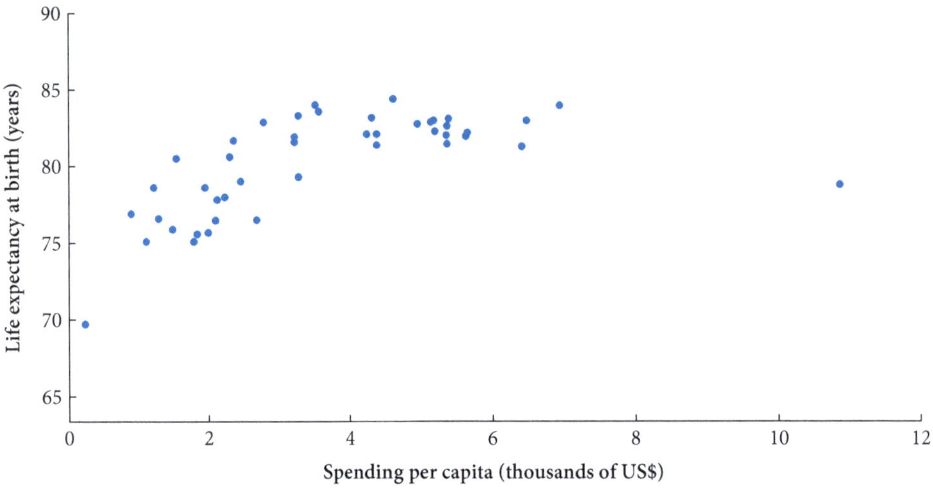

Figure 23.3 Life expectancy at birth plotted against spending per capita on healthcare (2019 data, from the OECD).

This data does not follow a clean, deterministic relationship between spending on healthcare and life expectancy, but we can see that, on average, as spending increases, life expectancy also seems to increase. When dealing with real economic data, we might assume that the observations of Y are generated using a data generating process, such as:

$$Y_i = \beta_0 + \beta_1 X_i + u_i$$

u_i can be thought of as all of the other factors that determine Y, and $\beta_0 + \beta_1 X_i$ can be thought of as the linear relationship between X and Y.

KEY DEFINITION: EXPLANATORY AND DEPENDENT VARIABLES

In econometrics, you will often hear economists discussing **explanatory variables** and **dependent variables**. Suppose that we are interested in estimating the relationship:

$$Y_i = \beta_0 + \beta_1 X_i + u_i$$

[1] This figure is an updated version of a figure from OECD (2015), *Health at a Glance 2015: OECD Indicators*, OECD Publishing, p. 47, https://doi.org/10.1787/health_glance-2015-en. The author has updated this figure using updated data from 2019. The data on health spending is freely available from https://data.oecd.org/healthres/health-spending.htm, whilst the life expectancy data is available from https://data.oecd.org/healthstat/life-expectancy-at-birth.htm. Data used to create this figure is available from Data sets and Exercises at the end of this chapter.

Then the Y_i variable is the dependent variable, and X_i is the explanatory variable. Intuitively, what we are saying here is that a change in the explanatory variable explains changes in the dependent variable. That is, changes in the Y_i variable are dependent on changes in the X_i variable.

In the example in Figure 23.3, we have treated:

- life expectancy as the dependent variable, and
- per capita spending on healthcare as the explanatory variable.

This makes sense because we might think that increases in spending will lead to higher life expectancy. However, even though we can see that there is a correlation between the two variables, we cannot conclude that there is a causal relationship.

To illustrate this, let's consider that there is a true relationship between a dependent variable, Y, and an explanatory variable, X, given by:

$$Y_i = 2 + 3X_i + u_i$$

A scatter plot of what the data might look like is illustrated in Figure 23.4. As you can see, if there are other inputs that determine our dependent variable, other than X, but there is a causal relationship between Y and X of the form $Y = 2 + 3X$, then we represent the other factors that determine Y as u_i. This is equivalent to the vertical distance between the observed value of Y and the true line.

The u_i is sometimes known as the error term. For each of the observations, the u_i is the vertical distance between the observed value of Y_i and the true line.

If the u_i is negative, then the observed value of Y will be below the line, and if the u_i is positive, then the observed value of Y will be above the line.

In reality, we will rarely know the true relationship between economic variables, and so we will need to estimate it, based on observing pairs of observations of the dependent and

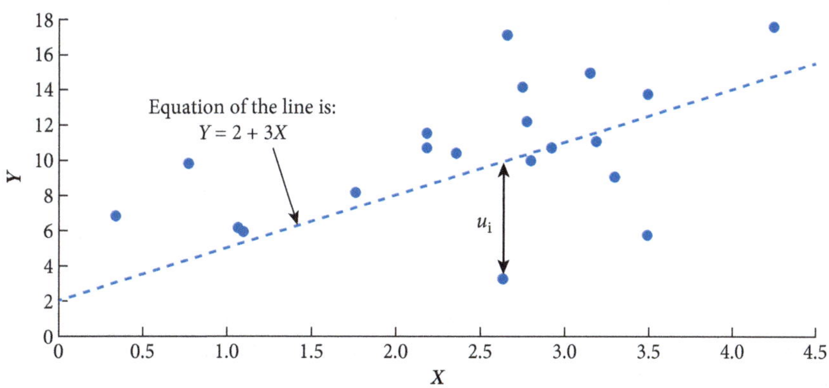

Figure 23.4 Scatter plot illustrating data generated with errors included.

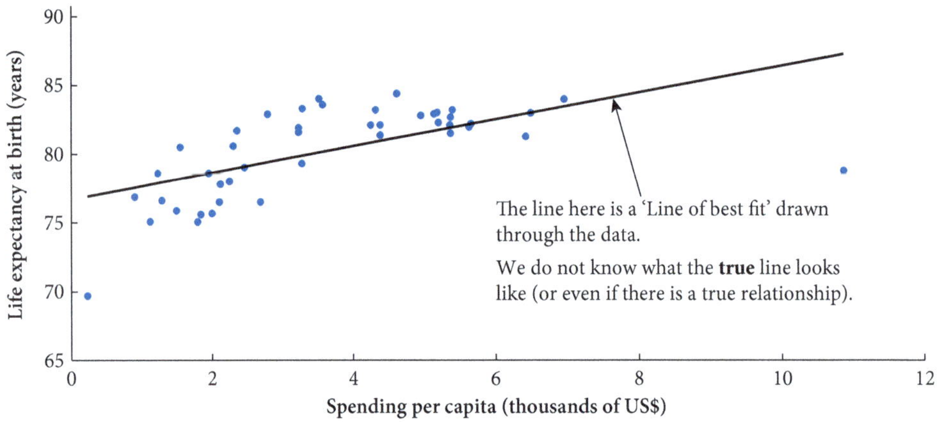

Figure 23.5 Scatter plot of life expectancy at birth against spending per capita on healthcare in 2019 with a line of best fit plot (data from the OECD).

explanatory variables. At its simplest, we can try to estimate the relationship between the two economic variables by drawing a line of best fit through the data.

To illustrate this, let's return to the OECD data on healthcare spending and life expectancy. Looking back at Figure 23.3, we can see that we do not observe any true line. All that we are able to see is pairs of observations of life expectancy and spending on healthcare for each country. However, we can use this data to try to estimate an underlying relationship between the two economic variables by estimating a line of best fit through that data.

A potential line of best fit is illustrated in Figure 23.5. Whilst it is possible to look at data, and draw a good straight line through data, it is unlikely that everyone will choose the same line to draw through a single plot of data, and so we need to formalize a method of drawing a line of best fit through our data using an estimator.

There are lots of estimators that could be used to choose our line of best fit, but the estimator that we will explore in this book is known as the ordinary least squares (OLS) estimator.

Using Excel to draw a line of best fit

Using the OECD data on healthcare spending and life expectancy, you can create a scatter plot and a line of best fit.

Step 1

Select the data representing 'Spending per capita (thousands of US$)' and 'Life expectancy at birth (years)'. Click 'Insert', and select 'Recommended Charts'. You can choose the formatting, but Excel will usually default to a scatter plot.

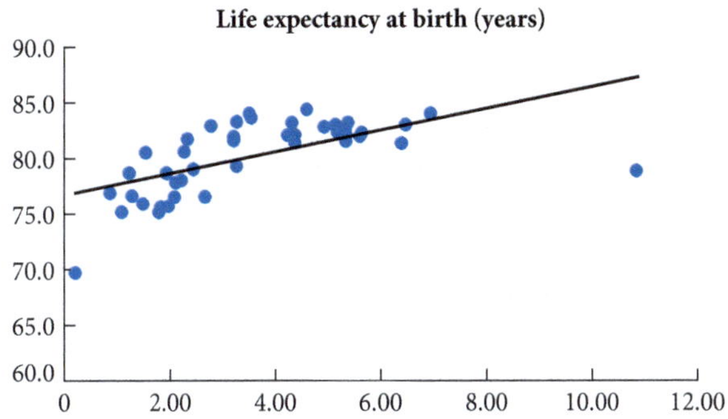

Step 2

Having produced the scatter plot, Excel can plot a line of best fit through the data.

Right-click on one of the points, and select 'Add Trendline'. This will insert a line of best fit, using the OLS estimator.

There is a range of options for the trendline: if you right-click on the trendline, and select 'Format Trendline', you can choose to display the equation of the line of best fit. In this example, the intercept of the line of best fit would be 76.685, with a slope of 0.9723.

The method that Excel uses to choose a line of best fit is the same method as we are going to examine in this chapter (i.e. OLS) and this methodology is simply creating a formal way of choosing a line of best fit. It should be noted that this is not the only way of choosing a line of best fit, and under certain circumstances is not the best way of choosing a line of best fit, but it is a good place to start.

DEFINITION: CAUSAL (NOT CASUAL) RELATIONSHIPS

Economists are interested in estimating causal relationships between economic variables. For instance, if we use the example of healthcare spending and life expectancy, the causal relationship would be the impact of an increase in healthcare spending on life expectancy keeping everything else fixed.

In reality, when we observe increases in spending on healthcare, there may be other factors that change at the same time; for example, the increase in spending may be due to the outbreak of a virus, such as COVID-19, which is also having an impact on life expectancy.

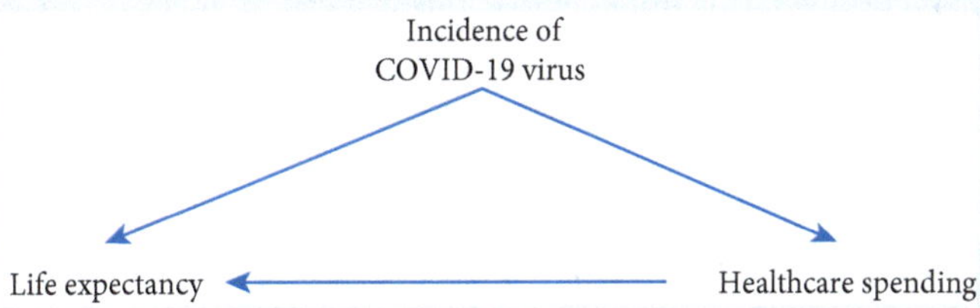

In this example, what we would be interested in is whether there is a direct effect of healthcare spending on life expectancy, but if we simply looked at the correlation between the two, because healthcare spending was increased by COVID-19, and life expectancy was reduced by COVID-19, it might look as if increasing healthcare spending actually reduced life expectancy.

In general, when you use OLS, the relationship that you estimate is merely a measure of correlation between the two economic variables, and not, necessarily, a causal relationship. However, there are two conditions where OLS will yield causal estimates of a change in an explanatory variable (X) on a dependent variable (Y):

1. In an experiment, where values of X are randomly assigned to individuals.
2. When the explanatory variable X is not experimentally assigned, but is unrelated to all of the other determinants of the dependent variable (Y).

In both of these examples, the key thing is that the value of X is unrelated to any of the other determinants of Y.

We will see, mathematically, why this holds in future chapters.

Returning to the healthcare data, when we fitted a line of best fit, using OLS, we implicitly began with the assumption that there was some true line that passed through the data, of the form:

$$life\ expectancy_i = \beta_0 + \beta_1 \times spending_i$$

β_0 is the intercept of the true line passing through the data, and β_1 is the slope of the true line passing through the data.

When we estimated this line of best fit using OLS, we obtained the following estimates:

$$\hat{\beta}_0 = 76.685$$
$$\hat{\beta}_1 = 0.9723$$

(Remember, the hats over the βs indicate that these are estimates of some population parameter.) Note that spending per capita is measured in thousands of US$. So, increasing the spending variable by 1 is equivalent to increasing spending by $1,000.

As such, we can think about the impact of increasing spending by $1,000 per capita as being related to an increase in life expectancy of 0.9723 years.

However, as mentioned, it is unlikely that this is a causal effect, as life expectancy and spending on healthcare are likely to be affected by a range of other factors, including the overall wealth of a country (richer countries may have higher life expectancy due to, for example, more consistent access to good sources of nutrition, and richer countries may choose to spend more on healthcare). The increase in life expectancy related to higher spending on healthcare would represent not just the impact of higher spending, but also the impact of the country being wealthier.

23.2 **Deriving OLS: Part 1—Assuming the line of best fit passes through the origin**

The line of best fit that we saw earlier in this chapter was generated using the OLS estimator, and this is a good starting point for understanding econometrics more generally.

Essentially, when we use OLS to try to estimate causal relationships, we begin with an assumption about the underlying relationship between two economic variables. As we have chosen to fit a straight line through the data, we have implicitly assumed that there is a linear relationship between the two economic variables. In the example in Section 23.1, we assumed that there was a **linear relationship** between life expectancy and spending on healthcare.

Important note

We can always draw a line of best fit through a scatter plot of data.

Just because we can estimate a line of best fit does not mean that there is any causal relationship between economic variables. As you study econometrics further, you will develop a stronger understanding of how we might estimate causal relationships.

The OLS estimator that we develop in this chapter provides an estimator for a line of best fit through the data. We will see, in future chapters, that if some very strong assumptions are true, then the OLS estimator can provide unbiased estimates of the causal relationship between two economic variables.

To derive the OLS estimator, let's begin with a simple example. Suppose that I am planning on driving 300 miles, and I want to estimate how much fuel I will need to complete the journey. To estimate this relationship, I would need to have data from previous journeys about how much fuel I used, and how far the journey was. The potential data of the population of journeys in my car is illustrated in Figure 23.6, with miles driven on the horizontal axis, and fuel used on the vertical axis.

We might begin with the belief that there is a linear relationship between fuel used, which for simplicity we will denote as $Fuel_i$, and distance driven, which we will denote as $Distance_i$. We might model this linear relationship as:

$$Fuel_i = \beta Distance_i$$

β here is the marginal effect of driving an extra mile on the amount of fuel that we use—that is, $\beta = \frac{dFuel}{dDistance}$. If distance increases by 1 mile, then fuel consumption would increase by β litres.

Note that we have explicitly made an assumption before we have even started estimating our relationship; that is, the (true) line passes through the origin. Intuitively, in this example, this means that if you drive zero miles you will use zero litres of fuel. This makes sense as unless you are either running the engine for a significant period when not travelling, or you have a petrol leak, then you wouldn't expect to see a reduction in your petrol when not travelling!

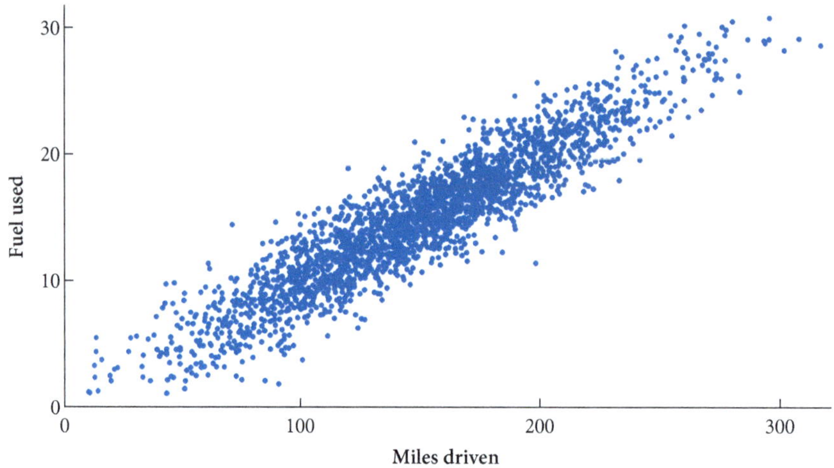

Figure 23.6 Scatter plot of fuel used across the population of journeys in my car.

When would we choose a model with a zero intercept?

In our example of using fuel, we have assumed that the appropriate underlying model would have a line that passes through the intercept (i.e. it crosses the vertical axis at $Y = 0$). In this example, it makes sense to do this, because when you drive 0 miles, you would expect to use zero fuel. As such, it seems appropriate to constrain the model so that the line passes through the origin, as shown in panel a) of Figure 23.7

In many examples, this would not make sense. Think back to our healthcare example. Suppose that a country spent nothing on healthcare. We wouldn't expect the life expectancy to drop to zero.

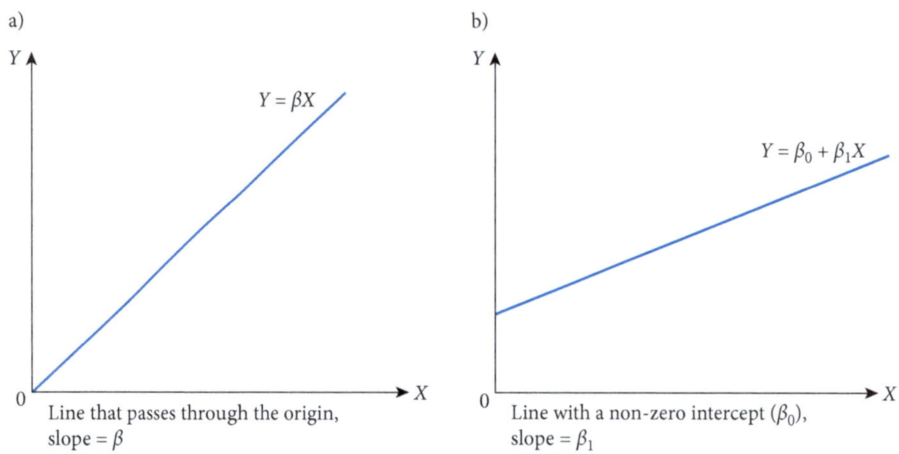

Figure 23.7 Comparing a line that passes through the origin with one that is allowed to have a non-zero intercept.

As such, in the example of life expectancy and healthcare spending, we would need to allow the model to have a non-zero intercept, as in panel b) of Figure 23.7. We will see, later in this chapter, how we can use data to estimate relationships with a non-zero intercept.

Of course, the relationship $Fuel_i = \beta Distance_i$ does not perfectly fit the data. We can see from Figure 23.6 that the data does not line up neatly in a straight line.

This is because it is extremely unlikely that the data generating process for our dependent variable (i.e. fuel used) is only determined by the single explanator (distance driven). Instead there are likely to be other factors, which we will represent as a simple error term, u_i, which also determine the amount fuel used.

We can write down an equation to represent the data generating process—that is, how miles driven contributes towards the amount of fuel used:

$$Fuel_i = \beta Distance_i + u_i$$

where $Fuel_i$ is the fuel used in journey i, $Miles_i$ is the number of miles driven, and u_i represents everything else that determines the amount of fuel used. For example, if you drive at a consistent speed (without much acceleration or braking), then you will likely use less fuel than driving in stop and start traffic. As such, if the journey is via motorways, you are likely to use less fuel than driving a similar distance in city-centre traffic, or even on country roads. Similarly, if you are driving into a headwind, you will end up using more fuel than if you have a tailwind behind you.

As we have seen above, it is unlikely that the amount of fuel used will be a simple linear function of the number of miles driven. Instead, there are likely to be other factors (represented by u_i here) which also determine the amount of fuel used.

Remember: We normally only see a sample from the population

In the scatter plot illustrated in Figure 23.6, we saw the population of car journeys. If we were to use this data, provided our assumptions about the shape of the relationship were true, we could construct the true marginal effect of distance driven on fuel used (i.e. β).

However, in reality, we rarely observe populations. We will normally only observe samples from the population, and so we will need to take into account **sampling variation**, which delivers variability in the estimates that we gain.

Suppose that we randomly sample ten journeys, and from each we have measured the distance driven and the amount of fuel used (Figure 23.8). We can use an estimator to construct an estimate of β. However, if we were to repeat this process, with a different random sample of ten journeys, we would have journeys of different length and different amounts of fuel used, and we would inevitably gain a different estimate of β. Because of sampling variation, every time we take a different sample, we gain a separate estimate, and so, we will also need to find a way of representing the variability of the estimator, which we will denote as the **standard error** of the estimator.

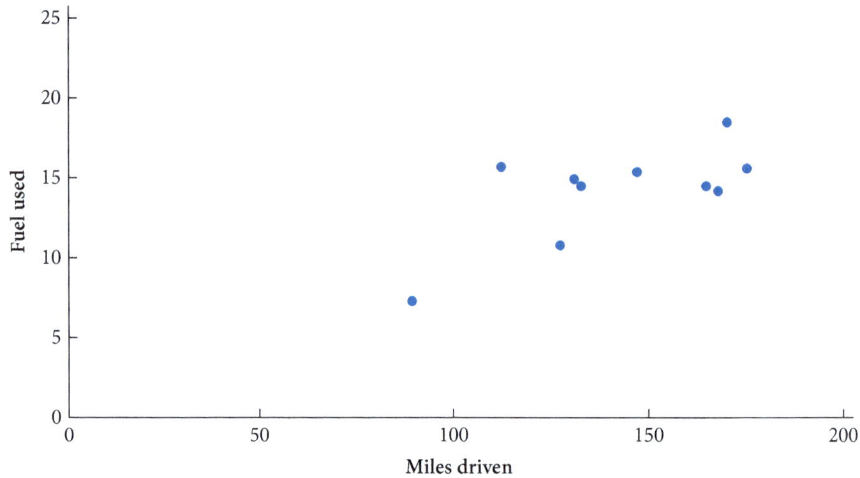

Figure 23.8 Random sample of ten journeys from the population.

23.2.1 How do we decide what is our line of best fit?

Suppose that we have randomly sampled ten observations from the population. Then if we are trying to estimate β in the relationship:

$$Fuel_i = \beta Distance_i + u_i$$

there are an infinite number of possible values that β could take. Four possible lines of best fit, through a sample of ten (pairs of) observations, are illustrated in Figure 23.9.

- Line 1 passes above all of the observations.
- Line 4 passes below all of the observations.
- Lines 2 and 3 pass through the data.

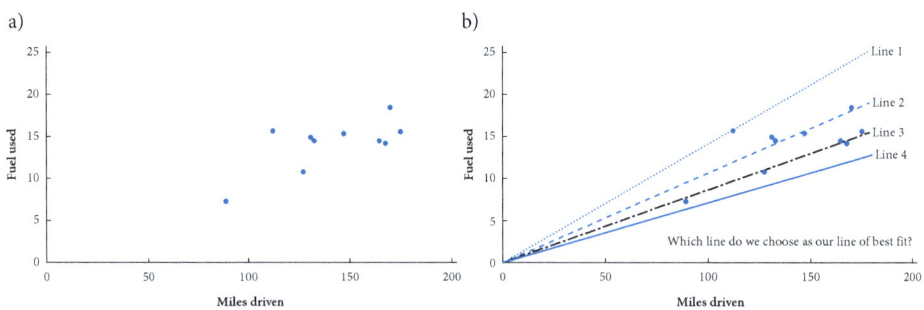

Figure 23.9 Possible lines of best fit through a sample of data.

However, we need a way to choose what line represents the best fit. We are going to start with a (hopefully) uncontroversial requirement that we want the line of best fit to pass through the data; this will eliminate lines 1 and 4. In fact, we are going to go further, and require that the line passes through the middle of the data.

When choosing our line of best fit, we are going to choose the line that is, in some sense, closest to the data that we observe. The OLS estimator chooses the line that minimizes the sum of squares of the vertical distances between the observed values of the dependent variable (litres of fuel used) and the predicted value, given by the **fitted line**.

To illustrate this, let's simplify our notation slightly, by defining our dependent variable as Y_i and our explanatory variable as X_i, and so the relationship that we are interested in is given by:

$$Y_i = \beta X_i + u_i$$

We are going to choose a line of best fit, with an equation $\hat{Y} = \hat{\beta} X$, where $\hat{\beta}$ is our estimate of β. When we construct the OLS estimator, we are going to minimize the sum of squares of the vertical distances between the observed values of Y and the predicted values of Y (which we will denote $\hat{Y}$), based on our line of best fit.

Vertical distances between the observed value of Y_i and the predicted value $\hat{Y}_i$

To choose our line of best fit, we try to choose the line which is closest to the data. However, there are many ways that we can define what it means for a line to be close to the data. For the sake of deriving the OLS estimator, we will define a line to be close to the data, based upon the vertical distances between the observed values of y_i and the predicted value based on the fitted line. This is illustrated in Figure 23.10.

Suppose that we observe a point, where $X = 10$. The chosen fitted line would predict that $\hat{y}_i = \hat{\beta} \times 10$. However, the true observed value when $X = 10$ is equal to y_i. As such, the vertical distance (denoted as $\hat{u}_i$) between the observed value y_i and the predicted value $\hat{y}_i$ is given as:

$$\hat{u}_i = y_i - \hat{y}_i$$

This $\hat{u}_i$ is also known as the **fitted residual**.

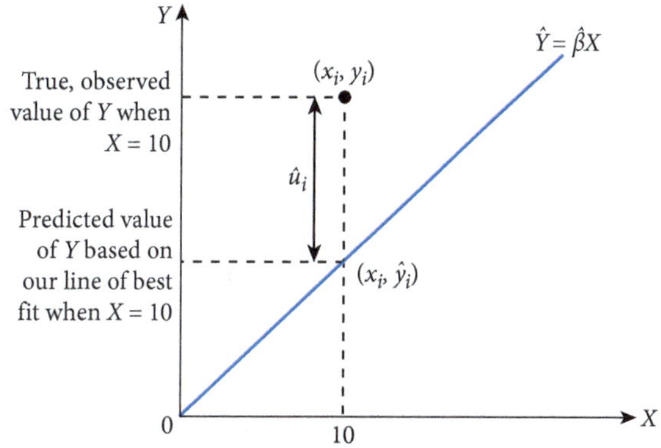

Figure 23.10 Finding the vertical distance between the observed outcome and the fitted line.

Note that we are using lower case y_i and $\hat{y}_i$ here to indicate that these are specific realizations of observations. If we are representing the overall random variable, we use capital letters, and for individual realizations, we use the lower case. In general, we will treat the individual observations as random variables, denoted by capital letters, Y_i and $\hat{Y}_i$.

Choosing the line of best fit using the fitted residuals

To illustrate what we are doing, consider the example in Figure 23.11. We have observed three observations of X and Y, with coordinates (x_1, y_1), (x_2, y_2), and (x_3, y_3), and we try to fit a line of best fit through the data. We have suggested two possible lines of best fit: the first with slope equal to $\hat{\alpha}$, and the second with a slope equal to $\hat{\beta}$, with $\hat{\alpha}$ greater than $\hat{\beta}$.

As you can see, as we change the slope of the line of best fit through the data, what happens is the size of the $\hat{u}_i$ changes. Moving from panel a) to panel b), the u_1 gets larger, whilst $\hat{u}_2$ and $\hat{u}_3$ get smaller. We want to choose a line that makes the average magnitude of these $\hat{u}_i$ as small as possible.

To choose a line that minimizes the magnitude of the deviations of the observations away from the line, we need all of the deviations to be positive, and as such, we will use a trick that we've already used several times in this book; that is, we will square each of those deviations. When we construct the OLS estimator, we will be choosing a line of best fit by choosing a value of $\hat{\beta}$ which minimizes the sum of squares of the fitted residuals (SSR).

That is, based on all of our observations, we choose the line which minimizes:[2]

$$SSR = \sum_{i=1}^{n} \hat{u}_i^2 = \sum_{i=1}^{n} (Y_i - \hat{Y}_i)^2$$

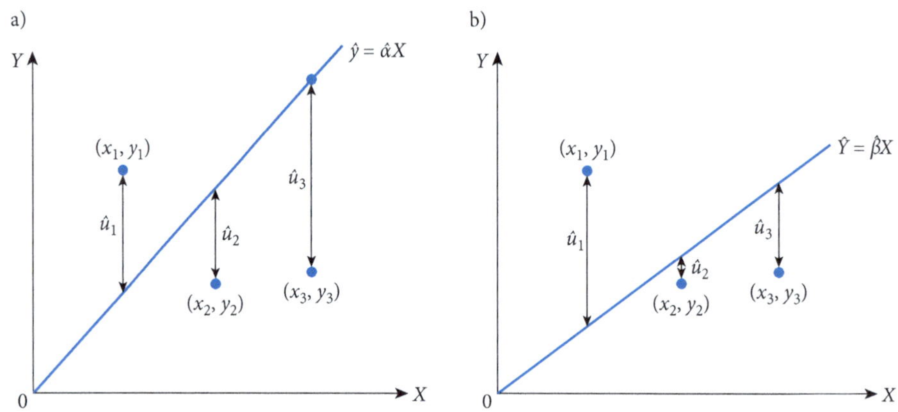

Figure 23.11 Two possible lines of best fit, based on three observations of X_i and Y_i.

[2] From now on, we are going to treat each observation as a random variable, to take account of the fact that if we were to repeatedly sample from the population, we would get variation in the pairs of observations of X_i and Y_i. For example, in one sample, you could observe $X_1 = 5$, whilst in another sample, you could observe $X_1 = 17$. This may seem a little confusing, but it will allow us to analyse the estimator more carefully in later chapters. Note that in constructing the SSR, we are treating Y_i, $\hat{Y}_i$, X_i and $\hat{u}_i$ as random variables here.

Table 23.1 Four pairs of observations of X_i and Y_i

Observation, i	$i = 1$	$i = 2$	$i = 3$	$i = 4$
X_i	1	2	3	4
Y_i	2	3	1	2

Worked example 23.1: Calculating the sum of squares of residuals

Suppose that we are interested in estimating a relationship between Y and X. Each observation that we take consists of an observation of an outcome of Y and a corresponding observation of X. We have observed four observations of X and Y, as represented in Table 23.1. For clarity,[3] the first observation, $i = 1$, corresponds to values of X and Y as $X_1 = 1$ and $Y_1 = 2$. Coincidentally, the four observations of X_i are 1, 2, 3, and 4.

In this simple example, we wish to choose a line of best fit through the data, making the assumption that the line passes through the origin. That is, we are imposing, in our relationship, that when $X = 0$, the underlying value of Y will also be equal to 1. This means that our line of best fit is defined as:

$$\hat{Y}_i = \hat{\beta} X_i$$

We have not yet constructed an optimal estimator, but two researchers have suggested candidates for the possible best 'slope' parameter as:

$$\hat{\beta} = 1$$

$$\hat{\beta} = 0.5$$

Based on three proposed slopes, this would yield two possible lines of best fit, as illustrated in Figure 23.12.

1. $\hat{Y}_i = 1 \times X_i$
2. $\hat{Y}_i = 0.5 \times X_i$

Ultimately, we consider a line of best fit to be better if the sum of squares of the fitted residuals is smaller. That is, a line of best fit is better, if it can be deemed to be 'closer', on average, to the observed data. Here we have two possible lines of best fit, and we would wish to choose the line with the smaller sum of squares of the residuals. To examine this, let's consider the two possible candidates in turn.

Candidate 1: $\hat{\beta} = 1$

We can construct the fitted residuals by comparing the true observed values of Y with the predicted values of $\hat{Y}$ based on the chosen line of best fit, where $\hat{\beta} = 1$.

[3] Note that we have added the observation number here, to make it easier to think about X_i in terms of X_1, X_2, X_3, X_4. Normally, when you see data, you will just see pairs of observations together, without a corresponding i. For example, the data set OECD Healthcare and Life Expectancy 2019.xlsx (available to download from Data sets and Exercises at the end of this chapter) does not explicitly include an i term.

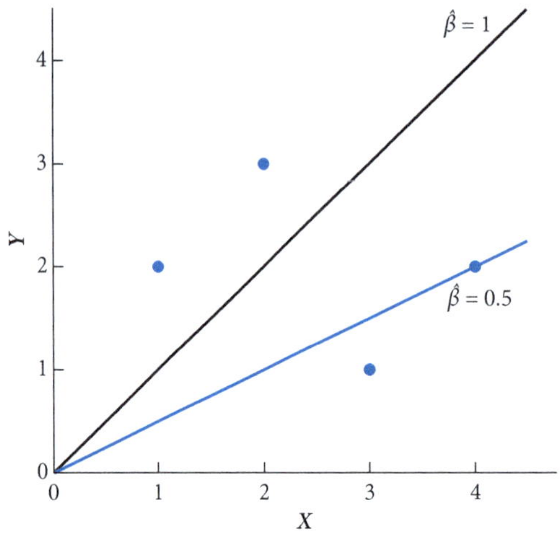

Figure 23.12 Two possible lines of best fit through our data.

The fitted residuals are just the difference between the observed value of Y, and the predicted value of $\hat{Y}$, based on our fitted line.

So, for instance, for $i = 1$, we know that:

- the observed value of $Y_1 = 2$
- the observed value of $X_1 = 1$

If $\hat{\beta} = 1$, then this means that the predicted value of $\hat{Y}_1 = \hat{\beta} \times X_1 = 1 \times 1 = 1$.

Thus, the fitted residual, as shown in Figure 23.13 (which is calculated as $\hat{u}_i = Y_i - \hat{Y}_i$) for $i = 1$ is just equal to:

$$\hat{u}_1 = Y_1 - \hat{Y}_1 = 2 - 1 = 1$$

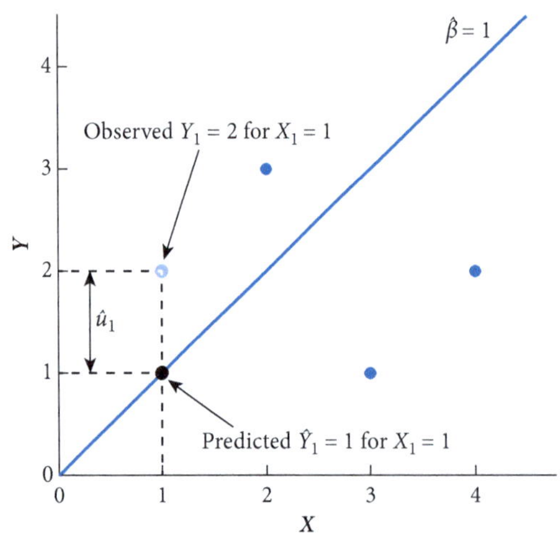

Figure 23.13 Calculating the fitted residual for $X_1 = 1$.

Table 23.2 Calculating the fitted residuals, $\hat{u}_i$ for $\hat{\beta} = 1$

Observation, i	$i = 1$	$i = 2$	$i = 3$	$i = 4$
X_i	1	2	3	4
Y_i	2	3	1	2
Fitted values				
$\hat{Y}_i = \hat{\beta} \times X_i$	1	2	3	4
$\hat{u}_i = Y_i - \hat{Y}_i$	1	1	-2	-2

We can repeat this for all four observations (see Table 23.2).

The four values for our fitted residuals are $\hat{u}_i = 1, 1, -2, -2$. As such, we can construct the sum of squares of the residuals (SSR).

$$SSR = \sum_{i=1}^{4} \hat{u}_i^2 = \hat{u}_1^2 + \hat{u}_2^2 + \hat{u}_3^2 + \hat{u}_4^2 = 1^2 + 1^2 + (-2)^2 + (-2)^2 = 10$$

Candidate 2: $\hat{\beta} = 0.5$

We can repeat this process for our second candidate, where $\hat{\beta} = 0.5$ (see Table 23.3).

Here we can calculate the sum of squares of the residuals as:

$$SSR = \sum_{i=1}^{4} \hat{u}_i^2 = 1.5^2 + 2^2 + (-0.5)^2 + 0^2 = 6.5$$

As such, we can see that the second candidate is a better fit than the first line, because the SSR is smaller (6.5 compared with 10).

However, we don't know whether this is the smallest possible value for the SSR. To construct our line of best fit, we will construct an estimator that minimizes this SSR.

Table 23.3 Calculating the fitted residuals, $\hat{u}_i$ for $\hat{\beta} = 0.5$

Observation, i	$i = 1$	$i = 2$	$i = 3$	$i = 4$
X_i	1	2	3	4
Y_i	2	3	1	2
Fitted values				
$\hat{Y}_i = \hat{\beta} \times X_i$	0.5	1	1.5	2
$\hat{u}_i = Y_i - \hat{Y}_i$	1.5	2	-0.5	0

23.2.2 Minimizing the sum of squares of the residuals

We wish to construct the estimator that minimizes the sum of squares of the fitted residuals—that is, the estimator that minimizes the sum of squares of the vertical distances between the observed value of Y_i and the predicted value of $\hat{Y}_i$, based on our fitted line of best fit.

Because we have assumed that the data generating process for Y_i is given by:

$$Y_i = \beta X_i + u_i$$

we are going to try to fit a line of best fit, with equation:

$$\hat{Y}_i = \hat{\beta} X_i$$

We know that the fitted residual is given by $\hat{u}_i = Y_i - \hat{Y}_i$ and, if we substitute in the equation of our fitted line, in place of $\hat{Y}_i$ gives us that:

$$\hat{u}_i = Y_i - \hat{\beta} X_i$$

As such, if we have n pairs of observations of X_i and Y_i, the SSR is equal to:

$$SSR = \sum_{i=1}^{n} \hat{u}_i^2 = \sum_{i=1}^{n} (Y_i - \hat{\beta} X_i)^2$$

If we wish to minimize the sum of squares of these fitted residuals (i.e. minimize the SSR), then we can differentiate this expression, and set the derivative equal to zero.

Since the way we are minimizing the SSR is by choosing the line that is closest to the data, we will therefore differentiate the SSR with respect to the parameters of the line that we are choosing. In this case, the equation of the line that we are fitting is:

$$\hat{Y}_i = \hat{\beta} X_i$$

Example: Differentiating a simple summation

Before we find the derivative in the general case, where we have n observations, let's begin with a simple example where we only have two observations. This will help us to understand the process of differentiating the SSR. With two observations, we can write the SSR as:

$$\sum_{i=1}^{2} \hat{u}_i^2 = \sum_{i=1}^{2} (Y_i - \hat{\beta} X_i)^2$$

Now, we can write this summation out, in terms of each observation, just by substituting $i = 1$ and $i = 2$:

$$\sum_{i=1}^{2} (Y_i - \hat{\beta} X_i)^2 = (Y_1 - \hat{\beta} X_1)^2 + (Y_2 - \hat{\beta} X_2)^2$$

We now have two terms: $(Y_1 - \hat{\beta} X_1)^2$ and $(Y_2 - \hat{\beta} X_2)^2$. Since the two terms are separate, we can easily differentiate the entire sum with relation to $\hat{\beta}$ by differentiating each term separately:

$$\begin{aligned} \frac{\partial}{\partial \hat{\beta}} \sum_{i=1}^{2} \hat{u}_i^2 &= \frac{\partial}{\partial \hat{\beta}} \sum_{i=1}^{2} (Y_i - \hat{\beta} X_i)^2 \\ &= \frac{\partial}{\partial \hat{\beta}} (Y_1 - \hat{\beta} X_1)^2 + \frac{\partial}{\partial \hat{\beta}} (Y_2 - \hat{\beta} X_2)^2 \end{aligned}$$

To find the derivative of each term, we will need to appeal to the chain rule. Remember that the chain rule tells us that if we have a function of a function, we first differentiate with relation to the outside function, and then multiply by the derivative of the inside function. So:

$$\frac{\partial f(g(X))}{\partial(X)} = \frac{\partial f(g(X))}{\partial g(X)} \times \frac{\partial g(X)}{\partial(X)}$$

Applying that to this example, we have $(Y_1 - \hat{\beta}X_1)^2$, which we wish to differentiate with respect to $\hat{\beta}$.

- We know that the derivative of Z^2 with respect to Z, we just multiply by the original power, and lower the power by 1; so the derivative would be $2Z$. In the same way, if we differentiate $(Y_1 - \hat{\beta}X_1)^2$ with respect to the inside of the bracket $(Y_1 - \hat{\beta}X_1)$, we will just get $2(Y_1 - \hat{\beta}X_1)$.
- We also know that when we find the partial derivative of $Y_1 - \hat{\beta}X_1$, we are treating Y_1 and X_1 as fixed with respect to $\hat{\beta}$. As such, the Y_1 and X_1 are like constants, and so this is equivalent to differentiating $-\hat{\beta}X_1$, which will be equal to $-(X_1)$:

$$\frac{\partial}{\partial\hat{\beta}}(Y_1 - \hat{\beta}X_1)^2 = 2(Y_1 - \hat{\beta}X_1) \times (-X_1) = -2(Y_1 - \hat{\beta}X_1) \times X_1$$

Since we have terms including X_1, Y_1 and X_2, Y_2, we will apply the chain rule in exactly the same way, giving us:

$$\frac{\partial}{\partial\hat{\beta}}(Y_1 - \hat{\beta}X_1)^2 + \frac{\partial}{\partial\hat{\beta}}(Y_2 - \hat{\beta}X_2)^2 = -2(Y_1 - \hat{\beta}X_1) \times X_1 - 2(Y_2 - \hat{\beta}X_2) \times X_2$$

But the first term of our derivative only includes Y_1 and X_1 terms (i.e. $i = 1$), and the second term only includes terms where $i = 2$. That is, both terms can be written in the form $-2(Y_i - \hat{\beta}X_i) \times X_i$. So, we can rewrite this as a summation:

$$= -2\sum_{i=1}^{2}(Y_i - \hat{\beta}X_i)X_i$$

This is the case for $n = 2$, but this rule generalizes to any sample size.

Returning now to the general case of n observations, we are trying to find the optimal $\hat{\beta}$ which minimizes:

$$\sum_{i=1}^{n}\hat{u}_i^2 = \sum_{i=1}^{n}(Y_i - \hat{\beta}X_i)^2$$

If we differentiate and use the chain rule in the same way, we will get:

$$\begin{aligned}\frac{\partial}{\partial\hat{\beta}}\sum_{i=1}^{n}\hat{u}_i^2 &= \frac{\partial}{\partial\hat{\beta}}\sum_{i=1}^{n}(Y_i - \hat{\beta}X_i)^2 \\ &= -2\sum_{i=1}^{n}(Y_i - \hat{\beta}X_i)X_i\end{aligned}$$

Since we are finding a minimum, we can set this derivative equal to zero, and we can indicate that we have implicitly defined the optimal estimator, by writing this as $\hat{\beta}^{OLS}$:

$$-2\sum_{i=1}^{n}(Y_i - \hat{\beta}^{OLS}X_i)X_i = 0$$

We can divide both sides by −2, and multiply out the brackets, giving us that:

$$\sum_{i=1}^{n}(Y_iX_i - \hat{\beta}^{OLS}X_i^2) = 0$$

Now, since this is a summation of a linear combination of terms, we can split this up into two separate summations, $\Sigma_{i=1}^{n}Y_iX_i$ and $\hat{\beta}^{OLS}\Sigma_{j=1}^{n}X_j^2$. Note that we have used j here rather than n, simply so that we can tell which summation each term relates to. As such, it will be the case that $\Sigma_{i=1}^{n}Y_iX_i - \hat{\beta}^{OLS}\Sigma_{j=1}^{n}X_j^2 = 0$. We can rearrange this to give that:

$$\sum_{i=1}^{n}Y_iX_i = \hat{\beta}^{OLS}\sum_{j=1}^{n}X_j^2$$

This is now simple to solve for $\hat{\beta}^{OLS}$ by dividing left and right by $\Sigma_{j=1}^{n}X_j^2$, giving us:

$$\hat{\beta}^{OLS} = \frac{\sum_{i=1}^{n}Y_iX_i}{\sum_{j=1}^{n}X_j^2}$$

KEY DEFINITION: OLS ESTIMATOR

We have constructed the OLS estimator, where we impose that the line passes through the origin. If we are estimating the relationship $Y_i = \beta X_i + u_i$, then the OLS estimator for β is given by:

$$\hat{\beta}^{OLS} = \frac{\sum_{i=1}^{n}Y_iX_i}{\sum_{j=1}^{n}X_j^2}$$

That is, the estimator is constructed based on the sum of the products of the pairs of observations of Y and X, divided by the sum of the squares of the observations of X_i.

23.2.3 Using the OLS estimator to estimate a slope parameter

In the previous section, we constructed the OLS estimator in general terms, but where this becomes really useful is actually using the estimator to estimate relationships between economic variables. In this section, we will consider two examples of how you can apply the OLS estimator.

Worked example 23.2: Calculating an OLS estimate based on four pairs of observations

Let's begin by revisiting the data we saw in Worked example 23.1. As before, we have four pairs of observations of X_i and Y_i, illustrated in Figure 23.14.

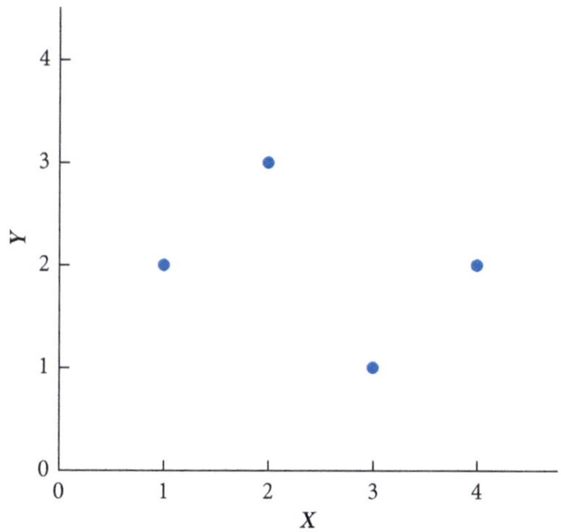

Figure 23.14 Four pairs of observations of X and Y.

The OLS line of best fit is defined as:

$$\hat{Y}_i = \hat{\beta}^{OLS} X_i$$

To find the OLS estimates, we need to apply the OLS estimator to our data:

$$\hat{\beta}^{OLS} = \frac{\sum_{i=1}^{n} Y_i X_i}{\sum_{j=1}^{n} X_j^2}$$

The numerator is the sum of products of the observed values of Y with their corresponding value of X. So, for $y_1 x_1$, we will substitute $y_1 = 2$ and $x_1 = 1$ to give 2×1. Similarly, the denominator is the sum of squares of the observed values of x_i. So, for instance, we will substitute $x_1^2 = 1^2$:

$$= \frac{2 \times 1 + 3 \times 2 + 1 \times 3 + 2 \times 4}{1^2 + 2^2 + 3^2 + 4^2} = \frac{2 + 6 + 3 + 8}{1 + 4 + 9 + 16} = \frac{19}{30}$$

So, the line of best fit for our relationship, using the OLS estimator, has a slope equal to 19/30 (see Figure 23.15). This implies that, based on our estimates, when X increases by 1, our estimated increase in Y is equal to 19/30.

Worked example 23.3: Estimating the fuel efficiency of a car

We began this section by thinking about the example of estimating the fuel efficiency of a car; that is, we were interested in estimating how much fuel we would use for varying different journeys. I currently drive a car that uses petrol, and I have randomly sampled ten journeys that I took, with the aim of estimating the average fuel consumption per mile. This is useful, as it then allows me to predict how much fuel I would need to be certain of not needing to refuel on a journey of (say) 200 miles.

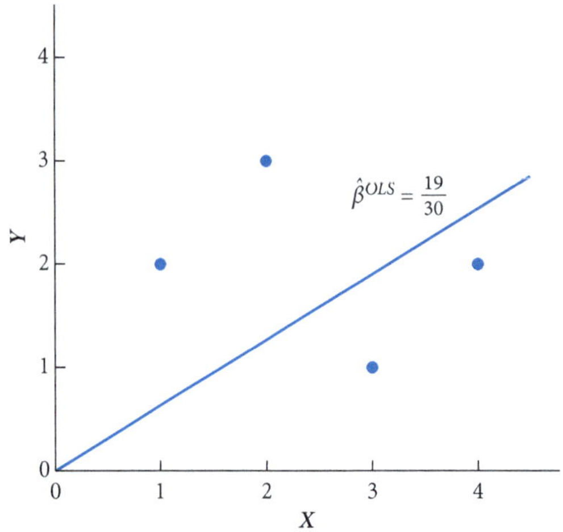

Figure 23.15 OLS line of best fit drawn through the data.

Ten (randomly drawn) pairs of observations of car journeys are illustrated in Table 23.4.

Table 23.4 Ten observations of miles driven and fuel used

Miles driven (x_i)	132.8	170.1	89.2	167.8	175.3	131.0	164.8	147.1	127.3	112.2
Fuel used (y_i)	14.5	18.5	7.3	14.2	15.6	14.9	14.5	15.4	10.8	15.7

As before, as we are trying to estimate β in the relationship:

$$Y_i = \beta X_i + u_i$$

We can use the OLS estimator we developed earlier in this section:

$$\hat{\beta}^{OLS} = \frac{\sum_{i=1}^{n} Y_i X_i}{\sum_{j=1}^{n} X_j^2}$$

Remember, to calculate the numerator, this is just the sum of the products of the pairs of observations of Y_i and X_i, or alternatively, fuel used and the distance driven. For the first observation, this product will just be equal to $y_1 \times x_1 = 14.5 \times 132.8 = 1{,}925.6$. Similarly, for the second term, $y_2 \times x_2 = 18.5 \times 170.1 = 3{,}146.85$.

- Using all ten observations, we can see that the sum of the products of the observations is equal to $\Sigma_{i=1}^{10} y_i x_i = 20{,}584.27$.

Similarly, the denominator (or bottom) of the estimator is the sum of squares of the observations of the explanatory variable. So, for the first observations, $x_1 = 132.8$, and so $x_1^2 = 132.8^2 = 17{,}635.84$. To find the denominator of the estimator, we simply add up the square of each of these values.

- Using all ten observations, we can see that the sum of squares of the observations of distance driven is equal to $\sum_{j=1}^{10} x_j^2 = 208{,}166$.

As such, our OLS estimate is given as:

$$\hat{\beta}^{OLS} = \frac{\sum_{i=1}^{n} y_i x_i}{\sum_{j=1}^{n} x_j^2} = \frac{20{,}584.27}{208{,}166}$$
$$= 0.0989$$

Our estimated relationship is illustrated in Figure 23.16. As we are estimating the relationship:

$$Y_i = \beta X_i + u_i$$

we can interpret β as the marginal impact of a change in X on Y. So, based on the data we have observed, our estimate of the marginal impact of an increase in X (miles driven) by 1 is to increase fuel used by 0.0989 litres.

Remember that the marginal impact is equivalent to the (partial) derivative of Y with respect to X, and the partial derivative is the derivative of Y on X, holding everything else constant. If we were to differentiate our relationship, then:

$$\frac{\partial Y_i}{\partial X_i} = \frac{\partial}{\partial X_i}(\beta X_i + u_i) = \beta$$

To reiterate, our estimated $\hat{\beta}$ is an estimate of the marginal impact of driving one additional mile on fuel consumed, keeping everything else constant.

Alternatively, you should remember that a derivative is a rate of change of Y with respect to X, evaluated at an infinitesimally small change in X. So, we could also represent the marginal change as $\frac{\Delta Y}{\Delta X} = \beta$ where ΔY is the change in Y and ΔX is the change in X. Because we

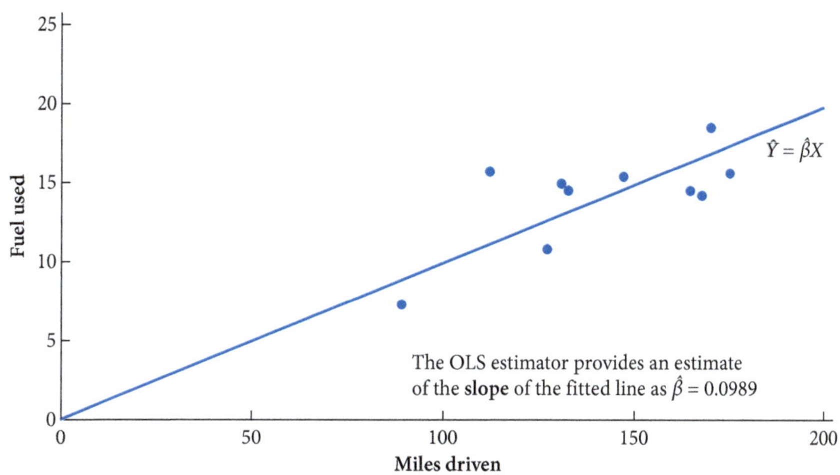

Figure 23.16 Estimating the relationship between fuel used and miles driven using OLS.

have estimated a straight line, the slope of the line is constant. Because we have this relationship, we can also write that:

$$\Delta Y = \beta \Delta X$$

That is, the change in Y is equal to β multiplied by the change in X. So, if we were to drive ten more miles ($\Delta X = 10$), then our estimated relationship suggests that we would use an additional $\hat{\beta} \times \Delta X = 0.0989 \times 10 = 0.989$ litres of fuel.

23.3 Deriving OLS: Part 2—Allowing the intercept to be non-zero

In the previous section, we saw how we can construct the OLS estimator (and estimate the estimator) if we are estimating the relationship:

$$Y_i = \beta X_i + u_i$$

When we estimate this relationship, we are imposing the condition that the fitted line, $\hat{Y} = \hat{\beta} X$, passes through the origin. That is, we impose that when $X = 0$, $\hat{Y} = 0$ as well.

However, more often than not, it is not appropriate to impose that the fitted line passes through the origin. To illustrate this, let's consider the data we saw earlier in the chapter on life expectancy plotted against spending per capita on healthcare from the OECD.[4]

We have illustrated this in Figure 23.17. However, note that we've plotted this with the scale on the vertical axis beginning at a life expectancy of 65.

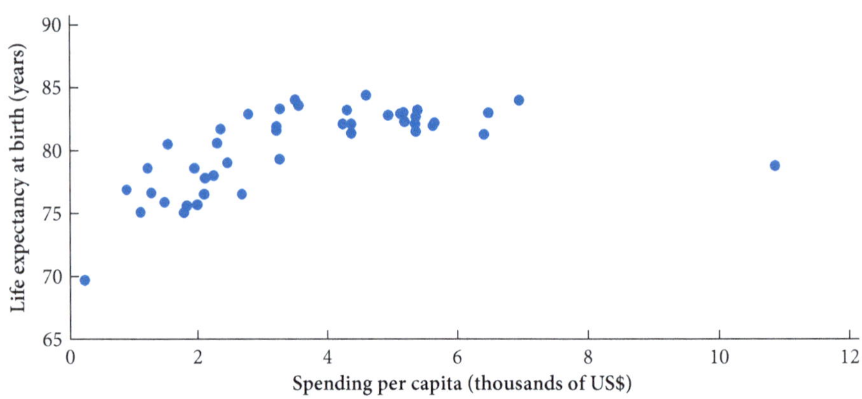

Figure 23.17 Life expectancy at birth plotted against spending per capita on healthcare (2019 data, from the OECD).

[4] As before, this is an updated version of a figure from OECD (2015), *Health at a Glance 2015: OECD Indicators*, OECD Publishing, p. 47, https://doi.org/10.1787/health_glance-2015-en. The author has updated this figure, using updated data from 2019. The data on health spending is freely available from https://data.oecd.org/healthres/health-spending.htm, whilst the life expectancy data is available from https://data.oecd.org/healthstat/life-expectancy-at-birth.htm. Data used to create this figure is available to download from Data sets and Exercises at the end of this chapter.

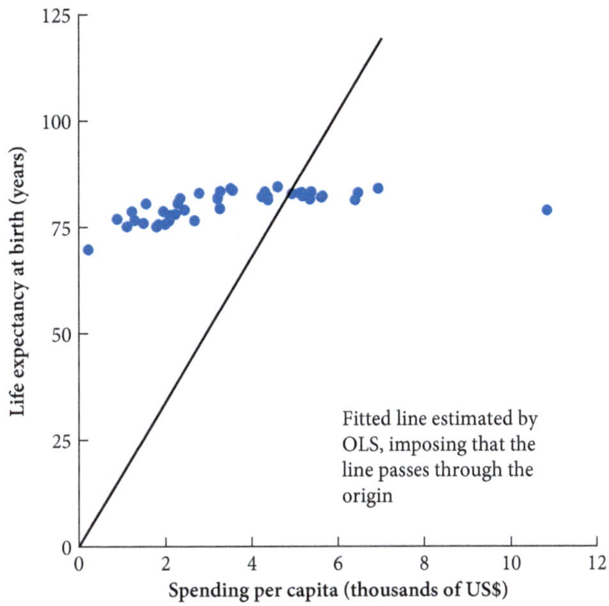

Figure 23.18 Estimating the relationship between life expectancy and spending on healthcare, imposing that the line passes through the origin.

Let's re-plot this data on a new set of axes, so that life expectancy begins at zero, and plot the line of best fit using the OLS estimator we have seen before. This is illustrated in Figure 23.18.

This line of best fit is much steeper than the slope suggested by the data, and most of the data points are nowhere near the line.

In fact, if we placed the restriction that the intercept is equal to zero, we would end up with a biased estimate of the impact of spending per capita on life expectancy, with the estimated marginal impact overestimated many times over.

There are two ways that we could try to address this: firstly, we could consider re-scaling all of our data, so that the data is centred around the origin, and secondly, we could use a different estimator.

If we rescale all of our data, so that the data is centred around the origin, this would mean that the line of best fit would automatically pass through the origin. To do this, we would need to subtract the sample mean of the life expectancy from all of the observed values of life expectancy, and subtract the sample mean of the spending per capita from each of the observed values of spending per capita. So, if we represent these as Y_i and X_i, respectively, we would rescale these for each observation as $Y_i - \overline{Y}$ and $X_i - \overline{X}$.

23.3.1 What happens when we rescale the data?

Having rescaled both the dependent variable and the explanatory variable, the data is now centred on the origin (see Figure 23.19). If we use the OLS estimator to estimate the relationship between these rescaled variables, as illustrated in Figure 23.20, then the line we have fitted looks much closer to the true trend of the data.

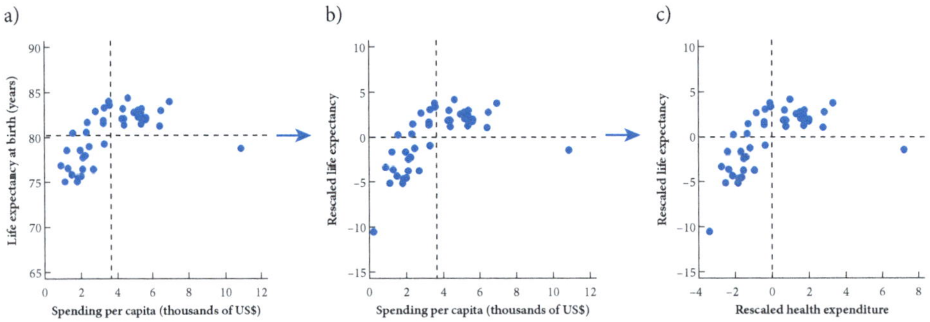

Original data.

The dotted lines here represent the **sample mean** of life expectancy (horizonal line), and spending per capita on healthcare (vertical line).

- Sample mean of life expectancy = 80.23 years
- Sample mean of spending per capita = 3.64341 ($3643.41)

Rescaled life expectancy.

We have rescaled the life expectancy here, by subtracting the sample mean. The shape of the data has not changed, but the position of the data has moved. The horizontal dashed line represents Y=0.

By subtracting the sample mean of the dependent variable, the data has moved downwards

Rescaled health expenditure

We have rescaled the health expenditure by subtracting its sample mean.

Again, the shape of the data is unchanged, but the data has shifted leftwards.

The data is now centred on the origin.

Figure 23.19 Re-scaling the data.

We can formalize this a little. Let's define life expectancy as Y_i and health expenditure as X_i. Then we can define two new variables, representing our rescaled variables. $y_i = Y_i - \overline{Y}$ represents the rescaled life expectancy (by subtracting the average life expectancy from each observation), whilst $x_i = X_i - \overline{X}$ represents the rescaled health expenditure. That is:

$$y_i = Y_i - \overline{Y}$$
$$x_i = X_i - \overline{X}$$

In Figure 23.20, we estimated the relationship between these rescaled variables, y_i and x_i, using the OLS estimator, imposing that the line passes through the origin:

$$\hat{\beta} = \frac{\sum_{i=1}^{n} y_i x_i}{\sum_{j=1}^{n} x_j^2}$$

Now, since we know that $y_i = Y_i - \overline{Y}$ and $x_i = X_i - \overline{X}$, we can substitute these in to write down a new OLS estimator in terms of the observed values of Y_i, X_i, and the respective sample means, $\overline{Y}, \overline{X}$, by substituting $Y_i - \overline{Y}$ in place of y_i and $X_i - \overline{X}$ in place of x_i. As such, the estimator will be:

$$\hat{\beta} = \frac{\sum_{i=1}^{n} (Y_i - \overline{Y})(X_i - \overline{X})}{\sum_{j=1}^{n} (X_j - \overline{X})^2}$$

When we estimate OLS, with the line constrained to pass through the (new) origin, the line is a much closer fit to the data than the unscaled version.

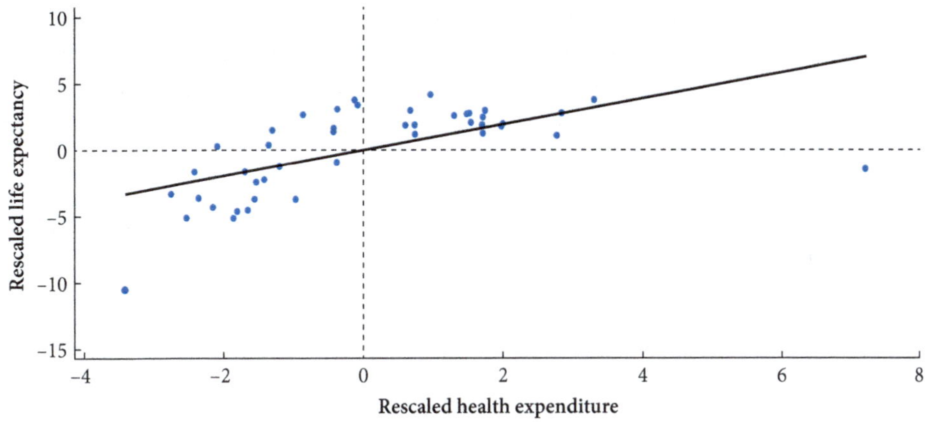

Figure 23.20 Estimating the relationship between the rescaled life expectancy and rescaled health expenditure (data from the OECD).

23.3.2 Can we estimate both an intercept and a slope?

So far, we have only considered estimating a slope parameter, but we will often want to estimate relationships with a non-zero intercept. Suppose that we were interested in estimating β_0 and β_1 in the following relationship:

$$Y_i = \beta_0 + \beta_1 X_i + u_i$$

β_0 is the intercept here, and β_1 the slope parameter (or the marginal impact of a change in X on Y). We can use exactly the same methods as we saw in Section 23.2.2 to estimate a relationship

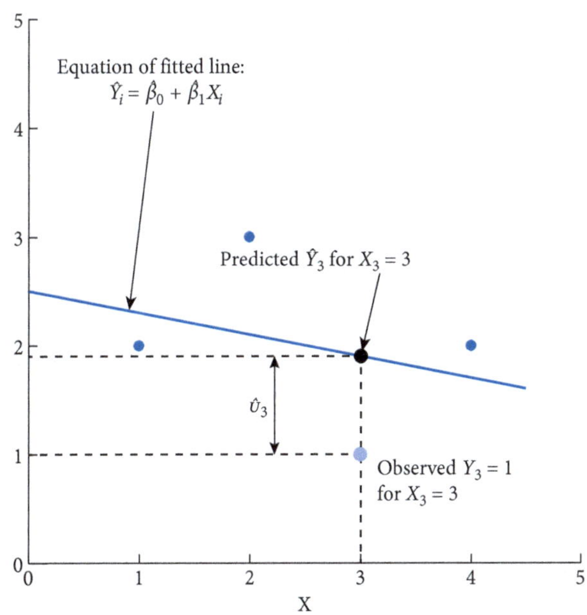

Figure 23.21 Finding the fitted residual when allowing the intercept to be non-zero.

which has both a non-zero intercept and slope. That is, we can choose a line which minimizes the sum of squares of the vertical distances between the observed points and the line. The only difference is that we will need two estimators: one for the slope, and a second for the intercept.

As such, we wish to estimate the β_0 and β_1, so we construct a line of best fit, with equation:

$$\hat{Y}_i = \hat{\beta}_0 + \hat{\beta}_1 X_i$$

where $\hat{\beta}_0$ is an estimator for the intercept, β_0, and $\hat{\beta}_1$ is an estimator for the marginal impact of X on Y. Just as earlier in the chapter, since the fitted residual is equal to the vertical distance between the observed value of Y_i, and the predicted value of $\hat{Y}_i$ based on the corresponding observation of X_i, we can write that:

$$\hat{u}_i = Y_i - \hat{Y}_i$$

These residuals are illustrated in Figure 23.21 for the data set based on four pairs of observations that we saw earlier in this chapter. $\hat{u}_3$ is the vertical distance between the observed point ($Y_3 = 1$) and the predicted value, based upon $X_3 = 3$. To construct the OLS estimator we will want to choose the optimal $\hat{\beta}_0$ and $\hat{\beta}_1$ which minimize the sum of squares of these vertical distances.

More formally, we can rewrite the fitted residual, $\hat{u}_i = Y_i - \hat{Y}_i$, by substituting in the equation of our fitted line, $\hat{Y}_i = \hat{\beta}_0 + \hat{\beta}_1 X_i$, so that:

$$\hat{u}_i = Y_i - \hat{\beta}_0 - \hat{\beta}_1 X_i$$

The principle of OLS is that we choose the optimal parameters that minimize the sum of squares of these vertical distances. Here, we are trying to choose the optimal $\hat{\beta}_0$ and $\hat{\beta}_1$ that minimize $\Sigma_{i=1}^{n} \hat{u}_i^2$. So, since we are trying to choose the optimal $\hat{\beta}_0$ and $\hat{\beta}_1$, we will need to (partially) differentiate our sum of squares of the fitted residuals with relation to both $\hat{\beta}_0$ and $\hat{\beta}_1$, equate both to zero, and solve, simultaneously.

We can write down the sum of squares of the residuals as:

$$\sum_{i=1}^{n} \hat{u}_i^2 = \sum_{i=1}^{n} (Y_i - \hat{\beta}_0 - \hat{\beta}_1 X_i)^2$$

Differentiating, first with respect to $\hat{\beta}_0$ gives us:

$$\frac{\partial}{\partial \hat{\beta}_0} \sum_{i=1}^{n} \hat{u}_i^2 = \frac{\partial}{\partial \hat{\beta}_0} \sum_{i=1}^{n} (Y_i - \hat{\beta}_0 - \hat{\beta}_1 X_i)^2$$

We use exactly the same method to differentiate this expression as we did in 23.3. Since this is a function of a function, we will need to appeal to the chain rule. Since every term in the summation is the same functional form of $\hat{\beta}_0$, we can effectively ignore the summation sign.

Step 1

We lower the power on $(Y_i - \hat{\beta}_0 - \hat{\beta}_1 X_i)^2$ by 1, and then multiply by the original power: $= 2(Y_i - \hat{\beta}_0 - \hat{\beta}_1 X_i)$.

Step 2

We then need to multiply the whole thing by the partial derivative of $(Y_i - \hat{\beta}_0 - \hat{\beta}_1 X_i)$ with respect to $\hat{\beta}_0$. Since the only term involving $\hat{\beta}_0$ is $-\hat{\beta}_0$, differentiating this expression will give us: $\frac{\partial}{\partial \hat{\beta}_0}(Y_i - \hat{\beta}_0 - \hat{\beta}_1 X_i) = -1$.

Therefore, the derivative of the sum of squares of residuals will be equal to:

$$\frac{\partial}{\partial \hat{\beta}_0}\sum_{i=1}^{n} u_i^2 = 2\sum_{i=1}^{n}(Y_i - \hat{\beta}_0 - \hat{\beta}_1 X_i) \times (-1)$$

Simplifying, and setting the expression equal to zero, gives us a first order condition:

$$-2\sum_{i=1}^{n}(Y_i - \hat{\beta}_0^{OLS} - \hat{\beta}_1^{OLS} X_i) = 0$$

Since we have set this equal to zero, then implicitly we have defined the $\hat{\beta}_0$ which minimizes the summation, and we will substitute in for $\hat{\beta}_0^{OLS}$ to indicate that this is the OLS estimator. Implicitly, because we are also going to optimize with respect to $\hat{\beta}_1$, the minimum will be achieved when we also substitute in $\hat{\beta}_1^{OLS}$.

The summation is made up of three elements, which we can split into three separate summations:

1. The sum of the Y_i terms: $\Sigma_{i=1}^{n} Y_i$.
2. The sum of the estimated intercepts: $\Sigma_{i=1}^{n} \hat{\beta}_0^{OLS}$.
   However, since $\hat{\beta}_0^{OLS}$ is, by definition, a constant, this can be rewritten as $n\,\hat{\beta}_0^{OLS}$.
3. The sum of the X_i terms $\Sigma_{j=1}^{n} \hat{\beta}_1^{OLS} X_j$. Since $\hat{\beta}_1^{OLS}$ is a constant multiplier of each of the X_j terms, we can take this outside of the summation, giving us $= \hat{\beta}_1^{OLS} \Sigma_{j=1}^{n} X_j$.

As such, the whole expression can be rewritten as:

$$-2\left[\sum_{i=1}^{n} Y_i - n\,\hat{\beta}_0^{OLS} - \hat{\beta}_1^{OLS}\sum_{j=1}^{n} X_j\right] = 0$$

We can then divide left and right by -2, and rearrange, to make $\hat{\beta}_0^{OLS}$ the subject of the equation, giving us:

$$n\hat{\beta}_0 = \sum_{i=1}^{n} Y_i - \hat{\beta}_1^{OLS}\sum_{j=1}^{n} X_j$$

Finally, we can divide left and right by n, giving us:

$$\hat{\beta}_0^{OLS} = \frac{1}{n}\sum_{i=1}^{n} Y_i - \hat{\beta}_1^{OLS} \times \frac{1}{n}\sum_{j=1}^{n} X_j$$

By definition, when we divide any sum by the number of observations, we will construct the sample mean, so we can rewrite $\frac{1}{n}\Sigma_{i=1}^{n} Y_i = \overline{Y}$ and $\frac{1}{n}\Sigma_{j=1}^{n} X_j = \overline{X}$:

$$\Rightarrow \hat{\beta}_0^{OLS} = \overline{Y} - \hat{\beta}_1^{OLS}\, \overline{X}$$

Now, we have constructed the estimator for the intercept $\hat{\beta}_0$. We will follow exactly the same mathematical process for the slope parameter. Remember, we will be differentiating the SSR with respect to $\hat{\beta}_1$, and setting the derivative equal to zero. The sum of squares of the fitted residuals is given by:

$$\sum_{i=1}^{n} u_i^2 = \sum_{i=1}^{n} (Y_i - \hat{\beta}_0 - \hat{\beta}_1 X_i)^2$$

The only thing that is different from the case above is that the partial derivative of $(Y_i - \hat{\beta}_0 - \hat{\beta}_1 X_i)$ with respect to $\hat{\beta}_1$ will be $-X_i$:

$$\frac{\partial}{\partial \hat{\beta}_1} \sum_{i=1}^{n} u_i^2 = \frac{\partial}{\partial \hat{\beta}_1} \sum_{i=1}^{n} (Y_i - \hat{\beta}_0 - \hat{\beta}_1 X_i)^2 = 2 \sum_{i=1}^{n} (Y_i - \hat{\beta}_0 - \hat{\beta}_1 X_i) \times (-X_i)$$

As before, we set this derivative equal to zero to find our first order condition (FOC), and in doing so, we have implicitly defined $\hat{\beta}_1^{OLS}$. We will also simplify the expression by dividing through by -2:

$$\Rightarrow \sum_{i=1}^{n} (Y_i - \hat{\beta}_0^{OLS} - \hat{\beta}_1^{OLS} X_i) X_i = 0$$

Since we already know that $\hat{\beta}_0^{OLS} = \overline{Y} - \hat{\beta}_0^{OLS} \overline{X}$, we can substitute this into our FOC, giving us the following expression:

$$\Rightarrow \sum_{i=1}^{n} (Y_i - \overline{Y} + \hat{\beta}_1^{OLS} \overline{X} - \hat{\beta}_1^{OLS} X_i) X_i = 0$$

Multiplying out the brackets and grouping terms gives us that:

$$\sum_{i=1}^{n} (Y_i - \overline{Y}) X_i - \hat{\beta}_1^{OLS} \sum_{j=1}^{n} (X_j - \overline{X}) X_j = 0$$

$$\Rightarrow \hat{\beta}_1^{OLS} = \frac{\sum_{i=1}^{n} (Y_i - \overline{Y}) X_i}{\sum_{j=1}^{n} (X_j - \overline{X}) X_j}$$

Now, it is possible to show[5] that:

$$\sum_{i=1}^{n} (Y_i - \overline{Y}) X_i = \sum_{i=1}^{n} (Y_i - \overline{Y})(X_i - \overline{X})$$

for any variables X, Y, and so, we can rewrite the OLS estimator for the slope parameter as:

$$\hat{\beta}_1^{OLS} = \frac{\sum_{i=1}^{n} (Y_i - \overline{Y})(X_i - \overline{X})}{\sum_{j=1}^{n} (X_j - \overline{X})^2}$$

[5] This is often referred to as the 'disappearing mean'. We prove this in the appendix to this chapter.

We have seen this estimator already, earlier in the chapter. This is the result for the estimator for the slope parameter when we rescaled the dependent variable (Y) and the explanatory variable (X) by subtracting the sample mean of the two variables.

KEY DEFINITION: OLS ESTIMATORS

When we are estimating the relationship $Y_i = \beta_0 + \beta_1 X_i + u_i$ (i.e. we are allowing the intercept to be non-zero), then the OLS estimators are given by:

$$\hat{\beta}_0 = \bar{Y} - \hat{\beta}_1 \bar{X}$$

$$\hat{\beta}_1 = \frac{\sum_{i=1}^{n} (Y_i - \bar{Y})(X_i - \bar{X})}{\sum_{j=1}^{n} (X_j - \bar{X})^2}$$

Worked example 23.4: Calculating an OLS estimate of both the slope and intercept, based on four observations

Let's repeat the simple example that we saw earlier, but this time we will allow the intercept to be non-zero.

The OLS line of best fit is defined as:

$$\hat{Y}_i = \hat{\beta}_0^{OLS} + \hat{\beta}_1^{OLS} X_i$$

Table 23.5 Four pairs of observations of X and Y

X_i	1	2	3	4
Y_i	2	3	1	2

To find the OLS estimates, we need to apply the OLS estimator to our data. Let's begin with the estimator for the slope parameter. It is easy to show that the sample mean of X is equal to 2.5, and the sample mean of Y is equal to 2:

$$\bar{X} = \frac{1}{4} \times \sum_{i=1}^{4} X_i = 2.5, \quad \bar{Y} = \frac{1}{4} \times \sum_{i=1}^{n} Y_i = 2.5$$

We can rescale our data by subtracting the sample means from our observations. For example, for the first observation $(X_i - \bar{X})$ is just equal to $1 - 2.5 = -1.5$. We do this for all four observations in Table 23.6.

If we substitute these into the OLS estimator for the slope parameter, $\hat{\beta}_1$, we have:

$$\hat{\beta}_1^{OLS} = \frac{\sum_{i=1}^{n} (Y_i - \bar{Y})(X_i - \bar{X})}{\sum_{j=1}^{n} (X_j - \bar{X})^2} = \frac{0 \times (-1.5) + 1 \times (-0.5) + (-1) \times 0.5 + 0 \times 1.5}{(-1.5)^2 + (-0.5)^2 + (0.5)^2 + 1.5^2}$$

$$= \frac{0 - 0.5 - 0.5 + 0}{2.25 + 0.25 + 0.25 + 2.25} = -\frac{1}{5}$$

Table 23.6 Re-scaling the observations by subtracting the sample mean

$(X_i - \overline{X})$	−1.5	−0.5	0.5	1.5
$(Y_i - \overline{Y})$	0	1	−1	0

Similarly, we can construct an estimate of the intercept as:

$$\hat{\beta}_0^{OLS} = \overline{Y} - \hat{\beta}_1^{OLS}\overline{X}$$

We know that $\overline{Y} = 2$, $\hat{\beta}_1^{OLS} = -\frac{1}{5}$, and $\overline{X} = 2.5$, and so:

$$\hat{\beta}_0^{OLS} = 2 - \left(\frac{1}{5}\right) \times 2.5 = 2.5$$

So, the estimated intercept is equal to 2.5, and the estimated slope is equal to −0.2. The slope suggests that the estimated marginal impact of an increase in X by 1 is to decrease Y by 0.2, whilst the intercept suggests that if $X = 0$, then the expected value of Y would be equal to 2.5 (see Figure 23.22).

As you can see, by allowing the intercept to be non-zero, we have seen a big change in the estimated marginal effect. When we imposed that the intercept was equal to 0, the estimated slope was 19/30, whilst when we allow the intercept to be non-zero, the estimated slope is −0.2. This suggests that, when we imposed that the intercept was equal to zero, we may have introduced some bias to our estimates. We explore the bias of the OLS estimators in future chapters.

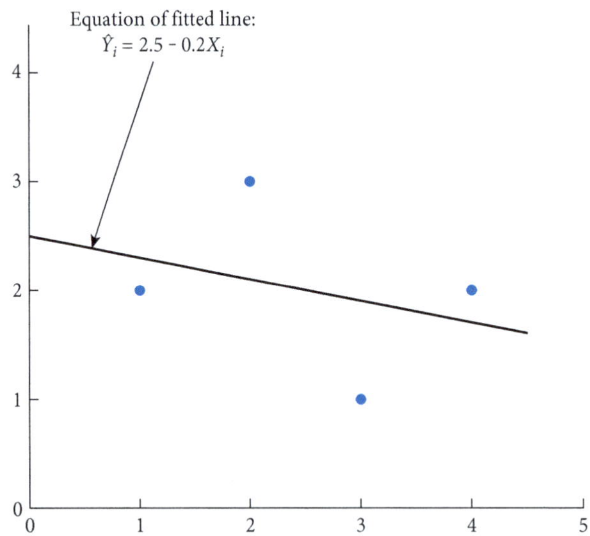

Figure 23.22 Fitted line, estimated by OLS through the four observations.

Table 23.7 Ten pairs of observations of miles driven, and fuel used

Miles driven (X)	132.8	170.1	89.2	167.8	175.3	131	164.8	147.1	127.3	112.2
Fuel used (Y)	14.5	18.5	7.3	14.2	15.6	14.9	14.5	15.4	10.8	15.7

Worked example 23.5: Estimating the fuel efficiency of a car

Let's quickly return to our example of how much fuel I use on a car journey. We had randomly sampled ten observations from the population of car journeys, and had the data shown in Table 23.7.

We are interested in estimating the relationship:

$$Y_i = \beta_0 + \beta_1 X_i + u_i$$

where Y_i is the dependent variable and represents the fuel used on journey i, and X_i is the explanatory variable and represents the miles driven on that journey. Whilst we could calculate the estimates of the slope $\hat{\beta}_1$ and the intercept $\hat{\beta}_0$ manually, it is often easier to use software packages (particularly when there are a large number of observations). Even with ten observations, the calculations can become fiddly, and as the number of observations increases, the chance of making an error also increases.

There is a wide range of software packages available that can estimate OLS for you. In the box, you will find step-by-step instructions for running OLS regressions within Microsoft Excel.

Step 1

When you first install Excel, its data analytics package is unlikely to be available. To install the data analytics package, you will need to click on the 'File' menu, and then select 'Options'.

Under Options, you will need to select 'Add-ins'. This will take you to a new menu, allowing you to add additional functionality to Excel:

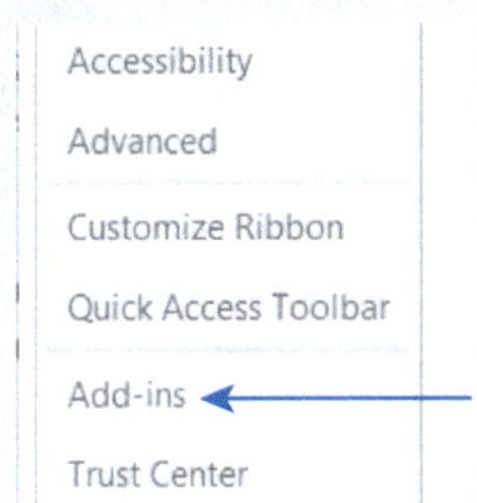

You will then need to select 'Excel Add-ins' under 'Manage', and then click 'Go'.

Under 'Add-ins', you will need to select 'Analysis ToolPak' (and 'Analysis ToolPak – VBA') and click 'OK'.

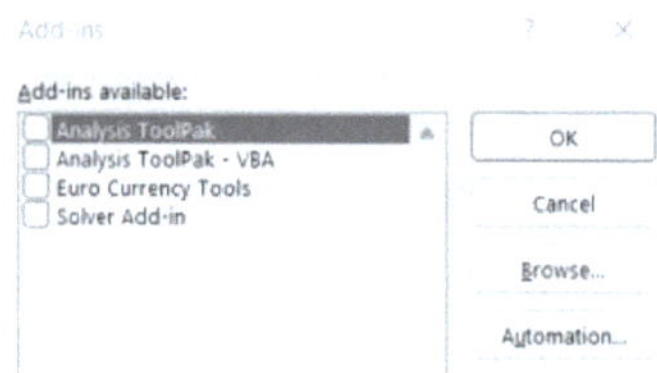

Having done this, under the 'Data' menu a new option will appear, called 'Data Analysis'.

Step 2

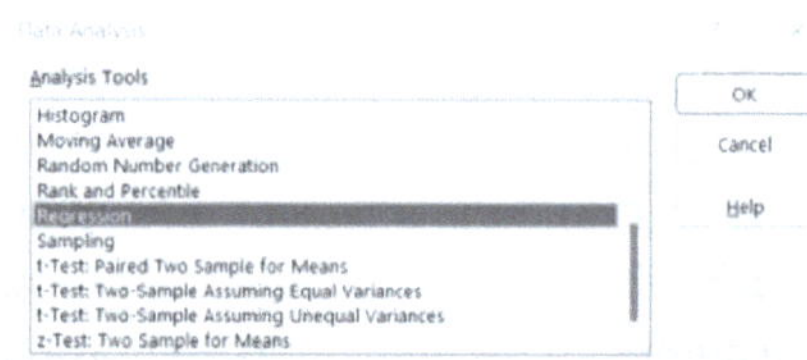

The Data Analysis toolpak has a range of tools available. As we wish to carry out OLS regression, we need to scroll down to select 'Regression', and then click 'OK'.

This will open a new menu, asking you to specify your regression.

Step 3

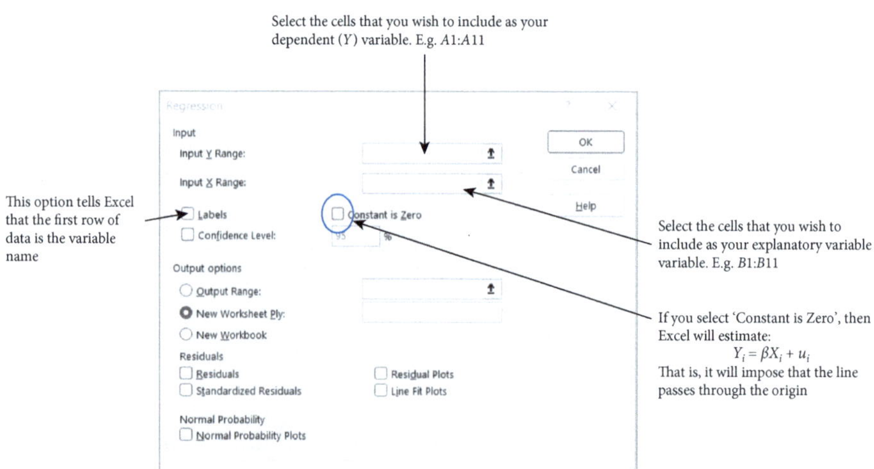

When you wish to carry out your OLS regression, you will need to select the cells that contain your dependent variable (in the example, this would be Fuel used), and explanatory variable (Miles driven).

There are a range of options. Labels indicates that the first row contains the name of the variable, and 'Constant is Zero', if selected, would impose that the estimated line passed through the origin.

Step 4

	A	B	C	D	E	F	G	H	I
1	SUMMARY OUTPUT								
2									
3	*Regression Statistics*								
4	Multiple R	0.693494424							
5	R Square	0.480934516							
6	Adjusted R Square	0.41605133							
7	Standard Error	2.333785296							
8	Observations	10							
9									
10	ANOVA								
11		*df*	*SS*	*MS*	*F*	*Significance F*			
12	Regression	1	40.37156462	40.37156462	7.412313558	0.026145106			
13	Residual	8	43.57243045	5.446553806					
14	Total	9	83.94399507						
15									
16		*Coefficients*	*Standard Error*	*t Stat*	*P-value*	*Lower 95%*	*Upper 95%*	*Lower 95.0%*	*Upper 95.0%*
17	Intercept	3.530046497	3.966320301	0.890005403	0.399435415	-5.616304519	12.67639751	-5.616304519	12.67639751
18	Miles driven	0.074844479	0.027490515	2.722556438	0.026145106	0.011451237	0.13823772	0.011451237	0.13823772
19									

Excel will output lots of information, which you will become more familiar with as you develop your understanding of OLS.

For now, the important information is highlighted—that is, the estimated coefficients. The estimated intercept ($\hat{\beta}_0$) is equal to 3.530, whilst the estimated slope parameter (i.e. the estimate of the marginal impact of miles driven on fuel used), $\hat{\beta}_1$, is equal to 0.0748.

To three decimal places, the estimated coefficients are:

$$\hat{\beta}_0 = 3.530$$
$$\hat{\beta}_1 = 0.075$$

Since we have been estimating the relationship:

$$Y_i = \beta_0 + \beta_1 X_i + u_i$$

then $\hat{\beta}_1$ is the (estimated) marginal impact of a change in X on Y (i.e. $\frac{\partial Y}{\partial X} = \beta_1$). The estimated coefficient suggests that an increase in X by 1 increases Y by 0.075. Or alternatively, driving an additional mile uses an additional 0.075 litres of fuel (see Figure 23.23).

The intercept ($\hat{\beta}_0$) is a little more tricky to interpret. In principle, we might think of the estimated intercept as the amount of fuel that we would expect to use if we drive zero miles. However, the estimated value of 3.530 doesn't make intuitive sense. If you drive zero miles, you would expect to use zero litres of fuel (or at least close to zero, as you might have some fuel evaporate).

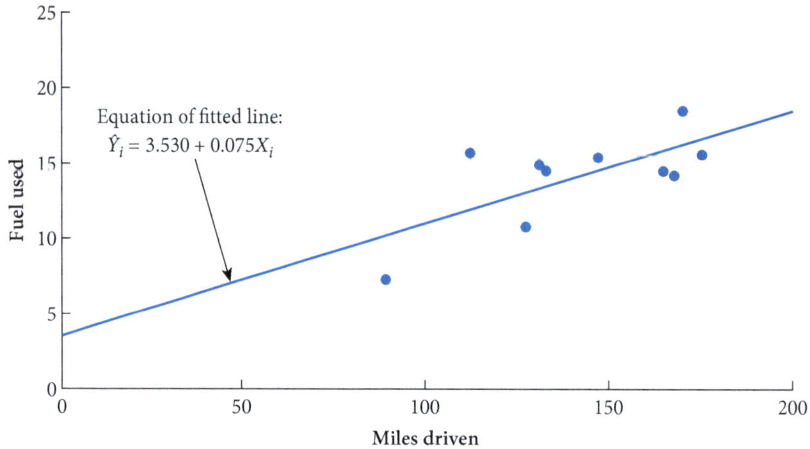

Figure 23.23 Estimating a fitted line with a non-zero intercept through the fuel data.

Part of the reason that we have this, apparently illogical, inference relates to the data that we have observed. All of the observations of miles driven are between 89.2 and 175.3. This data can tell us about what happens within that data range, but it will be less good for making predictions about where the line should lie outside of this range. For instance, it might be that, outside of this range, fuel usage is non-linear. As such, we cannot say anything (with certainty) about what happens to the line outside of this range (see Figure 23.24).

Remember also that $\hat{\beta}_1 = 0.075$ merely provides us with an estimate of the marginal effect of miles driven on fuel usage. If we took a different sample from the population, we would gain a different estimate (that might be larger, or smaller). However, if the slope changes

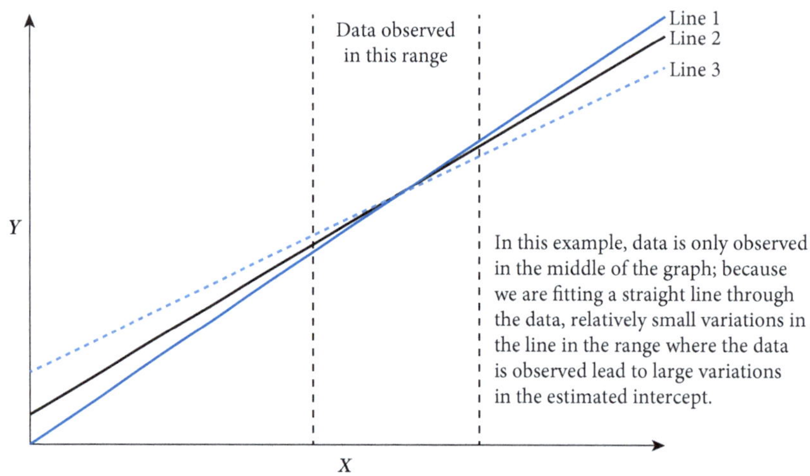

Figure 23.24 Extrapolating outside of the data range.

(with the average of the observations remaining constant), since the vertical axis is a long way from the observed data, we see big changes in the estimated intercept.

A further reason why it is difficult to make inferences about the intercept is that if we only observe data in a particular range, we have no idea what happens to the data outside of that data range. We may be able to make an inference that there is a straight-line relationship within the observed data range, but this may become non-linear when we move out of that data range! As a guide, if you want to have a good inference about what the fitted line does in a particular range for the explanatory variable, it is important to collect data around that data range.

Comparison of estimates

We have used two estimators to estimate the relationship between fuel used (dependent variable) and the number of miles we drive (explanatory variable). The two estimators produced slightly different estimates of the marginal impact of an additional mile driven on fuel usage.

Important note: Statistical significance

In previous chapters, we have seen how we can test hypotheses. For instance, we might wish to test whether the intercept is significantly different from zero.

We will introduce significance testing with OLS in future chapters, but it should be noted that in this example, whilst the point estimate of the intercept is equal to 3.530, we would be unable to reject the null hypothesis that the true intercept is equal to zero.

Whilst the point estimates (0.0989 vs 0.075) are different, these are of very similar magnitudes. It should not surprise us that we get slightly different estimates, because the models we are estimating are different.

Model 1

If we estimate the relationship $Y_i = \beta X_i + u_i$, then our estimate of the marginal effect is $\hat{\beta} = 0.0989$. That is, the estimated relationship suggests that:

$$\frac{\partial \hat{Y}}{\partial X} = 0.0989$$

The estimated impact of driving one additional mile is to use 0.0989 litres of fuel.

Model 2

If we estimate the relationship $Y_i = \beta_0 + \beta_1 X_i + u_i$, then our estimate of the marginal effect is $\hat{\beta}_1 = 0.075$.

That is, the estimated relationship suggests that:

$$\frac{\partial \hat{Y}}{\partial X} = 0.075$$

The estimated impact of driving one additional mile is to use 0.075 litres of fuel.

In this example, it is fairly obvious that the intercept should be zero (or very close to zero). Where the true intercept is equal to zero, then you should get very similar results if you estimate Model 1 (where you impose that the intercept is equal to zero) and Model 2 (where you allow the intercept to be non-zero).

Part of the reason that the coefficients are different is because, in statistics, there is always uncertainty about the true relationship. The estimate of the slope in Model 1 has uncertainty, whilst similarly, the estimate of the slope in Model 2 also has uncertainty. If you were to perform a test of statistical significance on the null hypothesis that $\hat{\beta} = \hat{\beta}_1$, it is unlikely that you would be able to reject the null that the two coefficients were equal.

However, the choice of model does matter when the true intercept is non-zero.

Worked example 23.6: The impact of healthcare spending on life expectancy

Let's return to the example that we began the chapter with to illustrate the decisions we need to make with OLS.

It is a reasonable assumption that increased spending on healthcare is likely to lead to improved overall health outcomes, and hence improved life expectancy. To investigate this relationship, we will consider a cross-section of observations, from the OECD, of 44 countries in 2019.[6] This data includes:

- the life expectancy (at birth)—our dependent variable, and
- spending on healthcare per capita (measured in thousands of US dollars).

Let's define our variables as $LifeExp_i$ to represent the life expectancy in country i, and $Spend_i$ to represent the spending on healthcare in country i.

The first question we need to ask is whether we should impose that our fitted line passes through the origin (Model 1), or whether we should allow the intercept to be non-zero (Model 2).

Model 1	**Model 2**
$LifeExp_i = \beta Spend_i + u_i$	$LifeExp_i = \beta_0 + \beta_1 Spend_i + u_i$

If we were to choose Model 1, we would be implicitly assuming that in a country with no spending on healthcare, the life expectancy would be zero.

Whilst it is certainly true that health outcomes (and life expectancy) would be expected to fall substantially if no healthcare were available, it is not plausible that life expectancy would be reduced to zero. After all, before any form of healthcare was available, people and animals managed to survive!

As such, we will only focus on Model 2:

$$LifeExp_i = \beta_0 + \beta_1 Spend_i + u_i$$

Using OLS, we get the following, estimated coefficients:

$$\hat{\beta}_0^{OLS} = 76.684$$
$$\hat{\beta}_1^{OLS} = 0.972$$

The interpretation of $\hat{\beta}_1^{OLS}$ is relatively straightforward, since $Spend_i$ is measured in thousands of US$, and increasing $Spend_i$ by 1 is equivalent to spending increasing by $1,000 per

[6] This is available to download from Data sets and exercises at the end of the chapter.

person. So, increasing $Spend_i$ by 1, the model would estimate that this would be associated with a 0.972 year increase in life expectancy. That is, the prediction of the model is that countries that spend $1,000 more on healthcare per capita have, on average, 0.972 years higher life expectancy.

Interpreting slope parameters

It's sometimes useful to think in terms of derivatives to interpret estimated slope parameters. If we have a relationship:

$$Y_i = \beta_0 + \beta_1 X_i + u_i$$

then, if we want to find the marginal effect of a change in X on Y, this is equivalent to (partially) differentiating the expression with respect to ΔX:

$$\frac{\partial Y_i}{\partial X_i} = \beta_1$$

Now, we can think of this derivative as being the change in Y (often denoted as ΔY) divided by the change in X (often denoted ΔX):

$$\frac{\Delta Y}{\Delta X} = \beta_1$$

This means that we can calculate the change in Y due to a change in X of size ΔX:

$$\Delta Y = \beta_1 \Delta X$$

So, if X increased by 2 (i.e. $\Delta X = 2$), then Y would increase by $\Delta Y = 2 \times \beta_1$.

Of course, if we model a non-linear relationship between X and Y, then this expression will only be approximately true. However, the approximation holds for relatively small changes in the explanatory variable.

Again, the intercept is trickier to interpret, as the literal interpretation is that it would be the life expectancy when countries spend nothing on healthcare. This indicates that the model predicts that, if a country spends nothing on healthcare, life expectancy would be 76.684 years.

Was a linear model appropriate?

Looking at Figure 23.25, we can see that we have fitted a straight line through the data, but the data appears to be curving. Thinking of economic theory, we wouldn't, necessarily, expect a linear relationship between spending on healthcare and life expectancy. At some point, we would expect to have diminishing returns—you cannot continuously increase life expectancy just by spending more money on healthcare!

The non-linearity can be seen in the data. Just by looking at the scatter plot of the data, we can see a non-linearity where life expectancies begin to flatten off as spending gets to about $4,000 per capita. As such, this suggests that maybe a linear model isn't the most appropriate model to consider here. Maybe we should try to introduce a model involving a quadratic term, as shown in Figure 23.26? Or maybe we should try to make use of logs to linearize the relationship?

We will see in subsequent chapters how we can estimate non-linear relationships between economic variables.

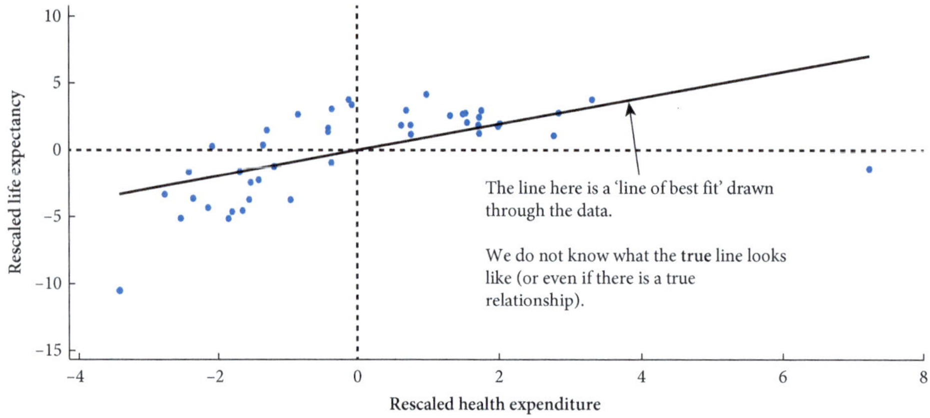

Figure 23.25 Life expectancy plotted against per capita spending on healthcare, with the OLS line of best fit included (2019 data, from the OECD).

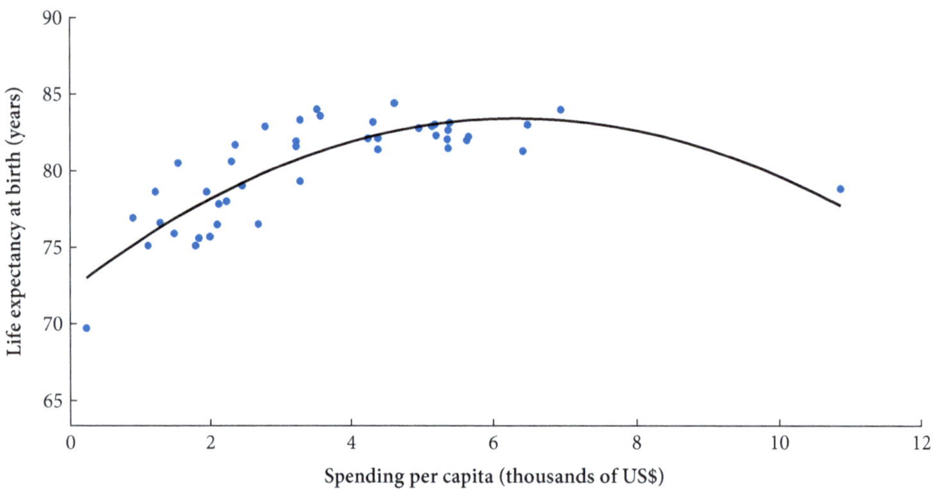

Figure 23.26 Life expectancy at birth plotted against spending per capita on healthcare, with a non-linear function fitted through the data.

Health warning: Sometimes the OLS estimates will not exist

On some occasions, when you have collected data, you will not be able to estimate OLS—for example, if you are interested in estimating:

$$Y_i = \beta_0 + \beta_1 X_i + u_i$$

but unbeknownst to you, all of the observations of X_i are constant (e.g. it might be that every observation was equal to 5). In this example, OLS would be impossible.

The reason for this comes from the formula for the OLS estimator:

$$\hat{\beta}_1 = \frac{\sum_{i=1}^{n}(Y_i - \overline{Y})(X_i - \overline{X})}{\sum_{j=1}^{n}(X_j - \overline{X})^2}$$

If every observation of X_i is a constant (say, equal to 5), then $\overline{X} = 5$ as well. Then, every term in the summation on the denominator will also be equal to zero: $\sum_{j=1}^{n} 0^2 = 0$. As such, the denominator of the estimator will be equal to zero, and $\hat{\beta}$ would be undefined.

- It is impossible to estimate this relationship using OLS, if all of the observations of X_i are constant.

However, even if one observation of X_i is different (e.g. if you had 99 observations of $X_i = 5$, and 1 observation of $X_i = 7$), then OLS could be estimated.

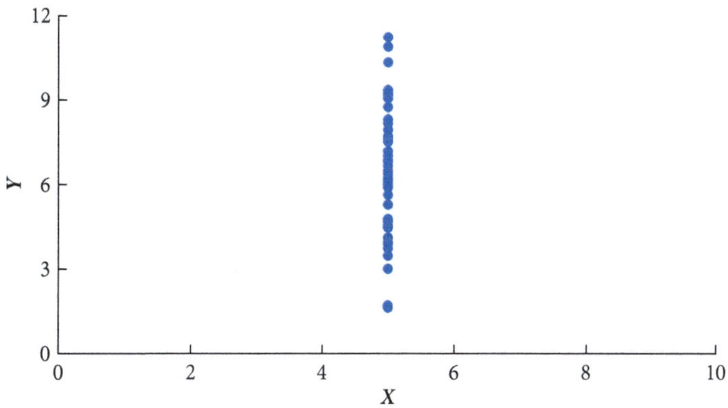

Summary

In this chapter, we have introduced the OLS estimators for estimating two types of relationship. The first type of relationship placed a restriction that the estimated line passed through the origin ($X = 0, Y = 0$), whilst the second allowed the intercept to be non-zero.

When choosing the appropriate estimator, it is important to think about whether it is likely that the true line will pass through the origin or not. If you have any doubt, then you should always err on the side of caution, and allow for the possibility of a non-zero intercept, as imposing that the line passes through the origin may cause bias. Implicitly, both of these estimators assume that there is a straight-line relationship between the two variables, which in some cases may be a poor assumption.

To summarize, suppose that we observe n pairs of observations of X_i and Y_i. The OLS estimators are illustrated in the key formulae below.

Key formulae

	1. Line passes through the origin	2. Line allowed to have non-zero intercept
Relationship being estimated	$Y_i = \beta X_i + u_i$	$Y_i = \beta_0 + \beta_1 X_i + u_i$
Estimator for the slope parameter (i.e. the marginal impact of a change in *X* on *Y*).	$\hat{\beta}^{OLS} = \frac{\sum_{i=1}^{n} Y_i X_i}{\sum_{j=1}^{n} X_j^2}$	$\hat{\beta}_1^{OLS} = \frac{\sum_{i=1}^{n}(Y_i - \bar{Y})(X_i - \bar{X})}{\sum_{j=1}^{n}(X_j - \bar{X})^2}$
Estimator for the intercept	Not applicable. The intercept is defined to be equal to 0 here.	$\hat{\beta}_0^{OLS} = \bar{Y} - \hat{\beta}_1 \bar{X}$
Notes	This estimator should only be used if you have very good reason to believe that the true line should pass through the origin. This might be because you know that when the explanatory variable is equal to zero, then the dependent variable will also be equal to zero.	If you have any suspicion that the intercept could be non-zero, then you should use this estimator. If the true intercept is non-zero, then estimating with the constraint that the intercept is equal to zero will lead to biased estimates of the marginal impact of X on Y.
Any necessary assumptions	OLS can be estimated, even if $var(X) = 0$. In this case, the OLS estimator will produce $\hat{\beta} = \bar{Y}$.	To estimate OLS, there must be variation in the explanatory variable: $var(X) \neq 0$. If all of the observations of X are the same, then OLS cannot be estimated.

Appendix

Proving the disappearing mean

In this chapter, we have used the property that $\Sigma_{i=1}^{n}(Y_i - \bar{Y})(X_i - \bar{X}) = \Sigma_{i=1}^{n}(Y_i - \bar{Y})X_i = \Sigma_{i=1}^{n} Y_i (X_i - \bar{X})$. This relationship is sometimes known as the disappearing mean, and it holds whenever you see a summation of two de-meaned variables.

Proof 1

1. Our initial relationship is the sum of the products of two de-meaned variables, X and Y (although this could be any pair of variables).	$\sum_{i=1}^{n}(Y_i - \bar{Y})(X_i - \bar{X})$
2. If we begin by multiplying out the brackets, we can rewrite this as:	$= \sum_{i=1}^{n}(Y_i X_i - \bar{Y} X_i - Y_i \bar{X} + \bar{Y}\bar{X})$

3. We can split this into two summations, splitting the four terms.	$= \sum_{i=1}^{n}(Y_iX_i - \overline{Y}X_i) - \sum_{j=1}^{n}(Y_j\overline{X} - \overline{Y}\overline{X})$
4. The first summation has a common factor of X_i, which we can take outside the brackets. Similarly, the second summation has a common term of $\overline{X}$, which as it is a constant, can be taken outside the summation.	$= \sum_{i=1}^{n}(Y_i - \overline{Y})X_i - \overline{X}\sum_{j=1}^{n}(Y_j - \overline{Y})$
5. The first part of this is just $\Sigma_{i=1}^{n}(Y_i - \overline{Y})X_i$, which is what we are aiming for. In the second part, we need to show that $\Sigma_{j=1}^{n}(Y_j - \overline{Y}) = 0$.	$\sum_{j=1}^{n}(Y_j - \overline{Y}) = \sum_{j=1}^{n}Y_j - n\overline{Y}$
6. However, since $\overline{Y} = \frac{1}{n}\Sigma_{j=1}^{n}Y_j$, we can rewrite the first term as $n\overline{Y}$.	$= n\overline{Y} - n\overline{Y} = 0$
7. So, going back to point 4:	$\sum_{i=1}^{n}(Y_i - \overline{Y})X_i - \overline{X}\sum_{j=1}^{n}(Y_j - \overline{Y})$ $= \sum_{i=1}^{n}(Y_i - \overline{Y})X_i - \overline{X} \times 0$ $= \sum_{i=1}^{n}(Y_i - \overline{Y})X_i$

Proof 2

1. Our initial relationship is the sum of the products of two de-meaned variables, X and Y (although this could be any pair of variables).	$\sum_{i=1}^{n}(Y_i - \overline{Y})(X_i - \overline{X})$
2. If we begin by multiplying out the brackets, we can rewrite this as:	$= \sum_{i=1}^{n}(Y_iX_i - \overline{Y}X_i - Y_i\overline{X} + \overline{Y}\overline{X})$
3. We can split this into two summations, splitting the four terms.	$= \sum_{i=1}^{n}(Y_iX_i - Y_i\overline{X}) - \sum_{j=1}^{n}(\overline{Y}X_j - \overline{Y}\overline{X})$
4. The first summation has a common factor of Y_i, which we can take outside the brackets. Similarly, the second summation has a common term of $\overline{Y}$, which, as it is a constant, can be taken outside the summation.	$= \sum_{i=1}^{n}Y_i(X_i - \overline{X}) - \overline{Y}\sum_{j=1}^{n}(X_j - \overline{X})$
5. The first part of this is just $\Sigma_{i=1}^{n}Y_i(X_i - \overline{X})$, which is what we are aiming for. In the second part, we need to show that $\Sigma_{j=1}^{n}(X_j - \overline{X}) = 0$.	$\sum_{j=1}^{n}(X_j - \overline{X}) = \sum_{j=1}^{n}X_j - n\overline{X}$
6. However, since $\overline{X} = \frac{1}{n}\Sigma_{j=1}^{n}X_j$, we can rewrite the first term as $n\overline{X}$.	$= n\overline{X} - n\overline{X} = 0$

7. So, going back to point 4:	$\sum_{i=1}^{n} Y\_i(X_i - \bar{X}) - \bar{Y}\sum_{j=1}^{n}(X_j - \bar{X})$ $= \sum_{i=1}^{n} Y\_i(X_i - \bar{X}) - \bar{Y} \times 0$ $= \sum_{i=1}^{n} Y\_i(X_i - \bar{X})$

- So, we have shown that $\Sigma_{i=1}^{n}(Y_i - \bar{Y})(X_i - \bar{X}) = \Sigma_{i=1}^{n}(Y_i - \bar{Y})X_i = \Sigma_{j=1}^{n}\bar{Y}(X_j - \bar{X})$.
- From this proof, it also follows that we can write $\Sigma_{i=1}^{n}X_i(X_i - \bar{X}) = \Sigma_{i=1}^{n}(X_i - \bar{X})^2$, as the second term is just equivalent to $\Sigma_{i=1}^{n}(Y_i - \bar{Y})(X_i - \bar{X})$ where $Y_i = X_i$.

Is the OLS Estimator Unbiased and Consistent?

24

Learning outcomes for this chapter

By the end of this chapter you will be able to:

- Evaluate the asymptotic bias for the OLS estimator, explain the likely source of bias from a simple OLS estimation, and understand the fact that correlation between the error term, u, and the explanatory variable, X, leads to estimates not being causal
- Evaluate the bias in general for the OLS estimator with a single explanatory variable
- Evaluate whether the estimator for the intercept is a consistent estimator

Mathematical tools

- Summations
- Algebra
- The law of iterated expectations

Introduction

In the last chapter, we introduced the OLS estimators, as a way of estimating a linear relationship between two variables. We know that the OLS estimator is constructed by choosing a line of best fit with the smallest sum of squares of the differences between the observed values of the dependent variable, Y_i, and the predicted values based on the fitted line $\hat{Y}_i$.

Suppose that we are estimating the following relationship, between a dependent variable Y and an explanatory variable X:

$$Y_i = \beta_0 + \beta_1 X_i + u_i$$

The OLS estimator for the marginal impact of a change in X on Y is given by:

$$\hat{\beta}_1 = \frac{\sum_{i=1}^{n}(Y_i - \bar{Y})(X_i - \bar{X})}{\sum_{j=1}^{n}(X_j - \bar{X})^2}$$

We wish to examine the properties of this estimator.

- Is the estimator unbiased?
- Is the estimator consistent?

In this chapter, we will examine the bias and consistency of the OLS estimator under various conditions. We will begin by analysing the OLS estimator in the most general circumstances, and then will investigate circumstances which will lead to OLS being both biased and inconsistent. Many textbooks will start with very strong assumptions, such as that the error terms are independent from the explanatory variable, which lead to OLS being both consistent and unbiased. These assumptions are often wrong, and it should be carefully noted that there are very many cases where OLS estimates will suffer from bias. In general, if you are presented with OLS estimates, you should be asking yourself where the bias will come from in those estimates.

In this chapter, we will begin by considering under what conditions OLS will be consistent, and hence what the asymptotic bias will be. We focus on the consistency of OLS, in part because the mathematics is easier to calculate, but also because you can gain a clear, intuitive understanding of what is going on in each case. We will then move on to examine the unbiasedness of the OLS estimator, and consider when the OLS estimator is unbiased.

In Chapter 25, we will go on to explore causes of bias and inconsistency within OLS, including:

- omitted variables bias
- specification errors
- measurement error.

Before we begin, it's useful to remind ourselves about the definitions of unbiasedness and consistency, and how these relate to estimators.

Revision: Definitions

1. Unbiasedness
An estimator is unbiased if on average it yields the 'true' population parameter. For any given realization of the estimator, the estimate will almost certainly not be the true population parameter, but if we were to repeatedly sample from the population, and apply the estimator to lots of different samples, if an estimator is unbiased, the average across all of our estimates would be equal to the true population parameter.
Formally, an estimator $\hat{\beta}$ of a population parameter β is unbiased if and only if:
$E(\hat{\beta}) = \beta$

2. Consistency
An estimator is said to be consistent if, as the sample size gets very large, the probability that any given estimate is within a very small distance of the true population parameter converges towards 1. What this means is that, if an estimator is consistent, with a very large sample size, the estimate should be (approximately) equal to the true population parameter being estimated.
Formally, an estimator $\hat{\beta}$ of a population parameter β is consistent if and only if:
$plim(\hat{\beta}) = \beta$

24.1 Is the OLS estimator consistent?

We will begin this chapter by considering the asymptotic bias and the consistency of the OLS estimator. Remember that the asymptotic bias is the bias of the estimator as the sample size tends towards infinity. Formally, the asymptotic bias of the estimator is given as:

$$\lim_{n \to \infty}[E(\hat{\beta}) - \beta]$$

That is, the asymptotic bias is the limit as the sample size tends towards infinity of the bias of the estimator. Now, provided the estimator converges in probability to some value, then this asymptotic bias is (in most cases) equal to the difference between the probability limit (plim) of the estimator and the true population parameter. That is, we can think of the asymptotic bias of an estimator $\hat{\beta}$, of a population parameter β as:

$$\text{Asymptotic bias} = plim(\hat{\beta}) - \beta$$

We will begin by making no assumptions about the data generating process, but as we progress, we will examine the implications of a number of assumptions.

KEY DEFINITION: PLIMS

If the probability limit of an estimator $\hat{\beta}$ is equal to β, then mathematically, we can say that:

$$\lim_{n \to \infty} P(|\hat{\beta} - \beta| < \varepsilon) = 1$$

That is, as the sample size tends towards infinity, the probability that $\hat{\beta}$ is within some arbitrarily small distance, ε, from the value β tends towards 1. If this condition holds, we can write that:

$$plim(\hat{\beta}) = \beta$$

We may also refer to this as $\hat{\beta}$ converging to β in probability.

An estimator is consistent if the probability limit of the estimator is equal to the true population parameter being estimated. As such, a good place to start might be to take the probability limit of our estimator. Remember that the probability limit examines what happens to the estimator as the sample size tends towards infinity. The probability limit of an estimator is, in essence, the value to which the estimator converges as the sample size tends towards infinity, but the convergence is in terms of probability rather than with certainty. That is, even if an estimator is consistent, and you have observed a very large sample, it is still possible to gain an estimate that is a long way away from the true value of β, but as the sample size tends towards infinity, the probability that you are infinitesimally close tends towards 1.

If an estimator is consistent then the probability limit or plim of the estimator will be equal to the true population parameter being estimated. This means that, as the sample size gets very large, the probability that the estimate, $\hat{\beta}_1$, that you obtain is within some arbitrarily small distance of the true population parameter, β_1, tends towards 1. We can analyse the consistency of $\hat{\beta}_1$ by taking plims.

$$plim(\hat{\beta}_1) = plim\left(\frac{\sum_{i=1}^{n}(Y_i - \overline{Y})(X_i - \overline{X})}{\sum_{j=1}^{n}(X_j - \overline{X})^2}\right)$$

We will use one key rule to evaluate this plim, namely the weak law of large numbers. However, before we can do that, we need to express the estimator in terms of sample means.

Weak law of large numbers

The weak law of large numbers states that if we randomly draw *n iid* observations from a population random variable X, where $E(X) = \mu_X$:

$$plim\left(\frac{1}{n}\sum_{i=1}^{n}X_i\right) = plim(\overline{X}) = \mu_X$$

If we were to divide top and bottom of the estimator by n (i.e. the number of observations), we could rewrite the plim as follows:

$$plim(\hat{\beta}_1) = plim\left(\frac{\frac{1}{n}\sum_{i=1}^{n}(Y_i - \overline{Y})(X_i - \overline{X})}{\frac{1}{n}\sum_{j=1}^{n}(X_j - \overline{X})^2}\right)$$

Dividing top and bottom by n makes no difference to the estimator; this is just equivalent to multiplying by 1. However, the numerator and denominator are now effectively sample means. The numerator, $\frac{1}{n}\Sigma_{i=1}^{n}(Y_i - \overline{Y})(X_i - \overline{X})$, is the sample mean of $(Y_i - \overline{Y})(X_i - \overline{X})$, whilst the denominator, $\frac{1}{n}\Sigma_{i=1}^{n}(X_j - \overline{X})^2$, is just the sample mean of $(X_j - \overline{X})^2$.

Rules of plims

Plims are a little like expectations and have their own specific rules. However, the rules of plims are much simpler than expectations.

• The plim of a sum of estimators is just equal to the sum of plims.	$plim(A+B) = plim(A) + plim(B)$
• The plim of a constant multiplied by an estimator is just equal to the constant multiplied by the plim.	$plim(aA) = a \times plim(A)$
• The plim of a product of estimators is equal to the product of the plims.	$plim(A \times B) = plim(A) \times plim(B)$
• The plim of a ratio of estimators is equal to the ratio of the plims (provided the denominator exists and is non-zero).	$plim\left(\frac{A}{B}\right) = \frac{plim(A)}{plim(B)}$
• The plim of a function applied to an estimator is equal to the function applied to the plim.	$plim(f(A)) = f(plim(A))$

The intuition behind why these rules work is simply that we are looking at what happens as the sample sizes get very large. By taking the plim overall, we are allowing the sample size to increase across the board. So, if we take the plim of a ratio, we are allowing the sample size to increase on both the numerator and the denominator.

From the rules of plims, we also know that the plim of a ratio is just equal to the ratio of the plims, so we can rewrite the probability limit of the OLS estimator as:

$$plim(\hat{\beta}_1) = \frac{plim\left(\frac{1}{n}\sum_{i=1}^{n}(Y_i - \bar{Y})(X_i - \bar{X})\right)}{plim\left(\frac{1}{n}\sum_{j=1}^{n}(X_j - \bar{X})^2\right)}$$

When we are taking the plim, we are allowing the sample size to tend towards infinity. This means that when we take the plim of the top of the fraction, then in effect, the $\bar{Y}$ and the $\bar{X}$ will also have plims taken. These are trivial, due to the weak law of large numbers, which tells us that the plim of any sample mean is equal to the expected value. So, within the plim, wherever you see a sample mean, this can be changed into an **expectation**.

$$\Rightarrow \frac{plim\left(\frac{1}{n}\sum_{i=1}^{n}(Y_i - \bar{Y})(X_i - \bar{X})\right)}{plim\left(\frac{1}{n}\sum_{j=1}^{n}(X_j - \bar{X})^2\right)} = \frac{plim\left(\frac{1}{n}\sum_{i=1}^{n}(Y_i - E(Y))(X_i - E(X))\right)}{plim\left(\frac{1}{n}\sum_{j=1}^{n}(X_j - E(X))^2\right)}$$

Finally, as the sample size tends towards infinity, the numerator (top) of the fraction is just the sample mean of $(Y_i - E(Y))(X_i - E(X))$, so as we take plims, this will become an expectation. Similarly, the denominator (bottom) of the fraction is just the sample mean of $(X_j - E(X))^2$, and so again, as we take plims, this will become an expectation. As such, the plim of the OLS estimator[1] can be written as:

$$plim(\hat{\beta}_1) = \frac{E(Y - E(Y))(X - E(Y))}{E(X - E(X))^2}$$

Hopefully, the numerator and denominator of this expression look familiar to you. We have seen previously that (by definition):

- $E(X - E(X))(Y - E(Y))$ is just the same as the covariance between X and Y, and
- $E(X - E(X))^2$ is just the same as the variance of X.

This means that, when the sample size becomes very large, the OLS estimator, $\hat{\beta}_1$, converges in probability to:

$$plim(\hat{\beta}_1) = \frac{cov(Y, X)}{var(X)}$$

To move any further, we need to start making some assumptions about how the observations of Y are generated.

Assumption 1

The true data generating process for our dependent variable Y is given by:

$$Y_i = \beta_0 + \beta_1 X_i + u_i$$

Assumption 2

The n pairs of observations of X_i and Y_i are drawn such that they are independent and identically distributed. It follows from this that all of the X_i have the same expectation, $E(X)$ and variance $var(X)$, and similarly, all of the Y_i have the same expectation $E(Y)$ and variance $var(Y)$.

It also follows that $cov(X_i, Y_i) = cov(X_j, Y_j) = cov(X, Y)$ for all possible observations, i, j.

Building on Assumption 1, because we are estimating the relationship $Y_i = \beta_0 + \beta_1 X_i + u_i$, we begin by assuming that this is how the observations of Y_i are generated. In this example, we are assuming that there may be a non-zero intercept, and there is a linear relationship (i.e. a straight-line relationship) between X and Y.

As we will see, if this assumption is violated, then OLS yields inconsistent (and biased) estimates of the marginal effect of X on Y.

[1] We have taken a shortcut here. We could have first shown that the numerator can be written as $\Sigma_{i=1}^{n} Y_i X_i - n\bar{X}\bar{Y}$ and the denominator as $\Sigma_{j=1}^{n} X_j^2 - n\bar{X}^2$, and then taken probability limits. We show this in the appendix to this chapter.

If this assumption is correct, then we can substitute this data generating process into the probability limit of our estimator to be able to evaluate the probability limit in more detail.

$$plim(\hat{\beta}_1) = \frac{cov(Y,X)}{var(X)} = \frac{cov(\beta_0 + \beta_1 X + u, X)}{var(X)}$$

Note that we have removed the subscript i from the X and the u because we are looking at the cov(Y,X). We can think of the population random variable Y as being generated by combining X and u in the same functional form as our assumed data generating process.

We can use the rules of covariances to evaluate the numerator. The two elements within the covariance are treated a bit like when we multiply two brackets together. We can look at the covariance between each term in turn.

Rules of covariances

If we have random variables X, Y, and Z, and constants a, b,and c, then:

1. $cov(a, X) = 0$
2. $cov(X, X) = var(X)$
3. $cov(aX, Y) = a \times cov(X, Y)$
4. $cov(aX, bY) = a \times b \times cov(X, Y)$
5. $cov(aX + bY, cZ) = a \times c \times cov(X, Z) + b \times c \times cov(X, Z)$

So, if we begin with the numerator, $cov(\beta_0 + \beta_1 X + u, X)$, we are finding the covariance between $(\beta_0 + \beta_1 X + u)$ and X. We can split this up into three separate covariances:

$$cov(\beta_0 + \beta_1 X + u, X) = cov(\beta_0, X) + \beta_1 cov(X, X) + cov(u, X)$$

Since β_0 is a constant, it automatically follows that $cov(\beta_0, X) = 0$. Similarly, we know that $cov(X, X)$ is just, by definition, the same as the variance of X, and so we can rewrite the expression as:

$$cov(\beta_0 + \beta_1 X + u, X) = 0 + \beta_1 var(X) + cov(u, X)$$

Combining the numerator and the denominator, we have:

$$plim(\hat{\beta}_1) = \frac{\beta_1 var(X) + cov(u, X)}{var(X)}$$

Since this is over a common denominator, $var(X)$, we can split this up into two fractions:

$$= \frac{\beta_1 var(X)}{var(X)} + \frac{cov(u, X)}{var(X)}$$

Since the first term has $var(X)$ on both top and bottom, this cancels, leaving us with:

$$plim(\hat{\beta}_1) = \beta_1 + \frac{cov(u, X)}{var(X)}$$

$\hat{\beta}_1$ will be consistent if $plim(\hat{\beta}_1) = \beta_1$. Since we've shown that (providing Assumption 1 is true), then $plim(\hat{\beta}_1)$ is equal to $\beta_1 + \frac{cov(u,X)}{var(X)}$, this means that if $\frac{cov(u,X)}{var(X)}$ is equal to zero, then the OLS estimator will be consistent. The only way that this can hold is if the error term, u, is uncorrelated with the explanatory variable, X—that is, if $cov(u, X) = 0$.

KEY DEFINITION: EXOGENEITY

An explanatory variable X is exogenous if the explanatory variable is independent from the error term. It would follow from this that $cov(u, X) = 0$. Intuitively, what this means is that we can observe changes in X without anything else changing within the model (i.e. a change in X is not related to a change in u).

As such, if X is an exogenous explanatory variable, it would also follow that $cov(u, X) = 0$, and that the OLS estimator would be consistent.

More formally, we can say that OLS will yield consistent estimates of the marginal effect of X on Y if:

1. We have correctly defined how the dependent variable Y is generated. In this example, this would mean that the data generating process is $Y_i = \beta_0 + \beta_1 X_i + u_i$.
2. The pairs of observations of Y and X are randomly drawn from the population.
3. The X is exogenous, meaning that $cov(u, X) = 0$.

Remember that the u_i term contains all of the other determinants of the dependent variable Y, other than the X variable that we have included, and controlled for. If any of those other determinants of Y are also correlated with the included X variable (i.e. if $cov(u, X) \neq 0$), then OLS will provide inconsistent estimates of the marginal impact of X on Y.

KEY DEFINITION: ASYMPTOTIC BIAS

If the probability limit of an estimator exists, then the asymptotic bias of an estimator is equal to the difference between the probability limit of the estimator and the true population parameter, so in this case:

$$\text{Asymptotic bias} = plim(\hat{\beta}_1) - \beta_1 = \frac{cov(u, X)}{var(X)}$$

If the asymptotic bias is equal to zero, then the OLS estimator will be unbiased in very large samples.

24.1.1 Under what circumstances might we have consistent (and inconsistent) estimates?

We can think about the process of OLS graphically. Suppose that we are estimating the relationship:

$$Y_i = \beta_0 + \beta_1 X_i + u_i$$

We are including X_i as an explanatory variable in the relationship, and we are treating everything else that is a determinant of Y_i as existing within the error term u_i. That is, we are not including any of the other possible determinants of Y_i in our model.

Suppose that there are elements of u_i which determine both the dependent variable, Y_i, and the (included) explanatory variable, X_i. This would mean that we have a relationship that looks something like Figure 24.1. This figure is a directed acyclic graph, which shows causal relationships between variables. Econometricians will often use directed acyclic graphs (DAGs) to map out relationships they are estimating, to help them think about possible endogeneity; that is, to think about where the exogeneity condition might be violated. Each arrow represents pathways.

Since we have not included u in our regression (we have only included X), if there is any relationship, or even correlation between X and u, then the estimated coefficient for a regression of Y on X would represent not just impact of a change in X on Y, but also the impact of u on Y, through the pathway $u \rightarrow X \rightarrow Y$. We have written this in Figure 24.1 as a causal relationship between u and X, but all that is required is a correlation between u and X for β_1 to represent both the direct impact of X on Y, and also the impact of any other determinant of Y that is correlated with X.

That is, the OLS estimator would be inconsistent, because whilst we haven't controlled for the effect of u on Y, since there is a pathway from u to Y through X, the estimated marginal effect, $\hat{\beta}_1$ would represent:

- the direct (marginal) impact of X on Y
- the impact of u on Y through the mediating variable, X.

It is not necessary for u to be a determinant of X for the OLS estimator to be inconsistent, merely that elements of the error term, u, are correlated with the explanatory variable, X. Mathematically, this can be represented as shown in Figure 24.2.

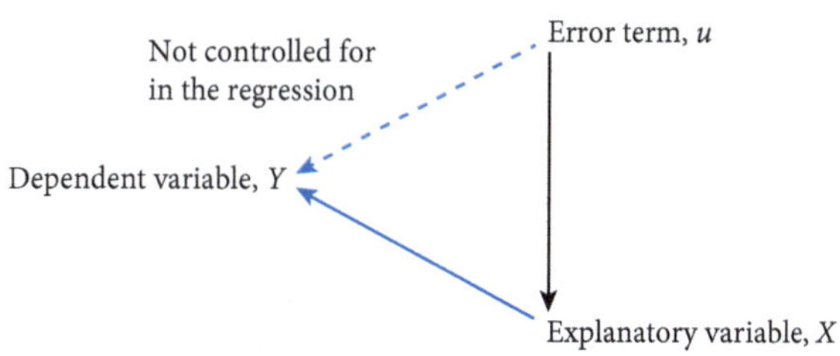

Figure 24.1 Directed acyclic graph (DAG), illustrating pathways in our model.

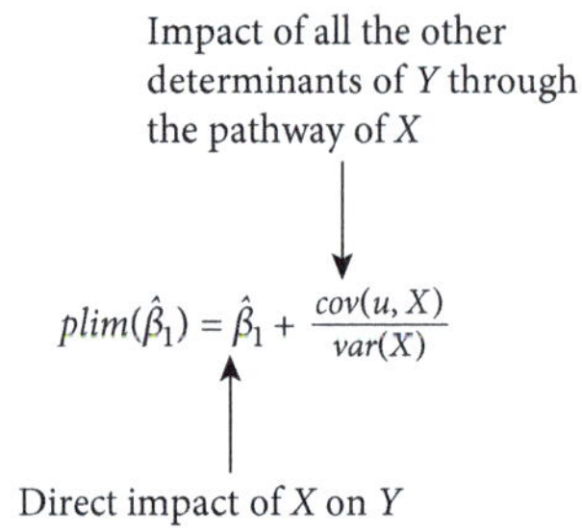

Figure 24.2 Decomposing the probability limit of $\hat{\beta}_1$

CASE STUDY 24.1 Spending on healthcare and life expectancy

To illustrate this, let's return to our example of the relationship between spending on healthcare and life expectancy. We used data from the OECD to estimate the relationship:

$$LifeExp_i = \beta_0 + \beta_1 Spend_i + u_i$$

where $LifeExp_i$ is the life expectancy in country i, whilst $Spend_i$ is the per capita spending on healthcare in country i. We saw in the last chapter that we obtained a positive estimate of the marginal impact of healthcare spending on life expectancy, $\hat{\beta}_1 = 0.972$. The estimated relationship is illustrated in Figure 24.3.

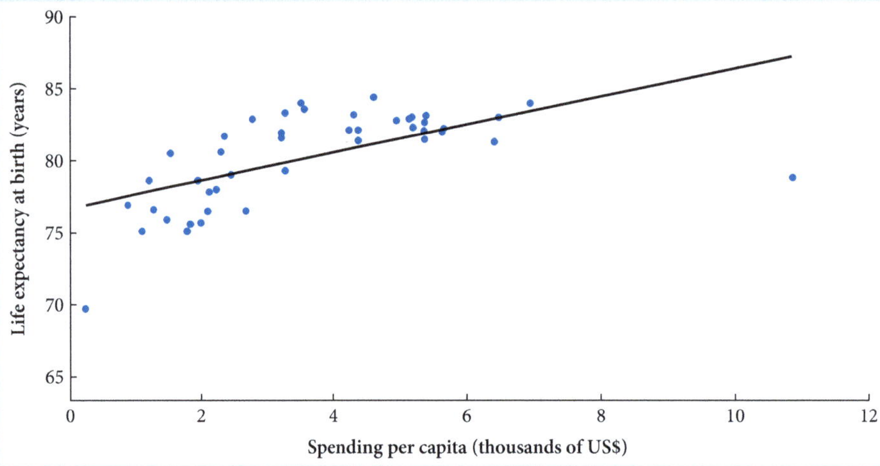

Figure 24.3 Estimating a linear relationship of the impact of healthcare spending on life expectancy (data from the OECD).

However, there are likely to be lots of other determinants of life expectancy in a country; for example, wealthier countries are likely to have higher levels of education, better diets, and also higher spending on healthcare. As such, the income of the country might be a key determinant of life expectancy that is not included within our model, but may be correlated with expenditure on healthcare. More formally, we might expect that GDP is contained within the error term u_i, and this may be correlated with the explanatory variable in the model.

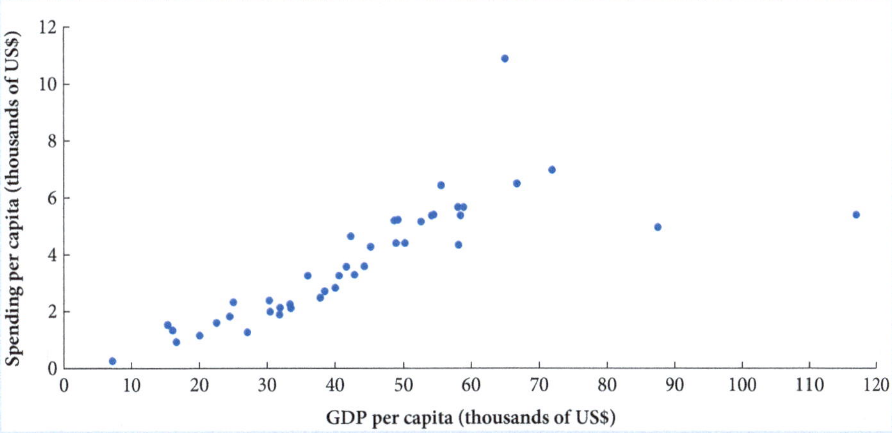

Figure 24.4 Scatter plot of spending per capita on healthcare against GDP per capita.

In fact, looking at the scatter plot between spending on healthcare and GDP in Figure 24.4, we can see a very strong correlation. The observations almost lie on a straight line (remember—if two variables are perfectly (positively) correlated, all the observations will lie on an upward sloping straight line). In this case, the correlation between the two variables is equal to 0.78.

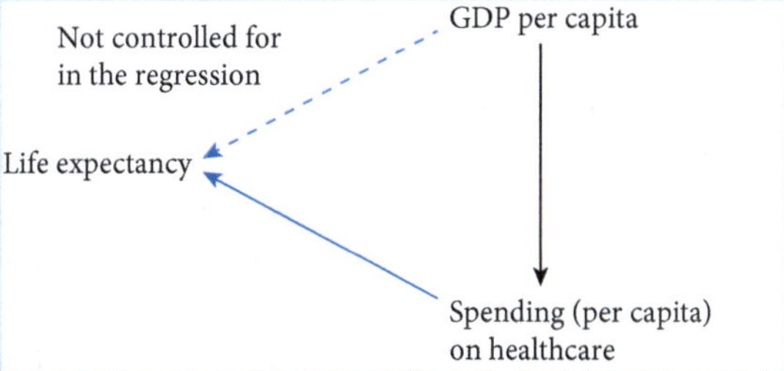

Figure 24.5 Simplified DAG representing the DGP for life expectancy

Again, we can visualize the potenvtial problem using a DAG, as illustrated in Figure 24.5. Based on this evidence, it appears that, since we might expect that GDP per capita is a determinant of life expectancy, and the correlation between GDP per capita and spending per capita on healthcare is so high, we would expect the estimated $\hat{\beta}_1$ to represent not just any causal impact of healthcare spending on life expectancy, but also the impact of GDP per capita on life expectancy as well.

As such, it is likely that, in this example, OLS will provide inconsistent estimates. Even if we collected lots more data, it is unlikely that the estimates will provide asymptotically unbiased, causal estimates of the impact of healthcare spending on life expectancy.

24.1.2 **Using OLS to evaluate experiments**

We've just seen that, in the example of estimating the impact of healthcare spending on life expectancy, the spending variable is likely to be correlated with elements within the error term, and as such OLS will likely produce inconsistent (and biased) estimates of the marginal impact of healthcare spending on life expectancy.

The most obvious place where we can obtain consistent estimates is through experimental means. For instance, suppose that we were interested in the impact of class sizes on student outcomes. If you merely observed a school, then the class sizes might actually be correlated with determinants of students' outcomes; for example, if the school has a priority on improving lower (prior-) attaining students, it may offer more resources to those students (and hence smaller class sizes). This would make it look like smaller classes were associated with lower levels of achievement.

An interesting example of an experiment was carried out in the United States Military Academy at West Point by Carter et al. (2017).[2] In their experiment, the authors were interested in whether having digital devices (such as laptops and tablets) in a classroom had any impacts on students' performance within the class. To evaluate this, they randomly assigned students to classrooms. In some classrooms, students were allowed to use digital devices, and in others, digital devices were prohibited. Students would be taught in the same classroom, either with digital devices permitted, or prohibited, for the entire term.

They then ran a regression of student exam performance against an indicator for whether students were in a classroom that allowed digital devices (or not).

Essentially, they estimated the following relationship:

$$Performance_i = \beta_0 + \beta_1 DigitalDevices_i + u_i$$

where $Performance_i$ is the performance of student i in their assessment, whilst $DigitalDevices_i$ is the indicator of whether the students were allowed digital devices (or not). u_i is the error term, containing all of the other determinants of student performance. The u_i term is likely to include factors such as the teacher in the classroom, the underlying ability of the student, and other characteristics of the student (such as their educational background).

So far, we have expressed the probability limit of the OLS estimator in terms of Y and X when we have been discussing regression specifications $Y_i = \beta_0 + \beta_1 X_i + u_i$, but in this instance, the Y_i term is just $Performance_i$ and the X_i term is just $DigitalDevices_i$. Therefore, if we take the probability limit of the OLS estimator,[3] we can write this as:

$$plim(\hat{\beta}_1) = \beta_1 + \frac{cov(DigitalDevices, u)}{var(DigitalDevices)}$$

[2] S. P. Carter, K. Greenberg, and M. S. Walker (2017), 'The Impact of Computer Usage on Academic Performance: Evidence from a Randomized Trial at the United States Military Academy', *Economics of Education Review*, 56, 118–132.

[3] When we ran a regression of Y against X, this was just $plim(\hat{\beta}_1) = \beta_1 + \frac{cov(X,u)}{var(X)}$.

So the asymptotic bias would be based upon the covariance between the error term, u_i, and whether a student is taught in a classroom allowing digital devices.

- If, for instance, all of the highest ability students were taught in a classroom that allowed digital devices, then this covariance would be positive. We would expect in that instance to see a big, positive estimate. However, the estimate would be inconsistent, and have a large (positive) asymptotic bias, because the observed effect would be due to the ability of the students, and not the impact of the digital devices.
- Similarly, if all of the best performing teachers (i.e. the teachers who gave the biggest improvement to students' performance) were allocated to classrooms where digital devices were prohibited, then we would expect a negative correlation between the error term and the digital device indicator. This would lead to negative bias. We might observe a negative estimate, but this would represent the impact of teachers on students, rather than digital devices.

Because the students are randomly assigned to classrooms, their individual characteristics would be independent of which classroom they are assigned to. This also means that their individual characteristics are uncorrelated with whether they are taught in a classroom where digital devices are allowed or prohibited. Similarly, the authors ensured that teachers for each class were randomly assigned to the groups to ensure that teacher characteristics were also uncorrelated with whether they were teaching in a digital device classroom or not.

Because of this, we can conclude that it is likely that the covariance (and hence correlation) between the *DigitalDevices* measure and the error term will be equal to zero:

$$cov(DigitalDevices, u) = 0$$

Because the students are randomly allocated to the digital devices classroom, we have argued that the covariance term will be equal to zero. Therefore, it is likely that the results are consistent.

The estimates the authors found showed that being taught in a classroom that allowed digital devices led to a reduction in performance of students in their examinations.

Sometimes, experiments can be ethically problematic to run, particularly if you have a prior belief that an innovation will significantly advantage (or disadvantage) either the treatment or control group. As such, where experiments are not practical, economists will often look for **natural experiments**. These often stem from policy changes, whereby a 'treatment' is introduced for one group, and is not introduced for another group, but there are areas where we can observe credibly random variation.

24.1.3 Natural experiments

Natural experiments exist where a treatment has been introduced and we can credibly argue that the treatment is uncorrelated with any of the other determinants of the dependent variable—that is, where the treatment is uncorrelated with the error term. Natural experiments are often seen when there is a new policy that is introduced only to a limited number of individuals, for instance at a geographic level, where there is a similar (often neighbouring) geographic area where the policy is not introduced. If the two geographic areas are sufficiently similar, then the untreated area can be thought of as a control group, and outcomes compared across the treatment and the control group. Of course, if the areas are substantially different, along dimensions that would lead to differences in the outcome variable, then the treatment would not be exogenous, and would be correlated with the error term.

A very famous example of a natural experiment was conducted by Nobel Prize winner David Card and Alan Krueger, who investigated the impact of the minimum wage on employment.

In 1992, the minimum wage was increased in New Jersey by 18.8 per cent, whilst in the neighbouring state of Pennsylvania, no such change occurred. Along the state border, there were a number of fast food restaurants (which customarily paid at the minimum wage), but otherwise, the environments in which the fast food restaurants existed were very similar, and there were no other contemporaneous changes. Card and Krueger took advantage of this, and used a method known as 'difference in differences' to argue that the only change that the New Jersey restaurants experienced (which the Pennsylvania restaurants did not) was the increase in minimum wage, and that they could then measure the changes in employment, using New Jersey as the treatment, and Pennsylvania as the control group.

The argument is that, when looking at changes in employment, because the restaurants were exposed to the same economic conditions, the 'error terms' (i.e. all the other determinants of changes in employment in the fast food restaurants other than minimum wage) were random (and uncorrelated with the increase). The authors found no significant impact of the minimum wage on employment, a result that has been replicated in many studies worldwide.

24.2 Bias in small samples

So far in this chapter, we have examined the asymptotic properties of the OLS estimator; that is, we have looked at what happens when the sample size tends towards infinity. In reality, we won't always observe infinite sample sizes, so we need to think about what happens in smaller samples. If an estimator is unbiased, then we are saying that on average, the estimator produces the correct estimate. Any given realization of the estimator is likely to not be the true population parameter, but, for an unbiased estimator, if we repeatedly sampled from the population, then the average of our estimates would be equal to the true population parameter being estimated.

Remember that, mathematically, an estimator $\hat{\beta}_1$ of a population parameter β_1 is unbiased if $E(\hat{\beta}_1) = \beta_1$. If we are estimating the following relationship:

$$Y_i = \beta_0 + \beta_1 X_i + u_i \qquad \text{Estimated model(1)}$$

then the OLS estimator for the slope is given by:

$$\hat{\beta}_1 = \frac{\sum_{i=1}^{n}(Y_i - \bar{Y})(X_i - \bar{X})}{\sum_{j=1}^{n}(X_j - \bar{X})^2}$$

We are going to use the same assumptions that we have made earlier in the chapter in order to analyse the bias (or otherwise) of this estimator.

Assumption 1

The true data generating process for our dependent variable Y is given by:

$$Y_i = \beta_0 + \beta_1 X_i + u_i$$

Assumption 2

The n pairs of observations of X_i and Y_i are drawn such that they are independent and identically distributed. It follows from this that all of the X_i have the same expectation $E(X)$ and variance $var(X)$, and similarly, all of the Y_i have the same expectation $E(Y)$ and variance $var(Y)$.

It also follows that $cov(X_i, Y_i) = cov(X_j, Y_j) = cov(X, Y)$ for all possible observations, i, j.

If we wish to analyse $\hat{\beta}_1$, a good place to start is to substitute in the data generating process for Y_i into our estimator. However, the first complication is that the estimator includes $(Y_i - \overline{Y})$, rather than just Y_i. It is trivial to show that, if $Y_i = \beta_0 + \beta_1 X_i + u_i$, then $\overline{Y} = \beta_0 + \beta_1 \overline{X} + \overline{u}$, and so we can write that:

$$(Y_i - \overline{Y}) = (\beta_0 + \beta_1 X_i + u_i) - (\beta_0 + \beta_1 \overline{X} + \overline{u})$$

The β_0 terms will cancel, and we can group our terms to give us that:

$$(Y_i - \overline{Y}) = \beta_1 (X_i - \overline{X}) + (u_i - \overline{u})$$

Therefore, we can substitute in our data generating process for Y_i as:

$$\hat{\beta}_1 = \frac{\sum_{i=1}^{n} (\beta_1 (X_i - \overline{X}) + (u_i - \overline{u}))(X_i - \overline{X})}{\sum_{j=1}^{n} (X_j - \overline{X})^2}$$

Multiplying out the brackets on the numerator allows us to rewrite this expression as:

$$\begin{aligned} \Rightarrow \hat{\beta}_1 &= \beta_1 \frac{\sum_{i=1}^{n} (X_i - \overline{X})^2}{\sum_{j=1}^{n} (X_j - \overline{X})^2} + \frac{\sum_{i=1}^{n} (u_i - \overline{u})(X_i - \overline{X})}{\sum_{j=1}^{n} (X_j - \overline{X})^2} \\ &= \beta_1 + \frac{\sum_{i=1}^{n} (u_i - \overline{u})(X_i - \overline{X})}{\sum_{j=1}^{n} (X_j - \overline{X})^2} \end{aligned}$$

By substituting in the data generating process, we have now been able to rewrite our OLS estimator as being equal to the true β_1 plus some other elements.

Disappearing mean trick

For any set of n observations of X_i and Y_i:

$$\sum_{i=1}^{n} (Y_i - \overline{Y})(X_i - \overline{X}) = \sum_{i=1}^{n} Y_i (X_i - \overline{X})$$

To make this easier to evaluate later, we will use the disappearing mean trick that we saw in the last chapter to rewrite the numerator of the second term as $\Sigma_{i=1}^{n}(u_i - \bar{u})(X_i - \bar{X}) = \Sigma_{i=1}^{n}u_i(X_i - \bar{X})$.

$$= \beta_1 + \frac{\sum_{i-1}^{n} u_i(X_i - \bar{X})}{\sum_{j=1}^{n}(X_j - \bar{X})^2}$$

If we wish to analyse whether $\hat{\beta}_1$ is unbiased or not, we need to take expectations of this expression:

$$E(\hat{\beta}_1) = E\left[\beta_1 + \frac{\sum_{i=1}^{n} u_i(X_i - \bar{X})}{\sum_{j=1}^{n}(X_j - \bar{X})^2}\right] = \beta_1 + E\left[\frac{\sum_{i=1}^{n} u_i(X_i - \bar{X})}{\sum_{j=1}^{n}(X_j - \bar{X})^2}\right]$$

We have used two rules here: the first is that the expectation of a sum is just equal to the sum of the expectations, and the second is that the expectation of a constant is just equal to a constant, so $E(\hat{\beta}_1) = \beta_1$. The second term is thus the bias that exists (in small samples) from OLS. If this bias is equal to zero, then OLS is unbiased, whilst if it is non-zero, then OLS is biased:

$$\text{OLS bias} = \beta_1 - E(\hat{\beta}_1) = E\left[\frac{\sum_{i=1}^{n} u_i(X_i - \bar{X})}{\sum_{j=1}^{n}(X_j - \bar{X})^2}\right]$$

This OLS bias is tricky to calculate, without knowing anything about the u_i and the X_i terms, because, unlike plims, the expectation of a ratio is not equal to the ratio of the expectations, and similarly, the expectation of a product is not equal to the products of the expectations. However, we can use the law of iterated expectations to make some progress with evaluating the bias.

Law of iterated expectations

If we know the conditional expectations of a random variable, X, given all of the possible values of Y, then the overall, or unconditional, expectation of X is given by taking the expectation over all possible values that Y can take of the conditional expectations:

$$E(X) = E_Y(E(X|Y = y))$$

This is equivalent to *weighting* all of the conditional expectations by the probabilities relating to each particular outcome of y.

Therefore, we can rewrite the OLS bias as:

$$E\left[\frac{\sum_{i=1}^{n} u_i(X_i - \bar{X})}{\sum_{j=1}^{n}(X_j - \bar{X})^2}\right] = E_{\{X\}}\left[E\left(\frac{\sum_{i=1}^{n} u_i(X_i - \bar{X})}{\sum_{j=1}^{n}(X_j - \bar{X})^2} \mid \{x_1, x_2, x_3, \ldots, x_n\}\right)\right]$$

The notation that we are using here, $E_{\{X\}}$, indicates that we are not just taking the expectation over all possible outcomes of one observation of X_i, but we are taking the expectation over all possible sets of n observations of X. That is, we are taking the expectation over all possible values that we could substitute in for $\{x_1, x_2, x_3, \ldots, x_n\}$.

This helps us, because if we are taking the conditional expectation of $\frac{\sum_{i=1}^{n} u_i(X_i - \bar{X})}{\sum_{j=1}^{n}(X_j - \bar{X})^2}$, we have conditioned on a particular set of observations, $\{x_1, x_2, x_3, \ldots, x_n\}$, and so we can treat all of the observations of X_i as *fixed* within the expectation. We can rewrite the conditional expectation as:

$$E\left(\frac{\sum_{i=1}^{n} u_i(X_i - \bar{X})}{\sum_{j=1}^{n}(X_j - \bar{X})^2} \mid \{x_1, x_2, x_3, \ldots, x_n\}\right) = E\left(\frac{\sum_{i=1}^{n} u_i(x_i - \bar{x})}{\sum_{j=1}^{n}(x_j - \bar{x})^2} \mid \{x_1, x_2, x_3, \ldots, x_n\}\right)$$

The lower case x_i and $\bar{x}$ indicates that these are no longer random X_i, but are now conditioned on by the expectation. The second thing to notice here is that the summation could be rewritten as follows:

$$\frac{\sum_{i=1}^{n} u_i(x_i - \bar{x})}{\sum_{j=1}^{n}(x_j - \bar{x})^2} = \sum_{i=1}^{n} \frac{(x_i - \bar{x})}{\sum_{j=1}^{n}(x_j - \bar{x})^2} \times u_i$$

That is, every observation of u_i is being multiplied by an $\frac{x_i - \bar{x}}{\sum_{j=1}^{n}(x_j - \bar{x})^2}$ term. However, since we have conditioned on the whole set of $\{X\}$ here, we can treat this entire element as a fixed multiplier for the u_i, and so we can take this outside of the expectation:

$$E\left(\frac{\sum_{i=1}^{n} u_i(x_i - \bar{x})}{\sum_{j=1}^{n}(x_j - \bar{x})^2} \mid \{x_1, x_2, x_3, \ldots, x_n\}\right) = \sum_{i=1}^{n} \frac{(x_i - \bar{x})}{\sum_{j=1}^{n}(x_j - \bar{x})^2} E(u_i \mid \{x_1, x_2, x_3, \ldots, x_n\})$$

Putting all of this together means that the bias from OLS is given by:

$$E\left[\frac{\sum_{i=1}^{n} u_i(X_i - \bar{X})}{\sum_{j=1}^{n}(X_j - \bar{X})^2}\right] = E_{\{X\}}\left[\sum_{i=1}^{n} \frac{(x_i - \bar{x})}{\sum_{j=1}^{n}(x_j - \bar{x})^2} E(u_i \mid \{x_1, x_2, x_3, \ldots, x_n\})\right]$$

Unless we know something about the conditional expectation of the error term, we cannot progress any further with this evaluation. Let's make a further, very strong assumption about the distribution of the errors.

Assumption 3

The error terms are independent from any of the observations of the X_i. That is, for any possible set of observations of $\{X\} = \{x_1, x_2, x_3, \ldots, x_n\}$, it will follow that:

$$E(u_i \mid \{x_1, x_2, x_3, \ldots x_n\}) = 0$$

This means that knowing any observed value of the set of $\{X\}$ will tell you nothing about the potential values of the u_i.

If the u_i is independent from all of the possible values of $\{X\}$, it follows that $cov(u_i, X_i) = 0$ for all possible values of i.

This is the strict definition of the explanatory variable being exogenous. Knowing any value of the explanatory variable tells you nothing about the particular value of the error term. Similarly, knowing any particular value of the error term tells you nothing about the value of the explanatory variable.

If we appeal to Assumption 3, we can write that for any set of n observations of $\{X\}$, $E(u_i \mid \{x_1, x_2, x_3, \ldots, x_n\}) = 0$ for all n observations. If we substitute this into the expectation, we have:

$$= E_{\{X\}}\left[\sum_{i=1}^{n} \frac{(x_i - \bar{x})}{\sum_{j=1}^{n}(x_j - \bar{x})^2} \times 0\right] = E_{\{X\}}\left[\sum_{i=1}^{n} 0\right] = 0$$

So, if the observations of X are exogenous, and independent from the observations of the u_i, then OLS is unbiased. In fact, it is possible to show that if our two assumptions are true, then both $\hat{\beta}_0$ and $\hat{\beta}_1$ are unbiased estimators of β_0 and β_1 respectively.

Strictly speaking, in order for $\hat{\beta}_1$ to be unbiased, it is not required that $E(u_i \mid \{X\})$ is equal to zero, but rather just that $E(u_i \mid \{X\})$ is equal to some constant—that is, provided the expectation of u_i is constant for all observations of i does not change.

It should be noted that, if $E(u_i \mid \{X\}) = 0$, it automatically follows that $cov(u, X) = 0$ as well. This means that, if this assumption holds, then not only is OLS unbiased, it will also follow that OLS is consistent. However, remember that the reverse does not hold. OLS can still be consistent, but suffer from bias, since $cov(u, X) = 0$ does not mean that u and X are necessarily independent from each other.

24.3 Consistency of the intercept

So far, we have focused on the consistency (or otherwise) of the slope estimator, $\hat{\beta}_1$, and we have largely ignored the OLS estimator for the intercept. If we estimate the following model:

$$Y_i = \beta_0 + \beta_1 X_i + u_i \qquad \text{Estimated model (1)}$$

then the OLS estimator for the intercept is equal to $\hat{\beta}_0 = \overline{Y} - \hat{\beta}_1\overline{X}$. Before we begin, we will need to make three assumptions about the model we are estimating:

Assumption 1

The true data generating process for our dependent variable Y is given by:

$$Y_i = \beta_0 + \beta_1 X_i + u_i$$

Assumption 2

The n pairs of observations of X_i and Y_i are drawn such that they are independent and identically distributed. It follows from this that all of the X_i have the same expectation $E(X)$ and variance $var(X)$, and similarly, all of the Y_i have the same expectation $E(Y)$ and variance $var(Y)$.

It also follows that $cov(X_i, Y_i) = cov(X_j, Y_j) = cov(X, Y)$ for all possible observations, i, j.

Assumption 3

The error terms are independent from any of the observations of the X_i. That is, for any possible set of observations of $\{X\} = \{x_1, x_2, x_3, \ldots, x_n\}$, it will follow that:

$$E(u_i | \{x_1, x_2, x_3, \ldots x_n\}) = 0$$

If we take probability limits of the estimator, this can be rewritten as:

$$plim(\hat{\beta}_0) = plim(\overline{Y}) - plim(\hat{\beta}_1\overline{X})$$

To evaluate this, we will need two rules: first, that the probability limit of a product is equal to the products of the probability limits, and second, the weak law of large numbers, which tells us that (provided the observations are *iid*), the probability limit of a sample mean is equal to the expected value:

$$= E(Y) - plim(\hat{\beta}_1)E(X)$$

To evaluate this further, we will need to make assumptions about the data generating process for Y. Let's begin by assuming that we have correctly defined the data generating process (Assumption 1). That is, every observation of Y_i can be written as $Y_i = \beta_0 + \beta_1 X_i + u_i$. This means that we can write down the expectation of Y:

$$E(Y) = E(\beta_0 + \beta_1 X + u) = \beta_0 + \beta_1 E(X) + E(u)$$

So, based on Assumption 1, we can rewrite the probability limit of our intercept estimator as:

$$plim(\hat{\beta}_0) = [\beta_0 + \beta_1 E(X) + E(u)] - plim(\hat{\beta}_1)E(X)$$

We already know that, if Assumption 1 is true, and the covariance between the included explanatory variable and the error term is equal to zero ($cov(u, X) = 0$), then $\hat{\beta}_1$ is a consistent estimator of β_1. Let's make a further assumption that $cov(u, X) = 0$, which will allow us to write that:

$$plim(\hat{\beta}_0) = \beta_0 + \beta_1 E(X) + E(u) - \beta_1 E(X) = \beta_0 + E(u)$$

If Assumption 3 is true, then it will automatically follow that $E(u) = 0$ and $cov(u, X) = 0$. If both Assumption 1 and Assumption 2 are true, then the OLS estimator for the intercept will be consistent:

$$\Rightarrow plim(\hat{\beta}_0) = \beta_0 + 0 = \beta_0$$

In reality, Assumption 3 is a very strong assumption, and the requirements for the OLS estimator to be consistent are slightly less strong, namely that:

1. We have correctly defined the DGP.
2. The OLS estimator for the slope, $\hat{\beta}_1$, is a consistent estimator of β_1 (this follows from 1 above and that $cov(u, X) = 0$).
3. The expectation of the error terms is equal to zero ($E(u) = 0$).

Summary

In this chapter, we have explored both the asymptotic bias, and the bias in small samples of the OLS estimator. If we are estimating the following relationship:

$$Y_i = \beta_0 + \beta_1 X_i + u_i$$

then provided we have correctly defined the data generating process, and the observations are *iid*, then the bias, and asymptotic bias, can be defined as follows:

Asymptotic bias of OLS (i.e. level of inconsistency)	Bias in small samples of OLS
$\frac{cov(u, X)}{var(X)}$	$E\left(\frac{\sum_{i=1}^{n}(X_i - \bar{X})u_i}{\sum_{j=1}^{n}(X_j - \bar{X})^2}\right)$

OLS will be consistent if the error term is uncorrelated with the explanatory variable, X. However, it is possible that OLS could be consistent, but still biased. That is, even if $cov(u, X) = 0$, it is possible that the bias in small samples could be non-zero:

$$E\left(\frac{\sum_{i=1}^{n}(X_i - \bar{X})u_i}{\sum_{j=1}^{n}(X_j - \bar{X})^2}\right) \neq 0$$

However, if the error terms and the explanatory variables are independent (that is, $E(u_i|\{x_1,x_2,x_3,\ldots,x_n\}) = 0$ for any set of possible observations $x_1,x_2,\ldots,x_n$), then OLS will be both unbiased and consistent.

We will explore in the next chapter what happens if our assumptions are violated. In particular, we will examine what happens if:

1. We have omitted a variable from the specification that is a determinant of the dependent variable.
2. We have mis-specified the model.
3. We have **measurement error** in the explanatory, or dependent, variables.

Appendix

Finding the probability limit of the OLS estimator from first principles

When we are estimating the relationship $Y_i = \beta_0 + \beta_1 X_i + u_i$, we know that the OLS estimator for the slope parameter can be written as:

$$\hat{\beta}_1 = \frac{\sum_{i=1}^{n}(Y_i - \bar{Y})(X_i - \bar{X})}{\sum_{j=1}^{n}(X_j - \bar{X})^2}$$

Now, we want to show that $plim(\hat{\beta}_1) = \frac{cov(Y,X)}{var(X)}$. This is easier to show, taking the numerator and the denominator separately, and then taking probability limits.

Numerator

We can rewrite the numerator by first multiplying out the brackets, giving us:

$$\sum_{i=1}^{n}(Y_i - \bar{Y})(X_i - \bar{X}) = \sum_{i=1}^{n}(Y_i X_i - Y_i \bar{X} - \bar{Y} X_i + \bar{Y}\,\bar{X})$$

Now, since this is a sum of sums, we can split this up into four separate sums; note that $\Sigma_{i=1}^{n}\overline{YX} = n\overline{YX}$:

$$= \sum_{i=1}^{n} Y_i X_i - \sum_{j=1}^{n} Y_j \bar{X} - \sum_{k=1}^{n} \bar{Y} X_i + n\overline{YX}$$

Now, within the summations $\bar{X}$ and $\bar{Y}$ are constants, so they can be taken outside the summation, giving us:

$$= \sum_{i=1}^{n} Y_i X_i - \bar{X}\sum_{j=1}^{n} Y_j - \bar{Y}\sum_{k=1}^{n} X_i + n\overline{YX}$$

We know that $\Sigma_{j=1}^{n} Y_j = n\overline{Y}$ and $\Sigma_{k=1}^{n} X_i = n\,\overline{X}$. So we can rewrite this as:

$$= \sum_{i=1}^{n} Y_i X_i - n\overline{Y}\overline{X} - n\overline{Y}\overline{X} + n\overline{Y}\overline{X} = \sum_{i=1}^{n} Y_i X_i - n\overline{X}\overline{Y}$$

Denominator

By the same logic, replacing Y_i with X_i, we can rewrite the denominator as:

$$\sum_{i=1}^{n} (X_i - \overline{X})^2 = \sum_{i=1}^{n} X_i^2 - n\,\overline{X}^2$$

So, we can rewrite the OLS estimator as:

$$\hat{\beta}_1 = \frac{\sum_{i=1}^{n} Y_i X_i - n\overline{X}\overline{Y}}{\sum_{i=1}^{n} X_i^2 - n\overline{X}^2}$$

If we wish to examine the consistency of the estimator, we will need to take plims. However, before we do so, it is often easiest to write the estimator in terms of sample means, so we can appeal to the weak law of large numbers. As such, if we divide top and bottom of the fraction by n, we will have:

$$\hat{\beta}_1 = \frac{\frac{1}{n}\sum_{i=1}^{n} Y_i X_i - \overline{X}\overline{Y}}{\frac{1}{n}\sum_{i=1}^{n} X_i^2 - \overline{X}^2}$$

Now, taking plims, we have:

$$plim(\hat{\beta}_1) = plim\left(\frac{\frac{1}{n}\sum_{i=1}^{n} Y_i X_i - \overline{X}\overline{Y}}{\frac{1}{n}\sum_{i=1}^{n} X_i^2 - \overline{X}^2}\right)$$

Now, the probability limit of a ratio is equal to the ratio of the probability limits:

$$= \frac{plim\left(\frac{1}{n}\sum_{i=1}^{n} Y_i X_i - \overline{X}\overline{Y}\right)}{plim\left(\frac{1}{n}\sum_{i=1}^{n} X_i^2 - \overline{X}^2\right)}$$

We also know that the probability limit of a sum is equal to the sum of plims. So we can split both the numerator and denominator into two separate plims.

$$= \frac{plim\left(\frac{1}{n}\sum_{i=1}^{n} Y_i X_i\right) - plim(\overline{X}\overline{Y})}{plim\left(\frac{1}{n}\sum_{i=1}^{n} X_i^2\right) - plim(\overline{X}^2)}$$

Taking each of these terms in turn:

1. $plim\,(\frac{1}{n}\Sigma_{i=1}^{n} Y_i X_i)$ is just taking the probability limit of the sample mean of YX. By the weak law of large numbers, this probability limit will just be equal to $E(YX)$.
2. $plim(\overline{X}\,\overline{Y})$ is the probability limit of a product of variables; this can be rewritten as $plim(\overline{X})plim(\overline{Y})$. By the weak law of large numbers, $plim(\overline{X}) = E(X)$ and $plim(\overline{Y}) = E(Y)$.
3. $plim(\frac{1}{n}\Sigma_{i=1}^{n} X_i^2)$ is just taking the probability limit of the sample mean of X^2. By the weak law of large numbers, this probability limit will just be equal to $E(X^2)$.
4. $plim(\overline{X}^2)$ can be rewritten as $plim(\overline{X})^2$ (as the square is a function applied to $\overline{X}$). We know that $plim(\overline{X}) = E(X)$, and so $plim(\overline{X}^2) = E(X)^2$.

Combining these gives us:

$$plim(\hat{\beta}_1) = \frac{E(YX) - E(X)E(Y)}{E(X^2) - E(X)^2}$$

However, the numerator is just equal to $cov(Y,X)$ and the denominator equal to $var(X)$:

$$\Rightarrow plim(\hat{\beta}_1) = \frac{cov(Y,X)}{var(X)}$$

Causes of Bias and Inconsistency in OLS

25

Learning outcomes for this chapter

By the end of this chapter you will be able to:

- Recognize where omitted variables bias is likely to exist, and evaluate the likely bias in estimated relationships based on intuition
- Recognize and evaluate the size of bias from mis-specifying the intercept
- Recognize the bias that is caused by using a linear specification to estimate a non-linear relationship
- Recognize and evaluate the bias that is caused by measurement errors in the explanatory variable
- Recognize that (random) measurement error in the dependent variable is not problematic, but that non-random measurement error will cause biased estimates

Mathematical tools

- Equations of straight lines
- Algebra and plims

Introduction

In the last chapter, we showed that, if three (very strong) assumptions were true, then OLS provided both unbiased and consistent estimates. That is, if we are estimating the relationship:

$$Y_i = \beta_0 + \beta_1 X_i + u_i$$

If the following assumptions are true, then OLS will be both unbiased and consistent:

1. The true data generating process for our dependent variable Y is given by $Y_i = \beta_0 + \beta_1 X_i + u_i$
2. The n pairs of observations of X_i and Y_i are drawn such that they are independent and identically distributed.
3. The error terms are independent from any of the observations of the X_i—that is, for any possible set of observations of $\{X\} = \{x_1, x_2, x_3, \ldots, x_n\}$.

In this chapter, we will explore what happens if these assumptions (in particular, assumption 1 and assumption 3) are violated. We will also explore what happens if we have measurement error in either the dependent variable or explanatory variable.

We will focus on causes of OLS being inconsistent. That is, we will focus on the probability limit of the estimator when the sample size becomes very large. The results that we see will be generalizable to the case of smaller sample sizes, but the intuition is much easier to understand when we are dealing with large samples.

25.1 Omitted variables bias

In the last chapter, we showed that if we are estimating the relationship $Y_i = \beta_0 + \beta_1 X_i + u_i$ by OLS, then provided we have correctly defined the data generating process:

$$plim(\hat{\beta}_1) = \beta_1 + \frac{cov(u, X)}{var(X)}$$

That is, the asymptotic bias is equal to $\frac{cov(u,X)}{var(X)}$. We began discussing under what conditions the covariance between the error term and the explanatory variable might be non-zero, and we introduced the idea, when estimating the relationship between life expectancy and healthcare spending, that the wealth of a country (as measured by the GDP) might be a determinant of life expectancy that is also correlated with healthcare spending.

This is an example of what is known as omitted variables bias, which we will explore in more detail here. Suppose that we wish to estimate the following model:

$$Y_i = \beta_0 + \beta_1 X_i + u_i \qquad \text{Estimated model (1)}$$

The error term contains all of the other determinants of the dependent variable, some of which may be correlated with the explanatory variable of interest, and others which may not be correlated with the explanatory variable.

Suppose that there is a second explanatory variable, Z, which is also a determinant of Y_i, such that the true data generating process (DGP) for Y_i is instead:

$$Y_i = \beta_0 + \beta_1 X_i + \beta_2 Z_i + e_i \qquad \text{True DGP(2)}$$

If we estimate model (1), then in essence, we can think of the 'true error term', u_i, in this model to be made up of the impact of Z on Y, and the e_i term. We can effectively write that:

$$u_i = \beta_2 Z_i + e_i$$

We saw, in the previous chapter, that when we estimate model (1) using OLS, the asymptotic bias of the OLS estimator is given by:

$$\text{Asymptotic bias} = \frac{cov(u, X)}{var(X)}$$

We can use this asymptotic bias to evaluate the impact of not including the variable Z within our estimated model. Since we can write that $u_i = \beta_2 Z_i + e_i$, we can substitute these into the formula for the asymptotic bias:

$$\frac{cov(u,X)}{var(X)} = \frac{cov(\beta_2 Z + e, X)}{var(X)}$$

Using the rules of covariances, we can rewrite this expression as:

$$= \beta_2 \frac{cov(Z,X)}{var(X)} + \frac{cov(e,X)}{var(X)}$$

Asymptotic bias caused by any correlation between e and X

$$\beta_2 \frac{cov(Z,X)}{var(X)} + \frac{cov(e,X)}{var(X)}$$

Asymptotic bias caused by omitting Z from our model

What we have done is effectively split the asymptotic bias into two components:

1. $\frac{\beta_2 cov(Z,X)}{var(X)}$ is the element that is caused by omitting Z from the model.

2. $\frac{cov(e,X)}{var(X)}$ is the element caused by any correlation between the explanatory variable, X, and the error term, e.

If we estimate the relationship, omitting Z from the model, this will cause bias if two conditions are met:[1]

1. Z has a direct impact on the dependent variable, Y (i.e. $\beta_2 \neq 0$).
2. Z is correlated with the included explanatory variable, X.

In the example we saw in the previous chapter, our three key variables were life expectancy (Y), spending per capita on healthcare (X), and GDP per capita (Z). We estimated the relationship:

$$LifeExpectancy_i = \beta_0 + \beta_1 Spending_i + u_i$$

By omitting GDP per capita, we would experience bias if GDP per capita were a direct determinant of life expectancy, and GDP per capita were correlated with spending in healthcare. Suppose, instead, the true data generating process was:

$$LifeExpectancy_i = \beta_0 + \beta_1 Spending_i + \beta_2 GDP_i + e_i$$

We saw that the correlation between GDP per capita, and per capita spending on healthcare, was equal to 0.78, indicating that $cov(Spending, GDP) \neq 0$, and we argued that we would

[1] Note: It is not necessarily the case that OLS will be unbiased and consistent if either of these two conditions are violated, as there is a second part to the asymptotic bias. You would also need that the explanatory variable, X, is uncorrelated with the error term, e.

expect an increase in GDP per capita to lead to higher life expectancy ($\beta_2 > 0$). As such, the asymptotic bias due to omitting GDP per capita would be:

$$= \beta_2 \frac{cov(GDP, Spending)}{var(Spending)}$$

All of the terms in this relationship are likely to be positive; that is:

- We would expect the covariance between GDP and spending on healthcare to be positive; we expect richer countries to spend more on healthcare (per capita) than poorer countries. This correlation is represented in Figure 25.1. As we can see a clear upward trend in the data (with much of the data close to a straight line), we can conclude that there is a positive covariance.
- We do not know what β_2 is, but again, it is reasonable to expect that richer countries have higher life expectancy than poorer countries. This may be due to better education, better sanitation, and better public health programmes. Therefore, it is reasonable to expect β_2 to be positive.
- We know that all variances are, by definition, positive.

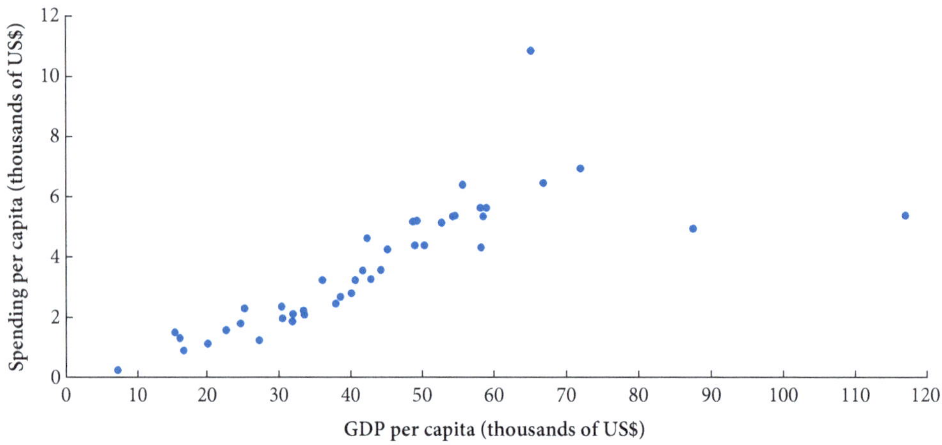

Figure 25.1 Scatter plot of per capita spending on healthcare and GDP (data from the OECD)

Since we have three elements multiplied together, each of which is positive, it is only possible that the overall product is also positive. This means that, by omitting GDP per capita, we would expect to overestimate the marginal effect of 'Spending on healthcare' on life expectancy. That is, the asymptotic bias due to omitting GDP would be positive.

Of course, this is not the entire asymptotic bias. By substituting the variable names in place of Y, X, Z, and e, we know that, if we only include $Spending_i$ as an explanatory variable, then the probability limit of the OLS estimator will be:

$$plim(\hat{\beta}_1) = \beta_1 + \beta_2 \frac{cov(GDP, Spending)}{var(Spending)} + \frac{cov(e, Spending)}{var(Spending)}$$

Positive or negative bias?

We will often talk about bias as being either positive or negative bias. This is merely an indication of the (mathematical) sign of the bias.

If the bias is positive this means that, on average, the estimator overestimates the population parameter. For example:

- If the true $\hat{\beta}_1 = 10$, you might gain an estimate of $\hat{\beta}_1 = 100$.
- If the true $\beta_1 = -20$, you might gain an estimate of $\hat{\beta}_1 = -2$.

In both of these cases, you have overestimated (i.e. your estimate is to the right on the number-line of the true population parameter).

If the bias is negative, then on average your estimate underestimates the population parameter. For example:

- If the true $\beta_1 = 2$, you might gain an estimate of $\hat{\beta}_1 = -20$.
- If the true $\beta_1 = -10$, you might gain an estimate of $\hat{\beta}_1 = -50$.

Worked example 25.1: Years of education

Because education teaches students skills that will be important in the workplace—such as numeracy, literacy, and more advanced skills, such as data analysis (and econometrics)—we would expect students with higher levels of education to have developed greater human capital, and hence gain a higher wage.

As such, using the 2019 UK Labour Force Survey, I have randomly sampled 500 observations, covering male full-time workers, aged 25 to 65. We have 500 pairs of observations of their gross weekly wage ($Wages_i$) and the age at which they completed their education ($Educ_i$). Whilst this is not a perfect measure, it will provide a measure of how many years of education the worker has gained.

As such, we are interested in estimating:

$$Wages_i = \beta_0 + \beta_1 Educ_i + u_i$$

where β_1 is the marginal impact of leaving education one year later. We gain the following estimates:

$$\hat{\beta}_0 = 167.99$$
$$\hat{\beta}_1 = 30.58$$

These estimates suggest that leaving education one year later increases earnings by £30.58 per week. However, it is highly likely that these results suffer from omitted variables bias. A key omitted variable is ability.

In 1973, Nobel Laureate Michael Spence identified that a second reason that individuals might gain more education was to signal their ability: individuals with higher ability want to signal to employers that they have higher levels of underlying productivity (and hence will receive higher wages).[2] His argument was that these higher ability workers find education relatively cheaper to obtain (in terms of the effort they need to put in to gain higher levels of education) than lower ability workers. As such, education can act as a signal of their ability. However, in Spence's model, it is not education that is causing the higher levels of pay, but instead, it is the ability of the worker, and the education level is merely acting as a signal of the underlying productivity of the worker.

In our model, we have not controlled for the ability of the worker. As such, the estimated impact of years of education on weekly wages ($\hat{\beta}_1 = 30.58$) will reflect not just the marginal impact of years of education on wages, but also the impact of ability on wages. The size of the asymptotic bias from omitting ability would be given by:

$$\text{Asymptotic bias} = \beta_2 \frac{cov(Ability, yrsed)}{var(yrsed)}$$

where β_2 is the marginal impact of ability on weekly wages.

- We would expect β_2 to be positive; that is, we would expect higher ability workers to be more productive, and receive higher wages.
- Similarly, if Spence's signalling model is correct, then higher ability workers would gain more education, and so $cov(Ability, yrsed)$ would also be positive.

Since $\beta_2 > 0$ and $cov(Ability, yrsed) > 0$, this would mean that (as variances are always positive), we would expect that the asymptotic bias would be positive. This means that the estimated $\hat{\beta}_1$ would likely be an overestimate of the true impact of education on earnings.

There is a range of studies that have tried to estimate the impact of additional years of education on earnings, but in order for the results to be convincing, the authors need to convince the reader either that they have successfully controlled for ability, or that they have managed to gain exogenous changes in the amount of school experienced by students. This means looking for changes in the number of years of education experienced, which are uncorrelated to the individual students' characteristics.

Colm Harmon and Ian Walker took advantage of policy changes in the UK which increased the school leaving age, first from 14 to 15, and second from 15 to 16.[3] Taking the first increase, their argument was that students leaving school at 14 before the reform would be sufficiently similar to students who left school at 15 after the reform to argue that the only thing that was changing was the number of years of schooling the students experienced. Their results suggest that an additional year of schooling is associated with more than a 15 per cent increase in earnings.

[2] M. Spence (1973), 'Job Market Signaling', *Quarterly Journal of Economics* 87(3), 355–374, https://doi.org/10.2307/1882010

[3] C. Harmon and I. Walker (1995), 'Estimates of the Economic Return to Schooling for the United Kingdom', *American Economic Review* 85(5), 1278–1286, http://www.jstor.org/stable/2950988.

25.1.1 Summary of omitted variables bias

Omitted variables bias occurs when you omit a determinant of the dependent variable that is correlated with an included explanatory variable. The direction of the asymptotic bias (i.e. positive or negative) is determined by the product of the marginal effect of the omitted variable on the dependent variable, and the covariance between the omitted variable and the included explanatory variable.

So, if the true data generating process for a dependent variable, Y, is:

$$Y_i = \beta_0 + \beta_1 X_i + \beta_2 Z_i + e_i \qquad \text{True DGP}$$

but we estimate a relationship with Y as the dependent variable, and only include X as the explanatory variable:

$$Y_i = \beta_0 + \beta_1 X_i + u_i \qquad \text{Estimated model}$$

then the size of the asymptotic bias caused by omitting the Z variable will be equal to $\beta_2 \dfrac{cov(Z,X)}{var(X)}$:

- If either $\beta_2 = 0$ (i.e. Z is not a determinant of Y), or $cov(Z,X) = 0$ (i.e. Z and X are not correlated), then omitting Z will cause no bias.
- If β_2 and $cov(Z,X)$ are the same sign (i.e. both greater than 0, or both less than 0), then the bias from omitting Z will be positive.
- If β_2 and $cov(Z,X)$ are different signs, then the bias from omitting Z will be negative.

25.2 Model mis-specification relating to the intercept

So far, we have seen two versions of the OLS estimator, depending on whether we impose that the intercept is equal to zero, or allow the intercept to be non-zero.

	Model that we are estimating	OLS estimator for slope parameter
1. Intercept is imposed to be equal to zero	$Y_i = \beta X_i + u_i$	$\hat{\beta} = \dfrac{\sum_{i=1}^{n} Y_i X_i}{\sum_{j=1}^{n} X_j^2}$
2. Intercept is allowed to be non-zero	$Y_i = \beta_0 + \beta_1 X_i + u_i$	$\hat{\beta}_1 = \dfrac{\sum_{i=1}^{n}(Y_i - \bar{Y})(X_i - \bar{X})}{\sum_{j=1}^{n}(X_j - \bar{X})^2}$

Suppose that we are estimating model 1that is, we are imposing that the line passes through the origin (i.e. $X = 0$ and $Y = 0$).

$Y_i = \beta X_i + u_i$	Estimated model

but, in reality the data generating process for Y_i is:

$Y_i = \beta_0 + \beta_1 X_i + u_i$	Actual data generating process for Y_i

The OLS estimator that we will use is $\hat{\beta} = \frac{\sum_{i=1}^{n} Y_i X_i}{\sum_{j=1}^{n} X_j^2}$. We want to know if this estimator will provide consistent estimates of the marginal effect of a change in X on Y. A good place to start is to take plims of the estimator:

$$plim(\hat{\beta}) = plim\left(\frac{\frac{1}{n}\sum_{i=1}^{n} Y_i X_i}{\frac{1}{n}\sum_{j=1}^{n} X_j^2}\right) = \frac{E(YX)}{E(X^2)}$$

A key question is what would be the result if we used this estimator when the true data generating process were $Y_i = \beta_0 + \beta_1 X_i + u_i$, where β_0 was not equal to zero. We can, intuitively, see the impact of this in Figure 25.2.

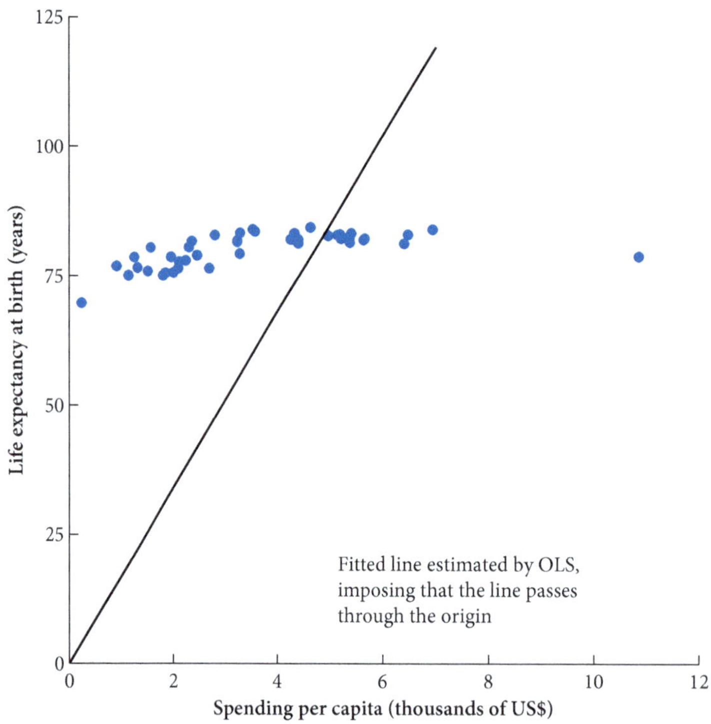

Figure 25.2 Estimating the impact of healthcare spending on life expectancy, imposing that the line passed through the origin (data from the OECD).

By imposing that the line passes through the origin, we have placed an additional constraint on the line which doesn't match the trend of the data. As such, it looks like our estimates would suffer from very strong positive bias (i.e. on average, our estimates would be much more positive than the true effect).

Mathematically, we can prove this by substituting the true data generating process into the probability limit, which will allow us to calculate the asymptotic bias

$$Y_i = \beta_0 + \beta_1 X_i + u_i \qquad \text{Actual data generating process for } Y_i$$

We know that $plim(\hat{\beta}) = \frac{E(YX)}{E(X^2)}$. If we substitute in the true data generating process for Y into the plim, we get:

$$plim(\hat{\beta}) = \frac{E[(\beta_0 + \beta_1 X + u)X]}{E(X^2)}$$

We can multiply out the brackets, and split the numerator up into three separate expectations, giving us:

$$= \frac{\beta_0 E(X) + \beta_1 E(X^2) + E(uX)}{E(X^2)}$$

Since we have a common denominator, we can split this up into three separate fractions, giving us:

$$= \beta_0 \frac{E(X)}{E(X^2)} + \beta_1 \frac{E(X^2)}{E(X^2)} + \frac{E(uX)}{E(X^2)}$$

The multiplier of the true effect, β_1 is $\frac{E(X^2)}{E(X^2)} = 1$, and so the plim of our estimator can be written as:

$$= \beta_0 \frac{E(X)}{E(X^2)} + \beta_1 + \frac{E(uX)}{E(X^2)}$$

The (asymptotic) bias can be thought of as the difference between the probability limit of our estimator and the true population parameter:

$$\begin{aligned} \text{Asymptotic bias} &= plim(\hat{\beta}) - \beta_1 \\ &= \beta_0 \frac{E(X)}{E(X^2)} + \frac{E(uX)}{E(X^2)} \end{aligned}$$

Revision: OLS assumption 3

So far, we've not made any assumptions about the distribution of the errors (u_i). For simplicity, we will assume that the all of the errors, u_i, are independent from the set of observations of $\{X\}$, and have conditional mean equal to zero.

$$E(u_i \mid \{x_1, x_2, x_3, \ldots, x_n\}) = 0, \text{for all } i \text{ and all possible observations } x_1, x_2, \ldots, x_n$$

What this means is that the error terms are independent of the Xs. We saw earlier in this book that, if two random variables are independent, then $E(uX) = E(u)E(X)$. Since the errors are assumed to have zero conditional mean, it will also follow that the unconditional mean is equal to zero. This means that $E(u) = E(uX) = 0$.

Using assumption 3, if the errors have zero conditional mean (when conditioning on any set of observations of the $\{X\}$), then it will follow that $E(uX) = 0$, and so the asymptotic bias can be rewritten as:

$$\text{Asymptotic bias} = \beta_0 \frac{E(X)}{E(X^2)}$$

The size of the asymptotic bias is related to two elements: the average of the X and the true β_0. If the true β_0 is equal to zero, then by estimating $Y_i = \beta X_i + u_i$, we would be estimating the correct specification, and as such, there would be no bias caused.

- i.e. if $\beta_0 = 0$, then the Asymptotic bias $= 0 \times \frac{E(X)}{E(X^2)} = 0$

25.2.1 The strange case of $E(X) = 0$

There is a second (very strange) case where we can still experience no bias. If the true intercept is non-zero, but $E(X) = 0$, then it will also follow that the asymptotic bias will be equal to zero.

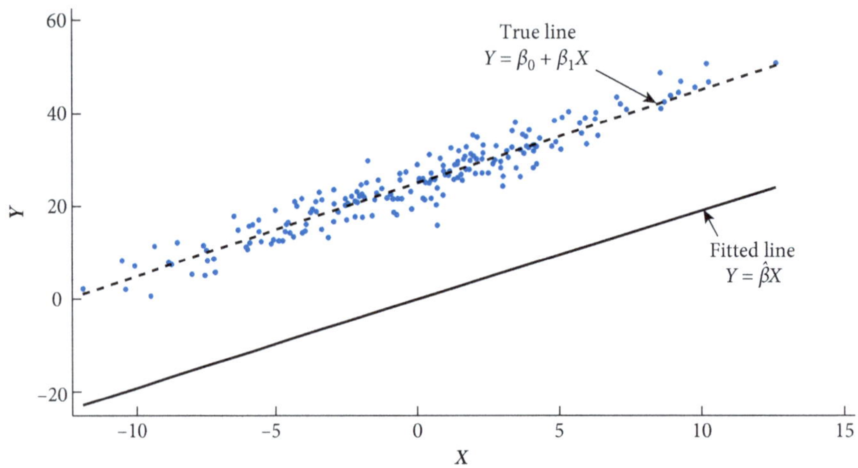

Figure 25.3 An example where $E(X) = 0$.

This is illustrated in Figure 25.3. In the case where $E(X) = 0$, in large samples the slope of the fitted line would be the same as the slope of the true line! However, the reason this a strange case is that the fitted line never passes through the data. In a very large sample, the fitted line will run parallel to the true line, but that fitted line will never cross the data. This, however, is a very special case, where $E(X) = 0$.

Worked example 25.2: Illustrating that when constraints are imposed, the OLS line might not pass through the data

Suppose that you observe the nine pairs of observations of X and Y shown in Table 25.1. It is easy to see that the sample average of X is equal to 0 here.

Table 25.1 Nine pairs of observations of X and Y

Y	3	4	5	6	7	8	9	10	11
X	−4	−3	−2	−1	0	1	2	3	4

If you plot the points on a set of axes (see Figure 25.4), you can see that all of the points lie on a straight line (indicated by the dotted line), and the intercept of the dotted line is equal to 7. Further, the slope of the line on which all of the points lie is equal to $\frac{\Delta Y}{\Delta X} = 1$.

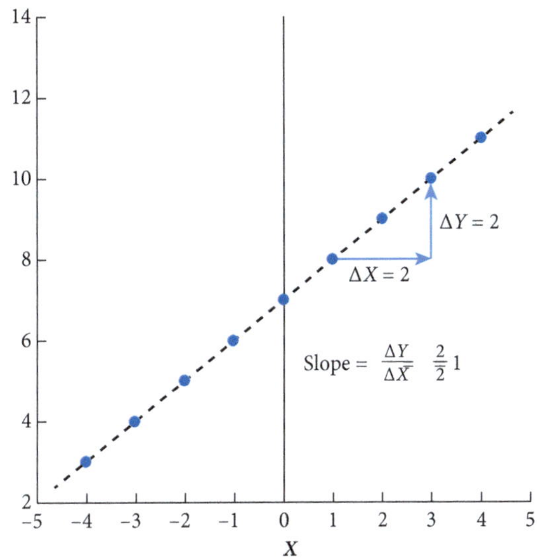

Figure 25.4 Plotting the data.

Suppose now, that we estimate the following relationship by OLS:

$$Y_i = \beta X_i + u_i$$

That is, if we assume that the line passes through the origin, then the OLS estimator is $\hat{\beta} = \frac{\sum_{i=1}^{n} Y_i X_i}{\sum_{j=1}^{n} X_j^2}$, and the estimate of the marginal effect of X on Y will be:

$$= \frac{[(3\times -4)+(4\times -3)+(5\times -2)+(6\times -1)+(7\times 0)+(8\times 1)+(9\times 2)+(10\times 3)+(11\times 4)]}{[(-4)^2+(-3)^2+(-2)^2+(-1)^2+0^2+1^2+2^2+3^2+4^2]}$$

$$= \frac{60}{60} = 1$$

So, if we use OLS, imposing that the intercept is equal to zero, we get an estimate of the slope of the line equal to $\hat{\beta} = 1$ (which is the same as the true slope). However, if we plotted the line, the fitted line would not pass through any of the observations. This is illustrated in Figure 25.5.

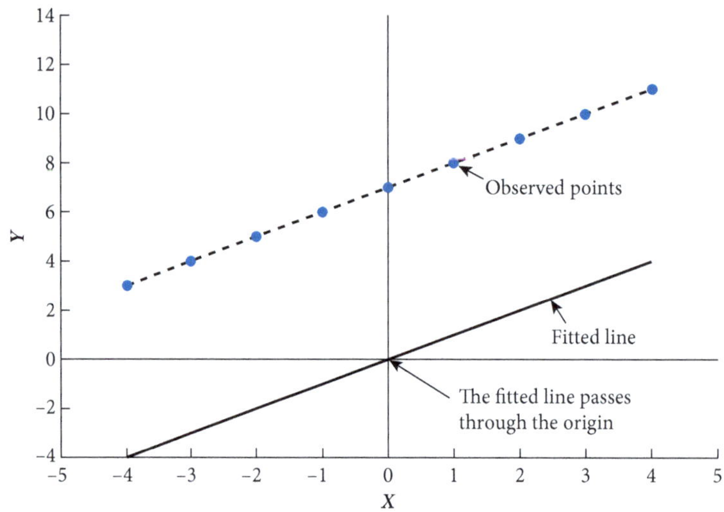

Figure 25.5 Plotting the fitted line when the average of the explanatory variable is equal to zero.

25.2.2 This form of bias can occur whenever we place a restriction on the intercept

In fact, this sort of bias occurs when you place any sort of restriction on the line that you are estimating. For example, we could have constructed our OLS estimator with the intercept conditioned to be equal to 50:

$$Y_i = 50 + \beta X_i + u_i$$

Then the fitted line we are choosing would have an equation $\hat{Y}_i = 50 + \hat{\beta} X_i$, and the fitted residuals would be equal to $\hat{u}_i = Y_i - \hat{Y}_i = Y_i - 50 - \hat{\beta} X_i$. As such, to construct the OLS estimator, we would try to find the optimal $\hat{\beta}$ which minimized:

$$\sum_{i=1}^{n} \hat{u}_i^2 = \sum_{i=1}^{n} (Y_i - 50 - \hat{\beta} X_i)^2$$

If we were to solve this, by choosing the optimal estimator $\hat{\beta}$, imposing that the intercept is equal to 50, the OLS estimator would be given by:

$$\hat{\beta} = \frac{\sum_{i=1}^{n} (Y_i - 50) X_i}{\sum_{j=1}^{n} X_j^2}$$

In general, if you wish to impose that the intercept is equal to k, then the OLS estimator would be:

$$\hat{\beta} = \frac{\sum_{i=1}^{n} (Y_i - k) X_i}{\sum_{j=1}^{n} X_j^2}$$

Whenever we impose a value for the intercept (or any parameter within the fitted line), unless that value is the true population parameter, we risk introducing bias.

To evaluate the asymptotic bias, we need to take plims of the estimator; as before, we can show that:

$$plim\left(\hat{\beta}\right) = plim\left(\frac{\sum_{i=1}^{n}(Y_i - k)X_i}{\sum_{j=1}^{n}X_j^2}\right) = \frac{E[(Y - k)X]}{E[X^2]}$$

Now, if the true data generating process for Y is $Y_i = \beta_0 + \beta_1 X_i + u_i$, we can substitute this into the probability limit, giving us:

$$= \frac{E[(\beta_0 + \beta_1 X + u - k)X]}{E(X^2)}$$

If we multiply out the brackets, and group terms, we get:

$$= (\beta_0 - k)\frac{E(X)}{E(X^2)} + \beta_1 + \frac{E(uX)}{E(X^2)}$$

As such, the asymptotic bias[4] from specifying that the intercept is equal to k is equal to $\frac{(\beta_0 - k)E(X)}{E(X^2)}$. Of course, if we have correctly specified the intercept, then this is not a problem.

25.2.3 Summary of model mis-specification relating to the intercept

Suppose the true data generating process for Y_i is equal to:

$$Y_i = \beta_0 + \beta_1 X_i + u_i$$

where β_0 is non-zero. Then, if you omit the intercept (i.e. you set $\hat{\beta}_0 = 0$), unless the true intercept is equal to zero, or the expected value of your explanatory variable is equal to zero, then your estimate of the marginal effect of a change in X on Y will be biased. The size of the (asymptotic) bias will be equal to $\beta_0 \frac{E(X)}{E(X^2)}$

More generally, if you impose a value (such as k) for the intercept, then:

Asymptotic bias from setting the intercept equal to $k = (\beta_0 - k)\frac{E(X)}{E(X^2)}$

[4] The $\frac{E(uX)}{E(X^2)}$ term relates to any correlation between the error term and the explanatory variable. We have ignored this here, but it may still cause bias.

This means that, if you specify the intercept, then it is likely that your estimates will be generated with bias. Your estimates will only have an asymptotic bias equal to zero if:

- $E(X) = 0$, or
- the true intercept is equal to k.

Of course, these are very singular conditions, and are unlikely to be realized in reality; if you have any doubt, you should always allow the intercept to be non-zero.

Note that in this section, we have only considered the asymptotic bias. The same pattern of results would emerge if we took expectations of our estimator.

25.3 Specification error—Incorrect model

Bias caused by inappropriately setting the intercept equal to zero is easy to avoid. Unless you have exceptionally good reason to do so, you should always allow the intercept to be non-zero.

However, other forms of specification errors are more likely to occur, which could lead to inappropriate estimates of the marginal effect of X on Y.

All of our models that we've estimated so far assumed a linear impact of X on Y. However, what if there was a non-linear relationship? For instance, suppose that we estimated:

$$Y_i = \beta_0 + \beta_1 X_i + u_i \qquad \text{Estimated model(1)}$$

but the true data generating process was:

$$\ln Y_i = \beta_0 + \beta_1 X_i + u_i \qquad \text{True DGP(2)}$$

In the estimated model, we assume that there is a linear relationship between X and Y. That is, a one unit increase in X is always associated with a β_1 increase in Y. However, in the true DGP, the relationship between Y and X is non-linear, such that an increase in X by 1 is associated with a β_1 increase in the natural log of Y.

To illustrate this, I have simulated a data generating process where $\beta_0 = -4$, $\beta_1 = 0.1$, and $E(u) = 0$. Each observation of Y is generated using the True DGP (2):

$$\ln Y_i = -4 + 0.1 \times X_i + u_i$$

The data we observe is illustrated in Figure 25.6. We can see that the data does not follow a nice straight line relationship; instead, the trend increases as the value of X gets larger.

However, if we estimate model (1) via OLS, we will not gain appropriate estimates of β_1. The reason for this is that the marginal effect of X on Y is changing. The line estimated by OLS and the true line are illustrated in Figure 25.7.

You can see that there is a single value of X where the slope of the fitted line is equal to the slope of the true line. However, this is only true in that one single instance, and the estimated line, in general, has a very different slope to the true slope.

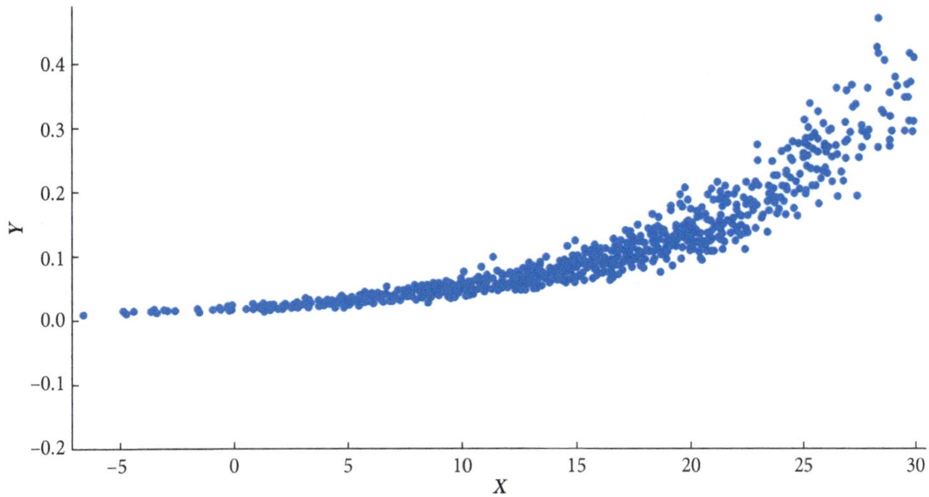

Figure 25.6 An example of observations of Y generated by a non-linear data generating process.

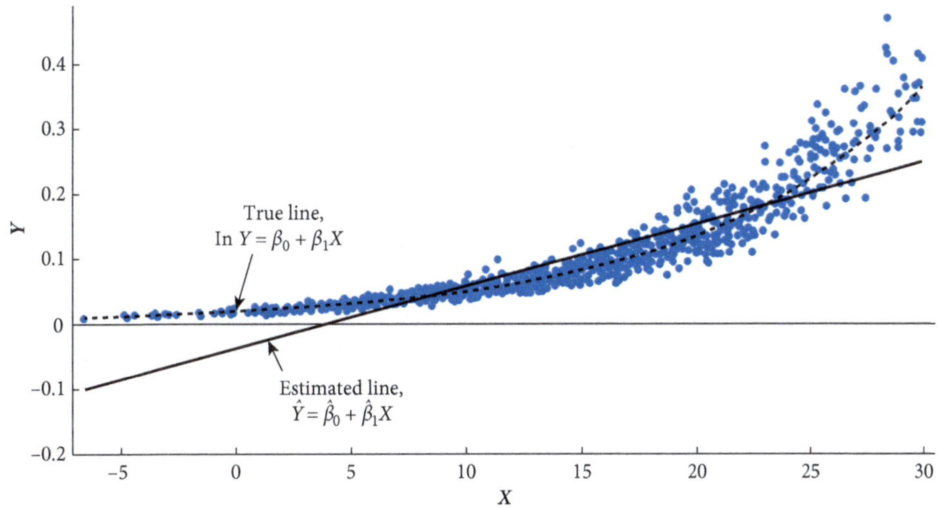

Figure 25.7 Comparing the estimated line (from OLS) and the true line for a non-linear data generating process.

When X is small, the fitted line underestimates the value of Y. When X is in the middle of the range, the fitted line overestimates Y, and in the largest observations of X, the line once again under-predicts the values of Y.

Most importantly, if we tried to estimate this (non-linear) relationship with a linear model, we would assume that the marginal effect of X on Y was constant, whereas in fact, the marginal effect is constantly changing.

25.3.1 More generally

In the previous section, we saw that, if we impose a linear model, but in reality, there is a non-linear relationship between X and Y, then OLS will produce inappropriate estimates. In the example we looked at, we considered a semi-log DGP, where the natural log of Y is related to the level of X.

However, this form of bias will exist whenever you try to fit a non-linear relationship to data where the true data generating process is non-linear. This can include a wide range of function forms for the data generating process. In each of the following cases, the relationship between X and Y would be non-linear:

- $Y_i = \beta_0 + \beta_1 X_i^2 + u_i$
- $Y_i = \beta_0 + \beta_1 \ln X_i + u_i$
- $Y_i = \beta_0 e^{X_i + u_i}$
- $Y_i = \beta_0 + \sin X_i + u_i$
- $Y_i = \sqrt{\beta_0 + \beta_1 X_i + u_i}$

The simple linear model, $Y_i = \beta_0 + \beta_1 X_i + u_i$, can be useful, as it can help us understand the average effect of a change in X on Y. However, to gain an accurate interpretation of the marginal impact of a change of X on Y, we would need to estimate the non-linear specification. We can do this by applying a transformation to either the explanatory variable, X, or the dependent variable, Y (or both!).

25.3.2 Summary

If we mis-specify the model by (for example) trying to fit a linear relationship to data generated via a non-linear relationship, then our estimates will be inappropriate.

This is due to the fact that, with a non-linear data generating process, the marginal effect of a change in X on Y will not be constant, but by fitting a linear relationship, we are assuming that the marginal impact is constant.

It is much more difficult to construct analytical values for the size of the bias, as this will change, depending on the value of X we are considering.

25.4 Measurement error in the explanatory variable

Often, when estimating relationships between economic variables, some of our observations may be measured with error; that is, we may not be able to observe the exact value of the explanatory (or dependent) variable. For example, earlier in this chapter, we used 'age completing education' as a proxy for the number of years of education obtained. However, this is likely to be measured with error for a number of reasons:

i) Students don't start school at birth; in the UK, students begin school in the school-year that they turn five-years-old.
ii) Some people leave education, and then return to education later. As such, even if we subtracted 5 from the age they left education, we might over-state the number of years of education they have obtained.

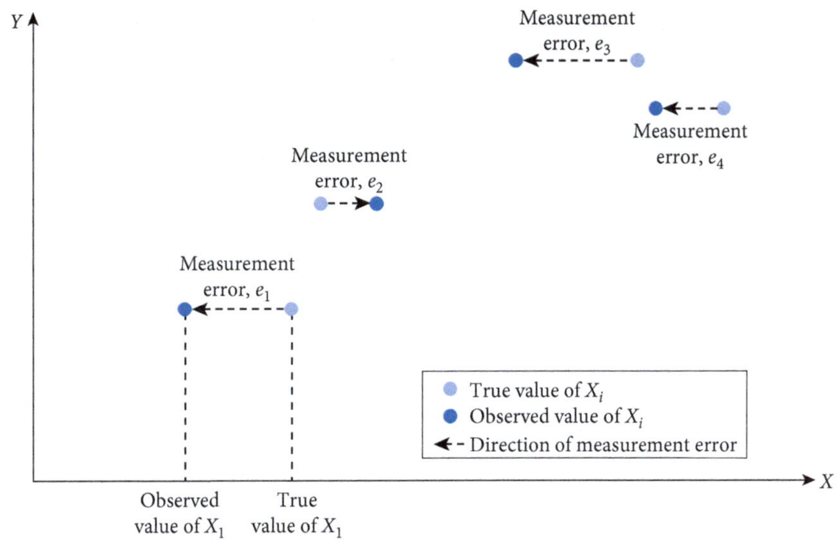

Figure 25.8 Example of measurement error in the explanatory variable.

In this section, we will examine whether measurement error in the explanatory variable causes bias in our estimates. For instance, does it matter if we observe that an individual has obtained 13 years of education, when in fact, they've only obtained 12.5 years? Does it matter if we observe that a country is spending \$4,000 per capita on healthcare, when in fact it is spending \$3,000? It is easy to assume that, as long as the measurement error is random, it won't cause any problems. However, this assumption is wrong.

In fact, if there is a random measurement error in our observed explanatory variable, then OLS will certainly suffer from bias, and the bias will be towards zero.

In Figure 25.8, the light blue dots represent the true values of X (with their corresponding observation of Y), whilst the dark blue dots represent the observed values. We can formalize this a little more. Suppose that we are interested in estimating:

$$Y_i = \beta_0 + \beta_1 X_i + u_i \qquad \text{True DGP(1)}$$

but, rather than observing X_i, we observe Z_i such that:

$$Z_i = X_i + e_i$$

For simplicity, we will assume that the measurement error, e_i, is purely random, such that $cov(X,e) = 0$, and we will also assume that the error term in the data generating process (1) is random with respect to both the observed values of X and the measurement error terms, so that $cov(X,u) = 0$ and $cov(u,e) = 0$.

Then the model that we estimate is:

$$Y_i = \beta_0 + \beta_1 Z_i + u_i \qquad \text{Estimated model (2)}$$

Because we are running a regression of Y against Z (rather than X), we need to replace X with Z in the OLS estimator:

OLS estimator for regression of Y against X	OLS estimator for regression of Y against Z
$\hat{\beta}_1 = \frac{\sum_{i=1}^{n}(Y_i - \bar{Y})(X_i - \bar{X})}{\sum_{j=1}^{n}(X_j - \bar{X})^2}$	$\hat{\beta}_1 = \frac{\sum_{i=1}^{n}(Y_i - \bar{Y})(Z_i - \bar{Z})}{\sum_{j=1}^{n}(Z_j - \bar{Z})^2}$

All that happens when we move from X to Z as our explanatory variable is that, wherever we had seen X in the OLS estimator, we replace that with Z. As such, if we estimate model (2) using OLS, then the probability limit of the OLS estimator can be written as:

$$plim(\hat{\beta}_1) = \frac{cov(Z,Y)}{var(Z)}$$

To evaluate this further, we need to think about the true DGP for Y (given in (1)), and also the effective data generating process for Z. That is, we need to substitute into this expression:

$$Y_i = \beta_0 + \beta_1 X_i + u_i$$
$$Z_i = X_i + e_i$$

Substituting these in gives us:

$$\Rightarrow plim(\hat{\beta}_1) = \frac{cov(X + e, \beta_0 + \beta_1 X + u)}{var(X + e)}$$

We can also expand out the covariance term and the variance term to give us that this probability limit can be rewritten as:

$$= \frac{\beta_1 var(X) + \beta_1 cov(X,e) + cov(X,u) + cov(u,e)}{var(X) + var(e) + 2cov(X,e)}$$

Based on our simplifying assumption that the measurement error, e_i, and the error term in the DGP, u_i, are random, we can drop the covariance terms (as these are all assumed to be equal to zero), and we can rewrite this plim as:

$$\Rightarrow plim(\hat{\beta}_1) = \beta_1\left[\frac{var(X)}{var(X) + var(e)}\right]$$

Now, since variances are always positive, it must be the case that the numerator of the multiplier ($var(X)$) is less than the denominator ($var(X) + var(e)$), and so the whole multiplier of the β_1 is going to be less than 1:

$$\left[\frac{var(X)}{var(X) + var(e)}\right] < 1$$

What this means is that (in large samples), the probability limit of our estimator, when we have random measurement error in the explanatory variable, is not equal to the true population parameter being estimated, but is instead equal to the population parameter, multiplied by a constant, which is less than 1. So, if there is random measurement error in the explanatory variable, you should expect your estimated coefficient to be closer to zero than it is in reality:

- For example, if the true β_1 were equal to 2, you might gain an estimated $\hat{\beta}_1$ equal to 1.5.
- Similarly, if the true β_1 were equal to −2, you might gain an estimated $\hat{\beta}_1$ equal to −1.5.

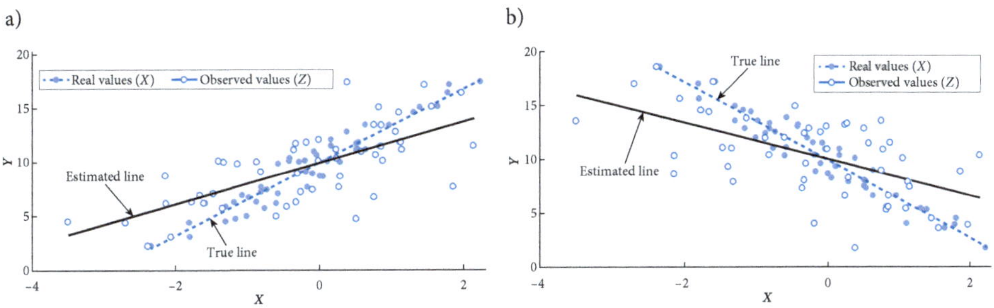

Figure 25.9 Illustrating the impact of (random) measurement error in the explanatory variable.

In both of these cases, the estimate is closer to zero than the true population parameter.

To illustrate this, I have run two simulations to demonstrate the impact of measurement error (see Figure 25.9). In panel a), the true β_1 is positive, and the estimated line is an underestimate of the true line. If you carried this out multiple times, with different samples from the population, you would systematically find that the estimated line is an underestimate of the true line.

In panel b) of Figure 25.9, the true β_1 is negative, and the estimated line is an overestimate of the true line. In both of these cases, the slope of the estimated line, $\hat{\beta}_1$, is closer to zero than it should be in reality. Intuitively, what is going on here is that when we observe Z, the values that we observe for our explanatory variable have a higher variation than the true explanatory variable, but there is no change to the variation in the Y variable. This is a bit like when you draw a diagonal line on a rubber sheet. If you stretch the sheet in only one direction, because the X-axis stretches (say), the line becomes shallower and close to flat. If you were able to stretch the sheet far enough, eventually the slope of the line would get shallower and shallower, and converge towards zero.

Classical measurement error

The measurement error that we have considered here is classical measurement error, such that the measurement error is additive. That is, we have treated the measurement error as simply being an error added on to the true value of X_i:

$$Z_i = X_i + e_i$$

There are other forms of measurement error that we will not consider in this book, including multiplicative measurement error, which causes similar effects, but will lead to measurement error that is correlated with the explanatory variable.

25.4.1 Non-random measurement error

There are a range of possibilities that could arise if the measurement error is non-random, and the impact of the measurement error is determined by the type of measurement error that we observe.

Systematic over- or under-measurement of the explanatory variable

Suppose that every observation of the explanatory variable is over-measured by the same amount. For example, in the case of using age leaving full-time education as a measure of years of education, this might be systematically equal to the total number of years of education plus 5.

To illustrate this, let's consider a simple example. Once again, we are interested in estimating the relationship between Y and X:

$$Y_i = \beta_0 + \beta_1 X_i + u_i$$

Unbeknownst to you, you do not observe the true values of X_i but instead observe Z_i, which is systematically one unit larger than X_i. That is, we can represent Z_i as:

$$Z_i = X_i + 1$$

In this case, the measurement error is constant (i.e. $e_i = 1$ for all i). It is trivial to show that $cov(X,e) = cov(e,u) = 0$. Because the measurement error is constant, all that happens is that each observation is shifted rightwards. That is, for every observation, the dependent variable is unchanged, but the observed explanator is one unit to the right. Intuitively, we can see that this will have no impact on the slope of the line that we estimate. This is illustrated in Figure 25.10, where the data has moved rightwards, and the estimated line has similarly moved rightwards by 1 unit. In fact, we can see, intuitively, that the only impact of this constant measurement error is to adjust the estimated intercept.

We can also show this mathematically. The key observation is that, if the measurement error is constant, it will also be the case that the variance of the measurement error is equal

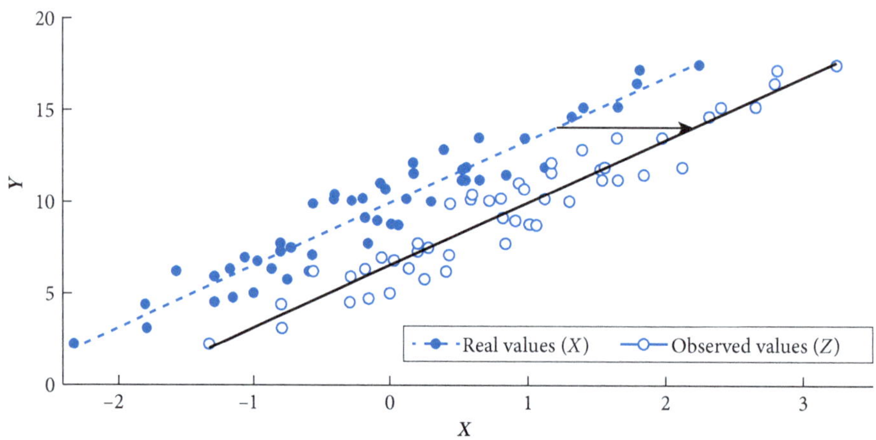

Figure 25.10 The impact of constant measurement error in X.

to zero: $var(e) = 0$. In this case, we can write that the probability limit of the estimator is equal to:

$$plim(\hat{\beta}_1) = \frac{\beta_1 var(X) + \beta_1 cov(X,e) + cov(X,u) + cov(u,e)}{var(X) + var(e) + 2cov(X,e)} = \frac{(\beta_1 var(X) + \beta_1 \times 0 + 0 + 0)}{var(X) + 0 + 2 \times 0}$$
$$= \beta_1$$

So, if the measurement error is constant for all observations, OLS can still yield consistent (and unbiased) estimates of the marginal effect.

Measurement error that is correlated with the explanatory variable

If the measurement error is non-random, and correlated with the true values of the explanatory variable, then OLS will be inconsistent (and biased). However, the direction of the bias will be determined by the correlations between the measurement error and the explanatory variable. For simplicity, let's assume that $cov(X,u) = cov(u,e) = 0$. Then we can write down the plim of our estimator, in the presence of this measurement error, as:

$$plim(\hat{\beta}_1) = \beta_1 \frac{(var(X) + cov(X,e))}{var(X) + var(e) + 2cov(X,e)}$$

To evaluate this, we would need to know about whether there was positive or negative covariance between the X and the e. If the covariance is positive, then the denominator would unambiguously be larger than the numerator, and so $\left[\frac{(var(X)+cov(X,e))}{var(X)+var(e)+cov(X,e)}\right] < 1$. This would yield the same result as when there is random measurement error, with the OLS estimator biased towards zero (although the shrinkage factor will be different). However, if the covariance is negative, the result is uncertain, and will depend on the relative sizes of the covariance between the explanatory variable and the error term, and the variance of that error term.

25.4.2 Summary of measurement error in the explanatory variable

We have seen that, in the case of classical measurement error, OLS will be biased, with the estimated (slope) coefficient biased towards zero. That is, if each observation of the explanatory variable is measured with some (random) measurement error, then the estimated slope coefficient will be closer to zero than the true value.

More precisely, if we are estimating $Y_i = \beta_0 + \beta_1 X_i + u_i$, but rather than observing X_i we observe:

$$Z_i = X_i + \varepsilon_i$$

where ε_i is a random measurement error, such that $cov(X,\varepsilon) = cov(u,\varepsilon) = 0$, then OLS is inconsistent (and biased),[5] with the probability limit of the estimator given as:

$$plim(\hat{\beta}_1) = \beta_1 \left[\frac{var(X)}{var(X) + var(e)}\right]$$

[5] It is a little trickier to prove the size of the bias for the estimator (in small samples), but the same general message will be true; if you have random measurement error, the estimator will be biased towards zero.

With non-random measurement error, the result is a little more nuanced. If the measurement error is constant, then the OLS estimator for the slope parameter will be unbiased and consistent, but the estimated intercept will be biased. However, if the measurement error is correlated with the explanatory variable, then the size of the correlation will affect the bias of the estimator:

$$plim(\hat{\beta}_1) = \beta_1\left(\frac{var(X) + var(X,e)}{var(X) + var(e) + 2cov(X,e)}\right)$$

25.5 Measurement error in the dependent variable

Measurement errors in the dependent variable are much less of an issue than measurement errors in the explanatory variable. Unlike in the explanatory variable, if you have random measurement error in the dependent variable, there is no impact on the bias (or otherwise) of the OLS estimator.

Mathematically, we can prove this in the same way as before. Suppose that we are interested in estimating the following relationship:

$$Y_i = \beta_0 + \beta_1 X_i + u_i \qquad \text{True DGP(1)}$$

but, rather than observing Y_i, we observe W_i such that:

$$W_i = Y_i + \varepsilon_i$$

For simplicity, we will assume that the measurement error, ε_i is purely random, such that $cov(X,\varepsilon) = 0$, and we will also assume that the error term in the data generating process (1) is random with respect to both the observed values of X and the measurement error terms, so that $cov(X,u) = 0$ and $cov(u,\varepsilon) = 0$.

Then the model that we estimate is:

$$W_i = \beta_0 + \beta_1 X_i + u_i \qquad \text{Estimated model (2)}$$

The probability limit of the OLS estimator for estimating (2) is given by:

$$plim(\hat{\beta}_1) = \frac{cov(W, X)}{var(X)}$$

We can substitute in for the data generating process of W_i, which gives us:

$$plim(\hat{\beta}_1) = \frac{cov(Y + \varepsilon, X)}{var(X)} = \frac{cov(Y, X)}{var(X)} + \frac{cov(\varepsilon, X)}{var(X)}$$

Provided $cov(X,u) = 0$, we saw earlier in this chapter that $\frac{cov(Y,X)}{var(X)} = \beta_1$, and if the measurement error, ε, is random with respect to X, then $cov(\varepsilon, X) = 0$, and so:

$$plim(\hat{\beta}_1) = \beta_1$$

If the measurement error is non-random, and is correlated with the explanatory variable, X, then OLS will be biased and inconsistent.

Summary

In this chapter, we have discussed various forms of bias that exist in OLS. Whilst much of the discussion has focused on asymptotic bias, the same lessons can be taken for bias in small samples (although the maths is slightly trickier to work through).

We have also not covered all of the possible forms of bias that you might experience. For example, if two variables are determined simultaneously, with each affecting the other, then it will also follow that OLS will be biased, as the error term will be correlated with the explanatory variable. An example where you may experience this might be in trying to estimate a demand curve; price and quantity are simultaneously determined based on the equilibrium of supply and demand. One way to try to estimate the shape of a demand curve might be to look for exogenous shocks to supply that don't affect demand (e.g. an oil shock) to evaluate the impact of a change in price on quantity demanded.

Problem	Summary (impact on $\hat{\beta}_1$)
1. The explanatory variable is **endogenous**. That is, the explanatory variable is correlated with the error term	OLS is both biased and inconsistent. The direction of bias will depend on whether the correlation between the explanatory variable and the error term is positive or negative: $\text{Asymptotic bias} = \frac{cov(u, X)}{var(X)}$
2. Omitted variables bias. The explanatory variable is correlated with a separate determinant of Y	OLS is both biased and inconsistent. The direction of the bias will depend on both the correlation between the included variable X and the omitted variable Z, and the marginal effect of a change in Z on Y: $\text{Asymptotic bias} = \beta_2 \frac{cov(X, Z)}{var(X)}$
3. Specification error (inappropriately setting intercept equal to zero)	If the true intercept is non-zero, and $E(X) \neq 0$, then OLS is both biased and inconsistent. This bias is caused by forcing the line to pass through the origin, even though the data may not. Provided the observations of X_i are exogenous: $\text{Asymptotic bias} = \beta_0 \frac{E(X)}{E(X^2)}$
4. Random measurement error in the explanatory variable, such that we observe $Z_i = X_i + e_i$ instead of X_i	OLS is both biased and inconsistent if there is random measurement error in the explanatory variable, with the bias directed towards zero. In asymptotics: $plim(\hat{\beta}_1) = \beta_1 \frac{var(X)}{var(X) + var(e)}$

Problem	Summary (impact on $\hat{\beta}_1$)
5. Random measurement error in the dependent variable	OLS is both unbiased and consistent if there is purely random measurement error in the dependent variable, conditional on the Xs being exogenous.
6. Measurement error in the dependent variable, where the measurement error is correlated with X	OLS is both biased and inconsistent. The size of the bias is related to the level of correlation between the measurement error (ε_i) and the explanatory variable (X): $\text{Asymptotic bias} = \frac{cov(\varepsilon, X)}{var(X)}$

Constructing the Variance of the OLS Estimator

26

Learning outcomes for this chapter

By the end of this chapter you will be able to:

- Appreciate that since the OLS estimator is itself a random variable, it has a corresponding variance
- Recognize that, under very strong assumptions, OLS is the best linear unbiased estimator
- Evaluate appropriate methods to improve the precision of the OLS estimates
- Use an appropriate estimator to construct estimates of the variance and standard error of the OLS estimator

Mathematical tools

- Equations of straight lines
- Algebra
- Summation algebra

Introduction

In the last two chapters, we have seen that, under some very strong assumptions, the **ordinary least squares (OLS)** estimator is both unbiased and consistent. We have also begun to interpret point estimates from OLS, but we haven't been able to make any conclusions about the population, because we haven't been able to test hypotheses.

In order to test hypotheses about the population, we will need to know what the variance of the OLS estimator is. In this chapter, we will discuss the **variance** of the OLS estimator, and how we might make our estimates more efficient, and how we might go about estimating the variance of the OLS estimator. In the next chapter, we will go on to use this, to test hypotheses about the population.

26.1 Variance of the OLS estimator

The first thing for us to think about is the variance of the OLS estimator; because the OLS estimator is an estimator, it is itself a random variable. What this means is that whenever we take a separate sample from the population, we will get different estimates of the population parameter.

As an example, suppose that we were interested in estimating the relationship between years of completed education and weekly earnings. I randomly sampled 100 observations of male full-time workers from the 2019 UK Labour Force Survey,[1] and estimated the relationship:

$$Wages_i = \beta_0 + \beta_1 Educ_i + u_i$$

Just as in Chapter 25, $Wages_i$ is the gross weekly wage of worker i, whilst $Educ_i$ is the age at which individual i left education. Based on the initial sample of 100 observations, I gained an estimate of $\hat{\beta}_1 = 79.98$, indicating that leaving education one year later is associated with an increase in weekly earnings of £79.98. However, when I repeated the process, and took a different random sample from the population, I obtained a very different estimate of the marginal effect, with $\hat{\beta}_1 = 30.44$.

This variability is represented in Figure 26.1, where we can see that the estimated line is much steeper for sample 1 than for sample 2.

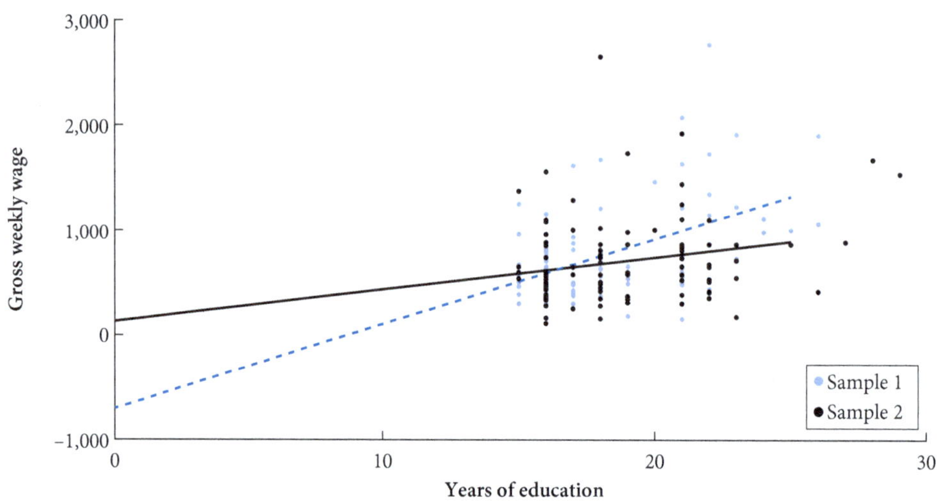

Figure 26.1 Scatter plot and fitted lines illustrating two random samples from the UK Labour Force Survey.

[1] The data can be downloaded from Data sets and exercises at the end of this chapter.

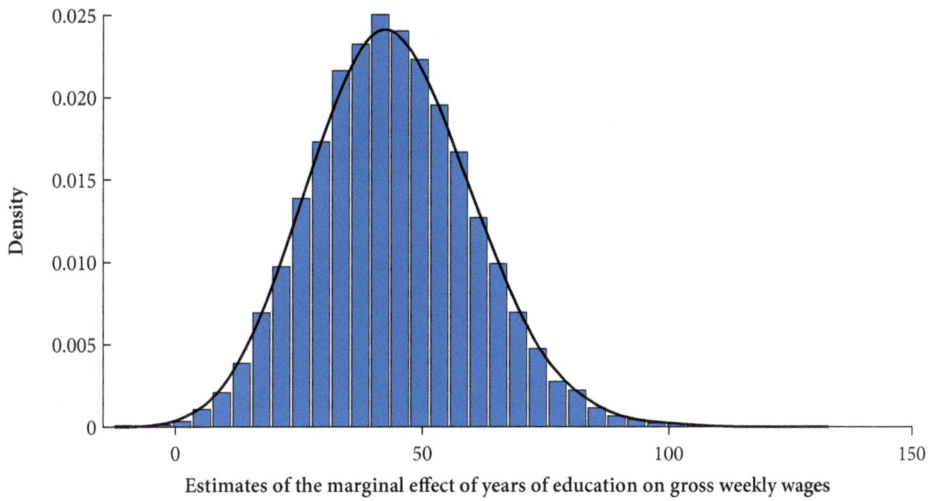

Figure 26.2 Distribution of estimates of $\hat{\beta}_1$ from Monte Carlo simulation.

Does this mean that one of these estimates is wrong? Have we made a mistake in calculating one of the estimates? Remember that every time we take a different sample from the population, we would expect to gain a different estimate of the population parameter, due to sampling variation.

In fact, we could do this repeatedly, each time sampling a different 100 observations from the population, until we have a very large number of estimates, based on 50,000 samples, each with $n = 100$ observations. This is represented in Figure 26.2, which uses a **Monte Carlo simulation**.

There is wide variability of estimates from our 50,000 random samples. Whilst the average of the estimates is equal to 44.07, there is a very wide range of estimate, ranging from $\hat{\beta}_1 = -12.54$ up to $\hat{\beta}_1 = 132.90$. In a way, this is concerning because depending on what sample from the population we observe, we obtain very different results.

However, the fact that there is variability in the estimates across different samples shouldn't come as a surprise. We know that estimators are, themselves, random variables, with an **expectation** and a variance. Because the estimator is itself a random variable, we never know anything for certain about a population parameter. We can only really discuss probabilities.

Suppose that we are interested in estimating the following relationship by OLS:

$$Y_i = \beta_0 + \beta_1 X_i + u_i$$

If we know the variance of the OLS estimator, we can use our estimates to test hypotheses about the true population parameter, and to construct **confidence intervals** around our point estimates. To construct the variance of the OLS estimator, we will make a number of assumptions about the data that we have observed.

Assumption 1	The model is correctly defined. That is, the true data generating process is $Y_i = \beta_0 + \beta_1 X_i + u_i$.
Assumption 2	The pairs of observations of X_i, Y_i are **independent and identically distributed**.
Assumption 3	The explanatory variables are **exogenous**; that is, they are independent from the values of the error term $E(u_i \mid \{x_1, x_2, x_3, \ldots, x_n\}) = 0$ for all i and any set of observations $\{x_1, \ldots, x_n\}$.
Assumption 4	The variance of the error terms are constant, $var(u_i) = \sigma^2$.
Assumption 5	The observations of X_i are **fixed in repeated samples**.

We have seen that, if the first three assumptions are true, then OLS is an unbiased and consistent estimator of β_1. That is, $E(\hat{\beta}_1) = \beta_1$ and $plim(\hat{\beta}_1) = \beta_1$.

There are additional implications of assumptions 2 and 3. If the observations are independent and identically distributed, and the error terms are independent from the values of X_i, it also follows that each observation of the error term will be independent and identically distributed. This will mean that $cov(u_i, u_j) = 0$ for all $i \neq j$.

To make the mathematics easier, we further assume that the variance of the error terms is constant (assumption 4), and that the observations of X_i are fixed in repeated samples (assumption 5). This final assumption is a very unrealistic assumption to make, but it makes finding the variance much easier mathematically.

These assumptions are not necessary to construct the variance of the OLS estimator, but if assumptions 1–5 are true, then the variance of the OLS estimator is given by:[2]

$$var(\hat{\beta}_1) = \frac{\sigma_u^2}{\sum_{i=1}^{n}(X_i - \bar{X})^2}, \quad var(\hat{\beta}_0) = \frac{\sigma_u^2 \sum_{i=1}^{n} X_i^2}{n\sum_{j=1}^{n}(X_j - \bar{X})^2}$$

26.1.1 What happens if assumptions 1–5 are not true?

As you progress through later courses in econometrics, you will explore what happens to the OLS estimators when you relax the assumptions.

When assumption 2 (i.e. that the observations are *iid*) is relaxed and the observations are not independent and identically distributed, we can experience something known as serial correlation. The implication of this is that $cov(u_i, u_j) \neq 0$. We often see serial correlation when looking at data over time. For instance, if you are looking at the stock market price of a firm, yesterday's closing price is highly likely to be a strong predictor of today's closing price.

When assumption 4 is relaxed (i.e. that $var(u_i) = \sigma_u^2$ for all possible values of i), the errors might suffer from heteroskedasticity. The implication of this is that $var(u_i) \neq var(u_j)$ for $i \neq j$.

Both of these are beyond the scope of this book, but the implications of these are that the variance of the OLS estimator would be different.

[2] A proof of the construction of the $var(\hat{\beta}_1)$ is presented in the appendix of this chapter.

You may come across papers where authors try to correct for serial correlation, using methods such as:

- Heteroskedasticity and Autocorrelation Consistent Standard Errors (HACSEs)
- different estimators such as the Newey West estimator.

26.2 Gauss Markov theorem

OLS is a form of linear estimator in terms of Y_i. A linear estimator is one that can be written as a linear function of our dependent variable, in the form:

$$\hat{\beta} = \sum_{i=1}^{n} a_i Y_i$$

where a_i are a series of multipliers of each observation so Y_i, which are either constants or functions only of the explanatory variables. That is, for a linear estimator the a_i cannot be functions of the Y_i.

KEY DEFINITION: SIMPLE EXAMPLE OF A LINEAR ESTIMATOR—THE SAMPLE MEAN

The sample mean, $\bar{Y} = \frac{1}{n}\sum_{i=1}^{n} Y_i$, is an example of a linear estimator, as it can be written in the form:

$$\bar{Y} = \sum_{i=1}^{n} a_i Y_i$$

In this case, a_i is equal to $\frac{1}{n}$ for every observation.

Returning to OLS, we are interested in estimating the relationship:

$$Y_i = \beta_0 + \beta_1 X_i + u_i$$

Using the 'disappearing mean', the OLS estimator can be written as:

$$\hat{\beta}_1 = \frac{\sum_{i=1}^{n}(Y_i - \bar{Y})(X_i - \bar{X})}{\sum_{j=1}^{n}(X_j - \bar{X})^2} = \frac{\sum_{i=1}^{n} Y_i(X_i - \bar{X})}{\sum_{j=1}^{n}(X_j - \bar{X})^2} = \sum_{i=1}^{n}\left[\frac{X_i - \bar{X}}{\sum_{j=1}^{n}(X_j - \bar{X})^2}\right] \times Y_i$$

That is, in the OLS estimator, every observation Y_i is multiplied by $\frac{X_i - \bar{X}}{\sum_{j=1}^{n}(X_j - \bar{X})^2}$. This means that we can express OLS as a linear estimator in terms of Y_i, where $a_i = \frac{X_i - \bar{X}}{\sum_{j=1}^{n}(X_j - \bar{X})^2}$. That is, the estimator is the weighted sum of Y_i, where each observation of Y_i is weighted by a_i.

The Gauss Markov theorem states that, provided assumptions (1), (2), (3), and (4) are true, then OLS is the Best Linear Unbiased Estimator (BLUE estimator) for estimating the relationship between Y and X.

We know that OLS is a linear estimator, and provided assumptions (1), (2), and (3) are true, then OLS is also unbiased. What the Gauss Markov theorem adds is that of the class of estimators that are both linear estimators and unbiased, OLS is the 'best' estimator. In this context, 'best' means that it has the smallest variance.

The variance of the estimator matters because the higher the variance, the greater the variability of the estimates across samples. This means that for an estimator with a high variance, even if the estimator on average produces the correct estimates (i.e. is unbiased), a high variance would mean that any given realization of the estimator could be a long way from the true population parameter being estimated. An unbiased estimator which has a small variance will, on average, produce the correct population parameter, and any given realization of the estimator will be close to the true population parameter.

26.3 How can we improve the efficiency of the OLS estimator?

From the analytical result that $var(\hat{\beta}_1) = \frac{\sigma_u^2}{\sum_{i=1}^{n}(X_i - \bar{X})^2}$, we can start to make some inferences about how we can improve the estimates that we achieve. Based on the Gauss Markov theorem, provided our assumptions are correct, OLS is the BLUE estimator, but, we may be able to improve the estimates (i.e. lower the variance) by collecting alternative data.

We saw in the appendix to Chapter XX the variance of the OLS estimator can be rewritten as:

$$var(\hat{\beta}_1^{OLS}) = \frac{\sigma_u^2}{(n-1)s_X^2}$$

where s_X^2 is the unbiased estimator for the variance of X.

Intuitively, what this tells us is that there are two methods we can use to lower the variance of the estimator (and hence make out estimates more efficient):

1. Increase the sample size. As the variance is inversely proportional to the number of observations (n), as we increase n, the variance of the estimator will decrease.
2. Increase the signal to noise ratio—that is, increase the variance of X compared to the variance of u_i. s_X^2 is the unbiased estimator of the variance of X, and we can rewrite the expression for the variance as:

$$var(\hat{\beta}_1) = \frac{1}{n-1} \times \frac{\sigma_u^2}{s_X^2}$$

If you can increase the variance of X within your sample (i.e. increase s_X^2) without increasing the variability of the u_i, then you can decrease the variance of your estimator (i.e. you can gain more efficient estimates).

26.3.1 Why does the variance of the explanatory variable matter?

There are a number of ways that we might see a lack of variability in the explanatory variable. One way is when we restrict the characteristics of observations.

Suppose that you were interested in the impact of the age completing education on earnings. If you restrict your population to only those individuals who have gained degrees, then most of the population will have values for the explanatory variable of age 21 or 22. That is, you will only have very limited variability in the explanatory variable.

If you wanted to increase the variance of the explanatory variable, you could simply remove the restriction, and consider the effect of age leaving education on all individuals.

It should be noted, however, that this may have other consequences. Suppose that university education has the effect of raising earnings by 5 per cent per year of education, whereas high school education has the effect of raising earnings by 10 per cent per year of education. If you suspect that there are differing returns, then you may not want to include both high school and university education together.

To illustrate the impact of this, consider Figure 26.3. Both of these scatter plots represent data generated using the same data generating process:

$$Y_i = 2.5 + 3 \times X_i + u_i \qquad \text{Data generating process of } Y$$

The fitted line is then estimated using OLS. The only difference between the two diagrams is that in panel a), the X variable is constructed with variance equal to 0.1, whilst in panel b), the X variable is constructed with variance equal to 10. In both cases, the variance of the u_i is equal to 25.

In panel a), because there is very little variation in the X_i, there is very little information about the overall trend of the data. This can be seen, clearly, when comparing the shape of the data in panels a) and b). In panel b), because there is much more variation in the explanatory variable, we get a much clearer indication of the overall trend.

By chance, we can also see that, for this example, the estimate of the marginal effect of X on Y is much closer to the true $\beta_1 = 3$ when we have a large number of observations.

The key reason for this is that, in panel a), the signal from the data about the relationship between X and Y is drowned out by the variation within the error term. Even if we zoomed into the graph, we wouldn't get a good signal about the relationship.

If we were to repeat the process we used to generate the data in panel a), it is possible that we would get an estimate of the marginal effect that is close to 3, but this is much less likely when we have a small variance than if we have a large variance of the explanatory variable.

26.3.2 Monte Carlo simulations of the variance of the OLS estimator

All that being said, this doesn't stop the OLS estimator being unbiased. If we repeated the process from the previous section a very large number of times, we would still expect that the average of our estimates would be equal to 3 (i.e. the true β_1) whether we have used $var(X) = 0.1$, or $var(X) = 10$.

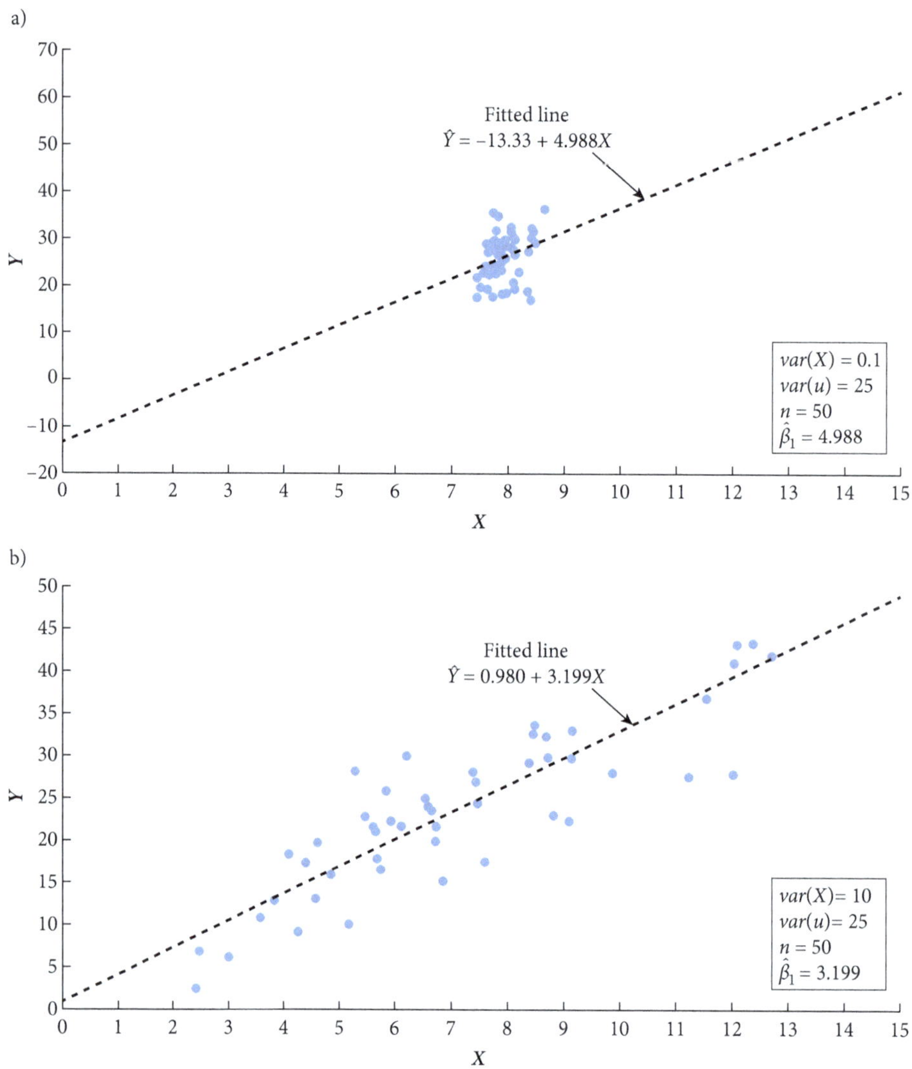

Figure 26.3 An explanatory variable with a small and large variance.

Monte Carlo simulations

In a Monte Carlo simulation, we repeatedly use random sampling from the population to examine the full range of outcomes that we would gain from an estimator. The use of repeated sampling allows us to observe the (experimental) distribution that the estimator follows.

In a Monte Carlo simulation, we specify the expectation, variance, and other population characteristics, and we can compare our estimates with the *known, true* values.

To illustrate this, let's consider a set of three Monte Carlo simulations, designed to investigate the properties of the OLS estimator under three different circumstances:

1. $var(X) = 0.1$
2. $var(X) = 1$
3. $var(X) = 10$

In each of the Monte Carlo simulations, we are going to randomly sample 50 observations of X (with the variance specified), and 50 corresponding, random, observations of u_i, where $var(u_i) = 1$ in all cases. It follows that, since the u_i and X_i are randomly chosen, independently from one another, it also follows that the X is exogenous in our data generating process.

Using these 50 observations of X_i and u_i, we can also generate 50 observations of Y_i, using the data generating process:

$$Y_i = 2.5 + 3X_i + u_i$$

Based on the 50 observations of Y_i and X_i we have now obtained, we can use the OLS estimator to construct an estimate of $\hat{\beta}_1$. We will then repeat this process 1,000,000 times, to gain a distribution of estimates under the three cases. Note that, because of the way that we have constructed the observations of Y_i, the true β_1 is equal to 3 in each of the cases.

The distribution of estimated $\hat{\beta}_1$s is illustrated in Figure 26.4. Firstly, we can see that in each of the cases, the average of the $\hat{\beta}_1$s is equal to 3; the distribution is centred on 3 in each case. This shouldn't be surprising, as we have constructed the data in such a way that $E(u_i|\{X\}) = 0$, and so OLS will be unbiased. What is interesting, though, is the variance (or variability) of the estimates.

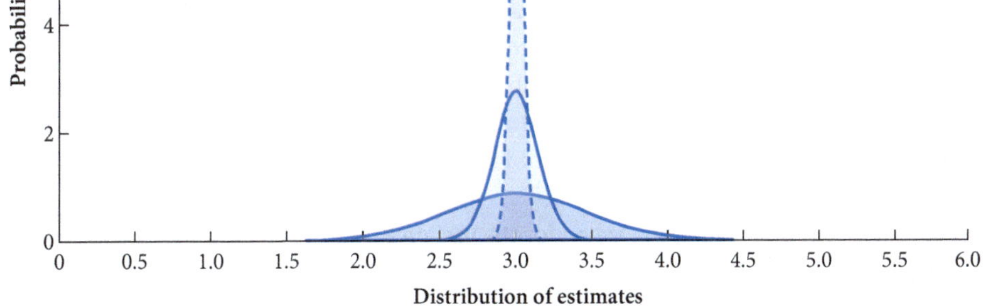

Figure 26.4 Distribution of estimates of $\hat{\beta}_1$ from a Monte Carlo simulation using different variances of the explanatory variable, where the true $\beta_1 = 3$.

Table 26.1 Percentiles of estimates of $\hat{\beta}_1$ from the Monte Carlo simulation

	1st	5th	10th	25th	50th	75th	90th	95th	99th
$var(X) = 0.1$	1.91	2.24	2.41	2.69	3.00	3.31	3.59	3.76	4.08
$var(X) = 1$	2.66	2.76	2.81	2.90	3.00	3.10	3.19	3.24	3.34
$var(X) = 10$	2.89	2.92	2.94	2.97	3.00	3.03	3.06	3.08	3.11

As we increase the variance of the explanatory variable, the variance of our estimates drops proportionately. When we increase the variance of X from 0.1 to 1, the variance of our estimates drops by a factor of 10. Similarly, when we increase the variance of X from 1 to 10, the variance of our estimates again drops by a factor of 10. To see the full impact of the increasing variance of X, it is useful to consider the percentiles of the distribution of our estimates (see Table 26.1).

Remember that, in the probability density plot, the height of the curve represents the relative likelihood of outcomes. When $var(X) = 0.1$, 50 per cent of our estimates of $\hat{\beta}_1$ are either below 2.69 or above 3.31. This corresponds to a probability of 0.5 of gaining a $\hat{\beta}_1$ more than 0.31 away from the true population parameter of $\beta_1 = 3$.

- When we increase the variance of the explanatory variable by a factor of 10, to $var(X) = 1$, the probability of gaining estimates more than 0.31 away from the true population parameter drops to approximately 4 per cent; that is, 96 per cent of the estimates of $\hat{\beta}_1$ are now within ± 0.31 of the true β_1.
- Similarly, when $var(X) = 10$, the probability of gaining a $\hat{\beta}_1$ more than 0.31 away from the true β_1 drops to approximately zero. In our simulation, we didn't see any $\hat{\beta}_1$ estimates outside of this range.

Intuitively, what this means is that, when the variance of X is low, the probability of gaining an estimate that is a long way from the true population parameter is relatively high, but as the variance of the explanatory variable increases, the probability of gaining an estimate far from the true parameter decreases. This ties in with our intuitive understanding from Figure 26.3.

When the variance of X was low, we gained little information about the *true* trend between Y and X, and our estimated marginal effect was a long way from the true β_1 (which was equal to 3 in our simulation). We can see from the Monte Carlo simulation that when $var(X) = 0.1$, there is a much higher probability of observing an estimate a long way from the true β_1. As the variance of the explanatory variable increases, the estimator converges towards the true β_1; the probability of gaining an estimate a long way from the true β_1 gets much smaller.

If we look back at the equation we had for the variance of the OLS estimator, this shouldn't be a surprise:

$$var(\hat{\beta}_1) = \frac{1}{n-1} \times \frac{\sigma_u^2}{s_X^2}$$

Since s_X^2 is an unbiased estimator of the variance of X, we'd expect that, if the variance of X were to double, the variance of the OLS estimator would halve. Similarly (as we've seen here), if the variance of X were to increase by 100 times, the variance of the OLS estimator would drop by a factor of 100.

The second factor that affects the variance of the OLS estimator is the sample size. We can repeat the Monte Carlo simulation that we saw earlier in the chapter, but this time, rather than considering three different variances for the explanatory variable, we can keep the variance of the explanatory variable fixed, and allow the sample size to vary.

Let's consider a Monte Carlo simulation to investigate the properties of the OLS estimator under three different sample sizes:

- $n = 25$
- $n = 100$
- $n = 500$

Just as before, we constructed our observations of Y_i such that the following data generating process is followed:

$$Y_i = 2.5 + 3X_i + u_i$$
$$var(X) = 1$$
$$var(u) = 1$$

Similarly, as before, the X_is and the u_is are independently drawn, and so the X variable is exogenous. The distribution of the estimated $\hat{\beta}_1$ is illustrated in Figure 26.5.

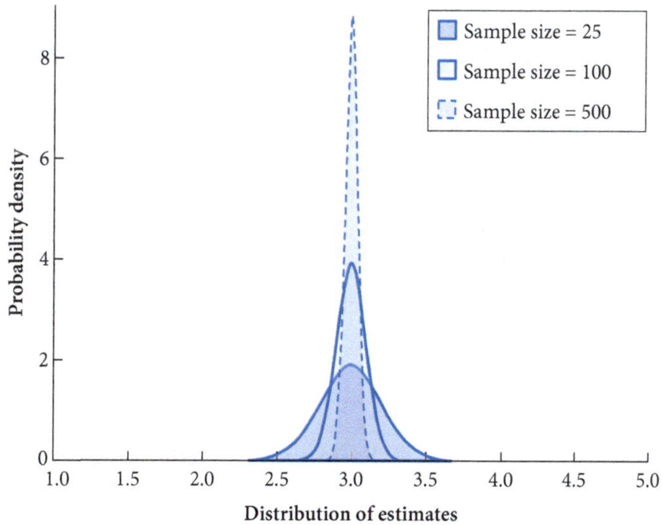

Figure 26.5 Distribution of estimates of $\hat{\beta}_1$ from a Monte Carlo simulation using different sample sizes, where the true $\beta_1 = 3$.

The key takeaway is that, as the sample size increases, the variability of our estimates drops. When the sample size is small, there is a high probability of gaining an estimate a long way from the true population parameter; when the sample size is large, that probability drops to approximately zero.

From both of these sets of Monte Carlo simulations, and our analytic result, if we wish the OLS estimator to be efficient (i.e. have a small variance), then we need to ensure that we have sufficiently large variation in the explanatory variable, and large enough sample sizes. When either of these is small, the OLS estimator can become inefficient, and yield very imprecise estimates of the true population effect.

Central limit theorem

Provided the sample size is large enough, the OLS estimators will follow an approximately normal distribution, centred on the expectation of the estimator, with variance equal to $var(\hat{\beta}_1)$:

$$\hat{\beta}_1 \sim N(E(\hat{\beta}_1), var(\hat{\beta}_1))$$

A further takeaway that we can see from these Monte Carlo simulations is the shape of the distributions of $\hat{\beta}_1$s. The distributions follow our (now very familiar) bell-shaped curve. In fact, just as with the sample mean, the central limit theorem will apply here. Provided the sample size is large enough (larger than about 30), the OLS estimators will follow an approximately normal distribution.

26.4 Estimating the variance of the OLS estimator

Knowing the distribution of the OLS estimators allows us to test hypotheses about the population parameter. For example, if we obtain a $\hat{\beta}_1 = 2.4$, we might be interested in testing the null hypothesis, H_0: $\beta_1 = 3$. Since we know that $\hat{\beta}_1$ will follow a normal distribution, we can test hypotheses in the same way as we have relating to the sample mean.

However, one obstacle still stands in our way before we can carry out statistical tests; that is, whilst we might know that the variance of the OLS estimator can be written as:

$$var(\hat{\beta}_1^{OLS}) = \frac{\sigma_u^2}{\sum_{i=1}^{n}(X_i - \bar{X})^2}$$

because we never observe the true u_i, we have no idea what the σ_u^2 term will be. As such, we will need to estimate it.

Unbiased estimator for variance of the u_i

Whilst we do not observe the true u_i, we can use the **fitted residuals** from OLS as proxies for the true errors. Remember, if we are estimating $Y_i = \beta_0 + \beta_1 X_i + u_i$ then we can construct the fitted residuals as:

$$\hat{u}_i = Y_i - \hat{\beta}_0 - \hat{\beta}_1 X_i$$

We saw that $s_X^2 = \frac{1}{n-1}\sum_{i=1}^{n}(X_i - \overline{X})^2$ is an unbiased estimator for the variance of X. We divide by $n-1$ as a **degrees of freedom** adjustment, because we have used $\overline{X}$ as an estimate of $E(X)$ in our expression.

When we estimated the variance of u_i, we used two estimates: $\hat{\beta}_0$ and $\hat{\beta}_1$. As such, when we construct an estimator for the variance of u_i, we will need to divide by $n-2$ to take account of the fact that we have lost 2 degrees of freedom by using estimates.

We will represent the unbiased estimator for the variance of the error terms as $\widehat{var}(u) = \hat{\sigma}_u^2$:

$$\widehat{var}(u) = \left[\frac{1}{n-2}\right]\sum_{i=1}^{n}\hat{u}_i^2 = \left[\frac{1}{n-2}\right]\sum_{i=1}^{n}(Y_i - \hat{\beta}_0 - \hat{\beta}_1 X_i)^2$$

You might ask why we use $\sum_{i=1}^{n}\hat{u}_i^2$ rather than $\sum_{i=1}^{n}(u_i - \overline{\hat{u}})^2$. The reason is that the sample mean of the fitted residuals will be equal to zero. We prove this in the appendix to this chapter.

Therefore, an estimator that we can use for the variance of $\hat{\beta}_1$ is:

$$\widehat{var}(\hat{\beta}_1) = \frac{\left[\frac{1}{n-2}\right]\sum_{i=1}^{n}(\hat{u}_i)^2}{\sum_{j=1}^{n}(X_j - \overline{X})^2}$$

Having seen that an estimator for the variance of the OLS estimator is given by:

$$\widehat{var}(\hat{\beta}_1) = \frac{\left[\frac{1}{n-2}\right]\sum_{i=1}^{n}(\hat{u}_i)^2}{\sum_{j=1}^{n}(X_j - \overline{X})^2}$$

you might be worried that this is going to be complicated to calculate whenever you wish to test hypotheses relating to the OLS estimates. However, statistical software packages, including Microsoft Excel, can automatically calculate the OLS estimates, and will construct estimates of the variance (or more particularly the standard error of the estimator). Remember, the estimated standard error is just equal to the square root of the estimated variance:

$$\widehat{s.e.}(\hat{\beta}_1) = \sqrt{\widehat{var}(\hat{\beta}_1)} = \sqrt{\frac{\left[\frac{1}{n-2}\right]\sum_{i=1}^{n}(\hat{u}_i)^2}{\sum_{j=1}^{n}(X_j - \overline{X})^2}}$$

The estimated standard error will be important when we come to test hypotheses relating to the OLS estimates. However, just as with tests of equality of means, whenever we use estimates of the standard error, we will need to consider the number of degrees of freedom.

26.4.1 Degrees of freedom

When we are thinking about the degrees of freedom within our regression models, we are thinking about the number of linearly independent values of $\hat{u}_i$ we have.

Because we have used $\hat{\beta}_0$ and $\hat{\beta}_1$ to construct the $\hat{u}_i$, we have effectively lost two of the observations. That is, if we observed $n - 2$ of the observations of $\hat{u}_i$, $\hat{\beta}_0$ and $\hat{\beta}_1$, we could construct what the final two observations must be.

As a good rule, when you estimate a relationship, the number of degrees of freedom is simply equal to the number of observations, less the number of coefficients you have estimated. When we estimated:

$$Y_i = \beta_0 + \beta_1 X_i + u_i$$

we estimated $\hat{\beta}_0$ and $\hat{\beta}_1$; that is, we estimated two coefficients. As such, we will have $n - 2$ degrees of freedom.

Similarly, had we estimated:

$$Y_i = \beta X_i + u_i$$

we would have only estimated one coefficient ($\hat{\beta}$). As such, we would have had $n - 1$ degrees of freedom. As a simple rule of thumb, the number of degrees of freedom in OLS estimators is equal to the number of observations, less the number of coefficients we have estimated.

Summary

In this chapter, we have introduced the variance of the OLS estimator, and we have shown that, provided the Gauss Markov assumptions are true, then the variance of the OLS estimator is given as:

$$var(\hat{\beta}_1) = \frac{\sigma_u^2}{\sum_{i=1}^{n}(X_i - \bar{X})^2}$$

An estimator is more efficient if it has a smaller variance. We have seen that there are two key ways to improve the efficiency of the OLS estimator:

1. Increase the number of observations. As with most estimators, the more information that we use to generate our estimates, the more precise the estimate is. In the case of the OLS estimator, the more observations we use, the smaller the variance.

2. Increase the variance of the explanatory variable. We need substantial variation in the explanatory variable to be able to observe the effect of a change in X on Y. The more variability there is in the explanatory variable, the more precision we have in our estimates.

Since we never observe the error terms (and we do not know the true variance of the error terms), to construct a measure of the variance of the OLS estimator, we will need to estimate these. We have seen that an estimator for the variance of the OLS estimator is:

$$\widehat{var}(\hat{\beta}_1) = \frac{\left[\frac{1}{n-2}\right]\sum_{i=1}^{n}(\hat{u}_i)^2}{\sum_{j=1}^{n}(X_j - \bar{X})^2}$$

Because $\hat{u}_i$ is constructed based on an estimated $\hat{\beta}_0$ and $\hat{\beta}_1$, the estimator has $n - 2$ degrees of freedom, where n is the number of observations.

In the next chapter, we will use this result to test hypotheses about the relationship between economic variables, based upon OLS.

Appendix

Constructing the variance of the OLS estimator

Suppose that you are using OLS to estimate the following relationship:

$$Y_i = \beta_0 + \beta_1 X_i + u_i$$

Then the OLS estimator for the slope parameter is:

$$\hat{\beta}_1 = \frac{\sum_{i=1}^{n}(Y_i - \bar{Y})(X_i - \bar{X})}{\sum_{j=1}^{n}(X_j - \bar{X})^2}$$

Assumption	Description
1. Data generating process	We have correctly defined our data generating process: $Y_i = \beta_0 + \beta_1 X_i + u_i$
2. *iid*	The observed pairs of X and Y are independent and identically distributed. It follows from this that u_i and u_j are also independent, for **all** $i \neq j$.
3. Exogeneity	The conditional expectation of the error term given any set of X is equal to 0: $E(u_i \mid \{X\}) = 0$
4. Homoskedasticity	The variance of the error terms is constant (irrespective of the value of X_i): $var(u_i \mid \{X\}) = \sigma_u^2$ for all values of i
5. Fixed in repeated samples	We will treat the set of {X}s as *fixed* in repeated samples (i.e. they are treated as non-stochastic). This is a very bad assumption, but it makes the mathematics easier, and more intuitive.

We have already seen that, if assumptions 1 and 2 hold, then OLS is unbiased. However, we will also need to think about the variance of the OLS estimator.

In the previous chapter, we were able to show that, provided the true data generating process (DGP) is $Y_i = \beta_0 + \beta_1 X_i + u_i$, then, by substituting the DGP into our estimator, we can rewrite this as:

$$\hat{\beta}_1^{OLS} = \beta_1 + \frac{\sum_{i=1}^{n}(X_i - \bar{X})u_i}{\sum_{j=1}^{n}(X_j - \bar{X})^2}$$

So, if we wish to find the variance of the OLS estimator, we merely need to find:

$$var(\hat{\beta}_1^{OLS}) = var\left(\beta_1 + \frac{\sum_{i=1}^{n}(X_i - \bar{X})u_i}{\sum_{j=1}^{n}(X_j - \bar{X})^2}\right)$$

However, since β_1 is a constant, and the variance of any random variable plus a constant is just equal to the variance of the underlying random variable:

$$\Rightarrow var(\hat{\beta}_1^{OLS}) = var\left(\frac{\sum_{i=1}^{n}(X_i - \bar{X})u_i}{\sum_{j=1}^{n}(X_j - \bar{X})^2}\right)$$

For simplicity, let's substitute in $a_i = \frac{X_i - \bar{X}}{\sum_{j=1}^{n}(X_j - \bar{X})^2}$:

$$\Rightarrow var(\hat{\beta}_1^{OLS}) = var\left(\sum_{i=1}^{n} a_i u_i\right)$$

Since the Xs are treated as fixed in repeated samples, we can also treat the a_i as fixed in repeated samples. To illustrate this, we can denote:

$$a_i = \frac{x_i - \bar{x}}{\sum_{j=1}^{n}(x_j - \bar{x})^2}$$

We use lower-case x_i terms to indicate that these are no longer random variables, but instead are treated as fixed:

$$\Rightarrow var(\hat{\beta}_1^{OLS}) = var\left(\sum_{i=1}^{n} a_i u_i\right)$$

Rules of variances

For random variables X and Y, and constants a and b:

$var(a + X) = var(X)$

$var(aX) = a^2 var(X)$

$var(aX + bY) = a^2 var(X) + b^2 var(Y) + 2ab\,cov(X,Y)$

We have a variance of a sum here, where the a_i are being treated as fixed (constant) multipliers of the u_i. Thus, we can rewrite this as:

$$var(\hat{\beta}_1^{OLS}) = \sum_{i=1}^{n} a_i^2 var(u_i) + 2\sum_{j=1}^{n-1}\sum_{k=j+1}^{n} a_j a_k cov(u_j, u_k)$$

Since the pairs of X and Y are *iid*, it follows that $cov(u_j, u_k) = 0$ for $j \neq k$:

$$var(\hat{\beta}_1^{OLS}) = \sum_{i=1}^{n} a_i^2 var(u_i)$$

Since $var(u) = \sigma_u^2$, we can rewrite this as:

$$var(\hat{\beta}_1^{OLS}) = \sum_{i=1}^{n} a_i^2 \sigma_u^2$$

$$a_i^2 = \left(\frac{(x_i - \bar{x})}{\sum_{j=1}^{n}(x_j - \bar{x})^2}\right)^2 = \frac{(x_i - \bar{x})^2}{\left(\sum_{j=1}^{n}(x_j - \bar{x})^2\right)^2}$$

$$var(\hat{\beta}_1^{OLS}) = \sigma_u^2 \frac{\sum_{i=1}^{n}(x_i - \bar{x})^2}{\left(\sum_{j=1}^{n}(x_j - \bar{x})^2\right)^2}$$

But the denominator is just the square of the numerator:

$$var(\hat{\beta}_1^{OLS}) = \frac{\sigma_u^2}{\sum_{i=1}^{n}(x_i - \bar{x})^2}$$

More generally, this means that we can write the variance of the OLS estimator for the slope parameter as:

$$var(\hat{\beta}_1^{OLS}) = \frac{\sigma_u^2}{\sum_{i=1}^{n}(X_i - \bar{X})^2}$$

One observation is that the unbiased estimator of the variance of X is defined as:

$$s_X^2 = \frac{1}{n-1}\sum_{i=1}^{n}(X_i - \bar{X})^2$$

As such, we can substitute in for the denominator of the variance of $\hat{\beta}_1^{OLS}$ to give:

$$var(\hat{\beta}_1^{OLS}) = \frac{\sigma_u^2}{(n-1)s_X^2}$$

Proving that the average of the fitted residuals is equal to zero

Note: Had we constrained that the intercept were equal to zero, this constraints would hold.

1. The average of the fitted residuals is equal to zero.

$$\frac{1}{n}\sum_{i=1}^{n}\hat{u}_i = 0$$

When we estimated the following relationship:

$$Y_i = \beta_0 + \beta_1 X_i + u_i$$

the equation of the fitted residuals was given by:

$$\hat{u}_i = Y_i - \hat{\beta}_0 - \hat{\beta}_1 X_i \qquad \text{Fitted residuals (1)}$$

We constructed the OLS estimator by minimizing the **sum of squares of residuals (SSR)**, by differentiating with respect to $\hat{\beta}_0$ and $\hat{\beta}_1$. If we examine the **first order condition (FOC)**, with respect to $\hat{\beta}_0$:

$$\frac{\partial}{\partial\hat{\beta}_0}\sum_{i=1}^{n}\hat{u}_i^2 = -2\sum_{i=1}^{n}(Y_i - \hat{\beta}_0 - \hat{\beta}_1 X_i) = 0 \qquad \text{FOC1}$$

But we can see that the equation for the fitted residuals ($\hat{u}_i = Y_i - \hat{\beta}_0 - \hat{\beta}_1 X_i$) is included in FOC1, so we can rewrite FOC1 to give us:

$$= -2\sum_{i=1}^{n}\hat{u}_i = 0$$

This must mean that $\sum_{i=1}^{n}\hat{u}_i = 0$, and hence the sample mean of the fitted residuals is also equal to 0. The implication of this is that the fitted line passes through the middle of the data.

Testing Hypotheses with OLS

27

Learning outcomes for this chapter

By the end of this chapter you will be able to:

- Test hypotheses relating to both the slope and intercept of OLS regression output, computing appropriate degrees of freedom
- Use Excel to carry out OLS regressions
- Construct confidence intervals relating to the OLS regression line
- Construct hypotheses other than $\beta = 0$
- Interpret measures of goodness of fit, including the R^2

Mathematical tools

- Equations of straight lines
- Algebra

Introduction

So far, we have seen estimates derived from OLS, but have not been able to make any conclusions about the population as a whole. Just as when we used the sample mean to estimate the population average, we need to have a way to make conclusions about relationships between economic variables in the population. For that reason, we need to carry out statistical testing relating to our OLS estimates.

In the last chapter, we introduced the variance of the OLS estimator, and in this chapter, we will see how to carry out statistical tests using OLS results. In addition, we will also begin to discuss how well the line we have estimated fits the data that we observe.

27.1 Statistical testing with OLS estimates

When we derived the OLS estimators in Chapter 23, we estimated the impact of per capita spending on healthcare on life expectancy, using 2019 data from the OECD (see Figure 27.1), and obtained the following (estimated) relationship:

$$\widehat{LifeExp_i} = 76.684 + 0.972 Spend_i$$

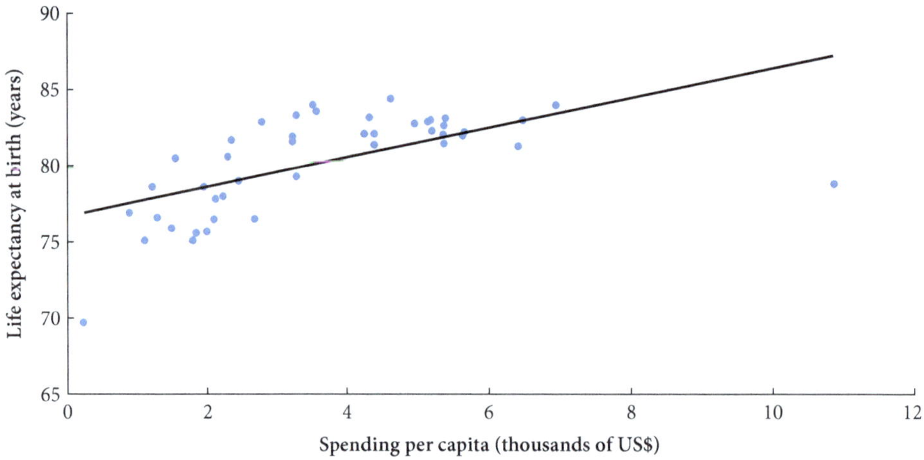

Figure 27.1 Life expectancy plotted against per capita spending on healthcare, with the OLS line of best fit included (2019 data, from the OECD).

Note that we have a 'hat' on $\widehat{LifeExp_i}$ to indicate that this is the estimated relationship, and our estimated coefficients were $\hat{\beta}_0 = 76.684$ and $\hat{\beta}_1 = 0.972$. That is, our estimated marginal effect of a change in healthcare spending on life expectancy is that an increase in spending by \$1,000 per capita is associated with a 0.972 year increase in life expectancy.

However, this is only a single sample of the data. It is possible that, if we took a different sample (based on either different years or a different sample of countries), we would gain a different estimate. That is, due to sampling variation, we would expect the estimated coefficients to change whenever we take a different sample.

We don't really know anything about the true relationship yet. We could have simply obtained a coefficient of $\hat{\beta}_1 = 0.972$ by chance, and in reality, there is no impact of spending on healthcare on life expectancy. Similarly, it could be the case that the true effect of spending on healthcare could be much larger than the estimated effect and, by chance, we have underestimated the effect.

This uncertainty is due to sampling variation, and just as in the statistics we saw earlier in this book, whilst we cannot know anything for certain about the true relationship, we can carry out statistical tests relating to the relationships.

To motivate this, let's consider a simpler example. Suppose that we are interested in estimating the relationship between a dependent variable, Y, and an explanatory variable, X. We therefore estimate the following relationship by OLS:

$$Y_i = \beta_0 + \beta_1 X_i + u_i$$

and based on our estimates we wish to test whether X has any impact on Y (or not). If X has no impact then this will be equivalent to β_1 being equal to zero. That is, the marginal effect of a change of X would be to lead to zero change in Y. This is equivalent to $\beta_1 = 0$. As such, we want to test the following hypotheses:

$$H_0: \beta_1 = 0$$
$$H_A: \beta_1 \neq 0$$

To test these hypotheses, we can use the same sorts of techniques we saw when we introduced statistical testing; that is, we can consider what the distribution of the test statistic will be if the null hypothesis is true, and then consider whether the observed $\hat{\beta}_1$ is an unlikely outcome. If the estimated $\hat{\beta}_1$ lies in the most unlikely k per cent of the distribution (where k is our significance level), then we can reject the null hypothesis.

By the central limit theorem, provided we have a large enough sample (usually more than about 30 observations), then the OLS estimator will follow an approximately normal distribution.

In addition, we know that, if the following four[1] assumptions are true:

Assumption 1	The model is correctly defined.
Assumption 2	The observations are independent and identically distributed.
Assumption 3	The explanatory variables are exogenous: $E(u_i \mid \{x_1, x_2, x_3, \ldots, x_n\}) = 0$ for all i and all possible sets of $\{X\}$.
Assumption 4	The variance of the error terms is constant, $var(u_i) = \sigma^2$.

- The OLS estimator is an unbiased and consistent estimator of the population slope parameter, β_1. That is, $E(\hat{\beta}_1) = \beta_1$.
- The variance of the OLS estimator is given by:

$$var(\hat{\beta}_1) = \frac{\sigma_u^2}{\sum_{i=1}^{n}(X_i - \bar{X})^2}$$

We can now combine these elements to write down the distribution of $\hat{\beta}_1$, subject to the four assumptions being true:

$$\hat{\beta}_1 \sim N\left(\beta_1, \frac{\sigma_u^2}{\sum_{i=1}^{n}(X_i - \bar{X})^2}\right)$$

Since $\hat{\beta}_1$ is an estimator that follows the normal distribution, we can standardize the distribution of the estimator by subtracting the expected value, and dividing through by the standard error of the estimator. (Remember, the standard error of an estimator is just equal to the square root of the variance of the estimator.)

As such, if we use our estimator, $\hat{\beta}_1$, we can standardize the test statistic to a normal, with expectation 0 and variance 1:

$$Z = \frac{\hat{\beta}_1 - E(\hat{\beta}_1)}{s.e.(\hat{\beta}_1)} \sim N(0,1)$$

[1] When constructing the variance of the OLS estimator, we considered a fifth assumption that the Xs were fixed in repeated samples. This assumption is not strictly necessary, but made the mathematics easier.

Substituting in the formulae for $E(\hat{\beta}_1)$ and $s.e.(\hat{\beta}_1)$, we would have:

$$Z = \frac{(\hat{\beta}_1 - \beta_1)}{\sqrt{var(\hat{\beta}_1)}} = \frac{(\hat{\beta}_1 - \beta_1)}{\sqrt{\frac{\sigma_u^2}{\sum_{i=1}^{n}(X_i \quad \overline{X})^2}}} \sim N(0,1)$$

Now, there are potentially two problems with carrying out this test:

1. We don't know what the true variance of the error terms is. As such, we need to use an estimator for the variance. We saw, in the previous chapter, that an estimator for the variance of $\hat{\beta}_1$ is:

$$\widehat{var}(\hat{\beta}_1) = \frac{\left[\frac{1}{n-2}\right]\sum_{i=1}^{n}(\hat{u}_i)^2}{\sum_{j=1}^{n}(X_j - \overline{X})^2}$$

2. As we will be using an estimator for the variance of the OLS estimator, our standardized test statistic will not follow the normal distribution, but instead will follow the t-distribution. Since

$$\hat{u}_i = Y_i - \hat{\beta}_0 - \hat{\beta}_1 X_i$$

we are constructing our estimate of the variance of σ_u^2 (i.e. the variance of the u_i) based on two estimated parameters ($\hat{\beta}_0$ and $\hat{\beta}_1$). Because we use two estimates in the construction of our estimate of the variance of $\hat{\beta}_1$, we effectively lose 2 degrees of freedom. Therefore, if we have n observations, then the standardized test statistic will follow the t-distribution with $n - 2$ degrees of freedom.

We have only discussed the slope parameter here, but to carry out a test relating to the **intercept**, we would use exactly the same technique. The only difference is that we would use a slightly different estimator for the variance of $\hat{\beta}_0$:

$$\widehat{var}(\hat{\beta}_1) = \frac{\left[\frac{1}{n-2}\right]\sum_{i=1}^{n}(\hat{u}_i)^2}{\sum_{j=1}^{n}(X_j - \overline{X})^2}, \quad \widehat{var}(\hat{\beta}_0) = \frac{\widehat{var}(\hat{\beta})\sum_{i=1}^{n}X_i^2}{n}$$

On the face of it, these estimators look horrible to calculate. However, in reality, we rarely have to calculate these by hand, because statistical software packages (such as Microsoft Excel) will do the hard work for you.

27.1.1 Interpreting results in published papers

In published papers, econometrics results will usually be arranged in tables, like the one we see in Figure 27.2.

	Results
Spending on healthcare	0.972
	(0.193)
Constant	76.685
	(0.805)
Number of observations	44

Notes: Dependent variable is the life expectancy at birth in country i. Estimated standard errors are reported in parentheses.

Estimated coefficient on 'Spending on health care' $\hat{\beta}_1 = 0.972$

Estimated standard error for $\hat{\beta}_1$ $\widehat{s.e.}(\hat{\beta}_1) = 0.193$

Corresponding estimates for $\hat{\beta}_0 = 76.685$, and $\widehat{s.e.}(\hat{\beta}_0) = 0.805$

Figure 27.2 Annotated OLS results in the format of a published paper.

It is important to always read the notes under the table, as this will specify key information. As a standard, in economics papers, the estimated $\hat{\beta}$s will be placed alongside the variable name; so here, $\hat{\beta}_1 = 0.972$ and $\hat{\beta}_0 = 76.685$. Similarly, the estimated standard errors of our estimates will normally be placed in parentheses (brackets) underneath the coefficients. So, the estimated standard error for $\hat{\beta}_1$ is equal to $\widehat{s.e.}(\hat{\beta}_1) = 0.193$.

However, some authors and some journals place t-statistics in parentheses underneath the estimated coefficients. These t-statistics would be for testing the hypothesis that, say, $\beta_1 = 0$. Some journals go further and require that rather than t-statistics, p-values will be included.

In this book, we use the standard economics notation, and include estimated standard errors in parentheses underneath the estimated coefficient. When you see results in other textbooks, or in journal articles, you should check carefully what the numbers in parentheses actually are!

27.1.2 Testing hypotheses related to the slope parameter

Let's return to the OECD data on healthcare spending and life expectancy. We wish to estimate the following relationship:

$$LifeExp_i = \beta_0 + \beta_1 Spend_i + u_i$$

where $LifeExp_i$ is the life expectancy at birth in country i, and $Spend_i$ is the spending on healthcare per capita (in thousands of US\$) in country i, whilst u_i is a (random) error term. For simplicity, we make the assumption that spending is exogenous, so that OLS is unbiased. The results, based on 2019 data from the OECD, are illustrated in Table 27.1. When you see results of regressions in published journals, they will normally be organized in a column like this. To explain what we are seeing here, we have estimates for the marginal effect of spending on healthcare on life expectancy, and an estimated intercept:

- The estimated slope parameter, $\hat{\beta}_1$, is equal to 0.972.
- The estimated intercept, $\hat{\beta}_0$, is equal to 76.685.

Table 27.1 Results from a regression of life expectancy against (per capita) spending on healthcare (data from the OECD)

	Results
Spending on healthcare	0.972
	(0.193)
Constant	76.685
	(0.805)
Number of observations	44

Note: Dependent variable is the life expectancy at birth in country *i*. Estimated standard errors are reported in parentheses.

Similarly, we have estimates of the standard errors of our estimates:

- The estimated standard error of $\hat{\beta}_1$ is $\widehat{s.e.}(\hat{\beta}_1) = 0.193$.
- The estimated standard error of $\hat{\beta}_0$ is $\widehat{s.e.}(\hat{\beta}_0) = 0.805$.

Finally, the table tells us that there are 44 observations. When we come to carry out tests on the population parameters, since we have estimated $\hat{\beta}_0$ and $\hat{\beta}_1$ in our model (i.e. we have estimated two coefficients), there will be $44 - 2 = 42$ degrees of freedom.

Relevant hypotheses to test

The first hypothesis you might wish to test is to ask the question about whether your explanatory variable has any significant impact on the **dependent variable**.
If we are estimating the relationship:

$$Y_i = \beta_0 + \beta_1 X_i + u_i$$

and the **explanatory variable** has no significant impact, then this would be equivalent to $\beta_1 = 0$. As such, if we test the hypothesis:

$$H_0: \beta_1 = 0$$
$$H_A: \beta_1 \neq 0$$

this is equivalent to testing the hypothesis that X_i has no impact on our dependent variable, Y_i. This is often the first test that economists carry out when faced with empirical results, but it is not the only test that might be of interest.

Let's begin by testing the hypothesis that spending on healthcare has no impact on life expectancy:

$$H_0: \beta_1 = 0$$
$$H_A: \beta_1 \neq 0$$

Remember, when we test a hypothesis, we begin with the assumption that the null hypothesis is true, and look at whether the result we have obtained is an unlikely one (or not).

We would construct the t-statistic by taking the estimated $\hat{\beta}_1$, subtracting the expectation of $\hat{\beta}_1$ (assuming that the null hypothesis is true), and dividing through by the (estimated) standard error of $\hat{\beta}_1$.

$$t = \frac{\hat{\beta}_1 - E(\hat{\beta}_1 \mid H_0 \text{ is true})}{\widehat{s.e.}(\hat{\beta}_1)}$$

There are three elements that go towards this t-statistic:

1. $\hat{\beta}_1$	This is just the estimated slope parameter. From Table 27.1, we know that this is just equal to $\hat{\beta}_1 = 0.972$.
2. $E(\hat{\beta}_1 \mid H_0 \text{ is true})$	This is the expected value of the estimator if the null hypothesis is true (i.e. if $\beta_1 = 0$). Given our assumption that the explanatory variable is exogenous (i.e. independent from the error terms), then OLS will be unbiased and $E(\hat{\beta}_1) = \beta_1$. Therefore, if the null hypothesis is true, then $E(\hat{\beta}_1 \mid \beta_1 = 0) = 0$. As a shortcut, when carrying out statistical tests, we normally just substitute the hypothesized value in here. However, you should remember that this is explicitly assuming that the estimator is an **unbiased estimator**. In this case, if OLS were biased, then it would not be appropriate to substitute 0 in here.
3. $\widehat{s.e.}(\hat{\beta}_1)$	This is just the estimated standard error of the OLS estimator; in this case, this is provided, and is equal to 0.193. As with the expected value of $\hat{\beta}_1$, the standard error is only correct based on the Gauss Markov assumptions. If these assumptions are violated, then the standard error would be incorrect.

So, we can substitute these into our t-statistic:

$$t = \frac{0.972 - 0}{0.193} = 5.036$$

Now, we saw earlier that we have 42 degrees of freedom here. We have implicitly assumed that this is a two-tailed test (our alternative hypothesis allows for β_1 to be either positive or negative). As such, we need to compare our test statistic with the **critical value** from the t-tables.

Table 27.2 Critical values from the t-distribution for a two-tailed test with 42 degrees of freedom

Significance level	Critical value, t_{42}
10%	1.682
5%	2.018
1%	2.698

As you can see from Table 27.2, the t-statistic we have constructed is larger than the critical value at the 10 per cent, 5 per cent, and 1 per cent significance levels. This means that we can reject the null hypothesis at each of these significance levels, in favour of the alternative.

P-values

The p-value associated with a t-statistic is the probability of achieving a t-statistic at least as far away from 0 as we have, if the null hypothesis were true.

Suppose that we have obtained a t-statistic of 1.4. Then the p-value would be the probability of achieving a t-statistic either greater than +1.4 or less than −1.4, if the null hypothesis were true.

$$\text{p-value} = P(|T|>1.4|H_0 \textit{ is true})$$

The p-value is often much more informative than a simple rejection of a null hypothesis, as it gives a real intuition of the likelihood of a particular outcome.

Calculating the p-value in Microsoft Excel

Microsoft Excel can calculate p-values associated with individual t-statistics. The formula:

$$=\text{T.DIST.2T}(x, df)$$

will calculate the probability of randomly drawing an observation from the t-distribution with df degrees of freedom with magnitude greater than x.

Note that this is a two-tailed test (indicated by the .2T in the formula). If you are interested in only the left-hand tail probability, you can use the formula =T.DIST(x, df), whilst for the right-hand tail probability, =T.DIST.RT(x, df).

We could go further here, and look at the p-value associated with the t-statistic. Excel can produce the appropriate p-value using the formula:

$$= \text{T.DIST.2T}(5.036, 42)$$

This command will find the probability of randomly observing a t-statistic (based on 42 degrees of freedom) either greater than 5.036 or less than −5.036 if the null hypothesis is true.

The p-value in this example is equal to 0.0000095. That is, if the null hypothesis is true, the probability of gaining a t-statistic whose magnitude is greater than 5.036 is equal to 0.0000095. For context, this is approximately equal to the probability of gaining 17 consecutive heads when flipping a fair coin. Whilst this is unlikely, you might have questioned whether the coin was actually fair if this happened!

P-values have an explicit link to traditional significance level, as if the p-value is less than 0.05, this is equivalent to saying that you reject the null hypothesis at the 5 per cent significance level. Similarly, if the p-value is less than 0.01, you would reject the null hypothesis at the 1 per cent significance level.

In this example, the p-value is so small, you would reject the null hypothesis at the 5 per cent, 1 per cent, 0.1 per cent, 0.01 per cent, and 0.001 per cent significance levels. This does not mean that the null hypothesis is definitely false, but the likelihood of gaining a t-statistic as impressive as the one we have is so low that it is almost certain that the null hypothesis is false.

27.1.3 Testing hypotheses relating to the intercept

We can use exactly the same methodology as in Section 27.1.2 to test hypotheses about the intercept, and statistical software packages will carry out tests relating to β_0 in exactly the same way as for β_1 (see Table 27.3).

If we have estimated:

$$LifeExp_i = \beta_0 + \beta_1 Spend_i + u_i$$

then we can test the hypotheses:

$$H_0: \beta_0 = 0$$
$$H_A: \beta_0 \neq 0$$

The method for testing this hypothesis is exactly the same as testing hypotheses about the slope parameter. We just need to use the estimated standard error relating to the intercept:

$$t = \frac{\hat{\beta}_0 - E(\hat{\beta}_0 \mid H_0 \text{ is true})}{\widehat{s.e.}(\hat{\beta}_0)} = \frac{76.685 - 0}{0.805} = 95.261$$

Again, we can compare this with the critical values from the t-tables (at the 5 per cent significance level, recall, the critical value with 42 degrees of freedom is 2.018, so we can reject the null hypothesis).

Again, we can calculate the p-value associated with this t-statistic. Using Excel, this will be calculated as:

=T.DIST.2T(95.261, 42)

This provides a p-value equal to 1.05×10^{-48}, which is so close to zero as to be practically equal to zero. We would be able to reject at *any* reasonable level of significance that the intercept is equal to zero.

Table 27.3 Results from a regression of life expectancy against (per capita) spending on healthcare (data from the OECD)

	Results
Spending on healthcare	0.972
	(0.193)
Constant	76.685
	(0.805)
Number of observations	44

Note: Dependent variable is the life expectancy at birth in country *i*. Estimated standard errors are reported in parentheses.

This isn't really a surprise though, as we had argued in previous chapters that it was very unlikely that an appropriate intercept would be equal to zero.

27.1.4 Important statistical health warning: Standard statistical testing assumes that the estimator Is unbiased.

All of the tests that we have carried out explicitly assume that OLS is unbiased. Suppose that we have tested the hypotheses that:

$$H_0: \beta_1 = 0$$
$$H_A: \beta_1 \neq 0$$

We have used $E(\hat{\beta}_1 \mid H_0 \textit{ is true})$ and the hypothesized value under H_0 interchangeably, so in the hypothesis we would substitute in $E(\hat{\beta}_1 \mid H_0 \textit{ is true}) = 0$.

If OLS is biased, then $E(\hat{\beta}_1) \neq \beta_1$, and so, if we wished to test this hypothesis, $E(\hat{\beta}_1 \mid H_0 \textit{ is true}) \neq 0$.

Thus, standard tests will be invalid if OLS is biased. However, if the estimator is biased but consistent, the tests will still be valid in large samples.

It should be noted that the tests we have seen in this chapter are implicitly assuming that the OLS estimator is unbiased. However, as you saw in the last two chapters, it is highly unlikely that our estimates from a regression of life expectancy against spending on healthcare are unbiased, because:

1. It is highly likely that there is some omitted variables bias.
2. We might have mis-specified the relationship. We have fitted a straight line through the data. In reality, it might be the case that a non-linear relationship is more appropriate.

As such, the results of our tests are likely to be incorrect. The examples that you see in this chapter provide an exemplar for the methodology, but you should be equally cautious when reading the results of statistical tests, particularly when you have good reason to believe that the OLS estimates are biased.

This is particularly a problem if the bias is away from your hypothesized value—for example, if $\hat{\beta}_1$ is positive, but you know that there is also likely to be positive bias. If you are testing

$$H_0: \beta_1 = 0$$
$$H_A: \beta_1 \neq 0$$

Since there is positive bias, the magnitude of $\hat{\beta}_1$ would be expected to be larger than the real β_1. This will also mean that the t-statistic will be of a larger magnitude. If the bias is away from zero, you are more likely to reject the null hypothesis, even when the null hypothesis is true.

This is really important to know, particularly when using statistical software. Often, when estimating relationships using OLS, the statistical software will produce t-statistics assuming that the estimator is unbiased.

27.2 Using Excel to carry out OLS regressions (revisited)

In Chapter 23, we saw that we can use Microsoft Excel to estimate OLS, using the 'Data Analysis' tool in Excel. When you run an OLS regression, you will be presented with a table much like the one in Figure 27.3.

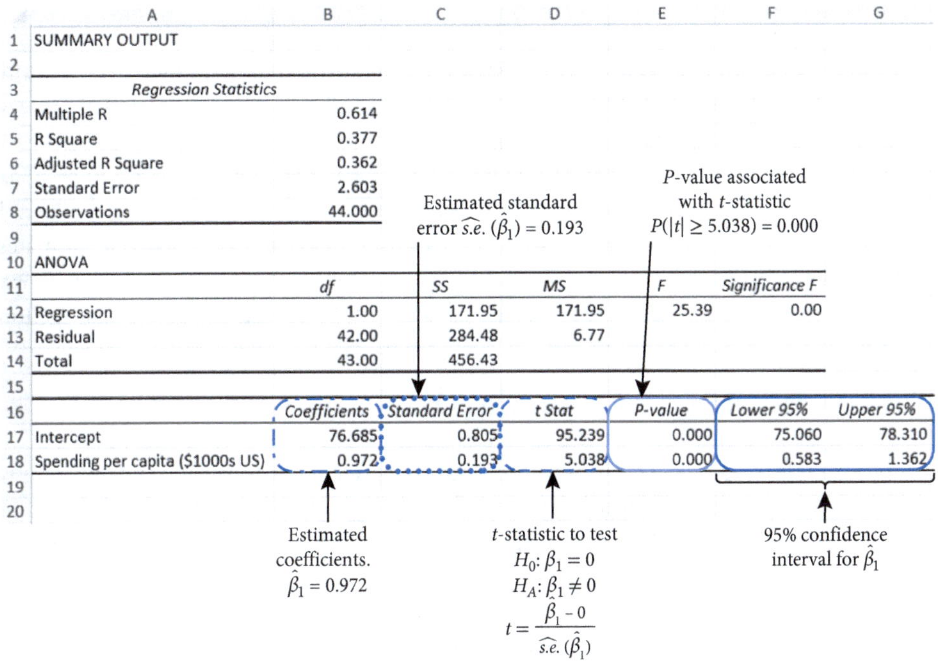

	A	B	C	D	E	F	G
1	SUMMARY OUTPUT						
2							
3	*Regression Statistics*						
4	Multiple R	0.614					
5	R Square	0.377					
6	Adjusted R Square	0.362					
7	Standard Error	2.603					
8	Observations	44.000					
9							
10	ANOVA						
11		*df*	*SS*	*MS*	*F*	*Significance F*	
12	Regression	1.00	171.95	171.95	25.39	0.00	
13	Residual	42.00	284.48	6.77			
14	Total	43.00	456.43				
15							
16		*Coefficients*	*Standard Error*	*t Stat*	*P-value*	*Lower 95%*	*Upper 95%*
17	Intercept	76.685	0.805	95.239	0.000	75.060	78.310
18	Spending per capita ($1000s US)	0.972	0.193	5.038	0.000	0.583	1.362
19							
20							

Figure 27.3 Annotated output from Microsoft Excel when estimating a relationship by OLS.

These results relate to the regression of life expectancy against per capita spending on healthcare:

$$LifeExp_i = \beta_0 + \beta_1 Spend_i + u_i$$

The key results are contained within rows 17 and 18 of the worksheet.

- Row 17 relates to the estimated intercept, $\hat{\beta}_0$.
- Row 18 relates to the estimated coefficients about 'Spending per capita' on healthcare, $\hat{\beta}_1$.

We will focus primarily on the results relating the slope parameter, but you can make the same inferences relating to the intercept as well. Similarly, the annotations in Figure 27.3 relate to the slope parameter, $\hat{\beta}_1$.

Focusing on row 18, the first number (in column B) is the estimated coefficient, so $\hat{\beta}_1 = 0.972$. The next column provides us with the estimated standard error of our estimator, so $\widehat{s.e.}(\hat{\beta}_1) = 0.193$.

In column D, we are presented with the t-statistic. Excel (and other software packages) will automatically construct a t-statistic to test the null hypothesis that $\beta_1 = 0$. That is, just as we saw in Section 27.2.1, the t-statistic corresponding to an estimated $\hat{\beta}_1 = 0.972$ and estimated standard error of $\widehat{s.e.}(\hat{\beta}_1) = 0.193$ is:

$$t = \frac{0.972 - 0}{0.193} = 5.038$$

Further, in column E, we are presented with the p-value associated with the t-statistic in column D. This is telling you $P(|t_{42}| \geq 5.038) = 0.000$ if the null hypothesis is true. This indicates that if the null hypothesis were true, the probability of gaining a t-statistic at least as impressive as 5.038 would be 0.000 ($3dp$).

Finally, the numbers in columns F and G provide the 95 per cent confidence interval for our estimate. This is the range of population values for which we would fail to reject the null hypothesis at the 5 per cent significance level. This indicates that, based on these estimates, at the 5 per cent significance level, we would fail to reject the null hypothesis that β_1 was anywhere between 0.583 and 1.362. We will discuss confidence intervals in the next section.

27.3 Confidence intervals in OLS

In the example in Section 27.2, you will see that Excel calculates confidence intervals for us on our estimates. The confidence interval tells us the range of values that we would fail to reject the null hypothesis at the relevant significance level. So for example, the 95 per cent confidence interval provides us with the range of possible hypothesized values that we would fail to reject as population parameters at the 5 per cent significance level. In a sense, this gives us a set of possible values of β_1 (or β_0) that are consistent with the estimated $\hat{\beta}_1$ (or $\hat{\beta}_0$).

To construct the confidence interval, we will use exactly the same method as we did in Chapter 18. The 95 per cent confidence interval based on our estimates is just equal to:

$\hat{\beta}_1 \pm t_{CV} \times \widehat{s.e.}(\hat{\beta}_1)$	95% confidence interval for β_1
$\hat{\beta}_0 \pm t_{CV} \times \widehat{s.e.}(\hat{\beta}_0)$	95% confidence interval for β_0

Table 27.4 Results from a regression of life expectancy against (per capita) spending on healthcare (data from the OECD)

	Results
Spending on healthcare	0.972
	(0.193)
Constant	76.685
	(0.805)
Number of observations	44

Note: Dependent variable is the life expectancy at birth in country i. Estimated standard errors are reported in parentheses.

Returning to the example of spending on healthcare (see Table 27.4), we have 44 observations, and have estimated two coefficients, so we have 42 degrees of freedom. The critical value from the t-distribution at the 5 per cent significance level, with 42 degrees of freedom, is equal to 2.018. Therefore, we can construct the 95 per cent confidence interval for our estimates as follows.

27.3.1 The 95 per cent confidence interval for β_1

$$= \hat{\beta}_1 \pm 2.018 \times \widehat{s.e.}(\hat{\beta}_1)$$
$$= 0.972 \pm 2.018 \times 0.193 = (0.583, 1.362)$$

Remember that what this tells you is that based on our estimates you would fail to reject the null hypothesis that β_1 was anywhere between 0.583 and 1.362. This gives us an indication that the range of values of β_1 that are consistent with our estimates are anywhere between 0.583 and 1.362.

We can repeat this process for the intercept.

27.3.2 The 95 per cent confidence interval for β_0

$$= \hat{\beta}_0 \pm 2.018 \times \widehat{s.e.}(\hat{\beta}_0)$$
$$= 76.685 \pm 2.018 \times 0.805 = (75.060, 78.310)$$

Because we have a 95 per cent confidence interval for both the intercept and the slope parameter, we can also construct a 95 per cent confidence interval for our fitted line. In effect, what happens is that we allow the intercept to take the values between the lower and upper confidence interval (i.e. 75.060 and 78.310), and at the same time, allow the slope parameter to take the values between the lower and upper confidence interval (0.573 and 1.362).

This is illustrated in Figure 27.4. The shaded area represents the set of lines according to which we would fail to reject the null hypothesis, based on our data. The narrower the plotted confidence interval, the greater precision we have over our estimates.

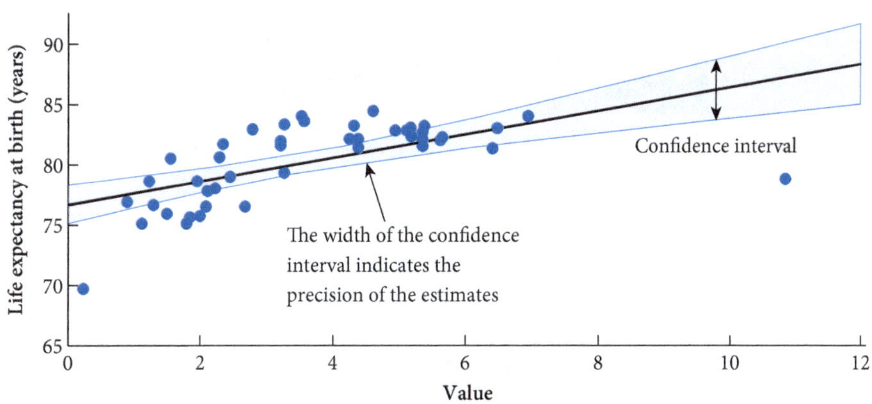

Figure 27.4 95 per cent confidence intervals plotted around the fitted line.

27.4 Testing hypotheses other than $\beta_1 = 0$

So far, all of the tests we have carried out are of a null hypothesis that the population coefficient is equal to zero. However, there's nothing particularly special about this as a test, other than that it tells us whether the explanatory variable has any significant impact on the dependent variable. However, we may be interested in other hypotheses.

Suppose that we estimate the following relationship:

$$LifeExp_i = \beta_0 + \beta_1 Spend_i + u_i$$

where $Spend_i$ is per capita spending (in thousands of US\$) on healthcare. We may have reasons (e.g. from economic theory) to believe that the true population parameter is $\beta_1 = 1$, for example—that is, that an extra \$1,000 per capita spent on healthcare is associated with an extra year of life expectancy. We will see how we can test this, based on the results in Table 27.5.

We begin by formally stating the null and alternative hypotheses.

H_0: $\beta_1 = 1$

H_A: $\beta_1 \neq 1$

If the null hypothesis is true, this is equivalent to $\beta_1 = 1$. We can thus construct our t-statistic in the normal way. We have implicitly assumed that $\hat{\beta}_1$ is an unbiased estimator of β_1. If this assumption is incorrect, then our t-statistic will also be incorrect.

$$t = \frac{\hat{\beta}_1 - E(\hat{\beta}_1 \mid \beta_1 = 1)}{\widehat{s.e.}(\hat{\beta}_1)} = \frac{0.972 - 1}{0.193} = -0.145$$

We get a t-statistic of –0.145.We saw earlier that the two-tailed 5 per cent critical value from the distribution with 42 degrees of freedom is 2.018. Since our t-statistic is smaller (in magnitude) than 2.018, we would fail to reject the null. This shouldn't be a surprise, as we saw earlier that the 95 per cent confidence interval around $\hat{\beta}_1$ was (0.583,1.362), meaning that we would fail to reject a null hypothesis that β_1 was equal to any value in that range (see Figure 27.5).

Table 27.5 Results from a regression of life expectancy against (per capita) spending on healthcare (data from the OECD)

	Results
Spending on healthcare	0.972
	(0.193)
Constant	76.685
	(0.805)
Number of observations	44

Note: Dependent variable is the life expectancy at birth in country *i*. Estimated standard errors are reported in parentheses.

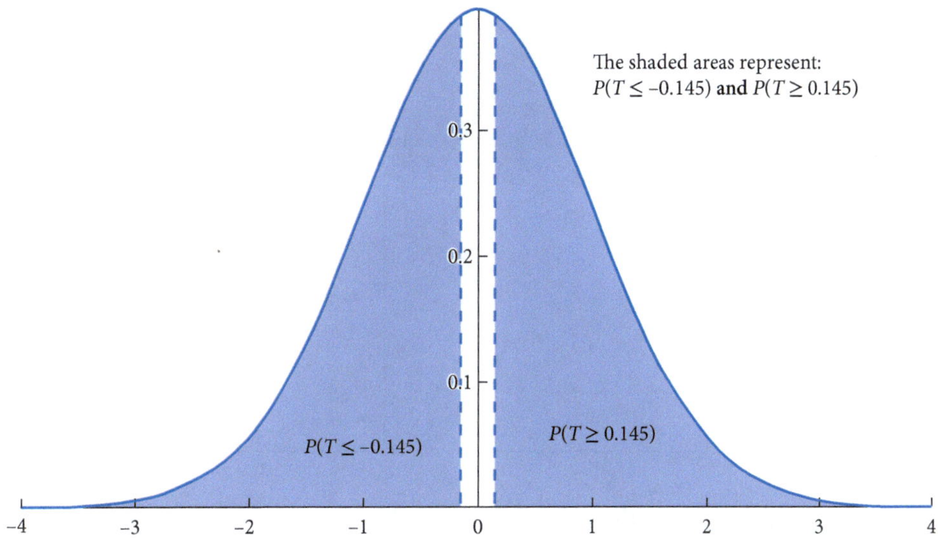

Figure 27.5 The p-value for a t-statistic of −0.145.

We can be a lot more informative about our test though by considering the p-value. Remember that the p-value tells us the probability of achieving a t-statistic at least as impressive as the one we have, if the null hypothesis is true. In this case, the p-value is equivalent to the probability of either gaining a t-statistic in the left-hand tail, to the left of −0.145, or in the right-hand tail, to the right of +0.145. We can calculate the appropriate p-value (using Excel, or equivalent software package), and we find that $P(|T_{42}| \geq 0.145) = 0.885$. This means that, if the null hypothesis is true, the probability of randomly observing a t-statistic 0.145 (or more) away from 0 is 0.885. In other words, this would happen 88.5 per cent of the time. This places this as a very likely outcome.

Remember though, just because we fail to reject the null hypothesis does not mean that the null hypothesis is true. If we have started with a good theoretical reason why we believe that $\beta_1 = 1$, then this would provide additional evidence, but it is perfectly possible that we are committing a type 2 error.

27.5 How well does the estimated line fit the data?

When we have tested the hypotheses that $\beta_1 = 0$, we have essentially been asking the question of whether the explanatory variable has any impact on the dependent variable. However, what this doesn't answer is how important that explanatory variable is for explaining variation in the dependent variable. To illustrate this, let's consider an example.

The data in Figure 27.6 are created by the same data generating process. In both cases, the observations of Y_i are generated through:

$$Y_i = 2 + 5X_i + u_i$$

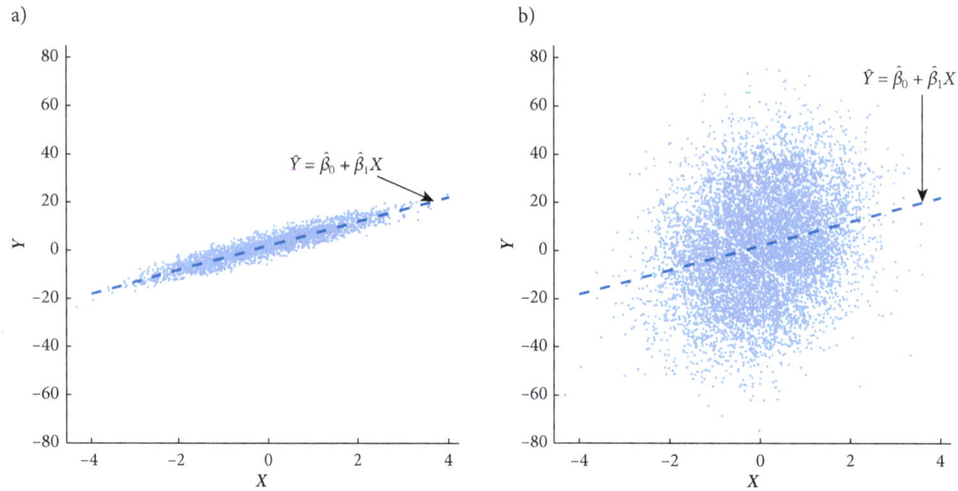

Figure 27.6 Different measures of 'fit' for a regression line.

When we use the pairs of observations of Y_i and X_i to estimate the relationship using OLS, we get a fitted line, with equation:

$$\hat{Y} = \hat{\beta}_0 + \hat{\beta}_1 X$$

However, we can see, very clearly, that the line fits the data much better in the case of panel a) than in panel b). That is, the data lies much closer to the line in panel a) than in panel b).

What this means is that we can see that variation in our explanatory variable is explaining much more of the variation in the dependent variable in panel a), whereas in panel b), there is a lot more noise that is unexplained by the model.

When we constructed OLS, we chose the line that minimized the sum of squares of the (fitted) residuals. However, unless all of the points lie directly on the straight line, this sum of squares will be non-zero. The magnitude of the deviations represents the noise in the model.

To see this mathematically, we can think of each observation of Y_i consisting of two parts: firstly, there is the prediction of the model $\hat{Y}_i$ corresponding with the observed value of X_i, and secondly, there is the unexplained residual (i.e. the $\hat{u}_i$). We can therefore write the observations of Y_i as:

$$Y_i = \hat{Y}_i + \hat{u}_i$$

This is further represented in Figure 27.7. We can think of the element $\hat{Y}_i$ as the element of Y_i that is explained by the model, but $\hat{u}_i$ is the element of Y_i that is unexplained by the regression line.

This is illustrated in Figure 27.7 with a single observation (although the regression line is necessarily constructed based on more observations). The estimated regression line is $\hat{Y}_i = \hat{\beta}_0 + \hat{\beta}_1 X_i$. If we observe a particular pair of observations, (x_1, y_1), then the regression model would predict that $\hat{y}_1 = \hat{\beta}_0 + \hat{\beta}_1 x_1$. The fitted residual would then be the difference

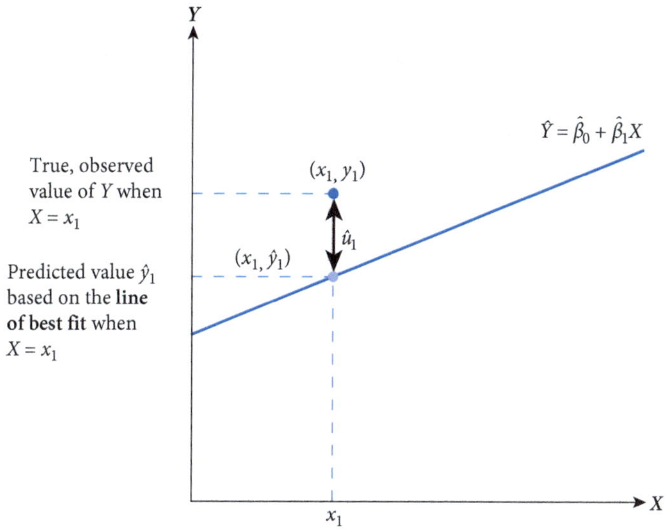

Figure 27.7 The fitted residual from OLS.

between the observed value of $Y_1 = y_1$ and the predicted value based on the observed value of $X_1 = x_1$. That is, $\hat{u}_1 = y_1 - \hat{y}_1$.

When interpreting regression results, it's important to think about how well we are explaining the variability in the dependent variable. Does the model provide us with a good insight about the values Y_i takes based on a particular value of X_i (e.g. in panel a)), or is there a lot of residual variation in the dependent variable that is unexplained by the model (e.g. panel b))?

There are a number of ways that we could try to measure how well the data fits the line. The first simply considers the residual terms. The standard error of regression (SER) is an (unbiased) estimate of the variance of the error terms, based on our fitted residuals:

$$SER = \sqrt{\left(\frac{1}{n-2}\right)\sum_{i=1}^{n}\hat{u}_i^2}$$

Remember that $\sum_{i=1}^{n}\hat{u}_i^2$ was the function that we minimized when we constructed the OLS estimators; the SER provides us a measure (in the units of the dependent variable) of how far, on average, the observed values of Y_i lie away from the fitted line. If the line was a perfect fit (i.e. it passed through all of the observed points), then the SER would be equal to zero, so a smaller value indicates a better fit of your model.

However, there are downsides to the SER, in that because this is measured in the units of the dependent variable, it can be difficult to compare models. For instance, if you were comparing how well a model of the impact of education on earnings fits the data for the UK compared with the USA, the dependent variable for the UK might be measured in British pounds whereas the dependent variable for the USA might be measured in US$. As such, the units of the SER would not necessarily be easily comparable.

A slightly easier method to consider how well our model fits the data would be to ask what proportion of the variation in our dependent variable Y is explained by our model $\hat{Y}$.

We can write the variance of our dependent variable as:

$$var(Y) = var(\hat{Y} + \hat{u}) = var(\hat{Y}) + var(\hat{u}) + 2cov(\hat{Y}, \hat{u})$$

It is relatively straightforward to prove that $cov(\hat{Y}, \hat{u}) = 0$, and so we can write that:[2]

$$var(Y) = var(\hat{Y}) + var(\hat{u})$$

Since we are interested in the proportion of the variance in the dependent variable that is explained by the model, let's divide left and right by $var(Y)$, to give:

$$1 = \frac{var(\hat{Y})}{var(Y)} + \frac{var(\hat{u})}{var(Y)}$$

There are two elements here:

$\frac{var(\hat{Y})}{var(Y)}$	This is the proportion of the variance of the dependent variable that is explained by our fitted model
$\frac{var(\hat{u})}{var(Y)}$	This is the proportion of the variance of the dependent variable that is not explained by our fitted model

We can rearrange the equation to give us that:

$$\frac{var(\hat{Y})}{var(Y)} = 1 - \frac{var(\hat{u})}{var(Y)}$$

The larger this first element is (i.e. the larger $\frac{var(\hat{Y})}{var(Y)}$ is), the better the line of best fit will be. If $var(\hat{Y}) = var(Y)$, then all of the observed values of Y_i will just be equal to the predicted values of $\hat{Y}_i$ for the corresponding values of X_i.

This is easier to see in Figure 27.8. When we estimate OLS, for every observation of X_i, we obtain a predicted value, $\hat{Y}_i = \hat{\beta}_0 + \hat{\beta}_1 X_i$, which lies on our fitted line. However, in many cases, the observed, corresponding, value of Y_i does not lie on the fitted line, and so there is a fitted, or predicted, residual $\hat{u}_i$. We can see in this model observed values of (x_1, y_1), (x_2, y_2), and (x_3, y_3), with corresponding predicted values of $\hat{y}_1$, $\hat{y}_2$, and $\hat{y}_3$.

If all of the observations lie on the straight line, then it will be the case that $y_i = \hat{y}_i$ for all of the observations, and it would also be the case that $var(Y) = var(\hat{Y})$. However, whenever any of the observed points lie away from the line, because there is now a 'noise element' to the observation of Y_i, it will be the case that $var(Y) > var(\hat{Y})$.

[2] This is proven in the appendix to this chapter.

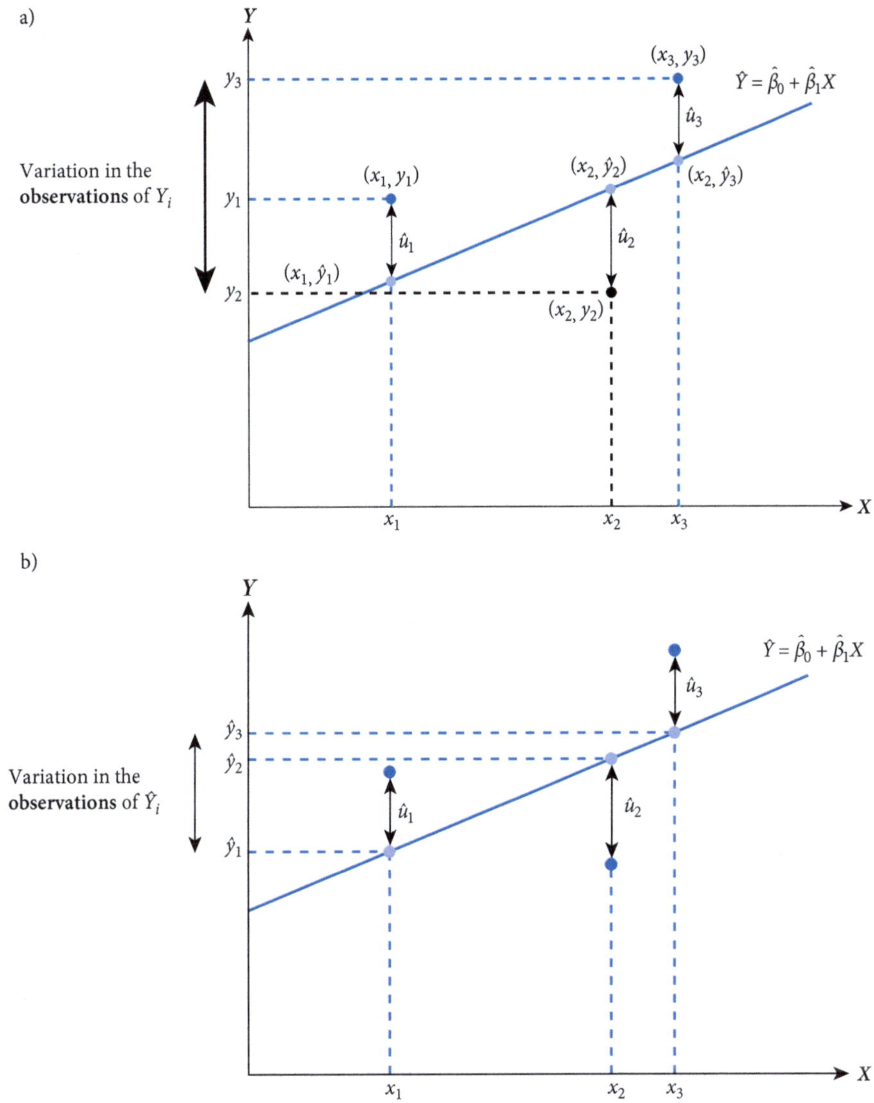

Figure 27.8 Difference between the variability in the true and the fitted observations.

Our second measure of how well the line fits the data is known as the R^2 **or R-squared**, and is a measure of the proportion of variance of our dependent variable that is explained by the model:

$$R^2 = \frac{var(\hat{Y})}{var(Y)} = 1 - \frac{var(\hat{u})}{var(Y)}$$

However, because we only ever observe a sample of the data, we do not know what any of these measures are, but we can estimate them using the unbiased estimator of the population variance, s^2_{n-1}. Constructing our estimates, we could write an estimate of the proportion of variance explained by the model as:

$$R^2 = \frac{\left(\frac{1}{n-1}\right)\sum_{i=1}^{n}(\hat{Y}_i - \overline{\hat{Y}})^2}{\left(\frac{1}{n-1}\right)\sum_{j=1}^{n}(Y_j - \overline{Y})^2} = 1 - \frac{\left(\frac{1}{n-1}\right)\sum_{i=1}^{n}(\hat{u}_i - \overline{\hat{u}})^2}{\left(\frac{1}{n-1}\right)\sum_{j=1}^{n}(Y_j - \overline{Y})^2}$$

Now, in each of the fractions, we have $\frac{1}{n-1}$ on the top and the bottom of the fraction, so these cancel. Further, it's trivial to prove that $\overline{\hat{Y}} = \overline{Y}$ and that $\overline{\hat{u}} = 0$. As such, we can write down the R^2 in a simpler form.[3]

$$R^2 = \frac{\sum_{i=1}^{n}\left(\hat{Y}_i - \overline{Y}\right)^2}{\sum_{j=1}^{n}\left(Y_j - \overline{Y}\right)^2} = 1 - \frac{\sum_{i=1}^{n}\hat{u}_i^2}{\sum_{j=1}^{n}\left(Y_j - \overline{Y}\right)^2}$$

This leads us to three measures that are often reported relating to regression results. The total sum of squares (TSS), the explained sum of squares (ESS), and the residual sum of squares (RSS). So, we can write the formula for the R^2 as:

$$R^2 = \frac{ESS}{TSS} = 1 - \frac{RSS}{TSS}$$

Total sum of squares (TSS)	$TSS = \sum_{i=1}^{n}(Y_i - \overline{Y})^2$	The TSS is the sum of squares of deviations of the observations of our dependent variable away from its average. This is a measure of the variability of Y_i.
Explained sum of squares (ESS)	$ESS = \sum_{i=1}^{n}(\hat{Y}_i - \overline{Y})^2$	The ESS is the sum of squares of deviations of the fitted values away from their average. This is a measure of the variability of fitted values of $\hat{Y}_i$ that is explained by the model.
Residual sum of squares (RSS)	$RSS = \sum_{i=1}^{n}\hat{u}_i^2$	The RSS is the quantity that we minimized when we constructed the OLS estimator. This is a measure of the variability of the unexplained elements of our dependent variable.

These measures are very similar to the measures we considered when looking at ANOVA tests in earlier chapters, and for very good reason. These measures can also be used to test hypotheses about our population, using an F-test.

To illustrate the difference between relationships with a low and a high R^2, consider Figure 27.9. Here, we can see scatter plots with a fitted line. Each dot represents an observation, and the line through the data is the fitted line from OLS.

[3] Again, this is proved in the appendix to this chapter.

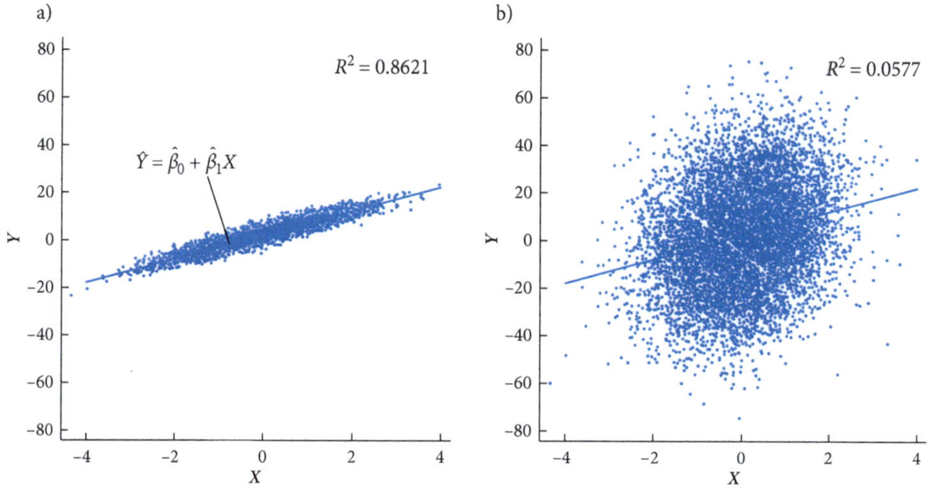

Figure 27.9 Comparing a relationship with a low R^2 and a relationship with a high R^2.

In the case where $R^2 = 0.0577$, you can see that the data is dispersed a long way around the fitted line; if the line wasn't there, it would be very difficult to pick out the trend in the data. However, when $R^2 = 0.8621$, the data is much closer to the line. In both cases, these relationships are based on 10,000 observations, but we can see that, when the R^2 is large, the data becomes much closer to the fitted line, and it is much easier to see a relationship just by looking at the data.

We can also visualize this by thinking about the distribution of the predicted values from the estimated model $\hat{Y}_i$ with the distribution of the true, observed, values of Y_i. Remember, the fitted or predicted values are constructed, based on an estimated $\hat{\beta}_0$, $\hat{\beta}_1$, and the observed value of X_i:

$$\hat{Y}_i = \hat{\beta}_0 + \hat{\beta}_1 X_i$$

This is illustrated in Figure 27.10. Panel a) compares the distribution of $\hat{Y}_i$ with the distribution of the true observations of Y_i for the example given in Figure 27.9, where $R^2 = 0.8621$. You can see that the two distributions are very similar. That is, much of the variation in the dependent variable is matched by very similar variation in the model (or the fitted $\hat{Y}_i$).

Conversely, in panel b), where $R^2 = 0.0577$, whilst the variability in the fitted $\hat{Y}_i$ is roughly the same as in panel a), there is much more variability in the dependent variable, Y_i. Because of this mis-match, much of the variation in the dependent variable is unexplained by the model. This means that the ratio between the variance of the $\hat{Y}_i$ and the variance of the Y_i will be very low.

One way of interpreting an R^2 in these two cases is:

- An R^2 of 0.8621 indicates that 86.21 per cent of the variation in the dependent variable (Y_i) is explained by variation in the model (i.e. variation in the $\hat{Y}_i$).
- An R^2 of 0.0577 indicates that 5.77 per cent of the variation in the dependent variable (Y_i) is explained by variation in the model, $\hat{Y}_i$.

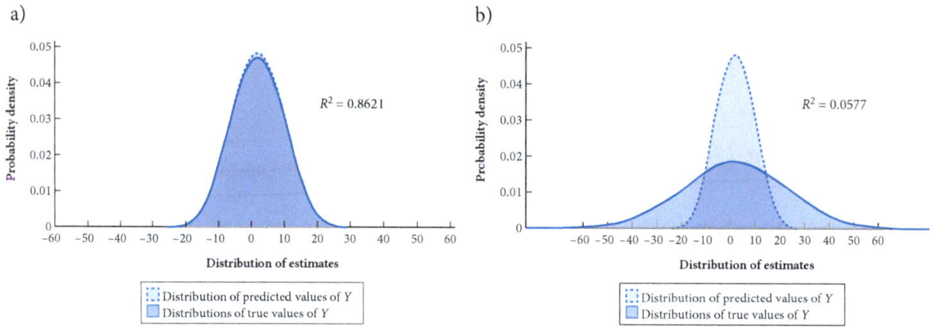

Figure 27.10 Comparing the distributions of $\hat{Y}_i$ and Y_i.

So, for $R^2 = 0.0577$, this is equivalent to:

$$\frac{var(\hat{Y}_i)}{var(Y_i)} \times 100 = 5.77\%$$

At its simplest, from Figure 27.9, we can see that the line fits the data much better in panel a) than in panel b). This is indicated by the fact that the data is much closer to the line, and that the variability in the predicted values is much closer to the variability in the dependent variable.

27.5.1 Measures of 'fit' in Microsoft Excel

When estimating OLS in Microsoft Excel, the key measures of how well the line fits the observed data are reported. To illustrate this, let's consider the regression of life expectancy against per capita spending on healthcare, based on OECD data that we saw earlier in this chapter. If you estimate this relationship in Excel, you will obtain output shown in Figure 27.1.

	A	B	C	D	E	F	G
1	SUMMARY OUTPUT						
2							
3	*Regression Statistics*						
4	Multiple R	0.614					
5	R Square	0.377					
6	Adjusted R Square	0.362					
7	Standard Error	2.603					
8	Observations	44.000					
9							
10	ANOVA						
11		*df*	*SS*	*MS*	*F*	*Significance F*	
12	Regression	1.00	171.95	171.95	25.39	0.00	
13	Residual	42.00	284.48	6.77			
14	Total	43.00	456.43				
15							
16		*Coefficients*	*Standard Error*	*t Stat*	*P-value*	*Lower 95%*	*Upper 95%*
17	Intercept	76.685	0.805	95.239	0.000	75.060	78.310
18	Spending per capita ($1000s US)	0.972	0.193	5.038	0.000	0.583	1.362
19							
20							

Figure 27.11 OLS regression output from Microsoft Excel.

Earlier in the chapter, we interpreted the estimated coefficients, but we also want to know how well the line we have estimated fits the data. All of this information is included in the top half of the output. Let's begin with rows 1 to 8, as illustrated in Figure 27.12.

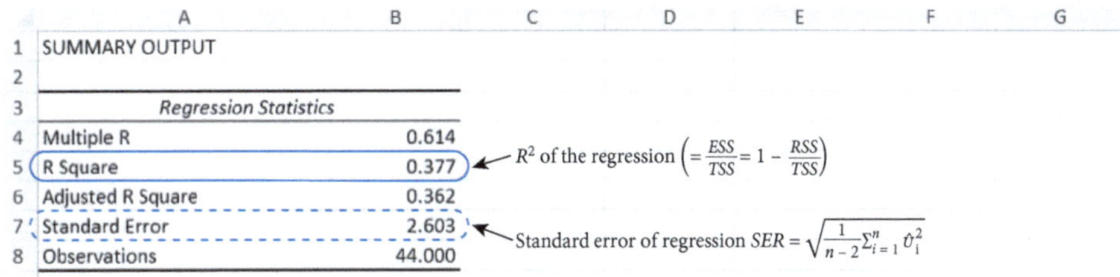

	A	B
1	SUMMARY OUTPUT	
2		
3	*Regression Statistics*	
4	Multiple R	0.614
5	R Square	0.377
6	Adjusted R Square	0.362
7	Standard Error	2.603
8	Observations	44.000

Figure 27.12 Annotated output relating to regression statistics from Microsoft Excel.

We can see that the $R^2 = 0.377$ (denoted R Squared). This indicates that 37.7 per cent of the variation in our dependent variable is explained by the model. Similarly, the standard error of the regression is given as 2.603. We can also see that the number of observations is 44.000 (i.e. we have 44 observations).

We can see where the numbers relating to the R^2 come from in the rest of the output. Remember that the R^2 is just equal to the ESS divided by the TSS. All of the relevant information is contained within the ANOVA section. You can hopefully see that there are columns headed by SS (meaning sum of squares) and MS (Mean of Sum of Squares). This is illustrated in Figure 27.13.

We can see that the ESS (which is denoted as the regression sum of squares in Excel) is 171.95, whilst the RSS is 284.48. Finally, the TSS is 456.43.

We can use these to calculate the R^2.

$ESS = 171.95, RSS = 284.48, TSS = 456.43$

So, we can calculate the $R^2 = \frac{ESS}{TSS} = \frac{171.95}{456.43} = 0.377$. Alternatively, we could calculate the $R^2 = 1 - \frac{RSS}{TSS} = 1 - \frac{284.48}{456.43} = 1 - 0.623 = 0.377$.

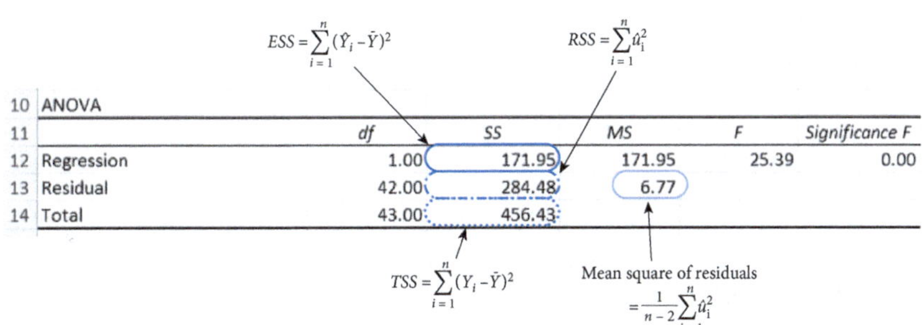

		df	*SS*	*MS*	*F*	*Significance F*
10	ANOVA					
11		*df*	*SS*	*MS*	*F*	*Significance F*
12	Regression	1.00	171.95	171.95	25.39	0.00
13	Residual	42.00	284.48	6.77		
14	Total	43.00	456.43			

Figure 27.13 Explained, residual, and total sum of squares.

F-tests based on OLS results

The Excel results also present the result of an F-test using ANOVA (see Figure 27.14). The explained sum of squares is much like the between group sum of squares, whilst the residual sum of squares is like the within group sum of squares in ANOVA.

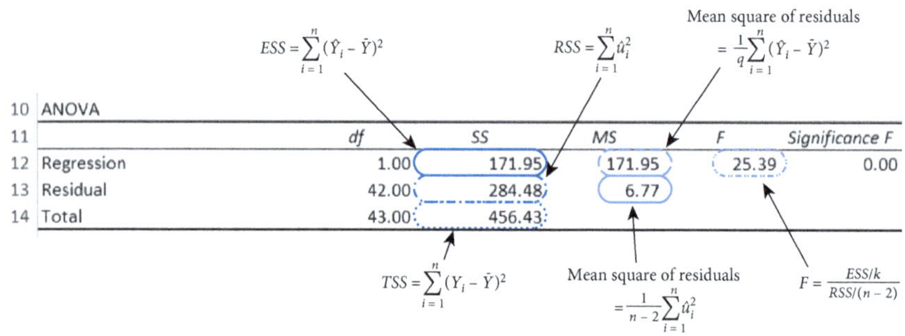

Figure 27.14 F-tests within Microsoft Excel.

The F-statistic presented here is testing the null hypothesis that the model does not explain the dependent variable. That is, the null hypothesis is that the coefficient on (all of) the explanatory variables is equal to zero.

$$F = \frac{ESS \,/\, k}{RSS \,/\, (n-2)}$$

k here is defined as the number of explanatory variables, excluding the constant. In this example, $k = 1$, but you will see examples as you study more econometrics with more than one explanatory variable. As such, our hypotheses are just:

$$H_0\!: \beta_1 = 0$$
$$H_A\!: \beta_1 \neq 0$$

The F-statistic is equal to 25.39, and would need to be compared with critical values from the $F_{q,n-2}$ distribution; alternatively, we could refer to the calculated p-value. If the null hypothesis were true, the probability of achieving an F-statistic greater than 25.39 would be equal to 0.00. As such, we can reject the null hypothesis at any reasonable level of significance.

Finally, look back at the estimated coefficient on per capita spending. You should see that the t-statistic is equal to 5.038. Interestingly, if we square this, we will obtain $5.038^2 = 25.39$. That is, when we square the t-statistic, we obtain the corresponding F-statistic.

27.5.2 Properties of the R^2

There are a range of properties of the R^2, which are useful to know, when either interpreting regression results, or reading published research that discusses the R^2 as a measure of how well the line fits the observed data.

1. Statisticians will often refer to the R^2 as telling us about how much variation in our explanatory variable explains variation in the dependent variable. This is because the fitted values, $\hat{Y}_i$, are just a linear function of the explanatory variables. Since the fitted values are constructed based on:

   $$\hat{Y}_i = \hat{\beta}_0 + \hat{\beta}_1 X_i$$

   then $var(\hat{Y}_i) = \hat{\beta}_1^2\, var(X_i)$. That is, the only variation within the fitted values of $\hat{Y}_i$ comes from variation in the X_i. As such, the R^2 provides us a measure of the proportion of variation in the dependent variable, Y_i, that can be attributed to variation in the explanatory variable.
2. Because the R^2 is a proportion, it will always be between 0 and 1. An R^2 of 0 indicates that variation in the explanatory variable explains none of the variation in the dependent variable, whilst an R^2 of 1 indicates that variation in the explanatory variable explains all of the variation in the dependent variable.
3. The R^2 has no units, so provides some ability to compare how well the model fits across different dependent variables.
4. When you are running a regression with a single explanatory variable, such as $Y_i = \beta_0 + \beta_1 X_i + u_i$, the R^2 is exactly equal to the square of the correlation coefficient between those two variables:

   $$R^2 = \hat{\rho}_{X,Y}^2$$

Note that this condition only holds when you have a single explanatory variable. As you study more econometrics, you will introduce multivariate regressions.

27.5.3 What makes a 'high' R^2?

A question that students of statistics often ask is 'what is a large R^2, and what is a small R^2?'. Unfortunately, the answer to this question is somewhat ambiguous. There is no set rule for when the R^2 is large, and when the R^2 is small. If the R^2 is close to 1 (say, 0.9), then it is unambiguously large. When the R^2 is close to zero (say, 0.01), then it is unambiguously small.

However, the context of the model matters. If you are estimating the impact of last year's GDP on this year's GDP, then the R^2 will automatically be high, because there are not, normally, large changes in GDP year-on-year. However, this will not be very informative, as it doesn't tell you why the changes occur year-on-year. If you are interested in the effect of years of education on gross weekly wages, the R^2 may be relatively low, but only because there is a wide range of other factors that determine wages. However, the results may be relatively informative.

As a good rule, if you are discussing the R^2, it can be useful to quantify the proportion of the variation that is explained by the model, but not try to state categorically that the R^2 is low or high.

Worked example 27.1: Interpreting the impact of age leaving education on wages

To illustrate how to interpret regression results, and how to carry out statistical tests, it's useful to consider a worked example.

I have randomly sampled 500 observations of female,[4] full-time workers aged 25–45 from the 2019 UK Labour Force Survey. I am interested in whether the age they left full-time education has any impact on their gross weekly wages.

We will estimate the following relationship for female workers:

$$Wages_i = \beta_0 + \beta_1 Educ_i + u_i$$

where $Wages_i$ are the gross weekly wages of individual i in their main job, and $Educ_i$ is the age at which they completed full-time education.

We represent the results from this regression in two forms here. Figure 27.15 shows the Excel output from a regression of $Wages_i$ against $Educ_i$, whilst Table 27.6 provides results formatted in the same way as you might see them in a published research paper.

In addition, Figure 27.16 shows the scatter plot of our observations, along with the fitted line, estimated via OLS, along with plotted confidence intervals. All of these suggest that there is a significant positive relationship between gross weekly wages and the age when completing full-time education.

There are three steps that we might wish to carry out when interpreting our regression results:

1. Ask how much of the variation in the dependent variable is explained by variation in the explanatory variable (i.e. what is the meaning of the R^2).
2. Ask whether the explanatory variable is statistically significant.
3. Explain what the meaning of the estimated coefficient is.

	A	B	C	D	E	F	G	H	I	J
1	SUMMARY OUTPUT									
2										
3	*Regression Statistics*									
4	Multiple R	0.289								
5	R Square	0.083								
6	Adjusted R Square	0.081								
7	Standard Error	292.536								
8	Observations	500								
9										
10	ANOVA									
11		*df*	*SS*	*MS*	*F*	*Significance F*				
12	Regression	1	3869914.604	3869914.604	45.221	4.839E-11				
13	Residual	498	42617638.778	85577.588						
14	Total	499	46487553.382							
15										
16		*Coefficients*	*Standard Error*	*t Stat*	*P-value*	*Lower 95%*	*Upper 95%*	*Lower 95.0%*	*Upper 95.0%*	
17	Intercept	1.180	90.976	0.013	0.990	-177.565	179.924	-177.565	179.924	
18	Age when completing full time education	30.593	4.549	6.725	0.000	21.654	39.531	21.654	39.531	
19										

Figure 27.15 Excel output from the regression of gross weekly wages against age leaving full-time education.

[4] In Chapter 25, we considered this for male, full-time workers aged 25–45. This is a different sample, considering the average wages within a different population. As such, we would expect to observe different results.

Table 27.6 Formatted results from a regression of gross weekly wages against age leaving full-time education

	Results
Age completing full-time education	30.593***
	(4.549)
Constant	1.180
	(90.976)
Number of observations	500
R-squared	0.083

Note: Dependent variable is the gross weekly wages of individual *i*. Estimated standard errors are reported in parentheses. *** indicates significant at the 1 per cent significance level, ** indicates significance at the 5 per cent significance level, * indicates significance at the 10 per cent significance level.

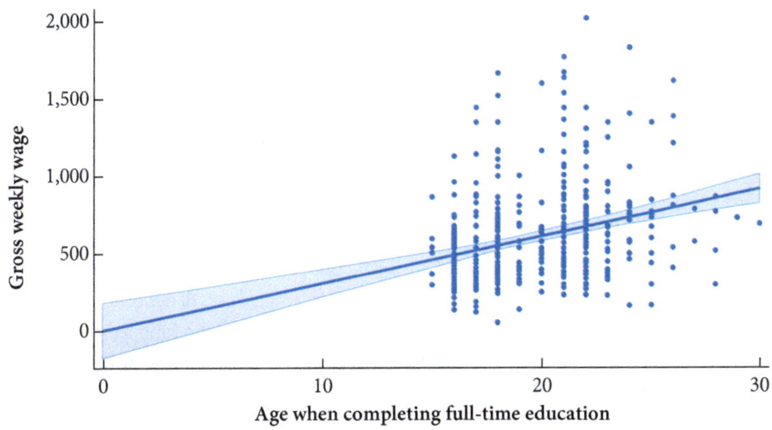

Figure 27.16 Scatter plot illustrating the estimated relationship with confidence intervals.

Let's begin with the first question; here the R^2 is equal to 0.083. This indicates that 8.3 per cent of the variation in the dependent variable is explained by variation in completed years of education. However, that also means that 91.7 per cent of the variation remains unexplained. This could be due to other factors that determine gross weekly wage, including experience not being included within the model.

We can then move on to test whether or not the estimated coefficients are statistically significant. Often authors ignore the estimated intercept (as they are only really interested in the marginal effect of the explanatory variable). Here, we will explicitly test the statistical significance of both the β_1 explanatory variable and the intercept.

Intercept	Explanatory variable
We wish to test the hypotheses: H_0: $\beta_0 = 0$ H_A: $\beta_0 \neq 0$ To test this, we begin by constructing the t-statistic. Remember that the t-statistic is constructed under the assumption that the null hypothesis (H_0) is true; i.e. assuming $\beta_0 = 0$. $t = \frac{\hat{\beta}_0 - E(\hat{\beta}_0 \mid \beta_0 = 0)}{\widehat{s.e.}(\hat{\beta}_0)}$ Substituting our estimated coefficient and standard error, and assuming that the OLS estimator is unbiased: $\Rightarrow t = \frac{1.180 - 0}{90.976} = 0.013$ We have 200 observations, but have estimated two coefficients ($\hat{\beta}_0$ and $\hat{\beta}_1$), so we have 500 – 2 = 498 degrees of freedom. The critical value at the 5% significance level is 1.96. As the magnitude of the t-statistic is less than 1.96, we would fail to reject the null hypothesis. Based on the Excel output, the p-value associated with $t = 0.013$ based on 198 degrees of freedom is 0.990. That is, when the null hypothesis is true, 99.0% of the time you would gain a t-statistic either above +0.013 or below −0.013. This is a large probability, indicating that it would not be an unlikely event. Based on this, we have insufficient evidence to conclude that the intercept is non-zero.	We wish to test the hypotheses: H_0: $\beta_1 = 0$ H_A: $\beta_1 \neq 0$ To test this, we begin by constructing the t-statistic. Remember that the t-statistic is constructed under the assumption that the null hypothesis (H_0) is true; i.e. assuming $\beta_1 = 0$. $t = \frac{\hat{\beta}_1 - E(\hat{\beta}_1 \mid \beta_1 = 0)}{\widehat{s.e.}(\hat{\beta}_1)}$ Substituting our estimated coefficient and standard error, and assuming that the OLS estimator is unbiased: $\Rightarrow t = \frac{30.593 - 0}{4.549} = 6.725$ We have 200 observations, but have estimated two coefficients ($\hat{\beta}_0$ and $\hat{\beta}_1$), so we have 500–2 = 498 degrees of freedom. The critical value at the 5% significance level is 1.96. As the magnitude of the t-statistic is larger than 1.96, we would reject the null hypothesis at the 5% significance level. Based on the Excel output, the p-value associated with $t = 6.725$ based on 198 degrees of freedom is 0.00000000005 (or more accurately 4.84×10^{-11}). That is, when the null hypothesis is true, 0.000000005% of the time, you would gain a t-statistic either above +6.725, or below −6.725. This is a very small probability. That is, randomly gaining a t-statistic this large would be an unlikely event. Because the p-value is less than 0.01, we can conclude that $\hat{\beta}_1$ is significant at the 1% significance level. Based on this, we can reject the null hypothesis that $\beta_1 = 0$.

We could also have used the F-test in the Excel output to test the hypothesis that $\beta_1 = 0$. We can see that the F-statistic is equal to 22.764. $k = 1$ here as there is only one explanatory variable, $ESS = 3{,}869{,}914.604$, whilst $RSS = 42{,}617{,}638.778$.

$$F = \frac{ESS/k}{RSS/n-2} = \frac{3{,}869{,}914.604/1}{42{,}617{,}638.778/498} = 45.221$$

The p-value associated with this F-statistic (based on an $F_{1,498}$ distribution) is equal to 0.00000355. You'll notice that this is exactly the same p-value as we obtained through our t-test.

As before, note that the t-statistic associated with the slope parameter is $t = 6.725\,(3dp)$. If we square the (unrounded) t-statistic, we obtain $t^2 = 45.221$. That is, the square of the t-statistic is once again equal to the F-statistic.

This shouldn't be a surprise based on the definition of the F-statistic and the t-statistic. Since an F-statistic is defined as the ratio of two chi-squared variables divided by their degrees of freedom:

$$F = \frac{\chi_q^2/q}{\chi_k^2/k}$$

Similarly, a variable following the t-distribution is defined as one based on the ratio of a (standard) normally distributed variable (Z), divided by the square root of a chi-squared variable (divided by its degrees of freedom, χ_k^2/k):

$$t = \frac{Z}{\sqrt{\frac{\chi_k^2}{k}}}$$

Therefore, if we square a variable following the t-distribution, we will have Z^2 divided by χ_k^2/k. However, by definition, the chi-squared distribution with q degrees of freedom is equal to the sum of q independent squares of standard normal variables. Thus, Z^2 will follow a chi-squared distribution with 1 degree of freedom:

$$\Rightarrow t^2 = \frac{Z^2/1}{\chi_k^2/k} = \frac{\chi_1^2/1}{\chi_k^2/k}$$

We have divided the numerator by 1, which makes no difference to the value, but allows us to write t^2 in terms of the definition of the F-distribution. Therefore, if we have a variable that follows the t-distribution, the square of that variable will always follow the F-distribution.

$$\Rightarrow t^2(k) = F_{1,k}$$

Finally, our estimated $\hat{\beta}_1 = 30.593$. We have estimated the following relationship:

$$Wages_i = \beta_0 + \beta_1 Educ_i + u_i$$

β_1 is therefore the marginal effect of leaving education one year later on gross weekly wages. Our estimates suggest that, by gaining an additional year of education, a female full-time worker increases her gross weekly wages by £30.593.

Important note

We have interpreted these relationships, assuming that the estimates are unbiased. Whenever you estimate a relationship using OLS, you should ask yourself about whether it is likely that the explanatory variable is exogenous. That is, are the observations of $Educ_i$ likely to be independent from the error terms?

In this example, it is highly likely that there is omitted variables bias. Remember, omitted variables bias occurs when there is some other variable that is a determinant of $Wages_i$, but is not included in the regression, and is correlated with the explanatory variable. If we have omitted a variable, Z_i, and the marginal effect of Z_i on $Wages_i$ is β_2, then in large samples, the (asymptotic) bias of omitting Z_i is:

$$= \beta_2 \frac{cov(Educ_i, Z_i)}{var(Educ_i)}$$

An example of Z_i might be the age of the individual. In general:

i) As individuals get older, their earnings tend to increase, as they increase their experience and seniority within a role.
ii) Similarly, there have been changes over the last 20 years in education levels. For example, more individuals are going on to higher education (e.g. university) than 20 years ago. As such, we would expect the older members of our sample to have left education at an earlier age than the younger members of the sample (on average).

Summary

In this chapter, we have introduced how to carry out statistical testing with OLS estimates when we have a single explanatory variable. Statistical software packages will carry out many of these steps for you, and will estimate coefficients, standard errors relating to those coefficients, and confidence intervals, calculate t-statistics and appropriate p-values, along with regression diagnostic tools, including the R^2, and F-tests relating to the regression you have estimated.

However, there are a number of questions that we haven't answered. In this chapter, we have only considered OLS regressions where we have a single explanatory variable. In the next chapter, we will introduce multivariate regressions, where we have more than one explanatory variable.

We have also only looked at the estimated effects in a very naïve way. When we've estimated the relationship:

$$Y_i = \beta_0 + \beta_1 X_i + u_i$$

we have thought of β_1 as the impact (on Y) of increasing X by 1. But is it reasonable for X to increase by 1? For example, X_i might be a proportion, where the minimum value is 0, and the maximum value is 1. Would it make sense to move from the minimum value to the largest possible value?

Similarly, even if increasing X by 1, is β_1 a large increase in Y? For instance, if $\beta_1 = 0.5$, but Y is UK GDP ($2.7 trillion in 2020), then the impact of a change in X by 1 is vanishingly small. This analysis is asking the question of whether the change is economically significant, and we will discuss this in more detail in later chapters.

Appendix

Properties of the fitted residuals

In this chapter, we have introduced the R^2. A key element in the construction of the R^2 is that the $cov(\hat{Y},\hat{u}) = 0$. That is, the covariance between the fitted $\hat{Y}$ and the fitted residuals, $\hat{u}$, is equal to zero. In this appendix, we will prove this, along with some other characteristics of the fitted residuals.

Summary of results	
$\frac{1}{n}\sum_{i=1}^{n}\hat{u}_i = 0$	The average (and sum) of the fitted residuals is equal to zero. This means that, on average, the fitted residuals will have positive and negative values that cancel out, meaning that the line passes through the 'middle' of the data.
$\frac{1}{n}\sum_{i=1}^{n}\hat{u}_i X_i = 0$	It follows from this property that the explanatory variable (and the fitted values of $\hat{Y}_i$) are uncorrelated with the fitted residuals.
$cov(\hat{u}, X) = 0$	The fitted residuals are uncorrelated with the observed values of X.
$cov(\hat{u}, \hat{Y}) = 0$	The fitted residuals are uncorrelated with the fitted values of $\hat{Y}$.
$\frac{1}{n}\sum_{i=1}^{n}\hat{Y}_i = \frac{1}{n}\sum_{i=1}^{n}Y_i$	Since the average of the fitted residuals is equal to the average of the observations of the Y_i, this means that our fitted line automatically passes through the point given by the average of the observations of the Y_i and the average of the observations of the X_i.

Proofs

1. The average of the fitted residuals is equal to zero. $\frac{1}{n}\sum_{i=1}^{n}\hat{u}_i = 0$

When we estimated the following relationship:

$$Y_i = \beta_0 + \beta_1 X_i + u_i$$

the equation of the fitted residuals was given by:

$$\hat{u}_i = Y_i - \hat{\beta}_0 - \hat{\beta}_1 X_i \qquad \text{Fitted residuals (1)}$$

We constructed the OLS estimator by minimizing the sum of squares of residuals, by differentiating with respect to $\hat{\beta}_0$ and $\hat{\beta}_1$. If we examine the first order condition, with respect to $\hat{\beta}_0$:

$$\frac{\partial}{\partial\hat{\beta}_0}\sum_{i=1}^{n}\hat{u}_i^2 = -2\sum_{i=1}^{n}(Y_i - \hat{\beta}_0 - \hat{\beta}_1 X_i) = 0 \qquad \text{FOC1}$$

But we can see that the equation for the fitted residuals ($\hat{u}_i = Y_i - \hat{\beta}_0 - \hat{\beta}_1 X_i$) is included in FOC1, so we can rewrite FOC1 to give us:

$$= -2\sum_{i=1}^{n}\hat{u}_i = 0$$

This must mean that $\sum_{i=1}^{n}\hat{u}_i = 0$, and hence the sample mean of the fitted residuals is also equal to 0. The implication of this is that the fitted line passes through the middle of the data.

2. The sum of the products of the fitted residuals and the observed values of X is equal to zero.

$$\sum_{i=1}^{n} \hat{u}_i X_i = 0$$

To prove this, we will consider a number of steps. First, we shall prove that the average of the products of $\hat{u}_i X_i$ is equal to zero.
We will begin by examining the second FOC

$$\frac{\partial}{\partial \hat{\beta}_1} \sum_{i=1}^{n} \hat{u}_i^2 = -2\sum_{i=1}^{n}(Y_i - \hat{\beta}_0 - \hat{\beta}_1 X_i)X_i = 0 \qquad \text{FOC2}$$

Again, we can see that the equation for the fitted residuals is included here, and so we can rewrite the second FOC as:

$$= -2\sum_{i=1}^{n} \hat{u}_i X_i = 0$$

This must mean that $\frac{1}{n}\sum_{i=1}^{n} \hat{u}_i X_i = 0$.

3. The fitted residuals are uncorrelated with the explanatory variable, $X cov(\hat{u}, X) = 0$.

To prove that the X are uncorrelated with the $\hat{u}$, we will also need to think about the definitions of the covariance:

$$cov(\hat{u}, X) = E(\hat{u}X) - E(\hat{u})E(X)$$

Now, we have proven for any sample size that:

$$\frac{1}{n}\sum_{i=1}^{n} \hat{u}_i X_i = 0$$

We can appeal to the **strong law of large numbers**, which tells us that as the sample size tends towards infinity, the sample mean will converge towards the expectation:

$$\lim_{n\to\infty} \frac{1}{n}\sum_{i=1}^{n} \hat{u}_i X_i = E(\hat{u}X)$$

But we know that, for any value of n, it follows that $\frac{1}{n}\sum_{i=1}^{n} \hat{u}_i X_i = 0$. It thus follows that $E(\hat{u}X) = 0$.
We can use the same argument for $E(\hat{u}) = \lim_{n\to\infty} \frac{1}{n}\sum_{i=1}^{n} \hat{u}_i$. We've shown that the sample mean of the $\hat{u}_i$s is always equal to zero, so it must also follow that $E(\hat{u}) = 0$. Thus, the covariance between $\hat{u}$ and X is equal to:

$$cov(\hat{u}, X) = E(\hat{u}X) - E(\hat{u})E(X) = 0 - 0 \times E(X) = 0 - 0 = 0$$

Thus, it follows that $cov(\hat{u}, X) = 0$.

4. The fitted values of $\hat{Y}_i$ are uncorrelated with the $\hat{u}_i cov(\hat{Y}, \hat{u}) = 0$.

Let's begin by showing that $\sum_{i=1}^{n} \hat{Y}_i \hat{u}_i = 0$. The $\hat{Y}_i$ are the fitted values, based on our estimated relationship, so we can write that:

$$\hat{Y}_i = \hat{\beta}_0 + \hat{\beta}_1 X_i$$

If we substitute this into the summation, we have:

$$\sum_{i=1}^{n} \hat{Y}_i \hat{u}_i = \sum_{i=1}^{n} (\hat{\beta}_0 + \hat{\beta}_1 X_i)\hat{u}_i = \hat{\beta}_0 \sum_{i=1}^{n} \hat{u}_i + \hat{\beta}_1 \sum_{i=1}^{n} X_i \hat{u}_i$$

Now, we already know that $\sum_{i=1}^{n} \hat{u}_i = \sum_{i=1}^{n} X_i \hat{u}_i = 0$, and so we can write that:

$$\sum_{i=1}^{n} \hat{Y}_i \hat{u}_i = 0$$

By the strong law of large numbers it also follows that $E(\hat{Y}\,\hat{u}) = 0$:

$$cov(\hat{Y}, \hat{u}) = E(\hat{Y}\,\hat{u}) - E(\hat{Y})E(\hat{u}) = 0 - E(\hat{Y}) \times 0 = 0$$

5. The average of the fitted values $\hat{Y}_i$ is equal to $\overline{Y}$.

$$\frac{1}{n}\sum_{i=1}^{n}\hat{Y}_i = \frac{1}{n}\sum_{i=1}^{n}Y_i = \overline{Y}$$

The equation of the fitted values is given as:

$$\hat{Y}_i = \hat{\beta}_0 + \hat{\beta}_1 X_i$$

We know that the OLS estimator for the intercept is given by $\hat{\beta}_0 = \overline{Y} - \hat{\beta}_1\overline{X}$, so we can substitute this into the equation for $\hat{Y}_i$:

$$\hat{Y}_i = \overline{Y} - \hat{\beta}_1\overline{X} + \hat{\beta}_1 X_i$$

To find the sample mean of $\hat{Y}_i$, we simply add up all the observations, and divide by the number of observations:

$$\overline{\hat{Y}} = \frac{1}{n}\sum_{i=1}^{n}\hat{Y}_i = \frac{1}{n}\sum_{i=1}^{n}(\overline{Y} - \hat{\beta}_1\overline{X} + \hat{\beta}_1 X_i)$$

We can split the summation up into three parts. However, $\overline{Y}$ and $\hat{\beta}_1\overline{X}$ are just constants in this summation, so this becomes:

$$= \overline{Y} - \hat{\beta}_1\overline{X} + \hat{\beta}_1 \times \frac{1}{n} \times \sum_{i=1}^{n} X_i$$

The final term is just equal to $\overline{X}$, so we can rewrite this as:

$$= \overline{Y} - \hat{\beta}_1\overline{X} + \hat{\beta}_1\overline{X} = \overline{Y}$$

Multivariate Regressions

28

Learning outcomes for this chapter

By the end of this chapter you will be able to:

- Explain how OLS estimates relationships with more than one explanatory variable
- Interpret multivariate regressions, and choose appropriate explanatory variables
- Evaluate estimated results in terms of economic significance
- Recognize key problems with multivariate regressions, including perfect multicollinearity
- Recognize the difference between perfect and imperfect multicollinearity, and understand that these require very different solutions

Mathematical tools

- Equations of straight lines
- Arithmetic
- Partial derivatives

Introduction

So far, in our discussion of econometrics, we have introduced the OLS estimator with a single explanatory variable:

$$Y_i = \beta_0 + \beta_1 X_i + u_i$$

However, as we saw in Chapter 25, if we have omitted a determinant of the dependent variable that is correlated with the explanatory variable, X_i, then our estimated $\hat{\beta}_1$ will be both biased and inconsistent.

A simple solution to this is to introduce multivariate regressions—that is, OLS regressions with more than one explanatory variable. We can use exactly the same methods as we have seen for a simple regression with a single explanatory variable to construct our estimators, and we can interpret the results in very similar ways.

During this chapter, we will also discuss what makes results economically significant. That is, based on an estimated coefficient, is the estimated effect large? Or is the estimated effect small? How can we tell?

28.1 How do we construct OLS with more than one explanatory variable?

Let's begin with a simple regression with a single explanatory variable. Suppose that we are interested in estimating specification (1) using OLS:

$$Y_i = \beta_0 + \beta_1 X_i + u_i \qquad \text{(1) Regression specification}$$

We have seen that OLS will be both biased and inconsistent, if $cov(X, u) = 0$. Suppose that, in reality, Y_i is determined not just by X_i, but also by some other variable, Z_i.

$$Y_i = \beta_0 + \beta_1 X_i + \beta_2 Z_i + e_i \qquad \text{(2) True DGP}$$

If the true data generating process is given by (2), then we have seen that if we try to estimate (1) using OLS, the resulting $\hat{\beta}_1$ will be biased, with the asymptotic bias due to omitting Z_i equal to $\beta_2 \frac{cov(X,Z)}{var(X)}$.

That is, if:

- Z is a determinant of Y ($\beta_2 \neq 0$), and
- X is correlated with the (omitted) Z variable ($\text{cov}(Z, X) \neq 0$),

then OLS will be biased and inconsistent.

So, we have seen that OLS can become biased if we omit an explanatory variable that is, itself, correlated with the explanatory variable of interest. However, so far, we have only dealt with OLS regressions relating to a single explanatory variable.

An obvious way to try to solve omitted variables bias would be to introduce a regression where we also include the omitted Z_i variable as a second explanatory variable. That is, we could try to estimate specification (3):

$$Y_i = \beta_0 + \beta_1 X_i + \beta_2 Z_i + e_i \qquad \text{(3) New regression specification}$$

Partial derivatives

In multivariate calculus, the **partial derivative** provides us the rate of change, holding everything else fixed. So, if:

$$W = 2Q + 3P$$

then $\frac{\partial W}{\partial Q} = 2$ is the rate of change of W with relation to Q, holding P constant.

Now, we can think about what is going on here mathematically by considering the partial derivative of our expression, first with relation to X_i, and then with relation to Z_i:

$$\frac{\partial Y_i}{\partial X_i} = \beta_1, \ \frac{\partial Y_i}{\partial Z_i} = \beta_2$$

So, β_1 can be interpreted as the marginal effect of a change in X on Y, holding Z constant, and similarly, β_2 can be interpreted as the marginal effect of a change in Z on Y, holding X constant.

To construct the OLS estimators with two explanatory variables, we would follow exactly the same approach as when we had one explanatory variable; we would choose the optimal $\hat{\beta}_0, \hat{\beta}_1$, and $\hat{\beta}_2$, which minimize the sum of squares of the residuals (SSR). In fact, this method of constructing OLS estimators is generalizable to any number of explanatory variables. We can estimate OLS with any number of explanatory variables, provided we have strictly more observations than we have explanatory variables.

28.1.1 Constructing the OLS estimators with two explanatory variables

If you are interested in estimating a relationship between a dependent variable, Y_i, and two explanatory variables, X_i and Z_i:

$$Y_i = \beta_0 + \beta_1 X_i + \beta_2 Z_i + e_i$$

The OLS estimator is constructed using exactly the same steps as in the case with one explanatory variable; we choose the optimal $\hat{\beta}_0, \hat{\beta}_1$, and $\hat{\beta}_2$ which minimize the sum of squares of the fitted residuals. That is, we are choosing the optimal $\hat{\beta}$s to minimize the following expression:

$$\sum_{i=1}^{n} \hat{e}_i^2 = \sum_{i=1}^{n} \left(Y_i - \hat{\beta}_0 - \hat{\beta}_1 X_i - \hat{\beta}_2 Z_i \right)^2$$

To do this, we can differentiate this expression with relation to $\hat{\beta}_0, \hat{\beta}_1$, and $\hat{\beta}_2$, and set these derivatives equal to zero, to construct the appropriate first order conditions (FOCs):

$$\sum_{i=1}^{n} \left(Y_i - \hat{\beta}_0^{OLS} - \hat{\beta}_1^{OLS} X_i - \hat{\beta}_2^{OLS} Z_i \right) = 0 \qquad \text{FOC1}$$

$$\sum_{i=1}^{n} \left(Y_i - \hat{\beta}_0^{OLS} - \hat{\beta}_1^{OLS} X_i - \hat{\beta}_2^{OLS} Z_i \right) X_i = 0 \qquad \text{FOC2}$$

$$\sum_{i=1}^{n} \left(Y_i - \hat{\beta}_0^{OLS} - \hat{\beta}_1^{OLS} X_i - \hat{\beta}_2^{OLS} Z_i \right) Z_i = 0 \qquad \text{FOC3}$$

It is possible (but mathematically involved) to show that the OLS estimators for β_0, β_1, and β_2 are given by:

$$\hat{\beta}_0^{OLS} = \bar{Y} - \hat{\beta}_1 \bar{X} - \hat{\beta}_2 \bar{Z}$$

$$\hat{\beta}_1^{OLS} = \frac{\sum_{i=1}^{n} (Y_i - \bar{Y})(X_i - \bar{X}) \sum_{j=1}^{n} (Z_j - \bar{Z})^2 - \sum_{k=1}^{n} (Y_k - \bar{Y})(Z_k - \bar{Z}) \sum_{l=1}^{n} (Z_l - \bar{Z})(X_l - \bar{X})}{\sum_{m=1}^{n} (X_m - \bar{X})^2 \sum_{p=1}^{n} (Z_p - \bar{Z})^2 - \left(\sum_{q=1}^{n} (Z_q - \bar{Z})(X_q - \bar{X}) \right)^2}$$

$$\hat{\beta}_2^{OLS} = \frac{\sum_{i=1}^{n} (Y_i - \bar{Y})(Z_i - \bar{Z}) \sum_{j=1}^{n} (X_j - \bar{X})^2 - \sum_{k=1}^{n} (Y_k - \bar{Y})(X_k - \bar{X}) \sum_{l=1}^{n} (Z_l - \bar{Z})(X_l - \bar{X})}{\sum_{m=1}^{n} (X_m - \bar{X})^2 \sum_{p=1}^{n} (Z_p - \bar{Z})^2 - \left(\sum_{q=1}^{n} (Z_q - \bar{Z})(X_q - \bar{X}) \right)^2}$$

In reality, it is unlikely that it will be useful to try to memorize these estimators, as statistical software packages can estimate OLS regressions with multiple explanatory variables.

28.1.2 Degrees of freedom

The number of degrees of freedom is the number of linearly independent $\hat{e}_i$ we have in the sum of squares of the residuals. Remember, the number of degrees of freedom can be thought of as the number of observations less the number of coefficients that we estimate. So, if we have k explanatory variables $(X_{1i}, X_{2i}, X_{3i}, \ldots, X_{ki})$, and estimate the following relationship:

$$Y_i = \beta_0 + \beta_1 X_{1i} + \beta_2 X_{2i} + \beta_3 X_{3i} + \ldots + \beta_k X_{ki} + u_i$$

then we have estimated k coefficients on our explanatory variables, and the β_0 for the intercept. As such, we have estimated $k + 1$ coefficients, and the number of degrees of freedom will be $n - (k + 1) = n - k - 1$.

It is often much easier to remember this as being equal to the number of observations less the number of coefficients estimated (including the constant). If we have estimated q population parameters, then we will have $n - q$ degrees of freedom.

CALCULATING THE NUMBER OF DEGREES OF FREEDOM

The number of degrees of freedom will always be equal to the number of observations minus the number of coefficients estimated. If you have k explanatory variables, and an intercept, in your model then:

$$\text{Degrees of freedom} = n - k - 1$$

28.1.3 How many explanatory variables can we include?

In the previous section, we have discussed the OLS estimator with two explanatory variables, but in principle, we can construct the OLS estimator for any number of explanatory variables, as long as we have more observations than coefficients we are trying to estimate.

If you tried to estimate OLS with fewer observations than coefficients, this is equivalent to trying to solve a simultaneous equation, where you have more unknowns than you have separate equations. Ultimately, this is impossible. This is easiest to see when we are trying to estimate the relationship:

$$Y_i = \beta_0 + \beta_1 X_i + u_i$$

The minimum number of observations needed to estimate both β_0 and β_1 is two. This is illustrated in Figure 28.1.

In order to determine a trend, we would need at least two observations, to draw a line of best fit through. When there is only one observation, we could choose any line that passed through the observation; that is, there would be an infinite number of lines of best fit, with an infinite number of intercepts and slopes.

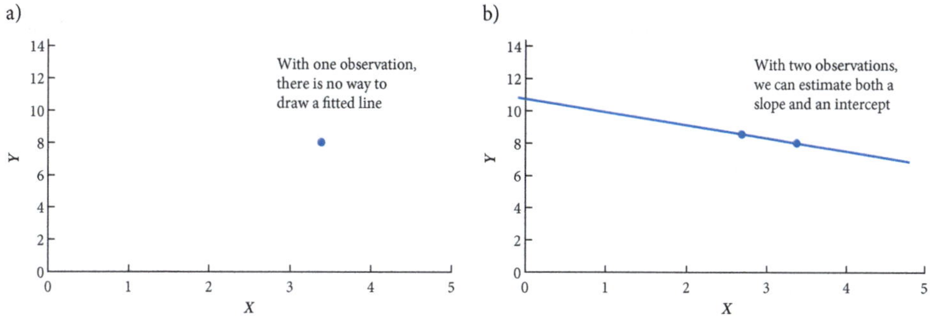

Figure 28.1 You need at least as many observations as the number of coefficients you are estimating.

As soon as we introduce two observations, we can choose a (single) line of best fit. However, this is still probably not a good estimate of the relationship between Y and X, as we would have zero degrees of freedom. If we took a different set of (two) observations, we would get very different line of best fit.

Remember, the number of degrees of freedom is equal to the number of observations, less the number of coefficients being estimated. It is impossible to estimate the relationship if the number of unknowns (i.e. coefficients) is less than the number of observations; that is, in order to estimate the relationship, you need to have at least zero degrees of freedom. Having said that, the estimate of the line will improve as the number of degrees of freedom increases; that is, as the difference between the number of observations and the number of coefficients estimated increases, the variance of the estimators decreases.

Irrespective of the number of explanatory variables, when we construct the OLS estimator, we are choosing the optimal set of coefficients to minimize the sum of squares of residuals, $\sum_{i=1}^{n} \hat{u}_i^2$.

As you include more explanatory variables, the OLS estimators will become more difficult to write down using summation notation,[1] but statistical software packages will usually carry out the calculations for you.

28.1.4 The impact of additional explanatory variables on R^2

The R^2 tells us the proportion of the variance of our dependent variable that is explained by our explanatory variables, so intuitively, we might expect that, if the R^2 increases as we add in additional variables, then it must mean that the new explanatory variables are adding explanatory power. Unfortunately, this intuition is not quite correct.

Whenever we add in additional explanatory variables, even if the variables add nothing more to the model, the R^2 will automatically get larger,[2] unless the new estimated $\hat{\beta}_k = 0$.

[1] As you advance in your study of econometrics, you may see the OLS estimator written in matrix notation. This is beyond the scope or the expectation of this book, but in matrix notation, you can represent the OLS estimator, with any number of explanatory variables as $\hat{\beta} = (X'X)^{-1}X'Y$ where $\hat{\beta}$ is a vector containing all of the $\hat{\beta}$s, and X is a matrix containing all of the explanatory variables. This notation is much more compact, but much less intuitive.

[2] We prove this in the appendix to this chapter.

As such, as we add in additional variables, we cannot look at the R^2 and state that an increased R^2 means the model is a 'better fit' for the data. A way of examining whether additional explanatory variables have any impact on the 'fit' of the model is to consider the adjusted R^2. This takes account of the fact that additional explanatory variables automatically increase the standard R^2, so give a clearer indication. So,

$$R^2_{Adj} = 1 - \frac{(1 - R^2)(n - 1)}{n - k - 1}$$

Once again, k is the number of explanatory variables in the model, so $n - k - 1$ is the number of degrees of freedom in the model. That is, it is the number of observations, less the total number of coefficients estimated (including the intercept).

28.2 Applying multivariate regression

In Chapter 23, we examined the relationship between life expectancy (as our dependent variable), and per capita spending on healthcare, and estimated the following relationship by OLS:

$$LifeExp_i = \beta_0 + \beta_1 Spend_i + u_i$$

When we estimated this relationship, we gained the results illustrated in Figure 28.2.

However, we noted that the estimated coefficients from this regression were likely to suffer from omitted variables bias. One candidate for an omitted variable that may cause bias is GDP per capita.

We may have reason to believe that the richer the country, the longer the life expectancy. For the sake of this analysis, we will assume that, if there is an effect, this is a direct effect, although in reality, this is likely to be an indirect effect (e.g. in richer countries, the populations might have better diets, better education, etc.).

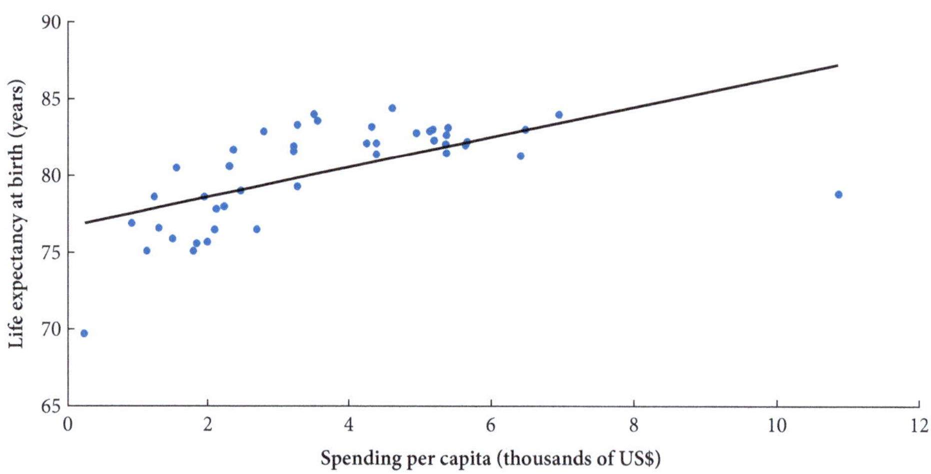

Figure 28.2 Results from a regression of life expectancy against per capita spending on healthcare (data from the OECD).

We can see from Figure 28.3 that there is a very strong correlation between the included variable ($Spend_i$), or per capita spending on healthcare, and per capita GDP.

If the true data generating process for life expectancy is:

$$LifeExp_i = \beta_0 + \beta_1 Spend_i + \beta_2 GDP_i + e_i$$

then in large samples, by the bias omitting the per capita GDP from our specification would be equal to:

$$\text{Asymptotic bias} = \beta_2 \frac{cov(Spend_i, GDP_i)}{var(Spend_i)}$$

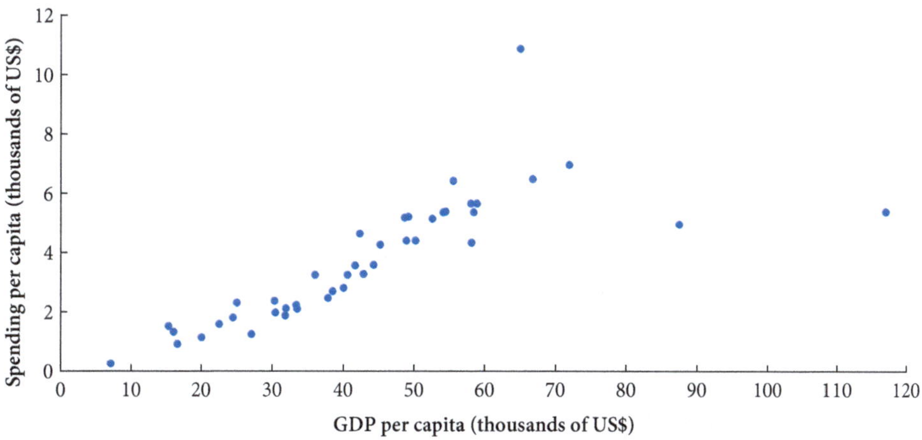

Figure 28.3 Scatter plot of per capita spending on healthcare against per capita GDP (data from the OECD).

We can see from Figure 28.3 that there is a strong relationship between $Spend_i$ and GDP_i; that is, as per capita GDP increases, on average per capita spending on healthcare also increases. The covariance will be strongly positive. As such, if GDP_i is a determinant of life expectancy (that is, if $\beta_2 \neq 0$), then omitting per capita GDP would cause bias. It is likely that richer countries (on average) have higher life expectancy, so we might expect β_2 to be positive, and as such, we might expect the bias from omitting GDP_i from the specification to be positive.

When we have two explanatory variables, it becomes a little more difficult to visualize what the data looks like. We now need to think about the data being plotted on three-dimensional axes, with each observation having three coordinates. The first two coordinates relate to the explanatory variables, per capita spending on health care and per capita GDP, whilst the final coordinate is the outcome variable, or life expectancy. These data are illustrated in Figure 28.4.

Similarly, since we are now thinking in three dimensions, we are no longer thinking about fitting a line through the data, but we are effectively fitting a plane through the data. It is rare to see scatter plots of data presented in this three-dimensional format in research papers, but it is useful to visualize what is going on here. When we estimate a relationship with more than one explanatory variable, we are thinking about the marginal impact of a change in that explanatory variable, keeping everything else fixed. You can think of the results as the estimated impact of a change in $Spend_i$, having chosen a particular value of GDP.

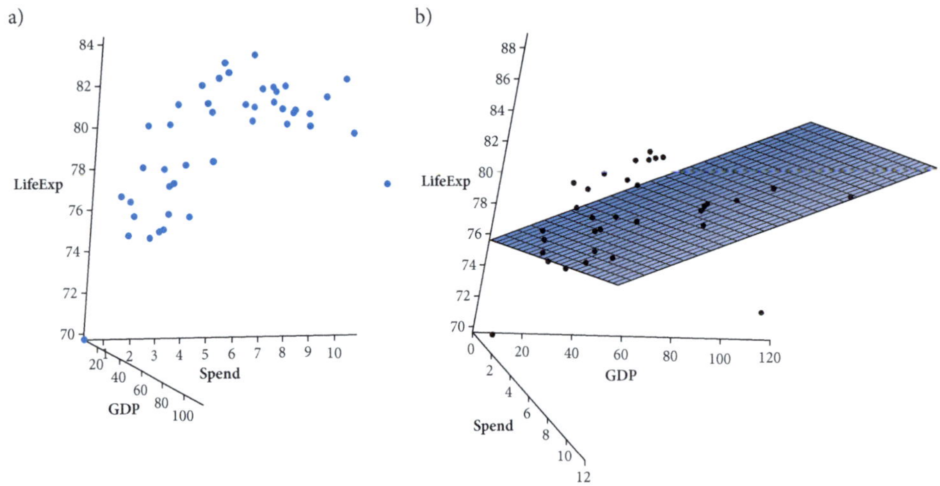

Figure 28.4 Scatter plots of life expectancy against spending on healthcare and GDP.

We will estimate regressions (1) and (2). Regression (1) is the specification we have previously examined, where we have only per capita spending on healthcare ($Spend_i$) as an explanatory variable, whilst regression (2) is our first **multivariate regression**, where we also include per capita GDP as a second explanatory variable.

$$LifeExp_i = \beta_0 + \beta_1 Spend_i + u_i \qquad (1)$$

$$LifeExp_i = \beta_0 + \beta_1 Spend_i + \beta_2 GDP_i + e_i \qquad (2)$$

These results are presented in Table 28.1. Column (1) shows the results that we have already seen, with only per capita spending on healthcare included as an explanatory variable, whilst

Table 28.1 Results from a multivariate regression of life expectancy against per capita spending on healthcare and per capita GDP

	(1)	(2)
Spending on healthcare per capita	0.972	0.458
	(0.193)	(0.292)
GDP per capita		0.068
		(0.030)
Constant	76.685	75.608
	(0.805)	(0.902)
Number of observations	44	44
R^2	0.3767	0.4465
Adjusted R^2	0.3619	0.4195

Note: The dependent variable is life expectancy at birth. Estimated standard errors are reported in parentheses.

column (2) includes both per capita spending on healthcare and per capita GDP as explanatory variables.

You will often see results presented in this way in journal articles, where authors begin with a very parsimonious specification, and gradually introduce additional explanatory variables to illustrate the impact of that new variable.

Reminder: Omitted variables bias

Remember that the asymptotic bias from omitting GDP as an explanatory variable in our model is equal to:

$$\text{Asymptotic bias} = \beta_2 \frac{cov(Spend, GDP)}{var(Spend)}$$

As such, the OLS estimator $\hat{\beta}_1$ will suffer from bias in specification (1) if GDP is a determinant of life expectancy ($\beta_2 \neq 0$) and GDP is correlated with spending on healthcare ($cov(Spend, GDP) \neq 0$).

When we compare the estimated coefficients on $Spend_i$ between specification (1) and specification (2), we can see that our estimates decrease from $\hat{\beta}_1 = 0.972$ in specification (1) to $\hat{\beta}_1 = 0.458$ in specification (2). That is, our estimated marginal effect of healthcare spending on life expectancy is reduced by approximately half by including the per capita GDP measure.

Since:

1. we have added in a variable that theory told us may be a determinant of life expectancy that was omitted in specification (1), and
2. the estimated coefficient on $Spend_i$ has changed substantially,

we can conclude that it is likely that specification (1) suffered from omitted variables bias (and that the bias was positive). That is, in specification (1), we might conclude that $E(\hat{\beta}_1) > \beta_1$.

How large is a large change?

A good question is how big a change constitutes a big change? We expect the estimated coefficients to change slightly whenever we add in additional explanatory variables, so how big a change tells us that there was omitted variables bias?

We might use a strict statistical test to test whether the estimated coefficients are statistically significantly different from each other, but this is tricky to carry out, as we would need to know the **covariance** between the two estimates.

A good rule of thumb is to compare the size of the change to the **standard error** of the estimates:

- If they change by more than twice the standard error (in this example, more than 2×0.193), you can be fairly certain that the initial regression suffered from **omitted variables bias**.

- If the change is small compared to the standard error (i.e. a small fraction of the standard error), then it is likely that the change is by chance.

This is merely a rule of thumb, and as a good economist, you need to anticipate where omitted variables bias might occur before even carrying out a regression. That is, you need to ask whether there are any variables that you have not included in your specification that:

1. Are determinants of the dependent variable and
2. Are correlated with one (or more) of the included explanatory variables.

Let's return to the results in Table 28.1. As we believe that specification (2) has removed omitted variables bias, let's re-examine the estimated impacts of spending on life expectancy.

When we examined specification (1), we constructed a t-statistic equal to $t = \frac{0.972-0}{0.193} = 5.036$, which was larger than the critical value. This suggested a statistically significant impact at the 1 per cent significance level of spending on healthcare on life expectancy, interpreted as an increase in spending on healthcare of \$1,000 per capita is associated with a 0.972 year increase in life expectancy.

However, we now also believe that specification (1) suffers from omitted variables bias. As such, the t-statistic can only tell us that there is a significant correlation between the two variables, rather than anything about any causal relationships between the variables.

Moving on to specification (2), our estimated relationship is:

$$LifeExp_i = \beta_0 + \beta_1 Spend_i + \beta_2 GDP_i + e_i \qquad (2)$$

The overall R^2 has increased from 0.3767 to 0.4465, but this is not sufficient to conclude that the model is a 'better fit', as the R^2 will mechanistically get larger whenever adding additional explanatory variables.

However, the *adjusted* R^2 also increases from specification (1) to specification (2), going from 0.3619 in specification (1) to 0.4195 in specification (2), indicating that adding in GDP has improved the fit of the model.

Moving on to statistical significance, based on the results of specification (2), we wish to test two hypotheses: firstly, whether spending on healthcare has a statistically significant impact on life expectancy, and secondly, whether GDP has any significant impact.

Does spending on healthcare have any impact on life expectancy?

If healthcare spending has no impact on life expectancy, this is equivalent to β_1 being equal to zero. So, we wish to test the hypotheses:

$$H_0: \beta_1 = 0$$
$$H_A: \beta_1 \neq 0$$

Does GDP per capita have any impact on life expectancy?

If per capita GDP has no impact on life expectancy, this is equivalent to β_2 being equal to zero. So, we wish to test the hypotheses:

$$H_0: \beta_2 = 0$$
$$H_A: \beta_2 \neq 0$$

We test this in the normal way, by constructing a t-statistic:

$$t = \frac{\hat{\beta}_1 - E(\hat{\beta}_1 \mid \beta_1 = 0)}{\widehat{s.e.}(\hat{\beta}_1)} = \frac{0.458 - 0}{0.292}$$
$$= 1.568$$

We test this in the normal way, by constructing a t-statistic:

$$t = \frac{\hat{\beta}_2 - E(\hat{\beta}_2 \mid \beta_2 = 0)}{\widehat{s.e.}(\hat{\beta}_2)} = \frac{0.068 - 0}{0.030}$$
$$= 2.267$$

There are 44 observations here, and we have estimated 3 coefficients (i.e. we have estimated $\hat{\beta}_0, \hat{\beta}_1$, and $\hat{\beta}_2$). As such, we have $44 - 3 = 41$ degrees of freedom.
Remember, if we have k explanatory variables, and a constant being estimated, we estimate $k + 1$. coefficients, and so the number of degrees of freedom is $n - (k + 1) = n - k - 1$.

We can consider the **p-value** associated with $t = 1.568$, when we have 41 degrees of freedom:

$$P(| T_{41} | \geq 1.568) = 0.1246$$

That is, if the **null hypothesis** is true, the probability of achieving a t-statistic whose magnitude is 1.568 (or larger) is equal to 0.1246.
This is not, by any reasonable definition, a rare event. Because the p-value is larger than 0.1, we would fail to reject the null hypothesis at even the 10 per cent significance level.

We can consider the p-value associated with $t = 2.267$, when we have 41 degrees of freedom:

$$P(| T_{41} | \geq 2.267) = 0.0287$$

That is, if the null hypothesis is true, the probability of achieving a t-statistic whose magnitude is 2.267 (or larger) is equal to 0.0287.
Since this p-value is smaller than 0.05, we would reject the null hypothesis at the 5 per cent significance level (but because it is greater than 0.01, we would fail to reject the null hypothesis at the 1 per cent significance level).

Alternatively, we could have compared our t-statistics with the critical values at the 10%, 5%, or 1% critical values (1.68, 2.02, and 2.70, respectively) and made the same conclusions.
These results suggest that, at the 5 per cent significance level:

- We cannot reject the null that per capita spending on healthcare has no impact on life expectancy.
- We reject the null that per capita GDP has no impact on life expectancy in favour of the alternative. This suggests that a higher per capita GDP leads to a higher life expectancy.

The estimated coefficient on GDP is $\hat{\beta}_2 = 0.068$. The GDP variable is measured in thousands of US$, and so if the GDP variable increases by 1, this is equivalent to GDP being increased by $1,000. Thus, having controlled for spending on healthcare, a 1 unit (or $1,000) increase in GDP is associated with a 0.068 year increase in life expectancy. This is equivalent to an approximately 3.5 week increase in life expectancy.

An important question is whether this is a 'large' or economically significant effect. Overall, the estimated impact seems very small. A 0.068 year increase in life expectancy due to a $1,000 increase in GDP sounds very small, especially when compared with the effects we obtained from our simple regression (specification (1)). We will explore economic significance in a little more detail later in this chapter.

28.2.1 Estimating multivariate regressions in Microsoft Excel

Just as with our simple regressions, it is possible to estimate multivariate regressions using Excel. The only thing to note is that, when estimating OLS with more than one

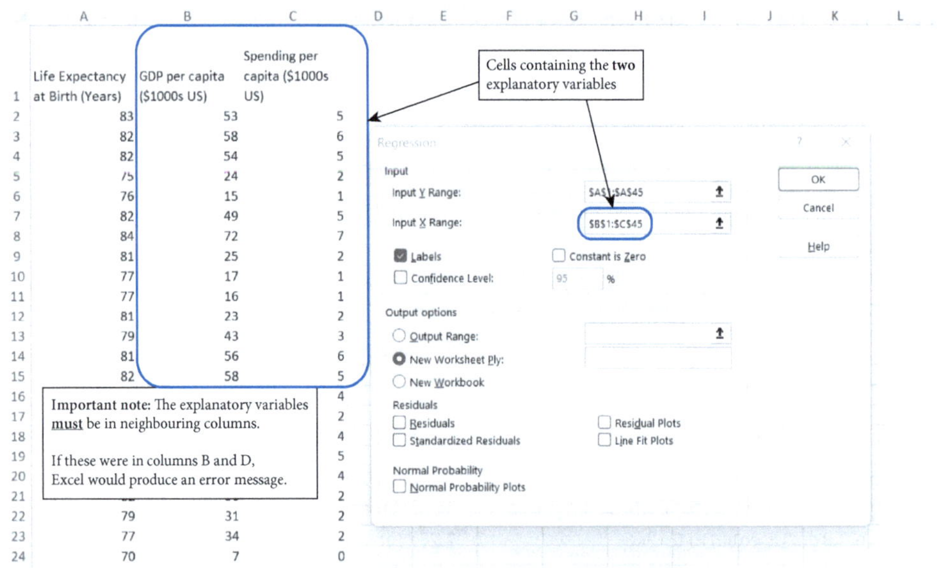

Figure 28.5 Using Microsoft Excel to estimate multivariate regressions.

explanatory variable in Excel, you need to ensure that the explanatory variables are in neighbouring columns.

For example, you could include the data for the two explanatory variables in columns B and C, and Excel would be able to estimate OLS for you, as shown in Figure 28.5.

However, if your data for the explanatory variables were in columns B and D, then Excel would produce an error (Figure 28.6) stating that the input range must be a contiguous reference.

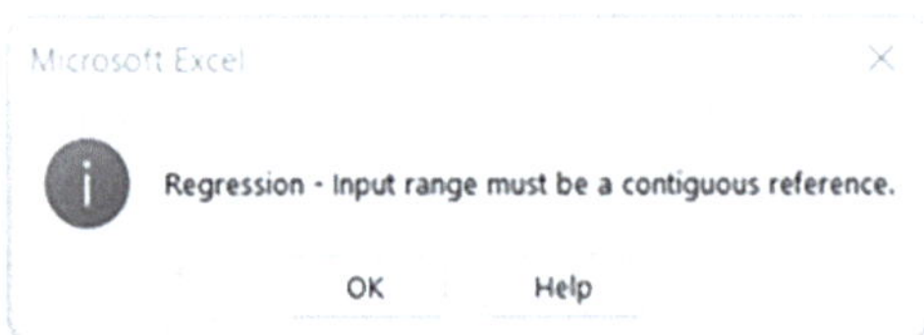

Figure 28.6 Error message in Excel.

The regression output in Excel for a multivariate regression is very similar to the simple regression case.

The estimated coefficients, standard errors, t-stats, p-values, and confidence interval are reported. The only key difference is that there are now three coefficients being reported (see Figure 28.7).

Further, under the ANOVA information, the F-statistic relates to a null hypothesis that none of the explanatory variables has any impact on the dependent variable—that is, in this example, that GDP per capita and spending per capita have no impact on the life expectancy.

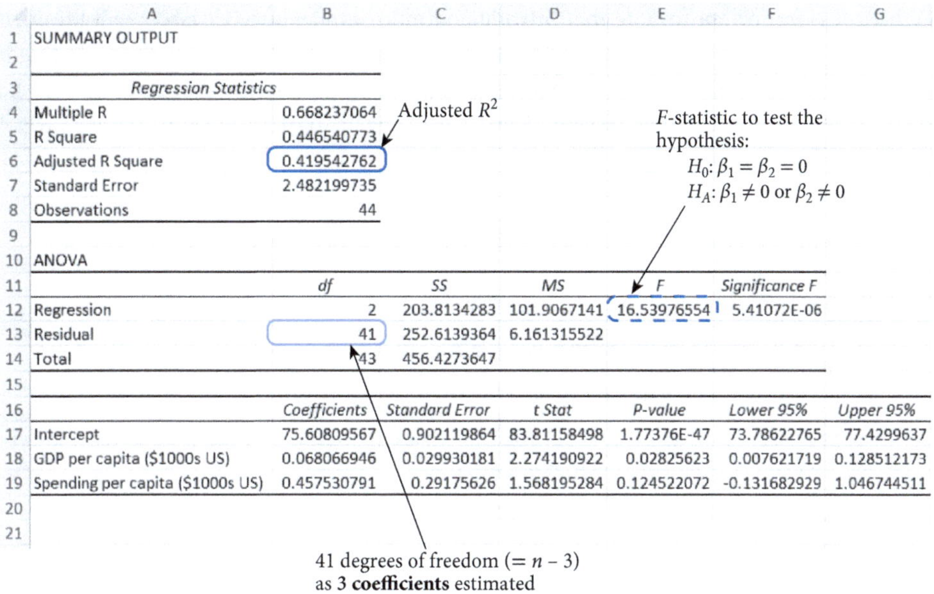

	A	B	C	D	E	F	G
1	SUMMARY OUTPUT						
2							
3	*Regression Statistics*						
4	Multiple R	0.668237064					
5	R Square	0.446540773					
6	Adjusted R Square	0.419542762					
7	Standard Error	2.482199735					
8	Observations	44					
9							
10	ANOVA						
11		*df*	*SS*	*MS*	*F*	*Significance F*	
12	Regression	2	203.8134283	101.9067141	16.53976554	5.41072E-06	
13	Residual	41	252.6139364	6.161315522			
14	Total	43	456.4273647				
15							
16		*Coefficients*	*Standard Error*	*t Stat*	*P-value*	*Lower 95%*	*Upper 95%*
17	Intercept	75.60809567	0.902119864	83.81158498	1.77376E-47	73.78622765	77.4299637
18	GDP per capita ($1000s US)	0.068066946	0.029930181	2.274190922	0.02825623	0.007621719	0.128512173
19	Spending per capita ($1000s US)	0.457530791	0.29175626	1.568195284	0.124522072	-0.131682929	1.046744511
20							
21							

Figure 28.7 Microsoft Excel output for multivariate regressions.

The F-statistic is calculated as:

$$F = \frac{ESS/k}{RSS/n - k - 1}$$

where k is the number of explanatory variables, excluding the constant. In this instance, $k = 2$, and so the F-statistic is just equal to:

$$F = \frac{203.8134/2}{252.6139/41} = 16.5398$$

If the null hypothesis is true, then the F-statistic will follow an $F(k,n - k - 1)$ distribution; that is, it will follow an F-distribution with k degrees of freedom in the first term, and $n - k - 1$ in the second.

28.2.2 Avoid kitchen sink regressions

We've seen that we can remove omitted variables bias by including the omitted variables in the regression. However, we don't know (for sure) what are the key omitted variables to include. As such, it might be tempting to include as many possible determinants of the dependent variable as you can measure. However, there are dangers associated with introducing increasing numbers of explanatory variables.

1. Every time you add an additional explanatory variable, you reduce the number of degrees of freedom, and hence the **efficiency** of your estimates. The more irrelevant explanatory variables (i.e. variables which are **not** determinants of your dependent variable) you include, the less precisely your estimated effects will be.

Whilst it is important to note that introducing more explanatory variables will lower the precision of your estimates, it is possible that you could also introduce bias by including irrelevant explanatory variables. An irrelevant explanatory variable would be one which has no impact on the dependent variable. That is, a change in an irrelevant explanatory variable would lead to no change in the dependent variable.

2. Suppose that your explanatory variable of interest, X_i is **uncorrelated** with the error term $(\text{cov}(X,u) \neq 0)$.
If you include an irrelevant explanatory variable, W_i, that:
   a) is correlated with the explanatory variable of interest $(cov(W,X) = 0)$ and
   b) is correlated with the error term $(cov(W,u) \neq 0)$,

   then by including W_i, you will introduce bias into your estimates by introducing a pathway between the error term and the X that didn't previously exist.

It can be tempting to include any possible explanatory variable you can think of (sometimes known as a 'kitchen sink regression') to try to avoid omitted variables bias, but this often will not solve the bias, and may lead to other problems, including introducing additional bias into your estimates.

For this reason, when deciding what variables to include in your regression, it's important to begin with theory; ask yourself what the theoretical justification is for including an additional variable.

If there's no theoretical reason that the explanatory variable should be a determinant of the dependent variable, don't include it in your regression!

28.3 Economic significance

In the previous example, in specification (2), a key question is what the meanings of the estimated coefficients are. We saw that whilst GDP per capita was statistically significant, per capita spending on healthcare was not significant. However, a result can be statistically significant, but not have any meaningful effect on an outcome. The question, therefore, is whether the estimated coefficients are 'large'; more formally, do they have economic significance?

In specification (2) we had two explanatory variables:

- per capita spending on healthcare
- GDP per capita.

If we attempt to naïvely interpret the estimated coefficient on GDP per capita ($\hat{\beta}_2 = 0.068$), this would indicate that an increase in GDP per capita by $1,000 is associated with a 0.068 year increase in life expectancy (approximately 3.5 weeks). Whilst we wouldn't normally do this for a statistically insignificant variable, if we did the same with the point estimate for spending on healthcare, it indicates that a $1,000 increase in spending per capita is

Table 28.2 Results from a multivariate regression of life expectancy against per capita spending on healthcare and per capita GDP

	(1)	(2)
Spending on healthcare per capita	0.972	0.458
	(0.193)	(0.292)
GDP per capita		0.068
		(0.030)
Constant	76.685	75.608
	(0.805)	(0.902)
Number of observations	44	44
R^2	0.3767	0.4465
Adjusted R^2	0.3619	0.4195

Note: The dependent variable is life expectancy at birth. Estimated standard errors are reported in parentheses.

associated with a 0.458 year increase in life expectancy (23.8 weeks). This makes it seem as if the income of the country has a very small impact on life expectancy.

However, the reason that the coefficient on GDP is much smaller is because the scale of the variation in the variable is much larger than for spending per capita. In this section, we will motivate how we might answer whether a coefficient is economically significant.

28.3.1 How do we evaluate economic significance?

Suppose that we are estimating a relationship between a dependent variable, Y, and two explanatory variables, X and W:

$$Y_i = \beta_0 + \beta_1 X_i + \beta_2 W_i + u_i$$

If we wish to find the marginal impact of X on Y, holding W constant, we can find the partial derivative of this expression with respect to X, giving us:

$$\frac{\partial Y}{\partial X} = \beta_1$$

A derivative looks at the rate of change, at a point—that is, where the change in X tends towards zero. Let's rewrite this to consider rates of change (with ΔY and ΔX representing the absolute changes in Y and X respectively). Here, we could reconsider the (partial) derivative as:

$$\frac{\Delta Y}{\Delta X} = \beta_1$$

This can be rewritten to give us $\Delta Y = \beta_1 \Delta X$. That is, the change in Y is equal to β_1 multiplied by the change in X. An important question is always what is a reasonable change in X?

Suppose that X were the GDP of a country (e.g. the UK GDP in 2020 was approximately \$2,700,000,000,000), then if we set ΔX equal to 1 (i.e. examined the impact of a \$1 increase in GDP), we wouldn't expect to see much of an impact, because relative to the size of GDP a \$1 increase would be inconsequential.

Similarly, if X were a proportion (say of left-handed people in a class), then the minimum possible value for X would be 0 (no one in the class was left-handed), and the maximum value would be 1 (everyone in the class was left-handed). In this circumstance, if we set $\Delta X = 1$, then we may expect to see an overly large effect, as this is the effect of moving from the lowest possible value to the highest possible value. In reality, we would not expect to see such large changes between classrooms.

As such, we need to consider what a reasonable change might be, and also what sort of change could be used to compare effects sizes across interventions. One metric that we could use is the standard deviation of our explanatory variable. The standard deviation gives us a measure of how much variation there is in the explanatory variable, and as such, provides us a standardized metric that we can use to measure the impact of a change in the explanatory variable.

Similarly, we may be interested in the impact of an intervention on various different dependent variables. For example, one study may look at the impact of an intervention on earnings in the UK (measured in pounds), and a second in the USA (measured in dollars); you may wish to compare the size of the effects. Again, one possibility is to compare the estimated effect size to the standard deviation of the dependent variable.

As such, this gives us a method to be able to evaluate the effect size in a simple, comparable way:

1. Consider the effect of a 1 standard deviation increase in the explanatory variable.
2. Calculate the number of standard deviations change in the dependent variable with which this is associated.

This is not the only way of discussing the size of the effect, but for linear specifications it provides a nice way of interpreting effects in a way that is comparable across a range of studies. However, for non-linear specifications (e.g. involving natural logarithms), it may be more appropriate to think in terms of elasticities, or percentage changes.

28.3.2 Does GDP per capita have an economically significant impact on life expectancy?

Let's return to the example of our estimated relationship between life expectancy, per capita spending on healthcare, and per capita GDP:

$$LifeExp_i = \beta_0 + \beta_1 Spend_i + \beta_2 GDP_i + e_i \qquad (2)$$

Remember, the estimated coefficients, $\hat{\beta}_2$, can be interpreted as the estimated marginal effect of a change in per capita GDP on life expectancy, holding per capita spending on healthcare fixed:

$$\frac{\partial LifeExp}{\partial GDP} = \beta_2 \Rightarrow \Delta LifeExp = \beta_2 \Delta GDP$$

Table 28.3 Results from a multivariate regression of life expectancy against per capita spending on healthcare and per capita GDP

	(1)	(2)
Spending on healthcare per capita	0.972	0.458
	(0.193)	(0.292)
GDP per capita		0.068
		(0.030)
Constant	76.685	75.608
	(0.805)	(0.902)
Number of observations	44	44
R^2	0.3767	0.4465
Adjusted R^2	0.3619	0.4195

Note: The dependent variable is life expectancy at birth. Estimated standard errors are reported in parentheses.

If we want to think about the impact of a change in per capita GDP, we can interpret this as follows. Since the marginal effect of a change in per capita GDP on life expectancy is β_2, we can think that the change in life expectancy due to a change in per capita GDP of ΔGDP will be $\beta_2 \times \Delta GDP$.

Let's look back at the results in Table 28.3. To interpret these results, we don't just need the estimated coefficients; we also need to think what a reasonable change in GDP per capita would be. One way of thinking about a reasonable change is to look at a 1 standard deviation (1 s.d.) increase in the explanatory variable.

Applying this, we will need to combine the results from Table 28.3 with summary statistics of the data from Table 28.4. We can see that:

- The estimated coefficient on per capita spending on healthcare is $\hat{\beta}_1 = 0.458$, and the standard deviation (from our summary statistics) in per capita spending is 2.06.
- The estimated coefficient on GDP per capita is $\hat{\beta}_2 = 0.068$, and the standard deviation is 20.05.

So, if we were to increase GDP per capita by 1 s.d., that would be equivalent to setting $\Delta GDP = 20.05$. Our estimated marginal effect $\hat{\beta}_2 = 0.068$, so a 1 s.d. increase in per capita GDP would be equivalent to:

$$\Delta LifeExp \cong 0.068 \times 20.05 = 1.36$$

Table 28.4 Summary statistics of the data (data from the OECD)

	Mean	Standard deviation	Number of observations
Spending per capita on healthcare (thousands of US$)	3.64	2.06	44
GDP per capita (thousands of US$)	43.37	20.05	44
Life expectancy at birth	80.23	3.26	44

So, a 1 s.d. increase in per capita GDP is associated with a 1.36 year increase in life expectancy.

Again, it is important to consider whether this is actually a large change (or not), so the second stage is to consider the (standardized) impact on the dependent variable. We have seen that a 1 s.d. increase in per capita GDP is associated with a 1.36 year increase in life expectancy, but is this a big number?

The standard deviation of life expectancy is 3.26 years. We saw that a 1 s.d. increase in per capita GDP was associated with a 1.36 year increase in life expectancy. If we find the ratio of these two numbers, this will give the number of standard deviations the change in life expectancy is:

$$\frac{\Delta LifeExp}{s.d.(LifeExp)} = \frac{1.36}{3.26} = 0.42$$

That is, a 1 s.d. increase in per capita GDP is associated with a 42 per cent of a standard deviation increase in life expectancy.

Standardizing the effect

Considering the number of standard deviations by which the dependent variable changes due to a 1 s.d. increase in the explanatory variable allows us to create a standardized metric, with which to compare effects across interventions.

There is no hard-and-fast rule for what makes a 'big' effect, but:

- If a 1 s.d. increase in the explanatory variable yields a 0.0001 s.d. increase in the dependent variable, this is a very small effect.
- If a 1s.d. increase yields more than a 1 s.d. increase in your dependent variable, this is a very large effect.

To answer whether the effect is big, you need to compare with estimates of other interventions.

Normally, we would not try to interpret the point estimate for per capita spending on healthcare, as the estimated coefficient is not statistically significantly different from zero (so we cannot reject the null that it has no impact on life expectancy). However, to demonstrate the comparison, let's naïvely try to interpret the estimated coefficient.

- The estimated coefficient, $\hat{\beta}_1 = 0.458$.
- The standard deviation of spending on healthcare is equal to 2.06.

So, if we calculate the estimated impact of a 1 s.d. increase in per capita spending on healthcare, then:

$$\Delta LifeExp = \hat{\beta}_1 \times \Delta Spend = 0.458 \times 2.06 = 0.943$$

This naïve interpretation suggests that a 1 s.d. increase in the spending variable is associated with a 0.943 year increase in life expectancy, or $\frac{0.943}{3.26} = 0.29$ of an s.d. of life expectancy.

What this demonstrates is that, because of the scale of the variables, even though the point estimate of the coefficient on per capita spending is much larger than for per capita GDP (0.458 vs 0.068), the economic impact of the estimated effect of GDP is larger.

DEFINITION: IMPERFECT MULTICOLLINEARITY

Later in this chapter, we will introduce a concept known as 'imperfect multicollinearity'. This occurs when you have two (or more) explanatory variables that are highly correlated, and the result is that you obtain very imprecise estimates of the estimated effect (i.e. the standard errors are large).

In this example, per capita GDP and per capita spending on healthcare have a correlation coefficient of 0.7759, meaning that our estimated effects are likely to be imprecisely estimated.

It could be that spending on healthcare does have a causal impact on life expectancy, but we have failed to reject the null hypothesis, because the coefficient is imprecisely estimated.

28.4 Perfect multicollinearity

One thing to note when estimating multivariate regressions is that, if you have perfect collinearity between one or more of your explanatory variables, then OLS cannot be estimated. Perfect collinearity is where you can write down a linear function which means that every observation of one explanatory variable can be written as a linear function of one (or more) of the other explanatory variables. That is, perfect multicollinearity exists when there is a systematic linear relationship between the explanatory variables that applies for every observation in your data.

For example, suppose that we are interested in estimating the relationship:

$$Y_i = \beta_0 + \beta_1 X_i + \beta_2 W_i + u_i$$

Our observations of X_i and W_i are illustrated in Table 28.5.

In this example, every observation of W_i is exactly double the observation of the X_i. So, for example, in the first observation, $X_i = 1.5$, whilst $W_i = 3$. This follows for all of the observations of X_i and W_i. So, we can write that, for all i:

$$W_i = 2X_i$$

Table 28.5 Example of data showing perfect multicollinearity

X_i	1.5	3	2	4	7	11	2.2	4	3	8.1
W_i	3	6	4	8	14	22	4.4	8	6	16.2

This is an example of perfect multicollinearity. Whenever you have perfect multicollinearity, it is impossible to estimate OLS. The reason for this is that, if you were to substitute $W_i = 2X_i$ into the OLS estimator:

$$\hat{\beta}_1^{OLS} = \frac{\sum_{i=1}^{n}(Y_i - \bar{Y})(X_i - \bar{X})\sum_{j=1}^{n}(W_j - \bar{W})^2 - \sum_{k=1}^{n}(Y_k - \bar{Y})(W_k - \bar{W})\sum_{l=1}^{n}(W_l - \bar{W})(X_l - \bar{X})}{\sum_{m=1}^{n}(X_m - \bar{X})^2\sum_{p=1}^{n}(W_p - \bar{W})^2 - \left(\sum_{q=1}^{n}(W_q - \bar{W})(X_q - \bar{X})\right)^2}$$

it is relatively straightforward to show that the denominator (and the numerator) are equal to zero here. Because we cannot divide by zero, it follows that the OLS estimator does not exist.

The intuition here is that whenever X_i increases, W_i also increases proportionately. As such, it is impossible to hold W_i fixed and allow X_i to vary.

There are a number of forms of perfect multicollinearity, and the only way to estimate OLS is to omit one of the variables that causes the multicollinearity.

28.4.1 Examples of perfect multicollinearity, and how to solve them

There are lots of cases where we might (inadvertently) create perfect multicollinearity. We will discuss one key cause, where we have data relating to categories, in the next chapter, but perfect multicollinearity occurs whenever two or more explanatory variables can be written as a linear combination of each other.

Suppose that we are interested in estimating the relationship between Y, X, W, and Z. We are interested in estimating the following relationship:

$$Y_i = \beta_0 + \beta_1 X_i + \beta_2 W_i + \beta_3 Z_i + u_i$$

We could experience perfect multicollinearity in some of the following ways:

Form of multicollinearity	Solution	Explanation
$W_i = aX_i$ where a is a constant	Omit either W_i or X_i from the regression	It's not possible to independently identify the impact of W_i and X_i on Y_i. It would be possible to estimate: $Y_i = \beta_0 + \beta_1 X_i + \beta_3 Z_i + u_i$ or $Y_i = \beta_0 + \beta_2 W_i + \beta_3 Z_i + u_i$ But your estimated $\hat{\beta}_1$ (or $\hat{\beta}_2$) will be the combined impact of both X_i and W_i.
$W_i = aX_i + bZ_i$ where a and b are constants	Omit one of X, W, or Z from the regression	Now, because there is a linear relationship between all three variables, if you hold X and Z fixed, it follows that W must **also** be fixed. It would be possible to estimate: $Y_i = \beta_0 + \beta_1 X_i + \beta_3 Z_i + u_i$ or $Y_i = \beta_0 + \beta_2 W_i + \beta_3 Z_i + u_i$ or $Y_i = \beta_0 + \beta_1 X_i + \beta_2 W_i + u_i$ However, you cannot include all three variables in the regression.

Form of multicollinearity	Solution	Explanation
$W_i = a + bX_i$ where a and b are constants	Omit W, X, or the constant from the regression	The collinearity in this example comes from collinearity between a combination of the explanatory variables, and the constant. The a term is just a constant multiplier of the intercept. As such, if we omitted the intercept, we would break the linear combination: It would be possible to estimate: $Y_i = \beta_0 + \beta_1 X_i + \beta_3 Z_i + u_i$ or $Y_i = \beta_0 + \beta_2 W_i + \beta_3 Z_i + u_i$ or $Y = \beta_1 X_i + \beta_2 W_i + \beta_3 Z_i + u_i$
$X_i = a$ where a is a constant	Omit either X_i or the constant from the regression	In this example, X_i is a constant and so would be collinear with the intercept. It would be possible to estimate: $Y_i = \beta_0 + \beta_2 W_i + \beta_3 Z_i + u_i$ or $Y_i = \beta_1 X_i + \beta_2 W_i + \beta_3 Z_i + u_i$

Perfect multicollinearity is not really interesting, as it simply stops you from estimating OLS. Most statistical software packages will detect when you have perfect multicollinearity between explanatory variables, and will automatically drop one (or more) of the explanatory variables. If this happens, you do need to be careful about *how* you interpret the estimated coefficients, but OLS cannot be estimated if there is perfect multicollinearity. However, if the collinearity breaks down, even for one observation, the OLS can be estimated.

For example, we saw an example earlier where every observation of $W_i = 2X_i$. Suppose instead that this relationship held for the first nine observations, but in the tenth observation this relationship broke down (see Table 28.6).

Table 28.6 Example of data demonstrating imperfect multicollinearity

X_i	1.5	3	2	4	7	11	2.2	4	3	**8.1**
W_i	3	6	4	8	14	22	4.4	8	6	**5**

In this example, there would not be perfect multicollinearity, as the relationship does not hold for every observation of X_i and W_i. However, we would have a potentially more serious problem, that of imperfect multicollinearity. We will discuss imperfect multicollinearity in the next section.

28.4.2 Illustrations of data sets exhibiting perfect multicollinearity

Suppose that you are interested in estimating the following regression:

$$Y_i = \beta_0 + \beta_1 X_i + \beta_2 W_i + \beta_3 Z_i + e_i$$

You have observed ten sets of observations of Y_i, X_i, W_i, and Z_i. What is the problem that causes perfect multicollinearity in each case? We have reported the observations of the explanatory variables, but not the dependent variable (Y_i):

Case 1: Simple multiples

In this example, we can see that every observation of $W_i = 3 \times X_i$. That is, for the first observation $X_1 = 1$ and $W_1 = 3$. For the second observation $X_2 = 2$ and $W_2 = 6$. Z_i does not have any systematic relationship with either X_i or W_i.

Solution

OLS cannot be estimated with both X_i and W_i in the regression. As such, we need to omit either X_i or W_i, and estimate one of the following two regressions:

$$Y_i = \beta_0 + \beta_2 W_i + \beta_3 Z_i$$
$$Y_i = \beta_0 + \beta_1 X_i + \beta_3 Z_i$$

Note that the estimated coefficient on X_i or W_i would represent the effect of a change of both X_i **and** W_i on Y_i.

X_i	W_i	Z_i
1	3	2
2	6	4
5	15	7
2	6	8
1	3	1
4	12	9
5	15	1
6	18	2
8	24	3
9	27	1

Case 2: Linear combinations

This example is a little more tricky to observe, but the key thing is that every observation of W_i is a linear combination of X_i and Z_i:

$$W_i = X_i + Z_i$$

(This would also mean that $X_i = W_i - Z_i$ and $Z_i = W_i - X_i$).

Solution

OLS cannot be estimated with all three regressors included in the regression. As such, we need to omit *one* of the explanatory variables:

$$Y_i = \beta_0 + \beta_2 W_i + \beta_3 Z_i + e_i$$
$$Y_i = \beta_0 + \beta_1 X_i + \beta_3 Z_i + e_i$$
$$Y_i = \beta_0 + \beta_1 X_i + \beta_2 W_i + e_i$$

Having omitted, say, the Z_i variable, we could not use the remaining data to write a systematic relationship between the X_i and the W_i. For example, for the first observation, $X_1 = 1$ and $W_1 = 2$, so the observation of W_1 is twice the value of the observation of the X_1. However, for the second observation, $X_2 = 1$ and $W_2 = 3$, so W_2 is three times the value of X_2.

So, by omitting the Z_i variable, we remove a route that creates perfect collinearity between the *included* explanatory variables.

X_i	W_i	Z_i
1	2	1
1	3	2
2	6	4
5	12	7
2	10	8
4	13	9
5	6	1
6	8	2
8	11	3
9	10	1

Case 3: Multicollinearity including the intercept

In this example, the multicollinearity includes the intercept. To illustrate this, the data includes a fourth column that is always equal to 1. This is because, when we estimate a relationship, the intercept is some constant, which is equivalent to having an explanatory variable that is equal to 1. So we are estimating:

$$Y_i = \beta_0 \times 1 + \beta_1 X_i + \beta_2 W_i + \beta_3 Z_i + e_i$$

In this example, the collinearity comes from the combination of the constant, the X_i and the W_i.

For every observation of X_i and W_i, we can write:

$$X_i = 1 - W_i$$

β_0	X_i	W_i	Z_i
1	1	0	1
1	1	0	2
1	0	1	4
1	1	0	7
1	0	1	8
1	0	1	9
1	1	0	1
1	0	1	2
1	1	0	3
1	0	1	1

So, for instance $X_1 = 1$ and $W_1 = 0$, so $X_1 = 1 - W_1$. Remember that the 1 is included as we have a constant included in our regression. As such, the multicollinearity in this example comes from including the constant, the X_i and the W_i together.

Solution

The solution to this is to estimate the relationship, omitting one of the X_i, the W_i, or the β_0 from the regression:

$$Y_i = \beta_0 + \beta_2 W_i + \beta_3 Z_i + e_i$$
$$Y_i = \beta_0 + \beta_1 X_i + \beta_3 Z_i + e_i$$
$$Y_i = \beta_1 X_i + \beta_2 W_i + \beta_3 Z_i + e_i$$

The third case is one that often confuses students of econometrics, but the key thing is that when estimating this third case, there is no way of writing any of the included variables as linear combinations of the other included variables.

28.5 Imperfect multicollinearity

Perfect multicollinearity is a curiosity. It is something that stops OLS from being estimated, and the only solution to perfect multicollinearity is to omit one of the variables that causes the linear combination to exist.

However, a much more common issue emerges through imperfect multicollinearity. Imperfect multicollinearity occurs when there is not a systematic relationship between two (or more) of the explanatory variables, but instead, there is a very high correlation between them, or alternatively there is an approximate relationship between the explanatory variables.

Consider, for example, that you are trying to estimate the relationship:

$$Y_i = \beta_0 + \beta_1 X_i + \beta_2 W_i + u_i$$

but there exists an approximate relationship between X and W, such that every observation of

$$W_i = X_i + \varepsilon_i$$

where ε_i is a (random) error term. If the variance of the error term is small, then the correlation between W_i and X_i will be very high, and the two variables will be approximately collinear. To illustrate the impact of this, consider a simulation to derive the bias and efficiency of the OLS estimator under both imperfect multicollinearity and no collinearity.

In this simulation, the data is generated so that X_i, W_i, and u_i have the same distributions under both the imperfect multicollinearity case and the no collinearity case.

To run the simulation (see Table 28.7), we generate 100 observations of Y, X, and W, using the data generating process described, and using that data, estimate the relationship:

$$Y_i = \beta_0 + \beta_1 X_i + \beta_2 W_i + u_i$$

We then save the estimated $\hat{\beta}_1$ and $\hat{\beta}_2$, and repeat the process 50,000 times for each of the imperfect multicollinearity and no collinearity cases.

Having done this, we can compare the distributions of the estimates (see Figure 28.8).

Our observations of Y_i are generated with the following data generating process:

$$Y_i = 1 + 2X_i + 3W_i + u_i$$

Table 28.7 Specifications for simulation

	Imperfect multicollinearity	No collinearity
Data generating process	$Y_i = 1 + 2X_i + 3W_i + u_i$	$Y_i = 1 + 2X_i + 3W_i + u_i$
Distribution of X_i term (observations are randomly drawn)	$X_i \sim N(0,1)$	$X_i \sim N(0,1)$
Distribution of u_i term (observations are randomly drawn)	$u_i \sim N(0,1)$	$u_i \sim N(0,1)$
Form of imperfect multicollinearity.	Every observation of W_i is constructed such that: $W_i = X_i + \varepsilon_i,\ \varepsilon \sim N\left(0, \frac{1}{16}\right)$ X_i and ε_i are independently drawn, so it follows that: $W_i \sim N\left(0, \frac{17}{16}\right)$	The W_i are randomly drawn, such that: $W_i \sim N\left(0, \frac{17}{16}\right)$
Correlation between W and X	$corr(W,X) = 0.9701$	$corr(W,X) = 0$

As such, we know that the true value of $\beta_1 = 2$, whilst the true value of $\beta_2 = 3$. Our simulation shows that, irrespective of whether there is imperfect multicollinearity or not, the OLS estimator remains unbiased. That is, the average of our estimates of β_1 is equal to 2.00 for both the imperfect multicollinearity and no collinearity cases, while the average of our estimates of β_2 is 3.00.

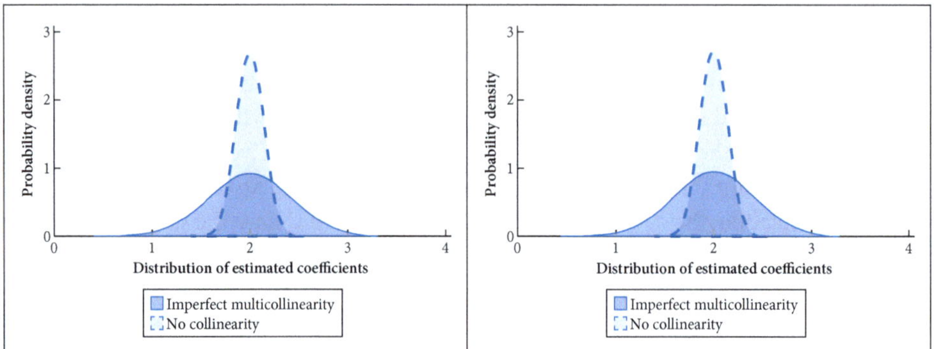

Distributions of estimates of β_1. True value is $\beta_1 = 2$

Distributions of estimates of β_2. True value is $\beta_2 = 3$

	Imperfect multicollinearity	No collinearity		Imperfect multicollinearity	No collinearity
Average of β_1	2.00	2.00	Average of β_2	3.00	3.00
Variance of β_1	0.176	0.010	Variance of β_2	0.166	0.010

Figure 28.8 Distribution of estimates from simulation.

However, where there is a difference is in the variation of the estimates. For both $\hat{\beta}_1$ and $\hat{\beta}_2$, the variance of our estimates is substantially larger in the presence of imperfect multicollinearity (between 16 and 18 times larger in this example). This means that our estimators are much less efficient when we have imperfect multicollinearity. In effect, this means that when there is imperfect multicollinearity, there is a high probability that our estimate of the marginal effect of (say) X on Y is a long way from the true effect.

28.5.1 Potential example of imperfect multicollinearity

Without realizing it, we have already seen a potential example of imperfect multicollinearity earlier in this chapter.

We have imperfect multicollinearity whenever we include an explanatory variable that has a strong correlation with one or more of the other explanatory variables.

When we estimated the relationship:

$$LifeExp_i = \beta_0 + \beta_1 Spend_i + \beta_2 GDP_i + u_i$$

we introduced a second explanatory variable, GDP, which was the per capita GDP in country i (see Figure 28.9).

We argued that omitting GDP per capita was likely to have caused omitted variables bias, when we estimated specification (1). This must mean that GDP per capita, and per capita spending on healthcare, are correlated. In fact, the empirical correlation between the two variables is equal to 0.7746.

This is a relatively high correlation, and we see that when we move from specification (1), where we included only the $Spend_i$ variable, to specification (2), where we include both the $Spend_i$ and the GDP_i variable, the estimated standard error, $\widehat{s.e.}(\hat{\beta}_1)$), increases from 0.193 to 0.292. Since the estimated standard error is the square root of the variance, this is equivalent to the (estimated) variance increasing from 0.037 to 0.085. Whilst this is not of the same magnitude as in the simulation in the previous section, this is still a substantial increase in the variance of our estimator.

	(1)	(2)
Spending on healthcare per capita	0.972 (0.193)	0.458 (0.292)
GDP per capita		0.068 (0.030)
Constant	76.685 (0.805)	75.608 (0.902)
Number of observations	44	44
R^2	0.3767	0.4465
Adjusted R^2	0.3619	0.4195
Note: The dependent variable is life expenditure at birth. Estimated standard errors are reported in parentheses.		

Figure 28.9 Results from a multivariate regression of life expectancy against per capita spending on healthcare and per capita GDP.

There are two reasons why this might have happened. Firstly, because the number of degrees of freedom has decreased from 42 to 41, the estimator automatically becomes less efficient, but secondly, because of the strong correlation between our two included explanatory variables, we experience imperfect multicollinearity.

28.5.2 Examples of imperfect multicollinearity, and how to solve them

In Section 28.5.1, we stated that the only solution to perfect multicollinearity was to omit one of the problematic variables. However, hopefully, you're already realizing that this is not an option with imperfect multicollinearity, if you also want unbiased estimates of the marginal effects.

Suppose that you estimate the following regression:

$$Y_i = \beta_0 + \beta_1 X_i + u_i$$

but the true data generating process is:

$$Y_i = \beta_0 + \beta_1 X_i + \beta_2 Z_i + e_i$$

If there is a strong correlation between X_i and Z_i, then we have two potential problems:

- If we omit Z_i from our regression, we will experience omitted variables bias in $\hat{\beta}_1$, whose asymptotic bias will be equal to $\beta_2 \frac{cov(Z,X)}{var(X)}$.
- If we include Z_i in our regression, then we will remove the omitted variables bias, but because this new variable is strongly correlated with X_i we will introduce imperfect multicollinearity, and whilst our estimates may be unbiased, they are likely to be very imprecisely estimated (i.e. they will have very large standard errors).

We can't omit the Z_i variable, as doing so would cause bias, but if we include it our estimates will be very imprecise. So, how do you solve a problem like imperfect multicollinearity?

If you think back to the simple OLS estimator, we showed that the variance of the OLS estimator was equal to:

$$var\left(\hat{\beta}_1^{OLS}\right) = \frac{\sigma_u^2}{(n-1)s_X^2}$$

Whilst the formula for the variance of the OLS estimator with more than one explanatory variable is a little more complicated than this, the same inference can be taken; as you increase the sample size (n), the variance of the OLS estimator will decrease. As such, if you are faced with imperfect multicollinearity, the solution is often to simply try to collect more data, to allow your estimates to be made more precisely.

Comparing sources of perfect and imperfect multicollinearity

The sources of imperfect multicollinearity are much like those with perfect multicollinearity, but with the adjustment that rather than a perfect systematic relationship, there might be a random error term added in.

Suppose that we are estimating the following relationship:

$$Y_i = \beta_0 + \beta_1 X_i + \beta_2 W_i + \beta_3 Z_i + u_i$$

Table 28.8 provides comparisons of different sources of perfect and imperfect multicollinearity.

Table 28.8 Comparing perfect and imperfect multicollinearity

Example of perfect multicollinearity	Example of imperfect multicollinearity
Every observation of X_i is a linear function of the observations of W_i $X_i = aW_i$ where a is a constant.	Every observation of X_i is *approximately* a linear function of the observations of W_i $X_i = aW_i + \varepsilon_i$ where ε_i is a random error term.
X_i is a constant (i.e. X_i is perfectly collinear with the intercept).	X_i has very little variance. This might come from most of the observations of X_i being constant, with a small number with variation, or alternatively just very small amounts of variation in the explanatory variable.
Every observation of X_i can be written as a linear combination of the observations of W_i and Z_i $X_i = aW_i + bZ_i$ where a and b are constants.	Every observation of X_i is approximately a linear combination of the observations of W_i and Z_i $X_i = aW_i + bZ_i + \varepsilon_i$

28.5.3 Illustrations of data sets exhibiting imperfect multicollinearity

Suppose that you are interested in estimating the following regression:

$$Y_i = \beta_0 + \beta_1 X_i + \beta_2 W_i + e_i$$

You have observed ten sets of observations of Y_i, X_i, and W_i. What is the problem that causes imperfect multicollinearity in each case?

Case 1: Simple multiples

In this example, we can see that every observation of W_i is approximately equal three times the value of the observation of X_i. The correlation between these two variables is equal to 0.99952.

In this example, OLS can be estimated, but the coefficients will be estimated very imprecisely (i.e. they will have very wide confidence intervals).

Solution

If both W_i and X_i are determinants of the dependent variable, Y_i, then omitting either the X_i or the W_i variable will lead to omitted variables bias.

The key solution is to try to collect more data.

X_i	W_i
1	3.2
2	5.7
5	15.3
2	6.2
1	2.8
4	12.2
5	15.1
6	17.5
8	24.1
9	26.9

Case 2: Little to no variation in the explanatory variable

In this example, nine of the observations of X_i are equal to 5, with the 10th equal to 7. There is variation in the X_i variable, and there is no systematic relationship between X_i, W_i, or Z_i.

However, the lack of variation in the X_i variable means that it is imperfectly collinear with the intercept.

The denominator of the OLS estimator will be close to zero, and as a result, the variance of the OLS estimator will be very large.

Solution

In this example, omitting X_i would not cause any bias to the estimated coefficient on W_i, but if you omitted the X_i variable from your regression, you would not be able to identify the impact of X on Y. Again, if you want to precisely estimate the impact of X on Y, you will need to collect more data, with more variation in the explanatory variable.

X_i	W_i
5	1
5	3
5	5
5	2
5	4
5	7
5	9
5	1
5	2
7	0

Ultimately, whilst imperfect and perfect multicollinearity sound like very similar problems, they have very different solutions.

- Under perfect multicollinearity, OLS cannot be estimated. The only option, if you wish to estimate OLS, is to omit one of the variables (or the constant, if relevant) that causes the linear function to exist. The estimated coefficients will reflect the impact of both the included and excluded variables.
- Under imperfect multicollinearity, OLS can be estimated. Omitting one of the variables will likely cause omitted variables bias, and as such should be avoided. The solution to imperfect multicollinearity is to collect more data.

Intuitively, the reason that imperfect multicollinearity is a problem is that, to identify the effect of more than one explanatory variable, you need to be able to consider the impact of a change in one explanatory variable, holding the other explanatory variable fixed. Where there is a very strong correlation between two (or more) explanatory variables, when you hold one variable fixed, you are only going to be able to generate a very small amount of variation in the other explanatory variable.

Summary

In this chapter, we have introduced multivariate regressions, where we have more than one explanatory variable in our model.

When we include additional explanatory variables in the model, we often state that we are controlling for other aspects. So, for example, when we estimated:

$$LifeExp_i = \beta_0 + \beta_1 Spend_i + \beta_2 GDP_i + u_i$$

then $\hat{\beta}_1$ could be expressed as the estimated impact of per capita spending on healthcare, having controlled for the per capita GDP. Mathematically, what is happening here is that we are estimating the effect of $Spend_i$ on $LifeExp_i$, holding GDP_i fixed.

Just as with simple regressions, statistical software packages will estimate OLS with more than one explanatory variable, but it's important to remember that when carrying out statistical testing, the degrees of freedom will be equal to the number of observations, minus the number of coefficients estimated. In the model, we would estimate 3 coefficients (β_0, β_1, and β_2), so if we have n observations, we would have $n - 3$ degrees of freedom.

In Chapter 29, we will build upon multivariate regressions, and also:

- introduce the concepts of dummy variables
- build upon the F-tests to formalize tests of multiple hypotheses.

Appendix

Proof that R^2 can only increase as we add additional explanatory variables

Whenever we add additional explanatory variables, we will automatically increase the R^2 as a result of reducing the residual sum of squares.

Suppose that we are considering two possible models:

$$Y_i = \beta_0 + \beta_1 X_i + u_i \quad (1)$$
$$Y_i = \alpha_0 + \alpha_1 X_i + \alpha_2 Z_i + e_i \quad (2)$$

In specification (1) we have one explanatory variable (X) and in specification (2) we have two explanatory variables (X, Z). Note that we have only used β and α to allow for us to easily distinguish between the coefficients in the two models.

The R^2 is defined as:

$$R^2 = \frac{ESS}{TSS} = 1 - \frac{RSS}{TSS}$$

Let's focus on the second formation. For a given dataset, the total sum of squares is fixed, as it is just constructed based on the observed value of Y_i,

$$TSS = \sum_{i=1}^{n}(Y_i - \bar{Y})^2$$

So, the only thing that will be affected is the residual sum of squares (which is what we minimized when we constructed OLS). The smaller the RSS, the larger the R^2.

We can write down the RSS for each of these cases:

$$RSS_1 = \sum_{i=1}^{n}\hat{u}_i^2 = \sum_{i=1}^{n}(Y_i - \hat{\beta}_0 - \hat{\beta}_1 X_i)^2 \quad (1)$$

$$RSS_2 = \sum_{i=1}^{n}\hat{e}_i^2 = \sum_{i=1}^{n}(Y_i - \hat{\alpha}_0 - \hat{\alpha}_1 X_i - \hat{\alpha}_2 Z_i)^2 \quad (2)$$

When constructing the OLS estimates in model (2), we have a starting point, which is model (1). We chose $\hat{\beta}_0$ and $\hat{\beta}_1$ to minimize $RSS_1 = \sum_{i=1}^{n} \hat{u}_i^2$.

Similarly, in model (2), we are minimizing the sum of squares of the residuals: $RSS_2 = \sum_{i=1}^{n} \hat{e}_i^2$.

There are two possible cases to consider:

1. $\hat{\alpha}_2 = 0$
2. $\hat{\alpha}_2 \neq 0$

Case 1 $\hat{\alpha}_2 = 0$ (Trivial)

If $\hat{\alpha}_2 = 0$, then $RSS_2 = \sum_{i=1}^{n} \hat{e}_i^2 = \sum_{i=1}^{n} (Y_i - \hat{\alpha}_0 - \hat{\alpha}_1 X_i - 0 \times Z_i)^2 = \sum_{i=1}^{n} (Y_i - \hat{\alpha}_0 - \hat{\alpha}_1 X_i)^2$. When we constructed the OLS estimators with a single explanatory variable, we chose the optimal $\hat{\beta}_0$ and $\hat{\beta}_1$ that found a global minimum for $RSS_1 = \sum_{i=1}^{n} \hat{u}_i^2 = \sum_{i=1}^{n} (Y_i - \hat{\beta}_0 - \hat{\beta}_1 X_i)^2$.

However, if $\hat{\alpha}_2 = 0$, the minimization problem for RSS_2 is exactly the same as the minimization problem for RSS_1. If we were able to find an $\hat{\alpha}_0$ and $\hat{\alpha}_1$ such that $RSS_2 < RSS_1$, then RSS_1 would not be the global minimum, and we would have a contradiction. As such, in this circumstance, the only possibility is that $RSS_1 = RSS_2$.

This also means that $R_1^2 = R_2^2$.

Case 2 $\hat{\alpha}_2 \neq 0$

We now have a base case, where $\hat{\alpha}_2 = 0$. We are seeking to minimize RSS_2, by choosing an optimal $\hat{\alpha}_0$, $\hat{\alpha}_1$, and $\hat{\alpha}_2$.

$$RSS_2 = \sum_{i=1}^{n} \hat{e}_i^2 = \sum_{i=1}^{n} (Y_i - \hat{\alpha}_0 - \hat{\alpha}_1 X_i - \hat{\alpha}_2 Z_i)^2$$

If there existed a solution to this minimization problem, where $\hat{\alpha}_2 \neq 0$ and $RSS_2 > RSS_1$, then this would not be a global minimum, as a lower residual sum of squares could be achieved by setting $\hat{\alpha}_2 = 0$.

As such, if $\hat{\alpha}_2 \neq 0$, it must be the case that $RSS_2 \leq RSS_1$, and hence $R_2^2 \geq R_1^2$.

Dummy Variables and F-tests

29

Learning outcomes for this chapter

At the end of this chapter, students will be able to:

- Recognize that dummy variables can be used to represent categorical variables in regressions, but that this introduces a danger of multicollinearity
- Use dummy variables to test equality of outcomes across groups
- Interpret results based upon regressions with multiple dummy variables
- Construct F-tests to evaluate whether groups of explanatory variables have an impact on a dependent variable
- Recognize that dummy variables change the intercept of regressions
- Use dummy variables and interaction terms to allow both the slope and the intercept of regression lines to change between groups.

Mathematical tools

- Equations of straight lines
- Arithmetic

Introduction

When we have estimated OLS up until now, we have estimated **linear relationships** between **explanatory variables** and **dependent variables**, and all of the variables we have considered have been quantitative. That is, all of the variables that we have considered have a strict numerical value that we can apply.

However, many relationships that we wish to estimate are not quantitative and linear. For example, suppose that we observed the highest academic qualifications that an individual had (e.g. doctorate, higher education, high school). We wouldn't necessarily expect a linear relationship between wages and the highest level of qualification. This means that we can't just translate these qualifications into a ranked numerical order, and we will need another way of including them within a regression.

In this chapter, we will introduce a number of ways to estimate **non-linear relationships**, and to take account of categorical variables. We will begin with introducing dummy variables, which allow us to control for characteristics that lie in two or more categories, and then will move on to asking how we can investigate whether different relationships exist for different groups of individuals.

29.1 Dummy variables

Often, economic explanatory variables do not take neat, numerical values; for example, we cannot just assign a number to the sex of an individual, or the industry in which an individual works, or in fact any categorical variable. However, these sorts of variable are often very important, as we might be interested in whether the industry you work in affects your wages, or even whether the colour of your eyes has any impact on the number of children that you have! Since we cannot just code these variables as a numerical value, we need an alternative route to include them in our regressions.

One route is through the use of dummy variables. Dummy variables are variables that take the value 1 if an individual belongs to a particular category, and 0 otherwise. So, for example, if we are interested in including whether an individual has gained a degree (or not), we could create a set of dummy variables as follows:

$$Degree_i = \begin{cases} 1, & \text{If individual } i \text{ has a university degree} \\ 0, & \text{Otherwise} \end{cases}$$

$$NoDegree_i = \begin{cases} 1, & \text{If individual } i \text{ does not have a university degree} \\ 0, & \text{Otherwise} \end{cases}$$

Here we have two potential categorical, or dummy, variables to represent whether an individual has a degree (or not). These allow us to model the two possible categories as 'Degree' or 'No degree' in a regression.

29.1.1 Dummy variables and perfect multicollinearity

In the previous chapter, we introduced perfect multicollinearity, which prevented OLS from being estimated. When we introduce dummy, or categorical, variables into our regressions, we run the risk of creating perfect multicollinearity.

For instance, suppose that we were interested in the impact of having a university degree or not. To evaluate this, we would have to collect data about whether each individual has a university degree or not. We could create two variables, $Degree_i$, which takes the value 1 when individual i has a degree and 0 otherwise, and $NoDegree_i$ which takes the value 1 if individual i does not have a degree and 0 otherwise. An example of this data is illustrated in Table 29.1.

Note, however, whenever $Degree_i = 0$, $NoDegree_i = 1$, and vice versa, if $Degree_i = 1$, then $NoDegree_i = 0$. That means that, for every observation, we can write:

$$Degree_i = 1 - NoDegree_i$$

Table 29.1 Example of data illustrating whether an individual has a degree or not

	$Degree_i$	$NoDegree_i$
Has a university degree	1	0
Has a university degree	1	0
No university degree	0	1
Has a university degree	1	0
No university degree	0	1
No university degree	0	1

Suppose then that we were interested in running the following regression:

$$Y_i = \beta_0 + \beta_1 Degree_i + \beta_2 NoDegree_i + u_i$$

where Y_i is some outcome, such as wages, of individual i. As we saw in the previous chapter, we would not be able to estimate this relationship, because the *Degree* variable is collinear with the combination of the $NoDegree_i$ variable and the intercept. If we wished to estimate this relationship via OLS, we would need to omit one of the problematic variables:

- $Degree_i$
- $NoDegree_i$
- the constant, β_0

As such, we could estimate the following regressions:

$$Y_i = \beta_0 + \beta_1 Degree_i + u_i \quad (1)$$
$$Y_i = \beta_0 + \beta_2 NoDegree_i + u_i \quad (2)$$
$$Y_i = \beta_1 Degree_i + \beta_2 NoDegree_i + u_i \quad (3)$$

However, the interpretation of our estimated coefficient changes depending on whether we estimate specification (1), (2), or (3). The group that we omit provide us with a comparison group:

- In specification (1), the β_1 tells us how much higher Y_i is for individuals with a degree, compared to those without degrees.
- In specification (2), the β_2 tells us how much higher Y_i is for individuals with no degree, compared to those with a degree.
- Specification (3) is a little different, because β_1 provides us with an average for those with a degree, whilst β_2 provides us with an average for those without a degree.

We will illustrate this in Section 29.2 using an example.

29.2 Using OLS with dummy variables to test equality of means

Suppose that we are interested in testing whether there are any differences in terms of pay, based on the sex of a worker. We saw in Chapter 20 that we could construct a t-test to test the equality of means between two separate groups. Let's repeat the process, but this time we will use OLS, and dummy variables.

Using data from the 2019 UK Labour Force Survey,[1] we have randomly sampled 400 full-time workers, aged 25–35. The sample is such that we observe 150 male workers and 250 female workers.

Recall from Chapter 20

When we used a t-test to test the difference of means, we tested:

$$H_0 : E(Y_{male}) - E(Y_{female}) = 0$$
$$H_A : E(Y_{male}) - E(Y_{female}) \neq 0$$

Our test statistic was constructed based on the difference of the sample means. The observed sample average for the male workers was $\overline{Y}_{male} = 668.2267$, whilst the sample mean for female workers was $\overline{Y}_{female} = 569.032$.

To test the hypothesis, we constructed the difference of the two sample means:

$$\overline{Y}_{male} - \overline{Y}_{female} = 668.2267 - 569.032 = 99.1947$$

When we assumed that the variance of wages was the same for male and female workers, we obtained a t-statistic equal to $t = 2.97$, and rejected the null hypothesis at the 10%, 5%, and 1% significance levels.

We wish to repeat this test, but instead of using a t-test of equality of means, we want to use OLS. The data only includes workers who are either male or female.

As such, to estimate the difference in wages we will use a categorical (or dummy) variable in our regression. However, because the data only contains individuals who are either male or female, due to the potential for perfect multicollinearity, we can only include either a dummy variable representing male workers, or a dummy variable representing female workers.

Let's begin by defining two possible dummy variables:

$$Male_i = \begin{cases} 1, & \text{If individual } i \text{ is male} \\ 0, & \text{Otherwise} \end{cases}, \quad \begin{cases} 1, & \text{If individual } i \text{ is female} \\ 0, & \text{Otherwise} \end{cases}$$

[1] This is the same sample from the UK LFS that we used in Chapter 20.

Table 29.2 Regression of gross weekly wages against a dummy variable for male using data from the UK LFS

	Results
Male	99.1947***
	(33.390)
Constant	569.032***
	(20.447)
R^2	0.0217
Number of observations	400

Note: Dependent variable is the gross weekly wage. Male is a dummy variable that takes the value 1 if individual is male and 0 otherwise. Estimated standard errors in parentheses. *** indicates significant a 1% significance level, ** indicates significance at 5% significance level.

We will begin by considering the following regression specification:

$$Wages_i = \beta_0 + \beta_1 Male_i + u_i \qquad (1)$$

where $Wages_i$ are the gross weekly wages of individual i, whilst $Male_i$ is the dummy variable. The results of the regression (estimated by OLS) are illustrated in Table 29.2.

We present the results of this regression here. The estimated intercept is equal to 569.032, whilst the estimated coefficient on $Male_i$ is equal to 99.1947.

Hopefully, you have noticed that we have seen these numbers before:

- £569.032 was the average wages for females in the sample.
- £99.1947 is the difference between the average wages.

Whenever you are dealing with dummy variables representing different categories, you will need to choose a group against which you will use as a comparison group; the comparison group is the group that you omit from the regression. In this example, there are two possible dummy variables we can include (based on the observed data). By omitting $Female_i$ from the regression, our results allow us to compare male (average) earnings with female (average) earnings).

In general, we can represent the fitted relationship as:

$$\widehat{Wages}_i = \hat{\beta}_0 + \hat{\beta}_1 Male_i$$

The interpretation of the magnitude of the (estimated) coefficients is a little different when we include dummy variables than when we have used a continuous, or numerical, explanatory variable. Because the dummy variable takes the value 1 (if the individual is male) in this case, or 0 (if the individual is not male), the coefficient provides us with a comparison, compared with the control group. To illustrate this, let's see what happens to the fitted relationship when we substitute in the two possible values for the $Male_i$ dummy variable.

$$\text{If } Male_i = 0 \quad \widehat{Wages_i} = \hat{\beta}_0 + \hat{\beta}_1 \times 0 = \hat{\beta}_0$$
$$\text{If } Male_i = 1 \quad \widehat{Wages_i} = \hat{\beta}_0 + \hat{\beta}_1 \times 1 = \hat{\beta}_0 + \hat{\beta}_1$$

$\hat{\beta}_0$ therefore gives us an estimate of the average wage for female (full-time) workers, whilst $\hat{\beta}_1$ provides us with an estimate of the difference between the average wages for male full-time workers and female full-time workers.

Mathematically, these estimates are the same as the ones we used in Chapter 20, whereby $\hat{\beta}_0 = 569.032$ is just the sample average of wages for female (full-time) workers, whilst $\hat{\beta}_1 = 99.1947$ is the difference between the male and female average wages, $\overline{Y}_{male} - \overline{Y}_{female}$.

Other than the interpretation of the magnitude of the estimated coefficients, we can interpret much of the results in exactly the same way as we have previously. We might start by looking at the $R^2 = 0.0217$. This indicates that 2.17 per cent of the variation in gross weekly wages is explained by the sex of the individual. Further, we can test the statistical significance of the intercept and the 'slope'.

$H_0 : \beta_0 = 0$
$H_A : \beta_0 \neq 0$
We can test this using a t-test in the usual way:

$$t = \frac{\hat{\beta}_0 - E(\hat{\beta}_0 \mid \beta_0 = 0)}{\widehat{s.e.}(\hat{\beta}_0)} = \frac{569.032 - 0}{20.447} = 27.83$$

We have 400 observations, and have estimated two coefficients; we therefore have 398 degrees of freedom.
The p-value associated with 27.83 from the t-distribution with 398 degrees of freedom is 2.06×10^{-95}. To give a sense of the likelihood, this is equivalent to gaining 315 heads in a row when we flip a fair coin. As such, we would reject the null hypothesis at *any* reasonable level of significance.

$H_0 : \beta_1 = 0$
$H_A : \beta_1 \neq 0$
We can test this using a t-test in the usual way:

$$t = \frac{\hat{\beta}_1 - E(\hat{\beta}_1 \mid \beta_1 = 0)}{\widehat{s.e.}(\hat{\beta}_1)} = \frac{99.1947 - 0}{33.390} = 2.97$$

We have 400 observations, and have estimated two coefficients; we therefore have 398 degrees of freedom.
The p-value associated with 2.97 from the t-distribution with 398 degrees of freedom is 0.003. Because this is smaller than 0.1 (10%), 0.05 (5%), and 0.01 (1%), we would reject the null hypothesis at the 10%, 5%, and 1% significance levels.
If the null hypothesis is true, there is a 0.3% chance of randomly gaining a t-stat at least 2.97 times the standard error away from the expected value.

Interestingly, the t-statistic for the test H_0: $\beta_1 = 0$ is exactly the same as the t-statistic we obtained ($t = 2.97$) when testing the equality of means in Chapter 20. This is reassuring, because essentially, we are testing the same hypothesis. Since β_1 can be interpreted as how much higher male wages are compared with the comparison group (female wage), then if $\beta_1 = 0$, this is equivalent to saying that there is no difference between male and female average wages.

Table 29.3 Estimating the three separate specifications

	(1)	(2)	(3)
Male	99.1947***		668.227***
	(33.390)		(26.397)
Female		-99.1947***	569.032***
		(33.390)	(20.447)
Constant	569.032***	668.227***	
	(20.447)	(26.397)	
R^2	0.0217	0.0217	0.7805
Number of observations	400	400	400

Note: Dependent variable is the gross weekly wage. Male is a dummy variable that takes the value 1 if individual is male and 0 otherwise. Estimated standard errors in parentheses. *** indicates significant a 1% significance level, ** indicates significance at 5% significance level.

We can repeat this for the three possible methods of estimating the relationship, omitting $Female_i$, $Male_i$ and then the constant from the regression in turn:

$$Wages_i = \beta_0 + \beta_1 Male_i + u_i \quad (1)$$
$$Wages_i = \gamma_0 + \gamma_1 Female_i + u_i \quad (2)$$
$$Wages_i = B_1 Male_i + B_2 Female_i + u_i \quad (3)$$

We have already seen specification (1) in Table 29.2. However, the numbers we see in specification (1) also provide a basis for all of the other numbers in the table (see Table 29.3). When we estimate specification (2), our estimated 'slope' coefficient, $\hat{\gamma}_1 = -99.1947$. This can be interpreted as how much *higher* female wages are (on average) compared with male wages. Notice that $\hat{\gamma}_1 = -\hat{\beta}_1$. This shouldn't be surprising, because whilst β_1 is a measure of how much higher average male wages are than female wages, γ_1 is a measure of how much higher average female wages are than male wages.

If, on average, female workers are paid £100 more than male workers, then it must also be true that, on average, male workers are paid £100 less than female workers.

Finally, in specification (3), the estimated coefficients are equal to the average wages for males and females, respectively. We have already seen the estimated coefficients in specifications (1) and (2): the estimated coefficient on $Male_i$ is the intercept from specification (2), whilst the coefficient on $Female_i$ is the intercept from specification (1). This is because the intercept provides us with a measure of the 'average' of the comparison group. In specification (1), the omitted variable is $Female_i$, and so the comparison group is female workers. In specification (2), the omitted variable is $Male_i$, and so the comparison group is male workers.

One thing to note here is that the R^2 appears much larger than specifications (1) and (2). It should be noted that the R^2 in a regression without a constant cannot be interpreted in the same way, so be careful not to assume that this means that we are seeing a better 'fit' to the model.

29.2.1 Interpreting dummy variables, in general

Suppose that you have a dependent variable Y_i, and an explanatory variable X_i, whereby X_i is a dummy variable that takes two possible values, $X_i = 1$ and $X_i = 0$.

We are interested in estimating the following relationship:

$$Y_i = \beta_0 + \beta_1 X_i + u_i$$

One way of examining this relationship is to consider the conditional expectation of Y_i, conditioning on the potential values of X_i. In general, if we condition that $X_i = x$:

$$\Rightarrow E(Y_i \mid X_i = x) = E(\beta_0 + \beta_1 X_i + u_i \mid X_i = x)$$

Since this is the (conditional) expectation of a linear combination of terms, we can break this up into three constituent components. Further, since β_0 is a constant, the expectation will just be equal to β_0. Similarly, $E(\beta_1 X_i \mid X_i = x)$ will just be equal to $\beta_1 x$ since β_1 is a constant multiplier, and can be taken outside of the expectation. Similarly, if we are conditioning that $X_i = x$, that must mean $E(X_i \mid X_i = x) = x$. As such, we can rewrite the expression as:

$$E(Y_i \mid X_i = x) = \beta_0 + \beta_1 x + E(u_i \mid X_i = x)$$

For simplicity, we will assume that $E(u_i \mid X_i = 0) = E(u_i \mid X_i = 1) = 0$. Now, we have two circumstances that we are interested in: the case where $X_i = 0$, and the case where $X_i = 1$.

Now, we substitute in the two possible values, $X_i = 1$ and $X_i = 0$. Let's start with $X_i = 0$:

$$\begin{aligned} E(Y_i \mid X_i = 0) &= \beta_0 + \beta_1 \times 0 + E(u_i \mid X_i = 0) \\ &= \beta_0 + 0 + 0 = \beta_0 \end{aligned}$$

Similarly, conditioning that $X_i = 1$, we have again assumed that $E(u_i \mid X_i = 1) = 0$, and so:

$$E(Y_i \mid X_i = 1) = \beta_0 + \beta_1 \times 1 + 0 = \beta_0 + \beta_1$$

So,

- when $X_i = 0$, the (population) average of Y_i is equal to $E(Y_i \mid X_i = 0) = \beta_0$
- when $X_i = 1$, the (population) average of Y_i is equal to $E(Y_i \mid X_i = 1) = \beta_0 + \beta_1$

That is, the difference between the two cases is equal to β_1. This ties in with the example in section 29.3, where we saw that the estimated intercept was equal to the average for the group where $X_i = 0$, whilst the estimated slope parameter was equal to the difference between the average for the group indicated by $X_i = 1$ and $X_i = 0$.

29.2.2 Dummy variables with experiments

Dummy variables are not just useful for controlling for characteristics of individuals, but are often used when estimating the impact of experiments.

In 2016, an experiment was carried out in the US Military Academy,[2] where students were randomly assigned to classrooms. Some of these classrooms allowed students to use computers, whilst others prohibited the use of any digital devices within the classroom.

[2] S. Carter, K. Greenberg, and M. Walker (2017), 'The Impact of Computer Usage on Academic Performance: Evidence from a Randomized Trial at the United States Military Academy', *Economics of Education Review*, 56, 118–132.

The students in the classrooms where computers were allowed can be described as the treatment group, and the students in the classrooms where digital devices were prohibited can be described as the control group.

We can represent this treatment using a dummy variable, $Treat_i$, that takes the value 1 if student i is in a treatment classroom, and 0 otherwise. This can then be used to estimate the following relationship:

$$Y_i = \beta_0 + \beta_1 Treat_i + u_i$$

where Y_i represents the score that student i gained. The results suggested that students taught in classrooms that permitted computer usage scored 0.21 **standard deviations** less than students who were taught in classrooms that prohibited digital devices.

Causal inference

A question that economists are always interested in is whether estimates are causal and unbiased; that is, in the example, does being taught in a classroom where computers are permitted cause you to score 0.21 standard deviations worse than in a classroom that prohibits digital devices?

When we are using dummy variables, it is often easy to evaluate whether estimates are causal (or not). If everything else is the same across the treatment and the control group, then the only difference between the two groups is the treatment. Since the u_i represents everything else that is a determinant of Y_i, this is equivalent to saying that $E(u_i \mid Treat_i = 1) = E(u_i \mid Treat_i = 0)$.

If this condition holds, then it will also be the case that the u_i and the $Treat_i$ variables are independent from each other (and hence uncorrelated). This is equivalent to the conditions we saw in Chapter 21, that provided $E(u_i \mid Treat)$ is a constant, then OLS is unbiased and consistent.

However, in many cases, it may not be the case that the treatment (or the value of the dummy variable) is independent from the error term. In these cases, there are a range of strategies that we might use, some of which are beyond the scope of this book:

- If we suspect that the differences amongst the groups can be controlled for (e.g. if the individuals in different groups work in different firms), then you could control for this using a multivariate regression.
- If you suspect that you have two groups that are quantitatively different, but are following similar trends over time, you can use a method such as difference in differences. Difference in differences uses a control group to ask how much the outcome variable would have changed in the treatment group if the treatment had not been instigated. The 'causal effect' is then the difference between the predicted change and the actual change.

If you have a variable that is correlated with the treatment variable, but is neither a determinant of the dependent variable nor correlated with any of the omitted determinants of the dependent variable, then you could use an instrumental variable to generate **exogenous** variation in the explanatory variable.

29.3 Multiple dummy variables

So far, we've only represented dummy variables representing variables where there are only two categories, but in reality, we will often be interested in variables where there are multiple categories; for example, we could be interested in the impact of the highest qualification gained on earnings, or we could be interested in whether the colour of an individual's eyes has any effect on their eyesight, or we could be interested in the impact of the country people live in on life expectancy.

In each of the earlier examples, there are multiple possible values for the variable we are interested in. If we are interested in the effect of highest qualification in England and Wales, this could include GCSEs (at age 16), A-levels (at age 18), undergraduate degree, vocational qualifications, and more.

Just as with the examples in the previous section, we can represent these kinds of categorical variables using dummy variables. However, we will need to include multiple dummy variables in our regression to represent the different categories.

When we observed two categories in the data, we cannot include both categories as dummy variables and the intercept. We would need to omit one of the categories to provide a comparison group. When we have more than two categories, the same rules apply. If we attempted to include all of the categories as dummy variables, we would experience perfect multicollinearity. As such, we always need to omit one of the categories. That is, if we have k categories, we could include $k - 1$ dummy variables, and the coefficients would reflect the comparison with the omitted group.

Worked example 29.1: Dummy variables representing the nations of the UK

The UK is made up of four constituent countries: England, Wales, Scotland, and Northern Ireland. You might be interested in estimating the relationship between which country of the UK individuals were born in, and their earnings at (say) age 25.

We can't just include country of birth as a single explanatory variable because:

1. The country of birth does not have a numerical value.
2. There is no way, *ex-ante* to code these to apply a numerical value to them.

As such, if we wish to estimate this relationship, we will need to use dummy variables. As shown in Table 29.4, we can have four possible dummy variables—being born in England, Wales, Scotland, or Northern Ireland. So for example, the Northern Ireland dummy would take the value 1 if the individual was born in Northern Ireland and 0 otherwise.

The first thing to note is that, as we increase the number of dummy variables, the more observations we are going to need in order to have meaningful variation in the explanatory variables to avoid imperfect multicollinearity as a problem. For instance, if you have a very large number of categories, you may have some categories with only one or two observations. This can lead to imperfect multicollinearity, and hence very imprecise estimates.

Table 29.4 Using dummy variables to represent the nations within the UK

Country of birth	$England_i$	$Scotland_i$	$Wales_i$	$NIreland_i$
Scotland	0	1	0	0
Wales	0	0	1	0
N. Ireland	0	0	0	1
England	1	0	0	0
Scotland	0	1	0	0
England	1	0	0	0
N. Ireland	0	0	0	1

The second thing to note is that, just as with categorical variables that take only two possible values, if we were to include all of the country dummies (along with a constant), OLS could not be estimated due to perfect multicollinearity.

As such, we need to omit one of the dummy variables, which then provides our comparison group. So, for instance, we would be able to estimate:

$$Y_i = \beta_0 + \beta_1 Scotland_i + \beta_2 Wales_i + \beta_3 NIreland_i + u_i$$

The interpretation of the coefficients would be:

- β_0 provides us the average level of Y_i for the omitted country. In this relationship, β_0 would be the expected Y_i in England.
- β_1 tells us the expected difference in Y_i between Scotland and England; that is, it tells us how much higher, on average, Y_i is in Scotland than England. If β_1 is positive, this means that Y_i is higher (on average) in Scotland than England, and conversely, if β_1 is negative, this means that Y_i is lower in Scotland than England.
- Similarly, β_2 tells us the expected difference in Y_i between Wales and England and β_3 tells us the expected difference in Y_i between Northern Ireland and England.

In each of these cases, because $England_i$ has been omitted from the regression, we are comparing outcomes in Scotland, Wales, or Northern Ireland with England. It should be noted that in this example we have omitted England, but we could equally have omitted Scotland or Wales or Northern Ireland. The key thing is that we omit one of the categories.

29.3.1 Simple estimation of the returns to different qualifications

To illustrate this, we will try to estimate the returns to different educational qualifications. To that end, I have collected a new data set of 500 full-time workers, aged 25–50, randomly sampled from the UK Labour Force Survey. Included in this data set, we have the sex of the worker and the highest educational qualification achieved. It should be noted that we will expect the estimated difference between average male and female earnings to be different in this sample than the one considered earlier in the chapter, because:

(i) We are effectively considering a different population. In the previous example, we were considering 25 to 35 year olds. In this example, we have widened that age range to 25 to 50 year olds.

(ii) Even if we were considering the same population, because we have taken a different sample from the population, due to sampling variation, we would expect a different estimates.

In terms of the highest qualifications, we have six categories: degree level qualification, some higher education, A-levels, GCSEs grade A*–C, other qualifications, and no qualifications. Let's define six dummy variables to represent these different categories of highest level of qualifications.

$$Degree_i = \begin{cases} 1, & \text{If individual } i \text{ has an undergraduate degree} \\ 0, & \text{Otherwise} \end{cases}$$

$$HE_i = \begin{cases} 1, & \text{If individual } i \text{ has some HE (but not a degree)} \\ 0, & \text{Otherwise} \end{cases}$$

$$ALevel_i = \begin{cases} 1, & \text{If individual } i \text{ has A} - \text{levels} \\ 0, & \text{Otherwise} \end{cases}$$

$$GCSE_i = \begin{cases} 1, & \text{If individual } i \text{ has GCSEs graded A} * -\text{C} \\ 0, & \text{Otherwise} \end{cases}$$

$$Other_i = \begin{cases} 1, & \text{If individual } i \text{ has other qualifications} \\ 0, & \text{Otherwise} \end{cases}$$

$$None_i = \begin{cases} 1, & \text{If individual } i \text{ has no qualifications} \\ 0, & \text{Otherwise} \end{cases}$$

Table 29.5 Illustrating the structure of the data for the dummy variables representing highest qualification

Highest qualification	$Degree_i$	HE_i	$ALevel_i$	$GCSE_i$	$Other_i$	$None_i$
Degree	1	0	0	0	0	0
Other	0	0	0	0	1	0
None	0	0	0	0	0	1
Some HE	0	1	0	0	0	0
Degree	1	0	0	0	0	0
GCSE	0	0	0	1	0	0
A-level	0	0	1	0	0	0

Because these are the highest levels of qualifications, individuals can only lie within one of the group; that is, an individual whose highest qualification is a degree will not be included in the group whose highest qualification is A-levels (or some higher education, or any other group). The structure of the data is illustrated in Table 29.5.

Even though there are six groups, we face the same potential issues as we did with simple dummy variables: if we were to include all six categories as dummy variables, our regression would suffer from perfect multicollinearity. As such, in order to estimate this relationship, we would need to omit one of the variables, which would provide us with a comparison group.

In the previous section, we estimated the gender pay gap using dummy variables. We will begin by repeating this process.

We will regress gross weekly wages first against a dummy variable $Female_i$ that takes the value 1 if individual i is female, and 0 otherwise (specification (1)), and then will move on to include dummy variables for the highest educational qualification achieved (specification (2)):

$$Wages_i = \beta_0 + \beta_1 Female_i + u_i \tag{1}$$

$$Wages_i = \beta_0 + \beta_1 Female_i + \beta_2 HE_i + \beta_3 ALevel_i + \beta_4 GCSE_i + \beta_5 Other_i + \beta_6 None_i + u_i \tag{2}$$

Table 29.6 Results from estimating specifications (1) and (2)

	(1)	(2)
Female	−170.631***	−205.175***
	(35.643)	(33.405)
Some higher education		−198.031***
		(65.591)
A-levels		−267.215***
		(43.580)
GCSEs grade A*–C		−297.215***
		(47.912)
Other qualifications		−381.637***
		(66.471)
No qualifications		−466.077***
		(123.813)
Constant	756.606***	915.7627***
	(22.711)	(27.640)
Number of observations	500	500
R^2	0.0440	0.1846

Note: Dependent variable is gross weekly wage in main job. Estimated standard errors are in parentheses. *** indicates significant at 1% significance level, ** indicates significant at 5% significance level, * indicates significance at 10% significance level.

When we include the dummy variables for highest qualification achieved, we need to choose which category to omit. Here we have chosen to omit the $Degree_i$ dummy variable; this means that we are comparing gross weekly wages against individuals with a degree. That is, β_2 is telling us how much higher (or lower) gross weekly wages are for those with only *some*

HE compared with those who have completed a degree. The results from estimating specifications (1) and (2) are shown in Table 29.6.

When estimating specification (1), we get an estimate of the (unconditional) gender gap between male and female workers. The estimates suggest that female workers are (on average) paid £170.631 less than male workers per week.

However, this is an unconditional estimate. That is, because $Female_i$ is the only explanatory variable, we haven't controlled for any of the other determinants of gross weekly wages. One possibility is that this estimate of the gender gap suffers from omitted variables bias. Education is likely to be a determinant of gross weekly wages, and if educational level is correlated with the sex of the worker, then we would yield biased results in specification (1).

In fact, within this data set, 45 per cent of males gain a degree, whilst 56 per cent of females gain a degree. As such, there is evidence of strong correlation between gaining a degree and the sex of the worker. This is shown in Table 29.7, where we can see that female full-time workers are also more likely to have some higher education, whilst male full-time workers are more likely to have lower levels of qualifications.[3]

Because females are likely to gain higher levels of education, and higher levels of education are expected to lead to higher earnings, by omitting the level of education, we may have positive bias when estimating specification (1). That is, the magnitude of the conditional gap between male and female earnings might be even larger than estimated here.

Table 29.7 Distribution of highest level of education, by sex

	Male	Female
Degree	45.45%	56.16%
Higher education	6.73%	7.39%
GCE A-level or equivalent	22.56%	15.27%
GCSE grades A*–C	15.49%	14.29%
Other qualification	7.07%	6.40%
No qualification	2.69%	0.49%

In specification (2), we introduce the highest education level dummies as additional explanatory variables. This creates a new estimate of the gender pay gap, having conditioned upon the highest level of education gained. The first thing to note is that the coefficient on $Female_i$ changes from specification (1) to specification (2); in fact, as we predicted, the magnitude of the difference gets larger, to $\hat{\beta}_1 = -205.175$. This suggests that, having conditioned

[3] To a certain extent, this difference may be due to selection, but in general, in the UK population, females are more likely to attend university. The UK Census in 2021 showed that (in total) 28.5 per cent of females in England and Wales had achieved at least some higher education (or a degree), whilst the equivalent figure for males was 26.6 per cent. These figures are different from the ones in our sample, because the census relates to the entire population, whilst we have restricted ourselves to only full-time employees aged 25–50.

for the education level, female full-time workers, on average, are paid £205.175 less per week than male workers.

We have seven coefficients that are of interest here. For brevity, we will not formally test the individual significance of each of the estimated coefficients, but we have tested the statistical significance of the higher education variable.

Testing the statistical significance of the dummy variables

For brevity, we will only test the statistical significance of the 'Some Higher Education' variable here. You can use exactly the same methodology to test the statistical significance of the other estimated coefficients, so I leave that as an exercise for you to work through.

$$H_0: \beta_2 = 0$$
$$H_A: \beta_2 \neq 0$$

We construct our t-statistic in the usual way:

$$t = \frac{\hat{\beta}_2 - E(\hat{\beta}_2 \mid \beta_2 = 0)}{\widehat{s.e.}(\hat{\beta}_2)} = \frac{-198.031 - 0}{65.591}$$
$$= -3.02$$

We have 500 observations, and have estimated 7 coefficients. As such, we have $500 - 7 = 493$ degrees of freedom.

The critical values from the t-distribution with 493 degrees of freedom are 1.648 (10 per cent), 1.965 (5 per cent), and 2.586 (1 per cent).

The magnitude of the t-statistic (= 3.02) is larger than the critical value at the 5 per cent significance level, so we would reject the null at the 5 per cent significance level, but smaller than the critical value at the 1 per cent significance level, so we would fail to reject the null at the 1 per cent significance level.

Note that the p-value associated with −3.02 is $P(|t_{493}| \geq 3.02) = 0.00266$. So, if the null hypothesis were true, the probability of achieving a t-stat at least as large as ±3.02 is about 0.266 per cent.[4]

Interpreting the estimated coefficients on the dummy variables

In fact, all of the coefficients are statistically significant at at least the 5 per cent significance level. However, what is more interesting is the economic interpretation of the estimated coefficients.

When interpreting the coefficients, it is important to begin by thinking about what are the omitted categories. We have two sets of categorical variables:

- The first relates to the sex of the individual. Since the data only includes individuals who are either male or female, we have included a dummy variable for female, and omitted the male variable. Therefore, the coefficients relating to sex are comparing against the earnings for males.

[4] To add context, this is roughly equivalent to flipping nine heads in a row.

- The second group of categorical variables relates to the highest educational qualification. Here, we have omitted the dummy for degree. This means that all of the coefficients relating to education are comparing against individuals with a university degree (or equivalent).

This means that the intercept is providing us with an average wage for the omitted categories. That is, males with a degree earn, on average, £915.7627. Another way of thinking about this is that the intercept gives us an average for wages where all of the dummy variables are equal to zero; again, this would then correspond to males with a degree.

Moving on to the estimated coefficients associated with the highest educational qualification, each of the estimated coefficients is the estimated difference in the expected wages compared with a degree (see Table 29.8).

As in previous examples, it can be useful to interpret these estimated effects in terms of the standard deviation of wages. From the data, an estimate of the standard deviation of wages is £399.90. To gain an interpretation of the impact, in terms of standard deviations, we can divide the estimated effects by the standard deviation of wages, giving us the interpretation shown in Table 29.9.

As before, converting the effects into standard deviations makes it much easier to answer whether the estimated effects are large (or not). In fact, the difference between those with a degree, and those with no qualifications, at 1.1654 standard deviations is a very large effect.

Of course, these estimated effects are still unlikely to be causal. There are still likely to be lots of elements in the error terms that are correlated with both the highest level of educational qualification and the level of earnings. It is possible that individuals are choosing their education level as a way of signalling their underlying human capital, which also helps to determine their level of earnings. In this case, it might be the underlying human capital that

Table 29.8 Interpreting the estimated coefficients

Variable	Coefficient	Explanation
Some higher education	$\hat{\beta}_2 = -198.031$	Workers with some higher education (but not a degree) earn £198.031 less per week (on average) than workers with a degree
A-levels	$\hat{\beta}_3 = -267.075$	Workers with A-levels (but no higher education) earn £267.075 less per week (on average) than workers with a degree
GCSEs grade A*–C	$\hat{\beta}_4 = -297.215$	Workers with GCSEs grade A*–C (but no further education) earn £297.215 less per week (on average) than workers with a degree
Other qualifications	$\hat{\beta}_5 = -381.637$	Workers with other qualifications earn £381.637 less per week (on average) than workers with a degree
No qualifications	$\hat{\beta}_6 = -466.077$	Workers with no qualifications earn £466.077 less per week (on average) than workers with a degree

Table 29.9 Interpreting the estimated effects in terms of standard deviations

Variable	Size of effect	Explanation
Some higher education	−0.4952	Workers with some higher education earn 0.4952 standard deviations (or 49.52% of a standard deviation) less, on average, than those with a degree
A-levels	−0.6679	Workers with A-levels earn 0.6679 standard deviations less, on average, than those with a degree
GCSEs grade A*–C	−0.7432	Workers with GCSEs grade A*–C earn 0.7432 standard deviations less, on average, than those with a degree
Other qualifications	−0.9543	Workers with other qualifications eran 0.9543 standard deviations less, on average, than those with a degree
No qualifications	−1.1654	Workers with no qualifications earn 1.1654 standard deviations less, on average, than those with a degree

causes both the level of education and the level of earnings, rather than the education level itself causing changes in earnings.

One question that might occur to you is that we have included a range of dummy variables to control for education, but even though we can test the individual significance of particular qualifications, compared with gaining a degree, we haven't been able to test whether education, as a whole, has any impact on our dependent variable (gross weekly wages).

Because education spans a number of explanatory variables, we cannot simply test this with a t-test. Instead, we will need to consider a different type of test. In the next section, we will introduce an F-test, that allows you to test multiple hypotheses simultaneously.

29.4 F-tests

We have introduced multivariate regressions, and in the last section, we introduced regressions with multiple dummy variables. In particular, we controlled for both the sex of the individual and the highest level of educational qualification gained.

An interesting question in these circumstances is to ask whether education has any impact on gross weekly earnings at all? In our second specification, we estimated the following relationship:

$$Wages_i = \beta_0 + \beta_1 Female_i + \beta_2 HE_i + \beta_3 ALevel_i + \beta_4 GCSE_i + \beta_5 Other_i + \beta_6 None_i + u_i$$

If education has no impact on earnings, then individuals would gain the same level of earnings, irrespective of whether they had a degree, some HE, A-levels, GCSEs, other qualifications, or no qualifications. Because β_2 to β_6 can be interpreted as the difference from an individual with a degree, then if education has no impact whatsoever on earnings, it would be the case that $\beta_2 = \beta_3 = \beta_4 = \beta_5 = \beta_6 = 0$.

As is the way with statistics, we want to develop a way of testing the hypothesis that education has no impact on earnings, but we cannot simply construct a single t-statistic to test this hypothesis; we could test each of the individual coefficients. However, a t-test can only be used to test a single hypothesis. That is, we could test that $\beta_2 = 0$, or we could test that $\beta_3 = 0$, but a t-test cannot be used to test the hypothesis that $\beta_2 = 0$ and $\beta_3 = 0$.

29.4.1 Do any of the explanatory variables have a significant impact on the dependent variable?

Before we consider the question of whether any of the education variables have a significant impact on earnings, let's begin with a more general question: do any of the explanatory variables included in the model have an effect on the dependent variable? To motivate this, suppose that you estimate a relationship between Y_i and k explanatory variables, $X_{1i}, X_{2i}, \ldots, X_{ki}$ plus a constant, β_0:

$$Y_i = \beta_0 + \beta_1 X_{1i} + \beta_2 X_{2i} + \ldots + \beta_k X_{ki} + u_i$$

Then, we can test the null hypothesis that none of the explanatory variables has any impact on Y_i:

$$H_0: \beta_1 = \beta_2 = \beta_3 = \ldots = \beta_k = 0$$
$$H_A: \beta_1 \neq 0 \text{ or } \beta_2 \neq 0 \text{ or} \ldots \text{or } \beta_k \neq 0$$

Explained sum of squares	$ESS = \sum_{i=1}^{n}(\hat{Y}_i - \bar{Y})^2$
Residual sum of squares	$RSS = \sum_{(i=1)}^{n}\hat{u}_i^2$
Total sum of squares	$TSS = \sum_{i=1}^{n}(Y_i - \bar{Y})^2$

You may recognize these sums of squares as being similar to the total, within, and between sums of squares we saw when using ANOVA in Chapter 22. In fact, the motivation behind these, and the way that we construct tests with them, is exactly the same.

As with ANOVA, we can use the ESS, RSS, and TSS to construct F-statistics. In this example, we have k explanatory variables, and we have estimated $k + 1$ coefficients. This means that the ESS will have k degrees of freedom, whilst the RSS will have $n - (k + 1)$ degrees of freedom (or $n - k - 1$) degrees of freedom. The F-statistic is then given as:

$$F = \frac{ESS/k}{RSS/(n-k-1)} \sim F_{k,n-k-1}$$

Remember that the F-distribution is defined as the ratio of two chi-squared variables, divided by their respective degrees of freedom.

Calculating the degrees of freedom

Remember that the number of degrees of freedom is the number of linearly independent elements within the summation. For the RSS, calculating the number of degrees of freedom is relatively straightforward. We know that:

$$RSS = \sum_{i=1}^{n} \hat{u}_i^2$$

Now, each $\hat{u}_i$ is constructed based on the observed values of Y_i and the estimated coefficients. So, we can write each $\hat{u}_i$ as:

$$\hat{u}_i = Y_i - \hat{\beta}_0 - \hat{\beta}_1 X_{1i} - \hat{\beta}_2 X_{2i} - \ldots - \hat{\beta}_k X_{ki}$$

Remember, for each additional estimate that we include in the RSS, we essentially lose a degree of freedom. Since we are using $\hat{\beta}_0, \hat{\beta}_1, \ldots, \hat{\beta}_k$, we have $k + 1$ estimates included—that is, the estimated coefficients on k explanatory variables, and the intercept. As such, if we have n observations, we will have $n - (k + 1)$ or $n - k - 1$ degrees of freedom.

For the ESS, the number of degrees of freedom is a little less straightforward. Beginning with $\hat{Y}_i$, this is constructed based on $k + 1$ elements:

$$\hat{Y}_i = \hat{\beta}_0 + \hat{\beta}_1 X_{1i} + \hat{\beta}_2 X_{2i} + \ldots + \hat{\beta}_k X_{ki}$$

As we see different observations of the explanatory variables, we will get different realizations of $\hat{Y}_i$. The number of degrees of freedom is the number of linearly independent elements within the $\hat{Y}_i$. However, once we know all of the $\hat{\beta}$ terms, we could construct any value of $\hat{Y}_i$ based upon the realized observations of the other $\hat{Y}_i$s. This is easiest to see when $k = 1$, as illustrated in Figure 29.1.

When we have one observation of $\hat{Y}_i$, we cannot make any conclusions about any of the other values of $\hat{Y}_i$. However, since the relationship between X_i and $\hat{Y}_i$ is a linear relationship, as soon as we have two observations, we can draw a straight line between the observations, and every subsequent observation of $\hat{Y}_i$ will lie on that line. As such, as soon as we know $\hat{Y}_1$ and $\hat{Y}_2$, then $\hat{Y}_3$ will be certain to lie on the same straight line between the observations. That

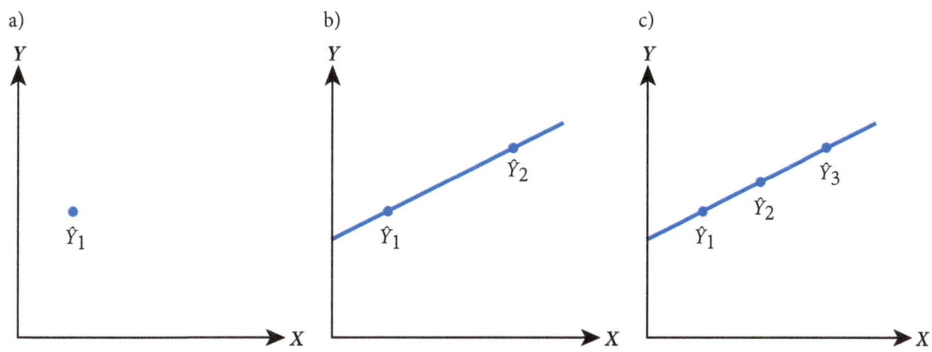

Figure 29.1 Degrees of freedom of $\hat{Y}$.

is, any subsequent $\hat{Y}_i$ can be written as a linear combination of $\hat{Y}_1$ and $\hat{Y}_2$. This means that, if $k = 1$, then there are only 2 degrees of freedom in $\hat{Y}_i$.

More generally, if we have k explanatory variables, if we are estimating $k + 1$ coefficients, then $\hat{Y}_i$ and we will have $k + 1$ degrees of freedom.

IIowever, the explained sum of squares is not just based upon the sum of the $\hat{Y}_i$ but also includes the sample mean of the observations of Y:

$$ESS = \sum_{i=1}^{n}(\hat{Y}_i - \bar{Y})$$

Since $\bar{\hat{Y}} = \bar{Y}$, this sample mean is itself just a linear combination of the $\hat{Y}_i$s. As such, we lose an additional degree of freedom here. This means that the total degrees of freedom for the ESS are just the number of degrees of freedom of $\hat{Y}$ less 1 to take account of the $\bar{Y}$. Thus, there are $(k + 1) - 1$ degrees of freedom, or more simply, k degrees of freedom (see Table 29.10).

Table 29.10 Degrees of freedom of the ESS, RSS, and TSS

Measure	Mathematical formula	Degrees of freedom
Explained sum of squares	$ESS = \sum_{i=1}^{n}(\hat{Y}_i - \bar{Y})^2$	The degrees of freedom will be equal to the number of explanatory variables $(= k)$
Residual sum of squares	$RSS = \sum_{(i=1)}^{n}\hat{u}_i^2$	The degrees of freedom will be equal to the number of observations, less the number of coefficients estimated $(= n - k - 1)$
Total sum of squares	$TSS = \sum_{i=1}^{n}(Y_i - \bar{Y})^2$	The degrees of freedom will be equal to the number of observations minus 1 $(= n - 1)$

Recall that the F-distribution is constructed based on the ratio of two variables following chi-squared (or χ^2) distributions, each divided by its relevant degrees of freedom. So, if you have two variables, following χ_a^2 and χ_b^2, respectively, then:

$$\frac{\chi_a^2/a}{\chi_b^2/b} \sim F_{a,b}$$

Since the ESS effectively follows a χ_k^2 distribution, and the RSS effectively follows a χ_{n-k-1}^2 distribution, then if we construct the F-statistic here:

$$F = \frac{ESS/k}{RSS/(n - k - 1)} \sim F(k, n - k - 1)$$

We can also write this F-statistic in terms of the R^2. If we were to divide top and bottom of the fraction by the TSS, we would have:

$$\frac{\frac{ESS}{TSS}/k}{\frac{RSS}{TSS}/(n - k - 1)}$$

We have seen two ways of calculating the R^2, using the ESS and the RSS. We know that:

$$R^2 = \frac{ESS}{TSS}, \text{ and } R^2 = 1 - \frac{RSS}{TSS}$$

Therefore, we can write the F-statistic as:

$$F = \frac{\frac{ESS}{TSS}/k}{\frac{RSS}{TSS}/(n-k-1)} = \frac{R^2/k}{(1-R^2)/(n-k-1)} \sim F_{k,n-k-1}$$

Worked example 29.2: Testing the hypothesis that none of the explanatory variables have any impact on the dependent variable

Let's return to the example we introduced earlier in the chapter; that is, suppose we are interested in estimating the relationship between weekly earnings, the sex of an individual, and their highest level of educational attainment.

We saw the results as illustrated in Table 29.11. The first thing that we may wish to do is to test whether any of the explanatory variables has any impact on the dependent variable.

Table 29.11 Results from a regression of gross weekly wages against sex and highest level of education

	(2)
Female	−205.175***
	(33.405)
Some higher education	−198.031***
	(65.591)
A-levels	−267.215***
	(43.580)
GCSEs grade A*–C	−297.215***
	(47.912)
Other qualifications	−381.637***
	(66.471)
No qualifications	−466.077***
	(123.813)
Constant	915.7627***
	(27.640)
Number of observations	500
R^2	0.1846

Note: Dependent variable is gross weekly wage in main job. Estimated standard errors are in parentheses. *** indicates significant at 1% significance level, ** indicates significant at 5% significance level, * indicates significance at 10% significance level.

Intuitively, since we can see that all of the estimated coefficients are statistically significant at the 1 per cent significance level, we would expect to reject that null hypothesis.

That is, we have estimated the relationship:

$$Wages_i = \beta_0 + \beta_1 Female_i + \beta_2 HE_i + \beta_3 ALevel_i + \beta_4 GCSE_i + \beta_5 Other_i + \beta_6 None_i + u_i \qquad (2)$$

and we may wish to test the hypotheses that:

$$H_0 : \beta_1 = \beta_2 = \beta_3 = \beta_4 = \beta_5 = \beta_6 = 0$$
$$H_A : \beta_1 \neq 0 \text{ or } \beta_2 \neq 0 \text{ or } \beta_3 \neq 0 \text{ or } \beta_4 \neq 0 \text{ or } \beta_5 \neq 0 \text{ or } \beta_6 \neq 0$$

We have just seen that we can construct the F-statistic as:

$$F = \frac{R^2/k}{(1-R^2)/(n-k-1)} \sim F_{k,n-k-1}$$

where k is the number of explanatory variables, and n the number of observations. In the regression results in Table 29.11, we can see that $n = 500, R^2 = 0.1846$, and $k = 6$. Similarly, the number of degrees of freedom in the RSS will then be equal to $500 - 6 - 1 = 493$.

As such, we can construct the F-statistic as:

$$= \frac{0.1846/6}{(1-0.1846)/493} = 18.60$$

If we look at the tables for the 5 per cent critical values of the F-distribution, based upon 6 and 493 degrees of freedom, we find a critical value of 2.12. Since the F-statistic is larger than the critical value, we can reject the null hypothesis.

We could also construct the F-statistic using data on the Explained and Residual Sum of Squares, as obtained from Microsoft Excel, as illustrated in Figure 29.2.

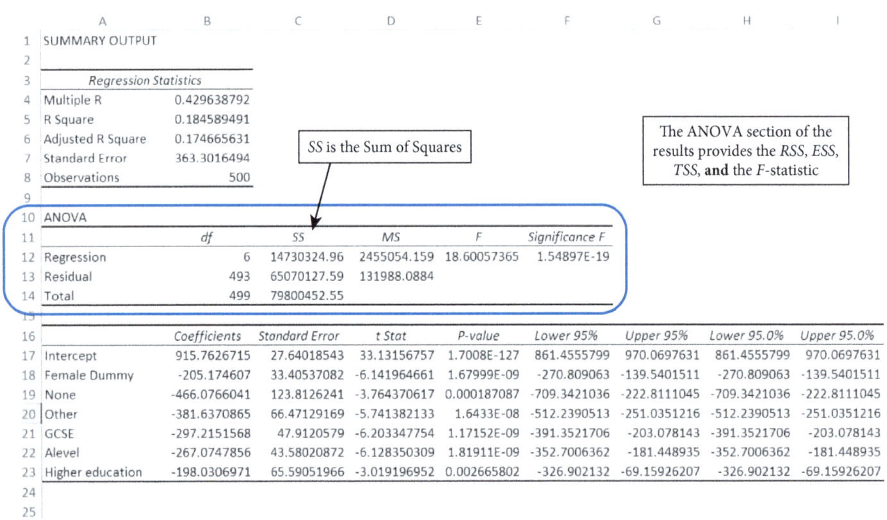
SUMMARY OUTPUT

Regression Statistics	
Multiple R	0.429638792
R Square	0.184589491
Adjusted R Square	0.174665631
Standard Error	363.3016494
Observations	500

ANOVA

	df	SS	MS	F	Significance F
Regression	6	14730324.96	2455054.159	18.60057365	1.54897E-19
Residual	493	65070127.59	131988.0884		
Total	499	79800452.55			

	Coefficients	Standard Error	t Stat	P-value	Lower 95%	Upper 95%	Lower 95.0%	Upper 95.0%
Intercept	915.7626715	27.64018543	33.13156757	1.7008E-127	861.4555799	970.0697631	861.4555799	970.0697631
Female Dummy	-205.174607	33.40537082	-6.141964661	1.67999E-09	-270.809063	-139.5401511	-270.809063	-139.5401511
None	-466.0766041	123.8126241	-3.764370617	0.000187087	-709.3421036	-222.8111045	-709.3421036	-222.8111045
Other	-381.6370865	66.47129169	-5.741382133	1.6433E-08	-512.2390513	-251.0351216	-512.2390513	-251.0351216
GCSE	-297.2151568	47.9120579	-6.203347754	1.17152E-09	-391.3521706	-203.078143	-391.3521706	-203.078143
Alevel	-267.0747856	43.58020872	-6.128350309	1.81911E-09	-352.7006362	-181.448935	-352.7006362	-181.448935
Higher education	-198.0306971	65.59051966	-3.019196952	0.002665802	-326.902132	-69.15926207	-326.902132	-69.15926207

Figure 29.2 Results of OLS from Microsoft Excel.

All of the important information for calculating the F-statistic can be seen in the 'ANOVA' box in Excel. One thing to note, however, is that Excel represents the 'Explained Sum of Squares' as the 'Regression sum of squares'. So, in Figure 29.2, we can see that:

- $ESS = 14{,}730{,}324.96$
- $RSS = 65{,}070{,}127.59$

Similarly, you can see that the degrees of freedom for the ESS is given as 6, and for the RSS is given as 493, as before. Using the formula for the F-statistic, based upon the ESS and the RSS, we can see that:

$$F = \frac{ESS/k}{RSS/(n-k-1)} = \frac{14{,}730{,}324.96/6}{65{,}070{,}127.59/493} = 18.60$$

In fact, if you look back at Figure 29.2, you will see that the F-statistic, 18.60057365, is reported. Whenever you run a regression using most popular software packages, the package will automatically calculate this F-statistic to test the hypothesis that none of the explanatory variables has any impact on the dependent variable.

29.4.2 Constructing a specific F-test

In the previous section, we introduced the idea of testing the hypothesis that none of the explanatory variables has any impact on the dependent variable. However, often, we might be interested in whether a subgroup of variables has any impact on the dependent variable. For instance, thinking back to the example where we ran a regression of weekly earnings against a female dummy, and dummies for the highest level of education, we might be interested in whether the education variables jointly have any impact on the dependent variable.

More generally, suppose that we are interested in the following relationship of Y_i against k explanatory variables, $X_{1i}, X_{2i}, \ldots, X_{ki}$

$$Y_i = \beta_0 + \beta_1 X_{1i} + \beta_2 X_{2i} + \ldots + \beta_q X_{qi} + \beta_{q+1} X_{(q+1)i} + \ldots + \beta_k X_{ki} + u_i$$

and we hypothesize that the first q explanatory variables $(X_{1i}, X_{2i}, \ldots, X_{qi})$ have no impact on the dependent variable. This would be equivalent to testing:

$$H_0 : \beta_1 = \beta_2 = \beta_3 = \ldots = \beta_q = 0$$
$$H_A : \beta_1 \neq 0 \text{ or } \beta_2 \neq 0 \text{ or} \ldots \text{or } \beta_q \neq 0$$

To test this, we could compare two separate regressions:

- In the first, we would impose that the null hypothesis is true (restricted specification).
- In the second, we would allow the alternative hypothesis to be true (unrestricted specification).

In this example, the restricted specification would impose that the coefficients β_1 to β_q would be equal to zero. We could achieve this by omitting $X_{1i}, X_{2i}, \ldots, X_{qi}$ from the regression.[5]

[5] This is equivalent to running a regression of $Y_i = \beta_0 + 0 \times X_{1i} + 0 \times X_{2i} + \ldots + 0 \times X_{qi} + \beta_{q+1} X_{(q+1)i} + \ldots + \beta_k X_{ki} + u_i$.

$$Y_i = \beta_0 + \beta_{q+1}X_{(q+1)i} + \ldots + \beta_k X_{ki} + u_i$$ Restricted specification

$$Y_i = \beta_0 + \beta_1 X_{1i} + \beta_2 X_{2i} + \ldots + \beta_q X_{qi} + \beta_{q+1}X_{(q+1)i} + \ldots + \beta_k X_{ki} + u_i$$ Unrestricted specification

Essentially, when we test this sort of joint hypothesis, using an F-test, we use measures of fit from the restricted and unrestricted models to ask the question about whether the unrestricted model is a better 'fit' for the data than the restricted model. That is, by allowing the βs to be non-zero, have we improved the model's fit through the data?

There are a number of ways that we can measure how well the model fits the data, but a good start would be the R^2. Remember that the R^2 is a measure of how much of the variation in the dependent variable that is explained by the model:

$$R^2 = \frac{ESS}{TSS} = 1 - \frac{RSS}{TSS}$$

For a given set of data, the total sum of squares is fixed (as it is determined by the set of observations of the Y_i). There are therefore three measures that we can use to examine whether the unrestricted model is a 'better fit' for the data than the restricted model:

1. The R^2 itself; as the R^2 increases, the model will show a better fit.
2. The explained sum of squares. As the ESS increases, the R^2 also increases. A larger ESS indicates a better fit for the model.
3. The residual sum of squares. As the RSS decreases, the R^2 increases. A smaller RSS indicates a better fit for the model.

From the restricted specification, we can obtain the

- explained sum of squares (ESS_r),
- the residual sum of squares (RSS_r)
- the R-squared (R_r^2)

Similarly, from the unrestricted specification, we can obtain the

- explained sum of squares (ESS_u),
- the residual sum of squares (RSS_u)
- the R-squared (R_u^2)

Note that, since the observations of Y_i do not change between the unrestricted and the restricted specification, the TSS is the same in both specifications:

$$TSS = \sum_{i=1}^{n}(Y_i - \bar{Y})^2$$

- If the null hypothesis is true, then the difference between the measures of fit will be (approximately) equal to zero:

  $$ESS_u - ESS_r \approx 0,\; R_u^2 - R_r^2 \approx 0,\; RSS_r - RSS_u \cong 0$$

- If the alternative hypothesis is true (and the q additional explanatory variables do have a significant impact on the dependent variable), then:

  $$ESS_u - ESS_r > 0,\; R_u^2 - R_r^2 > 0,\; RSS_r - RSS_u > 0$$

Note: It is not sufficient to merely find that $ESS_u > ESS_r$, or that $R_u^2 > R_r^2$, or that $RSS_u < RSS_r$. Whenever we add additional variables, the RSS mechanically gets smaller, and the ESS gets larger (and hence the R^2 also gets larger. As such, even if the new variables have no impact on the dependent variables, these differences will be numerically greater than zero. We need to formalize a test that allows us to see whether this difference is significant or not (or whether it is just random chance). The test that we can use here is the F-test.

Remember, by definition of the F-distribution, if you have two variables that follow a χ^2 (chi-squared) distribution, with q and k degrees of freedom respectively, then:

$$\frac{\chi_q^2/q}{\chi_k^2/k} \sim F_{q,k}$$

Since we have added an additional q variables in the unrestricted case, we can think of $ESS_u - ESS_r$ having q degrees of freedom in this measure. Similarly, RSS_u will have $n - k - 1$ degrees of freedom. As such, if the null hypothesis is true, it is possible to show that:

$$F = \frac{(ESS_u - ESS_r)/q}{(RSS_u)/(n-k-1)} \sim F_{q,n-k-1}$$

It should be noted that q is the number of restrictions that we are imposing in the restricted specification. In this example, we are imposing that $\beta_1 = 0$ and $\beta_2 = 0$ and . . . and $\beta_q = 0$. That is, we impose q separate restrictions. Similarly, $n - k - 1$ is the number of degrees of freedom in the unrestricted model, as we saw in Section 29.4.1.

By comparing the F-statistic to the critical values from the F-distribution (or calculating the appropriate p-value), we can test our hypothesis. Remember that the F-test is a one-tailed test though, so if you are looking for the appropriate critical value, you are looking for the most extreme cases in the right-hand tail!

Three different formulations of the F-statistic

There are three versions of the F-statistic that you might come across:

$$F = \frac{(ESS_u - ESS_r)/q}{(RSS_u)/(n-k-1)} \quad F = \frac{(RSS_r - RSS_u)/q}{(RSS_u)/(n-k-1)} \quad F = \frac{(R_u^2 - R_r^2)/q}{(1 - R_u^2)/(n-k-1)}$$

It is trivial to prove that each of these is equal to the others,[6] on the basis that $TSS = ESS + RSS$, and that $R^2 = \frac{ESS}{TSS}$.

Most textbooks will only look at the second or third version of this F-statistic formula, but it is useful to remember that the first version is very similar to the ANOVA formula you saw in Chapter 22 (see Figure 29.3).

[6] We prove this in the appendix to this chapter.

Algorithm for carrying out an F-test

Step 1
Specify your null (and alternative) hypothesis. For example, if you are estimating:

$$Y_i = \beta_0 + \beta_1 X_{1i} + \ldots + \beta_q X_{qi} + \beta_{q+1} X_{(q+1)i} + \ldots + \beta_k X_{ki} + u_i$$

H_0: $\beta_1 = \beta_2 = \ldots = \beta_q$
H_A: $\beta_1 \neq 0$ or $\beta_2 \neq 0$ or ... or $\beta_q \neq 0$

Step 2
Estimate the relationship with the null hypothesis imposed. Obtain the R_r^2, the RSS_r, or the ESS_r from this model. This is known as the **restricted specification**. In the example here, the restricted specification is:

$$Y_i = \beta_0 + \beta_{q+1} X_{(q+1)i} + \ldots + \beta_k X_{ki} + u_i$$

Step 3
Estimate the relationship allowing the **alternative hypothesis to be true**. Obtain the R_u^2, the RSS_u, or the ESS_u from this model. This is known as the **restricted specification**. In the example here, the restricted specification is:

$$Y_i = \beta_0 + \beta_1 X_{1i} + \ldots + \beta_q X_{qi} + \beta_{q+1} X_{(q+1)i} + \ldots + \beta_k X_{ki} + u_i$$

Step 4
Using the results from steps 2 and 3, construct the *F*-statistic:

$$F = \frac{(R_u^2 - R_r^2)/q}{(1 - R_u^2)/(n-k-1)} \quad \frac{(ESS_u - ESS_r)/q}{RSS_u/(n-k-1)} \quad \frac{(RSS_r - RSS_u)/q}{RSS_u/(n-k-1)}$$

Step 5
Compare the F-statistic obtained in step 4 with the critical values from the $F_{q,n-k-1}$ distribution.

Alternatively, calculate the **p-value** associated with the F-statistic. Excel will calculate this, for an F-statistic of *x* with *q*, *k* degrees of freedom: = F.DIST.RT(*x*, *q*, *k*)

Notes: *q* is the number of restrictions, whilst $n - k - 1$ is the number of degrees of freedom in the **unrestricted** model. As a good reminder, *q* is the number of equals signs in your null hypothesis, whilst $n - k - 1$ is the number of observations, less the number of coefficients estimated in the unrestricted model.

It is also important to note that you need to use the **same observations** in the **restricted** and **unrestricted** models.

Figure 29.3 Algorithm for carrying out an F-test.

Worked example 29.3: Does highest education level, jointly, have a significant impact on weekly earnings?

In the abstract, the F-test seems quite complicated, so it is often easier to think about this in terms of a concrete example. Let's return to the example of asking whether education level has any impact on wages. We are interested in the impact of the sex and the highest educational attainment of an individual, and so, using data from the UK Labour Force Survey, we estimated the following relationship:

$$Wages_i = \beta_0 + \beta_1 Female_i + \beta_2 HE_i + \beta_3 ALevel_i + \beta_4 GCSE_i + \beta_5 Other_i + \beta_6 None_i + u_i$$

Suppose that we wanted to test the hypothesis that the highest level of educational attainment had no impact on the weekly wages. That hypothesis would be equivalent to setting the coefficients on each of the education levels equal to zero. That is, we would be testing:

$$H_0: \beta_2 = \beta_3 = \beta_4 = \beta_5 = \beta_6 = 0$$
$$H_A: \beta_2 \neq 0 \text{ or } \beta_3 \neq 0 \text{ or } \beta_4 \neq 0 \text{ or } \beta_5 \neq 0 \text{ or } \beta_6 \neq 0$$

In this case, if we wanted to test that $\beta_2 = \beta_3 = \beta_4 = \beta_5 = \beta_6 = 0$, this would be equivalent to testing five separate hypotheses simultaneously—that is, testing that $\beta_2 = 0, \beta_3 = 0, \beta_4 = 0, \beta_5 = 0$ and $\beta_6 = 0$ simultaneously. We cannot test this.

Similarly, as we saw, both in Chapter 28 and earlier in this chapter, Excel automatically produces a F-statistic relating to the test that all of the explanatory variables have no (statistically) significant impact on the dependent variable.

1. **Restricted specification**

When we impose the null hypothesis to be true, we are explicitly placing a restriction on the model; the restriction is that all of the coefficients relating to education are equal to zero. As such, we define the specification where the null hypothesis is imposed to be true as the restricted specification:

$$GrssWk_i = \beta_0 + \beta_1 Female_i + u_i$$

2. **Unrestricted specification**

When we allow the alternative hypothesis to be true, we are not placing any restrictions on the coefficients or the model. We are allowing the $\hat{\beta}$s to take on any value. As we are not placing any restrictions on the coefficients, we define this as the unrestricted specification.

$$GrssWk_i = \beta_0 + \beta_1 Female_i + \beta_2 HE_i + \beta_3 ALevel_i + \beta_4 GCSE_i + \beta_5 Other_i + \beta_6 None_i + u_i$$

So, the restricted (1) and unrestricted (2) specifications are given by:

$$Wages_i = \beta_0 + \beta_1 Female_i + u_i \quad (1)$$

$$Wages_i = \beta_0 + \beta_1 Female_i + \beta_2 HE_i + \beta_3 ALevel_i + \beta_4 GCSE_i + \beta_5 Other_i + \beta_6 None_i + u_i \quad (2)$$

We have presented the OLS regression results from the restricted specification (specification (1)), and the unrestricted specification (specification (2)) in Table 29.12.

Table 29.12 Restricted and unrestricted specifications for carrying out an F-test

	(1)	(2)
	Restricted specification	Unrestricted specification
Female	−170.631***	−205.175***
	(35.643)	(33.405)
Some higher education		−198.031***
		(65.591)
A-levels		−267.215***
		(43.580)
GCSEs grade A*–C		−297.215***
		(47.912)
Other qualifications		−381.637***
		(66.471)
No qualifications		−466.077***

(continued)

Table 29.12 *(continued)*

	(1)	(2)
	Restricted specification	Unrestricted specification
		(123.813)
Constant	756.606***	915.7627***
	(22.711)	(27.640)
Number of observations	500	500
R^2	0.0440	0.1846
Total sum of squares	79,800,452.6	79,800,452.6
Residual sum of squares	76,289,727.8	65,070,127.6
Explained sum of squares	3,510,724.8	14,730,324.0

Note: Dependent variable is gross weekly wage in main job. Estimated standard errors are in parentheses. *** indicates significant at 1% significance level, ** indicates significant at 5% significance level, * indicates significance at 10% significance level.

We wish to see whether the unrestricted specification provides a better fit for the data than the restricted specification.

We will use the F-test to test the joint hypotheses:

$$F = \frac{(ESS_u - ESS_r)/q}{(RSS_u)/(n - k - 1)}$$

q is the number of restrictions. Here we are imposing that five coefficients are jointly equal to zero, so $q = 5$. Similarly, k is equal to the number of explanatory variables in the unrestricted specification. So, the F-statistic is equal to:

$$F = \frac{(14{,}730{,}324.0 - 3{,}510{,}724.8)/5}{65{,}070{,}127.6/(500 - 6 - 1)} = 17.001$$

Note

We have calculated the F-statistic here using the same formulation as we used in Chapter 22. We will get exactly the same value if we use either of the other two formulations of the F-statistic:

$$F = \frac{(R_u^2 - R_r^2)/q}{(1 - R_u^2)/(n - k - 1)} = \frac{(0.1846 - 0.0440)/5}{(1 - 0.1846)/(500 - 6 - 1)} = 17.001$$

$$F = \frac{(RSS_r - RSS_u)/q}{RSS_u/(n - k - 1)} = \frac{(76{,}289{,}727.8 - 65{,}070{,}127.6)/5}{65{,}070{,}127.6/(500 - 6 - 1)} = 17.001$$

The only difference you might observe would come from rounding errors. For instance, the R^2 is often only displayed to 4 significant places, whilst the RSS, ESS, and TSS are often displayed to 10 (or more) significant places. This means that the RSS, ESS, and TSS are more accurately reported than the R^2.

The p-value associated with an F-statistic of 7.51 is equal to:

$$P(F_{5,493} > 17.001) = 1.6 \times 10^{-15}$$

As the p-value is very small,[7] we would reject the null hypothesis at any reasonable level of significance (the p-value is less than 0.01, so we would reject the null at the 1 per cent significance level). This allows us to conclude that education levels have an impact on gross weekly wages.

Alternatively, we could have calculated the critical value at the 5 per cent significance level from an F-distribution, based on 5 and 493 degrees of freedom, which is equal to 2.232. Since the F-statistic is larger than the critical value, we would reject the null. Similarly, the critical value at the 1 per cent and 0.1 per cent significance levels would be 3.05 and 4.18 respectively. Again, we would reject the null at these significance levels.

In this example, we have motivated F-tests in the case of multiple dummy variables. However, you are not restricted to carrying out F-tests relating to dummy variables. In fact, if you wish to carry out a test of joint hypotheses relating to any explanatory variables (whether continuous, discrete, or categorical), you can use an F-test.

Using Excel to find a p-value of an F-statistic

Excel can calculate the p-value relating to an F-statistic using the formula:

$$=\text{F.DIST.RT}\left(\text{F}, \text{q}, \text{df}\right)$$

where q is the number of restrictions imposed, and df is the number of degrees of freedom in the unrestricted specification. This command calculates:

$$P(F_{q,df} > F)$$

29.5 Dummy variables change the intercept

A key question you might be asking is why we would want to use OLS, rather than simply using a t-test for the difference of means? The key reason for using OLS is that you are able to include other control variables.

For example, if you wanted to investigate pay discrimination, you might be concerned that the industry that individuals work in is a determinant of weekly wages, and that the industry worked in is correlated with the sex of the individual. By using OLS, we can control for multiple characteristics of the individual (and the job) to evaluate whether the differences in wages are being driven by the sex of the individual, or by some other, observable characteristic.

Similarly, we can use dummy variables to remove omitted variables bias when we are interested in the impact of a (continuous) variable on a dependent variable. By including dummy variables, what we effectively do is allow for there to be different intercepts for different groups. To illustrate this, we will revisit a relationship we saw in Chapter 25, and we

[7] This is roughly equivalent to gaining 49 heads in a row from a fair coin.

will investigate whether there is a relationship between age leaving full-time education and the sex of the individual.

In Chapter 25, we investigated the relationship between gross weekly wage ($Wage_i$) and age leaving education ($Educ_i$), using 500 randomly sampled male full-time workers aged 25–65 from the UK Labour Force Survey.

To illustrate how we can combine dummy variables and numerical variables, we have taken the original 500 full-time male workers, and randomly sampled an additional 500 female full-time workers, again aged 25–65. We will repeat the analysis we saw in Chapter 25, but this time we will also include a variable to control for the sex of the individual. As before, because the data only contains individuals whose sex is either male or female, we will need to omit one of the categories to construct a comparison group. This time, let's omit the male group and include a dummy variable that takes the value 1 if the individual is female, and 0 otherwise. As such, we will estimate:

$$Wages_i = \beta_0 + \beta_1 Educ_i + \beta_2 Female_i + u_i$$

Recall that $Educ_i$ is the age at which individual i completed their education, whilst $Wages_i$ is the gross weekly wages in their main job.

Since there are two values that $Female_i$ can take, let's substitute in $Female_i = 0$ and $Female_i = 1$ to see what happens to the relationship that we are estimating:

When the worker is female, $Female_i = 1$. This means that the estimated relationship is:	When the worker is not female, $Female_i = 0$. This means that the estimated relationship is:
$Wages_i = \beta_0 + \beta_1 \times Educ_i + \beta_2 \times 1 + u_i$ $= \beta_0 + \beta_2 + \beta_1 Educ_i + u_i$	$Wages_i = \beta_0 + \beta_1 Educ_i + \beta_2 \times 0 + u_i$ $= \beta_0 + \beta_1 Educ_i + u_i$

In this example, the marginal effect of leaving education one year later (β_1) is the same for males and females. What differs is the intercept. Having substituted in the values for $Female_i$, we can think of the intercept as any coefficient that is not multiplied by a variable.

- When $Female_i = 0$, the intercept is equal to β_0.
- When $Female_i = 1$, the intercept is equal to $\beta_0 + \beta_2$.

To illustrate this, let's return to our empirical example. Using the 1,000 observations from the UK Labour Force Survey, we will estimate the following relationship:

$$Wages_i = \beta_0 + \beta_1 Educ_i + \beta_2 Female_i + u_i$$

The results are illustrated in Table 29.13. The estimated marginal effect of leaving full-time education one year later is $\hat{\beta}_1 = 22.244$, which indicates that leaving education one year later is associated with an additional £22.244 per week in a main job. However, it is not this return that we are interested in here; we are really interested in what the estimated relationship looks like.

By including the $Female_i$ dummy, we have allowed for the possibility that males and females have a different relationship. The only thing that is being affected here is the intercept,

Table 29.13 Results from a regression of gross weekly wages against age leaving full-time education, and a dummy variable for female

	(6)
Age when completed education	22.244***
	(3.232)
Female	−158.841***
	(22.567)
Constant	325.987***
	(63.295)
Number of observations	1,000
R^2	0.0855

Note: Dependent variable is gross weekly wage in main job. Estimated standard errors are in parentheses. *** indicates significant at 1% significance level, ** indicates significant at 5% significance level, * indicates significance at 10% significance level.

and we have two estimated intercepts. Remember, the data contains 500 individuals who are male and 500 individuals who are female:

- Estimated intercept for males = $\hat{\beta}_0 = 325.987$
- Estimated intercept for females = $\hat{\beta}_0 + \hat{\beta}_2 = 325.987 - 158.841 = 167.146$

However, this is easier to understand visually. Figure 29.4 shows a scatter plot of the data for male and female workers, and the fitted lines we estimate for the two groups.

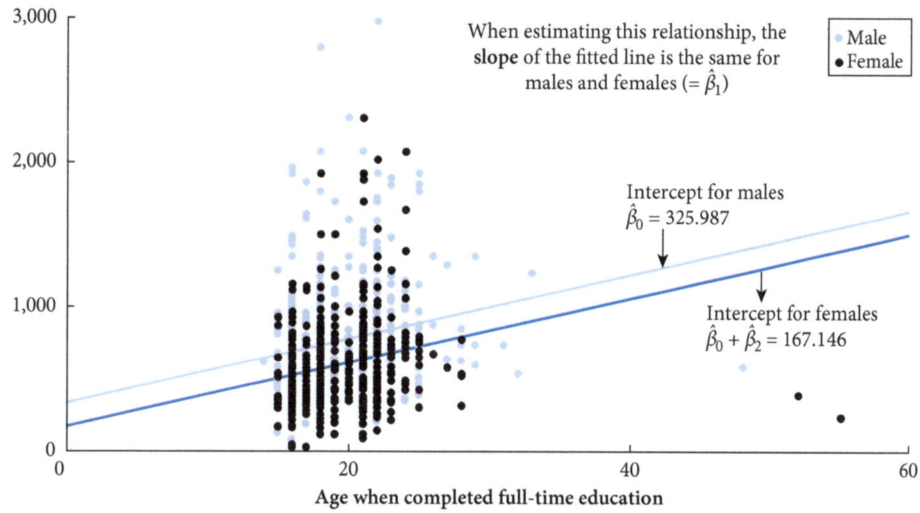

Figure 29.4 Estimated relationship between gross weekly wage and age when completing full-time education, allowing the intercept to be different for males and females.

What we see is that, when estimating this relationship, the fitted lines remain parallel for both males and females. This is because we only have a single coefficient on $Educ_i$, which is giving us a return to education that is the same for males and females.

What does change is the intercept for males and females. By introducing the female dummy variable, we are, in essence, allowing the intercept to change. This difference in intercept can be interpreted as the difference in the average wages for males and females, having conditioned for the age at which they left full-time education. If $\hat{\beta}_2$ is statistically significant, we are effectively saying that the intercept is statistically significantly different for male and female workers.

Worked example 29.4: Testing whether the intercept is equal for male and female workers

We can test whether the intercept is equal for male and female workers using our standard t-test. If the intercept is the same for males and females, then $\beta_0 = \beta_0 + \beta_2$, which will only occur if $\beta_2 = 0$. As such, if we wish to test that males and females have the same intercept, this is equivalent to testing whether the coefficient on the $Female_i$ dummy variable is equal to zero:

$$H_0: \beta_2 = 0$$
$$H_A: \beta_2 \neq 0$$

Using the data from our results, we have $\hat{\beta}_2 = -158.841$ and $\widehat{s.e.}(\hat{\beta}_1) = 22.567$. As such, our t-statistic is equal to:

$$t = \frac{\hat{\beta}_2 - E(\hat{\beta}_2 \mid \beta_2 = 0)}{\widehat{s.e.}(\hat{\beta}_2)} = \frac{-158.841 - 0}{22.567} = -7.04$$

We have 1,000 observations, but have estimated three coefficients. As such, we have 997 degrees of freedom. We could use the t-statistic here to calculate the p-value:

$$P(|t_{997}| > 7.04) = 3.57 \times 10^{-12}$$

As the p-value[8] is much smaller than any reasonable level of significance, we can safely reject the null, indicating that the intercept for males and females is different.

Note that, in the results, we have indicated significance at the 1 per cent significance level with ***. Software packages will often implicitly calculate the t-statistics for you, and so we do not always report the calculations of the t-statistics. However, it is often important to be aware of the process, and if you are sitting an econometrics exam, it is often worth demonstrating that you know how to carry out the appropriate t-tests!

29.5.1 Important note—Dummy variables change the intercept, but not the slope of the relationship

One thing that is important to note is that by introducing dummy variables, all we are doing is allowing for the intercept to change between our groups. In the example, we have allowed for a different intercept for males and females in our regression.

[8] For context, this is the same probability as gaining 38 heads in a row when we flip a fair coin.

Dummy variables on their own do not allow the slope of the relationship to vary across groups. We could include as many dummy variables, representing as many groups, as we liked. This would allow the intercept to change for each group, but each group would still have the same slope. In some circumstances, we may believe that explanatory variables have different marginal impacts on different groups.

As an example, suppose that you are interested in the effect of the number of police on the street on crime. There may be different marginal effects in different countries (or even in different cities), depending on the overall respect (or fear) of the police. Simply including dummy variables would not allow us to estimate different marginal effects across countries but merely different intercepts.

If you want to examine whether different groups have different slopes, there are a number of routes you could consider. One route, which we will discuss in the next section, is to use interaction terms. By introducing interaction terms, we can allow the slope of the estimated relationship to differ across groups.

29.5.2 Why do we need to worry about the intercept?

So far, we have not really asked the question why we need to allow the intercept to change across different groups, but this is an important question. The key thing is that if we impose that the intercept is the same across groups, then we may end up with omitted variables bias. This would occur whenever the allocation to groups is correlated with both the treatment and the dependent variable.

Example of allocation to groups causing omitted variables bias

Suppose that you are interested in the impact of the amount of work that students do on their performance in mathematics examinations at age 16. To investigate this, you go into a school, and observe three separate maths classes.

The school follows strict a strict streaming policy, so the students who performed best at age 13 are in group 1, the students with middling performance at age 13 in group 2, whilst the lowest performing are in group 3.

Alongside this, the teachers of the three groups want all of the students to perform their absolute best, so the teacher of group 2 encourages the students to engage in more work than those in group 1. Similarly, the teacher of group 3 knows this and encourages group 3 to do even more work.

Without any intervention, we would expect (based on prior attainment) students in group 1 to outperform the students in group 2, who would outperform the students in group 3.

However, as we will see, because the amount of work that students are doing is correlated with the group they are in, if we do not control for the group the students are taught in, we will gain biased estimates of the effect of doing more work on student outcomes. In fact, we would end up with a negative bias.

To illustrate this, I have simulated data for a dependent variable, Y, and an explanatory variable, X. The data has been generated so that there are three distinct groups, each of which has a different intercept. However, the data is generated so that in each group, the marginal effect of a change in X on Y is equal to 1. That is, for an increase of X by 1, on average Y increases by 1.

The data is generated as follows for each group:

Group number	Data generating process	Average of X within the group
1	$Y_i = 9 + 1 \times X_i + u_i$	$E(X \mid Group = 1) = 4$
2	$Y_i = 3.5 + 1 \times X_i + u_i$	$E(X \mid Group = 2) = 6$
3	$Y_i = -2 + 1 \times X_i + u_i$	$E(X \mid Group = 3) = 8$

So you can see that the data is generated such that the true intercept for group 1 is equal to 9, for group 2 is equal to 3.5, whilst for group 3, it is equal to −2. Further, the value of X is correlated with the group: the average of the observations of X in group 1 is equal to 4, in group 2, the average of X is 6, whilst in group 3, it is 8.

The simulated data, split by group, are illustrated in Figure 29.5.

There are three distinct groups within this data, which we've imaginatively called group 1, group 2, and group 3, but this could equally be data from three separate countries (e.g. UK, France, and Germany).

Group membership appears to have a determining factor on the dependent variable (Y), as on average Y appears highest for individuals in group 1, then group 2, and finally group 3.

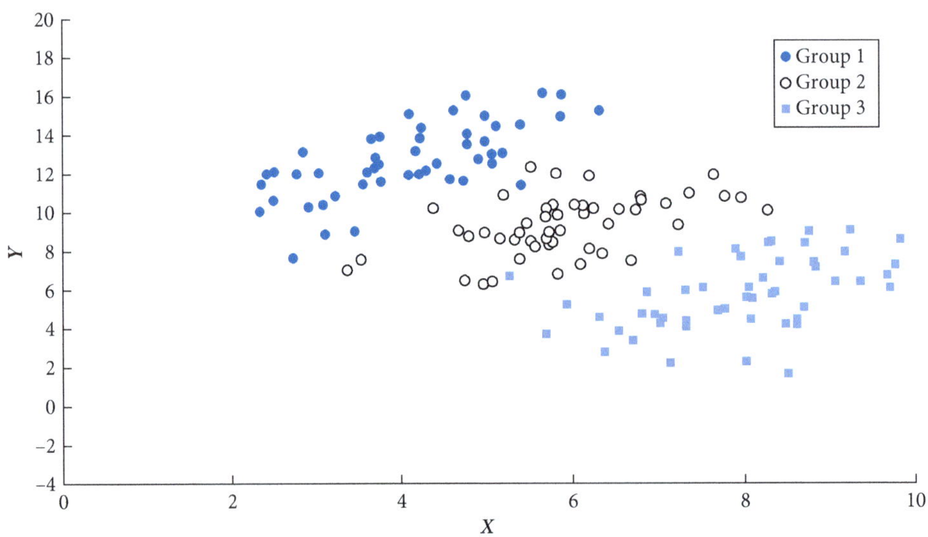

Figure 29.5 Scatter plot of the simulated data across three groups.

Suppose that we were to ignore the fact that these data are split into three distinct groups, and we simply estimated a single straight line through the data. Then what would the relationship look like? That is, if we estimated:

$$Y_i = \beta_0 + \beta_1 X_i + u_i$$

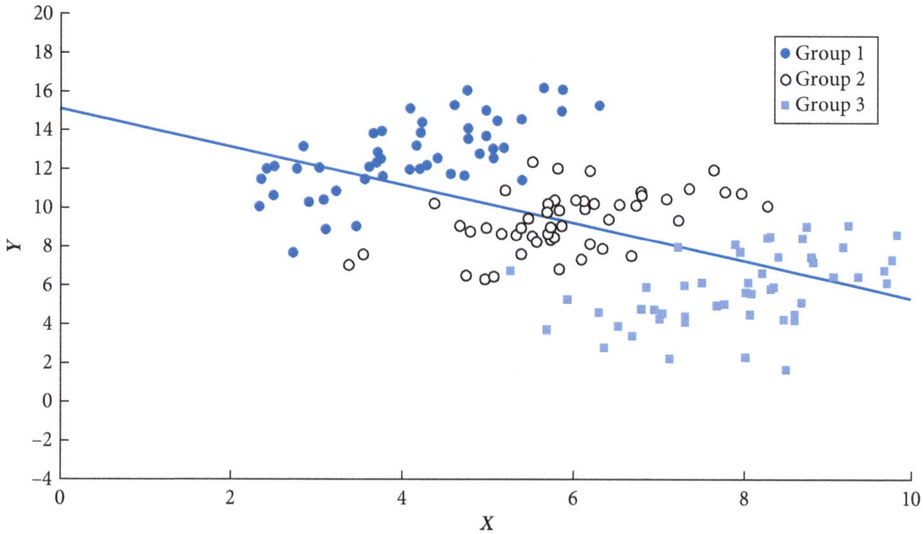

Figure 29.6 Result of estimating OLS with a single intercept across the three groups.

The estimated line we plot through the data is illustrated in Figure 29.6. Worryingly, even though we know that the true marginal effect of X on Y is $\beta_1 = 1$, the estimated relationship is downward sloping. In fact, based on the data that we observe here, we obtain a (statistically significant) estimate of $\hat{\beta}_1 = -0.98$.

Because group membership is correlated with the observed values of X (and because group membership appears to be (correlated with) a determinant of Y, by omitting group membership, we experience negative bias. In fact, the bias is so extreme here that, where we know that the true DGP of Y is such that a one-unit increase in X leads to a one-unit increase in Y, we have observed an estimate of the marginal effect being such that a one unit increase in X is associated with a 0.98 unit decrease in Y.

Now let's see what happens when we introduce a control for each group, to allow the intercept to be different within the three groups. That is, we will estimate:

$$Y_i = \beta_0 + \beta_1 X_i + \beta_2 Group1_i + \beta_3 Group2_i + u_i$$

where *Group1* is a dummy that takes the value 1 if individual i is in group 1 and 0 otherwise, whilst *Group2* is a dummy that takes the value 1 if individual i is in group 2.

The estimated relationship is illustrated in Figure 29.7. By allowing the intercepts to be different across the three groups, we remove the bias. In fact, in this case, the estimated marginal effect of X on Y is equal to $\hat{\beta}_1 = 0.932$ (with a 95 per cent confidence interval between 0.701 and 1.163). By including the controls for the group, we have allowed the intercept to

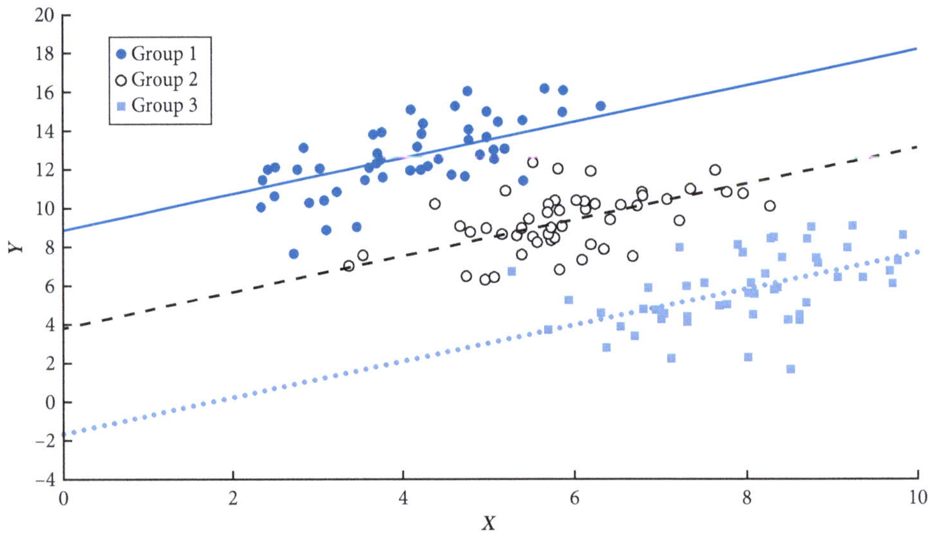

Figure 29.7 Simulation, allowing the intercepts to be different across groups.

change across the three groups, and we have removed the bias. By including the dummy variables, in effect, we are allowing the underlying values of Y to vary across the groups, and this avoids the omitted variables bias that occurs by requiring all of the relationships to have the same intercept.

A brief introduction to fixed effects

Often, researchers will discuss the use of fixed effects in regressions. In essence this means that they are including a dummy variable for different groups, where they observe those groups multiple times in the data.

In the example, we have effectively included fixed effects for the sex of the individuals. By including the dummy variables, without knowing anything more about the characteristics of males and females, the dummy variable acts to control for anything that is fixed within the group.

This is a very useful strategy if you are repeating groups, or individuals, repeatedly within a data set, but there are fixed characteristics that are unobservable about the individual.

For example, if you wanted to know the impact of hours of studying on exam marks, it is highly unlikely that hours of study is going to be exogenous. Instead, the hours of study is likely to be correlated with characteristics of the individual (such as ability, or determination) that cannot be easily measured. As such, if we cannot control for them, we are likely to have omitted variables bias in our regressions.

However, if you were to observe the students' hours of study across multiple modules, and their corresponding marks in those modules, you could include fixed effects for each of the students in your regression. In essence, this would be equivalent to including a dummy variable to allow for the intercept to be different for all of the students in your data.

This feels like a bit of a 'cheat'. You haven't been able to observe the fixed characteristics, but the impact of the fixed effect (or dummy variable) is to control for anything that is fixed within the individual, and the estimated effect is due to variation within group. In effect, by including fixed effects, we are able to remove omitted variables bias, not by observing the characteristics of the individual (or group), but instead by including a dummy variable that automatically controls for anything fixed within the group.

Fixed effects are regularly used whenever there are groups of observations from particular places, or individuals, where there are unobservable similarities within the group, which have an impact on the dependent variable. This could be similar levels of income, or similar levels of ability, or similar inputs (such as having the same teacher for a subject).

Fixed effects are used in a wide range of settings. Wherever you see groups of observations with some fixed underlying characteristics, you can control for these with fixed effects.

Fundamentally, the key element of fixed effects relationships is that the researcher is allowing for each individual, or each group, to have a separate intercept.

This is precisely what we did in our previous example, illustrated in Figure 29.8. By including the dummy variables, we allowed for the intercept to change across the groups, because each group had an underlying (set of) characteristics that impacted on the value of Y.

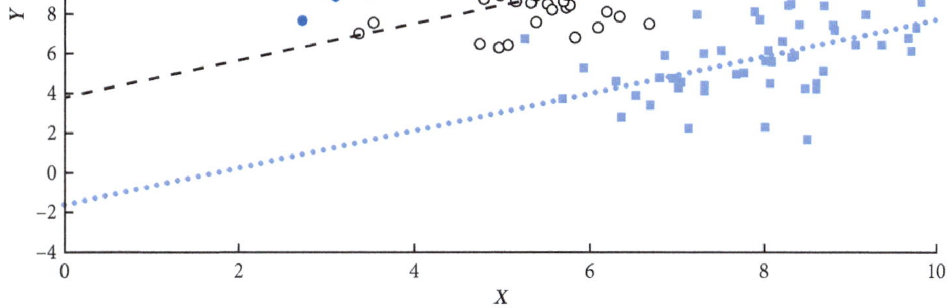

Figure 29.8 Simulation, allowing the intercepts to be different across groups.

29.6 Interaction terms

In the previous section, we introduced dummy variables as a way of changing the intercept across groups (illustrated in Figure 29.9). However, the marginal effect of a change in the explanatory variable (in this case, years of completed education) is treated as being equal across the two groups.

Including a dummy variable simply allows the intercepts to differ across groups, but we have effectively imposed that the slope, or the marginal effect of a change in age leaving school on weekly earnings, is the same for both male and female workers:

$$Wages_i = \beta_0 + \beta_1 Educ_i + \beta_2 Female_i + u_i$$

In reality, having the same slope across different groups may be inappropriate. It may be that different groups gain more from education than others. That is, there may be different marginal effects between groups. We can analyse these sorts of differing marginal effects using interaction terms. An interaction term is simply included to allow us to investigate the possibility that the slope changes between groups, and we estimate these by multiplying together the explanatory variables. To allow for the slopes to differ across groups, we would need to multiply together the explanatory variable we are interested in (in this example, years of completed education) and the dummy variable(s) we are interest in. In this simple example, we only have two groups (males and females), but you can use this methodology to estimate different slopes (and intercepts) across multiple groups.

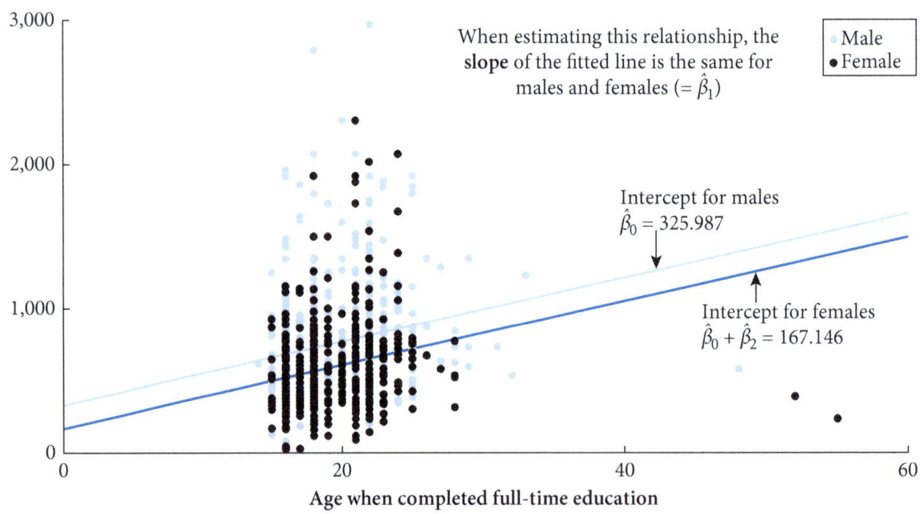

Figure 29.9 Estimated relationship between gross weekly wage and age when completing full-time education, allowing the intercept to be different for males and females.

To allow for the slope to differ across groups, we need to begin by creating a new variable which is known as the interaction term, between the $Female_i$ variable and the age completing full-time education, $Educ_i$. Interaction terms simply involve multiplying the two variables together:

$$\text{Interaction term} = Female_i \times Educ_i$$

Since the female dummy only takes the values 1 or 0, we can see in Table 29.14 that when the individual is female, the interaction term simply takes on the value of the age when completing education. Similarly, when the individual is not female, since the female dummy is equal to zero, when we multiply the completed years of education by the female dummy, we will gain an observation of 0.

Table 29.14 Example of data with an interaction term

$Female_i$	$Educ_i$	$Female_i \times Educ_i$ **(Interaction term)**
1	18	18
0	21	0
0	19	0
1	16	16
1	17	17

We can include this new interaction term variable in our OLS regression in the normal way. Normally, when you include an interaction term, it is important to include both the original variables (in this example, the female dummy and the age when completing full-time education) and the interaction terms:

$$Wages_i = \beta_0 + \beta_1 Educ_i + \beta_2 Female_i + \beta_3 Female_i \times Educ_i + u_i \qquad (1)$$

To interpret what this relationship will look like, let's begin by considering males and females separately. For males, the female dummy variable, $Female_i = 0$. We can substitute this into the relationship that we are estimating to give us:

$$Wages_i = \beta_0 + \beta_1 Educ_i + \beta_2 \times 0 + \beta_3 \times 0 \times Educ_i + u_i$$
$$\Rightarrow Wages_i = \beta_0 + \beta_1 Educ_i + u_i$$

So, for males, the intercept is equal to β_0, whilst the slope coefficient is equal to β_1. Similarly, for females, the female dummy variable, $Female_i = 1$. As such, we can substitute this into the relationship we are estimating to give us:

$$Wages_i = \beta_0 + \beta_1 Educ_i + \beta_2 \times 1 + \beta_3 \times 1 \times Educ_i + u_i$$
$$\Rightarrow Wages_i = \beta_0 + \beta_1 Educ_i + \beta_2 + \beta_3 Educ_i + u_i$$

In this relationship, we can group terms: we have two terms which are not multiplied by a variable (β_0, β_2), which correspond to the intercept of the model, whilst we have two coefficients that are multiplied by the variable $Educ_i$:

$$\Rightarrow Wages_i = (\beta_0 + \beta_2) + (\beta_1 + \beta_3) \times Educ_i + u_i$$

$$Wages_i = \beta_0 + \beta_1 Educ_i + \beta_2 Female_i + \beta_3 Female_i \times Educ_i + u_i$$

Including the dummy variable $Female_i$ allows the **intercept** to change for **males** and **females**.

β_2 can be interpreted as the **difference** in the intercept for male and female workers

Including the interaction term $Female_i \times Educ_i$ allows the **marginal effect** of years of education on gross weekly wages to differ between **males** and **females**

β_3 can be interpreted as the **difference** in the marginal effect for male and female workers

Figure 29.10 Explaining the meaning of the interaction terms.

That is, if we estimate this relationship, the intercept for female workers will be $\beta_0 + \beta_2$, whilst the slope (i.e. the marginal impact of $Educ_i$) will be $\beta_1 + \beta_3$.

In effect, we are using male workers as a control group, and the coefficient on the dummy variable tells you the difference in the intercept for female workers (compared with male workers), whilst the coefficient on the intercept term tells you the difference in the slope for female workers compared to male workers. Figure 29.10 explains the meaning of interaction terms.

Of course, the only reason why the male group is seen as the control group is because this is the omitted category.[9] We could have omitted the female dummy, and used a dummy that takes the value 1 if the individual is male; then the comparison group would be female workers.

In estimating this relationship, we have introduced a dummy variable and an interaction term:

- The impact of the dummy variable is to allow the intercept to change across groups.
- The impact of the interaction term allows the slope to vary across groups.

Table 29.15 shows the numerical results, whilst Figure 29.11 illustrates the fitted relationship between gross weekly wages and age when completing full-time education for full-time workers. The light blue line indicates the estimated relationship for male workers, whilst the dark blue line indicates the estimated relationship for female workers.

We can see that the intercept for male workers is less than the estimated intercept for female workers. This is illustrated in Table 29.15: as the coefficient on the female dummy is positive, the impact of a positive coefficient on a dummy variable is to shift the intercept upwards.

Similarly, the slope for female workers is less steep than for male workers. This is because the coefficient on the interaction term is negative. The interpretation of this coefficient is how much steeper the relationship is for female workers than male workers. Since $\hat{\beta}_3$ is negative, this means that the line is less steep for female workers than male workers.

The estimated constant, $\hat{\beta}_0 = 167.988$, provides us with an estimate of the intercept for male workers, whilst the coefficient on the $Female_i$ dummy variable ($\hat{\beta}_2 = 156.4364$) provides us with an estimate of the difference between the intercept for male and female workers. This provides us with an estimate of the intercept for female workers as $\hat{\beta}_0 + \hat{\beta}_2 = 167.9879 + 156.4364 = 324.424\,(3dp)$.

[9] This is because the data only contains individuals who are either male or female.

Table 29.15 Results from regression with interaction term

	(1)
Age completing full-time education	30.5815***
	(4.580)
Female	156.4364
	(125.088)
Interaction term (*Female*$_i$ × *Educ*$_i$)	−16.5190**
	(6.447)
Constant	167.9879
	(88.241)
Number of observations	1,000
R^2	0.0915

Note: Dependent variable is gross weekly wage in main job. Estimated standard errors are in parentheses. *** indicates significant at 1% significance level, ** indicates significant at 5% significance level, * indicates significance at 10% significance level.

Figure 29.11 Estimated relationship between wages and age when completing full-time education for male and female workers.

Similarly, the coefficient on age leaving full-time education ($\hat{\beta}_1 = 30.5815$) provides us an estimate of the marginal effect of education on gross weekly wages for males, indicating that one additional year of education is associated with an additional £30.58 per week for male workers.

For female workers, to calculate the estimated marginal effect, we need to add together the estimated coefficient on age completing full-time education, and the estimated coefficient on the interaction term: $\hat{\beta}_1 + \hat{\beta}_3 = 30.5815 - 16.5190 = 14.063\,(3dp)$. This indicates that our regression results suggest that an additional year of education is associated with an increase in gross weekly earnings of £14.06 for females.

All of this being said, we have carried out a very naïve analysis here. We haven't tested whether the coefficients are statistically significant. Remember that we have estimated the following relationship:

$$Wages_i = \beta_0 + \beta_1 Educ_i + \beta_2 Female_i + \beta_3 Female_i \times Educ_i + u_i \qquad (1)$$

1. Are the intercepts the same for males and females?

If the intercepts are the same, this is equivalent to the coefficient on $Female_i$ being equal to zero. We can test this:

$$H_0 : \beta_2 = 0$$
$$H_A : \beta_2 \neq 0$$

We would construct the t-statistic in the usual way:

$$t = \frac{\hat{\beta}_2 - E(\hat{\beta}_2 \mid \beta_2 = 0)}{\widehat{s.e.}(\hat{\beta}_2)} = \frac{156.436 - 0}{125.088}$$
$$= 1.25$$

We have 1,000 observations, but we have estimated four coefficients. As such, we have 996 degrees of freedom.

The critical value at the 5% significance level, with 396 degrees of freedom, is approximately 1.96. As the magnitude of the t-statistic is smaller than the critical value, we would fail to reject the null hypothesis.

Alternatively, we could calculate the p-value:

$$P(|t_{996}| \geq 1.25) = 0.2116$$

That is, if the null hypothesis is true, the probability of achieving a t-statistic with magnitude equal to or greater than 1.25 is 0.2116.

It is possible that we are making a **type 2 error** here, but we have insufficient evidence to conclude that the intercepts are not the same for males and females.

2. Are the slopes equal for males and females?

If the slopes are the same, this is equivalent to the coefficient on the interaction term being equal to zero. We can test this:

$$H_0 : \beta_3 = 0$$
$$H_A : \beta_3 \neq 0$$

We would construct the t-statistic in the usual way:

$$t = \frac{\hat{\beta}_3 - E(\hat{\beta}_3 \mid \beta_3 = 0)}{\widehat{s.e.}(\hat{\beta}_1)} = \frac{-16.519 - 0}{6.447}$$
$$= -2.56$$

We have 1,000 observations, but we have estimated four coefficients. As such, we have 996 degrees of freedom.

The critical value at the 5% significance level, with 396 degrees of freedom, is approximately. As the magnitude of the t-statistic is larger than the critical value, we reject the null hypothesis.

Alternatively, we could calculate the p-value:

$$P(|t_{396}| \geq 2.56) = 0.011$$

That is, if the null hypothesis is true, the probability of achieving a t-statistic with magnitude equal to or greater than 2.56 is 0.011.

Since this is smaller than 0.05 (5%), we would reject the null hypothesis at the 5% significance level (but not the 1% significance level). This suggests that the returns to an additional year in full-time education are higher for males than females. Of course, we may be making a **type 1 error**.

We have tested two hypotheses. That is:

1. That the intercept is the same for both males and females.
2. That the slope is the same for both males and females.

We rejected the second hypothesis at the 5 per cent significance level, but not the first hypothesis. This suggests that the intercept may be the same for males and females, but the slope (i.e. the return to spending an additional year in full-time education) may be different.

Important note

The t-statistics we have calculated assume that the estimates are unbiased. It is unlikely that these are purely unbiased and causal results, because:

1. There may be omitted variables bias, or some other correlation with the error term.
2. There may be selection, or measurement errors, which also cause bias.

If the OLS estimator is biased, then the t-statistics only tell us about the significance of the (conditional) correlation, but not about any causal relationship between gross weekly wages and education.

This may seem strange, not least as the magnitude of the coefficient $\hat{\beta}_2 = 156.436$ is very large (and is comparable in magnitude to the average difference between male and female earnings that we saw earlier in this chapter).

One of the reasons that we failed to reject the first hypothesis is that when we introduced the interaction term, our estimates became much less precise than when just including a dummy variable. To illustrate this, let's compare the two sets of results:

$$Wages_i = \beta_0 + \beta_1 Educ_i + \beta_2 Female_i + \beta_3 Female_i \times Educ_i + u_i \quad (1)$$
$$Wages_i = \beta_0 + \beta_1 Educ_i + \beta_2 Female_i + u_i \quad (2)$$

The results from these specifications are shown in Table 29.16. As you can see, specification (1) includes the interaction term, whilst specification (2) provides a comparison, by omitting the interaction term.

The key thing to note is that the standard errors of our estimates are much larger in specification (1) than specification (2). This is particularly noticeable for the coefficient on $Female_i$, where the standard error changes from 22.567 in specification (2) to 125.088 in specification (1). Unfortunately, this is a potential consequence of introducing interaction terms; by construction, they are likely to have a non-trivial correlation with another included explanatory variable, leading to potential imperfect multicollinearity. This highlights the importance of collecting sufficient data to test whether the slopes are equivalent across groups.

Table 29.16 Comparing regressions when we include, and omit, the interaction term

	(1)	(2)
Age completing full-time education	30.5815***	22.244***
	(4.580)	(3.232)
Female	156.4364	−158.841***
	(125.088)	(22.567)
Interaction term ($Female_i \times Educ_i$)	−16.5190**	
	(6.447)	
Constant	167.9879*	325.987***
	(88.241)	(63.295)
Number of observations	1,000	1,000
R^2	0.0915	0.0855

Note: Dependent variable is gross weekly wage in main job. Estimated standard errors are in parentheses. *** indicates significant at 1% significance level, ** indicates significant at 5% significance level, * indicates significance at 10% significance level.

Health warning

In circumstances like the one in Section 29.6, where we observe that the intercepts are not statistically significantly different from each other, it might be tempting to think that it is better to re-estimate the relationship, omitting the $Female_i$ dummy (but keeping the interaction term).

However, what this would do is to impose that the intercept for the male and female lines would be the same. As we saw earlier in this chapter, if the intercept is different for the two groups, by imposing that the intercept is the same, we could end up with bias in our estimates.

In this case, the big issue appears to be imperfect multicollinearity, so to gain more precise estimates, we would need to collect more data in order to gain better indications of the true relationship.

29.6.1 Testing whether the relationship is the same across two (or more) groups

What we might be interested in testing is not whether the slope or the intercept, separately, is different for males and females, but whether the relationship is, more generally, different for males and females. That is, we might want to test whether the same fitted line is appropriate for males and females, or whether we are better fitting separate lines for males and females.

If the relationship is the same, then there will be a single intercept and a single slope that applies to both males and females, but if the relationship is different, it might be that the intercept is different, or the slope is different, or that both the slope and intercept are different.

In specification (1) we estimated:

$$Wages_i = \beta_0 + \beta_1 Educ_i + \beta_2 Female_i + \beta_3 Female_i \times Educ_i + u_i \quad (1)$$

If there is a single relationship for both males and females (say of the form):

$$Wages_i = \beta_0 + \beta_1 Educ_i + u_i \quad (3)$$

then this is equivalent to β_2 and β_3 both being equal to zero. Therefore, if we want to test whether there is a single relationship that fits for both males and females, this is equivalent to testing whether $\beta_2 = \beta_3 = 0$. As such, we can write down a formal null and alternative hypothesis:

$$H_0 : \beta_2 = \beta_3 = 0$$
$$H_A : \beta_2 \neq 0 \text{ or } \beta_3 \neq 0 \text{ (or both)}$$

Because we have two hypotheses that we are trying to jointly test, we cannot test these with a t-test. Instead, we can appeal to an F-test to test this. Remember, in an F-test, we compare a restricted specification where we impose the null hypothesis to be true, and an unrestricted specification where we allow the alternative hypothesis to be true. In this case, we can write down our restricted and unrestricted specifications:

$$Wages_i = \beta_0 + \beta_1 Educ_i + \beta_2 Female_i + \beta_3 Female_i \times Educ_i + u_i \quad \text{Unrestricted specification}$$

$$Wages_i = \beta_0 + \beta_1 Educ_i + u_i \quad \text{Restricted specification}$$

To test our null hypothesis, we will need to estimate the restricted and unrestricted specifications, and compare the measures of fit (i.e. the R^2 or the RSS) formally, using the F-test formula:

$$F = \frac{(R_u^2 - R_r^2)/q}{(1 - R_u^2)/(n - k - 1)} = \frac{(RSS_r - RSS_u)/q}{RSS_u/(n - k - 1)} = \frac{(ESS_u - ESS_r)/q}{(RSS_u)/(n - k - 1)}$$

The results from estimating the restricted and unrestricted specifications are shown in Table 29.17.

Remember that q is the number of restrictions that we impose. A shortcut to find this is to count the number of equals signs in the null hypothesis. In this case, we are restricting that $\beta_2 = 0$ and $\beta_3 = 0$, so that's equivalent to $q = 2$ restrictions.

Similarly, $n - k - 1$ is the number of degrees of freedom in the unrestricted specification. We have 1,000 observations, but we have estimated four coefficients. This means that we have 1,000 – 4 = 996 degrees of freedom. (Alternatively, we have $k = 3$ explanatory variables, and a constant, which accounts for the –1 element, meaning that we have $n - k - 1 = 1{,}000 - 3 - 1 = 996$ degrees of freedom in the unrestricted specification.)

Table 29.17 Restricted and unrestricted specifications

	Restricted specification	Unrestricted specification
Age completing full-time education	21.351***	30.5815***
	(3.308)	(4.580)
Female		156.4364
		(125.088)
Interaction term ($Female_i \times Educ_i$)		−16.5190**
		(6.447)
Constant	263.610***	167.9879*
	(64.178)	(88.241)
Number of observations	1,000	1,000
R^2	0.0401	0.0915
Residual sum of squares	133,037,978	125,910,163
Explained sum of squares	5,554,876.28	12,682,691.6

Note: Dependent variable is gross weekly wage in main job. Estimated standard errors are in parentheses. *** indicates significant at 1% significance level, ** indicates significant at 5% significance level, * indicates significance at 10% significance level.

Substituting the numbers into the F-statistic, gives us:

$$F = \frac{(R_u^2 - R_r^2)/q}{(1 - R_u^2)/(n - k - 1)} = \frac{(0.0915 - 0.0401)/2}{(1 - 0.0915)/996} = 28.175$$

The p-value associated with an F-statistic of 28.175 from the F-distribution, constructed based on 2 and 996 degrees of freedom, is equal to:

$$P(F_{2,996} > 28.175) = 1.25 \times 10^{-12}$$

That is, the probability of randomly observing an F-statistic to the right of 28.175 (if the null hypothesis is true) is equal to[10] 0.00000000000125. Since this is smaller than 5 per cent (0.05) we would reject the null hypothesis at the 5 per cent significance level. This suggests that there is a difference in the relationship between male and female workers.

[10] This probability is equivalent to the probability of flipping a fair coin approximately 40 times, and achieving a head every time.

Summary

In this chapter, we have introduced dummy variables as a way of controlling for categorical variables, and doing so allowing intercepts and slopes to vary across groups.

We have seen four key elements in this chapter:

1. Whenever we have a set of categories, or characteristics, that we wish to control for, if we have k different groups, we would need to include a maximum of $k - 1$ dummy variables to control for the differences. The omitted dummy variable would provide us with our comparison group.
2. Dummy variables act to change the intercept for each different group. If we have other (continuous) explanatory variables in the model, dummy variables on their own do not allow you to estimate different slopes for different groups.
3. Interaction terms are created by multiplying together dummy variables with (continuous) explanatory variables. Interaction terms allow you to estimate different slopes for different groups.
4. We can use F-tests to test multiple hypotheses relating to OLS estimates. These can be useful when testing if a group of explanatory variables have any impact on the dependent variable (e.g. whether the educational level of an individual has any impact on earnings), or F-tests can be used to test whether there are differences in relationships across groups.

Key formulae

We can construct the F-statistic for a joint test by estimating a restricted specification, and an unrestricted specification, and obtaining the ESS, RSS, or R^2. If we have q restrictions, and $n - k - 1$ degrees of freedom in the unrestricted specification:

$$F = \frac{(R_u^2 - R_r^2)/q}{(1 - R_u^2)/(n - k - 1)} = \frac{(ESS_u - ESS_r)/q}{RSS_u/(n - k - 1)} = \frac{(RSS_r - RSS_u)/q}{RSS_u/(n - k - 1)}$$

Note: If you are testing that none of the explanatory variables has a significant impact on the dependent variable, this is equivalent to testing that $\beta_1 = \beta_2 = \ldots = \beta_q = 0$. In this case, $ESS_r = R_r^2 = 0$.

$$F = \frac{(R_u^2)/q}{(1 - R_u^2)/(n - k - 1)} = \frac{(ESS_u)/q}{RSS_u/(n - k - 1)}$$

Appendix

Proving the equality of the three F-statistics

In this chapter, we stated that there were three methods to calculate the F-statistic, based on our restricted and unrestricted regressions:

$$F = \frac{(R_u^2 - R_r^2)/q}{(1 - R_u^2)/(n - k - 1)} = \frac{(ESS_u - ESS_r)/q}{RSS_u/(n - k - 1)} = \frac{(RSS_r - RSS_u)/q}{RSS_u/(n - k - 1)}$$

We wish to prove that these are equal to each other. To prove this, we simply need to apply three simple rules:

1. The equation for the $R^2 = \frac{ESS}{TSS}$
2. We can write the explained sum of squares as $ESS = TSS - RSS$
3. The total sum of squares will be equal across the restricted and unrestricted specification, as the observations are just the same: $TSS = \sum_{i=1}^{n}(Y_i - \bar{Y})^2$

Let's begin with:

$$F = \frac{(R_u^2 - R_r^2)/q}{(1 - R_u^2)/(n - k - 1)}$$

Substituting in for $R_u^2 = \frac{ESS_u}{TSS}$ and $R_r^2 = \frac{ESS_r}{TSS}$ gives us:

$$= \frac{\left(\frac{ESS_u}{TSS} - \frac{ESS_r}{TSS}\right)/q}{\left(1 - \frac{ESS_u}{TSS}\right)/(n - k - 1)} = \frac{\frac{1}{TSS}(ESS_u - ESS_r)/q}{\left(\frac{TSS - ESS_u}{TSS}\right)/(n - k - 1)}$$

Now, working with the denominator, we know that $TSS - ESS_u = RSS_u$, so we can rewrite this as:

$$= \frac{\frac{1}{TSS}(ESS_u - ESS_r)/q}{\frac{RSS_u}{TSS}/(n - k - 1)}$$

Since we have a factor of $\frac{1}{TSS}$ on the top and bottom of the fraction, we can cancel these, to give:

$$= \frac{(ESS_u - ESS_r)/q}{RSS_u/(n - k - 1)}$$

We have now proven that $\frac{(R_u^2 - R_r^2)/q}{(1 - R_u^2)/(n - k - 1)} = \frac{(ESS_u - ESS_r)/q}{RSS_u/(n - k - 1)}$. To convert this into a relationship just including the RSS_u and RSS_r, we need to go back to the relationship between ESS, TSS, and RSS

We can write that:

$ESS_u = TSS - RSS_u,\ ESS_r = TSS - RSS_r$

Substituting these in gives:

$$= \frac{((TSS - RSS_u) - (TSS - RSS_r))/q}{RSS_u/(n - k - 1)}$$

The *TSS* will cancel, leaving us with:

$$= \frac{(RSS_r - RSS_u)/q}{RSS_u/(n - k - 1)}$$

Logs, Polynomials, and Other Non-linear Relationships

30

Learning outcomes for this chapter

At the end of this chapter, students will be able to:

- Estimate and interpret relationships including polynomials of the explanatory variables, and make judgements about the appropriate number of powers to include
- Estimate and interpret relationships using natural logarithms within multiple regressions, and make judgements about the most appropriate model to consider

Mathematical tools

- Logarithms
- Polynomials
- Differentiation

Introduction

Economists will often be interested in relationships other than simple linear relationships. For instance, an economist may be interested in the price **elasticity** of demand for a good. Remember that the price elasticity of demand is the percentage change in the quantity demanded due to a 1 per cent increase in the price. Mathematically, the price elasticity of demand, η_p can be defined as:

$$\eta_p = \frac{\text{Percentage change in quantity}}{\text{Percentage change in price}} = \frac{\Delta Q/Q}{\Delta P/P}$$

Suppose that the price elasticity of demand was constant, and equal to –0.5. This would mean that, whatever the price of the good, a 1 per cent increase in price would be associated with a 0.5 per cent decrease in demand. However, this will not be a linear relationship between price and quantity, and as such, we need a way of estimating these sorts of non-linear relationship. A demand curve, based on a constant price elasticity of demand of $\eta_p = -0.5$, is illustrated in Figure 30.1.

Elasticities aren't the only reason for being interested in non-linear relationships; for example, there might be non-linear returns to inputs in a production process. For instance, we

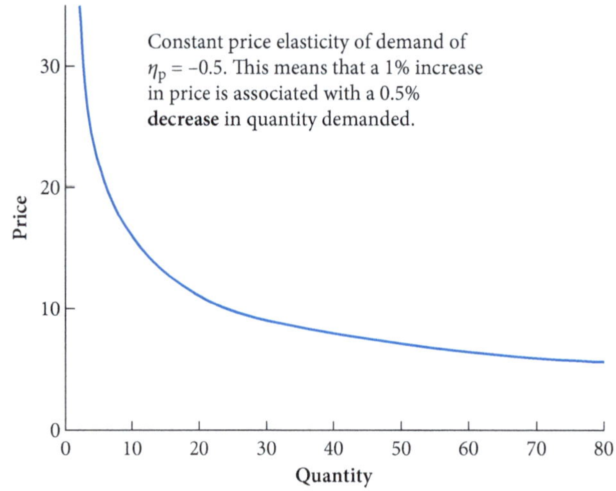

Figure 30.1 Demand function illustrating a constant price elasticity of demand of $\eta_p = -0.5$.

might expect to find diminishing returns to inputs, where each additional unit of input leads to less additional output than the previous unit. Similarly, there may be parts of the relationship where there might be increasing returns.

An example might be revising for an exam. The first hour of revision may have little impact, other than to increase your familiarity with the material, but the second hour of revision may have more impact than the first hour, as you start to get deeper into the subject. However, once you've done lots of revision, there's diminishing amounts of additional material that you need to master, and as such, you'd expect each additional hour to have less extra impact on your exam grade than the previous hour. Of course, at some point, we'd expect an additional hour of study to lead to zero impact on your grade, not least because there's usually a maximum mark that you are able to achieve!

In this chapter, we will introduce two key methods of estimating non-linear relationships. Firstly, we will introduce the use of polynomials, and then will discuss the use of (natural) logarithms, and how we estimate relationships with these non-linear specifications.

30.1 Estimating polynomial relationships

When we estimate relationships with dummy variables, even if the dummy variables represent *ranked* outcomes for the explanatory variable, we are essentially allowing for a non-linear relationship between the dependent variable and the explanatory variable.

If you have a quantitative or numeric explanatory variable, there are other ways you can estimate non-linear relationships. For instance, we might believe that there are diminishing returns to revision for an exam. The 10th hour of revision might have much more impact on your exam mark than the 100th hour. Alternatively, an extra \$1,000 spent on healthcare might have more impact on life expectancy when spending is very low, compared to when spending is very high.

One way that we can estimate a non-linear specification is to use polynomials—quadratics, cubics, etc. Figure 30.2 illustrates an example of a cubic relationship, where the values of Y are determined by X^3, X^2, and X terms.

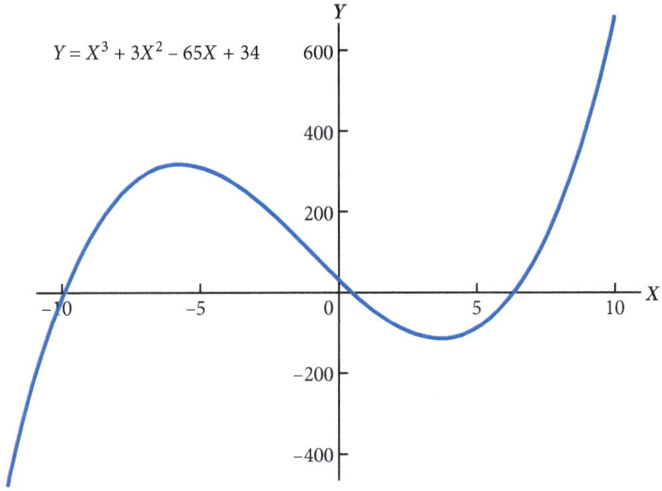

Figure 30.2 Cubic relationship between X and Y.

Let's begin by thinking back to the impact of spending on healthcare on life expectancy, based on OECD data that we began looking at in Chapter 23. A scatter plot of this data, across countries, is illustrated in Figure 30.3.

Figure 30.3 illustrates the scatter plot of life expectancy at birth against spending (per capita) on healthcare. Just looking at the data, we can see that when spending is low, initially an increase in spending seems to be associated with a big increase in life expectancy, but as we move to countries with higher spending on healthcare, the extra returns to life expectancy seems to level off. This suggests that there might be a non-linear relationship between life expectancy and healthcare spending.

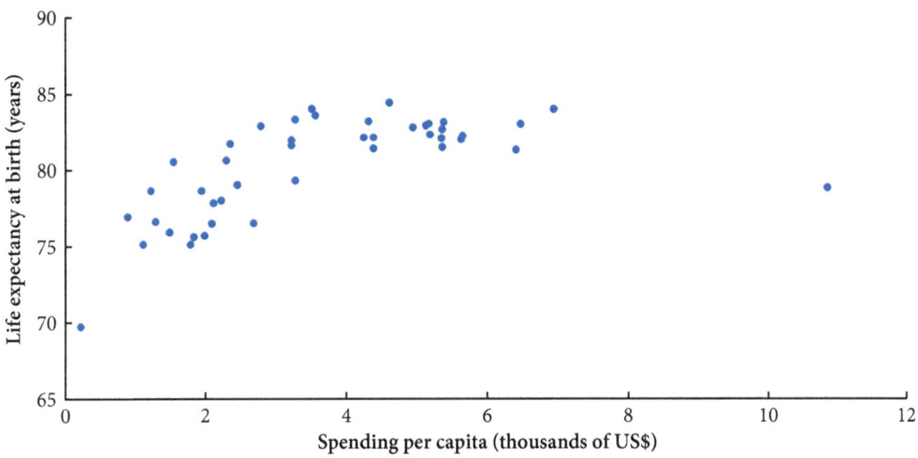

Figure 30.3 Life expectancy at birth plotted against spending per capita on healthcare (2019 data, from the OECD).

We could investigate this by estimating a quadratic relationship in terms of spending:

$$LifeExp_i = \beta_0 + \beta_1 Spend_i + \beta_2 Spend_i^2 + u_i$$

where $LifeExp_i$ is the life expectancy at birth in country i, whilst $Spend_i$ is the spending per capita on healthcare (measured in US$). Further, $Spend_i^2$ is just the square of spending in country i. So, if a country spends $2,000 per capita, the $Spend_i$ variable would take the value 2, whilst the $Spend_i^2$ variable would take the value 4.

Before we discuss the estimated results of this relationship, it's worth thinking about what the coefficients actually mean in this example, because we cannot just think about β_1 being the marginal impact of a change in $Spend_i$, and β_2 being the marginal impact of a change in $Spend_i^2$, as it is impossible to independently allow one of these variables to change, allowing the other to remain constant.

As such, to find the marginal effect of spending on healthcare on life expectancy, we need to (partially) differentiate the above specification with relation to spending on healthcare:

$$\frac{\partial LifeExp_i}{\partial Spend_i} = \beta_1 + 2 \times \beta_2 \times Spend_i$$

That is, if β_1 and β_2 are non-zero, then the marginal effect of spending on life expectancy depends on three factors—β_1, β_2, and the level of spending on healthcare. This is important, as it means that the marginal effect changes depending on the level of spending, so it becomes more difficult to evaluate. As a way of simplifying the interpretation, economists often choose an appropriate value of the explanatory variable to evaluate the marginal effect; this is often the mean (average) of the explanatory variable.

How to include a non-linear term

If we want to include a non-linear term into our relationship, we will need to create a new variable. In this example, since we want to evaluate the non-linear effect of per capita healthcare spending on life expectancy, we will need to create a new variable which is the square of the spending variable. So, suppose that we have observed $Spend_i$ taking the values 1, 2, 3, 4, and 5. Then we would need to construct a new variable, $Spend_i^2$, which takes the value equal to the square of each of these values.

$Spend_i$	$Spend_i^2$
1	1
2	4
3	9
4	16
5	25

We could then estimate the non-linear relationship by including both $Spend_i$ and $Spend_i^2$ as explanatory variables in an OLS regression.

Before we look at the numerical estimates, let's consider, visually, how this non-linear relationship fits our data. Remember, we are fitting a quadratic relationship, which means that the relationship will follow a parabola. The quadratic relationship is illustrated in Figure 30.4. A quadratic model allows for us to estimate the non-linearity of the relationship, and the non-linear model seems to fit the data much better than the simple, linear model we estimated in previous chapters.

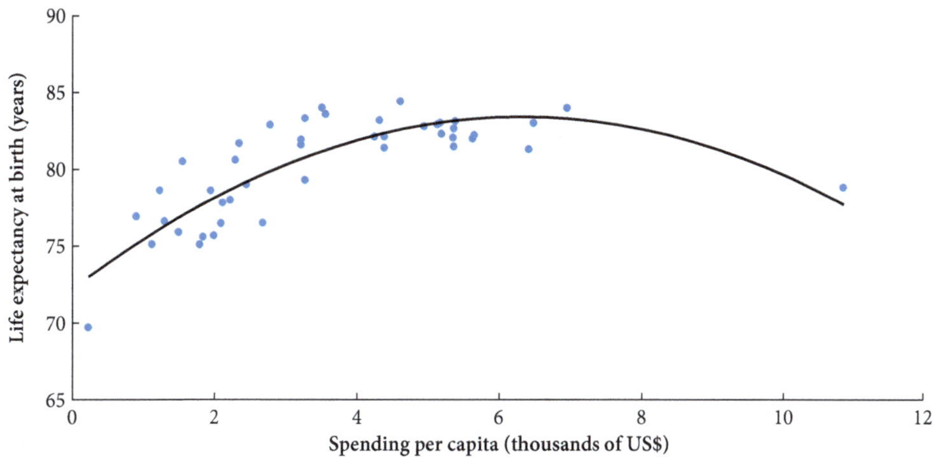

Figure 30.4 Fitting a quadratic relationship.

Based on economic theory, we generally might expect to have diminishing returns to spending on healthcare. There is a natural limit to life expectancy, and if you continuously increase the spending on healthcare, you would eventually expect increases to have no additional impact. That is, we might expect there to be diminishing returns to spending, where every additional dollar spent on healthcare has less impact on life expectancy than the previous one. This is exactly what this relationship looks like for spending levels less than about $6,000 per capita.

What we would not necessarily expect is for increased spending to actually lead to a reduction in life expectancy; rather we would expect to see life expectancy converge to some theoretical maximum. That is, we might expect the marginal effect of spending on healthcare to converge towards zero. However, that's not what the estimated relationship looks like. Instead, beyond $Spend_i$ = $6,000, the relationship starts to slope downwards. That is, the estimated relationship has an area where there is a negative marginal effect.

Unfortunately, this is one of the perils of using a quadratic specification to estimate a non-linear relationship. Any parabola has a single turning point where either the relationship moves from a positive marginal effect to a negative marginal effect, or vice versa.

In many cases this won't matter, because the curve will become negative outside of the data range. However, we have included one observation in the specification which is a substantial outlier—the USA. The USA has a substantially higher per capita spend on healthcare, and a below OECD-average life expectancy. Were we to only consider the other 43 countries in the data, we would allow for the non-linearity, but would not experience the downward sloping part of the relationship.

Now, we wish to interpret the marginal effect of per capita spending on life expectancy. To interpret the results, we will also consider the linear relationship we considered in Chapter 23, and we will try to evaluate which relationship is more appropriate for the data we have observed.

That is, we will estimate the following relationships:

$$LifeExp_i = \gamma_0 + \gamma_1 Spend_i + u_i \quad (1)$$

$$LifeExp_i = \beta_0 + \beta_1 Spend_i + \beta_2 Spend_i^2 + u_i \quad (2)$$

In specification (1), the marginal effect of healthcare spending on life expectancy is just γ_1. However, for specification (2), when we fit a quadratic relationship, we need to be a little more careful, as the marginal effect (i.e. the slope of the estimated relationship) will change, depending on the value of the $Spend_i$ variable. That is, if we find the (partial) derivative of specification (2) with relation to healthcare spending, we have:

$$\frac{\partial LifeExp_i}{\partial Spend_i} = \beta_1 + 2 \times \beta_2 \times Spend_i$$

The results from specifications (1) and (2) are presented in Table 30.1.

We have already interpreted specification (1), with an increase of per capita spending on healthcare by $1,000 associated with a 0.972 year increase in life expectancy. However, visually, it looked from Figure 30.4 that a quadratic relationship may be a better fit than the simple linear relationship. As such, we want to ask ourselves a few questions:

1. Is the quadratic relationship a better fit than the simple linear relationship? That is, is specification (2) superior to specification (1)?
2. Does spending have any impact on life expectancy in specification (2)?
3. If spending has an impact, can we quantify that impact?

Table 30.1 Results from the regression of life expectancy at birth against per capita spending on healthcare

	(1)	(2)
Spend	0.972 ***	3.5187 ***
	(0.193)	(0.3829)
Spend^2		−0.2774 ***
		(0.0392)
Constant	76.685 ***	72.2367 ***
	(0.805)	(0.8331)
R^2	0.3767	0.7194
Number of observations	44	44

Note: Dependent variable is life expectancy at birth. Standard errors in parentheses. *** indicates significance at 1% level, ** indicates significance at 5% level, * indicates significance at 10% level.

30.1.1 Is the quadratic relationship a better fit than the linear relationship?

Let's begin with the first question. Essentially, we are asking whether the quadratic relationship is a better fit than the linear relationship. Remember, we estimated the relationship:

$$LifeExp_i = \beta_0 + \beta_1 Spend_i + \beta_2 Spend_i^2 + u_i \qquad (2)$$

If the relationship between life expectancy and spending on healthcare is linear, then none of the non-linear terms should have any impact on the dependent variable. The only non-linear term we have included is the square of (per capita) spending on healthcare.

As such, if $\beta_2 = 0$, a linear relationship would have been more appropriate.

Let's test the hypothesis that the non-linear terms have no impact:

$$H_0: \beta_2 = 0$$
$$H_A: \beta_2 \neq 0$$

There are two ways that we could test this hypothesis. Since this is a single hypothesis, we could test this either using a t-test, or using an F-test. A t-test is usually easier to calculate, so let's focus on the t-statistic first.

$$= \frac{\hat{\beta}_2 - E(\hat{\beta}_2 | \beta_2 = 0)}{\widehat{s.e.}(\hat{\beta}_2)} = \frac{-0.2774 - 0}{0.0392} = -7.08$$

Now, we have 44 observations, and have estimated three coefficients, so we have 41 degrees of freedom (i.e. $n - k - 1 = 41$), and the 5 per cent critical value from the t-distribution with 41 degrees of freedom is 2.02. As the magnitude of the t-stat is larger than the critical value, we would reject the null hypothesis, concluding that the relationship is non-linear.

Alternatively, we can calculate the p-value as:

$$P(|t_{41}| > 7.08) = 1.28 \times 10^{-8} = 0.0000000128$$

That is, if the null hypothesis were true, then the probability of achieving a t-stat as large as we have is 0.000000012. This is a vanishingly small probability, and gives us good confidence that it is likely that the relationship is non-linear.

Repeating the test using an F-test

Our null hypothesis was that the coefficient on the squared term, $\beta_2 = 0$. If we impose the null hypothesis, we are essentially imposing a linear relationship between life expectancy and per capita spending on healthcare. However, we have already estimated this relationship as specification (1). As such, we have the restricted and unrestricted R^2, as shown in Table 30.1. Similarly, we know that we have $q = 1$ restriction and 41 degrees of freedom in the unrestricted model. This gives us an F-statistic of:

$$F = \frac{(R_u^2 - R_r^2)/q}{(1 - R_u^2)/(n - k - 1)} = \frac{(0.7194 - 0.3767)/1}{(1 - 0.7194)/(44 - 3 - 1)} = 50.07$$

If we calculate the p-value associated with this, $F_{1,41} = 50.07$, we get:

$$P(F_{1,41} > 50.07) = 1.28 \times 10^{-8}$$

Reassuringly, this is the same p-value as we obtained via the t-test, and as the p-value is smaller than 5 per cent, we would reject the null hypothesis at the 5 per cent significance level. As we have seen earlier in this book, the F-statistic is also the square of the t-statistic. This will always be the case when we are testing a single hypothesis.

30.1.2 Does spending on healthcare have any impact on life expectancy?

Let's now move onto the second question. This second test is asking the question of whether jointly the spending on healthcare variables has any impact on life expectancy. If it has no impact, then this would be equivalent to $\beta_1 = \beta_2 = 0$. So, we wish to formally test:

$$H_0\colon \beta_1 = \beta_2 = 0$$
$$H_A\colon \beta_1 \neq 0 \, or \, \beta_2 \neq 0 \, (or \; both)$$

Because we have two hypotheses that we are testing here ($\beta_1 = 0$ and $\beta_2 = 0$), we cannot test these with a t-test, and need to appeal to an F-test instead.

Remember, in an F-test, we compare the R^2 from a restricted specification, where we impose the null hypothesis, and the unrestricted specification, where we allow the alternative hypothesis to be true. If we impose the null hypothesis to be true here, this is equivalent to running a regression of life expectancy against a constant.

$LifeExp_i = \beta_0 + \beta_1 Spend_i + \beta_2 Spend_i^2 + u_i$	Unrestricted specification
$LifeExp_i = \beta_0 + u_i$	Restricted specification

It is possible to show that,[1] when you run a regression of a variable against a constant only, the R^2 will always be equal to zero (and $ESS = 0$). This means that $R_r^2 = 0$. We also know, from Table 30.1, that $R_u^2 = 0.7194$. We are imposing two restrictions under the null hypothesis; that is, $\beta_1 = 0$ and $\beta_2 = 0$. Therefore, $q = 2$, and we have 44 observations, but have estimated three coefficients in the unrestricted model, so $n - k - 1 = 44 - 3 = 41$:

$$= \frac{(R_u^2 - R_r^2)/q}{(1 - R_u^2)/(n - k - 1)} = \frac{(0.7194 - 0)/2}{(1 - 0.7194)/41} = 52.56$$

We could either look up the critical value from the F-tables based on 2 and 41 degrees of freedom (5% critical value = 3.23), or calculate the p-value ($P(F_{2,41} > 52.56) = 4.8 \times 10^{-12}$),

[1] We do not prove this in this book, but it is easy to understand intuitively. Remember that R^2 is equivalent to the ratio of $\frac{var(\hat{Y})}{var(Y)} = R^2$. If you run a regression of Y against a constant only, then you are only going to get a single fitted value for $\hat{Y}_i$, for all of the observations. This means that $var(\hat{Y}) = 0$. As such, R^2 must also be equal to zero. I leave it as an exercise for you to prove that $ESS = 0$. Hint: Show that $\hat{Y}_i = \overline{Y}$ when you estimate the relationship $Y_i = \beta_0 + u_i$.

but in both cases, we would reject the null hypothesis. The probability of gaining an F-statistic as large as 52.56 is vanishingly small if the null hypothesis were true. This allows us to be very confident that spending on healthcare is strongly related with life expectancy.

How do we quantify the effect of per capita spending on life expectancy?

In general, if you estimate the relationship:

$$Y_i = \beta_0 + \beta_1 X_i + \beta_2 X_i^2 + u_i$$

then the marginal effect of a change in X on Y will vary depending on the value of X_i. We can see this when we differentiate Y with relation to X, and we obtain:

$$\frac{\partial Y_i}{\partial X_i} = \beta_1 + 2\beta_2 X_i$$

That is, the change in Y is itself a function of X_i. In order for us to interpret the marginal effect of a change in X on Y, we therefore need to choose a value of X_i to help us evaluate the relationship. You could evaluate this at various values of X_i to illustrate the change in the marginal effect, or you could choose a 'typical' value of X_i. For example, you could evaluate this marginal effect at the median or the mean of X.

Returning to the example of per capita spending on life expectancy, let's consider specification (2) from Table 30.2.

It is easy to show in specification (2) that all of the estimated coefficients are statistically significant, and we have particularly tested that $\beta_2 \neq 0$. We showed earlier that (provided our specification is correct), the marginal effect of increasing spending on life expectancy is given by:

$$\frac{\partial LifeExp_i}{\partial Spend_i} = \beta_1 + 2 \times \beta_2 \times Spend_i$$

Table 30.2 Results from the regression of life expectancy at birth against per capita spending on healthcare

	(1)	(2)
Spend	0.972 * * *	3.5187 * * *
	(0.193)	(0.3829)
Spend^2		−0.2774 * * *
		(0.0392)
Constant	76.685 * * *	72.2367 * * *
	(0.805)	(0.8331)
R^2	0.3767	0.7194
Number of observations	44	44

Note: Dependent variable is life expectancy at birth. Standard errors in parentheses. *** indicates significance at 1% level, ** indicates significance at 5% level, * indicates significance at 10% level.

We have an estimated $\hat{\beta}_1 = 3.519$ and an estimated $\hat{\beta}_2 = -0.277$. As such, we can represent the estimated marginal effect of an increase in spending on life expectancy as:

$$\frac{\partial LifeExp_i}{\partial Spend_i} = \hat{\beta}_1 + 2 \times \hat{\beta}_2 \times Spend_i = 3.519 + 2 \times (-0.277) \times Spend_i$$

So, the marginal effect of an increase in spending on life expectancy is equal to $3.591 - 0.554 \times Spend_i$, but this is not, in and of itself, very informative, as the marginal effect *changes* depending on the value of $Spend_i$.

Table 30.3 Summary statistics

	Mean	Standard deviation	Number of observations
Life expectancy	80.23	3.258	44
(Per capita) spending on health care (in thousands of US$)	3.643	2.057	44

One way of illustrating the impact would be to calculate the marginal effect, evaluated at the (mean) average of the explanatory variable. To help us, Table 30.3 provides summary statistics for the data on both life expectancy and per capita spending on healthcare.

We are told that the mean of spending is 3.643 (or \$3,643 per capita), so we can substitute this into our marginal effect to give us:

$$= 3.591 - 0.554 \times 3.643 = 1.573$$

So, our estimated effect, evaluated at the average of spending, indicates increasing $Spend_i$ by 1 (remember this is equivalent to increasing spending by \$1,000 per capita) is associated with a 1.573 year increase in life expectancy at birth.

Even this is not the end of the story, as we really want to know whether:

a) A \$1,000 per capita increase is a large increase (or a small increase).

b) The increase in life expectancy is a large (or small) increase.

As such, we can evaluate the impact of a 1 standard deviation (s.d.) increase, again evaluating this at the mean of spending. The standard deviation of spending is 2.057 (or \$2,057), so if we increase spending by 1 s.d., the impact would be:

$$\Delta LifeExp_{iSpend_i=3.643} \approx 1.573 \times \Delta Spend_i = 1.573 \times 2.057 = 3.235$$

So, a 1 s.d. increase in spending is associated with a 3.235 year increase in life expectancy. However, we still want to know whether this is a large or a small increase. We are finally told that the standard deviation of life expectancy is 3.258 across countries. As such, the estimated marginal effect of a 1 s.d. increase in spending (evaluated at the mean of spending) gives us a $\frac{3.235}{3.258} = 0.99$ s.d. increase in life expectancy. When we see a 1 s.d. increase in an explanatory variable being associated with anything close to a 1 s.d. increase in the dependent variable, this indicates a very large effect.

However, since the coefficient on the squared term is negative, we can see that there are diminishing marginal returns to spending. This suggests that, whilst increasing spending for the average country may have a very economically significant impact on life expectancy, the impact for countries that already spend very high amounts will be low.

Important note: Causal inference

It is important to note that we have not established causality here. In fact, as we saw in earlier chapters, since we have not included any other determinants of life expectancy (such as GDP, or education, or other factors, which may also be correlated with life expectancy), we are likely to suffer from **omitted variables bias**. As such, we cannot establish causality based on the results we have observed here.

If we wanted to establish causality, we would need to observe some form of **exogenous** changes to healthcare spending that are unrelated to other determinants of life expectancy.

One way that you *may* be able to develop causality would be to observe the 44 countries over a period of time, and look at the impact of variations in healthcare spending over time on life expectancy within those countries (whilst also controlling for changes in factors such as GDP or education).

You could try to estimate these sorts of effects using fixed effects regressions (which we saw in the previous chapter), to control for anything that is fixed (such as culture) within the country.

We'll talk more about causal inference relating to this problem later in the chapter.

30.1.3 More general specifications

If you suspect that there is a non-linear relationship between a dependent variable Y_i and an explanatory variable X_i, you are not just limited to a choice between a linear relationship or a quadratic relationship. In fact, we can use OLS to estimate polynomials with many different power of X included. For example, you could estimate:

$$Y_i = \beta_0 + \beta_1 X_i + \beta_2 X_i^2 + \beta_3 X_i^3 + \beta_4 X_i^4 + \ldots + \beta_k X_i^k + u_i$$

In this example, we have allowed for k powers of X_i to be included. In principle, you can keep on adding as many powers of X as you like, with only a simple constraint.

The constraint is that, for each additional explanatory variable (or power) that you introduce, the number of degrees of freedom is reduced by 1. If you have n observations, then the maximum number of powers that you could include would be $n - 1$. However, because as we lower the degrees of freedom, the precision of the estimates reduces, you should avoid including too many powers.[2]

[2] There are models, such as the Akaike Information Criterion, that can help to determine what the optimal order of polynomial is to include when estimating a non-linear relationship.

Degrees of freedom

Remember that the number of degrees of freedom is the number of linearly independent equations for $\hat{u}_i$ you have. The number of degrees of freedom is given by $n - k - 1$ where k is the number of explanatory variables (and n indicates that you have included a non-zero intercept).

As the degrees of freedom decrease, the precision of your estimates also decreases (meaning your standard errors increase). If you were to include $n - 1$ explanatory variables, then you would have zero degrees of freedom, and hence would have infinite standard errors. You cannot estimate a relationship with more coefficients than you have observations.

Dangers of overfitting

Related to the problem of degrees of freedom is the problem of overfitting. If you include too many powers, then you may well be able to explain much (or even all) of the variation in your dependent variable, but this may be due to a functional form that passes through your data, rather than anything meaningful relating to the shape of the data.

If you use enough powers, you can actually draw a line that will pass through every observation. However, this is likely a case of trying to over-fit your relationship, rather than any true relationship between your dependent and explanatory variables.

If you have n observations of Y_i and X_i, then if you estimate a relationship with $n - 1$ powers of X_i (and a non-zero intercept) in your model, then you can guarantee that the line that you estimate will pass through every point you have observed.

To illustrate this, I have randomly chosen six observations of Y_i, and six observations of X_i. There is no relationship between X_i and Y_i, and we have estimated the following relationship:

$$Y_i = \beta_0 + \beta_1 X_i + \beta_2 X_i^2 + \beta_3 X_i^3 + \beta_4 X_i^4 + \beta_5 X_i^5 + u_i$$

On the face of things, you might think that this is a really good model to fit, as the line we have estimated passes through all of the observations, as shown in Figure 30.5.

However, there are two things that cause us major problems. Firstly, and most obviously, the model predicts values for Y that are way outside the true range of Y. In this example, the observations of Y are between −1.95 and 1.91, yet, the model predicts values for Y between −20 and +25.

Secondly, this is only going to be the model that appropriately fits this set of six observations of Y and X. When we take a different set of six observations of Y and X (again the observations of Y and X are chosen completely at random, with no relationship between Y and X), and attempt to fit our polynomial, we estimate a completely different relationship, as illustrated in Figure 30.6.

The reason for these problems is that we have overfitted our model. The more powers that we include, the closer we can fit the model to the observed set of data. However, this means that the model will be much less generalizable to other samples from the population. If you are dealing with big data, where you have very large frequencies of data (e.g. in stock trades,

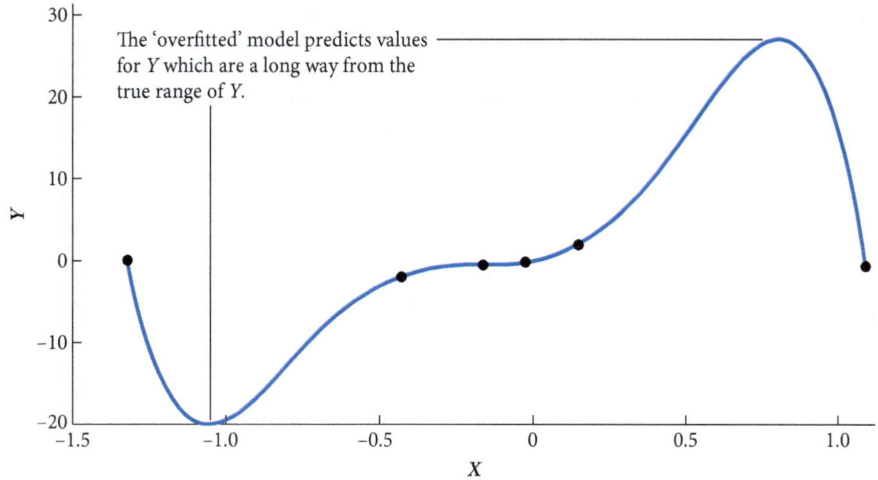

Figure 30.5 Estimating a relationship based upon six observations, with five powers of X included.

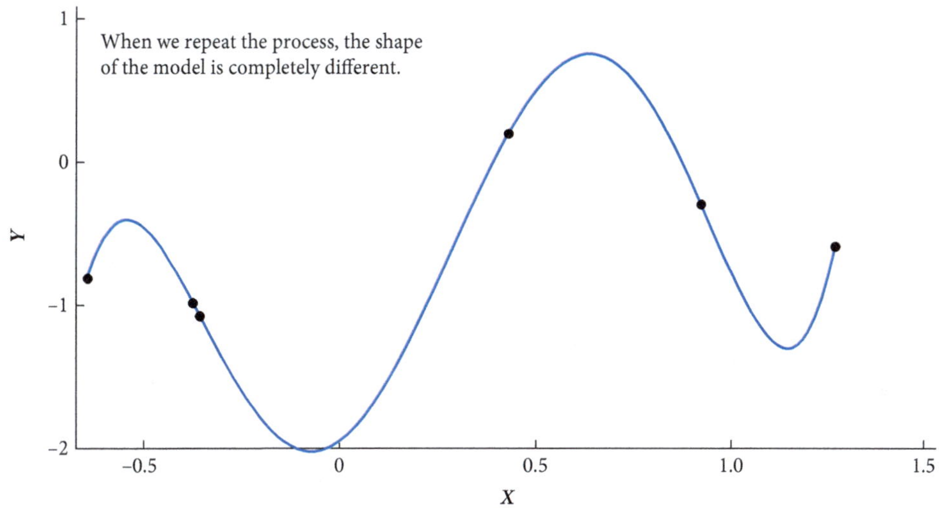

Figure 30.6 A second estimated relationship, based on the same data generating process as in Figure 30.5.

which happen continuously over time), you may want to include a complicated power series, but for many economic models, a quadratic (or possibly a cubic) will normally suffice to allow you to consider non-linearities.

In practice, economists often use 'information criteria' to help inform what the optimal number of powers to include is, although these are beyond the scope of this book.

30.1.4 Testing whether a (general) polynomial is a better fit than a linear relationship

Having estimated a non-linear specification, a good question to ask is whether a non-linear specification was appropriate in the first place. Suppose that you have estimated the following relationship:

$$Y_i = \beta_0 + \beta_1 X_i + \beta_2 X_i^2 + \beta_3 X_i^3 + \beta_4 X_i^4 + \ldots + \beta_k X_i^k + u_i$$

All of the powers greater than 1 (i.e. $X_i^2, X_i^3, \ldots$ etc.) are the non-linear terms here. If the relationship between Y and X is really a linear relationship, then the coefficients on all of these non-linear terms would be equal to zero, so we can test whether these non-linear terms have any impact on Y:

$$H_0\colon \beta_2 = \beta_3 = \beta_4 = \ldots = \beta_{k-1} = \beta_k = 0$$
$$H_A\colon \beta_2 \neq 0 \, or \, \beta_3 \neq 0 \, or \ldots or \, \beta_k \neq 0$$

You could test these using an F-test, where the restricted model would be a linear specification, and the unrestricted model would be the non-linear polynomial:

$Y_i = \beta_0 + \beta_1 X_i + \beta_2 X_i^2 + \beta_3 X_i^3 + \beta_4 X_i^4 + \ldots + \beta_k X_i^k + u_i$	Unrestricted specification
$Y_i = \beta_0 + \beta_1 X_i + u_i$	Restricted specification

Here, we would have $q = k - 1$ restrictions (as we have $k - 1$ non-linear terms in the unrestricted specification), and since we estimate $k + 1$ coefficients in the unrestricted model, we would have $n - k - 1$ degrees of freedom in the unrestricted model. As such, if the null hypothesis is true:

$$F = \frac{(R_u^2 - R_r^2)/(k-1)}{(1 - R_u^2)/(n-k-1)} = \frac{(ESS_u - ESS_r)/(k-1)}{RSS_u/(n-k-1)} = \frac{(RSS_r - RSS_u)/(k-1)}{RSS_u/(n-k-1)} \sim F_{k-1,n-k-1}$$

30.1.5 Multivariate regressions with non-linear terms

Just as with simple linear models, you can control for other characteristics using multivariate regressions. So, in the example of spending on healthcare, we could include a non-linear term for spending, and other controls, including the (per capita) GDP of the country:

$$LifeExp_i = \beta_0 + \beta_1 Spend_i + \beta_2 Spend_i^2 + \beta_3 GDP_i + u_i$$

Figure 30.7 shows this non-linear specification fitted through the data. Because we have included a non-linear term relating to spending on healthcare, this allows the slope to change as spending increases. As we can see, just as in the simple case, as spending on healthcare increases, the estimated marginal effect decreases.

The way that we have constructed this specification, there is a single linear estimate of the marginal effect of (per capita) GDP on life expectancy. This is the estimated slope, as we increase GDP_i for a given, or fixed, value of spending on healthcare.

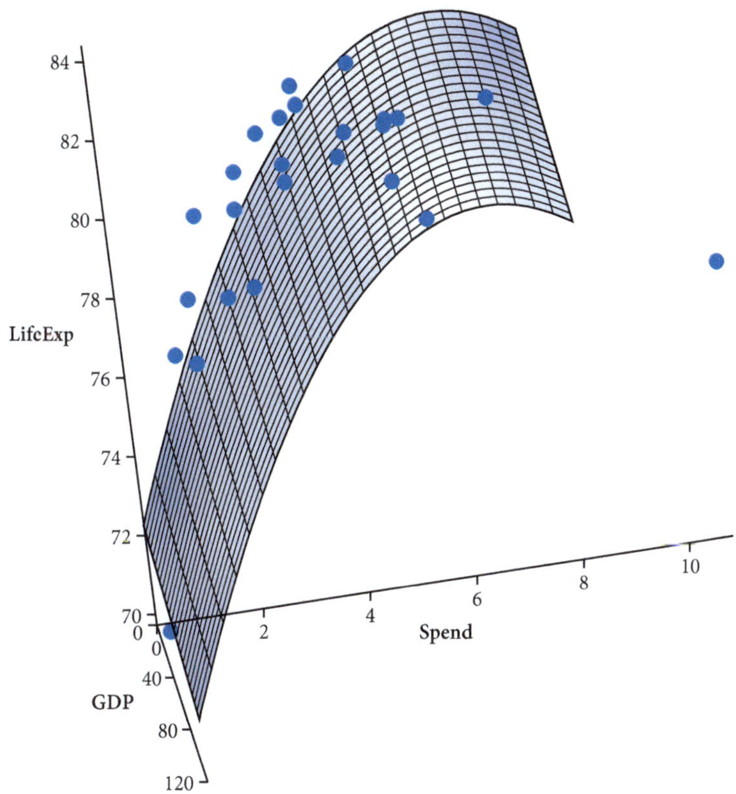

Figure 30.7 Relationship involving non-linear terms with more than one explanatory variable.

We have now estimated four specifications relating to this data, and it is important to examine these models in turn to evaluate what we have found.

$$LifeExp_i = \beta_0 + \beta_1 Spend_i + u_i \quad \text{(A)}$$

$$LifeExp_i = \beta_0 + \beta_1 Spend_i + \beta_3 GDP_i + u_i \quad \text{(B)}$$

$$LifeExp_i = \beta_0 + \beta_1 Spend_i + \beta_2 Spend_i^2 + u_i \quad \text{(C)}$$

$$LifeExp_i = \beta_0 + \beta_1 Spend_i + \beta_2 Spend_i^2 + \beta_3 GDP_i + u_i \quad \text{(D)}$$

The first specification (A) was the initial, naïve, specification that we estimated in Chapter 23, with only per capita spending on healthcare ($Spend_i$) as an explanatory variable. However, we suspected that this may suffer from omitted variables bias, so we introduced per capita GDP (GDP_i) as an additional explanatory variable in (B), and saw a substantial change in the estimated coefficient on $Spend_i$.

Specification (C) was our first non-linear specification, and specification (D) is included to investigate whether specification (C) suffered from omitted variables bias. See Table 30.4 for results from the four specifications.

Table 30.4 Results from our four specifications using OLS

	(A)	(B)	(C)	(D)
Per capita spending on healthcare (thousands of US$)	0.972***	0.458	3.519***	3.649***
	(0.193)	(0.292)	(0.383)	(0.552)
Square of per capita spending on healthcare ($Spend_i^2$)			−0.277***	−0.285***
			(0.039)	(0.046)
Per capita GDP (thousands of US$)		0.068**		−0.008
		(0.030)		(0.025)
Constant	76.685***	75.608***	72.237***	72.247***
	(0.805)	(0.902)	(0.833)	(0.843)
Number of observations	44	44	44	44
R^2	0.3767	0.4465	0.7194	0.7202

Note: Dependent variable is life expectancy at birth. Standard errors in parentheses. *** indicates significance at 1% level, ** indicates significance at 5% level, * indicates significance at 10% level.

As noted in earlier chapters, we believed that specification (A) might suffer from omitted variables bias, as there were likely other determinants of life expectancy that were correlated with per capita spending on healthcare. We thought that one of these might be per capita GDP, and when we introduced this in specification (B), we found a big change in the estimated coefficient.

However, another possibility was that we had mis-specified our model. That is, rather than a linear relationship between life expectancy and spending on healthcare, there may be a non-linear relationship between life expectancy and spending on healthcare, which we investigated in specification (C). However, when we now include per capita GDP as a further explanatory variable (specification (D)), there is little to no impact on the estimated coefficients for $Spend_i$ and $Spend_i^2$, indicating that having omitted GDP from specification (C), there was little evidence of bias, and further, the GDP variable isn't even statistically significant.

This seems like a contradiction, but in fact what it identifies is that the biggest problem that was experienced in specification (A) was not, in fact, omitted variable bias, but instead that we had imposed a linear relationship, when a linear relationship was not appropriate.

However, this should have been obvious to us, just by looking at the data. We can see that there doesn't appear to be a linear relationship between spending per capita and life expectancy. We can also see that, since the coefficient on GDP_i is not statistically significant, estimating specification (D) has not improved the fit of our relationship.

More on causal inference

Even though we have found that there is a strong non-linear association between spending on healthcare and life expectancy, we have not established causality. We have already suggested that there are likely to be lots of other determinants of life expectancy that we haven't been able to control for included in the error term. Even though we now suspect that GDP was not one of these, there may be many others, such as culture or education.

Further, there may be other complicating factors, such as life expectancy actually influencing healthcare spending (as a population with a longer life expectancy may have a greater number of individuals with complicated and long-term health needs simply due to aging).

There are a range of possible obstacles to causal inference:

- Omitted variables bias: there are likely to be other factors that are determinants of life expectancy that are correlated with healthcare spending, which have not been included in our model.

We have discussed OV bias in detail in this book, but there are a range of other factors that could lead to us gaining inappropriate estimates of the marginal effects of spending on healthcare on life expectancy.

- Reverse causality: it could be that healthcare spending has zero marginal impact on life expectancy, but in reality, increased life expectancy places higher demand on healthcare, which results in higher levels of spending.
- Simultaneity: whilst healthcare spending may have an impact on life expectancy, it could be that life expectancy simultaneously has an impact on healthcare spending.
- Model misspecification: if the quadratic model is inappropriate.

These are a sample of possible reasons why we may not identify causal estimates of the marginal effect. Econometrics has a range of tools to try to correct for these problems, which you will develop as you gain a stronger understanding of the subject. These include:

- difference-in-difference,
- regression discontinuity design, and
- instrumental variables.

We will discuss some of these strategies in the next chapter, to help you to understand published research in economics.

30.2 Estimating non-linear specifications using logarithms

Another way that economists estimate non-linear relationships is through the use of logarithms. Logarithms are often used when, rather than there being constant marginal effect on a dependent variable, a marginal effect has an effect on the growth rate of a devpendent variable.

Suppose you have a random variable, Y, that takes the value 2 when $X = 0$. So, when $X=0$, $Y=2$. Then for each increase of 1 in X, Y increases by 10 per cent. A 10 per cent increase in Y from 2 would be equivalent to multiplying Y by 1.1, so when $X = 1$, Y would be equal to 2.2.v

Similarly, a further 10 per cent increase in Y would make a total of 2.42, so when X is equal to 2, Y would be equal to 2.42, and so on. With this kind of constant proportional growth rate, there would be a non-linear relationship between Y and X. A growth rate like this is often referred to as exponential growth, and in this case, we can model the relationship between X and Y using exponentials. For example, we could represent Y as:

$$Y = 2e^{0.1X}$$

However, these kind of non-linear relationships are not easy to directly estimate, and so a trick to try and estimate this using OLS would be to take logs of the relationship:

$$\ln Y = \ln(2e^{0.1X})$$

Rules of (natural) logs

Remember that there are simple rules relating to natural logs:

1. The log of a product is equal to the sum of the logs:

$$\ln(XY) = \ln X + \ln Y$$

2. If you multiply a log by a constant (a), this is equivalent to raising the variable by the power a:

$$a \times \ln \mathrm{X} = \ln X^a$$

3. The natural log is the inverse of the exponential function.

Using the rules of logs, we can rewrite this as:

$$\Rightarrow \ln Y = \ln 2 + \ln e^{0.1X} = \ln 2 + 0.1X$$

That is, whilst there is a non-linear relationship between Y and X, there is a linear relationship between the natural log of Y and X. This is illustrated in Figure 30.8.

- Panel a) plots Y against X, where $Y = 2e^{0.1X}$. As taking the exponential of X is applying a non-linear function, we can see that there is a non-linear relationship between Y and X.
- However, panel b) presents the plot of the natural log of Y against X. By taking the natural log, we have created a linear relationship between the variable on the vertical axis ($\ln Y$), and the variable on the horizontal axis (X).

Exponentials are often used to model growth rates. In this example, Y is growing by 10 per cent for every one unit increase in X. If we suspect that a change in X is associated with a constant growth rate in Y, we can linearize the relationship by taking logs of the dependent variable.

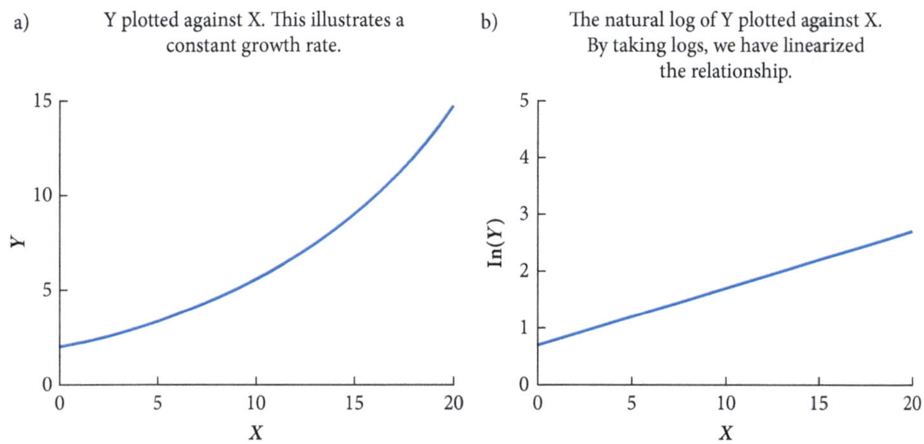

Figure 30.8 Using logs to linearize relationships.

This trick of creating a linear relationship by taking logs is referred to as 'log-linearization', and is often used by economists to try to create linear relationships where we suspect that the underlying relationship between the economic variables may be related to a growth rate. When you are dealing with data, you will not know what the underlying relationship is between the economic variables (otherwise there would be no point in econometrics!). However, economic theory might tell you to expect economic relationships to be related to growth rates.

For example, we might expect years of education, or experience, to be associated with a proportional growth in earnings. Similarly, the number of police on the street may have a proportional relationship to a reduction in crime. As such, if we are interested in these sorts of relationship, we might wish to carry out a log-linearization.

So far, we have only really discussed taking logs of the dependent variable, but there is no reason that you couldn't also consider taking logs of the explanatory variable (or even taking logs of both the dependent variable and the explanatory variables). However, the interpretation of the estimated coefficients changes in each case, which may help shape your choice of which model to choose.

Let's suppose that we have made 100 observations of Y_i and X_i, and suspect that there is a non-linear relationship between the variables, and we decide that we are going to try to linearize the relationship using natural logarithms. There are three possible models we could consider:

$\ln Y_i = \alpha_0 + \alpha_1 X_i + u_i$	Case 1—taking logs of the dependent variable
$Y_i = \beta_0 + \beta_1 \ln X_i + e_i$	Case 2—taking logs of the explanatory variable
$\ln Y_i = \gamma_0 + \gamma_1 \ln X_i + \varepsilon_i$	Case 3—taking logs of both the dependent and explanatory variables

We will go through the mathematics of how to interpret each of these relationships in the appendix, but let's walk through what each of the specifications means intuitively.

30.2.1 Taking logs of the dependent variable

If you estimate a semi-log specification, where you have taken logs of the dependent variable, and the explanatory variable is included as a level (i.e. you have not taken logs):

$$\ln Y_i = \alpha_0 + \alpha_1 X_i + u_i$$

then, α_1 can be interpreted as the proportional change in Y_i due to a one unit increase in X_i. This is equivalent to saying that if you increase X_i by 1, the (approximate) increase in Y_i would be to multiply Y_i by $1 + \alpha_1$. So, for example, if $\alpha_1 = 0.2$, that would indicate that a one unit increase in X would be associated with a 20 per cent increase in Y_i.

Of course, because $\ln(Y)$ only exists for positive values of Y, if the dependent variable, Y, is either equal to zero ($Y=0$), or negative $Y<0$, you would need to make a choice. You would have to either:

1. Omit observations where the natural log does not exist; or
2. Consider a different model.

It is often preferable to consider a different model if you observe negative, or zero, observations of Y, because if you are estimating:

$$\ln Y_i = \alpha_0 + \alpha_1 X_i + u_i$$

and any observations of Y_i are zero (or negative), you know that this cannot be the true data generating process. By attempting to estimate this relationship, you may suffer from specification bias. In practice, economists often may drop a small number of observations in these circumstances, because of the power of the specification in linearizing a non-linear relationship.

What if X_i is a dummy variable?

The approximation above is relatively good if we are looking at a small (relative) change in the explanatory variable. However, if X_i is a dummy variable, it is impossible to have a small change in the explanatory variable—as the variable only takes the values 0 and 1. Many economists will still interpret the estimated coefficient as a proportional change (and we will do that later in the chapter). However, if you want to be a little more precise, you might want to use e as the inverse of a log.

With dummy variables, the only feasible change is from the smallest possible value for that variable to the largest possible value for that variable (0 to 1). As such, the approximation begins to break down.

One way to interpret this might be to think about the expression we are estimating:

$$\ln Y_i = \alpha_0 + \alpha_1 X_i + u_i$$

Mathematically, we could try to find the impact of X on Y by trying to rewrite this expression with Y as the subject; that is, we could use the inverse of a log, and raise e to the power of the expression:

$$\Rightarrow Y_i = e^{\alpha_0 + \alpha_1 X_i + u_i}$$

This is a little cumbersome to deal with, but remembering the rules of powers, if we have Z^{a+b} this is equivalent to $Z^a Z^b$:

$$\Rightarrow Y_i = e^{\alpha_0} \times e^{\alpha_1 X_i} \times e_i^u$$

There are two possible options for X_i, with $X_i = 0$ or $X_i = 1$. We can rewrite the expression by substituting in these two values:

If $X_i = 0$	If $X_i = 1$
$\Rightarrow Y_i = e^{\alpha_0} \times e^0 \times e_i^u$	$\Rightarrow Y_i = e^{\alpha_0} \times e^{\alpha_1} \times e_i^u$
but $e^0 = 1$, and so this can be rewritten as:	
$\Rightarrow Y_i = e^{\alpha_0} \times e_i^u$	

These two expressions are almost identical, but for the inclusion of e^{α_1} in the second expression; that is, when $X_i = 1$, Y_i is e^{α_1} times larger than when $X_i = 0$.

So if $\alpha_1 = 0.2$, then we could write that Y_i would be $e^{0.2} = 1.22$ times as large (or an increase in Y by 22 per cent from $X_i = 0$ to $X_i = 1$). Even here, using α_1 as an approximate proportional change is a reasonably good approximation.

However, if $\alpha_1 = 0.8$, then $e^{0.8} = 2.226$; that is, Y would be 2.226 times as large (or an increase of 122.6 per cent).

Health warning

When we have estimated relationships using OLS, the $\hat{\alpha}_1$ may be an unbiased estimate of the marginal effect of X_i on $\ln Y_i$. When we raise $e^{\hat{\alpha}_1}$, we are effectively applying a non-linear transformation to the estimates, and the impact of this is to create a biased estimate of the proportional impact of X on Y. (This proof is beyond the scope of this book, but is related to Jensen's inequality.)

Many economists, when confronted with a regression with a log on the left-hand side and a dummy variable on the right-hand side will simply interpret this as the proportional change in the dependent variable Y.This is a good approximation if the coefficient is relatively small, but becomes an increasingly bad approximation as the coefficient gets larger.

30.2.2 Taking logs of the explanatory variable

If you estimate a semi-log specification, where you have taken logs of the explanatory variable, and the dependent variable is included as a level (i.e. you have not taken logs):

$$Y_i = \beta_0 + \beta_1 \ln X_i + e_i$$

then β_1 can be interpreted as the marginal effect on Y_i of a proportional change in X. For example, if $\beta_1 = 10$ and X were to increase by 10 per cent (equivalent to a proportional increase of 0.1), then this would be equivalent to Y increasing by $10 \times 0.1 = 1$.

Semi-log specifications with a log on the right-hand side (only) are rare, but not unknown. Wherever you expect a proportional increase to have a linear impact on a dependent variable, you could use this form of regression.

For example, if you are interested in the impact of GDP on, say, outcomes, you might take logs of the right-hand variable, as you may be more interested in the impact of the growth of GDP on education.

There are occasions when you cannot take logs of an explanatory variable. If any of the observations of X_i are zero (or negative), then the natural log will not exist.

30.2.3 Taking logs of both the dependent and explanatory variables

If you are estimating a relationship where both the dependent and explanatory variables are included as logs:

$$\ln Y_i = \gamma_0 + \gamma_1 \ln X_i + \varepsilon_i$$

then γ_1 can be interpreted as an elasticity. So, γ_1 is the percentage change in Y due to a 1 per cent increase in X.

For example, if $\gamma_1 = 0.4$, then this tells us that a 1 per cent increase in X is associated with a 0.4 per cent increase in Y. Often, we might estimate a demand function using a log-log specification, as we often think of movements along the demand curve in terms of elasticities.

KEY DEFINITION: ELASTICITY

An elasticity provides you the percentage change in one variable due to a 1 per cent increase in another variable. For example, the price elasticity of demand (η_p) is defined as the percentage change in quantity demanded due to a 1 per cent increase in price.

Mathematically, this is equivalent to:

$$\eta_p = \frac{\%change\ in\ quantity}{\%change\ in\ price}$$

Worked example 30.1: Estimating the impact of length of job tenure on earnings

To illustrate the impact of different specifications, we will attempt to estimate the relationship between gross weekly wages and the number of years of continuous employment for an individual (full-time) worker. It is not obvious whether increasing the time within a job is likely to be related to higher or lower wages, as we can tell a story that might explain a relationship in either direction:

1. Individuals who gain more experience in a job are likely to be promoted within the firm and to gradually become more senior, thereby gaining higher wages.
2. Highly productive workers (who would normally be paid higher wages) may be head-hunted by external firms to take on higher-paid jobs. As such, it might be that the newest workers within a firm are the highest paid workers.

Whatever happens, it is likely that the relationship between wages and tenure within a job will be non-linear. We will investigate this using logarithmic relationships.

To estimate this, we have randomly sampled 1,000 full-time workers aged 25–65 from the 2019 UK Labour Force Survey. Our sample consists of 500 male workers and 500 female workers. To assist with interpreting the estimated relationship, summary statistics are available in Table 30.5. The years of continuous employment is an *almost* continuous variable, constructed based upon the observed number of months continuous employment. So, if an individual had six months of continuous employment, this variable would take the value 0.5, representing half a year. We will denote the years of continuous employment as the length of tenure of the individual.

To help remove some potential bias, we will also include controls for the sex of the individual by including a female dummy along with controls for the highest education level achieved. We will begin by estimating a baseline linear specification, and then use the same controls in each of the subsequent regressions to illustrate the change in the estimates.

Part 1: Linear specification

The first specification we consider is a simple linear specification, where each variable is included either as a level, or as a dummy variable. As such, we will estimate:

$$Wages_i = \beta_0 + \beta_1 Tenure_i + \beta_2 Female_i + \beta_3 HE_i + \beta_4 ALevel_i + \beta_5 GCSE_i + \beta_6 Other_i \\ + \beta_7 None_i + u_i$$

- where: $Wages_i$ is the gross weekly wages of individual i in their main job, and $Tenure_i$ is the number of years of continuous employment;
- $Female_i$ is a dummy variable that takes the value 1 if individual i is female, and 0 otherwise;

Table 30.5 Summary statistics

	Gross weekly wage	Years of continuous employment
Mean	665.503	9.335
Standard deviation	345.565	9.256
Number of observations	1,000	1,000

- HE_i, $ALevel_i$, $GCSE_i$, $Other_i$, and $None_i$ are dummy variables to control for individual i's highest level of educational qualification. The omitted group is $Degree_i$, so the estimated coefficients will be comparisons with those with a degree. These are defined in more detail in Chapter 29.

However, as with previous examples, we will begin with a very parsimonious specification, and will add in additional explanatory variables, firstly with a control for the sex of the worker (the $Female_i$ dummy), and then with controls for the education level.

The results are presented in Table 30.6. When estimating specification (1), we gain an unconditional estimate of the marginal effect of tenure on gross weekly wages. This suggests that one extra year in continuous employment is associated with an increase in wages by £2.779 per week. We can see that this is statistically significant at the 5 per cent significance level (the t-statistic is 2.36).

Table 30.6 Results from a simple linear specification

	Specification (1)	Specification (2)	Specification (3)
Tenure	2.779**	2.520**	4.117***
	(1.179)	(1.143)	(1.059)
Female		−170.897***	−181.638***
		(21.144)	(19.419)
Some higher education			−201.276***
			(33.664)
A-levels			−216.803***
			(26.246)
GCSEs grade A*–C			−282.291***
			(27.710)
Other qualifications			−351.953***
			(41.476)
No qualifications			−446.499***
			(55.309)
Constant	639.565***	727.426***	866.645***
	(15.489)	(18.535)	(19.834)
Observations	1,000	1,000	1,000
R^2	0.0055	0.0667	0.226

Note: Dependent variable is gross weekly wage in main job. Estimated standard errors are in parentheses. *** indicates significant at 1% significance level, ** indicates significant at 5% significance level, * indicates significance at 10% significance level.

However, this is an unconditional measure, and is *at best* indicative of a statistically significant correlation. It is likely that there is omitted variables bias.[3] Specifications (2) and (3) try to remove some potential omitted variables bias, by controlling first for the sex of the worker, and then for the highest educational qualification achieved.

Whilst controlling for the sex of the worker makes little difference to the estimates (indicating that the sex of the worker is not correlated with the length of tenure), we do see a substantial change in the estimate when we control for the highest educational qualification. Controlling for the level of education, we see that a one-year increase in the years of continuous employment is associated with a £4.117 increase in gross weekly wages.

Of course, this isn't the full story, as we don't know whether a one-year increase is a large or a small change. One way of trying to interpret whether the effect is economically significant is to ask the following question:

> If we increase the explanatory variable by 1 standard deviation, by how many standard deviations does the dependent variable increase?

We know from Table 30.5 that the standard deviation of tenure is 9.256 years. Therefore, we will ask, given that $\hat{\beta}_1 = 4.117$, what is the impact of increasing tenure by 1 standard deviation, $\Delta Tenure = 9.256$?

$$\hat{\beta}_1 \times \Delta Tenure = 4.117 \times 9.256 = 38.107$$

We now compare this with the standard deviation of $Wages_i$, which again from Table 30.5 is equal to 345.565. Therefore, we can standardize the effect to say that a 1 standard deviation increase in tenure is associated with a $\frac{38.107}{345.565} = 0.110$ standard deviation increase in $Wages_i$. Relatively, this is quite small, when you consider that specification (3) suggests that female workers earn, on average, $-\frac{181.638}{345.565} = -0.526$ standard deviations less than male workers. The effect is not, however, trivially small.

So far we have just treated the variables as linear variables in the way that we have previously. It is not unlikely that there is a non-linear relationship between tenure and wages; individuals may expect to gain rapid advancement in the early years of a job, but salaries may be less likely to continue rising throughout a career. As such, we want to investigate some non-linear relationship between weekly wages and tenure.

Part 2: Semi-log specification (taking logs of the dependent variable)

Our first non-linear relationship using logarithms will be a semi-log specification, where we use the natural log of wages as the dependent variable (rather than just using wages). We saw earlier in the chapter that when we have a semi-log specification, the interpretation of the estimated coefficients changes. The estimated coefficient now becomes a proportional change in the dependent variable due to a one-unit increase in the explanatory variable.

[3] It is also likely that this estimate suffers from other sorts of bias, such as reverse causality. For example, it might be that the wages that an individual gains are a determinant of whether they are likely to regularly move firms. For example, an individual in a high paid job, with very high levels of skills, might be in high demand by other firms. As such, they might be more likely to move to another firm when they receive a good (external) offer.

Again, we will gradually build up the specifications from a very parsimonious specification with only tenure as an explanatory variable, and gradually add in controls for the sex of the worker, and the highest level of educational qualification:

$$\ln Wages_i = \beta_0 + \beta_1 Tenure_i + \beta_2 Female_i + \beta_3 HE_i + \beta_4 ALevel_i + \beta_5 GCSE_i + \beta_6 Other_i + \beta_7 None_i + u_i$$

The results are presented in Table 30.7. The most parsimonious specification produces an estimate of the marginal effect of tenure of $\hat{\beta}_1 = 0.0055$. This is statistically significant at the 1 per cent significance level (the t-statistic is equal to 3.24). It may be quite surprising, but the estimated coefficient has changed markedly when we use the natural log of the dependent variable, compared with when we used the level of gross weekly wages.

Interpretation of semi-log specifications

When we estimate a relationship:

$$\ln Y_i = \beta_0 + \beta_1 X_i + u_i$$

the β_1 can be interpreted as approximately a proportional change in Y_i due to a one-unit increase in X_i. So, for example, if $\beta_1 = 0.2$, this indicates that a one-unit increase in X_i is associated with a 20% increase in Y_i.

So, for example, Y_i might increase from 1 to 1.2, or from 5 to 6. These are both equivalent to 20% increases in Y_i.

This interpretation is only an approximation, and if β_1 or ΔX is large, then the approximation begins to break down. A better interpretation in those cases would be that the proportional change is equal to:

$$e^{\beta_1 \times \Delta X} - 1$$

However, this is also a biased interpretation.

The estimated $\hat{\beta}_1 = 0.0055$ in specification (1) indicates that a one-year increase in tenure is associated with a $0.0055 \times 100 = 0.55\%$ increase in earnings. Similarly, we can convert this into the effect of a 1 standard deviation increase in $Tenure_i$, $\Delta Tenure = 9.256$, to give us that, from specification (1), the estimated effect of a 1 standard deviation increase in Tenure is equivalent to:

$$\hat{\beta}_1 \times \Delta Tenure = 0.0055 \times 9.256 = 0.0509$$

That is, a proportional increase in wages of 0.0509. To convert this into a percentage, we can multiply by 100, giving us that a 1 standard deviation increase in tenure is associated with a 5.09 per cent increase in weekly wages.

However, we may be worried that specification (1) suffers from omitted variables bias. If we move to specification (3), where we have conditioned for the sex of the worker, and the

Table 30.7 Results from a semi-log specification, with the natural log of gross weekly wages as the dependent variable

	Specification (1)	Specification (2)	Specification (3)
Tenure	0.0055***	0.0050***	0.0075***
	(0.0017)	(0.0017)	(0.0015)
Female		−0.268***	−0.285***
		(0.031)	(0.028)
Some higher education			−0.302***
			(0.048)
A-levels			−0.309***
			(0.038)
GCSEs grade A*–C			−0.433***
			(0.040)
Other qualifications			−0.529***
			(0.060)
No qualifications			−0.711***
			(0.080)
Constant	6.325***	6.463***	6.671***
	(0.023)	(0.027)	0.029
Observations	1,000	1,000	1,000
R^2	0.0099	0.0802	0.2531

Note: Dependent variable is the natural log of the gross weekly wage in main job. Estimated standard errors are in parentheses. *** indicates significant at 1% significance level, ** indicates significant at 5% significance level, * indicates significance at 10% significance level.

highest educational qualification, we can see that $\hat{\beta}_1 = 0.0075$. I will leave it as an exercise for you to calculate the t-statistics, but you can also see that all of the explanatory variables are statistically significant. If we want to interpret the estimated coefficients in specification (3), remember that the estimated coefficient is approximately the proportional change in weekly wages due to a one-unit increase in the explanatory variable:

i. Tenure	$\hat{\beta}_1 = 0.0075$. This indicates that a one-year increase in tenure is associated with a $0.0075 \times 100 = 0.75\%$ increase in wages. If we convert this to a 1 standard deviation increase, $\Delta Tenure = 9.256$, this gives an estimate of $\hat{\beta}_1 \times \Delta Tenure = 0.0075 \times 9.256 = 0.069$. This is equivalent to a 6.9% increase in wages, due to a 1 standard deviation increase in tenure.

ii. Sex of worker	The omitted category here is *Male*$_i$, and so the coefficient is providing an estimate of female wages, compared with male wages. $\hat{\beta}_2 = -0.285$. Since *Female*$_i$ is a dummy variable, it can only change from 0 to 1. A simple way of interpreting this coefficient is that it tells you (approximately) the proportional difference between male and female wages. This suggests that, having controlled for tenure and educational qualifications, female full-time workers earn approximately 28.5% less than equivalent male workers. Because this is merely an approximation, a better interpretation might be to consider $\hat{e}^{\beta_2} - 1 = e^{-0.285} - 1 = -0.248$. That is, using the second interpretation, female workers earn approximately 24.8% less than male workers. Neither of these approximations are perfect interpretations, and both provide biased estimates. However, when $\hat{\beta}_2$ is small, the two approximations will provide good, and approximately equivalent, interpretations of the estimated coefficient.
iii. Highest education qualification	The omitted category is *Degree*$_i$, and so each of the coefficients is providing an estimate of the difference compared to an individual with a degree. We will not go through each of the estimates, but we will look at $\hat{\beta}_4 = -0.309$, relating to gaining A-levels as the highest qualification. A naïve interpretation would be that having A-levels (only) would be associated with a 30.9% reduction in wages compared with having a degree. However, we might be a little more precise by considering: $e^{-0.309} - 1 = -0.266$ In other words, the estimated effect is approximately to reduce earnings by 26.6%.

Part 3: Semi-log specifications (taking logs of the explanatory variable)

We will now examine what happens when we take logs of the explanatory variable(s). The first thing to note is that we can only take logs of the $Tenure_i$ variable, as all of the other explanatory variables are dummy variables. Since the (natural) log of zero does not exist, we cannot take natural logs of the dummy variables (which only take the values 0 and 1).

The coefficients with a specification with a log only on the right-hand side are a little more difficult to interpret, as they represent the impact on the dependent variable, due to a proportional increase in the explanatory variable.

Again, we will gradually build up the specifications from a very parsimonious specification with only tenure as an explanatory variable, and gradually add in controls for the sex of the worker, and the highest level of educational qualification:

$$Wages_i = \beta_0 + \beta_1 \ln Tenure_i + \beta_2 Female_i + \beta_3 HE_i + \beta_4 ALevel_i + \beta_5 GCSE_i + \beta_6 Other_i + \beta_7 None_i + u_i$$

The results are presented in Table 30.8. The most parsimonious produces an estimate of the marginal effect of tenure of $\hat{\beta}_1 = 22.210$. This is statistically significant at the 1 per cent significance level (the t-statistic is equal to 2.77). Again, having moved to this slightly different specification, our estimated coefficient has changed significantly.

Table 30.8 Results from a semi-log specification, with the natural log of tenure as an explanatory variable and gross weekly wages as the dependent variable

	Specification (1)	Specification (2)	Specification (3)
Natural log of tenure	22.210***	18.861**	26.511***
	(8.008)	(7.777)	(7.185)
Female		−169.444***	−180.045***
		(21.155)	(19.456)
Some higher education			−196.830***
			(33.567)
A-levels			−215.943***
			(26.259)
GCSEs grade A*–C			−277.995***
			(27.629)
Other qualifications			−348.053***
			(41.510)
No qualifications			−447.947***
			(55.381)
Constant	630.356***	720.377***	860.582***
	(16.710)	(19.721)	(20.884)
Observations	1,000	1,000	1,000
R^2	0.0099	0.0676	0.2253

Note: Dependent variable is the gross weekly wage in main job. Estimated standard errors are in parentheses. *** indicates significant at 1% significance level, ** indicates significant at 5% significance level, * indicates significance at 10% significance level.

Interpretation of specifications with logs on the right-hand side only

When we estimate a relationship:

$$Y_i = \beta_0 + \beta_1 \ln X_i + u_i$$

the β_1 can be interpreted as approximately the change in Y_i due to a proportional increase in X_i. This is often very confusing, so let's consider a couple of examples.

Suppose that $\beta_1 = 20$. This indicates that if X_i increases by 100% (i.e. a proportional change, $\frac{\Delta X}{X} = 1$), then Y_i would increase by 20. However, it is rare that we would want to know the impact of a 100% increase:

- If X increases by 20%, that is $\frac{\Delta X}{X} = 0.2$, then $\beta_1 \times \frac{\Delta X}{X} = 20 \times 0.2 = 4$. If $\beta_1 = 20$, then a 20% increase in X is associated with a 4 unit increase in Y.
- If X increases by 50%, then $\beta_1 \times \frac{\Delta X}{X} = 20 \times 0.5 = 10$. That is, a 50% increase in X is associated with a 10 unit increase in Y.

This leaves the question of what a reasonable, proportional increase in X is. You might consider the ratio of the standard deviation divided by the average of X. In the case of $Tenure_i$, the mean and standard deviation are approximately equal to 9. Thus a reasonable change (1 standard deviation) would be (approximately) equivalent to increasing an observation from the mean by 100%.

However, if $\overline{X} = 100$ and $s.d.(X) = 2$, then it might only be appropriate to consider a $\frac{2}{100} = 0.02$ or 2% increase in X.

All of the coefficients are statistically significant at the 5 per cent significance level (you can check this by calculating the t-statistic, and comparing with the critical values from the t-distribution).

- In specification (1), $\hat{\beta}_1 = 22.210$, indicating that a 100 per cent increase in $Tenure_i$ is associated with a $22.210 \times 1 =$ £22.210 increase in weekly wages. The standard deviation of gross weekly wages is 345.565, so this indicates that a 100 per cent increase in tenure is associated with a $\frac{22.210}{345.565} = 0.064$ standard deviation increase in gross weekly wages (or 6.4 per cent of a standard deviation).

Specifications (2) and (3) introduce dummy variables to control for the sex of the worker, and the highest educational qualification. Because these we do not take logs, these can be interpreted as in the linear case; that is, in specification (3), $\hat{\beta}_2 = -180.045$ indicates that, having controlled for tenure and highest educational qualification, female workers earn £180.045 less than male workers.

What we are really interested in is the conditional estimate of the impact of the natural log of tenure on gross weekly wages, having controlled for the sex and the highest educational qualification of the worker (specification (3)).

- $\hat{\beta}_1 = 26.511$ indicates that a 100 per cent increase in tenure is associated with approximately a £26.511 increase in gross weekly wages.
- Similarly, a 200 per cent increase in tenure is associated with approximately a $26.511 \times 2 =$ £53.022 increase in gross weekly wages.
- Similarly again, a 50 per cent increase in tenure is associated with approximately a $26.511 \times 0.5 =$ £13.2555 increase in gross weekly wages.

Part 4: Log-log specifications

The final type of specification we will consider including logs is a log-log specification. That is, we will take logs on both the left- and right-hand side. As in part 3, it is not possible to take logs of dummy variables, so we will include the dummy variables as levels as before.

We will estimate the following relationship, again beginning with a very parsimonious specification, and gradually add in additional controls:

$$\ln Wages_i = \beta_0 + \beta_1 \ln Tenure_i + \beta_2 Female_i + \beta_3 HE_i + \beta_4 ALevel_i + \beta_5 GCSE_i + \beta_6 Other_i + \beta_7 None_i + u_i$$

The results are presented in Table 30.9. All of the estimated coefficients are statistically significant at the 1 per cent significance level. (It would be a good exercise for you to check this by calculating the t-statistics.) Where we have included dummy variables, the interpretation is exactly the same as in part 2, as the dummy variables are included in the regression as levels, whilst the dependent variable is in logs. That means that we

Table 30.9 Results from a log-log specification

	Specification (1)	Specification (2)	Specification (3)
Natural log of tenure	0.041***	0.036***	0.048***
	(0.012)	(0.011)	(0.010)
Female		-0.266***	-0.282***
		(0.031)	(0.028)
Some higher education			-0.293***
			(0.048)
A-levels			-0.307***
			(0.038)
GCSEs grade A*–C			-0.425***
			(0.040)
Other qualifications			-0.522***
			(0.060)
No qualifications			-0.714***
			(0.080)
Constant	6.311***	6.452***	6.661***
	(0.024)	(0.029)	(0.080)
Observations	1,000	1,000	1,000
R^2	0.0124	0.0811	0.030

Note: Dependent variable is the natural log of gross weekly wage in main job. Estimated standard errors are in parentheses. *** indicates significant at 1% significance level, ** indicates significant at 5% significance level, * indicates significance at 10% significance level.

can consider (from specification (3)), a naïve interpretation that female earnings are approximately 28 per cent less than male earnings (having controlled for tenure and highest educational qualification).

Interpretation of log-log specifications

When we estimate a relationship:

$$\ln Y_i = \beta_0 + \beta_1 \ln X_i + u_i$$

the β_1 can be interpreted as an elasticity. That is, we can interpret β_1 as:

$$\beta_1 = \frac{\text{Percentage change in } Y}{\text{Percentage change in } X} = \frac{X}{Y}\frac{\partial Y}{\partial X}$$

Suppose that $\beta_1 = 0.2$. This indicates that if X_i increases by 1%, then Y_i would increase by 0.2%. Often relationships, such as supply and demand curves, are estimated to represent an elasticity.

So, in specifications (1) to (3), the estimated $\hat{\beta}_1$ is an estimate of the elasticity of gross weekly wages with relation to tenure.

- In specification (1), the estimated elasticity is $\hat{\beta}_1 = 0.041$, indicating that a 1 per cent increase in tenure is associated with a 0.041 per cent increase in gross weekly wages. Similarly, a 100 per cent increase in tenure is associated with a $0.041 \times 100 = 4.1$ per cent increase in wages.

I will leave it as an exercise for you to interpret the other coefficients.

Which specification is preferred?

Of course, we have used four different routes to estimate the impact of tenure on gross weekly wages, but we haven't discussed which is the most appropriate specification. Fundamentally, you will need to appeal to economic theory to determine which specification is most appropriate.

There are tests that help you evaluate whether a specification is appropriate (or not); for example, if you estimate a linear relationship (i.e. specification (1)), you could use a test known as the Ramsay RESET test to test whether a non-linear relationship is more appropriate.[4]

However, the tests themselves are not magic. The first step in determining the appropriate specification is to use core theory. Would you expect a linear relationship between tenure and gross weekly wage and earnings? If you have a linear relationship, then it would suggest that every additional year of tenure has the same effect as the previous year; this is probably unlikely. Probably, an elasticity is more appropriate.

[4] The mechanics of this test are beyond the scope of this book, but specialist statistical software such as R or Stata will be able to calculate this for you.

Similarly, when we have the absolute values of gross weekly wage as the dependent variable and a female dummy variable as an explanatory variable, this suggests that females earn a constant amount less than males (on average), irrespective of where you are in the earning distribution. If there were discrimination in terms of pay, you might expect this to be proportional, rather than an absolute difference. As such, a log specification may be more appropriate.

Summary: Estimating relationship using logarithms

We have seen three different types of specifications using natural logarithms. It is important to understand how you interpret the coefficients in each case. Mathematical derivations of these interpretations are set out in the appendix to this chapter.

	Semi-log specification (1)	Semi-log specification (2)	Log-log specification
	$\ln Y_i = \alpha_0 + \alpha_1 X_i + u_i$	$Y_i = \beta_0 + \beta_1 \ln X_i + e_i$	$\ln Y_i = \gamma_0 + \gamma_1 \ln X_i + \varepsilon_i$
Interpretation	α_1 is the proportional change in Y due to a 1 unit increase in X. We can convert that proportional change into a percentage change by multiplying by 100. **Example:** If $\alpha_1 = 0.4$, then if X increases by 1, Y would increase by 40%.	β_1 is the (linear) impact of a proportional change in X. **Example:** If $\beta_1 = 4$, then if X increases by 10% (which is equivalent to increasing by one tenth (a factor of 0.1), Y would increase by 0.4.	γ_1 is an elasticity. That is, γ_1 is the percentage change in Y due to a 1% increase in X. **Example:** If $\gamma_1 = 0.5$, then a 1% increase in X (e.g. from 100 to 101, or from 200 to 202) is associated with a 0.5% increase in Y.
Additional notes	This relationship can only be estimated when Y_i takes on positive (non-zero) values.	This relationship can only be estimated when X_i takes on positive (non-zero) values. It cannot be estimated when X_i is a dummy variable.	This relationship can only be estimated if both X and Y are positive and non-zero.

Summary

In this chapter, we have introduced two key ways of estimating non-linear relationships using OLS. The first was using polynomials of the explanatory variable, whilst the second involved logarithms.

The key learning outcome for this chapter is to be able to interpret relationships that use these sorts of non-linear tricks when presented within published research, but you may also need to estimate relationships yourself.

Non-linear specifications using polynomials are very powerful, as by using increasing powers of X they can represent different underlying relationships in different areas of the data. However, this is also a weakness of the approach: as you increase the number of powers, you automatically reduce the number of degrees of freedom, leading to the danger of overfitting your relationship to the data.

Similarly, logs are very useful when you believe that the relationship between variables is linked to proportional changes. However, if the relationship is more complicated, logs may not have enough versatility to reflect changes in the marginal effects.

Appendix: Deriving the interpretation of coefficients in logarithmic specifications

Before we dive into deriving the interpretation of coefficients, we need to revise the chain rule of differentiation. We will use the chain rule to evaluate the impact of a marginal change in X on Y when we have logarithms included.

Revision of mathematical techniques—The chain rule

To interpret the impact of a change in the explanatory variable in relationships using logarithms, it is mathematically useful to appeal to the chain rule.

If we have a relationship that is a function (f) of a function (g) of a variable x, then, if we wish to differentiate this relationship with relation to x:

$$\frac{d}{dx}[f(g(x))]$$

Then this derivative is equivalent to the two stage process of:

1. Differentiate $f(g(x))$ with respect to $g(x)$.
2. Multiply this derivative by the derivative of $g(x)$ with respect to x.

So, that means that the overall derivative can be written as:

$$\frac{d}{dx}[f(g(x))] = \frac{df(g(x))}{dg(x)} \times \frac{dg(x)}{d(x)}$$

Sometimes, you might see this written as:

$$\frac{d}{dx}[f(g(x))] = f'(g(x)) \times g'(x)$$

So, if we are trying to differentiate the following expression:

$$\ln Y_i = \beta_0 + \beta_1 X_i + u_i$$

then, differentiating the expression with respect to X_i would give us:

$$\frac{\partial \ln Y_i}{\partial X_i} = \beta_1$$

However, we are really interested in the left-hand side, as Y is a function of X, and we have applied a function to Y (by taking logs). As such, we can use the chain rule to rewrite the derivative as:

$$\frac{\partial \ln Y_i}{\partial Y_i} \times \frac{\partial Y_i}{\partial X_i} = \beta_1$$

That is, we can differentiate the $\ln Y_i$ term with respect to Y_i, and then multiply by the derivative of Y with respect to X_i.

In other words, we can rewrite the initial derivative as:

$$\frac{\partial \ln Y_i}{\partial X_i} = \frac{\partial \ln Y_i}{\partial Y_i} \times \frac{\partial Y_i}{\partial X_i} = \beta_1$$

This helps us, because $\frac{\partial \ln Y_i}{\partial Y_i} = \frac{1}{Y_i}$, so we can interpret β_1 in terms of rates of change of Y with respect to X:

$$\Rightarrow \frac{1}{Y_i} \times \frac{\partial Y_i}{\partial X_i} = \beta_1$$

Taking logs of the dependent variable

If we are estimating:

$$\ln Y_i = \alpha_0 + \alpha_1 X_i + u_i$$

to interpret the slope coefficient, we need to think about marginal effects of a change in X on Y.

It is trivial to show that the marginal effect of a change in X on $\ln Y$ is equal to α_1. That is, if we differentiate the relationship with relation to X, then:

$$\frac{\partial \ln Y}{\partial X} = \alpha_1$$

However, this is not really interesting, as this is telling us the rate of change of X on the log of Y, but what we are interested in is the impact of a change in X on Y.

So, we need to use the chain rule to rewrite $\frac{\partial \ln Y}{\partial X}$ as a function of $\frac{\partial Y}{\partial X}$.

$$\frac{\partial \ln Y}{\partial X} = \alpha_1 \Rightarrow \frac{\partial \ln Y}{\partial Y}\frac{\partial Y}{\partial X} = \alpha_1$$

That is, if we wish to differentiate $\ln Y$ with respect to X, we can first differentiate $\ln Y$ with respect to Y, and then multiply by the derivative of Y with respect to X. However, $\frac{\partial \ln Y}{\partial Y} = \frac{1}{Y}$, so we can rewrite this as:

$$\frac{1}{Y}\frac{\partial Y}{\partial X} = \alpha_1$$

Remember, we denote a change in Y as ΔY (delta Y), and a change in X as ΔX. The derivative is just defined as the limit of $\frac{\Delta Y}{\Delta X}$ as ΔX tends towards zero:

$$\frac{dY}{dX} = \lim_{\Delta X \to 0} \frac{\Delta Y}{\Delta X}$$

and similarly, if we are holding everything else constant, then:

$$\frac{\partial Y}{\partial X} = \lim_{\Delta X \to 0} \frac{\Delta Y}{\Delta X} |\textit{Holding everything else constant}$$

Since we know that $\frac{1}{Y}\frac{\partial Y}{\partial X} = \alpha_1$, we can convert the ∂Y and ∂X into ΔY and ΔX to represent the changes in X and Y. The relationship we will write down will not be an exact relationship, because the relationship between X and Y is non-linear; as such:

$$\frac{1}{Y}\frac{\Delta Y}{\Delta X} \cong \alpha_1$$

Multiplying left and right by ΔX gives us:

$$\frac{\Delta Y}{Y} = \alpha_1 \Delta X$$

- $\frac{\Delta Y}{Y}$ is just the proportional change in Y
- ΔX is the absolute change in X

So, α_1 can be interpreted as the proportional change in Y due to a one-unit increase in X (i.e. if $\Delta X = 1$). So, if $\alpha_1 = 0.4$, this indicates that a one-unit increase in X would be associated with a 40 per cent increase in Y.

Taking logs of the explanatory variable

If we are estimating:

$$Y_i = \beta_0 + \beta_1 \ln X_i + u_i$$

to interpret the slope coefficient, we need to think about marginal effects of a change in X on Y.

It is trivial to show that the marginal effect of a change in $\ln X$ on Y is equal to β_1. That is, if we differentiate the relationship with relation to $\ln X$, then:

$$\frac{\partial Y}{\partial \ln X} = \beta_1$$

However, this is not really interesting, as this is telling us the rate of change of the log of X on Y, but what we are interested in is the impact of a change in X on Y.

So, we need to use the chain rule to rewrite $\frac{\partial Y}{\partial \ln X}$ as a function of $\frac{\partial Y}{\partial X}$:

$$\frac{\partial Y}{\partial \ln X} = \beta_1 \Rightarrow \frac{\partial Y}{\partial X}\frac{\partial X}{\partial \ln X} = \beta_1$$

That is, if we want to differentiate Y with relation to $\ln X$, this is the same as differentiating Y first with relation to X, and then multiplying that by the derivative of X with respect to $\ln X$. However, $\frac{\partial X}{\partial \ln X} = \frac{1}{\partial \ln X / \partial X}$. We know that the derivative of the natural log of X is just equal to $\frac{1}{X}$ and so $\frac{\partial X}{\partial \ln X} = X$. Therefore, we can rewrite the marginal effect as:

$$\beta_1 = \frac{\partial Y}{\partial X} X$$

Remember, we denote a change in Y as ΔY (delta Y), and a change in X as ΔX. The derivative is just defined as the limit of $\frac{\Delta Y}{\Delta X}$ as ΔX tends towards zero:

$$\frac{dY}{dX} = \lim_{\Delta X \to 0} \frac{\Delta Y}{\Delta X}$$

and similarly, if we are holding everything else constant, then:

$$\frac{\partial Y}{\partial X} = \lim_{\Delta X \to 0} \frac{\Delta Y}{\Delta X} \,|\, \textit{Holding everything else constant}$$

Since we know that $X\frac{\partial Y}{\partial X} = \beta_1$, we can convert the ∂Y and ∂X into ΔY and ΔX to represent the changes in X and Y. The relationship we will write down will not be an exact relationship, because the relationship between X and Y is non-linear; as such:

$$\beta_1 \cong X\frac{\Delta Y}{\Delta X} \Rightarrow \beta_1 \frac{\Delta X}{X} = \Delta Y$$

- $\frac{\Delta X}{X}$ is just the proportional change in X
- ΔY is the absolute change in Y

That is, if X were to increase by 10 per cent (i.e. $\frac{\Delta X}{X} = 0.1$), and β_1 were equal to 4, that would indicate that Y would increase by (approximately) 0.4.

Taking logs of both the dependent and explanatory variables

If we are estimating:

$$\ln Y_i = \gamma_0 + \gamma_1 \ln X_i + \varepsilon_i$$

to interpret the slope coefficient, we need to think about marginal effects of a change in X on Y.

It is trivial to show that the marginal effect of a change in $\ln X$ on $\ln Y$ is equal to γ_1. That is, if we differentiate the relationship with relation to $\ln X$, then:

$$\frac{\partial \ln Y}{\partial \ln X} = \gamma_1$$

However, this is not really interesting, as this is telling us the rate of change of the log of X on the log of Y, but what we are interested in is the impact of a change in X on Y.

So, we need to use the chain rule to rewrite $\frac{\partial \ln Y}{\partial \ln X}$ as a function of $\frac{\partial Y}{\partial X}$. This is a little more complicated than the previous cases, but we can use the same steps. First of all, we can split $\frac{\partial \ln Y}{\partial \ln X}$ into two (partial) derivatives multiplied together:

$$\frac{\partial \ln Y}{\partial \ln X} = \frac{\partial \ln Y}{\partial Y}\frac{\partial Y}{\partial \ln X}$$

Intuitively, we can see that these expressions are equal, as we can think of the ∂Y terms as cancelling out. However, this still does not involve the rate of change of Y with relation to X. As such, we'll use the same trick with the second element to give us:

$$\frac{\partial \ln Y}{\partial \ln X} = \frac{\partial \ln Y}{\partial Y}\frac{\partial Y}{\partial X}\frac{\partial X}{\partial \ln X} = \gamma_1$$

We know that $\frac{\partial \ln Y}{\partial Y} = \frac{1}{Y}$ and that $\frac{\partial X}{\partial \ln X} = X$, and so, we can rewrite this as:

$$\frac{\partial \ln Y}{\partial \ln X} = \frac{X}{Y}\frac{\partial Y}{\partial X} = \gamma_1$$

You may already recognize $\frac{X}{Y}\frac{\partial Y}{\partial X}$ as an elasticity (i.e. the percentage change in Y due to a 1 per cent increase in X), but we can show this by using the trick we used in the previous two cases; that is, converting our ∂Y and ∂X into changes in X and Y:

$$\frac{X}{Y}\frac{\Delta Y}{\Delta X} = \gamma_1 \Rightarrow \frac{\Delta Y}{Y} = \gamma_1$$

$\frac{\Delta Y}{Y}$ is the proportional change in Y, and $\frac{\Delta X}{X}$ is the proportional change in X, so if we were to multiply these by 100, we would convert these into percentages (e.g. if X increases proportionally by 0.1, this is equivalent to a 10 per cent increase in X).

As such, we can see that a 1 per cent increase in X would be associated with a γ_1 per cent increase in Y. If γ_1 is equal to 0.3, then we could say that a 1 per cent increase in X is associated with a 0.3 per cent increase in Y.

In a log-log specification, the estimated coefficient is an elasticity.

Causality and Estimating Causal Relationships

31

Learning outcomes for this chapter

At the end of this chapter, students will be able to:

- Understand that whenever the error term is correlated with an explanatory variable, results from OLS will not be causal, and be able to identify sources of endogeneity
- Recognize identification strategies that are used in empirical research—including natural experiments, RDD, twin studies, difference in differences—and identify potential problems with those strategies.

Mathematical tools

- None required, but summation algebra is needed to interpret the appendices

Introduction

Econometrics is interesting in estimating **causal relationships** between economic variables. For example, if we increase interest rates, what is the impact of this change on inflation? If someone stays in school for an extra year, what is the effect on their earnings? If you increase spending on healthcare, what effect does this have on life expectancy? We introduced the **ordinary least squares (OLS) estimator** as a way of trying to estimate these sorts of relationships, but OLS only produces causal estimates of the impact of (a change in) one economic variable on another under very strong assumptions.

In this chapter, we will introduce the idea of causal relationships, and discuss some of the reasons why we may fail to obtain causal estimates. We will then briefly discuss the principles that lie behind some common identification strategies that can be used to try to obtain causal estimates, and discuss where weaknesses exist with those strategies.

The key aim of this chapter is to provide you with the toolkit to be able to understand why researchers have used particular methodologies to identify the (causal) impact of a policy change. We do not go into much detail about how to estimate these models based upon data, but the intuition developed will allow you to critique and evaluate research which tries to estimate causal relationships.

31.1 Examples of relationships which are not causal

The ultimate goal of empirical economists is to evaluate causal relationships between economic variables. In order for us to estimate causal relationships using OLS, it needs to be the case that the explanatory variable(s) are exogenous. So, for example, if we were to try to estimate the following relationship using OLS:

$$Y_i = \beta_0 + \beta_1 X_i + \beta_2 W_i + \beta_3 Z_i + u_i$$

then the OLS estimator for β_1 will provide causal estimates of the marginal impact of a change in X on Y if $E(u \mid \{X, W, Z\}) = 0$. That is, if the error term, u, is unrelated to any of the explanatory variables, X, W, Z, then the estimated $\hat{\beta}_1^{OLS}$ will provide unbiased estimates of the marginal effect of a change X on Y.

However, because we often rely on observational data, explanatory variables are often endogenous. Remember, if an explanatory variable is endogenous—that is, it is correlated with the error term—OLS will yield biased and inconsistent estimates of the marginal effect of a change in the explanatory variable on the dependent variable. Whenever this happens we can say that the results we obtain are not causal.

In reality, when we estimate relationships based upon observational data, the exogeneity assumption is often violated. When we use OLS as an estimator, in essence, we are only measuring a correlation between two variables. OLS on its own cannot tell us whether the results are causal or mere correlations.

Within this book, we've seen details of violations of this assumption through:

- omitted variables bias
- measurement error
- selection bias
- model mis-specification.

However, there are many more reasons that we could fail to gain causal estimates. For example, it could be the case that we have effectively estimated the wrong relationship. If we try to estimate a relationship with Y as our dependent variable and X as our explanatory variable—that is, we try to estimate

$$Y_i = \beta_0 + \beta_1 X_i + u_i$$

—but in reality, the direction of causation is that Y causes X, OLS would still probably find a statistically significant relationship between X and Y. Remember, just because you find a statistically significant correlation, this does not mean that there is a causal relationship. Correlation does not mean causation.

Because OLS alone cannot tell us whether the relationship that we have estimated is causal (or not), we need to know about the possible threats to causality. We have already discussed a number of threats, including omitted variables bias and measurement error, and we will now introduce two further threats, through reverse causality and simultaneity. These threats to causality sound very similar, but have subtle differences between them.

31.1.1 **Reverse causality**

Reverse causality is where the true direction of causality runs in the opposite direction to the direction that we are estimating (see Figure 31.1).

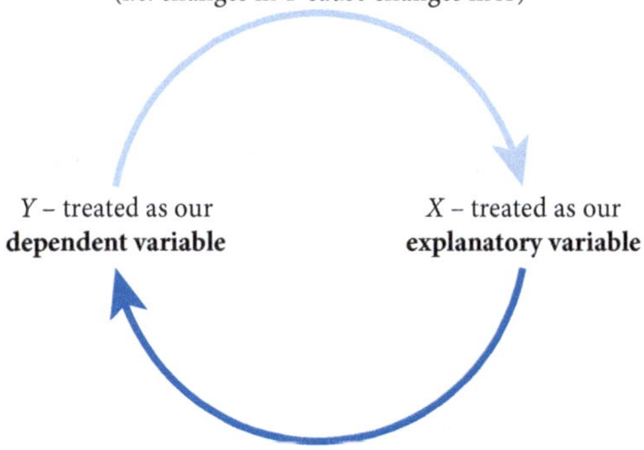

Figure 31.1 Reverse causality.

So, for example, we might have a prior that the level of debt taken on within a country may be related to economic growth. The rationale for this belief might be that as government borrowing increases, the likelihood of defaults would also increase, leading to investors requiring higher returns to lend money. This would mean that the government could less easily borrow money, so it may have to cut expenditure, leading to a contraction in the economy.

As such, we might try to estimate the following relationship:

$$growth_i = \beta_0 + \beta_1 debt_i + u_i$$

where $growth_i$ is the growth rate of country i, and $debt_i$ is the level of debt held by country i. If we were to estimate this relationship, we would likely find a negative relationship.

To illustrate this, I have collected data from the OECD[1] on countries' debt and nominal GDP, and constructed a data set, illustrating the growth in nominal GDP and the government debt (as a proportion of GDP). This is illustrated in Figure 31.2. The fitted line shows a negative relationship between growth and GDP.

Government debt is often reported as a percentage of GDP, as this gives the opportunity to compare the affordability of the debt across countries:

$$\text{Debt as a percentage of GDP} = \frac{\text{Stock of debt (\$)}}{\text{Nominal GDP (\$)}} \times 100$$

As such, there are two main ways for a government to decrease its debt. Firstly, it could reduce the stock of debt (i.e. the amount that it owes, in real terms, by running government

[1] OECD (2022), Gross domestic product (GDP) (indicator), doi: 10.1787/dc2f7aec-en (accessed 5 December 2022). OECD (2022), General government debt (indicator), doi: 10.1787/a0528cc2-en (accessed 5 December 2022).

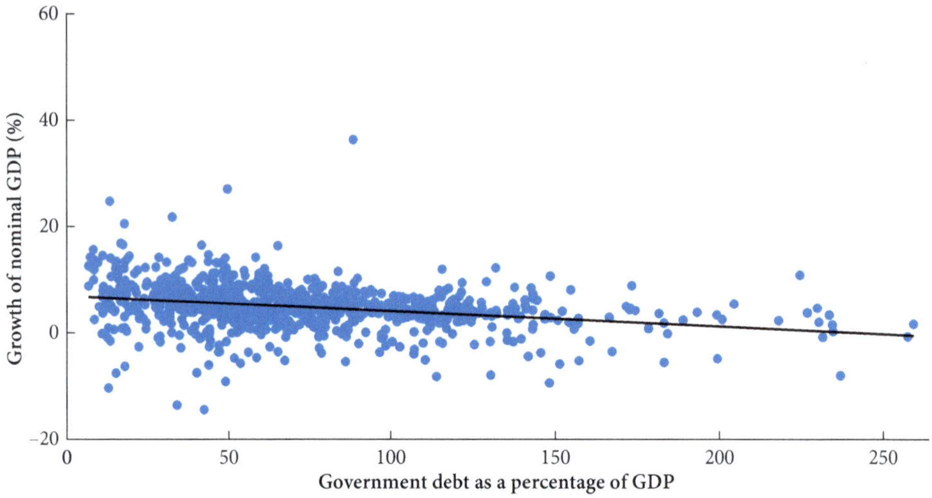

Figure 31.2 Growth in nominal GDP vs government debt.

surpluses). Secondly, because debt is reported as a percentage of GDP, it could stimulate growth, leading to nominal GDP increasing, and the debt falling as a percentage of GDP. Similarly, where growth is negative (i.e. the economy is contracting), or growth is low (less than the growth of debt), we would expect to see debt as a percentage of GDP increasing.

That is, if growth is low (e.g. negative growth), we could expect to see debt being **high** as a percentage of GDP. So, rather than high debt causing low growth, it could be that low growth causes high debt. That is, our initial specification may have been backwards! In other words, the true data generating process may look as follows:

$$debt_i = \alpha_0 + \alpha_1 growth_i + e_i$$

Where we mis-specify the relationship this way (i.e. having the dependent variable and the explanatory variable the wrong way round), the estimated effects will not be causal. However, if there is a strong significant relationship in the true causal direction, we would expect to see a statistically significant relationship when we estimate the relationship the 'wrong way around'. That is, in our example, if the true direction of causation is that low levels of growth cause high levels of debt, and there is a strong significant relationship, then we would equally expect to find a statistically significant relationship when we use growth as the dependent variable and debt as the explanatory variable.

Remember, correlation is not the same as causation, and just because you find a statistically significant result does not mean that there is a causal relationship between economic variables!

31.1.2 Simultaneity

The second case we can consider here is simultaneity. Simultaneity is where two economic variables cause each other in both directions. In the example in Section 31.1.1, it is possible

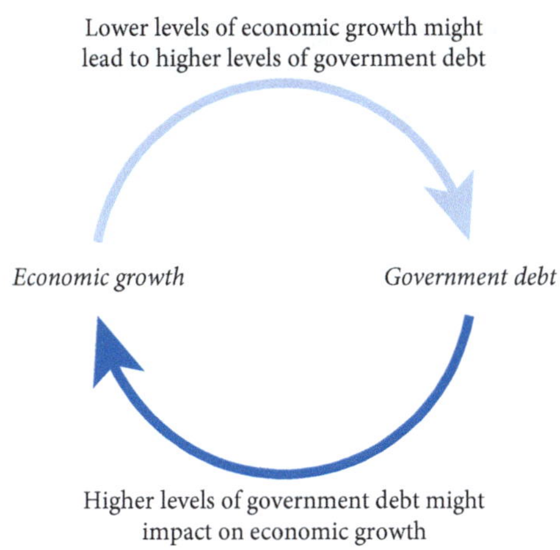

Figure 31.3 A possible example of simultaneity.

that low levels of economic growth could cause high levels of debt, and for high levels of debt to cause reductions in economic growth. That is, in reality, observations of $debt_i$ and $growth_i$ might be simultaneously determined by a pair of data generating processes:

$$growth_i = \beta_0 + \beta_1 debt_i + u_i \quad (1)$$
$$debt_i = \alpha_0 + \alpha_1 growth_i + e_i \quad (2)$$

In the case of variables which are simultaneously determined, we cannot gain causal estimates of either (1) or (2) by simple OLS. Simultaneity is illustrated in Figure 31.3.

31.1.3 Summary of threats to causality

Suppose that we are interested in estimating the relationship:

$$Y_i = \beta_0 + \beta_1 X_i + u_i \quad (A)$$

Then there are a number of reasons that OLS could yield biased and/or inconsistent estimates of the marginal effect of X on Y. In all of the following cases, suppose that we try to estimate (A) using OLS. In each of the cases, the estimated $\hat{\beta}_1^{OLS}$ will be biased and inconsistent. This list is not exhaustive, but provides you with an intuition for when results are unlikely to be causal.

We have already gone through the maths relating to omitted variables bias and measurement error in previous chapters. The maths for reverse causality and simultaneity is discussed in the appendix to this chapter, but I would encourage you to have a go at solving for these values. That being said, the key learning objective is to notice that, when estimating $Y_i = \beta_0 + \beta_1 X_i + u_i$, by design, it must be the case for both reverse causality and simultaneity that $cov(X,u) \neq 0$, and as such, OLS will produce biased and inconsistent results.

In all of the cases shown, if we tried to estimate the relationship using OLS, we would fail to obtain causal results. There are very many threats to our ability to gain causal results, and these are just a selection of possible threats.

Type of bias	Description
Omitted variables bias	There are determinant(s) of Y_i that are omitted from the model, which are correlated with the explanatory variable, X. For example, if the true data generating process is $Y_i = \beta_0 + \beta_1 X_i + \beta_2 Z_i + e_i$ assuming that $cov(Z,e) = 0$, if we try to estimate (A) using OLS, then the results will be biased and inconsistent, with the bias in large samples equal to: $\text{Bias} = \frac{\beta_2 cov(X,Z)}{var(X)}$ More generally, since the u_i term contains all of the determinants of Y_i other than X_i, the bias in large samples can be written as: $\text{Bias} = \frac{cov(u,X)}{var(X)}$
Measurement error in the explanatory variable	Suppose that rather than observing the true value of X_i, we observe $\tilde{X}_i = X_i + \varepsilon_i$, where ε_i is a random measurement error term, such that $cov(X,\varepsilon) = cov(u,\varepsilon) = 0$. If X is an exogenous variable $(cov(X,u) = 0)$, and we try to estimate (A) using our mis-measured observations $\tilde{X}_i$ as the explanatory variable, then in large samples: $plim(\hat{\beta}_1) = \beta_1 \left[\frac{var(X)}{var(X) + var(\varepsilon)}\right]$ Since $var(X) + var(\varepsilon) > var(X)$, it follows that $\hat{\beta}_1$ will be biased towards zero.
Non-random measurement error in the dependent variable	Suppose that, rather than observing the true value of Y_i, we observe $\tilde{Y}_i = Y_i + e_i$ where $cov(e_i, X_i) \neq 0$. If X is exogenous $(cov(X,u) = 0)$, and we try to estimate (A) using our mis-measured observations of the dependent variable, $\tilde{Y}_i$, then in large samples: $plim(\hat{\beta}_1) = \beta_1 + \frac{cov(X,e)}{var(X)}$ That is, the bias in large samples will be $\frac{cov(X,e)}{var(X)}$
Reverse causality	The true direction of causality is that Y causes X. That is, the true relationship between Y and X is: $X_i = \alpha_0 + \alpha_1 Y_i + e_i$ X is not a determinant of Y (i.e. the true value of $\beta_1 = 0$). If $\alpha_1 \neq 0$, then OLS will yield biased estimates of the marginal effect of a change in X on Y. The bias in large samples is given by $\text{Bias} = \frac{\alpha_1 var(Y) + cov(e,Y)}{\alpha_1^2 var(Y) + var(e) + 2\alpha_1 cov(Y,e)}$
Simultaneity	Causality works in both directions. That is, Y causes X, and X causes Y. $Y_i = \beta_0 + \beta_1 X_i + u_i \quad (A)$ $X_i = \alpha_0 + \alpha_1 Y_i + e_i \quad (B)$ With simultaneity, $\beta_1 \neq 0$ and $\alpha_1 \neq 0$ in the data generating process. The bias, in large samples, from estimating (A) using OLS is given by: $plim(\hat{\beta}_1) - \beta_1 = (1 - \alpha_1\beta_1)\frac{(\alpha_1 var(u) + cov(e,u))}{(\alpha_1^2 var(u) + var(e) + 2\alpha_1 cov(u,e))}$

31.2 Potential solutions to endogeneity—Identification strategies

In the previous section, we have explored a range of possible threats to obtaining causal estimates of the relationship between economic variables. When estimating a relationship between economic variables, it is always important to begin by thinking about these threats to causality. These threats are known as identification problems. That is, they are problems which create difficulties in identifying the causal effect of one economic variable on another.

In medical trials, treatments are randomly assigned to individuals, with non-treated individuals receiving a placebo. Provided your sample size is large enough, by randomly assigning individuals, you ensure that the other factors that are likely to be determinants of the outcome variable are unrelated to the treatment. For example, suppose you are testing a treatment for the cold virus. Some individuals may have naturally strong immune systems that means they always recover from colds quickly, whilst others may take longer. If the treatment were only offered to those with strong immune systems, then it would appear that the drug was associated with a faster recovery time from a cold. By randomly assigning individuals, we ensure that there is no systematic relationship between the treatment and the individual characteristics. In a well-designed experiment, those with naturally fast recovery times would be equally likely to receive the treatment as those with naturally slow recovery times. In terms of the mathematical language of econometrics, we could define recovery time as Y_i, assignment for treatment as X_i, and the data generating process:

$$Y_i = \beta_0 + \beta_1 X_i + u_i$$

If individuals are randomly assigned to the treatment, then, by design, $cov(X,u) = 0$; that is, the treatment is uncorrelated with the other determinants of recovery time.

However, in economics, we often try to evaluate economic relationships based upon observational data, rather than experiments. Because of this, it regularly occurs that we have explanatory variables which are related to the error term. When our explanatory variable is endogenous (i.e. $cov(X,u) \neq 0$), we need to develop techniques to generate exogenous variation in the explanatory variable; that is, we need to generate variation that is unrelated to the error term.

The act of generating exogenous variation of observational data sounds challenging. We can't simply change the values of the explanatory variable (because these have already been observed). As such, instead, economists look for **natural experiments** that allow them to effectively examine the impact of a change in the explanatory variable, in effect, keeping everything else fixed. These strategies used by economists are known as **identification strategies**, and are used to try to estimate causal relationships between economic variables.

Before we start talking about different identification strategies, let's begin by thinking about what an experiment would look like, and why identification strategies might be necessary.

31.2.1 Experiments in economics

Suppose that you wanted to estimate the impact of years of completed schooling on earnings in the workforce. You might have some prior beliefs that if you spend more years in school, then you develop more human capital, and hence increase your productivity, leading to higher wages.

If we were to try to estimate the following relationship:

$$Wages_i = \beta_0 + \beta_1 Educ_i + u_i$$

where $Wages_i$ is the gross weekly wages of worker i, and $Educ_i$ is the age individual i completed full-time education, based upon observational data, it is almost certain that there would be correlation between the u_i term and the age when leaving full-time education.

Winner of the 2001 Nobel Prize, Michael Spence[2] argued that years of education not only acted increase human capital, but may also work as a signal of individuals' productivity (i.e. their ability). Highly productive individuals may find it easier to obtain more years of education, and use that education to signal to employers that they have higher ability.

As such, the choice of years of education is not random. It will instead be correlated with ability, which we believe may be a determinant of gross weekly wages. This is one potential omitted variable that could cause bias, and cause us to fail to estimate causal relationships.

So, how could we use an experiment to estimate the causal relationship between years of education and gross weekly wages? What we would need to do is to allocate years of education to individuals in a way that is uncorrelated with their other characteristics which determine their weekly wages. In this circumstance, we would need to randomly allocate an age when individuals leave education; that is, at the start of their educational journey, we would need to randomly choose how many years of schooling each individual would be allowed to complete, before moving into the workforce. By randomly assigning the number of years of education, it would not be possible for the age at which workers left full-time education to be correlated with the error term (or in this example, ability), and thus, we would gain causal estimates. In effect, by randomizing the number of years of education, we would have generated exogenous variation in the explanatory variable.

Of course, this raises a much trickier question; an ethical question. Given the life-long impact of this random allocation, and the fact that we have a very strong prior belief that increasing years of schooling increases earnings, it would not be ethical to try to carry out this sort of experiment. For example, suppose that an individual who would otherwise have gone on to university, and then studied for a PhD, was allocated a school leaving age of 16. This allocation would completely change this individual's life direction, and could have significant negative effects on their life as a whole. Because these experiments are being carried out on live humans, and they have significant long-term life impacts on those individuals, ethical concerns would normally prohibit these sorts of experiments.

Instead, if we wanted to observe the impact of increasing the years of schooling on individuals' outcomes, we would need to try to find cases of natural experiments, where we can obtain exogenous variation in our explanatory variable, without ethically problematic treatments.

[2] M. Spence (1973), 'Job Market Signalling', *Quarterly Journal of Economics*, 87(3), 355–374.

Examples of experiments in economics

Whilst some experiments might be ethically problematic, there are a growing number of experiments being carried out by economists, with growing use of experiments in the economics of education. These sorts of experiments would normally take the form of a treatment being randomly assigned to one group of students, with the other students receiving the 'standard' educational treatment.

To be ethically viable, the researchers would need to have no prior beliefs that the treatment would have a significant negative effect on the participants, and often participants would be given the right to cease participation at any stage of the experiment.

Estimating the impact of allowing computers in classrooms

There is an ongoing debate about the impact of computers being allowed in classrooms. That is, does allowing use of computers have any short- or long-term impacts on students' educational outcomes? Does the ability to type notes help your ability to process information within lectures?

To investigate this, as part of an introductory economics course, researchers at the US Military Academy[3] randomly assigned students to classrooms. In some of the classrooms students were allowed to bring laptops and/or tablets, in some of the classrooms students were allowed to bring in tablets, whilst in a (control) classroom no digital devices were allowed, and the researchers investigated the impact of the type of classroom students were taught in on educational outcomes (see Figure 31.4).

It is highly likely that if students were allowed to choose whether they use laptops or not, this would be affected by their own individual characteristics (which may be determinants of their educational outcomes).

By randomly assigning the students to classrooms, where three separate treatments are allocated, the treatments will be uncorrelated with individual characteristics. This may mean that the treatment (i.e. whether students are in classroom type 1, type 2, or type 3) will be uncorrelated with the error term. It should be noted though that, even with students randomly assigned to different treatments, it is possible that there may still be **endogeneity** through teachers' behaviours being correlated to the type of classroom they teach in.

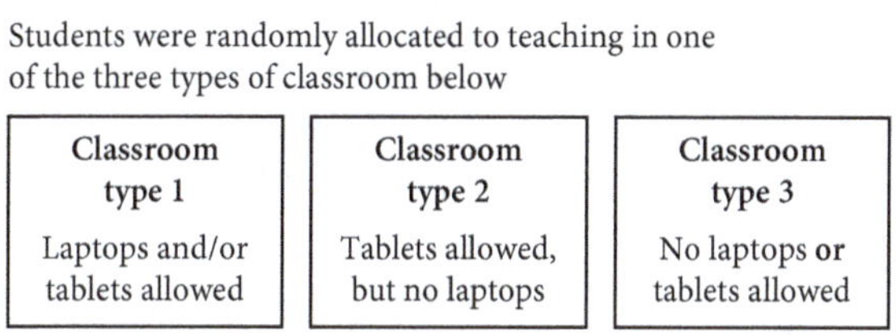

Figure 31.4 Structure of the experiment.

[3] S. P. Carter, K. Greenberg, and M. S. Walker (2017), 'The Impact of Computer Usage on Academic Performance: Evidence from a Randomized Trial at the United States Military Academy', *Economics of Education Review*, 56, 118–132.

Their key results showed that students who were educated in classrooms that allowed computers performed 0.18 standard deviations lower than students who were educated in classrooms where no digital devices were allowed.

31.2.2 Natural experiments

Where pure experiments are unavailable, economists often look for natural experiments. A natural experiment is where an exogenous change is made to individuals (or companies, or countries) that is unrelated to their individual characteristics. Government changes in policy often provide us with the opportunity to examine the impact of natural experiments.

Returning to the example of estimating the return to years of schooling, whilst it would be unethical to carry out a pure experiment where we allocate students different levels of schooling, it is possible to estimate the marginal effect of length of schooling through observing policy changes.

As we saw earlier in this chapter, the difficulty of estimating the return to years of schooling is that individuals choose the number of years of education that they complete, and this choice is likely to be correlated with individuals' characteristics, such as their underlying ability or productivity. Observational data would suffer from omitted variables bias. As such, any natural experiment would need to cause an exogenous change to the number of years of schooling that students experience.

In the UK, the age at which students could legally leave school was increased from 14 to 15 in 1947, and further to age 16 in 1973. Colm Harmon and Ian Walker[4] used these increases in school leaving age to estimate the impact of additional years of schooling on earnings.

So, in 1947, a student who would have chosen to leave school at age 14 would now gain one extra year of schooling, and similarly, in 1973, a student who would have chosen to leave school at age 15 would now have to gain an additional year of schooling. The students are not choosing to gain an extra year of schooling, so this shock is unrelated to their own characteristics. As such, the increase in schooling is an exogenous shock to the years of schooling. In this way, Harmon and Walker were able to compare the average impact of the extra year of schooling on students' outcomes. Overall, their results suggest that an extra year of schooling increases earnings by approximately 15 per cent, which is a significant, non-trivial result.

Ultimately, Harmon and Walker use a method known as instrumental variables to estimate the causal relationship between years of schooling and earnings. The details of how instrumental variables are estimated is beyond the scope of this book, but in essence the method is about generating exogenous variation in the explanatory variable that will be unrelated to the characteristics of the individual.

In the rest of this chapter, we will introduce a number of other methods that can be used to estimate causal relationships. In each case, the causal relationship can be estimated by generating exogenous variation in the explanatory variable, to evaluate the impact of a change.

[4] C. Harmon and I. Walker (1995), 'Estimates of the Economic Return to Schooling for the United Kingdom', *American Economic Review*, 85(5), 1278–1286.

31.2.3 Regression discontinuity design models

Another form of natural experiment can be assessed through what is known as a regression discontinuity design (RDD). An RDD can be applied when individuals receive some form of economic treatment, depending on the value they have on some continuous characteristic. The treatment could be eligibility for benefits, or it could be access to particular schools, access to medication, etc.

In order for an RDD model to be applied, there needs to be a sharp discontinuity in treatment, so that individuals on one side of the threshold are effectively not treated, whilst individuals on the other side of the discontinuity receive the treatment.

Let's illustrate this with an example, based upon David Lee and Justin McCrary's[5] analysis of the impact of sentencing severity on crimes in the USA. It is often hypothesized that if criminals face harsher sentences when convicted, then this will have a deterrent effect on crime. So, for example, researchers may be interested in estimating whether handing out longer prison sentences has a causal impact on crime. One of the issues with estimating this relationship is that there does not tend to be exogenous variation in sentencing. For example, there may be simultaneity. That is, the level of crime in a state or a country may influence the severity of sentences. Governments may respond to a spate of crimes by increasing the sentencing guidelines, to create a disincentive.

Lee and McCrary (2017) make the observation that, in the USA, criminals under the age of 18 are tried in juvenile court, whilst those over 18 are tried in adult courts, where penalties are harsher. Thus in the two groups, the under 18s are the untreated group, with relatively lenient penalties, and the over 18s are the treated group with relatively harsher sentences.

Thus, this creates a discontinuity in treatment. Individuals who commit exactly the same crime will get a different sentence depending on whether they are just under 18, or just over 18. Because individuals who are just above or just below 18 are likely to be quantitatively, and qualitatively, similar, the discontinuity in treatment is likely to be exogenous. That is, it is not likely to be the case that those individuals who are a few days short of their eighteenth birthday are fundamentally more (or less) likely to commit crimes than those who are just a few days after their eighteenth birthday.

Therefore, if we can compare the actions of individuals just above and just below the age of 18, their characteristics will be qualitatively and quantitatively similar. What is different is the fact that committing a crime (and getting caught) above the age of 18 is associated with being tried in an adult court, and potentially harsher sentencing.

The over-18s are treated with harsher sentences and the under-18s are effectively the control (comparison) group to whom we are comparing the treatment group. In essence, an RDD examines what happens at the discontinuity. Does the number of crimes increase? Does the number of crimes decrease? Or do they stay exactly the same?

The idea behind an RDD is that the individuals just above and just below the discontinuity are quantitatively and qualitatively the same. That is, in the example, potential criminals aged just over 18 are effectively equivalent to potential criminals in the same town who

[5] D. S. Lee and J. McCrary (2017), 'The Deterrent Effect of Prison: Dynamic Theory and Evidence', in M. D. Cattaneo and J. C. Escanciano (eds), *Regression Discontinuity Designs: Theory and Applications*, Emerald.

are aged just under 18. Thus, in this example, you can compare the number of crimes committed by individuals who are just after their 18th birthday with the number committed by individuals who are just before their 18th birthday.

Lee and McCrary (2017) found that the impact of the increased sanctions was to lower the likelihood of a potential criminal committing a crime by approximately 2 per cent.

How do we carry out RDD models in practice?

Researchers normally estimate an RDD using a simple estimation technique, such as OLS. To take account of the fact that the dependent variable may have a non-linear relationship with the variable that defines the treatment, the researchers would fit a polynomial between the dependent variable and the variable that defines the treatment. For example, you could include a polynomial relationship in terms of age. In addition, the researchers would include a dummy variable that takes the value 1 if the individual receives the treatment, and 0 otherwise.

To apply this to the example, we might estimate the following relationship:

$$Crime_i = \beta_0 + \beta_1 Age_i + \beta_2 Age_i^2 + \beta_3 Age_i^3 + \beta_4 Age_i^4 + \beta_5 Over18_i + u_i$$

where $Crime_i$ is the number of crimes committed by individual i, Age_i is the age of the individual, and $Over18_i$ is a dummy variable that takes the value 1 if an individual is aged 18 or over (and hence receives the tougher sentence—that is, they are treated in our model), and 0 if the individual is under the age of 18. β_5 would provide us with the causal estimates of the impact of the tougher sentences.

This is illustrated, through simulated data, in Figure 31.5. The horizontal axis represents the distance of observations below, or above, the discontinuity in treatment. We have fitted a polynomial relationship through the data, with a dummy variable included for observation to the right of the discontinuity. The coefficient on the dummy variable is then the causal

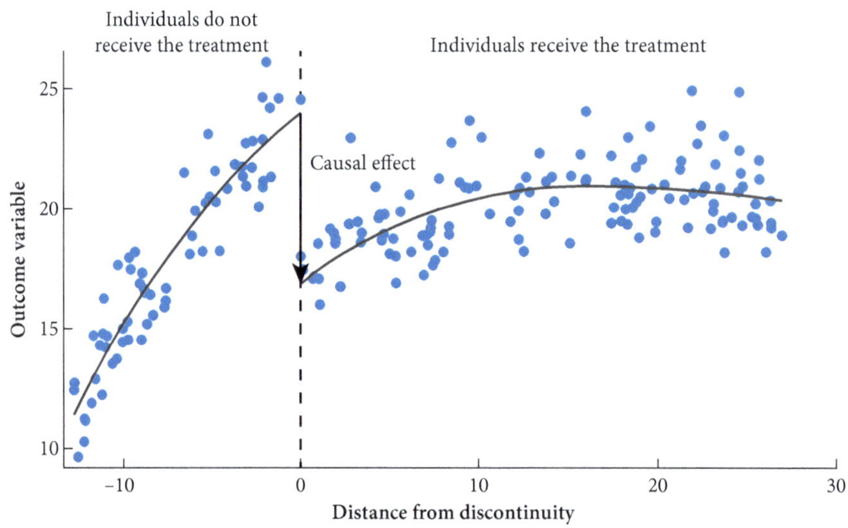

Figure 31.5 Simulation to illustrate RDD in action.

impact of the treatment. It is how much higher or lower the relationship is shifted due to the treatment being introduced. The vertical distance between the fitted lines at the discontinuity is equivalent to $\hat{\beta}_5$, our estimate of the causal impact of the treatment.

Usually, an RDD model will focus on data either side of the discontinuity; the further the observations are from the discontinuity, the more likely that the endogenous factors will cause bias in our results.

When is an RDD used?

Regression discontinuity designs can be considered whenever there is a discontinuous treatment across a range. This could include:

- Age: lots of papers use discontinuities in treatments for individuals based upon their age. We have seen that in the USA, sentences for crimes have a discontinuous treatment, depending on whether individuals are under or over 18. Some benefits are conditional upon age. Laws allowing purchase of cigarettes and alcohol are often dependent upon age. All of these allow for treatments that have a sharp discontinuity.
- Distance (or where you live): sometimes treatments are discontinuous depending on how close you live to the treatment. For example, schools sometimes use 'catchment zones'. Suppose there is a good school. If you live within the catchment zone, you can attend that school, and if you live outside of that catchment zone, you cannot. If you are interested in the impact of 'good schools' on house prices, you could compare house prices just inside and just outside of the catchment zone, as the only difference between the areas should be the availability of the good school.[6]
- Time: where a policy is implemented nationwide on a particular date, if the policy has 'quick' effects, it may be possible to observe the impact of the policy by comparing the outcomes before and after the policy is implemented. Of course, in the case of many government policies (e.g. the UK's decision to leave the European Union), the impact of the policy takes a long time to play out. In that time, other policies and other economic changes may affect the outcome variable, so RDDs cannot be easily used to compare longer-term impacts.

In fact, any continuous variable where a treatment is imposed at (and beyond) some threshold may help us to estimate an RDD model. These might include income, house prices, exam grades, wealth, and more.

Problems with RDD models

With any identification strategy, there are potential problems that you need to overcome. Firstly, we are only estimating a causal effect for a certain group of individuals. In the example, we would only be estimating the causal effect for young people (aged 17–19). We wouldn't be able to make conclusions about older potential criminals, because they may

[6] See, for example, S. Gibbons, S. Machin, and O. Silva (2013), 'Valuing School Quality Using Boundary Discontinuity', *Journal of Urban Economics*, 75, 15–28.

react differently to incentives. Maybe for 40-year-old criminals there would have been a larger fall in crime from increasing sentences? As such, this sort of methodology might be useful to identify causal effects, but it is only useful around the discontinuity.

Secondly, it needs to be the case that there are no other changes at the discontinuity, which are related to the dependent variable. It is certainly not the case that turning 18 only affects the sentencing related to a crime. At the age of 18, many things change; for example, people can move out of their parental home, they can get married,[7] they can take out credit cards. If any of these are related to the likelihood of an individual committing a crime, then the results will be biased.

These limitations of RDD models mean that they can only be used when very strong conditions are true. If there are any other changes that take place at the discontinuity, then it would not be possible to disentangle the impact of the multiple policies.

However, when treatments are discontinuous, there may be other routes to investigate the causal impact of the treatment.

31.2.4 Twin studies, synthetic controls, and matching models

One of the problems we have discussed with RDD models is that if there are any other changes across the treatment threshold, then it is not possible to disentangle the causal effect of one treatment from another. One way of trying to solve this problem is to ask what would have happened had the treatment we are interested in not happened?

Suppose we wanted to know the impact of the UK leaving the European Union. Whilst the UK voted to leave the EU in 2016, the actual act of leaving took place on 31 January 2020.

If we simply observed UK GDP before and after the UK left the EU in 2020, there were a range of factors that were likely to have affected UK GDP during that period; for example, economies worldwide were affected by COVID-19, which had a negative impact on GDP during the same time-period. As such, if we simply compared GDP before and after the UK left the EU (see Figure 31.6), we might conclude that Brexit had a stark, negative impact on UK GDP. However, in reality, just by looking at this data, we wouldn't be able to disentangle the impact of leaving the EU from the impact of COVID-19.

The important question is therefore not what happened to GDP before and after leaving the EU. Instead, you could break the question into two parts:

1. What would have happened to GDP if the UK had remained within the EU?
2. What additional impact (if any) did leaving the EU have on UK GDP?

In a matching model, we would try to estimate models by starting with the question of what would have happened had the policy change not occurred. To do this, we need a counterfactual—that is, a prediction of what would have happened had the treatment not occurred. We would obtain this by finding a control group with characteristics matching the

[7] Other than in Nebraska (19), District of Columbia (16), and Mississippi (21). Marriage Age by State 2023 (worldpopulationreview.com).

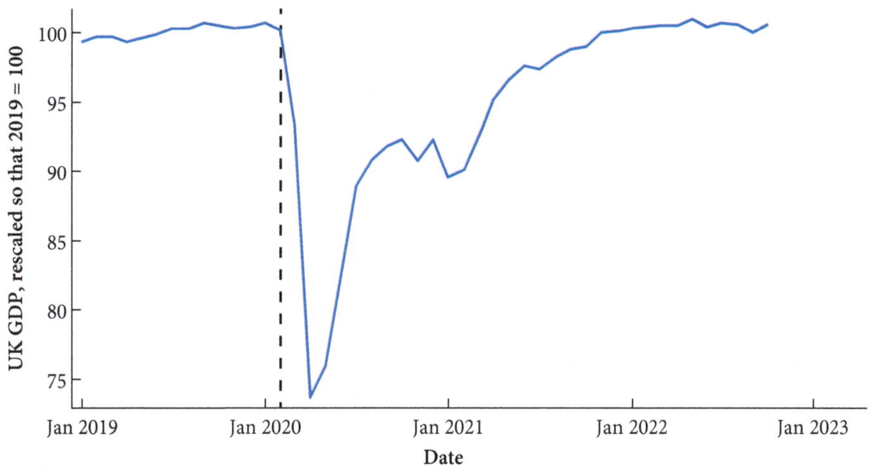

Figure 31.6 UK GDP between 2019 and 2023 (rescaled so that GDP in 2019 = 100) (data from the ONS).

treatment group, to allow us to identify what would have happened, had the treatment not been introduced.

Figure 31.7 illustrates the use of a counterfactual. The dotted line represents what would have happened if the treatment had not occurred; this is our counterfactual. The solid line, after the treatment, illustrates the observed outcomes after the treatment has been imposed.

In the example here, we can see that the observed outcome is lower than the counterfactual. This means that there was a negative impact of the treatment on the outcome variable.

The problem is, therefore, constructing our counterfactual. In a matching model, we essentially match the characteristics of a control group to the individuals (or countries) within our treatment group. Since the characteristics of the two groups are, in theory, identical, it

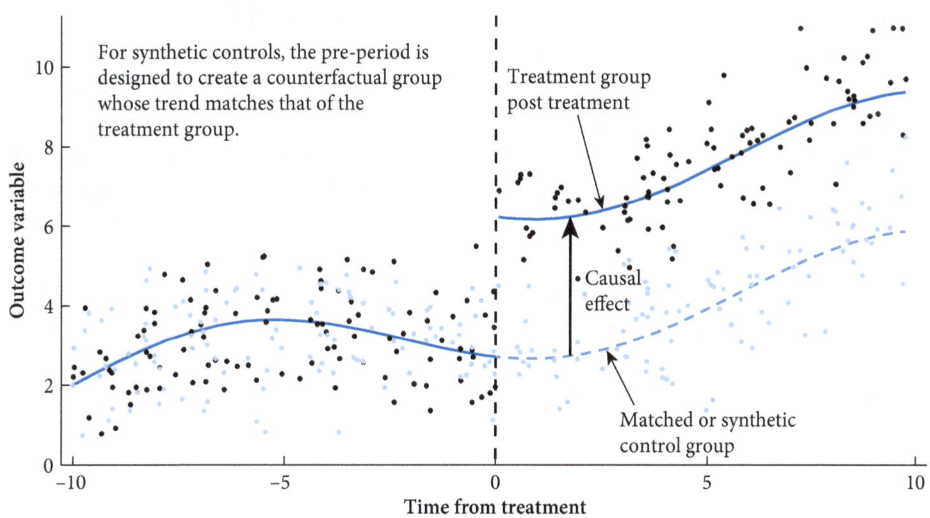

Figure 31.7 Using a counterfactual to estimate the causal effect.

should also be the case that without the treatment, the outcomes for the two groups are also identical.

In a matching model, the control group provides a counterfactual. Researchers would compare the outcome of interest between the control group and the treatment group.

Twin studies

The simplest form of matching study is through 'twin studies'. Because twins are genetically identical, and (it is assumed) they have the same upbringing, in principle, if one member of the twin is treated, and the other not treated, then the non-treated twin would tell us what the outcome variable is likely to have been for the treated twin, had they not been treated; as such, the difference would provide us with the causal estimate.

For example, Ashenfelter and Krueger (1994)[8] use pairs of twins to evaluate the impact of the number of years of schooling on wages. As we've discussed earlier, observational studies of the impact of years of education on wages can suffer from omitted variables bias (such as omitting the underlying ability of the students, which may be a determinant of both their wages and their completed years of schooling).

By using pairs of twins, the characteristics of the twin-pair should be identical (up to a certain point in life). In principle, when the authors observe variation in the number of years of schooling that the two members of the twin-pair gain, this should not be correlated with individual characteristics. The argument is that the two members of the twin-pair are otherwise identical.

Their results suggested that an additional year of schooling is associated with between 12 and 16 per cent increase in wages.

Other forms of matching models

Of course, twin studies are often either not feasible or just not possible. However, this doesn't stop matching models being considered.

One way to carry out a matching model would be to construct a treatment and a control group, based on choosing individuals with matching observable characteristics.

A second way of constructing a matching model is through synthetic methods. For example, returning to the economic impact of Brexit (the UK's leaving of the European Union), a range of studies tried to analyse the impact of the initial vote to leave the EU on UK economic growth by constructing a synthetic UK, based upon observations of other countries.

To do this, the researchers initially calibrated a model based on the pre-treatment period. They observed GDP growth across a range of countries, along with the UK. To initially calibrate their model, they then constructed a set of weights to be applied to the 'control countries' such that the new synthetic control matched the pre-treatment GDP growth in the UK.

[8] O. Ashenfelter and A. Krueger (1994), 'Estimates of the Economic Return to Schooling from a New Sample of Twins', *American Economic Review*, 84(5), 1157–1173.

Having constructed this 'synthetic UK' based upon observations of other countries' GDP, the same weightings could be applied to those other countries' GDP after the treatment occurred to provide a prediction of what would have happened to the UK, had the UK voted to remain within the EU.

One of the earliest studies to do this was written by John Springford of the Centre for European Reform in 2018.[9] The UK had voted to leave the EU in 2016, and he wanted to estimate the impact on UK GDP of that vote itself. The overall result was that, even by 2018, the UK had grown 2.1 per cent less than the synthetic model predicted.

Problems with matching models

Ultimately, any form of matching model depends on how well the control group matches the treatment group. If there is any unobserved heterogeneity that is both a determinant of the dependent variable and correlated with the treatment, then matching models will still suffer from bias.

Even with twin studies, it is not certain that you will obtain causal results. In the example, one member of the twin-pair has decided to spend longer in education than the other. What is it that determines that decision? If that decision is correlated in any way with differences in their underlying ability, or differences in their experience growing up, then the control group may not give an accurate indication of a true counterfactual.

31.2.5 Difference in differences

Often it won't be possible to observe a control group that exactly matches the characteristics of the treatment group, but there are still methods that we can use to construct a counterfactual, in order to estimate a causal relationship.

Remember, we are using the counterfactual to tell us what would have happened had the reform not happened. In the treatment group, we can think of the change after the reform as being made up of two parts:

1. The change in the outcome that would have occurred, even if the treatment hadn't been implemented.
2. The impact of the treatment.

One method that we can use to construct a counterfactual is known as Difference in Differences (DiD). In a DiD model, the control and treatment group need not be identical, but what matters is that the two groups follow the same trend before the treatment is implemented.

If the two groups (the treatment and the control group) follow the same trend, then we can use how much the control group changes to predict what would have happened in the treatment group, had there been no treatment. This is illustrated in Figure 31.8. The light blue solid line represents the outcome over time for the control group. Similarly, the dark blue solid line represents the outcome over time (before the treatment) of the treatment group.

[9] J. Springford (2018), 'What's the Cost of Brexit So Far?', *CER Insight*, 23 June.

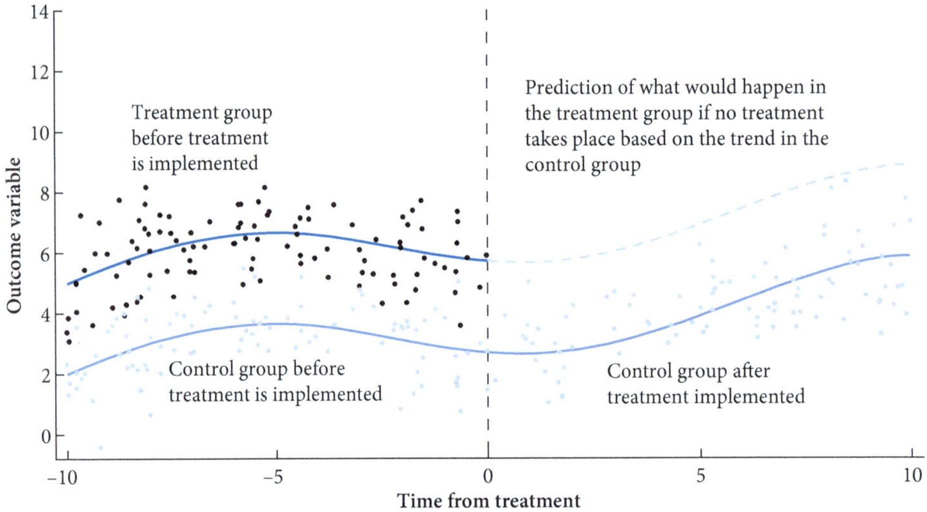

Figure 31.8 Predicting what would have happened in the treatment group if they had not received the treatment.

Key to this strategy is that the trends of the treatment and control groups are the same. That is, the two lines are parallel. Because of this, if the trends are parallel, we can make the assumption that had the treatment not occurred, then the outcome measures would continue to be parallel. As such, we can use the observed outcomes in the control group to predict what would have happened if there had been no treatment. This prediction is represented by the dotted line.

To estimate the causal effect of the treatment, we consider how much higher or lower the observed outcomes in the treatment group are than the predicted values.

In Figure 31.9, we illustrate the causal effect. The solid blue line (representing the observed outcomes for the treatment group) is higher than the predicted (dotted) line. This indicates that the treatment has had a positive impact on the outcomes for the treatment group.

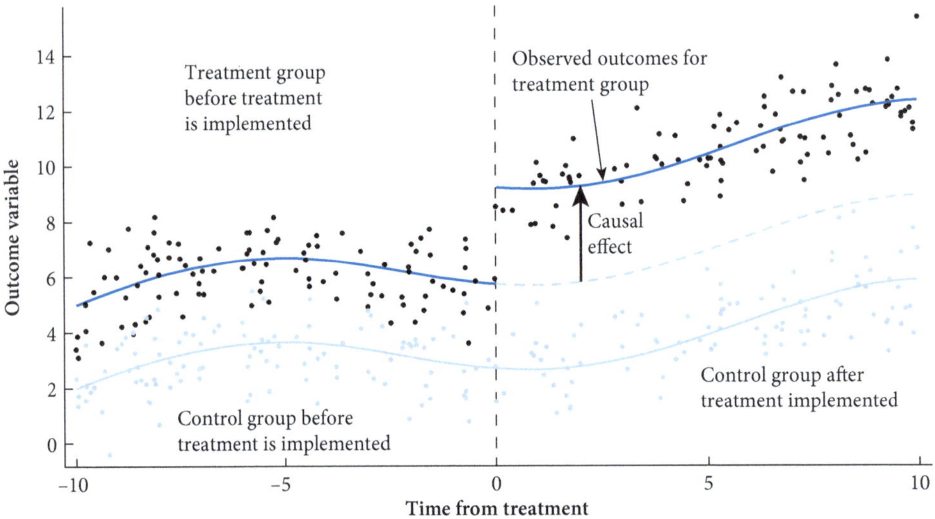

Figure 31.9 Estimating the causal effect.

So why is this called difference in differences?

An important question that you might ask is why this method is called difference in differences. This comes from the fact that the estimate of the causal effect is calculated by effectively comparing the difference between the treatment and control groups before the treatment, and the difference between the treatment and control groups after the treatment.

Figure 31.10 illustrates the differences between the treatment group and the control group after (A) and before (B) the treatment is implemented. To find the estimate of the causal effect we would need to compare how much larger or smaller (A) was than (B). That is, the estimate of the causal effect is just equal to:

$$\text{Causal effect} = (A) - (B)$$

Mathematically, we can calculate this by calculating the average outcome for the treatment and control groups during the two periods. For simplicity of notation, let's define the outcome of interest in the treatment group as Y, and in the control group as X. To calculate the causal effect, we would calculate four averages:

1. the average outcome in the treatment group after the treatment, $\overline{Y}_{after}$
2. the average outcome in the control group after the treatment, $\overline{X}_{after}$
3. the average outcome in the treatment group before the treatment, $\overline{Y}_{before}$
4. the average outcome in the control group before the treatment, $\overline{X}_{before}$

The estimate of the causal effect can then be calculated as:

$$\text{Causal effect} = (\overline{Y}_{after} - \overline{X}_{after}) - (\overline{Y}_{before} - \overline{X}_{before})$$

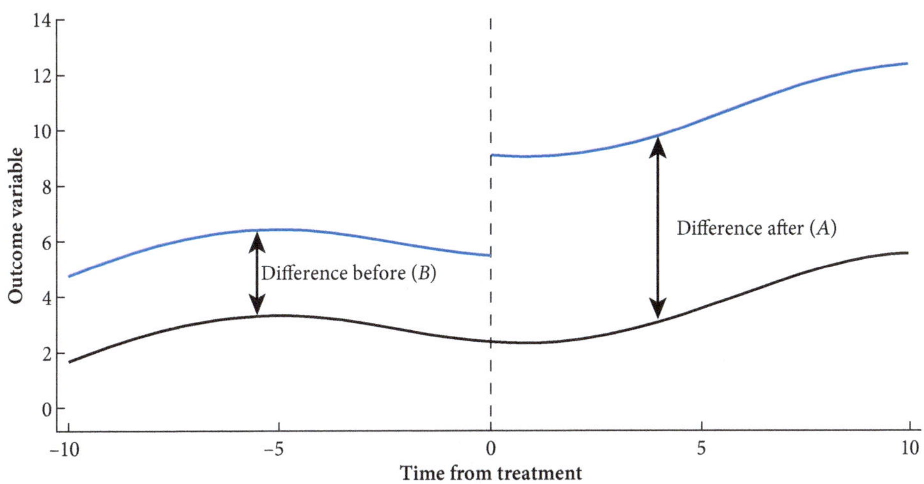

Figure 31.10 Differences between treatment and control groups.

We can see here that what we are doing is comparing the difference in the average outcomes between the treatment and control groups after the treatment is implemented with the difference in the average outcomes before the treatment is implemented. Hence we have calculated the difference of the differences.

Example: The effect of the minimum wage

One of the seminal examples of DiDs was to estimate the impact of a change in the minimum wage on employment. Nobel Prize winner David Card, along with Alan Krueger,[10] used a policy change in New Jersey to estimate the impact of increasing the minimum wage on employment.[11]

Figure 31.11 illustrates a very simple, traditional view of the impact of a minimum wage. Left to the free market, the wages in the economy should reach an equilibrium, where supply of labour offered is equal to the labour demanded, and there should be no unemployment.

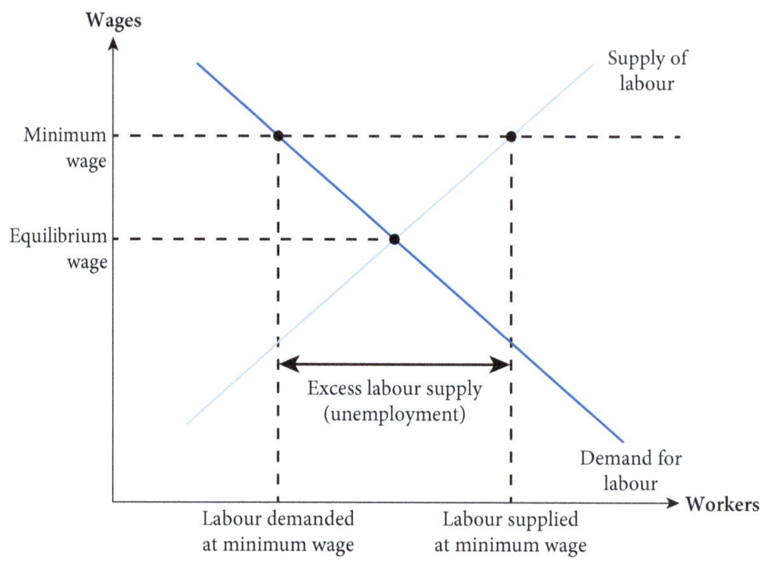

Figure 31.11 A traditional theoretical model of the impact of the minimum wage.

The traditional view of the labour market is that if there is a minimum wage set above the equilibrium wage, then the quantity of labour demanded will decrease, and the quantity of labour that workers are willing to supply should increase. This leads to excess supply of labour, and hence unemployment. The key prediction of the model is that if we increase the minimum wage, therefore, we should expect to see a reduction in employment, and an increase in unemployment.

[10] David Card won the Nobel Prize in 2021. Alan Krueger had sadly passed away in 2019. Many believe that had he survived he would have shared the Nobel Prize with David Card.

[11] D. Card and A. Krueger (1994), 'Minimum Wages and Employment: A Case Study of the Fast-Food Industry in New Jersey and Pennsylvania', *American Economic Review*, 84(4), 772–793.

Card and Krueger (1994) made use of an increase in the minimum wage in New Jersey from \$4.25 to \$5.05 per hour, whilst in the neighbouring state of Pennsylvania, no change was made to the minimum wage. We would only expect changes in the minimum wage to affect employment in low-paid industries (where equilibrium wages are below the minimum wage), so Card and Krueger focused upon the impacts of the increase in the minimum wage in fast-food retailers, as many workers would be paid at, or close to, the minimum wage in fast-food establishments.

To analyse the impact, Card and Krueger collected data on employment in fast-food retailers close to the border between New Jersey and Pennsylvania, before the increase in the minimum wage and after the minimum wage was increased. Their data is illustrated in Table 31.1.

Table 31.1 Employment before and after the increase in minimum wage in Pennsylvania and New Jersey

Average number of workers employed per store	Pennsylvania (Control)	New Jersey (Treatment)
Before the increase in the minimum wage	23.33	21.17
After the increase in the minimum wage	20.44	21.03

Before the reform, the average fast-food restaurant in Pennsylvania employed 23.33 employees, and New Jersey 21.17. We can use this data to calculate the estimate of the causal impact of the increase in the minimum wage. Using our equation from earlier:

$$\text{Causal effect} = (\overline{Y}_{after} - \overline{X}_{after}) - (\overline{Y}_{before} - \overline{X}_{before})$$

we can substitute in the numbers to give us:

$$\text{Causal effect} = (21.03 - 20.44) - (21.17 - 23.33) = 2.75$$

That is, the estimated causal effect of the increase in the minimum wage was to increase employment by 2.75 workers per restaurant. That is, counter to our theoretical prediction, the estimated causal effect was to actually increase employment in New Jersey.

This is a slightly counterintuitive result, when we look at the data, because we can see that employment actually fell in New Jersey during this period (from 21.17 workers per store to 21.03 workers per store). This illustrates the importance of a counterfactual. The data from Pennsylvania (where there wasn't a change in the minimum wage) indicates that, had New Jersey not increased their minimum wage, we would have expected employment to fall by 2.89 workers per restaurant. This reduction in employment could be attributed to changing economic conditions that would be expected to affect neighbouring states equally.

Of course, the key condition that is needed for these results to be causal is that there are no other changes in the same time period that affect New Jersey and Pennsylvania differently.

When is difference in differences used?

Difference in differences can be considered as a method to obtain causal estimates whenever there is a treatment that is applied to one group within the population, and not applied to a (quantitatively similar) group, to construct a counterfactual.

There have been a very large quantity of research carried out in recent years using DiD models, including topics as diverse as:

- the impact of football tournaments on students' academic outcomes
- the impact of competition between hospitals on the quality of healthcare provision
- the impact of unemployment benefits on job matches
- the impact of publishing school league tables on the quality of schools.

Problems with difference in differences models

Ultimately, as with all identification strategies, DIDs only provide causal estimates of a treatment if the underlying assumptions are true.

The first assumption is that the only asymmetric change that takes place when the treatment is introduced is the treatment that we are interested in. In the example of the minimum wage, if the increase in the minimum wage was also accompanied by greater support for people to find jobs in New Jersey (but not in Pennsylvania) at the same time, we wouldn't be able to distinguish between the impact of the increase in the minimum wage and the impact of the job-search support.

The second assumption is much more likely to fail—that is, the assumption that the control and treatment group have common trends before the treatment is introduced. This is important, because we are using the trend of the control group to predict what would have happened in the treatment group if there had been no treatment. To illustrate the impact of the control and treatment groups having different trends, consider Figure 31.12.

In Figure 31.12, the treatment has no impact on the treatment group. We can see this as, effectively, the trend and the level of the outcomes in the treatment group are unchanged before and after the treatment is introduced.

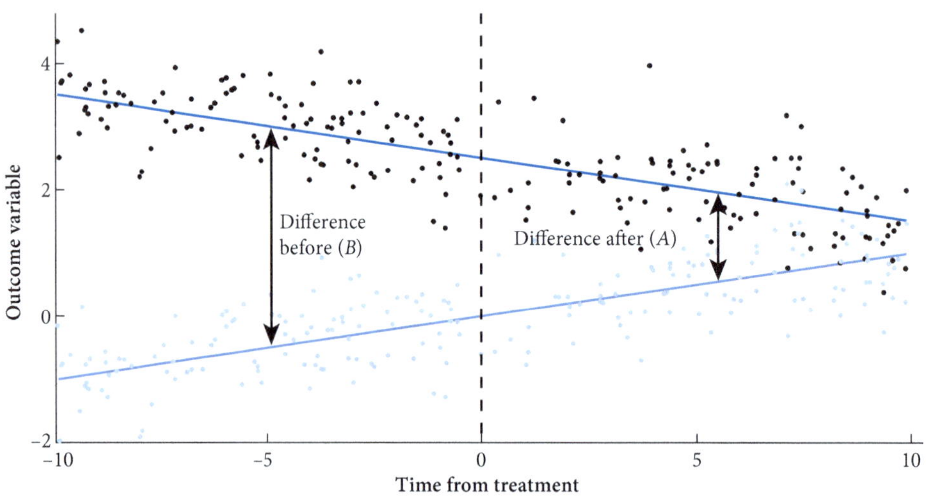

Figure 31.12 Difference in differences with the common trend assumption violated.

However, we can see that the difference between the treatment and control group gets much smaller after the treatment occurs than before. This is simply because the trend of the control group is that the outcome is increasing over time, whilst in the treatment group, the outcome is (slightly) decreasing over time. As such, DiDs would suggest that the impact of the treatment would be to reduce the outcome for the treatment group, whereas in reality, this treatment has no impact on the outcome variable of interest.

Summary

We have introduced a number of ways of estimating causal relationships, including using experiments, regression discontinuity design, matching, and difference in differences. Ultimately, other than pure experiments, all of the identification strategies rely on natural experiments, where we can observe an exogenous change in the explanatory variable, and evaluate the impact of that exogenous change on the dependent variables.

There are a wide range of other identification strategies that we could have considered in this chapter, but the aim of this chapter was to introduce you to the concepts of identification strategies, and to inspire you to look for natural experiments that might allow you to estimate causal relationships.

The most important thing to remember is that, just because OLS provides a statistically significant result, this does not mean that you have found a causal relationship. OLS as a tool provides a way of calculating a correlation; to determine whether the results are causal or not, you need to be able to conclude whether you have actually generated exogenous variation in your explanatory variable, or not.

Appendix

Constructing the size of the bias for different forms of endogeneity

When explanatory variables are exogenous, knowing the value of the variable tells us nothing about the value of the error term, and similarly, knowing the value of the error term tells us nothing about the value that the explanatory variable takes.

We know that if the explanatory variable is endogenous, then knowing the value of the explanatory variable provides us information about the value of the error term (and vice versa). As such, if we can show that there is a simple, deterministic relationship between the explanatory variable and the error term, then it also follows that the explanatory variable is necessarily endogenous.

So, for example, if we are estimating the relationship:

$$Y_i = \beta_0 + \beta_1 X_i + u_i \qquad (A)$$

if we can show that $X_i = \gamma_0 + \gamma_1 u_i + \varepsilon_i$ where $\gamma_1 \neq 0$, then it also automatically follows that u_i is a determinant of X_i, and hence $cov(X,u) \neq 0$. More generally, if $X_i = f(u_i)$ where f is any general functional form, then we can write that X is endogenous in specification (A).

Reverse causality

Suppose that you are interested in estimating the relationship:

$$Y_i = \beta_0 + \beta_1 X_i + u_i \tag{1}$$

However, the true relationship between Y_i and X_i works in the opposite direction. That is, the data generating process for X_i can be written as:

$$X_i = \alpha_0 + \alpha_1 Y_i + e_i \tag{2}$$

If the direction of causality only moves in the direction defined by equation (2), that is equivalent to saying that X has no causal impact on Y, and hence $\beta_1 = 0$. Thus, we can write that:

$$Y_i = \beta_0 + u_i \tag{3}$$

That is, every observation of Y_i can be written as a combination of some constant term and some error term (u_i). We have no idea what determines the value of u_i, but we merely wish to show that u_i will be correlated with X_i.

Substituting (3) into (2) provides us with:

$$X_i = \alpha_0 + \alpha_1(\beta_0 + u_i) + e_i$$
$$\Rightarrow X_i = \alpha_0 + \alpha_1\beta_0 + \alpha_1 u_i + e_i \tag{4}$$

From equation (4), we can see that provided Y_i is a determinant of X_i (i.e. $\alpha_1 \neq 0$), then u_i is a determinant of X_i, and thus it automatically would follow that $cov(X,u) \neq 0$.

Therefore, if we estimated specification (1), we would gain biased and inconsistent estimates of the marginal causal impacts of X on Y.

Proof of size of bias

We know that the probability limit of the OLS estimator for estimating the relationship between Y and X (equation (1)) is given by:

$$plim(\hat{\beta}_1) = \frac{cov(Y,X)}{var(X)}$$

Since the true value of $\beta_1 = 0$, Bias $= plim(\hat{\beta}_1) - \beta_1 = plim(\hat{\beta}_1) = \dfrac{cov(Y,X)}{var(X)}$.

We also know that the data generating process for X is given by:

$$X_i = \alpha_0 + \alpha_1 Y_i + e_i \tag{4}$$

We can rewrite the bias by substituting in (4) to give:

$$= \frac{cov[(\alpha_0 + \alpha_1 Y + e), Y]}{var(\alpha_0 + \alpha_1 Y + e)}$$

We will apply our rules of covariances and variances:

- α_0 is an additive constant on both the numerator and denominator; the variance of a constant term is zero, as is the covariance with any constant term. As such, we can drop this term from the numerator and denominator. Similarly, β_0 in the numerator.

$$= \frac{cov[\alpha_1 Y + e, Y]}{var(\alpha_1 Y + e)}$$

The numerator simplifies to $cov[\alpha_1 Y + e, Y] = \alpha_1 cov(Y, Y) + cov(e, Y) = \alpha_1 var(Y) + cov(e, Y)$. Similarly, the denominator simplifies to $var(\alpha_1 Y + e) = \alpha_1^2 var(Y) + var(e) + 2\alpha_1 cov(Y, e)$.

Therefore, the bias can be written as:

$$= \frac{\alpha_1 var(Y) + cov(e, Y)}{\alpha_1^2 var(Y) + var(e) + 2\alpha_1 cov(Y, e)}$$

Simultaneity

In the case of simultaneity, it is the case that both X causes Y, and Y causes X. That is, the data has two data generating processes that work simultaneously:

$$Y_i = \beta_0 + \beta_1 X_i + u_i \quad (1)$$

$$X_i = \alpha_0 + \alpha_1 Y_i + e_i \quad (2)$$

This sort of problem occurs when variables are determined in equilibrium. For example, price and quantity are determined simultaneously, due to the equality of supply and demand.

We may be interested in estimating only the impact of a change in X on Y. That is, we might be interested in estimating relationship (1).

If X is endogenous in (1), then it would follow that knowing the value of u_i tells us something about the value of X_i. As such, if we substitute the data generating process for Y (1) into the data generating process for X (2):

$$X_i = \alpha_0 + \alpha_1(\beta_0 + \beta_1 X_i + u_i) + e_i$$

If we multiply out the brackets, and group terms, we have:

$$\Rightarrow X_i(1 - \alpha_1\beta_1) = (\alpha_0 + \alpha_1\beta_0) + \alpha_1 u_i + e_i$$

$$\Rightarrow X_i = \frac{\alpha_0 + \alpha_1\beta_0}{1 - \alpha_1\beta_1} + \left(\frac{\alpha_1}{1 - \alpha_1\beta_1}\right)u_i + \frac{e_i}{1 - \alpha_1\beta_1} \quad (3)$$

We can see that, as long as $\alpha_1 \neq 0$, then u_i will once again be a determinant of X_i. As such, X_i would be correlated with the u_i term, and so if we tried to estimate (1) using OLS, then X_i would be endogenous, and hence the estimates would be biased and inconsistent.

Proof of the size of the bias

We know that the data generating process for Y is given as $Y_i = \beta_0 + \beta_1 X_i + u_i$. If we substitute this into the OLS estimator, and take probability limits, then the resulting plim can be written as:

$$plim(\hat{\beta}_1) = \beta_1 + \frac{cov(X,u)}{var(X)}$$

Therefore, the bias is equal to $\frac{cov(X,u)}{var(X)}$. However, we can evaluate this further by considering the data generating process of X_i in terms of the u_i and the e_i terms:

$$\text{Bias} = \frac{cov(X,u)}{var(X)} = \frac{cov\left(\left(\frac{\alpha_1}{1-\alpha_1\beta_1}\right)u + \frac{e}{1-\alpha_1\beta_1}, u\right)}{var\left(\left(\frac{\alpha_1}{1-\alpha_1\beta_1}\right)u + \frac{e}{1-\alpha_1\beta_1}\right)}$$

We can take the $1-\alpha_1\beta_1$ terms out of both the numerator and denominator to give:

$$= \frac{\left[\frac{1}{1-\alpha_1\beta_1}\right]cov(\alpha_1 u + e, u)}{\left[\frac{1}{1-\alpha_1\beta_1}\right]^2 var(\alpha_1 u + e)} = (1-\alpha_1\beta_1)\left[\frac{cov(\alpha_1 u + e, u)}{var(\alpha_1 u + e)}\right]$$

Now, the covariance and variances on the numerator and denominator expand to give:

$$= (1-\alpha_1\beta_1)\frac{(\alpha_1 var(u) + cov(e,u))}{\left(\alpha_1^2 var(u) + var(e) + 2\alpha_1 cov(u,e)\right)}$$

A Brief Introduction to Big Data

32

Learning outcomes for this chapter

At the end of this chapter, students will be able to:

- Understand how computers store data, and the challenges of storing big data
- Recognize the benefits of big data in answering complex questions

Mathematical tools

- None

Introduction

Throughout this textbook, we have been dealing with relatively small data sets, all of which either contain simple numeric data (such as spending, income, years of education), or could be treated as numeric data (through dummy variables, or equivalent).

Small data sets with relatively simple variables are relatively easy to store and analyse. However, over the last 50 years (and particularly since the birth of the internet), there has been a growth in 'big data'.

Data takes on many forms. Every video that is posted on YouTube or TikTok contains data about individuals; every post made on Facebook or X (formerly Twitter) contains data about individuals; and every transaction you make, whether financial or non-financial, includes data Every interaction you make, or firms make, or governments make online, and offline, is potentially valuable data to someone. How often have you received offers from supermarkets for goods you've never bought before, but realize that you actually really like? How often have you been recommended videos on YouTube from creators you've never interacted with, but who produce content that really interests you? All of this is because of big data, which firms can use to build a profile of you.

Big data is really a catch-all term for the vast quantities of data that firms and governments are able to collect, including data about consumer behaviour, search histories, and even qualitative characteristics and interactions, and may consist of millions or billions (or even more) of observations. Firms, political parties, campaigners, and governments can then use this data to target individuals with advertising, promotions, and political campaigning.

In this chapter, we will introduce the concepts behind big data, and will motivate why big data can be so powerful. We will also use the example of Google Flu Trends to illustrate where big data can fail.

32.1 How do computers store data?

Big data usually needs to be managed in a very different way to traditional data. To understand the challenges that are posed by big data, it's useful to begin by thinking about how data is stored in computers. At its simplest, data is stored in a computer in binary format; the simplest form of binary is a single outcome that takes the value 1 or 0. The data stored in this single binary digit is then known as a 'bit' (short for binary digit). For a computer, a binary digit is easy to interpret, as it represents either 'on' or 'off'.

32.1.1 A brief introduction to binary

We are most used to looking at numbers represented in base 10. In base 10, each digit, from the right-hand side, represents numbers of powers of 10. So for example, the number 237 is made up of:

- $7 \times 10^0 = 7$
- $3 \times 10^1 = 30$
- $2 \times 10^2 = 200$

So each digit represents a different power of 10. In 237, there are seven lots of 10^0s, three lots of 10^1s, and two lots of 10^2s. In decimal, we would use the ten digits 0–9 within the number.

Of course, there's no reason we need to be restricted to the digits in a number representing powers of 10. The digits within a number could represent any power. In binary, we restrict the digits that we use to either 0 or 1, and each digit represents a power of 2. So, for instance, an 8-digit binary number 11111111 is illustrated in Figure 32.1.

So, from the right-hand side, the first digit represents the number of 2^0, the second digit represents the number of 2^1, and so on. So in the example, there is one lot of 2^0 (= 1), one lot of 2^1(= 2), one lot of 2^2, one lot of 2^3, and so on. So, to convert the 8-digit binary number 11111111 to decimal notation, we would have:

$$1 \times 2^7 + 1 \times 2^6 + 1 \times 2^5 + 1 \times 2^4 + 1 \times 2^3 + 1 \times 2^2 + 1 \times 2^1 + 1 \times 2^0$$
$$= 1 \times 128 + 1 \times 64 + 1 \times 32 + 1 \times 16 + 1 \times 8 + 1 \times 4 + 1 \times 2 + 1 \times 1 = 255$$

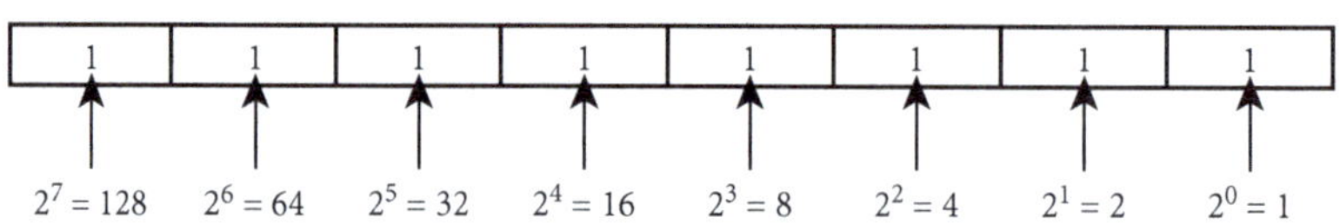

Figure 32.1 Explaining binary notation.

Table 32.1 ASCII codes for letters of the alphabet

65	**66**	**67**	**68**	**69**	**70**	**71**	**72**	**73**	**74**	**75**	**76**	**77**
A	B	C	D	E	F	G	H	I	J	K	L	M
78	**79**	**80**	**81**	**82**	**83**	**84**	**85**	**86**	**87**	**88**	**89**	**90**
N	O	P	Q	R	S	T	U	V	W	X	Y	Z

We can uniquely represent any decimal number in binary by simply breaking down the number into the sum of powers of 2. So, for instance, we can represent 37 as the sum of 32, 4, and 1. That is, $32 = 2^5, 4 = 2^2$, and $1 = 2^0$:

$$37 = 32 + 4 + 1 = 1 \times 2^5 + 0 \times 2^4 + 0 \times 2^3 + 1 \times 2^2 + 0 \times 2^1 + 1 \times 2^0$$

Whenever we multiply the power of 2 by 1, that turns the relevant digit into a 1, and similarly, when we multiply by 0, it turns the digit into a 0. So, in binary (base 2), we can represent 37 as 100101.

Why does this help us understand how computers store data?

If we think about an 8-digit binary number, we can represent any number between 0 and 255. One way that computers store alpha-numeric data is through American Standard Code for Information Interchange (or ASCII). ASCII assigns an 8-digit binary code for any letter or symbol. The ASCII codes for letters of the alphabet, represented in base 10, are shown in Table 32.1.

So, for example, in ASCII the character capital K is represented by the decimal number 75, which can be represented as the 8-digit binary number 00100111. When storing data, computers effectively convert each character into a storing of 8 binary digits (or bits), and each set of eight binary digits is then known as a byte. That is, a single character takes 1 byte to store.

One of the simplest ways of storing data is through 'comma separated values' (CSV) files. CSV files consist of each entry, separated by a comma, whilst each separate entry consists of a separate line.

So, suppose you had a data set representing individuals' eye colour:

Name	Eye colour
Arzhang	Brown
Briony	Blue
Cuthbert	Green
Dongyu	Hazel
...	...

In CSV format, this would be represented as:

```
Name,Eye Colour
Arzhang,Brown
Briony,Blue
Cuthbert,Green
Dongyu,Hazel
...,...
```

So, to store this data set, a computer would normally need to represent every character (including the commas and the line breaks) as an 8-digit binary number. Thus, the computer would store this data as a long string of 1s and 0s. (Spaces are added to show each separate byte of data.)

The data set in Figure 32.2 contained four observations (and the header with the variable names), and two (relatively simple) variables, and would take up 77 bytes of space to store. Had we 1,000 observations, the data set would be approximately 200 times larger (15.4kB), with 1,000,000 observations.

Suppose that you have a large but very simple data set, consisting of one billion characters. (i.e. 1 followed by 9 zeros). How big would your storage need to be to store this simple data set?

Remember, each character that a computer stores takes up one byte's worth of space. As such, if you wanted to store a data set containing 1,000,000,000 characters, this would take up one billion bytes (see Table 32.2). This isn't very informative, but for context, it's important to think about scale.

```
01001110 01100001 01101101 01100101 00101100 01000101 01111001 01100101 00100000 01000011
01101111 01101100 01101111 01110101 01110010 00001010 01000001 01110010 01111010 01101000
01100001 01101110 01100111 00101100 01000010 01110010 01101111 01110111 01101110 00001010
01000010 01110010 01101001 01101111 01101110 01111001 00101100 01000010 01101100 01110101
01100101 00001010 01000011 01110101 01110100 01101000 01100010 01100101 01110010 01110100
00101100 01000111 01110010 01100101 01100101 01101110 00001010 01000100 01101111 01101110
01100111 01111001 01110101 00101100 01001000 01100001 01111010 01100101 01101100 00001010
11100010 10000000 10100110 00101100 11100010 10000000 10100110
```

Figure 32.2 Data stored in binary.

Table 32.2 The amount of data that can be stored in different sizes of storage

Size of storage[1]	Number of bytes	Number of bits	Number of characters that can be stored
1 byte	1	8 bits	1 character
1 kilobyte (kB)	1,000	8,000	1,000
1 megabyte (MB)	1,000,000	8,000,000	1,000,000
1 gigabyte (GB)	1,000,000,000	8,000,000,000	1,000,000,000
1 terabyte (TB)	1,000,000,000,000	8,000,000,000,000	1,000,000,000,000

Simply to store the one billion characters,[2] we would need a gigabyte of space on a storage device. Whilst this is not a large amount of space in the context of modern computers (many off-the-shelf computers offer several terabytes of disk space), the data set we have described is not particularly complex, as whilst it contains 1,000,000,000 entries, each entry represents a single character, which is not realistic of most data sets.

In the context of big data, it would not be unusual for a data set to contain several billion observations (and for each observation to be made up of multiple characters). For example, in the London Stock Exchange, there are several million transactions carried out each day, and over the course of a year, it would not be unusual to have over half a billion transactions.

As such, data sets with a large number of (complicated) observations grow very large very quickly. The implication for big data is that standard storage solutions become impractical, and the data sets also become unwieldy to analyse in standard statistical programmes.

32.1.2 What is big data?

We have been talking about 'big data' in this chapter, without ever really defining what we mean by 'big data'. Generally speaking, big data is characterized by at least one of three characteristics:

- volume
- velocity
- variety.

[1] Note: sometimes, you will see these sizes as powers of 2, so that 1kB = 1,024 bytes = 2^{10} bytes. Similarly, 1 MB is often represented as 2^{20} bytes, 1GB as 2^{30} bytes, and 1TB as 2^{40} bytes. These make small but noticeable differences.

[2] The data that we are representing here is text data. For numeric data, it is more efficient for computers to store the data as a numeric value, rather than relying on strings to represent the characters in the data. When you read more about data storage, you will hear about string data, which represents data stored as alpha-numeric text, and numeric data that is stored as a number.

Volume simply relates to the number of observations (and variables) within a data set. In the example of the London Stock Exchange, if we are interested in analysing all of the trades made within a single year, then we would be looking at several hundred million trades.

Velocity relates to the speed and regularity that data arrives in a big-data context. Whilst in standard data sets, we might collect a sample of data, and then analyse that sample to make conclusions about a population, with 'big data', the data is constantly arriving. This means that analysis of big data needs different forms of server that can cope with hundreds or thousands of new observations arriving every minute.

The third characteristic, variety, relates to the fact that 'big data' can take a wide range of different forms. Big data can relate to simple numeric data, but it can also relate to written posts, or videos, or audio-files. The growth of the internet has led to a wide range of opportunities for retailers and other firms to collect data in a wide range of formats.

32.2 Benefits of big data

One of the biggest benefits of big data is that the scale of the data means that we don't need to worry (so much) about distributional issues. Whenever we carry out statistical testing based upon a (relatively small) sample from the population, we have to worry about sampling variation; that is, every time we take a different sample from the population, we will get a different estimate of the population value.

So, for instance, provided the observations are *iid*, we saw that the sample mean, $\overline{X}$, was an unbiased estimator of the population average ($E(X)$), but that the variance of the sample mean was equal to:

$$var(\overline{X}) = \frac{var(X)}{n}$$

Now, the first observation is that, as the sample size gets larger, the variance of the estimator gets smaller; with big data, we may be able to make inferences much more easily about populations, as we are implicitly observing a population. However, it should also be noted that it is important to define what population we are looking at.

If, for instance, the big data is generated by a social media platform (e.g. Facebook or X), then the population we are observing is the population of individuals who have social media accounts. Generally speaking, this may only be generalizable to the population we are observing; so for example, it may only be generalizable to the population of individuals who have social media accounts.

32.2.1 Collecting and analysing big data

Some of the statistical tools that we have learnt about in this book are less relevant when it comes to big data, as data first of all represents populations (rather than samples from the population), and secondly, because of the variety of the types of data (e.g. qualitative data, mixed in with quantitative data). Firms make use of machine learning, and develop algorithms to analyse the data.

We could begin by thinking about a traditional, bricks and mortar, supermarket. Every time you purchase goods in the supermarket, you are providing data to that firm. At its simplest, if you purchase goods in cash, then you are contributing to the supermarket's analysis of demands for goods, and by looking at what is purchased together, the supermarket can develop models of goods that are likely to go together.

However, as soon as you buy something where you can be identified, and purchases matched, you provide much more data, and much more power to the supermarket. Supermarket loyalty cards were an early attempt to be able to collect data about you, with the quid pro quo that you would receive discounts or vouchers for that store. The data that the supermarkets collect allows them to build a profile of all of their loyalty card holders, and use the observed data from other shoppers to predict goods that will come in handy.

A simple example would be that, if the supermarket observed a customer suddenly buying vitamin D and folic acid (often recommended as supplements to take during pregnancy), the supermarket may then be able to predict that this customer is pregnant, and then based on the observed spending habits of other customers, could start sending vouchers for, or recommendations for, products like nappies up to nine months later.

When we buy goods and services online, it becomes much easier for firms to track us, without the need for loyalty cards; most online stores encourage (or even require) customers to set up accounts, which can then keep track of purchases, or tracking cookies within your browser can be used to keep track of what pages you have looked at, to build a more in-depth profile of you as an individual. Once again, this can be used to create a model of you, and what goods and services may be of interest to you.

Of course, it is not just shops that are interested in the interests of individuals; during elections, political parties and campaigns are interested in trying to target individuals who may be willing to vote for them. Advertising that is sent to everyone (e.g. traditional television advertising, or banners shown to everyone in newspapers) is expensive, and not very effective. Instead, political parties want to be able to target their advertising towards individuals with similar views (e.g. in US elections, political advertising may be targeted towards voters who float between Democrat and Republican).

Almost everything we do in the modern world can create a digital footprint that is valuable in the world of big data. Our mobile phones can track where we are (and where we have been). CCTV can further track our movements, and face recognition and automatic number plate recognition (ANPR) technology can allow governments and police forces to further track individuals. Our spending on credit and debit cards, and our use of loyalty cards, allows firms to build profiles of individuals, and our activities online can be used to build a profile. Every time you share a post on social media, every time you purchase something (online, or in person), every time you read an article on a website, every time you search for something on Google, you are potentially creating new data that can be used to build a profile of you, and that profile is valuable; with careful analysis, this data can be used to target advertising, promotions, or political campaigns.

32.2.2 Google Flu Trends

Big data isn't just useful for analysing individual behaviour, but it can also be useful for providing insight into the world as a whole. By observing the behaviour of a large enough number of people, you can create predictions and insights about behaviour in the world.

One of the most famous (or possibly infamous) uses of big data was through Google Flu Trends. This was an application whereby Google used big data, based upon search terms, to predict when influenza outbreaks would occur. Every time that anyone searched for websites on Google, then that search term was recorded, along with identifiers, such as the IP address of the computer, which could be used to also identify where the computer was located in the world.

When people start feeling ill, they may search for remedies or for online diagnoses based upon symptoms. What Google Flu Trends attempted to do was to use historical observations of search patterns in local areas, and tie those in to historic flu outbreaks. For example, Google looked for search terms such as 'fever' or 'cough' to help predict whether a flu outbreak was ongoing. Having observed peoples' behaviour, they could use an algorithm to predict, based on search activity in a particular city, state, or country, whether a flu outbreak was likely or not.

In principle, this is a good idea, but it relies on two key elements:

1. It relies on behaviour being relatively homogeneous; that is, the population doesn't change their behaviour year on year. For example, if over time, the population becomes more likely to search for symptoms (even when they have relatively minor illnesses like the common cold), this may increase the likelihood of the algorithm (incorrectly) predicting a flu outbreak.
2. Because flu outbreaks don't take place in the same parts of a country every year, in essence, Google was using data from other parts of a country (or the world) to make predictions about behaviour; if there are differences across cities in search behaviour, then the algorithm may not be useful.

Google Flu Trends was relatively successful until 2013, when it overestimated the likelihood of a flu outbreak by over 140 per cent.[3] Following this, the service was quietly retired. Lazer et al. (2014) argued that the reason for the failure was an over-reliance on big data; that is, big data was being used as a replacement for traditional data sources rather than as a complement.

As in any data analysis, it is important to think about how relevant the data is, and how informative the data will be for answering the question that you are asking.

[3] D. Lazer et al. (2014), 'The Parable of Google Flu: Traps in Big Data Analysis', *Science*, 343, 6176.

Summary

Big data is all around us; everything we do may be contributing to big data somewhere. In this chapter, we have focused on big data related to individuals, but techniques relating to big data can be used wherever we are collecting data that is large in volume, has a variety of formats, or is arriving rapidly. For instance, weather forecasting is a successful application of big data; weather forecasters can use data from a wide range of sensors and observations, and historical observations, to predict the future.

Big data does, however, come with a number of potential dangers. Where we are looking at human behaviour, there may be lots of things that change over time, meaning that observations of the past may be less useful for forecasting future behaviour. Further, big data can be misused by campaigners and alien governments to try to shape behaviour, or to direct mis-information to individuals who may be most susceptible to fake news.

Afterword

In this book, we have built a foundation from which you can understand probability and can carry out statistical tests based on single variables, and also related to economic relationships between variables.

Hopefully, this isn't the end of your journey. In the final third of this book, we have introduced econometrics, the scope of which is far too vast to include in a single book. Ultimately, much of the econometrics we have discussed is about identifying correlations between variables, but we have also been worried about causality throughout as well.

As your journey in econometrics continues, you will build upon techniques (particularly those seen in Chapter 31) to develop your understanding of how you can use observational data to estimate causal effects. In addition, there are lots of things that we have not discussed, which you are likely to see in further texts.

For instance, whilst we saw dummy variables as explanatory variables, you can also use binary outcome variables as dependent variables. However, you need to use different methods to be able to gain 'correct' estimates of the marginal effect, which have further underlying assumptions. Similarly, you will get the opportunity to explore different types of data. In this book, we have largely concentrated on cross-sectional data; that is, data which is taken from a single snapshot of time. However, this is not the only type of data you can use. Many economists (and particularly those with an interest in finance) are interested in data that comes from a single source over a sustained time period. For example, you might be interested in the share price of a particular firm on the New York Stock Exchange over a one-year period. Time series raise all sorts of interesting questions, as it is highly unlikely that the sets of observations are 'random', since prices move relatively smoothly over time; similarly, because two shares might be increasing at the same time, this doesn't mean that they are intrinsically linked, but you may instead be observing spurious correlations. You can also combine cross-sectional data with time series data to construct panel data, where you observe the same cross-section of observations repeatedly over a set time period. Again, there is a wide range of specific tools that you can use to analyse these sorts of panels of observations.

One of the most important things you will develop is an appreciation of how to estimate relationships to establish causal relationships between economic variables. You will need to be able to:

- identify appropriate identification strategies to create causal estimates
- apply these identification strategies
- be able to understand when these identification strategies either have not worked, or are purely not valid.

A good, applied economist will be able to use a toolkit of identification strategies to try to estimate causal relationships between economic variables. They will also be able to critically evaluate the methods used, and to identify where fundamental assumptions break down.

Good luck with all of your future endeavours. This book should provide the solid foundations for the rest of your econometrics journey. Econometrics can open many interesting doors, and this book is just the first of them.

References

Agresti, A., and Coull, B. (1998), 'Approximate is Better Than "Exact" for Interval Estimation of Binomial Proportions', *American Statistician*, 52(2), 119–126.

ASCII Table, https://www.ascii-code.com/ (accessed 12 August 2025).

Ashenfelter, O., and Krueger, A. (1994), 'Estimates of the Economic Return to Schooling from a New Sample of Twins', *American Economic Review*, 84(5), 1157–1173.

Bayes, T., and Price, R. (1763). 'An Essay towards Solving a Problem in the Doctrine of Chance. By the late Rev. Mr. Bayes, communicated by Mr. Price, in a letter to John Canton, A.M.F.R.S', *Philosophical Transactions of the Royal Society of London*, 53, 370–418.

BBC News (2023), 'How Much Do Women Footballers Get Paid?', https://www.bbc.co.uk/news/business-62378095 (accessed 29 July 2023).

BBC News (2023), 'What Has Happened to Pay in the UK?', https://www.bbc.co.uk/news/business-64944262 (accessed 16 July 2023).

Beyer, M., Lapkin, A., Gall, N., Feinberg, D., and Sribar, V. (2011), '"Big Data" Is Only the Beginning of Extreme Information Management' (gartner.com).

Bodmer, W., Bailey, R., Charlesworth, B., Eyre-Walker, A., Farewell, V., Mead, A., and Senn, S. (2021), 'The Outstanding Scientist, R.A. Fisher: His Views on Eugenics and Race', *Heredity*, 126, 565–576.

Britton, J., Dearden, L., Shephard, N., and Vignoles, A. (2016), 'How English Domiciled Graduate Earnings Vary with Gender, Institution Attended, Subject and Socio-economic Background', IFS Working Paper W16/06.

Butler, S. (1872) *Erewhon; Or, Over the Range*, Sanage.

Card, D., and Krueger, A. (1994), 'Minimum Wages and Employment: A Case Study of the Fast-Food Industry in New Jersey and Pennsylvania', *American Economic Review*, 84(4), 772–793.

Carter, S. P., Greenberg, K., and Walker, M. S. (2017), 'The Impact of Computer Usage on Academic Performance: Evidence from a Randomized Trial at the United States Military Academy', *Economics of Education Review*, 56, 118–132.

Cochran, W. (1934), 'The Distribution of Quadratic Forms in a Normal System, with Applications to the Analysis of Covariance', *Mathematical Proceedings of the Cambridge Philosophical Society*, 30(2), 178–191.

De Moivre, A. (1718), *The Doctrine of Chances*, Woodfall.

Dinnes, J., Deeks, J. J., Berhane, S., Taylor, M., Adriano, A., Davenport, C., Dittrich, S., Emperador, D., Takwoingi, Y., Cunningham, J., Beese, S., Domen, J., Dretzke, J., Ferrante di Ruffano, L., Harris, I. M., Price, M. J., Taylor-Phillips, S., Hooft, L., Leeflang, M. M. G., McInnes, M. D. F., Spijker, R., and Van den Bruel, A. (2021), 'Rapid, Point-of-care Antigen Tests for Diagnosis of SARS-CoV-2 infection', *Cochrane Database of Systematic Reviews*, Issue 3. Art. No.: CD013705, doi: 10.1002/14651858.CD013705.pub2 (accessed 1 July 2023).

Fisher, R. A. (1958), *Statistical Methods for Research Workers*, 13th edn, Oliver and Boyd.

Gibbons, S., Machin, S., and Silva, O. (2013), 'Valuing School Quality Using Boundary Discontinuity', *Journal of Urban Economics*, 75, 15–28.

Gov.uk (2023), 'Statutory Guidance Overview', https://www.gov.uk/government/publications/gender-pay-gap-reporting-guidance-for-employers/overview#:~:text=Equal%20pay%20means%20that%20men,holiday%20entitlement (accessed 11 November 2023).

Harmon, C., and Walker, I. (1995), 'Estimates of the Economic Return to Schooling for the United Kingdom', *American Economic Review*, 85(5), 1278–1286, http://www.jstor.org/stable/2950988.

Jensen, J. L. W. V. (1906), 'Sur les fonctions convexes et les inégalites entre les valeurs moyennes', *Acta Mathematical*, 30(1).

Lazer, D., Kennedy, R., King, G., and Vespignani, A. (2014), 'The Parable of Google Flu: Traps in Big Data Analysis', *Science*, 343, 6176.

Lee, D. S., and McCrary, J. (2017), 'The Deterrent Effect of Prison: Dynamic Theory and Evidence', in M. D. Cattaneo and J. C. Escanciano (eds), *Regression Discontinuity Designs: Theory and Applications*, Emerald.

Mengel-From, J., Wong, T., Morling, N., Rees, J., and Jackson, I. (2009), 'Genetic Determinants of Hair and Eye Colours in the Scottish and Danish Populations', *BMC Genetics*, 10(88).

Newcastle United (2023), 'Gender Pay Gap Report 2022–23', https://www.nufc.co.uk/media/75582/pay-gap-report_march2023.pdf (accessed 29 July 2023).

OECD (2022), 'General government debt (indicator)', doi: 10.1787/a0528cc2-en (accessed 5 December 2022).

OECD (2022), 'Gross domestic product (GDP) (indicator)', doi: 10.1787/dc2f7aec-en (accessed 5 December 2022).

OECD (2019), *Health at a Glance 2019: OECD Indicators*, OECD Publishing, https://doi.org/10.1787/4dd50c09-en (accessed 11 August 2025).

ONS (2019), 'Average weekly earnings in Great Britain: April 2019', https://www.ons.gov.uk/employmentandlabourmarket/peopleinwork/employmentandemployeetypes/bulletins/averageweeklyearningsingreatbritain/april2019 (accessed 11 August 2025).

ONS (2023), 'Gender pay gap in the UK: 2023', Office for National Statistics (accessed 11 November 2023).

Reinhart, C., and Rogoff, K. (2010), 'Growth in a Time of Debt', *American Economic Review*, 100(2), 573–578.

Satterthwaite, F. E. (1946), 'An Approximate Distribution of Estimates of Variance Components', *Biometrics Bulletin*, 2(6), 110–114.

Saw, J. G., Yang, M. C. K., and Mo, T. C. (1984), 'Chebyshev Inequality with Estimated Mean and Variance', *American Statistician*, 38(2), 130–2.

Selvin, S. (1975), 'A Problem in Probability (letter to the editor)', *American Statistician* 29(3).

Shakespeare, W., 'Richard III', in B. Mowat, P. Werstine, M. Poston, and R. Niles (eds), *The Folger Shakespeare*. Folger Shakespeare Library, https://www.folger.edu/explore/shakespeares-works/richard-iii/ (accessed 11 August 2025).

Sheppard, W. F. (1903), 'New Tables of the Probability Integral', *Biometrika*, 2(2), 177–190.

Spence, M. (1973), 'Job Market Signaling', *Quarterly Journal of Economics*, 87(3), 355–374.

Springford, J. (2018), 'What's the Cost of Brexit So Far?', *CER Insight*, 23 June.

Stewart, I. (1977), 'Gauss', *Scientific American*, 237(1), 122–131.

Stone, L. D., Keller, C. M., Kratzke, T. M., and Strumpfer, J. P. (2014), 'Search for the Wreckage of Air France Flight AF447', *Statistical Science*, 29(1), 69–80.

Student (1908), 'The Probable Error of a Mean', *Biometrika*, 6(1), 1–25.

Taleb, N. (2008), *The Black Swan: The Impact of the Highly Improbable*, Penguin.

Welch, B. L. (1947), 'The Generalization of 'Student's' Problem When Several Different Population Variances Are Involved', *Biometrika*, 34(1/2), 28–35.

Bibliography

This list contains books that have been consulted as part of the preparation of this textbook.

- Angrist, J., and Pischke, J. (2014), *Mastering Metrics*, Princeton University Press.
- Cortinhas, C., and Black, K. (2012), *Statistics for Business and Economics*, Wiley.
- Crawshaw, J., and Chambers, J. (2001), *A Concise Course in Advanced Level Statistics*.
- Dougherty, C. (2016), *Introduction to Econometrics*, OUP.
- Gujurati, D. (1995), *Basic Econometrics*, McGraw Hill.
- Murray, M. (2003), *Econometrics: A Modern Introduction, International Edition*, Pearson.
- Stock, J., and Watson, M. (2019), *Introduction to Econometrics, Global Edition*, Pearson.
- Wooldridge, J. M. (2019), *Introductory Econometrics: A Modern Approach*, Cengage Books.

Glossary

Adjusted R^2 A measure of how well a fitted model fits the data. This is adjusted to take account of the number of **explanatory variables** used in the model.

Alternative hypothesis (H_A) In statistical testing, this is our hypothesized value when the null hypothesis is false.

ANOVA Analysis of **variance**. This is a test for the equality of means across multiple populations.

ASCII American Standard Code for Information Interchange. A set of codes used by computers to encode numerical values for letters and other characters.

Asymptotic bias The size of the bias as the sample size tends towards infinity.

Asymptotic variance The value to which the variance converges as the sample size tends towards infinity.

Bayes' rule A rule that allows you to make conclusions about individuals, based on observed characteristics of that individual.

Bernoulli trial A **discrete random variable**, with possible values 1 and 0, with the probability of the outcome 1 being equal to p. Independent Bernoulli trials can be combined to form a variable following the **Binomial distribution**.

Between sum of squares The sum of squares of group averages away from the overall sample average. This is used in **ANOVA**, and in **F-tests** more generally.

Between variance The average variability between groups.

Bias The difference between the average of estimates (from a large number of realizations) and the true population parameter being estimated. An **unbiased estimator** will have a bias equal to zero.

Binomial distribution A discrete random variable, based on the sum of n Bernoulli trials, each with probability of success equal to p.

BLUE estimator The Best Linear Unbiased Estimator. Best indicates that the estimator has the smallest variance, linear indicates that the estimator is linear (in terms of the explanatory variable), unbiased indicates that, on average, the estimator yields the *correct* estimate. If the observations are *iid*, then the sample mean is the BLUE estimator for the population average.

Causal relationship A relationship where a change in one variable causes a change in another variable.

Central limit theorem A theorem that tells us about the distribution of the sample mean. For a large enough sample, the sample mean will be approximately normally distributed.

Chi-squared (χ^2) distribution A continuous random variable, constructed based on the sum of squares of k independent random variables, which follow a standard normal distribution

Classical measurement error bias The bias that occurs from random measurement error of the **explanatory variable**. This causes the **OLS estimator** to be biased towards zero.

Conditional probability The probability of an outcome occurring given that you have observed another outcome (relating to a second random variable).

Confidence interval The range of population values that are consistent with a given estimate.

Consistent estimator An estimator is consistent if, as the sample size gets very large, the estimates converges in probability towards the correct population value.

Continuous random variable A random variable where outcomes are defined along a continuous range, with an infinite number of possible outcomes. The probability of any given outcome is zero, and the likelihood of outcomes is determined by a probability density, rather than a probability mass.

Convergence (absolute) An estimator converges in absolute terms if, as the sample size gets large, the estimate gets closer and closer to a particular value, k.

Convergence (in probability) An estimator converges in probability to a value, k, if as the sample size gets large, the probability that the estimates are within an arbitrarily small distance of k tends towards 1.

Correlation A standardized measure of the covariance, indicating how well the two variables covary together. A correlation of +1 indicates that all of the observations lie on an upward sloping straight line. A correlation of −1 indicates that all of the observations lie on a downward sloping straight line.

Covariance A measure of how much two variables deviate from their expected values together. A positive covariance indicates that as one variable increases, on average, the other variable also increases.

COVID-19 A novel airborne virus that caused a pandemic in 2020.

Cumulative distribution function The probability of seeing an outcome less than (or equal) to a particular value of the **random variable**.

Degrees of freedom The number of **linearly independent** elements within a sample.

Dependent variable In regression analysis, the variable that we are trying to explain.

Derivative The rate of change of one variable in relation to another.

Discrete random variable A random variable with a finite set of possible outcomes, with non-zero probabilities.

Dummy variable A variable that can only take the values 1 or 0. Dummy variables are often used to replace categorical data (e.g. the sex of an individual, or the country in which they live, or whether they have an undergraduate degree).

Economic significance The economic significance of a result is determined by the magnitude of the estimated effect. There is no fixed metric that determines if an effect is economically significant, so it is often useful to compare effect sizes with other, estimated effects in the literature. For example, if you are interested in the effect of an additional year of schooling on earnings, you might compare this with the impact of being taught by a good teaching, compared with a bad teacher.

Elasticity The percentage change in one variable due to a one percent increase in another variable.

Endogenous In regression analysis, where an explanatory variable is correlated with the error term.

Error term Other factors, other than included explanators, that determine the value of the dependent variable.

Estimate A single realization of an estimator, based on an observed set of data.

Estimated intercept The estimated point at which the fitted line crosses the Y axis.

Estimator A mathematical function, applied to data, to yield an estimate of an (unknown) population parameter. An estimator is itself a random variable, with an expected value, variance, and distribution. For large enough samples sizes, many commonly used estimators will be normally distributed (by the **central limit theorem**). Where the estimator is not normally distributed, other testing strategies will be necessary.

Exogenous An explanatory variable is exogenous when it is unrelated to the error term. When a variable is exogenous, it will be uncorrelated with the error term.

Expectation The expectation, or expected value, of a random variable tells you the (population) average of that random variable.

Experiment In an experiment, treatment is randomized, so that unobserved characteristics are uncorrelated with the treatment of interest. In a well-designed experiment, the treatment will be **exogenous**.

Explanatory variable(s) In regression analysis, the variable(s) that we are using to try to explain the dependent variable.

F-distribution A continuous random variable, constructed based on the ratio of two **chi-squared distributions**, divided by their relevant **degrees of freedom**.

Fitted line A line passing through the data, produced by an estimator.

Fitted residual The vertical distance on a scatter plot between the observed point and the fitted line.

Fixed in repeated samples We sometimes make the assumption that the explanatory variables are fixed in repeated samples. This means that, if we repeatedly sampled from the population, we would choose observations, such that the values of the X variable were the same every time. For example, you might sample the data such that your X values are 1,2,3,4,5,6,7,8,9,10. This is generally a very bad assumption, as in reality, we will never observe the explanatory variable being fixed, and if it is, it may cause implications for the other assumptions we make in OLS.

FRED Federal Reserve Economic Data.

Frequency histogram A graphical representation of data, with the height of bars representing how often observations occur within that range

F-test A statistical test, where (when the null hypothesis is true), the test statistic follows an F-distribution.

Gauss Markov theorem The Gauss Markov theorem states that, under strong assumptions, OLS is the Best Linear Unbiased Estimator to estimate the linear relationship between two (or more) economic variables.

Heteroskedasticity The **variance** of the **error term** varies.

Homoskedasticity The **variance** of the **error term** is constant.

Identification strategy A method that is used to find causal relationships between economic variables.

Independence **Random variables** are independent if knowing the value of one realization of a random variable tells you nothing about the likely value of another random variable.

Independent and identically distributed An assumption often made about sampling, where every observation is randomly drawn from a constant population, and each observation is independent from all of the other observations.

Interquartile range The distance between the 25th and 75th percentile.

Joint probability The probability distribution showing the likelihood of pairs of outcomes, across two random variables, occurring.

Kurtosis A measure of how much weight is in the tails of the PDF of a random variable.

Law of iterated expectations A rule that allows you to make conclusions about the overall population average, based upon a set of conditional expectations.

Linear combination For a pair of random variables, a linear combination is achieved by adding together some multiple of one random variable to a multiple of the second random variable.

Linear estimator A linear estimator is one that can be written as a linear function of the observations of the dependent variable.

Linear independence Data within a sample are linearly independent if, having observed $n-1$ observations you cannot, with certainty, write down the nth observation.

Linear relationship A relationship that can be represented as a straight line.

Linear transformation For a random variable, a linear transformation will transform every outcome by applying a fixed rule using addition of a constant, or multiplication by a constant. The related probabilities remain unchanged. The overall shape of the distribution following a linear transformation will be unchanged, but the position of the distribution and the overall spread of the distribution may change.

Marginal probability The (unconditional) probability of an outcome occurring. For example, the marginal probability of obtaining a head when flipping a fair coin once is equal to 0.5.

Mean A measure of the 'centre' of a sample. This is constructed by adding together all of the observations, and dividing by the number of observations.

Measurement error An error that occurs when the observed value of an observation is different from the true value.

Median A measure of the 'centre' of a sample. This is constructed by observing the middle value when observations are lined up from smallest to largest.

Mode The modal average is a measure of the 'centre' of a sample. This is constructed by observing the most common outcome. Continuous random variables do not have an explicit mode, but, in a population, you might describe the mode as the outcome with the highest probability density.

Monte Carlo simulation A simulation designed to find the distribution of estimators based upon repeated sampling from a known distribution.

Multivariate regression Regression analysis with more than one explanatory variable.

Natural experiment In a natural experiment, researchers observe conditions that allow the treatment to be considered as credibly random. Examples of natural experiments might be looking at outcomes of workers along the state boundary, when the minimum wage is increased in one state, but not in the neighbouring state.

Non-linear relationship A relationship that is represented with a curved line.

Normal distribution A continuous random variable where the PDF follows a distinctive, symmetric, bell-shaped curve.

Null hypothesis In statistical testing, our prior belief. When testing relating to relationships between economic variables, our prior is often that there is no relationship (or a null relationship) between variables.

OECD The Organisation for Economic Co-operation and Development.

Omitted variables bias Bias that affects regression analysis when omitting a potential explanatory variable.

One-tailed test A statistical test, where we only reject the null hypothesis if the test statistic lies in a (pre-specified) tail of the distribution (either the left- or the right-hand tail). Tests using the F-distribution are usually one-tailed tests.

ONS Office for National Statistics.

Ordinary least squares (OLS) An estimator that we can use to estimate relationships between economic variables. It should be noted that this is not the only estimator you can use.

Outlier An observation that lies a long way from the rest of the data.

Paired t-test A test for equality of means across two populations, where each observation in one population is paired with an equivalent observation in a second population. For example, each pair of observations might have been taken on the same date.

Partial derivative The rate of change of one variable with relation to another, holding everything else constant.

Percentile The *n*th percentile represents a value below which *n* per cent of the observations lie.

Population The population contains all of the possible individuals. Populations can be finite (such as the population of students within a university) or infinite (such as the outcomes from rolling a single dice). Where a population is infinite, this does not mean that there are an infinite number of possible outcomes, but instead that there are an infinite number of possible times that you could (for instance) roll a dice.

Power of a test Probability of correctly rejecting the null hypothesis. This can be calculated as 1 minus the probability of a **type 2 error**.

Probability A measure of the likelihood of an event occurring.

Probability density function For a **continuous random variable**, the probability of any given outcome is equal to zero. The probability density function tells you the relative likelihood of outcomes in a given range.

Probability limit The probability limit of an estimator is equal to the value that the estimator converges to in probability as the sample size gets very large.

Probability mass function The probability mass function for a **discrete random variable** tells you the probability of each possible outcome of that random variable.

P-value The probability of gaining a test statistics at least as impressive as the one observed, randomly, if the **null hypothesis** were true.

Quartile Values that split the sample (or population) into four equally sized groups when the data is sorted from smallest to largest. These values are the 25th, 50th, and 75th percentiles.

Random variable A variable with a range of outcomes, the likelihood of each outcome being determined by the **probability mass function** for discrete random variables, and **probability density function** for **continuous random variables**.

Rejection region For a statistical test, the rejection region is the set of values for the test statistic for which we would reject the **null hypothesis**.

Reverse causality In regression analysis, where the model that you have specified follows the wrong direction of causality. That is, the **dependent variable** causes changes in the **explanatory variable**.

R-squared (R^2) A measure of how well a **fitted line** fits the data. The interpretation of the R-squared is the proportion of variance in the **dependent variable** that is explained by the model.

Sample A subset of a population.

Sample variance An **estimator** for the variance of a **population**, based on a sample of data.

Sampling variation The variability in estimates that you observe when taking repeated (different) samples from a population.

Scatter plot A graphical representation of data, with the coordinates of each point representing the Y and X values of each observation.

Serial correlation There is systematic correlation between observations of the error term.

Significance level of a test The probability, set by a researcher, to determine what is seen as an 'unlikely' event in a statistical test. The significance level determines the rejection region for a statistical test. See also **size of a test** and **type 1 error**.

Simultaneity In regression analysis, where the direction of causality works in both directions. That is, changes in the dependent variable cause changes in the explanatory variable, and changes in the explanatory variable cause changes in the **dependent variable**.

Size of a test The probability of a **type 1 error**. This is the same as the **significance level of a test**.

Skew A measure of asymmetry of the **probability density function** of a **random variable**.

Standard deviation A measure of the variability of the **random variable**. This is equal to the square root of the **variance**.

Standard error The standard deviation of an **estimator**.

Standard normal distribution A **continuous random variable** that follows a normal distribution with **expectation** 0 and **variance** 1.

Statistical significance A result is deemed statistically significant if it is unlikely to occur, when the **null hypothesis** is true. The chosen significance level determines the probability that we deem as 'unlikely'. Economists often use 5 per cent as a default size of the test.

Strong law of large numbers As the sample size gets very large, the sample mean converges towards the expected value.

T-distribution The ratio of a standard normal variable, divided by the square root of a chi-squared variable, divided by its relevant degrees of freedom.

Total sum of squares The sum of squares of deviations of observations from the (overall) sample mean. This is used in **ANOVA**, and in **F-tests** more generally.

True line The true line is an unknown line, indicating the underlying relationship between two variables. In general, we do not even know if the 'true line' exists, or what the specification of the true line is.

T-test A statistical test where the **variance** of the underlying estimator is estimated. The test statistic is compared with the **t-distribution**.

T-test for equality of means A statistical test for whether the expected value is equal across two populations.

Two-tailed test A statistical test where the **rejection region** lies in both the right- and left-hand tail of the distribution. For a test at the 5 per cent significance level, this would mean that the rejection region contains the most extreme 2.5 per cent of outcomes in the left-hand tail, and the most extreme 2.5 per cent of outcomes in the right-hand tail.

Type 1 error A false positive for a test, i.e. rejecting the **null hypothesis** when it is true. The probability of a type 1 error is set by the significance level of the test.

Type 2 error A false negative for a test, i.e. failing to reject the **null hypothesis** when it is false.

Unbiased estimator An estimator is unbiased if, on average, the estimator produces the correct population value.

Uniform distribution A **continuous random variable** where the **probability density function** is constant for all possible outcomes, and zero everywhere else.

Variance A measure of the variability of the **random variable**.

Weak law of large numbers As the sample size gets very large, the probability that the sample mean is within any arbitrarily small distance from the expectation tends towards 1, i.e. the probability limit of the sample mean is equal to the expected value.

Welch's t-test A statistical test for equality of means, where the variance of the two populations is assumed to be different.

Within sum of squares The sum of squares of deviations of observations from the (within group) sample mean. This is used in **ANOVA**, and in **F-tests** more generally.

Within variance The variability within a group.

Z-test A statistical test where the variance of the underlying **estimator** is known. The test statistic is compared with the **(standard) normal distribution**.

Index

D

E

J

N

O

P

T

U